King of the World

Louis XVIII
Pillars of Monarchy
The Eagle in Splendour: Inside the Court of Napoleon
The Court of France, 1789–1830
Sultans in Splendour: Monarchs of the Middle East, 1869–1945
Constantinople: City of the World's Desire
The French Emigrés in Europe (co-edited with Kirsty Carpenter)
Paris between Empires
Prince of Europe: The Life of Charles Joseph de Ligne
Dressed to Rule: Royal and Court Costume from
Louis XIV to Elizabeth II
Levant: Splendour and Catastrophe on the Mediterranean
Monarchy and Exile: The Politics of Legitimacy
(co-edited with Torsten Riotte)
Aleppo: The Rise and Fall of Syria's Great Merchant City

PHILIP MANSEL

King of the World

The Life of Louis XIV

THE
UNIVERSITY
OF CHICAGO
PRESS

The University of Chicago Press, Chicago 60637
© 2019 by Philip Mansel
The author has asserted his moral rights.
Published 2020
Printed in the United States of America

29 28 27 26 25 24 23 22 21 20   1 2 3 4 5

ISBN-13: 978-0-226-69089-6 (cloth)
ISBN-13: 978-0-226-69092-6 (e-book)
DOI: https://doi.org/10.7208/chicago/9780226690926.001.0001

First published by Allen Lane, an imprint of Penguin Random House UK, 2019.

Library of Congress Cataloging-in-Publication Data

Names: Mansel, Philip, 1951– author.
Title: King of the world : the life of Louis XIV / Philip Mansel.
Description: Chicago : University of Chicago Press, 2020. | Includes bibliographi-
    cal references and index.
Identifiers: LCCN 2019037186 | ISBN 9780226690896 (cloth) |
    ISBN 9780226690926 (ebook)
Subjects: LCSH: Louis XIV, King of France, 1638–1715. | France—
    History—Louis XIV, 1643–1715.
Classification: LCC DC125 .M358 2020 | DDC 944/.033092 [B]—dc23
LC record available at https://lccn.loc.gov/2019037186

♾ This paper meets the requirements of ANSI/NISO Z39.48-1992
(Permanence of Paper).

You are destined to command the entire universe.
Jean-Baptiste Tavernier to Louis XIV, 1676

Contents

List of Illustrations

pp. 206–7 Israël Silvestre, perspective view of Versailles from the south showing, left to right, the garden, the orangery (foreground), the palace and the Grand Commun, from *Album Perelle*, 1687. Musée du Louvre, Paris. © *RMN-Grand Palais (musée du Louvre) / Michel Urtado*.

pp. 228–9 Israël Silvestre, perspective view of the town, the palace and the gardens of Versailles from the west, from *Album Perelle*, 1687. Musée du Louvre, Paris. © *RMN-Grand Palais (musée du Louvre) / Michel Urtado*.

Plates

1. Pierre Mignard (attr.), *Louis XIV during his minority, c.* 1643. Château de Champs-sur-Marne, France. *Bridgeman Images*.
2. Philippe de Champaigne, *The Virgin Mary offers the Crown and Sceptre to the young Louis XIV, attended by his mother Anne of Austria and brother Philippe, Duc d'Anjou*, 1643, detail. Hamburger Kunsthalle, Hamburg. *Bridgeman Images*.
3. French school (seventeenth century), *Gaston, duc d'Orléans in Roman dress*. Châteaux de Versailles et de Trianon, Versailles. © *RMN-Grand Palais (Château de Versailles)/image RMN-GP*.
4. Copper token struck in Paris satirizing Cardinal Mazarin, 1651, reverse. *CGB Numismatics, Paris/www.CGB.fr*.
5. Antoine Herisset, *Louis XIV holding a 'lit de justice' in the Grand' Chambre of the Parlement de Paris*, 1651. Châteaux de Versailles et de Trianon, Versailles. © *RMN-Grand Palais (Château de Versailles)/ image RMN-GP*.
6. Gobelins manufactory, workshop of Jean-Baptiste Mozin, *The Coronation of King Louis XIV*, tapestry from the series *The History of the King*, 1665–71. Châteaux de Versailles et de Trianon, Versailles. © *RMN-Grand Palais (Château de Versailles)/Christian Jean/Jean Schormans*.

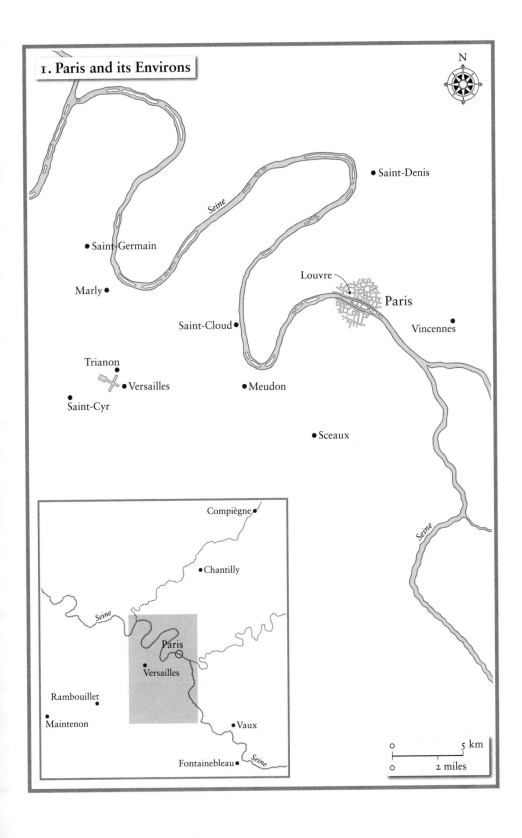

1. Paris and its Environs

N

Saint-Denis

Saint-Germain

Marly

Louvre

Paris

Vincennes

Saint-Cloud

Trianon

Versailles

Meudon

Saint-Cyr

Sceaux

Seine

Compiègne

Chantilly

Seine

Paris

Versailles

Rambouillet

Maintenon

Vaux

Fontainebleau

Seine

5 km

2 miles

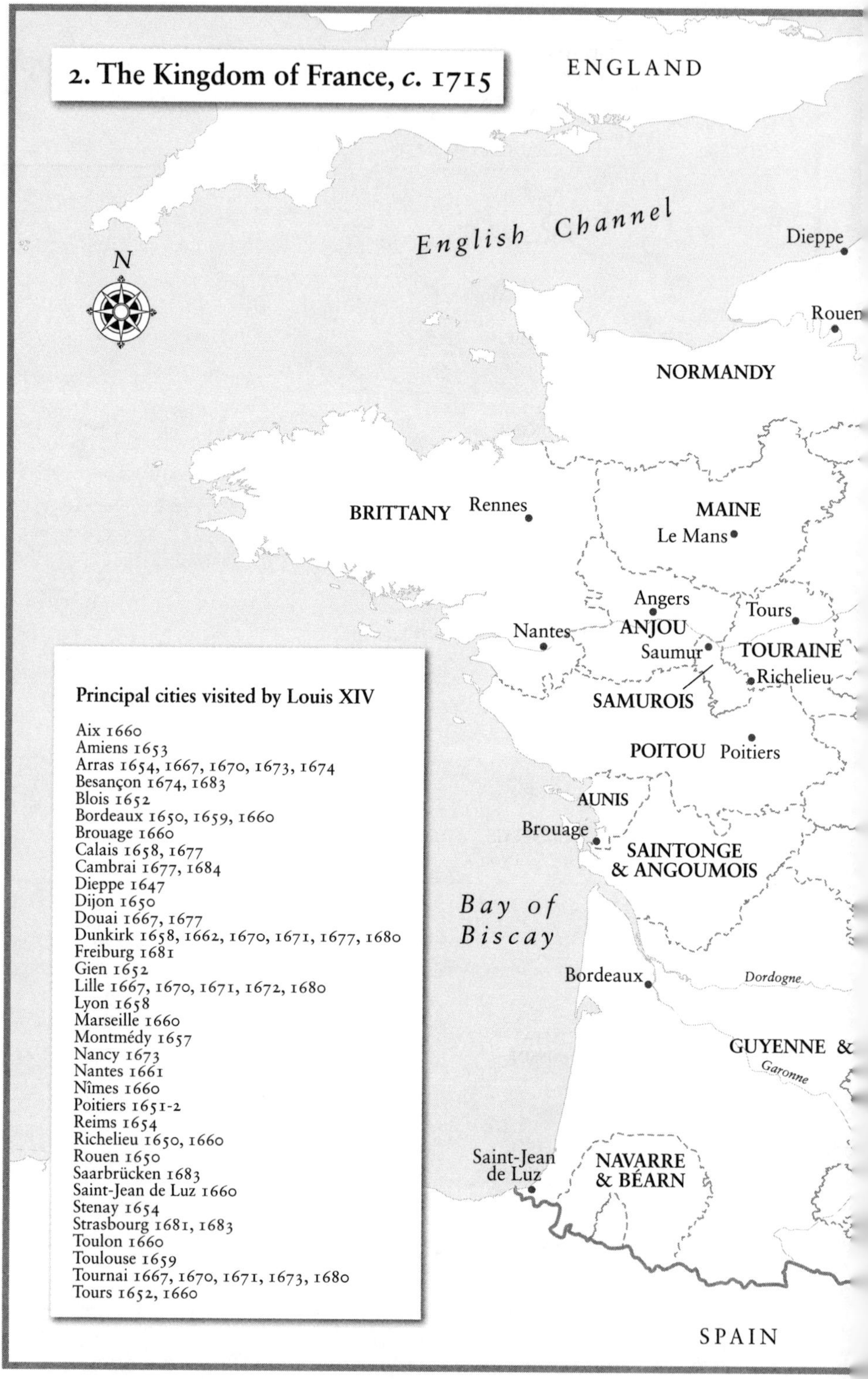

2. The Kingdom of France, *c.* 1715

ENGLAND

English Channel

Dieppe

Rouen

N

NORMANDY

BRITTANY · Rennes

MAINE
Le Mans·

Angers
Nantes · ANJOU · Tours
Saumur· TOURAINE
·Richelieu
SAMUROIS

POITOU Poitiers

AUNIS

Brouage·

SAINTONGE
& ANGOUMOIS

*Bay of
Biscay*

Bordeaux·   *Dordogne*

GUYENNE &
Garonne

Saint-Jean
de Luz   NAVARRE
& BÉARN

SPAIN

Principal cities visited by Louis XIV

Aix 1660
Amiens 1653
Arras 1654, 1667, 1670, 1673, 1674
Besançon 1674, 1683
Blois 1652
Bordeaux 1650, 1659, 1660
Brouage 1660
Calais 1658, 1677
Cambrai 1677, 1684
Dieppe 1647
Dijon 1650
Douai 1667, 1677
Dunkirk 1658, 1662, 1670, 1671, 1677, 1680
Freiburg 1681
Gien 1652
Lille 1667, 1670, 1671, 1672, 1680
Lyon 1658
Marseille 1660
Montmédy 1657
Nancy 1673
Nantes 1661
Nîmes 1660
Poitiers 1651-2
Reims 1654
Richelieu 1650, 1660
Rouen 1650
Saarbrücken 1683
Saint-Jean de Luz 1660
Stenay 1654
Strasbourg 1681, 1683
Toulon 1660
Toulouse 1659
Tournai 1667, 1670, 1671, 1673, 1680
Tours 1652, 1660

FLANDERS
& HAINAUT

Dunkirk
Calais
Ghent
Brussels
Cologne

Lille
Tournai

ARTOIS
Douai
Arras
Cambrai

Amiens
PICARDY

Frankfurt

Mainz

METZ &
VERDUN
Trier

Montmédy
Stenay

Saarbrücken
(Saarlouis)

ÎLE DE
FRANCE

Reims
Metz

Paris

CHAMPAGNE
& BRIE

Troyes

Nancy
TOUL
LORRAINE
& BAR

Strasbourg

ALSACE

Freiburg

ORLÉANAIS
Orléans
Gien

Blois

Dijon
Besançon

Basel

Bourges
NIVERNAIS
Nevers

BERRY
BOURBONNAIS

MARCHE

BURGUNDY

FRANCHE-
COMTÉ

SWISS
CONFEDERATION

Geneva

LYONNAIS
Lyon

Rhône

LIMOUSIN
AUVERGNE

PIEDMONT

Grenoble

GASCONY

DAUPHINÉ

Durance

COMTAT
VENAISSIN

Nîmes
Avignon

Toulouse
Montpellier
Aix
PROVENCE

LANGUEDOC
Marseille

0   50   100 miles

0   100   200 km

FOIX

Toulon

Perpignan
ROUSSILLON

Mediterranean
Sea

HOLY ROMAN EMPIRE

Heidelberg

Meuse

Moselle

Rhein

Seine

Loire

Saône

Rhône

Rhône

Lorraine was occupied by French troops
between 1670 and 1697.
The Comtat Venaissin belonged to the Papacy.

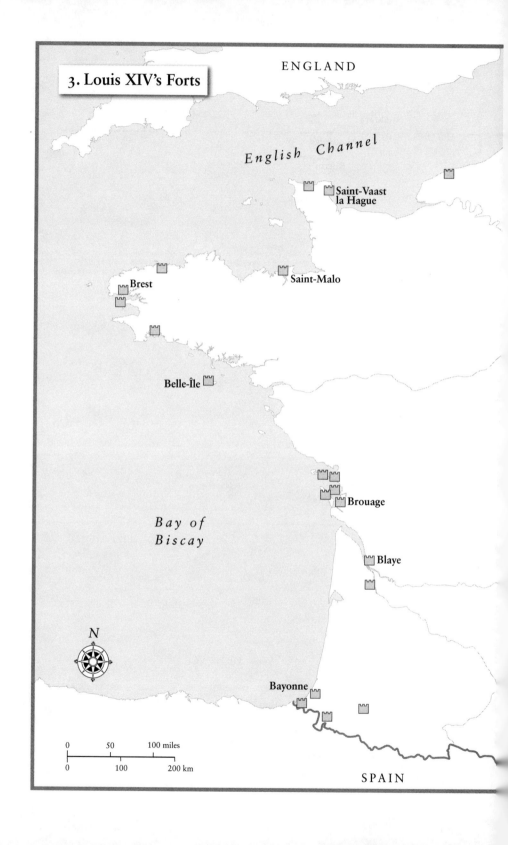

3. Louis XIV's Forts

ENGLAND

English Channel

Saint-Vaast
la Hague

Brest

Saint-Malo

Belle-Île

Brouage

Bay of
Biscay

Blaye

N

Bayonne

0   50   100 miles
0   100   200 km

SPAIN

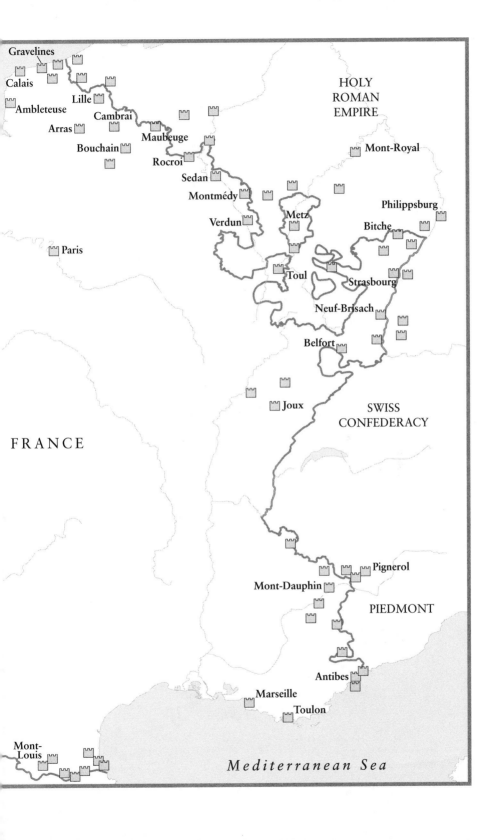

Gravelines

Calais

Ambleteuse

Lille

Cambrai

Arras

Bouchain

Maubeuge

Rocroi

Sedan

Montmédy

Verdun

Metz

Toul

HOLY
ROMAN
EMPIRE

Mont-Royal

Philippsburg

Bitche

Strasbourg

Neuf-Brisach

Belfort

Paris

Joux

FRANCE

SWISS
CONFEDERACY

Pignerol

Mont-Dauphin

PIEDMONT

Antibes

Marseille

Toulon

Mont-
Louis

Mediterranean Sea

4. The Eastern Frontier

N

North Sea

Amsterdam

Rijswick

Utrecht

Nijmegen

Ostend

Dunkirk

Ghent

Calais

Cassel

Ypres

Oudenarde
(1708)

Brussels

Maastricht

Saint-Omer

Courtrai

Ramillies
(1706)

Aachen

Lille

Tournai

Mons
(1691)

Charleroi

Meuse

FLANDERS

Valenciennes

Malplaquet
(1709)

Namur
(1692)

Arras

Hurtebise

Denain
(1712)

Maubeuge

Cambrai

Bouillon

Amiens

Luxembourg

FRANCE

Reims

Verdun

Metz

Marne

Paris

Toul

Nancy

Fontainebleau

Seine

Troyes

| 0 | 50 | 100 miles |

| 0 | 100 | 200 km |

FRANCHE-
COMTÉ

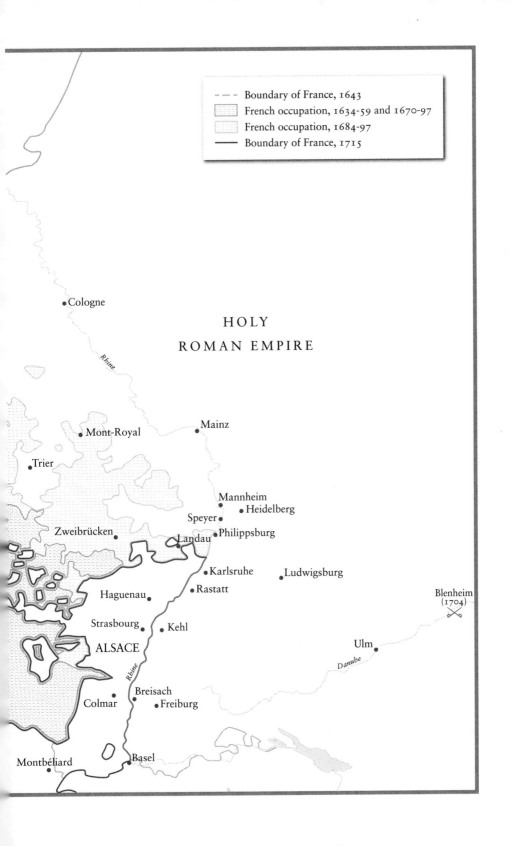

Boundary of France, 1643
French occupation, 1634-59 and 1670-97
French occupation, 1684-97
Boundary of France, 1715

HOLY
ROMAN EMPIRE

Cologne

Rhine

Mont-Royal

Mainz

Trier

Mannheim
Heidelberg
Speyer
Zweibrücken
Landau Philippsburg

Karlsruhe
Ludwigsburg
Haguenau
Rastatt

Blenheim
(1704)

Strasbourg
Kehl

ALSACE

Ulm

Rhine

Danube

Breisach
Colmar
Freiburg

Montbéliard
Basel

5. Europe after the Treaty of Utrecht

N

SCOTLAND

Edinburgh

North Sea

DENMRK - NORWAY

IRELAND

Boyne

Dublin

GREAT BRITAIN

WALES

ENGLAND

London

Amsterdam

Utrecht

HANOVER

Copenhagen

Hamburg

English Channel

Elbe

HOLY

Cologne

SAXONY

Rhine

ROMAN

PRAGUE

Seine

Paris

EMPIRE

Loire

Danube

BAVARIA

Munich

Berne

Zurich

SWISS CONFEDERATION

TYROL

FRANCE

Rhône

Milan

Venice

PIEDMONT

Genoa

Florence

Ebro

Saragossa

PAPAL STATES

PORTUGAL

Villaviciosa

CATALONIA

Corsica

Rome

Lisbon

Toledo

Barcelona

SPAIN

Almanza

Valencia

Minorca

Naples

Sardinia

Mediterranean Sea

Gibraltar

Algiers

Palermo

Sicily

Tunis

Malta

Boundary of the Holy Roman Empire
House of Habsburg
House of Bourbon

0   100   200   300   400 miles
0   200   400   600 km

SWEDEN

Stockholm

St Petersburg

LIVONIA

Riga

RUSSIAN   EMPIRE

Baltic Sea

Königsberg
Danzig
PRUSSIA

BRANDEN-
BURG

LITHUANIA

Warsaw
POLAND

Dresden

Krakow

BOHEMIA

Kosice

Vienna
AUSTRIA

Buda

HUNGARY   TRANSYLVANIA

Belgrade

Danube

Black Sea

OTTOMAN

Constantinople

NAPLES   Salonica

EMPIRE

Athens

Aleppo

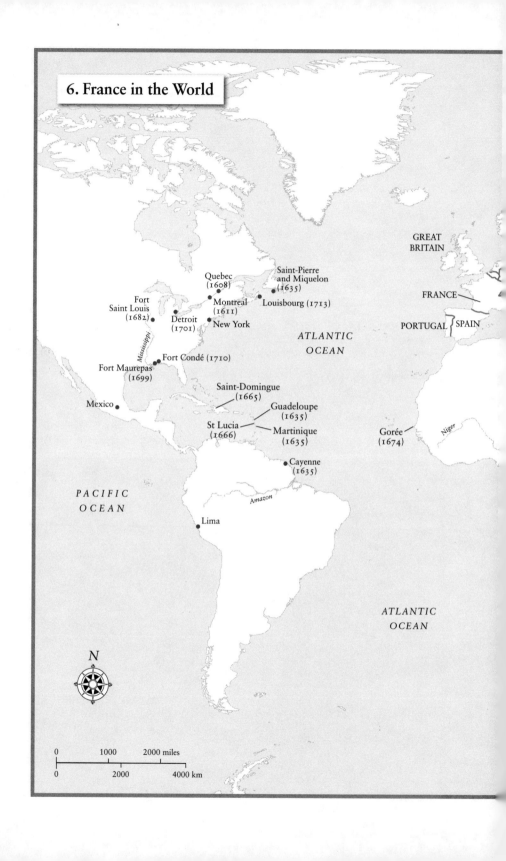

6. France in the World

GREAT BRITAIN

FRANCE

PORTUGAL   SPAIN

Quebec (1608)

Saint-Pierre and Miquelon (1635)

Louisbourg (1713)

Fort Saint Louis (1682)

Montreal (1611)

Detroit (1701)

New York

Mississippi

Fort Condé (1710)

ATLANTIC OCEAN

Fort Maurepas (1699)

Mexico

Saint-Domingue (1665)

Guadeloupe (1635)

St Lucia (1666)

Martinique (1635)

Gorée (1674)

Niger

Cayenne (1635)

PACIFIC OCEAN

Amazon

Lima

ATLANTIC OCEAN

N

0   1000   2000 miles
0   2000   4000 km

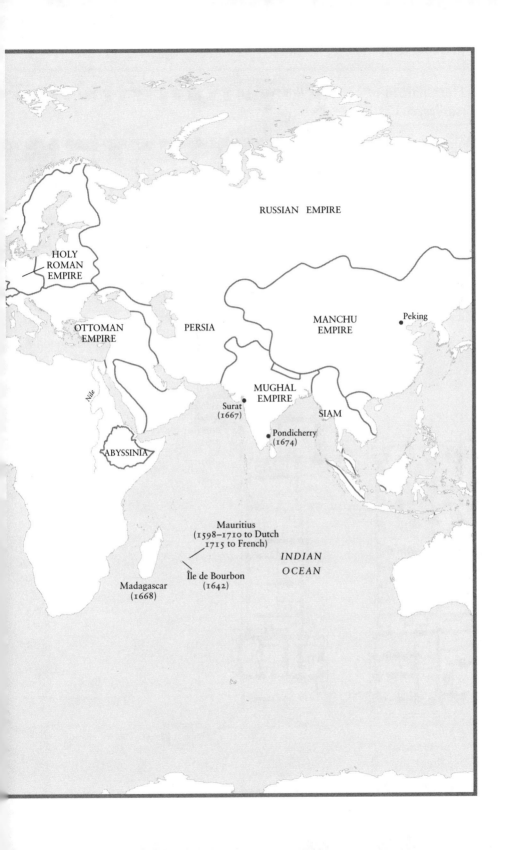

RUSSIAN EMPIRE

HOLY
ROMAN
EMPIRE

OTTOMAN
EMPIRE

PERSIA

MANCHU
EMPIRE

Peking

Nile

ABYSSINIA

MUGHAL
EMPIRE

Surat
(1667)

Pondicherry
(1674)

SIAM

Mauritius
(1598–1710 to Dutch
1715 to French)

INDIAN

OCEAN

Île de Bourbon
(1642)

Madagascar
(1668)

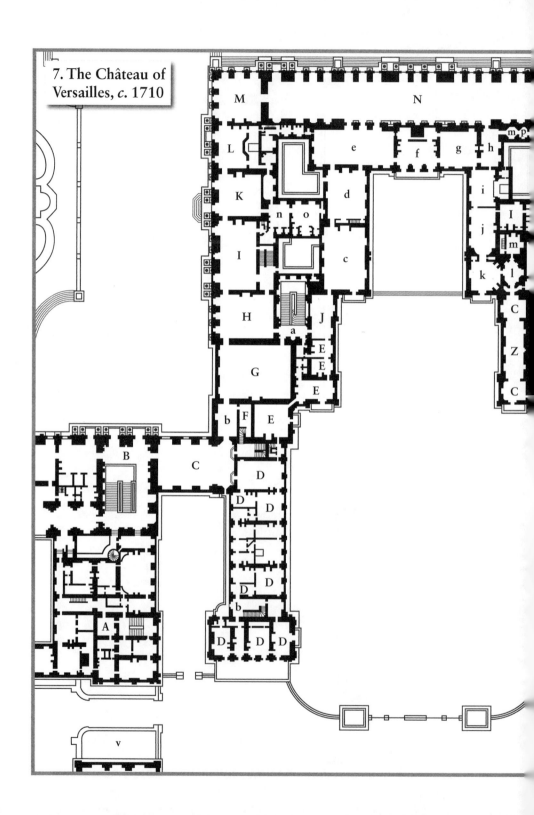

7. The Château of Versailles, *c.* 1710

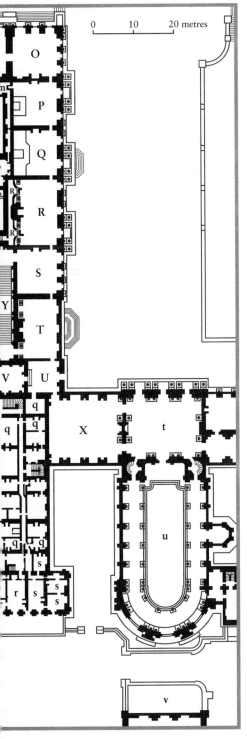

A. Pavillon d'Orléans
B. Staircase of the Princes
C. Salons
D. Apartments of the Children of France
E. Apartment of Madame de Maintenon
F. Staircase
G. Grand Hall of the Guards
H. Hall of the Queen's Guards
I. Antechamber of the Queen
J. Vestibule of the Marble Staircase
K. Grand Cabinet of the Queen
L. Bedchamber of the Queen
M. Salon of Peace
N. Grand Gallery
O. Salon of War
P. Salon of Apollo
Q. Salon of Mercury
R. Salon of Mars
R1. Tribunes for Musicians
S. Salon of Diana
T. Salon of Venus
U. Salon of Abundance
V. Cabinet of Medals
X. Salon of Hercules
Y. Ambassadors' Staircase
Z. Little Gallery
a. Marble Staircase
b. Passage
c. Hall of the King's Guards
d. Antechamber of the King
e. Grand Antechamber of the King, or Œil-de-Bœuf
f. Bedchamber of Louis XIV
g. Cabinet of Louis XIV
h. Cabinet of Wigs
i. Cabinet of Dogs
j. Cabinet of Agates
k. Cabinet of Jewels
l. Oval Salon
m. Cabinet
n. Bathroom
o. Chamber of Baths
p. Closet
q. Apartment of the Governor of the Château
r. Bureau of the Domain of Versailles
s. Apartment of the King's Confessor
t. Vestibule of the Chapel
u. Chapel
v. Wings of the Ministers

1. The Houses of France and Savoy

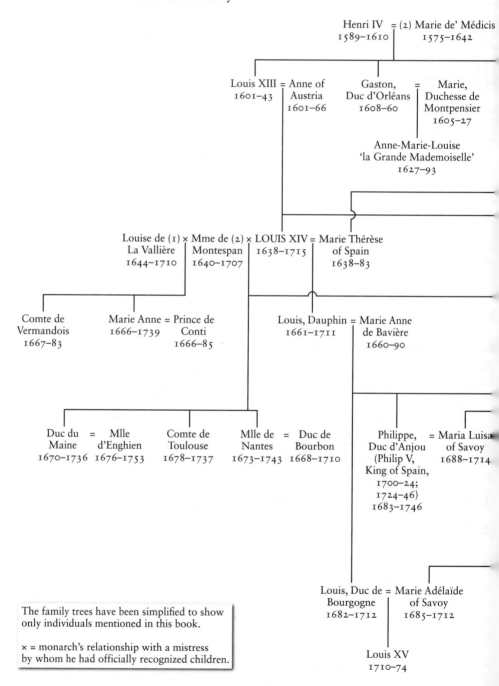

Henri IV = (2) Marie de' Médicis
1589–1610   1575–1642

Louis XIII = Anne of   Gaston, = Marie,
1601–43   Austria   Duc d'Orléans   Duchesse de
           1601–66   1608–60   Montpensier
                                         1605–27

Anne-Marie-Louise
'la Grande Mademoiselle'
1627–93

Louise de (1) x Mme de (2) x LOUIS XIV = Marie Thérèse
La Vallière   Montespan   1638–1715   of Spain
1644–1710   1640–1707   1638–83

Comte de   Marie Anne = Prince de   Louis, Dauphin = Marie Anne
Vermandois   1666–1739   Conti   1661–1711   de Bavière
1667–83   1666–85   1660–90

Duc du   = Mlle   Comte de   Mlle de = Duc de   Philippe,   = Maria Luisa
Maine   d'Enghien Toulouse   Nantes   Bourbon   Duc d'Anjou   of Savoy
1670–1736 1676–1753   1678–1737   1673–1743 1668–1710   (Philip V,   1688–1714
                                                              King of Spain,
                                                              1700–24;
                                                              1724–46)
                                                              1683–1746

Louis, Duc de = Marie Adélaïde
Bourgogne   of Savoy
1682–1712   1685–1712

Louis XV
1710–74

The family trees have been simplified to show
only individuals mentioned in this book.

x = monarch's relationship with a mistress
by whom he had officially recognized children.

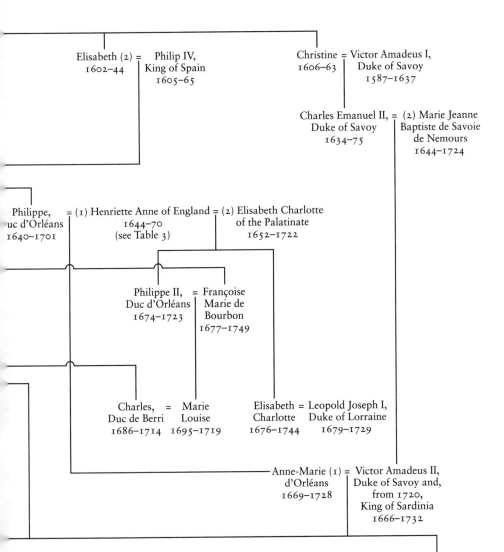

Elisabeth (2) = Philip IV,
1602–44 | King of Spain
1605–65

Christine = Victor Amadeus I,
1606–63 | Duke of Savoy
1587–1637

Charles Emanuel II, = (2) Marie Jeanne
Duke of Savoy | Baptiste de Savoie
1634–75 | de Nemours
1644–1724

Philippe, = (1) Henriette Anne of England = (2) Elisabeth Charlotte
uc d'Orléans | 1644–70 | of the Palatinate
1640–1701 | (see Table 3) | 1652–1722

Philippe II, = Françoise
Duc d'Orléans | Marie de
1674–1723 | Bourbon
1677–1749

Charles, = Marie
Duc de Berri | Louise
1686–1714 | 1695–1719

Elisabeth = Leopold Joseph I,
Charlotte | Duke of Lorraine
1676–1744 | 1679–1729

Anne-Marie (1) = Victor Amadeus II,
d'Orléans | Duke of Savoy and,
1669–1728 | from 1720,
King of Sardinia
1666–1732

Charles Emanuel III,
Duke of Savoy
and King of Sardinia
1701–73

2. Bourbon Cousins: The Houses of Vendôme, Condé and Soissons

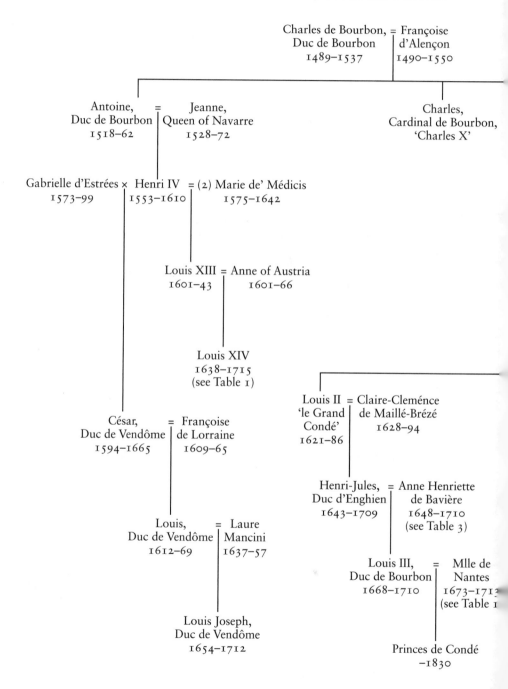

Charles de Bourbon, = Françoise
Duc de Bourbon | d'Alençon
1489–1537 | 1490–1550

Antoine, = Jeanne,
Duc de Bourbon | Queen of Navarre
1518–62 | 1528–72

Charles,
Cardinal de Bourbon,
'Charles X'

Gabrielle d'Estrées × Henri IV = (2) Marie de' Médicis
1573–99 | 1553–1610 | 1575–1642

Louis XIII = Anne of Austria
1601–43 | 1601–66

Louis XIV
1638–1715
(see Table 1)

Louis II = Claire-Cleménce
'le Grand | de Maillé-Brézé
Condé' | 1628–94
1621–86

César, = Françoise
Duc de Vendôme | de Lorraine
1594–1665 | 1609–65

Henri-Jules, = Anne Henriette
Duc d'Enghien | de Bavière
1643–1709 | 1648–1710
(see Table 3)

Louis, = Laure
Duc de Vendôme | Mancini
1612–69 | 1637–57

Louis III, = Mlle de
Duc de Bourbon | Nantes
1668–1710 | 1673–171?
(see Table 1

Louis Joseph,
Duc de Vendôme
1654–1712

Princes de Condé
–1830

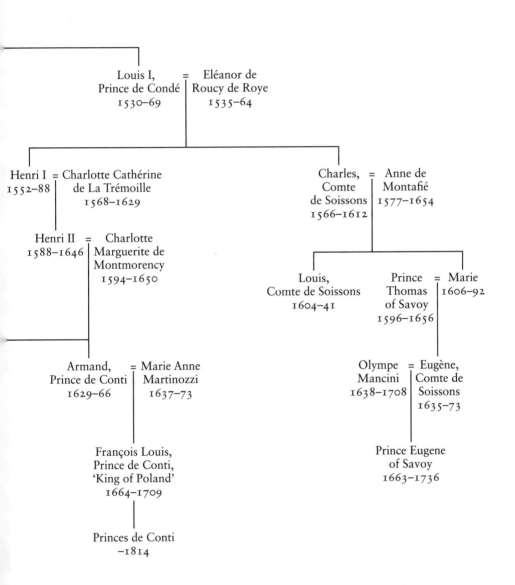

Louis I,
Prince de Condé
1530–69
= Eléanor de
Roucy de Roye
1535–64

Henri I
1552–88
= Charlotte Cathérine
de La Trémoille
1568–1629

Charles,
Comte
de Soissons
1566–1612
= Anne de
Montafié
1577–1654

Henri II
1588–1646
= Charlotte
Marguerite de
Montmorency
1594–1650

Louis,
Comte de Soissons
1604–41

Prince
Thomas
of Savoy
1596–1656
= Marie
1606–92

Armand,
Prince de Conti
1629–66
= Marie Anne
Martinozzi
1637–73

Olympe
Mancini
1638–1708
= Eugène,
Comte de
Soissons
1635–73

François Louis,
Prince de Conti,
'King of Poland'
1664–1709

Prince Eugene
of Savoy
1663–1736

Princes de Conti
–1814

3. The English Succession

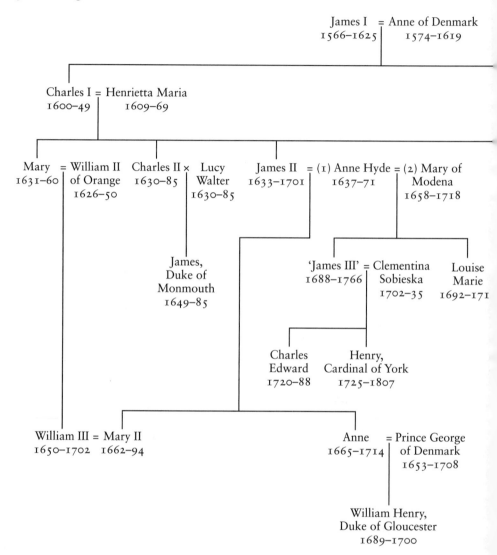

James I = Anne of Denmark
1566–1625   1574–1619

Charles I = Henrietta Maria
1600–49   1609–69

Mary = William II   Charles II × Lucy   James II = (1) Anne Hyde = (2) Mary of
1631–60 | of Orange   1630–85   Walter   1633–1701   1637–71   Modena
1626–50   1630–85   1658–1718

James,
Duke of
Monmouth
1649–85

'James III' = Clementina   Louise
1688–1766   Sobieska   Marie
1702–35   1692–171

Charles   Henry,
Edward   Cardinal of York
1720–88   1725–1807

William III = Mary II   Anne = Prince George
1650–1702   1662–94   1665–1714 | of Denmark
1653–1708

William Henry,
Duke of Gloucester
1689–1700

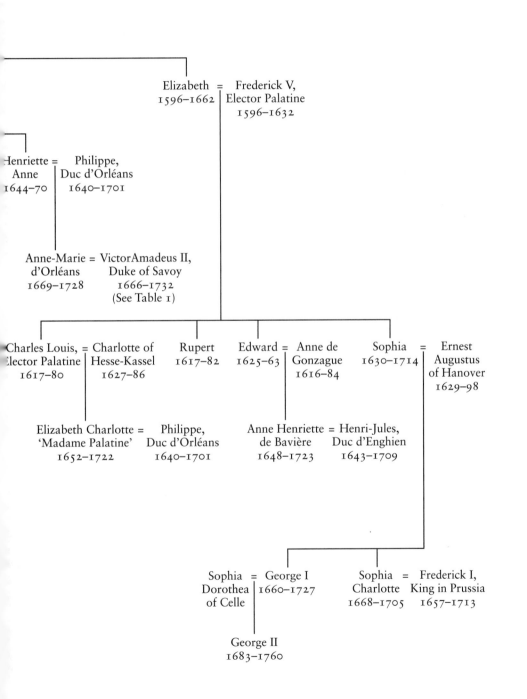

Elizabeth = Frederick V,
1596–1662 | Elector Palatine
1596–1632

Henriette = Philippe,
Anne | Duc d'Orléans
1644–70 | 1640–1701

Anne-Marie = VictorAmadeus II,
d'Orléans | Duke of Savoy
1669–1728 | 1666–1732
(See Table 1)

Charles Louis, = Charlotte of
Elector Palatine | Hesse-Kassel
1617–80 | 1627–86

Rupert
1617–82

Edward = Anne de
1625–63 | Gonzague
1616–84

Sophia = Ernest
1630–1714 | Augustus
of Hanover
1629–98

Elizabeth Charlotte = Philippe,
'Madame Palatine' | Duc d'Orléans
1652–1722 | 1640–1701

Anne Henriette = Henri-Jules,
de Bavière | Duc d'Enghien
1648–1723 | 1643–1709

Sophia = George I
Dorothea | 1660–1727
of Celle

Sophia = Frederick I,
Charlotte | King in Prussia
1668–1705 | 1657–1713

George II
1683–1760

4. The Spanish Succession

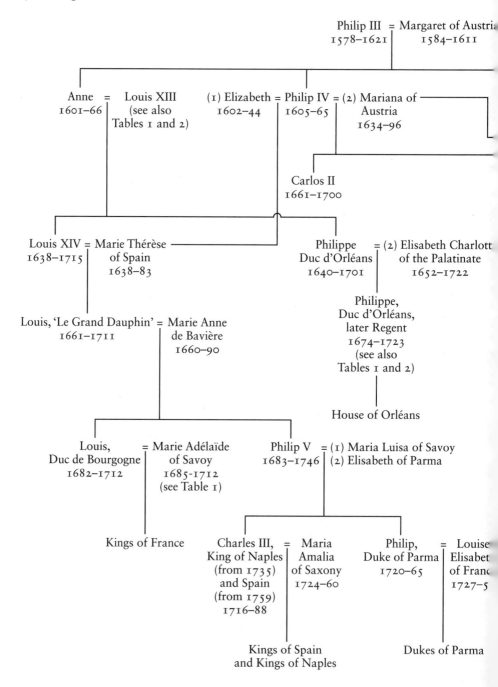

Philip III = Margaret of Austria
1578–1621   1584–1611

Anne = Louis XIII   (1) Elizabeth = Philip IV = (2) Mariana of
1601–66   (see also   1602–44   1605–65   Austria
        Tables 1 and 2)   1634–96

Carlos II
1661–1700

Louis XIV = Marie Thérèse   Philippe = (2) Elisabeth Charlotte
1638–1715   of Spain   Duc d'Orléans   of the Palatinate
             1638–83   1640–1701   1652–1722

                                          Philippe,
                                          Duc d'Orléans,
Louis, 'Le Grand Dauphin' = Marie Anne   later Regent
       1661–1711   de Bavière   1674–1723
                          1660–90   (see also
                                          Tables 1 and 2)

                                          House of Orléans

Louis,   = Marie Adélaïde   Philip V = (1) Maria Luisa of Savoy
Duc de Bourgogne   of Savoy   1683–1746   (2) Elisabeth of Parma
1682–1712   1685-1712
                   (see Table 1)

Kings of France   Charles III,   = Maria   Philip,   = Louise
                   King of Naples   Amalia   Duke of Parma Elisabeth
                   (from 1735)   of Saxony 1720–65   of France
                   and Spain   1724–60   1727–5
                   (from 1759)
                   1716–88

                   Kings of Spain   Dukes of Parma
                   and Kings of Naples

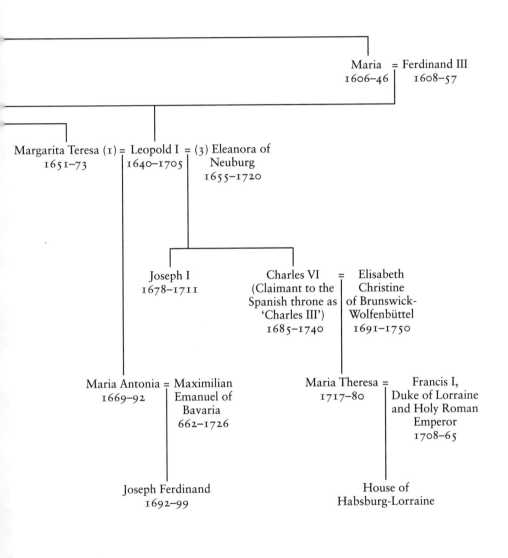

Maria = Ferdinand III
1606–46 | 1608–57

Margarita Teresa (1) = Leopold I = (3) Eleanora of
1651–73 | 1640–1705 | Neuburg
| | 1655–1720

Joseph I
1678–1711

Charles VI = Elisabeth
(Claimant to the | Christine
Spanish throne as | of Brunswick-
'Charles III') | Wolfenbüttel
1685–1740 | 1691–1750

Maria Antonia = Maximilian
1669–92 | Emanuel of
| Bavaria
| 662–1726

Maria Theresa = Francis I,
1717–80 | Duke of Lorraine
| and Holy Roman
| Emperor
| 1708–65

Joseph Ferdinand
1692–99

House of
Habsburg-Lorraine

5. The Colbert Family, with offices and dates held

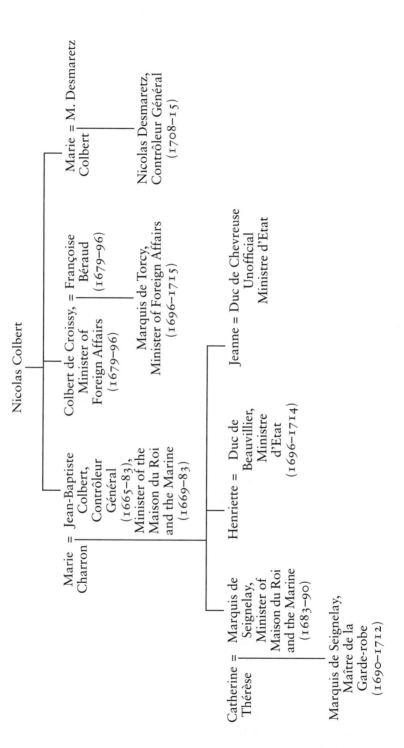

Introduction: A Thousand Years of France

Louis XIV was both King of France and a global ruler with global ambitions. He founded colonies in America, Africa and India, tried to seize Siam (as Thailand was then known), sent missionaries and mathematicians to the Emperor of China and launched the struggle for France's global markets which continues to this day. The motto he adopted early in his reign, in 1662, expressed his hopes and desires: 'Nec pluribus impar' (literally 'Not unequal to more'), meaning 'not incapable of ruling other dominions', as well as 'not unequal to many enemies'.

Louis was a man in pursuit of glory, a king devoted to dynastic aggrandizement and a leader bent on national expansion. He is also an argument. How could such a civilized man, exceptionally considerate to women (he built the best girls' school of the age, near Versailles at Saint-Cyr), order acts of barbarism against French Protestants and France's neighbours? Was Louis le Grand, as he was called from 1680, master or instrument of his court, his ministers and his financiers? Did he leave France stronger or weaker? He dominated his age and, since he chose the sun as his symbol, later became known as *le roi soleil* – the Sun King. Did he deserve the name?

The present biography has benefited from a surge of new books on his palaces,[1] household,[2] finances,[3] diplomacy,[4] ministers,[5] armies,[6] fortresses,[7] enemies,[8] Catholic faith[9] and health,[10] from the recently published complete correspondence of his second wife, Madame de Maintenon,[11] and from an account of his itinerary throughout his life,[12] as well as from the many books published in 2015 to mark the 300th anniversary of his death.[13]

Thanks to these and numerous other works, as well as my own researches in archives in Paris and London, this biography can take Louis out of Versailles (his main residence for less than half his reign, and never the only one) and show the view from Lille, Besançon and Strasbourg, as well as from London, Madrid, Constantinople and Bangkok. Multiple perspectives are needed for, in addition to working for the expansion of

France on the Rhine, the Mississippi and the Mekong, Louis pursued goals outside France. They included the restoration of his Stuart cousins to the thrones of England, Scotland and Ireland; the election of a French prince as king of Poland and grand duke of Lithuania; and the preservation as great powers of France's allies the Ottoman Empire and Sweden. Louis' greatest single mistake, the Revocation in 1685 of the Edict of Nantes which had permitted Protestant worship in France, was triggered not only by internal French forces, and his own Catholic zeal, but also by his rivalry with the House of Austria for the leadership of Catholic Europe.

Similarly, Louis' most famous single building, Versailles, was created not only for France but for the world: to attract and impress foreign visitors, and to surpass all other palaces, past and present. It was a bid for global fame, as well as his personal combination of royal residence, government and military headquarters, art gallery, music and ballet festival, and show-place for French products.

The end of Louis' reign would be dominated by pursuit of another global ambition, the Spanish succession. After his marriage in 1660 to the Infanta María Teresa, elder daughter of Philip IV of Spain, he hoped that one of their descendants, rather than one of the King's cousins in Vienna, would inherit the entire Spanish monarchy, including its global Empire stretching from Mexico to Sicily. Unlike in France, the Spanish monarchy could pass through the female line, and his brother-in-law Carlos II, King of Spain from 1665, was a childless invalid.

When Carlos died in 1700, Louis accepted his decision to leave the Spanish monarchy to Louis' second grandson, instead of observing international treaties which proposed to divide the monarchy and give France more territory. Philippe, Duc d'Anjou became El Rey Don Felipe V. Louis had put Spain before France, his family before his country. Fighting to keep Philip on the throne of Spain against a European coalition, he brought France close to collapse. Nevertheless, the present King of Spain, Philip VI, is a descendant of Louis XIV.

Louis XIV was able to play a global role because of the power of the kingdom of France. His reign and personality were conditioned by the geography, history, demography and traditions of the country he ruled. When he inherited the throne in 1643, the French monarchy was over a thousand years old. Between 481 and 511 Clovis, King of the Franks, one of the barbarian tribes which had invaded the Roman Empire, ruled what is now northern France and part of northern Germany. Around 497 Clovis converted to Christianity, and was baptized in Reims, north-east of Paris in the Frankish heartland.

In 751 Childeric III, the last of Clovis's Merovingian dynasty, had been confined to a monastery by his Mayor of the Palace, Pepin, who became the first king of the Carolingian dynasty. From 768 to 814 one of the great rulers in European history, Pepin's son Charlemagne, extended the Frankish kingdom into an empire stretching from the Elbe to the Ebro, and from the Baltic to the Mediterranean. He was crowned emperor by the Pope in Rome in 800.

The Treaty of Verdun in 843 divided Charlemagne's Empire between his three grandsons. King Charles the Bald ruled the west, called Francia after the Franks, although most of the population was of Celtic or Gallo-Roman stock. The middle land, stretching from the North Sea to Italy, was called Lotharingia after its ruler, the eldest grandson the Emperor Lothar, who reigned from Charlemagne's old capital Aachen in the Frankish heartland, near the Rhine. The east was ruled from Regensburg by King Louis the German. Absorbing most of Lotharingia after its disintegration in the tenth century, by 962 the rulers of the eastern kingdom had become emperors. Their territory had begun its evolution into the collection of around 300 semi-independent principalities, bishoprics, cities and counties known, in Louis XIV's reign, as the Holy Roman Empire of the German Nation.

After the death of the last Carolingian king of Francia or France, one of his relations, a prominent noble called Hugues Capet, was elected king by other great nobles in 987. His own domains included only the region around Paris, known as the Île de France, stretching from Compiègne north of Paris to Orléans to the south. Other regions of France formed autonomous fiefdoms under rival dynasties, supported by local interests and loyalties. Their allegiance to the king of France was little more than nominal.

Slowly, however, the kings of France extended their control. One of their principal advantages was the prestige of coronation at Reims. The ceremony was partly based on that of the kings of Israel, as described in the first book of Samuel in the Old Testament. Like them, the king of France was not only crowned but anointed with holy oil. A dove was believed to have descended from heaven to Reims bearing a container or 'holy ampulla' full of oil. The king of France was considered a sacred figure, with the power to heal, by his royal touch, men and women suffering from scrofula.

Other weapons were the growth of their capital Paris into the largest city north of the Alps, able to supply an army and administration; a growing sense of national identity and pride in France, and in being and speaking French (a literary language before Italian, English or German);

and the exceptional fecundity of Hugues Capet's descendants, the House of France. Rival dynasties died out. The many branches of the House of France multiplied.

After the conquest of England by the Duke of Normandy in 1066, the kings of England became the principal rivals of the kings of France. In the second half of the twelfth century Henry II of England and his sons also ruled the duchies of Guienne in the south-west and Poitou, Anjou and Normandy in the west of France. The Louvre began as a fort built in 1190–1202, at the same time as the city wall, by King Philippe Auguste, to protect Paris from English attacks. By 1204, however, as a result of English dissensions as well as his own strength, Philippe Auguste had conquered all the French possessions of the King of England, except the area around Bordeaux.

The French monarchy further increased in power and prestige in 1226–70, during the reign of King Louis IX, who would later become its revered patron saint, St Louis. After the 'Albigensian Crusade' in 1209–29 against the heretical Cathars, Toulouse and Languedoc were annexed to the royal domain. The population of the kingdom of France reached 17 million in 1300, more than any other country in Europe.

The power and attraction of France were shown by the submission of the Archbishop and city of Lyon to French rule in 1312, although Lyon had been part of the Holy Roman Empire. In 1349 Humbert II, the last ruler of Dauphiné, sold his province, also part of the Holy Roman Empire on the east bank of the Rhône, to the French crown. Henceforth, as he had stipulated, the eldest son of the king was called the Dauphin, the traditional first name of rulers of the province.

The kings of England remained half French in culture and ambitions. The Salic Law restricting the French crown to men descended from previous kings in the male line was invented in 1337–40 in a vain attempt to stop Edward III of England claiming the throne of France, through his mother Isabella, daughter and sister of kings of France.

By the 1360s the ambition of Edward III of England to rule France had been thwarted: he was left with the south-west corner around Bordeaux, and Calais. The Louvre expanded into a fortified palace under the cultivated King Charles V, who reigned from 1364 to 1380, and also built another fortified palace at Vincennes east of Paris. In 1420, after a string of victories, another king of England, Henry V, tried to create a composite Anglo-French monarchy. He was declared heir to the mad King Charles VI of France, but died in 1422, the same year as Charles himself. For a time his son Henry VI ruled northern France, as well as England. In 1429, however, an illiterate peasant called Jeanne d'Arc took Charles VI's son

Charles VII from his power-base south of the Loire, defeated English forces besieging Orléans and led him to be crowned king in Reims. The French monarchy was proving stronger than its foes.

The recapture of Bordeaux by Charles VII in 1453 signalled the end of the first Hundred Years War between the kings of France and England (the second would begin under Louis XIV). Tudor monarchs, however, still hoped to conquer slices of France. The kings of England continued to use the title king of France, and to quarter the fleurs-de-lys of the kings of France in their coat of arms, until the Treaty of Amiens between George III and the French Republic in 1802.

To the north lay another rival of the French monarchy: the Duchy of Burgundy. Until the reign of Louis XIV, the kings of France followed contradictory dynastic strategies, simultaneously expanding their domain and diminishing it, by assigning provinces known as appanages to younger sons, in order to support them and enhance their status. Monarchy remained a family business. In 1369 Philip the Bold, youngest brother of Charles V, who had been created duke of Burgundy, married Margaret of Burgundy, heiress of the provinces of Flanders, Brabant, Artois and the Franche-Comté in the Holy Roman Empire. Further advantageous marriages by his descendants led to the creation of a wealthy composite monarchy, a revived Lotharingia called 'Burgundy'. It soon ruled most of the coveted 'middle land' between France and the Holy Roman Empire, a tangle of small states without clear political, linguistic or geographical frontiers, stretching from the North Sea through the fertile provinces of the Southern Netherlands and the wooded hills of the Ardennes to Lorraine, Alsace and the confederation of cantons beginning to be known as Switzerland.

Philip's great-grandson Charles the Bold, Duke of Burgundy (who had hoped to unite his dominions into a single Kingdom of Burgundy), died in January 1477, his corpse devoured by wolves after his defeat outside Nancy, capital of the Duchy of Lorraine, which he had hoped to conquer. The Duchy of Burgundy, encouraged by its local assembly or Estates, returned to French rule. Flanders, however, and the neighbouring provinces, as well as the Franche-Comté, remained united under the Duke's daughter Mary. She married the Holy Roman Emperor Maximilian I, head of the House of Austria. The rivalry between their descendants and the kings of France would dominate Louis XIV's reign and last until the French Revolution and beyond.

Meanwhile the kingdom of France continued to absorb outlying provinces. In 1481, after the death of the last Count of Provence, Provence and Marseille, formerly owing allegiance to the Empire, acknowledged the

suzerainty of the King of France, while retaining much of their adminis-
trative autonomy; until 1789 French laws would be promulgated in
Provence in the name not of the King of France but of the 'King of France,
Comte de Provence'.

The Duchy of Brittany had been semi-independent since the ninth century, with its own language, laws, parliament (known as Estates since it
contained representatives of the three estates – church, nobility and Third
Estate) and dynasty. In 1491 the heiress to Brittany, Duchess Anne,
although dedicated to Breton independence, was obliged to marry Charles
VIII, King of France, who had invaded her duchy. After his death, she
married his cousin and successor Louis XII. In 1532 under François I,
son-in-law of Anne of Brittany, the personal union between the Duchy and
the kingdom was replaced by a perpetual administrative union, although
the Duchy, like Provence, was allowed to retain many independent institutions. In 1527 after the rebellion of the Constable de Bourbon, a descendant
of the fifth son of St Louis, his duchy of the Bourbonnais was also united
to the crown domain. As a further unifying gesture, François I by the Edict
of Villers-Cotterêts of 1539 decreed that official documents such as parish
registers should be henceforth kept in French, rather than Latin or other
languages like *langue d'oc*, the language of the south.

By the Treaty of Cateau-Cambrésis signed with the King of Spain in
1559, François I's son Henri II abandoned his claims to the Duchy of
Milan and the kingdom of Naples, for which kings of France had been
fighting since 1494. However, he won control of three cities between Lorraine and Alsace – Metz, Toul and Verdun. He thereby reasserted the
French monarchy's desire for expansion eastwards into the middle land,
a region which Louis XIV would get to know extremely well, as it would
be the scene of most of his wars.

After the dynasty, the court was another unifying institution, as central
to France's development as Parliament to England or the army to Prussia.
In addition to the King and Queen, other members of the royal family had
households of their own, drawn from most classes and regions. The court
was not only a constellation of households and departments but also a
dynamic force, strengthening and celebrating royal power and driving
cultural and religious change. More than any other court, perhaps because
of a long succession of forceful queens consort and queens regent since
Isabeau de Bavière, wife of the mad King Charles VI in the early fifteenth
century, the French court was also a female power-base. *The Book of the
City of Ladies*, one of the first defences of women's rights, and one of the
first French books by a woman, was written around 1400 by one of Isabeau de Bavière's servants, Christine de Pisan. The first Protestants in

France were encouraged by François I's sister Marguerite, Queen of Navarre (another woman writer), and his mistress the Duchesse d'Etampes.[14]

At least since the marriage of Charles VIII to Anne, Duchess of Brittany, the Queen's household and apartments had been almost as large and magnificent as the King's. It was Queen Anne, wrote the French chronicler Pierre de Brantôme, author of *Vies des dames galantes*, who introduced 'la grande cour des dames' and asked for noblewomen to enter her household in order to educate them and increase her own importance. A court without women, he wrote, was like a garden without flowers.[15]

Anne of Brittany's son-in-law François I, who reigned from 1515 to 1547, spent much of the year away from Paris, surrounded by women in his favourite hunting palaces of Fontainebleau, in a forest south-east of Paris, and Chambord, in a forest near the Loire. The former was an ancient royal castle which he expanded and had redecorated by Italian artists like Primaticcio and Cellini. The latter was a vast new palace and hunting lodge of 440 rooms which he built in 1519–47, possibly from designs by Leonardo da Vinci.[16]

Long before Louis XIV's creation of Versailles, François I made the French court a synonym for splendour. In 1544 the Mantuan Ambassador wrote: 'If you have not seen the court of France, you have not seen what grandeur is.'[17] This grandeur came not only from the number of courtiers (perhaps 10,000 in all) and the size of the palaces, but also from the luxury of the objects inside: pictures, jewels, furniture, tapestries. The court was always on the move, particularly between the many royal residences in the Île de France and the valley of the Loire, in search of safety, revenue, food and hunting.[18] Sometimes, it needed 12,000 horses to transport it. One shocked Italian bishop wrote to Cosimo de' Medici: 'this court is like no other ... here one thinks of nothing but hunting, women, banquets and moving house.'[19] Louis XIV's grandfather Henri IV would later boast that he had never slept in the same place two nights running.[20]

Both when the King was a minor and after he reached maturity, his mother publicly exercised or shared his authority. François I's daughter-in-law Catherine de Médicis, widow of his son Henri II, served as regent or a member of the council in 1560–88 during the reigns of her sons Charles IX and Henri III. So did Marie de Médicis, widow of Henri IV, in 1610–17 and 1620–30 during the reign of her son Louis XIII, and Anne of Austria in 1643–61 during the early reign of her son Louis XIV. Anne had the largest household of any queen of France (701 members in 1646), larger at times than her son's.[21] Under Louis XIV women would enjoy greater power than at any time before the Fifth Republic.

*

The most important section of the king's household, far larger than in other royal courts, was his guard. The Gardes du Corps, companies of mounted gentlemen, had been founded in 1419, when half of France was occupied by English troops. So little trusted were the French by the future Charles VII that he raised a company of Scots archers 'ordonnez à la garde du corps du roy': Scotland was a trusted ally in the wars against England.[22] Three more companies of French Gardes du Corps had been added by 1514, as well as a company of Swiss guards.[23] King Ferdinand of Aragon said: 'no one in all Christendom had such a guard, nor one which was so well ordered.'[24]

Throughout his reign Louis XIV would devote particular attention to his guard. His court was distinguished by 'the incessant aspect of force', wrote the Venetian Ambassador in 1684: 'never was a sovereign guarded with more diligent vigilance,' both inside and outside Versailles, and along its corridors and staircases.[25] The Captain of the Gardes du Corps on duty was always beside him, responsible for his security, and for granting permission to individuals who wished to speak to him.[26] Gardes du Corps would surround Louis at his coronation in Reims on 7 June 1654, and escort his coffin in the funeral procession from Versailles to Saint-Denis on 9 September 1715.[27]

For the king of France, and Louis XIV in particular, was a military leader as well as a sacred monarch. When he was crowned, he was given 'the Sword of Charlemagne' and golden spurs as well as the crown, orb, sceptre and hand of justice. One proverb said: 'Qui retire l'épée, perd le sceptre': 'Who sheathes the sword, loses the sceptre.'

The 'wars of religion' which devastated France after 1560 confirmed that royal power was based on force as well as religion. Great nobles like the La Trémoille and La Rochefoucauld families, and the King's Bourbon cousins the King of Navarre and the Prince de Condé, turned Protestant, as did an arc of cities stretching from La Rochelle on the Atlantic coast down to Nîmes and up to the Protestant stronghold of Geneva. Protestant forces under Condé tried to 'surprise' or kidnap the court at Meaux on 28 September 1567. It was saved only by the speed of its horses and carriages as it fled to Paris at two in the morning, and by the loyalty of Swiss mercenaries.[28] In reaction to growing insecurity, the Gardes Françaises, a regiment of 1,000 foot soldiers, had been formed to help guard François I's grandson Charles IX in 1563. On 24 August 1572, as hatred rose between Catholics and Protestants assembled in Paris to celebrate the future Henri IV's marriage to Marguerite de Valois, sister of Charles IX, the regiment led the St Bartholomew's Eve Massacre of Protestants in the streets of Paris and the courtyards of the Louvre.[29]

In 1576 the Duc de Guise, Grand Maître de France or head of the King's household, and a cousin of the Duke of Lorraine, had formed the Catholic League. He claimed descent from Charlemagne and, with the financial support of Philip II of Spain, had designs on the throne of Charles IX's brother and successor Henri III. On 12 May 1588 barricades made of barrels and paving stones were erected in the streets leading up to the Louvre itself by Parisians infatuated with the Duc de Guise. Royal troops lost control of the capital. As Henri III fled to Chartres on 13 May, he cursed Paris, which he had once loved more than his wife, and said he would return only through a breach in the walls.[30]

Through the *taille*, or land tax on non-nobles, and the *gabelle*, or salt tax, the French monarchy had greater permanent annual revenues than other monarchs. Since the fourteenth century, the States General, a national parliament assembling deputies of the clergy, the nobility and the third estate, had been occasionally summoned when the crown needed more money. The size of France limited this institution's usefulness, unlike the many local assemblies in provinces like Brittany and Provence. Thanks to the Salic Law, France lacked the disputed successions needing validation by a national institution which in England in the fifteenth and sixteenth centuries increased the importance of Parliament.

Now, in desperation at his loss of power, Henri III summoned the States General to the royal chateau of Blois on the Loire. They too, however, favoured the League and the Duc de Guise. More aggressive than the English Parliament, they demanded control of appointments to the King's court and his council – in other words, a share of executive power. They also imposed Catholicism as a condition of succession to the throne.[31] The King decided to eliminate Guise.

The King used not his Gardes du Corps, since they had been infiltrated by the League, but another force he had created in 1584 'for his most reliable and faithful guard'. Mainly bachelor nobles from the south-west, *les quarante-cinq* or *les gentilshommes ordinaires du roi*, as they were called, were directly under the King's authority (since Guise and his brother the Duc de Mayenne controlled much of the royal household through their offices of *grand maître* and *grand chambellan*), and guarded him day and night.[32] On the morning of 23 December Guise – ignoring warnings with the boast 'whom God guards is well guarded' – was summoned from the council chamber, where he could impose his wishes on the King, through the King's bedroom to the Cabinet Vieux. There the *quarante-cinq* overpowered and killed the Duke.[33]

As he contemplated his enemy's corpse, Henri III is said to have remarked, 'My God, how tall he is! He is even taller dead than alive.'[34]

Most of France rose in rebellion. The King's execution of Guise's brother the Cardinal de Guise, who had crowned and anointed him at Reims in 1575, was considered especially shocking. The university of Paris, the Sorbonne, deposed 'ce misérable bougre de roi', as 'the former king' was known, and released his subjects from their oath of allegiance. His name was deleted from public prayers.[35] Members of the League wrote that 'the people make kings, not kings the people.'[36] Henri III retained control only of the royal heartland of the Loire, Bordeaux and the Dauphiné. Tours became the de facto capital of France, as Bourges had been in the previous century when the King of England had ruled northern France.[37]

On 1 August 1589 Henri III was stabbed to death in a revenge assassination by a Dominican friar called Jacques Clément, at Saint-Cloud outside Paris, which he was besieging. The King had received him in private, on the commode, because the friar claimed to have secret information for Henri's ears only.[38] In Paris Guise's sister the Duchesse de Montpensier, one of the leaders of the League, declared, 'my only regret is that he did not know before his death that I had ordered it.' She then drove through the streets in her carriage, proclaiming, 'Good news, my friends! Good news! The tyrant is dead!'[39]

Henri III's childlessness had been a source of weakness. Under the Salic Law his heir was his distant Protestant cousin, Louis XIV's grandfather Henri, King of Navarre, a descendant of the fifth son of St Louis, Robert Comte de Clermont, founder of the Bourbon branch of the House of France. Navarre was a small kingdom in the western Pyrenees, founded in the ninth century by Visigoths fleeing the Arab conquerors of Spain. Henri had inherited it from his mother Jeanne d'Albret, Queen of Navarre; the southern part, which Navarrese autonomists still regret today, had been taken by Castile in 1512.

Although France and Navarre were legally united in 1620, their separate coats of arms – the three golden fleurs-de-lys on a blue background of France and the golden wheel on a red background of Navarre – were thenceforth constantly reproduced (joined under a common crown and surrounded by the collar of the royal Order of the Holy Spirit founded by Henri III in 1578) on the walls of French royal palaces, on the King's official documents and on his personal seal.

In 1589 part of the court and four-fifths of France refused to serve the new King of France and Navarre, because he was Protestant. Many nobles regarded his accession primarily as an occasion to bargain for more favours, including regular meetings of the States General. Dreams of provincial independence revived. The Duc de Mayenne, while governing as 'lieutenant-general of the kingdom' in Paris, hoped to become duke of an independent Burgundy, his cousin the Duc de Mercoeur to be duke of Brittany, and the Duke of Savoy to annex Provence and Dauphiné. Paris was 'purified' by repeated religious processions. Although the supreme French law court, known as the Parlement of Paris, defended the Salic Law as the basis of all others, the Council of Sixteen ruling the city asked for Philip II of Spain or his daughter the Infanta Isabella (whose mother had been a daughter of Henri II) to ascend the throne, and admitted a Spanish garrison. Pamphleteers called leaders on both sides vipers and scorpions feeding on the corpse of France.[40]

Henri IV had to besiege Paris twice, to prove himself an invincible hero in battle and to convert to Catholicism (the sixth time that he changed religion) before he could finally enter his capital, on 22 March 1594. Later that day he watched the last Spanish and Neapolitan soldiers leave Paris by another gate. He too had been helped by foreign forces, German Protestant mercenaries and above all English loans, ships and soldiers: to his Surintendant des Finances Maximilien de Sully, he later described Elizabeth I as 'a second self'.[41] After his entry into Paris, he felt obliged to visit every parish church in the capital, to reassure Parisians he was neither a Protestant nor the devil incarnate.[42]

By 1598, when he made peace with Spain, Henri IV controlled the same extent of territory as Henri II and Henri III. Despite his apparent triumph, he had felt obliged to buy nobles' and factions' submission: the Guise family for example received 4 million livres in 1593.[43] By the 'perpetual and irrevocable' Edict of Nantes of 1598, guaranteeing Protestants the right to worship in public in certain localities, he bought their submission. Echoing an edict of Henri III in 1576, he had also given them the right to garrison certain fortresses as *places de sûreté* (Saumur, Nîmes, Montpellier, Grenoble and other cities). In areas where they could worship in public, he also established mixed Catholic–Protestant courts. By secret clauses, the King even agreed to pay Protestant pastors, teachers and some of their garrisons. Later, contrary to the terms of the Edict banning Protestant services in and around Paris, he permitted Protestant services at Charenton just east of Paris. French Protestants, although forming no more than around 6 per cent of the population, ran the equivalent of a state within the state, with separate assemblies and armed forces.[44]

In 1598–1610 France enjoyed a rare interval of peace. The King could concentrate on building projects in Paris and the Île de France. Louis XIV would be taught to regard him as 'Henri le Grand', a hero as well as one of the greatest kings of France.

However, Henri IV's heart often ruled his head. In 1610 he planned war with Spain, partly in continuation of the traditional French struggle with the House of Austria, but also in pursuit of Charlotte de Montmorency, Princesse de Condé (later Louis XIV's godmother), who had been taken to Brussels, capital of the Spanish Netherlands, by her husband to enable her to evade the King's advances.[45] On 14 May 1610, Henri IV was stabbed to death in his carriage in a crowded Paris street, by Jean François Ravaillac, a Catholic fanatic convinced that the King was still at heart a Protestant hostile to the ultra-Catholic House of Austria: Ravaillac had been encouraged by books and sermons arguing, as in the reign of Henri III, that, for a good Catholic, 'tyrannicide' was no crime.[46] Gardes Français, who under their commander 'le brave Crillon' had helped Henri IV recapture his kingdom, kept order in Paris after his murder.[47]

Thus antiquity, heredity, coronation and the widely proclaimed belief that the kings of France were representatives and images of God himself did not protect them from rebellion or assassination. France was a monarchy on a knife-edge. For a time Parisians had favoured a king from the Houses of Austria or Lorraine. Both Henri IV's son Louis XIII and his grandson Louis XIV would be threatened by repeated revolts and haunted by fears of new religious wars and acts of regicide.

I

The Gift of God

Even by royal standards, the family into which the future Louis XIV was born on 5 September 1638 was a nest of vipers. Louis XIII had many reasons to fear his closest relations. His mother Marie de Médicis, and his weak and treacherous brother and heir Gaston, Duc d'Orléans, frequently rebelled or plotted against him. Gaston joined at least six separate conspiracies. Rebellion remained a French disease. As Louis XIII's chief minister the Cardinal de Richelieu wrote, Protestants behaved as if they shared the King's sovereignty; great nobles as if they were not his subjects; and governors of provinces as independent rulers.[1] His wife also conspired.

In Bordeaux cathedral on 25 November 1614, at the age of thirteen, Louis XIII had married Anne of Austria, a daughter of Philip III, King of Spain, of the same age as her husband. At the same time his sister Elisabeth of France had married Anne of Austria's brother, the future Philip IV of Spain. The two princesses had been exchanged at a formal ceremony at the exact midpoint between their two countries: on the Island of Pheasants, a tiny uninhabited islet of dried mud in the middle of the Bidassoa, the river which runs along the frontier between France and Spain down to the Bay of Biscay. However varied the kingdoms and provinces they ruled, dynasties in Europe retained an acute sense of nationality.

Marriages in Louis' mother's family the House of Austria helped create many of the states of Europe. In 1506 after the death of Philip the Handsome, son of the head of the House of Austria the Holy Roman Emperor Maximilian I and Mary of Burgundy, his son the future Emperor Charles V (1519–55) had inherited the Netherlands or 'Burgundy', the ancient rival of France. Through his mother Juana the Mad, daughter of Ferdinand, King of Aragon, Naples and Sicily and Isabella, Queen of Castile, Charles V also inherited those four kingdoms in 1516. After Maximilian I's death in 1519, he was in addition elected Holy Roman emperor: the title, in theory elective, had in practice become hereditary in the House of Austria. Under Charles V, Spain also conquered what are now Mexico and Peru.

After his abdication in 1555, his son Philip II inherited Spain and its global Empire and the Netherlands: because Spain was ruled by a branch of the House of Austria, Louis' mother, although an infanta of Spain, was called Anne 'of Austria'. Charles V's younger brother Ferdinand had become king of Hungary and Bohemia, by marrying the heiress to those thrones. He also ruled the family's hereditary lands in and around Austria and was elected Holy Roman emperor after Charles V's abdication. The lands of the House of Austria surrounded France and spread across the globe.[2] Hence the motto adopted by Charles V: 'Plus ultra' – 'Nothing beyond'.

The Franco-Spanish marriages of 1610 had been intended as guarantees of peace, prosperity, glory and alliance between the two most powerful, and most Catholic, kingdoms in Europe; hitherto they had often been enemies.[3] To her Première Femme de Chambre, Madame de Motteville, one of the many French courtiers who wrote political memoirs, Louis XIII's wife Anne of Austria was a heroine. One of the beauties of the age, she was particularly admired for the 'extreme whiteness' of her hands.[4] Her charm and familiarity won her courtiers' devotion.[5]

Nevertheless for Louis XIII and Richelieu she was a traitor. In 1626 she had confessed to the King's council her knowledge of 'the conspiracy of Chalais' (so named after the chosen assassin the Comte de Chalais, Maître de la Garde-robe du Roi) to kill the King and the Cardinal and marry her to her husband's brother Gaston. For twenty-two years, moreover, she had failed in the essential duty of a royal consort, to produce an heir. A fall on 14 March 1622, running down the long gallery of the Louvre with her ladies-in-waiting, had contributed to one miscarriage, and she would suffer three more. The Queen's prayers, pilgrimages and many vows to the Virgin Mary and the saints (Francis, Teresa of Avila, Anne 'la royale' and more) had no effect.[6]

One of Richelieu's greatest triumphs had been the fall of the Protestant stronghold of La Rochelle, despite naval and military support from England, after a thirteen-month siege in October 1628. The following June, after more fighting, the Edict of Nîmes ended the Protestants' state within a state, and their right to garrison towns and hold political assemblies. Thereafter Louis XIII and Richelieu pursued an increasingly anti-Spanish foreign policy.

Desire for peace with Spain, and resentment at her declining influence in the King's council, led to Marie de Médicis' break with Richelieu. After a violent scene in the Luxembourg, her palace in Paris, on 11 November 1630, Marie de Médicis believed she had persuaded the King to dismiss the

Cardinal. Richelieu, however, had remained in power by obeying Louis XIII's order to follow him to Versailles, his hunting lodge 5 miles south of Saint-Germain. His mother had not gone there herself, since she feared the boredom and discomfort.[7] After more disputes, she fled to the Spanish Netherlands in July 1631. In 1642 she would die in Cologne in the house of her favourite painter Rubens (who had decorated the gallery of the Luxembourg with pictures of her triumphs), abandoned by most of her household.

To the horror of devout Catholics, in 1631 France allied with the leading Protestant power Sweden, which was fighting the House of Austria in the Empire.[8] In 1633 French troops occupied Lorraine, in 1634 part of Alsace.[9] In 1635 Louis XIII declared war on Anne's brother Philip IV. France planned to break up the Southern Netherlands, then ruled by the King of Spain. France would take western Flanders and all French-speaking areas (present-day Wallonia), the United Provinces (as the northern Netherlands were then called) the rest.[10]

Security as well as territory would be secured by French expansion. As repeated invasions by English or Spanish armies had shown, no natural barriers defend Paris from armies invading from the north and the east. In what de Gaulle would call the 'fatal avenue' between France and Germany, every other town or village is the site of one battle, or more.* To this day farmers harvest weapons and bones, as well as crops.

In 1646 Richelieu's successor, Cardinal Mazarin, would write that acquisition of the Spanish Netherlands, Lorraine and Alsace – the heart of former 'Lotharingia' and 'Burgundy' – 'would form an inexpugnable bulwark for the city of Paris and it would then be truly called the heart of France and it would be placed in the most secure location in the kingdom. Its frontiers would have been extended as far as Holland, and in the direction of Germany, which is where one can also have much cause for fear, as far as the Rhine, by keeping Lorraine and Alsace.'[11] Louis XIV would also dream of making France's eastern boundary the Rhine.

Louis XIII and Richelieu often invoked the 'the good of the state' when defending their policies and condemning their enemies. 'The state' was a term much used in France since the dynastic instability and political anarchy of the period 1570–1600 had threatened the country's survival. 'The state' could refer not to the government and administration of France, but in reality to the King's will and policies. Louis XIII, when refusing to follow Marie de Médicis' pro-Spanish policies, said that, while he respected his mother, he had greater obligation to his state. In 1637 he told the Paris

---

* For example, Ramillies, Oudenarde, Malplaquet, Denain in Louis XIV's reign; later, to name only a few, Waterloo, Sedan, Ypres, Verdun, Dunkirk.

Parlement that new taxes were needed for 'my State', not for himself.[12] Participants in the innumerable conspiracies and revolts, both popular and aristocratic, of Louis XIII's reign thought that in practice his wars, by increasing taxation, public misery and revolts, weakened France and 'the state'. War with Spain was pursued and Richelieu's political rivals executed, imprisoned or exiled, not to strengthen 'the state' but to strengthen Richelieu, and his domination of the King.[13] After 'the year of Corbie' in 1636, when a Spanish army had crossed the Somme and taken Corbie 70 miles from Paris, the tide of war turned in France's favour. Just before capturing Arras, capital of Artois, in August 1640, Louis XIII himself, lamenting 'the destruction of the people', claimed to the Venetian Ambassador that he made war only to limit the power of the House of Austria and give peace to Christianity.[14]

After the outbreak of war in 1635, Louis XIII's sister Elisabeth of France, Queen of Spain, showed herself passionately Spanish, selling jewels to raise soldiers for her husband's army.[15] The Queen of France, however, favoured her own dynasty. In August 1637, despite taking communion and swearing on the holy sacrament that she had not secretly corresponded with 'enemies of the state', Anne of Austria had been forced by Richelieu and the Chancellor Séguier (who had foraged for incriminating letters in the Queen's bodice) to sign a confession admitting that she had. Using the convent she had founded at Val-de-Grâce on the rue Saint-Jacques in 1624 as a letter drop, she had secretly corresponded over many years in Spanish or in cipher with Philip IV, with another brother the Cardinal Infante Ferdinand, Governor General of the Spanish Netherlands and with her exiled favourite the Duchesse de Chevreuse (one of those with the Queen in the Louvre when she had a miscarriage), and had tried to prevent agreements being concluded between France, England and Lorraine. One of her husband's *premiers valets de chambre*, Pierre de La Porte, acted as her encrypter.[16] She had to write to Richelieu and Louis XIII to ask forgiveness, while admitting she did not deserve it. They forgave her because repudiation would have caused a scandal, and the King needed an heir. Thenceforth, all her letters were sealed by ladies-in-waiting chosen by her husband, and she was forbidden to visit Val-de-Grâce.[17]

Despite the Queen's treason, miscarriages and advanced age (she was thirty-seven), Louis XIII's confessor, and his confidantes Louise de La Fayette and Marie d'Hautefort, urged him to continue trying to father children. Between 9 November and 1 December the King and Queen were together in the Château Vieux of Saint-Germain, 11 miles west of Paris, built by François I in 1540–47 (and covered with his symbols of the letter

F and the salamander) on the foundations of a twelfth-century chateau. Saint-Germain is a tall, forbidding, five-sided castle constructed around a courtyard, now the Museum of National Archaeology, conveniently close to a forest where the King could go hunting.[18] On 1 December, since it was the beginning of winter, the royal couple moved to Paris.

Their son's conception may date from 30 November at Saint-Germain; the story of a conception after a storm out hunting had driven the King to accept last-minute hospitality in the Queen's apartment in the Louvre on 5 December is unproven. On 30 January her pregnancy was made public. Parisians reacted as if the Messiah was about to be born.[19]

Paris under Louis XIII and Louis XIV was so Catholic that it was called 'the second capital of Christendom'. It contained ten abbeys, eighty-four monasteries, eleven priories, fifty-nine parish churches and ninety chapels.[20] No Protestant services had been held there since the massacre of St Bartholomew's Eve. A visitor from Sicily wrote of the city: 'I have never seen a more devout people, better-behaved priests, a more organized clergy or monks giving a better example.'[21] Parisians regarded the Queen's conception as a miracle, a reward for the King's dedication of France to the Virgin Mary in 1637, in gratitude for her protection of his kingdom from the Spanish army in 1636.[22]

On 10 February 1638 Louis XIII formally published his *dédication*, declaring the 'Very Holy and Very Glorious Virgin Mary' France's 'special protectress', to whom he consecrated 'our Person, our State, our Crown and our Subjects' (the order is revealing – in France state and crown were already considered separate). He solemnized his *dédication* or vow by registering it in the supreme law court of the kingdom, the Parlement de Paris, and building a new high altar in Notre-Dame de Paris, the great cathedral with a façade decorated with statues of twenty-eight kings (whether of France or Judah is unclear) symbolizing the union of church and crown. His portrait by Philippe de Champaigne was placed on the altar. It shows the dark-faced King, in coronation robes and watched by angels, offering on his knees his crown and sceptre to the Virgin, who holds Jesus Christ after his descent from the cross.

Another portrait by Philippe de Champaigne – of the young Louis XIV offering his crown and sceptre to the Virgin and Jesus Christ, watched by his mother and brother – as well as the two life-size marble statues of Louis XIII and Louis XIV still on either side of the high altar of Notre-Dame, offering their crowns to Jesus Christ and the Virgin, also commemorate the vow of Louis XIII. For most Frenchmen in the reigns of Louis XIII and Louis XIV, Christianity and monarchy were similar cults of hierarchy and obedience.[23] Louis XIV would write to his son that all authority was ordained by God, whose lieutenants kings were. The king of France was known as 'the Most Christian King' and 'the Lord's Anointed'. For his part Jesus Christ, 'Son of God', was 'King of kings'. The Virgin, 'Mother of God', was 'Queen of heaven', frequently depicted seated on a throne and wearing a crown. Until the fall of the monarchy, the vow of Louis XIII would be honoured on the king's orders by processions throughout France on the feast day celebrating the Assumption of the Virgin into heaven. The 15th of August is still a national holiday in France today.[24]

As the Queen's pregnancy advanced, the King requested public prayers throughout France to implore God to bless 'la royale et très heureuse grossesse de nostre très-grande et très-Auguste Reyne' ('the royal and very fortunate pregnancy of our very great and very August Queen') with a son and heir. The holy sacrament was exposed day and night in churches: a dauphin would prevent the King's brother Gaston from ascending the throne. Jacqueline Pascal, sister of the philosopher Blaise Pascal, declaimed in front of the pregnant Queen verses praising the 'invincible son of an invincible father', who even in his mother's womb, by his kicks, 'makes himself feared and desired'.[25] She hoped that his kicks were a foretaste of the blows he would strike against France's enemies.[26]

The Queen moved to the Château Neuf of Saint-Germain, built in 1594–9 by Henri IV 200 yards east of the Château Vieux. Spectacular gardens, grottoes and fountains descended on a series of colonnaded terraces from the palace down to the Seine. The site combined the advantages of salubrity, proximity to hunting forests and 'the finest view in the world', a 180-degree panorama of Paris and the entire surrounding plain.[27]* Sometimes called 'the mountain of good air', in contrast to the fumes and smells of the capital, Saint-Germain was the Queen's main country residence. In a sign of their mutual distaste, if the Queen stayed in the Château Neuf, the King moved to the Château Vieux, and vice versa.

In the Château Neuf of Saint-Germain, at 11 a.m. on 5 September 1638, after a labour of twelve hours, the miracle occurred. At the age of thirty-eight, in the presence of praying nuns, holy relics, Princesses of the Blood, the King's brother and the King himself, the Queen gave birth to a healthy boy. 'Sire, c'est un dauphin!' a midwife told Louis XIII.[28] Te Deums, processions and fireworks were arranged throughout France in celebration. So much wine flowed in fountains at Saint-Germain that guards had to be posted at the entrance of the town to check the flood of people coming to drink it.[29] As far away as Constantinople, the French Ambassador

---

* Now blocked by the skyscrapers of La Défense.

fired so many cannon in celebration that the ladies of the imperial harem assumed that Christians had risen in revolt.

Prints commemorated 'the joy', 'the happiness' and 'the hopes of France'. The King and 'la reine notre très chère épouse' were depicted presenting the Dauphin to the Virgin in heaven.[30] His birth was compared to that of Jesus Christ – also born after a miraculous conception. One print called Jesus Christ, Son of God, 'the Dauphin in the skies' – Jesus thus named after the French Prince, not the other way round. Richelieu wrote to the King that 'God having given him to you, he has given him to the world for great things.'[31] On 6 March 1639 Louis' birth was further celebrated, in a manner especially appreciated at the French court, by a *Ballet de la Félicité* danced before the King and Queen.[32]

The Dauphin's Governess, the Gouvernante des Enfants de France, was called Madame de Lansac. She was a protégée of Richelieu, and daughter of the Maréchal de Souvré, who had been Louis XIII's governor. A portrait survives of Louis, tightly swaddled in accordance with French practice, round his neck the blue ribbon of the grandest French royal order, the Order of the Holy Spirit. One large naked breast of his wet nurse, 'dame Longuet de la Geraudières', wife of a royal tax official, is near his lips. The young Louis was voracious, with strong teeth, and hurt his wet nurses' nipples: he would run through eight nurses in all. The Swedish diplomat Grotius remarked that 'the neighbours of France should beware such a precocious rapacity.' In September 1640 his mother bore the Dauphin a brother, named Philippe, Duc d'Anjou (known as Monsieur, like Gaston before him, after Louis XIII's death in 1643).[33] The *Gazette de France* referred to Louis and his brother as 'these columns destined to assure our conquests'.[34]

Starved of affection by her husband, the Queen adored her elder son and, far more than most royal mothers of the day, brought him up herself. One observer noted in April 1639, 'The Queen hardly leaves him. She takes great pleasure in playing with him and in taking him out in her carriage when the weather is fine. It is her whole amusement; so there is no other in her court.'[35] Another witness wrote that he made a 'maddening noise in the bedchamber of the Queen but that does not bother Her Majesty'.[36]

For his part Louis XIII complained in a letter to Richelieu that the Dauphin preferred the company of women: 'from the moment he sees me, he cries as if he saw the devil, he always cries for maman. He must . . . be taken from the Queen at the earliest possible moment.' The King followed Richelieu's advice and threatened to send his son to Versailles. Four days later, proving the Queen's survival instinct, he wrote: 'my son demanded forgiveness on his knees and played with me more than one long hour. I gave him some toys to play with; we are the best friends in the world.' The following day: 'since that time he cannot bear to be without me' and followed the King everywhere.[37] Even at the age of two, Louis was a pawn in his parents' marriage. His feelings and manners were used as political weapons.

Louis XIII was a soldier king. Gédéon Tallemant des Réaux, author of a celebrated collection of anecdotes on the French court entitled *Historiettes*, remarked of Louis XIII's control over the guard and army that he was 'more jealous of that than of anything else'.[38]The French royal guard had been strengthened by Louis and before him by Henri IV with smaller units of Chevau-légers (1593), Gendarmes (1611) and Mousquetaires (1622) de la Garde, later known as the Maison du Roi or Household Cavalry, 'of which the King is extremely fond and which he puts on duty in front of his residence in the palaces where he goes'. The King himself was captain of each unit, and sometimes chose to serve as a sentry on guard duty at night. Louis XIII also added, during a rebellion by his cousin the Prince de Condé in 1616, a regiment of 3,000 Swiss Guards.[39]

Numbering 6,000 in all, the guards not only protected the King but acted as a training school for officers and as a shock force on the battlefield where Louis XIII, like Henri IV, spent much of his life. Louis XIII had also used his guards to kill another overmighty subject, the Queen Mother's favourite Concino Concini, Maréchal d'Ancre, outside the Louvre in April 1617. Concini's corpse was hung on the Pont Neuf, where it suffered 'every indignity' at the hands of jeering Parisians, before being dragged through the streets. On hearing news of the murder, Louis XIII had exclaimed, 'praise be to God, I am now king.'[40]

Guards were 'a mark of sovereignty', as the States General had declared in 1614 when asking for them to be reserved to the King and his family alone.[41] Only Richelieu's particular combination of authority and vulnerability after the conspiracy of Chalais in 1626 had persuaded Louis XIII to grant him the unique privilege of maintaining his own foot and horse guards – about 420 well-paid and magnificently uniformed Chevau-légers, Gendarmes and Mousquetaires. They not only guarded his residences, but accompanied him wherever he went, through the streets of Paris and to the King's palaces (although they were not allowed to follow him into the King's apartments). There was a ceremonial changing of the Cardinal's guard every morning in front of the Palais Cardinal, the present Palais Royal north of the Louvre, like that of the King's guard in front of the Louvre.[42]

Louis XIII devoted more time to his guard and his army than to his court. Richelieu complained to him of its loss of splendour. 'Foreigners who visited France were often surprised to see a State raised so high and a household so debased . . . everything in it was in confusion from the kitchens to the study . . . entry to your study has been permitted to everyone.' The courts of Spain and England, he continued, were not only more dignified but more secure.[43]

In 1642, when the Dauphin was four, yet another 'court tempest' (*orage de la cour*) hinged in part on the guards. It showed, as the murder of the Duc de Guise had done in 1588, that at the French court every nuance of human relationships, and every inch of the royal apartments, could have political consequences. The court was a zone of negotiation, and a school of psychology, as well as a battlefield. Since 1637 Louis XIII had been besotted with the Marquis de Cinq-Mars, handsome, witty and well built, who, at nineteen, was half his age. M. de Chavigny, a secretary of state, had written: 'never has the King had a more violent passion for anyone.'[44] In 1638 Cinq-Mars was appointed one of two *maîtres de la garde-robe*, in charge of the King's clothes, with constant access to his person. In 1639 he rose to be *grand écuyer de France* – 'Monsieur le Grand' in the language of the court – a vital post placing him in charge of the royal horses and carriages on which the King's security depended. Henri III had been able to flee from Paris to Chartres in May 1588 only because he could use the horses and stables which he kept beside the Tuileries garden outside the city walls, beyond the control of the master of Paris, the Duc de Guise.[45]

Louis XIII complained to Richelieu, who had favoured the rise of Cinq-Mars, of the impertinence, extravagance and bad temper of 'Monsieur le Grand'. Cinq-Mars snapped at the King, said he smelt and continued visiting mistresses in Paris. After their quarrels, he and the King would sign treaties, guaranteed by Richelieu, promising 'to be perfectly contented and satisfied with each other' (26 November 1639), or not to lose their tempers with each other (9 May 1640). Tallemant des Réaux claimed that at night Cinq-Mars would 'oil himself for combat' with the King.[46]

Encouraged by the King's confidence, and by his frequent complaints about Richelieu, Cinq-Mars launched a plot to kill the Cardinal, enter the council and make peace with Spain. Fellow conspirators included the Duc de Bouillon, Captain of the Cent-Suisses of the Guard, Gaston, Duc d'Orléans and perhaps the Queen. In January 1642 a treaty promising peace and an end to France's alliances with Protestant powers, such as Sweden and the Netherlands, was signed by Cinq-Mars' agent Fontrailles with Philip IV.[47]

In June that year, however, possibly through Anne of Austria (who as a reward retained control of her sons), or more likely through an intercepted Spanish courier, Richelieu made a 'marvellous discovery': a copy of the treaty with Philip IV.[48] At that point Cinq-Mars had seemed in higher favour than ever. The King was showing him increasing 'warmth'. Richelieu feared assassination and the Papal Nuncio predicted his fall.[49] Cinq-Mars had developed the habit, when Richelieu was away from the court, of attending council meetings standing behind the King's chair in his capacity as Monsieur le Grand, literally inching his way to power: the embodiment of the court official trying to dominate the government – as, earlier in Louis XIII's reign in 1617–21, another of his handsome courtier favourites, the Duc de Luynes, one of Concini's assassins, had done.[50]

On 12 June, returning from the capture of Perpignan, the King was staying in the palace of the Archbishop of Narbonne. Chavigny and Sublet de Noyers, two secretaries of state, showed the recently intercepted treaty to the King in an inner council room, when Cinq-Mars was, briefly, not beside him. They convinced him to sign an order for Cinq-Mars' arrest. In a crisis the council – the state – proved more powerful, and more trusted by the King, than the court.[51]

Even so Cinq-Mars was arrested only with difficulty. For hours he hid in the recesses of the Archbishop's palace. After his capture, he was entrusted to John Seton, one of the last Gardes du Corps of Scottish origin, presumably because the King's French guards were considered unreliable.[52] As in previous conspiracies, Gaston, Duc d'Orléans betrayed everyone in return for a pardon.

The King had 'le coeur fort serré', a heavy heart beset by 'l'acrimonie des humeurs'. Richelieu was furious, as he suspected that the King, tiring of the Cardinal's dominance, had listened to plans for his assassination and had appeared to favour them: after seventeen years, this old couple knew how to torture each other. The King admitted in a letter to Chancellor Séguier that Cinq-Mars had proposed such a plan and had offered to kill Richelieu himself.[53] He had not, however, given Cinq-Mars an order in writing.

Cinq-Mars and his adviser de Thou said they had acted only on the King's orders. Richelieu offered to retire to Le Havre, where his niece the Duchesse d'Aiguillon was governor, but the King refused to accept his resignation. 'Knowing of the King's consent he will always be afraid ... as long as those who had been destined for the execution [of the plot against his life] will be present [at court],' wrote Richelieu in a secret letter on 6 November; he also referred to 'matters one cannot write'. For a time the Cardinal refused to visit Louis XIII at Saint-Germain, fearing the hostility of guards 'implicated in the past machinations of Monsieur le Grand'. Finally, much against his will (they were immediately recalled on the

Cardinal's death), the King dismissed Troisville, the trusted commander of his Mousquetaires, and three officers of the Gardes Françaises, suspected of having also offered to kill Richelieu. Richelieu won increased powers and the right to enter the King's apartment with his own armed guards.[54]

Richelieu had achieved in 1642 what Guise had not in 1588: control of the King's guard. As the Venetian Ambassador wrote on 25 November: 'the court is thus purged and Monsieur le Cardinal in the most brilliant authority.'[55] But Richelieu was already dying. The epitome of the over-mighty minister, he dared to sit in an armchair in the presence of the Queen as if he were her equal, when she visited him in his splendid chateau of Rueil, halfway between Saint-Germain and Paris, to enquire after, or gloat over, his health.[56] Richelieu died, widely detested, on 4 December. When asked to forgive his enemies, he said he had none but those of the state. The day before, Louis XIII, worried for the safety of his sons after his death, as he told members of the Parlement, had determined to exclude Gaston d'Orléans from any future regency council. In a letter to the Parlement of 9 December he announced that there would be 'no change' in his policies.[57] He chose as his new principal minister a protégé of Richelieu, an Italian called Giulio Mazarini.

The fierce sense of nationality in seventeenth-century Europe did not exclude flexible identities, as two powerful diasporas of the reign of Louis XIV, the Huguenots and the Jacobites, would demonstrate. Europe was, for some, an open market, in which states bid for talent as companies do today. The French monarchy, despite its commitment to territorial expansion, sometimes preferred to employ foreigners, such as its Scots and Swiss Guards. Mazarin, himself an outstanding example of this preference, would call foreign troops 'the surest support of the state'.[58] A new regiment of foreign guards, the Gardes Ecossaises, was raised in 1642.

The French court also employed Italians. The Gondi family from Florence, originally court officials (one had attended the council meeting which decided on the Massacre of St Barthomew's Eve), had been bishops, then archbishops, of Paris since 1602.[59] Mazarin himself was born in Rome in 1602, of a Sicilian father from the minor nobility and a Genoese mother. But he put into practice the popular saying *al galantuomo ogni paese è patria*: 'to a gentleman every country is a fatherland.'[60] In December 1639, at the age of thirty-seven, this brilliant papal diplomat had been persuaded by Richelieu to entered French service. Twice, in April 1639 and October 1643, in return for 'commendable and important services', he received letters of naturalization making him legally French. However, he continued to acquire property in Rome, to speak French with an Italian accent (pronouncing both 'union' and 'oignon' as 'ougnon') and to be hated as a foreigner.[61]

Mazarin was called to the council on 5 December 1642, the day after Richelieu's death. On 16 December the Venetian Ambassador wrote of the King's favour, esteem and confidence enjoyed by the man he called 'notre très cher cousin le Cardinal Mazarini': the Pope had made Mazarin a cardinal in order to honour Louis XIII's new favourite. He showed 'singular industry' and cleverness, 'instructed as he has been in the school of Rome and in the practices of the court'. The Princes of the Blood and the public were hostile, but Louis XIII appeared fonder of Mazarin than he had been of Richelieu.[62] The new Cardinal often dined with the King in his favourite hunting lodge, Versailles.

The King, however, was wasting away, losing weight by the day, through a combination of tuberculosis, intestinal problems (including worms), Crohn's disease and abcesses. Princes and great nobles, with their followers, gathered 'in very large numbers' round the royal deathbed. In January Gaston, on bended knee, begged the King's forgiveness. Louis replied that, for the sixth time, he had forgiven and forgotten.[63] When the Queen assured him she had never joined the Chalais conspiracy in 1626 or desired his death, he answered that in the state he was in he was obliged as a Christian to forgive her, but not to believe her.[64]

On 13 April 1643 Mazarin appointed the man who would be his most faithful ally, and father of the famous minister Louvois, Michel Le Tellier, as secretary of state for war. On 20 April in the presence of the royal family, ministers, marshals, officials and dukes, the King declared his desire for Anne to be regent. Her council would be presided over jointly by Gaston and the next heir to the throne, their second cousin the Prince de Condé:[65] the two heirs next in line to the throne, if the King's sons were to die, were to counterbalance each other. Anne agreed, but, characteristically, sent to a Paris notary a secret protest invalidating her agreement. Influential members of the Parlement also told her they secretly supported her. The court was divided between partisans of Queen and Gaston. The Queen, in the Château Vieux, held the trump-card, her sons.

According to the *Gazette de France*, the official newspaper founded by Richelieu in 1631, Louis XIII, looking from Saint-Germain towards Saint-Denis, said: 'Voilà ma dernière maison où je me prépare pour aller gaiement.' Convinced that Anne would be more generous or more malleable than the King, courtiers looked sad when his condition improved, cheerful when it worsened.[66]

All eyes turned to the Dauphin. In 1643 at the Cène – the annual ceremony on the Thursday of Holy Week when the King of France washed the feet of twelve poor men, as Jesus Christ was believed to have done for the Apostles, before helping to serve them a meal inspired by the Last Supper – the four-year-old Dauphin, replacing his father, was praised for his 'piety, grandeur, vigour and beauty'.[67] His formal baptism took place on 21 April that year, in the magnificent mid-thirteenth-century chapel which survives today in the Château Vieux of Saint-Germain. Like his father and his successors, he was named Louis, after St Louis, the revered patron saint of the French monarchy. Instead of the Pope (who had been godfather to Louis XIII) or his uncle Gaston, the 'most eminent personage Cardinal Mazarin' was selected by Louis XIII to be his godfather. His godmother was his second cousin the Princesse de Condé, the 'celestial' beauty for love of whom Henri IV had been planning in 1610 to invade the Spanish Netherlands.[68] In the words of the official account of the ceremony, the Dauphin was 'beau comme un ange, modeste et retenu [reserved]'. In his name his mother three times renounced Satan and all his works.[69]

On 23 April, on the King's orders, his own declaration of 1 December against Gaston (written in Richelieu's lifetime) was torn out of the registers of the Parlement so that he could be named a member of the regency council.[70] As he lay dying, he forgave all his enemies except the Queen's friend the Duchesse de Chevreuse, whom he regarded as a devil because she had launched so many plots against him.[71] According to his *valet de chambre* Marie Dubois, he addressed his family, and 'messieurs du parlement' who were also present, 'with remarks so touching that they could not console themselves'. When he officially declared Anne the future regent, everyone, including Anne herself, wept.

They saw this King 'charged with victory' (his cousin the Duc d'Enghien, son of Condé, would win the battle of Rocroi against the Spanish army on 19 May), leaving his sceptre and crown 'with as little regret as if he was leaving only a bale of rotten hay'. Looking at his wasted body, he said, 'my God, how thin I am.'[72] During what was called a 'conference', Anne talked to him alone for hours: he was giving her his last words of advice, probably to trust Mazarin and not to allow him to retire to Rome.[73] Nine years later Mazarin would remind Anne that the dying King had 'twice recapitulated to her my promise which I had made to him and told her that he made me godfather of his son to oblige me even more not to leave him and begged her strongly to uphold me against all the attacks which infallibly people would make against me, to disgust me and oblige me to retire'.[74] Then she brought their sons to receive their father's blessing. 'Airs of devotion' were sung as, in great pain, the King received the last rites. On 14 May he died.[75]

The great preacher and organizer of public charities Vincent de Paul (canonized nearly a century later), whom the King had summoned to his deathbed, declared: 'since I have been on this earth I have never seen anyone die in such a Christian manner.'[76] Mazarin, who had bought property in Paris close to the royal palaces the day before the King's death,[77] wrote to Richelieu's brother: 'it is impossible to imagine a greater spirit in a weaker body.' The younger brother of the Duc de Bouillon, Turenne, later one of Louis XIV's best generals, wrote to his sister: 'it is true that no one on earth has ever made such a fine and constant end. As for affliction at court, it has been very mediocre there.' Indeed there was an explosion of joy at the King's death and the prospect of Anne of Austria's regency.[78]

Fearing a coup by the large number of followers accompanying Gaston and Condé to court, Anne appointed the Duc de Beaufort as commander of the guard, and ordered the Swiss Guards to be ready. Beaufort was the second son of Henri IV's illegitimate son the Duc de Vendôme: a bastard line with no chance of succeeding could be more trusted than princes who might wish to eliminate lives standing between themselves and the crown.[79]

On 15 May the new King made a state entry from Saint-Germain into Paris. It was the first time he had seen his capital. He was surrounded by his French and Swiss guards, Gendarmes, Chevau-légers, Mousquetaires, Gardes du Corps and princes, and was preceded by the Duc de Saint-Simon, Premier Ecuyer and a former favourite of his father, carrying his sword. Royal power was based on force but strengthened by emotion. The city authorities came outside the walls to present Louis XIV with the keys of Paris watched by 'an innumerable multitude of people who received him with great cries and acclamations of joy and happiness', according to the parish registers of Saint-Germain.[80] The Queen promised to tell her son he should display benevolence to his peoples.[81] The procession then advanced through the city to the main royal palace, the Louvre.

Olivier d'Ormesson, a judge in the Parlement de Paris and member of a legal family which still possesses the Château d'Ormesson near the city, recorded in his diary the emotional charge, close to physical love, which could pass between the king of France and his subjects: 'there was a very great shout of Vive le roi as he passed. He displayed great joy to see so many people and was not surprised by it although he had not been in Paris [before]. I did not see him, but only Monsieur who is the handsomest prince you could possibly see. Everyone yearned to see these two princes and they argued together over which was the handsomer.'[82] The King's first contact with Paris had gone well.

2

Our Good City of Paris

Cities were among Louis XIV's most persistent adversaries: provincial cities with republican aspirations like Marseille and Bordeaux; Protestant trading capitals, like Amsterdam and London; enemy cities whose bombardment he ordered, such as Algiers, Genoa and Brussels. Despite the acclamations at his entry, however, the most dangerous city of all to Louis XIV would be his own capital, 'notre bonne ville de Paris', as it was referred to in royal edicts.

Louis XIV's Paris was not one city, but four. Inscriptions on maps described it as 'la cité, ville, université et faubourgs de Paris'. The city's multiple identities help explain its rebelliousness and Madame de Motteville's remark, echoed by other admirers, that it was 'an entire world'.[1]

The *cité* was the Île de la Cité, the island in the middle of the River Seine, where kings of France had built a palace in the eleventh century, the period when Paris became the capital of France: the Gothic masterpiece the Sainte-Chapelle and some turrets of the Conciergerie prison are the palace's last physical remains today.[2] By the seventeenth century the kings had left 'le Palais', as it was called. But their law courts remained: the oldest, largest and most independent law courts in France: the Chambre des Comptes (checking government accounts), the Cour des Aides (dealing with taxation) and the Parlement de Paris. The Parlement de Paris had jurisdiction over most of the kingdom except the south. It applied the 'coutumier de Paris', the local laws first codified in 1510, which was later the principal source of the Code Napoléon.[3]

The Parlement's location is so convenient that the highest French law courts are still there today: 'le Palais' remains a synonym for 'the law courts'. About 140 judges and probably 5,000 clerks, lawyers and others worked there in the reign of Louis XIV. The building's halls and courtyards were among the main meeting places and shopping centres in the city, ten minutes' walk from the Louvre, on the right bank to the west, which by 1550 had become the principal royal palace in Paris. In 1644 the diarist John

Evelyn, one of many Englishmen who lived in France during the English Civil War, saw in and around the Palais the stalls of booksellers, engravers, goldsmiths, watchmakers and sellers of 'a thousand exotic extravagances', as well as a food market.[4] The Palais was equally close to two other power-centres, the Hôtel de Ville or town hall, to the east, where it stands today; and the cathedral of Notre-Dame de Paris, on the same island.

The Parlement also included a Cour des Pairs in which sat the peers of France – about fifty bishops, dukes and Princes of the Blood: a court which some of its members would have liked to become as powerful as the House of Peers in England. The Parlement of Paris was called a 'sovereign court', like the Cour des Aides and Chambre des Comptes, since it shared aspects of royal sovereignty. The Parlement had the right to verify, to register and to present remonstrances about royal laws and decrees. The *lit de justice*, the ceremony performed when the King came to the Parlement to register royal decrees, was the most important state ceremony in France. The Parlement was also used to register and validate the King's will. The Parlement's judgments in 1593 that the French crown must descend to the King's nearest male heir, and that he must be Catholic, had both lessened the House of Lorraine's chances of gaining the throne and helped persuade Henri IV, in the same year, to convert to Catholicism.

The Parlement's importance rose in the sixteenth century. It had the advantage of being a permanent institution, in contrast to the royal family, which was vulnerable to the hazards of dynastic biology – child kings, sickbeds and death. The Parlement was not subject to contested succes-sions, and developed better archives than the monarchy. In practice its right of remonstrance became the right to modify royal edicts and to assume police powers. It even acquired the power to break the king's testa-ment.[5] It also began to have ambitions to become a national political mediator, both serving and censuring the government. In 1597 Henri IV forbade it to deliberate on affairs of state.[6] In 1635, when it petitioned for the return of exiled judges, Louis XIII complained to Richelieu of 'the gentlemen of the Parlement who behave so insolently'. Nevertheless, as we have seen, some were present at his deathbed.[7] The conflict between crown and Parlement was also a conflict between two concepts of sover-eignty: absolute and collegiate, executive and judiciary. It would affect Louis XIV's reign and would last until both institutions were destroyed in the French Revolution.

The Parlement regarded itself as the French equivalent of the Roman Senate. Venality was its strength. Its members had bought or inherited their posts. They could be exiled, but the institution itself could not be prorogued or dissolved like the English Parliament. It sat all the year round, not for short sessions within the year. Omer Talon, Avocat Général of the Parlement, one of many French partisans of limited monarchy, claimed in 1648: 'the Parlement was the head of the people with the character of sovereignty, in order to manage their interests and represent their necessities, and with that quality it may oppose the will of kings, not however by provoking their anger but by imploring their justice by remonstrance.'[8] The Parisians, Madame de Motteville wrote in her memoirs, regarded each judge in the Parlement as an angel sent from heaven to protect them from Mazarin's tyranny.[9] The Parlement also considered itself the protector of the liberties of the Gallican church from interference by the Papacy.

The *ville* was the ancient trading city, which thanks to its position on the right bank of the Seine, and the proximity of the royal government on the Île de la Cité, had by 1200 become the largest city north of the Alps. It was built behind large grey stone boulevards or bulwarks, on the site of the present *grands boulevards*, about 6 feet thick and 28 feet high, and protected by a ditch.[10] The total population of Paris, 250,000 in 1564, had risen to about 500,000 by 1640, partly as a result of the growth in trade. The Seine is deep and navigable – hence the ship on the city's coat of arms to this day. As the English traveller Robert Dallington wrote around 1590, 'it supplieth wonderfully all the wants of Paris, a city that in people and in abundance of all things exceedeth far all other cities whatsoever within the scope of Christendom.'[11]

The principal official of Paris, the Prévôt des Marchands, or Provost of the Merchants, in theory elected, was in reality selected by the king. Based in the Hôtel de Ville, he was assisted by *échevins*, or aldermen, and by elected parish councillors. Out of municipal taxes, Paris paid for its own militia, formed by property owners in different quarters of the city: hence their name *quarteniers*.[12] Many of the sixteen colonels of the militia were also judges in the Parlement.[13]

Paris was part of the financial as well as the political machinery of the monarchy. Since 1522 the crown had issued bonds through the Hôtel de Ville, known as the *rentes sur l'Hôtel de Ville*. They provided permanent interest payments, paid out of both government and municipal taxes – although the government sometimes varied, or even suspended, the payments. The judges of the Parlement not only invested in these bonds, but tried to supervise their sale and rate of interest. By making themselves leaders of the investors in the *rentes*, they increased their own power.[14]

The left bank of the Seine had been dominated since 1200 by the largest and oldest university north of the Alps. It contained about sixty colleges: the Sorbonne, the Collège de France, the Jesuit Collège de Clermont, the

Collèges de Navarre, d'Harcourt and others. They attracted students from outside as well as within France – 'but they in nothing approach ours at Oxford for state and order,' wrote John Evelyn.[15] The left bank was called the Quartier Latin, as so many professors and students there spoke Latin, still the international language of scholarship. Such was its prestige that Henry VIII had turned to the Sorbonne, rather than to Oxford or Cambridge, to seek annulment of his marriage to Catherine of Aragon.[16]

Outside the walls of both the *ville* on the right bank and the *université* on the left were a series of *faubourgs*, literally 'false cities'. Workers lived in the Faubourgs Saint-Antoine and Saint-Marcel to the east, 'the nobility and persons of best quality' in the Faubourgs Saint-Honoré and Saint-Germain in the west.[17] Paris was also an aristocratic capital, containing the residences of many of the leading princes, nobles and judges (most of whom acquired noble status) in France – as well as what two visiting Dutchmen in 1656–7 called 'the enchanted houses and gold mines of the financiers'.[18] By then known as 'the queen of cities', Paris had replaced Venice as the centre of printing and bookselling in Europe, and had won a reputation as the best place in which to learn manners, dancing and horsemanship. Julien Bordeau described it in 1669 as 'the capital of the kingdom, the centre of the state, the usual residence of the kings and their court, the seat of the first and oldest Parlement, of the Court of Peers, the source of all law, the common fatherland of all Frenchmen, the [magnetic] pole of all the world's nations, the France of France'. Madame de Sévigné, one of the great letter writers of Louis' reign, often visited his court, but preferred Paris: she wrote, 'on ne guérit pas de Paris': 'one does not get over Paris'. Paris was already an addiction.[19]

Like the court itself, Paris was also the paradise of women. Writing towards the end of the century, a Sicilian called Jean Paul Marana described it as a city of foreigners, freedom and pleasure: 'lovers barely sigh, jealousy torments no one, French soldiers treat death as a diversion . . . you find in Paris everything you can desire, and you find it immediately . . . always new sauces and unknown ragouts.' Women, he added, 'give and receive love easily, but do not love long or enough . . . women are happy in Paris.'[20] Paris was already Europe's fashion capital. Two English travellers in the 1660s wrote: 'the humour of observing modes must be satisfied, in both sexes, though their bellies pinch for it . . . [the women] have a Breeding so free, that in England we should esteem it immodest; the huguenot as well as popish ladies spot and paint their faces . . . Swearing and cursing, with the addition of obscene words, are customary in both sexes . . .'[21]

*

The concentration of state, ecclesiastical, judicial, academic, commercial, cultural and demographic power in Paris was unique. No other capital in Europe could rival it; London and Westminster were separate commercial and political capitals, and had no university. Vienna was a third the size and near the Ottoman frontier. Madrid was far smaller, and almost entirely dependent on the court which had selected it as the Spanish capital in 1561. Amsterdam was the commercial capital of the Netherlands, but the political capital was The Hague.

As well as being the capital of the monarchy, Paris could rise against it. As early as 1358 Etienne Marcel, Prévôt des Marchands and builder of the first Hôtel de Ville, claiming to be speaking for all the cities of France, seized the royal fortress of the Louvre and forced his way into the royal council. He was assassinated on 31 July 1358, on the orders of the future Charles V.[22]

The kings of France voted with their feet. Charles V often resided in the massive castle complex which he built at Vincennes 10 miles east of Paris. After 1420 kings of France had moved 150 miles to the south, to the valley of the Loire – not only because English troops occupied Paris in 1420–36, but because they feared Paris. The magnificence of the royal castles at Blois, Amboise and Chambord, where Louis XIV often stayed, shows how much time the court spent there. François I (1515–47) stayed in his capital for only 12 per cent of his reign. Meetings of the States General were held in Orléans, Tours or Blois, but not (except in 1614) in Paris.

However, after 1540 the Louvre had been transformed from a medieval fortress into a Renaissance palace: a staircase and a façade are still decorated with the crowned and interlocked HC monogram of Henri II (1547–59) and his wife Catherine de Médicis – which could also be read, by knowing visitors, as the HD monogram of the King and his mistress Diane de Poitiers. One of the most complex buildings in France, the Louvre has witnessed, over five centuries, royal marriages and balls, massacres and revolutions, tournaments and parliaments, until its present incarnation as a museum. Most rulers of France, including Louis XIV, have added to it.

Henri II and his sons had often resided in the Louvre. After he reconquered Paris in 1594, Henri IV spent about 40 per cent of his time there. However Henri IV's distrust of his capital was shown by his construction in 1595–1610, along the Seine, of the wing linking the Louvre to the Tuileries palace started by Catherine de Médicis to the west. It can be admired today (although rebuilt in the nineteenth century), still decorated with crowns and Hs. It was an extension of the palace, housing on the first floor the longest gallery (a third of a mile) in Europe, where the court could exercise in winter, and on the ground floor, on Henri IV's orders,

painters, sculptors, goldsmiths and other court artists, including royal
printers, freed, in a royal palace, from the legal restrictions imposed by
the Paris guilds. The wing provided the king with a potential means of
escape. It crossed the city walls at the exact spot where Henri III had fled
Paris on 13 May 1588.[23]

Henri IV also built the Place Royale (now the Place des Vosges) in the
Marais, and completed the Pont Neuf, linking *ville*, *cité* and *université*.
In the middle of it his widow Marie de Médicis had his equestrian statue,
sent from her native Florence, erected in 1614: the statue became one of
the sights of Paris, and the surrounding area attracted every day a 'conflu-
ence' of people and carriages. In cities as well as palaces, space was power.
Although the court did not dominate Paris as its Spanish counterpart did
Madrid, part of Paris was being transformed into a court city. A statue of
Louis XIII was erected in the middle of the Place Royale in 1639.[24]

Louis XIII spent much of his reign outside Paris, fighting local or
foreign enemies. Partly because of his wars, he became unpopular. On
6 July 1641 the King's cousin the Comte de Soissons, Grand Maître de
France, who had fled in 1636 and allied with Spain, was killed after defeating French troops. It was said that, had he survived, he could have led his
army to Paris and raised it against the King. By the time of his death Louis
XIII limited his visits to his capital, for fear of being cursed in the streets.[25]

Thus Louis XIV's capital was a cauldron of combustible institutions,
at once the support and rival of the monarchy. On 18 May 1643, three
days after his state entry into Paris, Louis proceeded from the Louvre
through the streets caked in mud and excrement, for which Paris would
remain notorious until the mid-nineteenth century, to the Parlement on
the Île de la Cité. In the Grand' Chambre the young King, overcome by
the shock of his accession, burst into tears when he tried to make a speech:
it was finished for him by Chancellor Séguier. Anne of Austria, draped in
widow's black, asked the Parlement for advice on securing 'the good of
the state'. Gaston renounced his share in the regency promised in Louis
XIII's will, but with the other Bourbon princes, by right of birth, became
a member of the council. Showing his innate flexibility, Chancellor Séguier
helped ensure that the Parlement nullified the King's will restricting the
Queen's powers as regent, which he himself had written and had registered. At his request she received 'full, entire and absolute authority' as
regent, without the obligation to follow the advice of the majority of the
council. He called the Queen, whom six years earlier he had interrogated
for treason, 'virtue itself'.[26]

At first, her charm, her charitableness and the feeling that she too had
been a victim of Cardinal Richelieu's persecutions made the Queen

popular. The Comte de La Fare wrote in his memoirs that she knew 'how to hold a court better than anyone in the world' – how to do and say the right thing, maintain appearances and avoid inappropriate favourites. It was said that the French language had been reduced to five words: 'la reine est si bonne.'[27]

She was happy to spend the evening with her tapestry and her sons, while courtiers amused themselves elsewhere.[28] To universal surprise her husband's adviser Cardinal Mazarin was appointed head of the council on 20 May. The Queen trusted him more than anyone else; as a cardinal of foreign origin he was not dependent on French factions or princes. Gaston was often late for council meetings, after gambling through the night.[29] In September this poem was popular in Paris:

> The Queen gives all.
> Monsieur gambles all.
> M. le Prince takes all.
> Cardinal Mazarin does all.
> The chancellor seals all.

The young King is not mentioned.

More civil than Richelieu, Mazarin paid calls on all council members, and on princes, dukes and senior officials. 'He is tall, with good features, a good-looking man, with chestnut hair, a lively intelligent expression, with great gentleness in his face,' wrote d'Ormesson in his diary. Soon he was no longer 'le Cardinal Mazarini' but, like Richelieu before him, 'M. le Cardinal'.[30]

In June 1643 the Queen dismissed Richelieu's protégée Madame de Lansac as *gouvernante des enfants de France*. The epitome of the over-zealous governess, she had on several occasions, under Richelieu, tried to separate the Queen from her sons, and was said to have told her to retire to a pleasant house while she herself looked after the children.[31] She was replaced by the Queen's Dame d'Honneur Madame de Sennecey, an enemy of Richelieu who had returned to court after eight years' exile. In October 1643 the court moved from the Louvre to the Palais Cardinal, where Richelieu had lived. It was renamed the Palais Royal.

Much changed, the Palais Royal is now seat of the Conseil d'Etat: some walls in the courtyard, however, still display, as they did in Louis XIV's time, sculpted naval trophies placed there by Richelieu, who had been Admiral of France. The palace had a fine garden where the King could exercise. Louis XIV and his brother slept in Richelieu's bedroom, Anne of Austria in her old enemy's summer apartment.

In theory the move was for the King's health and to avoid building works at the Louvre. Some Parisians, however, said that the move was to satisfy the Queen's wish to 'have more liberty with M. le Cardinal'. From November 1644 he also slept in the palace. Their apartments were adjacent and communicated directly by a small *passage dérobé*: architecture confirmed the intimacy of their letters.[32] Mazarin's own palace, just north of the Palais Royal, was designed by François Mansart in 1643–7; it contained a magnificent gallery with frescoes of scenes from classical mythology, by a painter imported from Rome called Romanelli, now used for exhibitions by the Bibliothèque Nationale.

Mazarin's rise was further confirmed when, in 1645 and 1646 respectively, he became *surintendant* both of the Queen's household and of the King's education.[33] He used these offices, as was customary, to enrich himself. Private and public money were intermingled; he profited from war not only through supplying French armies, but also through his share of the sale of goods captured on enemy ships. His fortune – the size of which still eludes historians, as it did even his most suspicious contemporaries – would become as large, in liquid assets alone (that is, excluding properties), as all the liquid funds in the richest bank of the day, the Bank of Amsterdam.[34]

Her biographer Claude Dulong believes that, as some pamphlets and the *passage dérobé* suggest, the Queen and Mazarin were lovers, or secretly married. In their surviving correspondence from 1650–51 and 1657 the Cardinal affirms the uniqueness of their incomparable, unshakeable and 'perfect' friendship: 'never has there been a friendship approaching that which I have for you.' Secret signs, numbers, asterisks and codes symbolized love and fidelity. 'I am until my last breath **,' wrote the Cardinal. The Queen, regretting that there was much she could not put in writing, declared, 'I will always be as I ought to be, whatever happens . . . a million times until the last breath.' A secret seal linked the initials ICM (Jules Cardinal Mazarin) and AA (Anne of Austria), to which were added four crossed Ss, a seventeenth-century symbol of love. Thus a priest from a minor Roman noble family and a queen of France formed a couple. She visited him in the evening and disliked his departure on campaign. He tried to reassure and control her, fearing signs of independence.[35] At times he found her devotion and bedside visits wearisome. He had no other known mistress, so probably had little sexual drive. The Queen's maids and confessor took their secrets to the grave.[36]

Concentrating her interests and emotions in her regency for 'the king my son', Anne forgot her loyalty to the House of Austria. As queen regent, she dropped the friends she had made as queen consort. Her former intimate the Duchesse de Chevreuse encouraged the handsome, popular Duc de Beaufort to plot Mazarin's assassination. Beaufort was sent to the Bastille, the Duchess to her chateau of Dampierre outside Paris.[37] Mazarin wrote to the French Ambassador in Venice: 'there has never been a princess more French by inclination than she, nor a mother with more passion for the glory of her son and the good of his affairs.'[38]

Few royal mothers and sons in any century have enjoyed such a close bond. Mazarin wrote of the Queen (who had already had smallpox once) in December 1647, after Louis had contracted the disease, 'throughout the King's illness, she could not be obliged to take any precaution, nor prevented from doing everything generally which was most likely to make her catch the disease again, continually serving the King in every duty which his lowest servants could have performed, and kissing or embracing him all the time.' She suffered from exhaustion for 'having passed entire nights without having shut her eyes'.[39] She sometimes mended his clothes herself. If he disobeyed her, however, she would threaten him with a beating. He would ask her forgiveness and declare that he had no will but hers.[40] They ate meals together, which was not then customary. Until her death she wore a bracelet containing strands of his hair.[41]

Louis was kind and modest as a boy, far less terrifying than he later became. He was intelligent, 'seeing and understanding everything', according to one of his *premiers valets de chambre* Pierre de La Porte, an enemy of Mazarin and admirer of the Queen: 'he was naturally good and human, and from that time there was every appearance in the world that he would be a great prince, but . . . he was not inspired often enough to show he was the master.' He 'was very docile and always yielded to reason', accepting all his doctors' 'extreme remedies' during his infection with *la petite vérole*: enemas, bleedings and incisions. Thereafter, miraculously, he remained in good health. Courtiers, who sometimes attended his lessons, had to discourage him from wearing plain clothes, or standing up when his older cousin the Prince de Condé came into the room.[42] He sometimes quarrelled with his younger brother Philippe, Duc d'Anjou. They urinated on each other's beds; but he signed one letter to Philippe: 'votre affectionné frère et bon petit papa Louis'.[43] He was already, as he would remain, 'very secretive', in the words of La Porte. For Olivier d'Ormesson, 'No prince has been more promising, either by the perfection of his body or by that of his mind.'[44]

Louis' private life was dominated by his mother. His public life was already an unending sequence of ceremonies. He visited churches for Te Deums to celebrate French victories; for masses, sermons, vespers and ceremonies such as the Adoration of the Cross; or for admission into

Catholic *confréries* such as that of Saint-Denis. He won universal admiration for his gravity, grace and *prestance* (presence).[45] He also gave audiences and reviewed troops. In April 1644, for example, at the age of six, he reviewed the regiments of Gardes Françaises and Gardes Suisses in the Bois de Boulogne.[46]

On 1 April 1645, accompanied by the court, the guard and the choir of the chapel royal, held in the arms of his Premier Ecuyer the Duc de Saint-Simon, he laid the foundation stone of the new convent and church of the Val-de-Grâce, replacing the former buildings, on the rue Saint-Jacques leading pilgrims from Paris to the shrine of Santiago de Compostela in north-west Spain. It was erected by Anne of Austria as an expression of gratitude for 'the favour of a long-desired king and a fortunate birth'. Covered with their crowned, interlaced monogram A L, it is dedicated to the Virgin Mary and the infant Jesus (in implicit comparison with Anne of Austria and Louis XIV). Designed by Mansart, frescoed by Mignard, with a baldacchino like St Peter's in Rome, it expresses the triumph of a queen mother. It also contained a gilded pavilion, or hermitage – more luxurious than the nuns' dormitories – in which she could rest, pray or sleep, far from the turmoil of the court.[47] Between 1643 and her death in 1666 she would visit Val-de-Grâce 537 times and spend 146 nights there.[48]

Spending winter in Paris, in the summer Louis XIV and his mother visited other royal palaces – Fontainebleau, south-east of Paris; Compiègne, halfway to the Spanish Netherlands, to the north; Chantilly, the great Montmorency chateau which Louis' godmother had brought into the House of Condé, also to the north – and nearby provincial cities like Chartres and Amiens. At Dieppe, in August 1647 Louis first saw the sea, and witnessed a mock naval battle.[49] More itinerant than other monarchs of the time, Louis XIV would come to know his kingdom extremely well.

England, and his English cousins, were already part of Louis' life. In November 1644, he went outside Paris with his mother to greet his father's sister Henrietta Maria, Queen of England, after she had fled in the wake of Parliamentarian victories. Out of politeness and respect for the English monarchy – which considered itself equal in sanctity and antiquity to the French – and for Henrietta Maria's rank as *fille de France*, Anne of Austria let her sister-in-law take precedence. They called each other 'ma soeur'. Louis called Henrietta Maria 'ma tante'. She called him 'Monsieur'.[50] She received a pension of 1,200 francs a day, an apartment in the Louvre and frequent invitations to court.[51] In June 1646 she was joined by her son the Prince of Wales, who would live in France for most of the following eight years. After his father's execution in January 1649 had made him Charles II, he was treated in public as Louis XIV's equal, walking on his right and sitting in a similar armchair.[52] He also received part of Henrietta Maria's pension. To advertise his Protestantism, both in 1646–9 and during his second stay in 1651–4, Charles II regularly attended Anglican services in a room in the Louvre. In 1646 Henrietta Maria's youngest daughter Henrietta Anne, in 1648 her second son the Duke of York, the future James II, and in 1653 her third son the Duke of Gloucester also joined her. Until 1655, York was a familiar figure in Paris, dancing in the same ballets as Louis XIV and serving in the French army. Like Charles II, however, he could not find a French princess willing to marry him: the Stuarts, like the many supporters who followed them to Paris, were regarded as ill-fated exiles.[53]

Henrietta Maria and Charles II, and their courtiers, sometimes spent the summer in the Château Neuf of Saint-Germain. Mazarin, however, disliked Henrietta Maria and her children, as they did him. Dominated by concern to win England as an ally in the war against Spain, he considered the Stuarts authors of their own misfortunes.[54] When Charles I was executed, the French government had made no more than a feeble protest.

While the King was beginning to lose the 'roses and lilies' of his youthful complexion, the French army, led by his cousin the Duc d'Enghien (Prince de Condé after his father's death in 1646), was winning victories against Spain: Rocroi in 1643, Lens in 1648; news of the latter battle, remarked the King, would annoy 'messieurs du Parlement'.[55] Dunkirk was conquered in 1646. The Spanish army was no longer the best in Europe, and the French army was conquering the middle land between France and the Rhine, acre by acre. Victory, however, was accompanied by poor harvests, rising taxation and increasing discontent, especially in Paris. The annual budget of the crown rose from 88 million livres in 1642 to 141 million in 1644. Those who could not pay their taxes had their properties confiscated.[56]

In France in the seventeenth century *traitants* or *partisans*, as private financiers were called, organized tax collection and military supplies. Soon they were blamed for every financial crisis and were denounced as parasites gorging off public money. They, in contrast, regarded themselves as efficient managers who kept the crown and its armies functioning and victorious. Glorious new chateaux advertised their wealth, such as Maisons to the west of Paris, where Louis XIV was sometimes entertained by René de Longueil, Marquis de Maisons, Président de Parlement and Surintendant des Finances. For John Evelyn, Maisons exceeded almost anything he had seen in Italy.[57]

A tax on new constructions in the *faubourgs* particularly infuriated

Parisians. Treasury officials themselves sympathized with the complaints of taxpayers. The taille was the main royal income tax, raised from members of the third estate, with the exception of inhabitants of privileged towns: nobles were exempt. From 1645 the *taille* was farmed out to *traitants*. They loaned back to the state part of the profits they made from collecting its taxes.[58] Crowds entered the Palais de Justice and yelled for the head of the Surintendant des Finances, d'Emery. The Avocat Général Omer Talon feared that 'an entire people' had been roused.[59] In March 1645 a deputation from the Parlement was received by Anne. She said she would die rather than let royal authority be diminished. The deputation left 'very confused'. On her way with Louis XIV to Notre-Dame in November, their carriage was surrounded by women screaming for bread and money. On another occasion they yelled to her that d'Emery was spending her son's inheritance.

The conflict between the Palais Royal on the right bank and 'le Palais' on the Île de la Cité, between the court and the Parlement, soon developed into a revolutionary situation. It was called the Fronde, after the *fronde* or sling which boys used to propel stones at their targets; sympathizers were *frondeurs*; to riot or complain was *fronder*.[60]

On 14 January 1648 when asked to register yet more taxes and offices, *parlementaires* blamed the government for the impoverishment of the kingdom and urged the need to relieve the 'poor people'. Louis XIV – as he had in 1643 – forgot his words and began to cry; once again his speech had to be continued by Chancellor Séguier. As he left the Palais, there were no shouts of 'Vive le roi!'[61]

Respected judges spoke out. Pierre Broussel called the Parlement the centre of the monarchy, referred to Tiberius' [that is, Mazarin's] tyranny over the Roman Senate and claimed that 'the sovereign is best served by being disobeyed.' Aymard-Jean de Nicolay, First President of the Chambre des Comptes, in which his family had served since 1506, accused the royal council of 'overthrowing the foundations of this state by breaking the links between the sovereign power and its subjects'. Omer Talon denounced public misery, and criticized French conquests which 'cannot nourish those who have no bread, who cannot count myrtle, palms and laurel wreaths among the fruits of the earth'. He feared another 1588. On 13 May the different courts formed a union among themselves in an attempt to control the monarchy. Anne of Austria accused them of trying to create a republic.[62] Indeed some Parisians cried 'À Naples! À Naples!' when the King left the Palais – suggesting that they wished to follow the example of Naples, which had risen against the Spanish crown in July 1647 under a fishmonger called Masaniello and later declared itself a republic.[63]

In June, with three other sovereign courts, the Parlement followed up the 13 May *arrêt d'union* and formed a revolutionary assembly called the Chambre Saint-Louis.[64] Measures were passed declaring that no one should be held in prison for more than twenty-four hours without charge; and that the *taille* should be reduced by one-eighth and be collected by government officials rather than private financiers. The Parlement was exploiting popular discontent in a bid to secure a share in the King's legislative and executive, as well as judicial, powers, and turn France into a 'mixed' monarchy, with representative institutions. It decreed that no new law should be enforced without its prior approval.[65] The French monarchy already permitted representative institutions with tax-raising powers, like the General Assembly of the French Clergy meeting every five years, and assemblies of representatives of the three orders (clergy, nobility, third estate), meeting regularly in certain provinces such as Languedoc, Burgundy and Provence.[66]

Gaston, Duc d'Orléans, who spoke well in public, emerged as a mediator between the court and the capital. Assuring investors that interest on government bonds, suspended that January, would be paid, the Queen accepted the concessions Gaston proposed, and allowed the Chambre Saint-Louis to continue its meetings.[67] The principal royal executive agents in the provinces, the *intendants*, introduced under Richelieu and detested by the public, were officially abolished on 13 July.[68] Accounts of Concini's death in 1617 were pasted on walls in the city – implying that another Italian favourite, Mazarin, could also be murdered.[69]

On 26 August, the day after the annual festival of the French monarchy, the feast of St Louis (also the saint's day of Louis XIV), while a Te Deum was being sung in Notre-Dame for the great French victory at Lens over the Spanish army of Flanders, on Anne's orders six Gardes du Corps arrested the leading *parlementaires* Broussel and René Potier de Blancmesnil. They were sent to be imprisoned in Le Havre. As in 1588, Parisians rose in fury. Crowds gathered in the streets, perhaps as many as 50,000, including most of the militia, shouting 'Vive le roi! Vive le Parlement! Vive monsieur Broussel!' Shops closed.[70] The number of barricades in the streets was estimated at 1,260. Particularly on the Île de la Cité and in the rue Saint-Honoré, only a few steps from the Palais Royal, they were considered more formidable than in 1588.[71]

Again as in 1588, Paris proved stronger than the royal guard, which was prevented from occupying the Palais. Observers were impressed by what Olivier d'Ormesson called a 'spirit of order and obedience' throughout the city. Robbery and violence were rare. Stolen property was returned.[72] Madame de Motteville wrote that the militia, which was armed, did its rounds 'with so much order that one can say that never was disorder so well ordered'.[73]

In the summer of 1648 Paris was a volcano waiting to erupt. Some *frondeurs* claimed that officials of the King's household and soldiers of the Gardes Françaises encouraged them to revolt. Inside every courtier, a *frondeur* was trying to get out.[74] Madame de Motteville writes: 'Everyone wanted change, more by disturbance in their brains than by reason ... The king was weak, the princes had too much power, the minister was discredited, and the Parlement made overambitious attacks on royal authority. Everything was outside its normal limits; order was overturned; and the French, for having too many masters, no longer recognized any.'[75]

On 25 August Chancellor Séguier, besieged for five hours in the Hôtel de Luynes, had nearly been lynched. Marie Dubois, one of the King's valets, called Parisians 'tigers' and exclaimed in his memoirs, 'Paris is such a terrible force, which could unleash 100,000 men to execute what it desired!' The Palais Royal was like an armed camp; in the streets outside, courtiers dared not bear arms for fear of being attacked. Some bourgeois shouted that they wanted the King 'in their hands to guard him themselves in the Hôtel de Ville'.[76] Mazarin lamented in his notebook that 'the Parlement has performed the functions of the king and the people have entirely deferred to it. It has given the king Broussel as an associate.' The Queen and Mazarin were attacked in pamphlets and posters with 'terrifying insolence'.[77] Between 1648 and 1652 at least 5,000 pamphlets and poems against him, known as 'Mazarinades', were printed.[78] One called him a 'bougre sodomisant l'état'. Another showed him mounting 'l'âne [donkey] d'Autriche' – that is, the Queen.[79] As a friend wrote to Mathieu Molé, Premier Président of the Parlement de Paris, 'these sacred names [of the King and Queen] are not capable of restraining them.'[80]

The Queen and Mazarin did not perceive the economic or political causes of discontent, nor did they understand that the strains of war (France and Spain had been fighting since 1635) and the effects of corruption, in particular Mazarin's uncontrolled rapacity, were undermining the monarchy. They regarded all attacks on royal authority as outrageous. Having survived Richelieu and her own husband, the Queen knew how to play the political game, making use of delay, 'sweet words', even her own person. On the evening of 26 August 1648, she allowed colonels, captains and bourgeois of the Paris militia to be presented to her in the Palais Royal. She thanked them for preventing popular disorders 'with many displays of benevolence, the king being seated in a chair beside the bed of the said lady, who suffered that many of these captains and bourgeois embraced her by the legs while kissing her hands'.[81]

Finally on 27 August, bowing to the combined pressure of the city and the Parlement of Paris – the Premier Président Molé warned that she might lose the entire kingdom – the Queen agreed to release Broussel and Blancmesnil. The following morning, when Broussel appeared back in Paris, crowds shouted, 'Vive le roi et Monsieur Broussel!' The King was cheered again when he attended mass in Paris churches.[82] On 30 and 31 August colonels and 'the principal captains of the city' were again, probably on Mazarin's advice, admitted to the palace, this time to the bedroom shared by the King and his brother, and were again showered with compliments and with assurances of the royal family's love for Paris.[83]

One modern biographer of Anne of Austria expresses amazement that a revolution did not occur. 'One Danton would have been enough to make the history of France jump one hundred and thirty years ahead.'[84] In contrast to 1789, the King's guards remained loyal, while the Paris militia enforced law and order. No guards mutinied like the Gardes Françaises who led the attack on the Bastille on 14 July 1789; no officials or soldiers were murdered to deter others from obeying orders.

Above all Paris was still a Catholic city, with a growing number of charitable and religious orders and fraternities, which helped make the lives of the poor slightly less intolerable. Of the ambitious and able Co-adjutor of the Archbishop of Paris, Gondi, later known as the Cardinal de Retz, Madame de Motteville wrote that he had 'great intelligence and knowledge and in addition a great heart and grandeur in his soul'. The curés of Paris obeyed him; he walked through the streets of Paris to appease sedition. In 1789, in contrast, clergymen like Sieyès, Fouché and Talleyrand, and the curé deputies in the first estate, helped radicalize the revolution.[85]

On 22 October 1648 a reforming declaration was issued by the royal government. The *taille* was to be cut by 20 per cent. An amnesty for *frondeurs* and immunity for *parlementaires* were promised. The Queen protested to Condé and Gaston that she had agreed only under duress, because of 'the necessity of the state'. Her son, she feared, might become no more than 'a king in a pack of cards'. Mazarin was furious that the Treaty of Westphalia, signed that autumn, passed almost unnoticed in Paris. It ended war between France and the Holy Roman Emperor, and confirmed French territorial gains in southern Alsace. But his failure at the same time to conclude peace with the King of Spain left France, to the dismay of most Frenchmen, still at war.[86]

The more concessions the Queen made, the more Parlement demanded. It voted laws ordering the bourgeois to remain armed and forbidding the royal army to come within 20 leagues of Paris.[87] It was no longer discussing laws, but attacking the monarchy's military power. It also decreed, on 23 October 1648, that no financiers, or their children, could buy judicial offices.[88]

Like Henri III in May 1588 and Louis XVI in June 1791, the court decided on flight. Mazarin and the Queen chose the night of 5/6 January 1649. It was the feast of Epiphany, traditionally a time when 'everyone would be engaged in debauchery', wrote Gaston's daughter Mademoiselle de Montpensier, whose memoirs are among the most direct of this period.[89] In those circumstances it would be easier to slip out of the city. That evening the Queen remained in her Petit Cabinet, watching her sons and courtiers enjoy 'choosing the king', by hunting for a bean in a special Epiphany cake. The only change Madame de Motteville noted was that she seemed more cheerful than usual. She told courtiers that the following day she would visit the Val-de-Grâce.[90]

Having retired for the night, she woke her sons at 2 a.m. They left by an *escalier dérobé*, or backstairs, accompanied by the King's Governor the Maréchal de Villeroy; the Duc de Villequier, Capitaine des Gardes du Corps in waiting; guards officers such as Comminges and Guitaut; and the Queen's Première Femme de Chambre in waiting, Madame de Beauvais. De Beringhen, the Premier Ecuyer, organized the journey – as in 1567, 1588 and 1791, the success of the King's flight depended on his coaches and horses. In the gardens of the Cours la Reine west of the Tuileries garden, they were joined by Gaston, Condé and Mazarin, the latter carrying some of his jewels. As the royal coaches left Paris, Mademoiselle remarked that she had never seen anyone as gay as the Queen. It was as if she had taken the city and hanged all her enemies.[91]

Since the move was a surprise, and furniture generally followed the royal family from palace to palace, in the Château Vieux of Saint-Germain nothing was ready except four camp beds which Mazarin had had the foresight to send ahead a few days earlier. All but the King and Queen, Mazarin and Anjou had to sleep on straw.[92]

Justifying the move in a letter referring to a plot 'to seize our own person' and *parlementaires*' 'pernicious plans' and alleged negotiations with Spanish agents, the government had hoped to win Parisians' support against the Parlement.[93] However, the two remained in alliance. In addition part of the court and the nobility, in the language of the Registres de l'Hôtel de Ville, 'embraced the party of the City and the Parlement'. They included the illegitimate descendant of Henri IV, the Duc de Beaufort, known as 'le roi des halles', the king of the markets; the Duc de Bouillon; the Duc d'Elbeuf, younger brother of the Duc de Guise; and the ducs de

Luynes and de Chevreuse. Their leadership helps explain why the Fronde remained socially conservative.

At this time women were often active politicians. The Duchesse de Longueville, sister of the King's third cousins the Princes de Condé and Conti, was a leader of the Fronde. Mazarin called her Nérontine. Madame de Motteville considered her 'the soul of the Parisian party'. To the cheers of a mob, the Duchess moved into the Hôtel de Ville, where she gave birth to a son called Charles-Paris. She then summoned from Saint-Germain her younger brother the Prince de Conti, who followed her blindly, to be generalissimo of the army of Paris and the Parlement 'pour le service du Roi' – in reality against him.[94]

In January 1649, in a direct insult to the crown, Conti removed the royal Governor of the Bastille, the towering fourteenth-century fortress in the east of the city which was its principal arsenal and prison, and replaced him with Broussel. Paris was again, as in the days of the Catholic League, a city with an army. There were regular war councils of colonels and *quarteniers* to discuss fortifications and barricades; the militia included great nobles, Gardes Français, *parlementaires* like Pierre Viole and bourgeois like the crippled playwright Paul Scarron, author of scurrilous verses attacking Mazarin.[95]

For a time, loyalty to the city outweighed loyalty to the monarchy. The sight of royal livery in the streets of Paris made the wearer liable to attack. One judge in the Parlement declared, 'I am a native of Paris and I offer myself to her, to carry out any order she wishes to give me.' The university donated 10,000 livres. Lawyers volunteered to join the army of Paris, as did some royal guards.[96] Dubois, trying to rejoin the court at Saint-Germain to perform his duties as one of the King's valets, found 'all the people supported the *parlement* and assassinated those who went to join the king's service; they called us "the Mazarins" because of the government of Cardinal Mazarin who was head of the council and greatly hated.'[97] The Parlement, which claimed to represent justice, condemned the Cardinal to exile without trial and confiscation of his property. It was declared legal to kill this 'enemy of the King and the state' if he did not leave France at once.[98] Court and capital were at war.

3

The Struggle for France

The four years between the flight of the court from Paris on 5 January 1649 and Mazarin's return to Paris on 3 February 1653 are among the most confused in French history. Paris is in uproar. Princes and provinces rebel. Cities shut their gates in the King's face. The countryside is devastated. Frenchmen claim that kings have a duty to their subjects, as well as subjects to kings, and that obedience to kings is conditional on their observance of the law.[1]

Some Frenchmen dreamed of the convocation of the States General and a royal council composed of representatives of all three estates, Church, nobility and non-nobles.[2] Nine times between 1648 and 1653 Anne of Austria promised to summon the States General. On several occasions deputies were elected. They never formally assembled. The possibility of a meeting, however, would appeal to many during Louis XIV's reign.[3]

The absence of an enemy leader capable of exploiting French weakness – in contrast to the second half of Louis XIV's reign when he faced three geniuses, William III, Marlborough and Prince Eugene – helped the French monarchy to survive. The Archduke Leopold William, Governor General of the Spanish Netherlands from 1647 to 1656, was an aesthete who preferred collecting pictures in Brussels to fighting battles in France.

Another reason for the monarchy's survival was that its agents were often more unpopular than the institution itself. Louis XIV's youth, by absolving him of blame for the government's acts, also sustained his popularity. The wave of love which had greeted his entry into Paris in 1643 often returned, although not as frequently as his mother and he would have liked.

Moreover, most Frenchmen were repelled by what pamphlets called 'the bad example', 'the unfortunate example', of England. In France the trial and execution of Charles I on 30 January 1649, and the proclamation of the Commonwealth, increased support for monarchy, and intensified fear of a republic.[4] Anne of Austria's belief that Charles I's dismissal of his chief minister Strafford, and Strafford's subsequent execution, had led to his downfall strengthened her resolve not to dismiss Mazarin.[5]

Above all the monarchy survived because it retained control of its own security. The Gardes du Corps, the French and Swiss guards and the Maison du Roi did not mutiny or desert. The King was never a prisoner or a puppet, like Louis XVI after the Paris National Guard took control of his person from the Gardes du Corps on 6 October 1789 and escorted him from Versailles to Paris. Louis XIV could arrest his enemies, or move residence, as he wished.

On two occasions, in 1648 and 1651, Anne of Austria personally dismissed *capitaines des gardes*: the first time because of a brawl outside a church between Gardes du Corps and Gardes Français while the King was inside; on the second because M. de Chandenier, Capitaine des Gardes, was an ally of Mgr de Retz, the dangerously ambitious leader of the Paris clergy.[6] Chandenier was replaced by M. de Noailles – a key stage in the ascent of the Noailles who would later become, thanks to Louis XIV, the most powerful of all French court families, and who still own estates outside Paris today.[7] In May 1650, when delays in their pay led Swiss guards to threaten to stop guarding the Palais Royal and return home, the council soon found the money to pay them.[8]

Mazarin stressed that the King should always be surrounded by a large number of Gardes du Corps, in case the princes were tempted to stage a coup. The *capitaine des gardes* and *premier gentilhomme* in waiting should always sleep in the King's bedroom.[9] To Anne of Austria the Cardinal wrote: 'the Queen should be very careful and only go out very heavily escorted.'[10]

The Duc de La Rochefoucauld, author of celebrated maxims such as 'we all have enough strength to bear the misfortunes of others', later regretted this failure to seize the King's person at the start of the Fronde: 'the gravity of the undertaking prevented him [the King's cousin the Prince de Condé] from recognizing its facility.' 'This easy and assured path' would have prevented the return of Mazarin and legitimized the Fronde.[11] At the height of *frondeur* power in Paris, Retz and Beaufort also urged seizing the King: 'there is no point in half-measures.' Probably the main reason this advice was not followed was not respect for the King but fear of his guards.[12]

Mazarin was detested for his corruption, his foreign birth, his 'secrètes et artificieuses négociations'.[13] With the help of his brilliant young Intendant, Jean-Baptiste Colbert, he made a fortune selling offices and tax farms while many royal officials remained unpaid.[14] He helped both to save the monarchy and to endanger it. For the Duchesse de Nemours his greed and unpopularity were the main causes of the Fronde.[15] Yet while all turned against him, the Queen remained loyal. She almost always followed his advice, sent by coded letter when he was in exile. His notes telling her what she should say and do survive: 'la Reyne dira que', and so on.[16] For example: 'the principle of their [Anne's and Louis XIV's] conduct should never be the passion of love or hate but the interest and advantage of the state and the maintenance of their authority.'[17]

Mazarin believed that the private ambitions of between twenty and thirty princes, ministers and nobles were as important in driving the Fronde as public issues of war, taxation and royal authority. However, if public issues were not also crucial, they would not have been adopted by Mazarin's enemies: hence Gaston supported the calling of the States General, while Condé had links with key *parlementaires*. More people paid court to Condé than to Gaston, although Condé was a third cousin, rather than the uncle, of the King. Condé was a revered war hero, who had won most of the French victories of the 1640s, and he had a son. Gaston had a weaker personality and only daughters.

Expressing the opinions of the Queen's household, one of her *premières femmes de chambre* Madame de Motteville wrote in her memoirs that some 'great movements in the world which destroy or establish empires' were in reality due to the 'secret intrigues of a few people', often over unimportant matters.[18] The Duchesse de Chevreuse's hatred of the Prince de Condé, for example, helped divide the Fronde.[19] La Rochefoucauld's support of the Fronde was partly driven by desire to win his wife the right to sit on a tabouret, or foot stool, at formal ceremonies in the presence of the Queen.[20] The passion of *mesdames fesses*, or *les dames assises*, for what was called 'the divine tabouret' inspired a poem entitled 'De la guerre des tabourets', telling 'infamous bottoms' to take the route of Sodom and go to Rome.[21] The court of France was not the only institution which used furniture to mark status. City corporations and cathedrals also did so, as did other countries. French prestige, and the security of French trade in the Ottoman Empire, the French Ambassador would write to Louis XIV in 1680, depended in part on knowledge in that Empire that he had the right to place his stool on the Grand Vizier's platform.[22]

Love, money, personal circumstances could decide allegiances, as much as the ideological division between supporters of an authoritarian monarchy and those who preferred one limited by the States General. The greatest French generals were ready to fight for the King of Spain: Turenne in 1650–51, Condé in 1651–9. Turenne returned to his native allegiance in August 1651 partly for family reasons: in exchange for ceding the strategic Protestant frontier fortress of Sedan to the crown, his brother was given the Duchy of Albret in the centre of France. Their family, the La Tour d'Auvergne, who claimed to date from before the time of Christ, won the coveted rank of *prince étranger*.[23] This gave a small group of members of foreign ruling dynasties – such as the princes of the Houses of Gonzaga, Lorraine and Savoy – precedence over dukes at court, although not in the Parlement.

In February 1649, however, Condé had remained loyal. He commanded the royal army of 6,000 besieging and blockading Paris, although food supplies were let through.[24] His brother Conti, commanding Paris for the Fronde, had written asking for help to the Archduke Leopold William in the Spanish Netherlands. On 11 March, pushed by financial necessity and fear of a Spanish invasion, a treaty was signed at Rueil, Richelieu's splendid chateau west of Paris, where the court often resided. Lionne, Secretary of State for Foreign Affairs, wrote to Abel Servien, the diplomat who had helped negotiate the Treaty of Westphalia: 'the truth of the matter is that we had to sign because of the arrival of the Archduke.' Without fear of invasion, 'we would not have abandoned the punishment or at least the exile of the factious.'[25]

In return for an amnesty, there were to be no further collective assemblies of the different law courts. Decrees against Mazarin were annulled. Throughout April 1649 deputations from the law courts, the curés and the guilds of Paris came to salute the court at Saint-Germain; but the court spent May to August at the ancient royal palace of Compiègne, 50 miles north of Paris.[26] Anne of Austria, through Louis XIV, asked 'ma cour de Parlement' to help enforce law and order in Paris.[27] At Compiègne, Madame de Motteville wrote that the court which had inspired 'the admiration of Europe was reduced to great misery'. Some of the crown jewels were pawned. Many court officials and servants left, as they were no longer paid.[28]

The Parlement appeared to have won. Mazarin feared it, as a permanent institution, more than princes and nobles, believing that it hoped to control the King even after he reached his majority.[29] However, the monarchy still held the trump cards of the King's popularity, and the royal guard and army. On 18 August 1649 the court returned to the capital. The King and royal family in a carriage, escorted by Mazarin and Condé, were greeted, on the plain between Saint-Denis and Paris, by the Provost and *échevins* of the city on bended knee. 'They were not capable, in the excess of their happiness, of explaining themselves more than very feebly,' said the Provost, overcome by emotion. The plain and the entire route to the Palais Royal were covered with people shouting 'Vive le roi!' and letting off fireworks.[30] Paris was a court city again. Even Mazarin was cheered.

Parisians drank his health, with money distributed to them by his servants.[31]

On 25 August, his own feast day as well as that of St Louis, the King went in procession to the new, baroque church of Saint-Louis in the Marais, 'as superior in appearance and grace as in birth and dignity'. He was again greeted by 'continuous acclamation', according to Olivier d'Ormesson, and constantly took off his hat to the ladies cheering him from their windows. Anne of Austria wept for joy, 'acknowledging to the right and left all the princesses, ladies and other persons of condition' with 'caresses and obliging words', since she wanted 'to make herself popular with the Parisians'.[32] Market women who had formerly cursed her cheered and blessed her, begging forgiveness, trying to touch her dress.[33]

The Fronde was marked by balls as well as battles. The monarchy and Paris not only remained in dialogue; they danced together. On 5 September at a ball in the Hôtel de Ville (which was required to provide, in advance, 'rooms and private places' in which the ladies of the court could 'coiff and adjust themselves'), the King opened the dance with his first cousin Anne-Marie, 'la Grande Mademoiselle', daughter of Gaston, Duc d'Orléans by his first wife, the heiress of the ducs de Montpensier.* The greatest heiress in Europe, she considered only the King of France or the Holy Roman Emperor worthy to be her husband. As his next partner, again showing the court's desire to woo Paris, he took Madame le Feron, wife of the Prévôt des Marchands: an act of condescension to which, when older, he would never have stooped. Social distinctions were still fluid: as a young man, Louis XIV hunted and dined with judges, financiers and Protestants, whom in old age he would spurn.[34]

On 8 December Louis XIV was confirmed in the chapel of the Palais Royal. That Christmas, in another gesture to Parisians, he made his first communion in the local parish church, Saint-Eustache, still today, like Saint-Louis in the Marais, one of the great churches of Paris. There were 'perpetual cries of "Vive le roi"' despite the curé being an ardent *frondeur*.[35]

Condé, to whom Anne of Austria had publicly expressed her gratitude for the court's safe return to Paris, was now the most powerful man in France. He faced the dilemma common to ambitious royal cousins. The order of succession was too well established for usurpation to be easy. However, portions of sovereignty might be within reach. As the victor of Rocroi and defender of the monarchy, this arrogant Prince demanded influence over royal patronage and policy, and an automatic seat in the

---

* Gaston was usually known as 'Monsieur', short for 'Monsieur, frère du roi'. His daughter's title was 'Mademoiselle': she was called 'la Grande Mademoiselle' as she was unusually tall.

council, by right rather than as a favour – as today some corporations consider themselves automatically entitled to influence a government whose election they have helped to engineer. Mademoiselle wrote that, since the princes were 'the people most interested in the good of the State . . . according to every probability, they should be its masters'.[36]

In October Mazarin signed a treaty promising 'not to decide anything in affairs of state without asking the advice of the Prince de Condé'.[37] The princes were to be consulted on senior appointments, and even on the marriages of the Cardinal's nieces, one of whom, recently arrived from Rome, had danced with the King at the ball of the Hôtel de Ville.[38] Condé also became semi-independent ruler of the fortress of Stenay, on France's crucial eastern frontier.[39]

Despite the apparent truce, the power struggle between the Queen, Mazarin and Condé was heightened by acts of discourtesy on the Prince's part. He encouraged one of his followers, a guards officer called the Marquis de Jarzé, to write love letters to the Queen.[40] She told him publicly that she would have felt insulted had he been the first 'joli galant' in his family to make himself ridiculous; his grandfather had already tried to declare love for Marie de Médicis.[41] Some thought Condé wanted to rule Guyenne, Burgundy or Navarre, or become constable of France, controlling the government.[42]

Condé, Conti (now back under his brother's influence) and their brother-in-law the Duc de Longueville, Governor of Normandy, ignored the Duchesse de Longueville's advice never to go to court at the same time. On the morning of 18 January 1650 in the Palais Royal, the young King told them, 'maman says we should go to the gallery.' There the princes were arrested by the Comte de Guitaut, an officer in the Gardes du Corps, and then sent as prisoners to the fourteenth-century castle of Vincennes, east of Paris. Clearly Louis was growing in self-confidence.[43]

Demonstrating that the royal government could also use the language of consent, the Queen justified her use of force in a letter to the Prévôt des Marchands and his officials as being 'for the good of our affairs'.[44] The rest of 1650 was spent making visits to rebellious provinces. They followed a pattern. The court arrived; the young King was displayed; the province, which had previously supported the princes, submitted. The presence of the royal army was balanced by pardons and renewals of privileges. The court, usually staying in the palace of the local bishop or archbishop, endured rounds of urban, religious, legal and academic rituals and orations. The King continued his education.

Visits of this kind were made to Normandy in February 1650; Burgundy in March–April; the Orléannais and Touraine in July; and Bordeaux and its environs in August to October.[45] Sometimes, for example outside Saintes near Bordeaux in October 1650, the King's court was 'so small that you could hardly imagine it', as one eyewitness called Philippe Fortin de la Hoguette wrote.[46]

The King was the key. When he entered Rouen, his doting confessor Père Paulin declared, 'such is his goodness and facility of humour, joined to the grace of his body and the sweetness of his glances, that I know no more powerful philtre to enchain hearts. All Normandy could not tire of the sight of him.' The Queen could conquer the entire universe, he continued, merely by displaying him.[47] Mazarin wrote with delight to the Premier Président on 13 April 1650 from Dijon in Burgundy, where the royal troops were fighting the *frondeurs* under Turenne and his elder brother the Duc de Bouillon: 'without flattery the King has behaved marvellously well during this entire voyage; the soldiers have been extraordinarily satisfied with him; if he had been allowed to, there would have been nowhere [on the battlefield] where he would not have gone.'[48]

The King was naturally serious, rarely laughing even when playing with his brother Philippe.[49] He was learning politics by personal experience. On 7 September 1649 at the age of eleven he had sat in the council for the first time. Olivier d'Ormesson was told that he 'gave his opinion there so judiciously that . . . His Majesty showed all his ministers and Councillors of State the marvels they should expect from Him at a more advanced age'.[50] As his composure before the princes' arrest in the Palais Royal on 18 January 1650 showed, he had also become an excellent actor.

Attendance at the council, and private meetings with Mazarin several times a day, gave the King a political education, both French and European. Venetian ambassadors noted his great affection and sympathy for the Cardinal, although some also claimed that Mazarin encouraged the King's love of dancing and sports in order to deter him from concentrating on affairs of state.[51]

In addition, under the supervision of his Governor the Maréchal de Villeroy, he received a thorough education in Christian doctrine from his preceptors Mgr de Beaumont and Mgr Hardouin de Péréfixe, later Archbishop of Paris, and Père Paulin who, like all his confessors, was a Jesuit. He also studied Latin, Italian (which he learnt to speak well, with the help of one of Mazarin's officials named Ascanio Amalteo), geography, grammar and mathematics – lessons sometimes observed by court officials.[52] His French history lessons emphasized the power and antiquity of his dynasty and the number of kingdoms it had ruled, including Poland, Hungary, Naples, Jerusalem and Constantinople. His grandfather 'Henri le Grand' was depicted in the biography written for Louis XIV by Hardouin de Péréfixe and dedicated to Mazarin as a kind and gentle hero. Henri IV's Edict of Nantes of 1598, giving Protestants freedom to worship in certain locations outside Paris, and the right to defend themselves, had been a necessity of state. Forced conversions were wrong.

Above all Louis XIV was taught that a king must, like Henri IV, exercise his authority himself, not leave it in the hands of his ministers: 'Royalty is almost all action.'[53] It is not true, as many of Mazarin's enemies asserted, and as the King himself sometimes claimed in old age, that his education was neglected. By the age of fourteen he had acquired enough skill to typeset a page of Commynes' memoirs (the first book of French political memoirs, describing the power struggle between Louis XI and the Duke of Burgundy, published in 1524), and had translated part of Caesar's commentaries on the war in Gaul.[54] His Latin exercises from 1651, signed 'Ludovicus', begin with a translation of the statement 'the principal duty of a Christian prince is to serve God and piety is the foundation of all royal virtues.' He also translated warnings that it was his duty to restrain his passions as if they were 'wild animals'. Otherwise the people might despise his orders.[55] At night his valets read him works of history and other books, for example *Le Roman comique*, a novel by Paul Scarron (whose widow, by then known as the Marquise de Maintenon, he would marry thirty years later).[56] His favourite sports were swimming, tennis, dancing and horsemanship, taught by another Italian called Lepidio Arnolfini. Returning from reviewing his troops at the age of nine, he controlled a rearing horse, as ladies screamed with fright, removing his feet 'without emotion' to avoid them getting caught in the stirrups.[57]

From the age of five he also drilled a troop of *enfants d'honneur* in the art of war. Wearing black velvet trimmed with grey, they were exercised by him in the garden of the Palais Royal, 'pike in hand and beating drums', remembered one of them, Henri de Brienne. A miniature fort with bastions, built in the Tuileries garden in 1650, would start the passion for siege warfare which would mark the King's entire reign.[58]

His main hero was not, as his tutors would have wished, one of the great figures of French history such as Charlemagne, St Louis or Henri IV, but Alexander the Great, who inherited a throne and conquered the world.[59] Like Alexander, Louis would be determined to win what he called, in a letter to the commander of his Gardes Francaises, the Maréchal de Gramont, 'the most exquisite praises of history'.[60]

The young Louis XIV might be, as his tutors said, the key to France's future. Yet French provinces returned to the princes' authority, and paid them taxes, the moment he left. Bordeaux gave the King a cold welcome when it finally opened its gates in October 1650. The real reason for its submission was the need to harvest grapes in peace, in order to make wine that autumn.[61]

Mazarin and the financiers were still detested. In Paris the coach of Louis XIV and Anne of Austria could be followed by investors in government bonds shouting for justice. Pressure from court officials to release the imprisoned princes, and the numbers of formal petitions by the Parlement and assemblies of nobles in Paris, increased. On 30 January 1651 Gaston and Condé signed a treaty of friendship. On 1 February Gaston and Mazarin quarrelled in the King's presence in the Palais Royal, when Mazarin compared the Paris Parlement to the English Parliament which had ordered Charles I's execution – a comparison still in French minds two years after the event. Further comparisons with Oliver Cromwell and the Parliamentarian General Fairfax so infuriated Gaston that he swore he would not remain a member of the council while Mazarin was in it.[62] According to the *frondeur* the Duc de La Rochefoucauld, even court officials, as well as judges of the Parlement, wanted Mazarin's arrest.[63]

One of the Queen's goddaughters Anne de Gonzague, Princesse Palatine, daughter of Charles de Gonzague, Duke of Mantua and Nevers, was another powerful woman politician. Mazarin admired her 'perfect knowledge of the humours and interests of those with whom she has to deal'.[64] She dominated her husband, Prince Edward of the Rhine, a handsome, insignificant younger brother of Prince Rupert, who had moved to Paris and converted to Catholicism. Since Edward's mother Elizabeth, Queen of Bohemia, 'the Winter Queen', was daughter of James I, she called herself 'a granddaughter of England'.[65] For Madame de Motteville, and another great memoirist, the Cardinal de Retz, she was the paragon of her sex, beautiful, intelligent and capable of winning the confidence of all sides.[66] The diarist Pierre Lenet wrote that she was more intelligent than all the politicians of the period put together.[67] In February 1651, encouraged by the Princesse Palatine, Mazarin himself took the order for the princes' release to Le Havre. Then, realizing that the alliance between Gaston and Condé, and popular discontent, made his enemies stronger than he was, at the formal request of the princes and the Parlement he left France, for the castle of Brühl in the electorate of Cologne, in the strategic interzone between France and the Rhine. The Queen felt obliged to agree to his departure, but, as we have seen, continued to correspond with him in code.[68]

Condé's route from Le Havre back to Paris on 16 February 1651 was lined with crowds cheering 'Vivent les princes et point de Mazarin!'

Gaston himself came out from the city to greet his cousin.[69] Hitherto a loyal supporter of royal authority Gaston, Lieutenant General of the kingdom and President of the Council of War, now forced the Queen to agree to summon the States General. They had heated disputes in the council over the date it should assemble. The King's person remained the key to power. Every evening in February Gaston sent the commander of his Swiss Guard, Monsieur des Ouches, to the Palais Royal to draw the curtains of the King's bed, to check that he was there and had not again fled to Saint-Germain. On his orders, the Paris militia, as well as royal guards, patrolled outside. To the disgust of the Queen, the militia's posts around the palace were so close to the royal guards that the two could speak to each other.[70]

For more than a month the King was almost his uncle's prisoner. People going in and out of the Palais Royal were searched. The Queen was suspected of wishing to leave Paris. On the nights of 9 and 10 February she had to allow Parisians to file through the King's bedroom and check for themselves that he was still there: Madame de Motteville says that the visitors' alarm turned to love and they gave the sleeping boy a thousand blessings.[71]

This intrusion into the King's bedroom was as revealing of French attitudes to the monarchy as the grandiose *levers* and *couchers* which Louis XIV would hold there thirty years later. Submission alternated with disrespect. Mademoiselle comments in her memoirs, 'to tell the truth these are matters which can hardly be forgotten.' Indeed the young King would not forget such humiliations.[72] The Maréchal du Plessis, Governor of his younger brother the Duc d'Anjou, remembered that the populace of Paris committed 'daily follies'.[73]

The French court tried to woo its rebellious subjects through dance. Catherine de Médicis had popularized ballets as court spectacles after 1560: her son Henri III had been said to devote more attention to ballets than to war.[74] With elaborate, choreographed steps and figures, and magnificent sets and costumes, ballet was not only considered good exercise, like riding or fencing, but also represented on stage that harmony and control which the French monarchy tried to impose in the kingdom. Margaret McGowan calls it 'a source of unsurpassed entertainment as well as an opportunity to indoctrinate audiences with royalist propaganda'.[75]

Dance was almost as popular as gym exercises are today. The two had similar functions, since dance was believed to strengthen the body: it also advertised the dancer's skill, grace, benevolence and good humour and taught him or her deportment. Like Louis XIII, who had often danced in public, both at court and in the Hôtel de Ville, Louis XIV had danced before the court as early as the age of seven, with the sister of the

Princesse Palatine, Louise Marie de Gonzague, before she left France to become queen of Poland. Even when he danced, wrote the *Gazette de France*, 'il sait bien même faire le roi' ('he knows well how to act the king').[76] No false steps. Successive dancing masters (Henri Prévost, Jean Renaud and Pierre Beauchamps) helped turn a shy young prince into a regal monarch of great physical dexterity and dignity of bearing.[77]

Having rehearsed for days, the young King danced for the first time in public in *Cassandre* with words by the poet Isaac de Benserade on 26 February 1651: his lines included the assertion 'je ne suis point à moi, je suis à l'univers.' Like his father before him, he continued to dance on stage in public, as well as at balls in private, until he was aged over thirty: a total of sixty roles in twenty-three ballets. Some lasted for five hours. In especially complicated ballets, he might be guided by better dancers like Bontemps, a *premier valet de chambre*, or by the Duc de Saint-Aignan, a favourite *premier gentilhomme de la chambre*.[78] Sometimes, again like his father, he danced female roles, for example Ceres goddess of fertility, a village girl or a shepherdess – proof of his versatility, demonstrating that the King was above human norms, capable of playing any part, majestic or burlesque.[79]

From the bitterness of exile, Mazarin complained that, rather than organizing entertainments, the King and Queen should act as prisoners.[80] Stating that 'it is only by arms that one can completely re-establish affairs and the authority of the king,' he planned to bring foreign soldiers into France.[81] Thanks to the loyalty of the guards, and to Anne of Austria's new alliance with Condé against Gaston, by April 1651 the royal family had recovered their freedom.[82] That summer, however, although frequently hunting and swimming outside Paris, the King always slept in his capital.[83]

Posters appeared saying 'every good citizen and Frenchman' supported Condé. Terms like citizen, *patrie* and *fraternité* thus became familiar long before 1789, as did desire for government accountability and hatred of corruption. Condé wooed Parisians, kneeling and kissing the relics of St Geneviève, the city's patron saint, when they were paraded through the streets.[84] This did not prevent him complaining that his Protestant grandfather had not been more bored by Huguenot preachers in the Protestant port of La Rochelle than he had become by Parisians' talk of Parlements, assemblies and the Hôtel de Ville.[85]

Condé tried to control army and ministerial appointments. His protégés were appointed governors of Guienne, Berri, Burgundy and Champagne and, on 18 July 1651, he obtained the dismissal of three key ministers, Lionne, Servien and Le Tellier.[86] Yet Condé shunned the court and on

31 July refused to descend from his own carriage as the King's carriage passed by, returning from a swimming expedition in the Seine (carriages, as we shall see, frequently provoked precedence battles). The King remarked that, if his guards had been with him, he would have charged Condé at their head.[87] Unlike Anne of Austria, Condé made no effort to cultivate Retz; on 21 August their followers came to blows in the Palais. Retz was almost crushed between two doors by La Rochefoucauld's soldiers.[88] The young King asked his uncle Gaston: 'do you want to be in my party or M. le prince's?'[89]

On 7 September, when Louis XIV was thirteen, and officially came of age, another brilliant ceremony, like those marking his entries into Paris in 1643 and 1649, was staged in an attempt to reassert the prestige of the monarchy. The King went in state to the Parlement in a 'glorious cavalcade', preceded by 800 nobles walking two by two without order of precedence, by governors of provinces, marshals of France and chevaliers of the Order of the Holy Spirit. He was surrounded by his guards and household, and followed by princes and dukes.[90]

The diarist John Evelyn, watching from the window of his fellow exile the philosopher Thomas Hobbes, admired the blue velvet coats, embroidered with gold, worn by the King's trumpeters, and the guards and grandees 'magnificently habited and mounted . . . covered with gold, jewels and rich caparisons' of black velvet or scarlet satin. In the 'glorious cavalcade' there was an 'abundance of footmen and pages of the King new liveried with white and red feathers'. The King himself 'like a young Apollo was in a suit so covered with rich embroidery that one could perceive nothing of the stuff under it; he went almost the whole way with his hat in hand, saluting the ladies and acclamators who filled their windows with their beauty and the air with *Vive le Roy*. He seemed a prince of a grave yet sweet countenance.'[91]

After mass in the Sainte-Chapelle, he opened a solemn *lit de justice* in the Grand' Chambre with the words: 'Gentlemen I have come to my Parlement to tell you that according to the law of my State I wish to take charge of its government myself; and I hope by the goodness of God that it will be with piety and justice. My Chancellor will tell you privately my intentions.' Then, after short speeches by Chancellor Séguier and Anne of Austria, Louis XIV turned to his mother: 'Madame, I thank you for the care you have been pleased to take of my education and the administration of my kingdom. I beg you to continue to give me your good advice. I desire that after me you should be head of my Council.'[92]

Yet the glorious ceremony hid profound conflicts. The King's brother

Philippe and uncle Gaston paid him homage, but Condé, fearing arrest by royal guards, had left Paris the day before; the King did not deign to open his letter of excuse.[93] On 22 September Condé arrived in Bordeaux where he seized royal revenues and began to raise troops, as if he was the King, rather than the Governor of the province.[94]

Copies of the deluge of orders, instructions, commissions sent by the royal government, in the King's name 'on the advice of the Queen Regent Madame my mother', all recorded in registers in the same clear secretarial hand, show its attempts to control events. On 6 September 1651 for example the Maréchal d'Aumont was instructed to make 'les troupes des princes' join the King's army. On 10 September all officers of the Armée de Flandre (previously serving under Condé) in Paris were to be imprisoned by the watchmen of Paris in the Bastille.[95]

On 27 September the court left Paris in pursuit of the rebel Prince. Most of that autumn and winter it spent in Poitiers, in the centre of France.[96] The official council under the Queen and Richelieu's old enemy M. de Châteauneuf, with Molé as *garde des sceaux* (keeper of the seals), was hostile to Mazarin.[97] To Mazarin's horror, Louis XIV publicly proclaimed him an outlaw and a criminal.[98]

This had been, however, a tactic in a moment of weakness, designed to reassure public opinion. On 1 December the King, against the wishes of most of his court, but no doubt at his mother's prompting, signed a secret order for Mazarin to return. The Maréchal du Plessis, his brother's Governor, commented, 'the king, delighted to be obliged to begin acting as master in a matter of consequence, did so well that, having himself searched for a writing table, he signed it without anybody noticing.'[99] By the age of thirteen, he had become independent, competent and secretive.

In January 1652 Mazarin returned with 4,000 troops, escorted by 'the great Mazarins', marshals d'Hocquincourt, La Ferté and d'Aumont. Louis and his brother came out from Poitiers to greet him. A favoured royal financier, a Protestant of German origin called Barthélemé d'Herwarth, lent the Cardinal money.[100] Despite Mazarin's return, the Fronde was not losing but gaining strength. Divine right did not outweigh public hostility. In the words of La Porte it was a 'poor and miserable court on which all the cities shut their gates'.[101] On 27 March 1652 the court left Poitiers for Blois – where Henri III had murdered Guise in 1588 – 'from fear of dying of hunger' in the words of a Paris writer called Guy Patin. That day Mademoiselle entered Orléans in triumph, at the head of her troops, while the Garde des Sceaux, preceding Louis XIV, was refused entry.[102]

For two weeks, from 2 to 15 April 1652, the court retreated to the great brick castle of Gien, overlooking one of the few bridges crossing the upper

Loire. Condé suddenly appeared at the head of 15,000 soldiers, after a march across southern France from Bordeaux: the King had only 12,000.[103] On 6 April the royal army was defeated at the battle of Bléneau: it is possible that the King was saved from capture by Condé only by the arrival of Turenne at the head of another royal army.[104]

Paris turned against the royal government, again tarnished, in its eyes, by Mazarin's return. Gaston had told the Parlement that Louis XIV had become a 'roi de Bourges' like Charles VII, when England had controlled Paris and northern France in the 1420s.[105] He also said that Condé and he would lay down their arms if Mazarin left France. Despite a decree placing the Cardinal's magnificent 40,000-volume library under the legal protection of the King, it was auctioned by the Parlement (in deliberately small lots, in order to ensure its dispersal). The proceeds were to be used to pay his future assassin. Paris booksellers fixed the prices in advance with the auctioneers, in order to resell the books at a profit. Mazarin called them Goths and Vandals.[106]

After Charles II's miraculous escape in disguise from England following his defeat by Cromwell at Worcester, he had returned to Paris in November 1651. The Louvre again lodged an English court in exile. Since he had to pay his Privy Council and a web of diplomats throughout Europe, at times Charles was so short of money that he was reduced to eating in taverns. Nevertheless in May and June 1652, at his own suggestion, he acted as a mediator with the Fronde.[107] Gaston discussed with the Parlement the peace proposals Charles brought from Louis, but turned them down.[108] However, Charles did, to the *frondeurs'* fury, help persuade their ally, his cousin the Duke of Lorraine, to withdraw his 8,000 troops from France.[109]

Paris prepared for battle. Condé had entered the city on 11 April, and soon his street gang under M. Penis, a financial official from Limoges, was terrorizing the city.[110] The court circled around Paris, between Saint-Germain, Saint-Denis and Pontoise. To Condé's envoys Louis XIV reaffirmed his support for Mazarin.[111] The Registres de l'Hôtel de Ville show that the city council and militia were asked by the royal government itself to guard certain areas.[112] The King was shocked by *frondeurs'* attacks on his guards at Saint-Denis, even though, on his personal orders, they provided escorts for bread and bakers to enter Paris, so that the city would not starve. *Frondeurs* spread rumours that the bread was poisoned.[113]

In May Condé and the popular Duc de Beaufort, by virtue of their royal blood, entered the Grand' Chambre of the Parlement and issued orders as if they had royal powers in Paris.[114] In the east of Paris on 2 July, the royal army of 12,000 under Turenne started fighting Condé's army of 4,000, which was helped by members of the Paris militia and Spanish troops, wearing the red St Andrew's cross of the dukes of Burgundy. The King and Mazarin watched the 'battle of the Faubourg Saint-Antoine', as it was called, from a hill above it, where the cemetery of Père Lachaise now lies.[115] Relishing her role as an independent commander, Mademoiselle, having obtained a written order from her father Gaston, seized the Hôtel de Ville. On her orders the gates of Paris were opened to Condé's army and the cannon of the Bastille, normally turned inwards on Paris, were turned outwards and fired on the royal army. The Cardinal's favourite nephew Paul Mancini, commanding the Chevau-légers de la Garde, died from a wound received while fighting Condé's troops.[116]

The court withdrew to Compiègne, but Condé threw away the fruits of victory. On 4 July some of his followers and soldiers attacked the Hôtel de Ville and installed an obedient municipality, with Broussel's son as provost. Those who did not wear straw in their hats and shout 'Point de Mazarin!' were attacked. At least thirty Parisians were killed, many wounded and robbed. Condé was declared commander-in-chief. Public opinion was shocked by what Jean Vallier, one of the King's *maîtres d'hôtel*, called the insolence of 'an enraged soldiery' and a 'furious populace excited by the hope of pillage'.[117]

On 20 July the Parlement declared the King to be a prisoner of Mazarin, and reappointed Gaston lieutenant general of the kingdom.[118] Exploiting cities' persistent desire for autonomy and hostility to the central government, on 29 July the Provost of Paris wrote to a hundred cities in France advocating 'fraternity' and 'correspondence with the other cities of the kingdom by means of the commerce by which they subsist'. They had no other purpose than the fall of the Cardinal, 'absolute master of the king and his council' and object of 'universal hatred by the peoples'. Then they would secure 'general peace'.[119]

Charles I's widow Henrietta Maria, living in the Louvre with Charles II, thought that France resembled England during the Civil War. She wrote to her sister Christine, Duchess of Savoy that such was the ferocity of the soldiers on both sides, and of marauding peasants, that 'if God does not take action, France will soon be ruined.'[120] Père Vincent de Paul agreed. He wrote: 'Paris is packed with poor because the armies have led the poor people of the countryside to come and take refuge there.' Soup was provided daily by charitable societies for 15,000 who would otherwise have starved. Vincent de Paul told the Queen and the Pope that in the country royal troops as well as rebels stole holy vessels, defiled the holy sacrament, violated nuns, burnt towns and villages. Peasants were being killed or left to starve.[121]

Public opinion – appalled by Condé's followers, and finding the Prince's approval of their violence 'insupportable' – finally began to return to the monarchy. Mazarin had the sense to leave France again on 19 August. On 6 September the law courts sent a letter to Anne of Austria begging for 'the honour of her presence in this city, on which all the happiness of this State depends'. Both sides spoke the same language of love and concern for the state.[122] Parisians demonstrated in favour of the King's return as the only remedy for their oppression and economic misery.[123] He instructed the Paris militia to occupy key positions in the city – using it as a means of hastening his return.[124] Retz, out of hatred of Condé, helped organize the King's arrival, calling kings, in a speech to Louis XIV at Compiègne, 'living images of the Divinity on earth'. However, he also believed that Gaston, who was still popular, could have opposed the King's re-entry if he had been truly determined.[125]

On 3 October there were cries of 'Vive le roi et la paix et point de princes!' when Gaston went to the Parlement. Two days later an assembly of all the colonels and officers of the militia of Paris asked for the return of the King; the Fronde had lost its military power-base.[126] On 13 October Condé left France for the Spanish Netherlands; one month later Philip IV made him generalissimo of the armies of Spain. Some members of the council still considered it dangerous for the court to return to Paris. However, Anne, Louis and their principal general Turenne were determined. The court needed Paris as much as Paris needed the court, Turenne remembered, since it could raise money to pay its army more easily there.[127]

On 21 October 1652, at the age of fourteen, Louis XIV made his ceremonial re-entry into Paris. He came by the Porte Saint-Honoré – not, as in 1649, sitting in his mother's carriage, but at the head of his guards, riding between his cousins Charles II and Prince Thomas of Savoy, followed by his mother and his brother in a carriage.[128] Rooftops, windows and streets were packed with cheering crowds. Retz and his clergy welcomed him at the entrance to the Louvre. That evening, as the Queen was congratulated at her circle in the Louvre on the warmth of Parisians' cheers, Turenne whispered to Retz: 'They made almost as many recently [on 2 June] for M. de Lorraine' – the *frondeurs'* friend.[129]

The next day Gaston, once the arbiter of Paris, withdrew on the King's orders to Blois, capital of the appanage or provinces he had been assigned by the crown for his support: he had long been negotiating his pardon with the royal government, with which on 28 October he signed a treaty guaranteeing his rights and pensions. His daughter Mademoiselle was exiled to her chateau of Saint-Fargeau in the Auvergne.[130]

Changes of location indicated changes in the balance of power. Louis

XIV and his mother chose to live not in the Palais Royal but in the better-fortified palace of the Louvre (Henrietta Maria and Charles II, in consequence, moved to the Palais Royal). For a *lit de justice* on 22 October, rather than going to the Parlement in the Île de la Cité, Louis XIV summoned it to the Grande Galerie of the Louvre. He granted a general amnesty, tearing up records of the recent 'movements' in order to extinguish all memory of them, and reinstalled the Parlement in Paris. However, he forbade it to discuss politics or finance without his permission, as it had during the Fronde, and exiled some leaders including Beaufort, La Rochefoucauld, Viole and Broussel.[131]

Louis was now a formidable young man, not afraid to show what Jean Vallier called 'une mine fière et hautaine'.[132] Retz's arrest in the Louvre on 19 December, on the personal orders of the King and his mother, was a further assertion of Louis' authority, and proof of his dissimulation. The operation had been approved from his place of exile, after some hesitation, by Mazarin. In a postscript to his written order, Louis XIV added in his own hand that, if the Cardinal resisted, the guards were to take him dead or alive.[133]

Like Guise in 1588 and Condé in 1650, Retz ignored warnings not to go to court. Like them, he believed that his popularity protected him. While talking of comedies in an antechamber with Retz and M. de Villequier, Capitaine des Gardes on duty (who had already received an order in writing), Louis whispered a few words in Villequier's ear, then left for mass. His confessor later wrote that on that occasion the King behaved 'with so much sense that it is difficult to express it. I will only maintain that there has never been a more refined politician who could have done it so well.'

Villequier arrested the Cardinal, gave him a meal, then accompanied him the length of the Grande Galerie to a carriage waiting in the Tuileries garden. From there he was escorted by Gendarmes, Chevau-légers de la Garde and Gardes Français to the castle of Vincennes. Villequier then returned to tell the King of the operation's success.[134] 'Rien ne branla dans la ville' ('Nothing moved in the city'), wrote the Cardinal sadly in his memoirs. Paris was as submissive as it had once been rebellious.[135] On 3 February 1653 another cardinal returned to Paris. The King and Monsieur went out of the city to greet Mazarin, and that evening entertained him to supper in the Louvre.[136] In the war since 1648 between Paris and the court, the court had won.

On 23 February, the court celebrated victory with a new ballet: the *Ballet Royal de la Nuit*, written by Isaac de Benserade. With beggars, demons and werewolves, and Molière in the role of Laughter, it was such a success that it would be repeated five times. Performances were open to all well-dressed members of the public. According to the Venetian Ambassador, the King had been practising since December, for six or seven hours a day.[137]

After dancing as an hour, as a game of cards and as a fury, Louis XIV finally appeared as Apollo, the rising sun, wearing a kilt of sunrays and a headdress of pink and white feathers, studded with rubies, diamonds and pearls. Surrounded by Honour (his first cousin James, Duke of York), Victory, Valour and Fame, he recited verses in which he claimed to illuminate the universe, having vanquished the 'terrible serpent' of rebellion. He finished with a promise of wars to come:

> Quand j'auray dissipé les Ombres de la France,
> Vers les climats lointains ma clarté paraissant,
> Ira victorieuse au milieu de Byzance,
> Effacer le Croissant.[138]

> ('When I have dispersed the Shadows from France,
> My light appearing to distant climates,
> Will go victorious to the heart of Byzantium,
> To efface the Crescent')

4

M. le Cardinal

On 4 July 1653, a year after the attack on the Hôtel de Ville by Condé's forces, the young King was entertained in the same building to a comedy and a magnificent dinner by the Provost and aldermen of Paris. Then there were fireworks and he threw gold coins to the cheering crowds outside. A year later a marble statue of the King, dressed as a Roman emperor in armour 'crushing rebellion', one foot resting on a many-headed dragon, was erected in the courtyard.[1]

The return of the King and the Cardinal, however, masked the fragility of their victory. The Fronde was partly caused by Mazarin's unpopularity and by the ambitions of a few powerful individuals: Gaston, Condé, Retz, certain *parlementaires*. However, its duration for five years suggested that many Frenchmen preferred to be ruled by judges, city councils or princes rather than by the King – and wanted government by consultation, with meetings of the States General, rather than by royal decree.

In Paris the King's mother and Regent had been insulted, his servants attacked in the streets, his 'sacred' person inspected in bed.[2] Twice he had nearly been taken prisoner, in Paris in 1651 and Gien in 1652. Divisions among the leaders of the Fronde, and Turenne's military genius, as much as its own strength and its subjects' loyalty, had preserved the French monarchy.

Even after the court's return to Paris, France remained on the edge of a precipice. Jean Vallier wrote in August 1653 that 'bad government was so general and so common that without a secret protection of God it was impossible that the government could survive much longer'. He was appalled that Mazarin used every occasion and every type of taxation, however small, to enrich himself, and to reward or buy supporters, 'advancing their private interests at the expense of general ones'. While crown jewels were pawned to the Swiss cantons to guarantee the payment of Swiss troops, forty ministers of state were appointed, with enormous salaries but few duties.[3] In retirement at Blois, Gaston expressed sympathy with the misery of local peasants and prophesied the end of the monarchy.[4]

Bordeaux continued to challenge both the royal victory and French unity. It was less loyal to the French monarchy than the Catalan capital, Barcelona. After the Catalan revolt of 1640, the Catalan Cortes had deposed Philip IV, elected Louis XIII Count of Barcelona, sworn allegiance to him, and later to Louis XIV, and resisted Spanish armies for twelve years until they recovered Barcelona in 1652.

Bordeaux, in contrast, resisted French armies and welcomed help from Spain and England. Manifestos and 'acts of union' almost as radical as their English equivalents were printed. A party known as the Ormistes, as they met under a group of *ormes* or elms, expelled royal officials from the Hôtel de Ville and defied the Parlement. They raised a citizen militia, and claimed to represent a tradition of municipal freedom dating back to the Roman Empire: *Vox populi, vox Dei*. The Prince de Conti, commander of Paris for the Fronde in 1649, commanded Bordeaux in the same cause from 1651 to 1653, encouraged by his sister-in-law the Princesse de Condé and his sister the Duchesse de Longueville.[5] The royal government was alarmed by the 'humeur républicaine' of Bordeaux, and the 'profound roots', both political and commercial, of its desire for an English alliance. Before 1453 it had been ruled by the kings of England and it was ready to accept English troops again. From 1651 to 1653 the English Council of State kept an agent, Colonel Sexby, with four gentlemen in the rebel city.[6]

On 3 August 1653, however, pushed by bourgeois attracted by a royal amnesty, Bordeaux surrendered to the royal army under the Duc de Vendôme – a royal bastard again proved more loyal than the royal cousins Condé and Conti.[7] While humble Ormistes were broken on the wheel, the Prince de Conti and the Duchesse de Longueville were allowed, by virtue of their rank, to withdraw to their estates. The Princesse de Condé sailed away to join her husband in the Spanish Netherlands. The Duchesse de Longueville's parting words to Conti were: 'you are unworthy of the blood of the Bourbons and of the honour of being so closely related to Monsieur le Prince.'[8]

Conti now became a zealous 'Mazarin'. Saying he would take any of the Cardinal's nieces, since it was the Cardinal he wanted to marry, on 22 February 1654 in the Queen's bedroom in the Louvre, in the presence of the King, the Prince de Conti married Mazarin's blonde young niece, Marie Anne Martinozzi. Her dowry was said to be 600,000 livres.[9] The marriage, defying differences of rank, was a success: husband and wife surpassed each other in good works.

The Duchesse de Longueville also turned to God. Switching from political to religious opposition, she became a protector of Jansenism, a particularly rigorous form of Catholicism, named after a professor of theology at the University of Louvain. Jansenists put the demands of the most austere Christian morality, and their own individual conscience, before obedience to religious or secular authority, which they distrusted. Their belief in salvation by God's grace alone, rather than by good works, faith or the sacraments, had a special appeal for Parisians with a spirit of opposition, who were no longer satisfied by traditional values based on honour. The movement's headquarters was the monastery of Port Royal, not far from the Val-de-Grâce. The King and their intellectual rivals the Jesuits detested them. The Papacy condemned them. Increasing numbers of Parisians and former *frondeurs*, however, including the Cardinal de Retz, admired them.[10]

Despite France's demographic superiority (a population of around 19 million, compared to 8 million in Spain), it was so weak and impoverished that it needed an ally to win the war. Mazarin's solution to the resilience of the Spanish armies under the Prince de Condé (as late as July 1656 he routed French forces outside Valenciennes) was to ally with Oliver Cromwell, Lord Protector of England. France had already, to Henrietta Maria's horror, established diplomatic relations with the English Commonwealth in December 1652.[11] England's population was only around 4 million, but it was rich, with an efficient army and navy. Cromwell wanted Dunkirk, to strengthen English control of the Channel. Strategy trumped legitimacy, *raison d'état* 'the family of kings'. Each leader used threats to push the other towards the alliance: Cromwell the possibility of England helping Bordeaux, Mazarin the fear of France aiding Charles II.[12]

During 1653 Charles II continued to be entertained by Louis XIV to hunts, ballets and dinners. On 29 May 1654, however, feeling less welcome in Paris and weary of 'the humours of the Queen [his mother, Henrietta Maria] who is not easily pleased', Charles bid farewell to Louis and left for Cologne. The arrears of his French pension would be paid only when he had left France. He soon moved to the Spanish Netherlands and allied himself, and his army in exile, to Philip IV.[13]

Mazarin was friendlier to Cromwell than to other allies, assuring him that French Protestants were loyal and well treated and that, if Cromwell took the title of king or emperor, Louis XIV would not complain.[14] He even proposed sending French royal guards to England if there were threats to Cromwell's authority.[15] His fondness for the Lord Protector may have been increased by his desire to obtain Henrietta Maria's jewels (including two famous diamonds, the Sancy and the Mirror of Portugal) and pictures at bargain prices. In 1657 France and England signed a formal alliance. When Cromwell died in 1658, Louis XIV and the entire court wore mourning for the English regicide.[16]

Meanwhile the church, the most independent institution in France, confirmed the limits of royal power. The Cardinal de Retz was feared by the royal government as 'the most dangerous enemy of the Monarchy'.[17] After his arrest, his curés often met together and prayed for his delivery. In March 1654 while he was in prison, the chapter of Notre-Dame dared to elect him archbishop of Paris; in August, to Mazarin's fury, he escaped from the castle of Nantes. Let down by a rope from the top of the walls, he fled on a waiting horse, and eventually found a boat to take him from the island of Belle-Île to Spain, later moving to Rome. An assembly of curés of Paris sent him letters of support.[18] Showing the extent of discontent and disobedience after the 'end' of the Fronde, his letters criticizing the government were secretly printed and pasted on the walls of the capital.[19] Even four years later, in April 1658, preaching a Lent sermon in front of Louis XIV while his mother and Mazarin were away, one priest repeated that all the sufferings of the people were due to Mazarin.[20]

On 30 May 1654 the King left Paris to be crowned in the magnificent Gothic cathedral of Reims, a shrine to monarchy filled with statues and effigies of kings. Despite his composure at formal ceremonies such as the declaration of his majority in 1651, Louis disliked them. He did not mark either his arrival in Reims or his return to Paris by ceremonial royal entries. He could not, however, curtail the grandiose rituals of coronation, essentially unchanged since the ninth century, by which the church sanctified the King in return for his promises to protect it from iniquity and injustice, and to expel heretics.[21] On 7 June 1654 he was anointed with holy oil from the 'Sainte ampoule' and crowned king with the 'crown of Charlemagne', brought from Saint-Denis for the occasion, by the Bishop of Soissons (the Archbishop of Reims, Henri de Savoie, Duc de Nemours, could not officiate, as he was not an ordained priest).[22] The tapestry-draped cathedral rang with cries of 'Vive le roi! Vivat rex in eternum!' Doves were released inside the cathedral. The King was given the orb, the sceptre, the sword of justice and golden spurs. He then received the homage of the peers of France.[23]

In engravings his mother and his aunt, the widowed queens of France and England, can be seen leaning on the edge of their special tribune to get a better view. The coronation was less elaborate than those of Louis XIV's successors, and was marred by the absence of the senior males of the royal family, Gaston, Condé and Conti.[24] Even at this sacred ceremony, an element of consent remained. The Bishop asked if the people accepted him as king, as if they had a choice. Although the ceremony began at 6 a.m., lasted eight hours and was followed by a state banquet, according to the official account 'in the evening the King invited the princesses to supper.' Louis XIV was already eager for female company. To commemorate his coronation, 6,000 prisoners were released.[25]

The official historian of his coronation called him 'the sun in the middle of all the stars' and 'the veritable father of the Arts and the Sciences'.[26] Such praise was, however, exceeded by a poem written by two Jesuits, who called him the equal of Jesus Christ:

> Jésus et Louis couronnés,
> Tous deux nous sont des Dieux donnez.
> L'un est le fils âiné, l'autre l'époux de l'église.
>
> ('Jesus and Louis crowned,
> Both are given to us by God.
> One is the eldest son, the other the husband of the Church').[27]

Both Christianity and the monarchy revered kings, the king of heaven and the king of France.

The Louvre continued to be the court's principal residence in the winter. After the Fronde, it did not withdraw from Paris. From 1653 to 1660 the King's and Queen's apartments in Henri IV's new wing in the Louvre were redecorated. Frescoes by the Roman baroque painter Giovanni Francesco Romanelli, who had helped decorate the Palais Mazarin, in the apartment of Anne of Austria (now filled with 'Antiquités romaines') show Religion and the theological virtues, Apollo and Diana, War and Peace, the Seine and the Rhône, and scenes from Roman history. Her bedroom was decorated with 'the virtues of the Queen': figures representing Temperance, Chastity, Piety and Religion, Magnificence, Liberality, Happiness and Majesty. On the ground floor her summer apartment had scenes from the lives of Old Testament heroines such as Judith and Esther, giving biblical authority to her political role in France. Thus the court brought Italian art to Paris, just as thirty years earlier Marie de Médicis had re-created in the Palais du Luxembourg some of the splendours of the Pitti Palace in her native Florence.[28]

On the first floor of the Pavillon du Roi, the former Antichambre du Roi and the King's bedroom were redecorated under the supervision of Louis Le Vau, First Architect to the King. Now moved to the colonnade wing, they still display magnificent gilded wood panels showing crowns, Ls, fleurs-de-lys, bound captives, 'la France triomphante' and, symbolizing its global ambitions, 'the French monarchy leaning on a crowned globe'.[29]

Throughout these years, Louis XIV went to church every two or three days. On 3 May 1655 he was admitted into another of the fraternities which strengthened Counter-Reformation Catholicism: the Confrérie du Saint-Nom-de-Jésus, founded to discourage blasphemy. The king of France was so sacred that, since the Middle Ages, he had been thought to have healing powers. On 16 May Louis touched 800 people for the King's Evil, or scrofula, in the Grande Galerie of the Louvre, as he had done the previous year in Reims after his coronation.[30]

On 13 April 1655, at the age of sixteen and a half, Louis XIV came to Paris for the day from the chateau of Vincennes, 9 miles to the east. Wearing an informal costume – a red coat with a grey hat – to show lack of respect for the Parlement, he held a *lit de justice* in the Palais, before the Parlement, which was wearing full dress, and annulled some recent laws. Then he personally declared, without speaking through his Chancellor, 'Everyone knows how much your assemblies have excited troubles in my State; and how many dangerous effects they have produced.' He forbade its members to debate royal edicts which had already been registered. Such edicts should be executed immediately.[31] Later writers alleged that he stated, 'l'Etat c'est moi.' But this is an invention, recorded by no contemporary observer. As his dying words would show, he had a strong sense of the state's independence and durability, compared to the transient life of a king.

The Parlement continued to annoy Mazarin. 'Favours do not make *parlementaires* more obedient. These messieurs are convinced that all is due to them and they owe nothing,' he wrote to Nicolas Fouquet, a member of the *noblesse de robe* or legal nobility of Paris who, through his loyalty to Mazarin and skill in raising money, had risen from the post of *intendant* to that of joint *surintendant des finances* in 1653. Some thought France was on the eve of another Fronde.[32] Nevertheless, throughout Louis XIV's reign the Parlement remained part of the state's administrative apparatus.[33] In 1659, when the court left Paris for several months, Mazarin wrote to Le Tellier: 'in addition to the orders the King will give M. le Chancelier and M. le Procureur Général to maintain everything in the order in which they should be during the journey of His Majesty, it can only be advantageous for you to order the sovereign courts to recommend them also through deputies to watch over public safety and peace during his absence.'[34]

Meanwhile, all eyes turned to the young King. Between the ages of fourteen and thirty, between the abjection of the Fronde and the intoxication of absolutism, he was affable, informal and Parisian. A gentleman from Rouen, Pierre Thomas, Sieur de Fossé, remembered of a visit to Paris in 1655:

> I also liked, young as I was, to go to the Louvre for the sole pleasure of seeing the king. I never tired of watching him either during his dinner, when I found the means of entering his chamber, or in the courtyard of the Louvre when he sometimes came down into it to arrange the harnesses of different carriage horses. I considered myself very fortunate when I could come close enough to him to see him entirely at my leisure, loving him, honouring him and perfectly respecting him.[35]

After a visit to Fontainebleau during the hunting season, Louis' aunt Henrietta Maria in October 1655 wrote to Charles II: 'the king is perfectly well and is so grown and become so handsome that nothing could be more so . . . I am so partial to the king that I am now almost in love with him. It is true that now he treats me like another person, and has become the most civil being in the world.' His relations, like his subjects, judged him partly by his manners.[36]

A year later at another hunting palace, another queen expressed admiration. Having abdicated the throne of Sweden and converted to Catholicism, Queen Christina had settled in Rome. She was visiting France to discuss with Mazarin a plan to become queen of Naples, where there was still a party opposed to Spanish rule: he promised help if, after her death, her throne passed to the Duc d'Anjou. She was welcomed by the court at Compiègne in September 1656, both as an ally and as a curiosity. Her clothes and manners were more like a man's than a woman's, her ladies resembled shop assistants and her conversation – she spoke French as if born in Paris – reflected 'libertine ideas'.[37]

She was convinced there was nothing 'criminal' between Anne of Austria and Mazarin, whose 'merveilleuse adresse' in conversation she admired. She wrote of Louis XIV, whom she found shy and silent: 'he is civil and courteous beyond anything one can imagine . . . until now he occupies himself with his fine clothes, with his horses, hunting and dancing, and succeeds marvellously in bodily exercises. He is tall, well built and handsome, although much less so than people say.'[38] In 1658 Mademoiselle, half in love, would call him the handsomest and best-built man in his kingdom.[39]

The King was increasingly interested in women. Paul Mancini, the Cardinal's favourite nephew, had been called by Parisian pamphleteers 'a monster and a miscreant' who had 'made every effort to instruct and lead him [the King] into every kind of vice and debauch'.[40] How far his efforts went is unknown: Mancini may be the suspect in the accusation by La

Porte, one of the King's *premiers valets de chambre*, in his memoirs and in a later letter, of a sexual assault on the King.[41] Mancini, as has been noted, died in July 1652, from wounds received in the battle of the Porte Saint-Antoine. A few months later four of his sisters arrived at court from Rome, after a period for education and polishing by their eldest sister Laure, Duchesse de Mercoeur, in Aix-en-Provence where her husband was governor. They provided far greater attractions.

Olympe, Hortense, Marie and Marie Anne Mancini were young, beautiful, cultivated and foreign. The King and his brother soon lived with them in what Hortense, many years later, remembered as 'a charming familiarity and sweetness'.[42] This familiarity astounded Mademoiselle in 1658 when she saw the King sitting with them at supper without a prescribed place. The Queen, who called the girls by their first names, explained that 'the King did not like ceremonies.'[43]

Olympe Mancini, one year younger than Louis XIV, was his favourite. Queen Christina wrote: 'he is in love with Mlle Mancini but with so much moderation and virtue that I do not think that for the three years he has been her servant he has ever allowed himself to touch the tips of her fingers. She is witty, adroit, knows marvellously how to act cruelly and takes pleasure in seeing one of the greatest kings in the world languishing at her feet.'[44] For a time this dimpled beauty, with white skin and eyes of fire, was the centre of court life. Another young woman, Mlle de La Mothe d'Argencourt, also attracted his attentions, but left to become a nun.[45]

In February 1657 Olympe married one of Louis' cousins, the Comte de Soissons, recently appointed colonel of the Gardes Suisses and nephew of the Comte de Soissons who had died fighting Louis XIII in 1641. After the wedding his wife was believed to 'possess all his [the King's] affections'. At a ball in 1658, she was the only woman to whom he was seen to talk.[46] Mazarin used her as a source of information, pushing her to remain the King's favourite, writing: 'You should allow anything from the king.'[47] That was how women rose at court: as intermediaries and weapons, mistresses and sources of news and entertainment. The King and the younger courtiers often gambled and talked with 'Madame la Comtesse' and 'Monsieur le Comte', as they were known, in the Hôtel de Soissons until three in the morning.[48]

Louis' court was at this stage, in contrast to his mother's, formal in public but unconventional in private. He played the guitar in concert with other musicians, and had his nurse sleep in his bedroom.[49] Many of his companions had been in the troop of *enfants d'honneur* whose captain he had been. One 'vicious' (that is, homosexual) young friend of the King, formerly in the troop, was the Marquis de Vivonne. At a party he gave, guests made fun of church ceremonies. Mass was said over a dead pig. Vivonne was exiled from court, at Anne's suggestion.[50]

Another wild young favourite who had also been in the troop of boy soldiers was the Comte de Guiche, handsome, witty and well built. He was described by an Italian gossip called Primi Visconti as 'the most corrupt man of the court', a man 'whom Love and Nature have enriched with a thousand delicate charms'. A lover of the Princesse Palatine, among many others, he was also suspected of sodomy. Mazarin noticed that he was 'assiduous' in attendance on the King's brother Philippe, Duc d'Anjou. Philippe was said to have been introduced to *le vice italien*, as homosexuality was often called in France, by Mazarin's other nephew, Philippe Mancini. On one occasion, Guiche defecated in the sleeve of a woman's coat and watched her put it on; on another he removed the hat which had hidden a woman's hand playing 'in a place which modesty forbids one to mention'. He was not punished.[51]

Anjou also enjoyed women's company, although he preferred men sexually. Pretty and talkative, he thought more of clothes and jewels than of war. When he attended a ball disguised as a gypsy girl, according to Mademoiselle, Guiche 'pushed him a lot in the dance and gave him kicks in the bottom . . . Monsieur enjoyed everything he did.' Anne forbade them to see each other alone. For his part, according to Mademoiselle, the King 'always wages war on Monsieur': mocking and denigrating, he said that no one would want to marry his brother.[52] Monsieur had the reputation for being 'governed' by the Princesse Palatine, whom Louis XIV disliked. Mademoiselle believed that Mazarin had encouraged his femininity in order to make him less dangerous to his brother. On the rare occasions that Louis, Anne or Mazarin mentioned him in their letters, they called him 'Monsieur le présomptif'.[53]

Except in 1659/60, Louis XIV spent the winter in Paris. In the summer, however, he was with his troops. More than the court, more even than women, the army would be the love of his life. During the Fronde, he had witnessed enough battles and forced marches to last a lifetime. Nevertheless in July 1653 he was serving near Saint-Quentin with the army of Picardy, to the delight of the soldiers.[54] Mazarin assured his mother that he was as safe as if he was in the Louvre.[55]

Immediately after his coronation Louis set out from Reims for the siege of Condé's stronghold Stenay: Condé did not defend it in person, as he was fighting in Flanders, for the King of Spain against France. It was Louis' introduction both to the middle land between France and the Empire, which he would visit almost every year for forty years until it was almost as familiar to him as the Île de France, and to the siege warfare which would become his passion. Remaining in Stenay from 11 July to 7 August, far longer than he had been in Reims for his coronation, he inspected the troops and trenches in detail, sometimes staying up until two in the morning, and finally received the town's surrender in person.[56] In the hot weather, he often swam in the Meuse.[57]

The *Gazette de France* reported, 'he finds the air of camps and armies more agreeable than that of the court.' In order to be near the fighting, the King stayed in provincial towns – Ham, Châlons, Sedan, Montmédy, Thionville – which few Parisians would willingly visit today. His doctor called Montmédy 'the most desolate and inconvenient place in the whole kingdom'.[58]

In 1655 Mazarin wrote to the Queen: 'the confidant [their code-name for the King] is indefatigable; he rode all day with the army and on arrival here instead of resting went to see all the advanced guard posts . . . he is not tired after fifteen hours on horseback.' His own household, unlike the King, detested the *tracas* or worries of army camps.[59] The same pattern was repeated in 1656, when the King's passion for his army again led him to spend weeks in army camps. Munitions and supplies were transported in his own carriages, and those of the Queen and the Cardinal.[60]

Louis' love of fighting even affected his health. As a young boy, he had been physically strong, although often catching cold during ballet rehearsals. Preferring to 'expose himself to extraordinary fatigue' in order to avoid being away from his soldiers, the King rode all day on horseback, rather than using a carriage, sometimes until the early morning. In 1655 one of his doctors, M. Vallot, noticed what he called in his journal 'a matter of a consistency between white of egg and pus', flowing 'almost at every moment without pain or pleasure' from 'the parts which serve for generation'. Although believing that the King was still 'chaste', he also called it 'corrupted and infected seminal matter', hinting at venereal disease. The stains were hard to remove from the King's underclothes.[61] The doctor blamed the condition on friction from constant riding and 'les exercices de l'académie', in other words horsemanship. Although Louis was only seventeen, Vallot noticed that the King's private parts were 'meurtries' – 'already very weak' – and feared that he might not be able to have children.

The court doctors were meant to be the best in their profession, and supervised all doctors throughout France. However, even by the standards of the time, Vallot was a charlatan. His medicines for the King included pills made of ground pearls; a brew of deer antlers and ivory; 'opiate of Provins roses'; and application to his private parts and chest of 'essence of ants'. The King was also subjected to enemas, purges, blood-letting and more. At one time, on his doctor's advice, he did not eat fruit or salad for eight months.[62] Soon his illness was being discussed throughout France. By 1656, however, after drinking massive quantities of water from the spa at Forges, Louis XIV was better. No more fears for his health were expressed, although occasionally he had worms.

The problem appears to have been a result of masturbation or secret encounters with women. It was long believed at court that Madame de Beauvais, one of his mother's *premières femmes de chambre*, who had the reputation of being 'more than gallant', had, as his sister in-law would write years later, taught him 'what he has learnt to do so well with women'.[63] Simone Bertière, biographer of Anne of Austria and Mazarin, thinks, probably correctly, that the King's appetites were 'discrètement satisfaits en coulisse' ('discreetly satisfied behind the scenes').[64]

Despite health problems, Louis XIV frequently reviewed or drilled his troops in Paris as well as on campaign. In April 1657 two young Dutchmen visiting Paris saw the King exercising his musketeers with their commander, Mazarin's surviving nephew Philippe Mancini: 'Certainly they are well-chosen men who are magnificently dressed as each one has a blue breastplate with great silver crosses with golden flames which end in fleurs-de-lys . . . he is a brave prince, well made and very tall for his age.'[65] Louis would talk for hours with his cousins about his guards and musketeers, and in 1661 would write to his mother of the latter: 'they serve me with so much zeal and punctuality that every day I have more reasons to appreciate them.'[66]

In these years Louis, Anne and Mazarin formed an emotional triangle. In a letter to the Queen in 1653, Louis wrote, in his own hand: 'I have seen the letter you have written [to Mazarin] and I am delighted by the tenderness you have for me. I beg you to believe that I will have it for you until death. It is M. le Cardinal who tells me what to write, but only after I have told him what my feelings are.'[67] Mazarin assured Anne that the King loved her more than anything in the world. To Louis he signed himself 'the most faithful, passionate and partial of all your servants and creatures'.[68]

Mazarin loved Louis like a father. In 1658, for example, just before Louis was twenty, he wrote to Anne: 'they say he wears his wig so well [after he lost hair during an illness], that he is so well dressed and gallant that I do not doubt that being the best-built man in the kingdom, the ladies will rush at him ['ne le courent à force' – a hunting metaphor], and I approve of everything provided that they don't keep him up too late.'[69] Wearing a wig was the first of the many fashions set by Louis. Many men began to wear one too, out of flattery rather than necessity.

The Queen and Mazarin wrote as if they could control the King's movements, but he had begun to make his own decisions. For example in 1658 Mazarin wrote to the Queen, 'if the confidant takes more pleasure in Compiègne, he can stay there without government business suffering for it; but if he believes that he can enjoy himself more at Fontainebleau, I beg you to make him take the resolution to go there.'[70]

The King and his mother sometimes quarrelled about whose dynasty was grander: Louis reminded his mother that his ancestors had been kings of France when hers were mere counts of Habsburg (although, more recently, which may explain part of his ambition, the Bourbons had been mere ducs de Bourbon when the Habsburgs were Holy Roman emperors and kings of Spain). Later, one of Louis XIV's most admired preachers, Bossuet, would claim that the crown of France was 'as much above the other crowns of the world as royal dignity surpasses private destinies'.[71]

Both mother and son, however, agreed on Mazarin's genius in government. Despite being a cardinal, Mazarin deplored the influence of religion on policy. He defended the English alliance on the grounds that, despite its Protestantism, it was better to have England with France than against it. 'Bad Frenchmen' opposed the alliance 'under the pretext of religion and piety to surprise the good people who in their simplicity do not see the heart of the matter'.[72] Despite protests from Catholic bishops, he continued to regard French Protestants as loyal subjects and to allow them to hold synods.

Helped by their English allies, French troops under Turenne had begun to beat Spanish forces under Condé. On 14 June 1658 French and English armies defeated Spanish forces at the 'battle of the Dunes', on the beaches of Dunkirk. It was a battle in the continuing French and English civil wars, as well as in the international war between France and Spain. Serving with the Spanish army, the Duke of York was nearly killed charging into the midst of English troops at the head of his own English horse guards. Condé led French, as well as Spanish, soldiers against the French army.[73]

Louis XIV had insisted on staying with his troops outside Dunkirk. Day and night he was on horseback. Anne's and Mazarin's warnings had no effect.[74] Dunkirk surrendered on 25 June. On the 30th, affected by the bad water and nearby marshes, and the proximity of dying soldiers, the King fell ill and was taken to Calais. The laxatives, emetics, blisters and blood-lettings doctors applied to him would have killed many stronger men.[75] His mother again nursed him round the clock. Throughout France churches offered prayers for his recovery. At one moment, calling Mazarin 'the best friend I have', he asked the Cardinal to tell him when he was in danger, as the Queen would not do so, for fear of alarming him. Some courtiers, including the Princesse Palatine, began to consider Anjou the future king.[76] Mazarin wrote to his confidential adviser and Intendant Colbert: 'the King is very strong but the disease is rampant.' To Turenne: 'if a disaster which I fear more than my death occurred, I think I can tell you . . . that the state of affairs would not change in any way; for although the inclination of the Queen would in that case be to withdraw, I am assured that Her Majesty will do what I will have the honour to advise her and I know positively that Monsieur would be entirely resigned to her wishes.'[77] Later, however, he suspected that Monsieur had listened to conspirators who had planned his arrest. Hence his remark to Anne: 'I am the very humble servant of Monsieur.'[78] Soon, however, by what Mazarin considered a miracle, the King felt better. By 20 July he was recovering in the comfort of Compiègne.[79]

While France was winning victories, Mazarin was making himself the richest man in Europe. In return for loans to the Gonzaga dukes of Nevers, who had needed a large dowry for Louise Marie de Gonzague, sister of the Princesse Palatine, when she married King Władisław IV of Poland, he acquired their duchies of Mayenne and Nevers.[80] He made money by trading in jewels, by supplying the French army through proxies, by selling offices in royal households and through the Queen herself. Anne of Austria gave him a ship, the *Anna*, a gift to her from Queen Christina. He then sold it to the French government, for a large sum.[81] Even Anne wondered about Mazarin's fortune, as a letter to him from Colbert in January 1653 confirms. Alerted to rumours of embezzlement by the Princesse Palatine, she asked Colbert if the Surintendant des Finances La Vieuville, who had just died, had made 'such great deals [de si grandes affaires] for your Eminence'. Colbert replied that everything had been done with public knowledge.[82]

Mazarin was also accumulating a celebrated collection of paintings (540, including Van Dycks, Titians, Poussins), statues, gems, porcelain and early trophies of the global trade in luxuries, such as two chests, covered in gold lacquer landscapes, made in Kyoto in 1640 for the Dutch East India Company.[83] He gave a party with a lottery in which every guest won a prize. One lieutenant won a diamond worth 4,000 écus. Mademoiselle said that she had never seen such magnificence.[84]

At the same time he was embellishing the Château de Vincennes. The castle had been a favourite royal residence since the reign of St Louis; in 1361–85 Kings Charles V and Charles VI had added massive turreted walls, the tallest keep in Europe and a Sainte-Chapelle modelled on that in Paris. In 1654–8 the large, severe Pavilion of the King (the Pavilion of the Queen Mother followed in 1658–60), designed by Louis Le Vau under

Colbert's supervision, was added, as were stables and a triumphal entrance decorated with Mazarin's arms. A fortress as well as a palace, Vincennes was the court's answer to the Fronde. Colbert had suggested Mazarin become governor of Vincennes in order to have 'a place of his own where he could put in safety a considerable sum'. Mazarin sent his treasures to the chateau in July 1658, when the King's life was in danger.[85]

The King's near death, and the fact that he was a young man of twenty, encouraged Anne and Mazarin to marry him off as soon as possible. From 14 October to 16 December 1658 the court stayed in Lyon, to discuss a possible marriage with his first cousin Princess Marguerite of Savoy, daughter of his father's sister Christine. The dukes of Savoy, ruling a compact territory on both sides of the Alps, had vast ambitions. They demanded *trattamento reale*, or treatment as the equals of kings, due to their self-invented claim to the titles of king of Jerusalem and Cyprus. They also had long-term ambitions to acquire the adjoining Duchy of Milan, or more. The court of Savoy was magnificent, but the Princess was ugly.[86]

A legend has arisen, due to overestimation of Mazarin's subtlety, that this visit was a feint to force Spain to make peace and offer Louis XIV Philip IV's daughter the Infanta María Teresa. In reality Spain's disastrous military and financial situation, and Philip IV's determination to suppress a rebellion in Portugal, of which he was still theoretically king, were the main reasons why on 2 December 1658 in Lyon, Don Antonio de Pimentel, formerly Spanish Ambassador to Queen Christina, asked to open peace negotiations. Spanish diplomats never refer in despatches to fear of a Savoy match, and had left for Lyon before they knew of it.[87]

France also wanted peace – particularly when Mazarin learnt that Condé and Retz were meeting in Brussels. Marriage to the Infanta was favoured by Anne of Austria: she would obtain an obedient daughter-in-law from her own family. The Duchess of Savoy and her daughter left Lyon in tears.[88]

In 1659 secret peace negotiations between Mazarin and Pimentel continued in Paris. The main points of contention were frontiers and the Prince de Condé. Spanish diplomats believed that the honour of Spain required that Condé be re-established in all his offices: he should not be seen to have suffered for serving their King. Honour was considered the foundation of states. Without it, they could not survive: with it, they could hope to recover what they had lost. Today it would be called credibility. Mazarin, on the other hand, did not want Condé to have improved his position by rebellion. Condé himself considered that, if he did not return to France, the sovereignty of the Franche-Comté – the county of Burgundy, which lay between the French duchy of Burgundy and Switzerland (see Map 2) and was ruled by the king of Spain – would be suitable compensation.[89]

After a truce had been declared in May, the final points were resolved directly between Mazarin and Don Luis de Haro, chief minister of Spain. Between August and November, they met in a pavilion on the Island of Pheasants in the middle of the River Bidassoa. The island, which still exists, covered in trees, is still ruled alternately by France and Spain every six months. It had long been protected by palissades in order to make it a suitable place for Franco-Spanish meetings. To preserve equality between the two monarchies, symmetrical corridors and bridges led from either side of the river to the island, which was declared neutral territory. A contemporary map shows a large Salle de la Conférence, a garden and several smaller rooms. Despite suffering from gout and stones, Mazarin had made the difficult journey from Paris, with a train of 200 gentlemen and officials. Lengthy discussion decided the gestures with which the Cardinal and the Grandee of Spain were to greet each other.[90]

In a sign of his dynastic and military prestige, Condé's fate occupied about a third of their negotiating time. In the end he was granted a pardon for himself and his followers, the return of his estates and the governorship of Burgundy. His great court office of grand maître de France, once occupied by the Duc de Guise, went to his son the Duc d'Enghien. France agreed to stop supporting the rebels in Portugal against Philip IV. It obtained Roussillon, Artois and small sections of Flanders, Hainaut, Namur and Luxembourg by 'right of conquest', and confirmation of its gains in Alsace. Discussing the peace terms in the council in Madrid, the Duke of Alba commented that Spain's situation was so desperate that it should thank France for not taking more.[91] Thanks to the acquisition of Roussillon, the French frontier henceforth cut Catalonia in two, despite its historic cultural and linguistic unity: a separation still resented today. The clauses about amnesties, and mutual restitutions of property and prisoners, make the Treaty of the Pyrenees, like the Treaty of Westphalia of 1648 between France, Sweden, the United Provinces and the Holy Roman Empire, a milestone in the history of diplomacy. The rights of states and individuals were being established by European diplomats under international law.

It was agreed that the Infanta María Teresa would renounce her claims to the thrones of Spain on condition that her dowry was paid: at the time this condition was not considered important, as she had two brothers alive. Spain's negotiators had played a weak hand well, resisting each

French demand step by step. They infuriated Mazarin by delaying the wedding from November 1659 to March 1660 and finally to June. To excuse the delay, he spread the story that it was due to the Spanish court's desire to commission new liveries for its guards.[92]

The Treaty of the Pyrenees was a high point of French power in Europe. France emerged larger by two provinces, and surrounded by allies. One nationalistic voice, however, opposed it. Monsieur de Saint-Evremond, a writer and soldier, said Mazarin should have taken advantage of Spain's weakness to conquer the entire Southern Netherlands. This might have been militarily possible. But Mazarin's desperation to marry the King to the Infanta of Spain, whom he called the greatest and most virtuous princess in Europe, and to avoid a matrimonial catastrophe, persuaded him to put dynasty before territorial expansion.

For, while settling the affairs of Europe, Mazarin also had to settle those of the King's heart. Louis XIV had fallen in love with another of Mazarin's nieces, Marie Mancini, perhaps after he heard that she had cried during his illness in July 1658. She was not only attractive but cultivated, strong-willed and unconventional. She made him read poems and romances. Possibly she told him secrets about his mother and Mazarin.[93] Even her enemies admitted that their romance made her look beautiful.[94] By the time of the court's visit to Fontainebleau that autumn, all the courtiers – 'the usual spies of the actions of kings' as Marie remembered – knew of the affair.[95] The freedom of the court's stay in Lyon, when the King, his mother and court officials lived in separate houses, allowed it to flourish. The King began to escort Marie back to her house after the evening's entertainment.

Mademoiselle's memoirs are usually reliable. She often saw the King, and wrote in the 1660s and 1670s, using correspondence to support her memory, rather than decades after the event.[96] She recounted: 'at the beginning he followed her carriage, then served as the coachman, finally he travelled inside.' Even in the presence of the royal family and the court of Savoy, he would spend hours talking to Marie. Furious at her admirer's betrayal, Marie's elder sister Olympe, 'Madame la Comtesse', became her (and perhaps his) enemy.[97] Back in Paris the King and Marie spent the winter of 1658/9 going from fête to fête. Once, in a forest, the King threw away his sword, because Marie had stumbled against the hilt.[98]

No doubt, since she was unmarried, she did not give what were then called 'the ultimate favours'. She was not sent away from court, to live with a governess in an isolated seaside fort called Brouage, near La Rochelle, until 23 June 1659 – exactly when Mazarin was signing peace preliminaries with Spain.[99]

The King and Marie continued to correspond, using musketeers and footmen as couriers, sometimes five times a day. If they had survived, the letters would probably show that Louis XIV was more romantic than most Romantic poets, and perhaps that, behind his mother's and Mazarin's backs, he was plotting marriage.[100] He may even have considered dismissing Mazarin. At court it was believed that he had gone down on his knees to the Cardinal, requesting permission to marry his niece, claiming that it was the best way he could show his gratitude to his minister.[101]

Mazarin's letters to the young King during this emotional hurricane are lessons in statesmanship. On 28 June 1659: 'Remember, I beg you, what I had the honour to tell you several times when you asked me the path you needed to take to be a great king. It was this: that you had to begin by making supreme efforts not to be dominated by any passion . . . for when this misfortune occurs, whatever good intention one has, one is incapable of doing good. I have spoken to you with the liberty that you have commanded.' On 29 June: 'it only depends on you to be the most glorious king there has ever been, God having given you all the qualities for that.'[102] On 6 July: 'I beg you for your glory, for your honour, for the service of God, for the good of your kingdom and for all which can touch you most, magnanimously to take control of yourself.'[103]

On 16 July he criticized the King's neglect of the court in order to write long letters to Marie, and told the Queen that he was so worried that he could not eat or sleep.[104] Mazarin condemned his niece's 'unmeasured ambition and contrary spirit', adding warnings which many subsequent monarchs would have done well to heed: 'God has established kings to watch over the good of others and the security and peace of their subjects, not to sacrifice that good and that peace to their private passions. When there have been some unfortunate enough to oblige divine Providence by their conduct, to abandon them, history is full of the revolutions and the disasters which they have attracted on their persons and on their subjects.' He reminded the King that he was not an individual but an institution: 'Although you are the master in a certain sense to do what you wish, nevertheless you owe an account to God of your actions for your salvation and to the world for the maintenance of your glory and your reputation.' He threatened the King not only with a change of mind by Philip IV, but also with his own retirement and departure with his family for Italy.[105]

Almost losing the self-control for which he was famous, the Cardinal accused the King of dissimulation. To the Queen he wrote that everything was at stake: 'il y allait de tout.' The King sent Marie a puppy born from one of his own dogs called Friponne, with the inscription on its collar: 'Je suis à Marie Mancini.' Possibly he was planning her abduction by sea with the help of her brother Philippe Mancini, commander of his beloved musketeers.[106] On 29 July, Mazarin told him: 'You are master of your conduct but not able to oblige me to approve of it. All Europe is discussing the passion you have and everyone is talking with a liberty which is detrimental to you. Even in Madrid the affair has erupted . . .'[107] Probably the King sent on Mazarin's letters to Marie, whose comments can be imagined.[108]

Finally, the King renounced her. Mazarin's threat to retire and break the treaty had worked. Private feelings yielded to public pressures. The monarch triumphed over the man. The delighted Cardinal wrote, 'I seem to realize that you will be entirely master of yourself, when you wish . . . the most glorious of kings and the finest and most accomplished gentleman.'[109] On 13 and 14 August Louis had persuaded his mother to permit two final interviews with Marie at Saint-Jean-d'Angély. They looked so unhappy when saying goodbye that Marie's youngest sister Marie Anne burst into tears.[110]

On 3 September Marie promised not to write to the King again. The Cardinal wrote to Marie's Governess to tell her to read Seneca and remember that he was planning a marriage for her.[111]*

While waiting for the Infanta, Louis XIV would have preferred to winter in Paris, but Mazarin used the delay to make him see 'the provinces on this side which you have not yet seen and where your presence is necessary to adjust certain matters' – in plain French, to assert royal power and obtain money from local Estates. Louis XIV travelled around the south of his kingdom for an entire year, from July 1659 to July 1660. The court generally travelled one day in four, 22 miles a day, over a total distance of almost 2,000 miles. Possibly 15,000 people and 10,000 horses accompanied it.[112]

The King visited sixty-three cities in twelve months. A pattern was soon established. The King generally refused a full ceremonial entrée, such as his father had received, but entered most cities through tapestry-lined streets, to the sound of church bells. He then received deputations, listened

---

* English royal love matches across class barriers, such as Henry VIII's to Anne Boleyn in 1532, or that of Louis XIV's cousin James, Duke of York to Anne Hyde (to the fury of the bride's father the English chief minister Lord Clarendon, as well as of the royal family) on 9 September 1660, a year after Louis XIV renounced Marie Mancini, were almost unthinkable in France. The exception was Henri IV, who had planned to marry his mistress Gabrielle d'Estrées before her sudden death in 1599, and had shortly after promised marriage in writing to another mistress, Henriette d'Entragues. In 1600, however, he too had made a dynastic marriage, to Marie de Médicis: Jean-Pierre Babelon, *Henri IV*, 1982, pp. 643–5, 651, 655, 664, 816.

to speeches, usually confirmed privileges, liberated prisoners, visited churches, gave audiences. He often stayed in the house of a judge or a financial official, facing directly on to the street, without the barrier of a courtyard – his mother went to the bishop's or archbishop's palace. Thus he was immersed in cities and street life, often walking to mass.[113] Presents of local produce were offered. In Bayonne, for example, the King and his court and family received 394 of the hams for which the city was already famous[114] For relaxation, he reviewed troops, watched plays performed by travelling companies following the court, rode or played tennis.

Far from cutting it off from the country, the splendour and comfort of the court – and the efficiency of its travel department, the Maréchaux des Logis du Roi – enabled the King and his family to visit the provinces more easily than most Parisians. The centre came to the periphery. Courtiers often travelled with their own furniture. Anne of Austria paid the Duc d'Epernon an exceptional compliment when she did not insist on her own bed, but used one of his, while staying at his magnificent chateau of Cadillac near Toulouse.[115]

Bordeaux, formerly so rebellious, already visited in September and October 1650, was the residence of the court from August to October 1659. Louis XIV supervised the construction of a citadel designed to overawe the city.[116] When the Infanta failed to arrive, the King moved to Toulouse, staying more than two months from October to December 1659. By its size and the number of people, shops and carriages, Toulouse seemed to Mademoiselle to have an 'air of Paris'.[117] The King had returned to Olympe, 'Madame la Comtesse'. An agent reported to Mazarin on 21 October: 'the king lives so well with Monsieur and Madame de Soissons that nothing could be better.' They travelled and dined together in the same carriage. Delighted to have recaptured her King from her sister, she devoted all her 'soins' or care to him – probably meaning she became his mistress. Her husband encouraged her.[118]

Such was the court's demand for money, and the devastation inflicted by royal troops, that most cities were relieved to see it leave: 'every new city traversed saw smiles of welcome transformed into grimaces of farewell.'[119] That winter the court moved quickly, via Carcassonne, Narbonne, Montpellier, Nîmes (where the King visited the classical monuments and the Pont du Gard) and Arles, to Aix-en-Provence, where it stayed from January to March 1660.[120]

There on 27 January, after eight rebellious years, the Prince de Condé returned to court. The King, raising the penitent Prince, said, 'my cousin, after the great services you have rendered my crown, I will take care not to remember an evil which has brought harm only to yourself.' Anne of

Austria, more blunt, said, 'As for you, Monsieur, I admit to you that I have desired to harm you greatly, and you will surely do me the justice to admit that I was right.'[121] Condé swore he would think only of serving well, in order to efface whatever in his past conduct had caused dissatisfaction. He left the court after a few days and never completely returned to favour.[122]

There was an interlude in Toulon – even today a remote port, pressed between mountains and the sea – between 4 and 21 February. There the King stayed in the Hôtel de Ville with its magnificent carved atlantes by the great Provençal sculptor Puget, celebrated carnival and went on boat trips. Possibly Mazarin wanted to enthuse him with the prospect of a maritime expedition to help Venice fight the Ottoman Empire, as the lines in *Le Ballet Royal de la Nuit*, about 'eradicating' the crescent, had suggested.[123]

Between Aix and Toulon, in February the court visited the magnificent Gothic church erected over the alleged site of the death of Mary Magdalene at Saint-Maximin, in the hills above the Mediterranean. It attended mass, and gave a pink porphyry container for her relics. The court also went on a pilgrimage to Notre-Dame de Cotignac, along a road still called *le chemin de Louis XIV*. Twenty years earlier the Queen had made a vow asking for Notre-Dame de Cotignac's intercession for the Dauphin's birth. In gratitude to the Magdalene, Louis XIV presented her shrine with his gold ring and blue cordon of the Order of the Holy Spirit.[124] Thus the royal family reaffirmed its belief in vows and visions.

A few days later a visit to Marseille was a reminder that the monarchy was based on force as well as religion. Through most of his reign there would be a series of deals or arrangements with nobles, as Mazarin's generous transactions with ex-*frondeurs* had shown. At a time when nobles' legal status in countries such as England and Sweden was declining, the King of France enhanced nobles' tax and status privileges, in return for commitment of their social, political and military skills to his service.

Marseille, however, shows that the French crown could prefer bourgeois to nobles. One of the largest cities in the kingdom, proud of its Greek and Roman past, with ambitions to be a free city state, Marseille had rebelled against taxation in 1658, later than Paris or Bordeaux. Led by local nobles, the city had expelled the Governor of Provence, the Duc de Mercoeur. In January 1660 some 6,000 troops, including French and Swiss guards, had retaken the city. The court was determined to celebrate its victory.[125]

On 2 March 1660 Louis entered Marseille as if he had taken it by assault, at the head of his guards through a breach in the walls, rather than through the royal gate. There was no confirmation of privileges, the King refused the golden keys ceremoniously presented by city authorities, and declined a visit to the Hôtel de Ville.[126] In Marseille, the two forts of Saint-Jean and Saint-Nicolas, designed by M. de Clerville, the celebrated military engineer, still impressive today (they survived allied bombardment in 1944), were built at the entrance to the port. Completed in the next two decades, they were, in Mazarin's words, 'absolutely necessary to bridle that city'. The city officials known as consuls were henceforth to be appointed by the King, rather than elected by the city.[127] Marseillais had their weapons removed, and nobles were excluded from municipal offices in the city. When the King departed on 8 March, he left behind a garrison of 3,500 including Swiss troops.[128] Years later travellers could still see the 'pillar of infamy' erected in front of the house of M. de Glandevès, the noble who had led the rebellion of 1658 and taken refuge in Barcelona.[129]

The court then moved west via Arles, Avignon, Montpellier, Perpignan, Carcassonne and Toulouse. Louis XIV arrived in the small Basque port of Saint-Jean-de-Luz on 8 May.[130] The wait for the Infanta was over.

5

The Power of Queens

Louis XIV's choice of Saint-Jean-de-Luz for his wedding was a snub to Bordeaux, the most rebellious city of his kingdom, where his parents had been married on 8 May 1615. Saint-Jean-de-Luz's location by the Spanish frontier, on the main road from Paris to Madrid, was its sole advantage.

Philip IV, now old and ill, and the Infanta María Teresa had left Madrid on 15 April 1660, travelling through the impoverished Castilian countryside, with a huge cortège, augmented by Grandees of Spain, and his daughter's trousseau of twenty-three *robes de grand gala*. They stayed in San Sebastián in houses prepared by the Governor of the province, the Baron de Watteville, who had been Spanish agent in Bordeaux during the Fronde.[1]

Velázquez, Aposentador Mayor de Palacio or Master of the Household, a favourite of Philip IV as well as his court painter, was in charge of the Spanish court's travel arrangements: he filled the Spanish side of the Salle de la Conférence on the Island of Pheasants with tapestries showing the Apocalypse.[2] Working day and night as a royal wedding planner killed him: he died two months later on 6 August 1660.[3] One of his French equivalents was Jean-Baptiste Colbert, Mazarin's Intendant, who found the money to pay for jewels, tapestries and food for the French court.[4]

From San Sebastián and Saint-Jean-de-Luz, Europe's two most spectacular courts began to inspect each other. Mademoiselle noticed, like other French observers, that at court in Spain there was 'an air of gravity and of majesty that I have found nowhere else'. In contrast French courtiers were always talking and pushing for better places – in her phrase, making 'beaucoup de presse'.[5]

Spanish courtiers came to Saint-Jean-de-Luz to watch the King touching for the King's Evil, dancing on the stage put up for French travelling theatres and dining in public. He lived at the substantial three-storey

Maison Lohobiague by the sea. Anne of Austria stayed in a nearby house belonging to the same family. Mazarin lived outside the town at Ciboure.[6]*

On 3 June the marriage by procuration took place in the cathedral of Fuenterrabía. Don Luis de Haro represented Louis XIV. All eyes then turned to the Island of Pheasants in the Bidassoa. Contemporary prints show the French side of the river lined with carriages and different companies of guards – 'of his eminence', 'of the queen' and 'of the king'. In addition there were groups of 'marchands et vivandiers suivans la Cour', who are shown running the seventeenth-century equivalent of snack bars. Mademoiselle saw one company of guards whose role even she, despite her preoccupation with the court, did not recognize: the *gentilshommes à bec de corbin*, a ceremonial unit founded in 1478 which appeared only on the most important occasions. Their name came from their halbards' resemblance to 'crows' beaks'.[7]

The two courts finally met on 4 June in the Salle de la Conférence. Anne of Austria tried to kiss the brother she had not seen for forty-five years but he withdrew his head in time. When she explained, 'I hope your Majesty will forgive me for having been such a good Frenchwoman. I owed it to the King my son and to France,' Philip IV replied that he respected her for it, and added that 'The Queen my wife did the same; for, although being French, she had in her soul nothing but the interest of my kingdoms and the desire to content me.'

They continued talking, sitting on chairs on the exact line in the room separating the two kingdoms. Louis XIV appeared in a doorway incognito, accompanied by twenty courtiers. Philip IV remarked that he had a handsome son-in-law. María Teresa blushed.[8] French courtiers were dismayed by her dress and jewels and coiffure, but admired her blue eyes, silvery-blonde hair, white skin and dignity. She looked like a younger but less majestic version of her aunt, Anne of Austria.[9]

On 6 June, under a burning sun, peasants in traditional dress danced beside the river. Royal guards lined both banks. The two kings, kneeling side by side, swore on their Bibles, in French and Castilian, to observe the peace treaty and the wedding contract – the terms of which two secretaries of state had just read out. Mazarin acted as interpreter. 'Sí, lo juro,' said Philip IV. 'Non seulement je jure la paix, mais aussi l'amitié,' replied Louis XIV. Members of each court were then presented to the other's monarch.[10]

---

* In a startling example of family continuity, the Maison Lohobiague is still owned by descendants of Jean de Lohobiague, the shipowner who built it in 1643 and received the King there in 1660.

On 7 June Philip IV handed over his daughter. María Teresa and Anne wept. Louis expressed delight and declared himself the vassal as well as the friend, ally and nephew of the King of Spain. When the Queen apologized for the exertions of the journey, Philip IV replied, 'I would have come on foot if necessary.' To Mazarin he declared, 'Christianity owes you peace.'[11]

The next day, Anne supervised the transformation of her daughter-in-law from a Velázquez infanta into a queen of France, from María Teresa to Marie Thérèse. She received the oaths of her ladies-in-waiting, including the Princesse Palatine, who was appointed *surintendante de la maison de la reine* despite Louis XIV's dislike of her: the post was a reward for services during the Fronde, and she was soon replaced by the Comtesse de Soissons. Whereas Anne of Austria had retained Spanish servants for years, Marie Thérèse's Spanish household was sent back, with the exception of her confessor, two doctors and a maid.[12]

On 9 June in the church of Saint-Jean-Baptiste, which still uses the organ installed for the occasion, the wedding service was performed by the Bishop of Bayonne. It lasted from noon to 4 p.m. The church was packed. Mazarin had written, 'All the other persons of quality can come freely to the court' – in addition to those with official positions. There were special benches only for secretaries of state, marshals and ambassadors (England, Denmark, the United Provinces, Venice, Savoy, Portugal, the Pope and Tunis).[13] No ranks were observed, nor seats reserved, for anyone else – not even, to their fury, for dukes or bishops.[14]

Despite the heat the new Queen, covered in diamonds and emeralds, wore a small crown and an ermine robe decorated with golden fleurs-de-lys, with a train borne by two daughters of Gaston and the Princesse de Carignan, mother of 'Monsieur le Comte'. The King wore a coat of gold brocade covered in black lace and diamonds. He and his bride then withdrew to the Maison Lohobiague. The King threw gold and silver coins to the crowds on what is now the Place Louis XIV.[15] After supper they went to their apartment and were undressed: there was no public 'bedding' as at other royal weddings, possibly because of Anne of Austria's memories of her humiliating public bedding in 1615. The Queen simply said to her ladies: 'presto, presto quel Rey m'espera': 'quick, quick, the King is waiting for me.'[16]

The next morning, according to his cousin Mademoiselle, 'the King appeared in the best mood possible; he laughed and jumped and went to talk to the Queen with signs of tenderness and friendship which were a pleasure to see.'[17] No longer was he 'cold and grave'. During the journey back to Paris the King and Queen shared the same bed and the same table, as they would for most of their married life.[18]

After the wedding's political significance as confirmation of peace between France and Spain, it was the participants' jewels and clothes which most fascinated contemporaries. The French government was so indebted that Anne had to pawn some of her own jewels to provide her new daughter-in-law with appropriately splendid presents, including a diamond-studded heart, earrings, bracelets, mirrors, boxes; Marie Thérèse also had the right to wear the French crown jewels.[19] All the guards wore new uniforms and breastplates. Madame de Motteville thought the blue and gold of the French guards looked more striking than the red and yellow of the King of Spain's.[20] Louis XIV's clothes alone, his Maître de la Garde-Robe estimated, cost 90,000 livres.[21]

The French court, however, could also laugh at itself. Writing of the courtiers' feathers and embroideries, the musician Mathieu Marais declared, 'it reeked of Le Grand Cyrus from a hundred miles' – a reference to a popular romantic novel which Louis XIV and Marie Mancini had read together.[22] When the King asked the aged Duc de Roquelaure what he thought of his clothes and jewels, the Duke replied in his Gascon accent: 'parbleu, Sire, it seems to me Moncrot [a rich war financier] is getting married.' All the courtiers laughed. The King looked pensive. Moncrot died later in prison, unable to pay the fines imposed by an official investigation into profiteering.[23]

The Duc de La Rochefoucauld, one of the few frondeurs whom the King never forgave, also expressed disdain: 'people speak only of the magnificence of the costumes of our court; it seems to me to be a bad sign for those who wear them, and that they should wish to be talked about also.'[24] For some courtiers, however, dress, far from being a 'bad sign', was the best sign of all, sending a reassuring message of wealth and fashion. The French monarchy still needed dress and jewels and embroidery – and soldiers and courtiers – to impress outsiders. Louis XIV could not afford to dress badly.

Moreover the French court was merely doing what other courts were trying to do, but more flamboyantly. Velázquez dressed as the nobleman that, by birth, he was not, wearing velvet trimmed with Milanese silver lace, covered in diamonds and other jewels.[25] Even Oliver Cromwell and his courtiers had started to dress fashionably.

Finally on 15 June the court left Saint-Jean-de-Luz, via Bordeaux, Richelieu – the chateau and town built by the Cardinal de Richelieu south of the Loire – Chambord, Orléans and Fontainebleau, for Vincennes, where it arrived on 20 July. From 29 June to 1 July, however, Louis XIV had insisted on making a detour, with Mazarin and Philippe Mancini, to Brouage, the residence of Marie Mancini the previous summer. Passion had survived separation. He slept, crying and sighing, in Marie Mancini's former bedroom. Then he returned to his role as king.[26]

At three in the afternoon on 18 August, the King and Queen reviewed the Paris militia on the plain between Vincennes and Paris. Preceded by musketeers and followed by *force noblesse*, the King rode up and down the lines, battalion after battalion, as the Queen did in her carriage. All Paris was watching. The official account states: 'the only sound was the cry "Vive le roi et la reine" repeated by a million mouths.'

The Paris militia – 8,000 well-disciplined soldiers – was no less obsessed with dress than the court. Every soldier was covered in plumes and ribbons, colour-coded by battalion.[27] Officers dressed like courtiers; one colonel, Président de Guénégaud of the Chambre des Enquêtes, wore gold brocade – breaking the dress code of the *noblesse de robe*, who normally wore black – and had six pages and twenty-four lackeys.[28]

Like Louis XIV's entry into Marseille in March, his entry into Paris four days later on 23 August was a piece of royal theatre designed to show the triumph of crown over city.[29] First the King and Queen took their places on a giant temporary double throne, surmounted by a dome on four columns, on what is now the Place de la Nation. For five hours they listened to speeches by Parisian deputations, from the curés to the Parlement – some of them on their knees. At around 2 p.m. they made the grandest of royal entries into Paris.[30]

Windows and balconies lining the rue Saint-Antoine were thick with spectators. The king, on horseback, was surrounded by the princes of the blood, his court and military household and followed by all the institutions of the capital – law courts, university, Hôtel de Ville. According to Madame de Motteville, the King looked 'like the men whom the poets describe as transformed into gods. His coat was embroidered with gold and silver, as fine as it should be, given the dignity of the person wearing it ... the grandeur which he showed in his person made him admired by all.'[31]

A friend of Marie Mancini, the widow of the playwright Paul Scarron, wrote that it took one hour for the household of Mazarin alone to pass by. Little anticipating that she would herself one day become the King's wife, she added that the Queen must have gone to bed happy to have chosen such a husband.[32]

The Queen, a timid young woman just emerged from a secluded upbringing in a foreign country, was paraded through the streets of Paris as a symbol of peace. Inscriptions and triumphal arches celebrated the virtues of the kings and queens, and the love, loyalty, obedience and gratitude of Paris and France.[33] Figures of peace, abundance, magnificence, piety and France and Spain joining hands decorated the route.[34] The 'triumphant Queen' had come to reign over the hearts of the French, 'losing the fine title of infanta without regret in the arms of the handsomest of kings'. Fountains flowed with wine. Prisoners were liberated. Racine wrote his first poem, 'Le Nymphe de la Seine à la Reine'. La Fontaine praised 'the bourgeoisie' for rivalling the luxury of the court.[35]

The procession stopped in front of a 'magnificent palace', the Hôtel de Beauvais in the rue François Miron, built by a royal architect Antoine Le Pautre in 1656–60 for Anne of Austria's Première Femme de Chambre, Madame de Beauvais. Still surviving today, its size and splendour proclaim the material benefits of court office. On the balconies sat Anne of Austria, Henrietta Maria, Mazarin, Turenne, Mademoiselle and the Princesse Palatine. This royal entry was marked not only by its splendour, but also by a significant omission. The King received the keys of Paris, but he did not confirm the city's privileges.[36]

Nevertheless the procession, like the review, celebrated Paris, not just the monarchy. It included, in addition to other institutions, 'the merchants of the city', 'the city council', 'the parishes' and 'the beggars'. The Prévôt des Marchands of Paris was still capable of giving lessons to the crown. For example: 'Sire, let us not hide the fact that your triumphs in war are much less agreeable to us than peace, and less advantageous to you.' In one display the King was praised as 'Ludovicus pacificus', liberator of the arts and sciences.[37]

Mazarin appeared to be at the height of his power. Making him Duc de Mazarin, the King praised his patience, his 'inconceivable flexibility of spirit and intelligence', and prophesied that in the future no one would imitate his policies, which he alone had invented.[38] Even the Parlement of Paris, which ten years earlier had organized the sale of his books in order to pay his assassin, sent him a deputation. He told Président Lamoignon that, if he did not deserve such praise in the present, equally he had not deserved such attacks and insults in the past, from those who ought to have helped pilot the ship of state instead of trying to wreck it.[39]

The emotional triangle between King, Queen Mother and Cardinal, meanwhile, was changing. Mazarin showed Anne less respect; she showed him less tolerance. The King, however, showed more love for his godfather than many sons for their father.[40] The Venetian Ambassador reported that all his affections seemed to go to the Cardinal, whom he saw several times a day, for many hours in private, and to whom he referred all political decisions and even 'the smallest matters'. Council meetings were held in Mazarin's apartment.[41]

But, at the age of fifty-nine, Mazarin was dying. Tormented by gout and stones, he began to look like his own ghost.[42] On 22 February he left Paris for Vincennes; public prayers were said for him in churches as if he were a member of the royal family. Throughout his final days the King, often in tears, remained attentive, checking his medicines, bringing him drinks.[43]

Mazarin made his last decisions about his fortune. His favourite niece Hortense and her husband the Duc de La Meilleraye, whom she married on 28 February and who inherited the title Duc de Mazarin, received the largest part, including the Palais Mazarin. Two other nieces, the Comtesse de Soissons and the Princesse de Conti, became *surintendantes* of the households of the Queen and the Queen Mother respectively; the Princesse Palatine retired with a large pension. Louis XIV and Anne inherited jewels and treasures including the eighteen diamonds known as 'les Mazarins', perhaps worth 4 million out of a total fortune of around 38 million livres.*

On 6 March the Cardinal read his last despatches. The King was crying so much, he was asked to leave the bedroom. He watched through the doorway as the Cardinal received extreme unction. The next day, surrounded by weeping courtiers, Mazarin died. His last words, according to Madame de Motteville, were: 'Ah holy virgin, have pity on me and receive my soul.' She added that, on receiving news of his death, Anne of Austria said that it was better not talk of it. The King needed distractions and should think of other matters.[44] In a letter to Philip IV, however, Louis called Mazarin's death 'one of the greatest afflictions I could feel'.[45]

Mazarin left France the leading power in Europe, but his accumulation of a vast personal gold reserve, as well as jewels and other treasures, had exacerbated France's financial problems. Madame de Motteville wrote that he was 'so mean that he wanted to make a profit out of everything', and his own allies, Colbert and Le Tellier, agreed.[46] During the Fronde he made many mistakes, not least ordering the arrests of Broussel and Condé. In foreign policy, he was often wrong – for example he could have obtained better peace terms, earlier, from Spain, and he had believed in the future of the Protectorate in England. When in November 1659 Charles II had travelled from Bruges, across France, to Saint-Jean-de-Luz to ask for help, Mazarin had refused to see him.[47]

In reality 1660 was a good year for monarchy. Cities with dreams of independence like Marseille, Naples and Paris itself had been subdued. In Denmark the crown became hereditary instead of elective: the King of

---

* One of these, known as 'le grand Mazarin', was sold at Christie's Geneva in November 2017 for $14,600,000.

Denmark was henceforth one of the most absolute monarchs in Europe, and was usually allied to France. On 29 May, Charles II had entered London in triumph. Henrietta Maria proclaimed to her sister in Turin that her son was more powerful than any of his predecessors and 'even the common people' in England were overjoyed.[48] Mazarin had to withdraw the French Ambassador, the Président de Bordeaux, from London, as his links to the Commonwealth made him unacceptable to Charles II.[49]

The restoration of a powerful Stuart monarchy, allied to Spain, meant that the number of Scots in the Gardes du Corps, already declining since the King of Scots had become king of England in 1603, further diminished. The regiment of Gardes Ecossaises was dismissed; its Colonel, Lord Teviot, became governor of Dunkirk for Charles II.[50]

The Stuart restoration also led to another royal wedding. In March 1661, soon after Mazarin's death, Monsieur married the sister of Charles II, Henriette Anne. Both mothers had favoured the match and Monsieur considered himself in love. Because of court mourning for Mazarin, what Louis XIV called in a letter to Charles II 'a new tie further tightening the knot of our friendship' was celebrated privately, in Henrietta Maria's chapel in the Palais Royal.[51]

The two brothers were opposites. Following the fashion for educated Frenchmen and women, particularly at court, to write portraits of their contemporaries, the Comtesse de Brégis had composed a portrait of the King around 1659 for Mademoiselle:

> His person serves infinitely to enhance his other advantages . . . he is the best built of all men . . . His hair is so fine and so abundant that it adorns him as much as a crown and makes him reign in places where sceptres would not always be obeyed. His face is not handsome . . . his arms and his legs and his feet are so perfectly well made that no one should regret that they are [made] to march on our heads; he has a marvellous facility and address in all exercises: He dances better than anyone . . . he is judicious, gallant and discreet . . . His temperament is a little reserved and disdainful but kind and generous.

She thought his hair was dark chestnut. He was also slightly marked by smallpox, and his skin was dark.[52]

M. Martinet, an official in the Ceremonies Department in the Maison du Roi, was also charmed by Louis:

> He is very tall, upright, open, robust, with a large chest and shoulders, big arms and legs of proportionate size, and perfectly well made; a countenance which is proud and gentle at the same time; when he chooses to disguise

himself, he is nevertheless recognized at once wherever he goes as the master, because he has the air, the carriage and all the marks discernible in other times on those said to be of the blood of gods, and to be the origins of all monarchies . . .

The white [of his skin] has remained complete [this must have been written before the trip to the south in 1659–60], to contrast with the coral of that precious and beautiful mouth, beside which roses are pale and from which continuously flow either oracles or favours.

At this stage he was distinguished, his subjects believed, by clemency, 'paternal tenderness', generosity, a preference for taking 'the part of the weakest' and complete discretion. He observed the fasts of the church 'like a Capucin'. Martinet thought that, for Louis, the only advantage for kings is 'to do good to everyone, to possess everything in order to give it away'. Like Mazarin, he believed that the King was the masterpiece of heaven, destined to be 'the honour and the example of the entire earth'.[53]

Of Monsieur, in contrast, a later, anonymous observer wrote, 'he applies himself only to looking beautiful and to dancing with ladies; as much as the King his brother is courageous and virile, he is all the more effeminate and more like a woman than a man, as can be seen by his cheeks which are red thanks to a certain artificial colour and for the most part filled with little black beauty spots.' As this account suggests, he reacted to his brother's virility by exaggerating his own femininity 'all the more'.[54] Part of the fascination of the court of France was that it permitted homosexuality, multiple mistresses, gambling – behaviour that was derided elsewhere. Nevertheless Louis, like many heterosexual brothers, mocked his homosexual brother, sometimes physically – and cut his inheritance.[55] On the death of their uncle Gaston, Duc d'Orléans on 2 February 1660, after following a procession of the holy sacrament in the rain, Monsieur inherited his title and part of his appanage, but neither his palaces of Blois and Chambord nor his government of Languedoc.[56]

Henriette Anne, the new Duchesse d'Orléans, in the words of her cousin Mademoiselle, imparted 'a charm which cannot be expressed to everything she did'.[57] In contrast to the reserve of Marie Thérèse and Anne of Austria, she was talkative, winning a reputation for being more human than other members of the royal family. Madame de Motteville wrote that she had a complexion of jasmine and roses. Soon she was considered the principal ornament of 'the great theatre of the court of France'.[58]

Her marriage, however, was a calvary. Monsieur's love quickly turned to spite. As his Premier Aumônier Daniel de Cosnac wrote, he was even more jealous of her intelligence than of her person: 'he appeared angry that she contributed by her wit and skill in everything to make herself loved and respected by the king and the whole court . . . As for Monsieur he had wonderfully well retained and augmented the reputation which he had so justly acquired of being incapable either of keeping a secret or of giving advice.' Monsieur often quarrelled with his wife – enraged that the Comte de Guiche paid more attention to her than to him. The King moreover showed that he preferred his sister-in-law to his brother.[59]

The marriages of Mazarin's nieces, like those of the King and his brother, were also political. After his marriage, the King had continued to see Marie Mancini, who had returned to Paris. The Papal Nuncio reported that the Queen 'feels great jealousy on seeing the King make new demonstrations of love to Mlle Marie Mancini . . . The Queen would like this person to leave as soon as possible.' On 11 April 1661 in the royal chapel in the Louvre, in the presence of the King and Queen, Marie Mancini married, by proxy, a leading Roman prince, the Constable Colonna. As her dowry, Mazarin had given her his Rome palace, the Palazzo Mancini. When she left for Rome, the King assured her that, wherever she was, he would always remember and protect her.[60]

The marriage was unhappy. When her husband reproached her with her low birth, she replied that none of her sisters had married worse than she had. After bearing their children, Marie refused to sleep with Colonna and in 1668 fled back to France. Louis XIV, while promising 'all possible tenderness', and providing her with a passport, advised her to live in a convent at a distance from Paris. He told the Ambassador of Savoy, laughing, that he had no desire to see her again.[61] Later she lived in Spain, Flanders and France, but never returned to court. Independent to the end, she died alone in Pisa in 1715, the same year as Louis himself.[62]

Continuing the round of royal weddings, on 19 April 1661 Mademoiselle's beautiful and unconventional half-sister Marguerite Louise was married, also by proxy in the chapel of the Louvre in the presence of the King and Queen, to the heir of the Grand Duke of Tuscany, Cosimo de' Medici. Despite the King's lavish wedding presents of jewels and furniture, she complained that he was a tyrant to force her to marry and leave France. When she said farewell to the court, however, she shed no tears.[63]

As these royal weddings showed, despite the prevalent patriarchy and belief that women were weak and prone to hysteria,[64] dynasticism could favour and finance female independence. A household's obedience to its mistress, reinforced by personal wealth in the form of a dowry, jewels or pensions, could provide a power-base. Once the perils of childbirth were over, women were shielded by their gender from duels, battles and, in most cases, prison. Thus the Princesse Palatine and the Duchesse de Longueville, among others, had been leading politicians during the Fronde. Mademoiselle, as she boasted in her memoirs, made her own decisions on campaign, as an independent general. She saw herself as a heroine, not a victim. Some women held office too: the Maréchale de Guébriant had been appointed *ambassadrice extraordinaire* in 1645 to escort Louise Marie de Gonzague de Nevers to marry King Władisław IV of Poland, of the Polish branch of the Swedish House of Vasa.[65]

More than most monarchs, Louis XIV personally encouraged women to play a part in court and public life. To the Comtesse d'Armagnac, another French ambassadress in her own right, sent to escort his cousin Françoise to wed the Duke of Savoy in 1663, he wrote, 'Never was a prince better served by an ambassador than I am by an ambassadress; also of all the ministers I have in foreign countries, there is not one whose despatches please me more than yours do.'[66] His second wife, Madame de Maintenon, would have more influence than most of his ministers.

One contemporary wrote of women, in *Le Triomphe des dames*, 'their cleverness and their cabals have a thousand times more effect on the fortunes of families than the efforts of men around Princes and Kings.'[67] Another book praising women, by the early feminist François Poullain de La Barre, *De l'égalité de deux sexes: discours physique et moral où l'on voit l'importance de se défaire des préjugés*, was published in Paris 'avec privilège du roi' in 1673, and with the King's personal monogram of enlaced Ls engraved on the title page as proof of royal approval. Embedded in a foreign court, French princesses and ladies-in-waiting could be more effective than French ambassadors or soldiers. They spread the language, customs and fashions of France, and usually supported its policy.[68]

Princesses étrangères often preferred foreign marriages, since they brought greater status and independence. For the French government they were useful substitutes when royal princesses were unwilling to marry abroad (like Mademoiselle, who refused the kings of England and Portugal). In Poland, for example, Louise Marie de Gonzague became an important ally for the French government. After the death of her first husband King Władisław IV in 1649, she married his half-brother and successor King John Casimir.[69] Foreign ambassadors regarded her as the dominant force in the monarchy, ruling her gigantic second husband as easily as an elephant driver guides an elephant.[70]

Brilliant and energetic, often making long journeys throughout the country, Louise Marie, Queen of Poland, generally (but by no means always) supported French policy. She helped save the Polish monarchy from Swedish invaders during the Great Northern War in 1655–60, attended council meetings and personally encouraged Polish soldiers at the battle of Warsaw in 1656 (after which, in gratitude for his victory, John Casimir declared the Virgin Mary queen of Poland). With her help the French Ambassador de Lumbres mediated the signature on 3 May 1660 of the Treaty of Oliva (a monastery outside Danzig). It ended the war between Sweden, Denmark, Poland and Brandenburg, maintaining France's ally Sweden as the dominant power in the Baltic, but restoring all Poland's lost territories except Livonia, which was acquired by Sweden.

However one of the inbuilt dangers of royal monogamy in Europe (avoided by polygamous monarchs outside it) is childlessness – as France had discovered during the Wars of Religion when neither François II nor Charles IX nor Henri III fathered legitimate sons. Louise Marie had no children by either husband.

In an attempt to maintain French influence in Poland, with the encouragement of Louis XIV, her sister the Princesse Palatine and her husband, Louise Marie tried to arrange the election of her friend the Prince de Condé, or his son the Duc d'Enghien, as heir to the Polish throne in the King's lifetime.[71] On 11 December 1663 in the Louvre Enghien married her niece Anne de Bavière, a daughter of the Princesse Palatine. It was another grandiose royal marriage, arranged by international treaty between John Casimir, King of Poland (who, as the Queen had long planned, had adopted Anne de Bavière as his daughter) and Louis XIV.[72] Enghien began to learn Polish.[73]

For her part, Louise Marie tried to increase royal authority, abolish Polish nobles' right of veto in the Diet and reduce their control of the Polish army. In a sign of the dangers of elective monarchy, the Polish constitution and Polish factions were already beginning to tear the country apart. Louis XIV gave pensions to Polish magnates, praised Louise Marie's 'great reserves of cleverness and knowledge of private and public affairs in Poland' and assured her: 'Whatever happens I will not abandon you.'[74] The marriage between the Duc d'Enghien and Louise Marie's niece 'was this latest alliance which unites us more and more'.[75] He called Polish affairs the most important in Christendom, but already feared its partition by three hungry neighbours, Brandenburg, Russia and Austria.[76]

In the 1660s Louis XIV considered sending 10,000 French troops by sea to Danzig to support Condé's or Enghien's candidature for the throne of Poland.[77] In 1665, and again in 1667 when he was already intervening in the Empire as a member of the League of the Rhine, he also planned to send Condé with 4,000 troops and horses in small groups by land across the Holy Roman Empire to Poland. Sweden promised support.[78] The difficulties of moving French troops to Poland, by either land or sea, would, however, prevent him from helping Poland effectively, as similar difficulties would later French governments.*

Moreover, when given the chance of leading French armies against Spain in the war of 1667, Condé lost his desire to rule Poland: he may also have preferred living as a prince in the magnificent chateau of Chantilly north of Paris to reigning as a king in Warsaw.[79] Louise Marie's death on 9 May 1667 deprived their candidacy of its impetus. Weakened by internal divisions – John Casimir had caused civil war through his attempts to get a French prince elected as his heir in his lifetime – and by the power of the magnates, Poland ceded Kiev and part of Ukraine to the rising power of Russia in 1667. In September 1668, John Casimir, broken-hearted by his wife's death, abdicated. With the help of the French Ambassador, he retired to Paris to become abbot of Saint-Germain-des-Prés, where his magnificent tomb can be admired today.

In both 1668 and 1674, despite French bribes and Louis XIV's flattering letters,[80] Polish nobles – with unhappy memories of their unpopular and ineffective French king Henri III in 1573–4 – preferred a Pole as king, and elected Michael Wiśniowiecki and John Sobieski respectively. Even at its height, therefore, Louis XIV's influence had limits. He never enjoyed hegemony in Europe.[81]

Under King John Sobieski, who reigned from 1674 to 1696 and defeated the Ottomans in front of Vienna in 1683, Poland remained a great power. He had visited Paris and later married a Frenchwoman, a former maid of honour of Louise Marie called Marie Casimire Louise de La Grange d'Arquien. She too was believed to have 'absolute power' over her husband, whose election to the throne she had helped to arrange. As Louise Marie had hoped, a degree of French influence remained in Poland. Their court in Warsaw was half French: the King employed a French secretary and orchestra, modelled the decoration of his bedchamber on Versailles, made Louis XIV godfather to one of his sons and signed a secret treaty with him in June 1675.[82]

The Queen of Poland's importance is confirmed by Louis XIV's choice of her brother-in-law the Marquis de Béthune as his ambassador to Poland for the unusually long period of sixteen years after 1676, although the two sisters came to hate each other.[83] At the Queen of Poland's request, Louis XIV adopted her as his daughter, while her daughters became his wife's goddaughters.[84]

---

* One reason for the question often asked in France in 1939: 'Mourir pour Danzig?'

His ambassadors told Louis XIV that, because of her 'absolute power' over Sobieski, he must ('il faut que Votre Majesté . . .') win Marysieńka, as Sobieski called her, by making both her father and her son dukes and peers of France, and giving her father a pension. But Louis XIV came to distrust the Queen and despise her father: he lived in Paris, accumulating debts, lawsuits and diseases. In the end, he moved to Rome, where in 1695, at the age of eighty-two, he was made a cardinal by an amenable Pope.[85]

Frenchwomen also spread French influence in other courts. In 1665 another *princesse étrangère*, Marie Jeanne Baptiste de Savoie de Nemours, had married her cousin Charles Emanuel II Duke of Savoy (on the death of his previous wife, a half-sister of Mademoiselle, Françoise Madeleine d'Orléans). Her sister Marie Françoise Elisabeth de Savoie de Nemours, helped by a dowry of 600,000 livres from Louis XIV, married Alonso, King of Portugal in August 1666. By 1666 the Queens of Poland and Portugal, the Duchesses of Modena and Savoy and the future Grand Duchess of Tuscany were all French.

Like her sister in Portugal, Marie Jeanne Baptiste, Duchess of Savoy, attended council meetings in her husband's lifetime. After his death, from 1675 to 1684 she was regent of Savoy for their son Victor Amadeus II. Authoritarian and industrious, she often attended council meetings for five hours at a time, and actively supported French influence, hoping to use it to delay handing power to her son. Under pressure from Louis XIV, she introduced French troops into Turin, and sent Piedmontese regiments to serve in the French army.[86] Excluded from power by her son in 1684, Madame Royale, as she was called, remained an important patron until her death in 1724 – as is suggested by the magnificent Palazzo Madama, which she built opposite her son's Palazzo Reale in Turin.[87]

Her sister Marie Françoise Elisabeth, Queen of Portugal, was the second French princess, after Louise Marie de Gonzague, so ambitious to remain queen of a foreign country that she married her brother-in-law. Her first husband Alonso VI was disabled, subject to fits, and fond, according to an English account, of 'Boys . . . pickt up out of the Streets . . . Grooms, Blacks and Moorish slaves', and 'lewd women'. In November 1667, backed by Schomberg, commander of the French troops stationed in Portugal (where, in contravention of the Treaty of the Pyrenees, they had been helping defend its newly recovered independence from Spain), and by a French fleet moored near Lisbon, but also driven by her own desire for power, the Queen fled from her husband's palace to the convent of Esperança.[88] When the King rushed to retrieve her, the convent gates were shut in his face.

At first she threatened to return to France with her dowry. However, speaking to members of the council through the grate in the convent door, 'very gay and cheerful', she organized, with the King's younger brother Dom Pedro, the repudiation, confinement and deposition of Alonso VI.[89] Dom Pedro was described as 'of wonderful strength and great activity of body', and they had already started an affair. The Queen's marriage was annulled on grounds of non-consummation (although she provided no proof, and Alonso VI swore he had done his best); and in April 1668 she married Dom Pedro. Thereafter he ruled as regent, and following his brother's death after sixteen years in prison in 1683, as King Pedro II.[90]

The Queen could not stop Portugal, against Louis XIV's wishes, making peace with Spain, in February 1668. However, she assured Louis that she had 'an entirely French heart', and that she informed him of her most secret projects. Louis called her conduct 'beyond all praise' and approved her 'établissement effectif' with her new husband. She told a Paris friend, the Princesse de Soubise, that she enjoyed 'all the freedom that I want to take', although she admitted it did not reach the level of 'French freedom'.[91] Portugal remained generally pro-French until her death in 1683 – the same year as her ex-husband.[92]

Dynastic marriages could change the fate of nations, as the union of different nations, by that means, into the composite monarchies of Spain, Great Britain and Austria proved. The right marriage was regarded as the equivalent of a victory on the battlefield. They could, however, be mixed blessings. The marriage of Charles I and Henrietta Maria in 1625, for example, by establishing a French royal chapel and French Catholic priests and friars in the heart of London had, despite their happiness, increased her husband's unpopularity and contributed to the outbreak of the Civil War. In time Henrietta Maria also contributed to her son James's conversion to Catholicism, and so to his downfall, thereby destroying the alliance with France which her marriage had been intended to confirm.[93] Louis XIV's own marriage to a Spanish princess, by fuelling his ambitions for Spanish territory, hurt Spain: he would call his first war against Spain, in 1667, 'the War of the Rights of the Queen'.

Some royal marriages backfired spectacularly. Marguerite Louise, Grand Duchess of Tuscany, came to loathe the plump and taciturn Cosimo III. Incompatible with her husband, indifferent to their three children, she told him that she preferred the most miserable hut in France to the 'prison' of Florence. Considering the Medici vastly inferior to her own dynasty, she refused to extend her hand to the ladies to whom her mother-in-law extended hers.[94] As early as 1664, she plotted her return to France. A typical letter to her husband informed him: 'I am the source of your unhappiness as you are of mine.' Using ill-health as a pretext, in

1675, after many letters to Louis XIV, she obtained his reluctant agreement that she should leave Tuscany. She had secured a pension from her husband, and removed the ornaments of one of the Medici villas as her 'wages'.

Residing in the abbey of Saint-Pierre in Montmartre, which she occasionally tried to burn down, she continued to ignore conventions. On visits to Versailles, she enjoyed gambling for high stakes; but, according to her half-sister Mademoiselle, was badly dressed, and talked about horses and servants like a provincial. Until her death in 1721 a conspiracy of silence, and Louis XIV's indulgence, covered her 'disgraceful excesses' with members of the Gardes du Corps. Rather than reinforcing French prestige, Marguerite Louise had diminished it. Her humiliated husband became an ally of the House of Austria.[95]

She was not the only wife whom Louis XIV, against the conventions of the day, helped to leave her husband. Hortense Mancini left her jealous, hyper-pious husband the Duc de Mazarin (who mutilated the statues he had inherited from Mazarin, as offences against modesty), with Louis' blessing, in 1668 and was escorted to Rome by two Gardes du Corps.[96] After more travels, she arrived in London in 1675 disguised as a page and accompanied by her slave Mustafa, a present from the Duke of Savoy. Helped by her 'conquering eyes', and prompted by her need for funds, she became a mistress of Charles II. The French Ambassador reported to Louis XIV that she was 'fort satisfaite' by their nocturnal 'conversations'. During her favour in 1675–7, she was supported by Whigs against his other French mistress, the hated Duchess of Portsmouth (see below), as she was believed to be opposed to Louis XIV's policies. Once the greatest heiress and beauty in Louis' court, the Duchesse de Mazarin died in Chelsea in 1699 aged fifty-three, alcoholic and, but for Mustafa, alone.[97]

Dynastic marriages could be biological, as well as personal and political, disasters. In order to maintain their prestige, European sovereigns almost always married cousins from within 'the family of kings', whose ties were so strong that they wore mourning for each other as relations even when they were at war.[98] Yet the products of inbreeding are predisposed to illnesses, including madness and infertility. Despite the evidence of animals as well as humans, and despite churches' bans on consanguineous marriages, this risk continued to be taken by royal families until the twentieth century. Both Queen Victoria and Franz Joseph married their first cousins, who were also cousins in other degrees.*

---

* Since 1900 the practice has become less common. The present King of Norway, Haakon VII, however, is a healthy son of first cousins, who were also cousins in other degrees.

While Henriette Anne was Monsieur's first cousin, Marie Thérèse was Louis XIV's double first cousin. His mother-in-law was also his aunt; his wife's mother-in-law was also her aunt. Whereas six of his eleven known children by his mistresses reached the age of fifteen, only one of his six children by his wife did so: the Dauphin Louis, born in 1661. Probably because of their parents' consanguinity, none of their five other children, Anne Elizabeth (b. 1662), Marie Anne (b. 1664), Marie Thérèse (b. 1667), Philippe (b. 1668) and Louis François (b. 1672), lived beyond the age of five.[99] The consanguinity in the Spanish marriage helped deprive Louis XIV of spare legitimate sons and daughters to serve as agents of French influence in Europe.

No dynasty practised intermarriage more frequently than the Spanish branch of the House of Austria. While Louis XIV married his double first cousin, Philip IV took as his second wife a niece, the Archduchess Mariana of Austria, who was also, many times over, his cousin. After his death in 1665, he was succeeded by their son Carlos II. Marie Thérèse's half-brother, he was an impotent invalid whose protruding jaw made it difficult for him to chew food.

The possibility that a French prince would succeed Carlos II on the Spanish throne was always a factor in Louis XIV's foreign policy. Indeed, before Carlos II's long-predicted death finally occurred in 1700, he named one of Louis XIV's grandsons as his heir. The resulting War of the Spanish Succession would dominate the last years of Louis XIV's reign, and bring France to the edge of the precipice.

6

Fouquet's Fall

One of the most famous parties in French history was given for the twenty-two-year-old Louis XIV in the chateau of Vaux, east of Paris, on 17 August 1661. The host was Nicolas Fouquet, Surintendant des Finances. Fouquet's ambitions to become principal minister were suggested by his motto 'Quo non ascendet?': 'Whither will he not ascend?' This was inscribed below his personal symbol, a red squirrel with a large bushy tail (Fouquet is Breton for squirrel), which can still be seen throughout Vaux, as can the two crossed Fs for Fouquet, on every surface: ceilings, walls, tapestries, firebacks and bookbindings.

Fouquet had been building Vaux, conveniently close to Fontainebleau for council meetings, since 1658. Soon 900 men were working on the site and a tapestry factory had been established near by. Fifteen windows wide, this magnificent moated chateau in the latest classical taste combines a black-tiled French *mansarde* roof with rooms with high coved ceilings in the Italian style. The triumph of the King over his enemies, and the wealth and loyalty of Fouquet, were its messages.

In the centre of the chateau a large oval salon, decorated with reliefs of Olympian gods and signs of the zodiac, was intended to represent the palace of the sun. The Chambre des Muses celebrated the victory of the muses over the satyrs and the triumph of fidelity. The Salon d'Hercule showed the god's labours and apotheosis. The Salon du Roi had a ceiling depicting the triumph of Truth, supported by Time. Fouquet's own bedroom showed Apollo lighting the world, reflecting the Surintendant's conviction that he was the 'light of royalty'. These frescoed and gilded rooms created one of the most sumptuous interiors in France, an early version of the 'Louis XIV' style – more vivid, and better executed, than the rooms later created by the same artists for the King at Versailles.

Whereas Mazarin and Anne of Austria used Roman artists like Romanelli to decorate their palaces, Fouquet preferred French court artists. They worked as a team: Louis Le Vau, Premier Architecte du Roi, was the architect. François Girardon and Pierre Puget worked on the sculptures. Charles Le Brun, soon to be Premier Peintre du Roi, painted or supervised the frescoes. André Le Nôtre, a royal gardener since 1635, Contrôleur Général des Bâtiments et Jardins du Roi since 1658, designed the garden, a masterpiece of avenues, statues and fountains, reflecting the shape of the chateau it surrounded. To French eyes, Vaux was superior to the finest gardens in Italy.

It became the talk of Paris. Mazarin and Colbert visited it in June 1659, on their way to negotiate the Treaty of the Pyrenees. The King came twice, with his mother and brother in July 1659, with his wife in July 1660. Fouquet gave a party there for Henrietta Maria, Madame and Monsieur in July 1661. The party on 17 August that year was for the King, his mother (his pregnant wife did not attend) and 3,000 guests.

On arrival around 6 p.m., although he had already seen it twice, the King was astonished by the splendour of Vaux that evening, filled with tapestries and pictures brought from Fouquet's other residences. The King's astonishment struck Fouquet himself. In the gardens guests walked, or were driven in small carriages, through what seemed liked walls of water, as the fountains played more than 35 feet high. They then went inside for an *ambigu* or informal banquet prepared by the great chef Vatel, 'maître d'hôtel de Monseigneur le Surintendant', while they were entertained by twenty-four violinists.

Back in the gardens, there was another concert and a *comédie-ballet* by Molière. Entitled *Les Fâcheux*, performed by torchlight, it was the first time that a play had included ballets. A young actress named Armande Béjart, who later became Molière's wife, emerged from a grotto to declaim a poem in honour of the King:

> Jeune, victorieux, sage, vaillant, auguste,
> Aussi doux que sévère, aussi puissant que juste.
>
> ('Young, victorious, wise, valiant, august,
> As gentle as he is severe, as powerful as he is just')

The party ended at one in the morning, with a firework display; the sky blazed with illuminated Ls and fleurs-de-lys. A thousand rockets were fired from the dome of the chateau. After a last meal, the King and the court returned to Fontainebleau.[1]

The cause of Fouquet's fall was not, however, his magnificent fête and chateau, but Fouquet himself. To the amazement of Louis' family, court and ministers, the day Mazarin died the King had announced, 'I am determined henceforth to govern my state by myself.'[2] He wanted no over-powerful minister or relation, not even his mother, challenging his control of the government. After Mazarin's death, Anne of Austria no longer attended the council of ministers. Nor did Séguier, the Chancellor of France. The members were restricted to Lionne for foreign affairs, Le Tellier for war, Fouquet for finance and the King.

According to the son of a secretary of state M. Loménie de Brienne, Louis XIV told the Chancellor and each minister to sign nothing without an order from himself. 'The scenery in the theatre has changed,' he said. 'In the government of my state, in the administration of my finances and in negotiations abroad, I will have different principles from M. le cardinal. You know my wishes, messieurs, it is up to you to execute them.' When the Président of the General Assembly of the Clergy asked with whom he should discuss ecclesiastical business after Mazarin's death, the King replied, 'With me, Monsieur l'Archevêque.'[3] Thus, however fond of Mazarin Louis XIV had been, his assertion of 'different principles' shows that many aspects of the Cardinal's government had dismayed him: in particular his habit of negotiating favours and appointments with applicants as an equal, rather than as the master.

Louis XIV had been judged by appearances, by his love of dancing, hunting and Marie Mancini, rather than by the hours he had spent working and talking with Mazarin and attending council meetings. Colbert, his favourite minister of the 1660s, wrote two years later that no one had believed that a handsome young man with 'une santé forte et vigoureuse' would be capable of showing the strength of character to devote himself to business rather than pleasure. A new personality had been added to Louis XIV's collection of contradictions. He was a mild youth, devoted to his mother, women and the guitar; a dedicated soldier and huntsman; and, in addition, a hard-working bureaucrat, giving almost as much time to his ministers as to his army.

Both Condé and Turenne had hoped that they could emerge as the dominant figure in the government, and were shocked to be sidelined by three bourgeois: Lionne, Le Tellier and Fouquet.[4] Turenne, who had been made marshal general of the army in April 1660, was also a minister of state, consulted informally by the King on 'all important matters', according to Colbert – particularly on military affairs and, as a Protestant, on relations with Protestant powers such as the United Provinces, England and Brandenburg. He sometimes wrote drafts of ambassadors' instructions or treaties.[5] He was not, however, called to the council. This was the King's method with loyal grandees. He might consult them individually, or summon Monsieur, Condé, Turenne and favoured marshals (Villeroy, Gramont, du Plessis) to a wider Grand Conseil to discuss specific issues. He did not give them a permanent place, by right, on the inner council.[6]

In addition to council meetings, the King would hold meetings with individual ministers, to see if their attitude was the same as had been expressed in the council, and frequently answered ambassadors' despatches himself. He was helped by his principal secretary, the Président Rose, a member of the legal nobility inherited from Mazarin, who could imitate Louis XIV's handwriting and his signature to perfection, and compose letters in the appropriate royal style. At the end of the reign the Foreign Minister Torcy also wrote some of the King's letters, in an approximation of the royal handwriting. In every palace the King had small *cabinets*, with desks where he kept his papers, in addition to the Grand Cabinet where he held council. Often, instead of using secretaries, he wrote *mémoires* or notes in his own hand.[7] Mazarin's remark in his letter of 29 June 1659 was proving prophetic: 'If you once take charge, you will do more in one day than someone cleverer than me could do in six months; what a king does on his own initiative is of another weight and makes a more striking impression than what a minister does, however authorized he may be.'[8]

In the months after Mazarin's death, Fouquet too had hoped to dominate the government. Fouquet was bourgeois by origin (from a family of Angers cloth merchants), noble by the fiefs he had purchased and the genealogy he had commissioned: his coronet as Marquis de Belle-Île still decorates the walls of Vaux. A pupil of the Jesuits, he was a charmer, with what his friend Madame de Sévigné called a 'mine riante'. Breaking the strict dress rules of the monarchy, he sometimes wore the bright silks of the court nobility rather than the black of the *noblesse de robe*. Even after his disgrace, the writers La Fontaine, Bussy-Rabutin and others remained his friends. He had 116 protégés investing in the French financial and fiscal system, compared to Mazarin's 114 and Colbert's 55. Led by Fouquet, government officials were themselves profiting from the government's loans and tax farms. Colbert, Mazarin's capable and ambitious former Intendant, accused the Surintendant des Finances of pillaging the state and stealing its revenues, as if Mazarin and Colbert themselves had not also done so, to an even greater extent.[9]

Fouquet had tentacles overseas as well as throughout France. One of Louis' long-term ambitions, in addition to his drives to modernize and enlarge France, and to become the arbiter of Europe, was to win France a global empire. Spain and Portugal were in part financed by their overseas empires. Since 1600 England and the Netherlands had been founding colonies from the Caribbean to the East Indies: Englishmen already inhabited much of the east coast of North America. France, however, despite its long seaboard, its many ports from Calais to Toulon and its large population – 19 million compared to around 8 million in Spain, 4 million in England and about 1.5 million in the Netherlands – had faltered. The Fronde had been an economic as well as a political catastrophe. Since the early seventeenth century France had possessed only a few Caribbean islands such as Guadeloupe and Martinique, and Quebec.

Anticipating France's bid for world trade, on 5 September 1658 Fouquet had bought through intermediaries the island of Belle-Île off the coast of Brittany, near Nantes and the mouth of the Loire, from the Duc de Retz, brother of the Cardinal, for 1.3 million livres. In August 1660 he bought, again in secret, under the name of his follower the Marquis de Feuquières, the office of 'Viceroy of America', giving him the possibility of controlling all French possessions in it, and the island of St Lucia. He planned that his ships would monopolize France's trade with America. From Belle-Île, which he was fortifying with 400 Dutch cannon, his privateers would prey on foreign shipping.[10] In April 1661, furthering Fouquet's global ambitions, the King himself had placed Fouquet in charge of a newly created Council of Commerce.[11]

Like some international corporations today, Fouquet was running a parallel network inside the state, with *obligés* embedded throughout the government. He kept lists. They included 'almost all the court officials' and the Premier Président of the Parlement de Paris.[12] Fouquet even offered Anne of Austria his 'good services' with her own son over the management of her charities, to which he contributed. Despite promises of discretion, he then told the King, who then told his mother not to trust Fouquet. He also kept lists of female conquests. Madame de Motteville writes that he rewarded them with showers of gold.[13] Madame du Plessis-Bellière, his principal confidante, was known as the Surintendante of the love affairs of the Surintendant. They corresponded in code and he wrote, 'I trust [her] in everything.' He had no secrets from her, and she profited from some of his transactions. In an emergency it was she whom his friends should 'consult in everything'.[14]

Fouquet was aiming to control and marginalize the King. He tried to influence the King's private life, as well as his government. Marie Thérèse's many virtues did not ensure her husband's fidelity. As far away as Reims, she had an unappealing reputation: one of its inhabitants wrote in his diary, 'heavy in nature, with little conversation, people say that she does not speak perfect French.'[15] Moreover she was often pregnant, and preferred visiting churches to dancing in ballets. The King turned elsewhere.

In April 1661 the court and part of the government had moved to Fontainebleau for the summer. Balls, plays, hunts and swimming parties broke
the routine of council meetings, religious ceremonies and receptions.[16] At
court women had more freedom, and could mix with men more easily,
than in any other public space. The households of Louis XIV's wife and
sister-in-law filled the court with attractive young ladies-in-waiting. The
household of Madame in particular was known as 'the nursery of mistresses'.[17] When the Duke of Pastrana, came from Spain to the court of
France in the following decade, he called it a real brothel.[18]

To mask a flirtation with Madame, the King began to pay attention to
one of her maids of honour, Louise de La Vallière, daughter of a country
gentleman from the Loire. Her blonde hair and languid blue eyes were
much praised by contemporaries. She also danced and rode well. Her
timidity and sincerity pleased the King; she was only sixteen. Towards the
end of July, they met in an attic lent by the Comte de Saint-Aignan, one
of the King's *premiers gentilshommes de la chambre*.[19] The court conspired to keep the pregnant Queen in ignorance.[20]

Characteristically, Fouquet approached Louise de La Vallière and told
her that, if she needed anything, she should ask him. Possibly he offered
her money, or courted her himself, which might explain the hatred with
which the King thenceforth pursued him. A contemporary wrote:

> L'impudent, le perfide, le traître!
> Quoi! vouloir devenir le rival de son maître![21]
>
> ('The impudent, the betrayer, the traitor!
> What! To want to become his master's rival!')

Louis XIV later explained in the memoirs he wrote, or had written, for
his son that his decision to arrest Fouquet was due to Fouquet's 'insolent
acquisitions', 'restless humour' and 'bad faith':

> the general calamity of my peoples demanded ceaselessly my exercise of
> justice against him. But what made him even more culpable in relation to
> me was that, very far from profiting from the kindness that I had shown
> him by keeping him in my councils, he had developed from it a further hope
> of deceiving me, and rather than becoming wiser as a result, he had merely
> tried to become more adroit . . . he could not stop himself from continuing
> his excessive expenditure, from fortifying castles, from decorating palaces
> [that is, Vaux], forming cabals, and placing under the names of his friends
> important offices which he bought for them at my expense [such as the post
> of viceroy of America] in the hope of soon making himself the sovereign
> arbiter of the State.[22]

The King did not exaggerate. Fouquet even sent an agent to Rome, a writer called François de Mauclair, to create his own party in the College of Cardinals.[23] Fouquet also asked for frequent private audiences with the King – to demonstrate to courtiers that he was in favour – which Louis felt obliged to grant so as not to arouse his distrust.[24] His biographer Jean-Christian Petitfils thinks that it was above all the reports the King received from agents of Colbert, of the fortification of the island of Belle-Île with 400 cannon, more even than Fouquet's growing networks, which decided him, towards the middle of June or earlier, to prepare to arrest the Surintendant.[25]

Colbert's hostility also precipitated Fouquet's downfall. Colbert, as methodical as Fouquet was chaotic, had been secretly undermining Fouquet since at least 1659. He accused his rival, without exaggeration, of peculation; confusion and 'facility' in government business; sending agents abroad; dining 'superbly'; and acquiring 'friends of every kind' – as if he was a *frondeur* leader about to rebel, as some of his wilder projects suggested that he was. Because of Fouquet, the King was receiving only 35 or 40 per cent of the value of French taxes.

Fouquet was in part a scapegoat for Mazarin's pillaging and mismanagement. Colbert denounced 'the great fortunes of financiers and war suppliers which inspire envy and jealousy in everyone and which are the cause of a prodigious augmentation of luxury'. In reality Colbert, as Mazarin's *intendant* and testamentary executor, was guilty of similar faults, as Fouquet knew. Colbert had covered his tracks by burning Mazarin's account books, not making a complete inventory of his possessions after his death and partly rewriting his will. (Daniel Dessert calls Mazarin and Colbert the worst predators of the Ancien Régime.)[26] The legendary intriguer the Duchesse de Chevreuse, still able to influence Anne of Austria, whom she received that June in her chateau of Dampierre, also turned against Fouquet. In 1667 her grandson, the Duc de Chevreuse, would marry one of Colbert's daughters.[27]

Fouquet was aware of Colbert's enmity. Indeed their rivalry was represented on the ceilings of the Cabinet des Jeux at Vaux, painted in 1660–61. They show vipers – symbols of wisdom, and Colbert's emblem – threatening the squirrels of Fouquet.[28] On his way to Bordeaux in 1659, Fouquet had Colbert's letters of denunciation to Mazarin intercepted, and copied them overnight with a clerk, in order to be able to rebut them. Mazarin often preferred Fouquet's expediency to the harshness of Colbert, praising the former for being ready to engage his last sol for the good of the state.[29] Fouquet later said, 'I re-established the situation and upheld it [the government's finances], however miserable it was. Not only have we not lacked for anything, but we have been superior to the others [Spain and the *frondeurs*].' He claimed not to have received one 'penny [*teston*] of *gratifi-cation*' from the tax farmers. This was untrue. Fouquet's accounts were in chaos: some financial registers had been burnt, others falsified. His private finances and those of the French crown were inextricably intertwined.[30]

As early as 1658, when Mazarin had begun to question his financial methods, Fouquet had written down a plan of action in case of an attempt to arrest him. It included armed resistance from fortresses commanded by friends, or a coup in Paris. He hid, and forgot, this megalomaniac project behind a mirror, when one of his mistresses entered the room in his house at Saint-Mandé, near Vincennes, in which he was writing.[31]

Another mistress was Madame d'Huxelles, a rival of Madame de Sév-igné for the reputation of best letter writer in Paris. From her letters it is clear that Fouquet was persuaded by the King to resign as *procureur général* of the Parlement in August 1661, believing that in the future he would 'be obliged always to be beside the person of the king', rather than serving the Parlement which would have protected him. He believed he was close to supreme power in the council. 'Without flattering you, people think you have total authority,' Madame d'Huxelles wrote. She also, however, warned him: 'you should even beware of the fine welcome and kind face of the King and the prospects held out to you of other things'.[32] State officials like Colbert and another enemy, Le Tellier, had more power than the many courtiers whom Fouquet 'obliged'. The fall of Fouquet, like that of Cinq-Mars eighteen years earlier, confirms the dominance in France of state over court. Colbert, the arch-manipulator, drafted the plan for Fouquet's arrest and the speech the King made after it.[33]

On 29 August the King left Fontainebleau for Nantes, the only major French city he had not visited. The Estates of Brittany were meeting and the King wished them to raise taxes. He stayed in the ancient moated castle of the dukes of Brittany (furnished especially for him by the citizens of Nantes), where François I had proclaimed the union of France and Brittany in 1532 and Henri IV had published the Edict of Nantes in 1598. Fouquet stayed outside the city, in a house of Madame du Plessis-Bellière, which had a tunnel leading to the banks of the Loire – so that, in a crisis, he could flee by boat to Belle-Île.

The Surintendant was considered so formidable that, instead of having him arrested in his residence by Gardes du Corps or Gardes Français on duty, the King used his trusted Musketeers. The man he chose to lead the operation was the celebrated officer Monsieur d'Artagnan, model for Alexandre Dumas' hero. As a former *gentilhomme ordinaire* of Mazarin to whom Colbert had lent money, he could be relied upon. The arrest took place on 5 September, the King's twenty-third birthday, after an early-morning meeting of the council.

Since the Musketeers were an external guard, d'Artagnan arrested Fouquet outside the castle, on the Place Saint-Pierre. Fouquet was in a sedan chair on his way to mass in the cathedral. D'Artagnan said, 'Monsieur, je vous arrête par ordre du roi.' Musketeers guarded Fouquet, and kept him incommunicado all the way from Nantes, via Angers, the town from which his family came, to the Bastille.[34] Louis XIV had chosen Nantes as most of the court, including Anne of Austria who liked Fouquet, were still at Fontainebleau.

Fouquet's trial revealed the mixed character of the French monarchy. On the one hand military force was the King's *ultima ratio*, as he showed by arresting and imprisoning Fouquet. A letter written on the day of the arrest to his mother confirms the King's fear of those around him: 'I am overwhelmed all day by an infinity of extremely alert people who at the least sign could dig much further into what is going on . . . I am very happy that they see that I am not such a dupe as they had imagined and that the best decision they can take is to attach themselves to me.' The King feared that his own servants could be more attached to Fouquet than to him, just as many of his mother's and father's had been more loyal to Richelieu than to either of them.[35]

On the other hand, France was not solely a military monarchy. Fouquet had a genuine trial. One member of each provincial Parlement was added to the court, to make it more representative. The court was presided over by Chancellor Séguier, who had performed the same task at the trial of Cinq-Mars in 1642.[36]

On news of Fouquet's arrest, his mother, a devotee of Père Vincent de Paul, had said that she should thank God as now her son had found a way to save his soul.[37] His wife and mother were able to sway in his favour sections of Paris opinion, including his judges, even though they had been secretly selected by Colbert.[38] On their knees they also pleaded with Louis XIV for mercy, after his public dinner and on other occasions, without effect: by 1661 the kind young man of the 1650s was hardening.[39] Away from the intoxication of the court, Fouquet lost his megalomania. D'Ormesson wrote that at his trial he spoke with 'great intelligence, honesty and freedom of spirit'.[40]

Paris, still partly a *frondeur* city, began to regard Fouquet as a victim. Born in 1626, called by her cousin the writer Bussy-Rabutin 'the delight of the human race',[41] Madame de Sévigné admired Fouquet. When she saw him on his way to his trial surrounded by musketeers, her heart beat so fast she could hardly stand.[42] Her letters express admiration for Fouquet's patience and the 'marvels' in his replies in court. She was not afraid of the letters being intercepted by the post and shown to ministers.[43]

From the point of view of the crown, the trial was badly conducted. Fouquet's houses had been searched by musketeers in the presence of Colbert, which enabled Fouquet to claim that other papers could have been inserted among his own.[44] Fouquet's strategy was to demand original documents and to sow disagreement among his accusers. His enemies, he said – meaning Colbert – were hard as stone, while he had always been 'generous'. He reminded the court of the Chancellor's treason during the Fronde.[45]

Fouquet also hinted at a dark secret relating to Mazarin's alliance with Cromwell, which he could tell only the King – that, the English Ambassador Lord Holles wrote, Mazarin 'did not have good intentions for his master'. This is fantasy. If Mazarin had been ill intentioned, he would have allowed Louis XIV to marry his niece. From the perspective of the 1660s, however, Mazarin's alliance with the regicide, perhaps also his acquisitions from the English royal collections, appeared outrageous.[46] The real secret was Fouquet's knowledge, as one of the Cardinal's executors, that Mazarin's will and inventory had been 'manufactured' by Colbert after his death, and his account books destroyed, to favour the crown. Fouquet would be joined in prison later by a masked man – the original of 'the man in the iron mask'. He may have been Eustache d'Auger, a valet of Mazarin's treasurer, imprisoned because he also knew too much about the rewriting of Mazarin's will, and his profiteering at the expense of Louis XIV, Henrietta Maria and the French taxpayer.[47] Fouquet also claimed to the court that all his measures and irregularities had been authorized and approved by Mazarin, and restrospectively pardoned in conversation by the King himself, after Mazarin's death.[48]

Another element in Fouquet's defence was to remind the court that he had been 'firm and unshakeable' throughout the Fronde. Those who had wanted to deprive the King of his crown – Condé and Turenne for example – were now in favour, while he was in jail. When in 1654 and 1656 Mazarin and Le Tellier were desperate for funds, he had saved and sustained the finances of the state, by advancing his own money and using his own and his friends' credit. Without his help, he claimed in a *mémoire* for the King, the state would have perished.[49] The real criminals were those who had sided with the *frondeurs* and Spain. 'All France learnt and admired this reply,' wrote Madame de Sévigné: 'nobody talked of anything else.' Séguier, however, reminded the court that Fouquet's 'plan de Saint-Mandé' involved declaring war on the King, raising provinces and fortifying places against him.[50]

The trial took a long time. In August 1663 Louis XIV summoned the judges to the Louvre to tell them, in both group and private audiences, that he was satisfied with their services; he wanted justice; but he also wanted 'diligence' – speed.[51] He showed relative restraint, unlike Richelieu who had executed the Maréchal de Marillac in 1632 for opposing his policies. Rather than looking for enemies, the King feared to increase their number. Women's letters to Fouquet were burnt. Registers of his dependants and their 'fidelity pacts' 'towards and against everyone' – that is, the King – were not exploited. No one who was mentioned in the 'plan de Saint-Mandé' was interrogated, not even Madame du Plessis-Bellière.[52]

Finally in 1665 the court's verdict of banishment and confiscation of property, rather than execution, was a blow to the King; in the best traditions of the Paris Parlement, it had stood up to the government.[53] Olivier d'Ormesson wrote in his diary of the 'uncontrollable joy' in all Paris, 'even among the humblest servants in the shops', at the news that Fouquet was not condemned to death, due to the 'hatred everyone has in their hearts against the present government'.[54]

Exceptionally, however, Louis XIV used his reserve royal judicial powers to aggravate, rather than to commute, a sentence. The explanation may be a combination of personal hatred and generic resentment of France's succession of overmighty chief ministers. The former Surintendant des Finances was condemned to solitary confinement in the castle of Pignerol in the Alps. He was not at first permitted to take exercise. Only in 1674, after thirteen years, was he allowed to exchange two letters a year with his wife. She and his family were not allowed to visit him until a year before he died.[55]

Louis XIV had shown a streak of cruelty, hitherto unsuspected, from which many thousands more, inside and outside France, would suffer in the future.* After eighteen years in prison, Fouquet died in 1680. The epitaph on his tomb in the convent of the Visitation in Paris – where his sisters were nuns – reflected the piety at the city's heart: 'From a man infatuated with what is grandest and vainest in the world, he became by the spirit of God perfectly instructed and moved by what is holiest in religion.'[56]

Much of Fouquet's fortune was confiscated, but his family was spared. His wife and son continued to live in the splendour of Vaux. Louis, however, confiscated some of the best statues and tapestries from Vaux. On the latter, he replaced Fouquet's squirrel and interlaced Fs with his own crown and interlaced Ls (themselves possibly inspired by Fouquet's interlaced Fs: Louis XIII had not used them). They would adorn a palace of his own, created by the same team which had worked for Fouquet at Vaux: Versailles.[57]

---

* Another example was the execution in 1662 of a former *frondeur*, the Baron de Fargues, despite the general amnesty of 1652.

7

Making France Work

'Work is the first object of His Majesty and he prefers it to everything else,' wrote Colbert. Colbert was right. Until the end of the reign the King almost never missed a council meeting, every morning from 9 to 11 from Monday to Friday, and held lengthy meetings about finances three times a week in the evening. In addition he worked alone with the secretaries of state: Lionne on Saturday and Sunday; Colbert (whom he made *contrôleur général des finances* and *ministre de la maison du roi* in 1665) on Wednesday and Thursday; Le Tellier, for war, on Tuesday. He also held council meetings in the evening before supper at 10. The King's hours were said to be as regular as a monk's.[1]

The *Gazette de France* assured its readers that the King's 'assiduity' would bring France to 'the highest point of glory and happiness that the most fortunate monarchies have yet enjoyed'.[2] When courtiers complained that the King was shut up much of the day, even after dinner, he was usually working with ministers, not dallying with mistresses.[3]

Even hard work, and the vast theoretical authority of his crown, however, did not guarantee Louis XIV total control of France. Keen to show that they are not deceived by royal propaganda, or by the inflated view of royal power enshrined in Louis XIV's memoirs written for the instruction of the Dauphin, many historians emphasize the constraints placed on the crown by the social and economic structures, the traditional institutions (especially the Church) and the conservatism of France.

Even at the height of his power, as Fouquet's trial showed, individuals and law courts could challenge or criticize the King. In 1662 the Chancellor and the Parlement of Paris would defeat his attempts to modify the composition of the royal family by adding the House of Lorraine to the French order of succession.[4] The monarchy could be stronger than the King. Christianity, as well as conservatism, could encourage disobedience to Louis XIV – as he would find after 1680, when despite bribes and threats many Protestants would refuse to convert to Catholicism.

There were also individual examples of disobedience. When Louis XIV wanted to make the Maréchal de Fabert a *chevalier du Saint-Esprit* in 1661, Fabert refused because he lacked the degrees of nobility required by the statutes of the Order. Louis XIV admitted defeat, while praising 'this rare example of honesty . . . which I admit that I regard as an ornament of my Reign'.[5] The Queen's *dame d'honneur* the Duchesse de Navailles, during the Fronde a trusted intermediary for correspondence between Anne of Austria and Mazarin, was determined to protect the Queen's maids of honour from seduction by the King. Despite the King's pleas, she told him, 'as a Christian and as a woman of honour', to 'look elsewhere than in the household of the Queen, which was her own, for the objects of his pleasures and his inclinations'. The King, however, spoke to Mlle de La Mothe Houdancourt through a crack in the wall of the maids' apartment. When men were seen searching its gutters and chimneys for means of entry, the Duchesse de Navailles had them covered by iron grilles. In June 1664 she was exiled from Paris with her husband. Madame de Motteville wrote that 'the fear of offending God was more powerful than the desire to be agreeable to the King' – words which could have applied to many other subjects of Louis XIV. The Duchesse de Navailles did not return to court until 1682.[6] A few months after her exile, the Duc de Mazarin, Grand Master of the Artillery and husband of Hortense Mancini, having fortified himself by taking the sacrament, told Louis in a private audience that his love affair with Mlle de La Vallière was scandalizing France. Louis replied that Mazarin had long been ill in the head and left the room.[7]

Humbler Parisians also criticized the King, as Colbert informed him, for spending too much money on pensions, horses and household troops, or 'marionettes': 'The exaggerated distinction between his [military] household and everyone else discourages all the other subjects.'[8] When Louis XIV reviewed his musketeers and bodyguards, their uniforms were admired by enormous crowds, but, d'Ormesson added, 'everyone complains, as the troops are obliged to bear these useless expenses themselves.' He also wrote that the government was so harsh and unjust that it could not last.[9] In April 1672, at the start of a major war, three marshals of France, Humières, Bellefonds and Créquy, refused to serve under the great Turenne. He was using his rank as a *prince étranger* to issue orders to his fellow marshals. Ignoring the 'absolute orders of His Majesty' to obey Turenne, they retired to their estates. Courtiers applauded their bravery in preferring disgrace, and the temporary loss of their marshals' salaries, to 'dishonour'.[10]

These were, however, exceptional individuals or situations. Most people obeyed the King most of the time. He had an unwritten bargain with the nobility. Provided they entered his service and obeyed his orders, he would guarantee, even expand, their tax privileges and job monopolies. Compared to the governments of other countries, and to its own past, Louis XIV's monarchy was remarkably stable and authoritarian.

English visitors, for example, were attracted by France's proximity and its court, capital and nobility, but considered Louis XIV's government 'wholly arbitrary'.[11] A Yorkshire royalist, Sir John Reresby, wrote that 'the French kings have a most absolute power . . . they dispose of all governments of all towns and countries . . . they lay what taxes they please upon the people . . . they dare scarce so much as reflect upon their past liberties . . . [the King] himself is the channel through which flow all the streams of favour while the poor countryman sinks under the weight of his oppression.'[12] The philosopher John Locke thought that provincial governors had 'no power at all . . . the intendants give constant intelligence of all things to the Court.' Provincial Estates dared not refuse the King's demands.[13]

On 31 January 1670 Louis XIV surrounded the Château Neuf of Saint-Germain with 400 Gardes du Corps. His favourite *capitaine des gardes*, the Comte de Lauzun, then entered and arrested Monsieur's lover the Chevalier de Lorraine, to whom Monsieur had promised the benefices of three abbeys, and whom the King detested. Monsieur withdrew, enraged, to his chateau of Villers-Cotterêts north-east of Paris. Madame complained that she was reduced to learning Italian to pass the time. Monsieur's departure, however, had no political effect, as it would have done in previous reigns. Three weeks later he was back. The Marquis de Saint-Maurice, Ambassador of the Duke of Savoy, wrote: 'everyone is submissive, out of duty and fear, the King is in his sovereign power, strong through money and troops, master of the Parlements, of fortresses and of everything which is in his kingdom.'[14]

From 1667 Parlements were forced to register royal edicts and new legal codes without making their traditional 'remonstrances', although the edicts might be modified in accordance with subsequent remonstrances.[15] Many *parlementaires* took jobs in the royal administration.[16] Money, as well as loyalty and fear, bound them to the crown: judges who registered royal edicts were accorded *gratifications* by the King, on Colbert's recommendation: 'I permit you to do what you think good about *gratifications* with regard to my service,' wrote the King.[17] Parlements and provincial Estates survived partly because they were useful for imposing laws and raising further loans and taxes. Royal control was advertised by the large number of guards who accompanied the King when he visited the Parlement of Paris to register edicts. Colbert wrote that the Parlement of

Brittany was 'the only company in the kingdom which resists the will of the king'.[18]

Mastering institutional and individual opposition, Louis XIV was able to devote himself to an ambitious reform programme to galvanize the economy and modernize the monarchy. For an anonymous observer, writing in 1664, the King 'has vast and ample projects . . . he is turning the whole State upside down, and if his projects succeed he will entirely renew it'.[19]

In Colbert he had one of the ablest ministers in the history of France. The Venetian Ambassador reported that he inspired 'general hate' (many even wanted Fouquet back); but the King 'likes him very much . . . he brings everything to His Majesty's notice', and he introduced 'an incredible economy' in 'the smallest details' of every department he controlled. The Ambassador called him a man 'like a rock of steel', capable of 'indefatigable work', sometimes eighteen hours a day.[20] In the same week he would rotate between the King's chateau at Versailles, his own at Sceaux, south of Paris – less magnificent than Fouquet's Vaux – and his principal residence, rue Neuve des Petits Champs in Paris. He also had houses at Fontainebleau and Saint-Germain. He probably travelled with a secretary in his carriage who read to him or recorded dictation in pencil – given the state of the roads, ink would have spilt.[21] No complaints by Colbert or other ministers, about time wasted on travelling, have been found.

Colbert became so powerful that at times he gave instructions to Louis XIV. For example, in the plan for Fouquet's arrest, he had used phrases such as 'the King must', and he had laid down on which days the King should meet which council.[22] D'Ormesson wrote sourly in his diary: 'his fortune is rising rapidly and he is the master, doing everything he wants.'[23] Louis XIV allowed ministers like Colbert to 'propose' orders, select officials and initiate policy, provided they kept him informed.

The cumbersome and unjust tax system was one target of Louis XIV and Colbert. Through the special law court which had tried Fouquet, Colbert also helped the King recover money from financiers and war suppliers. Contracts signed with financiers since 1635 were annulled, and replaced by contracts with Colbert's supporters. Many previous tax farmers had to pay fines. All nobles had to have their titles verified. Many new offices were abolished. After the privatizations of the previous twenty years, the state was biting back.[24] New rules were introduced for tax farms, to ensure that they were auctioned competitively and that the crown received a higher percentage of their income: the government recived a total of 63 million of 95 million livres in 1665, compared to only 36 million of 80 million in 1660. In peacetime its negotiating position was stronger than in wartime, when its need for cash was more urgent.[25]

Colbert took over the register of secret expenses from Mazarin's Protestant banker Barthélemé d'Herwarth and began to keep an accurate
account of all revenues, reserves and expenditure.[26] He taught Louis XIV
elements of accounting; well-thumbed small red-leather *abrégés des
finances*, sometimes written for the King in gilt ink, listing income and
expenditure, debts and repayments, for the years 1662 to 1680, survive
in the Bibliothèque Nationale. They enabled the King to understand the
state of his finances at a glance. The main sources of his income were the
taille, levied on non-noble households according to the amount of land
they owned or farmed; the *gabelle* or salt tax; and the *aides* or indirect
taxes on other products such as wine. In 1663, after the fall of Fouquet
when the King had lowered taxes, expenses were approximately 47 million
livres, income was for once higher at 48 million. In 1670 expenses were
77 million livres, income 74 million. In 1680 expenses were 96 million,
income 92 million. All three were peace years. Figures were 30 per cent
higher in war. In 1674, for example, expenses were 107 million, income
106 million. Even in peacetime, war and fortifications absorbed over 50
per cent of income.[27]

Colbert, the voice of reason, repeatedly pleaded with the King, usually
in vain, to base his expenditure on his income rather than his desires.
Colbert could never control war expenditure, much as he tried.[28] Nevertheless the King continued to trust Colbert. He once wrote: 'as for finances,
I always approve what you do, I am happy with it.'[29]

Colbert often told the King about the misery inflicted by his taxes on his
subjects, especially the hated *gabelle*, which obliged everyone over the age
of seven, in certain provinces, to buy 7 livres of salt a year from the government, which had a monopoly on salt production and fixed the price.
Both knew that in almost all parishes wealthier taxpayers adjusted the
tax registers to make the poor pay more than their share. The King repeatedly expressed his desire for 'the relief of his peoples'.[30] The amount of
money raised through the *taille*, a tax which fell most heavily on the poor
and from which nobles were exempt, fell from 53 million livres in 1657
(a war year) to 35 million in 1680, when France was at peace.[31] Thereafter,
however, taxes rose unceasingly. Louis XIV wrote in the margin of a letter
from Colbert: 'the poverty gives me great pain. We must do everything
we can to relieve the people. I hope to be able to soon.' Colbert assured
intendants that the 'pain' the King felt when ordering a tax rise showed
his 'goodwill' towards his peoples. Taxes continued to rise.[32]

Sometimes Colbert tried to favour 'the weak' at the expense of 'the
strong'.[33] Dovecotes were one battleground. The possession of a large,
turret-shaped *colombier* or dovecote, built to breed pigeons for eating,

was a privilege, in some provinces, of certain nobles. In other provinces, the more land owned, the more pigeons a landowner was allowed to keep. Pigeons' habit of eating seeds and wheat in the surrounding countryside was naturally resented by peasants and tenants, who, since they owned small amounts of land, could keep few pigeons. Colbert sided with peasants against nobles, and wanted to abolish large dovecotes, as an abuse of power. He wrote that 'there is no greater servitude for the people.' In the end, however, dovecotes were simply listed and taxed. By 1682, even before Colbert's death, the government regarded almost every human activity as a potential source of revenue.[34]

The reformation of justice was another of Louis XIV's and Colbert's projects. The King had vast legal powers to issue laws, *ordonnances* and edicts, and to imprison or exile a subject without legal procedure, by *lettre de cachet*: 'legislative power in this kingdom resides in the person of the sovereign alone,' declared the preamble of one *ordonnance*. Nevertheless there were different legal systems in different provinces. In Normandy the Parlement still condemned witches to death.[35] In the remote and impoverished province of Auvergne in the centre of France, some nobles, often former *frondeurs*, lived as if they were above the law, starting private wars, as well as committing other crimes, with impunity.

A *conseil de justice* to improve laws, and facilitate procedures, was established in 1665. It included the King (at least for the first sessions), the Chancellor, the ministers and members of the Conseil d'Etat and the Parlement de Paris, meeting regularly in the King's Grand Cabinet in the Louvre, or at Fontainebleau. They planned to reduce all France to 'one same law, one same measure and one same weight', as Louis XI had intended in the fifteenth century and Henri III in the sixteenth, and as the National Assembly would finally achieve after 1789.

Despite meetings lasting several hours, Louis XIV took a personal interest, often asking lawyers and ministers to express their opinions directly to him, not through commissioners. He declared his desire 'to make justice reign in my kingdom', even to deliver his subjects from legal costs and make law cases 'entirely free': 'a prince who is ambitious should devote himself to difficult matters.' He, and others like La Reynie, future Lieutenant de Police de Paris, also wanted to discuss the legal privileges and exemptions of the church and the nobility.

One lawyer M. Hotma said that, as the oldest state in Christendom, France had no need of new laws; it already had too many. Colbert, the voice of government, declared that 'the phrase sovereign court is a vain and useless phrase.' The King was less authoritarian, assuring his audience that 'during his life remonstrances [by the Parlement] would cause no harm because he would well know how to cut out [*retrancher*] the useless and tumultuous ones and keep those which would be respectful and reasonable.'[36]

The French system of justice was improved. From September 1665 to January 1666, during the 'grands Jours d'Auvergne', 1,360 legal cases in that province were reviewed by judges from outside it. There were 357 death sentences, and twenty-three executions, including six nobles. Many accused fled to Spain.

A new code of civil law, the Code Louis, was issued in 1667. The King went to Paris from Saint-Germain to register it in person in a *lit de justice* in the Parlement. An *ordonnance* reforming legislation on forests and waterways was issued in 1669; a criminal law *ordonnance* in 1670; a new commercial code in 1673; and an *ordonnance* on the navy in 1681.[37] Judicial procedures, including the use of torture as a means of interrogation, and appeals to superior courts, were codified. Slowly, thanks to the Code Louis, the 'law of Paris', relatively egalitarian since it encouraged the division of property among siblings rather than primogeniture, spread through northern France, although cumbersome systems of feudal law continued to complicate many aspects of rural property. Most provinces in southern France continued to apply Roman law, based on the codes of the Emperor Justinian from the sixth century.[38]

Louis XIV played his part as 'the fount of justice' in deed as well as word. He not only sat through debates about law codes in 1665. For two months in 1672, after the death of Chancellor Séguier, he acted as his own chancellor of France. Holding the seals of office, he worked on legal cases on Mondays with the Conseil d'Etat. The Queen attended one session to plead for a criminal's pardon. The King said 'that the supplicant was from a good enough family for it to be accorded to her'.[39]

Louis XIV and Colbert also devoted their energies to promoting French trade. The King was merchant as well as judge. He ordered the Grand Maréchal des Logis, the official in charge of courtiers' accommodation, to lodge 'conveniently at our court and on journeys every merchant who will have business at court, during the entire time they will be obliged to stay there . . . in a house which will be called the house of commerce'. Whether such accommodation was always provided is unknown; probably they found their own, or came for the day from Paris.[40] In addition the court's own privileged merchants, such as the *marchand de vins*, the *cabaretier suivant la cour* (who had been present at the King's wedding festivities in 1660) and the *imprimeur ordinaire du roi*, followed it wherever it went: Versailles would contain on the first floor a special Salle des Marchands for them to sell their wares.[41]

The Conseil de Commerce met once a fortnight in Louis' presence. In 1664 the King invested in the West and East India Companies, which he had just founded, and ordered his family and courtiers, and the judges and merchants of France, to do so too. The two queens invested 60,000 livres each, Condé 38,000, the King 3 million. Condé wrote to the Queen of Poland, 'there is not one person who wants to pay court to the King successfully who does not invest'.[42] Meetings of the council of the East India Company were held by the King in the Louvre or the Tuileries. After 1665 French merchant ships regularly sailed to and from the Indian Ocean, where the French navy had begun to seize ports and islands: Mauritius and Réunion in 1664; Surat on the west coast of India in 1667 and Pondichéry on the east, the base for the French bid for an Indian empire in the eighteenth century, in 1673. Spices, porcelain and other luxuries were imported, French products exported.[43] Louis XIV's plan was, Colbert wrote in 1669, to 'stimulate the industry of his subjects everywhere and to spread to the furthest corners of his kingdom, even the most distant, purchases of merchandise [as opposed to the common practice of bartering], coach transport and the new establishments and factories'.[44]

No trade was more dependent on the court than the dress trade, which employed about a third of wage earners in Paris.[45] In 1663 Colbert wrote a memorandum in which he advocated 'assisting with protection and money all the drapery factories inside the kingdom . . . to prompt them to make fine materials with which to clothe the king', by giving them prizes, and he urged the King to wear 'bright colours'.[46] French cloth of *serge de Berry* was substituted for grey English cloth as the dress of the French infantry, and high tariffs were put on English cloth. In his determination to encourage French cloth, on one occasion Louis XIV gave orders that his son's coat of English cloth should be burnt, and that no coats were to be worn except those made of 'the cloth of the new manufacture of France'.[47]

The King also visited clothes, glass and lace factories, at Colbert's instigation, in order to encourage them. In 1670, for example, he wrote to Colbert, like the obedient pupil he was: 'I will go to the factories of Abbeville and Beauvais [which made cloth and tapestries respectively] and will speak as I believe I should do and as you tell me.'[48]

Louis encouraged French lace, much used in his reign on clothes and cravats, as can be seen on his own portraits. In 1665 foreign lace, cloth and trimmings were banned in France. Royal lace factories making *point de France* – generally less flamboyant than Italian lace – were founded in Arras, Reims and elsewhere. Venetians were brought over and given French nationality to teach the French to improve their lace. It became so good that two of these instructors were later murdered by Venetian agents.[49] The King wrote to the Governor of Sedan ordering that all Sedan lace be sent to France, since 'the establishment of the manufacture of *point de France* is of such great consequence for the good of my peoples,' protecting them from the 'malice' of merchants accustomed to order lace from Venice.[50] Louis spent 18,491 livres on French lace in July 1666 alone: his lace, like his palaces, was covered in his emblems – sunbursts, Ls intertwined with MTs, fleurs-de-lys.[51]

Lace spread on women's as well as men's clothes. Louis insisted on ladies wearing *grand habit* at court, even in chapel. It consisted of a stiff, boned, décolleté bodice, a skirt, a train and detachable lace sleeves. He used his mistress Madame de Montespan, wearing a dress covered in *point de France* lace, as 'a triumphant beauty to display to all the ambassadors', in the words of Madame de Sévigné. The lace was almost as much on display as Montespan herself.[52] By then French lace, thanks to Louis XIV and Colbert, had become the most fashionable in Europe.

The French dress trade was helped by the spread of engraved fashion plates, often printed from drawings by the King's Dessinateur Ordinaire du Cabinet Jean Bérain, and of fashion dolls wearing the latest French fashions. They enabled foreigners to see what was worn at court and in Paris. *Le Mercure Galant*, a magazine with news of the latest fashions founded in 1672 and 'dedicated to Mgr. le Dauphin', became monthly after 1677. It offered advice on how to dress and which Paris shops were best for clothes, materials and accessories like fans, lace and ribbons, and on the need to change fashions or colours before everyone else.[53] For the *Mercure Galant*, fashions spread from the ladies of the court to the ladies of Paris, next to rich bourgeoises (who 'think they are in fashion but never are'), then to the provinces, finally abroad.[54] By 1687 the magazine could claim, 'you have to be in fashion for fear of being considered ridiculous or mean.'[55] The first volume had been dedicated to Louis XIV in the usual style ('Vos actions, Sire, qui passent de bien loin celles des plus grands héros . . .') and after 1684 it received an annual government subsidy.[56]

Louis XIV used dress as a political as well as a commercial weapon. In 1664, he instituted the *justaucorps à brevet*, which honoured fifty favoured nobles by allowing them to wear gold and silver lace and embroidery – forbidden by law to others – in a special pattern on a blue coat lined with scarlet. In February 1665, as a 'particular sign of his benevolence' it was awarded, via a brevet signed by a secretary of state, to the Prince de Condé. Perhaps in order to advertise his return to royal favour, Condé had himself and his son painted in this costume (see Plate 21).[57] Around 1670 the King restricted the right to wear red heels to male members of the nobility sufficiently well born or well connected to be presented at court. The red heels of France were soon imitated by the courts of Europe. They are prominently displayed in portraits not only of Louis XIV and his courtiers, but also of enemies such as William III, George I and their ministers.[58]

Even after his death Louis continued to be a fashion model for other monarchs. In 1717 Augustus II, Elector of Saxony and King of Poland, although opposed to French foreign policy, insisted on wearing at parties 'a coat such as the deceased King of France wore at great ceremonies, such as his marriage, *en marteau pourpoint et rhingrave*. It will not be enough to send a drawing of this costume; but he must have a doll exactly dressed in this kind of coat.'[59]

Regulations poured out of Colbert's office in these years, encouraging, protecting and rewarding trade. Inspectors general were established to check the quality of French goods. Colbert wrote to the Prévôt des Marchands of Lyon about manufacturers' marks; to Madame de La Petitière, 'directrice de la manufacture de dentelles à Auxerre' – an early example of a female CEO – about women workers; to others about slaves (if they were too well fed, Colbert believed, they might work less hard) or the Levant trade.[60]

Colbert's global outlook led him to try to 'transplant to France the best industries of each country'. The Château de Madrid in the Bois de Boulogne, built by François I after his return from prison in that city, became a workshop for makers of silk stockings 'in the English style'.[61] Carpet makers copied designs from Persia. Mirror manufacturers, as well as lace makers, were imported from Venice (their glass factory still exists at Saint-Gobain), cloth workers from the Netherlands and furniture makers from Germany as they were considered more skilful than their French counterparts. The Dauphin's toys, for example, had been imported from Augsburg, since French ones were not good enough.[62]

Using craftsmen from Fouquet's tapestry factory at Maincy, in 1662 the Gobelins factory was established in the Faubourg Saint-Marcel, in south-east Paris, where it still stands. Like Saint-Gobain, it was a court factory. A protégé of Colbert, the King's Premier Peintre Charles Le Brun became its director in 1663, and the King visited it in 1667. Several hundred workers were employed making furniture, clocks and tapestries. Series of tapestries, surmounted by the royal coat of arms, showed scenes from the life of the King (his visits to the Academy of Sciences, and the Gobelins for example), views of his palaces or the exploits of Alexander the Great. Soon Le Brun had established control over much of the artistic production in Paris. The elaborate furniture, made of combinations of ebony, gilt bronze, silver, mother of pearl and turtle shell, often decorated with the King's profile or statue – the 'style Louis XIV' – was partly created at Gobelins by foreign workers, with names like Cucci, Slodtz, Caffieri or Van Riesen Burgh. Some products were sold, others were used as diplomatic gifts, presented to foreign sovereigns or ambassadors.[63]

Paris began to recover from Rome, Florence and Venice, and from Augsburg and Antwerp, the role as the centre of luxury and innovation in Europe which it had held before its marginalization by the Italian Renaissance and the Wars of Religion. Massive purchases of luxury goods were made in Paris for the coronations of Charles X of Sweden in 1654, Charles II of England in 1660, Charles XI of Sweden in 1675 (dressed as Phoebus in one portrait, Charles XI looks like Louis XIV) and his wife Ulrika Eleonora in 1680.[64] Foreign princes began to maintain, often to the annoyance of their official diplomats, special agents in Paris with the mission to purchase luxury products in the latest fashion, from cosmetics to carriages, for their master and his family: Daniel Cronström and Nicodemus Tessin were buyers for the King of Sweden, Martin Mayr and Baldassare Pistorini for the Elector of Bavaria. Hence the many luxury objects in the Louis XIV style now adorning palaces and museums in Stockholm and Munich.[65]

Paris tailors were welcome even in hostile capitals, such as London. In the comedy *The Man of Mode* (1676), by George Etherege, one character wears 'nothing but what are originals of the most famous hands in Paris'.

In order to promote French trade, Colbert encouraged what he called a 'money war against all the states of Europe'.[66] By 1660 the Netherlands, France's main rival, dominated world trade from America to Japan. The Dutch, Colbert's brother Colbert de Croissy complained to the French envoy in The Hague, M. de Pomponne, owned 15,000 (in reality nearer 9,000) of the 20,000 trading vessels in the world – meaning the West – while the French had only 500 or 600.[67] Amsterdam, wrote Colbert's son the Marquis de Seignelay during a European tour in 1671, was 'the city in the world with the most trade'. It provided a third of the ships in the Dutch navy and would be both the financial and intellectual heart of European coalitions against Louis XIV.[68]

Coenraad van Beuningen, son and grandson of burgomasters of Amsterdam, had helped make the French–Dutch treaty of 1662, and returned to France as ambassador in 1664–8. Even according to a fellow Francophobe, the English diplomat Sir William Temple, however, van Beuningen was 'not always so willing to hear as to be heard; and out of the abundance of his imagination is apt to reason a man to death'. His growing 'insolence' made Louis XIV and Colbert turn against him, as Charles II already had.[69] One of many people who were repelled, rather than seduced, by Louis XIV and his court, he would request his own recall. Subsequently he would help to organize alliances against Louis XIV, fearing French plans to conquer the Low Countries.[70]

Louis XIV and Colbert wanted to obtain Dutch trading secrets. Colbert imported M. van Robia from Holland to work in Abbeville as he had 'a particular secret for making hangings in black', and Dutch sugar workers to establish sugar refineries. Mainly for economic reasons, the Franco-Dutch alliance, dating back to the reign of Henri IV, began to fall apart. In 1667 new French tariffs deliberately penalized Dutch exports to France, by far their largest market.[71] In retaliation, imports of French wine were, at van Beuningen's suggestion, forbidden in the Netherlands. Colbert predicted that 'the imprudence and folly of sieur van Beuningen' would cause his country untold harm.[72]

The Compagnie du Nord, based in La Rochelle from 1669, was intended to bypass Dutch ships and merchants and trade directly with Sweden and the Baltic. However, it had to be dissolved in 1675 as French exporters themselves preferred Dutch freighters, and the Dutch were able to fight back by dumping low-priced goods on the French market.[73] Nevertheless French trade continued to grow. A total of 273 ships left La Rochelle in 1670–79, and 411 left in 1680–89; there were similar increases in other ports.[74]

The expansion of French trade under Louis XIV is symbolized by a book published in 1675: *Le Parfait Négociant, ou Instruction générale pour ce qui regarde le commerce des marchandises de France et des pays étrangers* ('The Perfect Merchant, or General Guide Concerning the Commerce in Merchandise of France and Abroad') It is no less characteristic of France under Louis XIV than the memoirs of his court officials. The author was a wealthy cloth merchant, and former protégé of Fouquet, called Jacques Savary. His guide contained details of products, weights and measures, customs rates and currencies throughout the world, which he had assembled while helping to prepare the commercial code of 1673. It also provided advice on how to trade, how to stop nobles accumulating debts and how to write business letters and negotiate credit in foreign countries. It became a global business handbook, frequently revised in French, soon translated into English, Dutch, German, Italian and Russian.[75]

Far from being indifferent to the sea, as is often alleged, Louis XIV and Colbert also focused their energies on the navy. In 1661 it had ill-disciplined crews and unseaworthy ships, under the incompetent leadership of the Duc de Vendôme, who had been made *amiral de France* as a reward for his loyalty during the Fronde.[76] Only after 1650 – later than the Dutch or English, let alone the Portuguese and Spaniards – had French navigators learnt techniques of navigation, and the use of prevailing winds in order to sail longer distances at greater speeds.[77]

In his memoirs Louis XIV would boast of Frenchmen's eagerness to abandon their homes to serve in his army and navy. In reality, as he wrote in a letter to Vendôme's son the Duc de Beaufort, there was what he called 'an almost insurmountable aversion among seamen to engaging themselves in the service of my vessels'. They preferred to serve in the merchant navy. The situation improved when press gangs were replaced by *inscription maritime*, a form of recruitment which guaranteed half-pay when sailors were on land.[78]

Because of the 'connection of commerce with the navy', after Vendôme's death in 1669 Louis appointed Colbert as France's first secretary of state of the marine, and they worked together every Friday afternoon.[79] The navy budget rose from 300,000 livres a year in 1661 to 10 million in 1670. Throughout his reign, Louis and his ministers issued streams of orders about masts, ropes, press gangs, how to train ships' carpenters and how much rice and meat to feed to the galley slaves.[80] In London and Amsterdam French ambassadors and agents learnt of new skills and techniques from officers in the Dutch and English navies.[81]

The navy became a massive consumer of wood and metal. One hundred and ten new warships were built with wood from the forests of Burgundy, or bought from Denmark, Sweden, the Netherlands or Genoa. By 1672 the French navy had reached the total of 120 ships of the line and 74 smaller boats, and would fight well in the wars of that decade.[82] In the 1680s it numbered 258 ships. On average four or five new ships were built every year.[83] Colbert wrote triumphantly to his cousin Colbert de Terron, Intendant at the new naval base of Rochefort, 'our navy is now established.'[84] France finally had a navy worthy of its long coastline, and could communicate with the outside world through ships as well as armies and embassies.

In the interests of trade, Louis XIV and Colbert also encouraged the growth of French ports – despite their record of hostility to the monarchy during the Fronde. In November 1662, after protracted bargaining, Louis XIV paid to Charles II, already short of funds two years after his restoration, 5 million livres for Dunkirk. Dunkirk shows the difference between the two cousins. Charles II, despite the port's proximity to England and his love of sailing in his royal yachts, never visited it. Immediately after its purchase, Louis XIV made the lengthy 200-mile journey from Paris in winter. In the space of two days, on 4 and 5 December, he received the keys of the city, confirmed its privileges, followed the holy sacrament in the rain in celebration of the town's delivery from the heretical English, attended mass, inspected the port's fortifications and dined in public – a pattern of 'sovereignty affirmation' which he would later repeat in other newly acquired cities, and which in Dunkirk produced 'a marvellous effect'. The King of France seemed to the people of Dunkirk 'less proud than any Spanish captain'. He visited the city six times in all, in 1658, 1662, 1670, 1671, 1677 and 1680.[85] He freed it of all customs dues and called it 'a city I regard as my own work'.[86] For Colbert Dunkirk was 'the most important of all the works of the king . . . which will make most noise and will win most fame in foreign countries'.[87]

His visit in 1680 was the only occasion that he inspected a working warship, *L'Entreprenant* with fifty cannon. He wrote to Colbert, 'I saw the vessel in every way, and performing all the manoeuvres, for combat as well as navigation. I have never seen such well-built men as the soldiers and sailors.'[88] Colbert's brother the Intendant Colbert de Maulévrier wrote, 'His Majesty yesterday spent nearly two hours on the vessel of the Chevalier de Lhéry, unable to stop admiring its beauty and magnificence.' The ships were a 'spectacle for all the court'.[89]

With 5,000 mainly Flemish-speaking inhabitants, Dunkirk was the only French port on the North Sea. Louis constructed magnificent sea and land defences – networks of canals, moats and forts, including underwater stacks of wood and stones, to protect the only navigable channel between Dunkirk and the sea, through the wide, white sand dunes on which the Battle of the Dunes had been fought in 1658 (and from which in May 1940 more than 300,000 allied troops would be rescued from encircling German troops).[90] He also added a hospital, an arsenal, a rope factory and a barracks, and made it a free port. The population rose to 10,515 in 1685 and to 14,000 in 1700.[91] The proud inscriptions on Louis XIV's medals – 'Dunquerca recuperata, providentia principis . . . Freti Gallici decus et securitas – Dunquerca munita et ampliata – Dunquerca illaesa' – did not exaggerate.[92]

Dunkirk would become a base for attacks on England and Scotland. The deposed James II came in 1696, for a planned attack which never took place. His son 'James III', the Old Pretender, would sail from Dunkirk in 1708 and 1715, in two attempts to win his crowns.[93] The principal French naval bases were now Dunkirk, Le Havre, Brest, Rochefort, Bayonne, Marseille and Toulon. Thus Louis XIV's government, far from ignoring the provinces, intervened in the furthest corners of the kingdom.

If Dunkirk became France's gateway to the north, Marseille had long been its port for the east. Colbert wrote: 'Marseille is the city necessary to us to wage continuous economic warfare against all trading cities and especially against the English and the Dutch who have long encroached on all Levantine commerce.' In 1669, in order to attract international trade, Marseille, like Dunkirk, was made a free port. Despite opposition

LOVIS·XIV·DANS·SA·MINORITÉ

1. Louis XIV during his minority, *c.* 1643, by Pierre Mignard. From an early age, Louis' poise and gravity struck all who met him.

2. Louis XIV offers his crown and sceptre to the Virgin, by Philippe de Champaigne, 1643. The Holy Family was a source of royal authority as well as an object of daily devotion for Louis and his court throughout his reign.

3. Gaston, Duc d'Orléans, Louis' uncle and a crucial figure during his minority.

4. This token, minted by the city of Paris in 1651, shows one of the slings or *frondes* from which the Fronde took its name. The inscriptions say that Mazarin would be attacked by stones hurled from slings, and suffer the fate of tyrants.

5. The young Louis XIV holding a *lit de justice* in the Grand' Chambre of the Parlement de Paris, 1651. Many Frenchmen hoped that the Parlement would permanently limit the King's authority.

6. Louis XIV's coronation and anointing with holy oil at Reims on 7 June 1654 confirmed the sacred nature of his monarchy. This is one of the many tapestries Louis commissioned from the royal Gobelins tapestry factory on the edge of Paris.

7. Louis XIV as La Guerre in the ballet *Les Noces de Pélée et de Thétis*, 1654. Louis had a passion for dancing, in public until he was thirty, in private until over sixty.

8. Nicolas Fouquet, above his squirrel emblem, 1661. Fouquet was Surintendant des Finances in 1653–61. Arrested by Louis in 1661, he was kept in solitary confinement until his death in 1680.

9. Fouquet's chateau of Vaux outside Paris, *c.* 1661, the magnificence of which astonished his guests, including the King.

10. The arrival of Anne of Austria and Philip IV on the Island of Pheasants on the Bidassoa, dividing France and Spain, 4 June 1660.

11. The meeting between Louis XIV and Philip IV on the Island of Pheasants, 4 June 1660. *Left to right*: Turenne (looking left), Lionne, French Foreign Minister, Monsieur, Anne of Austria, Mazarin, Louis XIV, Philip IV, the chief Spanish minister Don Luis de Haro, María Teresa in Spanish dress, unknown and Velázquez. In the middle is the dividing line between the French and Spanish halves of the island.

12. The Comtesse de Soissons on horseback, *c.* 1668. Olympe Mancini, a niece of Mazarin, married Louis XIV's cousin the Comte de Soissons. One of their sons was Prince Eugene of Savoy.

13. Louise de La Vallière on horseback, *c.* 1668. Louis XIV's mistress since 1661, Louise de La Vallière retired to a convent in 1674 after years of neglect.

14. Hortense Mancini (*left*) and her sister, Marie Mancini, whose fortune she is telling, *c.* 1670. Hortense, the most beautiful of Mazarin's nieces, left her husband the Duc de Mazarin in 1668, and after a stay in Rome (where this picture was probably painted) settled in London, where she died in 1699. Marie, Louis XIV's first love, also left her husband, and died in Pisa in 1715, four months before Louis.

15. Marie Thérèse of Austria, Queen of France. When Louis XIV was on campaign, she often acted as regent.

16. Françoise d'Aubigné, later Madame Maintenon, attributed to Pierre Mignard, c. 1671. The pearl symbolizes purity and rarity.

17. Madame de Montespan, Louis' principal mistress from 1667 to 1678, reclining c. 1676 in front of the gallery of the Château de Clagny, which the King had recently built for her near Versailles.

18. Louis XIV is here sculpted as Hercules crowned by victory, on the Porte Saint-Martin, erected in 1675 by the City of Paris to celebrate his conquest of Franche-Comté.

19. On this ceiling painting from the Galerie des Glaces at Versailles, c. 1680–84, by Charles Le Brun, Louis is shown as Jupiter with thunderbolts, to commemorate his capture of Ghent in January 1678 in six days.

from the local chamber of commerce, all duties were abolished and replaced by one tax, the *cottimo*, on ships entering and leaving the port. Marseille became a global port, trading with Africa, America and China, as well as throughout the Mediterranean.[94]

The ancient French alliance with the Ottoman Empire, dating from the reign of François I, who had allied with Suleyman the Magnificent against Charles V, was the foundation of the city's prosperity. The Chambre de Commerce de Marseille, founded in 1599, paid the salary of the French Ambassador in Constantinople. The city began to attract Muslims, Armenians and Jews from the Ottoman Empire. Armenians brought knowledge of the silk trade and in 1672 founded the first café in France (before the Café Procope in Paris) and a printing press. Workmen produced soap, fabrics, shoes and hats for export, mainly to the Ottoman Empire and North Africa. By 1677 the trade of Marseille surpassed that of its rival Mediterranean free port, Livorno in Tuscany.[95]

Urbanization as well as commerce helped the crown to impose its authority. From 1670 Marseille expanded from 175 acres to 480. New streets were laid out by royal officials on a grid plan around a large central area, now called the Cours Belsunce. The Hôtel de Ville, on the quay, directly facing the ships and galleys in the port, begun in 1656, was finished and decorated in 1673 with a bust of the King in Roman armour by Pierre Puget, a symbol of his role as a protector of trade which can still be admired today. Behind the royal façade were rooms for the Bourse de Commerce.[96]

Colbert's main agent in Marseille was Nicolas Arnoul, also a member of the *petite noblesse*, who served as *intendant général des galères* in 1665–71. He did not like the Marseillais, he wrote to Colbert, calling them a 'beast with a hundred heads', but he thought that Marseille deserved 'to be loved and caressed as the most likely city in the entire kingdom to make his [the King's] greatness appear in everything and that is your sole aim'.[97] The royal galleys moved from Toulon to Marseille in 1662. Other Mediterranean powers, such as Genoa and Malta, also used galleys, but they were instruments of prestige as much as weapons of war. By 1672, Louis XIV had 120 galleys based in Marseille, rowed by galley slaves – often North Africans or Turks who were considered 'extremely vigorous', but also Russians or Greeks. Others were native Americans, Africans, army deserters, smugglers or criminals with the letters 'GAL' branded on their forehead.[98]

Mademoiselle had written, describing the court's visit to Marseille in 1660, that 'this multitude of naked men', in chains and blackened by the sun, inspired horror and pity. Courtiers fainted or vomited at the sight.[99]

Nevertheless galley slaves were allowed to work in the city; some had little shops on the quays. Many had lovers on shore, whom the authorities tried in vain to prevent spending nights on the galleys.[100] The 'continual Noise and rattling of Chains' which accompanied them in the city, made the English traveller Ellis Veryard compare Marseille to 'the Suburbs of Hell'.[101] The galley slaves also worked in a vast arsenal by the quays. It was a city within the city erected in 1669, where workers made not only ships and rope but textiles copying the cloth of Alexandria and Smyrna.[102] By 1690 a total of 18,000 men, many of them slaves, were working there. Given the growing uselessness of galleys in naval warfare compared to sailing ships, the galley slaves probably spent more time working in the arsenal than rowing at sea.[103]

Other ports which Louis XIV and Colbert helped to found or expand in these years, through tax privileges, through the construction of naval dockyards and through labour provided by soldiers and sailors, were Sète, on the coast of Languedoc; Rochefort, on the coast of Poitou, founded in 1666–9; and Lorient on the south coast of Brittany, a naval base and headquarters of the Compagnie des Indes from 1666.[104] Toulon remained a major naval base. All the naval stores and shipyards, forges and rope factory were placed in one great walled arsenal there in 1670–86. The central building was decorated with sculpture by Pierre Puget.[105]

One of the great engineering projects of the reign, the *canal royal de communication des mers* between the Mediterranean and the Atlantic, was part of Colbert's programme of public works to link distant provinces by road and river to Paris.[106] It was a major achievement, compared at the time to those of the Roman Empire, and carried out, despite local opposition, by women as well as men.[107] It was inaugurated in 1681, having been financed partly by the government and partly by the Estates of Languedoc, the southern province through which it runs. They were among those provincial Estates which Colbert condemned, in a letter advocating their suppression, as 'always very expensive for the people and of little help to His Majesty', but which retained considerable independence until their abolition in 1788.[108]

Colbert became the King's most trusted minister, with responsibilities of every kind. He not only directed the works at the Louvre and Versailles, to be discussed in the next chapter, but also supervised the King's library. He sent agents to the monasteries of Provence and the Levant, to buy old manuscripts (not only Greek and Latin, but Hebrew, Syriac, Arabic) for his own and the King's library in Paris.[109] Once in 1667 Louis XIV said at his *coucher* that no kingdom had ever been as well regulated or as rich as his own. To Colbert he wrote in 1673, 'I can promise myself everything from your zeal and industry.'[110]

Since the King's public and private lives were entwined, he also used Colbert, more than his most trusted court officials, to help run his secret love affair. Colbert and Madame Colbert supervised the pregnancies of Louise de La Vallière, fetched doctors, arranged the secret birth and baptism of the two illegitimate children (to avoid shocking Anne of Austria) and removed them at night through a back door of the Palais Royal. Louise de La Vallière was still a *fille d'honneur* of Madame, whose residence the Palais Royal was.

Well-informed Parisians such as Olivier d'Ormesson, however, learnt at once what had happened. Louise looked 'fort pale' when she reappeared in public, he wrote in his diary, on 19 December 1663, the day of the birth, and 'no one doubts any more that she has been delivered of a son.' The Colberts brought up Mlle de Blois and the Comte de Vermandois, as they were later called, with their own children.[111] When she was not bearing the King's children, Louise de La Vallière could be seen riding and shooting. She was such a good horsewoman – considered better than any other at court – that she could jump on to a moving horse and ride it.[112] In 1664 an English visitor, Edward Browne, saw her driving to Paris with the King in a *chaise roulante*, 'habited very prettily in a hat and feathers and a justaucorps'.[113]

At times the King saw Louise de La Vallière every day. Writing in 1664, the Papal Nuncio expressed the belief that he had been faithful to her for three years.[114] However, her position was under constant threat. The court of France was 'the paradise of women', many of whom imagined themselves in love with the King, or were groomed by their family to seduce him. The Duc d'Enghien wrote that all ladies were 'extremely jealous' of Louise de La Vallière.[115] The Queen, Mademoiselle noted, sometimes felt so jealous that she vomited.[116]

Louis XIV's love for Louise de La Vallière, however, probably affected him less than the death of his mother. After his marriage, mother and son had continued to see each other frequently and to share most meals.[117] During the first stages of her cancer in April 1663, Louis XIV visited her eight or ten times a day. He rose earlier than usual, was present in her bedroom at all consultations, treatments and bleedings (the usual seventeenth-century treatment for illnesses) and at night would send messengers to obtain the latest news.[118]

During her final illness in 1666 he often slept fully dressed on a mattress at the foot of his mother's bed. 'He helped her always with unbelievable application, changing her bed, and serving her better and more adroitly than all her women.' (Praise indeed given that one of them, Madame de Motteville, is writing.) To the daughter of another *première femme de chambre*, Madame de Beauvais, the King said of his dying mother, 'look how beautiful she is. I have never seen her looking so beautiful.' Clearly she was one of the loves of his life.

Paris churches filled with people praying for her recovery.[119] She had wanted to die in her private paradise, the Val-de-Grâce, but at the beginning of 1666 the King and the doctors brought her back to the Louvre, partly to enjoy the carnival season and the wedding on 9 January of a confidante of the King and Louise, Mlle d'Artigny, which was celebrated by a ball and a ballet with six entries.[120] In her last months gangrene, ulcers and a pierced abcess prompted the Queen Mother to tell Madame de Motteville that 'there is no part of my body in which I do not feel very great pain.' The Queen Mother who had loved perfumes had to endure the smell of her own abcess. The King would drop in on his way to the council. When she grew worse, he abandoned his plans to hold military reviews outside Paris in order to stay with her, day and night.

After her confession and communion, her bedroom overflowed with people crying, or reading from works of piety, including the Princesse Palatine. Marshals and the trusted Protestant financier Barthélemé d'Herwarth also entered her bedroom; she asked the latter to convert. She begged her sons and daughters-in-law to love each other 'for love of me'. When told that she was leaving an earthly for a heavenly crown, she said that she had always considered her earthly crown 'as mud'.

Finally, around 6 p.m. on 19 January 1666, the men of her family and court went to the parish church of Saint-Germain l'Auxerrois to escort the sacrament to the dying Queen Mother. Madame de Motteville felt the Queen Mother's sons and daughters-in-law were not weeping enough. As she was dying, the Queen Mother looked at Louis XIV and said 'with the majesty of a Queen and the authority of a mother', 'Do what I told you: I tell you again, with the holy sacrament on my lips.' She was perhaps referring to the need to pardon Fouquet, or the Duc and Duchesse de Navailles. Her weeping son said he would.[121]

Monsieur, who was also constantly with their mother, said that the only matter in which he would disobey the King would be an order to leave her deathbed. Louis XIV often wept 'furiously' and fainted. She died at 7 a.m. on 20 January 1666, universally regretted. After her death, unable to endure the sight of 'the place where it had happened to me', Louis at once left Paris for Versailles.[122] Later he opened his heart to an intimate, the brother of Louise de La Vallière: 'what I have suffered in losing the Queen, madame my mother, surpasses anything you can imagine.'[123]

8

The Pursuit of Immortality:
The Louvre and Versailles

The trauma of his mother's illness and death in Paris prompted Louis to spend more time in Saint-Germain and Versailles. Nevertheless for the next five years, he continued to reside for part of the year in Paris. The city was still called, in official documents, 'the capital of the kingdom and the normal place of residence' of the King, as well as 'the most beautiful, the richest and the largest city of France'.[1]

With the help of Colbert and M. de La Reynie (appointed to the new position of *lieutenant de police de Paris* in 1667, as part of the King's programme of law reform), the King made Paris one of Europe's most modern cities as well, with the best shops and post service. Public carriages able to take up to eight passengers began on certain routes in 1662. The city walls were demolished after 1669 and turned into tree-lined boulevards.[2] An English visitor in 1672 called Francis Tallents was impressed by the 'wondrous clean and handsome' streets, the 'great and excellent order' and the lack of beggars.[3]

Women also enjoyed greater freedom than in other cities. Provided they were well dressed, they could go alone to the Tuileries, the formal garden west of the Louvre which Louis XIV adorned with statues, benches and shaded alleys. There they often invited gentlemen to 'a promenade, conversation or light refreshment'.[4] If its trees could talk, it was said, they would have many adventures to recount.[5]

In 1667 Louis XIV also introduced public lighting to Paris – the first city in Europe to have it, before Amsterdam and London. Lamps, hanging 15 feet above the street, from ropes attached to buildings on each side, made the city safer, encouraging Parisians to go out at night. There were 5,400 such lights by 1702.[6]

Louis XIV's and Colbert's most original achievement was the expansion of the Louvre into the 'palace of the arts' which it remains to this day. On 31 October 1660 an *ordonnance* referred to his plan to join the Louvre and the Tuileries palace to the west, 'according to the old and magnificent design which has been made by the kings his predecessors'.[7] This 'magnificent design', begun by François I in 1547 and continued by Catherine de Médicis, Henri IV and Louis XIII, also advanced under Louis XIV. In 1659 to 1662 Louis Le Vau and François d'Orbay added a northern wing to the Tuileries palace, containing the largest opera house in Europe, and a pavilion to balance the Pavillon de Flore at the end of the Grande Galerie. Decorated with a fresco of Louis XIV as Jupiter 'chaining Mars and protecting Hymen', the opera house opened with a performance of *Ercole amante* by Cavalli on 6 February 1662.[8]

Louis XIV confirmed his love of the Louvre by constructing the Galerie d'Apollon in 1662 to 1677, after a fire. It is on the first floor, above his mother's apartment and outside his own. A frescoed ceiling, partly by Charles Le Brun, celebrates the signs of the zodiac, the labours of Hercules, Apollo and the triumphs of Cybele and Neptune. It is enlivened by thirty-six stucco sculptures of gods, heroes and cupids, and decorated with the crowned arms of France and Navarre, images of the sun and Ls. This symbol of the King's Parisian youth today contains objects from the personal collection which he later assembled in Versailles: jewelled and gold-lined cups and jugs of jade, onyx and sardonyx, and Roman cameos, as well as a few of his grandest diamonds. The panache of the Galerie d'Apollon, like the elegance of Vaux, shows why, under Louis XIV, Paris painters and architects felt they were no longer inferior to Italians.[9]

From the Louvre Louis XIV launched a campaign to assert French precedence over the other powers of Europe. Taking precedence – the act of coming before others in a street or a palace – was a public demonstration of superiority. As Denzil Holles, Charles II's Ambassador to Louis XIV, wrote in 1664: 'ceremony is substance and he who carries it in that will carry it in the essentials.' Carriages, a relative novelty introduced in processions in the sixteenth century, often led to confrontations. The most violent occurred in London.[10]

On 30 September 1661, at the procession for the ceremonial entry into London of the Swedish Ambassador, the carriage of the Spanish Ambassador, the Baron de Watteville (who had been Spanish agent in Bordeaux during the Fronde), preceded the carriage of the French Ambassador, the Comte d'Estrades (royalist Mayor of Bordeaux since the Fronde). In the ensuing 'carriage war' between the French and Spanish ambassadors' retinues, the London crowd, paid and organized in advance, sided with Watteville: he had planned the French humiliation, even lining his horses' harnesses with iron so they could not be cut.

Six Frenchmen were killed and thirty-three wounded, including the Ambassador's son. Louis XIV withdrew his Ambassador to Philip IV and demanded an apology. On 23 March 1662 in the Louvre, in the presence of all foreign ambassadors serving in Paris as well as senior French officials, he recived a formal guarantee from the Count of Fuensaldagna, the 'Ambassador Extraordinary' sent by Philip IV for this purpose, that henceforth no Spanish ambassador in any court in Europe would compete for precedence with any French ambassador at any function. The official account of the ceremony was signed by four secretaries of state. De Watteville was withdrawn from London.[11]

On 5 and 6 June 1662 a splendid carousel in the square in front of the Tuileries palace, which is still today called the Place du Carrousel, celebrated both the birth of the Dauphin the previous year and the French court's cult of horsemanship: Louis XIII had also held a *ballet des chevaux*, in what is now the Place des Vosges, in April 1612. Horsemanship, shown in complicated steps such as courette, pirouette, pesade, levade, was much admired as a sign of masculinity, skill and domination, and often proved indispensable to survival on the battlefield. That is why Louis XIV commissioned so many equestrian portraits and sculptures of himself.[12]

In June 1662 some 800 knights on magnificently caparisoned horses in five rival teams, dressed in costumes designed by the King's *dessinateur du cabinet* Henri Gissey, as Romans, Persians, Turks, Indians and Americans, were led to the courtyard in front of the Tuileries palace by the King, Monsieur, the Prince de Condé, the Duc d'Enghien and the Duc de Guise. They tilted against each other, rode with their lances at a ring (a favourite court entertainment, at which the King was especially skilled), threw javelins at a Gorgon's head and exercised their horses in time with music, in front of the two queens, watching with their ladies from the central pavilion of the Tuileries. Thousands more watched from windows, balconies, rooftops and specially constructed wooden stands. The King, dressed as a Roman emperor, for the first time publicly chose the sun as his symbol. Again showing Louis XIV's concern for Paris, like his state entry in 1660 and unlike other court carousels in Dresden, Munich and Vienna, the knights' routes through the streets of Paris to the carousel were announced in advance, in order to give the public as many opportunities as possible to watch.[13]

The public could also wander in and out of the courtyards of the Louvre and its apartments, even in the evening after dinner. As Anne of Austria was dying, for example, Paris workmen came to her guard room in the Louvre to learn the news.[14] A visiting Italian called Sébastien Locatelli (whose description is confirmed by other contemporaries) wrote in 1665: 'the King wants all his subjects to enter freely so that he can be informed if necessary of very important events like rebellions, treasons and threats of revolt.' Inside the Louvre, Locatelli would not at first have recognized the King, as Condé and some other nobles were better dressed.

Locatelli also saw the Dauphin, aged four, whom he described as the handsomest child of his age and whom he had watched drilling soldiers in the courtyard of the Louvre with a miniature baton of command in his hand. The Queen brought him a cup of milk, and forced 'mon mignon' as she called him to pardon a soldier accused of insulting him.[15] He admired the Queen's blonde hair and white skin, but noted that she had black teeth from eating fruit 'to excess' and was 'melancholic, all for God'. When she went to Notre-Dame to give thanks for recovery from an illness, 'the cries of joy of the people, who had not seen her for three months, showed me how much everyone adores her.'[16]

Saint-Maurice, Ambassador of the King's first cousin the Duke of Savoy, called the sight of the court 'the most beautiful thing in the world'. At the King's *lever* 'there were three rooms full of people of quality and an unbelievable crowd which made it virtually impossible to enter the bedroom of His Majesty. And more than eight hundred carriages in front of the Louvre.'[17]

On 20 August 1662 another French Ambassador's suite fought another battle – this time in Rome, with the Pope's Corsican guards, who had picked a fight with the Ambassador's servants. The French embassy was besieged, the Ambassador and his wife were fired at; several people were killed, including a French page. At Fontainebleau on 29 July 1664, Louis XIV received another formal apology, from Cardinal Chigi the Legate sent by the Pope, with a promise to erect, on the site, a 'pyramid of shame' with an apologetic inscription. The scene is commemorated in a spectacular Gobelins tapestry now in one of the 'Louis XIV' rooms in the Louvre. In the royal bedroom, watched by courtiers, the proud young King stares ahead; with bowed head, the Cardinal reads out the Pope's apology.[18]

As a final sacrifice, the Pope reluctantly agreed to allow his own architect, sculptor and designer, Gian Lorenzo Bernini, the most famous in Europe, to leave Rome to work for Louis XIV (as Leonardo da Vinci and Cellini had left Italy to work for François I).[19] Bernini's visit shows that, as Colbert told him, the King would spare nothing to make the arts flourish in France; but in this domain, as in many others, his power was limited by his ministers and his court.[20]

On his way to Paris, Bernini was treated like royalty. He received special deliveries of ice because of the heat, and for part of the way rode in the carriages of the Duc d'Orléans. He arrived on 2 June 1665.[21] The journal of a *maître d'hôtel du roi*, Paul Fréart de Chantelou, who knew Italian and was chosen to guide Bernini round Paris, describes the resulting clash of personalities, cities and courts.

For Bernini nothing in Paris matched Rome. He complained – to Louis himself – that the style of French painters and architects was 'small and sad'; the Vatican surpassed the Louvre, but he would redress the balance.[22] Paris buildings, he declared, looking down from a tower of Notre-Dame, resembled the teeth in a dirty comb.[23] He also told Louis XIV that, for someone who had not seen the buildings of Italy, he had remarkably good taste.[24]

For their part French architects and courtiers laughed at the 'genius' from Rome. Bernini was right to say there was a conspiracy against him.[25] For the writer Charles Perrault – and his brother the architect Claude Perrault – Bernini was a bad architect, knowledgeable only about theatre decoration and machinery. Even worse from the point of view of a French courtier, Bernini's plans for the Louvre included 'admirable galleries' and 'everything which gives majesty to a great palace' but – the heart of the matter for French courtiers – 'the king will be obliged to sleep in such a small bedroom that half the lords and officers who have the right to enter it will not fit.' Nor were there plans for court officials' apartments. Such details, according to Perrault, were beneath Bernini. He showed his plans, uttering the phrase 'io sono entrato in pensiero profondo' ('I have entered into deep thought') so emphatically that it seemed 'as if he had descended into the depths of hell'. He did not understand the court.[26]

Colbert also complained that in Bernini's plans there was not enough room in front of the palace for the King's guards to manoeuvre.[27] There must be apartments for four secretaries of state, a room for the council and a large apartment for the King.[28] His arguments confirm that, for contemporaries, the court was a joint venture, which existed to please courtiers as much as the King: 'there was a large number of persons of quality who would be very annoyed to be anywhere other than in the very place where the king himself was to be found, that such was the character of the French and the custom of France.' A magnificent King's bedroom was essential.[29] Colbert also reminded Bernini that, to avoid smells, 'at each floor the discharge of excrement needs to be well managed. This issue must be considered one of the most important of all, for the health of the royal family depends on it.'[30]

Some details are recorded in diplomats' letters, but not in Chantelou's diary, as if they were too familiar. When Bernini began to work on plans for the Louvre, the King was so curious that he peered round a door to have a look. Bernini claimed to recognize the 'stranger' (who had already sent Bernini his portrait) solely by the grandeur and majesty of his face:

'that is the king!' He also told the King – music to royal ears – that he needed a palace more magnificent than Saint-Germain. The King wanted to preserve 'the work of my predecessors', but agreed that 'as far as money is concerned, there need be no restriction.'[31]

During one sitting for his bust, Louis let Bernini run his hands through his hair to make it look better. He was extremely cordial, even though he found it difficult not to laugh when Bernini 'stalked' stealthily around him, to catch every detail of his head and hair. He said that Bernini's sketch of him was the best he had seen.[32]

Bernini noted that on either side of his face Louis XIV's cheeks, nose and mouth were slightly different. One side of his nose was larger than the other and he had a small mark by one eye: 'the beauty of the king was a mixed beauty.' His eyes were 'a little dead, he hardly opened them . . . his mouth often changed'.[33] A year earlier Locatelli had noted further details: dark-blue eyes, an aquiline nose, a high forehead, a fine mouth, strong shoulders and olive-coloured skin. He embodied 'the secret force of royal majesty'.[34]

Bernini's bust (see Plate 25), was too large to go into the apartment of Anne of Austria, for which it was intended. Courtiers admired it, when it was first displayed in public, for showing the King with the stern expression he had assumed as he strode into the Parlement in 1655. Bernini said that it had been executed with such love that it was his least bad work, and that the King's mind was even more elevated than his rank. He then, in what was perhaps a calculated display of sensibility, burst into tears and left the room.[35]

As an unprecedented sign of favour, Louis XIV himself showed Bernini some of the crown jewels, and the Queen's.[36] However, the King, as well as his courtiers, felt that Bernini was prejudiced against everything French. Bernini's designs for the façades of the Louvre would not ultimately be adopted. On 17 October 1665, in the presence of French courtiers and architects, as well as Bernini himself, the King laid the foundation stone of the new east wing of the Louvre. Trumpets sounded. The King struck medals. Workmen were given money to drink his health. Three days later Bernini left for Rome: on both sides, no doubt, there was a sense of relief. At Bernini's farewell audience, the King had inclined his head and expressed his esteem. He and his brother rightly feared, however, that, although Bernini said he was returning only to see his wife, in reality he had departed discontented.[37] On 15 July 1667 Colbert had the pleasure of writing to Bernini to report that the outbreak of war prevented the King from carrying out his 'beautiful design' for the Louvre: 'His Majesty reserves the possibility of carrying out your design at a later date.'[38]

The main results of Bernini's visit are a Roman baroque baldacchino for the high altar at the Val-de-Grâce; the King's bust; and an equestrian statue of Louis XIV, sent by Bernini from Rome twenty years later in 1685. By then, however, the French court had lost any taste it had had for Bernini and Roman baroque. The equestrian statue was reworked in Paris by the fashionable French sculptor Girardon, who transformed the King from 'Hercules Gallicus' into a representation of the Roman hero Marcus Curtius, and banished it to the far end of the lake on the left of the park of Versailles. A copy by I. M. Pei now decorates the main entrance to the Louvre.[39]

In July 1665 Christopher Wren had arrived in Paris with Henrietta Maria and her household, leaving London to escape the Great Plague. Staying until February 1666, he studied every building he could. He wrote:

> the Louvre for a while was my daily Object; where no less than a thousand Hands are constantly employed in the Works; some laying in mighty Foundations, some in raising the Stories, Columns, Entablements etc with vast Stones, by great and useful Engines; others in Carving, Inlaying of Marbles, Plastering, Painting, Gilding etc Which altogether make a School of architecture, the best probably at this day in Europe.

Colbert came to inspect the work every Wednesday.[40] Slabs of the yellow-white stone of the Île de France, cut in quarries south-west of Paris, were so large that they needed a special machine to raise them to their positions at the top of the east façade.[41]

Instead of Bernini's baroque plans, for the east wing of the Louvre Louis XIV chose a tall straight façade, lavishly decorated at his personal suggestion with a colonnade of coupled Corinthian columns, designed by Claude Perrault and François d'Orbay, and covered in Ls, crowns and sunbursts. Finished in 1677, one of the most famous palace façades in Europe, it is more imposing, with more rhythm, than Louis Le Vau's monotonous north wing, or Perrault's sober southern façade added in 1667.

Its triumphant monumentality defies the restless city of Paris – even more so under Louis XIV, when Paris streets and houses were smaller.[42] Many contemporaries, including Louis XIV himself, considered it finer than the classical temples about which they read in Latin literature. They were convinced that, like Le Brun's Galerie d'Apollon, it showed that Frenchmen could now surpass both modern Italians and the masters of antiquity.[43]

The Louvre's fortress-like lower walls and moat also reflected political and military realities. With unusual frankness Colbert wrote that the palace needed to be built not only for magnificence and convenience, but also for 'security'. In 'the largest and most populated city of the world

subject to all kinds of revolutions' (that is, revolutions of fortune, including
political upheavals), its character should 'contain people in their due obedience . . . let the whole structure stamp respect in the spirit of peoples
and leave them an impression of his force'.[44] It became an inspiration for
other massive city palaces, also built partly for defence in 1700–1740, in
Berlin, Stockholm and Madrid.[45]

Reflecting Louis XIV's and Colbert's ambitions, the Louvre was to be
a global as well as a French palace. Perrault wanted it to contain reception
rooms, 'in Italian, German, Turkish, Persian styles, in the manner of the
Mogul, of the King of Siam, of China etc, not only because of the beauty
that such a curious and strange diversity would create, but in order that
when ambassadors from all those countries came here, they will see that
France is like a summary of the world'. Unfortunately these rooms were
never created. In all between 1664 and 1679, as much as 10.6 million livres
was spent on the Louvre and the Tuileries.[46]

Although his plans for the Louvre were not adopted, Bernini helped the
French government establish the Academy of France at the Villa Medici
in Rome above the Spanish Steps – as part of Louis XIV's search for
immortality. Although convinced that French architects could surpass
Italians, Louis XIV and Colbert realized that training in Rome would
also help French architects, painters and sculptors to establish his fame
and transmit it to posterity and would 'encourage young Frenchmen to
form their style and taste on the original and models of the greatest masters
of antiquity and of modern times'. Like the Louvre and the Gobelins, the
Academy of France in Rome has lasted to this day.[47]

The Tuileries palace, running north from the end of the long gallery
of the Louvre, served as Louis XIV's Paris residence from 1667 to 1671
when the Louvre was being rebuilt. In the decade after 1660, it had been
enlarged, refaced with columns and redecorated inside. The wings and
the two pavilions at each end of the palace were made symmetrical. A
Grand Appartement for the King was installed by Louis Le Vau along the
east side of the first floor, facing the Louvre, with a gallery 500 feet long
in which ambassadors could be received. Apartments for the Queen, the
Dauphin and Colbert were also created.

As in the Galerie d'Apollon, the decoration was mythological. The
King's apartment was decorated by Charles Le Brun and Jean Nocret with
scenes from the life of Hercules, Apollo crowned by victory, and Mercury
and Neptune offering Louis XIV the empires of land and sea; the Dauphin's with pictures by Jean-Baptiste de Champaigne of the education of
Achilles.[48]

The Tuileries garden to the west of the palace still has some of the statues installed for Louis XIV by Le Nôtre in 1665 to 1667. Before 1671 Parisians were delighted to see the King there:

> Chacun courut aux TUILERIES,
> où notre ROI victorieux
> Sera mieux logé que les dieux![49]

> ('Everyone rushed to the Tuileries,
> where our victorious king
> will be better housed than the gods!')

In 1672 the Académie Française, of which Colbert was protector, began to meet in the former royal council chamber in the Pavillon du Roi in the Louvre, where it also housed its library, started with spare copies of books from other royal libraries.[50] As Colbert wrote, expressing the French court's passion for the arts, 'royal majesty and belles lettres should have only one and the same palace.'[51]

From 1685 the Académie des Inscriptions, and from 1692 the Académies Royales de Peinture et de Sculpture and d'Architecture, founded to raise artists' status and free them from the authority of the guilds, moved their sessions to the Queen's apartment in the Louvre. Thus they met in a royal palace, among pictures and sculptures from the royal collection. From 1699 the Académie de Peinture also held an annual display of recent paintings in the Salon Carré, where the King had once given court balls – hence the expression *salon* to mean a painting exhibition. The Académie des Sciences and other collections, archives and institutions were also housed in the Louvre. On the ground floor, the Salle des Caryatides, built under Henri II in 1551–7, displayed part of the magnificent royal collection of classical sculptures, augmented in 1665 by bequests from Mazarin.[52]

Artists such as Jean Nocret the painter, the engraver Jean Berain, Carlo Vigarani the theatre designer from Modena, François Girardon the sculptor and the cabinet maker André-Charles Boulle lived above and below the gallery of the Louvre, which itself was used to display models of the forts of France. Boulle made his luxurious clocks, desks and cupboards, using a new technique inlaying horn, ivory and tin on wood, in a workshop in the former apartment of Anne of Austria.[53]

Thus long before the Louvre opened in 1793 as a museum, it was a palace of the arts. No other royal palace housed artists, their workshops and academies in apartments designed and decorated for the King and Queen. (The Royal Society, founded in London by Charles II in 1660, met in Arundel House, not in a royal palace.) Moreover Louis XIV's collections of sculpture and paintings in the Louvre, his furniture in the Garde-meuble, the royal library and the Gobelins factory could be visited by members of the public, if they were well dressed.[54] Thus the court of France inspired and financed creativity, gave artists space in which to work and displayed the results to the public.[55]

Even a writer of fairy tales like Charles Perrault, author of the classic versions of *Little Red Riding Hood*, *Cinderella* and *The Sleeping Beauty* ('les Contes de Perrault'), worked for the court. Perrault, a protégé of Colbert, was the first secretary of an academy founded in 1663 to manage Louis XIV's glory and reputation – his public image – called the Académie des Inscriptions. The academy's job included writing inscriptions for his medals and deciding how he was to be represented in paintings and sculptures. Perrault wrote in his memoirs:

> all these great exploits [of the King] having to be mixed with diversions worthy of the prince, with fêtes, masquerades, carousels and other similar entertainments, and all these matters needing to be described and engraved with intelligence, in order to be understood in foreign countries, where the way in which they are treated brings hardly less honour than the events themselves, he [Colbert] wanted to assemble a number of writers and have them beside him to be consulted on these matters and form a sort of small council for everything concerning belles lettres.

They began to meet twice a week in Colbert's house to 'review and correct works in praise of the king'.

Louis visited the academy, soon after its foundation, making a brief speech which defined its role: 'you can judge, messieurs, the esteem I have for you, because I entrust to you what is most precious to me in the world, which is my *gloire*.* I am sure that you will achieve wonders; for my part I will endeavour to furnish you with material which deserves to be made into works of art by people as skilled as you are.'[56]

Pursuing his campaign for *gloire*, Louis XIV gave pensions to foreign as well as French artists and scientists, 'to show the respect he has for your merit and as an assurance of the support which you can expect from his royal magnanimity'. They included, among many others, the astronomer Johannes Hevelius in Danzig; the poet Girolamo Graziani in Modena; the Dutch astronomer Christiaan Huygens, who perfected watchmaking while living in Paris from 1666 to 1680. The King persuaded Huygens to remain even when France and the United Provinces were at war.[57]

The Louvre was not the only building which transformed the

---

* The word 'gloire' can mean reputation as well as glory.

appearance of Paris under Louis XIV. In 1657 Mazarin and the Company of the Holy Sacrament had started the construction of the Hôpital de la Salpêtrière for poor invalids, women and children, in the south-east of the city. A massive complex of grandiose simplicity, 75 acres in size, designed by Louis Le Vau, it is sixty windows wide. Parts are still used as a hospital today (in the nineteenth century it was called 'the Versailles of pain'). It is built around three courtyards. In the middle is the chapel of Saint-Louis, finished in 1678, with three naves meeting in an austere, domed central space above the altar.[58]

From 1667 to 1681 an astronomical observatory was built on a hill to the south of Paris, now the southern point of the Luxembourg garden, in a similar austere, functional style. The Hôtel Royal des Invalides is the most impressive of all Louis XIV's buildings in Paris, and one of the largest in Europe. With fifteen courtyards laid out on a grid plan like the Escorial (prints of which helped inspire it), it was a separate, military city on what was then the south-west edge of Paris, as the Salpêtrière was a medical city on the south-east.[59]

The main façade, as monumental as the east façade of the Louvre, is decorated with Roman trophies, armour and helmets. Above the entrance is a statue, by Coustou, of Louis XIV on horseback, in Roman armour, between figures of Prudence and Justice, above the inscription 'Ludovico magno militibus regali munificentia in perpetuum providens 1675' ('Louis the Great, caring for his soldiers with royal generosity in perpetuity, founded this building in 1675').

The complex housed old or invalided officers and soldiers, wearing a blue uniform lined with scarlet. The intention was not only to provide them with somewhere to live, but also to take them off the streets, where they might cause trouble, and give them the intense religious life they had lacked in the army. Every detail of their food, accommodation, health care and religious services was minutely regulated.[60] A *cité idéale* two and a half centuries before Le Corbusier, it originally contained a barracks, monastery, hospice, pharmacy, vegetable garden, bakery and factory: soldiers in good health were meant to make uniforms or bookbindings. By the end of the reign there were 4,000 'invalids'. The four giant dining rooms are still lined with pictures showing 'Conquêtes du Roi Louis le Grand aux années 1676 – 1677 – 1678'. The Invalides has survived revolutions and wars relatively unscathed. Like the Salpêtrière, part of it still contains a hospital: 'Centre médico-chirurgical pour anciens combattants et grands invalides'. In addition it now houses the headquarters of the military division of Paris; the residence of the chief of staff of the French army; and, since the departure of the old soldiers in 1896, a military museum.

Two chapels at the heart of the building celebrate the alliance of God, the monarchy and the French army. The southern chapel, facing what was then the countryside, with repeated pairs of entwined SLs and Ls carved on the walls and the marble floor, and frescoes of Clovis, Charlemagne, St Louis and Louis XIV, was for the King. The more austere northern chapel, on the Paris side, was for the soldiers. In the middle a baroque high altar with a gilded baldacchino can be seen from both chapels, but is shielded by a glass screen from the soldiers' chapel. The dome of the chapel floats above the Paris skyline like the dome of St Peter's above Rome. Its gilded spire and ornaments led General de Gaulle to write in his memoirs, describing the liberation of Paris in 1944, that it still gleamed with the splendour of the Sun King.[61]

For John Northledge, an Englishman visiting Paris in Louis XIV's reign, the Invalides was 'their fairest and finest foundation of all. It far outdoes the Chelsea college' (the Royal Hospital, Charles II's and Wren's brick imitation, built a decade later, which still houses old soldiers today).[62] The Marquis de Sourches, Grand Prévôt de France, the official in charge of law and order at court whose diary is one of the key sources of the reign, wrote: 'nothing was more magnificent than this establishment, nothing greater, nothing more charitable, nothing more useful, nothing more worthy of the king, nor more glorious for him.' Louis XIV himself considered it the principal monument of his reign. Unlike Versailles, it is mentioned in his will. He often visited it. On 14 July 1702, he and his family watched the invalids eating their supper. His visit on 28 August 1706 for the inauguration of the chapel was the last time he saw Paris.

That day the King heard a low mass and Te Deum and congratulated not only the architect, Jules Hardouin-Mansart (Surintendant et Ordonnateur Général des Bâtiments, Arts et Manufactures de Sa Majesté and Premier Architecte du Roi, and great-nephew of François Mansart), but also his wife. Showing his personal respect for women, in an act to which no other monarch of the time would have stooped, he approached Madame Mansart in the crowd and said, 'Madame, seeing you there, I cannot stop myself from making you my compliment on the share you ought to take in the glory that your husband receives today.'[63]

Despite the institutional grandeur of the Louvre, the Invalides and the Salpêtrière, the King devoted more time and passion to a more personal building, with which he will always be associated: Versailles. In 1631–4 Louis XIII had transformed the original hunting lodge into a small square brick and stone chateau thirteen windows wide. He had planned to go there from Saint-Germain in 1643, if he recovered.

At Versailles Louis XIV was not merely following fashion or building what he thought a king of France should build. Unlike other monarchs, he decided every aspect of the plan and decoration, and often visited the building site. It was his personal creation, not a refashioning of a traditional royal palace, like the baroque state apartments which Charles II was creating inside Windsor Castle in the same years.[64] Versailles touched a nerve in the King. Perrault claims that, whenever his architects dared suggest changes to his father's original chateau, the King said 'in a loud voice and which appeared inflected with anger: do what you please, but if you destroy it, I will have it rebuilt as it is and without changing a thing in it'.[65]

Louis XIV's personal love of the countryside, and his association of Paris with his mother's death, contributed more to his move to Versailles than any political will to 'assert royal power' or 'tame the nobility'. He had been equally determined to assert royal power in 1652–71, when living partly in Paris, as thereafter, when avoiding it.[66]

From 1661 he began to enlarge the gardens at Versailles. Soon he added two separate wings in front of the chateau to house his ministers. Then he began to plan 'the envelope', enclosing his father's brick chateau in stone-faced extensions. Louis Le Vau was the main architect. André Le Nôtre supervised the gardens. Charles Le Brun, who, despite having worked for Fouquet at Vaux, had accumulated the offices of *premier peintre du roi*, director of the Gobelins factory, and chancellor and director of the Académie Royale de Peinture et de Sculpture, was in charge of the decoration. By 1665 the three main avenues radiating from the palace to Sceaux, Paris and Saint-Cloud had been laid out.[67]

Versailles was not the first gigantic royal palace, either in France or Europe. Louis XIV visited François I's vast hunting palace of Chambord nine times, and every autumn went to the even larger palace of Fontainebleau, south-east of Paris, to hunt.[68] In 1650 and 1660 he had visited Richelieu, the rectangular model town 30 miles south of the Loire, at the gates of the huge country house built in 1630–40 by the Cardinal (of which, since the revolution, only two gatehouses and part of the stables remain). Inside were paintings glorifying Louis XIII as a new Alexander, triumphant over heretics and the House of Austria.[69]

Spain provided two examples of prodigy palaces: the Escorial of Louis XIV's great-grandfather Philip II, built in 1563–86, was a combination of monastery, shrine (with 7,000 saints' relics), library (40,000 books), royal residence and necropolis, set in the plain outside Madrid, from which he had ruled his global empire (although government offices and almost all officials were in Madrid). With 4,000 rooms, it was the largest royal residence in Europe.[70] Second was the Buen Retiro, built nearer Madrid for Louis' uncle Philip IV in 1632 to 1633. Its 'hall of realms' was decorated with the arms of the kingdoms of the Spanish monarchy, and with pictures of Spanish victories throughout the world.[71]

In 1659, some 6 miles outside Turin, Louis XIV's first cousin Charles Emmanuel, Duke of Savoy had begun a massive 'palazzo di Piacere e di Caccia' called Venaria Reale, decorated with pictures and sculptures of hunts, and surrounded by a small residential town. His Ambassador Saint-Maurice claimed that both the palace and the parties the Duke gave there inspired Louis XIV.[72] Massive palaces with surrounding court cities accorded with both the spirit of the age and the traditions of the French monarchy. Only the scale of Versailles, and Louis XIV's use of it as a seat of government and residence of officials and officers as well as courtiers, would be new.

As early as 1665, however, when work was only just beginning, Versailles provoked a counter-blast from Colbert to the King. It is the state reprimanding the court, the treasury the spending departments, the capital the country and a teacher a pupil twenty years younger than himself. It confirms that Versailles, like the Louvre and the Invalides, reflected Louis XIV's personal desire for immortality, and for a new country residence, as well as his political project to create buildings celebrating France and the monarchy.

> Your Majesty has returned from Versailles. I beg him to allow me to say to him on this subject two words of reflection, on which I often dwell, and concerning which he will please forgive me for my zeal. This house is more to do with the pleasure and diversion of Your Majesty than his glory . . . However, if Your Majesty is good enough to search, in Versailles, for more than five hundred thousand écus which have been spent there in the last two years, he will certainly have difficulty in finding them. If he desires to reflect that people can always see in the accounts of the Treasurers of his Buildings that, while he has spent such great sums on this house, he has neglected the Louvre, which is assuredly the most superb palace in the world, and the most worthy of the grandeur of Your Majesty . . . Your Majesty knows that, in the absence of great deeds of war, nothing reveals more the grandeur and spirit of princes than buildings; and all posterity measures it on the scale of these superb houses which they have erected during their lives. Ah, what a pity that the greatest and most virtuous prince, with the real virtue which makes the greatest princes, should be measured on the scale of Versailles! And yet there is reason to fear this misfortune![73]

He was afraid that Le Nôtre and Le Vau 'will drag Your Majesty from scheme to scheme to render their works immortal if he is not on guard against them'. Versailles should receive a fixed annual sum. Then, if peace lasted, the King should concentrate on the Louvre and on building 'public monuments which will carry the glory and grandeur of Your Majesty', further than those of ancient Rome did their builders'.[74]

In a private memorandum, not for the King's eyes, Colbert called Versailles an architectural monster, like a small man with arms which are too long. Colbert hoped that this 'pitiful' building would fall down. In the end, however, it would be Versailles that killed him, not the other way around.[75]

In its early days some courtiers also disliked Versailles, claiming that the King took no trouble on their behalf and there was nowhere to stay. There was 'a great solitude' during the carnival parties in 1667; only three or four carriages came from Paris.[76] Long before Saint-Simon's denunciations of Versailles as 'the saddest and most unrewarding place in the world', courtiers damned it as 'a favourite without merit'. They preferred Paris 'avec grande passion', at least in winter, since their families, friends and occupations were there.[77]

From the start Versailles could also arouse popular revulsion. Workers on the site were paid only 30 livres a year, or between 15 and 50 sols a day (in comparison the Premier Architecte Le Vau received 6,000 livres a year) and many left in disgust, saying that their wages were not enough for their families to live on.[78] Many considered that the Surintendance des Bâtiments under Colbert and Mansart kept wages too low, thereby encouraging craftsmanship of bad quality. D'Ormesson and Saint-Maurice both report in July 1668 the insults levelled at the King by a woman whose son had died working on the construction of machines bringing water from the hill behind Versailles. It was a moment of truth. 'She shouted insults at the king calling him whore-monger, *roi machiniste*, tyrant and a thousand other stupidities and extravagances which made the king in his surprise ask if she was speaking to him.' Many condemned the severity of her punishment: whipping and incarceration in a lunatic asylum. Everyone heard of the number of deaths on site. In 1678 Madame de Sévigné claimed that cartloads of dead workers were being removed every night, as from a hospital.[79] But the King could show concern for the fate of the workers. He added at the end of one note to Colbert about Versailles: 'I forgot to tell you yesterday that something must be given to poor Brottin who works on the pumps . . . he is to be pitied.'[80]

Nevertheless with his mother, one or two women and his army, Versailles was one of the loves of Louis XIV's life. It stayed in his mind when he was away on campaign. In 1672 when Colbert asked him how long his reports on Versailles should be, he replied with a phrase which could be a motto for his reign: 'detail in everything'.[81]

After 1668 an 'envelope' of stone, containing larger apartments for the King and Queen, was built around the original chateau, thereby trebling its size. The white, pink, green, grey and purple marbles which line the walls and floors of the state apartments of Versailles came from Carrara, by boat via Genoa, the Languedoc canal around the Atlantic coast and up the Seine, and above all from newly opened quarries in Languedoc and the Pyrenees.[82] French marbles were used, both inside and outside the palace, to show that they were as good as Italian marbles.[83] The state apartments of Versailles were perhaps inspired by the gilded and frescoed rooms created by Pietro da Cortona in the Pitti Palace in 1641–7, glorifying the King's Medici cousins and the gods of Olympus. Like them the rooms at Versailles were named after Mars, Venus, Diana, Mercury, Apollo, Jupiter and Saturn.[84] The marble clashes with the large gilt bronze trophies on the walls. However, the size of the rooms, what Anthony Blunt calls their 'unparalleled richness and impressiveness', as well as 'the delicacy of the detail', made them particularly suitable for court ceremonies and entertainments.[85]

Louis XIV began to spend more time at Versailles and by 1669, at the latest, he had decided to make it his principal residence, housing courtiers and ministers as well as the royal family. In 1670 Colbert wrote to the King that, of the two carpentry workshops at Versailles, one worked by day, the other by night.[86] Thereafter Versailles cost far more annually than the other main residences, Saint-Germain or the Louvre and the Tuileries in Paris.

From 29 November 1670, with a break for Christmas and New Year at Versailles and Saint-Germain, Louis XIV spent a last winter, unwillingly, in the Tuileries. On 10 February 1671 he left 'for ever', as the Ambassador of Savoy wrote that day to his Duke, never spending a night in Paris again.[87] He continued to regulate life in his capital from a distance, but visited it only eighteen times in the following forty-five years. Like his desire to marry Marie Mancini, his 'extreme aversion for Paris', as Sourches called it, confirms Louis XIV's unconventionality: no other monarch in Europe has shunned his capital for so long.[88] Versailles was not the cause of the separation from Paris. Until 1682, as work continued on Versailles, his main country residence remained Saint-Germain. The separation reflected his desire for more freedom with his mistresses, more space in which to drill troops and, above all, his growing love of country pleasures – hunting, riding, gardening, walking. His doctor wrote in 1687 that riding and hunting in the country was 'what he loved most in the world'.[89]

More than other country palaces, French or foreign, Versailles was planned as a government centre as well as a royal residence and hunting lodge. In order to create a 'considerable town' around it, the King gave courtiers land on which to build houses, and legal privileges, such as exemption from the duty to provide accommodation to court officials and, until 1713 – to the fury of the Parlement de Paris – from seizure of properties for unpaid debts.[90]

In 1670 the Comte de Soissons, the ducs de Créquy and de Noailles and the Maréchal de Bellefonds were the first of many courtiers, ministers and servants to build their own houses in the town, lining the Avenue de Paris and other streets closer to the palace. At the King's wish they built in the same style as the palace, often using his architect, Jules Hardouin-Mansard.[91] The foundation stone of the magnificent baroque church of Notre-Dame (the royal family's parish church) was laid on 10 March 1684 by 'Louis le Grand . . . le Conquérant, le Belliqueux' himself, as an inscription proclaimed.[92] The town acquired a hospital for the workers on the building sites, and inns for visitors without houses or apartments of their own: by 1700 there were 120 inns in Versailles.[93]

As the town expanded, Louis XIV made the palace the machine for *divertissements* – entertainments – which it remained for the rest of the reign. The choice of Versailles as a setting for his entertainments, even when it was a site of frequent building works, shows how greatly he preferred it to Saint-Germain. Descriptions of early parties confirm that courtiers' complaints of neglect were usually unjustified. As Colbert recorded on 14 October 1663:

> every day balls, ballets, comedies, music for voices and instruments of every kind, violins, promenades, hunts and other diversions have followed one after the other, and what is very special in this house is that the King wanted every apartment for his guests to be furnished; he also feeds everyone and provides fuel and candles in all the bedrooms which has never been the habit in any of the royal residences.[94]

For Mademoiselle, Versailles in 1666 was 'very agreeable', above all because guests were with the King from morning until evening. She was never bored when she was with him. All women were a little in love with him; all men courted his favour.[95] The Duc d'Enghien wrote, 'At a great ball at Versailles all the ladies have been grandly dressed and everyone was much diverted.' The King opened one ball wearing a half-Persian, half-Chinese costume. Another lasted until six in the morning.[96] Enghien called Versailles 'the most agreeable place you could imagine', one more-over which 'is most liable to produce dramatic events' – since the King was so accessible there.[97]

In May 1664 Louis gave a week-long party for 600 at Versailles entitled 'Les plaisirs de l'île enchantée'. His *premier gentilhomme* the Duc de Saint-Aignan – who had helped arrange early meetings with Louise de La Vallière, and supplied him with gossip – organized the details. It was based on a story from one of the most popular poems of the period, Ariosto's *Orlando Furioso* of 1516.

Alcine has enchanted Roger (played by the King) and other knights. They have to break the spell. Melissa gives a magic ring to Roger, thereby freeing him from the spell. Finally there was a ballet enacting the storming of Alcine's magical palace by knights, dwarves, demons and monsters. This time Roger was played by a professional actor, to enable the King to watch.

In a theatre on the main lawn Molière and his troupe performed a play *La Princesse d'Elide* (Elysium) with a ballet of the same name. In addition to the tournament and the play, there were balls, fireworks and supper parties in different locations in the garden – for hundreds of guests, watched by thousands of spectators.

An illuminated manuscript recording the party survives, covered in crowns and Ls. Each knight was commemorated with flattering verses: the Duc de Noailles for example is called 'gifted for politics, for writing, for combat, as he is active both in peace and war'.[98] In addition books of illustrations of these parties, and of Versailles itself, printed by the Cabinet du Roi, were distributed by French ministers and ambassadors to the courts of Europe, where they were eagerly awaited.[99]

As a result of recent improvements in candles, torches and fireworks, more entertainments could be held outdoors at night – further demonstration of the King's wealth and his power to turn night into day.[100] The magic of the fireworks and illuminations was doubled by their reflection in the Grand Canal and the fountains, as prints confirm.[101] At 1 a.m. on the last night of another great series of entertainments, *Les Divertissements de Versailles*, held between 4 July and 31 August 1674 to celebrate the conquest of the Franche-Comté, more than 24,000 candles illuminated fountains and terraces in the park.[102] The account by the art philosopher André Félibien, one of the royal historiographers, describes the Grand Canal turning into a sea of flame, lit by a thousand rockets, hissing like furies escaping prison; other rockets traced the King's monogram of inter-laced double Ls in the sky. Le Brun and Le Vau did the sets in the park, creating temporary 'enchanted palaces'. Carlo Vigarani from Modena organized the temporary theatres; Molière directed the plays.[103]

At supper in one of the groves in the park called 'the *bosquet* of the Star', on 18 July 1668, during the Grand Divertissement Royal to celebrate the end of the War of Devolution (see next chapter), food was part of the spectacle. Orange trees bearing candied fruit stood between mountains of jams and marzipan, castles of sweets, pyramids of fruit; 'the magnificence of the King shone on all sides.' The 'food scramble' at the end, when members of the public were allowed to pillage the mountains of food, added to courtiers' amusement.[104]

Most ambassadors left early, however, after they had been jostled by hordes of unruly guests, as they often were at the French court. The Gardes du Corps could not or would not control them. The Queen herself had to wait half an hour before she could enter the theatre, while the King had to ask gentlemen to leave, to ensure that she and other ladies were given seats. Some guests said that he should have given the money he spent on the fête to his soldiers. The Marquis de Saint-Maurice, Ambassador of the Duke of Savoy, ended the long account written for his court: 'There has never been such great disorder ... with madmen one must be a madman.'[105]

The fireworks and illuminations in the park, however, which continued until two in the morning were the finest spectators could remember. The intention was to show, as the official account of the 1668 fêtes proclaimed, that France was 'no less great and magnificent in peace than conquering and glorious in war, since its sceptre has been placed in the hands of a monarch all of whose days are filled with marvels which have no example in the past and will have nothing similar in the future'. The purpose of Versailles could not have been more clearly stated.[106] It was a showcase for France as well as a residence for the King.

9

Conquering Flanders

On the right bank of the Seine, the Louvre celebrated the French monarchy's love of the arts. On the left bank, the elegant, domed semi-circle of the Collège des Quatre Nations commemorated its conquests. Built between 1662 and 1688 with money bequeathed by Mazarin, today it houses the Académie Française, but still contains much of his magnificent library, as well as a tomb, showing him accompanied into the afterlife by Victory, Prudence, Peace, Religion, Fidelity and Vigilance. Adding another college to the university, it was intended to house sixty students from four regions or 'nations' conquered during his ministry – Artois, Alsace, Pignerol in the Alps (where Fouquet was imprisoned) and Roussillon. Education in Paris would, it was believed, turn them into what Louis XIV called 'bons français'.[1]

Louis XIV was described by Colbert in 1663 as 'avidement désireux de conquête'.[2] Other kings of France, from Charles VIII to his own father Louis XIII, had led armies south, to conquer Milan, Naples or Catalonia, to which they believed they had claims. Mazarin too had hoped to win Naples for a French prince. With his innate strategic sense, however, Louis XIV – like his brilliant fifteenth-century predecessor Louis XI, who had annexed the Duchy of Burgundy and occupied Franche-Comté – led his armies east and north-east.

At this stage, he was more interested in territorial expansion for France than in dynastic claims to the Spanish monarchy. Saint-Maurice wrote, 'he has the wind behind him, it is to be presumed that he wants to profit and acquire from the Low Countries everything which will be to his country's advantage, seize the gates through which the Spanish have often entered there, and thus protect his kingdom and Paris from their invasions.'[3]

As had been confirmed by the Spanish invasion of 1636, and the threat of another in 1649, France's most vulnerable border, to which Paris was dangerously close, was with the Low Countries. Flanders, in particular, was not only close, and one of the richest and most densely populated provinces in Europe, it had also, until François I's renunciation of the link in 1529, owed allegiance to the French crown; its language of government was French, and the city of Tournai, a former Frankish capital, was called the 'eldest daughter of the Kings of France'.[4] In 1663 Louis wrote to his Ambassador in The Hague, the Comte d'Estrades: 'the expulsion of the Spaniards from Flanders, since they have possessed it, has always been the aim of the kings my predecessors, and myself.'[5]

The 1660s were a favourable time for French expansion. Under the leadership of Jan de Witt, Grand Pensionary of Holland, the regents governing the Netherlands preferred their ancient ally France to the hated commercial rival England. Charles II was, moreover, uncle to their political enemy the Prince of Orange, whom they had excluded from all his ancestors' public offices such as stadtholder of Holland and Zeeland. Indeed, in accordance with the 1662 French–Dutch treaty, Louis had, in January 1666 during the second Anglo-Dutch War, declared war against his cousin Charles II. He sent French troops to attack England's ally and the Netherlands' enemy the Bishop of Münster.[6] France's rivals the Holy Roman Emperor Leopold I and the sickly child king of Spain Carlos II were weak. Many German princes were members of the pro-French League of the Rhine, founded by Mazarin in 1657, renewed by Louis XIV in 1664. That year Louis sent French troops to help another member of the League, the Elector of Mainz, against the city of Erfurt, and the Elector of Cologne against the city of Cologne.[7] Louis XIV had also renewed treaties of alliance with Denmark, Sweden, the Swiss Confederation and Portugal.[8]

His wife Marie Thérèse, rather than being a 'dove of peace', provided a pretext for war. In the 1659 marriage treaty she had renounced her claims to the Spanish monarchy in return for a dowry which had never been paid. Two views of monarchy were in conflict. The Spanish monarchy was treated by its dynasty as private property, where succession could be governed by the king's personal decisions and royal wills, rather than – as in the kingdom of France – by state laws such as the Salic Law, limiting the succession to heirs through the male line.

Also treating the Spanish monarchy as private property, in 1667 the King and his lawyers argued that, according to the law of 'devolution' observed in the Southern Netherlands, Marie Thérèse, as child of the first wife of Philip IV, rather than her half-brother Carlos II, child of the King's second wife, should inherit part of it. In his proclamation of 8 May 1667 Louis claimed Brabant, Limburg, Namur, Hainaut, Antwerp and much else. Marie Thérèse loved her husband and willingly supported his claims.

Dynasticism then had such a deep hold on hearts and minds that Louis preferred not to admit in public that conquest was a motive. Guy Joly, another *frondeur* turned royalist, wrote a *Traité des droits de la Reyne très chrétienne sur divers estats de la monarchie d'Espagne*, printed in Paris at the Imprimerie Royale.[9] Protesting too much, he claimed that 'it is neither the ambition to possess new states nor the desire to acquire glory through arms which inspires the Most Christian King with the design to uphold the rights of the Queen his Wife.'[10]

The King left for another campaign on the north-east frontier. He was accompanied by far more people than he had been in the 1650s: his wife and her ladies; ambassadors, courtiers, servants, guards; provision wagons and cannon. On 16 May 1667 he slept in the chateau of the Président de Molé at Champlâtreux. By 2 June he had reached Charleroi in what is now southern Belgium.[11] Thanks to Saint-Maurice, Ambassador of Savoy, we can follow the court's progress. On 11 June he wrote: 'the king sleeps on a bed of straw, is working very hard, does everything with good grace, without rush and *en maître*; he appears proud but gives orders very gently.'

The rising star was the young Marquis de Louvois, who had inherited the office of secretary of state for war from his father Le Tellier in 1664. 'I have never seen a man work so hard,' commented Saint-Maurice.[12] Louvois 'was always followed by 100 officers asking to be employed'. That was where power lay: with ministers, more than with princes or generals.[13] In these years Louvois made the army a disciplined, well-fed, well-clothed and well-armed force. He ensured that regiments were regularly inspected to check on numbers, uniforms, supplies and weapons, and built barracks, munitions stores and later hospitals throughout France.[14]

At first he had behaved as a protégé, who wrote that he felt obliged to inform Turenne of 'everything which happens at court on every kind of matter'.[15] By 1667, however, Louvois could decide, or help the King decide, the movements of generals of the highest rank, including Condé and Turenne.[16] Like many others, Turenne complained to Louis XIV of Louvois' haughtiness, rudeness and brutality. He wrote that, even if he was the most incapable man in France, he should not receive precise orders from such a distance, and won the right to correspond with Louis XIV directly, rather than through the minister.[17] Courtiers, Parisians and officers (whose thefts of soldiers' pay and rations Louvois tried to prevent) came to loathe Louvois. They rejoiced when the King reprimanded him in public, and blamed him for French mistakes.[18]

On campaign the King changed his habits. He talked and gave money to soldiers, and every evening had fifteen or twenty officers to dinner.

Sometimes they kept their hats on – a rare exception to the rule of uncovering in the presence of the King (the King himself removed his hat in the presence of Turenne). He became thin and suntanned, with his hair tied back. Even on campaign, however, he held a *lever* and remained obsessed by his appearance. Sometimes, wrote Saint-Maurice, 'he spends half an hour in front of the mirror arranging his moustache with wax; here he wears a cravat, a cloth shirt, a plain jacket; despite this, here and with the army he spends more than an hour and a half getting dressed and seated [on the commode]; it is true he does not get bored as everyone talks to him and they tell him many witty stories that make him laugh.'[19]

On 24 June Tournai surrendered, on 6 July Douai. Everywhere the King and Queen were greeted by triumphal arches, magistrates on bended knee offering the keys of the city and speeches of welcome and oaths of loyalty.[20] They then withdrew to the comfort of the royal palace at Compiègne, where the King stayed from 8 to 19 July. As the French army gathered in early August outside Lille, capital of Flanders, soldiers complained that there were not enough cannon or boats to assist them; and that they had not been paid.[21] Nevertheless victory was certain: 50,000 French troops faced 20,000 Spanish. The King was constantly inspecting his troops, often exposed to enemy fire, sometimes spending the night in the bivouac: his presence in the trenches before Tournai would be commemorated in a Gobelins tapestry. On 27 August, after seventeen days' bombardment – the preferred combat method of Louis XIV and Louvois – Lille surrendered to avoid further loss of life. On 28 August the King entered Lille and thanked God in the church of Saint-Pierre.[22] By 7 September he was back at Saint-Germain.

However, the King's triumphs displeased many of his contemporaries. The Dutch Ambassador van Beuningen, although he had negotiated the treaty between Louis XIV and the Netherlands in 1662, turned violently anti-French. He complained that the King 'devoured' countries.[23] 'If the King does not make peace,' he said at Saint-Germain, 'the Dutch will not allow him to make new conquests in Flanders.' They wanted to make a European league in opposition to the King of France, 'as it is well known that he is aiming for universal monarchy'.[24] The phrase 'universal monarchy' implied supreme influence as the preponderant power in Europe, capable of preventing any hostile moves or alliances against itself, rather than unlimited territorial expansion.

M. de Lisola, another anti-French diplomat bent on uniting Europe against Louis XIV, came, like Watteville, from the Habsburg province of Franche-Comté, between Burgundy and Switzerland. In 1665, as Imperial ambassador in Spain, he had arranged the marriage of Marie Thérèse's younger sister the Infanta Margareta to the Emperor Leopold I, thus reinforcing the Austrian Habsburgs' claim to the Spanish monarchy. In 1667 he published in Brussels *Bouclier d'estat et de justice contre le dessein manifestement découvert de la Monarchie Universelle, sous le vain prétexte des prétentions de la reyne de France*, a pamphlet denouncing Louis XIV's ambitions and praising Leopold I as the defender of European liberty.[25] He was one of a generation of diplomats and lawyers who wanted to apply the growing body of international law to European politics, to stop states devouring each other like lions and tigers. His pamphlet, banned in France, spread panic in the Netherlands, and was at once translated into English and other languages.[26]

Thus from the start of Louis XIV's wars, he learnt, like Napoleon I and Wilhelm II after him, that the virus of conquest produced the antivirus of hostile European alliances. In reality Louis was too realistic to hope for 'universal monarchy'. He already knew that there were limits to his power to intervene in Poland. Unknown to his contemporaries, he had signed a secret treaty in January 1668 with the Holy Roman Emperor Leopold I, cousin (and in his own mind, and by the will of Philip IV, heir) of Carlos II, agreeing to divide the Spanish monarchy between them. The Holy Roman Emperor or a son would obtain Spain, its colonies, and Milan. Louis XIV would receive the Southern Netherlands, Naples, Sicily and (for commerce with Asia) the Philippines. At this stage Louis was sufficiently moderate to accept the principle of dividing the Spanish monarchy, to which he considered his son the Dauphin the legitimate heir.[27]

The triple alliance signed by England, the Netherlands and Sweden in February 1668 was the first anti-French coalition of the reign. Despite Charles II's protestations of friendship for Louis XIV, when pushed by public Francophobia and his need for money from Parliament, he could turn hostile: moreover they had fought on opposite sides during the recent Anglo-Dutch War. The same month Louis conquered Franche-Comté. Finally, by the Treaty of Aix-la-Chapelle of May 1668, France expanded deeper into the Spanish Netherlands, acquiring land along the coast as far as Furnes, and the cities of Lille, Douai, Oudenarde, Tournai, Charleroi and Philippeville; but Franche-Comté was restored to Spain.[28]

By then the young William III, Prince of Orange, grandson of Charles I and nephew of Charles II, was a rising star and had become first noble of Holland: the 'bourgeois republic' contained many nobles like Zuylestein, Ginkel and Keppel, eager to lead its armies into battle, as Louis XIV would learn to his cost. Like his ancestors, William III maintained, out of his personal income from estates and investments, an ambitious and cultivated court based in The Hague – a political rival to the States

General and the city of Amsterdam. As at many other courts in Europe, courtiers not only spoke French (without a foreign accent, in William III's case) but also dressed and danced in the French style.[29] William danced in a 'ballet de la paix', representing, among other figures, a peasant girl and Mercury, working for the glory of the fatherland.[30]

William III was Louis XIV's first cousin once removed: Henrietta Maria was both Louis XIV's aunt and William III's grandmother. They corresponded as cousins and allies.[31] Nevertheless William III was already a potential rival, as yet another 'carriage war' had demonstrated. On 6 May 1664, the French Ambassador in The Hague, the Comte d'Estrades, encouraged by his victory over the Spanish Ambassador in London in 1661, had refused to let his carriage give way to the Prince of Orange's carriage along the Lange Voorhout, the principal avenue in The Hague, even though William claimed precedence as a grandson of Charles I with a place in the English succession, rather than as prince of Orange. On the advice of Jan de Witt, William III had been obliged, before a large crowd, to order his carriage to turn back, and to continue his journey on foot. His feelings of rage and humiliation can be imagined.[32] Louis began to hate the Dutch for their republicanism, their 'ingratitude' in helping by means of the Treaty of Aix-la-Chapelle of 1668 to limit his conquests (when he had fought as their ally against Charles II in 1666), as well as – while French overseas companies faltered – their commercial success.[33]

He had, however, secured Lille and the surrounding area. Under the Spanish crown, which had ruled the towns of Flanders since the accession of Philip II in 1555, they had been almost self-governing, paying minimal taxes. Although many inhabitants of Flanders spoke French, many preferred the light hand of Spain to the harshness of France, whose armies had so often devastated their country. In public processions and prayers in Lille in August 1667, the inhabitants had implored the city's patron saint, Notre Dame de la Treille, for protection, and had declared that their hearts were Spanish and Burgundian, not French.[34] Even today the brick architecture of the city's magnificent central square, as well as its geography, ensure that Lille is closer to Brussels than to Paris.

The diary or 'Chronique immémoriale des choses mémorables' of a Lillois called Pierre-Ignace Chavatte records his continued admiration for the King of Spain and the Holy Roman Emperor, in contrast to 'les français', who 'pillaged' fellow Catholics. He deplored the decline in morals since the arrival of French soldiers and the 'peace without joy as we remained under the King of France': few people attended the Te Deum.[35] To avoid brawls with French soldiers Lillois were forbidden to go out at night. In 1670 the Spanish Ambassador was cheered in the streets.[36]

Royal visits were part of Louis' strategy for making his conquests French, as he had shown by his dash to Dunkirk in 1662. After his triumphal entry in 1667, the court returned to Lille on four occasions: in 1670 when Louis tossed gold coins 'several times' to the crowds and there were fireworks, illuminations, fountains of wine and *fêtes galantes* at night; in 1671 when he brought musicians, a choir and tapestries for the procession of the Fête Dieu; in 1672 when the Queen stayed there, while the King was on campaign; and in 1680 when the inhabitants of the marketplace placed candles in their windows at night, and there was a play with Jupiter (that is, the King) destroying giants. In addition grandiose church services in Lille celebrated French royal births, deaths and victories.[37]

By her piety, as well as her dynastic claims, the Queen was an instrument of French policy. On her visits to churches and convents she impressed congregations by the fervour of her prayers. Even Chavatte admired her 'piety towards God, her charity towards the poor, her love for the King, her tenderness to her children and her kindness to the officers of her household'. When she died, the bells of Lille rang three hours a day for forty days, and her *chapelle ardente* (memorial service) was the finest he had seen.[38]

In addition to royal visits, French rule also meant, despite the change in sovereignty, respect for local customs. Louis XIV felt no humiliation in swearing to observe the customs and traditions of Flanders and other provinces. Unlike the French Republic and Empire after 1792, the French monarchy did not try to impose all its laws and regulations on all its conquests. Flexibility and diversity were in its nature. French Flanders kept its laws and privileges (including exclusion from the main French customs zone, and from the Edict of Nantes legalizing Protestant services and law courts), which Louis XIV swore to respect on the holy gospel and relics of the cross, the day he entered Lille. He subsequently signed a lengthy treaty listing the city's rights and privileges.[39]

As in other conquered cities, an *intendant* from Paris, however, became the main official. He supervised municipal finances, arbitrated taxation disputes and regulated the economy.[40] On 24 May 1670, the King, in his role as chief merchant of France, received the principal merchants of the city in the Hôtel de Ville and asked what were the needs of commerce. Roads to Paris were improved, and the area of the city expanded. A Parlement, acting as an instrument of French law and sovereignty in Flanders, was installed in a newly built Palais de Justice in the nearby city of Tournai.[41] Another result of French rule, caused by the King's relentless desire for money, would be to make all municipal offices venal and semi-hereditary, which they had not been under Spanish rule. Thereby the crown acquired revenue and local elites a vested interest in French rule.[42]

Above all, French rule meant French soldiers. 'The queen of citadels', a vast seventeenth-century pentagon on the edge of Lille, designed to withstand a siege of sixty days, demonstrated the King's determination to keep Lille French. Covering 90 acres in all, it was built with 60 million bricks, by a local master mason called Simon Vollant, according to a design by the King's favourite engineer Vauban, who had helped organize the siege in 1667. Massive brick bastions, named after the King, the Queen, the Dauphin, the King's second son the Duc d'Anjou and Turenne, surrounded neat rectangular barracks, with room for thousands of soldiers. Suns with shining rays and royal fleurs-de-lys decorate the entrance and the walls.[43]*

While conquering a new province, the King was also conquering a new mistress. Louise de La Vallière had held him, against relentless competition, for six years.[44] In May 1667 – it would have been unthinkable while Anne of Austria was alive – she was created Duchess de Vaujours (the first such creation for an unmarried woman: François I had rewarded his mistress Anne de Pisseleu by making her husband Duc d'Etampes). At the same time their daughter was formally recognized by the Parlement de Paris as Mlle de Blois, 'Légitimée de France'. The King was said to have called La Vallière's ducal patent a *folie*; it may in reality have been a farewell present.

That year Saint-Maurice noted that the twenty-two-year-old La Vallière, still very pretty in 1665, had lost her looks. Her cheeks were hollow, her mouth and teeth bad, her nose too large, her face too long. She had also begun to look at people 'de haut en bas'.[45]

One of the Queen's ladies, travelling during the 1667 campaign in the same carriage, said, when La Vallière's unwanted arrival on campaign was mentioned, 'God forbid that I should be mistress of the King; but if I was, I would be very ashamed in front of the Queen.' Her name was Madame de Montespan.

Louise de La Vallière was the daughter of a country gentleman from Touraine. Madame de Montespan, a Rochechouart and daughter of the Duc de Mortemart, came from the highest nobility in the land: according to the family motto, before the sea was in the world, the Rochechouart were on the waves. Her words hid, or advertised, her desire to win the King. In 1661, she had come to court at the age of twenty-one. Like Louise, she began as a *fille d'honneur* of Madame. In 1663 she had married the

---

* Even today, after many wars and sieges, while the surrounding moat and land form a peaceful landscape park, the citadel retains a military function, as HQ of a NATO rapid reaction force.

Marquis de Montespan, from a family in western France less ancient and less well connected than her own. In 1664 she had entered the household of the Queen in the new post of *dame du palais*. These posts were particularly coveted since *dames du palais* were companions, rather than officials with household duties. Montespan had a legitimate reason thereby for seeing the King, or travelling in the same carriage.[46]

Already Enghien and Saint-Maurice had noticed that the King was attracted to her. Writing on 5 November 1666, Enghien added: 'in truth she would indeed deserve it [royal notice] for it is impossible to be more beautiful or wittier than she is.'[47] Another of her techniques, in order to convince the Queen of her morality and the King of her availability, had been to laugh at aspiring lovers at the Queen's *coucher*. She warned her husband of the King's growing interest; he remained blind.[48]

During the campaign in Flanders, probably when the court was at Avesnes between 9 and 14 June 1667, the guard posted on the staircase between the King's and Madame de Montespan's bedrooms was removed. The King began coming to the bed he still shared with the Queen early in the morning. When the Queen asked why, he replied that he was working late on despatches. Mademoiselle found him 'of an admirable gaiety'.[49]

In August Saint-Maurice wrote to the Duke of Savoy that the King 'has no more thoughts except for the Montespan'. He made sure that she sat in his carriage and diverted his wife's attention by encouraging her jealousy of La Vallière.[50] Inevitably in October 1667 someone sent a letter to the Queen. She replied, 'I am not such a dupe as they imagine, but I am prudent. I see things clearly.'[51]

The precise weight of personal and political factors in Louis XIV's decisions is impossible to assess. He may, however, have been deflected from making more territorial conquests by desire for sexual conquest, as well as by his belief that Carlos II would soon die, and he would win more territory without fighting. Saint-Maurice thought the King had made three mistakes in 1667: to have attacked Flanders with too few troops; to have returned, for ten days in the middle of the campaign, to visit his wife and her ladies at Compiègne; and, for the same reason, to have finished the campaign early, instead of taking more territory.[52]

Montespan was not the King's only target. Bussy-Rabutin, who had been exiled to the country in 1665 for writing a pamphlet describing the court's love affairs, called Louis XIV 'the most gallant prince on earth . . . whose example incited courtiers to make love', that is to make declarations of love.[53] The Italian observer Primi Visconti believed that every woman at court hoped to become the King's mistress.[54] Louis XIV himself wrote that they attacked his heart like a military objective.[55]

The King was known to like women who were young and appetizing (*ragoûtantes*),[56] and was believed to enjoy them like post-horses, 'which you ride only once and then never see again'. The physical arrangement of such encounters is never described. Perhaps trusted court officials such as Saint-Aignan guarded a room or a secluded corner in a garden, and later rewarded the woman concerned.[57] Sometimes there were children, for whose upbringing the King paid.[58]

The number of his mistresses is unknown. The Princesse de Soubise was said to wear emerald earrings during her husband's absences, as a signal that the King could visit her. She was considered 'highly capable of conducting great affairs', and became, like Madame de Montespan, a *dame du palais de la reine*.[59] When she was seen on a balcony with La Vallière and Montespan, a courtier said: 'there is the past, the present and the future.'[60] By the end of the reign, her husband's family the Rohan were one of the most powerful clans at court, with the rank of *princes étrangers*. Her husband became captain of the Gendarmes de la Garde in 1674. The looks and manners of their younger son Gaston de Rohan, born the same year, encouraged rumours that he was the King's son. He became bishop of Strasbourg in 1704 and *grand aumônier de France* in 1713. Both posts became semi-hereditary in the Rohan family.[61]

Another of the King's mistresses was the Princesse de Monaco, as attractive and sensual as her brother the Comte de Guiche: Madame de Sévigné called her 'the torrent'. According to Saint-Maurice, she complained, when the King deplored her size, 'that although his power was great, his sceptre was very small': a remark which, if true, may explain his eagerness to advertise his mistresses. She died in 1678, disfigured by a disease which was described as a warning to all those tempted to imitate her conduct.[62]

One of her lovers was the Comte de Lauzun, an insolent debauchee feared by other courtiers as a snake. On one occasion the King had arrived for an assignation with the Princesse de Monaco but found her bedroom door locked: Lauzun had locked the door and removed the key, and was watching with glee from a hiding place. A spell in the Bastille was his punishment. On another occasion, Lauzun 'accidentally' trod on the hand of Madame de Monaco during a gambling party. The King himself had to intervene to prevent a duel between Lauzun and her brother.[63] Sourches wrote that, despite his acts of insolence, the King retained 'a great penchant to favour M. de Lauzun'.[64] He used Lauzun, Saint-Maurice alleged, to 'observe' women whom he considered taking as mistresses.[65]

Lauzun's independence, like Marie Mancini's, appealed to Louis XIV. In June 1669 Lauzun, already *colonel général des dragons*, became one of the four *capitaines des gardes du corps du roi*. Lauzun was a confidant who not only arrested the King's brother's lover (see above, p. 113) but in March 1670 smuggled out of Saint-Germain his first son by Madame de Montespan, the future Duc du Maine, into the waiting arms of the friend she had chosen as his governess: Madame Scarron, the impoverished widow of the *frondeur* poet Paul Scarron.[66]

Madame de Montespan became a companion for Louis XIV as well as a mistress. To mark her status as a *maîtresse déclarée*, likely to bear royal children – and to protect her from her outraged husband – a sentinel was placed outside her door.* Gardes du Corps sometimes escorted her carriage. As with the Queen, only women were allowed to eat at her table. By 1668 it was said that the King could not bear to be parted from her. She was witty, intelligent and forceful. In her desire to make the King laugh, she spared no one. Madame remembered that no one felt bored in her company. Confidence added to her charm. For Madame de Montespan the Bourbons might be more illustrious than her own family the Mortemart, or the La Rochefoucauld, but they were not more ancient.[67]

The Marquis de Montespan, however, refused the role of complaisant husband. He insulted Louis XIV and threatened his wife. Louis regarded him as a dangerous madman. He had Montespan imprisoned, won the Marquise a legal separation, then exiled the Marquis to Poitou. There Montespan consoled himself by erecting a pair of cuckold's antlers above the gate of his chateau.[68]

After the campaign of 1667 the King had been 'extremely cold' towards La Vallière, although the accounts of the Bâtiments du Roi show that large sums continued to be spent on her apartment at Saint-Germain.[69] In February 1669 their two-year-old son was legitimized as Comte de Vermandois and made admiral of France. Known as 'les dames de la faveur', La Vallière and Montespan were constantly together. The King's affair with the former was, in theory, finished. Yet in 1670, to the fury of Madame de Montespan, she was again pregnant.[70]

Montespan, however, had won the King's heart. She was so forceful that in November 1673 she ensured the abolition of the 'hydra' of the chamber of the *filles d'honneur de la reine*, all of whom were potential rivals.[71] Beside the park of Versailles Louis XIV built the chateau of Clagny for Montespan, with its own gallery, chapel and marble-paved orangery; it was so magnificent that even the Queen came to inspect.[72] A

---

* One memento of their affair is the octagonal bath, cut from a single block of purple marble, with steps and an inner bench seat, which she and the King used in her apartment at Versailles, now displayed in the Orangery. See Antonia Fraser, *Love and Louis XIV: The Women in the Life of the Sun King*, 2006, p. 145 and n.

portrait by Montespan's favourite painter Henri Gascar shows her reclining on a sofa at Clagny, dress parted to display a gleaming white breast. Cherubs draw back curtains, covered in royal fleurs-de-lys, to reveal the gallery, adorned by the most luxurious furniture of the day, two Japanese lacquer cabinets on gilt stands, crowned with blue and white Chinese porcelain.[73] She was also a patron of Molière, Racine and La Fontaine, and helped Racine and Boileau become royal historiographers in 1677.[74]

She literally outshone the Queen, being given jewels not only by Louis, but also, showing the French monarchy's global reach, by ambassadors from the King of Benin, on the west coast of Africa. In 1676 she was described by Madame de Sévigné as wearing 'a dress of gold on gold, embroidered in gold, lined in gold and covered in swirled gold, enhanced with a gold mixed with another gold which makes the finest material which has ever been imagined'.[75]

The Marquis de Montespan was not alone in refusing to accept the affair. Inside France, an alternative power obeyed Jesus Christ and his 'vicar on earth' the Pope, as well as the King. The French Catholic or Gallican church was more powerful and more courageous in the seventeenth century than in the twentieth. It could challenge Louis XIV through its hold on his subjects' hearts and minds, and through the independently elected Assembly of Clergy, on whose 'free gift', voted every five years, the crown relied for revenue. At times the Gallican church acted as an unofficial opposition to Louis XIV.

However pious the King showed himself to be, however often he visited churches and followed processions, the Gallican church or the Papacy occasionally thwarted his desires. The King was unable to restrict the number and size of the monasteries which owned so much land and in Colbert's opinion weakened the economy. Of the 266,000 clerics in France, 181,000 were monks or nuns.[76] The King was also stopped by the Papal Nuncio from issuing declarations to limit the number of men taking monastic vows. All that was done was to abolish seventeen religious holidays.[77]

Priests were prepared to attack the King to his face. A famous preacher called Jacques-Bénigne Bossuet denounced the morals of the court in sermons in front of the King, urging him to worship God alone, not the false idol of the God of love.[78] The poor were dying of hunger: he should relieve their suffering, since he was born for the public, not for himself alone.[79] Another preacher, Louis Bourdaloue, attacked gambling at court, the reduction of peasants to the state of animals and the King's 'commerce' with his mistresses.[80] On 11 April 1675 another priest would refuse

Madame de Montespan absolution before taking the Easter sacrament, as she was guilty of double adultery, against the Queen and against her own husband.[81] Priests also encouraged Louise de La Vallière to leave the King.

Increasingly pious, she had long wanted to do so, but wrote, 'I am weakness itself.' Convents, however, provided havens for women determined to escape the power of men. Donations ensured their economic independence. Of Fontevrault, a massive royal convent near Saumur, which Madame de Montespan's sister ruled as if she was 'the queen of abbesses', it was said that wherever there was wind or rain, the Abbess of Fontevrault owned a farm. More than Paris, or chateaux in the provinces, convents were the real anti-Versailles.

Paris alone contained over forty, many built since 1600 in a surge of Counter-Reformation piety, and out of a desire to encourage women's education and charity work. New orders for women included Feuillantines, Bernardines, Visitandines (who started the cult of the Sacré Coeur in the reign of Louis XIV), Capucines and many more.[82] By 1700, thanks to their expansion throughout the kingdom, there was one poor house, often staffed by nuns, in every French town with more than 5,000 inhabitants.[83]

As early as February 1662 Louise de La Vallière had bolted to the convent of the Dames de la Visitation at Chaillot, until the King himself came to bring her back. In February 1671 she fled there again. This time the King sent Colbert to persuade her to return: she was still needed as a screen for his affair with Madame de Montespan.

The King, briefly, showed more *empressement* or eagerness, and she continued to hunt with him. In reality she already wore a hair shirt as an act of repentance, to mortify her flesh.[84] Another mortification, in December 1673, was to stand as godmother to the first daughter of Louis XIV and Madame de Montespan, Mlle de Nantes. She was also obliged to help at Montespan's toilette, as if she was an attendant, and on journeys, in a refinement of cruelty, to sleep in an adjoining bedroom.[85]

Pious friends and relations encouraged her to leave. The convent she chose as her refuge was the Couvent des Carmélites Déchaussées, a particularly austere order in the Faubourg Saint-Jacques, which had often been visited by Anne of Austria. The King and Madame de Montespan considered her decision ridiculous, but consented. On 19 March 1674 she wrote: 'at last I am leaving the world, it is without regret, but not without pain.' On 18 April, during a farewell audience to ask the Queen's forgiveness, the Queen raised and kissed her, saying she had long been forgiven. That day she had a farewell audience with the King, and a last supper with Madame de Montespan.[86]

The following day Louise de La Vallière attended her last service in the chapel at Versailles. A slight redness was seen in the King's eyes. Radiant with relief, she then left for the convent. After a year as a novice, in June 1675 she took her vows of chastity, poverty and obedience as a nun, before a congregation which included the Queen, Monsieur, Mademoiselle and half the court. Bossuet preached, acknowledging that he had no need to say anything: 'things speak enough by themselves.'[87] La Vallière led a life of extreme self-mortification, performing menial tasks, sometimes refusing to drink water, in memory of Christ's thirst on the cross.

The Queen and Madame de Montespan came to visit. Montespan asked what message she had for the King. La Vallière's reply showed her contempt: 'anything you wish, Madame, anything you wish.'[88] When Madame de Sévigné visited the convent in January 1680, she observed of 'soeur Louise de la Miséricorde': 'as for her modesty, it is not greater than when she brought the princesse de Conti [as her daughter had become] into the world . . . in truth this nun's habit and this retreat are a great dignity for her.'[89] Her rejection of the King and the court was a form of victory. When told that her son the Comte de Vermandois had died at the age of sixteen, Soeur Louise commented, 'I ought to weep for his birth far more than for his death.' She died in her convent in 1710, at the age of sixty-six.[90]

In the church of Saint-Louis-en-l'Île on the island behind Notre-Dame, named after the patron saint of the French monarchy, visitors can see the *bénitier*, or holy-water stoup, decorated with the head of a winged angel, which Soeur Louise gave to the convent at Chaillot where she had first taken refuge from the court. Beside it is the inscription: 'Souvenir de la Pénitence de Soeur Louise de la Miséricorde 1675'.

IO

Fighting the Netherlands

While enjoying Madame de Montespan's company in Saint-Germain and Versailles, the King had also been planning war with the Netherlands. War was supported by Condé, Turenne and the Secretary of State for War, Louvois. Louvois, Louis' new favourite, entered the council in February 1672 at the age of thirty-one. He was then considered, in the words of Saint-Maurice, 'far stronger than anyone else'. His rival Colbert opposed war, since he wanted to cut expenditure; but he was losing favour and was often ill.[1]

War was not undertaken solely for the sake of conquests. The King enjoyed it, and, even more than the court itself, war was considered a necessity to tame and satisfy the French nobility, as Lisola had warned in his pamphlet of 1667.[2] There were ten times more officers in the army than in the royal households. War increased nobles' chances of promotion, money, fame and emotional satisfaction. It justified, to themselves and the public, their prestige and privileges. In 1667 Saint-Maurice had claimed that the King went to war 'to amuse all the young men of the court'.[3] In 1683 the Marquis de Sourches would write in his diary of the joy in the army and at court at the prospect of 'war, which everyone desires'.[4] Ladies of the court, often at their own request, also followed the King on campaign. They were called *les dames du voyage*. In the evening, the King worked in his study. They played cards as if they were at Saint-Germain or Versailles.[5]

Like most contemporaries, Louis XIV believed that nobles shared 'an instinctive attraction for command'. Throughout his reign, the King showed a preference for officers of noble birth. By 1693, about half of all able-bodied nobles in France were serving in his army.[6] Death in battle could be courted almost as eagerly as royal favour: the Duc de Longueville, for example, died leading a charge at Tolhuis by the Rhine in June 1672, crying 'Kill! kill! no quarter!'[7] Jean Martinet, Lieutenant Colonel of Louis XIV's favourite Régiment du Roi, founded in 1662, was such a dedicated inspector of troops, with such high standards of discipline and smartness, that he gave the word 'martinet' to the French and English languages. He too died in battle in 1672.[8] Louis wrote that he was 'very upset because he had greatly contributed to putting my infantry on a sound footing'. D'Artagnan died leading the Grey Musketeers in their attack on Maastricht the following year. In November 1673 the Comte de Guiche, who had recovered the King's favour by his bravery in battle, died after losing some troops in a skirmish: the King was at his deathbed.[9]

The King too was often dangerously conspicuous thanks to his white horse, the plumes on his hat or the large numbers of courtiers following him. On occasion pages were killed beside him when he was visiting siege trenches. Turenne once threatened to leave the army unless he exposed himself less.[10] Turenne himself would be killed in battle in July 1675 – and, on Louis XIV's orders, received the honour of burial in Saint-Denis, near the Bourbons.[11]

In addition to Louis XIV's and his nobles' love of war, his personal exasperation with the Netherlands in general and van Beuningen in particular drove him to fight in 1672. All major events of Louis XIV's reign, from his birth to his death, were commemorated by medals, 318 in all. Inspecting and arranging his collections of antique and modern medals, in gold, silver and bronze, on over 300 trays in twelve specially built medal cabinets in his private gallery in Versailles would be one of the King's favourite pastimes. Inscriptions, such as 'Felicitas temporum' (1663), 'Disciplina militaris' (1666), 'Rex dux et miles' (1667), 'Aeternitas imperii Gallici' (1683), linked his medals, like his many portraits and statues dressed as an emperor, to the Roman Empire: many are echoes of lines in Ovid or Virgil. The King himself sometimes supplied words – adding 'providentia' for example to an inscription commemorating the fall of Philippsburg in 1688.[12] Medals could, however, be causes of conflict, as well as means of self-congratulation.

In 1669–70, as twelve medallions of the sun (Louis XIV) were being placed on the garden façade of Versailles, Coenraad van Beuningen, or some of his friends, commissioned or planned a medal showing Joshua (van Beuningen), leader of the people of Israel, stopping the sun in the middle of the sky. 'Stetit sol in medio coeli' was the inscription. Despite van Beuningen's denials, he was widely believed to be responsible. He enraged the sun, as other Dutch medals glorifying the defeat of England enraged Charles II.[13]

Moreover in 1668 the States General had commissioned another medal, with a wider circulation and an inscription boasting of having 'assured the Laws, reformed the abuses of Religion, assisted, defended and reconciled Kings, restored the Freedom of the Seas, brought about a glorious Peace by force of arms and re-established the repose of Europe'. Louis in turn denounced the Netherlands for having 'even now the insolence to aim at setting itself up as sovereign arbiter and judge of all the potentates'. His subsequent peace demands would include the despatch, in perpetuity, of an annual embassy to France bearing a gold medal proclaiming gratitude for French help in winning Dutch independence from Spain.[14]

Personal feelings could drive public events. In Louis XIV's private 'Mémoire sur la campagne de 1672', in the war archives at Vincennes, he repeatedly stated that the 'ingratitude, ignorance and insupportable vanity' of the Netherlands, 'cette altière et ingrate nation', were the cause of his decision to attack it. He also defended his feelings of glory and ambition, and 'my desire to revenge myself for the insult I had received from the Dutch', against the condemnation of posterity. His feelings, he wrote, were understandable in a young monarch 'as well treated by fortune as I was'. Moreover he needed to maintain 'the glory and the reputation of my kingdom'. Thus he both knew and revealed himself.[15]

A wooden fort called Fort Saint-Sébastien near Saint-Germain now became a training ground, where the King exercised and reviewed his troops, and instructed them in trench and siege warfare; he was as much a military monarch as the Hohenzollerns would be later. Like Frederick William I of Prussia, he too had his dominions searched for tall men for favourite regiments: finding them was another of Colbert's duties.[16]

Louis XIV also demonstrated his love of war by making his guards the shock troops of the army, and increasing their discipline, pay and privileges. Under his personal supervision, they became an officers' training corps, a 'School of Mars', men whom he considered 'incapable of a bad action'.[17] He abolished venality in his Gardes du Corps in 1664, increased their numbers from 100 to 360 in each company and gave them a separate staff organization. After 1671 all the units of his foot and horse guards together were known as the Maison Militaire du Roi.[18] Jean de Plantavit de La Pause, a young provincial noble, was dazzled by the magnificent uniforms and plumed hats of the Gardes du Corps and regretted that he was too poor to join them.[19]

A unit of Grenadiers à Cheval was added to the Maison Militaire in 1676. Louis XIV promoted officers from his Maison Militaire to higher ranks in the army, as he considered them better disciplined. By 1700 half the colonels of regiments of the line had previously served in the Maison Militaire.[20]

Nearly every day, if the King was in residence, Versailles or Saint-Germain enjoyed the military spectacle, and music, which London experiences once a year at the Trooping of the Colour. The *Gazette de*

France wrote on 10 November 1674: 'every day the King rides out to see the gentlemen recruited from different provinces and assigns them himself to the companies of Gardes du Corps.' Officers were chosen partly for their build, often from the royal pages.[21] Van Beuningen's successor as Dutch ambassador, Peter de Groot, called them 'very fine, vigorous and robust, all well dressed and disciplined'.[22]

The King remained an army officer on active duty to the end of his life: the inscriptions on two of his medals, 'Rex dux et miles' and 'Disciplina restituta', did not lie. He often reviewed his troops, man by man, horse by horse, on the plains and avenues around his palaces, and sometimes on the terrace at Versailles after dinner. 'He is more strict than any commissary,' wrote one of his favourite courtiers, the Marquis de Dangeau, a gambler who also kept one of the most accurate and informative diaries of the reign. Sometimes he forbade courtiers to follow him, in order to be alone with the troops.[23] He reviewed his Maison Militaire particularly often, since so many died in battle, or were promoted to commands in line regiments, that he needed to test their replacements. Those who were not of the regulation height were dismissed.[24]

The philosopher John Locke, visiting France in 1678, saw the King review his Maison Militaire, 'all lusty, well horsed and well clad'. They marched 'so narrowly . . . in file man after man just before him, and [he] had the number in each squadron, as they passed, noted down, compiling in the meantime a strict survey of their horses and them'. At another review in 1679, as the King passed the end of each line,

> the officers at the heads of their companies and regiments in armour with pikes in their hands saluted him with their pikes and then with their hats, and he very courteously put off his hat to them again, and so he did again when he, taking his stand, they marched all before him. He passed twice along the whole front of them forwards and backwards, first by himself, the Dauphin etc. accompanying him, and then with the Queen, he riding along by her coach side.[25]

By such ceremonies the emotional bonds between the dynasty and the guard were reinforced throughout the year, every year.

Saint-Maurice was impressed: 'Never have you seen so much regularity and discipline and never has an army been so well regulated.'[26] Peter de Groot warned his government, on 22 January 1672, of 'the certitude of a very violent war . . . we will need all the favour which God has so often shown us on such occasions'. On 5 February: 'one [meaning the King] wants here at any price whatever to become master of the Low Countries.'[27] He blamed England as 'the sole cause of all the evil'.

For, perhaps remembering Mazarin's alliance of 1657, and showing unusual caution, Louis XIV chose to attack the Netherlands in alliance with Charles II and the Elector of Cologne. Louis' principal weapon in securing the English alliance, after money, was his sister-in-law. Charles II had long been writing to Madame in private letters that Louis XIV could count on his 'eternal friendship as long as I live'; but he wanted 'to find my account in it as it is reasonable they should find theirs'. He wanted money and territory.[28]

Encouraging the friendship between the two kings (although, as Louis XIV suspected, putting her brother before her brother-in-law), Madame had been the first, in 1665, to propose a secret correspondence and treaty between them. The Secretary of State for Foreign Affairs Lionne (who drafted some of her letters to Charles II), a French Protestant diplomat called Ruvigny, the French Ambassador in London Colbert's brother Colbert de Croissy, the English Ambassador in Paris Ralph Montagu and the English minister Lord Arlington were in the secret, as were English Catholics like Sir Thomas Clifford, Lord Arundell of Wardour and the Abbé Montagu, the latter for fifty years an intermediary between the two courts.[29]

The presence of Henrietta Maria's household at her estate in Colombes near Paris, after her return in June 1665, gave an excuse for frequent journeys between London and Paris.[30] In 1667 she had helped negotiate peace between Louis XIV and Charles II.[31] After her death at Colombes in September 1669, although she was Queen Dowager of England, she was buried in Saint-Denis, beside her father Henri IV. To the fury of Monsieur, Charles II inherited all her possessions, except her pearls and her house and furniture at Colombes, which went to Madame.[32]

Charles II was not, as Louis XIV knew, invariably pro-French. He had fought France in 1656–9 and 1666. Louis' ambassadors kept him informed of the force of Francophobia in England.[33] Charles II wrote, 'Messieurs, I am not so absolute in my state as the king my brother is in his. I have to humour my people and my parliament.' With a well-justified reputation for unreliability, he was ready to switch allies, as he had in 1668 when he signed the Triple Alliance with the Netherlands and Sweden.[34]

Nor did Louis XIV inevitably support Charles II. He had signed a treaty with the Netherlands in 1662 and supported them in the Anglo-Dutch War of 1665–7. Alarmed if Charles II and his Parliament agreed with each other, or with the Netherlands, he would be prepared to subsidize members of the English republican opposition, like Algernon Sidney, in order to weaken Charles II.[35]

Charles wanted money from Louis, whose revenue was five times larger than his own. Louis XIV, despite the progress of his own navy, wanted the English navy on his side. Charles also promised to support Louis' claim to the Spanish succession, provided he himself obtained most of Spain's overseas empire. Both Louis and Charles were motivated by desire to seize Dutch territory and trade, as well as by fury with Dutch 'insolence'.[36]

On 24 February 1670 Madame and Monsieur returned to Saint-Germain, three weeks after their departure following the arrest of the Chevalier de Lorraine. Madame and Louis began to prepare a treaty with Charles II in a private room in the chateau.[37] In May 1670, while Louis and the court were inspecting Lille, Madame, accompanied by a 'reduced' household of 237, visited Charles in Dover Castle. According to the English Ambassador Ralph Montagu, Monsieur had slept with his wife every night, to try to make her pregnant in order to prevent the visit.[38] Nevertheless the Treaty of Dover was signed on 1 June. Its terms remained secret until the following century.

In return for a subsidy of £150,000 or around 1.5 million livres a year (equivalent to seven weeks of the English revenues), Charles II promised to declare war on the Netherlands in alliance with Louis XIV. The war was to be led by France on land, by England on sea. In addition, he promised to declare himself Catholic and to improve the legal status of Catholics in his three kingdoms. Thus the Anglo-French alliance became linked to the Stuarts' conversion to Catholicism which would destroy it. The Duke of York revered Turenne, under whom he had served from 1651 to 1656, as 'the greatest and most perfect man he had ever known and the best friend he had ever had'.[39] In 1669, a year after Turenne converted to Catholicism in France, the Duke of York ceased attending Anglican services in England. In 1673 he became openly Catholic.

On the other hand Charles II's plans to convert to Catholicism may have been, rather than an act of piety, a calculated gesture to rid himself of a reputation for unreliability and insincerity, woo Louis XIV and extract more money.[40] The timing was left to Charles, and the 6,000 French troops promised if Charles declared himself Catholic were too few to be useful. It was a secret clause of a secret treaty. Until his deathbed conversion to Catholicism, induced as much by illness and York's pressure as by his own piety, Charles II remained a practising Anglican. On his orders, York's daughters Mary and Anne, the heirs to his throne (and future enemies of Louis XIV), were educated away from their father as Anglicans.[41]

On 29 June 1670, two weeks after her triumphant return from Dover, the toast of two courts, Madame died at Saint-Cloud. Louis XIV, who was present, shed more tears than her husband. She was only twenty-six, and the speed of her death invited accusations of poison: the Chevalier de Lorraine was suspected. In reality, as an autopsy showed, peritonitis and a perforated ulcer were the probable causes. Saint-Maurice wrote, 'the court and the kingdom have lost their finest ornament and the ladies will no longer know where to show themselves as the Queen hardly holds court': Marie Thérèse disliked society.[42] In his funeral oration Bossuet told the congregation that Madame had been distinguished by her merit even more than her rank; her kindness had won all hearts, despite 'the divisions all too ordinary in courts'; but, whatever her achievements on earth, 'vanity of vanities, all is vanity.'[43]

Despite her death, Anglo-French intimacy deepened. That summer the Duke of Buckingham and Charles II's illegitimate son the Duke of Monmouth were more 'caressed' by the King with balls, reviews, private audiences and mock battles on the canal at Versailles than any foreigners before them.[44] At times, wrote Henry Savile, an English envoy, Louis XIV used expressions of friendship for Charles II more passionate than 'I ever heard from any man in my whole life. In good earnest I doe hardly see how hee can say much more to his mistresse.'[45]

Madame's diplomacy was continued after 1670 by another female diplomat, one of her *filles d'honneur*, Louise de Kéroualle, a penniless young Bretonne with whom Charles II had fallen in love. At Charles's insistence, and with Louis' encouragement, she moved to England to serve as one of his wife's maids of honour. After a mock wedding in October 1671 'the French bitch', as Londoners called her,[46] became Charles's principal mistress. Created Duchess of Portsmouth in 1673, she was the richest and most important power-broker at court. Her French and British pensions of £40,000 a year were not her only financial rewards. Ministers cultivated her friendship; the French Ambassador treated her as a colleague.[47] The twenty-four-room apartment in Whitehall Palace of 'dearest, dearest fubs', as the King called her, was 'the true Cabinet Council', according to Lord Halifax, one of its shrewdest members, where ministers and courtiers discussed policy and patronage with the King. Decorated with tapestries depicting Louis XIV's palaces, lacquer cabinets and silver vases, it was both politically and aesthetically a corner of France.[48]

Louis was diverted by despatches recounting her quarrels with Charles over his other mistresses; her infection with venereal disease by the King; and his propitiatory offering of a pearl necklace. Louis himself gave her a pair of diamond earrings. His letters to 'ma cousine la duchesse de Portsmouth' express 'esteem', 'affection' and gratitude for her efforts, throughout Charles II's reign, to promote 'parfaite intelligence avec le Roi de la Grande Bretagne'. Her replies expressed determination to promote his interests 'as much as it depends on my small amount of power'. As a reward for her services in England, in 1682 he made her Duchesse d'Aubigny in France – the only woman to have become a duchess in her own right in two kingdoms.[49]

While Madame and Louise de Kéroualle had secured Charles II, Louis' foreign minister Lionne and Louvois had won an alliance with the Elector of Cologne, Maximilian Henry of Bavaria: one of those German sovereigns who, far from being minor figures, helped decide the fate of Europe. This Elector not only ruled a strategic area of the middle land along the Rhine, but was also Sovereign Bishop of Liège. His territories provided a corridor for the movement of troops from France to the Netherlands, bypassing the Spanish Netherlands.

Lionne was helped by the principal French agent in the Holy Roman Empire, a member of a prominent South German dynasty called Wilhelm Egon von Fürstenberg. A friend of Louis' Foreign Minister Lionne and lover of Madame de Lionne, Fürstenberg had had a written contract since 1658 obliging him to further 'all the plans and interests of His Majesty' in the Holy Roman Empire, whose leading personalities he knew well. He was rewarded with French nationality and benefices worth 90,000 livres a year (including the Abbey of Saint-Germain-des-Prés – hence the name given to the rue de Furstemberg beside it). His brother, known as 'Bishop Bacchus' as he ate and drank so much, was principal minister of the Elector of Cologne. Both represented the spirit of Rhineland Francophilia, already expressed in Mazarin's League of the Rhine (and later in Napoleon's Confederation of the Rhine), which would be epitomized in one of the fathers of modern Europe, Chancellor Adenauer, under whom Bonn, on the Rhine, would become capital of West Germany.[50]

In January 1672 the Dutch Ambassador had protested to Louis XIV about his preparations for war, suspecting the Netherlands was the target. The King replied that he would raise even more troops and would then do everything which his interests and his reputation dictated.[51] On 6 April the two kings declared war on the Netherlands. On 27 April Louis left Saint-Germain. On 4 May he wrote to Colbert, 'I find a great part of the troops in the best state in the world; I hope they will soon make themselves and me talked about.' On 5 May he reached Charleroi.[52]

The French army marched in good order – foraging, not pillaging – down the Meuse towards the Rhine. As in 1667, Saint-Maurice praised the King's military professionalism. The King, he wrote on 13 May, 'does everything himself alone, without haste, without a harsh word to anyone; he orders marches, organizes encampments, marks the places for the guards, visits them and makes more effort than any other officer.' In contrast to his elaborate meals at court, on campaign he ate what other officers ate.[53] By 20 May he was outside Liège. On 21 May Saint-Maurice continued: 'The king is constantly on horseback; he takes great care that his army lives and marches in order; he keeps an eye on everything and does not rush, and one would say that he no longer gives a thought to the beauties he has left near Paris . . . he always has the map of the region to hand and speaks to all the officers, listens to everyone and gives orders without consulting anyone . . . Never has a man been more dedicated.' He even provided meals for watching ladies, both bourgoises and peasants. He himself instructed favourite officers such as the Duc d'Enghien, son of the grand Condé, his friend and cousin the Comte de Soissons and the great engineer Vauban.[54]

Moving down the Rhine, on 7 June he was received at Rheinberg by his ally the Elector of Cologne. On 9 June he crossed the Rhine near Wesel. On the 12th, at the suggestion of the Comte de Guiche, French cavalry forded the Rhine at Tolhuys near Nijmegen, swords clenched between their teeth, hands clutching their horses' manes – it was not the deep, German Rhine, but a shallower, Dutch version, with a depth of about 3 feet.[55] The King was infuriated by the cowardice of the Duc de Chevreuse, commander of the Chevau-légers de la Garde, who paid to cross the river by boat.[56]

In what is still remembered in the Netherlands as Rampjaar or disaster year, towns and villages were devastated by French forces. Government bonds could not find buyers. The price of stocks in the Dutch East India Company fell by half. Some merchants moved their business to Hamburg.[57] The Dutch army offered little resistance. Garrisons surrendered without a fight. On 23 June a Dutch general named Godard van Ginkel wrote to his father: 'our whole country for which our forefathers fought for 80 years is on the brink of being lost . . . without even having strongly resisted the enemy.'[58] The condition of the Netherlands was described as *redeloos* (irrational), *radeloos* (desperate) and *reddeloos* (hopeless).[59]

Utrecht, with a population about a third Catholic, refused either to admit William III and his troops or to resist the French army; the French entered on 24 June.[60] Louis XIV had been staying in a succession of Dutch country houses, including Ginkel's house at Amerongen. He arrived outside Utrecht on 1 July, but, wary of unexploded mines in cellars, would not enter until his brother told him it was worth a visit. The Chevalier de Lorraine, returned to favour on account of his military talents and often accompanying Louis, had given a party there for Monsieur and Monmouth. On 3 July Louis XIV rode into Utrecht through streets lined with

Gardes Français, but did not dismount. Nor did he enter the cathedral (the only church that the French returned to Catholic use), where on 30 June his Grand Aumônier, Turenne's nephew the Cardinal de Bouillon, had celebrated the first mass since the Reformation. A boy cried 'Vive le prince!' but no one cried 'Vive le roi!'

For ten days, until 10 July, Louis XIV stayed outside Utrecht in a camp in the park round the castle of Zeist – the furthest he would ever travel from France. His camps, prepared by his favourite officer M. de Chamlay, Maréchal Général des Logis, were like small cities, with their own hospitals, supplies and orderly rows of tents.[61] The city librarian Everard Booth called it the Camp of Mars. The King's bedroom in his tent became 'la chambre du roi' – as in a French palace, you had to take off your hat to the royal bed. Booth also noted that the King had his pet dogs with him.[62]

French officers, however, had failed to retain control of Muiden, 9 miles from Amsterdam, briefly occupied on 20 June and the key to Dutch water defences. Estrades' advice to keep Muiden (as former French Ambassador in The Hague, he understood dykes) had arrived too late. On 22 June the Dutch commanders opened the sluices in the dykes, putting a vast lake, stretching from Rotterdam to Amsterdam, between Zeeland and Holland and the French army. Louis XIV was cheated of the main prize.[63]

Many observers blamed him for following the advice of Louvois rather than Condé. On 28 June the young English diplomat Sydney Godolphin, attached to French headquarters, wrote to Lord Clifford: 'if the king went back to Paris and left the Prince de Condé his army to prosecute the war, I believe you would soon hear of him at Amsterdam or the Hague.' The cautious King always put his army first, confirming that his wars were fought for it, as well as by it. He 'very seldom fails to reward those who deserve it before they expect it', and was 'very careful to provide for the convenience of his soldiers, always marching on horseback in the heat and in the rain'.[64] Louis preferred sieges, followed by triumphal entries into cities, to risking defeat, and soldiers' lives, in pitched battles.

Errors of diplomacy and the emergence of an unexpected rival further disrupted Louis' triumph. On 26 June Dutch negotiators offered to cede him Maastricht and northern Brabant. They could have been useful bargaining counters for territory nearer France. Again following the advice of Louvois, on 2 July he held out, in addition, for Utrecht, Overijssel, Groningen, Limburg and Guelders; forts on the Rhine; better trade terms; legal rights, including the right to hold public office, for Catholics throughout the United Provinces; an indemnity of 24 million livres; and the annual despatch of a gold medal expressing contrition for past Dutch hostility.[65] In the end he would obtain none of these. Another French mistake – which he attributed in his memoir on the war to 'excessive indulgence' – was that of allowing 20,000 Dutch prisoners of war to be released, in return for payment of their ransoms: their return increased the size of the Dutch army.[66]

Above all Louis XIV faced his first nemesis: his first cousin once removed, William III, Prince of Orange. In July 1672, in his moment of truth, William III put his country before his dynasty or, as he expressed it, his obligations before his interests. He refused the suggestions of Louis XIV and Charles II that, in return for agreeing to their conquests of Dutch territory, he should become sovereign of Holland and Zeeland. The Duke of Buckingham asked him, 'Surely you see that everything is lost?' William III's reply added a phrase to the English language: 'My lord, my country is indeed in danger but there is one way never to see it lost and that is to die in the last ditch.'[67]

The duel between Louis XIV and William III had begun. Louis' invasion handed power to his worst enemy. On 4 July William was elected stadholder by the Estates of Holland and Zeeland (as he would be later in three other provinces). On 6 July the States General of all seven United Provinces appointed him captain general of the Dutch army and admiral general of the navy for life.[68] William III was now not only Prince of Orange in southern France; Count of Nassau in the Holy Roman Empire; and grandson of Charles I with a place in the English succession; but also Stadholder in the Netherlands.

Amsterdam, like Rotterdam and The Hague, was more anti-French, and pro-William III, than the rural provinces of the Netherlands. On 7 July, Louis XIV's personal enemy van Beuningen, who had become a member of Amsterdam city council and an adviser of William III, persuaded the States General, in a famous speech, that their condition was far from desperate and they should break off negotiations with Louis.[69]

On 25 July the Holy Roman Emperor Leopold I allied with the United Provinces, through his envoy in The Hague, the inveterately anti-French Baron de Lisola (whom Louvois wanted to have kidnapped and killed). A second anti-French European alliance, after that of 1668, had been created.[70] Until the end of his life, William III, who soon took charge of Dutch diplomacy, saw his destiny as not only to defend the Netherlands, but also, as he wrote, 'to restore and preserve the liberty of Europe', against the ambitions of Louis XIV to be 'a sovereign arbiter in Christendom'.[71]

Meanwhile, on 10 July Louis had begun his return to France, via Amerongen and Arnhem. Arriving in Saint-Quentin at dawn on 1 August, he was, thanks to relays of horses, back in Saint-Germain by 10 o'clock the same evening, having covered over 80 miles in one day.[72] He had once been a gentle youth who cried easily, and called mercy 'the most royal of all the virtues'. In letters to Queen Christina and Philip IV protesting against attacks on French diplomats in Rome in 1662, he had invoked 'le droit des gens' and 'l'humanité'.[73] In 1666 the Venetian Ambassador had called humanity and horror of bloodshed and cruelty his shining gift.[74]

By 1672, however, he had changed. In the Dutch countryside, on Louvois' orders, French troops unleashed a reign of terror. 'I dare not tell you what excesses pillaging has reached,' wrote their commander the Maréchal de Luxembourg to Louvois on 12 August. Some soldiers were hanged for their crimes.[75] But the policy was repeated in following years, in order to terrorize the inhabitants into paying 'contributions'. Louvois wrote to an army *intendant* to have everything possible burnt, and to the Comte de Calvo: 'you must burn entire villages.'[76]

Louis XIV and Louvois were as surprised by Dutch resistance in 1672, as Wilhelm II and his generals would be by Belgian resistance in 1914. Both monarchs were blinded by power. In the words of Herbert Rowen, biographer of Jan de Witt and of Louis XIV's Foreign Minister M. de Pomponne, the King chose 'brutal methods which repeatedly led precisely to the result he was seeking to avert'.[77] This is not just a twentieth-century view. Even Condé, famous for his ruthlessness, warned Louis XIV of 'the cruel aversion we have attracted to ourselves' through the behaviour of French troops; 'I do not know if it is in the interest of France to continue.'[78] The Marquis de La Fare would complain that France, by its own efforts, had lost 'the domination of Europe' in exchange for its hatred.[79]

In the villages of Zwammerdam and Bodegraven, 2,000 houses were burnt with people inside them. Louvois wrote to Condé: 'all the Dutch who were in the village were grilled . . . not one was allowed to leave the houses.' Other villages also suffered.[80] These atrocities inspired prints entitled *The Mirror of French Tyranny*, published by Romeyn de Hooghe in Amsterdam in 1673. Abraham de Wicquefort, a *frondeur* long established in Amsterdam (who also acted as a French spy), wrote the text. Europe thus wrote and engraved against Louis XIV, as well as fighting back. The Dutch army also massacred and plundered civilians without mercy: Ginkel wrote of 'many atrocities' in the Electorate of Cologne. French propagandists, however, did not publicize them.[81]

William III's power in the Netherlands had been confirmed by the murder of Jan de Witt. In July 1672 de Witt had resigned as grand pensionary of Holland. Many Dutchmen considered him responsible for their defeat, even a traitor – he had orchestrated the 'perpetual exclusion' from politics of the House of Orange since 1650, had been Louis XIV's principal Dutch ally and was still in contact with French diplomats. In a classic political lynching, on 20 August Jan de Witt and his brother Cornelis were led from a prison in The Hague, where they had already been tortured. To cries of 'Oranje boven! de Witt onder!' they were publicly beaten, stabbed and shot by members of the militia, while pastors praised 'the Lord's work'. Their corpses were partly skinned and disembowelled. Fingers, ears and other 'scraps' were sold as souvenirs, or roasted and eaten: the fingers had to be punished for signing the edict of 'perpetual exclusion' against the House of Orange. The corpses were left hanging on the public scaffold as a warning to William III's enemies. To rebut charges of complicity, William III had the same morning left The Hague to visit fortifications east of the city at Woerden. Clearly he had planned the murders, and gave jobs and pensions to some of the perpetrators.[82]

Until the Treaty of Nijmegen in 1678, every year Louis XIV followed a similar pattern. From Saint-Germain or Versailles he left to join his army in late winter or spring, for two or three months.[83] In this war he spent a total of 647 days on campaign.[84] The Queen was regent in his absence: he wrote her long descriptions of his campaigns, intended to be read by others. She presided over some council meetings, including the Conseil Royal des Finances, signing financial and political documents and receiving ambassadors, for three to four months during the campaigning season in 1673, 1675, 1676 and 1677, and was praised for her prudence, directness and application.[85]

Each campaign was planned in detail in advance by the King, Louvois and a few favoured officers. Sometimes Louis XIV himself drafted an *ordre de marche* for troops, of which Chamlay later made a fair copy. In this golden age of French cartography, *géographes du roi* were making increasingly accurate maps of France and abroad, usually dedicated to the King.[86] The Maréchal de Luxembourg called Chamlay 'a living map', and he soon became Louis XIV's chief of staff, and chief military cartographer.[87]

Louis XIV also controlled campaigns through detailed memoranda to his generals, usually discouraging pitched battles, although he was capable of leaving decisions to the commander in the field. When not on campaign, he continued his normal routines: work with the ministers; supervising building projects; hunting and entertaining; attending mass; and giving audiences to high officials and ambassadors.

Each year the French army had a different target. In 1673 it was one of the strongest fortresses in Europe, Maastricht, 'the bulwark of the Netherlands', in the southern extension of the country, and guarding a

crucial bridge (still there today) across the Meuse. Maastricht was protected by a panoply of moats, counterscarps, palisades, ramparts, walls
and outworks. Condé and Turenne were sent to command armies in the
Netherlands and Germany respectively. Louis XIV wanted sole credit for
the fall of Maastricht.[88]

On 11 June 1673, Louis XIV laid siege to the city with an army of
24,000 men: the first major siege organized by Vauban. A magnificent
bird's-eye view by Jean Paul shows the King's sumptuous tent south-east
of the city, far from the action, near the village of Woerle. Surrounded
by rows of French army tents like regiments on parade, as far as the eye
could see, Maastricht had little hope. At this high point of the Anglo-
French alliance, the Duke of Monmouth, commander of the Life Guards,
commanded an English regiment in French service called the Royal Anglais
(8,700 English troops in all were fighting with the French army), and
would receive one of the five quarters around the city, the Quartier de
M. de Monmouth: the others were the Quartiers du Roi, de Monsieur,
des Ministres and de M. de Louvois. In his account of the siege Louis XIV
would single out Monmouth for praise.[89]

In addition to firing upon the city walls with cannon, Vauban ordered
a subterranean labyrinth of trenches to be dug up to the walls, not directly
but in zigzag patterns, perhaps learnt from the Turkish attack on the
Venetian town of Candia in 1669. These trenches made it more difficult
for the defenders to see and fire on the enemy and, in addition, allowed
miners to approach the base of the fortifications and plant mines.[90]

The French and English, after some difficult fighting, crossed the moat
and seized a crescent-shaped fortification which would become the scene
of the toughest fighting of the siege. The Dutch recaptured the crescent
soon afterwards, but when the Duke of Monmouth rallied his troops to
a second assault, fighting in water up to their knees, the Dutch were driven
back once more. Finally, Louis XIV ordered the artillery into action. The
Dutch surrendered with the honours of war, leaving with drums beating
and flags flying.[91]

On 3 July 1673, after only three weeks, as Vauban had predicted, Louis
XIV made a formal entry into Maastricht. He could have stayed in the
magnificent town hall finished in 1664 – a miniature version of the town
hall of Amsterdam – but, as at Utrecht in 1672, preferred to live in tents
outside the city. Vauban added several lunettes to Maastricht, improved
the canal system and made provision for countermines.

John Churchill was then serving in the Royal Anglais regiment under
French overall command. Partly as a reward for his courage in the attack
on Maastricht (he was wounded while protecting Monmouth), 'the

handsome Englishman', as he was called, became a lieutenant colonel, master of the robes and gentleman of the bedchamber of James, Duke of York. He was also formally presented to Louis XIV and, already an English colonel, was promoted to the same rank in the French army in March 1674. Continuing to serve in the Royal Anglais under Turenne, he learnt to consider sieges a waste of resources and to appreciate the advantages of a war of movement, as Louis XIV would learn to his cost during the War of the Spanish Succession.[92]

From 31 July to 24 August and 8 to 30 September 1673 the King lived in Nancy, capital of the Duchy of Lorraine, which had been occupied by French troops since 1670 – possibly with the intention of ultimate annexation. Its location between France and the Empire made it strategically vital, and Louis XIV had already in 1661 secured the right to send French troops along 'military roads' through the duchy. Every day, while the Queen visited churches and convents, Louis inspected the bastions and ramparts which French troops were building around the city. It was in Nancy, for the first time, that on 10 August he appeared with a complete wig: hitherto he had only added strands of hair to his own.[93]

He received few cheers, for the people of Lorraine remained loyal to their exiled duke, Charles IV. After Charles IV's death in 1675, his son reigned in exile from Vienna as Duke Charles V, continuing the ancient enmity between the Houses of France and Lorraine, and joining the growing list of Louis XIV's personal enemies: Watteville, Lisola, van Beuningen, William III. In August 1673 an alliance between Austria, Spain and the Netherlands aimed to return France to the frontiers of 1659.[94]

In the same month, continuing the absorption of Alsace which he had been planning since 1664, Louis XIV installed French garrisons in ten towns in the province, including Colmar, Sélestat and Breisach.[95] City walls were razed and militias abolished. Venality was introduced for public offices, thereby linking officials' fortunes to France. The French language was imposed for use in official documents. A brief reoccupation by Imperial troops in 1674–5 reinforced the inhabitants' acceptance of French rule.[96]

That autumn French forces retreated from their last outposts in the Netherlands, except Maastricht. Luxembourg had failed to take Amsterdam, even though the water barrier protecting it had frozen over in the winter of 1672/3. The ice proved too thin to support his soldiers.[97] In November 1673 William of Orange, who had increased the size of the Dutch army to 80,000, took Bonn, capital of Louis XIV's ally the Elector of Cologne.[98]

On 6 October 1673, French forces took Trier, capital of another powerful Archbishop Elector of the Holy Roman Empire; the excuse was that this prevented the Spanish army from doing so. Pomponne, the new Foreign Minister who favoured moderation, Colbert and Turenne had opposed the attack, but Louvois had supported it. The move horrified M. de Gravel, French envoy to the Imperial Diet at Regensburg. French diplomats, left deliberately uninformed, felt betrayed. His generals warned Louis XIV against harsh methods in warfare; his diplomats warned him against harsh phrases in French declarations: 'fury against France is the dominant passion and virtually the universal distemper in Germany,' wrote Gravel. Trier was recaptured in 1675 by Charles V of Lorraine.[99]

Again showing the power of private feelings in public affairs, the war was fuelled not only by the King's rage against the Netherlands, and French nobles' love of fighting, but also by his passion for Madame de Montespan, as is shown by letters he wrote to her in 1673 from the siege of Maastricht. From Brussels Lisola gloated to Chancellor Hofer in Vienna, 'we have intercepted four letters to Madame de Montespan written in the king's hand, they are filled with countless blandishments . . . that fully reveal the abjectness of this prince and the nature of his ruling passion. But the most loathsome thing is that the letters contain detailed descriptions of the siege as if they were intended for one of his generals. How far from such shameful softness is our Emperor!' Monsieur's second wife, often called Madame Palatine to distinguish her from her predecessor Madame Henriette, later claimed that the reason Louis XIV left the army in 1672 had been his desire to see Madame de Montespan after the birth on 20 June 1672 of their child, Louis-César.[100] When she was pregnant – in the language of the day, 'her powder ignited quickly' – Louis delayed his departure for the front.[101] One historian sees the King's love of war as stemming from his 'need to demonstrate his virility to Madame de Montespan and to himself'.[102] In 1676 they timed her return to court from taking the waters at Bourbonne-les-Bains to coincide with his return from fighting in Flanders.[103]

The King also discussed Madame de Montespan in letters to Colbert: 'you have told me nothing in all the letters you have written to me, about the work at Saint-Germain concerning the terraces of the apartment of Madame de Montespan.' Detailed instructions followed about cages and fountains for her birds, so that they could drink water when they wanted. A few months later he was still concerned: 'she recommended me to take care that the reservoir should not lack water so that the fountain plays when she wants.'[104] Phrases in letters to Colbert such as 'After having seen it [a plan] with Madame de Montespan, we both approve that,' and 'I am not yet replying about this as I want to know what Madame de Montespan thinks,' show that they functioned as a couple, in which Montespan often took the decisions.[105] For her part Madame de Montespan would show her interest in war by commissioning as a present for the King a magnificent illuminated manuscript of views of the cities he had captured in 1672, bound in gilded leather, with texts by Racine and Despréaux.

In February 1674, proving that he was not Louis' puppet, Charles II made peace with the Netherlands. English officers and diplomats had been dismayed by the poor performance of the French navy against Dutch ships, and by French atrocities in the Empire. From London, Colbert de Croissy told his brother that trying to maintain the Anglo-French alliance was like sailing against the wind and the tide.[106]

English regiments continued to serve in the French army, even though Louis XIV considered they provided a bad example. Churchill left French service in 1676, when he was refused promotion on the grounds that he was 'too devoted to pleasure' (in other words to his future wife Sarah, and to Lady Castlemaine, the mistress he shared with Charles II).[107]

On 31 March 1674, the Diet of the Empire in Regensburg voted to help the Emperor and the Elector Palatine, whose strategic territory on the middle Rhine was being devastated by French troops. Turenne would 'ruin' thirty-two villages in the Palatinate in July 1674.[108] The Empire itself was, for the first time, at war with France (although the rulers of Bavaria, Mainz and Cologne remained French allies). Louis XIV was denounced as the Monster of the Apocalypse, the enemy of the human race, the new Attila.[109] By the end of 1674, France was fighting alone against an alliance of the Emperor, Spain, Brandenburg, Denmark, the Netherlands and Lorraine.

After Utrecht and Amsterdam in 1672, and Maastricht in 1673, in 1674 Louis' principal target was Franche-Comté, between Burgundy and Switzerland. Although tempted, like many areas in the middle zone, to 'turn Swiss' and join the Swiss Confederation, the Francs-Comtois, loyal to the Spanish monarchy and their own autonomy, resisted more fiercely than in 1668. Like the Dutch, they were spurred by the cruelty of French troops, who burnt alive a hundred villagers from Arcey who had taken refuge in their church. Finally on 15 May, after a four-week siege, Louis made a formal entry into the largest city in the province, Besançon, with the Queen and the Dauphin. Like Lille, it has been French ever since. They stayed for twelve days; by 19 June they were on the road to Fontainebleau.[110]

Resistance – 'la petite guerre' – by 'loups de bois' continued for years: into the eighteenth century some Francs-Comtois preferred to be buried face down, to avoid seeing the French sun.[111] Many priests, especially Capuchin monks, were reported as still 'favouring the service of the King of Spain'.[112] However, Louvois supervised the integration of the province, with the help of three key officials: the Governor, the Duc de Duras, a nephew of Turenne; the Intendant, Michel Camus de Beaulieu, a relation of Colbert; and a local man, Claude Boisot, *greffier* (clerk) in the Parlement, who was convinced, as he wrote to a cousin in 1674, that 'we are French for ever.'[113]

Louis XIV favoured Besançon, to compensate it for its loss of its status as a Free Imperial City. In 1676, in return for a payment of 300,000 livres, he transferred the Parlement, and in 1691 the university, of Franche-Comté from Dole to Besançon. Besançon was formally made capital of the province in October 1677. Provincial Estates were maintained in Artois and Flanders, but the King did not, despite many requests, revive them in Franche-Comté.[114] As in Lille, 'becoming French' meant royal visits; the introduction of venality, almost unknown under the House of Austria, into local office-holding; and the construction of another massive citadel by Louis' favourite engineer Vauban, a walled military city looking down on Besançon from a hill above. The moats are wide enough to serve, today, as the local zoo. In addition Vauban added bastions to every corner of the city walls.[115]

Louis XIV's government varied its system of control to suit different cities and provinces. In Marseille and Franche-Comté it favoured new men, in Lille and Alsace traditional elites. It usually favoured cooperation over confrontation. It allowed local officials and judges increased prestige, better costumes and buildings and more secure exercise of their authority. Since their fortunes were invested in their offices, interest as well as necessity made them French.[116]

In 1675 a conspiracy and two revolts showed that, if the Fronde had been defeated, its spirit survived. Conspirators included the Chevalier de Rohan, a younger son of the Duc de Montbazon and former gambling partner and Grand Veneur of the King. In 1669 he had been forced by his debts, or his audacity in competing for women with the King, to sell his court post. A fallen favourite from a grand family, he wanted revenge on the King – 'ah, if you knew him as I do, you would not like him.' Other participants included Franciscus van den Enden, an atheist who had taught philosophy to Spinoza in Amsterdam before moving to Paris; a noble from Normandy called de Lautréamont; and a Protestant friend of van Beuningen, Jean-François de Paule, Chevalier de Sardan, a bankrupt who called himself 'Syndic général des confédérés de la province de Languedoc'. The Queen Regent of Spain, William III (who signed a treaty with Sardan in April 1674) and the Governor General of the Spanish Netherlands supported the conspirators.

The conspirators' intention, given what they called the 'public misery', was to create a 'free republic' in Normandy with Dutch and Spanish help and a 'corps protestant' in the south. The States General, in accordance with Anne of Austria's promise of 1651 – still remembered by some after twenty-three years – were to be summoned. A reign of terror was planned a hundred years before 1793. Frenchmen declared 'traîtres à la patrie' were to have their goods confiscated for the 'general good' – in other words, revolutionaries would kill their enemies and enrich themselves. A Dutch fleet appeared near Noirmoutier and Fouquet's former stronghold at Belle-Île.

French spies in William III's entourage, however, had kept Louvois and Louis XIV informed. Most of the plotters' plans had been fantasies. Sixty men were arrested: four executed, including the Chevalier de Rohan himself, in front of the Bastille, on 26 November 1675. In the hope of a pardon he had revealed everything. Rohan's death was a reminder that, under Louis XIV as under Louis XIII and Henri IV, the King's friends could betray him.[117]

In the same year there were revolts against taxation. Bordeaux remained, as Colbert had complained in 1663, a city 'which had always started seditions and revolts'.[118] A revolt on 26 March 1675 led to the billeting of eleven regiments on the city. They caused such havoc that many people left. The magistrates referred to 11,000 abandoned houses: 'we are the magistrates of a desolated city.' The Parlement was exiled. A new citadel was built at Bordeaux's expense on the site of a famous Roman amphitheatre, known as the Palace of Gallienus, which was demolished.[119] The city's 'seditious spirit' turned to resignation:

> Pourquoi plaignez vous tant,
> Ces piliers qu'on détruit?

asked a poet.

> Bordelais, Louis règne.
> Obéissez sans bruit.[120]

('Why lament
These fallen columns?
Bordelais, Louis reigns.
Obey without protest.')

In Rennes on 18 April 1675, another revolt broke out, provoked by the increase in paper money and taxation. Tax offices were sacked. Some of the local militia sided with the rebels. Peasants attacked chateaux. Fifteen people died, including the Intendant. The King sent the new Capitaine Lieutenant of his musketeers M. de Forbin, at the head of 6,000 men, to restore order. Trees sagged under the weight of rebels hanged from their branches. Madame de Sévigné declared: 'we are all ruined.'[121]

William III had, however, been deluding himself when he wrote to Fagel, Grand Pensionary of Holland, on 10 August 1675 that 'everyone' in France was discontented and the King would be obliged to make peace. The war continued. As Lisola had fuelled Francophobia with *Le Bouclier d'estat* in 1667, so did Sardan in 1677 by another incendiary pamphlet, *L'Europe esclave, si l'Angleterre ne rompt ses fers*. It was soon translated into German, English (as *Europe a Slave unless England Break her Chains*) and Flemish.[122]

In 1676 the King missed another chance of proving himself a great general. On 10 May at Hurtebise near Valenciennes, his army was waiting to attack the far smaller army of the Prince of Orange. However instead of ordering an advance, Louis hesitated and asked for advice. A council of war including Louvois, marshals d'Humières, de Schomberg and de La Feuillade, perhaps sensing what Louis and Louvois wanted to hear, advised the King not to command a pitched battle in person. Only the Maréchal de Lorges favoured an immediate attack.

Louis XIV functioned as an institution, as the King bound to listen to official advisers, rather than as the heroic individual part of him would have liked to have been. He said, 'as you all have more experience than I, I yield but with regret.' Putting caution before courage, letting others take the responsibility for decisions, he was too proud to risk defeat, his generals too frightened to risk his person. La Fare later blamed Louvois, 'as fearful as he was insolent'. Louis 'listened too much to prudent counsels when more audacious ones would have placed him above everyone'.[123]

Louis too regretted this missed opportunity. Twenty-three years later, in 1699, the Marquis de Dangeau, who knew him well, recorded a conversation with courtiers in the gardens at Versailles. Louis XIV dropped his mask of royal authority and admitted 'tout bas' that he could be influenced and make mistakes. Again he showed that he knew himself: 'it was the day of his life when most mistakes were made, that he never thought of it without extreme sorrow, that he dreamt of it sometimes at night and always woke up in anger, because he had missed a certain opportunity to defeat the enemy. He put most of the blame on a man that he named to us [M. de Louvois] and even added: he was an unbearable man at all times.'[124]

In contrast to the King's timidity at Hurtebise, his brother Monsieur, helped by Luxembourg, won a decisive victory over William III at Cassel near Saint-Omer on 11 April 1677. William III lost his personal gold and silver services and his maps. Revealingly, Louvois asked the Maréchal de Luxembourg not to send him the Prince's silver or plate, 'but his maps which I ask you to hide well so that you are not obliged to present them to anyone' – probably meaning the King. Maps were power.[125]

According to Visconti, Monsieur went to battle made up (*fardé*), as if going to a ball. His horse was shot under him in the fight. Again in contrast to his brother, he continued to live in Paris, in the Palais Royal, as well as in his own country palace at Saint-Cloud, and at Saint-Germain and Versailles. He was generous and talked to 'everyone'. As a result, 'you had to see the joy of the Parisians for the victory of Monsieur, for the city of Paris loved him greatly.' Visconti implies that Paris loved the King less.[126]

Years later Monsieur's second wife wrote, 'the King was not a coward but . . .' This may be a literary device to suggest what she pretends to deny. With age the King was becoming both more cautious, and more jealous. Monsieur never received a field command again. One of the ablest French diplomats, who knew the King well, M. de Courtin, also an enemy of Louvois, once warned Condé, in a private letter, that winning a victory over the Dutch would be 'the shortest route to Chantilly': in other words, to retirement in his country house. The King wanted victories for himself, his son and grandsons, but feared successful generals in junior branches of his dynasty.[127]

Valenciennes, where Turenne had been defeated by Condé in 1656, fell on 17 March 1677 after an eight-day siege. On the King's express orders, to the dismay of his troops, the city, despite its support for the King of Spain, was spared pillage.[128] One of the strongest forts in the Southern Netherlands, Cambrai had resisted French troops in 1649 and 1657. On 19 April 1677, after a siege of twenty-nine days, Louis XIV entered in triumph. Like other conquests that year, it has remained French to this day (and still owns the magnificent portrait of the King by Hyacinthe Rigaud, which he gave to the city, and paintings of the siege by van der Meulen). Carts went round the city to remove inhabitants' weapons, which they had been told to stack at their front doors.[129] As in other conquered cities, Valenciennes and Cambrai received confirmation of their privileges and exemptions, and visits by Louis, sometimes with the Queen, through streets lined with tapestries, ending with a Te Deum and fireworks. Each city was also obliged to pay for the construction of a new citadel.[130]

The remark made of the dukes of Savoy, that they devoured Lombardy like an artichoke, leaf by leaf, could also have been made of Louis XIV and the Southern Netherlands. On 11 and 25 March 1678 respectively, Ghent and Ypres, both within 50 miles of Lille, terrified by French bombardments, surrendered to his armies after short sieges, undertaken not in order to secure more conquests but in order to force the Netherlands to make peace. Only a minority in the Netherlands now wanted to continue fighting.[131]

As French armies won cities and battles, Charles II again proved unreliable. With his consent, on 4 November 1677 William III married his first cousin Mary, daughter of the Duke of York, in St James's Palace – to please Parliament and perhaps to unite two claims to the throne (since William considered the Duke of York's children by his first marriage to Anne Hyde morganatic). Louis XIV, rightly, regarded the marriage as equivalent to losing an army: it brought his worst enemy closer to the throne of England.[132] For the next five years Charles, trapped in the hysteria of the Popish Plot and the Exclusion Crisis (when more than forty English Catholics were executed on trumped-up charges), was more anti- than pro-French. Even the Duke of York, more pro-French than his brother, said to a committee of MPs, 'nothing could be more evident than that France intended an universal monarchy and nothing but England could hinder them and that without it [war with France] the king would endanger his crown.' Charles signed a treaty of alliance with the Netherlands in July 1678.

Finally peace with the Netherlands was signed in the Dutch town of Nijmegen, on 10 August 1678, although not with the Empire until 5 February 1679. Chosen because it was on the Rhine near Louis' army's crossing-place in 1672, with good communications, Nijmegen showed that the Netherlands played a central role in diplomacy as well as trade. The main French envoy was the Comte d'Estrades, a veteran of the Congress of Münster in 1648, who had also been ambassador in London and The Hague.[133]

William III was so bellicose that four days later, on 14 August, he attacked the French army under Luxembourg at the battle of Saint-Denis, in the hope of breaking the peace which he knew had been signed. Five thousand more soldiers were killed. William III and Monmouth, who had switched sides and was now serving against Louis XIV, fought bravely in hand-to-hand combat, but the battle ended without a clear victor.[134]

Thanks to French victories, and agents such as Fürstenberg and the Elector of Cologne, French influence in the Empire was at its apogee. By the Treaty of Nijmegen, the Elector of Brandenburg was forced to return recently conquered territory to Louis XIV's ally Charles XI of Sweden. France won the Franche-Comté, and the town of Freiburg on the far side of the Rhine; kept Cambrai, Valenciennes and Ypres; but had to evacuate Maastricht and Ghent and cede Courtrai and Furnes. Such territorial gains were

relatively small compared to the Dutch offers of 1672, and to Louis XIV's
ambitions. As he wrote in his 'Relation de la campagne de 1678', he had
hoped to make the campaign more 'useful' than previous ones, to keep
Mons, Ghent, Brussels and Luxembourg and 'to finish the conquest of the
whole country'.

Louis XIV's wars were, however, ends as well as means. They were
designed to conquer time as well as space, immortality as well as territory.
He wrote in his memoirs, 'a well-brought-up heart is difficult to content
and can only be fully satisfied by glory but also this sort of pleasure over-
whelms it with happiness by making it believe that it alone was capable
of the undertaking and worthy to succeed.' He added, 'Glory is not a
mistress which can be neglected.'[135] In 1673 he had taken Maastricht,
rather than the capital of the Spanish Netherlands Brussels, because, as
he told one of his commanders, Maastricht was a famous citadel, which
had in the past resisted other armies for months; its fall made Parisians
light bonfires.[136] So far from France, it was unlikely to be retained at a
peace treaty.

In the official histories written by Chamlay and Racine, and in innumerable *éloges historiques*, Louis XIV was called the terror and delight
of the human race. He had become 'the victor and arbiter of all Europe
which had united against him'; his acts were 'never equalled in the past
and impossible to repeat in the future'.[137] Colbert compared him to Julius
Casear (who had taken Besançon 1,700 years earlier), and thanked God
for having been born under 'a king who will have no more limits to his
power than those of his will'.[138]

Louis XIV commemorated his campaigns in detailed historical
accounts, including marching instructions, cavalry and infantry regulations, correspondence with generals and with Louvois. They show that
he was a better military administrator than general. Used to teach his
successors, his accounts were published in 1806, by Général de Grimoard,
to whom Louis XVI had entrusted them before the revolution.[139] They
attribute all initiatives to himself, and diminish the roles of Turenne,
Condé and Louvois.[140]

In addition illuminated manuscript records of Louis XIV's campaigns
and sieges, bound in green and gold leather, were prepared for his private
library, where he could peruse them in winter. Now in the Bibliothèque
Nationale, they represent his campaigns as disciplined progresses. Villages
and camps, guns, helmets, flags, trophies, fauns and dragons are beauti-
fully painted.[141] The marching instructions and passwords are recorded:
Saint-Pierre et Rome, Saint-Jean et Blois, Saint-Louis et Paris. Louis XIV
is depicted as a Roman emperor, his soldiers as centurions.

Typical sentences include: 'A squadron of Gardes du Corps will march at the head of the Treasury which will be followed by the hospital, supplies, the carriages of the Quartier du Roi and after by all those of the Army'; 'Soldiers will be forbidden to touch peasants for three leagues around the camp or to enter places under safeguards, under threat of death.'[142] The King is represented as all powerful, his army as perfectly disciplined. After the fall of the town of Condé in April 1676, for example, 'the King had all the works of trenches and lines erased, chose the troops and officers whom he wished to compose its garrison, and gave all the orders necessary for the safety of this city. Nothing escaped the foresight of His Majesty that day.' At night he went from bivouac to bivouac, checking that all was in order.[143] In 1677 the panegyrist of the conquest of Valenciennes and Cambrai writes of 'the King, whose prudence fatal to the prince of Orange has always [sic] annihilated his designs'.[144] In the history of the 1678 campaign a figure symbolizing the French monarchy is pulled on a triumphal carriage by lions and cherubs, while the French cock drives the Belgian lion into a cave.[145]

In addition to inspiring panegyrics, Louis XIV's campaigns received more tangible commemoration. A marble relief by Coysevox, executed in 1673 for the Salon de la Guerre in Versailles, shows the King on horseback trampling over his enemies at the moment of crossing the Rhine, while Clio, the Muse of History, records the event. On the ceiling, painted by Charles Le Brun, France, armed and sitting on a cloud, is surrounded by Victories and the King's three conquered enemies: the Empire, Spain and the Netherlands. Bellona, goddess of war, subdues Rebellion and Discord – acknowledgement that external war could be used to solve internal problems.[146]

Wars also inspired monuments in Paris. The less time the King spent in his capital, the more sculptures of him were erected there, as if in compensation for his absence. The city paid for two magnificent arches, to celebrate the war of 1672–8. The Porte Saint-Denis, built by François Blondel in 1672–3 across the rue Saint-Denis – then the city's main north–south artery – is adorned with Roman trophies: armour, helmets, scabbards and triumphant sculptures and, at the King's suggestion, the inscription 'Ludovico magno'. Holland, sculpted by Michel Anguier, is represented both as a terrified old woman and as a skinned lion; the Rhine as a stricken river god. On the north side of the arch the bewigged King, on horseback, represented as a triumphant general rather than a divine-right monarch, accepts the surrender of Maastricht. An inscription boasts that in 1672 the French army had crossed the rivers Rhine, Waal, Meuse and Issel and conquered three provinces and forty fortresses in sixty days. It does not mention the French retreat a year later.

To the right the more austere Porte Saint-Martin, across the rue Saint-Martin, boasts of the King twice taking Besançon and Franche-Comté and 'breaking' the German, Spanish and Dutch armies: 'Et fractis Germanorum, Hispanorum Batavorumque exercitibus 1675'. Sculptures by Martin van den Bogaert and Pierre Bullet show Louis XIV both as a Roman emperor in armour and as a naked Hercules with his club.

In reality they sculpted too soon. Enemy armies had not been 'broken'. Far from being a terrified old woman, the Netherlands would later help to create European coalitions against Louis XIV, which would bring France to its knees.

11

To the Rhine

After the Netherlands, Louis XIV turned to the Rhine. For many French-
men, including the King, the Rhine was France's natural eastern frontier.
'Quand Paris boira le Rhin, toute la Gaule aura sa fin' ('When France
drinks the Rhine, all Gaul will have found its limits'), the poet Jean le
Bon had written in 1568.[1] Vauban believed that the 'natural limits' of
France included the 'two oceans', the Pyrenees, the Alps and the Rhine.[2]
To many Germans, however, 'old Father Rhine' was a symbol of their own
country, as its prominence in the medieval *Song of the Nibelungen*
suggested.[3]

Along the Rhine, Alsace was a natural target for Louis XIV. By the
Treaty of Westphalia in 1648, France had acquired territory in the south
and ill-defined rights over some other areas. But the province remained
part of the Holy Roman Empire. M. du Val, a *géographe du roi* who visited
it in 1662, considered it one of the wealthiest provinces in Europe. Its
rivers were well stocked with fish, it had mines of silver, copper and lead,
excellent pasture and no fallow land. 'Alsace wine is very agreeable to
drink and so much is produced that it is transported to Switzerland, to
Swabia, to Bavaria, to Lorraine, to Flanders and even to England.' While
most of the population spoke Alsatian dialects, nobles had begun to wear
French clothes and speak French.[4]

There were other tempting prospects along the Rhine. Heidelberg, with
an ancient university, was capital of the Palatinate, ruled by Charles Louis,
Elector Palatine, a first cousin, through his mother 'the Winter Queen' of
Bohemia, of Charles II of England. The last coup of the aged Princesse
Palatine, widow of Charles Louis' brother Edward, had been to arrange
the wedding of her niece, the Elector's daughter Elizabeth Charlotte, to
Monsieur, as his second wife, in November 1671.[5]

Her marriage was a political and sexual disaster. Like the first Madame,
she was tormented by her husband's lovers. French armies devastated her
homeland, the Palatinate, in the summer of 1674. Writing that 'the army

of the Emperor and the laws of war had forced him to do it against his own inclination and against the desire he has always had to spare the lands of the Empire,' Louis XIV apologized for his soldiers' cruelty.[6]

Further down the Rhine lay the prosperous cities of Coblenz, Mainz and Cologne, capitals of the three ecclesiastical electors of the Holy Roman Empire, the Archbishops of Trier, Mainz and Cologne – hence the Rhine's medieval English name 'Priest Street'. The Archbishop of Trier resided in Coblenz, as it is strategically situated at the confluence of the Rhine and the Moselle. Cologne had in 1288 driven out its Archbishop. He resided in Bonn, while Cologne became a Free Imperial City. A sign of the electorate of Cologne's importance and close links with France had been its selection, both by Marie de Médicis in 1641–2 and by Mazarin in 1651–2, as their place of exile: in the 1680s its absorption by France was one of Louis XIV's long-term aims. Master of the most terrifying army in Europe, with a total size, in theory, at the beginning of 1678 of over 250,000 soldiers, Louis XIV seemed to have the middle land between France and the Rhine in his grasp.

After the Treaty of Nijmegen, Louis decided to use French laws, backed by French troops, as an instrument of expansion in the middle land. The fact that inhabitants spoke German dialects now called Alsatian, Letze-burgisch, Francique, Lotharingien or Rhenish was then of minor importance. Whatever their language, Louis believed he could transform them into Frenchmen, like his Catalan, Provençal and Flemish subjects. In October 1679 he established three sovereign law courts known as *chambres de réunion*. One was attached to the Parlement of Besançon, covering Franche-Comté and its neighbours; another to the Conseil Souverain of Breisach, for Alsace; a third to the Parlement of Metz for Lorraine and the three bishoprics of Metz, Toul and Verdun. Their task was to examine treaties, registers, estate deeds and other documents concerning sovereignty, allegiance, jurisdiction and land ownership. They then summoned existing sovereigns or their representatives to provide documentary proof of their rights. If they could not do so, their lands were declared French territory by *arrêts de réunion*. In other words, the *chambres de réunion* provided a façade of legality for annexation by France.[7] The policy had the enthusiastic support of Louvois, who as secretary of state for war was responsible for Alsace and the three bishoprics.

On 9 August 1680 lawyers proclaimed full French sovereignty over all Alsace, from the principality of Montbéliard in the south to the cities of Landau, Wissembourg and Haguenau in the north. Protests from the princes and cities concerned to the Diet of the Empire had no effect. France was close and strong; the Diet, sitting in Regensburg on the Danube, was weak and distant. Many began to fear that Louis XIV's ambitions extended beyond Alsace to the other side of the Rhine.[8]

Saarbrücken was declared a French city – in the strategic interzone, now called the Saarland, which France would rule again in the periods 1792 to 1815, 1918 to 1936 and 1945 to 1956. In 1680 Louis gave orders to build a citadel on the banks of the River Saar, on a site chosen by Vauban called Sarrelouis. In 1683 Louis XIV visited it with his court and granted a coat of arms showing the sun dispersing clouds, below three royal fleurs-de-lys.[9] Declared a fief of the Bishop of Metz by the *chambre de réunion* in 1680, the principality of Zweibrücken was also annexed to France, although its sovereign was Louis XIV's ally Charles XI of Sweden. Refusing Louis XIV's offers to buy his rights, he began to turn against Sweden's French alliance.[10]

France also advanced up the valley of the Moselle, along the route which Louis XIV and his army had taken in 1672. The fortifications of Trier were demolished, despite the Elector's protests. A fortress called Mont Royal was built on a strategic point, east of Trier, dominating the valleys of both the Meuse and the Moselle in order, wrote Sourches, 'to make all Germany tremble': 'Germany' was already being used as shorthand for the Holy Roman Empire. Louvois claimed that Mont Royal would make the Electors of Cologne, Trier, Mainz and the Palatinate so dependent on France that that frontier would be more secure than the frontier with Flanders.[11]

Further north, half of the duchy of Luxembourg – 3,000 square miles with about 100,000 people – was annexed village by village, *seigneurie* by *seigneurie*, either through the *arrêts de réunion* of the *chambre de réunion* or by force. Law officers were sent out by the *chambres de réunion*, with armed escorts, to enforce their decrees and exact acts of homage to the King of France. For example, law officers from Metz forced their way into the abbey of Chiny, despite a struggle with monks at the door, and declared it French. The Marquis de Bissy, commander of French troops, wrote to Louvois: 'although the change is sudden, the region is in a state of total obedience.' Another Frenchman gave villagers a barrel of beer with which to drink Louis XIV's health and forget the past.[12]

In an extreme example of a common procedure, in 1683 M. Ravaux, Procureur of the Parlement of Metz, claimed the annexation of the entire duchy of Lorraine as a feudal dependency of the bishop of Metz. On a visit that year (his fifth to this vital garrison city) Louis told the Parlement of Metz: 'I have great pleasure in seeing you and your company here; I am satisfied with the services which it renders me and will remember them on occasions.'[13]

Lorraine, Alsace and the Saar were desirable. Strasbourg, with over 20,000 inhabitants, was the prize. The Sieur de l'Hermine had called it 'one of the largest and finest cities in Germany . . . one of the strongest in Europe . . . governing itself as a republic'. Having seized control from its Bishop in the thirteenth century like Cologne, Strasbourg was a prosperous Free Imperial City, with the tallest cathedral (the towers are 465 feet high) in Europe, an impressive arsenal and defence system, prosperous printers and silversmiths, an ancient university and its own mint. It had long been allied to Berne and Zurich: in 1576, a cauldron of porridge prepared in Zurich had arrived in Strasbourg by river eleven hours later, still warm, an edible token of proximity. It was one of those semi-independent cities, once as confident as monarchies, which had dominated the Holy Roman Empire and northern Italy, and which in France itself before 1660, in the cases of Bordeaux, Marseille and Paris, had even challenged Louis XIV.[14] Moreover, Strasbourg controlled a crucial bridge across the Rhine, built in 1388. In 1674–6 the city had permitted Imperial armies fighting Louis XIV to use the bridge, and had considered joining the Swiss confederation.[15]

In Strasbourg Louis XIV showed himself a statesman. Wary of reaction in the Empire, keen to keep his armies intact, he had resisted his generals', and Fürstenberg's, pressure to attack the city as early as 1678.[16] Instead he pursued a policy of combined intimidation and seduction. The key is revealed in the diary of the Marquis de Sourches, written without hindsight, at once critical and accurate. In April 1682, commenting on the King allowing the canons of Strasbourg to choose their own bishop, rather than imposing his own (they chose the pro-French Wilhelm Egon von Fürstenberg to please him), Sourches wrote: 'he had to do everything not to repel the other cities of Germany from entering under his domination.' As Ulm and Cologne feared, 'the other cities', and bishoprics, in the Empire were the next targets.[17]

An earlier letter of M. de La Vauguyon of 6 June 1681 to Louis XIV claimed that, if the chapter of Strasbourg was treated well, France would attract 'the ecclesiastical princes, who are continually anxious and oppressed, for lack of protection, and who all together, it seems to me, would not abhor the sovereignty of Your Majesty if they were assured that they would keep under their domination the same privileges that they possess under the Empire and that they should not fear that after some time their subjects would be charged with *tailles* and other taxes with the result that they could no longer draw anything from them themselves'. Privileges and taxes, as well as language and religion, could decide national loyalties: perhaps France could absorb the electorates of Mainz, Cologne and Trier.[18] The Elector of Mainz assured a French diplomat that he preferred the King of France as his neighbour to German Protestants.[19]

Christophe Günzer, the secretary of the Strasbourg city council, had been won in advance, as were the Catholic canons of the cathedral.[20] An economic blockade was started in 1680. The war of 1672 to 1678, when Louis XIV had taken so many Flemish cities, showed the futility of other cities opposing the French army. Moreover, Turckheim and Haguenau, north of Strasbourg, had been sacked and burnt by French troops in 1677.[21] The terror Louis XIV used on campaign facilitated his later annexations. From July 1681 he and Louvois prepared to take Strasbourg.

Realizing its weakness, the Senate of Strasbourg wrote to the Emperor Leopold I in Vienna that it preferred to bow to the 'terrible power of His Most Christian Majesty' rather than to risk their lives and their city by 'imprudent stubbornness'. They had 'to submit [themselves] to the will of God and accept what conditions His Most Christian Majesty will deign to prescribe'. At the same time they assured Louvois of their city's readiness to accept the King's 'sovereign protection'.[22] In Vienna, according to the French envoy M. de Sébeville, the government was prepared to accept all losses beyond the Rhine, 'as long as he [Louis XIV] stayed there and did not pass this river'.[23]

The French occupation of Strasbourg may have been hastened by the news that the Emperor had come to an agreement with rebels whom Louis had been subsidizing in Hungary, thereby releasing troops to help Strasbourg.[24] By 17 September, as shown by a letter from Louvois to a French commander, M. de la Frégeolière, the decision to move on Strasbourg had been taken. On 26 September, instead of going hunting at Chambord as planned, Louis XIV announced his departure for Strasbourg.[25]

On 28 September the local French commander M. de Montclar advised 'MM. de Strasbourg' that he wanted to 'agree with you about everything à l'amiable' – in plain French, they should not resist.[26] On 29 September the French Resident in Strasbourg M. Frischmann wrote to Montclar that the magistrates had removed powder from the cannon on the walls, so no one could use them 'imprudently'. The guilds favoured a show of resistance, only in order to achieve a more honourable 'accommodation' with the King. At night there was not a sound in the street.[27] Desire not to be seen to oppose the winning side prevailed over dreams of independence. Louvois, who had arrived near the city, told the Senate to open the gates to the King's troops immediately, or he could not guarantee their good behaviour. In any case, he could take the city when he wished.[28]

Having consulted with 'all the bourgeoisie', the Senate of Strasbourg dropped its ideals in exchange for a deal. By a treaty probably drafted by

the Senate itself, which Arsène Legrelle, its best historian, has compared
to a marriage contract, on 30 September 1681 it recognized Louis XIV
as the city's 'sovereign lord and protector'. In return, as in Lille in 1668,
all the city's privileges, rights and customs were confirmed. Louis again
showed a light touch. An urban republic was absorbed in a monarchy; but
the Senate and magistrates, colleges, law courts and mint stayed as they
were. The bourgeois continued to enjoy tax exemptions. The Lutheran
university continued to teach German as well as French law – and would
later, for that reason, be attended by Herder and Goethe (a rival Catholic
university would be founded near by in 1703). The only church of which
Lutherans lost control was the cathedral, returned to the Catholics from
whom it had been taken in 1560. The bourgeois of the city were allowed
to keep their weapons, as was not the case in other towns.[29] To protect
the commerce of the city, there was no diminution of the tolls it was
allowed to levy. To remove memories of opposition to Louis, registers of
the Senate's debates before the French occupation were destroyed, as those
of the Parlement de Paris during the Fronde had been.[30]

The King, meanwhile, delighted by Strasbourg's submission 'to my
obedience', was on his way, in a procession of 400 carriages.[31] To distract
courtiers from the journey's horrors – Sourches wrote that they would
long remember their night in the village of Germiny – the King allowed
them to gamble for high stakes. He himself, however, grown serious with
middle age, every evening had 'very long conversations with madame de
Maintenon'. Madame de Maintenon, governess of his elder children by
Madame de Montespan, was now a declared favourite – not yet, perhaps,
a mistress. She had been appointed second *dame d'atours* of the new
Dauphine in 1680: a post especially created to justify her presence at court,
and her apartment in the central block of Versailles.[32]

As well as his hours alone with Madame de Maintenon, the King's
insistence on being accompanied by large numbers of ladies, even to the
furthest corners of his kingdom, showed his addiction to their company.[33]
In 1681, instead of going straight to Strasbourg, he first inspected Breisach
and Freiburg in Breisgau on the far side of the Rhine, conquered in 1648
and 1678 respectively. Breisach controlled a bridge over the Rhine and
was considered the door into Germany.[34] On 18 October Sourches noted
that the King, after inspecting the troops and the fortifications at Breisach,
'gave dinner to all the ladies of the court . . . in the evening he supped
again with the ladies and the next day he returned to see the citadel . . .
After having seen Fribourg with extreme pleasure, the King again dined
there with the ladies.'[35]

At Ensisheim on 20 October he gave a formal reception for

twenty-three ambassadors of the Swiss cantons. After hearing their respectful speeches and salutations, he assured them:

> seeing you so well intentioned, I am delighted to have come to this region to see you and to confirm to you that I am more than ever determined to maintain the alliance and the treaties which have for so long been concluded between France and the Swiss and the more I am your neighbour [a reference to his new fort at Huningue on the Rhine, at the gates of Basel] the more marks of my friendship and affection I will give you.[36]

Then he advanced to Strasbourg.

The Bishop, the French agent Franz Egon von Fürstenberg, had already entered the city on 20 October in a triumphal chariot escorted by French cuirassiers, as well as his own bodyguards. He began to redecorate the cathedral, but told Louvois that cannon and 30,000 French troops would do more to convert the city than missals and rosaries.[37] A famous preacher, Fléchier, an *aumônier* of the Dauphine, wrote that he had never heard so many drums and trumpets. 'What a city, mademoiselle! Fine streets, good houses, rich merchants, handsome people, everything there breathes well-being.'[38]

The weather for Louis XIV's state entry on 23 October was excellent. The King, greeted by repeated cannon salutes, was accompanied by the Queen, Monsieur and Madame, the Dauphin and Dauphine in a carriage drawn by six grey horses; by court officials and ladies, including both Madame de Montespan and Madame de Maintenon; Gardes du Corps, Mousquetaires, guards of the Prévôté and Swiss guards. Troops lined the streets. The keys of the city were presented. Church bells rang. Immediately after he arrived at the residence of the Margrave of Baden-Durlach, he went with Louvois and Vauban to inspect the site between the city and the Rhine chosen for the new citadel. The presence in Strasbourg of what Sourches called 'a very great assembly of German princes', including the widowed Electress Palatine, mother of Madame, the rulers of Baden and Württemberg and envoys from other princes, showed that they too, like Strasbourg, were turning towards France. Opinion in the Empire was horrified. Leibniz, the German philosopher and genealogist who had become a political adviser to the House of Hanover, lamented that the Rhine, once in the middle of the Empire, now marked its frontier.[39]

On 24 October the King and Queen gave thanks at a Te Deum in the cathedral, kneeling and kissing the cross after they had entered. At the head of the clergy of his diocese, Fürstenberg, Bishop of Strasbourg, blessed the King, comparing himself to Simeon saying his Nunc Dimittis in the New Testament. He too could now depart in peace, having seen 'the man' in the Temple of the Lord: Jesus Christ in Simeon's case, Louis XIV in Fürstenberg's. That afternoon Louis inspected the bridge over the Rhine at Kehl and the new citadel, giving 2,000 louis to the soldiers digging the foundations. Louvois and others ordered some of the silverwork for which the city was famous.[40]

The King left Strasbourg on 27 October. On the way back he inspected forts and towns, such as Saverne, Phalsbourg, Sarrebourg, Nancy, Thionville and Longwy. Between Longwy and Longuyon on 4 November the guides got lost; the Queen and the princesses were separated from their maids and had to use what linen the King could spare. The Queen wept for fear of being kidnapped by Spanish troops from Luxembourg. They slept in a farmhouse, surrounded by animals: Madame de Montespan slept on straw. The Dauphine and the Princesse de Conti (the King's daughter by Louise de La Vallière), however, were 'delighted with this disorder'. Long afterwards, the women complained of the 'incommodities' they endured on the journey, although they were only a fraction of what their male relations suffered every year on campaign.[41] By 13 November Louis XIV and the court were back at Saint-Germain.

The annexation of Strasbourg was one of the apogees of the reign. It went like clockwork. Not a drop of blood was shed. Thereafter Strasbourg and Alsace continued to enjoy a treble identity, French, German and Alsatian. They spoke and speak three languages (French only became fully dominant after 1960), enjoyed three cultures and practised three forms of Christianity: in 1697, of Strasbourg's 26,481 inhabitants, 19,839 were Lutheran, 5,119 Catholic and 1,523 Calvinist.[42]

Protestants continued to enjoy freedom of worship in this province of Catholic France. From 1684 a legal arrangement called the *simultaneum* allowed Catholics and Lutherans in Alsace to use the same churches at different times, as in some churches they still do. Catholics used the choir, Protestants the nave.[43] Their coexistence continued despite Louis XIV's persecution of Protestants elsewhere in the kingdom. Louvois wrote to a magistrate on 11 December 1682: 'His Majesty wants liberty of conscience to be total in Strasbourg.'[44] This attitude persisted among French officials. The Contrôleur Général wrote in the margin of a letter from the Maréchal d'Huxelles in 1701: 'il ne faut point toucher aux usages de l'Alsace.'[45] Collaboration worked.

Strasbourg did, however, in time become more French and more Catholic. In 1683 Louis XIV returned to see the great fortress built by Vauban between the city and the Rhine. A commemorative medal was struck with the famous but unfortunately inaccurate inscription 'Clausa Germanis Gallia' – 'Gaul closed to the Germans'. Louis XIV allowed an Imperial engineer to inspect the new citadel, and even to be given a copy of its plan, and to review the enormous garrison, in order to convince the Emperor of the permanence of French sovereignty.[46]

Chamilly, the French military commander in the city, gloated in his letters about the obedience of the people of Strasbourg, 'timid, ignorant and afraid of everything'. His surprise may indicate how disobedient Louis XIV's officers found French towns. On 28 December 1681 he wrote to Louvois that with only 300 men the King would be as much master of Strasbourg as of Paris.[47] He ensured that large numbers of soldiers were on duty to prevent disorders during the Christmas fair. Thieves would be hanged on the spot.[48]

The crown favoured Catholics. From 1685 all legal acts had to be in French, from 1687 Catholics were to alternate with Lutherans in municipal offices. In practice until 1750 there were too few Catholics to hold any but the most junior offices. Calvinists and Jews remained marginalized.[49]

Different individuals followed different trajectories. In 1684 Frédéric Ulrich Obrecht, a Protestant professor and *avocat de la ville*, was converted to Catholicism by Bossuet. Two years later he became *préteur royal*, one of the government's officials in the city. However, despite interviews with Bossuet and Louvois, and offers of financial rewards (part of a government campaign to convert prominent Protestants), Dominique de Dietrich, an *Ammeister* or alderman, a personal enemy of Obrecht, refused to convert. He was imprisoned and not allowed to return to Strasbourg until 1685: even then he remained under house arrest until his death in 1692. His descendants, however, while still Lutheran, would become French patriots, sponsoring the first performance of the 'Marseillaise' in 1792 and founding one of the most famous French iron firms, still flourishing today.[50]

After Strasbourg, the Spanish Netherlands – not evacuated by French troops until June 1679 – became the King's next target. Here he practised *petite guerre*. While denying warlike intentions, French troops inflicted on Spanish territory every form of intimidation: deportations, requisitions, 'ravaging' and fires, in order to ruin the country 'from top to bottom', as its government complained. In the end the Spanish Governor General in Brussels, after many protests against French treaty infractions, declared war again on 11 December 1683.[51]

On 23 November 1683, after the Turkish defeat outside Vienna, Louvois had written to the Maréchal d'Humières: 'the intention of His Majesty is to torment the Spanish as much as possible during the winter.' Bruges and Mons were bombarded, Oudenarde reduced to ashes, Courtrai,

Dixmude and Ghent occupied. Louis XIV, who could be as hypocritical as a modern dictator, declared his desire for 'la tranquillité de toute l'Europe'.[52] Pierre-Ignace Chavatte, the Lillois whose diary has already been quoted, reflected widespread disgust, and admiration for the House of Austria: 'the French took to their arms to go and pillage in Flanders while the Emperor and the King of Poland and Spain were afflicted with the Turks and Vienna was besieged . . . and the poor peasants did not know what to do or whom to obey and from there were pillaged and burnt.'[53]

The following year French forces turned on Luxembourg. It was one of the strongest citadels in Europe, constructed since 1544 on a salient between the Alzette and Pétrusse rivers. It had been the base from which Spain had reconquered the Southern Netherlands after 1577, and would be a German stronghold in 1815–67, 1914–18 and 1940–44. French troops had already blockaded it once, from September 1681 to March 1682. The blockade was lifted only for fear of reproaches from fellow Catholics that the Most Christian King was helping his Ottoman ally as it prepared to besiege Vienna. However, the blockade soon resumed. The inhabitants were reduced to 'the worst misery'. Many died of hunger.[54]

On 28 April 1684 the siege of Luxembourg formally began, followed in detail by Louis XIV and Louvois.[55] On 6 June it surrendered. The garrison was allowed to leave with 'the honours of war', drums beating and flags flying. Vauban commented, 'At last that terrible Luxembourg has been reduced as you wished; I rejoice for it with all my heart for the great good it will do to the King's service. It is the finest and most glorious conquest which he has ever made in his life and one which best assures his interests on all sides.' The fall of Luxembourg, coming soon after that of Strasbourg, terrified France's neighbours.[56]

In reports to Brussels, the Prince de Chimay said he had done everything possible to put the city in a state of defence; the city magistrates, however, blamed his contradictory orders and counter-orders for stopping them from behaving 'as veritable Luxembourgeois with their customary fidelity'. They had dug trenches day and night without any help from the soldiers in the garrison.[57] In reality, since 20,000 French troops were besieging a garrison of 2,000, the result was a foregone conclusion.

Vauban immediately began to fortify the citadel, employing 3,000 workmen, some from as far away as the Tyrol. Stronger ramparts and bastions, and new barracks, were built. By 1687 it was ready for inspection. Louis arrived on 21 May, after an eleven-day journey via Châlons and Verdun, leaving five days later. Ladies of the court again accompanied him. Every day he visited a different church and distributed money. Racine, his official historiographer, wrote to Boileau: 'The King has taken a liking to his conquest and is not displeased to examine it at leisure. He has already inspected all the fortifications one after the other, has even entered in the countermines of the covered passage, which are impressive, and above all has been very pleased to see those famous redoubts between the two covered ways which have given M. de Vauban so much difficulty.' Crowds cried, 'Fif le roi!' At one church an old woman shouted that she had seen him ten years earlier and he had changed a lot. He smiled and walked on.[58] Although many inhabitants continued to yearn for rule by the King of Spain, France was not oppressive. Large sums were spent by the garrison and the Ministry of War. The King himself paid for the festivities, gave money to hospices and convents, and compensated inhabitants for damage done by the Spanish garrison.[59]

By 1687 Louis XIV had given France a new north-eastern frontier. A straight line went from east of Dunkirk south-east to Mons. Then, changing from its present position, the frontier went due east, incorporating southern Namur, advancing up the valley of the Moselle towards Trier, then south-east as far as the Rhine, incorporating much of what is now Saarland. To the south all Alsace and all Franche-Comté had become French.

The towns and fortresses Louis had won included, along France's eastern frontier, Dunkirk, Lille, Mons, Ypres, Montmédy, Luxembourg, Strasbourg, Colmar, Huningue, Belfort, Besançon. In the middle land, outside his normal environment, he showed his prophetic vision. For his acquisitions did not merely consist of land and people. They were also, in a way today's demilitarized mentality has difficulty understanding, strategic assets, sited on coasts, besides rivers or mountains, across plains, where they could hold up invading armies. He understood geography better than Napoleon, who believed that France extended to the Elbe and the Tiber.

One of the men most respected by the King was Sébastien de Vauban. A minor noble from Burgundy, he had become one of the greatest engineers of his day, and *commissaire général des fortifications*. Since 1661, travelling constantly along French coasts and frontiers, he supervised the fortification, by the corps of *ingénieurs du roi*, of 150 cities and strongholds, including, among many others, Dunkirk, Lille, Douai, Tournai, Breisach, Montmédy, Philippsbourg, Strasbourg and Roussillon. The entire eastern frontier became a building site. In all about 8 million livres a year were spent on fortifications between 1682 and 1691, about 3 million a year thereafter. The fortifications of Dunkirk alone cost 2 million livres, as much as a small palace.[60]

Vauban had many meetings with the King, and after Louvois' death in

1691 would work directly with him. Vauban wanted to give France a logical frontier. As he wrote, in a famous letter to his patron Louvois, in January 1673, 'Seriously, monseigneur, the king should think a little about making his field square. This confusion of friendly and enemy places *pêle-mêle* displeases me.'[61]* The King's passion for fortifying his frontiers would be celebrated in a medal struck in 1692: 'Securitati perpetua', 'security perpetuated'.[62] Fortresses' star-shaped brick ramparts, bastions, 'contrescarpes', 'demi-lunes', moats and battlements, giving French artillery multiple lines of fire against the enemy, are as characteristic of Louis XIV as the marble halls of Versailles. He built not only for personal glory but also for the defence of France.

Louis XIV's fortresses would prove more effective than their twentieth-century equivalent, the Maginot Line (which included some of his forts, for example Maubeuge, Bitche and the Fort de Joux near Switzerland, 250 years after their construction). Many were used as barracks until the Second World War. The citadel of Lille resisted for eight weeks after the fall of the city in 1708. Huningue, constructed by Vauban in 1679–81, resisted a siege of four months in 1813–14. Maubeuge, built in 1679–85, suffered sieges in 1814, 1815, 1914 and 1940. Belfort resisted a German siege between 3 November 1870 and 18 February 1871, making it a celebrated symbol of French defiance. Vauban's citadel in Calais, protected by vast ramparts, held off German attacks on 23–26 May 1940 (as did other Vauban forts at Gravelines, Maubeuge and Bouchain), thereby helping the escape of French and British soldiers from the beaches of Dunkirk.[63]

Louis XIV and his advisers knew that danger would come from Germany. On 28 June 1684 Louvois wrote Vauban a letter which would take 200 years to make sense. In the future, he wrote, attacks would come from 'the Germans who should from now on be considered our veritable enemies and the only ones who could do us harm if they had an Emperor who wanted to get on his horse'.[64]

While Louis XIV was securing conquests along the Rhine, in France he was completing a conquest of another kind: a palace rather than a chain of fortresses. In the 1670s, although Versailles was still a building site, he began to spend longer there. Saint-Germain was increasingly cramped and dilapidated. From the camp before Cambrai, he wrote to Colbert in 1677: 'inform me sometimes in detail of what is happening at Versailles'; 'you can be sure that I will go to Versailles to spend the summer there.' Three

---

* Despite the money spent on fortifying them, Charleroi, Courtrai and Maastricht were abandoned in 1678, since they were far from the French frontier.

years later: 'there is no time to lose for I will certainly be at Versailles on 1 September.'[65]

Between 1678 and 1682 Colbert, as *surintendant des bâtiments*, raced to complete Versailles for his demanding master. He sent detailed instructions about doors, windows and avoiding the smell of paint. In March 1678 Colbert wrote to Louis XIV: 'yesterday I spent the whole day at Versailles . . . the new buildings are advancing rapidly . . . so I hope, Sire, that all Your Majesty has ordered will be ready to give him pleasure and some relaxation after his great and glorious conquests.' The King replied from outside Ghent, during its siege: 'I am very pleased with the account you give me of the state of Versailles . . . the new buildings must again be hastened, so that they are completed at the time I said.' He added, 'You are doing wonders with the funds and every day I am more pleased with you, I am very happy to tell you this.'[66]

Versailles reflected the King's personal tastes and desires: he even gave instructions about the decoration of the mantelpiece in his bedroom.[67] Versailles alone cost more than the entire fortification programme, roughly 8 million livres a year, rising to a peak of 15 million in 1685. (According to a memorandum of 1690, the total cost had been 81 million livres, excluding free labour provided by the army.)[68]

From 1678 the Galerie des Glaces, then called the Grande Galerie, replaced the terrace between the King's and Queen's apartments, which were almost finished. One side was lined with seventeen windows looking on to the garden; the other with mirrors made by the Manufacture Royale – thereby advertising the French glass industry. It is 35 feet wide and 240 feet long. The gallery, decorated with classical statues and silver furniture, at once became the most famous, as well as the largest, room in the palace.[69]

Palaces need galleries: long spaces for exercise, processions or meeting people, free from the rules of etiquette observed in state apartments. Galleries in other palaces, many of which would have been familiar to Louis XIV through prints, books or ambassadors' accounts, were used to display and celebrate maps (the Vatican); books or battles (the Escorial); ancestors (the Residenz, Munich); the virtues and victories of the monarchy (Buen Retiro and the Royal Palace, Stockholm); hunting (Venaria Reale); or the gods and heroes of Olympus (the most common theme, in the Galerie François I in Fontainebleau, Mazarin's gallery in his Paris palace, Louis XIV's own Galerie d'Apollon in the Louvre and, perhaps most influential of all, Monsieur's recently completed Galerie d'Apollon in Saint-Cloud, with frescoes by Le Brun's rival Mignard).[70]

Indeed the Premier Peintre Le Brun originally planned to illustrate the ceiling with the labours of Hercules. The King, however, insisted that he himself should be the main subject: the council warned, unsuccessfully, that nothing in the frescoes should wound foreign powers.[71] Like Marie de Médicis' 1621 commission of a cycle of self-glorifying pictures by Rubens for her Palais du Luxembourg in Paris, Le Brun's thirty frescoes on the ceiling, surrounded by cupids, satyrs, trophies in gilt lead or stucco, and gilded columns in the 'French order', provide a triumphant allegorized history of the reign of Louis XIV between 1661 and 1678. 'The King governs by himself' (1661) was in the middle. Others included 'the acquisition of Dunkirk' (1662); 'order restored in finances' (1662); 'protection accorded to the fine arts' (1664); the crossing of the Rhine (1672); the establishment of the Invalides (1674); and the taking of Ghent (1678). The King is always shown in Roman armour, and his personal motto 'Nec pluribus impar', 'Not unequal to more', frequently appears. It was boastful, but less so than the motto of the kings of Spain since the conquest of the new world under Charles V: 'Plus ultra', 'Nothing beyond'. The gallery was inaugurated on 15 November 1684.[72]

Whereas the Galerie des Glaces was devoted to the King, the rest of the palace, in accordance with French tradition, distinguishing it from palaces in other countries, housed his relations and courtiers. In 1679 the three-storey Aile des Princes to the south of the main palace, looking like a baroque barracks with columns, was added for the royal family, matched in 1684 by the equally enormous (both are almost 1,000 feet long) Aile du Nord, to the north, for courtiers.[73] Both façades are marked, like the east façade of the Louvre, by repeated pairs of columns. Nowhere is there a dominant central dome or pediment, as in the Louvre or the Invalides. The palace looks relatively informal. When completed, it contained 189 apartments for court officials; twenty for members of the royal family; and a total of 1,840 rooms.[74] Versailles was larger than any other palace in Europe, with the possible exception of the Escorial, much of which was a monastery.

From 1679 to 1682 Mansard extended the two ministers' wings to the east of the palace, each of which became the size of a large chateau (with basements containing rooms for the Gardes Français and Gardes Suisses on duty). He also designed two royal stables, the Grande Ecurie and the Petite Ecurie, opposite them, and added a great square block, the Grand Commun, to the south of the palace, for royal staff and kitchens in 1682–6.[75]

In early 1682, as the palace was nearing completion, Colbert's letters to his son d'Ormoy, his potential successor as *surintendant des bâtiments* (who in his father's opinion was lazy, ignorant and too fond of Paris), became frantic. On 12 February 1682, he wrote, 'the King [who checked everything] did not find the works as advanced as they should be.' On 25 March he told d'Ormoy to get up between 5 and 6 every morning to check all the carpenters', locksmiths', window-makers' and painters' workshops, and their bills. On 11 April he was furious that the 'small balustrade' for the King's bedroom was still not in place, although he had been asking for it for two months.[76]

A month later Sourches' diary is the main source for the King's installation at Versailles. Contrary to what many history books claim, there was no official decree. 'On 6 May 1682 the King left Saint-Cloud to go and establish himself at Versailles, where for a long time he had wished to be, although it was still full of building workers [d'Ormoy had not done his job], with the intention of staying there until the delivery of Madame la Dauphine, who was obliged to change apartment on the second day after her arrival because the noise stopped her sleeping. He loved this house with a boundless passion,' despite its 'very ugly situation'.[77]

Versailles became the King's principal – but not his only – residence. Saint-Germain had been dethroned: the King never slept there again. But he continued to reside in Compiègne (seventy-five visits between 1643 and 1699), often holding military reviews and 'camps' near by; and in Fontainebleau, for one or two months most autumns. In addition he visited recent conquests (Besançon and Strasbourg in 1683, Cambrai and Valenciennes in 1684, Luxembourg in 1687) and Chambord (1685), and in the summers of 1691, 1692 and 1693 went on campaign in the Southern Netherlands. Age and the pressures of work then made him choose a more sedentary life at Versailles.[78]

However, the Menus Plaisirs (the department dealing with the props and decors needed for royal ceremonies and entertainments), the Mousquetaires, Gardes Françaises and Gardes Suisses – much of the outer court – stayed in Paris, only sending detachments to serve at Versailles. The embassies, law courts, academies and many government offices also remained in Paris. Ministers, courtiers, visitors sped between Paris and Versailles, and other royal residences, even more often than wealthy modern Parisians between Paris and the country at the weekend.[79]

Versailles and Paris were in symbiosis. The Premier Médecin du Roi in daily attendance at Versailles was in charge of the Jardin des Plantes, as was the Grand Aumônier of the Hospice des Quinze-Vingts, both in Paris. The King's doctors were allowed to live in Paris provided they attended the *lever* and *coucher*.[80] The Premier Peintre du Roi, Charles Le Brun, the stylemaster of Versailles, also worked for Paris clients and churches, and lived in Paris at the Gobelins. André Le Nôtre, who designed the gardens at Versailles, lived in a house by the Tuileries garden in Paris, surrounded by collections of antiquities, paintings and porcelain, frequently praising 'the good humour of his master'.[81] There was no style war between Paris and Versailles; financiers' houses in new squares such as the Place Louis le Grand or the Place des Victoires were decorated in the same style as the palace of Versailles, often by the same craftsmen.

Members of the royal family also constantly visited Paris. The Dauphin was even more popular in the capital than the King's brother Monsieur. He knew Paris well from his frequent visits to the opera (he made love to the singers 'without distinction'). The *Mercure Galant* declared that 'every day his praises are in the mouth of the people.'[82]

The King too remained in dialogue with Paris: they were separated, not divorced. In 1680 the city of Paris formally proclaimed him Louis le Grand – a title which survives today in the name of one of the largest and most famous schools in France, the Lycée Louis-le-Grand. The school inherited the site (on the rue Saint-Jacques) and name of the old Collège Louis-le-Grand, as the Jesuit Collège de Clermont was renamed, on Louis XIV's prompting, in 1682.* He was well received on the rare occasions he visited Paris (1682, 1683, 1687, 1692, 1701, 1702, 1706). The royal government continued to encourage the modernization of the city. The Pont Royal was rebuilt in stone in 1685–9; the Place des Victoires and the Place Louis le Grand (now Vendôme) were started at the same time.[83]

The departure of part of the court relieved Parisians of the pressures on living accommodation, and the obligation to provide it at special rates to court officials. Perhaps the growth of its luxury industries, aristocratic residences and foreign visitors lessened Paris's need of the court. Although shocked by the city's poverty and the number of monks and convents, in 1698 the English doctor Martin Lister noted that there were 700 mansions with portes cochères for the carriages of the wealthy, and so many new buildings that it had become 'in a manner a new city this past forty years'.[84]

The birth of the King's first grandson, four months after Louis moved to Versailles, marked its inauguration as a dynastic shrine (until 1789 all members of the French royal family were born there). Indeed Sourches' diary entry – 'with the intention of staying there until the delivery of Madame la Dauphine' – suggests that Louis XIV moved to Versailles for this very reason. The Dauphin had married Marie Anne Victoire, sister of the Elector Max Emanuel of Bavaria, in 1680: shared enmity to the

---

* It has educated, among other famous pupils, Voltaire, Robespierre, Victor Hugo, Baudelaire, and Presidents Poincaré and Pompidou. It still has a picture of *The Family of Darius before Alexander the Great* by Jouvenet, presented by Louis XIV.

House of Austria had long made allies of France and Bavaria, as well as France and the Ottoman Empire.[85] As she lay pregnant, the Dauphine said that she wanted to have a portrait of the King always before her eyes, so that her son would resemble him: he was so touched that he sent her a jewelled coverlet.[86]

The King and Queen slept on mattresses in her bedroom in order to be present at the moment of birth. The bedroom was bursting with other relations and courtiers. A son was born on 22 August 1682.[87] The moment the bedroom doors opened and the news was announced, 'such a shout of joy arose in the palace that it was at once heard to the end of the town,' wrote Sourches. The King allowed himself to be embraced by anyone who was present. The guards lit bonfires in the courtyards: the King let them burn what they wished 'as long as they do not burn us'. The flames were reflected in the gilded ornaments on the palace roofs. 'Fountains of wine' were set up. Nobles and servants joined in the same dances. The Gouvernante des Enfants de France, the Maréchale de La Mothe, repeatedly showed the baby at the window to satisfy the crowds arriving from Paris. In Paris the Grande Galerie of the Louvre was illuminated for an 'inconceivable influx of people'. Churches throughout France, including Lutheran churches in Strasbourg, held services of thanksgiving.[88]

For the first time since François I, the succession to the crown was assured by two generations of princes. Rather than being called duke of Brittany like François I's grandson, Louis, to the horror of the Spanish court, named his grandson duke of Burgundy: a sign that Louis considered him heir to the dukes of Burgundy, whose immense dominions, stretching from the Channel to the Alps with their capital in Brussels, had dominated the middle land in the fifteenth century. Louis XIV had already in 1680 obliged Carlos II of Spain, their senior descendant, to remove the title of duke of Burgundy from his list of titles and the arms of Burgundy from his heraldry.[89] The first royal birth in Versailles, like the *réunions* and the annexation of Strasbourg, confirmed the King's ambitions to make the Rhine French.

Challenging Louis XIV's official world of monarchy and piety at Versailles was a counter-culture of 'abominations'. At its head was the King's brother Monsieur, living mainly in the Palais Royal in Paris, and in his country palace west of Paris, Saint-Cloud. After he had rebuilt it between 1677 and 1688, with a Galerie d'Apollon frescoed by Mignard, it was almost as majestic as Versailles. His collections, his entertainments and his fountains also rivalled his brother's.[90] Unlike Versailles, Saint-Cloud, which many preferred, has views of Paris, where he and his family continued to spend part of the year. Once, when the King invited him to see new fountains at Versailles, he replied that he was going to see a new opera in Paris.[91] With well over 1,000 posts and benefices available, Monsieur's household (which was larger than the Queen's), appanage, estates and regiments provided an alternative career structure to Versailles.[92]

Alternative pleasures were also offered. In theory homosexuality, particularly sodomy, was a capital crime. Homosexuals were burnt alive on the Place de Grève in the heart of Paris in 1662, 1671 and 1677.[93] Others were imprisoned in the Bastille, as Louis XIV well knew: the police reports which were read out to him spared few details of their 'criminal abominations', often in the Tuileries or Luxembourg gardens.[94] Suspected atheists or *libertins* could also be executed, as eighteen were between 1636 and 1650.[95]

As with gambling and illegitimacy, however, what was punished elsewhere flourished at court. Indeed Sourches called the court 'une petite Sodome'. In June 1682, only a month after the move to Versailles, several young courtiers, including princes of Rohan, Lorraine and Monaco, were exiled for what were termed *débauches ultramontaines* (so called since homosexuality was, in France, termed 'the Italian vice' or *les plaisirs d'Italie*).[96]

The King's fifteen-year-old son by Louise de La Vallière, the Comte de Vermandois, was questioned by his father. He admitted his 'crimes' and denounced 'a long list', including the Prince de Conti, the ablest, handsomest and most popular of the Princes of the Blood.[97] Some had tried to 'debauch' the Dauphin, as well as Vermandois.[98]

After a whipping in his father's presence, Vermandois said that he would repent. Monsieur, however, never hid his nature. He continued to be covered in jewels, bracelets, ribbons, perfume and rouge.[99] The Chevalier de Lorraine, handsome, well built and brave, and Monsieur's Premier Ecuyer the Marquis d'Effiat, the greatest sodomite in France (and nephew of Louis XIII's favourite Cinq-Mars), were his principal lovers.[100]

They gave orders in his household and 'tormented' Madame. Monsieur, according to Saint-Simon, allowed no limits to his pleasures 'in number or time'.[101] He had younger lovers – whom Madame called 'buben' – allowing himself, she wrote, 'to be ruled by these lewd boys', and showering them with gold. She wrote to her aunt Sophia, Duchess of Hanover, that she knew she would be poisoned like the first Madame. Instead of fearing death, however, she desired it.[102] When Monsieur died, Madame burnt their love letters.

Monsieur had described Lorraine as 'the best friend that I have on the earth', in a letter to Colbert in 1670 complaining of the Chevalier's arrest – and of his treatment by the King 'all his life' – and signed 'votre bien bon ami, Philippe'.[103] Lorraine had since returned to favour, but in June 1682, when he asked to join the King's hunt, he received the reply: 'as they did not take the same pleasures, it was not right that he should come to share the pleasures of hunting the stag.'[104]

Finally Lorraine would oblige Monsieur to 'content the King in everything'. In other words, to the disgust of Madame, since such a marriage dishonoured their son Philippe, Duc de Chartres, Monsieur would tell Chartres to marry the King's illegitimate daughter Mlle de Blois in 1692. Her dowry of 2 million livres would help make the Orléans one of the richest families in France until the 1970s. In return Lorraine would frequently receive the honour of entertaining the King in his chateau of Frémont, on the road between Versailles and Fontainebleau.[105] Thus in order to marry one of his illegitimate daughters to his nephew, Louis XIV sanctioned the homosexual bond between his brother and Lorraine. In private life, as in public affairs, he was not as absolute as he claimed.

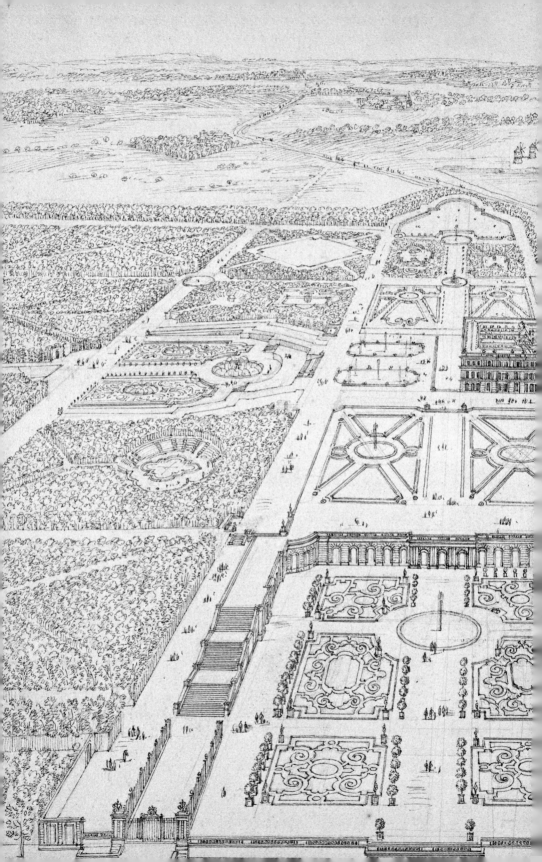

12

The King Outdoors

Most of Louis XIV's victories have been forgotten. His citadels are ivy-covered ruins. Millions, however, still identify him with Versailles. Three chapters are necessary to describe it since Versailles was, Charles Perrault wrote in *Le Siècle de Louis le Grand* in 1687, not a palace but an entire world:

> Ce n'est pas un palais, c'est une ville entière,
> Superbe en sa grandeur, superbe en sa matière.
> Non, c'est plutôt un monde, où du grand univers
> Se trouvent rassemblés les miracles divers.

> ('It is not a palace, it is an entire city,
> Superb in its grandeur, superb in its nature.
> No, it is rather a world where the diverse miracles
> Of the entire universe are gathered.')

Versailles, moreover, reflected Louis XIV's private personality, as well as his public roles as king and France. Versailles was his personal property, decrees proclaimed, 'to be enjoyed separately'. Unlike the other royal palaces, it did not belong to the crown. Its governor was not a great noble, but one of the King's *premiers valets de chambre* or confidential servants, M. Blouin.[1]

The King's outdoor life will be described first; life inside Versailles in the following chapter; finally the King's private life with his families, mistresses and ministers.

Like many other royal palaces, Versailles owed its existence to hunting. In 1623 Louis XIII built his first hunting lodge at Versailles, because it was close to forests full of game. Louis XIV himself first visited Versailles, in April 1651, in order to hunt there.[2]

Hunting had, and in some cases still has, a particular appeal for royalty.

It was not only a source of pleasure and exercise. It was also a visible assertion of domination over landscape and animals. Hunting was also believed – until the Second World War by some officers – to be a school of war. It helped teach courage, horsemanship and the ability to read the lie of the land and charge the enemy.[3]

In his book *La Vénerie royale* ('The Royal Hunt'), dedicated to Louis XIV in 1655, Robert de Salnove praised hunting as 'such a noble exercise that it is almost the only one to which Princes devote themselves as they do to the apprenticeship of war, that most illustrious of arts and most generous of professions, which has the same ruses and the same fatigues; so much so that there is little difference between the hunter and the warrior . . . the same God who has given us kings rightly reserved the stag for them.'[4]

Hunting also helped the court fulfil one of its essential functions: increasing and institutionalizing sociability. A royal hunt could occupy hundreds of people, across a large stretch of land: guards, spectators, hunt servants, musicians, keepers, beaters and finally the monarch himself and his courtiers, huntsmen and grooms. Royal hunts were the outdoor equivalent of a court ball, and were often, particularly under Louis XIV, followed by ladies.

In France since 1533 all hunting rights in theory derived from the King, and all non-nobles who were not owners of noble fiefs were forbidden to hunt.[5] Louis XIV was addicted to hunting. In his correspondence with Condé and others, he asked for canvas screens with which to trap deer, or game with which to restock the royal forests of Versailles and Boulogne.[6] In 1664 he sent Charles II a present of 100 head of deer.[7] By Louis' hunting *ordonnance* of 1669 he renewed all traditional regulations for hunting and forest law, while abolishing the death penalty for hunting offences.[8]

One of the great annual entertainments of his court, the Fête de Saint Hubert, linked (and in parts of France still links) hunting to Christianity. St Hubert, patron saint of hunters, was a seventh-century Frankish prince who, after a vision of a stag with a cross between its antlers, had given hunting a set of rules: for example, to kill old stags, and spare the young. For the Fête de Saint Hubert in November 1665, the Prince de Condé and the Duc de Verneuil, as well as the King, brought their hounds to Versailles. After an open-air mass in honour of the saint, and the blessing of the hounds with holy water, a lavish hunt, with four packs of hounds hunting at the same time, 'gave the Court the greatest pleasure in the world'.[9]

Louis XIV's hunts were run by the court department called the Vénerie, under the Grand Veneur the Duc de La Rochefoucauld, with a staff of around 100 loaders, beaters, huntsmen and grooms, and 200 horses. It was based in the Hôtel du Grand Veneur, on the Avenue de Paris. Still bearing scars from fighting against Louis in the Fronde, La Rochefoucauld, who was also Grand Maître de la Garde-robe, was a particularly dedicated courtier. He rarely missed one of Louis' *couchers* or *levers*, or slept away from the palace where he was in residence. The King, in return, frequently paid his debts.[10] The Vénerie hunted deer. The King also had separate equipages, used less frequently, for hunting boar or wolves, and for falconry.[11]

The Vénerie provided Louis with shooting in the Petit Parc around Versailles and hunting in the Grand Parc enclosing the Petit Parc and Saint-Cyr, to the south and west of the chateau. It was surrounded by a 26-mile-long wall, to keep game in.[12] In the Petit Parc thousands of pheasants and partridges, reared on a massive scale in *faisanderies* in the Grand Parc, and then released, provided the King and his relations and favourites with superb shooting. On 16 August 1685 for example, he released 5,000 partridges and 2,000 pheasants.

Louis XIV had started shooting young. After a bet with Mazarin at the age of nineteen, he shot 112 rabbits in five hours at Vincennes.[13] Soon he was considered the best shot in France. Saint-Simon wrote, 'no man in France shot so well, so adroitly or with such grace'.[14] Louis hunted or went shooting on 182 days in 1689, on 138 in 1707 and on 118 in 1708, roughly two days a week, at least two or three hours a time, usually on Wednesdays and Saturdays. When he had gout, he went shooting in a sedan chair carried by four valets.[15] Sometimes he went hunting and shooting on the same day.[16]

Both parks were planted in the 1670s and 1680s with beech, oak, elm and lime trees, to give the game cover as well as to beautify the landscape. Louis, irritated by the slow growth of young trees, transported forests of mature trees to Versailles from Flanders, the Île de France and Normandy.[17] The figures are phenomenal. Orders exist for 2,870,000 beech and 604,000 willow to be transported from the valley of the Eure. At times fully grown trees were transported to Versailles in special pots on wheels. Many died.[18]

The forest at Fontainebleau is even better for hunting than the land around Versailles – 74,000 acres of ancient woodland, well stocked with game, compared to the Grand Parc of 27,000 acres around Versailles.[19] Louis spent in all six years of his life there, hunting almost every day during his visits in the autumn. Despite the plays and operas with which they were entertained at Fontainebleau, more frequently than at Versailles, many courtiers preferred the forest to the palace.[20] In the evening ladies enjoyed going into the forest, to hear the sound of rutting stags.[21] The *curée* or ceremonial feasting on the dead deer by the hounds, by the light of torches and to the music of hunting horns, was an unforgettable spectacle: one evening in 1714, in front of the King, 200 dogs devoured the carcasses.[22]

After bad falls out hunting in 1681 and 1683, Louis XIV preferred to follow the hunt in a light, two-wheeled carriage called a *soufflet*. According to Saint-Simon, he drove it 'very fast with a skill and precision which the best coachmen did not have'.[23] In 1706, at the age of sixty-eight, when a stag charged straight at his carriage, he drove it off with the flick of a whip.[24]

The royal family shared Louis' passion for hunting. The Dauphin hunted even more than his father. Most of his letters to his son Philip V in Spain are about hunting.[25] At the end of his life Philip V could still remember every hunt he had attended, fifty years earlier, at Fontaine-bleau.[26] The Dauphin hunted wolves so vigorously, with his own pack of wolfhounds, that he cleared them from the Île de France. Louis XIV often discussed hunting with another passionate royal huntsman, his illegitimate son Toulouse, who became *grand veneur* in 1714 after the death of La Rochefoucauld.[27] Toulouse's brother the Duc du Maine had the 'most magnificent equipage ever seen', with which the King sometimes preferred to hunt, to the dismay of his own.[28]

Under Louis XIV Versailles was filled with the sight and sound and smell of dogs. In 1662, he boasted to his huntsmen that he was creating 'a pack of the finest and best dogs which it is possible to find'.[29] By 1700 there were around 400 in the King's kennels at Versailles, as well as in kennels belonging to the princes' hunts. Madame, who wrote that in France she preferred dogs to people, and filled her study with them, claimed there were 1,000 dogs in Versailles.[30] Louis loved dogs, although he did not sleep with them on his bed, like his father or his cousin Charles II. The chasm between animals and humans was less absolute then than now. Love of animals was sanctified by Greek myths, and by Aesop's and La Fontaine's fables, in which animals teach lessons to humans.

Whereas he commissioned no portraits of courtiers or servants, Louis was the first king of France to commission portraits of his pointers and spaniels, by François Desportes. The dogs are life-size, with their names written on the picture in large gold letters: Diane, Folle, Blonde and many others. They hung in an antechamber in Marly and in the Cabinet des Chiens du Roi in Versailles, a small room on the first floor of the palace, between the *cabinet* for the King's wigs and the *cabinet* for his jewels. [31]

There with his favourite gun-bearer Antoine, he would feed his *levrettes de la chambre* biscuits after dinner – thereby improving their obedience in the hunting field.[32] The familiar world of guns and dogs and horses – of carefully selected stags tracked for hours through the forest, until they emerged in alleys to be caught by hounds – of pheasants flying above the guns – freed the King, for a few hours, from cares of state: no despatches to read, no documents to sign, no ministers.[33]

The King's horses came from the royal stud farms in Normandy and the Île de France, which he established in 1665, partly to supply the army, and by purchase from North Africa and Europe. In addition, other monarchs sent Louis presents of horses, as he did them: black horses from the King of Spain, bay horses from the Elector of Brandenburg, white Oldenburgs from the Duke of Hanover. The magnificent harnesses, saddles and saddle cloths which Louis sent with twelve white horses to Charles XI of Sweden in 1673 can still be admired in the Royal Armoury in Stockholm today.[34] The horses included riding horses, parade horses, chargers, war horses, carriage horses and cart horses. Portraits of Louis' horses, with their own and their donors' names (for example 'le Bacha Turc Ville de Namur', 'le Géant anglais Ville de Cambrai'), can be seen in the Musée Tessé in Le Mans.[35] Already, however, England was beginning to replace France, as before 1600 France had replaced Italy, as the centre of horsemanship. In February 1683 Louis XIV watched the Duke of Monmouth win the first horse race near Paris, on an English horse.[36]

The stables were the elegant, horseshoe-shaped buildings, decorated with horse sculptures, which still exist between the three avenues opposite the main palace of Versailles. An English guidebook called them 'so regular and beautiful that few royal palaces exceed them'.[37] The King's horses and equerries were housed nearer to him than his guards, who were billeted in inns or private houses, or in barracks in Versailles and Paris.[38]

On the right the Petite Ecurie (formed by Henri III in 1582, in order to preserve direct control over his own transport), under the Premier Ecuyer, ran the King's personal carriages and horses.[39] One *premier écuyer*, Claude de Saint-Simon, father of the memoir-writer, had won Louis XIII's favour in 1627, as a young equerry from Poitou, by teaching him a new method of changing horses – sliding directly from saddle to saddle – without dismounting. Such dexterity, and his ability to sound a hunting horn without spitting, had encouraged Louis XIII to make Saint-Simon a duke and peer, and governor of the palaces of Saint-Germain. However, he fell from favour in 1636, when he warned an uncle of his impending arrest.[40]

Louis XIV was a skilled horseman, who on the same day, 19 September 1661, rode from Fontainebleau to Vincennes, then to Paris, on to Saint-Cloud to see Louise de La Valliere, then back to Fontainebleau again.[41]

He often chose his horses himself, writing to his Premier Ecuyer M. de Beringhen, 'you will find considerable increase in numbers in my stables when you return to your post.'[42]

On the left, the Grande Ecurie was ruled by the Grand Ecuyer, known at court as 'M. le Grand', the post once held by Louis XIII's favourite Cinq-Mars. It supplied horses and carriages for the court and part of the army, and ran the royal stud farms (a prerogative which Louis XIV preserved for it from the minister in charge of trade). The number of horses in both stables rose from 228 in 1664 to 382 in 1680, to 550 in 1700 and to 648 in 1715. They cost more to maintain than the servants who looked after them.[43]

Louis XIV's Grand Ecuyer for most of his reign was the Comte d'Armagnac, a prince of the House of Lorraine whose brother was Monsieur's favourite the Chevalier de Lorraine: he often played billiards with the King in the evening, kept open house both in Versailles and Paris and would act as a link between the King and his cousin the Duke of Lorraine.[44] The Grand Ecuyer also ran a school for eighty pages, young nobles of proven pedigree sent to Versailles by their parents at the age of fourteen to learn horsemanship, fencing, dancing, draughtsmanship and manners, as well as mathematics, Latin, history and geography, before starting careers in the army.[45] As he boasted in his memoirs, Louis increased their number by half and ensured that they were more carefully selected and educated, with more opportunities to serve him personally. Thereby, in the King's opinion, they would become better and more devoted officers.[46]

Both stables also contained riding schools which taught princes, courtiers and pages how to ride and control a horse, and provided accommodation for equerries and grooms.[47] They also housed carriages for the King and the court – from the gilded and sculpted mobile saloons in which the Queen entered conquered cities, to the sedan chairs which carried courtiers through the gardens and courtyards of Versailles. Only the royal family's sedan chairs could enter the palace itself.

Carriages, horses, embroidered saddle cloths and gleaming harnesses and spurs were an essential aspect of court splendour. In October 1699 an English officer called Richard Creed, travelling with Lord Exeter, was impressed by the sight of the court moving from Fontainebleau back to Versailles. Twenty miles of roads were 'filled with vast trains of equipages': 300 carriages with six or eight horses, and 'a world of princes and dukes and ladies of the court'. The King himself leant out of his carriage window, 'called me and asked me particularly' with whom he, Creed, was travelling, repeating the word 'Exeter' until he could say it correctly: 'he was pleased to be very free and civil to me.'[48]

In addition to the royal carriages, from 1669 public *coches* or carriages with places for hire, and private carriages for hire, had started to operate between Paris and Versailles, even when the court was not in residence. You could also go by boat from Paris to Sèvres and then by coach to Versailles.[49]

In addition to hunting, shooting and riding, gardening also drew Louis XIV out of doors. It was, Sourches wrote, 'one of the King's great passions . . . he is always ordering some beautification in the gardens'.[50] Dangeau wrote on 5 November 1695: 'The King walked all day in his gardens where he is happier than ever.' He often walked in the garden, at Versailles, Marly or Trianon, after dark, even when he was over sixty – if the moon was bright, until after midnight;[51] he also sometimes hunted by moonlight.[52] Neither cold nor rain kept the King indoors. In February 1701 Dangeau wrote that, despite the bad weather, the King 'went to walk at Trianon where he is changing many things in the gardens'.[53] On 20 December 1704 he walked all day in the gardens, although the frost and ice were so 'violent' that his dogs could not go out: the King was the toughest animal in his court.[54]

André Le Nôtre, 'Jardinier ordinaire du roi, dessinateur des plans et jardins du roi, contrôleur général des bâtiments, arts et manufactures de France', called Louis XIV the 'greatest gardener in the world'. Neither King nor gardener could endure a finite view. Together they created at Versailles a garden of multiple avenues, with perspectives stretching to the horizon, unfolding as the walker advanced from viewpoint to viewpoint. They were created with the help of optical and geometrical instruments and of the famous astronomer and mathematician the Abbé Picard, author of *Traité du nivellement* (1684, on the science of levelling). Under Le Nôtre was an army of gardeners, planting, raking, removing dead leaves, trimming topiary into new shapes.[55]

Louis XIV constantly added new fountains, statues and pavilions to the gardens at Versailles. Believing that, as the *Mercure Galant* wrote, courts should contain 'everything which is rarest on earth', in 1663–8 Louis XIV also established a menagerie about a mile from the palace. In pavilions grouped around a domed octagon, visitors could see pelicans, ostriches, porcupines, *demoiselles de Numidie* (a species of crane) and *coqs de Constantinople*. An elephant was sent by the Queen of Portugal in 1668, a tigress by the Sultan of Morocco in 1682.[56]

Between 1668 and 1672 the present Grand Canal was dug west of the palace. It was so large and deep that Louis XIV kept there *chaloupes* from the Bay of Biscay; *galiotes* from le Havre; two English yachts, especially built as a present for him by Charles II's master yachtsman Matthew Deane; and a small galley.[57] These boats were manned by 200 boatmen in red and blue uniforms under the Admiral of the Canal, M. de Langeron. In 1679 more boatmen brought gondolas presented by the Doge of Venice. They lived in houses by the canal which are still called the Petite Venise.[58] The flotilla on the canal tested new boats for the navy, as well as transporting courtiers from one end of the park to another.[59] On one occasion when the King proved 'a very bad pilot' at the helm of a boat, Louvois was frightened of being thrown into the lake.[60]

In 1678–83 the 22-acre Potager du Roi was created south-east of the palace. Now called the Ecole Nationale Supérieure de Paysage, and still a fruit and vegetable garden, it was run by M. de La Quintinie, who had been placed in charge of all fruit trees in the royal gardens in 1670. He wrote in his dedication to Louis XIV of *Instruction pour les jardins fruitiers et potagers avec un traité des orangers, suivi de quelques réflexions sur l'agriculture* (2 volumes, 1690) that the King himself was 'the most perfect of nature's works'. Twenty-nine sections for different kinds of fruit surrounded a central vegetable garden, fertilized by droppings from the royal horses.

La Quintinie boasted that he gave the King 'new pleasures' through his asparagus and figs. In the summer 700 fig trees produced 4,000 figs a day, varieties with names such as Grosse Blanche, Petite Blanche and Grosse Violette. Sometimes the King permitted courtiers following him to pick and eat the fruit. Two foreign visitors, Nicodemus Tessin from Sweden in 1687 and Martin Lister from England in 1698, as well as M. de La Quintinie, record that the King would sometimes tend trees and bushes with his own hands. Like many other courtiers, La Quintinie was given a plot of land in Versailles on which to build a house, in addition to his official residence inside the *potager*. Fruit and vegetables considered unfit for the court were distributed to the Versaillais.[61]

In 1678–85 a vaulted stone orangery, designed by Jules Hardouin-Mansart, was built beneath the south terrace of Versailles, between two colossal stone staircases. It housed a thousand or more orange and lemon trees in winter, as it still does. Orange and lemon trees were an equivalent of silver furniture: supreme status symbols because of their cost and, in northern Europe, rarity. In summer they were moved outside, or into the palace. The main gallery of the orangery, with bare, unadorned walls and vaults, was so long and tall (510 feet by 70, twice the length of the Galerie des Glaces) that it was compared by Martin Lister to 'the naves of so many churches put together'.[62] If the stables were palaces for horses, the orangery was a palace for orange trees – one which, said ambassadors from Siam in 1686, many kings would be happy to live in themselves.[63]

While the orangery is to the left of the palace, the main garden stretches in front of it, sloping down to the canal. It was distinguished by its size (230 acres by 1715), its fountains and its sculptures in dazzling white marble. There were then at least 1,000 pieces in the park and on the façades of the palace, the largest collection of modern sculptures in Europe.[64] In 1674 alone a *grande commande* was issued by Colbert to twenty-three sculptors for sculptures of the elements, the seasons, the four continents, the four temperaments and the four types of poetry.

Four French masterpieces, Girardon's *Apollo Served by the Nymphs* and *The Abduction of Proserpina by Pluto*, and Pierre Puget's *Milo of Crotona* and *Perseus and Andromeda*, were carved for Versailles, and carefully placed at special sites in the park.[65] In Versailles, observed the *Mercure Galant* in 1684, sculptures 'seem to grow like plants and form there alleys which arouse the admiration of the cleverest and most inquisitive'.[66] The modern French sculptor Girardon, who also 'restored' many ancient statues for Louis XIV, was considered even more illustrious than the ancient Athenian sculptor Phidias.[67]

Between the palace and the Grand Canal a web of groves with pools and fountains – *bassins* and *bosquets* – are linked, through densely planted oak, beech and ash trees, by long gravel paths lined with statues. One of the most spectacular groves is called the Ballroom. Gilded vases and candelabra decorate a circular stone amphitheatre, decorated with sea-shells from the Indian Ocean, with seats for spectators, and for musicians to play for dancers in the round open-air ballroom. Others were the colonnade (surrounding Girardon's statue of the *Abduction of Proserpina by Pluto*); the labyrinth, decorated with statues of the animals mentioned in Aesop's fables; and *bassins* of Apollo, Neptune and the Nymphs.[68] The fountains of Neptune and the Dragon contain baroque sea monsters and winged dragons.[69]

Unlike its rivals Vaux-le-Vicomte and Saint-Cloud, Versailles lacked a good water supply. Yet it needed 222,000 cubic feet of water an hour to make the fountains play.[70] Sourches wrote in 1682 that the fountains and gardens were surprisingly magnificent, but that every fountain needed a river to make it flow; Versailles did not have a drop of water except what came from a 'nasty pond'.[71]

The fountains were turned on by the *fontaniers* (working under M. Denis, *commandant en chef des fontaines du roi à Versailles*) only if the King or important guests were in the garden. The King himself established the order in which they were to be turned on. The *fontaniers* whistled to each other, as they still do, to synchronize opening the taps in order to provide enough pressure to bring water to the fountains. When the King could no longer see the fountains, the taps were turned off and the fountains ran dry.[72]

On 19 October 1684 Louis XIV announced at the *lever* his plan to divert and canalize part of the River Eure, 40 miles to the west, in order to bring more water to the reservoirs and improve water pressure at Versailles. Since France was then at peace, in the following years thirty-six battalions of infantry and six squadrons of dragoons – perhaps as many as 35,000 soldiers – were employed levelling hills, building aqueducts, roads and bridges, in addition to the hundreds of civilians already working on the palace and park. Remains of the Aqueduct of Maintenon can be seen near the chateau of that name, showing, as the King intended, that he could emulate the arcaded aqueducts of ancient Rome: it looks like a section of the Pont du Gard. Some 1,500 soldiers died during the operations. More fell ill from the marshy air and bad water, and later spread diseases among other troops.[73]

Vauban, the voice of reason, was appalled, criticizing the King in a letter to Louvois on 29 June 1685 for trying to surpass the Romans while ruling only a tenth of their Empire: 'the King will be accountable to all nations and to posterity.'[74] As with the construction of Versailles on a bad site, the difficulty of the enterprise was part of its attraction. Louis XIV wanted to demonstrate omnipotence.

Eventually, however, thanks to the establishment of massive lakes and reservoirs over a large area, watered by the River Bièvre – shown being visited by Louis XIV and Louvois in a painting by Jean-Baptiste Martin le Vieux – and to the creation of another aqueduct, vaulted reservoirs under the park and almost 40 miles of pipes and drains, the fountains could run for a few hours, enough to astonish and delight visitors.[75] The Dragon fountain, among the highest in Europe, can reach 88 feet in height, the Obelisk fountain, with 232 jets of water, 75 feet.[76]

In addition to Versailles, Paris was being encircled by parks, with similar fountains, statues, orangeries, *tapis verts*, terraces and sweeping perspectives. In 1669–73 at Saint-Germain, Le Nôtre had laid out the magnificent Grande Terrasse, 2,600 yards long, above the Seine. It was intended to continue the Champs-Elysées, laid out for Parisians after 1670 as a park and avenue to the west of the Tuileries garden, and still the defining axis of western Paris today.[77] In addition to his parks and gardens at Saint-Germain, Versailles, Marly, Trianon, Compiègne and Fontainebleau, Louis also encouraged his relations and courtiers to create or extend their own, and he often suggested improvements during his visits: the Dauphin at Meudon; Monsieur at Saint-Cloud; the Prince de Condé at Chantilly; the Duc du Maine at Sceaux; the Comte de Toulouse at Rambouillet; and many more. He never, however, revisited the first of them all, Fouquet's garden at Vaux.

In addition to the main garden at Versailles, Louis XIV created two other gardens, around pavilions called Trianon and Marly. They expressed his tastes and personality even more than Versailles itself, which partly reflected his ambitions for the monarchy and for France.

In 1668–70 a church and village north-west of the chateau of Versailles called Trianon were demolished, to make place for the Trianon de Porcelaine. Covered in blue and white Dutch and French tiles in the Chinese style, it was a lovers' retreat. One of the three rooms was called the Chambre des Amours, where the King met Madame de Montespan in private in the daytime.[78] It was his creation. He wrote to Colbert in 1670, 'Hurry on with Trianon, for it must be perfect when I arrive.'[79] The tiles on the outside, however, often broke in winter. After the celebrations held there in July 1685 for the marriage of their elder daughter Mlle de Nantes to Condé's grandson the Duc de Bourbon, when a pyramid of fire with 7,000 lights was erected at the other end of the Grand Canal, it was demolished.[80] Marriage to Bourbon, 'very considerably shorter than the shortest men' (his mother's dwarf was widely blamed) according to Saint-Simon, with a ferocious temper, livid yellow skin and delusions that he was a dog, was unpleasant, but gave his wife the rank of Princess of the Blood.[81]

In the autumn of 1687, a new Trianon of marble, personally designed by the King with the help of Mansart, was started. The King worked in a tent near by, so that he could check on its progress. In January 1688 he dined there for the first time. The new Trianon de Marbre was completely original: two one-storey, elongated, flat-roofed Palladian villas of about thirty rooms, including council and music rooms. They were connected by an open colonnade, with views of the gardens and the canal and were lined on the garden side by eighty columns and pilasters of pink Languedoc marble.[82]

Whereas Versailles was a garden of statues and fountains, with a few flowerbeds near the palace, Trianon was a garden of flowers. Louis XIV loved flowers, like music and ballet, more than any other king of France. The King himself had been compared to a great and immortal flower, whose perfume scented all Europe, when he danced as Spring in the *Ballet des Saisons* (1661).[83] He was also compared to a sunflower, an orange tree or a lily.[84] In the winter of 1669, on the last occasion the King danced in public, in the *Ballet Royal de Flore* in the Tuileries palace where it joined the end of the Grande Galerie of the Louvre, Flora, goddess of flowers, told him that the flowers should no longer regard her as their queen, since they recognized no one but him as their Sovereign. The section of the palace where the ballet was performed was renamed the Pavillon de Flore, a name it has kept to this day.

Flowers decorated the King's carpets, tapestries, furniture and pictures, as well as his gardens.[85] Tuberoses, hyacinth and jonquil were imported for Trianon from Normandy, Marseille and Toulon. In 1682, in addition to the royal nursery and the Jardin des Plantes already flourishing in Paris, a special nursery was created at Toulon solely to grow Mediterranean plants for the King. In 1683 a total of 65,000 tuberoses were sent from Toulon to Versailles.[86] In 1686 some 20,000 jonquil bulbs and in 1687 more than 5,300 violets and 2,000 iris were sent to Trianon from Toulon, while 20,000 narcissus bulbs were sent from England.[87] In 1687, according to the Swedish architect Nicodemus Tessin – and similar figures can be found in the garden accounts – 200,000 potted plants were being prepared near Trianon (in a special hot house called Châteauneuf de Trianon) for the royal gardens 'in order to make the changes in decoration which His Majesty desires'.[88]

Flowers, like fountains and gardens, showed the King's power. Through flowers, he turned winter into spring.[89] The garden of Trianon had a special Cabinet des Parfums with heavily scented jasmine, tuberose and hyacinth. According to Saint-Simon, confirmed by a letter from Madame de Maintenon, 'all the flowerbeds changed compartments of flowers every day and I have seen the King and all the Court be forced to leave them by the smell of the tuberoses, whose scent embalmed the air but was so strong from their quantity that no one could remain in the garden, although it was vast and on a terrace above an arm of the canal.'[90] A contemporary guidebook states that the scent of the thousands of flowers in the 'enchanted place' of Trianon made visitors 'ravished as if they were in ecstasy'.[91]

The garden at Trianon also had fountains and statues like Versailles. Part of it, however, was wild, separated from the Grand Parc by early examples of ha-has. Beside one wing was the Jardin des Sources, a romantic garden of rivulets snaking through woods and bushes, to create islets where ladies could play cards or sew.[92] The King loved Trianon. He once wrote to his son, 'The weather is marvellous and I am very happy to enjoy the beauties of this place, which I find greater every day; that is why I do not know when I will leave it.'[93]

Trianon could be visited by courtiers and members of the public. Marly, however, was reserved for the King's guests. It was built in a secluded valley 5 miles north of Versailles, and 3.5 miles south of Saint-Germain. From June 1679 the King had a park cleared (twenty-two workmen died at Marly that year)[94] and from 1680 to 1684, as Versailles was being finished, built a square Pavillon Royal between two long *pièces d'eau*. Like Trianon, it was inspired by Palladian villas in Italy. It was surrounded by guard pavilions, two service buildings, twelve smaller pavilions (of Jupiter, Venus and other Olympian deities), pools, gardens and woods. To emphasize its fairy-tale character, ornaments on the façades, showing scenes from the life of Apollo, the Sun God, were painted in pink, blue and gold trompe l'oeil.[95]

In 1680–85 an engineer from Liège named Baron Deville created the Machine de Marly. It was the largest machine of its time, partly designed to impress by its scale and audacity. Two hundred and fifty-nine pumps and fourteen wooden wheels raised water 535 feet above the Seine to an aqueduct 710 yards long which supplied the palace, parks and neighbouring villages. Cuttings through the forest and the village – the Chemin de la Machine and the rue de la Machine – show where the machine once worked, before its destruction in 1817. Fountains could play all day at Marly, which they could not at Versailles.[96]

Louis spent a few nights in Marly in October 1683 – a year after his move to Versailles – and gave his first party there on 23 July 1684. Soon it became a passion. He went there eight times in 1687, sixteen in 1688 and twenty-seven in 1689. At first there were about thirty guests, after 1700 generally over 100.[97]

In the 1660s Louis had invited members of the bourgeoisie or the *noblesse de robe* – Madame Bignon, Madame Tambonneau, the Présidente Tubeuf – to entertainments at Versailles.[98] Attracted to intelligence, he had relatively low-born favourites like Vauban, Racine, and Madame de Maintenon herself. He liked to think that he valued merit, ability and hard work.[99]

At Marly after 1686, however, Louis invited only the *noblesse d'épée* (the few *nobles de robe* who appeared had to dress as *nobles d'épée* in bright silk or velvet court costumes rather than in their normal black costume: Lauzun called them fashion dolls). Rules for presentation and the right to sit in the King's carriages were tightened, making the court more exclusive.[100] In order to raise money, Louis XIV also ordered *recherches de noblesse*, and created new offices, throughout the kingdom in 1666–74 and 1696–1715, which penalized the *noblesse de robe* (whose offices thereby lost value), and, by raising the price of nobility, made proofs of ancient birth a source of wealth as well as pride.[101] Thus, at Marly and Versailles, Louis began the process of restricting the honours of the court to a caste of a few hundred ancient noble families, which would alienate many of the monarchy's natural supporters.

His first visits to Marly of three to four days were gradually extended to seven to ten days. After 1700 he spent three or four months a year there – in 1711, for example, 143 days. Even if he slept at Versailles, he might visit Marly for a few hours in the day.[102]

The park at Marly contained over a hundred Salles de Verdure or green rooms, opening into each other, or connected by long straight paths through woods. Decorated with fountains and statues, they had names like 'salon of the faun', 'vestibule of Hercules', 'basin of the vestal virgins', 'the baths of Agrippina'. Each 'room' was lined with topiary hedges, marble benches and trees in tubs. They often contained games, such as swings, an early version of croquet, a chess table or a wooden chariot on a slide called a *roulette*. The combinations of light, shadow, water, trees, grass, statues – and silence – made these gardens particularly seductive. Sometimes guests ate meals or played cards in them.[103]

The King was particularly proud of 'the river', which he had designed himself. It looked like a cascade, but was in reality fifty-two pools of water, lined with red, green and white marble, descending a hill opposite the Pavillon Royal. Some of the fountains at Marly sprayed water at each other continuously, making a sound like artillery fire.[104]

Another entertainment was to watch carp swimming in the pools. Louis XIV would come in the evening from Versailles especially to admire silver, gold or blue carp 'of extraordinary beauty', with names like 'the mask of gold', 'the crimson'; the biggest was called 'la royale'. However, carp need mud and he needed clear water to see them. Many died, or were replaced 'an infinity of times', in the words of Saint-Simon, by carp offered by loyal subjects; others, unmentioned by the Duke, survived in the ponds known as *la grande pièce* and *les nappes*.[105]

In 1702 the park at Marly was finished by placing at the entrance, beside a large pool where horsemen could wash their horses, two magnificent statues of winged horses by Coysevox, now in the Cour Marly in the Louvre. Madame called them the most beautiful statues in the world, in the most beautiful garden.[106] She was not alone in her opinion. Four years earlier, William III's Ambassador, the Earl of Portland, who was also 'surintendant' of his gardens, had admired the situation of Meudon, the magnificence of Versailles and the charm of Trianon. But, as he wrote to his master, Marly was 'the most agreeable garden I have seen, and it would greatly please Your Majesty', although he was shocked by the time and money spent on the Machine de Marly.[107] In the next reign an Ottoman ambassador, on seeing the beauty of Marly, exclaimed that the world was the paradise of the infidel but the prison of the faithful. In all, the creation of Marly cost about 11.7 million livres.[108]

At Marly Louis XIV could express his unconventionality. Despite all his experience of living in public, he was, according to Sourches, 'always [extremely gay] when he was accompanied by few people'. The few in this case (Sourches is describing a visit to Maintenon) were nineteen court officials in waiting, two ministers, a small number of *bas officiers de service* and the colonels of some regiments stationed near by.[109] Racine wrote from Marly in 1687: 'There are few people and the King selects those who should follow him [court officials came only if invited]. So all those who are there consider themselves very lucky to be there, and are in very good humour. The King himself is very free and very caressing there. One could say that at Versailles he is completely devoted to politics and in Marly to his pleasures and himself.'

Marly was a country house, not a palace. The King's bed had no balustrade, as it did in Versailles or the Louvre, to keep courtiers at bay. In the main salon of the Pavillon royal guests stretched out on chairs in the presence of members of the royal family, talking and playing cards with them almost as equals. They could address the King when they wished. Women wore *robes de chambre* rather than, as at Versailles, *grands habits*. Guests were fed and heated at the King's expense, which was not the case at Versailles. Meals were eaten together at round tables. The fashionable new drinks of tea and coffee were served, which they were not at the King's meals at Versailles. In 1705 Madame complained that men wore hats when walking with the King in the garden, and even the cleaners had started playing cards in the corridors: 'it no longer resembles a court at all.'[110]

Dangeau noted: 'The king, who wants courtiers to be completely at ease here, has ordered all sorts of liqueurs to be brought to the salon so that they do not think of leaving the château.' Courtiers should lack nothing.[111] Conversation in the salon at Marly spared no one. At Versailles the King's illegitimate daughters were admired for their grace and majesty; at Marly they exchanged insults.[112] The Princesse de Conti was heard to call her sister a wine sack; the Duchesse de Chartres replied by reproaching her with her multitude of lovers. Many Gardes du Corps had been sent away, because they had been, or might become, her lovers.[113]

The King remained a compulsive host, who did not wish his guests to be bored. In June 1701, despite his grief at Monsieur's death, he insisted that gambling continue at Marly.[114] Sometimes there were four balls during one visit to Marly, and the King, drinking as if in a cabaret, spent two hours at dinner with the ladies.[115]

At Marly even guests who had given up dancing, or were in mourning, were made to dance. For carnival, courtiers dressed as peasants, animals, amazons, Chinamen or the Ottoman Sultan and his court. Saint-Simon, who once danced dressed as a peasant, claimed that after he had refused to dance, he was no longer invited.[116] The King himself danced, aged sixty-five, in a mask, with a gauze dressing gown over his usual clothes, and allowed court officials to attend his *coucher* in masks.[117]

Strangely, as with ministers' ricochets between Paris and Versailles, no complaints from courtiers of the repeated journeys between royal chateaux have been found. Perhaps they enjoyed the relative quiet of the carriage. The King never kept still. In one day, 29 October 1699, for example, he went from Versailles to Marly, and then to Saint-Germain, and then via Marly back to Versailles.[118] On 2 November 1702, at the age of sixty-four, he went from Versailles to Marly, then to Saint-Germain, then back to Versailles.[119] By then however he was using, as he had done since an operation in 1686, an early example of a wheelchair, pushed from behind by two servants, for long walks in the park.[120]

His family also frequently moved between different places in the same day. On 4 December 1710 the Dauphin's daughter-in-law the Duchesse de Bourgogne went from Versailles to Meudon to dine with her father-in-law; they then travelled together to the opera in Paris; then back to Versailles for supper with the King.[121]

Louis XIV was proud of Marly, and used it as another instrument of control, like the *justaucorps à brevet* and the *divertissements*. Women attended the King's supper at Versailles, to show their desire to go to Marly, and have their names put on the next guest list.[122] Nobles asked for invitations the day before his departure, or on the morning itself, with the famous phrase, 'Sire, Marly?' The list of guests was not publicly announced until the last moment. Sometimes the King left earlier than announced in order to avoid courtiers' requests.[123] In 1687 Dangeau heard him say that, if Marly were as large as Fontainebleau, it would still not be big enough for everyone who asked to stay there.[124] More rooms were added, so he could invite more guests.[125]

Invitations began to be issued to ministers and even their wives, or as rewards to distinguished officers like the Maréchal de Bellefonds or Vauban.[126] Like Versailles, Marly too eventually became in part a working palace, with council meetings and regular military reviews held on an open space on the way to Versailles called the Hell Hole – *le trou d'enfer*. Sometimes, if the King was away, the gardens were opened to the public.[127]

The public was usually allowed into the gardens and palace of Versailles 'without distinction of sex, age or condition'. Only the dirty or diseased were stopped by the Gardes du Corps at the entrances.[128] Sometimes, however, the King preferred to be alone when giving orders to the garden-ers.[129] The garden was also closed if the King felt 'overwhelmed' by the multitude of people, 'above all from Paris'; 'la canaille', wrote Dangeau, damaged the statues and vases.[130] However, Louis XIV's sense of kingship trumped his love of privacy: the public was always allowed back. Without the public, the gardens would have lost their purpose. In 1704 the King ordered fences to be removed from the *bosquets* of Versailles so that the public could enjoy walking inside them (which it cannot now do, except on the few days the fountains are playing).[131]

Versailles was built for Europe, as well as for France. From the start, more than other royal palaces, it was intended to please not only the King and his courtiers, but also the growing number of foreigners making the Grand Tour. From 1674 detailed guidebooks by the court historiographer André Félibien and others were written, partly for foreigners, by order of the King and checked by the group responsible for managing his image, known as the Petite Académie. In addition prints of buildings and parties at Versailles were engraved by the Cabinet du Roi, and by counterfeiters, and the *Mercure Galant* regularly published accounts of buildings and receptions at Versailles.[132]

Favoured foreigners were given special tours of Versailles. The Spanish (1679), Russian (1682), Moroccan (1684), Algerian (1686), English (1698) and Tripolitanian (1704) ambassadors and the Doge of Genoa (1685) were taken round the gardens, and the palace, by officials of the Ministry of Foreign Affairs – and some also visited Marly. The King himself showed especially favoured guests and ambassadors around his gardens, for exam-ple Vauban in 1686; the Duchess of Modena in 1673, on her way to England with her daughter Mary, the bride whom Louis XIV had selected for the Duke of York; and Mary of Modena, back again in 1689, this time as England's exiled Queen.[133] That year Louis XIV wrote his own guide-book, *Manière de montrer les jardins de Versailles* ('The Way to Show the Gardens of Versailles'); he subsequently rewrote it six times. The tone is dry and commanding, like instructions for ballet movements: 'one will enter the small alley which goes to Flora, one will go to the Baths of Apollo, and one will walk round them to consider the statues, the cabinets and the bas reliefs . . . if one wants to see the Ménagerie and Trianon in the same day, after having paused beside Apollo, one will take a boat for the Ménagerie.'[134]

A few foreigners mocked Versailles; the poet diplomat Matthew Prior who served Louis XIV's enemy William III described it as 'something the foolishest in the world; he is strutting in every panel and galloping over one's head in every ceiling'. Or they hoped that its cost would

discourage Louis XIV from starting more wars.[135] Thousands more, however, were impressed. In another guidebook to Versailles, which gives as
much space to the gardens, Trianon and Marly as to the palace itself,
Piganiol de La Force called Versailles 'the admiration of the centuries to
come and the marvel of our own'.[136] French guidebooks boasted that Versailles showed that the King could conquer nature as well as provinces.
Forests and gardens had appeared out of nowhere.[137] Like Rome and
Venice, Versailles became one of the sights of Europe. By 1700 the future
George I of England, and two future kings of Poland, Augustus the Strong
of Saxony and Stanisław Leszczyński, had all visited it.

English visitors were particularly impressed. Even Matthew Prior,
despite his mockery, acquired prints and descriptions of Versailles.[138]
Another English visitor, Martin Lister, described Versailles as the most
magnificent palace 'in all Europe'. Both the Grand Appartement and the
King's and Dauphin's private apartments could be visited by ordinary
travellers as well as grandees, especially if they had a letter of recommendation and the King was away.[139] In 1701, John Northleigh, although
shocked by the number of beggars in Paris, also called Versailles 'the most
beautiful palace in Europe ... that [side] which fronts the Garden surpasses all that can be imagined sumptuous; its Roof glittering with Gold
affords a glorious Prospect at a Distance.' The garden, 'for statues, canals,
groves, grotto's, fountains, waterworks or what else may be thought
delightful, far surpasses any Thing to be seen of this kind in Italy'. Inside,
the great gallery was 'the noblest that I ever beheld in my Life'.[140]

In the same year another Englishman, Ellis Veryard, wrote that the
gardens and fountains in 'this Master-piece of Art ... in my opinion far
exceed those of Frascati and Tivoli so much boasted of in Italy'.[141] Writing
a guide to the Grand Tour in the 1740s, Thomas Nugent called the palace
'one of the finest in all Europe': 'The great marble staircase surpasses
anything in antiquity.'[142]

Versailles was not just a prodigy designed to impress by its scale and
beauty. It was also intended to promote pleasure. The gardens contain
statues of nymphs and satyrs, Venus and Ganymede. A Cupid guarded
the entrance to the Labyrinth. Plays performed at court, such as *L'Amour
médecin* (1665), *Les Amants magnifiques* (1670, a subject chosen by the
King), *Les Fêtes de l'Amour et de Bacchus* (1672) or *Le Triomphe de
l'amour* (1680), celebrated 'the adorable power of love', conqueror of
conquerors. In *Thésée* (1675), Venus, goddess of love, hopes to establish
her court in the gardens of Versailles.[143]

The memoirs of Jean de Plantavit de La Pause, an officer from the
provinces on leave, show that he (and no doubt others) did indeed 'court

Venus' in the gardens of Versailles. Plantavit de La Pause stayed for three days in an inn at Versailles in July 1699, making visits to Trianon where he attended the King's *lever* and enjoyed the 'brilliant company' and the gardens. A friend called M. de Berteuil organized a meeting for Plantavit and his brother-in-law with two women at 10 p.m. in the Allée du Dragon, beside a gate going straight from the town into the park, avoiding the guards and the palace. They waited in silence between marble statues.

When the women arrived, Berteuil, no doubt protected by trees, 'conversed for some time with the mother, for it was a mother and a daughter, while we kept the daughter. Then we gave him the daughter, while we kept the mother. They were quite amiable . . . the daughter was thin but she had fine eyes, a good figure and an inexhaustible love of pleasure. We spent an hour perfectly agreeably with them.' Then they escorted their companions back to the town of Versailles. Next day the adventure was the talk of the court.[144] The gardens continued to attract lovers. In August 1722, soon after the return of the court under Louis XV, three young courtiers would be exiled for committing 'abominations' in a *bosquet*.[145]

Versailles was intended by Louis not only to impress and entertain visitors, but also to surpass the palaces and gardens of Rome, both ancient and modern. The inscription on a print of 1683, like many others, proclaimed that he was heir of the Roman emperors:

> – Monde, viens voir ce que je voye,
> – Et ce que le soleil admire.
> – Rome dans un Palais, dans Paris un empire.
> – Et tous les Césars dans un roy.[146]

('World, come and see what I see, and what the sun admires, Rome in a palace, an empire in Paris, and all the Caesars in one king.')

Louis, more than other monarchs of his time, was sculpted as a Roman emperor, in Roman armour, cloak and boots and a full seventeenth-century wig, even in bronze effigies on pieces of furniture, as well as on triumphal arches in Paris. In the frescoes of the Galerie des Glaces, he was represented as Apollo, Mars or Jupiter with thunderbolts.

Many statues, both inside and outside Versailles and Marly, were either copies of Roman originals by modern French sculptors (the Apollo Belvedere, Laocoön and his children, Antinous) or were Roman statues inherited from Mazarin, bought in Rome or discovered in France and on the shores of the Mediterranean.[147] They included the Venus of Arles (discovered in the Roman theatre there in 1651); Jupiter and Juno from Besançon; Apollo from Smyrna; Modesty from Benghazi; twelve porphyry busts of Roman emperors in the Galerie des Glaces.[148] Confirming Versailles' identification with imperial Rome, eighty-four marble busts of Roman emperors decorate the façade facing Paris, in eloquent proximity to the French royal crowns and fleurs-de-lys in the balustrades.

Versailles helped free Frenchmen from their sense of inferiority towards the classical past and modern Rome. The King was assured that he was more glorious than Alexander, Caesar or Augustus, that Versailles would win him immortality.[149] M. Combes wrote that the peoples of the earth should come to Versailles: 'Versailles alone is enough to assure for ever to France the glory which it now has to surpass all other kingdoms in the science of buildings . . . You will see there ancient and modern Rome.'[150]

Charles Le Brun's cycle of stupendous pictures of Alexander the Great, such as *The Queens of Persia at the Feet of Alexander*, still hanging in Versailles today, was intended not only as an homage to the new Alexander, Louis XIV, but also as proof that French painters were as good as Italians. The creation of Versailles, boasted Madeleine de Scudéry in 1669 and Charles Perrault in 1687, meant that Italy must now yield supremacy in the arts to France.[151]

Louis XIV also bought Italian pictures for the Royal Collection, increasing their number from 200 to 2,000. In December 1681, on one of his rare visits to Paris, he selected around forty-five pictures in the Louvre for removal to Versailles, including works by Raphael, Titian, Rubens and Van Dyck. The *Mona Lisa*, acquired by Leonardo's patron François I, was placed in the King's private gallery, with many other treasures: the great Veronese *Supper in the House of Simon*, a present from the Doge of Venice, hung in the state apartments. The *Mercure Galant* in 1682, like later guidebooks, listed the pictures and sculptures in the palace among its attractions for visitors.[152] Unlike the Louvre today, Versailles was a royal palace, not a public museum. It too, however, could be visited by the public, and both palaces served the same purpose: to increase the attraction and prestige of France. In the words of the *Mercure Galant*, at Versailles Louis XIV 'does the honours of France and shows foreigners the magnificence of his court'.[153]

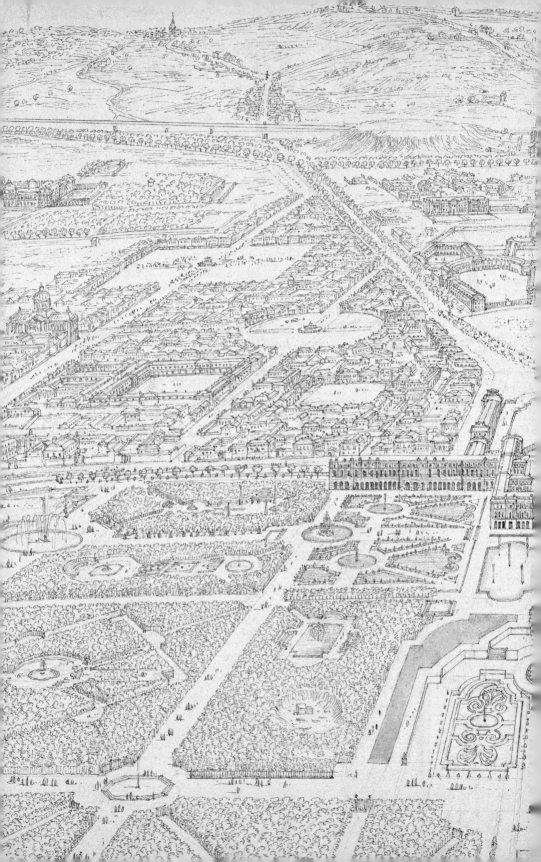

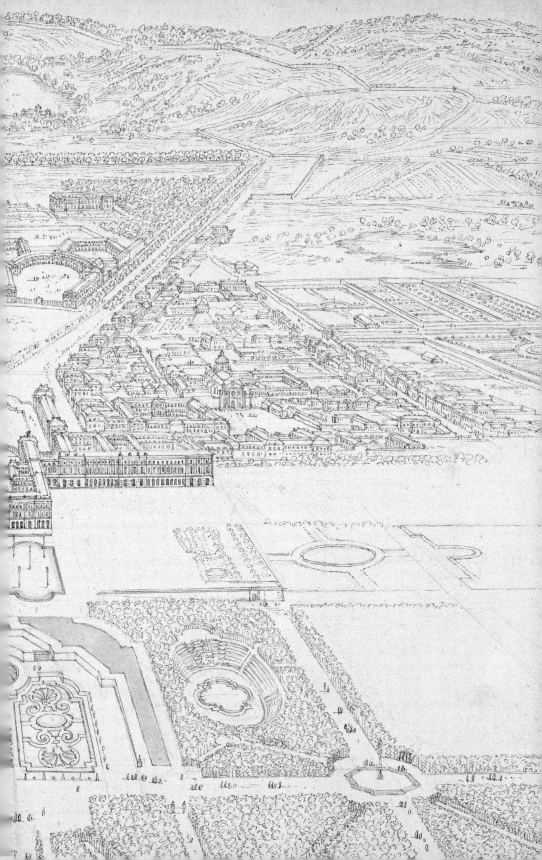

13

Inside Versailles

The King's day inside his palaces began and ended with the *lever* and the *coucher*. They were not only physical processes, when the King rose and retired, but also occasions when courtiers could watch him, talk to him and each other, and hear the latest news. Molière often watched, since he was 'very assiduous' during his turn of duty as one of the *valets de chambre tapissiers*, responsible for the King's furniture and making his bed, a post inherited from his father. In 1663 he described the *lever* as a battle. Men pushed like devils, elbowing aside their neighbours, to reach the front of the crowd.[1]

Like most aspects of his court, these ceremonies were not invented by Louis XIV, but were inherited from previous reigns. Since at least the sixteenth century, the king of France had been dressed and undressed by some of his highest court officials: the *grand chambellan, maître de la garde-robe* and *premier gentilhomme de la chambre*, and by princes of the royal family, if present. As Catherine de Médicis had informed her son Henri III, of his grandfather François I (reigned 1515–47): 'When he took off his shirt and other clothes, all the princes, lords, captains, knights of the order, gentlemen of the chamber, *maîtres d'hôtel* and *gentilshommes servans* then entered and he spoke to them and they saw him, which greatly contented them.'[2]

During Louis XIV's youth in Paris in the 1650s, his *lever* had been relatively simple, as Marie Dubois, one of his *valets de chambre*, recounts: prayers; study; half an hour on the commode; conversation with *grands seigneurs* to whom he 'talked in such familiar fashion, one after the other, that he delighted them'. Then the King washed, prayed again, finished dressing, worked with Cardinal Mazarin and left to practise fencing or dancing, or to go hunting.[3]

After 1661, Louis XIV's *lever* and *coucher* were more formal and better attended. Between 7.30 a.m. and 8.30 a.m., as the *valets de chambre* tidied the bedroom, its doors were opened by an *huissier de la chambre*, or usher, for his Premier Médecin, Premier Chirurgien and, until her death in 1688, Perrette Dufour, a peasant woman ennobled in 1653 for having been his wet-nurse.[4]

Apart from his moments of relaxation with Madame de Montespan, the King rarely had baths, except, reluctantly, *bains de la chambre* for medical purposes, on doctors' orders.[5] Instead, after he had risen, he was rubbed down, dressed and shaved (every two days) by valets. Then the *grandes entrées* were admitted. They included court officials such as the *premiers gentilshommes de la chambre*, *premiers valets de chambre* and Grand Maître de la Garde-robe; and the *lecteurs du roi*. The King washed his hands and read his prayers. Louis XIV also gave these *entrées*, much appreciated for the opportunities provided to talk to him informally, to a few personal favourites: his illegitimate sons, Lauzun in 1671 and after 1689, and at the end of his reign victorious generals such as Boufflers and Villars; but not to Princes of the Blood until after the death of Condé in 1686.[6]

Later, as the King's shirt and jacket were presented to him by the Premier Gentilhomme in waiting, or a prince, the third level of privileged subjects, the *entrées de la chambre*, were admitted. They included the elite of France: the Grand Chambellan and Grand Aumônier (the cardinal in charge of the royal chapels and religious life at court); bishops and chaplains; *capitaines des gardes*; marshals, admirals, lieutenant generals, ambassadors, cardinals, ministers, governors of provinces, *premiers présidents de parlement* and others.[7]

Sometimes there were as many as a hundred men at the *lever*, although court officials not in waiting were not obliged to attend.[8] In contrast to their respectful silence in his youth, courtiers continued talking even when the King was praying by his bed. John Locke was surprised in December 1678 'by the noise and buzz of the rest of the chamber which is full of people standing and talking to one another'.[9] Louis XIV occasionally announced a piece of news at a *lever* or *coucher*. In 1703 and 1712, for example, he read out despatches, praising and mentioning by name the officers and regiments who had distinguished themselves in the latest battle.[10]

Ambassadors were reluctant to attend the *lever* or *coucher*. In contrast to their formal Tuesday audiences with the King and the royal family, organized by the Grand Maître des Cérémonies and his department, they were pushed by courtiers 'in the crowds and in the press', as Ezechiel Spanheim, the Brandenburg minister, complained: an insult to their masters as well as themselves. At the end of the *lever* the King had his wig arranged, prayed at his prie-dieu and ate a quick breakfast of wine, soup and bread.[11] Finally he was handed his hat, gloves and cane, and gave his orders for the day to waiting officials.

Thus accessibility, like the *lever* and *coucher* themselves, distinguished the French from other European courts. Access was regulated by when courtiers were admitted to the King's bedroom, not where they were admitted in the state apartments. There were no *distinctions d'antichambre*, limiting certain ranks to certain rooms. Henri III's efforts to introduce them, and to regulate access, had increased his unpopularity.[12]

The court's informality lasted throughout the reign. Far from being an enclosed world, it was, as foreigners frequently remarked, more accessible, and less hierarchical, than other courts. Louis XIV himself disliked ceremonies and would write, in a famous phrase, 'if there is a singularity in this monarchy, it is the free and easy access of subjects to the monarch.'[13] The Italian Primi Visconti described Louis XIV's court as 'a real confusion of men and women'.[14] Another visitor from Italy, Antonio Farnese, wrote in 1698: 'when you want, you can see, talk with and almost touch the King.'[15] The King needed his cane not only for support, but to bar uninvited guests, or to fight to make room for the Queen and her ladies, or even for himself.[16] The court was not a slave, as Saint-Simon claimed, but a hydra. Not even Louis XIV, for all the fear and awe he inspired, was in total control.[17]

The same process, lasting about an hour and a half even when the King was on campaign, was repeated in reverse during his *coucher*, as the King retired to bed. Since it was late, however, there were fewer people. At the end the King gave the password to the commanders of the different forces on guard, and then told his Premier Valet de Chambre to pass the *bougeoir* – a candle on a plate – to whomever he wished to favour that evening. As the King boasted in his memoirs, one of the most visible effects of his power was to give 'an infinite value' to something which in itself was nothing.[18]

Thereafter, during what was called his *petit coucher*, wearing no more than his dressing gown, the King sat on his commode. Even during his most basic functions, the King received one or two courtiers 'by ceremony far more than by necessity'. They were proud recipients of the *brevet d'affaires*, named after his commode or *chaise d'affaires*, an honour which gave special opportunities to talk freely to the King and on occasion to ask for favours.[19] He then went to the Queen's bedroom, escorted by the Premier Valet de Chambre with a torch.

There were at least seven rooms elsewhere in the palace serving as public lavatories, while courtiers and members of the royal family would have their own *chaise percée* in a small *cabinet d'aisance* in their apartment. Madame nevertheless complained that it was impossible to leave her apartment without seeing people urinating. Staircases and galleries were especially popular.[20]

The only senior court posts created by Louis XIII had been military: the commanders of the Mousquetaires, the Chevau-légers and the Gendarmes of his guard. The only senior court post created by Louis XIV was in charge of his clothes: the *grand maître de la garde-robe* in 1669. With unconscious irony Louis XIV gave the post in 1672 to the Duc de La Rochefoucauld, whose father had, in private, been so critical of courtiers' dress in 1660.[21]

Louis XIV often wore plain clothes, particularly on campaign. However, he was a connoisseur of jewels. In 1674 he wrote to Colbert of his need to have a case of jewels for himself and Madame de Montespan, so that they always had enough to suit the colour of their clothes: 'it is necessary to have stones of all colours so that they can be changed.'[22] On great occasions, he was covered with jewels like the images of the Madonna carried in procession through the streets of Paris.[23] He would wear them on his coat, hat, sword hilt and cross of the Order of the Holy Spirit. Once his coat of gold brocade was so covered in diamonds that he seemed to the Chevalier d'Arvieux to be surrounded by light.[24]

Due to the King's massive purchases from jewellers such as Jean-Baptiste Tavernier and Jean Chardin, who travelled as far as India, the value of his personal jewels – as distinct from the crown jewels, which formed a separate collection – rose from 7 million livres in 1666 to 11 million in 1691. According to the inventory of 1691, Louis XIV owned rubies, emeralds, pearls and sapphires, and diamonds.[25] He already owned 1,911 diamonds in 1669. His jewel casket, smothered in raised gold filigree carvings (especially of sunflowers), made in 1675 by Jacob Blanck of Nuremberg, is one of the treasures of the Louvre's Louis XIV galleries. Jewels surrounded the crowned miniature portraits of himself, which he gave as diplomatic gifts.[26]

The Garde-robe was a separate department of the Maison du Roi. It included two *maîtres de la garde-robe*; four *premiers valets de la garde-robe* who served in rotation every three months; sixteen *valets de garde-robe*; and many other servants. They helped the King put on and remove his under-garments (courtiers did the rest), and ordered and looked after his clothes. The clothes themselves were kept in three rooms on the ground floor of the central block of the chateau of Versailles.[27]

With the expansion of the Garde-robe, the number employed at the Maison du Roi, including guards and tradesmen following the court, rose from 833 in 1663 (less than during the Fronde) to 1,139 in 1674; to 1,866 in 1683; and to 3,309 in 1702. In addition to the King's civil household there were other royal households – of the Queen (609 in 1683), of Monsieur (830 officers, excluding servants, in 1699), of Madame and of the King's grandsons. In order to reduce his independence, the Dauphin, in accordance with French court traditions, was obliged to use the King's household.[28]

The court was further expanded by the creation of households, with pages and court officials, for the King's illegitimate children. The total number, with the military household and courtiers' servants, may have reached 10,000, or more.[29] This was in contrast to the undignified court of his father's final years. It may have represented between 10 and 20 per cent of total government expenditure in an average year in peacetime – although this figure includes pensions, many of which were awarded to people without court offices.[30]

In one respect, however, Louis XIV reduced his household. Henri III had had over 700 gentlemen of the chamber. Henri IV and Louis XIII had continued to appoint them.[31] After 1661 Louis XIV stopped. He had no equivalent of the 300 or more chamberlains of the Holy Roman Emperor – who, however rarely they served at court, connected it to distant provinces. Perhaps he felt that, unlike his predecessors, he did not need to use this post to secure nobles' loyalties; perhaps he wanted to encourage ambitious nobles to serve in his military rather than his civil household.[32]

Instead of noble court officials, the court of France was distinguished by a multiplication of valets, *huissiers* and *garçons* in the Chamber and the Garde-robe. They were often well-educated men with aspirations to noble status, although the Parlement de Paris, in a rare display of independence, refused to register a royal edict giving it to them automatically.[33]

The most important were the four *premiers valets de chambre* – confidants who helped run Louis XIV's private life and funds, and had as much influence as more senior officials such as the Grand Ecuyer or Grand Aumônier. The Premier Valet de Chambre in waiting slept on a camp bed at the foot of the King's bed, guarded the doors of the council chamber, and held the keys to his chests of valuables. He also presented and helped reply to petitions to the King, and helped organize the allocation of apartments in the palaces. Jérôme Blouin, Premier Valet de Chambre, who before his death in 1665 helped organize the King's early land purchases at Versailles, was also a councillor of state.[34]

Access to the King's apartment was controlled by the Premier Gentilhomme de la Chambre. Outside his apartment, access to the King was the responsibility of the Capitaine des Gardes on duty, who always walked behind or beside him. By using the Premier Valet de Chambre's apartment and back stairs (known as *les derrières* or *les détours*) near the King's apartment, however, the King could bypass his court officials and receive people without their knowledge, including political figures and mistresses.[35]

A naval officer called the Comte de Forbin wrote of Bontemps, another *premier valet de chambre*, whom he used as an intermediary with the King and the ministers, that there was hardly any protection at court so useful and so sought after as his, and that few nobles had as much credit as he did.[36] Bontemps' father had been a *premier valet de chambre* of Louis XIII. Louis XIV trusted Bontemps so much that he also became governor of Versailles and *secrétaire général des Suisses et Grisons*, also running, as well as the regiment of Gardes Suisses, the Suisses du Château, often called *garçons bleus* from the colour of their livery, a private security service responsible directly to himself. They acted as the King's spies inside and outside the palace, checking comings and goings in corridors, staircases, galleries, courtyards and gardens.[37] Clearly they were effective. Ezechiel Spanheim called security at court 'excellent' – and he also admired its 'order and economy'.[38] On Bontemps' death in 1701, the *Mercure de France* praised him for being born 'less for himself than for his master'; for never speaking ill of anyone; and for serving the King with 'more exactitude than it was possible to say'.[39]

The *lever* and the *coucher* were not the only daily ceremonies when the King was on display. Public dining, with an array of silver and gold plate, and a silver or gold *nef* or vessel containing the monarch's eating utensils, often accompanied by music, was a ritual by which monarchs and grandees, throughout Europe, had long displayed their power, rank and wealth. Louis XIV, for example, ate in state in newly conquered cities in the Low Countries. 'The eloquence of the dining table' was understood by the public filing past it, wherever the King ate.[40]

The King usually had a quick meal around 1 or 2 p.m., with his brother or other members of his family. In the evening at around 10 p.m., with unusual regularity compared to his predecessors, and far more often than other monarchs, he supped *au grand couvert* – meaning in public, served, under the control of the Premier Maître d'Hôtel du Roi, by *maîtres d'hôtel* and *gentilshommes servans*. They tasted the food before it was served, to test it for poison.[41] The Capitaine des Gardes and twelve Gardes du Corps controlled security.

Usually Louis XIV ate with the Queen and other members of the royal family, at trestle tables set up for the occasion, in the room between her guard room and the Salle de l'Oeil de Boeuf called the Antichambre du

Grand Couvert. The food came from the Office Bouche on the ground floor of the Aile des Princes, in processions announced by the words 'Messieurs, à la viande du roi!' The King sat in the middle, members of his family on either side.[42]

Monsieur generally led the conversation. Madame claimed that after his death there was no general conversation at the King's table, and no one said more than a few words to their neighbours – like eating in a convent.[43] The meal was served, in the words of Spanheim, 'with calm and silence and without bother or rushing'.[44] In the King's last years, according to Madame, his way of showing favour was to offer a dish with the words 'Would you like some?'[45]

Many people, including provincials and foreigners, provided they were sufficiently well dressed to impress the *huissiers de la chambre* on the door or arrived early, took the opportunity of the public supper to watch the King eat.[46] While everyone else had to stand, duchesses, princesses and ambassadresses had the right to sit on tabourets or stools opposite the royal table. When she 'took possession' of her tabouret at the King's supper in 1696, the face of the Comtesse de Marsan shone with joy.[47]

The number of dishes (most which would subsequently have been consumed by the staff) demonstrated the display and abundance expected of a great court. The dishes served at the King's dinner, supplied by the Bouche du Roi, in which 324 people worked, on an average day included soup; *petits potages*; and four *petits potages hors-d'oeuvre*; entrées, *petites entrées* and *petites entrées hors-d'oeuvre*; twelve pigeons *pour tourte* (in a pie); six chicken fricassées and two minced partridges; two partridges; two young partridges; six turkeys, three chickens, four capons and four roast partridges; two fat capons; nine chickens, nine pigeons; four tarts; four *tourtes*; one capon, two woodcock; two *cercelles* (wood snipe) and five partridges as *petits plats hors-d'oeuvre*. The vegetables were not even listed. As the King's teeth decayed, fricassées and minced meat, soups and salads, appeared more frequently on the menu. On Fridays and fast days, when observant Catholics were obliged by church rules to eat fish, the Bouche used, for all the meals it served at court, twenty-two carp, 200 oysters, *écrevisses* (crayfish), two trout on spits; nine perch; twenty-six soles or salmon, ten carps, 100 eggs and much more.[48]

On Fridays and fast days, fish was rushed direct to Paris from the nearest ports on the Picardy coast on carts pulled by especially powerful horses, by what was called the *route du poisson*. The court naturally got the first.[49] Cooks could take offence as easily as princes. On Friday 24 April 1671 Condé's Contrôleur Général des Officiers de Bouche François Vatel, who had formerly worked for Fouquet, feared the day's catch would not arrive in time for supper at Chantilly (perhaps because heavy rain had affected the *route du poisson*), where the King was visiting the Prince for the first time. Seeing the lack of fish as an affront to his honour and his reputation, Vatel stabbed himself to death in his bedroom – just as the fish began to arrive. Mademoiselle claimed that its non-appearance had made Condé lose his temper with Vatel. Madame de Sévigné, however, wrote that he had visited Vatel in his bedroom to reassure him that nothing had been finer than the King's supper the day before. More clearly than the length of the royal menus, Vatel's suicide demonstrates the cult around royal dining. The King was shocked and said that in the future he did not want to cause so much *embarras*. Madame de Sévigné's letter, however, shows that the entertainment continued: 'dinner was very good, there was a collation and supper, an excursion, gambling, a hunt; everything was perfumed with jonquils, everything was enchanted.'[50]

The King ate with his fingers, long after the habit had become unfashionable, using a knife only to cut meat; he forbade his grandsons to use forks at his table.[51] His appetite was gigantic. Madame could remember him eating soup, a pheasant, a partridge, ham, mutton, pastries, salad and fruit in one meal. He was particularly fond of game, peas, figs and meringues. He drank little wine: at first champagne, after 1694 at his doctors' suggestion usually burgundy cut with water.[52]

Every occasion at Versailles led to the consumption of food. Even the King's confessor, each time he came to court and saw the King, was given a meal with, among other dishes, one capon, two partridges, three chickens and four pigeons.[53] Leftover food was shared among the servants.

Louis XIV's meals reflected the fashion, since 1650, for dining to become grander, cleaner and more elegant, with more elaborate table settings, more silver and a multiplicity of small dishes – as was shown in cookbooks like *Le Pâtissier français*, *Le Parfait Confiturier*, *Le Cuisinier royal*.[54] Such choice and abundance encouraged Louis XIV to eat more than he should, especially when visiting Fontainebleau, Marly and Meudon. His doctors particularly feared 'large meals during the long days of Marly and Trianon', and at *grands couverts* at Fontainebleau.[55] This led to indigestion, frequent visits to the Garde-robe, 'vapours' and rotting teeth. He got worms and may have become diabetic. His stool was minutely described by his doctors in their official diary, searching for evidence of undigested food.[56] They often made him take *lavements* (purges) and *bouillons purgatifs*.[57]

During dinner and supper, while the royal family was generally silent, favoured courtiers and members of the public filing past had opportunities to talk to the King, exchange news and ask for favours. The King asked travellers for news from foreign countries (see below, p. 281) or announced the latest news from the front. On 18 November 1704, for example, Sourches wrote, 'during his dinner the King announced to the public the truth about the affair of Breisach.'[58]

Indeed for some people the court was more important as a job and news centre than as a royal residence. As government became more centralized, great nobles lost their provincial power-bases and cut their households. The King became the principal source of patronage. All eyes turned to Versailles. Two ambassadors, Saint-Maurice and Spanheim, wrote that it was because the King was 'master of all favours' in the army, the administration and the church, and because he showered them on people working at or attending his court, that it was 'very large' and his courtiers extremely submissive.[59]

Versailles functioned as a national job centre, rather than as a gilded cage, for the nobility. Only 189 apartments in the palace were available for people outside the royal family (although there were more in the Grand Commun and Grande and Petite Ecuries). The Maison du Roi totalled around 2,000, of whom most were servants. Versailles alone could never have tamed the French nobility, which consisted of over 200,000 people.

The court was a marketplace which helped to channel the aggression and rivalries of the French nobility into the King's service. In return for protestations of love and loyalty, and obedience to the royal programme of grandeur and glory, Frenchmen who went to court, and were prepared to wait in antechambers or offices, obtained jobs, titles, honours, pensions. They also had opportunities to meet people and hear news: in other words, to network.

Advising his young cousin the naval captain Comte de Forbin, the Cardinal de Forbin-Janson, Grand Aumônier de France, wrote: 'you must have patience there [at court], ask at the right moment and do not lose heart when you do not at first obtain everything you ask for.'[60] A popular saying was 'sit down when you can; piss when you can; and ask for any job going.' Another was 'you must shoot at the right moment.'[61] The diaries of Sourches and Dangeau regularly include lists of the hundreds of new appointments made by the King, as part of court news.[62]

The King regarded job allocation as one of his principal duties. When someone asked for a dying treasurer's job, the King replied, 'the man is not yet dead and sixteen people have asked me for it.'[63] His gravity and reserve were adopted as a barrier not only against familiarity, but also against the daily deluge of requests for favours and jobs.[64] Louis often avoided or delayed decisions – over jobs or precedence, or which court official should hand him his coat – as a device, to keep courtiers panting (*en haleine*), like his dogs at feeding time.[65]

Some contemporaries also believed that the King spent time alone with Madame de Montespan, and later Madame de Maintenon, in their private apartment, partly as protection against courtiers' demands. The King and his ministers were determined to keep 'the direction of every matter and the distribution of offices'.[66]

If, as Marx would write, the July Monarchy of Louis-Philippe was 'nothing but a joint-stock company for the exploitation of France's national wealth', so was Versailles under Louis XIV. The money raised through taxes was used (sometimes, at the King's wish, against his government's financial interests)[67] to redistribute part of the wealth of France, through salaries, pensions and presents, to his nobles and officers. Similarly, lotteries at royal parties were frequent, and every guest won a prize – including treasures from Persia, China and India.[68]

He could not do too much for his favourites. To the Maréchal de Gramont, commander of the Gardes Françaises, for example, he wrote in 1673: 'when we are together you will only have to tell me what you want for me to do it with the greatest pleasure in the world.'[69] On his deathbed he would apologize to courtiers for not having 'done more' for them.

During the King's daily procession, through the Grande Galerie and the state apartment, to mass in the royal chapel, people presented petitions for jobs, pensions or promotion. The 103 placets presented to the King at Versailles on 12 June 1702, carefully listed and summarized by an official, confirm his role as the engine in a vast machine distributing jobs and money. Half the petitions concern promotions, pensions and payments in the army (53); the other half (50) deal with debts, jobs, food, law cases, vacancies in nunneries, compensation for losses suffered during fires.[70]

The King usually replied 'Je verrai' ('I will see'), and gave the petitions to be analysed by officials and ministers. A retired officer who had lost an arm once answered that, if he had said 'I will see' when told to join battle by his commanding officer, he would still have his arm and would not be presenting his petition: the King at once granted him a pension.[71]

Another officer named M. Quarré d'Aligny visited Versailles between campaigns. When the King did not at first reply to a request for promotion, Quarré d'Aligny, who had been wounded in battle, asked again, to receive the answer 'Ah! pour le coup, Monsieur, je verrai.' On another occasion the King said, 'Monsieur d'Aligny, I am very distressed by your wounds, I will look after you.' D'Aligny received an annual pension of 1,000 livres, but still had to sell some of his estates, to pay the expenses of army life.[72]

Another visitor to Versailles, Louis Monnier de Richardin, came three times between 1699 and 1707 to give the Minister of War petitions on behalf of the university of Douai. He often thought he would die of disappointment. However, he was delighted by the music in the chapel, and enjoyed watching the King's kindly behaviour to the Dauphin there. He viewed the whole palace, including the Dauphin's collections of porcelain and precious objects, watched the royal family dine in public (noticing they rarely used forks) and, thanks to an *huissier de la chambre*, obtained access to a *lever*. There he noticed the humble air of the Maréchal de Boufflers and other grandees, and the number of soldiers asking for medals, pensions or places in the Invalides. Finally in 1707 he obtained the longed-for edict, permitting medical studies at Douai.[73]

Women exercised power at the French court, not only as wives or mistresses, but also as job brokers or fixers. They could be more effective than men, as they were not distracted by wars or duels. Louis XIV's attempt in 1699 to forbid the purchase of 'protection' and 'favour' from courtiers and ladies suggests how widespread the practice had become.[74]

Lauzun put his desire for promotion before his respect for the King. In 1671, although he held the key office of *capitaine des gardes du corps*, he wanted the even more important office of colonel of the principal guards regiment, the Gardes Françaises. Madame de Montespan promised to help. On 26 October Lauzun hid under the King's bed, to check whether she was indeed advancing his candidacy to the King. He was enraged to hear her denigrating him. Later, to her horror, he told her what he had overheard, calling her 'bougresse de putain' and 'grosse tripière', among other epithets, and threatening her with revenge.

The King demanded he apologize to Madame de Montespan. He refused. On 25 November 1671, like Fouquet ten years earlier, he was escorted to the fortress of Pignerol by musketeers commanded by d'Artagnan. There he spent the next ten years, lost to the world, with only Fouquet for company. When Fouquet's family was allowed to visit him, Lauzun tried to seduce his daughter.[75] Another of the King's favourites, the Duc de La Feuillade (see below, p. 323), became colonel of the Gardes Françaises.

Gaspard Lallemand, Sieur de Blémont, visited Versailles and Fontainebleau, between the autumn of 1691 and the summer of 1692, to see M. de Refflers, *chef de bureau* under M. de Barbezieux, Minister of War responsible for Franche-Comté. He was representing the city of Dole in its efforts to obtain a reversal of the recent transfer of its university to its rival Besançon. Dole offered to pay the crown 150,000 livres.[76] Lallemand used the Princesse d'Espinoy and her mother Madame de Lillebonne, favourites of the Dauphin, at their suggestion, to 'attack' ministers on behalf of Dole. The latter promised to 'use everything'. During a carriage journey Madame d'Espinoy showed enough of her breasts to Lallemand 'to move an anchorite'. However, after weeks visiting ministers in Versailles and Paris, he concluded that the King decided everything alone with the Intendant and that they preferred Besançon, since they considered it more pro-French than Dole. Despite her failure Madame de Lillebonne, as she had planned, received from Lallemand 600 livres, recorded by her notary, collected by her equerry.[77]

No family profited from the court more than the Noailles – a success still resented by some French nobles today. They were an ancient noble family from the Auvergne, which had been serving the monarchy since the sixteenth century. In 1648 Anne, later first Duc de Noailles, acquired the key position of *capitaine des gardes du corps*, in which his descendants would continue to serve until 1830. His son Anne-Jules succeeded him in this post and became a marshal of France.[78]

Louis once wrote to Anne-Jules' widow, the Maréchale de Noailles, famous for her skill in advancing her children (four daughters married four dukes), 'believe me it is impossible to have more affection than I have for you.'[79] Her correspondence shows her power. She received letters asking for recommendations, favours, the payment of friends' pensions and news, from diplomats, generals and bishops, not only in France but in Spain and Italy. Her correspondents included the famous general the Duc de Vendôme, the Papal Nuncio (in cipher) and her old friend Madame de Maintenon.[80] So many Noailles served at Versailles that a corridor in the Aile du Nord was called the rue de Noailles.[81] The Noailles were also reputed to make fortunes by recommending officials and merchants to ministers. Saint-Simon accused them of 'pillaging', and lamented that they had become 'in every way' the most powerful, numerous and 'ardent' family at court.[82]

Even more than Paris, Versailles was at the centre of the web of France. Far from isolating the court from France, Versailles was a convenient base – perhaps less self-absorbed than Paris – from which to visit and study it. Most court officials served only three months in the year, or one year in four. Therefore they spent three-quarters of the year, or three years in four, away from the court. When the court was at Versailles, Paris did not become 'a desert', as contemporaries had complained when it was further away, at Fontainebleau.[83]

Court officials, as well as ministers, couriers and petitioners like Monnier and Lallemand, were constantly moving between Versailles and the rest of France, as the King himself had done before 1687. Colbert's son

Seignelay, Minister of the Marine, for example, toured much of Europe and all the ports of France, from Dunkirk in the north to Toulon in the south.[84] His nephew Torcy knew Europe from Lisbon to Stockholm. Louvois was on the road at least one day in fifteen, often more, on journeys of inspection: eleven journeys to the northern frontier alone. Once he went as far as Roussillon.[85]

The King's cousin the Duc d'Enghien, Condé's son, for example, had an apartment at Versailles, and as *grand maître de France* sometimes served the King at table.[86] However, he usually resided with his father at the great chateau of Chantilly, north of Paris, where they maintained their own cultivated and hospitable court, with a household of around 300 (and Enghien created in 1686–94 the Galerie des Actions de M. le Prince, which is as self-glorifying as the Galerie des Glaces). Enghien also regularly visited Dijon where, as semi-hereditary governor of Burgundy, he helped obtain regular subsidies, without bargaining, from the Estates – and to the King's delight, sent him detailed accounts of the province.[87]

Versailles was also a news centre, a palace of couriers as well as courtiers: not only the King's *courriers du cabinet*, but also ministers' and generals' couriers. On one day, couriers arrived from Flanders, Alsace and Languedoc; on another from Flanders, Dauphiné and Germany; on a third Sourches wrote that 'the news from Poland is more contradictory than ever.'[88] Ministers competed to employ the fastest couriers: in 1700 the War Minister's courier brought news of the death of the King of Spain to Fontainebleau before the Foreign Minister's.[89] 'Being at court you are informed of everything,' wrote M. Amelot, French Ambassador in Spain, to the Duc de Noailles, son of the Maréchal de Noailles, one of the *capitaines des gardes* at Versailles, who had become a general, provincial governor and confidant of Louis XIV.[90]

Versailles was also a centre of entertainment, inside the palace as well as in the gardens. The unceasing round of concerts, dances, plays and receptions reflected Louis XIV's tastes and character, and distinguished his court from others, as much as its size and accessibility. In 1680 the new Dauphine, a princess of Bavaria, was astonished by 'the trouble to which people go in order to divert themselves'. Being alone in a room with a servant, which she preferred, was considered unsuitable and undignified in France.[91]

Entertainment and conversation were regarded as beneficial in themselves, weapons against ignorance, bad manners and solitude. No one would complain of boredom at Versailles, as they did at Windsor or Schönbrunn. Madame, who loved talking to the King 'for he was very agreeable company', wrote that she was never bored at court: hunting, the theatre, conversation and society occupied her time 'and during the day one could be oneself as much as one liked.'[92]

On his Grand Tour, the son of the Elector of Saxony was advised to visit Versailles often, 'pour la conversation'.[93] At the end of the reign Ferenc II Rákóczi, Prince of Transylvania, enjoyed Versailles not only for the hunting, the flirtations and the games of cards, but also for the 'military, political or scholarly debates' he held there with courtiers.[94]

As part of his science of entertainment, in 1661 Louis had founded the Académie Royale de Danse to produce better dancers and dancing masters, to teach posture and physical discipline and to raise the prestige of dance. The foundation edict called dancing 'most advantageous and useful to the nobility and to the other people who have the honour of approaching us' – 'not only in the time of war in our armies but also in time of peace in our ballets'.[95] In 1675 he also encouraged Raoul Feuillet to invent choreography, the detailed system for recording patterns of dance steps on paper, like musical scores.[96] Often dedicated to Louis, books of dance steps were published in London soon after Paris, for French dances (*gavottes, menuets, sarabandes* and more) conquered Europe as easily as French fashions. The vivid French style of dance, with tiny, springing steps, became a new art form. Operas and plays at court often included ballets. *Le Bourgeois Gentilhomme* by Molière, for example, was called a 'comédie-ballet'.

Every day for twenty-two years Louis himself had lessons from Pierre Beauchamps, Directeur de l'Académie Royale de Danse et Compositeur des Ballets du Roi.[97] When alone with Madame de Montespan, the King was said to dance 'folies d'Espagne' until too exhausted to continue.[98] He also continued to dance in public until February 1670, when the physical strain of hours of rehearsal and performance began to make him ill. He continued to dance in private, however, until he was over sixty.[99]

Thereafter in most winters, there were balls every two or three days at court.[100] In the 1700 carnival season, for example, there were twenty-five balls in Versailles and Marly. Saint-Simon claims that for three weeks he never saw the light of day; he spent every night at a ball and slept all day.[101] Even in old age, Louis wanted Parisians to have extra days before Lent for balls and masquerades: Madame de Maintenon complained that he lacked 'the spirit of true penitence'.[102]

Louis preferred parties to ceremonies. He believed that shared pleasures bound some courtiers to him more strongly than rewards and favours. His parties, like Versailles itself, were also intended to impress 'all our subjects in general' and Europe.[103] The *Gazette de France* wrote that the 'belle manière de ces divertissements' showed that Louis XIV was the first monarch in the world. Louis wrote in his memoirs – pretending that parties were organized only for the good of his country, rather than also for his pleasure – that such fêtes made 'a very advantageous impression', on foreigners as well as Frenchmen, 'of magnificence, of power, of wealth and grandeur'.[104]

In 1682 he institutionalized his parties by the introduction of 'Appartement' at Versailles. Three evenings a week, on Mondays, Wednesdays and Thursdays, from 6 until 10, the state apartments of Versailles were open to *les gens de condition*: 'tout ce qu'il y a de plus considérable en France', anybody familiar and well dressed. Special invitations were not required. The Premier Gentilhomme in waiting and Bontemps were in charge.

The King was present and insisted that other members of the royal family also attend. In 1686 he told the unsociable Dauphine: 'madame, I want there to be Appartement and that you dance there. We are not like private people; we owe ourselves entirely to the public. Please do so with good grace.'[105] On the other three days plays were performed (there was a theatre in the Aile des Princes), and the alternating plays and Appartement, with balls in winter, continued until the end of the reign.[106]

In private audiences Louis XIV could intimidate even the boldest. In Appartement, however, moving from room to room through hundreds of guests, according to the Abbé Bourdelot, he was no longer 'the terrible of terribles . . . he is accessible to everyone'. Guests were obliged to remain seated when he approached their table.[107]

There was dancing and music in the Salon de Mars, where two tribunes for musicians were installed in 1687; singing in the Salon d'Apollon, since Apollo was god of music; cards and games with refreshments – buffets of coffee, chocolate, fruit, cakes, liqueurs and wines – in the Salons de l'Abondance and de Venus, where guests served themselves. The Salon de Diane was used for billiards, a game in which the Abbé Bourdelot called the King 'master in this as in everything'.[108]

Madame, although she neither danced nor gambled, enjoyed the freedom to wander from room to room; 'if I could describe the splendour with which these rooms are furnished and the amount of silver there is everywhere, I should go on for ever.' Quantities of solid silver mirrors, chandeliers, candle stands, tables, chairs, orange pots and vases, usually designed by Le Brun, had been especially ordered for the state apartments. In the Salon de Mercure, which served the function of royal bedroom in the state apartments, a solid silver balustrade separated the King's bed from the rest of the room. The throne in the Salon d'Apollon was of silver-plated wood, but was decorated with sculptures of solid silver.[109]

Repeated decrees forbade public gambling parties in Paris, and gambling by particular groups such as priests and officers. The decrees were usually ignored, and at court the King encouraged gambling for money, sometimes playing himself.[110] Card games such as lansquenet, brelan, reversis, piquet and others were played in the Salons de Mercure and de Mars. Men who did not gamble were called useless bits of furniture. The Dauphin himself gambled late into the night during Appartement, and the King always paid his losses. Gambling heightened the addictive power of the court, and its role as redistributor of wealth, as well as a centre of amusement. Cards became a means of entry to the court for 'every kind of rascal', Madame complained, if they had money. One of the King's favourites, the Marquis de Dangeau, Colonel of the Régiment du Roi and the most reliable diarist of the reign, was of relatively humble birth; but by concentrating on the cards while others were distracted, he made a fortune.[111] At Marly so much time was spent gambling, for such high stakes, that some guests left for Paris.[112]

When the King was in residence, Versailles was filled with the sound of music, conveying a message of power and triumph. In addition to the drums and trumpets of the Maison Militaire often playing in the courtyards, the King had three separate orchestras, each with its own musicians: the Musique-Chapelle for religious music in the chapel; the Ecuries for music during hunts and processions; and the Musique de la Chambre, with the famous twenty-four *violons de la chambre*, for music inside the palace.[113] The last also often accompanied the King on his journeys, for example to accompany Te Deums in conquered cities.[114]

The King personally supervised music at court, with the help of Jean-Baptiste Lully, Surintendant da la Musique du Roi, and Directeur de l'Académie Royale de Musique since 1661, who had come to Paris from Florence in 1646. A dancer and composer, who wrote music for the King's parties and operas at Versailles and Saint-Germain, he was such a favourite that he survived rivals' attacks as well as the King's disapproval of his love affair with a page (the page was whipped and sent to a monastery for two years). Lully dedicated most of his music to 'the Conqueror of a thousand nations, the Pacifier of Europe, the sovereign Arbiter of the world' – Louis XIV.[115]

No king of France loved music more than Louis XIV. In his youth the King played the guitar (his guitars are in the Gemeentemuseum in The Hague), the lute and the harpsichord, and composed songs. In 1660 the Florentine Resident wrote that 'the king's greatest taste at the moment is for Italian music, occupying him for three or four hours every evening.'

At concerts in his private apartments, even at the age of sixty, he occasionally sang with ladies-in-waiting, while his daughter the Princesse de Conti played the harpsichord.[116]

He remembered some opera tunes fifty years after he had heard them, and had his own music library, assembled by André Philidor.[117] He would also suggest subjects for operas (generally stories of love and chivalry, like Lully's *Amadis* in 1683 or *Armide* in 1685) and attend rehearsals.[118] If an opera was being performed in the evening, he did not go hunting in the day, to conserve energy and attentiveness for the performance.[119] Sometimes, on hot summer evenings, he and the royal family were rowed up and down the canal of Versailles in gondolas, followed by boats of serenading musicians, or he listened to their music from the terrace at Trianon.[120]

Thanks to Louis, Lully and also Lalande, who worked there from 1683 to 1723, the music in the French chapel royal became famous. Louis helped choose singers and musicians himself, often testing voices in the chapel where they would be singing. His taste was more Italian and less French than his courtiers'. His innovations included the accompaniment of mass, and of the psalms, epistles and gospels, by long and short motets, some by Lully, sung by soloists and alternating small and large choirs, with interludes of violin music.[121]

The King, who clearly shared the contemporary belief that music brought listeners closer to God, hoped that the choir of his chapel would inspire the cathedral choirs of France; sometimes the choir even included castrati and women (such as the wife and daughters of Lalande, and Mlle Couperin), which other choirs did not.[122] Visitors were transported. An envoy from Parma, Count Gianmaria, for example, wrote that the music was the best he had ever heard; even in Italy, it could not have been better.[123] Ambassadors said that, after the French court, you had to block your ears when you heard the music played at other courts.[124]

Versailles was synonymous with theatre as well as with gambling, ballet and music. There may have been as many as 1,200 performances of plays at Versailles (without counting those at Fontainebleau and other residences) between 1682 and 1715.[125] Plays were performed either by the professional troupes of the Comédie Française or the Comédie Italienne coming especially from Paris in a large theatre in the Aile des Princes, or by amateurs, often including members of the royal family, organized by the Princesse de Conti, the Duchesse du Maine or Madame de Maintenon and playing in their apartments.[126]

Molière was a living contradiction of his own saying 'Qui se donne à la cour se dérobe à son art' ('Who gives himself to the court diminishes his art'). From 1659 to his death in 1673, working primarily for the King, most of his plays, often containing ballets with music by Lully, were first performed at Versailles before they were seen in Paris. He described his vocation, in a petition to the King, as 'to bring laughter to the monarch, who makes all Europe tremble'.[127]

As with operas and concerts, Louis XIV himself sometimes suggested themes for plays, attended rehearsals, commented on performances, and in 1665 named Molière's players the Troupe du Roi, with a pension of 7,000 livres. In all, the troupe spent 333 days at court, Molière himself probably many more. The King and his court were part of the creative process.[128]

The King also on occasion danced and acted beside Molière, and in 1664 stood godfather to his son Louis. In 1669, after several years' delay, he allowed public performances of *Tartuffe ou l'Imposteur*, Molière's attack on religious hypocrisy, despite attempts by the Archbishop of Paris to ban it. It ends with praise of Louis XIV as:

> un prince ennemi de la fraude,
> Un prince dont les yeux se font jour dans les coeurs,
> Et que ne peut tromper l'art des imposteurs.

> ('A prince enemy of fraud,
> A prince whose eyes can see into hearts,
> And whom the art of impostors cannot deceive.')

Le Bourgeois Gentilhomme, first performed at Chambord in October 1670, partly reflected Louis XIV's desire to root out 'false nobles' – 'bourgeois gentilhomme' being, in theory, a contradiction in terms in France.[129] Since there had recently been a Turkish embassy, Louis XIV asked the Chevalier d'Arvieux, a consul and merchant working in the Ottoman Empire, who also served at court as equerry to the Gouvernante des Enfants de France, to supply details of Turkish manners and customs. Thus there were scenes with a false mufti, pretending that the Sultan wanted to marry the daughter of M. Jourdain – the *bourgeois gentilhomme* of the title. Other scenes mock M. Jourdain for trying to learn to dance, to dress and to 'faire la révérence' to ladies 'like gentlemen of quality'.[130] In the wake of the play's success, the King said, according to d'Arvieux's memoirs, 'I can see that the Chevalier d'Arvieux had a hand in it'; 'these obliging words coming from the mouth of such a great Monarch won me the compliments of the whole Court. They are holy water with which courtiers are not mean.'[131] The play continued to be performed at court, making members of the royal family cry with laughter, until the end of the reign.[132]

Racine was seventeen years younger than Molière, but equally determined to win the King's favour. His career as a courtier was as important to him as his vocation as a writer, which it transformed.[133] In *Bérénice* (1670), dedicated to Colbert, the figure of the Emperor Titus was partly modelled on Louis XIV. Hence the celebrated lines, praising Louis XIV:

> Qu'en quelque obscurité que le sort l'eût fait naître,
> Le monde en le voyant eût reconnu son maître.

> ('In whatever obscurity fate would have had him born,
> The world, on seeing him, would have recognized its master.')

As Louis XIV had renounced Marie Mancini, Titus feels obliged to renounce Bérénice: the laws of Rome are more important to him than love. Bérénice's line 'Vous êtes empereur, seigneur, et vous pleurez!' echoes the reproach of Marie Mancini ten years earlier: 'Vous êtes roi, vous pleurez et je pars.' Titus replies:

> Oui madame, il est vrai, je pleure, je soupire . . .
> Malheureux! Mais toujours la patrie et la gloire
> Ont parmi les Romains remporté la victoire.

> (Yes, Madame, it is true, I weep, I sigh . . .
> Unfortunate! But always glory and the fatherland
> Have won victory among the Romans.)

In 1677, helped by the supreme job fixer Madame de Montespan, Racine became an *historiographe du roi*, with a salary of 6,000 livres a year, required by the King, in his own words, 'to explain to posterity the great actions of His Majesty . . . the astonishment of the universe'.[134] Racine wrote *Eloge historique du roi Louis XIV sur ses conquêtes depuis l'année 1672 jusqu'en 1678*, and after 1684 helped polish the King's image as a member of the Petite Académie.[135]

Unlike the royal historiographer Pelisson, who had a moustache resembling a roasted omelette and was said to exceed all normal limits of ugliness, Racine became a favourite at court. As Spanheim wrote, 'for a man come from nothing, he has easily adopted the manners of the court.'[136] From 1689 Racine was invited to Marly. In 1694 he was given the *grandes entrées*, and in 1695 an apartment in the palace. Like other writers, he often talked to Louis during the Grand Couvert, and he read Plutarch's life of Alexander to the King when he was ill.[137] In addition to his salary as historiographer, Racine received a pension and regular *gratifications*, sometimes as much as 10,000 livres. In 1690 he became a *gentilhomme ordinaire du roi* (the position created in 1584 to guard the king, now mainly honorary), at 4,600 livres a year, with his son as *survivancier*, guaranteed the office on his father's death.[138]

His favour with the King raised the status of French writers in general, as Le Brun's raised that of French painters. His greatest triumphs at court were two religious tragedies, with songs and musical interludes to please the King: *Esther* (1689) and *Athalie* (1691). Based on stories in the Old Testament, they were acted and sung by the girls of Saint-Cyr (the school founded by Madame de Maintenon; see below) in front of the King. The latter ends with the lines:

> Que les Rois dans le Ciel ont un Juge sévère,
> L'Innocence un Vengeur, et l'orphelin un Père.

> (That Kings have in Heaven a severe Judge,
> Innocence an Avenger and orphans a Father.)

Louis XIV and Racine were on more intimate terms, for longer, than any other French monarch and writer. The King once said at a *lever*, 'I would praise you more, if you did not praise me so much.' When Racine died, the King praised him so highly that other courtiers said they wished they could die too.[139] At Marly no one talked of anything else.[140]

In addition to hunting for jobs and news, and enjoying *divertissements*, courtiers were occupied by writing, as was the King himself. The paper palace they constructed is as remarkable as the palace of stone and marble in which they lived. The pen was, if not mightier than the sword (over 5,000 Mazarinades suggest that most French writers had supported the Fronde), certainly as sharp: sharpened by tradition, competitiveness, desire to win the approbation of posterity, and malice. As Bernini was told, 'it was typical of court wits to . . . convert everything into venom.'[141]

Louis was aware that he was constantly criticized. As he would write to his grandson Philip V of Spain, 'it is impossible to deprive the public of freedom of speech . . . in France more than anywhere.'[142] Lauzun's audacity has already been mentioned. Another of Louis' favourites, the Comte de Guiche, was equally insolent. He called the King timid, miserly, boastful and (because of his love of embroidered clothes) 'the marquis of filigree', and had affairs with both Monsieur and Madame. Yet his courage in battle made the King forgive him.[143] Even in July 1672, at the height of Louis XIV's success, courtiers criticized his ministers, his generals and his policies.[144] By the end of the reign Madame de Maintenon was complaining that 'freedom of speech in our court has been taken to excess.' She too, however, criticized the King's wars and entertainments in letters to friends.[145]

Many courtiers wrote diaries or memoirs. Two of Louis XIV's valets, for example, Dubois and Laporte, wrote memoirs: the latter even accused Mazarin of a sexual assault on the young King. One of Anne of Austria's *premières femmes de chambre*, Madame de Motteville, in her memoirs could be brutal about Louis XIV and Anne of Austria. For example she wrote, unjustly, that he 'was so avid for glory that he did not want to leave even the crumbs to the Queen his mother, he wanted everything to refer to himself', and she blamed the Queen for the Fronde. In reality he often praised his mother as not only a great queen but worthy of being ranked among the greatest kings.[146]

For the instruction of the Dauphin, from 1661 to 1679 Louis XIV himself corrected and edited his secretaries' memoirs – an official, royal version of events – partly written to celebrate the King's industry and idealism. His claims that he was determined not to inspire fear in his neighbours nor to put his own glory before his subjects' 'repose' were disproved by his acts. However, he could be honest about his egotism and his distrust of his own court. He admitted that 'it seems to me to lessen some of my glory when it is possible [for others] to acquire it [glory] without me'; and, without illusions about his courtiers, that in 'the malignity of the court' there was little fidelity without self-interest. Favours were demanded or 'extracted' (*arrachées*) from the King.[147]

Letter writing also occupied the court. Saint-Simon for example frequently wrote and received letters: such was the fear of the government that even those written in cipher could not recount everything.[148] Officers and officials often kept their own records of events – for example, the bound volumes of correspondence (including letters from Louis, Louvois and Lionne) of the Maréchal de Créquy, covering his conquest of Lorraine in 1670, or the meticulously organized letter books of the Maréchale de Noailles and her son the Duke, now in the Bibliothèque Nationale.[149] The Marquis de Sourches, when he was in the provinces, continued to write his diary, from 'reliable letters' sent to him from the court. They were inspired to write, partly because, at court, they had so much to write about. So much changed so quickly at court that, if courtiers spent two days' away, they found the King and his ministers almost unrecognizable.[150]

Writing letters was the principal occupation of Monsieur's second wife, Madame Palatine; she may have written 90,000 during the fifty years she lived in France, from 1671 to 1722 – five or six a day, mainly to relations abroad. Once her children had grown up, eager to escape her husband's spies and lovers she spent much of her time alone in her study, reading, writing, playing with her beloved dogs and assembling collections of medals and popular songs. The latter she considered more truthful than official histories.[151]

At the heart of the French monarchy (she hunted with the King and handed the Queen her shift during her *lever*), Louis XIV's sister-in-law remained sceptical about it. Believing in freedom of conscience, she consoled herself by singing Lutheran hymns when she thought herself alone, and read the Lutheran Bible and Calvinist prayers.[152]

Louis' most influential critic was the Abbé de Fénelon. With eyes dancing and sparkling like a torrent, so magnetic that Saint-Simon wrote that you had to make an effort to stop looking at him, in 1689 he became tutor to the King's grandson the Duc de Bourgogne. His promotion was partly due to his friendship – 'like one soul' – with Bourgogne's Governor, the Duc de Beauvillier. Intelligent, honourable and popular, Beauvillier was another great noble, like Turenne and the Maréchal de Villeroy, who enjoyed political influence under Louis XIV, helped by his marriage to a daughter of Colbert. He was not only a *premier gentilhomme de la chambre*, and Governor of the King's grandsons, but also from 1685 chief of the Conseil Royal des Finances, and from 1691 a *ministre d'état*, sitting in the council. Sometimes he gave orders in the King's absence. Even more unusual, in this court of war, he was a man of peace.[153] Another son-in-law of Colbert, the Duc de Chevreuse, was also regularly consulted on political matters by Louis XIV and the ministers.[154]

Author of an influential book on female education, *De l'éducation des filles*, Fénelon had been a favourite adviser of Madame de Maintenon. He hoped she would guide the King. In December 1693, in the middle of a global war, Fénelon sent her an anonymous 'Letter to the King' (which Louis XIV probably never saw). He denounced the King for having a fatal bandage over his eyes. The war of 1672, he wrote, had been due to the King's vanity. Inside France he had raised government revenue to absurd heights, and substituted the King for the state. He had impoverished the country in order to favour 'remorseless and incurable luxury' at court. Commerce had been destroyed.

Abroad 'our name has been rendered odious and the whole French nation insupportable to all our neighbours' by the King's lust for glory and 'useless conquests' (which included, however, Cambrai, of which Fénelon would, thanks to Louis XIV, become archbishop in 1695). France had become one large hospital. Regular meetings of the States General, and a diminution of royal power, were the remedy.[155] Fénelon also denounced 'this great number of women who go freely everywhere at court' as 'a monstrous abuse to which one [Louis XIV] has accustomed the nation'.[156] Other courtiers may have inspired another incendiary pamphlet, also calling for the States General, *Les Soupirs de la France esclave, qui aspire après la liberté* ('The Sighs of Enslaved France, Which Aspires to Liberty').[157]

In 1697, Fénelon was dismissed from his post as tutor of Bourgogne and exiled to Cambrai for his support, in his book *Maximes des saints*, of the religious 'heresy' of quietism – the belief that Christians should abandon themselves to God through 'pure love' and 'inner crucifixion', bypassing the church hierarchy. Salvation came through grace alone, not good works. His inspiration, the ardent and 'sublime' Madame Guyon, was imprisoned in the Bastille in 1698 for five years. Regretting her previous enthusiasm for them, Madame de Maintenon became their enemy.[158]

Fénelon's novel *Les Aventures de Télémaque, fils d'Ulysse*, written to instruct the Duc de Bourgogne and published (allegedly without permission) in The Hague in 1699, became one of the most popular books of the eighteenth century. It denounces 'an unjust and too violent authority in kings' and 'luxury which corrupts manners'. 'They [kings] take and ruin everything, they alone possess the whole State . . . they sap the foundations of their power.' He also prophesied that Louis XIV's wars would cause revolts.[159]

Louis tried in vain to suppress it. The market was stronger than the monarchy. Rouen, where *Télémaque* and other *mauvais livres* on Jansenism or the court's *dames galantes* were printed, was a port city, the minister Pontchartrain complained, determined to 'protect the liberty of commerce against everything'.[160]

Despite Louis' hostility, Fénelon had many supporters at court. Beauvillier and Bourgogne, among others, regarded him as a potential saviour of France.[161] The Cardinal de Bouillon, Grand Aumônier de France, was dismissed in 1700, partly for corresponding secretly with him.[162] Thus the court, bringing so many intelligent and ambitious people together under one roof, fostered opposition as well as loyalty. La Fontaine and La Bruyère, for example, lived partly at court but criticized it in their writings.[163]

Saint-Simon used his years at Versailles to gather stories and information for memoirs extremely hostile to Louis XIV. Even Racine, while officially 'gathering materials for the life of the King', was also writing a sympathetic secret history of the Jansenist abbey of Port Royal. Tiring of what he called the 'horrible dissipation' of the court, he had begun to refuse invitations. He never finished his life of the King. His history of Port Royal, however, was published after his death.[164]

The energy and curiosity of Louis XIV himself, his passion for

entertainment and his eye for talent (which led him to employ such independent spirits as Bossuet, Fénelon, Racine) made Versailles a cultural
dynamo, comparable to Florence, Rome or Paris. Louis XIV inspired and
commissioned more artists, in more forms of creativity, than any other
monarch in European history, even his relations Cosimo and Lorenzo de'
Medici. He discussed music and ballet with Lully, gardens with Le Nôtre,
botany with La Quintinie, architecture with Bernini and Mansart, painting with Le Brun and Mignard, literature with Molière and Racine and
the drapery in a painting by Correggio with the Swedish Ambassador.[165]
His appreciation, generosity and interest electrified his artists.

Bernini himself had admired Louis XIV's 'fine and delicate taste'. He
interrupted a council meeting, and took his ministers with him, to admire
a picture in his bedroom by his Premier Peintre Charles Le Brun of *The
Raising of the Cross*. Admiring another of Le Brun's pictures, *Moses
Defending the Daughters of Jethro*, he told the ageing painter with sardonic Bourbon humour, 'don't die, Lebrun, to raise the prices of your
pictures. I esteem them enough for you not to do that.'[166] Even out hunting,
he thought of painting, encouraging the animal painter Desportes to
accompany him, and advising Desportes not only on what scenes to paint
(for example the King's favourite hounds), but also on how to compose
them.[167]

For once frescoes such as *Royal Magnificence and Magnanimity Inspir-
ing and Rewarding the Arts* in the Salon de l'Abondance, and *Apollo
Distributes Rewards to the Arts and Sciences, and Minerva Crowns the
Genius of France* in the King's Petite Galerie, reflected reality. Louis
XIV's Petite Galerie and *cabinets* on the first floor facing the Cour de
Marbre were filled with his private treasures: 21,000 medals, engraved
gems and cameos, ancient and modern, in special display cabinets; bronze
sculptures; medieval manuscripts like the *Livre de chasse* of Gaston
Phébus, as well as illustrated accounts of his own campaigns; rock crys-
tal, amethyst, sardonyx and lapis-lazuli cups and goblets; Chinese
porcelain; and a huge collection of porphyry.[168] If they had letters of
recommendation, travellers could usually visit the King's and the Dauphin's collections in their absence.[169]*

Louis XIV's interests were so broad, or his vanity so great, that he also
prepared medicinal remedies in his *cabinet*: for example a mixture of
chloric acid and wine as a treatment for hernias. They were described in
the *Mercure de France*, perhaps with a hint of irony: 'his royal hands,

---

* Visitors to the Dauphin's apartment were given *pantoufles* or slippers to wear, like modern
tourists.

which carry the sceptre so worthily, are sometimes used for the composition of private remedies known to him alone.'[170]

The court was a laboratory as well as a marketplace; a news centre; an art gallery; a year-round festival of music, dance and theatre; a fashion show; a trade fair; a hunt and riding school; and a parade ground. While the King was entertaining his court and his guests, he also raised the status of musicians, writers and painters, and helped create new kinds of music, opera, ballet and gardens. As the King's last Director of Buildings, the Duc d'Antin, Madame de Montespan's son by her husband, wrote in 1708, echoing words used by Colbert fifty years before: 'to make a reign illustrious, you must make the arts and sciences flourish, and it seems to me that the King has omitted nothing to do this.'[171]

14

Inside Louis XIV

Louis XIV's enjoyment of his court was heightened by his stupendous vitality. He could work six or seven hours a day, or more, in addition to performing the daily rituals of the *lever*, mass, public dinner and *coucher*, and following a strenuous outdoor routine of hunts, shoots and walks.

His stamina enabled him to survive frequent fevers and 'vapours', aggravated by the marshy, mosquito-infested atmosphere of Versailles – and, after 1685, bouts of gout, rheumatism and arthritis.[1] When in September 1683 he fell from his horse and broke an arm, he told his First Surgeon before the operation: 'Félix, don't spare me.' It was his courtiers, not the King, who fainted from shock at his suffering. He was soon riding again.[2] He was so determined to appear healthy that he often hid, or tried to hide, his fevers and sleeplessness from the court. Sometimes, however, council meetings were held in the King's bedroom, while he was in bed.[3]

Only a man of exceptional self-control and courage could have endured the extraction of his teeth by clumsy dentists in 1685 and a second horrific operation, when red-hot iron was applied to his jaw to cauterize the wounds left by the extraction. He showed at least as much heroism on the operating table as on the battlefield. Thereafter his expression became, in the words of Colin Jones, 'compressed, toothless and unsmiling'. He no longer needed to use a knife, since, with no teeth left, he ate minced meat (*hachis*) and fricassees.[4]

Louis XIV's warmth, charm and *joie de vivre* – what Saint-Simon called his 'incomparable grace and majesty' – strengthened the forces of power, fear, loyalty and ambition on which the monarchy normally relied. Madame de Motteville admired his 'air de maître et de souverain' ('air of master and sovereign'), Sourches the grace he knew how to put into all his actions.[5] He could use his manners to 'caress' or *gracieuser* his servants and increase their devotion. 'Never did anyone give with better grace, thereby augmenting the price of his favours,' wrote Saint-Simon. His manners were more than skin deep. 'Never was a man so naturally polite,'

Saint-Simon added: he raised his hat to every woman he met, even to the maids at Marly.[6]

Helped by his 'incomparable grace and majesty', Louis XIV made his family and court into an emotional community – unlike the venomous courts of the Stuarts, the Hanovers, the Romanovs and his own father, which were split by conspiracies and executions.[7]

One of the few monarchs of his day who shared his wife's bed, he was also present when she bore their children or was ill.[8] He loved their children. Even on campaign, he wrote frequently to his children's Governess about their health. In October 1670 he left Chambord for Saint-Germain earlier than planned, to see his second son who had a fever.[9]

On the death of their daughter Marie Thérèse in 1672, Saint-Maurice reported that the King had been constantly in her bedroom, in tears; he and his wife then retreated together to Versailles to hide their 'inconceivable affliction'.[10] When the Queen herself was dying in 1683 (largely from doctors' mistreatment of a fever), he was with her constantly, as he would be at the deathbeds of most members of his family, even to the point of endangering his own health. The Queen's last words were 'Monsieur, I am dying.'[11] Much loved for her charity and piety, her death caused 'inconceivable sadness' far beyond the court.[12] The King wept and said in public that, while he had given her a thousand causes for complaint, she had never given him any. Her death helped make him even more religious.[13]

Louis XIV's family feeling extended to all members of the dynasty. Even distant cousins such as the Duc de Bourbon had apartments in his palaces. The two exceptionally large wings of Versailles, to the north and south of the central block, with twenty apartments for princes or princesses, were built partly to accommodate them.[14] Louis XIV encouraged members of his family to talk about anything at meals – 'ne pas faire la mignonne'.[15] To his sister-in-law the first Madame, Louis XIV wrote in 1668 one of his most emotional letters: 'my heart is for you as it should be ... I love you as much as one can love.'[16] To his cousin Condé he declared in 1672, 'we are towards each other on such terms that whatever happens to one of us touches us both equally.'[17] He wrote to the Dauphin that he would feel 'bien seul' ('all alone') in Fontainebleau, where he was surrounded by relations and courtiers, if the Dauphin was not also there.[18]

In 1698 when his niece Elisabeth Charlotte d'Orléans left to marry Leopold I, Duke of Lorraine, the King, the royal family, courtiers, guards, ambassadors and 'the people' watching them shed 'fountains' of tears, as they had twenty years earlier at the departure of her half-sister Marie Louise to marry Carlos II of Spain, and would again at the departure of his grandson Philip V in 1700.[19] On the death of Monsieur a year later, both the court which he had done so much to entertain and the King were in tears. Louis XIV said that he could not get used to the idea of no longer seeing his brother, and could barely eat at dinner.[20]

Louis' ties to his brother were political as well as emotional. The French monarchy remained a family business, and Monsieur had become a diplomat like his first wife Madame Henriette, sometimes bypassing official channels. After Monsieur's death, the Ambassador of his son-in-law the Duke of Savoy praised him as 'a reliable and rapid intermediary whom I used to communicate much of our business to the king; for I doubted, less by ill will than by forgetfulness, whether the minister [of Foreign Affairs] would convey it exactly to the king.'[21]

Louis XIV ensured that all the dynasty shared in his glory. Princes and princesses increased the size of their households, stopped paying visits even to the grandest nobles unless they held court office and were accompanied everywhere by an officer of the Gardes du Corps.[22] Princes of the Blood felt they had risen in status and wealth under Louis XIV, compared to previous reigns, even though since 1576 all Princes of the Blood, however distantly related to the King, had precedence over all peers of France, however rich or powerful.[23] Louis, however, also increased differences of rank between the Princes of the Blood like the Condés and the Contis and the immediate royal family, including his controversial nephew the Duc d'Orléans.[24] The Condés devoted considerable time and energy, often in secret, to attempts to equalize their rank and dress (the length of their mourning trains, for example) at court ceremonies with the Orléans. From 1675 until the end of his life, Louis XIV also, in a series of carefully planned steps, began to insert his illegitimate children into the ranks of the Princes of the Blood.[25]*

The bitterness of the Duc de Saint-Simon was partly caused by the increased elevation of the royal family, including its illegitimate members, and other ruling dynasties such as the House of Lorraine, over non-royal dukes and duchesses, as repeated disputes at court and in the Parlement demonstrated.[26] When Saint-Simon had tried to precede a German prince called the Duke of Zweibrücken at Louis XIV's table, Madame, always proud of her German blood, shouted, 'Why is M. le Duc de Saint-Simon pushing the prince of Zweibrücken so much? Does he want to ask him to take one of his sons as a page?'[27]

Louis' sense of dynasty overruled his personal emotions, as he had

---

* Louis XIV's recognized adult illegitimate children were: by Louise de La Vallière the Comte de Vermandois and Marie Anne, later Princesse de Conti; by Madame de Montespan the Duc du Maine, the Comte de Toulouse, Mlle de Nantes and Mlle de Blois.

already shown in 1659 by abandoning Marie Mancini. In 1670 his cousin Mlle de Montpensier fell in love with his favourite *capitaine des gardes*, Lauzun. He was six years younger than she, but she admired his air of being 'the emperor of everyone'. Short, ugly, dirty and bald, looking more like a Tatar than a Frenchman according to Primi Visconti, Lauzun 'knew how to please ladies'. He kept collections of his mistresses' portraits (some with gouged-out eyes) and hair – some labelled 'taken in the right place'.[28]

On 10 December 1670 in the Tuileries Mademoiselle informed the King of her desire to marry Lauzun. She excused the difference in rank and fortune: 'the honour of being your subject makes me respect him more than any sovereign.' The King, occasionally a romantic, replied, according to her memoirs, 'I do not advise it, I do not forbid it, but I beg you to think about it . . . many people do not like M. de Lauzun.'[29] He liked Lauzun and desired 'not to disoblige the French nobility'. Four nobles formally thanked the King for the honour the marriage would bestow on their order.[30] For eight fatal days, however, ignoring friends' advice, Mademoiselle and Lauzun delayed in order to receive congratulations, prepare the ceremony and arrange a financial settlement to raise Lauzun's status.[31]

Thereby they gave the royal family, and public opinion, time to react. In England in 1660 the Duke of York had been allowed to marry Anne Hyde, his sister's maid of honour. But in France the royal family saw itself, and was seen by others, as a race apart. Moreover the royal family wanted to keep Mademoiselle's fortune for itself. Monsieur, who detested Lauzun as the man who had arrested the Chevalier de Lorraine, said that France was not Turkey, where the daughters of the Grand Seigneur married pashas. Madame de Montespan (perhaps already planning for her one-year-old son to be Mademoiselle's heir) agreed. Even the Queen, in the name of her husband's glory and reputation, protested.

On 18 December, to the joy of the court and the royal family, Louis summoned Mademoiselle to the Tuileries and forbade the marriage.[32] He feared appearing to advance Lauzun, who was widely considered to be his favourite.[33] The King admitted his change of heart, in a public letter circulated by Lionne to French ambassadors abroad. He told his cousin, 'kings should satisfy the public.' Two masks, those of Louis XIV's absolutism and of his firmness, fell simultaneously. Showing their intimacy, the two cousins then lay on the floor in the King's study, as she recounted, 'three-quarters of an hour, his cheek pressed against mine'. The King told her to beat him if she wanted: he deserved it.[34] Despite his tears, the King would not relent (although a secret marriage may have taken place later).

A year later, as we have seen, Lauzun was imprisoned in Pignerol, for threatening and insulting Madame de Montespan when she advised the

King not to make him colonel of the Gardes Françaises, and possibly also for treasonable conversations with Dutch diplomats. The King had a nosebleed – a sign of emotion which would recur on the death of his second son the Duc d'Anjou. For the first six years of his imprisonment, Lauzun was allowed no communication with the outside world.[35]

Louis XIV also showed his love for his family by his favours to his illegitimate children. For most of France bastardy was a stigma. However, while imposing punitive legislation on others' bastards (including a special tax on them in July 1697), he defied the law to favour his own. Over the years, he formally legitimized all his children by Louise de La Vallière and Madame de Montespan, married them into the Conti, Condé or Orléans branches of the Bourbons, and in 1694 gave his illegitimate sons the new rank of *princes légitimés*.[36] He loved his illegitimate daughters the Princesse de Conti, the Duchesse de Bourbon and the Duchesse de Chartres, often spent the evening with them and in 1693 ordered his Grand Maréchal des Logis (the officer in charge of accommodation) to give them apartments next to his own during journeys, in preference to all court officials except the Capitaine des Gardes on duty.[37]

The Duc du Maine was the King's favourite illegitimate child. He was married to a Condé princess so short (like her brother the Duc de Bourbon) that she was called a *poupée du sang* rather than a *princesse du sang* – and given the key offices of colonel general of the Swiss and Grisons, and *grand maître de l'artillerie*. Thanks to manoeuvres by the King and Madame de Montespan, who behaved like avaricious relations in a nineteenth-century novel, in return for Lauzun's release from prison in April 1682 Maine, instead of Lauzun, became principal heir to the vast fortune of Mademoiselle. Contrary to what Mademoiselle had been led to understand, Louis again refused to let them marry. Again her tears had no effect. Once released, Lauzun showed little desire for her company. In 1684, after many rows and physical assaults by Mademoiselle on her shorter and weaker lover, there was a final rupture. She later wrote that she wished she had never met him.[38]

In addition to his family, Louis XIV enjoyed life with his mistresses. They provided him with a second family: publicly declared mistresses, during their period of favour, were given escorts of Gardes du Corps, as if they were royalty.[39]

As the King's declared mistress from 1667, Madame de Montespan was a power at court. For example her enemy Lauzun was imprisoned for ten years, while her protégés Racine and Boileau became *historiographes du roi*. There was, however, an interlude from Easter to July 1675. Attacked by the preachers Bossuet and Bourdaloue – in public denunciations and private exhortations to both Montespan and the King – Madame de Montespan was refused the sacraments at Easter; the King promised to renounce physical intercourse. Bossuet told him that his greatest but most difficult victory would be a victory over his own heart. They met only in full view of onlookers.[40]

In August 1675, however, after his return from the front, Montespan resumed her sway. Madame de Sévigné wrote on 2 July 1677, after another temporary rupture: 'never has an empire been better restored.' She was again 'in triumphant possession' of the King, radiating 'prosperity and joy', covered in diamonds like 'a brilliant divinity', leaning her head on the King's shoulder as she gambled to her heart's content. The King always paid off her losses.[41]

The King had, however, begun, when Montespan was pregnant with their last children, Mlle de Blois and the Comte de Toulouse, to spend less time with her and to 'coquette with all comers', according to Madame de Montmorency.[42] In 1676 he fathered a child, baptized Louise de Maison-blanche, by one of Montespan's maids, Mlle des Oeillets.[43] Despite Montespan's apparent confidence, she wanted reassurance. Like the King's early love Olympe Mancini, Comtesse de Soissons, she had visited a cele-brated Paris sorceress called Mme Voisin. Voisin offered love potions, spells, pacts with the devil, to try to keep the King faithful – or, in Olympe's case, to win him 'back'. Both had entered a forbidden world of sorcery which would later help to destroy them.[44]

Madame de Montespan's friend Madame Scarron, whom she had selected as governess of their six eldest children, including the Duc du Maine, was another threat. As early as 1674, the two women had shown signs of 'antipathy' and 'aversion'. Born in 1635, Françoise d'Aubigné had spent a tempestuous childhood between prisons and convents; between Martinique (where she lived from the ages of five to eleven – the draughts in the King's bedroom at Versailles would remind her of Caribbean hur-ricanes) and Paris; and between Catholicism and Protestantism.[45] Her grandfather had been the Protestant historian Agrippa d'Aubigné. Her father had been a murderer and counterfeiter who spent part of his life in prison; the poet Paul Scarron, whom she had married in 1652 to avoid being obliged to enter a convent, was a drunk, a cripple and a *frondeur*. After Scarron died in 1660, she continued to see unsuitable friends such as the Cardinal de Retz.[46]

Nevertheless, with fine dark eyes, agreeable conversation and quick intelligence, she rose rapidly in the King's favour.[47] By 1674 she was no longer a secret governess subordinate to Madame de Montespan, but the recipient of *gratifications* from the King of 250,000 livres, which enabled her to buy the estate of Maintenon, west of Versailles. The Marquise de Maintenon, as she became, began to improve her park and her genealogy.[48] Unlike Montespan, Maintenon never lost her temper. Even Saint-Simon, who detested her, praised her graceful manners and conversation.[49]

In 1677 the King's affair with the beautiful Madame de Ludres, a canoness from Lorraine, and *fille d'honneur* of Madame, was acknowledged when duchesses started to stand as she entered a room: her connection with the King, and the possibility of bearing his child, overrode normal hierarchies.[50] Madame de Montespan, who was thirty-seven and beginning to lose her looks, made scenes. Having refused other offers of money, in January 1678 Madame de Ludres retired to a convent with a pension. When Monsieur told him the news, the King asked: 'is she not there already?'[51] A later mistress was yet another *fille d'honneur* of Madame, Mlle de Chausserais; she died rich, the Contrôleur Général des Finances and other ministers having refused her nothing.[52]

Always plump, Montespan now became enormous. Primi Visconti claimed that one of her thighs, glimpsed as she entered a carriage, looked as large as his waist. Some thought she was no more than a habit. After the birth of their sixth and last child the Comte de Toulouse, on 6 June 1678, the King may not have resumed physical relations.[53]

On 11 April 1679 the end of the affair was publicly confirmed when, after the resignation of the Comtesse de Soissons in return for 200,000 livres, Madame de Montespan was appointed *surintendante de la maison de la reine*. The post, which she had long desired, gave her the right to sit on a tabouret, which was called her *tabouret de remerciement* ('dismissal' or 'thank-you tabouret', like the rank of duchess given to Louise de La Vallière) – an honour to which she could not otherwise pretend, since the Marquis de Montespan refused to profit from cuckoldry and be made a duke. She was still visited by the King, after mass and after supper. However, others were always present. She wrote to the Duc de Noailles: 'it is much better to see each other a little with freedom than often with embarrassment.'[54]

Another reason for the end of the affair between Madame de Montespan and the King was his passion from October 1678 for yet another *fille d'honneur* of Madame, Marie Angélique de Scorailles de Roussille de Fontanges. She looked and moved like a goddess.[55] The *Mercure Galant* wrote: 'she is very beautiful. She is tall, blonde, with good skin, blue eyes and a thousand beautiful qualities of body and mind, despite her youth. M. le comte de Roussille, her father, is from Auvergne.' Of La Rochefoucauld's readiness to accompany the King on secret assignations with Mlle de Fontanges in the Palais Royal, Saint-Simon wrote that the huntsman had 'placed the animal in the trap'.[56]

In February 1679 both Fontanges and Madame de Montespan, the latter 'dans un fort grand négligé' with her children beside her, were observed, eyes raised in ecstasy, praying in front of the King, like rival divinities on opposite sides of the royal chapel.[57] The Duchess of Hanover thought that the King regarded Fontanges with greater devotion than the altar.[58] At one ball, she arrived covered in jewels and went straight to the King, without curtseying to the Queen. In March 1679 Montespan 'brusquely' departed from Saint-Germain, to avoid Fontanges' presence.[59]

In late 1679, however, Fontanges also left the court and in January 1680 suffered injuries from a stillbirth: wounded on active service, said Parisians. Montespan was amusing and intelligent, with many stories to keep the King entertained, but Fontanges won a reputation for vacuity. She was still in favour, and still astonishingly beautiful, in March 1680; Madame de Sévigné called her 'the grey carriage' because she had such a vehicle, pulled by eight horses, a number normally reserved for royalty.[60]

On 27 April 1680, however, she too received a *tabouret de remerciement* – the title of duchess, with a pension. Montespan wept with rage. Fontanges began to make retreats to convents, dying in the Jansenist stronghold the convent of Port Royal on 28 June 1681, at the age of nineteen. 'La belle Fontanges is dead. Sic transit gloria mundi,' wrote Madame de Sévigné.[61] The King founded an annual mass in memory of 'ma très chère et bien aimée cousine la duchesse de Fontanges'.[62]

Some, including the Duchesse de Fontanges herself, believed that she had been poisoned at the instigation of Madame de Montespan.[63] 'L'Affaire des Poisons' showed that the court, despite its outward piety, had links not only to a homosexual underworld, but also to another underworld of aphrodisiacs, abortions, poisons and, by some accounts, sacrilege, satanism and child sacrifice. The line in the ballet *Psyché* (1671), 'la cour où je règne est fertile en démons,' proved correct.[64] In April 1679, soon after Louis had ended his affair with Montespan, he appointed a special Chambre Ardente, sitting in the Paris arsenal, to investigate. By the time it was abolished in July 1682, there had been 194 arrests, thirty-four men and women had been executed, burnt alive or broken on the wheel, and two had died under torture.[65] More had been imprisoned. Some of the highest in the land had fallen under suspicion.

The Comtesse de Soissons had been one of the few friends allowed to talk relatively freely to the King: as late as 1678 she had accompanied him on campaign, in his carriage with the Queen and Madame de Montespan. However, she was implicated by some of the accused. On 24 January 1680, alerted by the King himself, she fled to Brussels – like London, a natural refuge for French exiles. She later admitted that she should have stayed to face her accusers. The King told her mother-in-law the Princesse de Carignan that one day he might have to answer to God and his peoples for his warning.[66] A month later Madame Voisin, principal supplier in Paris of love potions and poisons, was burnt at the stake, unrepentant.[67]

During the secret interrogations Madame de Montespan was mentioned by many witnesses. Some claimed that she had planned to poison the King and the Duchesse de Fontanges. To achieve her ends, 'black masses', using the blood of murdered children, had been held over her naked body. Madame de Montespan was extremely pious and would have been horrified by murder or a 'black mass', let alone regicide. The King, nevertheless, asked for further interrogations.[68]

Much of the testimony was dubious, possibly orchestrated by Louvois, Minister of War, an enemy of Montespan, or wrung – literally, by racks and other torture instruments – from unreliable witnesses. By making wilder accusations involving grander people, they may have hoped for mercy or reprieve from their torturers.[69] Montespan's maid des Oeillets had indeed bought *poudres d'amour* in 1667, which she may have believed would help Montespan win the King from Louise de La Vallière. It is possible that des Oeillets may later, when her child by him was not legitimated, have tried to harm the King – hence some of his fevers. However, she was never questioned. Most of the allegations have never been proved.[70]

In 1670, unlike many at court, Louis XIV had refused to believe that Madame had been poisoned. In 1679–82, he proved more credulous. Perhaps he was influenced by his headaches, fevers and insomnia; and by Louvois and La Reynie, the Lieutenant de Police, whom he trusted, and to whom he gave long, private audiences. La Reynie believed the allegations of infanticide.[71]

Colbert, however, the voice of reason, was sceptical – a scepticism increased by his rivalry with Louvois, by his many years' service as an intermediary between Louis XIV and Madame de Montespan and by his youngest daughter's marriage in October 1680 to Madame de Montespan's nephew the Duc de Mortemart. His agent Claude Duplessis, after going through the testimonies, wrote: 'His Majesty, who knows Madame de Montespan to the bottom of her soul, will never convince himself that she could have been capable of such abominations.' Murder would have been against her interests and her feelings. The accused were lying, or distorting visits to fortune-tellers. Another accusation, that Racine had poisoned his mistress, was absurd.[72] In the end the King adopted this view.

Louis' treatment of Louvois' enemy, Lauzun's replacement as *capitaine*

des gardes du corps the Maréchal de Luxembourg, showed a similar
scepticism. From 24 January 1680, accused of planning to poison his wife,
among others, and having signed a pact with the devil, Luxembourg voluntarily entered the Bastille to await trial in order to clear his name. For
three months he was confined not in one of the special apartments reserved
for prisoners of rank but, on Louvois' orders, in a narrow, unheated cell.
On 14 May he was tried and acquitted. His only crime was to have asked
a fortune teller how to make the King and a lady love him. After a year's
exile in the country, the King made amends by reinstating him as *capitaine
des gardes*. If what Luxembourg called the 'false, horrible and absurd
allegations' against him had been believed by the King, the King would
never again have entrusted Luxembourg with his personal security. Thereafter, when Luxembourg commanded an army, he was allowed to report
directly to the King rather than through Louvois.[73]

Parisians too remained sceptical. When the Duchesse de Bouillon, the
Comtesse de Soissons' youngest sister, appeared in court, escorted by
admiring friends, she prompted laughter by replying to La Reynie's question, as to whether she had seen the devil, 'No; but I see him now, he is
old, ugly and disguised as a councillor of State . . . Truly I would never
have believed that such sensible men could ask me so many stupid things.'
Her disdain may have been sharpened by her knowledge that her husband
and La Reynie were locked in litigation.[74]

The Affaire des Poisons probably developed for four reasons: hysteria
affecting both accusers and accused, as in the case of the executions of
'the witches of Salem' in Massachusetts twelve years later; ladies' obsession with the King; Louvois' and La Reynie's desire to frighten and
humiliate court nobles and friends of Colbert, especially the Comtesse de
Soissons and Louvois' former protégé Luxembourg; and Louis XIV's
desire to distance himself from Madame de Montespan. Saint-Maurice
the Savoy Ambassador, Feuquières the French Ambassador to Sweden, La
Fare, Visconti and Madame de Sévigné all believed that the affair had
been orchestrated by Louvois to serve his 'private passions' – his hatred
of Colbert and Luxembourg. The Affaire des Poisons subjected France,
even the King himself, to mockery in Europe, as French ambassadors
complained. In her book on the affair, Anne Somerset concludes that it
was the King's mind, not his body, which had been poisoned. In 1682 the
special court dealing with the accused was wound up, and Louis XIV
later burnt all his documents relating to it.[75]

The shame of the Affaire des Poisons, like the death of the Duchesse de
Fontanges, favoured the rise of Madame de Maintenon. She had become

too respectable to visit sorcerers, and had long planned to 'save' the King. Already in 1676 Madame de Sévigné had written that her standing was 'paramount' (*extrême*), while Montespan's was beginning to fade.[76] In late 1679 the King appointed Maintenon second *dame d'atours* of the new Dauphine, in order to give her an apartment in the palace. Madame de Montespan's rages, from which Maintenon had suffered so often, helped drive the King away, despite Colbert's efforts at reconciliation. Spanheim wrote that her temper made her detested. That autumn Louis did not receive the sacraments. It is possible that Maintenon now became his mistress.[77]

Madame de Sévigné was an observer in the crucial year 1680: 'the favour of Madame de Maintenon is increasing every day; there are infinite conversations with His Majesty' (20 March); the King's relations with Montespan had turned to 'extrême brouillerie' (25 May); Maintenon's conversations with the King from 6 to 10 in the evening in his apartment, on the other hand, were 'of a length which makes everyone wonder' (5 June). Ministers now courted her as much as they were courted by others (21 June). While he visited Montespan and Fontanges for only a few moments in the day, 'the favour of Madame de Maintenon is still supreme' (11 September).[78]

Madame de Maintenon was attractive and intelligent, and her health had not been wrecked by childbirth. Like some French men and women of the day, she believed that the mind had no sex, and men and women should be equal.[79] Religion, however, was the basis of her relationship with the King. Catholicism gave purpose, colour and drama to the King's year. Every day of his life, he said his morning and evening prayers with 'extreme devotion' and attended a low mass in his chapel. He also wore a small sachet containing holy relics, including a piece of 'the true cross'.

Unlike previous kings of France (including his father, who had generally prayed in a small private oratory), Louis XIV made his attendance at chapel in Versailles, at midday in his wife's lifetime, thereafter at 10 a.m., into a magnificent court ritual, like his meals. His procession through the Grand Appartement to the chapel included members of the royal family of both sexes, court officials and *maîtres des requêtes* to take petitions presented during the procession. Guards beat drums and played fifes as he entered the chapel. The King was included in the ritual as a priest, receiving incense and consecrated bread (*pain bénit*).[80]

In addition he attended a sung high mass, or sung vespers, on Thursdays and Sundays; and such great feasts as Christmas (when he attended six masses in two days), Epiphany, Easter, Whitsun, the Assumption of the Virgin and the Feast of the Immaculate Conception, when he took communion.[81] A community of Lazarists* was attached to the chapel at Versailles to say masses through the day, even when the King was not in residence; by 1710 twenty masses were being said there every morning.[82]

The King fasted during Lent, and encouraged courtiers to do likewise, and he listened to Lent and Advent sermons, by a variety of preachers (Bossuet, Bourdaloue, Massillon), some of whom criticized his private life with a frankness which few modern heads of state would tolerate.[83] In the course of his life, he attended around 30,000 masses and listened to 2,000 sermons.[84] Further demonstrating his piety – accompanied by an army of court officials, guards and pages holding candles in their hands – he also followed public processions on foot through the streets of Paris and later Versailles, hung with the finest tapestries of the crown, for Jubilees or the Fête Dieu. He also performed the ritual washing of the feet of twelve poor children every Thursday before Easter, in imitation of Jesus Christ washing the feet of the Apostles.[85] His Catholicism reflected both his belief in God and his belief in monarchy. He wrote to his son that Catholicism taught obedience to kings as lieutenants of God. Therefore, for reasons of prudence and common sense as well as faith, Catholicism should be 'the first and most important part of our policy'.[86]

Throughout his reign, from his coronation in 1654 to his death in 1715, even when he was ill, Louis (after taking communion) also performed the ritual of touching for the King's Evil (scrofula), usually in Versailles' ground-floor galleries, sometimes more than a thousand people in one day. At Whitsun, Easter, the Assumption, All Saints and Christmas, Versailles became the Lourdes of the seventeenth century, crowded with men and women with scrofula, some come from as far as Spain and Italy to be cured by the King of France. Supplicants were selected by the royal doctors. Their hands were held together by the Capitaine des Gardes in waiting to stop them harming the King. As the King touched their shoulder with his right hand, and traced the sign of the cross, he said, 'The king touches you; God heals you.' Each was given a coin. Between each touching, the King's hands were wiped with a wine-soaked cloth, to prevent infections. On 1 November 1685, for example, although barely able to stand from gout, he touched 300: a triumph of duty over ill-health. The total touched during his reign, Alexandre Maral estimates, may have reached 200,000.[87]

Between 1664 and 1680, Louis XIV did not take communion except

---

* The preaching order, founded by Père Vincent de Paul and favoured by Anne of Austria, which ministered to the court parishes of Versailles, Fontainebleau, Saint-Germain and Saint-Cloud.

at Easter, as he had no intention of giving up his mistresses.[88] After Easter 1680 Maintenon encouraged him to practise all the duties of a good Catholic, including fidelity in marriage. He regularly took communion – demonstrating that he was no longer, in the eyes of the Catholic church, in a state of sin.[89] He began to see more of his wife, perhaps to have more frequent sexual relations with her. In 1680 Sévigné wrote that the Queen was in favour at court.[90] In 1681 Sourches summarized what courtiers knew, that Madame de Maintenon had won the King's entire confidence and respect by her intelligence, her manners and her discretion. He showed her all possible friendship, and had long conversations with her every day. He no longer had 'commerce' with women and communicated regularly four times a year.[91] That October Louis XIV ended all forms of intimacy with Madame de Montespan, sending her his compliments, and assurances of friendship, via his trusted intermediary with his mistresses, Colbert.[92]

Soon after the Queen's death, Maintenon and Louis married, probably in October 1683, in the presence of the Archbishop of Paris, Louvois and the King's confessor. She was forty-seven, he was forty-five. For once Louis let the unconventional, emotional sides of his personality triumph over conventions. He married for love, breaking the rules limiting his dynasty's marriage to people of royal birth, which he had been forced to observe in 1660 and which he had imposed on Mademoiselle in 1670.[93] The marriage was full of contradictions. In public Maintenon remained *seconde dame d'atours* of the Dauphine, helping her to dress and do her hair, yielding precedence to ladies of apparently higher rank. Like the uncrowned Queen of France she had become, however, in their private apartments Maintenon stayed seated in the King's presence and began to visit enclosed convents – a privilege reserved for the Queen.[94] No one else had the right to a chair in her apartment, not even Madame, who therefore remained standing, rather than endure the humiliation of a tabouret. In the gardens at Versailles or at military reviews, the King would walk beside Maintenon's sedan chair, bending down to talk to her, showing more public deference than he had to the Queen.[95] The King's return to respectability made religion fashionable. Maintenon boasted to her brother of the 'conversion' of the entire court: every Sunday the chapel was now as full as it had formerly been only at Easter.[96]

At Versailles Madame de Maintenon had a fine apartment on the first floor,[97] and a house of her own in the town, just below the chateau in what is now the rue du Peintre Lebrun. Madame de Montespan, on the other hand, left her apartment in 1684, which the King then used for his art collections, and moved to the ground floor.[98]

After 1691, to universal relief, like Louise de La Vallière and the Duchesse de Fontanges before her, Montespan left court for a convent; in her case, the Filles de Saint-Joseph in the rue Saint-Dominique, of which she had been protectress since 1676. Montespan spent her days fasting, praying and organizing charity work. In a workshop attached to the convent, she organized poor girls for whose education she was paying, with the help of professional embroiderers, to embroider tapestries for the royal palaces (Louis had the largest collection of tapestries of any monarch since Henry VIII of England: 304 sets and 2,566 separate pieces). They showed, for example, Mlle de Nantes, her eldest daughter by the King, as Spring; their elder son the Duc du Maine as Fire; the King as Air. She also had the girls educated and given dowries to help them find husbands.[99]

Even her own convent, however, suffered from what nuns called her 'absolute, precipitous and changeable temper' and 'harsh injustices'. Montespan had helped celebrate their elder daughter's wedding to the Duc de Bourbon in 1685, and arranged a carnival party at Marly in 1686, but in 1692 was invited neither to their younger daughter's wedding to the King's nephew Duc de Chartres nor to the Duc du Maine's wedding to his cousin Mlle de Condé. By 1701, wrote Madame, her hair was white and her reddened face was covered in lines, like a piece of paper which had been folded and refolded. She died in 1707, expressing repentance for her sins to her servants (she had had herself painted as a repentant Mary Magdalene). No letters survive to give her version of her replacement in the King's favour by her former friend.[100]

While Montespan was excluded from the court, Maintenon and the King lived like the married couple they were. A few short notes from the King have survived the destruction of their correspondence, probably kept by Maintenon herself. They often arranged meetings in the day, in addition to their evenings in her apartment. For example this note, from the King about her beloved girls' school at Saint-Cyr (see below), in July 1693: 'if it is too late to come past the garden, inform me as then we will go to the main gate of the house, by which I mean the one that encloses the women in the courtyard.'[101] The most moving is from April 1691, eight years after their marriage: 'I always cherish you and I respect you, to an extent which I cannot express; and indeed, whatever affection [*amitié*] you have for me, I have even more for you, being with all my heart totally yours.'[102]

For the King, Maintenon entertained court ladies, although she hated ceremonies and entertainments and what she called the constraint and noise at court, as courtiers laughed and danced, in her phrase, with daggers in their heart. Sometimes, she wrote, the ladies talked of nothing but peas.[103] She called her life a martyrdom and wrote to the Archbishop of Paris that at Trianon – loved by the King and his family – 'you hardly feel anything there but sadness, fatigue and boredom and the more you look for pleasure, the more it eludes you'.[104] A natural pessimist, she was outraged by, as well as sceptical of, pleasure.[105] Ignoring how many men had helped her own dazzling ascent, from Paul Scarron to the men who built Saint-Cyr for her female pupils – and Louis himself – she wrote, 'men are unbearable when you see them at close quarters.' She herself, she complained, counted for nothing.[106]

She also acted as a surrogate mother and grandmother to the royal family. Although both the Dauphin and Madame hated and despised Maintenon as an ambitious intruder, they used her, as did ministers, ambassadors and generals, as an intermediary to convey requests or news to the King.[107] During the campaign of 1691, for example, Maine, her favourite, wrote to her comparing the King to a young madman who has to establish his reputation and prove he is not frightened, or to reassure her about the King's health. The Dauphin wrote to her almost daily, even claiming, falsely, 'no one is more for you than I am.'[108]

Madame de Maintenon remained a governess and teacher at heart. To please her, the King built near Versailles, at a cost of 1.4 million livres, a girls' school called the Maison Royale de Saint-Cyr, inaugurated on 2 August 1686. Two hundred and fifty girls of proven noble birth and impecunious background – officers' daughters were preferred – were taught history, geography, Latin, mathematics, music and sewing, to prepare them for married life. They danced and sang for the King during his visits.[109]

It became her private paradise, which alone enabled her to endure the pressures of Versailles. On 31 March 1698 she married her niece and heiress Mlle d'Aubigné to Adrien Maurice de Noailles, a member of the most influential family at court. Hundreds, both from the court and from Paris, including members of the royal family, had paid congratulatory visits to Madame de Maintenon, who gave the wedding dinner. As he said good night, the King had given each spouse a pension of 8,000 livres a year, in addition to the dowry of 800,000 livres he had already given Mlle d'Aubigné, on account of his 'considération particulière' for 'la dame Marquise de Maintenon'.[110] Adrien Maurice de Noailles became a confidant of Maintenon and the King.* In a letter of 4 March 1702, Maintenon wrote to him of 'the passion I have for Saint-Cyr' and 'the detail into which

---

* Later he would, by his own account, stop the King burning his papers, remove them and, still later, give them to the royal library in Paris: Abbé Millot, *Mémoires politiques et militaires pour servir a l'histoire de Louis XIV et de Louis XV*, 1839, pp. 227, 254, 255; Don Fader, 'La Duchesse de Bourgogne, le mécénat des Noailles et les arts dramatiques à la cour

I enter about the education of the girls who are there'. She was determined to occupy them from morning to night with 'beautiful and good subjects, or at least innocent ones'.[111] Often she spent the day at Saint-Cyr (as the King did at Marly), returning to Versailles in the evening. Even at Versailles she spent time with a reading group of pious ladies known as 'the court convent'.

The girls were taught that marriage was a tribulation, good husbands almost unknown. They should suffer, in silence. The only true happiness lay in conformity to the will of God. Men were masters: women should suffer with good grace. It was a royal school and in one of the educational dialogues she composed she makes 'Alphonsine' tell 'Placide', echoing what Louis himself and most of his subjects believed, 'without any prejudice the greatest dynasty we know is that of Bourbon which now governs us.'[112]

Saint-Cyr would later be imitated by court girls' schools in Vienna and St Petersburg. But Saint-Cyr also showed that, despite her intelligence, Maintenon lacked judgement. Frequent rows divided the school's teachers. Her friend Madame de Brinon, the first Director, was removed by *lettre de cachet* in December 1688: she had begun to have ideas of her own. Like Louise de La Vallière, Madame de Ludres, the Duchesse de Fontanges, Madame de Montespan and many others, Maintenon began to feel the call of the convent. In 1694, fearing 'impurity', Maintenon, against her original intention, made Saint-Cyr an Augustinian convent.[113]

The inscription on a gold cross that the girls at Saint-Cyr gave to Madame de Maintenon (composed by Racine) confirms her love of power:

> Elle est notre guide fidèle.
> Notre félicité vient d'elle.[114]

> ('She is our faithful guide.
> Our happiness comes from her.')

Contradicting her claim to be 'nothing', she soon played a political, as well as a religious, role. From 1691 the King began to meet ministers in her apartment, to which he later personally supervised extensions.[115] Maintenon became, more than Montespan before her, a crucial part of the Versailles power and patronage machine. Until the King's death, she was inundated with letters asking for jobs, pensions and favours.[116] She herself wrote that her apartment was like a church, with 'everyone' coming and going all day: ladies-in-waiting, bishops, generals, princes, ministers

autour de 1700', in Fabrice Preyat, ed., *Marie Adélaïde de Savoie (1685–1712): Duchesse de Bourgogne, enfant terrible de Versailles*, Brussels, 2014, pp. 175–90.

and the King himself. Ambassadors thought she was all powerful – although when approached by the Papal Nuncio, over a dispute between the Pope and the King, she claimed to be 'too feeble an instrument to enter into such matters'.[117]

Indeed her power had limits. She preferred peace, but could not stop the King going to war, exposing himself to danger in battle or refusing her candidate as his confessor.[118] Many people she disliked stayed at court: for example, the Duc de Beauvillier, a *premier gentilhomme* and a minister, even though they had quarrelled in 1697 over his continued admiration for Fénelon.[119] Her attempt in 1702 to help the Maréchal d'Harcourt enter the council failed. Torcy, whom she disliked, remained foreign minister until the King's death, and moreover held the key post of *surintendant des postes*, which gave him the opportunity to read her letters.[120]

Versailles represents both the triumph of the court over the state, in the move from Paris against Colbert's advice, and the triumph of the state over the court, in the pre-eminence of ministers, once the court had settled there. As we have seen, Louis XIV spent as much time with his ministers as with his family, his court officials or his mistresses. The ministers' wings, stretching east from Versailles with apartments and offices for the ministers of foreign affairs, war, the Maison du Roi and the marine, distinguish Versailles from other palaces as much as the courtiers' and princes' wings stretching to the north and south.[121]*

Versailles was a working palace. The Cabinet du Conseil where Louis XIV met his ministers was more important than the adjoining bedchamber, where he slept and held the *lever* and the *coucher*. At Versailles as at Saint-Germain, the council, composed of ministers of state, the Dauphin and after 1702 his son the Duc de Bourgogne continued to meet from 10 to 12 on Sunday, Wednesday, Thursday and every other Monday. This was the heart of government, to which ministers read reports on their department's activities. The Council of Finance met on Tuesday and Saturday, also from 10 to 12; the Council of Despatches met every other Monday to discuss internal affairs, with Monsieur and all ministers. The Council of State for legal affairs met on the ground floor, without the King, every Monday, as did a special council dealing with Huguenot affairs.[122]

---

* The Stadtpalais of Potsdam, for example, was constructed by the Elector Frederick William of Brandenburg at a similar distance from the capital, for similar reasons – love of the country and proximity to hunting forests – and at roughly the same date. However, it contained no ministers' wings. The council continued to meet in the palace in Berlin. Ministers came to Potsdam to see the Elector in the day, but returned to Berlin in the evening: Derek McKay, *The Great Elector*, 2001, pp. 235–6.

In addition to council meetings, Louis XIV spent many evenings working with individual ministers. A note returning files about the situation in
the Mediterranean to his minister Pontchartrain shows that one evening
in 1703, when the King was sixty-five, he was working at midnight.[123] The
state took priority over the court. 'The King goes neither to comedies nor
to Appartement except on extraordinary occasions. He spends his time at
Madame de Maintenon's apartment where he works with some of his
ministers,' reported Dangeau in 1698. To the King's annoyance, despite
the Dauphin's presence, there began to be 'very few women and even very
few men' at Appartement.[124]

Ministerial departments in Paris and Versailles were smaller than court
departments. There were fifty to a hundred clerks in most ministries –
fifteen to twenty-nine in the Foreign Ministry – compared to over 300 men
in both the Grande and Petite Ecuries.[125] The government as well as the
court was run by dynasties. The key ministerial dynasties – Colbert, Le
Tellier, Phélypeaux – were more powerful than even the grandest courtier
dynasties: Montmorency, Rohan, Noailles or Lorraine. Knowledge of their
characters, relationships and degrees of royal favour was as necessary to
navigate the court as knowledge of the map of Métro lines is to cross
modern Paris. Each ministerial dynasty represented a programme, as well
as a family: the Colbert advocated state intervention in the economy and
religious orthodoxy; the Le Tellier war and expansion. The Phélypeaux de
Pontchartrain, the most enduring ministerial dynasty in French history
(with nine members holding ministerial office between 1610 and 1781) had
a special interest in the Maison du Roi, the navy and overseas trade and
exploration, as the names Lac Maurepas, Fort Maurepas and Lac Pontchartrain in Louisiana suggest. They established an office of maps and plans
in the Ministry of the Marine in 1696, and supported wars against England
in the eighteenth century. Under Louis XIV Louis de Pontchartrain was
contrôleur général and minister of the marine and the Maison du Roi in
1689–99, and from 1699 chancellor. His son Jérôme de Pontchartrain
became minister of the marine and the Maison du Roi in his turn in 1699.[126]

The rivalry between Colbert and Louvois was probably encouraged by
the King in order, in Visconti's phrase, to 'faire ses affaires'. Distrusting
ministers' ambitions, he wanted to prevent them uniting to impose their
will on him. They not only strove to keep their sources of information from
their rivals, sometimes they quarrelled at council meetings in the King's
presence, for example over their departments' share of government expenditure.[127] Sourches thought that Maintenon played a role in balancing the
Louvois and Colbert families, although her heart was with the latter.[128]

Courtiers asked ministers for favours, not the other way round. Louvois

had helped put Luxembourg in the Bastille during the Affaire des Poisons –
a Montmorency, a *capitaine des gardes* and a victorious marshal of France.
When Luxembourg was released, he wrote his tormentor abject letters of
gratitude.[129] Ministers could enter the King's bedroom before the *grandes
entrées*, if they had important news.[130] The Maréchal de Villeroy said,
'hold a minister's chamber pot for him as long as he is in power – empty
it over his head when he loses power.' Unless you made yourself the valet
of a minister, wrote M. de Coligny, an army officer, it was a waste of time
to attach yourself to the King's service.[131] Another courtier, the Dauphin's
Governor M. de Montausier, complained that only ministers or mistresses
had power 'en ce pays-ci' – a phrase meaning at court.[132]

Ministers were so powerful that one of them usually attended the King's
private audiences: exceptional interviews, granted to a favoured few (816
French men and women in the whole reign) for fifteen or thirty minutes,
usually on Thursdays. Saint-Simon obtained an audience with the help of
his friend the Premier Chirurgien Mareschal, in order to try to convince
the King that he did not deserve his reputation as a troublemaker. He
admitted that on such occasions the King listened with patience, kindness
and a desire to learn the truth. Anything could be said, even by those the
King disliked, if it was said in the right way, with respect and an air of
submission.[133]

Ministers had more occasion to talk to the King than even the most
important court officials, with whom he was rarely alone. Ministers
brought bundles of papers with especially wide margins, on which Louis
XIV wrote his comments.*

Louis XIV also corresponded directly with certain senior officers and
officials – usually with, but sometimes without, the knowledge of his
ministers – for example with Vauban and Chamlay, and with ambassadors.
He frequently requested more detailed despatches from his ambassadors,
or from members of his family when they were serving in the army.[134]

Louis exchanged long letters with his Ambassador to Sweden in the
1670s, M. de Feuquières, about Hanoverian ambitions in northern Germany or Swedish senators' attitudes to foreign policy, for example, and
with his Ambassador to Spain in 1698–1700, the Marquis d'Harcourt,
about every detail of Carlos II's health and every nuance in Spanish

---

* As can be seen in surviving documents formerly in the archives of Colbert's descendants,
the ducs de Luynes, in the chateau of Dampierre, used by Inès Murat in her biography, and
in the Ministry of War and the Archives Nationales. Under Louis XIV some ministers'
archives began to be stored in official buildings and inventoried, rather than being left in the
hands of the ministers and their families: Thierry Sarmant and Mathieu Stoll, *Régner et
gouverner: Louis XIV et ses ministres*, 2010, pp. 179, 384.

attitudes towards a Bourbon succession or a partition of the Spanish monarchy. His correspondence proves the King's detailed knowledge of European personalities, issues, disputes and wars. He lived and breathed foreign policy.[135]

Similarly in his letters to Madame de Montespan's brother the Maréchal de Vivonne, commander of the galleys and Viceroy of Sicily during the revolt of Messina in 1676–8, he regularly expressed his desire for 'the pure truth without disguising or omitting anything'; and 'to be informed of everything and even by more than one route, in order to know the truth more distinctly and more profoundly'.[136] Fifteen years later a typical request to an officer in the field in Ireland was: 'give me your news as often as possible and tell me the exact situation.' Like Napoleon, Louis XIV always knew the state of his troops and his fortresses.[137]

Thus the King ensured that he was the best-informed man in his kingdom. In a 'Mémoire pour mon fils' of 1673, Colbert warned his son: 'you must be ready to give information to the King when he asks for it, otherwise you will regret it'; 'you must tell the King everything'; 'Every affair, great and small, important and bagatelles, is equally known by this prince, who loses no opportunity to be informed of everything, even down to the detail of his buildings.'[138]

Ministers were so important that some helped run the King's private life as well as public policy. We have seen how he used Colbert, despite his vast public responsibilities for the navy, the economy and the Maison du Roi, as a trusted intermediary with Monsieur, Madame de Montespan and Louise de La Vallière.[139] Occasionally, Colbert scolded his master about his failure to base government expenditure on income.[140] Their relations came to resemble a volatile love affair, and ambassadors sometimes thought Colbert's disgrace imminent. On 26 April 1671 the King wrote to Colbert:

> do not think that my friendship is diminishing, as your services continue; that is impossible, but you must perform them as I desire them and believe that I do everything for the best. The preference that you fear that I give others should not cause you any distress. I simply want to commit no injustice and to work for the good of my service. It is what will happen when you are all beside me. Believe in the meantime that I have not changed for you and that my feelings are as you would wish them to be.

He wanted his ministers to speak to him freely, but once he had made a decision he did not want it queried.

When Colbert was ill, the King paid him the unusual honour of coming to his house to work with him. Like many healthy people, Louis XIV thought other people's illnesses were in their minds: 'Sadness creates illness, be cheerful and you will be cured.'[141] Colbert could boast that 'the King is much more the father of my children than I am.'[142] Helped by royal favour, Colbert married three daughters to three dukes (Chevreuse, Beauvillier, Mortemart); one of his sons became grand master of ceremonies. His brother Colbert de Croissy became minister of foreign affairs in 1679 and was succeeded on his death in 1696 by his son Torcy. Colbert's own son Seignelay succeeded him in 1683 as minister of the marine. Seignelay's son became *maître de la garde-robe* in 1690. Colbert's nephew Desmarets would become *contrôleur général des finances* in 1708.

In 1683, as Colbert was dying, Louis XIV wrote loving letters to Seignelay about 'the particular friendship I have for him and for you and all his family'.[143] In reality by then Colbert may have lost the King's favour over building work at Versailles. Louis was said to have complained that it was strange that, being so generous, he was worse served than anyone else: with Louvois he had only to suggest something for it to be accomplished. At this Colbert took to his bed 'prey to the most extreme pains [or sorrows]', and died. The taxes he had imposed had made him so hated in Paris that his funeral procession had to be protected by guards from hostile crowds.[144]

Louis XIV's growing reliance on Louvois had been another reason for Colbert's sorrow. As well as being minister of war, and replacing Colbert, on his death, as *surintendant des bâtiments*, Louvois became, like Colbert before him, the King's friend and intimate. As *surintendant des bâtiments*, Louvois corresponded with Louis on such matters as the construction of the orangery at Versailles and the gilding in the royal bedroom: 'take more care of my bedroom than of the rest,' Louis wrote.[145]

In October 1683 he may have witnessed the King's wedding to Madame de Maintenon. On 18 November 1686 it was not a courtier, a relation or Maintenon, but Louvois who held the King's hand during the agonizing six-hour operation for the removal of his anal fistula. The only other people in the room were the surgeon, Monsieur, Madame, his eldest illegitimate daughter the Princesse de Conti and Madame de Maintenon.[146] In this matter of life or death, a minister enjoyed greater intimacy than any servant, court official or relation. The King's stamina and self-control were such that this prolonged torture, as the swelling was cut and removed, evoked no cries of pain, beyond two exclamations of 'Mon Dieu!' It barely interrupted his schedule of work, exercise and entertainment. The curved steel pincers (*bistoury à la royale*) used for the operation can be seen in the Musée d'Histoire de la Médicine in Paris.[147]

Louvois, like Colbert, accelerated his family's entry into court society. He entertained the King at his chateau of Meudon, as Colbert had at Sceaux, and he married his daughter to François de La Rochefoucauld, son of Louis XIV's Grand Maître de la Garde-robe, in November 1679 – a magnificent wedding attended, in the words of Madame de Sévigné, by 'toute la France'. Other relations married into the Villeroy and Aumont families, while his brother became archbishop of Reims. One son, the Marquis de Barbezieux, became minister of war; another, the Marquis de Souvré, a *maître de la Garde-robe*; a third, the Marquis de Courtanvaux, captain of the Cent-Suisses de la Garde, a post retained by his descendants until the 1770s.[148] Other ministers' relations who acquired senior court office included the Marquis de Dreux-Brézé, son-in-law of the Controleur Général Chamillart, who became *grand maître des cérémonies* in 1701, a post held by his descendants until 1830; and Chamillart's son the Marquis de La Suze, who became *grand maréchal des logis*.[149]

Sourches, Grand Prévôt de France, commented, with the bitterness of a powerless court official, 'great ministers like M. de Louvois have so much access and credit with their master, and have occasions to choose their moment so favourably, that they succeed in the most unlikely matters and that nothing is impossible to them; that is why a good courtier is never surprised to see them achieve objects for which they themselves would never have dared to hope.'[150]

Despite the King's hard work, and his access to information from non-ministerial sources, many believed that, as Saint-Maurice wrote in a despatch in 1668 and Saint-Simon asserted in his memoirs, he could be 'absolutely governed by his ministers'.[151] Absolutism could be a façade hiding the power of ministers and factions to persuade the King to take the decisions they wanted. He could be their instrument not their master. A historian of the eastern Pyrenees considers that the King merely endorsed decisions about that region which Louvois had already taken.[152] Sometimes Louvois overruled the King, for example over regimental regulations in 1675: 'your Majesty will permit me to tell him that the expedient which he proposes to change regimental companies does not suit this service for many reasons which would be too long to explain to him in a letter.'[153]

Ministers could get the King to revoke his own orders if they found them shocking – for example, an instruction that prisoners of war should be sent to work in his galleys.[154] On occasion his decisions depended on whom he had seen last, Colbert or Louvois. In the last years of the reign he sometimes told couriers to take despatches to a minister first, rather than to himself, so that the minister could report to him on their content.[155] Louis did not feel free to correspond directly with Vauban, whom he had known since the war of 1667, until the death of Louvois in 1692. Thereafter, however, Louis allowed Vauban many liberties in his letters. Vauban did not hesitate to tell the King of the disastrous situation of his kingdom.[156]

By 1680, in his own eyes, Louis XIV was master of France and arbiter of Europe. Colbert wrote that year, exaggerating government control, 'everything reflects total submission . . . the authority of the Parlement reduced to a point where only the shadow of it remains.' Even 'the misery and distress of the peoples' served royal power, since the King could control 'this proud and inconstant nation with the restraint of extreme necessity'. Law codes had been reformed without consulting Parlements or Estates. *Lettres de cachet* and extraordinary courts were used more often. Paris was better policed than most cities in Europe.[157] Versailles was considered the wonder of the world. Royal academies glorified the King, the monarchy and France. Louis XIV had won almost universal admiration as administrator, commander, patron and king.

Yet his achievements hid inner weaknesses. As a young man Louis had been considered kind and 'civil and courteous beyond anything one can imagine'.[158] By the age of forty, blinded by flattery, power, success, a new man had emerged. The Brandenburg minister Ezechiel Spanheim considered that Louis showed little charity, compassion, humility or moderation.[159]

Narcissism, tactlessness, lack of realism and failure to foresee consequences had become characteristics of Louis XIV. For example in 1672 the French invasion of the Netherlands had transformed his cousin William III, whose dynasty the House of Orange had previously been French allies, into a lifelong adversary. Louis later thought to win him by offering an illegitimate daughter's hand in marriage – only to receive the reply, 'in my family we marry the daughters of great Kings, not their bastards.'[160] In 1672, reflecting both the influence of Louvois and his own combination of caution and overconfidence, Louis failed either to seize Amsterdam or to accept favourable Dutch peace terms.

Louis XIV revealed his growing narcisissim in his own words. He wrote of the invasion of the Netherlands in 1672: 'I can praise myself for having let people see what France can do alone' (forgetting that France was not 'alone' but allied to Charles II and the Elector of Cologne).[161] Courtin, a valued adviser on foreign policy, warned as early as 1673 that the King would in the future find many opportunities, in his wars, to display his courage and virtue, but in doing so would ruin his subjects.[162] Desire to win praise, and to outshine both his rivals and his ministers, could be as important to Louis XIV as winning territory. He preferred sieges to battles, as the outcome was more certain, while the glory, in his eyes, was the same. The King's need for admiration was well known. In

1680, for example, there is a suggestion of irony and exasperation in the description of Louis XIV by his *premier gentilhomme de la chambre* the Duc de Saint-Aignan, in a letter to Bussy-Rabutin, as 'the King whose intelligence is infinite and who is no less great in his judgement than in his other admirable qualities'.[163]

Two remarkable memoirs by Claude Le Peletier, Contrôleur Général in 1683–9, a member of the Paris *noblesse de robe* and protégé of Louvois, were written in private after his resignation, perhaps for his family rather than for posterity. He criticizes both the magnificence of Louis XIV's palaces and the 'very bad' conduct of foreign policy. He blamed the King for trying to show 'all Europe' (his audience as much as France) that he did not need his ministers' advice. A few pages later he went to the heart of the man: 'the King flattered himself and liked to be flattered, reducing everything to his own convenience and wanting to persuade the whole world that he directed affairs by himself . . . the King likes to do more by himself than befits a prudent prince.' He blamed the influence of Madame de Maintenon rather than that of his protector, Louvois.[164]

The amount of information in every field on which Louis XIV insisted delayed government decisions, and generals' initiatives in the field, and made debates in the council less decisive. He also lacked a large personal secretariat to help him enforce decisions.[165] Registers of orders issued later in the reign by Pontchartrain, Ministre de la Maison, after discussion with the King, to the Lieutenant de Police de Paris confirm the King's absolute powers and attention to detail. For example, he gave instructions about disorders in the cul de sac of the Hôtel de Soissons; the imprisonment of vagabonds; the pardoning of galley slaves; 'insolent' conversations in Paris cafés and suburban cabarets, and 'insolent' pamphlets from Liège; illegal gambling parties of basset and pharaon; scandalous monks; and 'the insolence of the coachman of M. the ambassador of Venice'. Often a note is made that 'His Majesty did not want to make a decision,' because he had requested more information about 'all the circumstances'.[166] He controlled music in Paris as well as Versailles, down to the last detail. To the new Director of the Paris Opera, Pierre Guyenet, who later went bankrupt, Pontchartrain wrote, 'His Majesty will protect you on all occasions. With regard to Marais [a famous musician] he agrees that he should beat time as usual, and you could not do better than to use Beauchamp also for the dances.'[167]

The King's methods of government, and delusions about French power, would contribute to the disasters of the second half of his reign. Madame believed that all the luck and good fortune of France had died with the Queen in 1683. The death of Colbert in the same year had been a far greater loss to the country.

15

The Global King: From the Mississippi to the Mekong

On 1 September 1686 Louis XIV received an embassy from another world. Ambassadors from the King of Siam had been travelling for two years over a distance of 4,000 miles. That day they crossed the courtyards of Versailles, lined with French and Swiss guards. They then climbed the Escalier des Ambassadeurs 'to the sound of drums and trumpets, to imitate the manner of the king of Siam, who never enters the audience hall without this music'.

The Escalier des Ambassadeurs, built between 1672 and 1679 and designed by Le Brun on the right of the palace, was far grander than the Escalier de la Reine on the left, leading to the Queen's apartments. Lined with pink and green marble, and lit by a glass roof, the Escalier des Ambassadeurs led to the state apartments on the first floor. The walls were decorated with frescoes showing the admiring nations of the four continents (Asians, Africans, Americans and Europeans), and French victories at Cambrai, Valenciennes, Saint-Omer, Cassel. In the middle of the main wall where the staircase divided into two, was a bust by Jean Warin of the King as a Roman emperor.[1]

The ambassadors carried a letter from the King of Siam, written on gold leaf, placed in a gold casket on a gilded litter surmounted by parasols. They advanced through the state apartments into the Galerie des Glaces, lined with courtiers and silver furniture. Jean de Plantavit de La Pause noted that 'the crowd was unbelievable and seemed to shock and offend the king's majesty but in France our kings are used to being overwhelmed by the crowd which is their grandeur.'

At the end, sitting on his silver throne raised on eight steps, was the King, wearing a golden coat sewn with diamonds worth more, Sourches claimed, than the entire kingdom of Siam. Beside him were the royal princes, also covered in jewels, behind him the officers of his chamber and wardrobe. As the ambassadors advanced, they repeatedly prostrated themselves – kowtowed – almost to the floor, in 'respect and admiration'.[2]

At the foot of the throne, the ambassadors gazed at the King for several minutes, and made another prostration before him 'in their manner, to which the King replied by standing and raising his hat to them'. Then, after the King had sat on his throne again, 'the first ambassador made him a speech in Siamese [praising 'the very great king who had conquered all his enemies'], during which he made several profound reverences, to which the King replied by raising his hat.' After the speech they had a long conversation through the Abbé de Lionne, a missionary who had lived in Siam. Finally, after more bows, the ambassadors and their suite retired backwards through the gallery.

They then paid court to all the other members of the royal family in turn and displayed their presents, including gold and silver vessels and pieces of Chinese porcelain and Japanese lacquer.[3] In the following weeks they visited the sights of Paris and the fortresses on the northern frontier. After a private audience with the King in October, they began the long journey back to Siam, taking with them presents and such purchases as 4,264 mirrors from the Saint-Gobain factory. Before they left they declared that France was not a country but a world, where everything was possible; its people were not humans but angels. The Duc de La Feuillade, Colonel of the Gardes Français, who had provided them with escorts in Paris, bade them farewell with the words 'Qui n'était pas bon siamois n'etait pas bon français.'[4]

The Siamese embassy, like the Escalier des Ambassadeurs itself, was a sign that Versailles was a global palace for a global monarch. He was linked to the rest of the world through an elaborate hierarchy of ambassadors, envoys extraordinary, ministers plenipotentiary, residents and mere agents, whom he sent to and received from foreign governments.

Foreign diplomats came every Tuesday from Paris to pay court to Louis XIV: they were not allowed to live in Versailles, since Paris was still the capital. Their visits were organized by officials under the Grand Maître des Cérémonies, a post created by Henri III in 1585 when he was trying to increase the ceremonial impact of his court.[5] Full 'ambassadors extraordinary' were given, in some degrees, the rank of the crowned heads they represented, with precedence over princes, as French ambassadors repeatedly reminded William III before 1688 when he was only Prince of Orange. Versailles was designed to impress ambassadors as well as travellers. In an éloge of Colbert, the lawyer Barbier d'Aucourt praised the pomp and magnificence of the royal palaces 'filled with precious furniture which represent with such splendour the grandeur and majesty of the State to the ambassadors of all the kings in the world'.[6]

In addition to ambassadors from Europe, Louis XIV received

ambassadors from what an inscription in the Galerie des Glaces called 'the extremities of the earth': Muscovy (1668, 1685), the Ottoman Empire (1669), Morocco (1682, 1699), Algiers (1684), Siam as we have seen (1686), Tunis (1690) and Persia (1715).[7] He also occasionally received people or embassies from America and Africa. After 1683, for example, the Compagnie Royale de Guinée had begun to trade with Issinie, a kingdom east of Abidjan in what is now Côte d'Ivoire. Prince Aniaba, son of King Zena, was brought to France in 1688, possibly presented to Louis XIV and baptized Louis, as the King's godson, by Bossuet in 1691. A priest called Claude Chatelain claimed that the King told Aniaba that there was no more difference between them than between black and white. He became an officer in the Régiment du Roi, with a royal pension.[8] After he had returned to Issinie on a French boat in 1701, however, with a gold medal of the royal family and a picture of the Virgin, he showed himself in some way 'unworthy of the King's favours'. Having failed to use French power to make himself king, he died in exile in Togo after 1718.[9] In 1705 an American chief called Nescambiout was also received by Louis XIV at Versailles, and given a medal and a sabre.[10]

Conversation at Marly and Versailles could be about Aleppo, Siam or America.[11] During dinner, Louis XIV often talked about their journeys to French travellers and missionaries. He granted the former permission to dedicate books to him, and let the latter travel free on his ships.* He was continually curious. A Jesuit missionary called Père Pallu noted on 29 December 1684: 'His Majesty loves the sciences extremely and every kind of knowledge which one can acquire in foreign countries.'[12] In 1685 the King bade farewell to the first French embassy to Siam during dinner. He placed his hands on the shoulders of Père Bénigne Vachet and said, 'so you want to leave, Monsieur Vachet. I pray to Our Lord to grant a happy success to all our plans. I know they are good and I hope we will soon meet again.' Vachet replied, 'Sire, I indeed expect it. But if it please God, it will be in paradise and not in your kingdom.'[13] Louis also sponsored the voyages of Jean Richer in Acadia and Cayenne (1670), Jean Picard in Denmark (1671–2), de Varin in Africa and the Antilles (1681–3), Louis

---

* Books dedicated by travellers to Louis XIV, at his suggestion, include François Bernier's *Histoire de la dernière révolution des Etats du Grand Mogul* in 1670; Guy Tachard SJ's *Voyage de Siam des Pères Jesuites envoyés par le roy aux Indes et à la Chine* in 1687; Souchu de Rennefort's *Mémoires pour servir à l'histoire des Indes orientales* in 1688; and Barthélemy d'Herbelot's 1,000-page *Bibliothèque orientale, ou Dictionnaire universel contenant généralement tout ce qui regarde la connoissance des Peuples d'Orient* in 1697.

Econches Feuillée in the Levant and South America (1699–1711) and
Amédée Frézier in South America (1712–14).

Some travellers encouraged Louis XIV's dreams of a global empire.
Jean-Baptiste Tavernier, for example, who had travelled to Asia in search
of precious stones, had been received in audience by the King in 1668. His
account of the Ottoman court is a rhapsody of imperialism, dedicated to
Louis XIV. He found 'I know not what so grand and so extraordinary in
your sacred person that it seems to me that all the Kings of Asia and Africa
will one day be your tributaries and that you are destined to command
the entire universe. The more a true Frenchman has travelled, the more
he esteems his country . . . when you have the good fortune to see Your
Majesty you can no longer admire anything else.'[14] Other travellers also
told Louis XIV that he would rule the world. In 1689 the dedication of
a new description of the kingdom of Siam by the Jesuit missionary Guy
Tachard assured the King that 'posterity will count among the conquests
of LOUIS LE GRAND the Kings of Siam and China, submitted to the cross
of Jesus Christ.'[15]

Two gigantic plaster globes made by the Franciscan friar Vincenzo
Coronelli on elegant bronze and marble supports, given to Louis XIV by
Cardinal d'Estrées in 1683 and installed in Marly in 1704,* also symbolized his global ambitions. One is a celestial globe which shows the stars'
position on the day of his birth. The other is a terrestial globe, dedicated
'à l'auguste majesté de Louis le grand, l'invincible, l'heureux, l'étonnement
de tant de Nations' ('the invincible, the fortunate, the wonder of so many
Nations') – which he could have conquered if, to quote one of his adul-
ators' favourite phrases, his moderation had not equalled his glory.[16]

Under Louis XIV Frenchmen's communication with other countries,
across barriers of race, religion, distance and ignorance, was facilitated
by shared belief in monarchy and hierarchy, as common then as enthusiasm for human rights today.[17] Gestures, dress and ceremonial were used
to indicate levels of respect and friendship between monarchs. When an
Ottoman envoy called Süleyman Aga reached Saint-Germain in November
1669, he communicated with the King and his ministers through gestures
(advancing, sitting, standing or bowing), headgear (raising it or keeping
it on), dress, jewels, letters and position in processions.

The gallery at Saint-Germain was lined with courtiers, who were,
exceptionally, allowed to abandon the mourning dress they were wearing
for Henrietta Maria, in order to look more magnificent. The King, blazing

* They are now in a hall of the Bibliothèque Nationale, site François-Mitterrand.

with diamonds, would not advance to receive the Sultan's letter (as he would for the Siamese ambassadors), as Süleyman Aga was an envoy, not a full ambassador extraordinary. Both courts understood the difference. According to the Chevalier d'Arvieux, who interpreted for Louis XIV as he understood Ottoman Turkish, the King said 'that it was not his custom to stand to receive letters'. The envoy should give him the letter. Süleyman Aga, who had been unwilling to advance to give the letter, then kissed it and placed it on the knees of the seated King with what d'Arvieux calls 'un air chagrin'. The low rank, bad manners and dirty costumes of the Ottoman envoy and his suite shocked the French court. The embassy was not a success. It did, however, begin a fashion for coffee in Paris. By 1692 the King himself was sometimes drinking it, on his doctors' recommendation.[18]

The shared framework of monarchy, and the fact that European states had not yet reached their subsequent levels of domination over the rest of the world, encouraged a degree of open-mindedness. During the Siamese embassy of 1686, as well as filling thousands of pages of the *Mercure Galant* with news of Siam, the editor Donneau de Vissé reminded readers that the French must seem as barbarian to the Siamese as the Siamese did to the French: 'the colour black, brown or white has no bearing on the heart of a man.'[19]

The King's envoy in 1687–8, Simon de La Loubère, in his *Description du royaume de Siam*,[20] wrote: 'it would not be just to despise everything which does not resemble what we see today at the court of France.'[21] The descriptions of the kingdom of Siam by Guy Tachard SJ, published at Louis XIV's *commandement exprès*, with many prints of views of Siam, compared the French and Siamese courts. The King of Siam had 'much grace and majesty' and like Louis XIV had a throne and audience chamber.[22] The palace complex which he made his capital at Lopburi, 100 miles north of Bangkok, was known to later European travellers as the 'Siamese Versailles'.

La Loubère also compared the two kings. While the King of Siam's guards were foreign (Laotian, Indian or Japanese), 'as for the Chamber of the King of Siam, the true officers are women. Only they have the right to enter it. They make his bed and his food . . . they dress him and serve him at table.' La Loubère noted the King of Siam's interest in the mechanics of elective monarchy in Poland and the Empire. Whereas the King of Siam enjoyed despotic power, even blinding his own brothers, the King of France respected the law.[23] Another French missionary, Jacques de Bourges, considered the principal advantage of Siam to be that it had the most absolute government, with the most obedient subjects, in the Indies.[24]

French attitudes to 'the extremities of the earth' were framed by Catholicism as well as monarchism. Thanks to the Société des Missions-Etrangères (still today at 128 rue du Bac, on a site where it has been since its foundation in 1658), French priests spread through the Levant, Asia and Canada. French Capuchins, Carmelites and Jesuits had been preaching in the Ottoman Empire since 1625, in Siam since 1662.[25]

Catholicism was presented overseas, as in Europe, as a buttress of monarchy. One argument for conversion advanced to King Phra Narai of Siam, according to a missionary called Mgr Lambert, was that Catholicism was 'the most suitable religion to enable the princes who profess it to reign with supreme authority because by its laws it obliges Christians to be faithful and very obedient to their sovereigns or else they are damned'.[26] In 1681 Louis also praised Catholicism, in a letter to his 'très cher et bon amy' the 'Très haut, très excellent et très puissant Prince' the King of Siam, as 'the religion which was the highest, the noblest and above all the best suited to enable kings to reign absolutely over their peoples'. The sequence of words – the culminating 'above all' – reveals the King's order of priorities.[27]

Since the foundation of Quebec by the explorer Samuel de Champlain in 1608, there had been small French settlements in Canada, then known as New France. It was run by a chartered company, which had concentrated on the profitable fur trade instead of colonization. In 1664 Louis XIV granted the colony to a new company, sent out the Régiment de Carignan and thereafter corresponded directly with his military commander in Quebec about the necessity of encouraging colonization and Catholicization, defeating the Iroquois and treating other Native Americans with 'douceur' and justice.[28]

Louis also inspired one of the most ambitious acts of expansion in the history of European empires, comparable in intent if not in result to the Spanish conquests of Mexico and Peru in the previous century. In May 1678 a former Jesuit turned explorer called Cavelier de La Salle received a commission from the King to explore the western part of 'our land of New France' and establish forts there, on the model of Fort Frontenac, built in 1673 on Lake Ontario south of Montreal and named after the able Governor of New France (see Map 6). Accompanied by twenty-three Frenchmen and eighteen Native Americans, La Salle established forts around the Great Lakes and down the River Ohio: Fort Crèvecoeur in 1680 and Fort Prudhomme in 1682. On 9 April 1682, having travelled down to the Gulf of Mexico (then known in French as the Nouvelle Biscaye, after the sea between France and Castile), La Salle 'took possession'

20. Louis XIV as a general on horseback, 1668, by Charles Le Brun. A magnificent horse was a symbol of power and chivalry – hence the many equestrian portraits and sculptures of himself which Louis commissioned.

21. Louis de Bourbon, the 'Grand Condé', and his son Henri-Jules de Bourbon, Duc d'Enghien, *c.* 1666. Condé wears the *justaucorps à brevet*, a lace-covered coat awarded by the King to fifty courtiers, to prove that he had returned to favour after the Fronde.

22. François-Michel Le Tellier, Marquis de Louvois (1641–91), 1689. Louvois was one of the most influential, industrious and war-loving of Louis' ministers.

23. Colbert (*left*) presents to Louis XIV members of the Académie Royale des Sciences, founded by the King in 1666. To the right of the King is his brother Monsieur. Behind is the Observatory, built on a hill south of Paris in 1667 and still functioning today.

24. Monsieur, who commissioned this picture by Jean Nocret *c.* 1669 of the royal family as the gods of Olympus, is shown as the Morning Star, announcing the Sun, Louis XIV. His wife Henriette Anne, sister of Charles II (*right*), is Flora, goddess of flowers, their eldest daughter Marie-Louise a zephyr or wind. Henrietta Maria (*left*), widowed Queen of England, and Monsieur's aunt and mother-in-law, is Amphitrite, holding Neptune's trident, symbol of England's sovereignty over the seas.

25. Gian Lorenzo Bernini's 1665 bust, for which he had been allowed to study the King at close quarters, was greatly admired by courtiers.

26. The construction of the east façade of the Louvre, 1677. Although the Louvre continued to house officials and artists, the King abandoned it after his mother died there in 1666.

27. Versailles *c.* 1668, before Louis XIII's transformation of his father's hunting lodge. The ministers' wings are on either side of the courtyard. The layout of the town with three avenues meeting at the chateau is already apparent. The King's carriage was always, as in this picture, accompanied by guards and equerries.

28. A view of the stables at Versailles, from the Cour de Marbre, 1693. In the second courtyard can be seen Gardes Suisses in red on the left, Gardes Françaises in blue on the right. Beyond are (*left*) the Grande Ecurie and (*right*) the Petite Ecurie.

29. This delicate drawing by Sébastien Leclerc of the Galerie des Glaces at Versailles in 1684 shows Louis XIV's silver furniture, which in 1689, in a show of patriotic zeal, he melted down to help pay for the war.

30. Fireworks on the canal at Versailles, 18 August 1674. These fireworks, using the latest technology, celebrated the conquest of Franche-Comté earlier that summer.

31. A billiard party *c.* 1694, from a series of prints advertising the pleasures of Versailles. *Left to right*: the King's brother Monsieur; his cousin the Duc de Vendôme; his younger illegitimate son the Comte de Toulouse; Chamillart, later Contrôleur Général des Finances, with his back to spectators; Louis XIV; the Comte d'Armagnac, his Grand Ecuyer; unknown; and his nephew the Duc de Chartres, later Regent.

32. The chateau, park and forest of Fontainebleau, by Jean-Baptiste Martin,
c. 1700, in a contemporary frame with the initials of Louis XIV, who stayed there
almost every autumn.

33. Ponne, Bonne and Nonne, Louis' hunting dogs. The King commissioned these
life-size portraits of them by Alexandre-François Desportes for an antechamber at
Marly, c. 1702.

34. Louis XIV on horseback as a Roman emperor, between figures of Prudence and Justice, above an inscription reading 'Louis the Great, caring for his soldiers in perpetuity with royal generosity, founded this building in 1675', by Guillaume Coustou, north façade of the Invalides, 1732–3.

35. Mansart presents the keys of the Invalides chapel to Louis XIV, from the *Almanach pour l'année 1707*, during his last visit to Paris, for the chapel's consecration on 28 July 1706. This print gives the architect almost as much prominence as the King.

of the entire valley of the Mississippi 'au nom du Très Haut, Très Puissant, Très Invincible et Victorieux Prince Louis le Grand Par la Grâce de Dieu Roi de France et de Navarre, quatorzième de ce nom'. The ceremony, recorded by a notary, was celebrated by a Te Deum, shouts of 'Vive le Roi!' and the construction of a column, surmounted by a cross, decorated with the royal arms and the inscription 'Louis le Grand, roi de France et de Navarre, règne, le 9 avril 1682'.[29]

La Salle called the new territories Louisiane, after the King. He returned to France in 1684 to receive further instructions, and was given a commission 'to subject under our domination several savage nations and bring them the light of the faith and the Gospel' in the lands between Illinois and the Gulf of Mexico. However, in 1687 he was shot dead in a mutiny.[30]

The first account of this new conquest 'much larger than Europe', *Description de la Louisiane, nouvellement découverte au sud-ouest de la Nouvelle France*, was dedicated a year later to Louis by a member of La Salle's mission, a priest named Louis Hennepin. Hennepin claimed that the explorers' account of the power of their King and the 'love and felicity of his subjects' had helped convert 'ces barbares' to Christianity: he also said that their word for sun sounded like Louis. Henceforth, on French maps, the words 'Nouvelle France' and 'Louisiane' were written in large letters across most of North America.[31]

At Marly in 1698 Louis XIV chose officers, under d'Iberville, to explore the mouth of the Mississippi, explicitly motivated by the desire 'to stop the English establishing themselves there'. Blocking other powers' expansion, by forming pro-French confederations of Native Americans as well as by French colonization, could be as strong a motive for conquest as expansion itself. Explorers flattered the King by claiming that the Mississippi valley was 'the finest land in the world for pasture'. The cattle had better wool and hides than in France. Fort Louis de la Louisiane, now the city of Mobile, was founded in 1701. Also in 1701 Detroit (originally Fort Pontchartrain du Detroit, named after the Minister of the Marine, and the *détroit* or strait of Lake Erie) was founded by M. de Cadillac (after whom the car was later named) as a French trading post. Today Sainte-Anne-de-Détroit is the second oldest continuously operating Catholic parish in the United States.

That year, in a sign of its growing importance, Louisiana was separated from New France and given its own governor. Louis wrote: 'His Majesty has resolved to found a settlement at the mouth of the Mississippi . . . this has become an indispensable necessity to halt the advance which the English from the colony of New York have begun to make in the lands which lie between them and this river.'[32]

However, despite government subsidies for their journeys, and government efforts to send out unmarried Frenchwomen or *filles du roi* as potential wives, there were only around 300 colonists in Louisiana by 1715.[33] They found that in reality the climate was unhealthy, the soil bad, local inhabitants hostile. The French colonies in America won a bad reputation. Moreover many French peasants already owned land and, despite wars, famines and high taxation, preferred to stay in France. If Louis XIV had encouraged some of the Huguenots who fled France to settle in his colonies, rather than in hostile European countries (see Chapter 16), half of North America might be speaking French today. However, the Code Noir, promulgated in 1685, following a similar decree by Richelieu in 1627, forbade the exercise in French colonies of any religion other than Roman Catholicism.[34]

Above all because of the limited economic opportunities available, few Frenchmen settled in America. At most 10,000 Frenchmen crossed the Atlantic in the entire seventeenth century, compared to around 350,000 Spaniards in 1561–1650 and 100,000 British in 1660–1700 alone.[35] The total number of Frenchmen in North America rose from about 22,000 in 1670 to 45,000 in 1715; far fewer – roughly 7 per cent – than the number of British, which in the same period rose from roughly 300,000 to 550,000.[36] Slaves had to be imported from Africa to keep Louisiana alive.

Since 1664 the Compagnie des Indes Occidentales had run the sugar plantations of the French Caribbean islands of Guadeloupe, Martinique and St Lucia. There too labour was provided by slaves, despite denunciations in the 1680s by Capuchin monks and the Papacy. The slave population of Martinique, for example, rose from 2,642 to 10,656 between 1660 and 1684, largely supplied by Spanish and Dutch traders. The French slave trade itself did not start until the first French slave ships left Nantes for Africa in 1688.[37]

Soon 2,000 slaves a year were being shipped from Africa by the Compagnie de Guinée et du Sénégal, for labour in the French sugar plantations in the Caribbean. Africans from Cape Verde were preferred since they were 'much more vigorous than those of Guinea'.[38] To encourage the trade, the French government gave a 'bounty' for each slave transported across the Atlantic. Although slaves were legally their master's possessions, they were admitted by French law to have souls. Their rights to food, clothes, religious instruction and families, and a day of rest on Sunday, were enshrined in the Code Noir of 1685, less brutal than comparable English legislation. Their children were to be baptized. Miscegenation was accepted, torture theoretically forbidden.[39] In reality their lives were dominated by daily acts of violence and humiliation, often leading to suicide.

By 1715 there were about 77,000 slaves in the French colonies in America. They would be the principal cause of the astonishing prosperity of the white elite in Saint-Domingue (now Haiti) in the eighteenth century.[40] In France itself, however, both in theory and usually in practice under Louis XIV, as soon as slaves touched French soil they became free, on the ancient principle that 'there are no slaves in France.'[41]

The King wanted territory in Asia as well as America. The arrival of the grandiose Siamese embassy at Versailles in 1686 had been a sign of the friendship already developing between the two monarchies. Siam was already open to Portuguese, Dutch and English traders, and a Persian embassy had also arrived there in 1685, to encourage trade and Islam.

A first French embassy to Siam, led by the Chevalier de Caumont and the Abbé de Choisy, a transvestite courtier who travelled to Siam for adventure, had arrived in 1685. Behind the official expressions of benevolence, Jesuit missionaries like Guy Tachard and a brilliant, multilingual favourite of the King of Siam, a Catholic from Cephalonia called M. Constance, had a secret plan to convert the kingdom to Catholicism and establish a French protectorate, if necessary by force. In 1686 the splendour of the Siamese embassy to Versailles organized by Phaulkon (as Constance was known in Siam) had been part of the plan.

Of Phaulkon, who was fluent in Thai, Malay, English, French, Portuguese and Greek, the Abbé de Choisy wrote:

He was one of those in the world who have the most wit, liberality, magnificence, intrepidity, and was full of great projects, but perhaps he only wanted to have French troops in order to try and make himself king after the death of his master, which he saw as imminent. He was proud, cruel, pitiless and inordinately ambitious. He supported the Christian religion because it could support him; but I would never have trusted him in things in which his own advancement was not involved.[42]

Phaulkon corresponded in secret with Père Lachaise, the King's confessor, urging him 'by the entrails and wounds of Jesus' to persuade Louis XIV to send French soldiers to Siam. Louis XIV was led to believe that a grand French embassy to Siam, accompanied by soldiers, would encourage Phra Narai to convert to Catholicism.

The King of Siam was indeed impressed by the Jesuit astronomers and mathematicians (given the special title *mathématiciens du roi dans les Indes et la Chine*), and by the engineers who arrived from France and helped him build forts. He liked talking about religions and allowed the erection of Catholic churches. He was also interested in using foreign troops to increase his authority over his own mandarins.

However, rather than converting to Catholicism as Louis XIV suggested in his letters, the King of Siam gave the King of France a lesson in common sense and humanity. The month after the Revocation of the Edict of Nantes in France, he told Phaulkon, who relayed his words to the French Ambassador, that he could not suddenly change a religion (Buddhism) professed in Siam for 2,109 years: 'as [God] diversified all the works of nature, he wanted to do the same in matters of religion.' God had always wanted to be worshipped by 'an infinity of different religions'.[43]

Neither the cities nor the court of Siam impressed Louis' officials. Fifty musketeers would beat the King's guards easily, wrote the Abbé de Choisy. While the Siamese had been shocked by the noise and crowds around Louis, the French laughed at the Siamese custom of kowtowing. The French envoy the Chevalier de Chaumont preferred to bow 'à la française'. To honour him, as Louis had done to Siamese ambassadors at Versailles, Phra Narai advanced to take the letter from Louis and held it high above his head.[44]

By 1688, after the arrival in Siam of a second French embassy in six boats, which also brought back the Siamese ambassadors to the court of Louis XIV, there were 1,361 French troops and sailors, as well as French priests and merchants in Siam. Phaulkon was made a count and a chevalier of the Order of St Michel. In January 1687 in his instruction to La Loubère, Louis XIV's Minister of the Marine Seignelay (who had already organized the bombardment of Genoa) had written: 'his Majesty . . . has decided to attack Bangkok and to render himself master of it by the open use of force.' There were plans 'to bring terror to all places in the Indies'. Despite frequent references to religion, he admitted that 'the establishment of commerce is the basis of this affair'. The Chevalier de Forbin became governor of Bangkok, and a new French fort was built at the mouth of the Mekong. There were plans for another Frenchman, the Marquis de Ragny, to become *capitaine des gardes* of the King, commander of French troops and 'great judge'. Siam would become a French protectorate.[45]

In reaction against the growing French presence, on 18 May 1688 a prominent mandarin called Petracha, the King's milk-brother and commander of his elephants, seized the palaces. He was supported by some of the Siamese who had accompanied the embassy to Versailles two years earlier, and by mandarins and Buddhist priests fearful of French influence. Some of the King's brothers, sons and ministers were killed in front of him; the King, already ill, was taken prisoner and died heartbroken on 10 July 1688. Petracha became king and Phaulkon was executed. After a four-month siege in Bangkok, on 13 November the French sailed away for Pondichéry. French ambition and proselytizing Catholicism had led to an Asian triumph over European imperialism.

All the achievements of the Franco-Siamese friendship since 1662 were destroyed. Missionaries, artisans and soldiers were imprisoned in chains. Portraits of Louis XIV and Jesus Christ were burnt on the funeral pyre of King Phra Narai. Petracha, who had received help from the Dutch in Batavia, sent them some of the presents his predecessor had received from Versailles. Siam became a hermit kingdom, not reopening to the outside world until the nineteenth century.[46]

In contrast to the debacle in Siam, Louis XIV established peaceful and lasting links with China. The Trianon de Porcelaine, built in 1670 for meetings with Madame de Montespan, had first brought China to Versailles. Covered in blue and white Delft, Nevers and Rouen faience tiles 'façon de Chine', it had been partly inspired by Dutch prints of a porcelain pagoda near Nanjing. Soon France began to import, via the Netherlands, Chinese blue and white porcelain. A total of 5,520 pieces arrived in France in 1680, and 153,104 in 1683. Many were bought by the King, the Dauphin and the Prince de Condé.

Catholicism formed a stronger bond than porcelain. On 15 September 1684, the year that he received the first embassy from Siam, Louis XIV also received a Flemish Jesuit called Philippe Couplet, accompanied by a Chinese convert, wearing a green silk tunic with dragons, called Shen Fuzong or Michel Sin. Jesuits, mainly Portuguese arriving via the Portuguese colony of Macau, had been preaching in China, and learning the Chinese language, since 1579. Couplet had been in China since 1658, working as a missionary and scientist, and had begun the famous Jesuit 'accommodation' of Christianity with Confucianism and ancestor worship. He presented the King with Chinese books and a request for more missionaries.[47]

Louis was so eager to start conversation that he interrupted Shen Fuzong's kowtows (as he had the Siamese diplomats'; he liked flattery but not physical prostration). The next day Couplet and Shen Fuzong talked to him again during dinner; Louis made Shen recite in Chinese the Ave Maria, Paternoster and Credo. The royal family watched Shen use chopsticks to eat food from a golden plate especially brought for him. When Shen and Couplet visited the gardens, the fountains were turned on in their honour.[48] The first European book on Confucius, a translation of his works into Latin by Couplet, *Confucius sinarum philosophus, sive Scientia sinensis latine exposita* ('Confucius the Philosopher of the

Chinese, or Chinese Science Explained in Latin'), published in Paris in 1687, was financed by and dedicated to Louis XIV.[49]

True to his ambition to be a global monarch, Louis personally financed the despatch of six French Jesuits, mathematics teachers at the Collège Louis le Grand, to the Chinese court – competing with the Portuguese missionaries from the 'Vice-Province of China'. They left Brest in March 1685 with a stock of mathematical and astronomical instruments, arriving via Siam in China in July 1687 and in Beijing in February 1688. They captivated, and were captivated by, the Kangxi Emperor and his court: the Manchu dynasty was more open to the outside world than its Ming predecessors. French Jesuits saw the Emperor daily, teaching him mathematics and astronomy, drawing him maps of the earth and the skies, and translating French books on mathematics and medicine into Chinese. In 1692 an Edict of Toleration confirmed permission for them to preach Christianity and make converts. In 1693 they treated the Emperor with quinine to cure him of a fever. Père Joachim Bouvet returned to France on the Emperor's orders in 1697, in order to recruit more astronomers for China. He also brought Chinese manuscripts for the Bibliothèque du Roi, and published books on China.[50]

In November 1698 the first French boat to sail directly to China left La Rochelle. It carried eight more Jesuits and an Italian fresco painter called Giovanni Gherardini, who would decorate churches in Beijing and paint portraits for the court. The ship returned to Lorient in August 1700 with a cargo of porcelain. Soon more priests were despatched, bringing more knowledge of astronomy, cartography and mathematics, and French cannon for the Emperor.

Under Louis XIV a dialogue between courts – one monarchy speaking to the other across 4,000 miles – had been established, a hundred years before the despatch of the first, unsuccessful, British embassy to China in 1793. The two courts shared a taste for absolutism, magnificence, hunting, literature and science. The Beauvais factory made tapestries entitled *Histoire du Roy de la Chine*. The royal library acquired books in Mandarin. Père Lachaise corresponded with Jesuits in Beijing.[51] More French missionaries were sent in 1699, 1700, 1702 and 1703.[52] Portraits of the King and the royal family and of France's allies the kings of Spain and England ('James III'), and engravings of palaces, were displayed in the Jesuit mission in Beijing 'in order to reveal to the entire universe the magnificence of the court of France'.[53]

In his *Histoire de l'Empereur de la Chine présentée au roi* (1699), Père Bouvet compared the Kangxi Emperor to Louis XIV, calling him 'a prince who like you, SIRE, joins to a genius as sublime as it is solid, a heart even more worthy of the Empire'. Kangxi would be 'the most accomplished Monarch who has reigned on the earth in a long time, if his reign did not coincide with that of Your Majesty'. Like Siam for Jacques de Bourges, China for Père Bouvet was worthy of the respect and admiration of all nations, as it was distinguished by its marvellous art of government, and a moral code resembling Christianity.[54]

Both the Papacy and the Sorbonne, however, were dismayed by Jesuits' belief that the practice of Confucianism and ancestor worship were purely civil actions, compatible with Catholicism. Such flexibility was condemned by the Pope in 1704 and 1707.[55] Quarrels between missions, and differing views over the salvation of pagans, led to the detention of the Cardinal de Tournon in Macau, where he died in 1710. The Kangxi Emperor did not convert to Christianity, as his Jesuits had expected. However, needing foreign doctors, astronomers, cartographers and interpreters, he remained more tolerant of Christian missions than many of his bureaucrats. Despite Chinese resentment of Christianity's claim to exclusive truth, and the expulsion of Jesuits to Macau in 1724, two French missionaries Jean-Baptiste Régis and Pierre Jartoux would help map China for his successor: the maps would be printed in Paris in 1730–34.[56]

The rulers of Siam and China were not the only distant monarchs to whom Louis XIV sent emissaries. Sultan Moulay Ismaïl, ruler of Morocco, had sent his first embassy to Louis XIV in 1682. Moulay Ismaïl asked him to convert to Islam and to arrange an exchange of slaves, head by head. Louis preferred to buy back enslaved Frenchmen, rather than exchange them, thereby retaining the strongest Moroccan galley slaves for the French navy. Sometimes they were hidden from visiting Moroccan ambassadors. Moulay Ismaïl, who accused Louis XIV of not observing his treaties, wrote that he would have preferred the return of one Moroccan slave to all the King's presents: 'one of our greatest joys is the freedom of a slave.'[57]

Again, however, monarchy spoke to monarchy across barriers of religion and distance. Moroccan ambassadors compared Louis XIV to Süleyman, Chosroes and Alexander, and brought him gifts of horses.[58] The two kings shared a love of magnificent palaces with impatience at their pace of construction. A French envoy sent to Morocco in 1691, partly to buy back French slaves, was impressed by the Sultan's gardens, stables and horses.[59]

Links between the monarchs might have become even closer. In 1699 the Moroccan envoy was subjugated by the grace and beauty of Louis' daughter by Louise de La Vallière, the widowed Princesse de Conti, glimpsed at a ball at Saint-Cloud. The Sultan's request on 14 November

1699 for her hand in marriage – he said that he would be honoured to be Louis XIV's son-in-law and would guarantee her freedom of worship – was refused, unless the Sultan converted to Christianity. It did, however, inspire courtiers to write her poems saying that 'the conquests of your eyes reach further than those of Hercules' and 'Africa capitulates to you.'[60] The Sultan's request for French architects and engineers also received an evasive reply: the King said he would not force them to go anywhere.[61] Louis did not want to be seen to be helping a modernizing Muslim monarch.

The Ottoman Empire was strategically more important to Louis XIV than Siam, China and Morocco combined. The greatest power in Europe and the Levant, ruling from Hungary to Yemen, was also, after the Swiss Confederation, France's oldest ally. Since the capture of François I by Charles V in 1525, the two monarchies had been linked by a shared fear of the House of Austria and a desire for trade. François I had sent officers to advise the Ottoman army and navy, and in 1543–4 allowed the latter to winter in the port of Toulon. The call to prayer was heard from the towers of Toulon cathedral.

Sensitive to Catholic disapproval – pro-Habsburg pamphleteers called the King of France 'the most Christian Turk' – Louis XIV, like his predecessors, avoided the written treaty of alliance repeatedly demanded by the Sublime Porte. The Ottoman–French alliance, however, was accepted as a reality. Madame de Sévigné refers to 'our brother the Turk'. At Versailles the Venetian Ambassador teased the French Foreign Minister about it.[62] In an instruction of 10 June 1679 to his Ambassador Guilleragues, and a letter of 6 October 1681 to Admiral Duquesne, Louis referred to the 'alliance which I have with the Grand Seigneur'.[63]

The alliance was managed by Ottoman officials and by networks of French merchants, priests and interpreters, in Constantinople and other ports, as well as by capable French diplomats. Two of Louis XIV's ambassadors, Girardin and Ferriol, spoke Turkish, while Châteauneuf wore Turkish dress and slippers inside (but not outside) his embassy, considering them 'more likely to encourage the familiar relations he had with the Turks'. The Mufti of Istanbul, the senior Muslim cleric, to whom the King himself occasionally sent letters, was Châteauneuf's particular friend.[64]

Louis claimed that French friendship with the Ottoman Empire was conducted 'for the good of Christianity', and was justified by his success in protecting Christians (meaning Catholics) and Christian sites under Ottoman rule.[65] Capitulations governing French trade and worship in the Ottoman Empire, first confirmed in 1569, were renewed on favourable terms by his Ambassador the Marquis de Nointel in June 1673, partly because the Ottoman government was impressed by Louis' victories in the Netherlands. The capitulations confirmed 'complete freedom and safety' for French pilgrims and merchants, and French diplomatic protection of Catholic priests, who were constantly quarrelling with Orthodox priests over control of Christian shrines in Jerusalem and Bethlehem.

In 1674–5 Nointel travelled to Smyrna, Athens, Aleppo, Jerusalem, bringing copies of the capitulations, to ensure that local governors enforced them. The French–Ottoman alliance had cultural, as well as religious effects. The pictures Nointel commissioned from his accompanying artist Jacques Carrey, of himself in Athens and Jerusalem, surrounded by French and Ottoman escorts, are not only expressions of the French–Ottoman alliance, but also the first accurate representations of those cities and their monuments. Carrey's drawings of the Parthenon marbles (which Nointel had hoped to remove for Louis XIV) are their only accurate depiction before their damage by the Venetian bombardment of 1687.[66]

The French–Ottoman alliance had flourished since the reign of François I and was too important to fail. It survived Louis XIV's attempts to impress Catholic opinion by sending French troops to fight against the Ottoman Empire, for the Emperor in Hungary in 1664 (the French ambassadors claimed to the Ottomans that he was merely acting as Landgraf of Alsace), and for Venice in Crete, under the flag of the Papacy, in 1669. It also survived the occasional attacks of conscience, expressed in council meetings by the pious Duc de Beauvillier.[67]

Even the ravages of Christian and Muslim corsairs did not destroy it. The Knights of St John in Malta seized Muslim shipping and enslaved Muslims. In their turn ships from Algiers, Tunis and Tripoli, states which were in theory Ottoman vassals but in practice took little notice of orders from Constantinople, raided European ships and coasts, in order to seize people to work as slaves or to be sold back or exchanged for Muslim slaves. There were so many that two religious orders, the Mercedarians and Redemptorists, had been founded with the specific mission to 'redeem' Christian captives abroad.

French galley slaves included Maghrebis, Africans, Native Americans, Greeks, Russians and even Turks bought on the market in Constantinople, and in other cities and islands in the Levant, for 'the Most Christian King'.[68] At one time each French consul in the Ottoman Empire was expected to supply the French navy with fifty or more Turkish slaves a year, on pain of losing his post. The market was stronger than Muslim law, under which Muslim slaves were illegal.[69] In negotiations with Ottoman or Moroccan authorities, French officials were unwilling to exchange any but old or ill Muslim slaves. They insisted on keeping strong and healthy Muslim slaves, even if they were related to government officials.[70]

In July 1681 the French admiral Abraham Duquesne chased Tripolitanian ships, which had seized a French vessel off the coast of Provence, to the island of Chios off the coast of Anatolia. Thanks to the French–Ottoman alliance, Ottoman authorities and ships remained neutral. The Kaptan Pasha (commander of the Ottoman navy) obliged the Tripolitanians to return the French slaves on board. With the help of lavish French presents to the Sultan of mirrors, jewels, clocks and chairs, the alliance survived even Duquesne's bombardment of Chios on 23 July, which led to the deaths of 250 Muslims, and more Greeks, and the temporary blockade of the Dardanelles.

In order to free French slaves, and also to demonstrate to Europe that France was not allied to the Ottoman Empire, Duquesne went on to bombard other ports in North Africa, testing the amount of damage French bombs and cannonballs could inflict, from a newly invented vessel called the *galiote à bombes*. French *galiotes* bombarded Algiers in 1682, 1683 and 1684, and Tripoli in 1683, 1685, 1688 and 1692.[71] In a celebrated act of retaliation in July 1683, the French Consul in Algiers, an aged Lazarist monk named Père le Vacher, hitherto distinguished by his good relations with the Dey of Algiers and his success in buying back French slaves, was bound to the mouth of a cannon (thereafter known in French as *la consulaire*) which was then fired, reducing him to shreds. French bombardments inspired such terror that by a treaty of April 1684 the Dey of Algiers agreed to exchange French for Muslim slaves and to recognize French sovereignty over three ports on the Algerian coast, Bougie, Bône and Djidjelli.[72]

Between bombardments, however, there were exchanges of presents, as well as slaves: horses, lions and camels from Algeria for Louis XIV, guns, medals, clocks and tapestries from France for the Dey of Algiers.[73] Bombardments soon resumed. In July 1688 another French consul in Algiers was fired from *la consulaire*. Finally peace was signed in September 1689. Despite France's constant need to import grain from North Africa, the peace would be more faithfully observed by Algerian than by French commanders.[74]

The 1680s became Louis XIV's decade of megalomania. French ships bombarded Christian as well as Muslim cities. One of the richest cities in Italy, the great port of Genoa, 'La Superba', had been for the last 150 years a source of loans and shipping for Spain, and a base from which to transport men and money to fight in the Spanish Netherlands. France also had disputes with Genoa about debts and about trade with Algiers. Louis XIV, to whom a book was dedicated in 1683 praising the 'noble art' of throwing bombs, decided to bombard Genoa from the sea. It was the first city in Europe to suffer the experience.

Against established international law, the Genoese envoy in Paris was imprisoned in the Bastille. Then, between 18 and 28 May 1684, watched by the Minister of the Marine Seignelay, eager to see how his *galiotes à bombes* performed, 16,000 cannonballs and grenades were fired on the city from a French fleet of twenty galleys and fifty-four other vessels – again ignoring rules of diplomacy and humanity. Few were killed, since thousands of Genoese had already fled to the hills above the city. Moreover only 8,000 projectiles, according to Genoese estimates, landed on the city, the rest falling short and landing in the sea. Perhaps 1,000 houses were destroyed, of a total of 6,000 in the old walled city.[75]

For years afterwards, however, ruined houses could be seen near the harbour.[76] Many churches also were damaged; the *Dialogue of Genoa and Algiers, Cities Destroyed by the Invincible Arms of Louis le Grand*, published in Amsterdam the following year, listed thirteen. Most of the city's magnificent palaces and convents further up the hill, including the Palazzo Ducale itself, were damaged rather than, as French accounts boasted, destroyed.[77] Three thousand French troops under the Duc de Mortemart, Madame de Montespan's nephew and Seignelay's cousin, landed and set fire to a suburb, but were then compelled by Genoese and Spanish troops to re-embark. The ladders they had brought for scaling the city walls were never used. According to French sources, French merchants in Genoa, who had not been warned of the attack by their government, were killed in reprisal. Louis XIV later, by what he called a movement of piety, did not demand compensation for their loss, provided Genoa paid for the repair of the churches damaged by his ships.[78]

Adding insult to injury, the Doge of Genoa, obliged by Genoese law to remain inside the ducal palace during his term of office, was compelled by a treaty signed on 12 February 1685 to come to Versailles, in effect to apologize for Louis' attack on his city. On 17 May, although guards hit spectators to clear the way, it took the Doge in his crimson damask robes of state, accompanied by four senators in black, half an hour to advance from one end of the Galerie des Glaces to the other. 'You never saw such a great crowd nor so much disorder,' wrote M. de Plantavit de La Pause; there was 'an infinity of people of the first quality'. Finally the King himself descended from his throne 'to make the crowd retreat to the right and left and with the point of his cane opened a passage for the Doge who at last encountered the King'.[79]

The King said he would renew his friendship with the Republic if it behaved better in the future, and gave the Doge two sets of Gobelins tapestries, and his portrait set in diamonds.[80] The Doge remarked, after a round of receptions, balls and promenades in the park as fountains played in his honour, 'One year ago we were in hell and today we are in paradise.' He was reported as adding that 'the pain of leaving France so soon is almost as great as the pain he had suffered at being obliged to come here.'[81] Genoa had been humiliated. It continued into the eighteenth century to balance between the Bourbons and the Habsburgs. A Spanish fleet and troops were welcomed to Genoa, immediately after the French bombardment.[82] In the wars after 1689, however, Genoese merchants would help to supply starving France with grain.

Meanwhile the Emperor Leopold I and the Ottoman Sultan had again been at war since 1682. An Austro-Turkish war suited French policy. One ironical French diplomat called it 'this diversion so useful to [Louis XIV's] kingdom and so suitable to the veritable interests of the Catholic religion'.[83] From 1664 to 1687 Louis also supported a Hungarian rebellion, led by a Protestant noble called Imre Thököly allied to the Ottoman Empire. Leopold, who was also king of Hungary, had suspended the Hungarian constitution, deprived over 400 Protestant priests of their churches and sent sixty-seven to the galleys.[84] Louis XIV sent Thököly officers, subsidies and munitions (organized by the French Ambassador in Poland, and despatched via Danzig and Poland to Upper Hungary, in what is now eastern Slovakia), and in 1677 signed a treaty with him. Distance and qualms about helping Protestant rebels against their legitimate, crowned sovereign discouraged him from doing more.[85]

The Rhine dominated Louis XIV's policy on the Danube. His interest was, he wrote in April 1682 to his Ambassador in Constantinople, M. de Guilleragues, for Ottoman attacks on Austria and Hungary to 'prevent the Emperor from employing all his troops on the Rhine'. He did not want Vienna to fall to the Ottomans: French volunteers were allowed to serve in the Emperor's armies. Nor, however, did he want a triumphant Austria to force the Ottoman Empire to make peace. While Ottoman forces besieged Vienna in July–September 1683, Louis XIV continued to fight the Emperor's cousin the King of Spain in the Spanish Netherlands: peace was not signed until July 1684. He told the protesting Papal Nuncio that the days of holy wars were over.[86]

Meanwhile, to the dismay of the King and his diplomats, who did not want Austria to gain allies,[87] Poland had joined its war against the Ottoman Empire. In 1683, as Ottoman forces (helped by Thököly and the Hungarian insurgents) advanced on Vienna, the French Ambassador M. de Vitry was insulted in the streets of Warsaw.[88] King Jan Sobieski led a

Polish army on Vienna and on 12 September, with Austrian and Imperial forces, defeated the Ottomans outside the city walls. Thereafter, the Emperor's armies began to advance eastwards into Hungary. Almost overnight the Austrian monarchy, from being a poor cousin of the King of Spain, became a great power admired throughout Christendom, with an army of 120,000.

Austrian victories increased the Ottoman Empire's need for the French alliance. French diplomatic pressure on the Mufti, the Janissary Aga and the Grand Vizier was able, on several occasions, to dissuade the Sultan from making peace. In 1685, in a revealing change of etiquette, the French Ambassador recovered the right to have his stool placed on the Grand Vizier's raised sofa or platform, withdrawal of which in 1678 had infuriated Louis XIV.[89] The French Ambassador M. de Girardin wrote on 23 May 1686: 'they [the Ottoman government] have never yet refused me anything for which I asked.' French ships took over the carrying trade between Constantinople and Alexandria (since Ottoman ships might be attacked by Knights of Malta or Venetians).[90] In 1687 Louvois persuaded Louis XIV to keep a French agent with the Grand Vizier's army fighting Habsburg forces in Hungary.[91] From 1688 Louis XIV gave an annual pension of 2,400 livres to Mavrocordato, the Greek chief interpreter for the Ottoman government, who rendered many services to French merchants and diplomats in Constantinople. Mehmed IV wrote to Louis XIV to rejoice that 'the friendship, good will and good relations . . . that for long existed between your parents and great-grandparents and the Emperors my forefathers have since been augmented and fortified'.[92]

At the same time that he strengthened the French–Ottoman alliance, Louis XIV sent travellers and scholars on expeditions round the Ottoman Empire. At the height of its power, the Ottoman Empire facilitated French cultural imperialism on its territory. French agents, from Jean Michel Vansleben in 1671–5 to Paul Lucas forty years later, purchased quantities of Hebrew, Greek, Syriac, Arabic, Persian and Turkish manuscripts for the Bibliothèque du Roi. The King and Colbert wanted, as Colbert wrote to the Marquis de Nointel on 10 November 1674, to 'decorate our France with the remains of the Orient', and to make Paris 'a new Athens'. Christian manuscripts were also sought, to reinforce the Catholic position in debates with 'schismatics'.

In Smyrna, Aleppo and Cairo, as well as Constantinople, French consuls and scholars waited for imams and muftis to die, in order to purchase their manuscripts – although d'Arvieux complained from Aleppo, as early as 1682, that 'the English have emptied this land.'[93] In 1702 alone Paul Lucas sent several thousand medals and coins back to Paris, while another traveller Pitton de Tournefort was collecting rare plants for the King in Anatolia. Under Louis XIV Paris confirmed the role which it had established in the early seventeenth century, and retains to this day, as one of the world centres of oriental studies.[94]

One of the ablest French consuls in the Ottoman Empire, a believer in evolution who wrote that men descend from fish, was M. Maillet, Consul in Egypt from 1692 to 1708, author of an early *Description de l'Egypte* (2 volumes, 1735). A hundred and seventy years before the Suez Canal opened in 1869, Maillet proposed digging a canal between the Mediterranean and the Red Sea, where a French fleet would be stationed. At his suggestion young Copts were sent from Egypt to study in the Collège Louis le Grand.[95]

Partly at his instigation, and partly at the request of the Negus or Emperor of Ethiopia, who had a French doctor called Jacques-Charles Poncet, in 1705 M. Lenoir du Roule, French Vice-Consul in Damietta, then one of Egypt's main ports, was sent as French envoy to Ethiopia. His mission was meant to encourage French trade and the Negus's conversion to Roman Catholicism. However, it looked suspiciously grandiose. Accused of carrying treasures and practising magic, resented for not offering drinks to the wives of the Fung King of Sennar on the Blue Nile in what is now Sudan, and feared as protagonists of a Franco-Ethiopian alliance against Muslims, the envoy and his party were murdered in November 1705. No more French missions would be sent to Ethiopia until 1897.[96]

Louis XIV was in reality pursuing a three-sided policy towards the Ottoman Empire. On the one hand he maintained France's traditional alliance, repeatedly instructing his ambassadors to keep the Empire at war with Austria, even to tell Ottoman officials, orally, that he would not object if they took Vienna.[97] At the same time, without informing the Ottoman government, he was reinforcing French ties with local Christians. Already in 1649 the French government had, at Mazarin's initiative, extended its protection to 'all the Maronite Christians of Mount Lebanon' – the group of Arabic-speaking Christians who have acknowledged the authority of the Pope since the twelfth century, and who still look to France for protection today.[98]

In 1674 Louis XIV's Ambassador the Marquis de Nointel went in state to Syriac and Maronite churches in Aleppo, 'to the sound of trumpets and drums, surrounded by my household and followed by more than one hundred horsemen who composed the French nation', as he wrote to the Foreign Minister de Pomponne. In the Syriac church the Syriac Patriarch preached a sermon in praise of Louis XIV. Syriac, Armenian and

Orthodox patriarchs, as well as the chief of the Yezidis and some Lebanese Christians, told Nointel they wanted a French invasion of the Empire to 'liberate' its Christians.[99]

In 1675 Louis XIV declared himself protector of Catholics in the Aegean, although they too were subjects of his ally the Sultan. By 1700 – despite grand viziers' complaints about French interference with Ottoman subjects – this 'protection' had been unilaterally extended to all Catholics in the Empire. By then they included Syriac, Armenian and Greek Catholics, who kept their own rites but acknowledged the supremacy of the Pope.[100] The French Consul in Aleppo helped the Catholic candidate Athanasius III Debbas become Orthodox patriarch of Antioch, leading to the emergence of a separate Greek Catholic community. With the help of French consuls, some began to study in Paris, often at the Collège Louis le Grand.[101] A French-speaking Catholic elite in the Levant, which has lasted to this day, had been born.

At the same time that Louis XIV declared his 'friendship' for the Ottoman Empire and extended his 'protection' to its Catholics, he was contemplating a third policy: conquest. In 1672 the philosopher and Hanoverian councillor Leibniz came to Saint-Germain to present the King with a project to conquer Egypt, possibly in order to obtain a pension, or to deflect the King from attacking the Holy Roman Empire.[102] Eight years later Grelot's *Relation nouvelle d'un voyage de Constantinople* (1680), dedicated to the King, urged him to conquer the whole Ottoman Empire: 'Oui, Sire, les Peuples de Villes que ces Esquisses représentent, remplis du glorieux nom de LOUIS LE GRAND, s'estimeroient heureux de vivre sous le doux empire d'un souverain qu'ils considèrent avec raison comme le premier et le plus grand Monarque de l'Univers' ('Yes, Sire, the peoples of the cities represented in these sketches, filled with the glorious name of LOUIS LE GRAND, would judge themselves fortunate to live under the gentle sway of a sovereign whom they rightly consider the first and greatest Monarch of the Universe').

After 1683, as Austrian armies advanced deeper in the Balkans, the Ottoman Empire appeared close to collapse. Louis began to consider, in secret, what his share of the spoils should be. In January 1686 the new French Ambassador M. de Girardin arrived in Constantinople with a team of engineers, draughtsmen and geographers, led by a professional naval officer, M. d'Ortières, a former *intendant de la marine* in Dunkirk and *contrôleur général des galères* in Marseille. In 1686 and 1687 they travelled round the ports and islands of the Ottoman Empire – Salonica, Gallipoli, Smyrna, Naxos, Paros, Sidon, Alexandria (where they were attacked) and Tunis, drawing detailed maps and views, even showing houses and olive trees. They also tried to establish statistics on the number of Christians and the volume of local trade. All the time they were reminding Ottoman officials of the power of Louis XIV, whose conquests, in the familiar French phrase, were limited only by his moderation.[103]

Secret instructions of 31 October 1685, resembling those issued at the same time to French officers sailing to Siam, told them to 'reconnoitre the positions of the forts of His Highness and notice the means by which one can attack them' and 'make ourselves their masters', to examine defences and cannon, as well as to record the width and depth of harbours, the best moorings in them and the state of the country. Thanks to their missions, the archives of the Service Historique de la Défense in France contain the finest collection of views of the Levant in the seventeenth century.[104]

They were also asked to draw up a plan to evacuate the embassy staff, and local French merchants, before 'burning Constantinople following the instructions of His Majesty'. 'All the Turks', according to one passage, would be cut in pieces 'without quarter', except those saved to work in French galleys. The Ottoman navy would be too weak to oppose the French, who would need only thirty-five vessels. The government should not listen to Marseille's fears of ruin. Rhodes would be returned to the Knights of St John. France would take Constantinople, Smyrna, the Aegean, Syria and Egypt, other Christian princes the rest. The Sultan would withdraw to the Euphrates.[105]

In the event, diplomacy prevailed over brutality, the Ministry of Foreign Affairs over the Ministry of the Marine. In the autumn of 1688 desire to assist the Ottoman Empire, and to stop it making peace with the Emperor, would be a crucial factor in Louis XIV's decision to attack the Rhineland rather than the Netherlands. In the 1670s and 1680s, however, Louis XIV had started wars, bombarded foreign ports, annexed foreign territory, spent France's diplomatic capital. He had sown the wind. Soon he would reap the whirlwind.

16

The Huguenot Cataclysm

Louis XIV was the only king of France, perhaps the only French head of state before 1945, to enter a synagogue. On Saturday 23 September 1657, while staying in Metz for over a month, the King had visited the synagogue with his family and court in what the rabbi called 'pomp and splendour' to watch the ceremonies of the Feast of the Tabernacles (Succoth). The largest garrison city in France, situated on the frontier with the Holy Roman Empire, Metz was the only place in France where Jews had been encouraged to settle and allowed a synagogue. Arriving soon after the French annexation of the city in 1552, Jews had been favoured by the monarchy and army authorities, since they helped supply the garrison with horses, fodder, food and loans. By 1650 there were about 2,000.

Louis never returned on his four subsequent, but briefer, visits. However, he continued until his death to 'gratifier et traiter favorablement les Juifs' in Metz. He confirmed their privileges, approved their choice of rabbi and allowed them to wear black hats rather than, as hitherto, yellow. His visit had been a sign of protection, as well as curiosity.[1]

Local officials were more hostile. In 1669, while the Intendant Jean-Paul de Choisy was away, a Jew from neighbouring Lorraine (therefore not protected by French law) called Raphaël Lévy had been accused of the 'ritual murder' of a missing Christian child, tortured, condemned by the local Parlement and on 17 January 1670, after strangulation, burnt in the main square. When Louis was informed, too late, he exonerated Lévy and decreed that all such charges should henceforth be judged in Paris or before the King, not locally. None recurred. During the famine of 1709, the Jews of Metz would be rich enough to import grain and help save the city from starvation.[2]

As far as is known, Louis never visited a Protestant church. However, since the return of their strongholds to the crown in 1629, the Huguenots had switched from rebellion to submission. Unlike almost every group in the kingdom, including the royal family and the Parlement of Paris,

Huguenots had remained loyal during the Fronde: they regarded the crown as their safeguard against Catholic zealots. The Edict of Nantes was formally reaffirmed in 1629, 1643, 1653 and 1657.[3] Protestants and Catholics coexisted peacefully in most of France, sometimes attending each other's festivals. There was little friction in streets or law courts. The needs and exchanges of everyday life soothed the bitterness of religious difference.[4]

On 18 February 1658, after a long wait, Protestant deputies were introduced to the King by their Deputy General, the Marquis de Ruvigny. Louis XIV listened to a litany of complaints about infractions of the edict, promised that in future the Chancellor would ensure that it was observed and thanked them for their fidelity.[5] In 1661 Louis XIV boasted to his Ambassador in The Hague, the Comte d'Estrades, that he based 'the principal of my conduct and my actions on those of this great prince from whom I have the honour to descend': Henri IV. This was not written simply to impress Protestant opinion abroad. He repeated these sentiments to his *premier gentilhomme*, the Duc de Saint-Aignan, Governor of Le Havre, in 1666: 'not being less loyal to me than my other subjects, they should not be treated with less respect or kindness.'[6] Toleration remained a distinguishing feature – by some considered a strength – of the French monarchy.

Louis declared both to the Elector of Brandenburg and to Charles II 'on my royal word' that Protestants in France lived on a footing of equality with his other subjects. In 1661 he wrote that they should be reduced 'little by little', but nevertheless treated with 'justice and dignity [*bienséance*]', without 'extreme and violent remedies'. Colbert encouraged Protestant workers to enter France, not to leave it. They were not penalized, like Catholics in the Netherlands or England, but enjoyed the protection of the crown. Tavernier, one of Louis' favourite jewellers, and Petitot, his preferred miniature-painter, were both Protestant. Two Protestants, Turenne and Schomberg, were among his most trusted marshals. Protestant soldiers were admitted to the Invalides.[7]

Schomberg came from the region Louis XIV particularly coveted, the valley of the Rhine. The story of his life symbolizes Louis' break with Protestant Europe. He was born in Heidelberg in 1615, the son of a court official of the Elector Palatine and an English lady-in-waiting of the Elector's wife, Princess Elizabeth, daughter of James I. He spoke German, English and French, and had served in the Dutch, English and Swedish armies before choosing France after 1650. As a servant of the French and English crowns, he had led the Portuguese army in its war in 1662–8 to secure independence from Spain, becoming a Grandee of Portugal. Although he had led William II's unsuccessful coup against the city of Amsterdam in 1650, his Orangist past did not prevent him leading French armies against William III after 1672, and helping Louis XIV to win Ghent in 1678 and Luxembourg in 1684 – when he was placed under the 'ban of the Empire'. Naturalized French in 1664, he bought an estate outside Paris and was made a marshal of France in 1673. Louis XIV wrote to 'mon cousin' to express his 'particular satisfaction for the service you have accorded me in this last campaign'.[8] His sons also served the King, occasionally advising their father to moderate his zeal in holding public Protestant services on campaign.[9] As late as June 1685 his son Meinhardt was sent by Louis XIV on a mission to the Elector Palatine in Heidelberg.

Although they had produced subversive rebels and writers in the sixteenth century, after 1650 Protestants were at least as monarchical as Catholics: indeed, without the duty to obey a rival hierarchy of Pope, bishops and religious orders, often more so. Louis XIV's ally the King of Denmark, the most absolute monarch in Europe, was called by one preacher God on earth.[10] For Charles Ancillon, a French Protestant refugee, the Elector of Brandenburg was 'a mortal God', with 'the mark of the image of God'. He was called 'divus' in inscriptions, which Louis XIV was not.[11]

Despite his Protestant subjects' loyalty, however, and his earlier aversion to 'new rigours', Louis XIV became their persecutor. Dogma triumphed over pragmatism. As early as 1661, as part of the planned reduction 'little by little', Protestants had been forbidden to sing psalms in public, or even in their own houses, unless they sang so quietly that they could not be heard outside.[12] From about 1678, anticipating some of the horrors of the twentieth century, the doomed minority was first marginalized, then demonized, finally eliminated. Restrictions were imposed on Protestants' access to jobs, schools and hospitals, on the number and location of their churches (they had to move out of town centres to suburbs) and on their ministers.

With the naivety of wealth, the King thought he could buy foreign princes, although, like the Elector of Brandenburg, they often took his pensions without supporting his policies. After 1676 he also tried to buy French Protestants, through an institution with the self-contradictory name of Caisse des Conversions: if genuine, conversions would not have needed rewards from a *caisse*. It was run by an *historiographe du roi* called Paul Pellisson. A secretary of Fouquet who had spent 1661-5 in the Bastille, Pellisson was a former Protestant with the zeal of a convert. Entire families, Colbert's son Seignelay wrote to Louis XIV in 1680 from Rochefort, would be converted to Catholicism for one pistole. Converts were also relieved of debts to unconverted Protestants.[13]

The Caisse was financed by the revenues of vacant abbeys. Special 'converters' were paid by the numbers 'converted', their conversions certified by curés, bishops or intendants. Lists were drawn up, even shown to the King, but many Protestants – or Catholics pretending to be so – 'abjured' more than once, in order to make more money.

In 1680 mixed marriages were banned. The Intendant in Poitou, M. de Marillac, invented the *dragonnades*. Dragoons were mounted infantrymen, so called because their guns belched flames like dragons. At Marillac's instigation, they were billeted on particular houses or districts, to encourage or force the inhabitants to convert to Catholicism: hence the verb 'to dragoon', introduced into English at this time.[14] After troops had been billeted in Rouen, it looked like a town taken by assault. Many Protestants agreed to convert.[15]

The connection between France and England, which had made the Fronde more conservative, made the Huguenots more vulnerable. The Secretary of the Duchess of York, Father Edward Coleman, had travelled to France and corresponded with Louis' Ambassador in England, encouraging him to bribe English ministers and MPs to support an alliance with France. During the frenzy of anti-Catholicism in 1679–81 sparked by the mass delusion of the 'Popish Plot', he was found guilty of high treason and hung, drawn and quartered on Tower Hill. Forty people, including eighteen Catholic priests, were executed in the same years.

Such judicial murders of Catholics in England were used to justify the persecution of Protestants in France. An English envoy, Henry Savile, reported in 1679 that Louis' confessor Père Lachaise and the Archbishop of Paris had done 'all they can to make the King revenge the quarrel of the English Catholicks upon the French Protestants who tremble for fear of some violent persecution, and are ready to go into England in such numbers as would be a great advantage to the nation'.[16]

The most immediate reason for Louis' decision in October 1685 to revoke the Edict of Nantes, however, may have been his desire for a grand gesture to impress Catholic Europe and minimize his Ottoman alliance. After the Ottoman rout outside Vienna in 1683, Louis' rival Leopold I became a Catholic hero. The Emperor's conquests in Hungary were 'the greatest object of Europe', according to Sourches: 'No one talked of anything else anywhere.'[17] Thirty thousand troops from the Empire, led by the Electors of Bavaria and Saxony, joined his crusade.[18] His court in Vienna was becoming a centre for the King's enemies, including the exiled Charles V, Duke of Lorraine, who married the Emperor's sister, became governor of Tyrol and would command the army which recaptured Buda in September 1686.

Another personal enemy, who had arrived in time to fight in the Siege of Vienna, was the youngest son of the King's former intimate the Comtesse de Soissons. In July 1683 the Chevalier de Savoie left France for Austria, in disguise and without asking the King's permission (as all leading nobles had to).[19] In the words of the Marquis de Sourches the Chevalier had 'in France neither possessions nor consideration' and was regarded merely as 'the youngest of the brothers of the Comte de Soissons'. His father, who had been one of the King's closest friends and had built one of the first houses at Versailles, had died in 1673.[20] His eldest brother had lost favour owing to a secret mésalliance with another *fille d'honneur* of Madame (who had, moreover, attracted the King), and had failed to inherit their father's post of colonel of the Gardes Suisses. Furthermore the brothers had killed some men, in a brawl at night in Lyon in 1679.[21]

The Chevalier's tastes, as well as his family, displeased the King. According to Madame, he had 'acted the lady', giving himself to 'all comers', and was called 'Madame l'ancienne' or 'Madame Simon', after two Paris prostitutes.[22] Thus he was a younger son with a terrible reputation, from a disgraced and impoverished junior branch of the royal family. An audience with Louis XIV went badly. Despite repeated requests, he refused to give the Chevalier de Savoie command of a regiment or a benefice.

Having evaded couriers sent by Louis to bring him back, the Chevalier arrived in Austria, determined, as he wrote to Leopold I, to 'devote all my strength, all my courage and if need be my last drop of blood to the service of Your Imperial Majesty and to the welfare and development of your great House'; determined also no doubt, to avenge his rejection in France. He was rapidly given his own regiment in the Austrian army, and became famous under the name Prince Eugene of Savoy. He would prove an even more relentless enemy of Louis XIV than William III or the Duke of Lorraine.[23]

In July 1685 Louis' son-in-law the Prince de Conti, his brother the Prince de la Roche-sur-Yon and the Prince de Turenne, a nephew of the Marshal, also left France to fight as volunteers for the Emperor against the Ottoman Empire. Their secretive departure, without authorization from the King, seemed disrespectful. Letters addressed to Conti by his wife and their friends the Marquis d'Alincourt and two Comtes de La Rochefoucauld, hidden in the linings of a page's coat, were intercepted at Strasbourg.

The letters mocked the King and revelled in 'debauchery': 'in most of these letters there were great abominations of debauchery . . . infamies of ultramontane debauchery . . . And even cutting satires on the government . . . insulting the very person of the king'. He was called an ageing country gentleman with an old mistress: a 'theatre king' in public, and a checkmated king (*roi d'échecs*) on the battlefield. Some ladies 'of the highest rank' were accused of having written 'letters very far from the virtue of their sex'. The Princess complained that she was mortally bored by the entertainments at court. Soon after the letters' discovery, the Princess was seen leaving the King's study in tears. The King threw the letters on a fire. After fighting as volunteers in the Imperial army, the Conti brothers returned to France at the end of the campaign season.[24]

To remove the shame of his alliance with the Ottoman Empire, Louis XIV needed to prove himself to be more Catholic than the Emperor. From 1681 Leopold I had shown Protestants in Hungary (although not in Austria or Bohemia) relative tolerance. They were guaranteed partial religious freedom, despite some restrictions on public worship and the construction of new churches, and despite the obligation for public officials to take an oath to the Immaculate Conception. There were no *dragonnades*, no children taken from their parents. A quarter of the kingdom remained Protestant.[25]

Almost since its promulgation, the Edict of Nantes had been under attack. The clergy, the one group in France with its own national assembly, agents and income, a portion of which it offered the King as 'free gifts' in lieu of taxes, had been urging the proscription of Protestantism since 1614.[26] Protestants were often better educated than their Catholic rivals. In 1651 the Assembly of the Clergy had denounced 'this unfortunate liberty of conscience which destroys the true liberty of God's children'.[27] In 1665 the Assembly of the Clergy, reminding Louis XIV of his coronation oath to extirpate heresy, had called for revocation of the Edict of Nantes. In 1675 the Bishop of Uzès (a town with many Protestants) had demanded the 'extirpation' of the 'monstrous hydra' of heresy. Protestant churches were 'synagogues of Satan'.[28] After 1680 there were attacks on Protestant pastors in Paris.[29]

Louis XIV also needed the support of the French clergy, since he was in conflict with his personal enemy Pope Innocent XI, over the *régale* (income from vacant sees), the perennial problem of French diplomatic immunities in Rome, and what the King considered the Pope's pro-Austrian bias. Perhaps there was an unwritten bargain between the King and the clergy: he would eliminate the Protestants; they would support him against the Pope. In 1682 an *Avertissement Pastoral* by the French clergy, attacking the authority of the Pope over the *régale*, also threatened Protestant 'schismatics' with 'fatal and terrible misfortunes'. In 1688, from his refuge in Brandenburg, the Huguenot judge Charles Ancillon, formerly of Metz, would blame 'the clergy to whom everyone knows that these two actions should be imputed, for it suggested them to the King'.[30]

In addition to his desire to outshine Leopold I, and please the Assembly of Clergy, Louis was corrupted by piety. He believed that he was doing God's work, and that revocation would save Protestants' souls: 'I am persuaded that God will devote to his glory the deed which he has inspired in me,' he wrote to the Archbishop of Paris.[31] Louis XIV had been educated by a mother and a tutor who had practised a policy of mercy. Mazarin had written to the Duc de Mercoeur, 'My temperament leans rather to end matters by gentleness than by violence.'[32] But in his decade of megalomania Louis XIV preferred violence to gentleness.

Mgr d'Harcourt, Archbishop of Paris, was President of the Assembly of Clergy. Possibly also witness to the King's marriage to Madame de Maintenon in 1683, he was as assertive as his predecessor the Cardinal de Retz. Some called him 'the pope this side of the mountains'.[33] Louis XIV discussed the impending Revocation – 'the great declaration of which you have knowledge' – with d'Harcourt, and through him, in September, supplied bishops, with 'the money you consider necessary to facilitate and strengthen [sic] the conversion of heretics in their dioceses'.[34] Since July the text of the Revocation had been prepared by the King, Seignelay Minister of the Marine and the Maison du Roi, Harlay the Premier Président of the Parlement of Paris, and Le Tellier the Chancellor of France.[35]

Other ministers, including Louvois, and the King's confessor Père Lachaise were less ardent. A royal official called d'Aguesseau opposed Huguenots' persecution since it would damage the economy: 'in nearly all trades the most able workers and richest businessmen were Protestants.'[36] Louvois did not want to interfere with the army, or the economy, and told *intendants* not 'stubbornly to try to reduce everything' and to treat bankers and factory owners with care.[37] Despite or because of her Protestant background, many blamed Madame de Maintenon for their persecution. She had certainly, on her own initiative, kidnapped some of her young Protestant relations from their parents, in order to make them Catholic, but she probably preferred persuasion to persecution.[38]

The acceleration of persecution can be followed through the memoirs and letters of the Intendant of Béarn in the Pyrenees, Nicolas Foucault. In February 1685 he ordered the demolition of Protestant churches, writing to the Chancellor that there would be more converts if Protestant worship was forbidden. Père Lachaise wrote to him of the King's pleasure at news of conversions. From July all Protestant schools and assemblies were forbidden, all Protestant pastors obliged to leave the country. Converts received tax privileges. So many had converted that the government believed, with the same naivety that had led to the Caisse des Conversions, that the Edict of Nantes was no longer necessary, and should be revoked 'to efface entirely the memory of the troubles of the confusion and ills of the kingdom'.[39]

The correspondence of Seignelay shows that children were kidnapped from parents in order to convert them. Protestant women had their property confiscated or were sent to prison or the convent, as they were accused of 'dividing' families.[40] From May 1685 the King again authorized the forced billeting of soldiers on Protestants. On many occasions, as royal officials were told, hosts were injured, raped or killed by the soldiers. Old women would be dragged to Catholic churches by force, 'impénitents' hanged upside down by their feet. Soldiers seized by force what Protestants were ready to offer them voluntarily. *Intendants* sent lists of Protestant converts, by time and place, signed by priests and bishops, to Versailles: four converts on 1 October, 109 on 16 October and so on.[41]

Mgr d'Harcourt spent the week of 8–15 October at Fontainebleau: the Assembly of Clergy had already called for more demolitions of Protestant churches.[42] Dangeau's diary acquires a tone of exaltation: on 13 October, at Fontainebleau during the *lever*, courtiers learnt that 'all Poitou has converted ... at Grenoble also all the Huguenots have abjured.' On 16 October 'all Lyon has converted even before the arrival of dragoons.'[43]

On 19 October Louis XIV signed the Edict of Fontainebleau, revoking the Edict of Nantes and the 1629 Edict of Nîmes confirming it. On 22 October he asked Seignelay four times to check that the new edict had been registered by the Parlement of Paris.[44]

Thereby Louis XIV betrayed his grandfather Henri IV, his godfather Mazarin and his own younger self. He was allied to the Ottoman Sultan, curious about Confucianism and tolerant of Lutherans and Calvinists in Alsace. Yet in France he became a fanatic. All remaining Protestant churches and schools were destroyed, beginning with the Temple at Charenton a few miles east of Paris, and its surrounding graveyard. All Protestant assemblies and forms of worship were forbidden, all priests expelled. The possessions of all French Protestants abroad were confiscated. All Protestant children had henceforth to receive Catholic baptism and instruction or their parents would be fined. Even the graveyard for foreign Protestants outside Paris, to the horror of the Danish envoy, was destroyed.[45]

In theory there was no mass expulsion or imprisonment. As long as Protestants refrained from practising their religion, by Article 14 of the

Edict of Fontainebleau they could continue to trade in France without abjuring or being 'troubled under the pretext of religion', 'until it pleases God to enlighten them like the others'. Thus the King did officially accept the possibility of religious difference.[46]

Louis's acts contradicted his words, however. On 6 November he instructed the Duc de Noailles, commander in Languedoc, to tell Protestants there that they would enjoy 'no repose or pleasantness [*douceur*] at home as long as they remained in a religion which displeases His Majesty' and desired 'the foolish glory of being the last in it'. Many had their houses demolished. Protestant deserters from the galleys, the King wrote, should have only the tip of their nose cut off, rather than all of it, to ensure that they would continue rowing.[47] To the last Protestant duke, the Duc de La Force, as his wife and children were taken from him, Louis XIV wrote condemning a 'religion that I no longer wish to tolerate in my kingdom'. La Force was imprisoned in the Bastille until he converted.[48]

The King used the persecution of Protestants to reinforce his authority. On 2 November 1685 a bourgeois of Marseille recorded that 100 dragoons were going from house to house telling Protestants to convert 'or to go from now on to the galleys and their wife to America' (like the prostitutes sent there by the government). To ensure converts' presence at mass on Sunday, there was a roll call, to which all had to reply loudly 'suis isy.'[49] In some areas inspectors were placed at church doors to ensure that converts were attending. Nobles could be put in prison and their daughters in convents until they converted. Protestants caught meeting or praying together might be imprisoned, hanged or sent to the galleys.[50]

In Paris leading Protestant merchants were summoned to ministers' houses and told to sign acts of abjuration, which included a clause affirming that they were signing of their own free will.[51] The King personally ordered all former members of the Protestant consistory of Paris to leave for the provinces, and forbade visits from their wives or children.[52] All remaining Protestants were, in theory, expelled from Paris in January 1686. Two hundred and sixty-five were imprisoned in the Bastille until they abjured.[53] Any Protestants meeting in assemblies, wrote Louvois on Louis' orders in July 1686, should be executed.[54]

Louis soon believed that he had surpassed Leopold I as a champion of Catholicism. Bossuet hailed him as a 'new Theodosius' – the first Christian emperor to persecute pagans – for performing 'the miracle of our age'.[55] Despite – or because of – the brutality of their persecution, however, even in Paris Protestantism survived. Many *nouveaux convertis*, as they were called, conformed outwardly but remained secret Protestants. Children could be even more Protestant than their parents, who had to attend mass.

Many French Protestants would re-emerge after their status was legalized in 1787.[56]* Paris retained an inconspicuous minority of about 5,000 *nouveaux convertis*. From about 1705, provided they did not meet in assemblies, and made a show of outward conformity, they were rarely harassed. Mallet Frères, for example, functioned as a Protestant bank in Paris after 1713, until it closed in 2004.[57]

One of many Huguenots who stayed in France was another banker called Samuel Bernard. He waited until the last moment, November 1685, to convert to Catholicism. His wealth grew thereafter, partly due to the help he gave other Huguenots to move their capital abroad and to continue trading with France.[58] His international networks would enable him, even in wartime, to purchase grain in Danzig or Hamburg for the French government and help save the country from starvation when the harvest was bad. He also helped supply the funds with which to pay French diplomats abroad.[59]

To the surprise of the royal government, however, many Huguenots preferred to pay to leave France rather than to stay and be paid to become Catholic. The kings of Spain, when they had expelled Jews and Muslim 'nominal Christians' in 1492 and 1609–14 respectively, had allowed them to leave unharmed with some of their possessions; the crown even paid some transport costs for Muslims.[60] As early as August 1685, however, Louis had forbidden Protestants to leave without permission, which was rarely granted, on pain of prison, the galleys or death. Anyone who helped them leave was also threatened with the same penalties. He soon found, however, that while absolute in theory – as the Edict of Fontainebleau demonstrated – his powers over his subjects were limited in practice. As Louis' failure to alter the order of succession would also show (see below), absolutism was a façade masking the independence of institutions and individuals.

Frontiers were patrolled, local people encouraged to arrest and rob fleeing Protestants, ships fumigated in order to smoke out hidden passengers.[61] But frontiers were porous, and subjects disobedient, brave or venal. Despite naval and army patrols, *passeurs* – people-smugglers – were ready, for a fee, to help Protestants to escape.[62] Some swam out to rocks to be picked up by foreign ships.[63] The market proved stronger than the monarchy. When 'converted' Huguenot shipowners helped their co-religionists escape, Seignelay closed his eyes. Surveillance and persecution cost too much, and 'His Majesty does not want to spend anything.'[64] In

---

* They included the ancestors of, for example, Guizot, Pierre Loti and Gide. At present about 2.5 per cent of the French population is of Protestant origin.

1685–8 about 10 per cent of Huguenots, perhaps 130,000–150,000 in all (others died on the journey), managed to leave their 'Babylonian captivity' in France for what they called the 'Refuge' abroad; the word 'refugee' was first used at this time to describe them. The properties of departed Huguenots were confiscated and either given to Catholic relations, or sold to pay for Catholic education or pensions for Protestant converts, or allocated to Catholic institutions and charities.[65]

Thereafter Louis faced not only enemy rulers like Leopold I and William III, but the wrath of a Protestant diaspora. By driving Huguenots into exile, Louis XIV turned them from obedient subjects, who had been hoping their King's persecution would abate, into dangerous adversaries. From the safety of exile, they preached, wrote and fought back against their persecutor. Thousands of soldiers and officers and perhaps 15 to 20 per cent of the manpower of the French navy left, usually to fight for Louis XIV's enemies.[66] Louis proved implacable to Huguenots captured fighting in enemy armies. They were sent to the galleys or hanged, even if French generals had guaranteed their safety in order to persuade them to surrender.[67]

Two of Louis XIV's nemeses employed French Protestant secretaries: William III was served by Pierre du Moulin and Jean de Robethon, who later also worked as Hanoverian minister in London. With his ability to draft letters in English, and many English and Huguenot contacts, Robethon would help arrange the smooth succession of Louis XIV's enemy the Elector of Hanover to the British throne in 1714.[68]

Marlborough would employ Adam Cardonnel, son of a Protestant merchant from Caen, as a secretary, specializing in his relations with foreign armies (another Huguenot, Gabriel Delahaye, drew some of his maps). The Revocation may indeed have helped transform Marlborough from an ally (and former officer) of Louis XIV into his enemy. Beforehand, First Lord of the Bedchamber, Master of the Robes and Colonel of one of the three Troops of Life Guards of James II, he had supported his master's alliance with France. He had announced James II's accession to Louis XIV at Versailles in February 1685, and led James II's armies against Monmouth in June.[69] After the Revocation (and the attack in 1687 on the Church of England's privileges), however, he began to conspire with James II's enemies, and in 1688 would lead many officers over to William III's army.

By the Revocation, Louis XIV not only helped to unite Europe against France, but also transferred French cultural, commercial and technical leads to its rivals. The impact of even a small number of Huguenots outside France shows how advanced its culture and economy were, in comparison to other countries' – and that for some exile can lead to success as well as suffering.

They were helped by the French language. Long before Louis XIV's accession, French had become the language of Europe, boosted by the prestige of the French monarchy, of the city and university of Paris, and of the French-speaking court of Burgundy in the fifteenth century. At Nijmegen in 1678 French was the main language not only of the peace congress itself, but also of the foreign embassies attending it.[70] Attacking the use of Latin inscriptions on monuments, François Charpentier proclaimed in De l'excellence de la langue française (1683) that Louis XIV had brought French to a state of perfection and made it immortal.[71] An Englishman called John Northleigh noted that 'the French Tongue spreads itself mightily and becomes almost universal' – and 'a requisite for all princes'.[72] French was the preferred language of Louis XIV's enemies as well as his admirers, of William III and later of George I with his English ministers.

Huguenots went everywhere: from New York, where ancestors of Winston Churchill's mother Jennie Jerome settled in the early eighteenth century, to the Cape, where descendants of the first 400 Huguenots, arriving in 1687, live today.[73] Three countries in particular welcomed Huguenots: the Netherlands, Brandenburg and England.

About 35,000 French Protestants settled in the Netherlands. Amsterdam, already home to some of Europe's best cartographers and printmakers, became a centre of the French book trade. By 1700 Huguenot publishers had about a fifth of the market.[74] Huguenot writers in Amsterdam included Pierre Jurieu, 'the Goliath of the Protestants', who had taught in the Protestant academy in Sedan and believed that Louis XIV could be driven south of the Loire. Elie Benoist collected records of their religious persecution in France in Histoire de l'Edit de Nantes (5 volumes, Delft, 1693–5), thereby strengthening their sense of martyrdom and exceptional destiny.

After 1684 in his journal Nouvelles de la République des Lettres Pierre Bayle, formerly a Protestant pastor in France, taught that religion should be a matter for the individual rather than the state, and that everyone had the right to hold mistaken beliefs. After the death of his brother in prison in Bordeaux in 1685, he became more hostile to Louis XIV and Catholicism, writing, 'tolerance for Catholics is a state against nature.' He answered the Grand Dictionnaire historique (1674) of the Catholic Abbé Moréri with the Dictionnaire historique et critique (1695–7), a frequently reprinted precursor of the Encyclopédie. Voltaire called it 'the first dictionary which taught men to think'.[75]

Religious persecution and forced 'conversions' increased incredulity, not least in Bayle himself.[76] In 1719 a Huguenot writer Charles Levier would publish in Amsterdam, hidden in a life of Spinoza, an atheist manifesto called the *Traité des trois imposteurs*, probably written by the Irish Whig John Toland, denouncing Moses, Jesus and Mohammed as frauds.[77] Another influential Huguenot book was Bernard Picart's *Cérémonies et coutumes religieuses de tous les peuples du monde*, published in Amsterdam in ten volumes from 1727 to 1743 by another Huguenot Jean Frédéric Barnard, with more than 250 pages of engravings and 3,000 of text. The first global history of religion, it was one of the first to relativize Christianity and treat it in the same manner as other religions.

Huguenot refugees spread not only religious scepticism, but also hostility to the French monarchy. A violent attack on the Bastille was written by a Huguenot officer who had been imprisoned there for eleven years, Constantin de Renneville. *L'Inquisition française ou Histoire de la Bastille*, listing Louis XIV's prisoners in the Bastille and their sufferings, first published in 1715, was republished in six volumes in Amsterdam in 1724. It helped confirm the Bastille's reputation as a symbol of royal tyranny. Dedicated to George I, it praised the English Parliament as 'the only institution in Europe which has kept its antique liberty'.[78]

With domains stretching from the Rhineland to Lithuania, Frederick William, Elector of Brandenburg and Duke of Prussia, was considered the 'wisest fox' in the Empire, with its best army. He had been a French ally since 1664, receiving a total of 4 million livres in subsidies before his death in 1688, even making Louis XIV executor of his will.[79] In fact, as Louis and his Foreign Minister Colbert de Croissy suspected, he was playing a double game, mainly concerned to divert French support and subsidies from his rival Sweden.

He feared Louis XIV both as a Catholic and as a conqueror, believing, with reason, that he wanted to acquire 'the entire course of the Rhine'. Moreover he was uncle by marriage of William III, who visited him in Berlin in 1680. Appalled long before the Revocation by Louis' persecution of Huguenots, he welcomed them in his dominions, particularly since, while most of his subjects were Lutherans, they were Calvinists like himself.[80] (For the same reason, Charles XI of Sweden, since he was a Lutheran, discouraged their immigration.)

Huguenots helped unite Europe against Louis XIV through their diplomacy as well as through their publications, as the careers of Robethon and Cardonnel showed. One French Protestant pastor called François Gaultier de Saint-Blancard left for the Netherlands in 1683 when his church in Montpellier was demolished. There he not only published detailed accounts of the persecutions, but also won the confidence of William III.[81] On 8 January 1685 he had a 'very secret' audience with the Prince before leaving for Berlin, dressed as a cavalier rather than a pastor, to hide his role as the Prince's secret agent. In Berlin, created a court preacher, he had several audiences with the Elector.

Frederick William I was not only William III's uncle by marriage, but had recently married his son Frederick to Sophie Charlotte, a daughter of William's cousin Sophia, Duchess of Hanover, thereby giving him a remote claim to the crown of England (Frederick would also consider claiming the succession to the stadholderate in the Netherlands, as the Prince's nearest relation). Gaultier de Saint-Blancard suggested the creation of a league of Protestant princes and a general assembly of their ministers. In March 1685, even before the Revocation, the Elector wrote that, before James II had time to establish himself as king of England, William III should invade it with 10,000 men; through both his wife and his mother the crown should belong to him. Thus the first suggestion for the 'Glorious Revolution' in England came from Berlin.[82] In May 1685, encouraged by Gaultier and Pierre Jurieu, the Prince and the Elector signed an alliance to protect the Protestant religion.[83] Both Gaultier and Jurieu would run spy networks in France, which would provide information for Louis' enemies in the war of 1689–97.[84]

In response to the Edict of Fontainebleau, on 29 October 1685 Frederick William's Edict of Potsdam denounced the persecution in France and promised asylum and financial assistance to French Protestants who settled in the dominions of the Elector of Brandenburg. Ezechiel Spanheim, his minister in Paris, opened his embassy to them. More agents in Amsterdam and Hamburg helped their immigration.

Louis' able envoy to Berlin M. de Rébenac, who had distributed pensions and gifts to members of the Elector's court, complained. The Elector replied on Christmas Day 1685 to Spanheim – how much was conveyed to Louis is unknown – that, when the King of France did so much for his religion, 'how could he regard it as a crime by us not to be indifferent to our religion and to open our arms to our unfortunate co-religionists who sacrifice to their conscience all their goods and who prefer a life of misery to abjuration?'[85] After allying with William III in 1685, in March 1686 he signed a twenty-year military alliance with the Emperor. Frederick William I dreamed of an army of Dutch, Germans and Spaniards marching on Paris. The Parlement and the princes would rise against the King. 'Then we would no longer need to fear her,' he said of France.[86]

In August 1686 the Elector held military manoeuvres in Cleves near the Rhine with William III. Orders were given in French, probably because it was the only language common to the many nationalities of which William III's army was composed. Mockingly, he asked Rébenac to tell Louis XIV that he modelled his army on the King's, 'and there were garrisons in France which did not conform so rapidly to the regulations and commands of Your Majesty as his did.' He was imitating France in order to defeat it. What Sophia of Hanover called 'all the Huguenotterie' were at the manoeuvres, stimulating the rulers' anti-French zeal.[87] Even a humble country priest in the north of France, Alexandre Dubois, knew of Huguenots' role in forming alliances against France: he wrote in his diary that Louis XIV's 'religion triumphed over his interests'.[88]

In April 1687 the grandest Huguenot of all, the Maréchal de Schomberg, recruited to command the Elector's army with the help of the Huguenot Pastor Jean Claude, famous for his controversies with Bossuet and hostility to Louis XIV, arrived in Berlin. A year earlier, abandoning his country, his property and his career at the age of seventy, Schomberg had left France for Portugal. He retained his French pensions and in theory was on a mission from Louis XIV to encourage the King of Portugal Pedro II, widower of Queen Marie Françoise, to choose another pro-French bride. Louis had made Schomberg vow not to join the enemies of France, but many considered his departure a disaster. Sourches wrote that it was 'to the great regret of all France which lost in him the best and most experienced of its generals'.[89] Despite Schomberg's role in helping to win Portugal's independence twenty years earlier, and his rank as Grandee of Portugal, its Inquisition, like Louis XIV, would not allow him to hold Protestant services. He left for Brandenburg.

On his journey from Portugal to Brandenburg in January–April 1687, passing through England and the Netherlands, he had been horrified by James II, but impressed by his former adversary William III. He wrote to Henry Sidney, an English Whig who had joined William's service: 'Without doubt they will one day be established in England. There is nothing I would not sacrifice for that.'

Schomberg was appointed commander-in-chief of the Elector of Brandenburg's forces: as long as the Elector remained a French ally, Louis allowed Schomberg to retain his French pensions. He wrote, 'I hope that you will find there all the satisfaction that you deserve, until God disposes you to return to these countries where no one wishes more than I to have the honour to see you.' Rébenac assured the King that his zeal could not be doubted.[90] In reality Schomberg had long been planning to join Dutch service.[91]

Schomberg was not the only Huguenot officer in the Brandenburg army.

In 1687 the Elector formed two companies of Grands Mousquetaires, modelled on Louis XIV's musketeers but composed of Huguenot exiles (later the Elector also established his own Gardes du Corps and Cent-Suisses). Soon about 15 per cent or more of his officer corps, 600 officers, were of French origin, including General de Forcade, an officer in the Elector's Garde du Corps who later became military governor of Berlin. They had advantages of pay and conditions of service over native Branden-burgers. By 1698 there were probably around 15,000 French Protestants in the Elector's domains and 7,500 in Berlin alone, 20 per cent or more of the population. Protected by successive electors and kings, they were subject to their own laws, and had their own churches, hospitals and schools.[92] The French envoy noted that 'Berlin is full of French factories' (some of which made luxury goods for the court), while German shops were empty. Huguenots, he believed, missed France, and hoped for 'an impending revolution' there.[93]

The Französisches Gymnasium in Berlin, which still uses French as a language of instruction, is a descendant of the Huguenot 'collège fran-çais'.[94] The French church in Gendarmenmarkt was built, partly on the model of the Temple at Charenton, by Jean Louis Cayart, an engineer who had worked for Vauban.[95] The Huguenot judge Charles Ancillon also served the Elector as a historiographer and diplomat, and as director of the Académie des Nobles. The Bonnet brothers became Prussian residents in London in 1695–1720. Two Huguenots, his Governess Madame de Roucoulle and his tutor Jacques Duhan, would help give the Elector's great-grandson, the future Frederick the Great, his love of the French language and French literature.[96]

Rich, royal and close, London also became a favourite destination for Huguenots, including some who had worked for Louis XIV.[97] Already in July 1679, with the help of English diplomats in Paris, the Foubert family of *écuyers du roi*, esteemed as being among the best in Europe, had moved their Royal Riding Academy to London (eventually to what is still called Foubert's Place, off Carnaby Street). Foubert's Academy, and other Hugue-not academies, would train Englishmen, in horsemanship, fencing, dancing and mathematics, until the mid-nineteenth century.[98]

On 28 July 1681, again showing he was not Louis' puppet, Charles II issued a proclamation, encouraging, on the grounds of honour and con-science, the 'poor afflicted Protestants' from France to take refuge in his kingdoms, freeing their goods of import dues and facilitating the process of 'denization' (the equivalent of obtaining residence permits, preceding naturalization).[99] Thus Louis XIV knew that Huguenot refugees were being welcomed abroad. The bishops of the Church of England treated them more kindly than they did English Nonconformists.

James II, who succeeded Charles II in February 1685 nine months before the Edict of Fontainebleau, was less sympathetic than his brother, although the commander-in-chief of his army was a French Protestant, a nephew of Turenne called Louis de Duras, Earl of Feversham. Even James II, however, denounced the *dragonnades* as a persecution 'not to be equalled in any history since Christianity'. In April 1687 his Declaration of Indulgence (whose principles would be reaffirmed by William III in 1689) ended the need for Huguenot refugees to conform to Anglican sacraments. By 1695 about 20,000–30,000 had settled in London (and 50,000 throughout the country): an unprecedented influx for a city of 500,000, resented by some local tradesmen. After 1700, partly helped by the Huguenot influx, London's population for the first time surpassed that of Paris.[100]

The Marquis de Ruvigny, the former Protestant Deputy General at court and three times envoy from Louis XIV to Charles II (in 1660, 1667–8 and 1674–6), had often warned the King that his treatment of Protestants was the best way to antagonize England and impoverish his own kingdom. Like many others, he realized that his remarks made no impression. During one audience, the King said he would give one of his own arms if he could bring all his subjects back to the Catholic church.

In 1686, the same year that Schomberg left for Lisbon, Ruvigny again left for London, this time as a refugee.[101] Ruvigny's son Henri called their decision to leave 'the most difficult decision to take and to execute which you can possibly imagine', although, by a special privilege, they were allowed French passports and, for a time, to keep their estates in France. Religion had trumped nationality and property. Henri de Ruvigny later became, as Earl of Galway, a British general leading Huguenot forces invading the Dauphiné, British envoy to the Duke of Savoy, a promoter of Protestant settlement, domination and expropriation of Catholics in Ireland, and a spokesman for the Huguenots in England, as his father had been in France.[102] Another Huguenot, John Ligonier, born in Rouen in 1680, became commander-in-chief of the British army from 1757 to 1759.

After 1685 London attracted even more French workers in the luxury trades than it had before: cabinetmakers; silk weavers, cobblers and tailors; gunsmiths and armourers, who made English guns the best in Europe; watchmakers; engravers, cartographers and booksellers.[103] Bringing some of their tools and their capital, they often settled in Soho and Spitalfields, which until the 1730s remained partly French-speaking. They also included musicians, dance masters, doctors and silversmiths like Augustin Courtauld and Paul de Lamerie, who helped make English silver and gold plate as richly decorated as French. Courtauld's descendants would later turn to textiles, and found the famous company of that name.[104]

Despite their abhorrence of Louis XIV, Huguenots spread French styles and the French language at least as effectively as the court of Versailles. After 1685 English monarchs and courtiers slept in beds, sat on chairs, dined off silver, drove in carriages and used guns and watches made by Frenchmen in the latest French styles. Huguenots (like their Jacobite enemies in France after 1688), although driving the two countries apart politically, brought them closer culturally and commercially.

Daniel Marot, for example, was a Protestant who like his father Jean Marot had worked for Louis XIV: he engraved prints of ceremonies commemorating the birth of the Duc de Bourgogne in 1682 and the funeral of the Queen in 1683. Leaving France in 1684, he began to serve William III, helping to design his new palace of Het Loo. Marot became chief architect, decorator and garden designer for William III and his courtiers in the Netherlands, and from 1694 to 1697 in England.[105]

Huguenots were vanguards of globalization. In addition to an international market in books and ideas, they helped to create an international financial market. The Bank of England was originally founded in 1693 mainly to finance the war against Louis XIV. Seven directors would be of Huguenot origin, contributing around 15 per cent of its original capital. The first Governor, in 1694–7, was Sir John Houblon, from a Huguenot family. Showing how well integrated Huguenots could become, he was also an MP, Lord Mayor in 1695, a lord of the admiralty and a director of the East India Company (which was advised by another Huguenot, the great traveller Sir John Chardin, who left France in 1681). One brother, James Houblon, became an MP for London, another, Abraham Houblon, also became governor of the Bank of England.[106] Huguenots called Portal printed the first banknotes, as their descendants continued to do until the 1980s. Another Huguenot Jean Castaing ran a coffee house, called Jonathan's in the City, where, in 1698, stock and commodity prices, and exchange rates, were first regularly posted: an early form of stock exchange.[107]

A leading investor in the Bank of England was Esther d'Herwarth, Marquise de Gouvernet. She had much to invest, as her father had been Louis XIV's trusted banker Barthélemé d'Herwarth, to whom the King had written a letter in his own hand asking for 'the greatest sum of money you can provide' on the day of Fouquet's arrest: in gratitude for his services, Louis XIV had given her special permission to leave France with her fortune.[108] She is buried below a striking monument in the north transept of Westminster Abbey with her mother, known as the 'mother of the Huguenots'. Her brothers abjured their faith and stayed in France.

Her cousin Philibert, however, would become William III's ambassador to the Swiss cantons.[109]

Huguenots flooded London with accounts of their flight from France, which were repeated by English clergymen and writers. They also published works on the 'torments', 'sufferings' and 'persecution' of French Protestants, as well as the wickedness of Louis XIV.[110] Evelyn in his diary lamented that 'the utmost barbarity' of the French persecution exceeded even the heathen persecutions of the past.[111] In 1687 alone £42,000 was raised by voluntary subscriptions to help them. Many also received grants from the Privy Purse or Parliament.

In addition to blasting France, Huguenots helped to modernize England, like German and central European exiles in the twentieth century. Paul Rapin de Thoyras, a Huguenot nephew of Paul Pellisson, head of Louis' Caisse des Conversions, had accompanied William III to England. He became the first great Whig historian of England, praising 'the constant union of the Sovereign with his parliament' as 'the most solid foundation for the glory of the Prince and the welfare of his subjects'. His books include a *Dissertation sur les Whigs et les Tories* (1717) and *Histoire d'Angleterre* (1724–7, dedicated to George I).[112] The first regular general-interest magazine in England, the *Gentleman's Journal or Monthly Miscellany*, later called the *Lady's Journal*, written partly by as well as for ladies, was started in 1692 by a Huguenot called Peter Motteux. He also wrote articles in favour of the equality of men and women, and translated Rabelais and Racine.

Abel Boyer, a prolific journalist, translator and historian, naturalized English in 1706 (a sign that he had abandoned hope of return to France), was another Huguenot pioneer. As the English Parliament became more powerful, with more frequent sessions, and the press became more free, he was the first person, from 1711 to 1729, to print regular reports of Parliamentary debates.[113] Sometimes calling himself Gallo-Britannus, he also translated *Télémaque* and compiled French–English dictionaries (*Compleat French Master for Ladies and Gentlemen*, 1694; *Dictionnaire royal français et anglais*, 1699) which remained in print for a hundred years. They spread the French language in England, as other Huguenot dictionaries did in Brandenburg and elsewhere.[114] Huguenot booksellers, specializing in imported French books, maps and music, lined the Strand, unable to operate in the City of London owing to the opposition of the Stationers' Company.[115]

Leaving their country did not stop Huguenots trading with it – they changed addresses but not businesses (as, in reverse, many Jacobite exiles in France would continue to trade with England).[116] René Baudouin, born in Tours in 1650, moved to London in 1679 and prospered as a merchant until his death in 1728. His monument in the church of St Mary Aldermary in the City expresses horror that French Protestants had been 'cruelly persecuted for their Religion . . . in the reign of King Lewis the 14th', and gratitude for the 'true Christian Love and Charity of this Nation [England] which God for ever preserve'. It does not mention his impeachment and fine for importing silk from France in wartime. Other Huguenots, for example Peter Motteux who imported French luxuries for his shop in Leadenhall Street, the Two Fans, also continued trading with France, and, as we shall see, would help finance Louis XIV's wars.[117]

A Protestant convert called M. de Bonrepaus was sent by Louis XIV to London in January 1686 to try to tempt back, with offers of pensions, offices and the return of confiscated property, Protestants who had left for what the King called 'un caprice de religion'. The 'pretended persecutions' were described as 'exhortation'. Bonrepaus, however, lamented in 1686 'the establishment . . . in this kingdom of our best manufactures. It is not only people of the RPR [religion prétendue réformée] who come to work there but several Catholics': Catholic workmen had followed their Huguenot employers. Huguenots proved too frightened to return. He persuaded at most 500 to do so.[118]

Realizing its harmful consequences, a few Frenchmen, including royal officials, dared to criticize the Revocation. The great engineer Vauban told the King that his troops would be better employed digging canals than 'dragooning' Protestants, and that 'converted' Huguenots were no more Catholic than he was Muslim. After 1689 he wrote a mémoire advocating the recall of the Huguenots. All the measures against them had only made them more 'obstinate'. He lamented the depopulation of France, 'the ruin of the most considerable portion of trade'; the loss of 12,000 soldiers and 10,000 sailors; and the sharp pens in foreign countries 'cruelly unleashed against France and the person of the King'. Louis XIV probably never saw it.[119]

Vauban considered that one solution might be to 'exterminate them all from the first to the last'. However, seventeenth-century France was more Christian, and possessed fewer means of extermination, than twentieth-century governments. He continued: 'apart from the difficulties there would be in the execution, this action which would be execrable before God and man, would only serve to weaken us even more than before, to render us eternally odious at home and to our neighbours.' Protestants should stop being 'tormented' and the Edict of Nantes should be reinstated.[120]

The literary genius of the Duc de Saint-Simon is no guarantee of reliability: he wrote his memoirs forty years after events, many of which he did not witness. His bitterness and love of quarrels made it difficult for contemporaries, including Louis himself, to take him seriously. The Marquis d'Argenson, son of the Lieutenant Général de Police, called him 'odieux, injuste et anthropophage' ('odious, unjust and cannibalistic').[121] His claim to have been 'instructed of all matters great and small' should make the most admiring readers suspicious. He was an outsider, who did not hold office until Louis XIV's death. His memoirs – for example his claims that the King loved the bourgeois and desired to humiliate nobles, and his accounts of other people's conversations (at which he was generally not present) and motives – are in part delusions.[122] Alexandre Maral, reflecting the opinion of most historians, as well as Saint-Simon's contemporaries, believes that his memoirs should be used only with 'the greatest circumspection'.[123]

However, Saint-Simon had an outsider's independence of judgement. In his memoirs he was more critical of the Revocation than anyone else in France, even Vauban. He called it a 'general abomination born of flattery and cruelty', 'without the slightest pretext and without any need':

> this terrible plot which emptied a quarter of the kingdom, which ruined trade, which weakened it in every part, which placed it for so long under the avowed and public pillage of the dragoons, which authorized the torments and punishments during which they killed innocents of every sex in their thousands, which ruined so many, which tore apart families, which armed relations against relations in order to seize their properties and let them die of hunger, which made our factories move abroad, made their States flourish and expand at the expense of ours, which gave them the spectacle of such a prodigious group proscribed, denuded, wandering without crimes, looking for asylum far from the fatherland; which placed nobles, rich, old, people often highly respected for their piety, their knowledge, their virtues, people well off, weak, delicate . . . for the sole cause of religion [under the threat of being sent to prison or the galleys]. Everything echoed with the cries of these unfortunate victims of error.

Others bought their peace and kept their possessions by 'simulated abjurations'.[124]

Few others in France expressed such revulsion. The potential popularity of the Revocation may have hastened it. Like other persecutions of minorities, it gave part of the population the pleasure of joining in or watching what they considered patriotic acts, as well as opportunities to acquire, at low prices, the possessions of the persecuted. The diary of Etienne Borelly of Nîmes expresses admiration for our good King Louis XIV, 'may god preserve and bless him', and for the *dragonnades*, and hatred for the 'cursed race' of Protestants, who were either atheists or traitors, although even he felt their departure with 'immense sums' 'entirely ruined' the kingdom. His hatred did not stop him buying a cheap coat for his daughter at a sale of Protestants' possessions.[125]

As Pierre Bayle wrote from Rotterdam, 'you have thus all been complicit, in these crimes.'[126] Unlike many of the King's other policies, including his wars, his taxes, his treatment of the Parlements and the Jansenists, his persecution of Protestants aroused little criticism in France. Their execution and imprisonment continued after his death, even under a regent who barely believed in God, and whose mother, Madame Palatine, had Protestant sympathies.[127] Anti-Huguenot laws were formally reinforced in 1724; even Saint-Simon, so critical of the Revocation in order to discredit Louis XIV, in practice supported its continuation. A Protestant pastor was executed as late as 1762. In 1768 there were still fourteen Protestant women in chains in the Tour de Constance at Aigues-Mortes; one, Marie Durand, had been there for thirty-eight years. Protestant services had to be held in remote mountains, to escape persecution, like Catholic services in Ireland on the 'mass rock'. Official toleration of Protestant rights in France, finally reintroduced in 1787, would anger the Catholic clergy.[128]

Louis did not limit his persecutions to his own kingdom. In 1686 he sent troops to help his cousin the Duke of Savoy attack and 'convert' the Waldensians, a Protestant minority resident in the Alps. His general Catinat, despite a reputation for 'humanity', wanted them 'entirely extirpated'.[129] After courageous resistance expected by neither monarch, most Waldensians had been either been 'exterminated' (the word used by Madame de Sévigné),[130] converted, or – in the case of 2,000 diehards – allowed to leave for exile in Geneva.

In one of his cruellest letters Louis mocked the Waldensians' deaths from starvation or disease in the camps into which they had been herded: 'I see that diseases deliver the Duke of Savoy from the trouble caused by the need to guard the rebels from the valleys of Luzerne and I do not doubt that he easily consoles himself for the loss of such subjects, who make place for better and more faithful ones.'[131] In May 1689, when the Duke allied himself to William III, the exiles were allowed to return to Savoy in what was called the 'Glorioso Rimpatrio', a repatriation of which Protestant refugees from France dreamt in vain.

The popularity of the Revocation is also suggested by the many statues to the King erected at the same time, to public applause, throughout France. The supreme courtier the Maréchal Duc de La Feuillade had been subsidized by the King to buy the office of colonel of the Gardes Françaises in 1672. Allegedly at his own expense (although perhaps again with help from the King), from 1679 he began to plan, in the Place des Victoires which he created in Paris, a huge statue of the King in gilt bronze by Maurits van den Bogaert. Parisians said that desire to be forgiven for the money he had made selling posts in his regiment was one of his motives.[132]

The statue showed the King in coronation robes, crowned with laurels by a figure of victory, with a baton of command in one hand, crushing a three-headed dog, representing Rebellion, above the inscription 'Viro immortali' in golden letters. On the statue's marble base were four bronze plaques showing Spain recognizing the precedence of France; the passage of the Rhine; the Fall of Besançon; and the Peace of Nijmegen. Roundels showed further triumphs such as the construction of Versailles; the destruction of heresy; and the Siamese embassy. Round the base of the statue were statues of four bound slaves, representing the Empire, Spain, Brandenburg and Holland.

Bound slaves also surrounded the statues of Henri IV on the Pont Neuf, of Ferdinand I, Grand Duke of Tuscany, in Livorno and of Frederick William I in Berlin. They did not, however, represent defeated neighbours. Even some of Louis' subjects were shocked by the blasphemous inscription 'Viro immortali': 'to the immortal man'. Again the King showed his desire to conquer time.[133] Crowds attended the statue's inauguration by the Dauphin on 28 March 1686, escorted by La Feuillade's Gardes Françaises, to the sound of trumpets, drums and violins. The gilt statue reflected the light of candles burning, day and night, on the top of four immense columns surrounding it. A print of the statue called Louis XIV 'the Invincible, the Victorious, the perpetual Triumpher, the Tamer of Heresy, the Father of his Peoples, the Arbiter of Peace and War'.[134]

The King had already seen it in 1681, when he made 'a thousand obliging remarks' to La Feuillade, and he visited it again in 1687.[135] Only in 1699, after widespread criticism, did the King say that, in future, he would prefer 'what is wise and reasonable, and nothing in one word which recalls the idea of the bas-reliefs, slaves and inscriptions of his statue of the Place des Victoires'. The candles burning round it, on the King's order, were extinguished.[136]

Following government instructions to *intendants* of 5 August 1685, other statues were erected, usually depicting the King on horseback, according to officially approved designs, in eight other cities, including Poitiers, Lyon, Montpellier and Quebec. More were planned, but were abandoned on grounds of cost.[137] A second statue was unveiled in Paris on the Place Louis-le-Grand in March 1699: the King was portrayed as a

Roman emperor on his horse, 200 feet high. The inscription, 'À Louis le Grand, le Père et le Conducteur d'Armées Toujours Heureuses', confirmed French delusions of omnipotence. Even today, statues of Louis XIV dominate the Place Bellecour in Lyon, the Place du Peyrou in Montpellier and the Place des Victoires in Paris, despite their destruction during the Revolution, and replacement under Louis XVIII by less elegant versions. Nevertheless, at the time, some Frenchmen considered the debris of Protestant churches finer tributes to Louis XIV than his statues. In a speech to the Académie Française on 27 January 1687, the Abbé Tallemand called them 'fortunate ruins which are the finest trophies which France has ever seen. The triumphal arches and statues erected to the glory of the King cannot raise it any higher than this temple of heresy which has been destroyed by his piety.'[138]

On 30 January 1687 the King was cheered by crowds during a visit to the Hôtel de Ville for a ceremonial banquet, after a Te Deum in Notre-Dame, to give thanks for his recovery after his fistula operation. With gratified servility, the Prévôt des Marchands, who served the King at table, recorded that every time he refilled the King's glass of wine, the King touched his hat to him. They talked at length about Paris, and the King agreed to release some prisoners. Bread was thrown to crowds outside; fountains flowed with wine. The cheers grew louder when the King appeared at a window and threw fistfuls of gold coins. As he left, city councillors fell to their knees. The Prévôt's wife, who served the Dauphine at dinner, died of 'apoplexy' that evening: another death, like Vatel's in 1671, hastened by the cult of Louis XIV. After the banquet the King went to the Place des Victoires to examine his statue. He remarked that the chained slaves around it were 'fort beaux'.[139]

Many Frenchmen believed that they had entered a golden age. Panegyrics praised the King's immortal, divine or supernatural powers. Frenchmen's love for the King was compared to a second religion.[140] That year Charles Perrault wrote:

> Quel siècle pour ses roys,
> Des hommes révéré,
> Au siècle de Louis peut être préféré?
> De Louis qu'environne une gloire immortelle,
> De Louis des rois le plus parfait modèle.[141]

> ('What epoch for its kings,
> Revered by men,
> Can be preferred to the epoch of Louis?

Of Louis surrounded by immortal glory,
Of Louis the most perfect model of kings.')

On 9 July 1686, however, the Emperor Leopold I and the princes of the Empire, both Protestants and Catholics, had formed the League of Augsburg (one of the richest of the Imperial Free Cities) to halt French expansion on the Rhine. Leopold I's son Joseph was crowned hereditary king of Hungary in 1687 and elected king of the Romans, or heir to the Holy Roman Emperor, in 1688, on better terms than his father in 1658.[142] The House of Austria was recovering power and confidence. After the inauguration of the statue of the Place des Victoires, the Imperial envoy in Paris had told the French Foreign Minister, as reported by his English colleague, not as 'a Complaint but only to lett it be known he was not Insensible': his master 'was not in the condition of a Slave with his Hands tyed in Chaines'.[143] Louis XIV and his subjects would soon learn how misleading were the statue of the Places des Victoires and its inscription.

17

England Changes Sides:
The Flights of King James

In 1689, partly as a result of the Revocation of the Edict of Nantes, Louis XIV welcomed a visitor almost as surprising as the Siamese ambassadors three years earlier. At six in the evening on 7 January, in the Château Vieux of Saint-Germain, Louis XIV met his cousin the deposed King James II of England for the first time since 1655, when France's alliance with Cromwell had obliged the young Duke of York to leave France. The crowd was so great that it prevented Louis greeting his cousin until he had reached the top of the staircase. He said: 'Monsieur my brother, how happy I am to see you here! I cannot describe my joy at seeing you in safety.' He then accompanied James to the bedroom of his wife Mary of Modena, who had arrived the day before with their son the Prince of Wales, saying, 'I bring you a man whom you will be very happy to see.'

James recounted the details of his flight from England, admitting that William III had encouraged it by the deliberate negligence of the guards assigned to him. After half an hour, Louis XIV left, with the words 'Monsieur [not Your Majesty], we will be living together for more than a day, do not let us stand on ceremony, you will not see me out.' They treated each other as cousins rather than kings. However, in public assertion of their royal rank, James and his wife were henceforth guarded by Gardes du Corps, and received almost the same honours as Louis XIV himself.[1]

Four years earlier, when James II had succeeded Charles II on the throne of England, his flight to France had seemed inconceivable. The rebellion in June 1685 of Louis XIV's former protégé, Charles II's eldest illegitimate son the Protestant Duke of Monmouth, had been easily defeated. Parliament had voted James a large revenue which, with his expanding army and navy, made him appear the most powerful king of England since Henry VIII. From 1677 to 1681 Louis had tried to prevent 'accommodation' between Crown and Parliament, and English opposition to his conquests on the continent, by subsidizing opposition politicians, even appearing to favour the future James II's exclusion from the succession. The English monarchy, however, had since increased in wealth and independence.[2]

On 4 April 1687 James had issued a Declaration of Indulgence suspending all penal laws against Catholics and Dissenters, thereby threatening the Anglican monopoly of public office. James began to appoint Catholics to important posts, hoping to raise their status and encourage Protestant conversions. From the brave young officer he had been in the 1650s, however, James had become a weak old man, whose nosebleeds may have been symptoms of mini-strokes. He repeatedly displayed what Racine in *Athalie* (1691) would call:

> Cet esprit de vertige et d'erreur,
> De la chute des rois funeste avant-coureur.

> ('That spirit of panic and error,
> Fatal warning of the fall of kings.')

Louis himself had contributed to James II's downfall. The Revocation, and the preceding *dragonnades*, not only filled England with Huguenots denouncing Louis, but also showed the horrors which a proselytizing Catholic monarch could inflict on his Protestant subjects, and, to many minds, the nature of Catholicism. The Revocation weakened loyalties to James, while making it impossible for him to request assistance from Louis.[3]

In addition Louis' wars and annexations made William III eager to use England's army and navy to protect Europe from French ambitions. Without English help, he feared that Europe might be lost.[4] To use England to defeat France, he needed to replace the Stuarts. For the Stuarts, despite moments of hostility, usually reverted to a state of dependency on Louis XIV, as Charles II's treaties of 1670 and 1681 (when he recovered a French pension) had shown.

Louis XIV's old enemy van Beuningen had become burgomaster of Amsterdam in 1683. He too believed that 'without England acting powerfully alongside her, the Republic can enter into neither an open nor a cold war with France.'[5] By then, Louis XIV's brilliant Ambassador in the Netherlands the Comte d'Avaux had realized that William was hoping either to inherit or to seize the throne of England. In August 1687, d'Avaux told Louis that it was 'the principal matter he has in view'.[6] The following year, again thanks to d'Avaux, Louis would know in advance of the invitation which William had received from seven prominent Englishmen, of his naval, military and diplomatic preparations, and of his planned declaration in favour of the Parliament, laws and religion of England.[7]

If the Revocation weakened James II, it strengthened William III. Before the Revocation, thanks to d'Avaux's good relations with provincial Estates, especially in Groningen and Friesland, and with some regents of the city of Amsterdam, he could block William's attempts to expand the Dutch army. He was also helped by the favourable trade terms granted by France in 1678, when Colbert was alive. In those years, some Dutchmen preferred Louis XIV, who favoured trade, to William III, who preferred war.[8]

In August 1687, however, Louis XIV began a tariff war with the Netherlands. The herrings the Dutch exported to France would henceforth, he decreed, have to be salted in France with French salt. Dutch commercial interests, and the Amsterdam city council, became more anti-French. Commercial concessions to the Netherlands, which d'Avaux urged and which Louis XIV had willingly made in 1678, he now called 'a weakness little suited to my dignity'.[9]

The birth of a Catholic prince of Wales in London on 22 June 1688 was celebrated by James II's Ambassador in Paris Bevis Skelton with fireworks, fountains of wine, a concert and a banquet.[10] In England, however, Protestants were alarmed. Despite many Protestant eyewitnesses in the Queen's bedchamber in St James's Palace, rumours spread that he had been smuggled in a warming-pan by Jesuits into his mother's bed: hence his later title the 'Old Pretender'. One source was the King's daughter Princess Anne, then known as the Princess of Denmark as she had married Prince George of Denmark in 1682. She resented the arrival of a healthy Catholic half-brother for three reasons: as a Protestant; as a half-sister, whose place in the order of succession he demoted; and as a mother, whose own children were either stillborn or short-lived. She had already eliminated another half-brother, the Duke of Cambridge, in 1682, by accidentally giving him smallpox with a kiss. The letter sent, at William's insistence, by seven leading Englishmen on 10 July inviting him to invade England claimed 'not one in a thousand' of the population believed the Prince of Wales genuine.[11]

Acting both as (in theory) sovereign prince of Orange and as captain general and admiral general of the Netherlands, from July 1688 William began to assemble a fleet and an army in the port of Amsterdam. By 24 August 1688 d'Avaux, who had informers in the Amsterdam city council, the States General and William's household, was certain that William's expedition was directed against England not, as had been rumoured, the pirates of Algiers. On 9 September d'Avaux appeared before the States General and warned them that Louis XIV would regard an attack on James II as an attack upon himself.

Despite warnings from French and English diplomats, James refused to believe that William, his nephew and son-in-law, was preparing to invade.

On 4 September the French diplomat Bonrepaus, sent by Louis on a special mission, told him he was the only person in Europe who still rejected these reports.[12] Another reason for James II's disbelief was the apparent folly of transporting an army across the North Sea and the Channel. The dangers of such an attempt had been shown by the dispersion of the Spanish Armada by storms and enemy action a hundred years earlier to the month. News of the projected invasion would cause the second worst crash of the century on the Amsterdam stock market, after that triggered by the French invasion in 1672.[13] It ruined van Beuningen, who had advocated the expedition to England which caused it; he died deranged in 1693.

Between 7 and 10 September, as d'Avaux's spies informed him, William met his uncle the Elector of Brandenburg in secret, as guests of their mutual relation the Duke of Hanover at Minden. William prepared his alliances with German princes, in order to invade England, as sixteen years earlier in 1672 Louis and Louvois had prepared theirs, in order to invade the Netherlands. Gravel, the French envoy in Berlin, reported to Louis that German princes believed that William was 'the salvation of the Protestant religion' and were ready to loan him some of their regiments.[14] Troops from Brandenburg, Brunswick, Hesse-Kassel and Württemberg moved into position to guard the Netherlands from a possible French invasion, thereby calming Dutch fears and liberating Dutch forces to invade England.[15] A Dutch agreement with the Duke of Württemberg for 1,296 soldiers had already been signed on 25 July, showing how far in advance William had been planning.[16]

William III's second in command was none other than the Maréchal de Schomberg, whom he had selected because Schomberg alone was of sufficient rank and reputation to be a suitable commander-in-chief if William was killed or wounded. Moreover, with an English mother, he was half English. In September, after their meeting with William, the new Elector of Brandenburg Frederick I and Schomberg had proceeded to Cleves. They were alarmed by the presence of French troops in Cologne and by the election of the French protégé Fürstenberg as elector of Cologne on 19 July. From Cleves Schomberg had left to join William at Nijmegen.[17]

Schomberg managed his switch of loyalties from Louis XIV to William III to his own advantage. Bargaining with both rulers to secure his financial future, Schomberg had told the French minister in Berlin M. de Gravel in August that he could not help France, because of the end of his pensions. For his part the Elector Frederick I of Brandenburg had sworn he was a solid ally of France, but had been offended that the French court had not worn mourning for his father for even a day.[18]

In his last visit to Gravel before leaving Berlin, Schomberg 'insinuated several times that the kingdom was denuded of men and money' and 'the power of the king so weakened by the departure of the Protestants'. He blamed his own departure from France on 'the bad offices which he said Madame de Maintenon had rendered him'. Frederick I told Gravel that Schomberg had agreed to serve him only on the express condition that William III could employ him when he wished. On 24 September Schomberg's French pensions were re-established, but by then he already had an agreement with William to fight Louis.[19]

Sourches commented that all Schomberg had wanted was to live peacefully in France following his own religion, as the great Admiral Abraham Duquesne had been allowed to do: 'in truth we could have shown as much consideration for him as for Duquesne.' Schomberg's motive in switching loyalties was 'in some ways to revenge himself on France with which he was not content' because of the persecution of Protestants.[20]

Meanwhile, rejecting d'Avaux's offer of Louis' support, James II with his ministers declared that he was 'too great to need a foreign protection' and recalled his Ambassador from Paris. Only on 17 September did James finally accept that William was about to invade.[21]

Even then James refused French help. Instead he offered an alliance to the Netherlands, summoned a new Parliament and revoked most of his measures against the privileges of the Church of England. Thinking that James and his ministers were bewitched, Louis wrote to d'Avaux on 7 October, 'we could have easily dispersed all the [Dutch] forces if my vessels joined to those of the King of England had been ready to attack the fleet when she was at sea or in the Thames, but there is nothing to do now but to await events.'[22]

Louis, like James, had also acted against his own best intersts. Orange was the hereditary principality next to the papal territory of Avignon which gave William III the status of a sovereign prince 'by the grace of God'. Instead of allowing it to remain in William's possession, and thereby act as a French bargaining counter, Louis had annexed it in 1682. Three years later, to William's dismay, all Protestant churches in Orange were demolished by French troops. Dynastic status was almost as important to William as the Protestant faith. One of Louis' ambassadors later wrote, 'nor can anybody be more jealous than he [William III] is of everything relating to his rank.'[23]

Louis' trade war also made him enemies in the Netherlands. From July 1688 d'Avaux had warned the King of Dutch fears that he intended to destroy their religion 'and above all their commerce'. If he had stopped his trade war, the States General and the city of Amsterdam might not have supported William III's expedition.[24]

As a counter-measure, d'Avaux urged Louis either to invade the Spanish Netherlands or Liège, or to make trade concessions.[25] Instead on 27 September, by one of the great strategic errors of his reign, Louis launched an attack across the Rhine. French troops took Mainz on 17 October and the imperial fortress of Philippsburg on 29 October, soon followed by other cities on the Rhine: Speyer, Worms and Mannheim.[26] As in 1667 he was helped by claims arising from a royal marriage; in this case the claim, manufactured by French royal lawyers, of his sister-in-law the Duchesse d'Orléans to half the Palatinate, and family treasures, after the death of her brother the Elector Palatine in 1685. (In the Palatinate the war is still called the 'Orleansche Krieg'.)[27]

In his proclamations Louis also spoke of the necessity of recognition by the Emperor of the French candidate Fürstenberg as elector of Cologne; and of turning the truce of 1684 into a permanent peace with formal Imperial recognition of French sovereignty over all gains made since 1678.[28] D'Avaux commented sourly from The Hague on the French attack on the Rhine: 'never has any news made the Prince of Orange happier.'[29]

On 27 September 1688 Louis also impounded all Dutch ships and sailors in French ports, thereby removing Dutch merchants' last hesitations about supporting the invasion of England.[30] Dutch support for William was reinforced by news that Dutch sailors in French ports, if they refused to convert to Catholicism, were being sent to the galleys, embittering opinion 'to a point that I cannot describe', d'Avaux wrote to Louis.[31] Louis had alienated, while failing to intimidate, the Dutch. The sermons of Huguenot ministers had also strengthened Dutch support for the invasion of England, and the return of Protestants to France.[32] The city of Amsterdam had already agreed to give support. On 29 September the States of Holland and on 8 October the States General of the Netherlands did likewise.[33]

The real reasons for Dutch military and financial support for the invasion were fear of France, and fear of a pro-French Elector of Cologne (whom some French officials hoped to turn into a French tributary). Grand strategy was more important than religion or nationality. In July 1688 the ultra-Catholic Emperor Leopold I would renew his alliance with the ultra-Protestant William III, whom in early 1689 he would recognize as king of England, since both opposed Louis XIV. The Anglo-Austrian alliance, pivot of European coalitions against France until 1815, began in 1688 thanks to Louis XIV.[34]

Louis XIV had three motives for invading the Rhineland rather than the Netherlands. First his passion for expansion on the Rhine. Second his fear of Austria – which conquered the great Ottoman fortress city of

Belgrade on 6 September 1688. In reply to d'Avaux's plea for an attack on the Netherlands, he wrote that it would have taken too long to besiege the cities of Flanders. He wanted to conquer 'all the other cities and forts on the Rhine' before the end of the year: 'the necessity [sic] to prevent the evil designs of the court of Vienna did not leave me any other choice than that which I have made and which appeared to me the most suitable.'[35] He also wanted to oblige the Emperor to make a permanent peace recognizing all French *réunions* since 1678.

Perhaps the most important reason for his attack on the Rhine was his fear that the Empire might defeat or make peace with the Ottoman Empire, thereby weakening the French–Ottoman alliance and releasing Imperial armies to fight France on the Rhine. In a public '*Mémoire* of the reasons which have obliged the King to take up arms again', he claimed that, despite his own 'desire for public tranquillity', he was 'forced' to fight owing to the 'plan which the Emperor has long formed to attack France as soon as he has made peace with the Turks'.[36] In other words he felt obliged to make what today would be called a 'pre-emptive strike'.

Throughout the summer and autumn of 1688 Louis XIV had been receiving letters from Pierre de Girardin, his Ambassador to the Ottoman Empire, warning him of its impending collapse. Troops were unpaid, provinces in revolt. The Grand Vizier threatened to make peace with 'the Imperials' (Austria) since it was 'the unique remedy' for the Ottoman Empire's troubles.[37] Girardin wrote on 26 May that 'the contempt the militias and the people have conceived for the Sultan is increasing daily. If the Imperials advance as far as Constantinople, the route to which is open to them, nothing can guarantee this empire from total ruin.'[38]

At times the Ambassador, who helped organize the capital's grain supply despite Venetian attempts to blockade it, thought the Turks were so frightened they would leave Constantinople. Shops had shut. The city was 'a veritable desert'. Only beggars were left.[39] In October he prophesied that, through either 'internal revolutions' or external attacks, 'the fall and entire decadence of the Ottoman Empire is inevitable'.[40] He was told to follow the Grand Seigneur (the Sultan) if he withdrew to Asia.[41]

That summer the Ottoman government in effect blackmailed Louis, threatening to make peace with Austria even under the most unfavourable conditions unless he made war in Europe. It accused him of staying on the Rhine, 'with his arms folded', when he could win great advantages over Austria.[42] On 10 September Louis replied by promising to march his troops towards the Rhine and Italy.[43]

On 15 October he boasted to Girardin that his armies had mastered the entire course of the Rhine from Cologne to Basel, including most of the Palatinate: 'there is a general war in Europe,' from which the Turks should profit either by making a favourable peace or by recovering territory in Hungary.[44] On 2 December he told his Ambassador to 'use this information adroitly to stop the Turks precipitating a peace which in reality [sic] would be much more damaging to Christendom than to the Ottomans by giving the House of Austria the means to increase its power and ruin the Catholic states and the great sees of Germany'.[45] He wanted the Ottoman Empire to attack Hungary but to make peace with Poland. Austria's alliance with Protestant powers legitimized his own with the Ottoman Empire.[46] Louis denied even to his own diplomats that he wanted 'to excite the Turks against the Emperor', but continually did so.[47]

Thus the Danube, the Rhine, the Bosphorus and the Channel flowed into each other. Louis may, in secret, have welcomed William III's invasion of England. A civil war in England, which he believed would occupy William and Dutch forces for a long time, would facilitate French conquests on the Rhine. Louis overestimated James's support, and underestimated English anti-Catholicism.

That autumn, as Louis XIV began his hunting season – riding with the ladies of his court through the forest of Fontainebleau en cavalcade – William III continued to expand his forces. His army – possibly as many as 21,000 strong, larger, better trained and better armed than James II's – was truly European. It included 3,700 English and Scots troops in Dutch service, Dutch, Germans, Danes, Swedes, 800 Huguenot officers and 200 Africans from Surinam.[48]

Louis, meanwhile, had alienated the Pope as well as the Emperor. He complained in a letter to Cardinal d'Estrées of the Pope's prejudice against France and 'his natural leaning to the House of Austria'.[49] The old quarrel over diplomatic immunities revived. The entry into Rome on 25 November 1687 of the new French Ambassador, M. de Lavardin, with 700 guards had been deliberately provocative. The Pope refused to confirm Fürstenberg as elector of Cologne or the King's nominations to French bishoprics; he prepared to place France under an interdict and secretly excommunicated Louis. Louis for his part considered an invasion of the Papal States. Even if James II had deigned to request French help, he would have found that most of the French fleet was far away in the Mediterranean, preparing to attack Rome. The French navy had, in any case, been weakened by lack of investment. From 1685 to 1687 14 million livres had been spent on Versailles, Saint-Cyr and the Invalides, but only 7 million on the navy.

In France in the first days of November 1688 people cried for joy at news that 'all the Rhine' was in French hands, and that the Dauphin was 'adored' by his troops.[50] Then on 11 November, after one false start, the Dutch fleet, 463 ships in all, sailed in a convoy 20 miles long from the Netherlands for England. The elements – in the form of 'the Protestant wind' blowing down the Channel – favoured William III. James II's fleet under the Earl of Dartmouth suffered from contradictory orders and disloyal officers, and thought the Dutch would land near the Thames.[51] The convoy advanced unopposed down the Channel and on 15 November William landed at Brixham near Torbay in Devon.

William slowly advanced on London, gathering support as he went – while denying, with no less hypocrisy than Louis denying his Ottoman alliance, that he had any intention of deposing James II. Thousands of copies of his Declaration asserted that he wanted only to preserve 'the Protestant religion' and 'the laws and liberties of England' by calling 'a free parliament', elected 'according to the laws of England', and to investigate the birth of the 'alleged' Prince of Wales.

James's officers coordinated their desertion with William's advance. On 3 December James's general John Churchill led 400 other officers and troopers, including the King's son-in-law Prince George of Denmark and the dukes of Grafton and Ormonde, over to William's side. Churchill's treason had been planned since at least the spring of 1687, before the birth of the Prince of Wales. James's daughter Princess Anne also joined the rebellion.[52]

Louis thought James should stand and fight. He had written to his Ambassador Barillon on 1 November 1688, 'the more a king shows greatness of soul in peril, the more he strengthens the loyalty of his subjects. Let the King of England show the intrepidity which is natural to him and he will render himself redoubtable to his enemies.'[53]

However, James II failed as a king as he failed as a general. He had lost his youthful courage and was frightened that he would be deposed and killed like other kings of England, Richard II, Henry VI and his own father. Unlike William of Orange, he was not prepared 'to die in the last ditch'. On the night of 20/21 December James II, in the first of three flights between 1688 and 1690, fled London by boat disguised as a servant, dropping the Great Seal of England into the Thames as he left, believing that government would thereby come to a halt. In his absence London briefly fell into the hands of rioters, who sacked Catholic ambassadors' chapels.

James had written on 20 December to his commander-in-chief Louis de Duras, Earl of Feversham, who had proved as useless on land as his naval commander Dartmouth on sea, telling him not to resist 'a foreign army and poisoned nation'. Feversham resigned that day, formally disbanding James's army, to try to prevent more desertions to William.[54] To fill the power and military vacuum, and lessen panic, on 22 December a group of thirty peers met in the Guildhall and Whitehall, to show that they represented both city and court. They included the two archbishops and the Earl of Halifax (whose son had married a granddaughter of Louis XIV's Protestant banker Barthélemé d'Herwarth). They invited William III to London. Their position as peers of the realm and privy councillors gave them natural authority in the state as power-brokers which many French nobles would have envied. James was arrested by a group of fishermen at Faversham on the Kent coast, where he had been trying to flee to France. After four days of humiliating imprisonment, he was escorted back to London on 26 December by Life Guards sent by the peers. Londoners rang church bells, lit bonfires and cheered his return.[55]

William had arrived at Windsor on 24 December. The army changed sides. William Blathwayt, as secretary at war, and Churchill, as commander of the guards regiments and lieutenant general of William III's army, began to take his orders, and to purge the army of James II's supporters.[56] At 8 p.m. on 27 December, 6,800 troops from William's Dutch guards, and his English and Scottish regiments, entered London under his cousin Count Heinrich von Solms-Braunfels. As they took control of Whitehall (where some remained until 1698), on James II's orders the English guards on duty did not resist.[57] At 1 p.m. on 28 December James II again left Whitehall. He said that he did not know who were worse, the Dutch guards or his own. A few courtiers and his illegitimate son by Churchill's sister Arabella, the Duke of Berwick, accompanied him by boat down the Thames (the route chosen by William to prevent his uncle being cheered in the street) to Rochester, on the Kent coast.[58]

Meanwhile on the night of 19/20 December James II's wife Mary of Modena, with the Prince of Wales, had also fled London in disguise. James II was so distrustful of his own subjects and fearful of 'the Rabble' that, to escort his wife and son to France, he had chosen Louis XIV's former favourite Lauzun, who had arrived in England in mid-October, on a mission from Seignelay, Minister of the Marine.

On 20 December Mary of Modena, with the Prince of Wales, Lauzun and a few courtiers, sailed from Gravesend on the Kent coast, landing at Calais the following day. The haste and secrecy of the flights of James II and his wife show their awareness of their unpopularity. James later deplored 'so general a defection in my Army as well as in the nation amongst all sorts of people'.[59]

On Mary of Modena's journey from Calais to Saint-Germain, she was received according to the etiquette established for queens of England visiting France since the arrival of Henrietta Maria in 1644.[60] On 6 January

1689 Louis went in state with his court and guards, in a procession of a hundred carriages, as far as Chatou to greet her. Back in Saint-Germain he was impatient to see Lauzun, saying, 'Enter M. de Lauzun, you have only friends here'; they spent an hour talking together. As Madame de Sévigné wrote to her daughter, in yet another dramatic reversal of fortune Lauzun had returned to Versailles through London. He recovered his *grandes entrées*, and became one of the principal advisers of James II (and later of his son 'James III') in exile. Finally, in 1692, at the request of Mary of Modena, Lauzun, already created a Knight of the Garter by James II, would achieve his lifelong ambition to be made a duke by Louis XIV. Mademoiselle, whom he had abandoned in 1684, was infuriated.[61]

James spent five days in Rochester, in the house of the Mayor, Sir Richard Head, waiting for 'the Nation's eyes' to be opened. He received courtiers and letters from London; but preferred flight abroad.[62] His request for a refuge in the Spanish Netherlands was refused by the Governor General. At midnight on 1/2 January, without telling most of his servants and courtiers, James II left the house (now Abdication House, 69 High Street) by the backstairs, down to a waiting boat, with Berwick and his Master of the Robes, Richard Hamilton. He sailed to France in the morning, landing at Ambleteuse near Boulogne on 2 January, and reaching Saint-Germain, as we have seen, on 7 January.[63]

Meanwhile at 4 p.m. on 28 December, with Schomberg beside him in the carriage, William III had entered Westminster, while crowds waved oranges on sticks, crying 'An Orange! an Orange!' At the peers' request, William III formally took over the government of the kingdom. Plans for an investigation into 'the forgery of the belly' (the birth of the Prince of Wales) were dropped: the lie had served its purpose.[64]

On 13 February William III and Mary II, Louis XIV's greatest enemy and his wife, were proclaimed king and queen. England, an ally of France for most of the previous hundred years, from Elizabeth I to Charles II, had changed sides. Even before his formal accession, William had begun to send British and Irish regiments out of London and to summon more Dutch troops to Britain. He also sent British troops (many of whom mutinied) to defend the Netherlands, on which Louis XIV had already declared war in November.[65]

Most of Ireland still acknowledged James II's authority, and in March 1689 Louis despatched James there with French troops. James might have preferred to go to Scotland or to remain in France, hunting and attending mass.[66] Louis, however, wanted him in Ireland for French strategic reasons, even urging him to treat his Protestant subjects there as well as possible. His main advisers were Louis' Ambassador the Comte d'Avaux; Lauzun, whom James made captain general of his forces; and the Lord Lieutenant of Ireland, Richard Talbot, Duke of Tyrconnell and Marlborough's brother-in-law.[67]

James's arrival in Ireland, as well as news of the devastation of the Palatinate (see below, p. 346), increased English enthusiasm for war with Louis, which William declared on 17 May, and which he is said to have urged from the first day of his reign.[68] Already on 12 May William had signed a formal alliance with the Emperor Leopold I, intended to deprive Louis of all his conquests since 1659, and – because King Carlos II was childless and unhealthy – to ensure the succession of the House of Austria to the entire Spanish monarchy.

James II showed the same *esprit de vertige et d'erreur* in Ireland as in England. William III's army, in which some of the best troops were Huguenots, was commanded by Schomberg. Four years after bidding farewell to Louis XIV in Versailles, Schomberg had become an English duke, colonel of two English regiments, master general of the Ordnance and recipient of a salary of £10,000 a year and £100,000 compensation for his lost French estates. According to his Whig friend Gilbert Burnet, he also claimed that Louis lacked 'true judgement'. There was no way of dealing with him 'but by most abject flattery'; 'the chief maxim he has is to put nothing to hazard.'[69]

On campaign in 1690, however, many heard William, disappointed by Schomberg's generalship, cursing that he had paid too much for the marshal.[70] On 1 July, as he was trying to cross the Boyne to rally his troops, Schomberg, identifiable by his blue Garter ribbon, was shot dead by a French soldier, with the words 'So it is you, you old bugger.'[71] His sons continued to serve William III.

William fought at the Boyne with characteristic bravery. Perhaps encouraged by Lauzun, James II fled so fast from the battlefield that he was called in Gaelic 'Seamas an Chaka', 'James the shitter', because he was believed to have dirtied his breeches in fright. Four days later, after seventeen months in Ireland, he sailed for France.[72] The last French and Irish troops were evacuated following the Treaty of Limerick in 1691. Stiff anti-Catholic laws, including the theoretical prohibition of Catholic priests and Catholic worship, ensured Protestant and English domination of Ireland after 1690.[73] In Ireland as in France and England, the chasm between Protestants and Catholics had deepened.

James II returned dejected to Saint-Germain. Louis XIV felt sceptical about the extent of support in England for a king of whose 'excessive indulgence and irresolution in all the most important affairs' he himself had complained to the Comte d'Avaux in 1689, and whom in 1688 he had considered bewitched.[74] Nevertheless he allowed French policy to be distorted by his devotion to kingship and Catholicism, and committed French resources to invasion plans in 1692 and 1696. On both occasions James II and a large French and Irish force assembled on the French coast.[75] English control of the Channel thwarted both invasions. Incapable of blaming their repeated failures on her husband, her host or her religion, Mary of Modena preferred to attribute them to what she called 'almost supernatural mischances'.[76]

What remained was 'our court at Saint-Germain', in the Vieux Château abandoned by Louis since 1682, where James had already stayed between 1649 and 1652. The Stuarts had then been far less generously funded by the French government than they were from 1689.[77] The King and Queen each now employed a household of about ninety. James II's Secretary of State, James Drummond, Earl (later Duke) of Melfort, lived in the former apartment of Madame de Montespan; the Prince of Wales occupied the Dauphin's. Of two Jennings sisters who had been the toasts of the court of Charles II, Frances, Duchess of Tyrconnell served Mary of Modena as lady of the bedchamber at Saint-Germain; Sarah, later Duchess of Marlborough, was mistress of the robes to Anne, Princess of Denmark at Whitehall.[78]

James II maintained, in addition to his own household, a chapel with Italian musicians; medallists (Jacobite medals usually showed the effigy of the exiled King with the inscription 'Unica salus', or 'The only hope'); a lord chancellor and secretary of state; his own army of Irish regiments; a herald; and, at sea, Jacobite privateers to whom he issued letters of authorization. Louis XIV paid for almost everything, including the furniture in the palace.[79] The total number attached to the court, including courtiers' servants, was about 1,000. They learnt French, and often entered French service and took French nationality, but for many decades retained ambitions and connections across the Channel.[80]

The number of visits between the two courts suggests that Louis enjoyed having other crowned heads with whom to talk and hunt, especially Mary of Modena, whose mother, one of Mazarin's nieces, he had known as a boy. Louis treated the Prince of Wales and his sister Louise Marie – born in 1692 and known as 'la Consolatrice' – as his own children. If Louis had not liked the Stuarts, he would not have continued to fund them, nor refused to consider their expulsion during negotiations with William.[81]

Although the journey from Saint-Germain to Versailles took roughly two hours, the two royal families met on no fewer than 548 occasions

from 1689 to 1715, about every two weeks, Bernard Blasselle has calculated, including 193 visits by Louis to Saint-Germain. The English royal
family went 303 times to Versailles or Marly (which was nearer) and made
fourteen long, autumn visits to Fontainebleau. Louis XIV and the ladies
of the court would wait for the English court on their horses at the edge
of the forest of Fontainebleau, for James II and Mary of Modena were
usually late. They heightened Fontainebleau's *air de cour*, bringing, Madame de Maintenon complained, a 'redoublement de plaisirs': hunts,
concerts, card parties, Appartement. Fifty magnificently dressed ladies
attended Mary of Modena's morning toilette. As Saint-Simon wrote:
'nothing equalled the attention, the respect nor the politeness of the King
for them, nor the air of majesty and gallantry with which, every time, it
took place.'[82] If Mary of Modena felt ill, the King called twice a day to
ask for news.[83] Sometimes, during a military review, he rode beside her
carriage, explaining the troops.[84] James often accompanied the King to
reviews or ceremonies, and handed French princes their shirt on their
wedding night.[85]

Another reason for Louis' 'respect and politeness' was his desire for
applause. Mary of Modena said that, by his hospitality, he had made her
forget her misfortunes. James declared Louis to be the greatest gentleman,
as well as the greatest king, in the world.[86] Madame de Sévigné said Louis'
hospitality to James was 'in the image of the Almighty'; 'the beautiful soul
of the King enjoys playing this great part.'[87] Perhaps he felt that the presence of another anointed king added prestige and sanctity to his court.
James II frequently touched for the King's Evil at Saint-Germain.

The envoy of Mary of Modena's brother the Duke of Modena, however,
was appalled by James: 'he lives always surrounded by friars and talks of
his misfortunes with indifference as if he did not feel them or had never
been king. In this way he has entirely lost the respect of the French, and
those who knew him in Flanders [as a young officer] say he was quite
another man then.'[88] Madame called 'notre bon roi Jacques' 'the silliest
man I have met in my life'. He should move to Rome, where he could meet
as many priests and monks as he liked. The more she saw him, the more
she admired William III.[89] Madame de Sévigné also came to admire William III, a 'devil of a man', who 'alone puts all Europe in agitation. What
a destiny!'[90] She too despised James II: 'when you listen to him, you
immediately understand why he is here.' Courtiers called him 'a fool who
had lost three kingdoms for a mass', or 'without firing a shot in anger'.[91]

The Queen by contrast delighted Versailles. With her dark eyes, good
skin and figure, and 'perfection' of dress, she combined majesty, intelligence and good manners. Madame de Sévigné called her 'a very

self-possessed person who pleases greatly [*une personne fort posée qui plaît fort*]'.[92] She let French duchesses decide whether to be received by her in the English way – kissed, but obliged to stand; or in the French fashion – not kissed, but permitted to sit on a tabouret in her presence. They chose the latter.[93] To please Louis, French ladies 'very assiduously' paid court to Mary of Modena, at both Saint-Germain and Fontaine-bleau.[94] A queen of England suited Versailles better than Marie Thérèse or, in the eighteenth century, Marie Leszczyńska or Marie Antoinette, both of whom preferred entertaining a circle of friends to receiving the court. Implicitly criticizing his wife's memory, Louis said of Mary of Modena, 'this is how a queen should be, in both body and soul, holding her court with dignity.'[95] In time, having at first been almost a prisoner in France (Louis had given orders on 1 January 1689 not to let her leave, were James to summon her back to England), she came to dominate the Jacobite government, and to influence Louis more than his ministers desired.[96]

Mary also became a friend of Madame de Maintenon. One hundred and forty-five letters from the Queen survive, repeatedly assuring her 'best of friends' of her love and gratitude: 'wherever I am, I will be yours with all my heart to the end of my life': 'God has chosen you to do good to everyone.'[97] Maintenon always supported the Stuarts, even admiring their English style of wrapping babies loosely in swaddling clothes, rather than 'wrapped tightly in their mess like ours'.[98]

The Stuarts were popular in France. At this stage, the deposition of James II and the rise of Parliament inspired more revulsion than admiration (except in Madame, who wrote that no one had a right to call William an usurper, as the English people had called him to the throne).[99] William III's efforts to present himself as a liberator, who would free the French nobility and the Parlements from their chains, and 'relieve the people', had no more effect in the 1690s than in the 1670s.[100] In 1690 rumours of his death provoked joyful demonstrations throughout France, even in the courtyards of Versailles.[101] Louis and his officials were dismayed by what they called the 'insolence' and 'extravagances' of 'the people'. Twelve years later, when William was about to die, with his very long memory and revulsion for all popular demonstrations, however patriotic, the King took measures in advance to prevent similar 'extravagances', even among Jacobites. 'His Majesty intends that his will on this matter should be totally executed,' wrote the Minister of the Household to d'Argenson, Lieutenant de Police de Paris.[102]

The Jacobites were regarded, like the Free French in England in 1940, as gallant if occasionally exasperating friends in a world of enemies. The French clergy, whose assemblies met in the neighbouring Château Neuf of Saint-Germain, sent James II subsidies, and deputations extolling his virtues and prophesying his restoration. James II often visited Paris churches, made retreats to the exceptionally ascetic monastery of La Trappe in Normandy, and practised mortification of the flesh with 'an Iron Chain with little sharp points which pierced his skin'.[103] After his death some Parisians regarded him as a saint.

Behind Louis' façade of Catholic and monarchical solidarity, he may also have used the Stuarts as a means to pursue his long-term plan to divide England, Scotland and Ireland. Already in 1687 he had corresponded with the Lord Lieutenant of Ireland Richard Talbot privately through the Minister of the Marine, not through diplomatic channels, over plans to make Ireland and Scotland independent, if William succeeded to the English throne.[104] In England Louis was regarded as a tyrant, in Scotland and Ireland (and Hungary) as a potential liberator.

In contrast to James himself, the Jacobite diaspora proved almost as energetic as its adversary the Huguenot 'Refuge'. The stimulus of exile gave members of both groups more unusual careers than they might have enjoyed at home. Forty thousand Jacobites provided France with partial compensation for the loss of 130,000 Huguenots. The Jacobites' arrival, coupled with most Huguenots' decision to conform to Catholicism – at least outwardly – and remain in France, and the continued arrival of foreign Catholics to work in France (half the great 'French' furniture makers of the eighteenth century were German), ameliorated the impact of the Revocation on the French economy.[105]

The Stuart court and army, together with the galaxy of English, Scottish and Irish convents, monasteries and colleges established in France since the Reformation – such as the English Augustinians and Benedictines, 'the Blue Nuns of the Immaculate Conception', the Dames Anglaises, the Collèges des Irlandais and des Ecossais and many others – created an alternative England, Scotland and Ireland in France.[106] In Paris Jacobites congregated on the left bank, in the rue de Buci, the rue Jacob and the rue Saint-Jacques. The need to 'contain' their 'tumults', and end their scandals, was henceforth a regular item in the King's and ministers' instructions to the Lieutenant de Police de Paris.[107] In 1705 on the King's initiative, the Lieutenant de Police d'Argenson wrote to Mr Caryll, the Jacobite Secretary of State, 'the officers of police of Paris are more and more embarrassed by the large number of English who come there and stay there in complete freedom as if we were in the most profound peace.' After taking Mary of Modena's orders, an English priest should make a list of all 'faithful English' and 'suspect English' in Paris.[108]

Louis XIV's 'politeness' and 'attention' to the exiled Stuarts in France did not extend to their Protestant followers, about 10 per cent of the total. The proportion would have been higher if Louis had not told James and Mary he did not want them. Until his death, they were refused permission to hold services, including funerals (they had to be buried in fields). Yet again the King was more Catholic than the Pope, who had begun to relax restrictions on Protestant worship and burial in Rome. Louis personally expelled from Saint-Germain Dean Granville, a friend and adviser of James and Mary, who held Anglican 'assemblies', although the Queen protested that he was an 'homme de qualité', attached to the rightful King.[109] Louis XIV's intolerance and the Stuarts' ostentatious Catholicism in France harmed their cause in England and Scotland, where few realized that James II continued to believe in freedom of worship.[110]

The connection with Louis harmed the Jacobites at home, but helped their careers abroad. The Irish regiments (of Berwick, Clare, Dillon, Tyrconnell and others), the legendary 'wild geese', fought under flags inscribed 'Semper et ubique fidelis': 'Always and everywhere faithful'. In the 1690s there were 6,000 Irish troops in the French army and about 18,000 in James II's army in exile: organized by the King, who issued the officers' commissions, but ultimately under the control of the French Ministry of War.[111] After the peace of 1697, when Louis dismissed many of his French regiments, he did not dismiss the Irish, as a result of James's personal plea.[112]

In their red uniforms, a legacy of their Stuart origins, they would help win battles for France, at Cremona in 1702, Almanza in 1707 and Fontenoy in 1745. They paraded their loyalty to the Stuarts. In reality many were professional soldiers who would have chosen careers in the French army even if the Stuarts had stayed on the throne. Louis' army in the 1660s had already included four Irish and two Scottish regiments.[113]

Like the Huguenots, Jacobites influenced their new homeland. Anthony Hamilton, brother of James II's Master of the Robes, had served in the armies of Louis XIV and James II. In 1705–6, while living at Saint-Germain, Anthony Hamilton wrote *Mémoires du Comte de Gramont*, subtitled *Intrigues amoureuses de la cour d'Angleterre*. He pretended they were by his brother-in-law Philibert de Gramont, a French courtier described by Saint-Simon as a rabid dog with the freedom to say anything to the King about anyone, even about his ministers; Gramont's wife was also one of Louis' favourites.[114] The memoirs criticized the pious 1700s when, as Hamilton complained, courtiers spent half the day either praying or pretending to pray, from the perspective of the pleasure-loving 1660s. Like Madame de La Fayette, Hamilton depicted courtiers, both in France and England (which he considered similar in their elegance and love of pleasure), as dominated by emotions rather than ambitions. James, Duke of York's affair with Arabella Churchill, after she fell off a horse and revealed some of her attractions, was in contrast to the saintly way of life he had since adopted. Much admired for their concise, mocking style, the memoirs were frequently reprinted after publication in 1713.[115]

Written in French by an Irishman, the *Mémoires du Comte de Gramont* were translated into English a year later by a Huguenot, Abel Boyer. Both diasporas transmitted the culture of the country they had fled. Both also spread the subversive craft of freemasonry. Jacobites helped found the first masonic lodge in Paris in 1726, nine years after the first lodge had been established in England, with the help of Dr J. T. Desaguliers, a Huguenot from La Rochelle, who in England had become an Anglican preacher, lecturer to George I and his court in experimental philosophy and deputy grand master of the freemasons.[116]

In 1685–9 both France and England had become more monolithic. The flight of Huguenots from France, and Jacobites from England, made France more Catholic, England more Protestant, and both more hostile to each other. Incited by the two diasporas, the second Hundred Years War had begun.

18

France against Europe

'Ultima ratio regum', 'The final argument of kings', was the motto often inscribed on Louis XIV's massive bronze cannon, below the royal crown and coat of arms of three fleurs-de-lys. By 1688 the King owned at least 13,000 cannon: examples can be seen in the courtyard of the Invalides today. They were not only his 'final argument', but often his first argument too.[1] It was not (as commonly stated) Voltaire but Louis XIV's principal secretary, the Président Rose, who first wrote, 'God is on the side of the big squadrons and the big battalions against the small ones, and the same for armies.'[2]

In September 1688, when Louis decided to attack the Rhineland, his armed forces were at their peak. One of his officers, M. de La Colonie, remembered: 'nothing was talked about any more except war and the entire youth of the kingdom displayed such a great spirit of emulation that it dreamt only of following the torrents of the new levies that were being raised every day.'[3] From 20 November, tax registers were used as a means of finding one recruit (in theory) for every 2,000 livres of *taille* paid by a parish. In practice soldiers were recruited mainly through the attractions of enlistment 'bounties' and, as the economic situation worsened, regular supplies of food.[4] The provincial militias, reformed and strengthened by Louvois, provided another source of recruits for the army. A feudal 'ban' summoned nobles to arms, although they often commuted military service by paying higher taxes;[5] By 1693, the army reached around 320,000 men and 20,000 officers.[6]

Louvois, high in royal favour, had continued his modernization of the army. He was unusually hard-working, even for a minister of Louis XIV, and was helped by no more than thirty officials, working from rooms in the Hôtel de la Surintendance in Versailles, for he was also, after the death of Colbert, Surintendant des Bâtiments.[7] Systems of pay and promotion by seniority had been standardized. Regiments of carabiniers were introduced after 1680. By the 1690s around 160 barracks had been built, hospitals improved and uniforms standardized; the King's guards and personal regiments like the Régiment du Roi wore blue, line troops grey, the Swiss Guards red.[8] By 1705 muskets and pikes had been replaced by guns with bayonets. Officers were severely punished, or imprisoned, if caught diverting their soldiers' pay or rations to themselves.[9]

The Brandenburg Ambassador Ezechiel Spanheim, who won the reputation of being the most intelligent and erudite diplomat in Paris, admired the size, discipline and obedience of the army, and the excellence of the frontier forts. However, he knew that the navy was weak, and French cannon badly made. France had no allies, and had been weakened by the Huguenots' flight. He believed that Louvois had instilled in Louis a fatal overestimation of the power of France and the weakness of its enemies, and foretold defeat.[10] Without knowing of Louis XIV's promises to the Ottoman government, Spanheim wrote that war was undertaken in 1688 'de gaieté de coeur': it was not only cruel and unjust, but badly planned.[11]

Moreover, Louis XIV's army had become a machine for destruction. Spanheim called it 'more than barbarian', practising 'unexampled inhumanity'.[12] On 24 October, as William III was about to invade England, Chamlay, Louis' unofficial chief of staff, wrote to Louvois, who had already made a similar suggestion: 'I would dare to propose to you something that perhaps will not be to your taste, that is the day after we take Mannheim [in the Palatinate, which fell on 12 November] I would put the city to the sword and plough it under.'[13] The King and Louvois agreed. The immediate aim was to create beyond the French frontier a protective belt of territory which had been subjected to so much devastation that enemy armies gathering in the Empire would be unable to sustain themselves when they advanced to attack France. The ultimate aim was to impose the French candidate Fürstenberg as archbishop of Cologne, and in time turn the four Rhineland electorates (Mainz, Cologne, Trier and the Palatinate) into French vassals.[14]

On 15 November Louvois ordered generals in the Rhineland 'to destroy utterly [*faire bien ruiner*] the houses in a manner that not one stone stands on another'. On 13 January 1689, referring to Mannheim, he wrote, 'the King wills that all the buildings of the city be razed without leaving any structure standing,' before adding, 'His Majesty recommends that you ruin the places you leave.' Showing that these orders were unusual, Louvois insisted that they remain secret. Louis urged, without success, that Catholic churches be spared. He was not in full control of his war machine.[15]

From Düsseldorf in the north to Freiburg 200 miles to the south, Louis turned the valley of the Rhine into a vale of desolation. Cities, villages and farms in the Rhineland were burnt or blown up, their inhabitants expelled, their cattle, grain and wine seized. The cities included Koblenz, Heidelberg, Speyer, Mainz and many small towns and villages, Catholic and Protestant alike. When the inhabitants returned, they lived like savages in the cellars of their houses, if they could find them. Only two houses were left standing in the ancient medieval capital Heidelberg. The entire town had to be rebuilt, which is why visitors today see an eighteenth-century, rather than a medieval, city.[16] In March, in accordance with Louvois' orders, Mannheim too was razed to the ground. The Concordienkirche, built by the Elector Palatine in 1679 for all Christian denominations, was destroyed in the middle of a Sunday service. Anyone who tried to return, according to the French commander La Grange, was killed.[17]

Into the twentieth century local inhabitants would call a wild dog a Mélac, after the French commander who led the destruction and won a reputation for rape and hunting men with dogs. Already in 1672 he had, as he informed Luxembourg, burnt alive men, women 'and little children' in Dutch villages.[18] For his superior officers, however, as well as the King and the court, Mélac was one of the best officers in the French army, amiable and docile.[19] Saint-Simon calls him 'un bon et honnête homme, pauvre, sobre et frugal, et passionné pour le bien public'. Even Saint-Simon could be deceived by the masks men adopted far from the battlefield.[20]

Madame was appalled by the knowledge that such destruction was inflicted in her name – on the pretext that the King was claiming her inheritance in the Palatinate. Unlike the Queen, who had felt entirely French, Madame had retained a double identity. 'My name serves to ruin my fatherland,' she told the Dauphin's Governor before he left to command the army, ' . . . and one [the King] complains that I am afflicted by it, but it is stronger than I am.' She cried all night. By day she retreated to her study, seeking consolation in her medals and her spaniels.[21]

Destruction did not lessen Versailles' desire for diversion. On the Dauphin's return from the front (where he had acted, in his words, as Madame's chevalier), a ballet entitled *Le Palais de Flore* was danced in his honour at Trianon, with music by Delalande. The Princesse de Conti played Diane, Mlle de Blois Flore. 'Our spring lasts for ever,' sang the chorus.[22]

The Thirty Years War had seen similar acts of destruction. Since 1648, however, the laws of war had become stricter. The levelling of Dutch villages, and burning alive of many inhabitants, by French troops in 1672 and 1673 had been a propaganda disaster;[23] Louis' policy of 'ruin' in the Spanish Netherlands in 1683 and 1684 had been less brutal.[24]

In the Rhineland a huge area was methodically laid waste, without a declaration of war. French generals on the spot, such as Duras and Villars, were horrified. They warned Louvois of the 'terrible feelings of aversion' sweeping Europe.[25] Louis also waged war on the dead. On 31 May 1689 the tombs of the Holy Roman emperors in the Catholic cathedral of Speyer, one of the oldest in the Empire, and of the electors Palatine in the Heiliggeistkirche in Heidelberg, were opened and robbed by French soldiers.[26] The cathedral itself was mined and set alight. To make it burn better, inhabitants had been encouraged to store their possessions inside, with the promise it would not be destroyed. In the event, it burnt so quickly that French troops had to leave before they could destroy all the tombs (most tombstones can still be seen). Dangeau reported that Louis XIV later gave 100,000 livres to the Elector of Trier, claiming (falsely) that the cathedral had been set on fire against the King's orders, and despite precautions. It would not be rebuilt until the nineteenth century.[27]

The frenzy of destruction was publicized by the Dean of Speyer cathedral Heinrich Hartard von Rollingen, city councils and Palatinate officials in reports to the Reichstag of the Holy Roman Empire at Regensburg and the main German-language journal, *Theatrum Europaeum*. On 24 January 1689 the Empire declared war on France, the common enemy of all Germans, Catholic and Protestant alike. German pamphlets called on 'all Europe where we have been driven into exile' (some 'poor Palatines', as refugees from the Palatinate were called, settled in London) for 'Vengeance! Vengeance! Vengeance! for all eternity' against the French 'cannibals', or 'Turks'.[28] The 'wasting' of the Rhineland, following the persecution of the Huguenots, confirmed Europeans' view of Louis XIV as a 'new Attila'. Chamlay admitted that the Empire had never been more united than in its hatred of Louis XIV.[29] The destruction of the Palatinate was also publicized in sermons and pamphlets in England, in time to strengthen support for William III's declaration of war on Louis XIV on 17 May 1689.[30] At the same time Louis lost the support of his cousin and nephew by marriage the Duke of Savoy. Formerly a French ally who had sent regiments to serve in the French army and had allowed French garrisons on his territory, he too joined the anti-French coalition in early 1690.

Mainz on the Rhine, under siege since May 1689, was recaptured by Imperial armies, under Louis XIV's personal enemy Charles V of Lorraine, on 8 September that year, the rest of the Rhineland in 1690. The King and Louvois had failed in their aim to make the Rhineland a buffer zone protecting France. Nevertheless their action on the Rhine, by drawing away Imperial forces from attacking the Ottoman Empire in the Balkans, helped to preserve the latter, until it made peace with the Holy Roman Empire, two years after Louis, in 1699.

In 1689 French armies had been so busy wrecking the Rhineland that they had missed the opportunity to attack the Netherlands while William III was in Ireland fighting James II. In Flanders on 1 June 1690, however, the French army of about 30,000, commanded by the Maréchal de Luxembourg, won the battle of Fleurus over a British–Dutch–German force. Much of the Spanish Netherlands passed under French control. French forces behaved with more restraint than on the Rhine. No cities were burnt.

The number of enemy flags which Luxembourg sent to decorate the nave of Notre-Dame in Paris won him the name 'le tapissier de Notre-Dame', the decorator of Notre Dame. When the King was congratulated on French victories by the Prévôt des Marchands of Paris during his 1691 New Year visit to Versailles, the King tapped Luxembourg – standing beside him as *capitaine des gardes* on duty – with his cane and said, 'They are mostly due to you.'[31]

In 1691 the French besieged Mons, capital of the county of Hainaut in the Spanish Netherlands, south-west of Brussels, in a location so strategic that in 1914 it would witness the first battle between British and German armies, and in 1966 would be chosen as the site for NATO's headquarters. The King stayed in the nearby abbey of Bélian. On 14 March 1691 Dangeau wrote: 'the King is never for one moment not working.' He inspected French trenches around the city for six hours at a time and worked on political affairs in the evening.[32]

Mons had been steadily refortified since 1648. The panorama painted by J. B. Martin ('Martin des Batailles'), now at Versailles, shows the small walled city, dominated by the tallest belfry in the region (built to look out for advancing French armies), encircled by an ocean of French cannon, tents, bivouacs, in apparently perfect order. A print published by Nicholas Langlois, *La Prise de Mons capitale du Hainaut par le Roy en personne le VIII Avril*, shows the King gesturing from a trench towards the city as it is bombarded. He is surrounded by Monsieur, Chartres, the Dauphin, the Duc de Bourbon and, lying on the ground on the left, a soldier killed by a cannon ball, to prove that the King had risked his life.

French trenches went right up to the city walls. The Mousquetaires were especially brave. On 8 April the Mons garrison surrendered. From 7,000 they had been reduced to 4,500 – whereas the French had lost only about 300 men. William III called Mons 'an irreparable loss'.[33] The King was greeted at the main gate by magistrates offering him a golden key. He assured them of his clemency and esteem. In the day he inspected fortifications; in the evening he watched fireworks.[34]

As the war continued, perhaps surprised by the rapid loss of the Rhineland, Louis began to lose faith in Louvois. His brusque and arrogant manner, which did not always spare the King or other ministers, in whose work he often interfered, had made him many enemies. As with Colbert in 1683, a minister's loss of royal favour hastened his death.[35] Le Peletier, the former Controleur Général, wrote that the fall of Mainz to Imperial forces in September 1689 destroyed Louvois. 'The aversion of the King was at its culminating point.' Madame de Maintenon was believed to hate him, as he had stopped her following the King to the siege of Mons. His dismissal (some anticipated imprisonment in the Bastille) was only a question of time.[36] He died suddenly, probably having suffered a stroke after a testing audience with the King, on his commode at Versailles on 16 July 1691.[37] A few weeks later Madame wrote that she had not seen the King so cheerful for a long time.[38]

Perhaps to give the King greater personal control over the army, Louvois' son Barbezieux succeeded as war minister, at the age of twenty. He enjoyed far less influence, and took refuge in hunting and drinking. (William III commented that it was strange that Louis XIV had such a young minister and such an old mistress.)[39] Louis worked with Barbezieux many hours most days, dictating letters for the minister to write in his own name, or writing letters in his own hand.[40] Louis also wrote hundreds of letters about the war to princes, generals, army *intendants*, directly through his own secretaries, rather than through the Secretary of State for War. Many thought the King had become his own war minister.[41] He drew up plans of campaign, and selected and promoted officers himself.[42] Madame de Maintenon wrote that he was holding 'more councils than ever'. After two hours' hunting, 'when he can he returns at 6 and continues until 10 without stopping, reading, writing and dictating.' Even after supper with his daughters, he often went back to work.[43]

In his fifties, as in his youth, Louis devoted particular attention to his guards. He defended the independent power of their commanders against that of the Ministry of War, in order to reinforce his own ultimate authority.[44] In September 1691, after the death of the Colonel Général des Gardes Français the Maréchal de La Feuillade, Louis XIV himself briefly took the job, 'being very pleased to do it myself in order to regulate everything as I wish for the future' (as he had briefly acted as chancellor of France in March 1672).[45] Some letters he dictated to M. de La Cossière, one of the *premiers commis* in the Ministry of War, are twenty pages long, about marches or attacks. As he had for the construction of Versailles, he asked for 'the detail of everything which happens', and thanked M. de Boufflers, the new Colonel General, for his zeal and diligence in 'my service', defending 'my country' and 'my frontier'.[46] Gardes Français must look 'as they should to approach my person' (in other words, physically impressive). On

23 October he wrote to Boufflers: 'write now to M. de Barbezieux. I will order him to explain to you my intentions on policy in detail, reserving to do it myself on important occasions.'[47]

Louis XIV also used personal advisers, such as Vauban and Chamlay, as well as princes of his family, as his eyes and ears in his armies. For example, in 1693 the King wrote to Vauban, Surintendant Général des Fortifications de France, whom he knew well and saw often at Versailles and Marly: 'you can speak to me all the more frankly in that I will show your letter to nobody and it will remain between you and me.' In other words, once Louvois was dead, the Minister of War was bypassed.[48] Vauban wrote and spoke to Louis XIV freely; but even so he dared not send the King his *mémoire* demanding the recall of the Huguenots, asking Louvois and perhaps Madame de Maintenon to do so.[49] They too probably lacked the necessary courage.

Louis' critics, including Primi Visconti, Ezechiel Spanheim and Saint-Simon (three outsiders), said that, as supreme warlord, he hampered generals' actions in the field by micro-management from his office at Versailles. He was accused of waging 'la guerre de cabinet': the perennial cry of critics of wartime governments.[50] Nevertheless, as generals said at the time, he could be flexible, certainly less authoritarian than Louvois.[51] A capable general with a record of victories, like Luxembourg, Catinat or Villars, could resist or ignore his orders. It is not true that Louis XIV was afraid of talent. He used former *frondeurs* like Condé and Luxembourg because of their abilities, and promoted men like Vauban and Catinat, from relatively humble backgrounds, for the same reason.[52]

The King also allowed himself to be overruled. 'The King's service' was a flexible concept, leaving room for disobedience. In 1675 Turenne had sent the King a defence of disobedience in court language, where words like 'never' can mean their opposite: 'I will never disobey him except when I will believe, being far from Him, that He would reproach me, and that it would be entirely contrary to his service, were I to do things which He would not command me to do if he was on the spot.' In other words, the Marshal did what he thought best.[53]

Both Turenne and Luxembourg had been able, by their prestige and independence of spirit, to keep the King away from the scene of operations.[54] Luxembourg could also criticize the King's decisions to his face, for example about a proposed attack on Liège in 1693: 'Judge, Sire, if with many fewer troops [than suggested] it is possible to think of it.'[55]

Often generals asked the King for precise written orders, in order to escape responsibility in case of defeat. In 1691 the King wrote to Boufflers: 'I do not give you a positive order to undertake the surprise [attack] but only, if you consider it appropriate to do it, not to lose time': Boufflers did not attack.[56] In 1692 the King told Luxembourg that he sent advice only because he knew Flanders so well, from his many visits since 1654, 'and you know it even better than I, which is why I am persuaded that you will take all the measures necessary to ensure your safety.'[57]

The main difference between the King and his generals was that he considered the defence of France and the monarchy as important as victory in battle. In contrast to Napoleon or the generals of the First World War, for utilitarian rather than humanitarian reasons he preferred to preserve troops' lives, and not to take risks or fight battles on French soil. On 25 August 1692 he wrote to Luxembourg: 'the essential is that no accidents befall my army and even that there is no battle where losses [suffered by opposing armies] might be equal.'[58]

Namur in 1692 was Louis XIV's last siege. A seemingly impregnable citadel on a hill beside the town of Namur 40 miles south-east of Brussels had been fortified on the advice of 'the Dutch Vauban', Menno van Coehoorn. The siege began on 25 May. The Comte de Fiesques wrote to Madame de Maintenon that a bullet had almost killed the King, begging her 'to conjure the king to behave like a general [in reality French generals often risked their lives] and not a soldier'.[59] Despite the proximity of an army of 80,000 under William III, the city capitulated on 5 June, and the citadel on 30 June, on Vauban's advice, in order to avoid being stormed and sacked.[60] Vauban commented: 'may Heaven ensure that this August Prince always defeats his enemies with the same good fortune.'[61]

The fall of Namur was considered a French triumph. Le Peletier, however, wrote that the siege had been undertaken by Louis XIV for emotional rather than military reasons, to flatter himself: 'to show all Europe that without the help of M. de Louvois His Majesty on his own could execute a great design'.[62] Indeed Louis' own account confirms Le Peletier. He wrote that he was 'all the more satisfied by his conquest because this great expedition was entirely his own work [not Louvois']; he had undertaken it [guided] solely by his own judgement; executed it, so to say, with his own hands.' Moreover William III had not dared counter-attack.[63]

Perhaps for Louis XIV, as for many contemporaries, the purpose of war was war. France was at war for thirty-three of the fifty-four years of his personal rule after 1661. The army was by far the largest item in the French budget, usually consuming over 50 per cent of revenues, and in war years over 80 per cent.[64] The King used war as a means to expand French territory, but he also needed victories to control his subjects. A curious remark in memoirs written in the 1670s by Mademoiselle implies

that some courtiers desired French defeats, in order to be 'better welcomed' by the King.[65] Victories, on the other hand, increased the King's
prestige and his subjects' obedience. After the end of this war, he would
write in his memoirs (with the help of his historiographer Pellisson), 'for
almost four years France had been continuing a war against almost all
the powers of Europe, with a success very different from what his enemies
had expected.' To the French Ambassador in Turin he boasted that 'most
of the Princes of Europe had leagued themselves against me; from allies
they had become my enemies.' War with 'the Princes of Europe' could be
seen as an end in itself. For the King and many of his subjects, the number
of his enemies revealed his strength, rather than his unpopularity and lack
of diplomatic skills.[66]

Louis XIV even let the demands of war outweigh those of birth. In
1675 Louvois had introduced the rule of allotting military commands and
promotions by seniority, by date of entry into 'the service'. One reason for
Louis XIV's implacable dislike of the Duc de Saint-Simon, even more than
Saint-Simon's taste for inflaming precedence disputes, was his decision in
1702, at the age of twenty-seven, to leave the army. Ill-health was the
pretext. In reality, as a duke and a peer, he felt humiliated by the promotion, above himself, of men of lesser birth but greater seniority or ability.[67]
The Minister of War considered Saint-Simon a bad officer, who neglected
his regiment.[68] The King never employed him again. Saint-Simon took
revenge in his memoirs.

In 1693 Louis XIV went on campaign as usual. However, the French
war effort was weakened by his decision to fight on two fronts, in Flanders
and on the Rhine, as well as with smaller armies stationed along the Alps
and the Pyrenees. On 8 June that year, instead of continuing to focus on
Flanders, he sent troops to the Rhine, as he had in 1688 and 1690. The
decision enraged many of his officers. Luxembourg, the commander in
Flanders, wrote to the King on 22 June, as he had written to Louvois two
years earlier, that trying to do too many things at once often led to failure
in all of them. He wanted French forces concentrated under his command
in Flanders.[69]

The Dauphin was sent to the Rhine with 25,000 men but, indecisive
and a burden on the battlefield, made no gains for France. In Flanders, in
contrast, Luxembourg won another victory, at Neerwinden on 29 July. In
a letter to Monsieur, who was likely to broadcast its contents widely, the
King tried to justify himself. He wrote that progress in Flanders was
slowed by rivers and canals, while his decision to make war in the Rhineland would force his enemies to make peace. Like Richelieu before him,
he identified 'the State' with his own policies:

Finally I have yielded to the lively remonstrances which have been made to me, and to the movements of my own reason, and I have sacrificed with pleasure my taste and private satisfaction and what could most flatter me [victories in Flanders] to the good of the State, being convinced that this decision can more effectively procure the re-establishment of peace . . . You who love the State more than anyone, I am sure this decision will be to your liking.[70]

In reality there were no permanent gains on the Rhine, and peace was not made until four years later. For reasons which are unclear – age (he was fifty-five), gout, increasing workload, Madame de Maintenon – after 1693 Louis XIV never went on campaign again.

Meanwhile, French troops continued their devastation of the Rhineland even after Louvois' death, thereby showing that their brutality was as much Louis' responsibility as his minister's. On 22 May 1693 the palace of the electors Palatine on a hill above Heidelberg was mined and blown up. It was so well built that the sixteenth-century walls with their statues of Roman emperors, and German kings and electors (asserting, like the façade of Versailles, that the builders were heirs of the Roman Empire), still remain. A rival of the electors Palatine, Friedrich Ernich von Leiningen, gave a dinner for Marshal Tallard and Mélac across the river in Battenberg castle, during which they watched the palace burn. The dinner did not stop his guests burning Leiningen's own castle a few days later. Madame wrote that the King himself, who used to hate any disorder caused by his troops, admitted that he had given the orders 'to sack everything'. She blamed his cruelty on Madame de Maintenon.[71]

A dedicated soldier himself, Louis XIV ensured that most Bourbon princes served with the regiments of which they were colonel (Dauphin Cavalerie, Monsieur Infanterie, and so on). In 1689, at the age of seven, the Duc de Bourgogne, like his father the Dauphin before him, had drilled the Mousquetaires de la Garde in front of the King, later serving in the unit for a year.[72] At the Duc du Maine's first battle in 1690, which he told Madame de Maintenon he enjoyed, he was only twenty: his Governor was killed beside him.[73] In 1694 the ducs de Vendôme and du Maine were promoted in reward for their services on the battlefield. Maine became grand master of the artillery.[74] Both Orléans' son the Duc de Chartres and Maine's brother Toulouse, who started fighting at the age of thirteen, were wounded during the campaign of 1692. As bullets flew past, Toulouse said to his Governor, the Marquis d'O: 'Marquis, is that all?'[75]

One of the bravest soldiers in the family was the Prince de Conti. He was distrusted by Louis because of his service with the Imperial army and the letters mocking the King in 1685, but he often served under the Maréchal de Luxembourg. It was said that, whenever he appeared, victory swiftly followed. On 29 July 1693, after the victory of Neerwinden, Luxembourg wrote to the King, 'the princes of your house have surpassed themselves. As for me, Sire, my sole merit is to have executed your orders. You told me to attack a fortress and to fight a battle. I took the first and I won the other.'[76] Luxembourg, the idol of the army, died in January 1695. Despite repeated requests, Conti was not employed thereafter.

Louis XIV's eagerness for his family's glory did not always benefit France. In order to make him 'known to Europe', the King had given the Dauphin command of French forces on the Rhine in 1689 and 1690.[77] According to courtiers, he was popular with the troops, to whom he distributed large sums. However, in 1690 Louis XIV's military adviser Chamlay wrote to Louvois, complaining that each prince on campaign with his household consumed more fodder than an entire regiment. Of the Dauphin he wrote: 'Mgr goes out [on inspections] for too long, too often and with too much affectation,' both tiring the troops and putting himself in danger.[78] Some believed that Louis XIV discouraged generals from risking battles if his son was not present to share some of the glory.

War militarized the monarchy. In December 1689, the King had ordered silver in churches (except 'sacred vessels') and at Versailles, including the celebrated silver furniture in the Galerie des Glaces, to be melted down in order to raise money for the army. Horrified by the loss to the arts, Sourches declared that Colbert would never have allowed it.

Marly, built as a retreat from cares of state, began also to serve as a military headquarters. A barracks was built by the gates in 1689.[79] Louis XIV reviewed his guards and held manoeuvres on the fields outside the park.[80] Captured enemy flags were displayed in the salon, to impress foreign ambassadors.[81]

At Versailles in April 1693 the King, on his own initiative, founded the Order of St Louis – named after the patron saint of the French monarchy, who had died on crusade in Tunis in 1270. It was 'purely military', the edict of foundation stated, accorded to officers after ten or more years' military services, and it provided some chevaliers with a modest income from the 300,000 livres a year allotted to it.

Here again service took precedence over birth. If the recipient was not noble (up to 20 per cent of French officers were not), his Cross of St Louis ennobled him and his descendants. The King was head of the order but, despite pleas, princes of the royal family were not admitted until they had served ten years in the army.[82] Groups of chevaliers, on their knees in the

King's Grand Cabinet, swore to observe the statutes of the order, read out
by the Minister of War or the Marine. They were then knighted by the
King with his sword, embraced by him and given the cross of the order,
decorated with a portrait of St Louis hanging from a flame-coloured ribbon, with the words 'I make you Chevalier in the name of St Louis.'[83]

France continued its devastations. Showing that he had learnt nothing
from the reaction to the ravaging of the Palatinate, in August 1695 Louis
XIV ordered the bombardment of Brussels. He believed that 'tormenting'
the population would make it demand peace. He also hoped to prevent
the loss of Namur to William III and to retaliate for English bombardments of some of the Channel ports, Dieppe, Saint-Malo and Brest. As
with the siege of Namur in 1692, his true motive was to impress Europe.
'Il faut faire quelque chose d'éclat,' he wrote to the French commander,
his old friend the Maréchal de Villeroy.[84]

On 13 to 15 August 1695, after the inhabitants had been given time to
retire to surrounding hills, about a quarter of the city was destroyed, by
French cannonballs and by the fires they caused. In letters to the King,
Villeroy rejoiced over what he called 'a total conflagration of all the
city . . . the disorder we have caused in Brussels is beyond description'.
Many public and religious buildings (Louis had by now abandoned his
qualms about churches) and the city archives, as well as about 4,500 private houses, were destroyed.[85] Even French officers were shocked by the
bombardment: James II's son by Arabella Churchill, the Duke of Berwick,
compared it to the destruction of Troy.[86]

Far from being cowed, the inhabitants of Brussels remained hostile. A
pamphlet soon circulated, addressed to France by her 'humble and obedient
friend' the Devil, complaining that she had taken his job, leaving him no more
horrors to perpetrate: 'Having usurped all the princes on earth, bombarded
so many cities, you are going to take over my empire and send me further
than hell.'* The bombardment brought France no military advantage. Namur
surrendered to William III two weeks later, on 1 September 1695.

As if in retribution (as Madame believed it was, for the devastation of
the Palatinate), France was struck by a series of harsh winters, and by crop
failures, which were particularly common in the 'little ice age' which
climaxed at the end of the seventeenth century. Already in 1691, the Duc

---

* Brussels soon acquired a new Grand-Place that survives to this day, at least as impressive
as the Place des Victoires in Paris. It was rebuilt in record time, in under four years, by the
city guilds on the orders of the last Spanish Governor General of the Netherlands, Max
Emanuel, Elector of Bavaria: Arlette Smolar-Meynart, ed., *Autour du bombardement de
Bruxelles: désastre et relèvement*, Brussels, 1997.

de Bourbon had been appalled by the poverty he saw on his way to Dijon, to preside over sessions of the Estates of Burgundy. He wrote to Pont-chartrain, Minister of the Marine, 'in the villages on the road that I took I did not see a single inhabitant who did not ask me for alms.' People were dying with stomachs full of grass.[87] The curé Alexandre Dubois wrote in his diary of the terrible hunger felt by people living near Lille. Every parish had to feed its poor; 'we were truly tired of being alive.'[88] Hospitals were besieged by hordes of starving people desperate for food, like scenes from the Last Judgement.

In 1694 the relics of St Geneviève were taken in procession through the streets of Paris to invoke God's mercy. Sourches, whose Gardes de la Prévôté provided part of the escort, noticed beggars in the street 'whose faces worn out by hunger, were frightening to look at. Most were lying on straw or on the pavement, crying and dying of poverty.' The King stopped touching for the King's Evil at Versailles, to avoid catching 'mal-adies populaires'.[89] In all perhaps 1.3 million more people than usual died in 1693 and 1694: some 5 per cent of the population, more than in the First World War. In 1694 there were 25 per cent fewer births than in a normal year, 587,000 compared to 802,000.[90]

The crown reacted with relative efficiency. Thirty years of government by Louis XIV had accustomed his subjects to obedience. *Intendants* started programmes of government works, 'uniquely in the view of keep-ing the poor peasants alive and not to leave them in idleness'.[91] In the winter of 1693/4 thirty enormous ovens were set up in the courtyard of the Louvre to bake bread for the starving.[92] A Protestant shipowner in Rouen who had converted to Catholicism, Thomas Legendre, was helped by his continued contacts with Protestant merchants abroad to import grain from neutral Sweden and Denmark.[93]

The crown also increased fiscal pressure on its subjects, inventing new taxes and demanding more loans. In 1692, for example, the crown had created mayors in every city in the kingdom, except Paris and Lyon, to raise money rather than to promote municipal autonomy.[94] In addition bourgeois were encouraged to purchase patents of ennoblement. A radical new *capit-ation* or income tax started in January 1695. For the first time, everyone except the King and the clergy, which bought exemption, had to pay. Show-ing the true distribution of wealth and power in France, the first category of taxpayers included not only the Dauphin, princes and ministers but also tax farmers. Each category included nobles and non-nobles.[95]

France was at war at sea as well as on land. After a victory at Beachy Head on 10 July 1690, for the only time in history the French navy controlled the English Channel. In April 1692 James II again bade farewell to Louis XIV, hoping to return to England at the head of French and Irish troops. The battle of Cap La Hogue on 1 July 1692, however, which he watched from the coast of Normandy, was, as Louis had been warned it would be, a catastrophe. French ships were outnumbered and outgunned.[96]

The King suffered the consequences of his taste for brilliant appearances. His ships, of which fragments can be seen in naval museums in Paris and Toulon, were gilded and sculpted with crowns, fleurs-de-lys, Ls, sirens and sea gods trumpeting the glory of France. However, as officers often complained, they looked better than they sailed.[97] The King's impressive-looking galleys, for example, were not only cruel for the slaves rowing them, but obsolete, vulnerable to faster and better-armed warships.[98] At La Hogue the most magnificent of all Louis XIV's warships, *Le Soleil Royal*, built in Brest in 1668–70, the poop sculpted with an effigy of the King guiding the horses of the sea, was burnt, having served in battle only three times. Just one member of its 882 crew survived. Another over-decorated, overweight French ship *Le Royal Louis*, built in 1692, was sold in 1694 after only one campaign.[99]

The best officer in the French navy, with whom Louis worked for hours in his study, was Admiral de Tourville.[100] On 28 June 1693, off the Spanish coast, de Tourville captured or sank most of the eighty ships of the Anglo-Dutch 'Smyrna convoy', escorting merchant ships from Amsterdam and London to Smyrna, the main port of the Levant. It was considered the worst financial disaster in London since the Great Fire.

Thereafter, however, Louis did not have the financial or material resources to stop the decline of his navy, from 135 major ships in 1690 to 80 by 1715.[101] The army came first. The Ministry of the Marine turned to privateering, led by the legendary captain Jean Bart (born Jan Baert, to a family of Dunkirk fishermen). In July 1694 Bart seized a convoy of Dutch ships carrying grain from Poland and Russia and escorted it back to Dunkirk, thereby helping to save France from famine. He was ennobled in August 1694, as a sign of 'the particular consideration we have for his valour', and allowed to add to his arms a golden fleur-de-lys.[102] When his son slipped on the parquet floors of Versailles bringing the King captured Dutch flags, the King laughed and said, 'Messieurs Bart are better sailors than courtiers.'[103]

Peace negotiations, begun in The Hague in 1693, resumed near Brussels in the summer of 1697. To save time (and to avoid problems arising from Louis XIV's refusal to recognize 'le prince d'Orange' as king of England), they were conducted over the heads of official diplomats, between William

III's favourite Hans Willem Bentinck, Earl of Portland, and the Colonel of the Gardes Françaises, the Maréchal de Boufflers. They continued at William III's palace of Rijswijk, outside The Hague.[104] The arrangements in the main room for equal and symmetrical spaces for the diplomats of the two sides (with space for the Swedish mediators in the middle) were almost as precise as those on the Island of Pheasants in 1659 for the Treaty of the Pyrenees. Hoping to exploit Louis XIV's vanity, Portland assured Boufflers that his master regarded the King of France as not merely the greatest king, but the greatest man, in the world.[105]

Negotiations revealed that, when governments wanted peace, their interests proved stronger than those of the diasporas they were hosting. James II sent an agent called M. Dem to advance his case, protesting that his was the 'common cause of all Sovereigns' and denouncing negotiations with William, 'the Usurper of our Kingdoms'. No one listened. Pomponne, the moderate former Foreign Minister and enemy of Louvois, whom Louis had been consulting since Louvois' death, had long been urging him to disregard James II. Repeated failures to invade England, and William's success in maintaining himself on his new throne, showed James's limits as a French weapon.[106]

Similarly, Huguenots in the Netherlands had formed a secret committee, including Pierre Jurieu and Elie Benoist, to lobby diplomats to make their return to France a condition of peace. William III, whom they had once hailed as God's instrument for the destruction of the Antichrist (Louis XIV), ignored them. During peace negotiations Louis threatened to order his diplomats to leave if they were forced to listen to any demands 'in favour of His Majesty's subjects of the so-called reformed religion'.[107] Indeed the Huguenot convert M. de Bonrepaus, later sent to the Netherlands as Louis' ambassador, promised in the name of the French government that Huguenots could recover confiscated properties, and acquire their relations', only if they converted to Catholicism. About 700 did so in his embassy in 1697 and 1698. Provided they passed 'sincerity tests', they could then, to the horror of fellow Huguenots, return to France and recover their property. Some Huguenots from England and Brandenburg did the same.[108]

By the Treaty of Rijswijk signed on 20 September 1697, Louis XIV recognized William III as king of Great Britain. He promised, on the word and faith of a king, not to give William's enemies (that is, James II) any assistance 'directly or indirectly'. He insisted, however, on the grounds of honour, compassion and kinship, that James remain at Saint-Germain.[109]

The war with Louis XIV had, in the end, increased the power of the English monarchy. What it had lost in authority (until ministers like

Harley and Walpole learnt to manage Parliament on its behalf) by the revolution and Bill of Rights in 1688–9, it had gained in revenue – there was a three-fold increase in the 1690s – and the size of its army. Soon it would reach over 90,000 men.[110]

Moreover, as Vauban pointed out, for the first time since the loss of Piedmont by the Treaty of Cateau-Cambrésis in 1559, France had lost territory. The Empire recognized French sovereignty over Alsace and Strasbourg 'in perpetuity', but the strategic assets of Mons, Tournai, Luxembourg, Montroyal, Philippsburg, Landau, Freiburg and Breisach, fortified at great expense by France, were returned to their previous sovereigns. The great fortress of Pignerol in Piedmont, French since 1630, where Fouquet and Lauzun had been imprisoned, had already been ceded to Victor Amadeus II, Duke of Savoy by a separate treaty in 1696. French claims to the Palatinate and Zweibrücken were abandoned, to the Elector Palatine and the King of Sweden respectively. Eight thousand Dutch troops were allowed to garrison cities in the Southern Netherlands – Ostend, Mons, Namur, Charleroi and Luxembourg – as a barrier against France.[111] Barcelona, taken in August 1697, was returned to Spain. So many cities were handed back that Parisians said they were relieved that Paris was not among them. Many were reluctant to support official peace celebrations.[112]

Chamlay and Vauban were particularly incensed by the loss of Luxembourg, 'one of the finest and strongest positions in the world': 'with her we lose for ever the chance of having our frontier on the Rhine.'[113] The dream of a French Rhineland was over, until the French Republic conquered the left bank in 1792. Vauban told Racine that, having won their neighbours' aversion, the French would now lose their respect. It was a peace which dishonoured 'the king and the whole nation'.[114] Europe had beaten France.

Moreover the Treaty of Rijswijk restored to the Duke of Lorraine the duchy which, since his expulsion of Charles IV in 1670, Louis XIV had treated as a French province.[115] On 10 November 1698 Charles IV's grandson Leopold I, Duke of Lorraine, re-entered Nancy in triumph from Vienna, where he had been serving in the Imperial army. However, he had married Louis XIV's niece Elisabeth Charlotte, a daughter of Monsieur, at Fontainebleau a month earlier on 13 October, and French troops retained the right to use four routes through the duchy. Advised by Boffrand and Mansart, after 1702 the new Duke of Lorraine would run into debt creating a new palace and gardens at the small town of Lunéville, south of Nancy. Lunéville became de facto capital of his duchy, and his court a smaller, more domestic version of Versailles. Leopold's interlaced Ls decorating Lunéville are replicas of Louis' interlaced Ls at Versailles.[116]

Even French pre-eminence in royal splendour was challenged by William III's state entry into London on 26 November 1697, its grandest public spectacle since the coronation of Charles II. He was greeted with 'extraordinary acclamations of joy' by the greatest assemblage of well-dressed people he had ever seen.[117]

After 1660, in contrast, Louis XIV had always refused another state entry into Paris. Instead he expressed his power through his preferred methods of dynastic marriage and *divertissements*. In 1695 the Duke of Savoy had been detached from his alliance with William III by an offer of Pignerol and marriage between his daughter Marie Adélaïde and Louis XIV's grandson and ultimate heir the Duc de Bourgogne: a marriage which Louis XIV and Monsieur (the Princess's grandfather) had planned since her birth.[118] From the moment Marie Adélaïde de Savoie arrived at court in November 1696, she charmed the King and Madame de Maintenon.

The King told courtiers, on the day he met her at Montargis, after analysing her throat, figure and hands as if checking the 'points' of a horse or hound: 'I would not for anything in the world change any aspect of her appearance.'[119] In a letter to Madame de Maintenon he praised her red lips and white teeth. She was 'dressed fit to paint and coiffed the same', with 'the best grace and the finest figure I have ever seen'. He continued: 'she pleases and I see in everyone's eyes will please.' The King knew that he too had to please the public, like a professional actor: 'until now I have done marvellously. I hope I will maintain a certain air of ease which I have adopted until Fontainebleau where I very much wish to return. Not wishing to tell you what I am thinking, I give you one thousand good [here follow two effaced lines] . . . everyone seems truly satisfied.' The King again stresses her need to please the public: 'everything pleases except for her curtsey.'[120]

Madame de Maintenon continued the Princess's education, taking her to classes at Saint-Cyr and having supper with her every day. On 6 November Maintenon wrote to Marie Adélaïde's mother the Duchess of Savoy of their 'transports of joy at the treasure we receive'. On 1 July 1697 she continued: 'she is the sole delight of the king, she amuses him by her gaiety and her chatter . . . she dances very well and no one ever had so much grace.'[121] As Louis approached sixty, his court was rejuvenated. Two years later, annotating a note by Mansart about redecorating the Princess's apartment in the Ménagerie, he wrote, 'there must be youthfulness everywhere.'[122]

The marriage celebrations at Fontainebleau and Versailles in December 1697 were spectacular: fireworks, concerts, receptions, operas and a ball. Dangeau wrote, 'the merchants swear they have sold five millions' worth [of clothes and jewels].'[123] The court was proud of its economic function. At the ball in the Galerie des Glaces, wrote Sourches, there were eight pyramids of 150 candles, and such magnificence as had never been seen before in France. He continued, defensively, 'foreigners must admit that even if war had continued France would not have collapsed for lack of money.'[124] In the scramble for supper after the ball, Monsieur was knocked to the ground and trampled on. The King too was jostled, and had to use his cane to make space for the ladies. However, the Venetian Ambassador was impressed. 'At that hour when the glory and grandeur of France were made manifest, one can see how poor, how despicable are the imitations of other nations.'[125] Louis had overestimated his power, brought misery to France and the Rhineland and lost territory, but the court remained a showcase for France.

19

Spain Changes Sides:
The Accession of King Philip

At eleven in the morning on 16 November 1700 the doors of the Grand Cabinet du Roi at Versailles were opened to reveal the King and his blonde seventeen-year-old younger grandson the Duc d'Anjou. Courtiers entered and fell silent. Louis XIV then announced, 'Messieurs, here is the king of Spain. His birth called him to this crown, the late king also by his will. The whole nation desired it and begged me for it pressingly. It was the decree of heaven. I have accorded it with pleasure.' Then, turning to his grandson: 'Be a good Spaniard; it is now your first duty; but remember that you were born French, in order to maintain the union between the two nations. It is the way to keep them happy and to maintain the peace of Europe.'

Everyone crowded round to congratulate the new King, including the Papal Nuncio and the Venetian Ambassador. Louis had chosen to make the announcement on a Tuesday, when foreign ambassadors came to court. He said to the Spanish Ambassador, 'Monsieur, salute your king.' In tears, the Ambassador kissed the hands and feet of his new king and exclaimed, 'What joy! There are no more Pyrenees, they are destroyed and henceforth we are one.'[1]

The Spanish succession goes to the heart of Louis XIV as a man, a king and a country. His speech accepting the throne for Philip V cited many of the forces governing his life and reign: the rights and obligations of birth, a King's will, nationality, public opinion, the will of God and the peace of Europe. All contributed to Louis XIV's announcement of his acceptance of Carlos II's decision to leave Louis' grandson his thrones, although their precise influence is debated to this day. Not mentioned, but as important as any of them, was his rivalry with the House of Austria and his desire for the aggrandizement of the House of France.

Since the death of Philip IV in 1665, the Spanish succession had been a time bomb threatening the peace of Europe. Carlos II, Philip IV's son and successor, and Louis XIV's brother-in-law, was a warning of the

perils of intermarriage. Deformed, tormented with exorcisms by a confessor who believed him bewitched, he had long been near death.[2]

Three separate partition treaties, between Louis XIV and the Emperor
in 1668 (in secret), and between Louis XIV and William III in 1698 and
1700, had planned to divide the Spanish monarchy, to the dismay of its
government.[3] With some variations, the Emperor Leopold I's second son
the Archduke Charles was to be king in Madrid. The Dauphin would
receive the Spanish Netherlands, Navarre (showing that the French monarchy, like modern Navarrese autonomists, had not forgotten Spain's
annexation of the southern portion of Navarre in 1512), Naples, Sicily
and, in the interests of French commerce in Asia, the Philippines.

Dynastic and national interests, rather than being contradictory, could
complement each other. French interests would be further served by a plan
for the Dauphin to exchange Naples and Sicily for Piedmont and Savoy,
thereby giving France a massive extension to the south-east, and the Duke
of Savoy the royal crown for which he yearned. A similar exchange was
also discussed with the Duke of Lorraine: he would receive Milan, and
France would finally annex Lorraine. Like other monarchs in similar
circumstances, the Duke was willing to exchange his hereditary lands for
a larger and richer sovereignty.[4]

Vauban and Louis' ministers preferred territorial expansion for France
to Bourbon claims to Spain.[5] Louis himself had written in 1698: 'it is
more advantageous to my crown to acquire these provinces than to put
one of my grandsons on the throne of Spain while according Italy to
the Emperor and places in India and the Mediterranean to the English
and the Dutch.'[6]

Partition treaties, however, were rejected by the Emperor Leopold I,
more powerful in 1698 than when he had signed the first such treaty in
1668. He believed that his younger son, the Archduke Charles, should
inherit the entire Spanish monarchy, as William III and the States General
had agreed in a secret article of the treaty they had signed with Leopold
I in May 1689, and as Philip IV himself had desired by his will of 1665.[7]
His enemies accused Louis XIV of desire for 'universal monarchy', but
the House of Austria was equally or more ambitious. Since the fifteenth
century 'AEIOU' – 'Austriae est imperare orbe universo' ('Austria should
rule the whole world') – had been its motto.

Another alternative advocated by Louis XIV and William III (and
Queen Mariana, mother of Carlos II) 'in the general interests of Europe'
had been to make the Electoral Prince Joseph Ferdinand of Bavaria – son
of an archduchess, grandson of Leopold I, but neither Austrian nor
French – heir to the thrones of Spain, with Milan going to the Archduke

and Naples to the Dauphin.[8] Carlos II even made a will in Joseph Ferdin-
and's favour. However, the young Prince had died on 6 February 1699.

The partition treaties did not come into effect. But they did reaffirm
the possibility of collective security in the interests of what the English
Parliament called 'the freedom and balance of Europe' and 'the peace of
Europe', achieved by diplomatic agreements rather than imposed by uni-
lateral decisions.[9] At the same time, in contradiction to the partition
treaties and the policy of French territorial expansion, but reflecting his
role as head of his dynasty, Louis wrote to his ambassadors that he considered his son the legitimate heir to the Spanish monarchy through his
mother Queen Marie Thérèse. The choice of the Spanish/Burgundian
name of Philip for his second grandson already suggested his hopes. In a
letter of 25 July 1700 Madame wrote that, grave and serious in his speech
and movements, the Duc d'Anjou 'truly has the air of a King of Spain'.

Another factor favouring the choice of Louis XIV's grandson as king
of Spain, at least as important as Bourbon dynasticism in France, was
support for imperialism in Spain. Spaniards, both rich and poor, were
determined to maintain the unity of what Carlos II called in his will 'all
my kingdoms and dominions without exception': the entire Spanish global
empire, including the viceroyalties of New Spain and Peru; Castile, Aragon
and the Spanish Netherlands; and the kingdoms of Sicily and Naples.
Spaniards preferred to go to hell, it was said, rather than to allow the
monarchy to be dismembered.[10]

In a remarkable tribute to Louis XIV's political and military reputation, between 1697 and 1700, despite three Franco-Spanish wars since
1635, many Spaniards came to think of France as the state most likely to
maintain the territorial integrity of Spain's global empire. The Viceroy of
Catalonia, for example, wrote to him in 1700 that all 'are tired of the
disorders of the past and yearn for the good sense and policy which reign
in France'.[11] In addition many Spaniards, like Louis himself, supported
the succession of a French prince on the grounds that the Dauphin had
the best hereditary claim, since his mother Marie Thérèse was the elder
daughter of Philip IV. The regents of Spain wrote to Louis XIV on
3 November 1700 that a 'unanimous desire' favoured Anjou.[12]

The unpopularity of Carlos II's second wife, María Ana of Neuburg,
and of the Imperial Ambassador in Madrid Count Harrach, and the failure
of Austrian troops to prevent France taking Barcelona in 1697, also
encouraged Spaniards to turn to France. Louis wrote to his new Ambassador the Marquis d'Harcourt in December 1697 that 'the hatred that all
the nation has against the Germans . . . is the principal and perhaps the
sole foundation of the leaning which one now discovers in the nation

towards France.'[13] Even James Stanhope, Ambassador of Austria's ally England, admitted as early as 1698 that most Spaniards would prefer a French prince: their aversion to the Queen having set them against all her countrymen, 'it is scarce conceivable the abhorrence they have for Vienna.'[14] In contrast the Marquis d'Harcourt, hospitable, charming and Spanish-speaking, helped to win Madrid for a Bourbon. Madame d'Harcourt, generous to Spanish friends with dresses, fans and *objets de Paris*, also charmed Madrid. As she passed through the streets, people shouted, 'Ah qué linda, ah qué hermosa que está' ('How lovely, how beautiful she is!'). The English Ambassador called her 'a very proper person to manage a Court intrigue'.[15] Of Louis XIV's many brilliant ambassadors – d'Estrades, d'Avaux, Bonnac, Guilleragues – Harcourt would be the only one raised, by a grateful monarch, to the ranks of duke and marshal.[16]

In this golden age of diplomacy, ambassadors could change the fate of nations. If Harcourt helped win Spain for the Bourbons, Barillon, Louis XIV's Ambassador in England, had helped persuade James II to flee in 1688.[17] Embassies were beginning to resemble miniature courts, with their own throne rooms and chapels.[18] Ambassadresses too were rising in power and status: Louis XIV accorded foreign ambassadresses the honour of a royal audience on both their arrival and their departure, and the right to a tabouret. Madame de Guilleragues ran the Constantinople embassy for three months after her husband's death in 1685.[19]

Even Louis XIV appeared, by the Treaty of Rijswijk, to prefer diplomacy to war. He directed his envoys more carefully than his generals. When in December 1696 François de Callières had asked for freedom of action during negotiations in Amsterdam, because of the delays caused by the slowness of couriers, the King refused to let him make any changes to 'what I have informed you about my intentions'.[20]

In 1698 Callières replaced the aged Président Rose as *secrétaire du cabinet*. A bachelor art collector, Callières was a professional diplomat who believed that 'Secrecy is the soul of negotiation.' Even Saint-Simon admired his common sense, honesty and ability to tell the truth to the King and his ministers. His book *Manière de négocier avec les souverains*, published in 1716 and frequently reprinted, gave many details about the differences between ambassadors extraordinary and ordinary, envoys, ministers plenipotentiary, residents and agents, and would become a diplomat's bible.[21]

Louis XIV's new Minister of Foreign Affairs from 1696, a nephew of Colbert called the Marquis de Torcy, was a European who had visited Stockholm, London, Lisbon, Madrid, Rome and Vienna, and learnt Spanish, Italian and German.[22] Reflecting Louis' new-found preference for diplomacy, a memorandum by his adviser Chamlay deplored the decision for war in 1688 and blamed it on Louvois. Thus Louis XIV himself admitted that his ministers could influence his policy: in reality he was seeking to shift blame for a war which had not won total victory for France.[23]

By the summer of 1700 'Borbonistas' had defeated 'Austracistas' in the battle for the heart of Spain. All but one member of the Council of Castile accepted the choice of a French prince as king. The Pope and the Jesuits also supported a French prince, as did an unexpected ally, Marie Mancini. In another stage in her prolonged flight from her husband Prince Colonna, she had arrived in Madrid and regularly saw the Queen.

In principle Spain was a hereditary monarchy. In practice in Spain, as in other countries, some monarchs believed that succession to the crown, like a private estate, could be decided by the monarch's will rather than by heredity.[24] As we have seen, in his will of 1665 Philip IV had left the entire Spanish monarchy, after his son, to their Austrian cousins, and as late as September 1700 Carlos II had confirmed a will he had made leaving his crowns to the Archduke Charles, younger son of Leopold I.[25] That month, however, with the Pope's approval, Cardinal Portocarrero, Archbishop of Toledo, the leading pro-French minister, drew up another will, which left the monarchy to the Dauphin's second son, Philippe, Duc d'Anjou.[26]

On 2 October, Portocarrero and the rest of the council made the King sign the new will which contained the condition that the crowns of France and Spain were never to be united, and the advice that, in the interests of the peace of Europe, the Duc d'Anjou should marry an archduchess. If he refused the inheritance, it should be offered to the Emperor's younger son, the Archduke Charles.[27] Harcourt's replacement Blécourt wrote to Louis XIV of 'universal consent': the 'party of the Emperor in Spain is so weak that it is not worth talking about'.[28]

When the will, and the King's death on 1 November, were announced to Louis XIV on 9 November at Fontainebleau, long debates followed in the council. In the interests of peace, and French expansion, some ministers such as the Duc de Beauvillier preferred to remain loyal to the partition treaty – although no one in Spain or Austria accepted it, and it would need to be imposed by force. Beauvillier believed, wrongly, that Bourbon kings of Spain would prove as jealous of France as Austrian ones. The Chancellor Pontchartrain and Torcy, however, spoke in favour of Carlos II's latest will. The French government felt obliged to deprive the House of Austria of the dazzling prize of the Spanish monarchy, and to secure it for the House of France.[29]

Madame swore that 'la pantocrate' (Madame de Maintenon) attended the decisive council meeting, as she had occasionally done since 1698. Since many lengthy meetings on 9 and 10 November were held in her apartment, it could hardly have increased her influence further. Torcy denies it.[30]

Louis XIV was both a Frenchman devoted to national expansion and a king to whom the prospect of placing his grandson on the throne to which he had the best hereditary claim was irresistible, as it would have been to almost all his fellow monarchs. Moreover, one key member of his council agreed: the Dauphin.

Behind a façade of silent submission, which aged courtiers compared to that of Louis XIV under Mazarin, the Dauphin was tougher than he looked. He loved hunting, gambling and dancing. He was at the heart of carnival balls, for which he was happy to dress as a parrot or a mandarin. So many dancers came from Paris to a carnival ball he gave at Versailles in 1705 that they could not fit into his apartment.[31] He frequently took courtiers away from Versailles, to stay at his chateau at Meudon with its stupendous views of Paris: Saint-Simon writes of 'les Meudons' as well as 'les Marlis'.[32]

He had, however, also been a member of the council since 1691, discussed strategy at length with his father and corresponded in secret with some of his father's generals.[33] At the council meetings of November 1700, all sources agree that the Dauphin played a crucial role in persuading the council to abandon the partition treaty and accept the King of Spain's will. The dynasty was put before the state, and a Bourbon on the Spanish throne considered more important than the territorial expansion of France.* On 13 November, testing the waters, the King asked his daughters the Princesse de Conti and the Duchesse de Bourbon their opinion. They said that, from what they heard, the public supported acceptance.[34]

Louis believed, as he wrote on 14 November to his Ambassador in the Netherlands, that a partition treaty would have led to 'a war whose end was impossible to foresee', and to an archduke in Madrid.[35] He hoped that the succession of his grandson would instead lead to a close alliance and understanding between France and Spain.[36] Even in England public opinion preferred the King of Spain's will to the partition treaty, assuming the former easier to enforce. William III was dismayed. He felt that Louis had duped him and that England and the Netherlands faced ruin.[37]

After his proclamation on 16 November, Philip V of Spain, as he now was, stayed for two weeks with his family. There were three kings in

---

* A dynasty with relations on other thrones was also believed to strengthen the state.

Versailles: Louis XIV, Philip V and, continuing his regular visits, James II. Philip received royal honours from the Gardes du Corps, and occupied the state apartments. On the first occasion they attended chapel together, there was only one hassock set out for the King. Louis, with his usual presence of mind, kicked it away, so that, when they knelt, the kings of France and Spain did so as equals.[38]

Philip's farewell to the royal family at Sceaux on 4 December (bought earlier that year from Colbert's heirs by the Duc du Maine) admitted the public into the emotional theatre of the court. The road from Versailles to Sceaux was lined with people. Such crowds filled the hills around Sceaux, and the park, on foot, on horseback and in the trees, that the Duchesse de Bourgogne and Louis XIV were separated. Both kings wept so much that they could not see each other.[39] Dangeau writes of 'the entire royal house crying and even uttering cries of affliction'. Courtiers, guards and members of the public also burst into tears.[40]

Philip then began a slow journey down France, through Orléans, Blois and Bordeaux to Saint-Jean-de-Luz, along packed and tapestry-hung streets, to the sound of church bells and cannon salutes.[41] To show his brothers the ducs de Bourgogne and de Berri to France (their return journey would include Marseille, Grenoble and Lyon), and France to them, and to delay the final farewells, they accompanied Philip. The Maréchal de Noailles acted as *capitaine des gardes*, bringing twenty-four of his own musicians to entertain the princes. The 'Idylle de Sceaux' was sung at Mont-de-Marsan 'as if Lully had been there'.[42]

As they neared the frontier, Spanish courtiers began to appear: the Constable of Castile told Philip V that his Spanish subjects were waiting for him like souls in purgatory waiting for paradise.[43] At the moment of parting, both sides of the Bidassoa were packed with cheering crowds as far as the eye could see, and the brothers were drenched in tears.[44]

On the other side of the Pyrenees, Philip advanced through more cheering crowds to Madrid. The new King did not speak more than a few words of Castilian, and until his death in 1746 used French with his household and family.[45] Nevertheless, this French-born King was at once accepted by most of his new subjects, as he accepted Spain as his new *patrie*, showing little regret for France.

Philip appealed to his subjects not only because of French prestige and his dynastic rights, but also because he looked handsomer and healthier than his debilitated predecessors.[46] Like Louis XIV himself when young, Philip enjoyed what the Comte d'Ayen, son of the Maréchal de Noailles, called 'the strength of youth with the colours of health and all the graces of a majestic beauty'.[47] He began to attend bullfights. The pitiful state of his new carriage and servants, looking like clowns in yellow Burgundian liveries (which he soon changed to Bourbon royal blue), merely made him laugh.[48] Cheering crowds lined his route through Madrid, on 5 January 1701, to the royal palace. At a Te Deum at the shrine of Our Lady of Atocha on 19 February, the choir of the royal chapel was drowned out by the cheers from the public outside. He was also cheered at his swearing of an oath to observe the laws before the Cortes of Castile at the church of San Jerónimo on 8 May; on his departure from Madrid to visit Barcelona, Naples and Milan in September 1701; and on his return in January 1703.[49]

Philip was subject to *vapeurs*, serious mood swings, which may have amounted to depression and 'bipolar disorder'.[50] Sometimes he withdrew to his rooms, refusing to speak. However Princess Maria Luisa of Savoy, younger sister of the Duchesse de Bourgogne, whom he married at Figueres in Catalonia on 3 November 1701, could combat such moods by her emotional warmth. Although only thirteen and not beautiful, she was strong-willed, charming and intelligent. They fell in love.[51]

Because Philip could be influenced by his wife and others, many, including Louis XIV, dismissed him as weak. He certainly allowed his officials enormous influence in the running of the Spanish government. Blaming his inexperience in writing political letters, Philip admitted to Louis that his courtier Louville and later the Princesse des Ursins' equerry d'Aubigny, sometimes drafted his letters, even to his wife. D'Aubigny, who was Ursins' lover, also wrote some of her letters.[52] In Madrid's labyrinth of intrigues, letters were often written by someone other than the signatory, for public consumption, without reflecting the writer's or the signatory's feelings. Louis XIV's own letters to Philip were also often written or drafted by Torcy or Callières.[53] A dynasty was a joint enterprise, between a monarch, his relations and his officials.

Although Philip could be manipulated, he was also hard-working, dignified, popular and on occasion braver than Louis. Madame called him good-natured, generous and a man of his word, with no vices.[54] Like his grandfather, he loved the arts. He would found the Royal Library, the Spanish Academy and the Academies of History and Sciences, and brought thousands of French books to Madrid.[55]

War was probably inevitable. Already in June 1701 French, Spanish and Austrian troops had started fighting in northern Italy for control of the Duchy of Milan, which Austria had long planned to annex.[56] Leopold I refused to recognize Philip V and also wanted to reassert Imperial claims to suzerainty in northern Italy. In June 1697, after Prince Eugene's victory over the Ottomans at Zenta, Count Martinitz, Imperial Ambassador in Rome, had published a declaration summoning all fief-holders of the Holy

Roman Empire in Italy to Vienna within three months, to prove their rights to their possessions: an Austrian version of Louis XIV's *réunions* in the Rhineland.[57] French generals in northern Italy found widespread support for Imperial suzerainty and fear of 'the Germans'.[58]

From 1700 to 1710, or later, French and Spanish history are inseparable. At first, as Louis had promised, the French Ambassador and French courtiers and officials tried not to interfere in Spain. However, Cardinal Portocarrero agreed with Philip's French courtiers that most Spanish Grandees were ignorant imbeciles, loyal out of laziness or cowardice, but eager to exploit the monarchy.[59] French troops were sent to Spain, and at Portocarrero's suggestion Harcourt began to attend the council or to receive daily analyses of its discussions – a privilege which, under the House of Austria, the Imperial Ambassador had never enjoyed. Portocarrero consulted him on everything.[60] In effect he acted as a minister in Spain: another sign of the power of ambassadors under Louis XIV and the unity of the House of Bourbon.

Louis' innumerable letters to Philip, which took about a week to reach Madrid from Marly or Versailles,[61] show that he soon began to give advice, for example to trust the French marshals Marsin and d'Harcourt, and the new French Ambassador the Cardinal d'Estrées.[62] He also encouraged Philip to be his own master: 'I hope with all the ardour of which I am capable to see you as great a king as you can be, if you wish so.' Philip followed his grandfather's advice to leave the Queen in Madrid, when he went to Italy in 1702, to show he was not abandoning Spain, although chastity depressed him.[63] His reception in Italy in 1702 showed the continued prestige and popularity of the Spanish monarchy: there was less resentment of Spanish rule in Naples and Milan than of English rule in Dublin. Fighting Austrian forces for more than fourteen hours on 12 July 1702 at the battle of Santa Vittoria in Lombardy, Philip V displayed such bravery 'that all were encouraged by his energy and enthusiasm'.[64]

More French officials were sent by Louis XIV to galvanize the Spanish government. At the request of Portocarrero Jean Orry, a brilliant member of the Conseil de Commerce, who had also worked on the diversion of the waters of the Eure to Versailles, arrived to help reform Spanish finances and the royal household. Orry was criticized for making money out of army supplies. Spaniards came to detest both his manners and his reforms. However, he cut expenses and increased revenue.[65]

For his personal comfort, Philip brought about fifty French servants including his old nurse, his confessor and his barber Vazet, who made him laugh more than all Spain together (and through whom the French Ambassador was able to intercept and read Queen Maria Luisa's letters to her family in Turin).[66] This separate *casa francesa*, resented by the Spanish household, came to about 15 per cent of the whole household.[67]

The King's Spanish and French cooks waged food wars. The former, disobeying the King and his 'French dogs', poured away French soups and sauces, saying they might dirty their hands. Finally the Queen herself began to make, in her own apartment, dishes such as onion soup. French servants baked French bread for the King and Queen, Spanish servants Spanish bread for the household.[68]

Dynastic successions governed the fate of Europe. A knowledge of relationships within and between the royal families of Europe was as essential to diplomats as knowledge of relationships in ministerial and ducal families to courtiers. At the same time as Spain, Poland, although it was an elective monarchy, also suffered from a disputed succession involving a French prince, followed by an international war. When King Jan Sobieski died in 1696, three candidates for Poland's throne emerged. First, Sobieski's eldest son Jakub Ludwik, a godson of Louis XIV. Second, the handsome, wealthy and priapic Elector of Saxony Augustus II, devoured by the same passion for a royal crown as his fellow electors of Bavaria, Brandenburg and Hanover (see below), and the dukes of Württemberg, Lorraine and Savoy. All were competing for self-aggrandizement with each other and with their suzerain the Holy Roman Emperor.[69]

The third and apparently strongest candidate was Louis XIV's cousin the Prince de Conti. Perhaps because the Conti were the poorest princes in the dynasty, with no great estates to keep them in France, his brother had already been publicly suggested by Louis XIV as a possible king of Sicily in 1675.[70] Since 1693 the able and charming French Ambassador in Warsaw, the Abbé Melchior de Polignac, had been preparing Conti's election. Aided by the Cardinal Primate of Poland, who had lived in Paris, and the Grand Treasurer Hieronim Lubomirski, whom Conti had known in Vienna in 1685, and promises of future French subsidies, in addition to letters of exchange supplied via Danzig by the great French banker Samuel Bernard, Polignac won Conti a majority of votes in the Diet on 26 June 1697. Showing the jealousy many Polish nobles felt for the Sobieskis, it was the first time that a surviving son of the previous king of Poland had not been elected as his father's successor.[71]

On 11 July 1697 Louis XIV proudly presented Conti to the ladies in Madame de Maintenon's apartment with the words 'Here is a king I am bringing you.' Only Conti's pleas stopped the King treating his wife as queen of Poland. The King believed, or said he did, that in Poland the grandees, the nobles and the army were waiting for Conti.[72] Instead of leaving at once, however, Conti did not sail until 7 August, from Dunkirk in a fleet of five ships captained by Jean Bart. Perhaps fearing what Saint-Simon called 'the horrors of perpetual expatriation' in Poland, he may have preferred to remain in France, with his many lovers of both sexes (including the King's daughter the Duchesse de Bourbon), and the prospect of dominating the reign of his admiring cousin the Dauphin. He did not arrive off Danzig until 26 September.[73]

France finally seemed to have obtained what it had attempted in 1665–8 through the Duc d'Enghien, and had enjoyed a hundred years earlier in 1573–4, through Henri III: a French-born king of Poland, acting as a barrier in eastern Europe to the House of Austria. If Poland had been strengthened by a line of kings from a powerful foreign dynasty like the Bourbons, as it had been by its Vasa kings from Sweden in 1587 to 1668, its subsequent partitions, and its elimination as an independent state from 1795 to 1918, might have been avoided, and France's relative power in Europe enhanced.

Polignac, however, had exaggerated to himself and his government the solidity of Conti's support in the Polish Diet. As France's many subsequent failures to intervene in Poland would show, distance weakened its leverage.[74] France was far. Saxony (like Prussia later) and Russia were near. Moreover Louis, who had distrusted Conti since reading his mocking letters in 1685, gave him 2.4 million livres, but no troops or munitions. This had been the excuse Conti gave for delaying his departure, criticizing the King, apparently to his face: he had not wished to appear in Poland alone, as an 'unfortunate wanderer'.[75]

Augustus II of Saxony had visited Louis XIV during his Grand Tour in 1687. Guided by his Huguenot Ordonnateur du Cabinet, Raymond Leplat, he bought jewels, bronzes and 'toutes sortes de choses exquises' from France, and later created a state bedroom like Louis XIV's in his palace at Dresden.[76] If his tastes were partly French, however, his policies were not. He commanded the Imperial armies against the Ottomans in 1695–6, and on 2 June 1697, although head of the Lutheran bloc in the Reichstag, converted to Catholicism in Baden outside Vienna: like Henri IV, he said a kingdom was worth a mass. He did not change his religion, it was remarked, as he did not have one to change, and his certificate of conversion was sufficiently vague to facilitate a subsequent reversion to Lutheranism. Sure of Austrian support, he then left for Poland. The day after the Diet voted for Conti, it voted again for Augustus II, who had raised money in Saxony to buy their votes and had 5,000 soldiers stationed near by. On 15 September, eleven days before Conti arrived off Danzig, Frederick Augustus of Saxony was crowned king Augustus II of Poland in Cracow cathedral.[77]

None of Conti's promised Polish troops appeared. Polish arms, it was said, were raised to take his money rather than to support his claims. Despite her French birth, Sobieski's widow opposed Conti's candidature from her residence in the port of Danzig, which refused to admit Conti's ships: the city's Lutheran governing elite preferred Augustus II to a French prince. Conti himself, extremely cautious and receiving conflicting advice from his Polish supporters, went on shore only once for a few hours, at Oliva, site of the treaty between the northern powers which France had mediated in 1660. On 10 November he sailed back to France, and on 13 December reappeared at mass at Versailles, thinner, poorer and sadder than when he had left.[78]

Madame concluded that, in their attitudes to kings, the Poles were 'even worse than the English'. Even the most loyal courtiers began to criticize the King's judgement. Dangeau wrote in his diary that everything they had been told about Poland had proved a fairy tale: 'it is not thought to be in the King's interest that a prince of his blood should act on so much uncertainty'. Perhaps, however, the King had secretly intended the humiliation of the cousin who had dared mock him, or had used Conti's candidature as a means to pressure the Emperor to sign the peace treaty at Rijswijk. On his return from Poland, Polignac was exiled to the provinces.[79]

Together with France's territorial losses at Rijswijk, the election of Augustus II in Poland in 1697, following the accession of William III and Mary II in England in 1689, showed that Louis XIV was no longer the arbiter of Europe: the accession of Philip V was a partly Spanish decision, which would be secured with difficulty only after an international war lasting ten years. In the cultural sphere also, other courts were as eager to compete with France as to imitate it. The coronation of Augustus II's rival Elector, Frederick I of Brandenburg, for example, as first king in Prussia on 18 January 1701 reflected the Hohenzollerns' long-term ambitions, and their hostility to Louis XIV.[80]

The coronation was justified in the official account by the Master of Ceremonies Johann von Besser by the Elector's absolute sovereignty and dynastic grandeur; the size of his army and its role in the war against France; and 'the magnificence and renown of the court', which Frederick's father had already, in the opinion of French diplomats and travellers, made one of the most splendid in the Empire. One reason for the Emperor's consent to the Elector's elevation was his promise that he would commit 18,000 troops to fight in the next war with France, in which they would indeed serve well. The coronation was followed by a further increase in the grandeur of the court of Berlin.[81]

The fifty triumphant baroque palaces erected by Austrian nobles in Vienna after 1683 were totally different in style and conception to Versailles and Paris *hôtels*. Their principal architects Lucas von Hildebrandt and Fischer von Erlach were inspired by Rome rather than Paris, which neither of them visited.[82] The masterpieces are the Belvedere and the Winter Palace, built for Louis' enemy Prince Eugene of Savoy. He filled their dazzling interiors with books, some bound by a royal bookbinder lured from Paris; pictures by Jacques-Ignace Parrocel, nephew of one of Louis XIV's battle painters, of his victories over French and Ottoman armies; and statues, including the famous Greek statue beloved of homosexuals, the so-called 'Praying Boy', which he bought, like his print collection, from Fouquet's heirs. Prince Eugene's revenge on Louis XIV was cultural as well as military.[83]

The Emperor also began to build in Vienna on a scale surpassing Versailles in triumphalism: the country palace of Schönbrunn from 1696; thirty years later the stupendous Imperial Library (longer and higher than the Galerie des Glaces, 250 feet long and 60 feet high); the Riding School, also in the Hofburg in Vienna; and the massive monastery of Klosterneuburg outside Vienna, planned as an Austrian Escorial, each wing to be surmounted by the crown of a different Habsburg realm.[84]

Many other European architects also never visited France. The standard guide to Italy for Englishmen, *Nouveau Voyage d'Italie, avec un mémoire contenant des avis utiles à ceux qui voudront faire le même voyage* (The Hague, 1691; English edition 1695), takes readers through the Netherlands and the Empire over the Alps to Italy, avoiding France. The author Maximilien Misson could not have visited it, since he was a Huguenot refugee.

In 1698 Augustus II's ally the young Tsar Peter of Russia led his 'great embassy' of 250 Russians abroad, to learn how to modernize their country. They visited Amsterdam, London and William III, not Paris, Versailles and Louis XIV (who had already rejected Russian overtures in 1668, and would probably have refused to receive a ruler he considered a barbarian). St Petersburg, which the Tsar founded on the Baltic in 1703 as Russia's main port and 'window on Europe', would be partly modelled on Amsterdam. One district was called 'New Holland'. Its first architects and planners were Dutch or Italian. Like Vienna and Dresden, it owed little to France.[85]

From 1700 to 1721, in alliance with Saxony and Denmark, Peter was fighting the Great Northern War for control of the Baltic and Poland, against another dazzling young monarch, Louis' ally Charles XII of Sweden. Louis XIV had been taken by surprise by Russia's attack on Sweden.[86]

Against Augustus II, Charles XII supported another rival for the throne of Poland, Stanisław Leszczyński (who would be elected king on 12 July 1704, after promising to abdicate in favour of Sobieski's eldest son Jakub if he was released from prison by Augustus II).

Like Peter himself, Charles XII practised a style of monarchy opposed to Louis XIV's: despotic, economical, giving the army precedence over the court. After his victory over Peter at Narva on 30 November 1700, he spent his reign on campaign or in exile, far from his court and his capital. Without wife or mistresses, it was said that he was married to his army. Like an ordinary soldier, he wore a simple tight blue tunic, without braid or embroidery; and boots and breeches rather than buckled shoes.

His youth and simplicity, as well as his victories, won him the admiration of Europe. In 1701 Madame wrote, 'Everyone here admires the King of Sweden; for three days no one has talked of anything else.'[87] Dangeau, the voice of Versailles, noted in 1703, 'the King of Sweden is not yet twenty-one and he has already won four battles.'[88] Charles XII, like Peter the Great, wore his own hair. From being the cynosure of Europe, Louis XIV was becoming as outdated as his full-bottomed wigs.

In addition to the Spanish and Polish successions, the English succession also influenced European politics. William III had begun to plan his succession soon after his coronation, since both his wife and her sister Anne were childless. From Hampton Court on 28 April 1689 he wrote to the next Protestant descendant of James I, his cousin the Duchess (after 1692 Electress) Sophia of Hanover, the aunt and favourite correspondent of Madame: 'according to apppearances one of your sons will reign there one day.'[89] For ten years Anne's son the Duke of Gloucester, born in July 1689 and christened William Henry like his godfather William III, had appeared to remove that possibility. However Gloucester, always puny, died in July 1700.

The Act of Settlement, passed by Parliament on 12 June 1701, guaranteed the Electress Sophia and her heirs 'in communion with the Church of England' the succession to the throne. The Electress Sophia, who had spoken good English since her youth and whom William III had visited several times, was naturalized English and began to attend Anglican services (although herself a Calvinist), to receive more English visitors and to have her grandchildren taught English.[90] Louis' hope that William III might be succeeded by the exiled Prince of Wales was an illusion.[91]

Traumatized by fear of Louis XIV and the exiled Stuarts, both Tories and Whigs accepted the Protestant succession. It is glorified in one of the most spectacular rooms in England – the Painted Hall, or dining room,

in the Royal Hospital for Seamen in Greenwich built by public subscrip-
tion, and one of England's answers to the Galerie des Glaces, as the
Imperial Library in Vienna was one of Austria's. Designed by Wren and
Hawksmoor, it was painted between 1708 and 1727 by James Thornhill.
On the ceiling of the main hall King William and Queen Mary are
enthroned in heaven, below figures of Athena, Apollo and Hercules. Peace
hands an olive branch to William III, who gives a cap of liberty to Europe.
At his feet writhes a figure of tyranny, with the features of Louis XIV.
On the west wall of the upper hall is a fresco of the Electress Sophia,
George I and their descendants – described as a 'new race of men from
heaven' – embodiments of the Protestant succession. Other frescoes show
the arrival of William III in 1688 and Neptune surrendering his trident
to Queen Anne, in acknowledgement of Britain's dominion over the seas.

After making peace with William in 1697, Louis had cooperated diplo-
matically with his former enemy until late 1700. He showered favours on
William's Ambassador Lord Portland, whom he assured, in an extended
private audience, of his 'sincere intentions to maintain a strict and firm
bond of union' with his master.[92] Le Nôtre sent William designs for gardens
at Windsor, and William planned a Trianon of his own at Hampton Court.

Nevertheless, as Portland and later ambassadors noted in dismay, James
II and his family (including his illegitimate son the Duke of Berwick,
whom they suspected of having plotted to assassinate William) continued
to attend Louis' court. At a christening at Saint-Cloud English diplomats
on one side of the gallery looked at Jacobites on the other 'with civility
mixed with contempt'. On 30 August 1698 Matthew Prior, a secretary
with the English embassy, wrote: 'vive Guillaume! You never saw such a
strange figure as the old bully [James II] is, lean, worn and riv'led [wrin-
kled] not unlike Neal the projector [speculator]; the Queen looks very
melancholy but otherwise well enough; their equipages are all very ragged
and contemptible.' At Fontainebleau in October, he wrote, 'the two Courts
are inseparable,' with many cries of 'à boire pour le roi d'Angleterre!' 'All
the court is made to Queen Mary, everybody is at her court in the morning, from whence the King of France leads her to chapel; the two Kings
and the Queen in the midst sit at the head of the table at dinner.'[93]

In November that year William, objecting that 'there could not be two
kings of England', requested James's departure from France. Louis replied
with sardonic humour that he was 'merely alleviating the misfortunes of
his [William's] father-in-law . . . during the rest of the year he passes a
very lonely life at Saint-Germain . . . Some hunting parties given him for
twelve or fifteen days ought not to be a subject of reproach.'[94]

William, as we have seen, was outraged by Louis' acceptance of the will of Carlos II, contrary to the second treaty of partition, signed in March 1700. In addition, in the interest of what Louis called 'perpetual friendship and the most perfect correspondence' between France and Spain, letters patent of December 1700 formally kept Philip in the line of succession in France 'in the same manner as if he was still actually residing in our kingdom', and French princes in that of Spain. The two crowns were to remain separate, but the possibility was raised of a constant shuttle across the Pyrenees between French and Spanish Bourbons, succeeding to each other's thrones.[95]

Further alienating European opinion, on 5 and 6 February 1701 French troops peacefully evicted Dutch troops from the fortresses along the frontier of the Southern Netherlands, where they had been stationed since 1697 as a barrier against French attacks. In September 1701, working through the Minister of the Marine Pontchartrain and Admiral Ducasse, rather than the Minister of Foreign Affairs Torcy, French merchants in the Compagnie Royale de Guinée obtained the *asiento de negros*, the right to ship 4,800 slaves every year from Africa to the Spanish colonies, previously assigned to a group of Portuguese merchants.[96]

Although large numbers of slaves perished en route, many knew that, as the French Ambassador Harcourt had written when proposing the deal, 'this commerce is very advantageous.' It also helped French merchants to sell French products in Spanish America.[97] Louis, a major investor, said he was personally 'very satisfied'.[98] He showed his continued interest in trade by reviving the Conseil de Commerce in 1700 and honouring non-noble merchants like Samuel Bernard, Antoine Crozat (both of whom invested in the *asiento*), Jean Orry and Nicolas Mesnager with private audiences, official appointments, ennoblement and titles.[99] They were indispensable.

Some people on both sides, especially merchants, hoped for peace. In April 1701 England, soon followed by the Netherlands, recognized Philip V. However, the contradictions between Louis' treaty with William and friendship with James became evident at James's deathbed.

On 2 September 1701 James II collapsed at mass. Members of the French royal family paid many visits, especially the Duc and Duchesse de Bourgogne (his great-niece) and the Prince de Conti (Mary of Modena's nephew). Louis came three times. On 5 September the Queen asked him to recognize her son as king, on grounds of status not politics, 'that he might not be dishonoured and return to the state of a private individual'.[100] James had already appointed Louis and the Queen joint guardians and tutors of the thirteen-year-old Prince.

Louis replied that he would have to consult his council. The ministers, eager to preserve the peace, begged him not to. But as with the recognition of Philip V in November 1700, dynastic dynamics – the hidden wiring of the kingdom – proved more powerful than ministers' advice. Moreover Louis XIV enjoyed showing that he was not obliged to follow their advice, even when they were unanimous.[101]

In 1700 the Dauphin had favoured his son becoming king of Spain. In 1701 he insisted that his cousin be proclaimed king of England. Not to do so would be unjust, unbecoming and 'a great cowardice'.[102] The King and the royal family had seen for themselves that the majority of visiting Englishmen at court, at reviews and at the great military camp at Compiègne in 1698 shunned 'the late king', as they called James II.[103] Nevertheless the Bourbons put conscience and family feelings before *raison d'état*.

On his deathbed James II told his son never to abandon the Catholic faith, to obey his mother the Queen and always to stick to the King of France. He also told him, as the Dauphin and Bourgogne had also been educated to believe, that 'Kings are not made for themselves but for the good of the People'.[104] After the last rites, he urged all his Protestant followers to become Catholics and forgave his enemies, even the Prince of Orange, the Princess of Denmark (his daughter Anne) and the Emperor Leopold I. Louis XIV's final visit, on 13 September, lasted an hour. He told his dying cousin, 'Monsieur, after the death of Your Majesty, I will recognize him [his son] as king of England,' and promised the young Prince that he would be a father to him.

At these words, wrote James's courtier the Duke of Perth to his religious adviser Père de la Trappe:

> the bedroom which was full to the doors resounded with cries of joy mixed with tears and acclamations to see the King who had just committed the most generous act. Some threw themselves at his feet to kiss his shoes, others raised their hands to heaven to thank God . . . the acclamations, the applause, the tears mixed with cries of joy and finally the surprise of such agreeable news prevented the King from hearing the thanks of the dying King.

Like the great showman Louis was, he was more interested in hearing his courtiers' applause than his cousin's expressions of gratitude. They were as convinced as he was that 'James III' was the rightful heir to England. As Louis left, he told the guards officer on duty to pay the same honours to the son as he had to the father. James II died at half-past three in the morning on 16 September.[105]

When James had asked to be buried in his parish church of Saint-Germain-en-Laye, Louis had replied, 'Monsieur, that is suitable neither for you nor for me.'[106] Showing that Louis regarded him more as a saint than as an ally, he ordered James's body to be dissected and the parts dispersed like the relics of a saint (or a king of France), not buried intact like a king of England. His body was interred in the Convent of the Benedictines Anglaises on the rue Saint-Jacques, near the Val-de-Grâce; his heart in his wife's Couvent de la Visitation at Chaillot; his brains in the Collège des Ecossais, in what is now the rue du Cardinal-Lemoine, where the Duke of Perth erected a monument to 'the best of masters'. His entrails were divided between the parish church at Saint-Germain and the English College at Saint-Omer. The convent of English Augustinian nuns in Paris received an arm.[107]

Putting his conscience before his country, and piety before policy, Louis XIV's recognition of 'James III', like the Revocation of the Edict of Nantes, was one of the blunders of the reign. Mazarin would have avoided both. The Cardinal had been particularly appreciative of Huguenots, whom he called 'good and faithful servants of the king'.[108] In 1659 he had warned that French intervention on behalf of the Stuarts would harm both them and France: 'As for England, it seems to me one should rather think of the interest of France, which in my opinion is not to embrace the quarrel of this king [Charles II].' The slightest demonstration in his favour by France would unite all parties against him in England, as indeed happened in 1701.[109]

Louis told the Papal Nuncio that he knew that recognition would help William III, and excite England and all the Protestant princes against himself; but 'he would not change his conduct, hoping that God would protect his good intentions and the justice of his cause.'[110]

The Foreign Minister Torcy swore to William's Ambassador in Paris the Earl of Manchester, and to the French representative in London M. Poussin, that the recognition was not contrary to the Treaty of Rijswijk, that Louis XIV would not help 'le Roi d'Angleterre' recover his thrones or trouble William III. Then he admitted that all the ministers had been against it and only the Dauphin and Madame de Maintenon had favoured 'a right given him by nature which none could take from him'.[111]

Manchester too blamed 'a person who governs all here', that is Madame de Maintenon, said to have promised Mary of Modena her son's recognition. Her failure to call William anything but 'le Prince d'Orange' – whereas Louis had called him (as well as James II) 'le Roi d'Angleterre' – proved her Jacobite sympathies, and her opposition to official French diplomacy. She wrote to Philip, in a moralizing tone, that the death of James II had edified 'the greatest libertines of the court' and, in a detail recorded by no one else, that Gardes du Corps had dipped their handkerchiefs in the blood of the King's corpse as it was being dissected.[112]

Manchester wrote grimly to his minister that the French would have occasion to repent their 'impertinent discourses': 'there is no relying on anything this court says or does, after what we have seen . . . there never will be any treating with this court without great vigour and resolution and avec les armes à la main.' To Torcy he wrote on 2 October, 'the king my master having learnt that SMTC [Sa Majesté Très Chrétienne] has recognised another king of Great Britain does not believe that his glory or his service allows him to keep an ambassador with the king your master any longer.'[113]

Manchester left Paris without a farewell. At the gates of the chateau of Saint-Germain, 'Athlone Herald', cheered by courtiers and townspeople, proclaimed 'James III' king of England, Scotland and Ireland. He was then recognized by the Pope and Philip V,[114] and asserted his sovereignty by the creation of peers and Knights of the Garter.[115] Mary of Modena's claim that recognition by Louis would merely prevent her son becoming a private person had been a cover for her political goals.

William was disgusted by what he saw as Louis' perfidy. An alliance had been signed between England, the Netherlands and the Holy Roman Emperor on 7 September, even before Louis XIV's recognition of 'James III'. Later that year a clause was added stating that they would not make peace until Louis XIV had formally recognized the Protestant succession in England.[116] The recognition of 'James III' was not, however, the only cause of the European war. War had already broken out between French, Spanish and Austrian forces in northern Italy in 1701, and the Emperor refused to recognize Philip V.

William III, long in bad health, died on 18 March 1702. Queen Anne, his successor, was not recognized by Louis XIV, who called her the Princess of Denmark. In a further act of tactlessness he told the Dutch they had been restored to freedom. On 3 April 1702 an Act of Abjuration and Bill of Attainder were passed in Westminster against 'James III'. Louis XIV had helped to bring war closer in unfavourable circumstances, having so ruined his reputation with foreign governments as to make peace more difficult since almost none of them trusted him.[117]

War was formally declared on Louis XIV and Philip V (called the 'Duc d'Anjou') by England, the Netherlands and the Emperor on 15 May 1702. Jacobite medals minted in France depicted Louis XIV's sun dispelling the clouds over the hopes of 'James III'.[118] Queen Anne's coronation medal, designed by her Master of the Mint Isaac Newton, was equally belligerent. It showed her as Athena, striking down a monster with two heads: Louis XIV and 'the Pretender'.[119] The War of the Spanish Succession was also a war over the English succession.

20

The Triumph of Europe

Four years after his grandson was proclaimed king of Spain, Louis XIV enjoyed another dynastic triumph. At Versailles at 5.30 in the afternoon of 25 June 1704, after an agonizing nine-hour labour, the Duchesse de Bourgogne gave birth to a healthy son. Throughout, the King had remained at the foot of the bed, Madame de Maintenon at the head, other members of the royal family in the room, while 'an infinity' of courtiers filled the antechambers of the Queen's apartment, which the Duchesse de Bourgogne occupied. Her husband, unable to bear to watch or listen, waited in an adjoining room.[1]

Louis XIV was thus both the longest-reigning king in European history and the first to know, in his lifetime, three generations of heirs descended from himself: his son the Dauphin; his grandson the Duc de Bourgogne; and the Duc de Bretagne, as the King's great-grandson was called (he died on 16 April 1705: the Duchesse de Bourgogne was heartbroken, but bore a second Duc de Bretagne in 1707 and a Duc d'Anjou, the future Louis XV, in 1710). In April 1705 Louis wrote to the Cardinal de Noailles, Archbishop of Paris, that 'this long succession of Kings . . . without example in any of my predecessors' reigns . . . assures the perpetuation of the good fortune of my lands.'[2]

As it had for the birth of the King's eldest grandson the Duc de Bourgogne on 6 August 1682, France celebrated in a frenzy of Te Deums, fireworks, public balls and wine fountains. The curé of Rumegies, near Lille, wrote in his diary: 'This was a new addition of joy for France, it being very certain that princes have no army as effective as a numerous family.' The birth was a 'blessing from heaven, without precedent for any of the kings of France.'[3] In a print showing the scene, inscribed 'La bénédiction du ciel sur la postérité de Louis le Grand', the Duchesse de Bourgogne watches exhausted from her bed, as Louis gestures to the well-swaddled baby, held by the Maréchale de La Mothe, Gouvernante des Enfants de France, beside the Dauphin, the Duc de Bourgogne and

the Duc d'Orléans. Below are vignettes of victories in Piedmont and fireworks in Paris. Vauban wrote from Paris, 'it is such universal joy in this
city that people do nothing but drink and dance all night.' The move to
Versailles had not cut what Louis XIV called his family's 'sacred knot'
with his subjects.[4]

On 28 August 1704 on the King's orders the city of Paris gave a fête in
honour of the Duc and Duchesse de Bourgogne. From the windows of the
Louvre, they watched boat races on the Seine. Fireworks represented
the 'eternal union' of Spain and France, and the homage offered to the
Seine and the Tagus by the other rivers of Europe – the Thames, the Meuse,
the Scheldt, the Neckar, the Rhine and the Danube.[5]

The fecundity of the Bourbon dynasty emphasized its rivals' lack of
direct heirs. William III had died without children; none of Queen Anne's
lived beyond the age of eleven. The Emperor Joseph I, who succeeded
his father Leopold I in 1705, had only daughters, ineligible for election as
Holy Roman emperor – thereby, as was already anticipated by diplomats,
weakening his house, and eventually leading, in 1740, to the War of the
Austrian Succession.[6]

Joy, however, soon turned to tears. The fireworks showing the 'homage
of the rivers of Europe' proved to be as hubristic as the sculptures of bound
nations surrounding the King's statue on the Place des Victoires. News of
a French defeat beside one of the rivers arrived even before the fireworks
were displayed.

In 1702 and 1703 the War of the Spanish Succession had gone well for
France. In the summer of 1704 a French army under Marshal Tallard,
with the army of Louis XIV's ally the Elector Max Emanuel of Bavaria,
had planned to march down the valley of the Danube on Vienna. On 13
August 1704 Louis' two nemeses, John Churchill, Duke of Marlborough
and Prince Eugene of Savoy, swooped on this army at Blenheim (see Map
4) on the Danube: 40,000 French and Bavarian soldiers were killed or
captured.

It was a triumph of Europe over France. The allied armies included
troops from England, Scotland, Ireland, the Netherlands, Denmark, Han-
over, Prussia, the Palatinate (avenging the horrors of 1688–93) and the
Habsburg monarchy. Marlborough was not only Captain General of
Queen Anne's forces and her Ambassador to the States General, but also
a field marshal of the Holy Roman Empire and Deputy Commander-in-
Chief in the Netherlands. Prince Eugene was President of the Imperial War
Council, Field Marshal of the Holy Roman Empire, Governor General of
Milan and Imperial Vicar General in Italy. Allied officers included the
future kings George II of England and Frederick William I of Prussia and

(briefly and incognito) Augustus II of Saxony. Apart from Spain, Bavaria was France's only Christian ally.[7]

Allied victory was due to superior diplomacy as well as generalship. Marlborough, helped by what Lord Chesterfield called his 'engaging, graceful manner' and good looks, was as effective negotiating with his allies in The Hague, Berlin and Vienna as he was fighting on the battle-field. Huguenot and other agents supplied him with intelligence from France, via his Huguenot secretary Cardonnel.[8]

Prince Eugene was animated by reckless courage and an 'invincible hatred' for France, as Villars informed the King, as strong as when he had left the country of his birth in 1683. At Blenheim he led his men in charge after charge, always 'the first of the hunt', eyes lit up with fury: it was a miracle he survived.[9] Saint-Simon claims that French officers who talked to Prince Eugene during their subsequent captivity reported that the Prince relished the prospect of revenge for the King's contempt and his brother's failure to inherit their father's office of *colonel général des Suisses et des Grisons*. He wanted to divide France and force Louis XIV south of the Loire.[10]

Marlborough, like his first commanding officer Turenne, understood the need for speed and surprise. He had led his armies 200 miles down the Rhine to the Danube: in Winston Churchill's phrase, 'a scarlet caterpillar' crawling across the map of Europe.[11] French generals, in contrast, were immobilized by sieges, and by orders from Versailles. Villeroy's fawning words to the King, from the front, help explain French defeats: 'Your Majesty understands war better than those who have the honour to serve you.'[12]

France's military performance was weakened by its demographic and climatic catastrophes, such as the flight of the Huguenots and the loss of population in the winter of 1693/4. Allied soldiers tended to be stronger, and better fed and disciplined. Moreover they paid for supplies. Louis XIV's ill-paid troops, in contrast, pillaged their way across Germany, stoking the fires of Francophobia.[13] During his reign his soldiers' average height diminished, reflecting the impoverishment of much of the French population.[14]

Defeat was also due to the superiority of allied equipment. Only in 1703 had French infantry finally abandoned pikes and muskets for guns and pistols like their enemies.[15] Under the Duc du Maine, Grand Master of Artillery, the quality of the King's cannon did not match their quantity. Splitting cannon barrels wounded French artillerymen almost as often as their cannonballs did the enemy. Officers made profits out of supplying guns of low quality. Sometimes the navy returned its cannon as unusable. Guy Rowlands concludes: 'the biggest weapons system the world had ever seen did not work.'[16]

Allied artillery was also used more effectively, being fired by platoon rather than by line. Captain Robert Parker wrote of one British charge at Blenheim, 'the French fire was quite extinguished, they made not the least resistance, but gave way and broke at once. Our squadrons drove through the very centre of them which put them to an entire rout . . . they were almost all of them killed or drowned.'[17] At Kerkhoven near Oudenarde in 1708, he recorded that the French, on sight of the enemy, 'to the great surprise of all Europe and to the scandal of the French arms . . . without firing a gun . . . instantly dispersed and fled, leaving behind them upwards of forty pieces of cannon with a great quantity of powder and ball'.[18] Absenteeism, as well as corruption, weakened French armies. In 1706 the French Ambassador in Spain, M. Amelot, reported that 'in some [French] regiments there is neither a colonel nor a lieutenant-colonel nor a major nor an aide-major . . . however good the troops are that is very unfortunate on the eve of a great battle.'[19] The extension of venality throughout the French army, including the artillery in 1703, in order to raise revenue, led to French officers often being less capable than their enemies.[20]

The French commander captured at Blenheim, Marshal Tallard, blamed his defeat on the divided command and lack of coordination with the Elector of Bavaria. In reality French troops had lost their fighting spirit. Dangeau recorded Louis XIV's incomprehension that at Blenheim, while eleven French infantry battalions had been cut to pieces, twenty-six battalions, and four regiments of dragoons, had surrendered without trying to fight their way out.[21] Marshal Villars, a better general than Tallard, said that they made him blush for his country. Humiliated French officers asked in captivity, 'Oh what will the King say?'[22]

Louis' manners triumphed over his anger. Madame de Maintenon wrote to their friend the Maréchal de Villeroy, 'you know his firmness; his temper has not changed for one moment; his kindness has made him concerned for all the individuals we have lost and we can say without flattery [sic] that he is truly great.'[23]

Marlborough had inflicted on Louis XIV what the States General called, in its letter of congratulation, 'a blow the likes of which the reigning king has never felt in all his long reign'.[24] Louis' conviction that, when equally matched, French troops would always beat the enemy, as he had written to Luxembourg in 1691, and would do again in 1706 to Villeroy, had proved to be another delusion, like his belief that all French Protestants would convert to Catholicism.[25]

Louis' armies had been further weakened by another war, with Protestants from the Cévennes, the mountains north of Montpellier and west of the

Rhône. In 1702, in response to the outbreak of war and to increased persecution of 'Nouveaux Catholiques' – Protestant 'converts' to Catholicism identified by their refusal to take the sacrament during mass – some Protestants had risen in revolt. Mainly peasants or weavers, about 10,000 in total, they were known as Camisards from the shirt they wore (*camisa* in *langue d'oc*), in contrast to the uniforms of the French soldiers sent to defeat them.[26]

Louis believed them to be seditious fanatics, who burnt Catholic churches and killed Catholic priests. While Protestant villages were burnt and destroyed, mountains as bleak and remote as the Cévennes, as later French Resistance fighters would find, were ideal for guerrilla warfare, of which the Camisard risings were an early example. Camisards could elude French troops in the caves and valleys which they had known from birth and which are today regarded as shrines to their heroism. They proved so formidable, under a brilliant young cobbler's son called Jean Cavalier, that three marshals of France, Broglie, Marcin, Villars, were sent in turn to fight them, with thousands of troops. In nearby towns such as Uzès and Nîmes many inhabitants were disarmed as 'suspects'.[27]

The Camisards considered themselves 'Children of God', crossing 'the desert' to 'the promised land'. Some were convinced, by local prophets who were often women or children (since the pastors had been killed), of the imminence of the Apocalypse, or deliverance from persecution. Like other conventional generals facing other guerrilla wars, Villars was surprised by the resistance he met in this 'horrible region': 'never has a people so little resembled those I have known hitherto.' Camisards were killed, imprisoned or sent to the galleys, and their villages destroyed. French troops, however, were often defeated.[28] Villars came to consider 'les voies de douceur' more useful than violence.[29] On 6 May 1704 Cavalier, to the horror of many local Catholics, agreed to surrender to Villars in return for an amnesty: the twenty-two-year-old cobbler's son negotiated with the fifty-year-old marshal as an equal.[30]

In 1699 as *contrôleur général* and secretary of state for war Louis had chosen a man named M. de Chamillart, a former administrator of Saint-Cyr and protégé of Madame de Maintenon, who had been introduced to the King by the Duc de Vendôme, grandson of an illegitimate son of Henri IV, and the Grand Ecuyer the Comte d'Armagnac. The King liked playing billiards with him. He was called a hero at billiards and a zero in the ministry, and was said to love the King like a mistress. However, he proved unsuccessful: such a combination of jobs would have been beyond almost anyone.[31] He was also inhuman. In February 1703 Chamillart advocated a 'general massacre' of Camisards in order 'to uproot this great evil'. He used language that would become familiar in the twentieth century: 'although I am not cruel by nature, it seems to me that on occasion one must divest oneself of all humanity.' Louis, however, showed that his youthful mildness had not completely vanished. Chamillart complained of the King's 'great grief' at the destruction of Protestant villages: 'His Majesty has difficulty in consenting to go to the final extremities against his subjects.' In the end Louis refused to do so.[32] He could still show mercy. On another occcasion he pardoned deserters whom he met in a chain-gang on its way to the galleys.[33]

In 1704 Louis XIV met a French Protestant noble for the first time since the departure of Schomberg in 1686. The Baron d'Aigaliers, who had helped persuade Protestants in the Cévennes to submit to Villars, twice saw Louis XIV at Versailles in late June and early July, once in the Chambre du Conseil in the presence of all the ministers. It was a confrontation between two mentalities, as well as two faiths. Louis XIV saw men in terms of services and favours, while d'Aigaliers thought ideologically. 'His Majesty received me very kindly and told me he was content with the zeal for his service I had shown in Languedoc,' remembered d'Aigaliers. On 3 July the King told him, 'I would wish you were a good Catholic to have cause to grant you favours and thereby to put you in a position to continue to serve me.'[34]

D'Aigaliers said, according to his own account, that persecution merely confirmed Protestant zeal and despair. The King, with a shrug of his shoulders, replied, 'That is enough, speak no more about it.' When the Baron asked 'my King and the father of all his subjects' for his blessing, Louis laughed and said, 'M. de Chamillart would give me [d'Aigaliers] his orders.' Chamillart blamed him for showing 'a little too much zeal for your religion' and told him the King would rather see his kingdom overthrown than permit the free exercise of the reformed religion.[35] D'Aigaliers retired to Geneva in September 1704, returned to France and died in prison in 1708. In his last letter to Chamillart he wrote, 'Alas Monseigneur what have we done to the King, who wants to deprive us of the privilege of serving him, while serving God according to the light of our conscience? Have we in our religion any maxim against the good of society?'[36]

Cavalier also resisted the siren song of the court: 'Believe what you wish but perform the [outward] functions of Catholics.'[37] He and thirty-three followers were given passports to leave France. After many years in British service, rising to the rank of major general and governor of Jersey, he died in London in 1740.[38]

Persecution of heretics in areas affected by the Camisard risings became more brutal. Watched by Catholic crowds, some Camisards, both men and women, were broken on a wheel or hanged. A few were burnt for profaning the host (the wafer, which Catholics believe becomes the body of Christ during the sacrament of mass), as Catholics also were for the same crime. Two Camisards called Jean Ravanel and Abdias Maurel were tortured, then burnt at the stake in Nîmes in April 1705. In March 1706, on the esplanade outside the walls of Montpellier, so was Salomon Couderc, one of the murderers of the detested missionary the Abbé du Chayla in July 1702.[39]

More French defeats followed Blenheim and the campaigns against the Camisards. On 23 May 1706 at Ramillies, south-east of Brussels, 26,000 French and Bavarian troops under Villeroy were killed, wounded or captured by allied troops under Marlborough and Eugene. Even crack units broke and fled, and were cut down as they ran.[40] When Louis told courtiers of the disaster, wrote Sourches, 'he did not spare the reputation of his Gardes du Corps who had fought there'.[41] This was not an isolated debacle. In 1709 the sudden surrender of a French garrison at Ghent, with all its munitions, led the King to send the commander to prison.[42]

On 4 July 1706 Madame de Maintenon wrote to her friend and ally Madame des Ursins, 'the King has seen so clearly and so convincingly the little confidence the army has in him [the Maréchal de Villeroy] and the clamours of Paris have been so loud that he has been forced to make this change and would always have regretted it if he had not done so.'[43] Villeroy was dismissed with kind words. To Saint-Simon this former favourite appeared like a deflated balloon.[44] Maintenon pressed for peace. In July 1707 she told Madame des Ursins, 'what cruelty war brings and seeing all these princes persecuting each other and causing so many people to perish! I am in a great sadness and see nothing but horrors.'[45]

Even more than before, generals were paralysed by micro-management from Versailles. Working late into the night, the King sent frequent couriers to his generals, with demands for the smallest details of news, and counsels of prudence, as is clear from many letters in his hasty, sprawling handwriting. The King regarded the Low Countries in particular as his area of expertise. In 1706 Chamillart wrote to Vendôme, Villeroy's replacement, 'nothing is done in Flanders but under the eyes of His Majesty and by his orders, He himself regulates his armies and writes in his own hand the number of troops He wants to garrison each of his strongholds.'[46]

The King's choice of generals was as unfortunate as his direction of their campaigns. Tallard, La Feuillade and Villeroy were mediocrities who owed their commands partly to the King's friendship. Villeroy, whom

Louis XIV had known all his life, entertained him with gossip about Paris and the court.[47] In 1703 Victor Amadeus II, Duke of Savoy, had again changed sides, prompting a letter from Louis XIV in his best sardonic style: 'Monsieur, Since religion, honour, interest, the alliance and your own signature are nothing between us, I am sending my cousin the Duc de Vendôme at the head of my armies to explain my intentions to you.'[48] French armies occupied Piedmont. While besieging Turin, however, on 7 September 1706 they were beaten and scattered by a smaller allied army under Prince Eugene and his cousin Victor Amadeus. Louis had insisted on the siege against Vendôme's and Vauban's advice, and had put two generals in charge: the Maréchal de Marsin and his nephew the Duc d'Orléans.[49] Louis himself began to lose heart. At eleven one night he wrote to Chamillart, 'all the news is appalling.'[50]

The allied victory at Turin ensured Savoy's final escape from French domination: hence the central position given by Prince Eugene to a picture of it, dwarfing pictures of his other victories, in the central salon of his Winter Palace in Vienna. It would be commemorated by Victor Amadeus II, in fulfilment of a vow to the Virgin, by the domed basilica of La Superga, overlooking Turin. It is an architectural celebration of triumph over Louis XIV as emphatic as the Duke of Marlborough's Blenheim Palace, on which work had begun, at vast expense to the British government, in 1705.[51] Until Italian unification all rulers of Savoy would be buried in La Superga, where every 7 September a commemorative Te Deum is still held. The allies' victory at Ramillies gave them Brabant; Turin won them northern Italy.[52] Thereafter, claiming them as fiefs of the Holy Roman Empire, the Emperor annexed Milan, raised taxes in Genoa, Tuscany and Parma, prepared to seize the last two on the extinction of their dynasties, and in 1708, on the death of the last Gonzaga Duke, annexed Mantua. The Duchy of Mantua, long a pro-French outpost in the valley of the Po, ceased to exist.[53]

In answer to French medals celebrating Louis XIV's victories, medals were minted abroad, usually in Amsterdam, mocking his defeats. His favourite phrases and images were turned against him. 'Nec pluribus impar' became, on an enemy medal celebrating the destruction of his ship *Le Soleil Royal*, 'Nunc pluribus impar'. 'Gallia victrix' became, on a medal attacking the Franco-Turkish alliance, 'Gallia supplex'. On one medal the Duke of Savoy, as Jupiter, destroys Phaeton – the Sun King – with thunderbolts. On another Louis XIV was shown dancing to a tune played by Queen Anne. The message: 'you must know how to please ladies.' Other medals showed him vomiting, defecating ('Even gods do not resist necessity') or being devoured by dogs.[54]

The allies' atrocities, like their arrogance, began to rival Louis XIV's. By its brutality the English bombardment of Cadiz in 1702 had reinforced its loyalty to Philip V.[55] In 1704, to punish the Elector of Bavaria for allying with Louis XIV, Marlborough ordered 'the entire ruining' of his country, letting soldiers destroy everything they could not pillage. Outside Munich 2,000 Bavarians were massacred by Imperial troops.[56]

France turned to Vendôme to end the run of defeats. Despite his unashamed homosexuality, his victories made him a popular hero. Parisians booked seats eight days in advance if they knew he was going to the opera, where he would be greeted with 'astounding acclamations' of 'Vive Vendôme!'[57] When he was staying at his country seat at Anet south-west of Versailles, the road from Paris was packed with carriages and Anet resembled a 'little Marly'.[58]

In 1708, reflecting both his caution and his passion for military glory for his heirs, Louis made Vendôme share command of French forces in Flanders with his eldest grandson Bourgogne, who was accompanied by his younger brother the Duc de Berri. In contrast to Vendôme's boldness, Bourgogne preferred to consider all possible reasons for making decisions, and opposed reckless attacks. He lacked the killer instinct needed for victory. France's national army became more divided than Marlborough's European army. As relations between Vendôme and Bourgogne deteriorated, the King twice sent the Minister of War Chamillart (who had already visited the front in 1706) to assess the situation, and Berwick to advise Vendôme. Two princes, two generals, the Minister of War, no clear chain of command, contradictory orders from Versailles: like the siege of Turin, a model of how not to run a campaign.[59]

At Oudenarde south of Brussels on 11 July 1708, the French army, despite superior numbers, was again defeated by Marlborough, in one of the few defeats of Vendôme's career. Both Bourgogne and Vendôme left the field for the safety of Ghent – Bourgogne quicker than Vendôme, who fought like a tiger. To Fénelon, whom he still venerated, Bourgogne tried to justify himself against accusations of indecision, saying that the King, on Chamillart's observations, had withdrawn the order to attack, while Vendôme was a man of 'absolute presumption'.[60] Vendôme complained that his orders had not been followed. He could have won the battle if Bourgogne had not held back his troops. He implied that Bourgogne was a coward and also criticized the decision to send the princes to the front.[61]

Public opinion supported Vendôme. Popular songs accused Bourgogne of being a coward and a bigot. Others attacked his Savoyard wife as a traitor; the tone is almost as hostile as in verses against Louis XVI and Marie Antoinette eighty years later.[62] The curé of Rumegies wrote in his diary that the young Prince had 'destroyed the country and during the campaign did nothing but make mistake after mistake'.[63]

France soon suffered a further defeat. Despite a gallant defence under the Maréchal de Boufflers, on 22 October 1708, as Vendôme had predicted, the allies took the city of Lille, and on 10 December its citadel, the centre of the web of fortresses protecting France's northern frontier.[64] Again, despite superior French numbers (perhaps 120,000 French to 85,000 allied troops), disputes between Vendôme, Bourgogne and other generals, their fear of losing a pitched battle and failure to intercept allied convoys had helped Marlborough to outmanoeuvre them.[65] This time Louis XIV had wanted the French army to fight. He told Bourgogne that it was his duty to encourage his soldiers and take risks: 'it is on such occasions that those who are above others must encourage them by their example.' The implication was that Bourgogne had not.[66]

The Maréchal de Noailles was pessimistic. He wrote to his son the Duc de Noailles private letters lamenting the incapacity of officials in the Ministry of War, divisions among the generals, bad food supplies and the low quality of French troops, 'very different from what they were in the past and above all the officers'. Soldiers 'flee as far as they can, having thrown down their weapons according to the good habit they have learnt recently'. The King, whom he pitied with all his heart, was 'very badly served'.[67]

The public and the court, led by marshals Boufflers, d'Harcourt and Villars, turned on Chamillart. Either he or the state, it was said, must perish. Bourgogne admitted that 'society was too infuriated against Monsieur Chamillart for him to be able to be useful in this post.'[68] The King, despite his personal regret, felt obliged to dismiss him: as with Villeroy in 1706, public opinion was stronger than Louis XIV. In February 1708 Chamillart was replaced as minister of finance by Desmarets, a brilliant nephew and pupil of Colbert, and in 1709 as minister of war by Voisin.[69] Chamillart's remark to Desmarets shows the exhaustion Louis inflicted on his ministers: 'Monsieur you are giving me life; I am giving you death.'[70] Both the new ministers proved more capable than their predecessor.

Meanwhile the Duc and Duchesse de Bourgogne were becoming the centre of the court. The Duchess, affectionate, graceful and intelligent, seemed to be everywhere at once, like a whirlwind. She enjoyed hunting, riding and the theatre, and often stayed up all night, going from party to party in different apartments in the palace. Thanks to her, in the 1700s Louis' court was almost as lively as in the 1660s.[71] Like her grandmother the first Madame, she won courtiers' hearts by treating them as humans rather than as servants.[72] The second Madame considered she was allowed too much freedom and foretold disaster.[73] Indeed while Bourgogne was on campaign, she had enjoyed love affairs with the Abbé de Polignac and two handsome young officers, the Marquis de Nangis and de Maulévrier. Her adoring household protected her reputation.[74] Bourgogne probably never knew.

Perhaps compensating for his failures on the battlefield, Bourgogne avoided parties and spent much of his time in his study, devoting himself to mathematics, science, music and drawing.[75] He and his wife remained a united couple, both politically and physically, eager to sleep together at once if they had been parted.[76] Sometimes they wrote letters to each other in their own blood. He wrote more often.[77]

The Duchess spent many evenings, and sometimes the whole day, with the King: more time than with her own husband. Antonia Fraser thinks that Louis loved her more than anyone in his life, with the possible exception of his mother.[78] They both enjoyed the theatre. When she acted in a play in Madame de Maintenon's apartment, with other members of the royal family and the Noailles, the King sometimes sang in the chorus with the *dames du palais*.[79] Occasionally he declared that, rather than having supper with him every night, she must 'divert herself' elsewhere.[80] On 20 April 1708, however, in a celebrated scene described by Saint-Simon, for once an eyewitness, she had a miscarriage because, on Louis' orders, she had rushed to join him at Marly. He loved her so much, or was so selfish, that he could not bear to be there without her.[81] The Maréchal de Noailles commented, 'there is no doubt she miscarried, that is very unfortunate and should oblige [no person named] in the future to take much greater precautions.'[82]

Understanding in a second everything happening in a room, even what she was meant not to, the Duchesse de Bourgogne became her husband's most ardent defender after the debacles in Flanders. When she saw Vendôme in the salon at Marly – the court's conversational battlefield – she asked, 'Will I always see the enemy of my father and my husband?' Vendôme said, according to one of his admirers, a police official called Narbonne, 'if the king my master had let me act, I would have reduced your father to such extremities that he would no longer have been able to hurt anyone. And as for your husband, I would have wished him to acquire glory and it is not my fault if he did not.' She refused to play cards with him. To please her, Louis XIV stopped inviting this popular general to Marly and removed him from the army list. Vendôme retreated to Anet. The Dauphin, however, remained his friend.[83] By then the court had formed into three cabals: the King's most obedient servants and ministers around Madame de Maintenon, a war party around the

Dauphin and a group of reformers with the Duc de Bourgogne, piloted by Fénelon from his exile in Cambrai. They were known as the cabals of the ministers, of Meudon and of the nobles.[84]

France was weakened by the Stuarts' disasters as well as its own. The decade after the death of James II in 1701 was the golden age of the Jacobite court. 'James III' was braver and more intelligent than his father: even Matthew Prior, a servant of William III, considered him 'very lively'.[85] In May 1700, according to the Earl of Manchester, Ambassador of William III, his first communion, at the age of twelve, had been 'a great day here': 'the Prince of Wales, as they call him, went in great state to Notre-Dame and was received by the Archbishop of Paris with the same honours as if the French king himself had been there . . . all the English that are here run to see him.'[86]

Each time the young 'James III' danced at court, Louis XIV stood up, as for a reigning monarch.[87] His sister Louise Marie, 'la princesse d'Angleterre', was much admired. As heiress presumptive to the throne of England, she was even given precedence over her friend the Duchesse de Bourgogne.[88] When not with Louis XIV, the Duchesse de Bourgogne spent hours alone at Saint-Germain with Mary of Modena, whom she may have regarded as a second mother.[89] The Duke of Berwick, naturalized French in 1703, promoted marshal of France in 1706, often led French troops to victory, as did other Jacobite commanders such as Arthur Dillon and Count O'Mahony.[90]

Encouraged by Mary of Modena and Madame de Maintenon, as well as by Louis himself, on 17 March 1708 James III sailed to Scotland from Dunkirk in a fleet of thirty-three ships under the Comte de Forbin, carrying 6,000 troops, an orchestra and gold plate off which to eat.[91] An attack of measles, and the presence of English ships off Dunkirk, had delayed their departure. James hoped to exploit the unpopularity of the Act of Union of 1707 between Scotland and England, and to address his next letter to his mother, as he wrote to her, 'from the Palace at Edinburgh. I should be there by Saturday.'

On 11 April, however, three weeks after it left, the French fleet returned to port. Forbin had proved a bad navigator. When he finally reached the Firth of Forth, he had found, not welcoming bonfires, but ships of the Royal Navy. Despite James's pleas, Forbin had refused to land French troops.[92]

Despite a worsening military situation, in December 1709 Louis XIV planned another expedition to take James to Scotland, with 2,000 French troops, provided that the court at Saint-Germain – considered incapable of keeping secrets – was not informed until the moment of departure. Louis wrote two short memoranda in his own hand, listing the officers, ships and munitions to be chosen for the expedition. It never materialized.[93]

While Louis XIV was suffering defeats, Philip V (whom he encouraged to fight at the head of his troops) was winning victories. Philip shared Louis' belief in the indispensability of an effective royal guard. In May 1702 Philip had written to Louis: 'as long as I do not have troops devoted to myself and above all a regiment of guards on which I can rely, I will never achieve anything.'[94] In 1702–3, following plans drawn up by Orry, the traditional Spanish royal guards, composed of what were called 'the vilest artisans of Madrid', were dissolved. Two new guards regiments, the Spanish Guards and the Walloon Guards, were formed on the model of the French Guards and Swiss Guards of Louis XIV. In 1704 Philip also formed four companies of Gardes du Corps, 300 men strong, as in France. Again reflecting a belief that foreigners were more reliable than Spaniards, while two companies were Spanish, another was Italian and the fourth Walloon. Louis sent drill instructors and other officers to train the guards, and they had similar uniforms, in similar Bourbon livery colours of blue, silver and red, to their French models.[95]

In August 1705 Philip gave the Captain of the Gardes du Corps on duty the right to sit directly behind him, on a small bench or *banquillo*, during services in the chapel. In protest at this infringement of Grandees' privilege to stand directly behind the King, all Grandees – even two who were captains of companies of Gardes du Corps – refused to attend the chapel. Encouraged by Louis, the King stood firm. He also insisted, as in France, on giving orders directly to guards commanders himself rather than through court officials. By December 1705 the King had won and the Grandees were back in attendance in the palace chapel.[96]

Without this expansion of the royal guard, Philip V and his contemporaries felt, the monarchy would have perished. The Camarera Mayor, the lady in charge of the Queen's household with the right to enter her bedroom when she wished, wrote to Madame de Maintenon on 3 September 1705, 'The King of Spain cannot be the master until he is able to make himself feared by the grandees; and if he does not have guards he will never succeed in this.'[97] This large, privileged royal guard would prove its worth by defending Philip throughout the War of the Spanish Succession, and by maintaining his son Charles III on the throne during serious riots in 1766.[98]

The Camarera Mayor, Madame des Ursins, came from the most ambitious section of the French nobility, the *princes étrangers*. Born a La

Trémoille in 1642, in 1659 she had married a Talleyrand, the Prince de Chalais, from a *frondeur* family. His participation in a duel had led to their departure to live in Madrid (1663–70). In 1670, after his death, she had married the Duc de Bracciano, a Grandee of Spain of the powerful Orsini family of Rome, but was soon widowed again. Thereafter she had divided her time between Paris (1676–82 and 1687–95) and Rome, where she kept open house and was a leader of the 'French party'. She had influenced the Pope, whose election she was believed to have helped, in favour of Philip V. Although Louis XIV did not entirely trust her, he gave her a pension.[99] She enjoyed the triple advantage of friendship with Madame de Maintenon, since the days when she had been plain Madame Scarron;[100] ability to speak French, Spanish and Italian; and knowledge of Madrid and the rank of a wife of a Grandee of Spain. That is why Louis XIV and Philip V had selected her, at her own suggestion, as *camarera mayor* of the new Queen.[101]

Madame des Ursins would become as powerful in Madrid as Madame de Maintenon in Versailles or the Duchess of Marlborough in London. Saint-Simon, who knew her well, wrote:

> she was tall rather than short, dark with blue eyes which continually said whatever she wished, with a perfect figure, a fine neck and a face which without being beautiful was charming; an extremely noble air, something so majestic in her entire bearing and such continual and natural grace in everything, down to the smallest and most unimportant details, that I have never seen anybody approach it either in their body or in their intelligence, of which she had everything and of every kind, flattering, caressing, insinuating, controlled, wishing to please for its own sake and with charms from which it was impossible to defend yourself when she tried to win and seduce.

She soon won the confidence of the King and 'my young and marvellous queen', as she called Maria Luisa.[102]

In March 1702 she boasted to Torcy, 'I think I will always be sufficiently mistress to make her do everything I wish.'[103] Soon she was leading what she called 'the life of a convict', giving Philip his slippers and removing his *robe de chambre* at night, before he climbed into bed with the Queen, and opening the bedroom curtains and removing the royal chamber pot in the morning.[104] The young Queen's need for guidance, affection and amusement was the basis of Madame des Ursins' power. While the King was being acclaimed by his Italian subjects in 1702, with Madame des Ursins' encouragement the Queen spent six hours a day in the council, and subsequently served three times as regent. Together they helped run Spain.[105]

Encouraged by Louis, she also tried to soften the etiquette which kept
Philip and Maria Luisa prisoners in their own palace, and to introduce to
Madrid some of the *divertissements* of Versailles.[106] On Philip's return
from Italy, she began to redecorate the state apartments, to organize balls
and plays and to persuade Grandees to attend the toilette of the Queen.
The King began to dine in public, and hold Appartement three times a
week. The Queen imposed French fashions on Spanish ladies, although
some Grandees said that they would rather their wives died than showed
their feet.[107]

Convinced of her own reason and moderation, Ursins also began to
influence government appointments, supporting Orry and helping to
remove Portocarrero, her former ally, and Cardinal d'Estrées from the
Despacho, or council of ministers. In a private letter taken by Philip V's
courtier Louville directly to Louis XIV himself, she accused d'Estrées of
dark designs.[108] In April 1704, Louis XIV, increasingly annoyed by reports
of dissensions among French agents in Madrid, asked her to return to
Rome. Queen Maria Luisa pleaded in vain for her to stay.[109]

Madame des Ursins, however, was a match for Louis XIV. On her way
back, she obtained permission to rest in Toulouse. By persistent appeals
to Madame de Maintenon, she then received authorization to visit Paris.
Finally on 11 January 1705, she had a two-and-a-half-hour audience at
Marly with Louis himself. Her justifications were so persuasive, her
knowledge of Spain so evident, the pleas of Philip V and Maria Luisa so
heartfelt, that Louis changed his mind and ordered her to return to Spain.
Torcy and the French Ambassador in Spain were dismayed.[110]

Like the politician she was, Madame des Ursins drew up a treaty (now
lost), defining her powers in Spain, with Madame de Maintenon in her
bedroom in Marly. With her adviser Jean Orry on 29 April 1705 she
received the rare honour of an audience with the King, without the presence of a minister, and won the right to receive orders directly from
him.[111] At a ball at Marly, Louis XIV was seen to pet her lapdog: an
unheard-of honour, since no courtier was, in theory, allowed to bring
these detested animals into his presence.[112] She also wrote memoranda for
Torcy and suggested M. Amelot as next French ambassador in Spain.
Knowing the King's love of flattery, she later wrote to Madame de Maintenon that he was 'le plus honnête homme du monde' ('the greatest
gentleman in the world' – the same compliment James II and Mary of
Modena had paid him), and better company than anyone she had met in
France, Italy or Spain. She did not leave Versailles until 2 June.[113]

Her return to Spain after a year's absence was an apotheosis. Along the
route the Camarera Mayor, travelling in royal carriages with a suite of

eighty, received the homage of officers, clergy and magistrates, and 'the acclamations of the people'. She was assured that her return was the will of 'all the nation', and was entertained with bullfights and fireworks. On 3 August, despite the heat, the King and Queen, ministers and ambassadors, came out to welcome her back to Madrid. She entered the capital, according to the *Mercure Galant*, through a double row of carriages, with 'the most august, the finest and the most numerous cortège which has ever been seen, followed by all the people who shouted that they wished the Camarera Mayor to live a thousand years'. A lady-in-waiting publicly enjoyed the power and status of a chief minister.[114]

Later that year her enemy d'Estrées was replaced by a new ambassador, suggested by Ursins, from a *famille de robe*, the Marquis d'Amelot. Louis XIV made Ursins, Orry, Tessé and Amelot swear amity. Finally he had an effective team in Madrid. Amelot and Orry began to draft Philip V's instructions to his council. Thanks to Orry's reforms, soldiers began to desert to, rather than from, the Spanish army.[115] Grandees were excluded from high office, in accordance with Louis' belief that 'the power of the Grandees must be repressed in all instances where it can cause harm to government business and the good government of the State'. They should be compensated with 'prerogatives which only concern ceremonial'.[116]

Philip and Maria Luisa were invigorated by the return of the Princesse des Ursins. She wrote that he breathed war and swore that he would not cede an inch of territory. When he was on campaign, the Queen, with whom he was as passionately in love as his brother Bourgogne was with her sister, remained in Madrid as regent. She pawned her jewels and the Princesse des Ursins raised 'voluntary contributions' from cities and provinces in order to pay and feed the troops.[117] Some of her letters to Chamillart or Madame de Maintenon about army movements and appointments are those of a confident minister of war.[118]

However, Philip's Austrian rival 'Charles III', as the Archduke Charles was called by his adherents as well as by most of Europe, was a growing threat. Having been proclaimed king of Spain in Vienna in September 1703, he had travelled via England to Lisbon, where he resided between March 1704 and July 1705. Like another former French ally Savoy, Portugal had turned against France. Philip had deprived its merchants of the *asiento de negros*, while 'Charles III' made a secret promise to cede it Spanish territory, as he had already ceded Milan to the Emperor.

After England had guaranteed Catalonia's laws and privileges and an annual subsidy of £210,000 by the Pact of Genoa of 20 June 1705, the principality had revolted against Philip V. From 9 October that year 'Charles III' established his government, with English and Dutch support, in Barcelona. To this day he is celebrated as a symbol of Catalan independence.[119] Another memorial to the reign of 'Charles III', and an unintended gift of Louis XIV to Britain, is British control of Gibraltar. It was conquered, in Charles's name, by British, Dutch and Austrian forces on 4 August 1704. A year later it received its first British governor, and would help make part of the Mediterranean a British lake until the disbandment of the Mediterranean fleet in 1967.[120]

On 25 June 1706 Charles occupied Madrid, forcing Philip and Maria Luisa to flee. Toledo and Saragossa also acknowledged him. However, Madrid remained loyal to 'Philipismo'. Patriotic prostitutes slept with allied troops in order to infect them with diseases. On 5 August Philip recovered control of his capital.[121] The Queen wrote to Madame de Maintenon that they owed their crown, after God, to the people alone.[122] In contrast the loyalty of Grandees, even of Cardinal Portocarrero and the Admiral of Castile who had helped put Philip on the throne, wavered with every allied victory.

The Duke of Berwick won a great victory at Almanza near Valencia on 25 April 1707, over allied troops commanded by the Huguenot Henri de Ruvigny, Earl of Galway, including a regiment of Camisards under Jean Cavalier. Thereafter, confident that Philip V had come to stay, all Spaniards except judges renounced the traditional black *habit à l'Espagnole*. Instead, Amelot wrote to Louis, they adopted French dress, 'without anyone having been told the slightest thing on behalf of the King your grandson, to procure this change'.[123] To the benefit of the French dress trade, streams of fashion accessories crossed the Pyrenees to Madrid – cravats, hats, wigs and swords as well as clothes.[124]

In April 1707 news of the Queen's pregnancy prompted spontaneous illuminations in Madrid, where she was adored. Luis, Prince of Asturias, the eldest son of Philip V, was born on 25 August (St Louis' day) 1707 in Madrid, in the presence of Grandees as in France, rather than in private as hitherto in Spain. The Princesse des Ursins organized a grandiose public baptism. Crowds cheered frenetically when the Queen appeared on the palace balcony to show them 'Luizillo'.[125]

Already in late 1706, however, faced with repeated French defeats, Louis had warned Philip that he should abandon a 'badly placed resistance' and be prepared to accept what his accession had been intended to prevent: 'great dismemberments of the monarchy'.[126] France was running out of money as well as victories. In 1703 receipts were 105 million livres, expenses 171 million. In 1706 expenses reached 196 million livres, while revenue had sunk to 53 million.[127] By 1710 military and naval expenses, and the loans needed to pay for them, were absorbing more than 75 per cent of the budget.[128] Despite pleas from Samuel Bernard and his allies, however, the French government created no equivalent of the Bank of Amsterdam or Bank of England to issue notes and help finance the war. Such a measure was officially approved in early 1709, but abandoned in the face of opposition from other French bankers and Lyon.[129] The government avoided bankruptcy by short-term borrowing at disastrous interest rates (far higher than those paid by its enemies) and creating more offices to sell. By 1708 government debt would reach 2 billion livres and servicing it would absorb over 50 per cent of government expenditure: 470 of 756 million livres.[130] Europe's triumph over France was not only military and diplomatic, but financial.

21

Towards the Precipice

When Louis XIV wanted money, he forgot his prejudices. On 6 May 1708, during a financial crisis, he took the unusual step of himself showing Samuel Bernard round the gardens at Marly. Saint-Simon admired the contrast between the King's normal reserve and the flow of words, spoken with the grace which he could deploy so well when he wished, addressed to this non-noble banker and former Huguenot, and described it as 'cette espèce de prostitution'. Soon afterwards, however, the government secured loans with which to pay the troops.[1]

In all Samuel Bernard may have supplied the government with 200 million livres during the War of the Spanish Succession, almost entirely from borrowing abroad. Sometimes he charged the government 12 or 16 per cent interest. Putting business before religion, Huguenot bankers abroad also helped finance their persecutor in France.[2]

Another financier and currency speculator called Antoine Crozat, from a prosperous office-holding family of Toulouse, also lent money to the monarchy. Crozat created a global empire in coffee, spices, tobacco, textiles and slaves. One of his companies had the *asiento* for Spanish America and in 1712 Louis XIV would lease him a monopoly on trade with Louisiana. Despite attacks by the Royal Navy, Crozat and merchants from Saint-Malo (hitherto a modest fishing port), Nantes and La Rochelle traded directly with Spanish colonies in America; as a result 55 million livres of American gold and silver entered France between 1701 and 1717. Opposition from Madrid was defeated by bribing officials in the colonies.[3] In 1707 and 1709, thanks to Spanish ships choosing to sail to French ports, Louis XIV received more silver from Spanish America than Philip V. It helped him to avoid bankruptcy and to pay some of his soldiers.[4] Both Samuel Bernard and Antoine Crozat, with fortunes of 20 million livres or more, were as rich as the richest royal prince the Duc d'Orléans. Crozat lived in two houses in the Place Vendôme and married his children into the high nobility, not always with the intended result. What is now the Elysée Palace was built in 1707–20 by Crozat's son-in-law the Comte d'Evreux, son of Louis XIV's Grand Chamberlain, with the money of his wife's dowry. The moment it was finished, he sent 'the gold lingot', as his family called his wife, back to her father.[5]

French financiers, however, could not relieve the rigours of the winter of 1708/9, when France faced not only military defeat but climatic disaster. For eleven days the temperature was minus 15 or below, occasionally reaching minus 21. Rivers froze over, as did trees, plants, seeds in the ground and bottles of wine.[6] The Parlement de Paris suspended its sessions. The King, who normally walked in his gardens whatever the weather, stayed indoors, and stopped giving balls or going to Marly. The Dauphin moved to Versailles, as his own chateau of Meudon was too cold.[7]

In previous years there had been so much grain that France could export it; by 1708 there was so little that the country was on the verge of famine.[8] France was worse affected than it had been by the winter of 1693/4. The Lyon silk industry collapsed. Silk workers slept in the street, having sold everything in order to buy food.[9] The curé of Cindré in the Auvergne wrote to Desmarets, the Controleur Général, to warn that landowners were abandoning the countryside while most farmworkers had died; 'the rest resemble corpses which collapse along the roads and hedges and do not rise again.' There was neither money nor credit. In all around 630,000 Frenchmen may have died from cold and hunger.[10]

Madame de Maintenon's letters to the Princesse des Ursins and Adrien Maurice de Noailles show her awareness of the horrors outside the palace walls, and her growing panic and despair. On 23 December 1708 she wrote, 'France had expanded too far and perhaps unjustly . . . our nation was insolent and uncontrolled.' Perhaps such criticisms, including her remark that God 'wants to humiliate him in order to save him', were meant to be intercepted and read by the King.[11]

> 8 April 1709: the price of wheat is rising every day . . . famine is universal. It seems that God wants to reduce us to the last extremities.[12]
>
> 29 April: You think that it is better to perish than to surrender, I think that we must yield to force, to the hand of God who is visibly against us, and that the King owes more to his peoples than to himself.[13]
>
> 5 May: we are at Marly but you hear of nothing in this ravishing place but poverty. No labourer is as worried as we are about wheat and its price.[14]
>
> 14 July: Paris is very difficult to control. Bread is becoming more expensive there every day . . . we have seditions everywhere.[15]
>
> 30 July: our court is still very sad. We talk only of wheat, oats, barley and straw. One [Louis XIV] is very occupied with the relief of the people . . . there are ill-intentioned people who excite them.

26 August: the greatest misfortunes have often had smaller beginnings . . . The question of wheat will make me lose my head.[16]

4 November: I am used to living on poison . . . I am no longer good for anything.[17]

She assured all her correspondents that the King was in good health; but in May 1709 she prophesied that the younger members of his family would see 'bien des révolutions'.[18] Going from Meudon to Paris for the opera, the Dauphin was often stopped by crowds of women shouting for bread. He would order his servants to throw them coins, and his coachman to drive on.[19]

Two senior court officials, Bouillon and La Rochefoucauld, told Louis of 'extremely insolent posters' in Paris. One, stuck on a statue of Louis XIV, praised Ravaillac, the assassin of Henri IV. Another included a prayer which began, 'Our father who art in Versailles, your name is not hallowed, your kingdom is no longer great, nor is thy will done by land or sea. Give us this day our daily bread for we cannot buy it.'[20]

As the playwright Chamfort would write eighty years later, France was an absolute monarchy tempered by songs. One song expressed contempt for the royal family and desire for an English solution:

> The grand father is a braggart [*fanfaron*],
> The son an imbecile.
> The grandson a big coward.
> What a fine family!
> How I pity you, poor Frenchmen,
> Under their rule!
> Do as the English have done,
> That is enough to tell you.

Popular resentment, hunger and violence, always in the background, became so intense that there were more food riots and popular uprisings in France in 1709 than in any year that century before 1789: a total of 298 in 1709 as against 310 in 1789.[21]

The Venetian Ambassador wrote from Paris that everyone complained of the government's tyranny; he feared that the danger from within might be worse than from without. In the Ardennes the poor spoke only of pillage, while the rich barricaded themselves in their houses.[22] In Rouen there was a revolt with cries of 'Vive Marlborough!' and calls to attack the court and the Bastille. In the summer of 1709 flooding rivers, as well as hailstorms, ruined what few crops remained to harvest. Samuel Bernard himself defaulted on his debts. Fénelon said that despotism was the cause of all France's ills.[23] In a gesture of despair, the relics of the patron saint of Paris, Sainte Geneviève, were paraded through its streets.[24] Army pay was months late: there were mutinies and 'discours insolents et séditieux' by troops in Calais, Dunkirk and Sarrelouis.[25]

In contrast to 1789, however, the government did not waver. The monarchy was not the worn-out machine, close to collapse, that Fénelon and other critics alleged. Its power was more pervasive throughout France, and it was more resourceful than at the beginning of the reign. The book trade, for example, was regulated more effectively, by a system of government censorship and licences for privileged printers, supported by police raids on their premises to check on publications. Chancellor Pontchartrain established a census of all printers and booksellers, in order to control them. Few hostile pamphlets could be printed, although not even Louis XIV could prevent the circulation of handwritten songs.[26]

Desmarets had at first underestimated the crisis. However, with what his biographer calls the government's 'more pervasive presence' in the provinces, it managed to employ or feed some of the poor in the famine years of 1693–4 and 1709–10. Barley was sown as a substitute for wheat.[27] In addition a voluntary levy was instituted in May 1709 on the rich, including the King and the Dauphin, in order to help feed the poor.[28]

Louis had been fortunate in his choice in 1697 of the Comte d'Argenson as successor to La Reynie as *lieutenant général de police*. As respected as his predecessor, he proved just as effective in dealing with a potential revolution as with the usual police problems of irreverence at mass, 'indecent postures' on stage and illegal gambling parties.[29] Saint-Simon claimed that there was not one person in Paris whose daily movements he did not know, and that he had the ability, while always preferring mercy, to make even the most innocent tremble. The diarist Mathieu Marais considered that he had the political genius of Richelieu. D'Argenson himself regarded his duty as, in his own words, to serve the poor with all his heart.[30] To stop guns falling into the wrong hands, they were removed from manufacturers' houses and stored in the Bastille.[31] People who denounced grain hoarders were rewarded with half the hoard when it was found.[32] In addition to the forty-eight *commissaires de police*, d'Argenson had two men in each quarter charged with selling bread at the low price of two sols a loaf and a special tribunal to judge fraud in the wheat trade. With the Chancellor, the Contrôleur Général, the Prévôt des Marchands and the Premier Président, as well as court officials, he kept the King daily informed of the price and availability of bread in Paris.[33] Gardes Français, Gardes Suisses and Mousquetaires, moreover, had been kept back from the front, especially to 'contain the populace' in Paris.

On 4 May 1709, however, d'Argenson admitted that the markets had been emptied by eleven in the morning: 'today we would have had some strange problems without the help of the regiment of Gardes Français and if we were without it, certainly we would see only trouble and confusion' – as would occur eighty years later in 1789.[34]

When d'Argenson's house or carriage were besieged by famished women, he would mix with them, listen to them and distribute money. He wrote to the Chancellor: 'I try to appease the fire which is starting as best I can.' Soldiers were placed at the gates of markets to stop them being pillaged. The phrase 'the fire which is starting' (*le feu qui s'allume*), however, shows how alarmed this experienced police chief had become.[35]

While France starved and rioted, a 'union of ministers' hoped to oblige the King to make peace at any price.[36] Already in 1708 Louis had opened unofficial negotiations through Chamillart, with no result but to increase allied demands. In April 1709 the Foreign Minister Torcy, at his own suggestion, moved by the King's tears, travelled to The Hague to restart peace negotiations.[37]

French eagerness for peace encouraged allied diplomats, advised by Marlborough and Prince Eugene, to put forward humiliating demands: the loss of French Flanders and most of Alsace including Strasbourg; the demolition of the fortifications of Dunkirk; the occupation of four French forts as 'guarantees'; the expulsion of 'James III' and recognition of the Protestant succession in England; and the recognition of 'Charles III' in Spain and expulsion of Philip V, with Louis XIV's help. Madame de Maintenon and the ministers, except Desmarets, wanted Louis XIV to accept.[38]

The allies had become as arrogant and unrealistic as Louis at the height of his power. They ignored Castilians' passionate loyalty to Philip V and his determination to continue fighting, even from America.[39] Allied negotiators justified themselves by saying that Louis XIV had broken the partition treaty and could not be trusted to keep new ones. They forgot that the partition treaty had never been accepted by Spain and had therefore been unworkable; and that England and the Netherlands had also broken it, by recognizing Philip as king of Spain in 1701.[40]

Louis refused to dethrone his own grandson. Regarding the peace conditions as impossible, he resolved to fight on. In reaction to the allied peace terms, on 12 June 1709 he played an unexpected card: an appeal to the nation. The concepts of *la nation* and *la patrie* were familiar to him and his subjects. In 1649 a speech against Mazarin had referred to 'that natural affection which all men have for their fatherland'.[41] 'There is

nothing more glorious for the nation and for you than what has happened,'
Louis had written to Luxembourg after the victory of Neerwinden in
1693, as twenty-seven years earlier he had written, 'I like the glory of my
nation.'[42] Madame wrote that 'the French are more infatuated with their
fatherland than any other nation' – even her beloved Germans.[43]

Drafted by Torcy, a master of propaganda as well as diplomacy, the
appeal was in the form of a letter addressed to the Duc de Tresmes, Premier
Gentilhomme and Governor of Paris. In reality, it was intended for all
FRANÇAIS (in capitals in the appeal). Printed by the Imprimerie Royale,
it was read out to, and applauded by, soldiers in the field, and posted on
public buildings.*

The King talked not just of the obligations imposed by 'the crown which
God had given him', but also of 'my tenderness for my people . . . no less
strong than that I have for my own family'. He explained that a truce, more
dangerous than the war itself, would prevent peace rather than hasten it
and would give the allies access to the interior of the kingdom. Referring
to the obligation to dethrone Philip V, he continued: 'it is against humanity
to believe that they had ever thought they could persuade me to join such
an alliance.' Rather than accept 'conditions equally contrary to justice and
to the honour of the French name', the French should fight on.[44]

On 9 July 1709 Marlborough, perhaps misled by French deserters and
Huguenot informants, assured Anthonie Heinsius, Grand Pensionary of
Holland, that France could not continue fighting and would accept any
terms. French troops were in 'unbelievable misery', 'half starved and quite
naked'.[45] In reality Louis' public appeal to the French had elicited 'a cry
of joy and ardour' from his troops, and was also popular in Paris.[46]

Louis XIV was not prepared to dethrone Philip V by force. The humiliation, and the impracticalities, were too great. However, in his desperate
quest for peace, despite having devoted so much effort to putting his
grandson on the throne of Spain, in late 1709 and again in 1710 Louis
XIV asked him to leave it.[47] In contrast to 1700, he now put France before
his dynasty. In the summer of 1709, telling Philip V that he had to listen
to 'the voice of my peoples', Louis withdrew almost all French troops from
Spain, as he had begun to do in 1707. The 25,000 who remained no longer
obeyed Philip V or fought 'Charles III'. From 1 July 1709 the French
Ambassador stopped attending the Spanish council. In the interests of
peace, Madame de Maintenon also began to advocate the departure of
Philip V and accused Madame des Ursins, because of her support for him,

---

* It has been called 'l'appel du 12 juin', in anticipation of de Gaulle's 'appel du 18 juin' in
1940, also rejecting the shameful prospect of capitulation to the enemy.

of no longer being a good Frenchwoman. Ursins replied that she was a better Frenchwoman than anyone.[48] Since 1708 she had been warning against peace at any price. The King would always regret any treaty signed under such conditions.[49]

France remained on the edge of the precipice – a metaphor used at the time, for example by Torcy.[50] On 20 August 1709, for several hours, bakers' shops in the Faubourgs Saint-Antoine and Saint-Martin in Paris were looted, by workers from government workshops who had not been paid. French and Swiss Guards were attacked in the streets. They fired back, killing ten. A crowd of up to 15,000, men and women, armed with nothing but sticks, advanced west towards the Palais Royal, crying 'Bread or death!' The Maréchal de Boufflers, Colonel of the Gardes Françaises, and his son-in-law the Duc de Gramont, who happened to be in Paris, talked to the protesters in the street, gave them money and promised to tell the King that they were owed bread and wages. Crowds dispersed, crying 'Vive le Roi et du pain!' According to Madame (but no one else), who witnessed what she called the revolt, they also shouted that they wanted to burn Madame de Maintenon as a witch. Since there was so little wheat, bakers were obliged to add oats when making bread.[51]

In a despatch to his government, the Venetian Ambassador, informed by Gramont, made a prophetic remark, like d'Argenson's about the Gardes Français: 'if, in this crowd of malcontents, there had been one of the nobles irritated against the present government, and he had made himself leader of the sedition, a fatal rebellion would have started.'[52]

Some nobles did propose radical measures. Not only Fénelon and the reformers, but even the King's favourite the Duc de Vendôme had advocated summoning the States General to raise money for the war: 'the King is so absolute that he should not fear that an assembly of Estates would diminish his authority in any way and if that did happen, it seems to me that one should yield something with respect to one's subjects rather than let oneself by dictated to by one's enemies,' he had written to Chamillart, asking for his letter to be shown to the King.[53] A plan by Orry and Madame des Ursins to improve the government's credit and help it tap national wealth may also have contained suggestions for political changes 'for the good of my fatherland', Ursins wrote. It was considered dangerous. No copy survives.[54]

The Cardinal de Bouillon was arrogant and treacherous even by the standards of the *princes étrangers*, falsifying his genealogy to claim descent from the dukes of Aquitaine and demanding to dine at the same table as the royal family at the wedding of the Duc de Bourbon. In May 1710, saying that that his birth as a *prince étranger* gave him the liberty

to change sides, he returned his soiled ribbon of the Order of the Holy
Spirit to Louis. He then left France to join the enemy in the Netherlands.
Since the Bouillon were related to the princes of Orange, he hoped to make
his nephew, who had also deserted France, stadholder.[55]

Despite worse weather and higher taxation than in 1789, however,
nobles and bourgeois were too well rewarded with offices and privileges,
and too overawed by the King, either to start revolts or to fail to suppress
them. Moreover most of them accepted Louis XIV's ideology of monarchy
and military service. Even his conquests, Flanders, Alsace and Franche-
Comté, remained loyal.

Indeed Lille's experience of occupation by Dutch and English forces
after 1708 strengthened its French loyalties. The curé of the nearby village
of Rumegies denounced the murders, rapes and profanities of allied soldiers 'with faces breathing nothing but carnage'. The Day of Judgement
could not be more terrible. Allied troops took everything: 'it made us
regret that we were not still under the domination of France, when we felt
secure from that point of view.'[56]

Even Paris remained a theatre of hunger rather than rebellion. Madame
wrote on 26 October 1709 that as soon as you left the house you were
followed by people blackened with hunger, or saw them falling down and
dying in the street.[57] The curé of Rumegies finished his diary for the year
with the words: 'if I wanted to record all the calamities of the year 1709,
I would never finish. The poverty of the people is so terrifying that I cannot express it except by my tears.' The following year most people in his
village died of hunger.[58] When wheat appeared at markets in Normandy,
it was bought by speculators, in order to raise the price.[59]

France's global reach, however, as well as Louis XIV's firm government,
pulled it back from the edge of the precipice. As well as silver from Spanish
America, grain from the Ottoman Empire came to the rescue. The French
Ambassador in Constantinople M. de Ferriol regularly obtained permits
from the Grand Vizier to export as much grain as he could buy from the
ports of Sidon, Candia, Alexandria and elsewhere. Ferriol boasted that
he was refused nothing. In return he supplied the Ottoman fleet with
anchors.[60] Possibly as many as 1,000 shiploads of grain reached France
from the Ottoman Empire and North Africa between 1708 and 1710,
despite the efforts of the Royal Navy from its new bases in Gibraltar and
(after 1708) Minorca.[61] The Ottoman Empire helped save France in 1708–
10, as France had helped save the Ottoman Empire in 1688.

Meanwhile, partly due to Villars, 'French fury' began to reappear among
French soldiers. Louis allowed him, as he had previous favoured generals

like Turenne and Luxembourg, to make his own military decisions, and to disobey orders when he considered it necessary.[62] On one occasion he wrote to Villars, 'it is up to you, who sees matters at close hand, to take decisions; I give you an absolute power to do everything which you think will be good for my service.'[63] Villars did not hesitate to do so.

An enemy attempt to cross the Rhine was repulsed at Neubourg on 31 August 1709 (as an attempt by Prince Eugene to take Toulon had been in 1707). At Malplaquet in Flanders on 16 September, while 12,000 French troops were lost, allied losses were about 20,000: Villars considered it equivalent to a victory. Boufflers, who served as a volunteer under Villars, told the King that both Marlborough and Prince Eugene had described the charge of the Maison du Roi as 'beyond all humanity and all expression'. Villars himself was wounded.[64] That winter he was allowed to use the apartment of the Princesse de Conti in Versailles. The King made lengthy visits to him on his sickbed, without a *capitaine des gardes*, to discuss the war.[65]

Torcy's journal for these months, the only known journal by a minister in this period, shows Louis XIV, who turned seventy in 1708, as vulnerable and volatile. To the outside world he put on a mask of magnificent imperturbability. Even Saint-Simon was impressed by his 'male courage' and 'firmness of soul' and called him 'truly great' in defeat.[66] To his ministers however, who saw the man inside the monarch, he sometimes seemed in 'extraordinary depression and as if penetrated by sorrow'. He blamed his ministers, especially Torcy and Beauvillier, for making 'too lively arguments' for peace in May and June 1709 and himself for agreeing to them. He especially regretted his offer to cede Alsace.[67]

The financial situation remained desperate. Money had ceased to circulate, there was no credit, and many bankers were bankrupt. The government received only 30 per cent of its revenues, the rest staying in the hands of tax officials or being used to pay interest on loans. Samuel Bernard, back in business, sometimes received 20 per cent interest.[68] Louis' ministers feared that, at the next campaign, the allies would be at the gates of Paris and he would have to abandon Versailles. The grain was dying in the earth. General famine threatened for the second year running.[69] The Duc de Bourgogne wrote to Philip V on 21 October 1709 that peace had become indispensable. On 9 February 1710 he added that there was no money to pay the troops or to buy wheat. It was not certain that there would be a French army to oppose an enemy attack 'before the green [spring] has come'.[70] According to Torcy famished French soldiers looked like ghosts, while the few horses left could hardly stand.[71] In May 1710 even Villars, who had favoured fighting on in 1709, said that it was

impossible to 'expose the State' and risk everything in one battle: peace
was essential. France should submit to the allies' demand to force Philip
V off his throne.[72]

Maintenon was increasingly important as an intermediary with the
King and often saw official despatches.[73] She too begged the King to make
peace. But, showing the limits to her influence, the war went on.[74] As a
gesture, the King said he would follow Philip V's example and cut out 'all
expenses which I can avoid in order to be able to continue the war better'.[75]
Already in 1705 he had issued orders to the Lieutenant de Police de Paris
to stop merchants selling ladies' materials of a price 'higher than that
which is regulated by the *ordonnance*' for the dresses they wore to Marly.
He himself warned his courtiers against putting gilt paint on their carriages.[76] In 1709, 1710 and 1711, in an unprecedented break with routine,
the court did not go to Fontainebleau for the autumn.[77] In 1710, not only
did the King not give new-year presents himself, but he forbade the city
of Paris to do so – 'which was aiming rather high', wrote Dangeau. In
other words, Dangeau was surprised that the King dared stop the flow of
money to senior officials. Princes and courtiers sent their silver, the King
his gold plate, to the mint, to be melted and turned into coin.[78] The King
used silver, his courtiers blue and white Rouen faience.

A more drastic financial measure was the introduction in September
1710 by the new Contrôleur Général Desmarets, after many hours' prep-
aration with the King, of the *dixième*, another radical new income tax, like
the *capitation* of 1695, on all property owners, noble and non-noble alike.
For once the rich, not the poor, were the main target. It required declaration of the payer's wealth and respected no privileges except the clergy's:
the Dauphin himself, like other princes, had to pay.

It raised only about 22 million livres a year, less than expected, as it was
not applied rigorously, and many taxpayers understated their own wealth.
Nevertheless, Desmarets had the confidence of financiers. The government's position began to improve.[79] In July 1711 Villars reported to Torcy
that his army was again well paid, well fed and well disciplined.[80]

Despite token economies, and continued fighting, the court went on: concerts, balls at Versailles, new fountains at Marly, a new chateau at Meudon
for the Dauphin.[81] The Duc d'Antin, Madame de Montespan's son by her
husband, was a favourite of the King and Madame de Maintenon. When
the King criticized a line of chestnut trees in his park, he had it cut down
overnight. In 1708 he became *directeur des bâtiments du roi*, in charge
of Versailles and Saint-Germain, with the privilege of working directly
with the King.[82] The register of his orders and letters shows the King's

determination to go on building despite the war: orders for 1,500 squares of white marble, for example, were placed in Dieppe in 1710.[83]

Indeed, Versailles expanded. Work on a new and larger chapel, begun in 1682, was finished in 1710. It is a masterpiece by the great architect Germain Boffrand, covered with Ls, crowns and gilding like a royal apartment, with an image of the Holy Spirit as a dove hovering above the balcony opposite the altar, where Louis XIV normally stood.[84] On 9 June 1710 the Cardinal de Noailles, Archbishop of Paris, said the first mass there. Demonstrating the royal family's pride in Versailles' appeal to the public, like a modern chatelain boasting of visitor numbers, Bourgogne reported to Philip V: 'it is one of the finest specimens for its architecture and its frescoes and its sculptures. It appears to be very much to everyone's taste and every day recently there has been a great crowd of people to see it.'[85] The Bishop of Metz said that, instead of creating such splendour, the King would do better to pay his starving troops and help his overtaxed subjects. The King knew of the remark that evening; the Bishop was never forgiven.[86]

A month later, on 6 July, the first wedding to be celebrated in the chapel was between Bourgogne's youngest brother the Duc de Berri and Mlle d'Orléans, granddaughter of Monsieur. Against the opposition of the Dauphin and the young Prince himself, it had been arranged by Louis and the Duchesse de Bourgogne in order to avoid the problems arising from marriage to a foreign princess, or a princess of Condé, who would have been under the influence of her mother, the King's intelligent, independent daughter 'Madame la Duchesse'.[87] The chapel, filled with ladies sparkling with jewels, was, according to the Baron de Breteuil, 'one of the most magnificent and striking spectacles which you could ever see'. Twenty-eight members of the extended royal family, including Princes and Princesses of the Blood, joined the King for the wedding supper.[88]

The Duc and Duchesse de Berri's new households were criticized for their size and magnificence. Indulging her love of food, wine and men, the Duchesse de Berri soon made the royal family regret the marriage. She vomited or passed out at parties, and took lovers.[89] Her grandmother Madame commented, referring to the Duchess's other grandmother Madame de Montespan, 'like grandmother, like granddaughter': 'bon chien chasse de race'.[90] Parisians called her the first prostitute of France.[91] Like the duchesses de Bourgogne and du Maine, she continued the French court's tradition of independent princesses: she was more intelligent than her husband, whom she despised.[92]

While the court pursued pleasure, the allies pursued France. After Lille in October 1708, the allies took Tournai on 3 September 1709 (Louis

XIV's bust on the city gate was removed by Marlborough, to crown the top of the garden front of Blenheim Palace); Mons on 25 June 1710; Douai on 9 August; Béthune on 29 August; Aire on 19 November. Despite Vauban's forts and Villars' defensive lines and careful generalship, they were only a hundred miles from Paris. Louis saved himself by his resolution. The vanity and love of applause he had shown during his reign did not indicate lack of confidence. He did not bolt like James II in 1688, or withdraw to Blois as some of his advisers proposed.[93]

Meanwhile, during further peace negotiations conducted in the Netherlands in 1710 by the Maréchal d'Huxelles and Polignac, the allies added new conditions, including compensation for the ravaging of the Palatinate twenty years earlier. From 27 May they also insisted that Louis alone, without the help of allied troops, expel Philip V from Spain and its empire without compensation, within the space of two months. If he did not do so, war would resume.[94]

He was dissuaded from accepting allied peace terms by the conscience of the dynasty, the Dauphin. The Dauphin had been careful to continue to appear to remain obedient to his father: for example he wrote to Philip on 23 December 1708, 'always relying on the letters the King writes you, I never send you any news.'[95] However, despite appearances, he was, as Torcy wrote to Philip, 'neither docile nor easy to lead'.[96] Some diplomats believed that he had prevented his father from publicly declaring his marriage to Madame de Maintenon. Whereas the Duc de Bourgogne urged Philip to abdicate, in 1709 and 1710 the Dauphin opposed peace negotiations, and supported using French troops to keep his son on his throne.[97] On 16 July 1710 Louis XIV, recovering his pride, said that the peace conditions were impossible: if he had to continue fighting, he preferred to fight his enemies rather than his grandson. On 25 July Polignac and Huxelles left the Netherlands.[98]

However, in September Louis sent his confidant the Duc de Noailles (who had just repulsed another allied invasion at Sète, on the south coast) to Spain on a particularly delicate mission: to persuade Philip to abdicate voluntarily and retire to Sicily, Sardinia or France.[99] Philip, however, like Louis XIV himself in 1700 when he had announced his acceptance of Carlos II's will, based his rule on popular feeling as well as hereditary right. He refused to abandon his people, whose love and zeal surpassed all imagination and had been only increased by his misfortunes.[100] He wrote to his grandfather on 25 September 1710 (no doubt with help from Ursins and her lover/secretary d'Aubenton), at a time when he had again been temporarily (21 September to 6 November) driven from Madrid by the forces of 'Charles III': 'God has placed the crown of Spain on my head; I will wear it as long as I have one drop of blood in my veins. I owe it to my conscience, to my honour and to the love of my subjects' – as well as to 'the glory of our house and the interests of France'.[101]

Earlier that year Philip had summoned Vendôme to Spain, despite Bourgogne assuring him that Vendôme was lazy, rash and presumptuous: the King had appreciated Vendôme when they had fought together against Austrian forces in Italy in 1702.[102] Vendôme was accompanied by his favourite, a priest from Parma called Giulio Alberoni, whom he had met on campaign in the Po valley. As the Prince had risen from the commode on which he received visitors, Alberoni was said to have exclaimed, 'Culo di angelo!' ('The bottom of an angel!') and rushed to kiss it. Presents of macaroni and sausages helped win him friends in Versailles and Madrid, including the Princesse des Ursins.[103] He became Vendôme's agent in Madrid and was soon known among the French in Madrid as 'M. de Derrière', 'l'homme au derrière' or simply 'derrière'.[104]

Madame de Maintenon spat venom about Vendôme and Alberoni to Madame des Ursins: 'He has abandoned himself to the Abbé Alberoni, an Italian and his favourite, to dishonour M. le duc de Bourgogne. He keeps Alberoni beside him . . . and declares that he would be inconsolable if he lost him . . . M. le Maréchal de Boufflers says that you cannot command an army from a chamber pot, it is his most usual position.'[105] Unlike her favourites Villeroy or Bourgogne, however, Vendôme won battles. After his victory at Villaviciosa in northern Castile over the forces of 'Charles III' on 10 December 1710, Alberoni wrote that Vendôme had, by his courage, replaced the crown of Spain on Philip V's head.[106] Already in October that year, frustrated by their enemies' intransigence, Louis XIV had decided, instead of asking Philip to leave Spain, to send him military help again.[107] The situation in Spain was changing in his favour. It was about to do so in England too.

Nemesis Averted

'There cannot be too much division in England,' Louis had written to his Minister of the Marine Pontchartrain while planning the Jacobite invasion of 1708.[1] Indeed divisions in England would help him win an honourable peace. The issue of peace 'with' or 'without' Spain stoked hatreds in England between Whigs (many of whom profited from the war, and demanded 'no peace without Spain', meaning without the imposition of 'Charles III') and Tories. They began to detest each other almost as much as they did the French. In 1710 England was paying for 171,000 troops in the field (many of them German or Savoyard) and war was absorbing 80 per cent of government expenditure. England, like France, had also suffered bad harvests after the terrible winter of 1709. Public desire for peace was increased by French and Spanish resilience: many French forts still barred Marlborough's advance on Paris.[2] Tories like Robert Harley, although he had been educated at a Huguenot school (Foubert's Academy) and had helped draft the laws enforcing the Protestant succession, turned to France and their former enemies the Stuarts, to hasten peace, and from fear of the Hanoverians' determination to continue the war.

Elections in August 1710 had given the House of Commons a majority in favour of peace, including around fifty Jacobite MPs, who increased the political leverage of 'James III'.[3] The court also favoured peace. The break between Queen Anne and her domineering Mistress of the Robes, the Duchess of Marlborough, had been confirmed by a quarrel over how the Queen should wear her jewels on 19 August 1708, during the procession to St Paul's for the Te Deum for Oudenarde. The Queen complained of being 'teased' and 'tormented', both in conversation and in the Duchess's many angry letters. The Duchess looted the Privy Purse, threatened to publish the Queen's letters and encouraged Whig pamphlets alleging that the Queen had 'so great a passion' for her new Tory favourite and Woman of the Bedchamber, the Duchess's cousin and former protégée Lady Masham, who was also a cousin of Harley.[4]

At the same time, without telling his colleagues, Marlborough was trying to obtain from the Queen the unprecedented office of 'Captain General for Life', which could have given 'King John', as some enemies called him, lasting control over the armed forces. Normally parsimonious, Marlborough had offered the Electress Sophia, the heir to the throne whom he charmed during two visits to Hanover, a 'loan' of £20,000 in return for her signature on this commission, to be valid from the day of her accession.[5] He also hoped to become governor general of the Southern Netherlands for 'Charles III', and to continue the war until he reached Paris. Hitherto the Queen had supported the war with France. After 1709 her fear of Marlborough, and loathing of his wife, strengthened her desire for peace.

As a young princess, the future Queen Anne had been barely noticed by her cousin Louis XIV in 1668–70, when she had stayed with her grandmother Henrietta Maria at Colombes and her aunt the Duchesse d'Orléans at Saint-Cloud for eye treatment. Since he recognized 'James III', he continued to call her by her husband's name, the Princess of Denmark. She lived in 'perfect solitude' and worsening health, in a small brick palace in Kensington, or in a modest 'garden house' beside Windsor Castle, rarely using Charles II's state apartments.[6]

Yet her decisions were now crucial to Louis XIV. In 1710 Dangeau noted in his diary, beside news of the war, news of her dismissal of the Marlboroughs' daughters as ladies of the bedchamber, and of their son-in-law Sunderland as secretary of state. That August, after the Tory victory in the general election, Harley became the leading figure in a new administration.[7]

French generals had lost the war. French diplomats now won the peace. There was in London a French agent, more trusted than most ambassadors, called the Abbé François Gaultier (by coincidence the same name as that of the Huguenot pastor who had helped organize a coalition against Louis XIV; see above, p. 313). A former sacristan of the parish church at Saint-Germain, he had been refused a post in James II's chapel.[8] Having come to London in 1698 in the household of the French Ambassador Tallard, he had been instructed to remain behind at the beginning of the War of the Spanish Succession. He served in the chapel of the Imperial Ambassador Count Gallas, but since 1705 had maintained a secret correspondence with Torcy. Since March 1710 he had been predicting the Marlboroughs' disgrace.[9] In December, prompted by Lord Jersey, a former ambassador to Louis XIV, Gaultier wrote to Torcy that the British government, impressed by Philip V's victory at Villaviciosa, would not insist on imposing 'Charles III' on Spain, provided British commercial interests were secured. Defying their 'Grand Alliance' with the Emperor and the Netherlands, while still fighting France British ministers began to negotiate peace with it.[10]

Gaultier, who was discreet, a pleasant drinking companion and spoke good English, became Harley's channel of communication with Torcy. 'Le petit prêtre Gautier', as Dangeau called him, arrived in Versailles on his first secret mission from Westminster on 15 January 1711.[11] Torcy found him a man of sense, ready to convey correct information, and in August made him *agent du roi* in London.[12] From April Torcy had also been secretly negotiating with Heinsius, Grand Pensionary of Holland, through Jacques Basnage, a Huguenot pastor in The Hague; but Dutch demands for Huguenot rights in France were an insuperable obstacle. Louis XIV would not permit Huguenots, or their children who had taken foreign nationality, even to trade in France, let alone return there.[13]

Dynastic biology also favoured Louis XIV. The Emperor Joseph I died without sons, on 17 April 1711. On 30 May his brother 'Charles III' left Barcelona, and on 12 October he was elected emperor. The Emperor Charles VI, more hegemonical than Louis XIV, wanted to remain Charles III of Spain, as his English supporters like Marlborough also insisted. Charles VI would not abandon his claims to Spain until 1725. Feeling like an exile in his own homeland, he retained a Consejo Supremo de España and many Spanish servants in Vienna. A Spanish crown and coat of arms adorn his tomb in the city's Kapuzinergruft.[14]

France's resilience and its influence over Philip V made it more important to England than the Netherlands or Austria. Although still at war, the English and French ministries became almost as intimate as in the reign of Charles II. Churchill wrote: 'The Queen and the Lord Treasurer [Harley], aided and abetted by St John, saved France as surely, although scarcely as nobly, as Jeanne d'Arc.'[15]

Fearing the Elector of Hanover's revenge for their betrayal of the Grand Alliance, perhaps also to facilitate peace negotiations, Harley and the Francophile Secretary of State Henry St John (later ennobled as the Earl of Oxford and Viscount Bolingbroke respectively) even told Gaultier that they favoured the succession of 'James III'. Moving between London, Paris, Fontainebleau and Utrecht, Gaultier was a treble agent serving the French government, the British ministry (which trusted him more than its own diplomats) and 'James III'. He saw no contradiction in multiple loyalties: he wrote that together France and England should 'give the law to Europe'.[16] Gaultier was so determined for 'James III' to become Anglican and win the English crown that Torcy remarked that he should be made archbishop of Canterbury.[17] In reality – although this was hidden by Torcy and Gaultier from Oxford and Bolingbroke – 'James III' never considered renouncing Catholicism.[18]

Gaulter was not the only secret negotiator. In August 1711 Louis XIV and Torcy gave secret audiences to Matthew Prior (to whom the King had been particularly gracious in his farewell audience in 1699, saying he hoped to see him again): on one occasion Prior and Gaultier met Torcy at night in the garden of Fontainebleau.[19] In September Nicolas Mesnager, Comte de Saint-Jean, a Rouen merchant and economist often employed by Louis XIV, and already used in peace negotiations with the Netherlands in 1707, was received in secret by Queen Anne at Windsor.[20] He proved a brilliant diplomat. 'Preliminaries' signed there on 27 September promised Britain Minorca, Gibraltar and the coveted *asiento de negros* – the exclusive right to ship to Spanish America around 4,700 African slaves a year for thirty years, which France had enjoyed since 1701. Britain was confirmed as the supreme global trading power.[21] It won territories such as Acadia and Newfoundland, although France kept the island of Cap Breton, north of Acadia, on which in 1713 it began construction of the fort of Louisbourg. Louis agreed to recognize the Protestant succession and expel 'James III', and to 'dismantle' Dunkirk, and make its port inaccessible to large ships. In return, however, whereas in 1709 he had been prepared to cede Franche-Comté, Lille and Strasbourg and revert to the frontiers of 1648, in 1712 he retained almost all his conquests except Mons, Ypres and Tournai.[22]

Global trade was almost as important as European conquests. Peace between nations which considered themselves the height of civilization – France, England, Spain and the Netherlands – partly depended on the right to sell slaves to Spanish America. Louis XIV, Philip V, Queen Anne and George I, as well as kings of Ashante and Dahomey, invested in the trade on account of its spectacular profits, which made those in other trades seem modest.[23] In reality British companies had already begun to replace their French rivals in Spanish America, as they were more efficient. After 1713 French merchants never recovered the right to trade in Spanish America, although some continued to do so illegally. Particularly thanks to Saint-Domingue, however, which Louis had secured for France in 1697, French sugar and coffee production later overtook British. French colonial trade increased by 400 per cent by the 1740s, bringing prosperity to the ports of Nantes and Bordeaux, as their dazzling eighteenth-century architecture confirms.[24]

While suffering political defeats in England, Marlborough had continued to win military victories in France. On 12 September 1711, just as Mesnager was signing the secret preliminaries at Windsor, Marlborough broke through Villars' defensive lines at Vimy Ridge, site of a famous battle in 1917, and captured Bouchain, 108 miles from Paris.[25] He hoped the following year to date his despatches from the French capital. Nevertheless on 31 December 1711 he was dismissed by Queen Anne from all his offices.

In January 1712 about fifty delegations from throughout Europe – including one from *la nation catalane* still fighting Philip V – assembled in Utrecht, the city occupied by Louis XIV's forces in 1672 and 1673. Utrecht was chosen in part to satisfy delegates' status sensibilities. Its wide streets were suitable for ambassadors' carriages, and the town hall had rooms with doors of equal grandeur, through which rival ambassadors could enter at the same time.[26]

On 12 May 1712 the new British Commander-in-Chief in the Low Countries, the Duke of Ormonde, received 'restraining orders' from Queen Anne (possibly first suggested by Abbé Gaultier), 'restraining' him from fighting on the side of his allies Austria and the Netherlands. Prince Eugene was not informed, but Villars was. Britain was in effect helping French operations against its allies.[27] British troops halted within sight of the promised land – France – but were not allowed to taste its milk and honey. Hostilities between the two countries formally ended on 19 July.

Given a free rein by Louis, Villars won the battle of Denain on 24 July 1712, over Prince Eugene's superior Austro-Dutch forces. Prince Holstein, the allied Governor of Lille, was among Villars' prisoners. Louis XIV was so moved that he thanked his courtiers for the joy they showed at the news. Denain was followed by the recovery of French frontier fortresses such as Le Quesnoy, and on 28 July by a formal armistice.[28] Queen Anne wrote to congratulate Louis XIV on his victory over her allies.

Like Luxembourg in the 1690s, Villars became the hero of the hour. He received a *brevet d'affaires* to see the King whenever he wanted, even 'during his most secret actions' (that is, sitting on the commode), and was given use of the apartment of the Duc de Berri in Versailles. He renamed the chateau of Vaux, which he had bought from Fouquet's widow, Vaux-Villars, and filled it with pictures of his victories.[29]

The British government had become more friendly with its former enemy France than with its allies. During a visit to Paris in August 1712, Bolingbroke stayed with Torcy's mother. To win better terms, Torcy showed him letters from the Dutch revealing their desire for peace. Bibulous dinners ended with toasts by Torcy to Queen Anne, by Bolingbroke to Louis XIV. Louis gave Bolingbroke a diamond once worn by the Dauphin, and promised Prior a pension. The two nations, he said, were descended from the same blood and had been enemies only by necessity.[30]

Peace was finally signed (but not by the Emperor Charles VI or the Elector of Hanover) in Utrecht on 12 April 1713. One of the French negotiators was the Abbé de Polignac, restored to favour by Torcy's protection after the debacle in Poland.[31] On the evening of 14 April Torcy ushered M. de Beringhen, the Premier Ecuyer, into Madame de Maintenon's apartment with the news.[32] On 22 May, d'Argenson, Lieutenant de Police, led the heralds' procession proclaiming peace through the streets of Paris, and 'distributed money to the people'. The Duc and Duchesse du Maine threw coins from a balcony on the Place Royale. Louis walked all morning in his gardens, planning improvements.[33]

As a barrier against French invasions, the Netherlands recovered the right to garrison its troops in cities in the Southern Netherlands and to continue to block the Scheldt – thereby crippling Antwerp to favour Amsterdam. Victor Amadeus II of Savoy acquired more territory in northern Italy, including Montferrat, and became king of Sicily (later exchanged with Sardinia): a huge extension of power, finally giving his house the royal rank it had long claimed. Since 1690 British subsidies had helped him fight Louis, and British ships would carry him to Sicily to be crowned in Palermo cathedral on 24 December 1713. However, despite losing his Italian possessions and the Southern Netherlands to the Emperor, and Gibraltar and Minorca to Britain, and despite the obligation to renounce all claims to the French crown for himself and his descendants, Philip V remained king of Spain. In this crucial respect, Louis XIV and Philip V had won the War of the Spanish Succession.[34] As Polignac exclaimed, the difference between the peace terms of 1709 and 1713 was like that between night and day.[35]

The curé of Rumegies, near Lille, wrote in his diary of the 'general joy' at peace and being Louis' subjects again.[36] Forty years of French rule, and five years of allied rule, had turned the inhabitants into Frenchmen. After his entry with French troops into Lille on 4 June 1713, the Maréchal de Montesquiou wrote to the Minister of War:

> it would need an entire book to describe to you all the marks of rejoicing the people have given at the entry of the King's troops . . . there was such a resounding cry of Vive le Roi that they [welcoming magistrates] could not speak because you heard nothing. This Vive le Roi carried me with the same force to my house where I arrived almost drunk, because I could not refuse quantities of bourgeois who came out of their houses with bottles and glasses to make me drink to the King's health. I was in such a fine state that I could hardly stay on my horse.[37]

Utrecht was a victory for Europe and diplomacy. The defence of 'the freedom and the balance of Europe' had been proclaimed as the reason for the declaration of war on Louis XIV in 1702.[38] At Utrecht 'peace and calm in Christendom through an equal balance of power' was restated as the political ideal for Europe. Medals celebrated the return of peace and trade, and England's role, in its own opinion, as 'the protector of Europe'. Prints showed an Englishman, a Frenchman, a Dutchman, a Spaniard, a German and a Savoyard dancing 'le farandole européen'.[39] Some diplomats dreamt of a European army and assembly, with a Senate meeting in Utrecht.[40] Callières, Louis' secretary, would later write a manifesto for Europe: 'All the states of which Europe is composed have between them necessary liaisons and connections which mean that one can regard them as members of one same republic [in the sense of political body] and it is almost impossible for a considerable change to take place in any of its members without it troubling the repose of all the others.'[41]

In the interests of the peace of Europe, however, some nations were ignored or suppressed. The Southern Netherlands' independence had often been discussed. Louis had considered making them a republic with a guarantee of perpetual neutrality or a kingdom for the Elector of Bavaria, the last Spanish Governor General who, like other German electors, yearned for a royal crown.[42] They were, however, assigned to Charles VI (although, such was the attraction of Spanish pay and service, Spain continued to recruit soldiers there throughout the eighteenth century). They had to wait until 1831 for internationally recognized independence as the kingdom of Belgium. In addition the triumph of the Protestant succession kept Scotland and Ireland subordinated to England.

A year after Utrecht, on 7 March 1714, peace with Louis XIV's relentless enemy the Emperor Charles VI was signed at Rastatt in Baden. Peace had been negotiated by the Maréchal de Villars and Prince Eugene, who had served together in the Imperial army in the 1680s. Reaching the greatest extent in its history, Austria acquired Milan, Sardinia, Naples and the Southern Netherlands. However, the Empire did not, as it had hoped, recover Alsace and Strasbourg. Louis XIV's allies the Elector of Cologne and the Elector of Bavaria, moreover, who had been outlawed by the Empire, were restored to their dominions. Max Emanuel of Bavaria was reluctant to leave France, where he had lived for ten years and fathered many illegitimate children.[43] He had impressed the court (his sister's marriage to the Dauphin made him uncle to the Duc de Bourgogne and Philip V, almost one of the royal family) with his 'air fort noble', and had been a frequent guest at Compiègne, Fontainebleau and Marly as well as Versailles. He knew how to flatter Louis XIV, assuring him that 'the pleasure of having been attached to the greatest king in the world consoled him for all his misfortunes'.[44]

After 1715 he established in Munich and at his country palaces at Schleissheim and Nymphenburg the most elegant and Francophile court in the Empire, with a lavishly decorated French-style state bedchamber and furniture, sculpture, carriages, pavilions and gardens, designed by Paris-trained artists and craftsmen in what he called the 'latest tastes of France'. He also instituted French-style comedies, concerts, balls and Appartement.[45] The aim was to outshine the court of Vienna and show that he was worthy of winning, with French help, the royal crown which his former equals the electors of Saxony, Brandenburg and Hanover had already gained in Poland, Prussia and England respectively. Even more ambitious than his fellow electors, he intended his family the Wittelsbachs to succeed the House of Austria both as Holy Roman emperors and as kings of Bohemia.[46]

Another of Louis XIV's allies, however, did not return home. Louis XIV's support for anti-Austrian Hungarian malcontents under Emeric Thököly in 1675–8 and 1681–3, in cooperation with the Ottoman government, had revived during the War of the Spanish Succession. The principality of Transylvania had transferred its allegiance in 1686 from the Ottoman sultans to the Habsburg kings of Hungary. After June 1703, however, an insurrection 'with God for Fatherland and Freedom' led by Ferenc II Rákóczi, a wealthy landowner descended from five previous princes of Transylvania, had conquered most of Hungary. In July 1704 the Diet of Transylvania elected Rákóczi as prince. Driven by hatred of the Emperor's taxes and German favourites and officials, the insurrection briefly took Graz and threatened the Emperor in Vienna. Since 1700 he had been asking for Louis' help. Having previously been reluctant to support 'rebels against their legitimate sovereign' (the Emperor Joseph I had already been elected and crowned king of Hungary, and was supported by many Hungarians), Louis changed his ideology to suit his strategy. In March 1705, calling Transylvania 'a free nation', he recognized Rákóczi as sovereign prince of Transylvania, sent a professional diplomat the Marquis des Alleurs and French officers to advise him and provided a regular subsidy of 50,000 livres a month, paid through the French Ambassador in Warsaw. In June 1707, the Hungarian Diet deposed the House of Austria from the throne of Hungary, and thereafter organized under Rákóczi a new confederated state in Transylvania and Upper Hungary, with its own army and coinage. Toleration, love of liberty and respect for peasants' rights distinguished these allies of Louis XIV. Although himself a pious

Catholic, Rákóczi planned to make a Calvinist, the Crown Prince of Prussia, king of Hungary: Charles XII of Sweden, Augustus II of Poland and Max Emanuel of Bavaria were also offered the throne.[47]

To Louis' satisfaction, the war tied up about 50,000 Austrian troops, perhaps half the army. After August 1708, however, they began to defeat Rákóczi's irregular forces, which lacked both cannon and discipline. He later described himself as a blind man leading the blind. Louis' subsidies did not stop Hungary and Transylvania again falling under what Rákóczi called 'the heavy yoke of the House of Austria'. In May 1711 a compromise peace between Austria and the exhausted insurgents was signed. Transylvania preserved a semblance of autonomy. Having failed to win representation at Utrecht, Rákóczi and around 2,000 followers (more would follow) left Hungary and arrived, via Danzig and England, in Paris in January 1713.[48]

Tall and handsome, with imposing manners and good French, and a wife related to the wife of Louis' favourite the Marquis de Dangeau, the Count of Saros, as Rákóczi called himself, soon became popular at court. He was a frequent guest at Versailles, Fontainebleau, Rambouillet and Marly, where he often attended the *lever* and mass. Louis gave him a pension and audiences, lent him horses and allowed him to wear the uniform of the royal hunt, saying that the presence of a man like Rákóczi did it honour. His followers later formed the first hussar regiment in the French army. However, he left France in 1717, and died near Constantinople in 1735, still an ally of France and still planning a return to Transylvania. In Hungary today, he is considered a national hero.[49]

Having made peace with governments, Louis' final enemy was, in keeping with his long history of conflict with cities, the Catalan capital Barcelona. It had remained loyal to 'Charles III'. Despite repeated promises not to abandon Catalonia, England and the Emperor Charles VI (the former 'Charles III') did so at Utrecht.[50] The siege of Barcelona (already besieged by French troops in 1695–7) by French and Spanish troops under the Maréchal de Berwick started in May 1713, after the departure on a British ship of Charles VI's wife the Empress Elisabeth. The siege lasted for seventeen months, until the city's surrender on 11 September 1714. (Despite France's state of exhaustion, Louis could still fight a two-front war, against Catalonia in the south and the Emperor in the north.) Philip V did not forgive Catalonia's disloyalty, for he had extended its privileges when living there in 1701–2. After 1714 he abolished those privileges, closed Catalan universities, razed the walls of Barcelona and constructed the last great Louis XIV-style fortress, a detested symbol of Bourbon power overlooking Barcelona.[51] That was the end, for over 200 years, of Catalan autonomy. The 11th of September, the day of surrender, is now the National Day of Catalonia, when Barcelona's defenders against Bourbon troops are commemorated at the site of their mass grave, and hundreds of thousands of Catalans march through the streets, demanding independence from Spain.

Perhaps reflecting the influence of Callières, Louis asked his grandson to show to Barcelona the humanity which he himself had failed to show to Genoa, Heidelberg, Brussels and other cities he had bombarded. On 2 July and 1 August 1714 he asked Philip not to cause 'the total ruin of a considerable city': 'although rebels they are your subjects and you should treat them as a father ... Christianity should incline you to clemency.' Without Louis, Philip's vengeance on Barcelona might have been worse.[52]

While the fall of Barcelona was a triumph for the Bourbons, 'the cursed sluices of Dunkirk' symbolized the triumph of Britain. Dunkirk had been the jewel in Louis XIV's crown, subject of more medals than Versailles, its corsairs seizing more English ships (1,617 in all) than those from any other French port. Article 9 of the Treaty of Utrecht was, however, lethal: 'The Most Christian King will raze the fortifications of Dunkirk, fill in the port, ruin the sluices which serve to clean the said port, all at his own expense and within a space of five months from the signature and conclusion of the treaty.' In Dunkirk, Louis was no longer master in his own house.[53] To ensure enforcement of British demands 6,722 British troops were stationed in Dunkirk from July 1712 to August 1714 (thereby releasing the French garrison to fight Britain's Dutch and Austrian allies), and a British commissioner would remain in the port in peacetime until 1778. The pleas of a deputation sent by Dunkirk to London, for preservation of the harbour in the interests of trade between the two countries, had no effect.[54]

War almost resumed in 1714 and again in 1730, over French attempts to build a canal connecting the nearby port of Mardyck to the sea. In 1717, at British insistence, the Mardyck canal was destroyed. Dunkirk then revived as a centre for fishermen, smugglers, sugar traders and Jacobites. Much later, however, having become the third port of France, Dunkirk would connect, rather than divide, France and Britain. It was vital for supplying British troops in France in the First World War, and for evacuating, from its long sandy beaches, 338,226 French and British troops, in May 1940: an evacuation which owed part of its success to the French troops defending the city.[55]

*

While successfully negotiating peace abroad, Louis had suffered disasters at home. When the Dauphin caught *petite vérole* on 10 April 1711, the King was so worried that, ignoring the risk of contagion, he moved to Meudon. Council meetings were held there, so that the King could visit the Dauphin's sickbed more frequently: he was nursed by his adored half-sister the Princesse de Conti (one of the kinder members of the royal family – she had also nursed her mother Louise de La Vallière, and would help nurse Louis himself). Finally the Princess forced her father out of the room, saying that he should think only of himself. On 14 April, the Dauphin died. Since the royal doctor Fagon had been over-optimistic, the Dauphin had not had time to confess and receive the last rites. As the King's carriage left Meudon, members of the Dauphin's household threw themselves to the ground in front of it, begging him not to let them starve.[56]

Both the King and Paris, where the Dauphin had been 'adored', were inconsolable; Sourches writes of the 'terrifying sorrow' of Paris.[57] The King was often thought to be heartless. He had shown no regrets at the deaths of his former mistresses Fontanges, La Vallière or Montespan.[58] For his family, however, he cared deeply. When he tried to speak to his ministers, according to Torcy, 'his sorrow and his tears prevented him speaking each time he tried to express himself.'[59] Madame said that the King's grief would melt a stone. He always had tears in his eyes, and looked as if he was himself about to fall ill.[60] Fagon, the incompetent royal doctor, recorded that he was shaking all over and suffered violent heart tremors, from his 'inconceivable sadness'.[61] Torcy also wept, like his fellow ministers, but was sufficiently self-controlled to decide with the King that from that day the Duc de Bourgogne would be known as M. le Dauphin.[62]

The new Dauphin was more austere than his father. He attended mass every day, took the sacrament every Sunday, fasted frequently and had renounced dancing, gambling, concerts and the theatre. Despite the King's request, he refused to attend a ball at Marly, and stayed in his study, since it was the Feast of the Epiphany.[63] To the King's and Torcy's annoyance, he let himself be guided by his conscience when discussing policy at council meetings.[64] However, his honesty and industry – he spent hours working alone in his study – made him the hope of many Frenchmen. Helped by the excellence of French maps, the detailed reports on the provinces which all *intendants* had been asked to send him and the extensive provincial tour he had made in 1701 after escorting Philip V to Spain, he was said to know France as well as the gardens of Versailles. The King told his ministers to show him everything.[65]

The Dauphin's favourite maxim, which he announced even in the salon of Marly (and which Bossuet had taught his father), was that kings were born for their subjects and belonged to them, not the other way round. Unlike his father and grandfather, he disliked war (as the Oudenarde debacle showed) and luxury, and had plans to hold meetings of the States General every three years. He was a reformer who wanted to lower taxes and ensure that every regiment contained at least one non-noble officer.[66]

More royal deaths, however, were to devastate France. Louis' favourite, the new Dauphine, had never been strong. Madame de Maintenon thought that she had been married too young. On 7 February 1712 she caught a fever after eating cheesecakes she had cooked in the Ménagerie. She complained that the pain was worse than childbirth. Perhaps due to an abcess in her jaw arising from problems with her teeth, the fever grew worse and developed into a virulent form of measles. She died on 12 February, after a long confession to the parish priest of Versailles (having sent away her own confessor). She was followed by her inconsolable husband, from the same disease, six days later on 18 February; and by their eldest son the second Duc de Bretagne, briefly called M. le Dauphin, on 8 March.[67]

The Dauphine's Premier Ecuyer the Maréchal de Tessé wrote to the Prince de Monaco that she had been created to ensure the happiness of France. 'The King has retired to Marly in a state of collapse that inspires pity. Paris and the court are in extreme desolation.'[68] Madame de Maintenon wrote to the Princesse des Ursins that there was no more court: 'everything is missing, everything seems empty, there is no more joy or activity.'[69] Even Madame, who had disliked both the Duc and the Duchesse de Bourgogne, admitted that the Duchesse had been the King's comfort and joy. She was so young, and had such natural high spirits, that, however 'maussade' he was, she could always cheer him up. Bourgogne was a loss for the whole kingdom.[70] He would long be remembered as the reformer who might have transformed the monarchy and ensured the peace of Europe.[71]

On 2 April 1712 Madame de Maintenon again wrote to the Princesse des Ursins: 'I have never seen sorrow last so long at Court.'[72] This hecatomb was even more devastating for Louis than that of 1671–4, when he had lost six children, legitimate and illegitimate. He started to eat alone in the evening, and Dangeau feared, like Madame, that 'this new thunderbolt' would affect his health. As he had during the defeats of 1709–10, he showed astonishing resilience. On 27 October, however, Sourches noticed the first signs of senility: 'he mistook one thing for another' and, for the first time, fell asleep in the carriage taking him from Versailles to Marly.[73]

Nothing, however, could keep him from government business.[74] On 18

July 1713, Dangeau wrote: 'The King held the council of finances, then worked for a very long time with M. Desmarets. After dinner he worked with M. Voysin, then went to watch people playing mall.'[75] The King's youngest grandson and his wife, the Duc and Duchesse de Berri, tried to dissipate the gloom. Plays were performed three times a week to amuse the court. Sometimes their balls lasted till eight in the morning.[76] The Duchesse du Maine, wife of the King's favourite illegitimate child, also organized fireworks, balls, plays and operas at her husband's chateaux at Sceaux (where the King sometimes stayed when travelling between Versailles and Fontainebleau), Châtenay and Clagny. Les Grandes Nuits de Sceaux, as they were called, lasted through the night, to divert the insomniac Duchess. Often with herself in the leading role, the plays and operas attracted hundreds of guests, both from the court and from Paris. Some had biblical or classical themes; others were frivolous comédies-ballets, such as Dialogue de Flore et de Zéphir. In 1707 her carnival balls at Sceaux had been attended by up to 850 carriages, driving the 15 miles from Paris even in bad weather.[77] Her entertainments may also have been intended to attract support for her husband's political ambitions.

Once so proud of his family's fecundity, Louis was now running out of heirs. The throne of France depended on an old man of seventy-four, on the Duc de Berri and on a boy of two, the Bourgognes' third son, the Duc d'Anjou, now the fourth Dauphin in one year. Madame, probably correctly, believed that, if the doctors had been allowed near him, they would have killed him, as they had killed his parents and brothers. His Governess the Duchesse de Ventadour, by refusing to allow doctors to bleed him, keeping him under her care and feeding him on biscuits soaked in wine and water, probably saved his life.[78]

In England Queen Anne also faced problems arising from the succession to the throne. After 1712 she was victim of rumours alleging her support for the succession of 'James III', as baseless as the rumours which she herself had helped to spread in 1688, that he was suppositious. In reality Anne was a fervent Anglican, frequently and publicly reassuring both her Hanover cousins and the Houses of Parliament of her loyalty to the Protestant succession.[79]

Despite its secret negotiations with 'James III', of which the Queen never knew, the Tory ministry officially favoured the Protestant succession. At its request Louis XIV, who had refused similar requests from William III for the departure of James II, asked 'James III' to leave Saint-Germain. He moved to Châlons in September 1712 and to Bar in Lorraine (where he was well received by his cousin Duke Leopold) in February the following year.[80] Oxford and Bolingbroke, while also corresponding with the Elector of Hanover, corresponded with 'James III', even, via Gaultier, helping to draft his manifestos. In March 1714, to their apparent surprise, 'James III' told them that, since he intended when he became king to grant liberty of conscience to others, he saw no reason not to grant it to himself. He would remain Catholic.[81]

In France, Great Britain, Hungary and Catalonia, two views of monarchy were in conflict: the pragmatic view, based on royal wills and renunciations, international treaties and local laws, held that dynastic succession could be regulated for political reasons. Most English and Scots supported Parliament's Act of Settlement of 1701, settling the succession on the Electress Sophia and her Protestant heirs. Many Hungarians supported the deposition of the House of Austria by the Diet in 1707. Most Catalans supported 'Charles III'.[82]

The rival, dynastic view, especially strong in France, was that God had chosen lines of kings to lead his peoples; the sanctity of royalty was greater than the power of treaties. Torcy explained the Salic Law governing the French succession to his friend Bolingbroke in March 1712: 'this law is regarded in France as the work of he who has established all monarchies and we are persuaded in France that God alone can abolish it.' Most Frenchmen believed that the nearest relation in the male line automatically succeeded the previous king, and that a prince's personal renunciation did not apply to his descendants.[83]

Even Louis XIV, however, as well as his subjects, and Carlos II and his, had agreed that the same king could not rule Spain and France. Therefore they accepted the possibility of renunciation. The Dauphin and the Duc de Bourgogne had renounced, in favour of Philip V, their own and their descendants' claims to the throne of Spain. As Louis wrote to his Ambassador Bonnac on 22 April 1713, 'it is only by virtue of the renunciation which they [Philip V's father and elder brother] voluntarily made that the King my grandson reigns today in Spain.' If Philip had succeeded to France, he planned to renounce the throne of Spain in favour of one of his sons.[84]

At Louis' insistence, in the interests of European peace and equilibrium and in accordance with the Treaty of Utrecht, an elaborate theatre of renunciation was enacted in Madrid and Paris. In November 1712 Philip V had renounced in the Cortes in the presence of the British Ambassador 'for ever and always for myself and my heirs and successors' all claims to the crown of France. After his nephew the new Dauphin, and his younger brother the Duc de Berri, the crown of France, missing the Spanish Bourbons, should pass to the House of Orléans, then to the other Princes of the Blood.[85]

In reciprocity, in March 1713, watched by their French cousins and the Spanish and British ambassadors, Berri and Orléans renounced in the Parlement of Paris their claims to the crown of Spain. After Philip V and his descendants, it should go to the Duke of Savoy and his descendants, not to the Orléans, who were reserved for France. By speeches checked word for word on his copy by the British Ambassador the Duke of Shrewsbury as they were read out by princes and judges, 'the royal branch of France and all the branches of France' were separated for all time – in theory – from the 'branch of the royal blood of Spain', in the interests of 'the universal good and repose of Europe, and to establish an equilibrium between the powers and general peace'. Foreign powers were now influencing the French succession, as France had once influenced the English, Spanish and Polish successions. The renunciations were registered with the Cortes, the Parlement de Paris and the Cour des Comptes. An English suggestion that the States General should be summoned for the same purpose was ignored.[86]

Despite the return of peace, Louis XIV remained as authoritarian as ever. Only reluctantly in 1713 did he liberate 136 Huguenot galley slaves, at Queen Anne's special request.[87] When she asked for more, Torcy exclaimed, 'why do you, ministers of a monarch, continue to plead for rebels, mutineers etc and are not these Huguenots the worst enemies the King has? Nay are they not the worst the Queen has?'[88]

Louis also continued to persecute Jansenists, as innovators and republicans. First the King secured from the Pope a bull of dissolution for the convent of Port-Royal des Champs. His final confrontation with the French convents to which his mistresses had so often retreated took place on 29 October 1709. In what Saint-Simon would call a 'barbarism of ancient times', and others compared to despotism in Morocco, eighteen aged nuns were taken by force by d'Argenson and 200 soldiers from their convent at the Jansenist centre of Port-Royal des Champs and sent to other convents. Port-Royal was razed to the ground by royal troops.[89] Two years later even the graves at Port-Royal were destroyed, the corpses disinterred and the bones placed in a common grave.[90] In 1712 a royal decree declared that, if the relevant crimes were sufficiently serious, corpses too could be tried, in order to inspire terror in the living.[91]

Formerly opposed to papal authority, Louis XIV now used it, to the detriment of his royal prerogative, to continue persecuting Jansenists. The Bull Unigenitus, issued by the Pope at the King's request in September 1713, condemned yet more theological propositions, formerly considered orthodox, as 'Jansenist' and obliged priests to guarantee in writing their submission to the bull. This caused a political and religious earthquake. Despite Louis XIV's threats of imprisonment, it was publicly opposed as contrary to church discipline and theological orthodoxy by the Cardinal de Noailles, Archbishop of Paris (another of Madame de Maintenon's confidants who, like Fénelon and Beauvillier, turned against her), by the Parlement of Paris and by a majority of priests and teachers in Paris.[92] In 1714, for the only time in history, the Chancellor of France, M. de Pont-chartrain from the Phélypeaux family, resigned, because he refused to enforce the bull.[93] Maintenon began to regard Noailles as a heretic and to see Jansenists everywhere. Louis XIV planned to hold a *lit de justice* and a national church council in order to pursue his crusade against the Jansenists.

The Parlement's opposition to the crown after 1715 would be, in part, fired by Jansenism and Gallicanism. As well as atheism and indifference, another reason for the transformation of Paris from a bastion of Catholicism into Europe's capital of disbelief would be the persecution under Louis XIV and Louis XV of people suspected of Jansenism.[94] The refusal of the sacraments to dying supporters of Jansenism, who did not have tickets proving they had made their confession to an officially approved Catholic priest, led to a decline in Christian faith. In 1753 the minister d'Argenson, son of Louis XIV's Lieutenant de Police, believed that the number of communicants in the parish of Saint-Eustache in Paris (where Louis XIV himself had been confirmed in 1648) had declined by half.[95] The crusade against Jansenism created enemies for the French crown, and a desire for revenge which would contribute to the expulsion of its most ardent supporters, the Jesuits, from France in 1764.[96]

Louis XIV, and many at court, remained sympathetic to the Jacobites, but he was determined not to provoke another war with Britain. After Queen Anne's death at Kensington Palace on 1 August 1714, 'James III' dashed back to France, staying in a house at Issy outside Paris. Mary of Modena informed Madame de Maintenon and asked for recognition of her son as king. In 1714, however, in contrast to 1701, Louis put peace before war. As Matthew Prior wrote to George I, Louis sent Torcy to ask 'James III' to leave at once, and refused all requests for recognition, funds or the loan of soldiers from Irish regiments in French service.[97] In London the army and the Privy Council had already ensured the peaceful accession of George I. On 20 October 1714, when the Archbishop of Canterbury asked the congregation at George I's coronation in Westminster Abbey whether it accepted him as lawful king, the Countess of Dorchester, former mistress of James II, remarked, 'Does the old Fool think that Anybody here will say no to his Question, when there are so many drawn Swords?'[98]

Paris, Versailles and the French embassy in London, however, remained hives of Jacobite activity. Bolingbroke was terrified that the Whigs might impeach him for high treason for his secret peace negotiations and correspondence with 'James III' or for his role in the 'restraining orders'. He spoke such good French that Torcy, his host in Paris in 1712, wrote that 'the court of France did not seem foreign to him, as he himself did not appear foreign.'[99] Therefore with the help of the French Ambassador in London d'Iberville, Bolingbroke fled to Paris in April 1715, disguised as a French courier's servant. He often saw Torcy in Paris, and in July was appointed secretary of state by 'James III'.[100] On 30 July, possibly provoked by the Whig ministry, another Tory idol, the former Captain General the Duke of Ormonde, also fled to escape impeachment, and his own debts. He arrived in Paris on 7 August and saw Torcy and Bolingbroke. 'James III', who again secretly visited Paris at this time, selected him to command a future uprising in England.[101]

The 'Projet de Marly', discussed in that chateau during Louis XIV's last visit in June 1715 by Torcy, Berwick and the Swedish Ambassador Count Sparre (since George I had occupied Swedish territory at the mouth of the Elbe), was devised to foment uprisings in England and to persuade Sweden and Spain, in place of France, to help 'James III'. Philip V agreed, provided 'James III' promised to return Gibraltar and Minorca and to assist Spain to recover its dominions in Italy. In return for an English noble title, Crozat made a loan to 'James III'. In August Louis XIV's last letter to Philip V urged him to send funds to 'James III'.[102] Thus Louis left France at peace, but committed to three damaging crusades: against the Huguenots, against the Jansenists and, although more secretly, for 'James III'.

23

Funeral Games

In 1714 Matthew Prior had found the King 'as well as I have ever seen him since I have been in France', hunting, shooting or walking every day, and eating with 'a great appetite'.[1] He ate so much that Madame de Maintenon and his courtiers trembled for his health.[2]

On 19 February 1715, in a last show of global ambition and personal vanity, he arranged a reception in the Galerie des Glaces in honour of an ambassador from Persia, a country in which he had long been interested. Mehmet Reza Beğ was not an impostor, as was alleged by Saint-Simon and others, misled by his bad manners and paltry presents. He had been sent with a large suite from Isfahan to Paris to negotiate a new commercial treaty and to secure French naval help for a Persian attack on Muscat, whose Arab ruler was challenging Persian control of the Gulf.

A massive gilded throne was made for the occasion and Louis wore 12.5 million livres' worth of crown jewels on his coat; it was so heavy that he changed it immediately afterwards. In the Galerie des Glaces he walked close to the tiers of seats filled with ladies, 'who much wanted to see him in his magnificence'. The Elector of Bavaria, the son of Augustus II of Poland, and Prince Rákóczi were among the spectators, incognito. The Introducteur des Ambassadeurs the Baron de Breteuil, however, complained that the crowd behaved so badly, as usual, that it 'avilit le spectacle' ('degraded the spectacle'). Nevertheless the cries of 'Vive le roi!', when the King appeared on the palace balcony could be heard as far as the Avenue de Paris.[3] A commercial treaty with Persia was signed on 13 August 1715, although the joint attack on Muscat, and despatch of French engineers and architects, requested by Persia (like that requested by the Sultan of Morocco in 1699), never took place.[4]

Younger princes and princesses, complained Madame de Maintenon, enjoyed drinking, smoking and 'promenades nocturnes' at their private houses in the country.[5] However, peace had brought the return of army officers and foreigners to the court. Reflecting the court's pride in the number of visitors, Madame de Maintenon and Dangeau claimed that never had such crowds presented themselves for invitations to Marly ('the accommodation places limits on his kindness') or to see the apartments and watch the fountains play at Versailles. The King still enjoyed concerts and plays (including some by Maintenon's first husband Scarron) in the evening in her apartment.[6] He continued to review his troops, 'giants' of 'extraordinary beauty' in new uniforms.[7] On 8 June 1715, at the age of seventy-seven, despite a heat wave, he touched 1,700 people for the King's Evil.[8]

Dynastic problems, rather than foreign wars, dominated the last year of his life. On 5 May 1714 the King's youngest grandson the Duc de Berri had died from the effects of a hunting accident. After his surviving great-grandson the future Louis XV, his nearest legitimate male relation in France, and the natural future Regent, was now his nephew Philippe, Duc d'Orléans. Louis XIV had many reasons to distrust him.

As a young general in 1693 and 1694, the Duc de Chartres (as he was known until his father's death) had pleased Louis XIV by his application and the length and precision of his reports from the battlefield. By 1696, however, as Madame reported to his tutor and adviser the Abbé Dubois, the King was furious with his 'impertinent remarks' and 'bad conduct'.[9] The King's failure to employ him subsequently in the army infuriated Monsieur and may have led to a quarrel between the brothers and Monsieur's fatal heart attack in 1701, although Madame, normally eager to complain, does not mention this in her account.[10] Thereafter Orléans, as he had become, frequented what Madame de Maintenon called the 'worst company in the world', and lodged his mistress in his palace. Orléans' passion for his daughter Marie Louise Elisabeth would later make both her husband the Duc de Berri and her mother, Orléans' wife, jealous. He was impious as well as debauched. Louis XIV and Madame de Maintenon were appalled.[11]

Spurning hunting and dancing, Orléans conducted experiments in his private laboratory, bought 'powders' from a sorceress, tried to recreate the music of the ancient Greeks and composed operas.[12] He was also ambitious. In a secret display of independence, his father had reserved the Orléans' rights to the crown of Spain in November 1700, in a notarized document, on the grounds that his mother Anne of Austria's renunciation of the throne of Spain had been less absolute than Marie Thérèse's. In 1708–9, when commanding French troops in Spain, Orléans had interfered in Spanish internal affairs by requesting from Philip V a pardon for Valencia. In July 1709, when there was talk of Philip's abdication – at the suggestion of an English general James Stanhope, whom Orléans had previously met in Paris – he sent two of his officers, Flotte and Regnault, to recruit partisans to support his claim to the Spanish throne. In the words of his friend the Duc de Saint-Simon he was 'drunk with the prospect of a crown'.

On 12 July 1709 Philip arrested and imprisoned Flotte and Regnault, and would not release them until Louis himself requested it in 1715.[13] In his eagerness to satisfy allied demands for Philip's removal, Louis may have failed sufficiently to discourage Orléans' attempts to offer himself as an alternative monarch.[14] Louis begged Philip for secrecy, assured him that Orléans had never acted against his service and tried to suppress evidence of Orléans' 'imprudence'. Philip replied that Flotte said Louis had known everything.[15]

At Versailles and Madrid there were 'clamours'. The Dauphin demanded a criminal trial.[16] According to Torcy, the Dauphin told the King that Orléans wanted 'to exterminate them all', in order to win the crowns of both France and Spain. The rivalry between the Bourbons and the Orléans, which would contribute to the success of the revolutions of 1789 and 1830 in France, began in Spain.[17]

Orléans remained under suspicion. The sudden deaths of the Duc and Duchesse de Bourgogne in 1712, combined with his interest in chemical experiments, made many accuse him of poisoning them. Courtiers shunned him. When he went to pay his respects at Saint-Denis on 17 February, he was insulted by members of the public: 'Voilà l'assassin! Voilà l'empoisonneur de nos princes!'[18] Louis XIV was reassured only when his Premier Chirurgien certified that he had found no traces of poison.[19] Yet he feared to entrust his great-grandson to his nephew.

The King turned to his illegitimate sons the Duc du Maine, the Comte de Toulouse and their descendants. The legitimized princes were given places in the line of succession after the legitimate Princes of the Blood in July 1714 and the full rank and prerogatives of Princes of the Blood the following May. Louis XIV thereby broke both dynastic and religious rules.[20] Other dynasties gave bastards positions of responsibility. Anne of Austria and Mazarin, for example, had trusted the Vendôme family more than the Condé. No bastards since the fifteenth century, however, had been allowed a place in the succession – as Charles II's son Monmouth had learnt for himself in England in 1685, when he was executed after a failed uprising.[21] As the Chancellor Séguier had said in 1662, when Louis XIV had previously tried to break dynastic rules by making Lorraine princes Princes of the Blood in France and inserting them in the succession, in France you could only make new Princes of the Blood with the Queen.[22]

By the King's will, written at Marly on 2 August 1714, Maine was given command of the nerve centre of the monarchy, the royal guard and household, as well as supervision of the future King's education. 'All the officers of the Guard and the Household' were to obey him. Orléans was to be chief of the Council of Regency, but not regent.[23] He could not make decisions 'alone and by his sole authority', but only by a majority vote of the Council of Regency, which Louis ensured was composed of princes, secretaries of state and marshals de Villeroy, d'Huxelles, de Tallard and d'Harcourt, many of whom distrusted Orléans. By a codicil in 1715, Louis named as the future King's governor his oldest friend, the Maréchal de Villeroy. On the King's death Louis XV was to be taken via Paris to the Château de Vincennes. Although the court had not used Vincennes for fifty years, the air was good and, unlike Versailles, it was fortified.[24]

Louis claimed that, by increasing the numbers of 'our august House of Bourbon', he would avoid the 'division among the *grands seigneurs* of the Kingdom', and harm to the state, which would occur if it died out.[25] Instead, by dividing responsibilities among rival princes, he prepared conflict in the dynasty. His will, like his plan of campaign in 1708, was a lesson in mismanagement.

There were three factions again, as there had been before 1711: the Duc d'Orléans and his son; Maine and Toulouse; and Philip V who, reported the French Ambassador in Madrid, thought he would have a better claim than Orléans to the regency when his grandfather died, and was moving troops to the French frontier.[26] Philip's new Ambassador in Paris, Prince Cellamare, had orders to form a party in his favour, hopefully including Maintenon, Torcy and the Duc du Maine.[27] Philip had been informed, incorrectly, that 'all good Frenchmen', and all but one of the ministers, supported his claims to the regency.[28]

Exhausted by her husband's love-making, and her frequent pregnancies, Maria Luisa, Queen of Spain, had died on 14 February 1714. The Princesse des Ursins had shown an ambition for sovereignty typical of *princes étrangers* by demanding her own independent principality in Limbourg, Luxembourg or the Pyrenees, with an income of 30,000 livres a year, as Maria Luisa and Philip V had long promised her.[29] As governess of the King's children, Ursins built a special wooden corridor connecting her apartment to his, so that the inconsolable widower could visit his children more easily. She told Madame de Maintenon that it was her duty to 'support and amuse the King'. Others suspected that she wanted to keep him secluded. Until obliged by a letter from Louis XIV, Philip had refused to sign peace with the Netherlands unless Ursins received an independent sovereignty.[30]

Meanwhile a new wife had been selected for Philip V at the prompting of the Abbé Alberoni, who after Vendôme's death in 1712 had remained in Madrid: the Duke of Parma's daughter Elisabeth Farnese. While feigning devotion to Ursins, Alberoni, who remained a correspondent of the Duke of Parma, secretly groomed the future Queen to remove her. He ensured that he reached the Queen, on her journey from Parma to Madrid, before she did.[31]

The fall of the Princesse des Ursins in December 1714 was a particularly brutal example of the mechanics of disgrace, and encouraged Philip's growing independence from his grandfather. Reversing the roles of Queen Anne and the Duchess of Marlborough, in Spain the Queen lost her temper with the lady-in-waiting. When they met at the small town of Quadraque north of Madrid on 23 December, the Princesse des Ursins failed to show the new Queen sufficient respect. She entered a room at the same time, and criticized the Queen's clothes and failure to hasten to meet Philip V. No doubt she expected to dominate the new Queen as easily as she had her predecessor.

Coached by Alberoni, Elizabeth Farnese reproached the Camarera Mayor for trying to prevent her from meeting her aunt the Queen Dowager, widow of Carlos II, and intercepting their letters. A French agent reported their alleged conversation: 'To speak to me in that fashion, to me, Elisabeth!' Then, turning to the officer of the Gardes du Corps in waiting: 'Make this madwoman leave my presence!' She called the Princess 'une insolente' and 'une impertinente', and had her household arrested. After being shut in a bedroom with nothing to read or write, Ursins was escorted by fifty Gardes du Corps, through a snow blizzard, over the Pyrenees to France, sleeping on straw, with only one maid and a footman, and only eggs to eat. Her survival, she later wrote, was a miracle.

'Her Majesty dismissed me shamefully, while uttering insults,' Madame des Ursins wrote to Madame de Maintenon.[32] Philip V expressed regrets, but after the first night with his new wife, fell under her influence. On 27 March 1715 the Princesse des Ursins was granted a two-and-a-half-hour audience by Louis XIV at Versailles. The King gave her a pension, and wrote a letter in his own hand assuring her of his esteem and regret.

Indeed in 1709 and 1710 she had strengthened Spanish resistance and helped dissuade Louis from signing a humiliating peace. After farewell audiences with Louis and Madame de Maintenon at Marly on 6 August 1715, she left France for Genoa. Soon, both in Spain and France, she was as forgotten as Caesar or Pompey. Her last years, from 1719 until her death in 1722, would be spent in Rome at the court of the exiled 'James III', unable to live without what her friend Saint-Simon called 'the air of a court and the whiff of politics'.[33]

While Orléans had foreign enemies like the King of Spain and his new Queen, he also had foreign allies. George I favoured Orléans, his first cousin once removed, and an enemy of his enemy Philip V. In July 1715 Orléans' former tutor and confidential adviser the Abbé Dubois had a secret meeting with George's ambassador to France, Lord Stair (who had fought at Ramillies and Oudenarde, and was detested in France for his arrogance), at night in the Bois de Boulogne. They discussed 'James III' and the Mardyck canal. Stair hoped to use Dubois as a source of information about French policy and the plans of 'James III' to invade England.[34] He also had frequent audiences with Orléans, where they discussed future relations between the kingdoms.[35]

In June 1715 Louis XIV held what turned out to be his last 'Marly'. There were 107 guests, including the Orléans, the Princes of the Blood and the legitimized bastards; the Cardinals de Rohan and de Polignac; the Duchesse de Saint-Simon and the Prince of Transylvania. Apart from eating too many peas and strawberries, the King seemed well.[36] Still a relentless host, he had forced the Duchesse de Berri to quit deep mourning for her husband in order to 'lead the gambling' in the Grand Salon.[37] He also enjoyed placing statues from Rome in the garden. He continued to hunt and to hold reviews. At his review of the Régiment du Roi on 3 August, however, he shivered and put on a cloak; no one else felt cold.[38]

Gangrene, probably complicated by diabetes, had begun to spread, particularly in the left leg, so prominently displayed in his 1700 portrait by Rigaud. It gave him pain and he began to lose appetite.[39] At his public supper at Versailles on 12 August, two days after his return from Marly, Lord Stair wrote, 'he looked mighty ill, came late into the room with great pain supported upon a stick.' The following day: 'I saw the King dine, who looked exceedingly ill; spoke with a broken voice; and could not eat. He seemed uneasy to see me at the table. The courtiers looked hideously upon me.' Stair had quarrelled with Torcy, whom he considered a Jacobite, because he had failed to expel Ormonde and Bolingbroke from France or to persuade the Duke of Lorraine to expel 'James III'.[40]

Remembering afterwards the *coucher* on 12 August, Dangeau wrote: 'it seemed on seeing his body that his flesh had been melted away.'[41] That night the King felt that his stomach was on fire and kept waking his valets to bring him water to drink. Blouin, the Premier Valet de Chambre on duty, insisted that doctors be summoned from Paris to advise Fagon and the King's doctors, whom like most courtiers he distrusted. They did little except prescribe asses' milk.[42] Unable to walk, the King had to be carried in an armchair or pushed in a wheelchair. On 14 August he attended mass in the royal chapel, on the 16th received the ambassadors and on the 19th listened to music with Madame de Maintenon and her friends in her apartment, for the last time.[43] When he appeared in the chapel there were many shouts of 'Vive le roi!' The crowd in the gallery was so great that his procession had difficulty in making its way through.[44] He was still working with his ministers, discussing plans for buildings and gardens with the Duc d'Antin, talking to courtiers at meals and seeing Madame de Maintenon, 'les dames familières' and his family in the evening.[45] However, Madame wrote that his condition worried her so much that she felt ill and could barely eat or sleep.[46]

He had difficulty sleeping and was always thirsty. He said that he could tell from the looks on the faces around him how ill he was: 'I am really exhausted, but how could I be otherwise, suffering day and night without ceasing?'[47] He lost appetite and usually ate little except at supper on 21 August when he consumed forty figs.[48] Madame de Maintenon complained that he did not know how to obey doctors' rules.[49] His bedroom and his *cabinet* in the evening were packed with princes, court officials and ministers. D'Anthoine, one of his *garçons de la chambre*, writes that 'the pleasure of seeing the love and zeal of his courtiers gave him satisfaction and made him forget his pain.' They admired his courage, his piety and his application to government business.[50]

On 22 August he showed that he expected to live by asking for coats to be laid out so that he could choose a new one to wear at the end of court mourning for Prince François de Lorraine, who had just died.[51] By 24 August, however, the day he held his last council, he knew he was dying. He dined in public, but had lost feeling in his left leg, which had turned black with gangrene. He made his confession to Père Le Tellier at 11 o'clock that night.[52]

On 25 August, as it was the feast of St Louis, the violins and musicians of the Chamber and the bands of the Gardes Francaises and Gardes Suisses in the courtyard played for him.[53] He still worked with ministers and saw Madame de Maintenon and some ladies, and had a long private conversation with Orléans. However, he was so weak that, at the suggestion of the Maréchal de Villeroy and the Grand Aumônier the Cardinal de Rohan, who had rushed back from his diocese of Strasbourg to be with the King at Versailles, he received the sacraments of communion *en viatique* and of extreme unction. As he did so, surrounded by his household, he cried, 'Mon dieu, ayez pitié de moi . . . j'espère en votre miséricorde.' The princes and courtiers present were in tears.[54]

The churches of Paris filled with people praying for the King's recovery – as the crowds at Versailles also showed, he was not as detested as critics would later claim.[55] On 27 August a deputation from the Paris Parlement came to enquire about his health, but was not allowed into his bedroom by the Premier Gentilhomme in waiting, the Duc de Tresmes. He told them that they could judge the state of the King by the consternation they saw on people's faces.[56]

Amid tears and lamentations, on 25, 26, 27 and 28 August Louis made his farewells to his ministers, to his courtiers and, individually, to the princes of his family. He was particularly gracious to M. Desmarets, the Contrôleur Général, who had restored French finances and avoided bankruptcy. 'However great he has been in the glorious course of a reign of seventy-two years, he has made himself appear even greater in his death. His good sense and firmness did not abandon him for a moment,' wrote Dangeau.[57] The same could be said of his family and officials. Everyone did their duty. Despite the religious and personal feuds dividing them, and the trauma of losing the King they had known all their lives, they ensured a smooth transition to the next reign.

The most frequent visitors during the King's final days were his confessor Père Le Tellier; Madame de Maintenon, an almost invisible figure in a corner by the King's bed, often in prayer, escorted to and from the room (she slept at Saint-Cyr) by her nephew the Duc de Noailles; the Chancellor; Villeroy; the Duc du Maine. The Oeil de Boeuf, the antechamber to the King's bedroom, was used by servants and doctors. Courtiers filled the gallery, and those with the right *entrées* the council chamber. Such was the magnetism of the King and the monarchy that both soon became impenetrable. Crowds filled the palace courtyards and the surrounding streets.[58]

With the Chancellor the King added his final codicil to his will, naming Fleury, a protégé of Torcy, as preceptor of the Dauphin. It was an inspired choice: Fleury, as Louis XV's chief minister from 1726 to 1743, would give France and Europe two decades of stability. Louis XIV told Villeroy, particularly assiduous throughout these days, that he had been appointed the next King's governor, 'the most important job that I can give', and asked Villeroy to serve him after his death as faithfully as he had during his lifetime: 'Adieu, monsieur le Maréchal. I hope that you will remember me.' He had a final conversation with Orléans, who left bathed in tears.[59]

On 26 August to his five-year-old great-grandson the Dauphin his last words included: 'My dear child [or, according to Dangeau, Mignon], you are going to be the greatest king in the world. Never forget the obligations you have to God. Do not imitate me in my wars; try always to maintain peace with your neighbours, to relieve your people as much as you will be able to, which I have had the misfortune to be unable to do, due to necessities of State.' The King who had loved war admitted that he should have maintained peace. Dangeau and Breteuil also claimed that he said that he had continued his wars out of vanity. By order of Louis XV's Governess, the Duchesse de Ventadour, these words would be transcribed by a court calligrapher M. Gilbert, and placed on a wall by the young King's bed. In 1712 she had saved his life; after 1715 she tried to guide his reign.[60]

Louis' last words to his courtiers confirmed that the court of France was a joint venture between the dynasty and its servants: 'Messieurs, I ask your forgiveness for the bad example I have set you; I must thank you for the way you have all served me and for the attachment and fidelity that you always shown me.' He advised them to serve his successor with similar fidelity and obey his nephew. Even now on his deathbed, he felt an obligation to his courtiers: 'I am very sad that I have not done for you what I would have very much wished to do: the unfortunate times are the cause. Adieu messieurs, I count on you to remember me sometimes.' By another account, he added words which became famous: 'I am leaving, but the State will always remain. Be all united and in agreement; that is the union and the force of a State.' All, including the princes, burst into tears.[61]

To the members of his family he recommended that they remain united. To Madame he said goodbye so tenderly she almost fainted. He assured her that he had always loved her and apologized if he had occasionally caused her chagrin. He continued to give orders, she wrote, 'with a firmness of which you can have no idea. At each moment he gives orders as if he was simply going to leave on a journey.'[62]

On 27 August his last dialogue with Madame de Maintenon, recorded by their friend Dangeau, conveys their unity as a couple, his desire to please and her implacability:

'What will become of you, Madame, for you have nothing?' (In fact she had 4,000 livres a month.) She insisted, 'I am but nothing. Think only of God.' The King said he did not find death so difficult to face. She replied: 'This decision [to accept death] is difficult only when one has attachment to people, when one has hate in one's heart, restitutions to make.' The King said, 'As for restitutions, I owe none to any private people, but as for those I owe to the kingdom, I must trust in the mercy of God.'[63]

The same day, despite advancing gangrene, he assigned the apartments for the court's impending visit to Vincennes (which the Grand Maréchal des Logis had never visited) and gave orders to the Ministre de la Maison for the transport of his heart to the church of Saint-Louis in Paris, as calmly as if he was ordering a new fountain for Marly. With the Chancellor he burnt some of his papers.[64] Dangeau recorded that Louis referred to the Dauphin as the king. On 28 August to two weeping servants he said, 'Why are you crying? Did you think I was immortal?'[65]

Maine and the King's daughters reigned in his bedroom. At their insistence, despite the doctors' opposition, on 28 and 29 August the King took an 'elixir' brought by a quack from Marseille called Brun. He recovered briefly and ate a few biscuits. Thereafter his pulse continued to weaken.[66] Saint-Simon and Pierre Narbonne remembered that, each time the King appeared to recover, Orléans' apartment emptied of courtiers. Each time he worsened, it filled again. 'Voilà le monde.'[67]

On 30 August, as the King drifted in and out of consciousness, Madame de Maintenon left, as he had ordered, having distributed her few possessions at Versailles among her servants.[68] That day the Abbé Mascara, agent of Philip V, wrote that Louis' leg was black as coal up to his knee, and had lost all feeling. The King asked God to let him suffer as long as He wished. Dangeau writes that at 10.30 in the evening on 31 August the King could still say the creed and the Ave Maria mechanically, following the words of the priests in his bedroom. Then at 8.23 in the morning of 1 September, he died 'like a candle going out' in Dangeau's words.[69] By chance, it was the date on which London gamblers had long been betting.

From the palace balcony, the Grand Chamberlain the Duc de Bouillon cried: 'Le roi Louis XIV est mort. Vive le roi Louis XV!' All courtiers, male and female, rushed to pay their respects to the five-year-old Louis XV. He wept on hearing the words 'Sire' and 'Majesty'. At their head was Orléans who declared himself, on bended knee, 'the first and most obedient of your subjects'. Crowds cried 'Vive le roi Louis XV!' when he appeared on the balcony.[70]

The dead King's body, with a crucifix in his hands, was laid out on his bed. The Cardinal de Rohan began to recite the De Profundis. Fifty-six Gardes du Corps guarded the dead King, while others protected the living King, Louis XV. From 10 a.m. the doors were opened – by one leaf, to control the crowds, whom guards kept moving in a continuous flow.[71] Ministers, ambassadors and the Assembly of Clergy arrived to sprinkle holy water on the dead King.

The next day the body was opened and dissected. It was found to be gangrened, with inflamed tissues in a state of 'total dissolution'. In accordance with French royal tradition (also practised by the House of Austria and some private individuals), so that his body would not rot, the King's heart and entrails were removed from his corpse, which was then embalmed and put in a coffin.[72] For the next eight days the embalmed corpse was exposed in the Salon de Mercure in the Grand Appartement, with 'the finest furniture of the crown'. The bed on which he was laid had been specially made for Louis and Madame de Montespan; her face, embroidered on the bed canopy, stared down on her lover's corpse. The clergy sat on the right, court officials on the left. All day long, until eight in the evening, crowds filed past. Priests said mass at portable altars, and sprinkled the coffin with holy water. Musicians from the royal chapel played music composed for the prayers De Profundis and Miserere and for requiems.[73]

The King's entrails and heart, which had also been embalmed, and placed in lead caskets, were escorted by Gardes du Corps to Paris. The entrails were buried on 4 September beneath the choir of the cathedral of Notre-Dame; the heart ('sad but precious remains of the greatest and most powerful prince in the world', said the Cardinal de Rohan) was taken on 6 September to the church of Saint-Louis, founded by Louis XIII in 1627 in the Marais, where it was later suspended from an arch in a golden casket.[74]

Such was the force of heredity, and Orléans' political genius, that the transfer of power had already started, and Orléans had already begun to give orders, even before Louis' death. On 23 August George I's Ambassador Stair, interfering in Paris as readily as French ambassadors had once done in London, had met Dubois in the Tuileries garden and assured him of 'the King's [George I's] good intentions and firm resolution to support the duke of Orléans'. On 26 August, he offered Orléans whatever assistance he wished 'to make good his right to the regency, in exclusion of the King of Spain', or, if the Dauphin died, to the throne. Orléans told Stair not to worry, as he was sure of the Parlement and the troops.[75]

On 27 August, Orléans began to issue orders to d'Argenson the Lieutenant de Police de Paris, to officials of the Parlement and to officers of the Gardes du Corps.[76] Already on 22 August, as Maine was reviewing the gendarmerie at Marly, the Dauphin dressed in Gendarme uniform had arrived with Orléans – thereby showing that Orléans had the support of the Gouvernante des Enfants de France, Madame de Ventadour, a former dame d'honneur of his mother. The moment they arrived, all present turned to Orléans; Maine withdrew. The army was on Orléans' side.[77]

At the first meeting of the Parlement in Paris on 2 September, the Gardes Français lining the roads around it were commanded by Orléans' ally the Duc de Guiche.[78] Orléans claimed that the King had told him, in private conversations on 25 and 26 August, that his rights had been preserved and that he should make any changes to the will he judged appropriate.[79] There were no other witnesses to this conversation.

Orléans declared that anyone who had advised the King to give power

over the Maison du Roi (meaning both the royal household and the household troops) to someone other than himself should be punished. Despite
Maine's authority over the Maison du Roi granted by the King's will, and
his offices as grand master of the artillery and colonel general of the Swiss
Guards, Maine said that, if what had been concluded in the will in his
favour displeased the Duke and the Parlement, he would be very happy
to sacrifice his interests to the good of the state. He had a sense of public
duty. It was Maine, not Fredrick the Great as is frequently claimed, who
invented the precept 'it is always the State one serves and the King himself
is only its first servant.'[80]

In defiance of Louis' will, Orléans was declared regent, with full authority over the Maison du Roi as well as the government. His own words
made his bargain with the Parlement clear: 'Whatever right I have to the
Regency, I dare assure you, messieurs, that I will earn it by my zeal for the
King's service and by my love for the public good, above all aided by your
councils and your wise remonstrances.' In return for the Parlement's support, the Regent abrogated Louis XIV's edicts of 1667 and 1673 imposing
automatic registration by the Parlement of royal laws. Henceforth, with
disastrous consequences for the monarchy, the Parlement could discuss and
present remonstrances concerning royal laws before their registration.[81]

Thus Paris and the state reasserted their authority over Versailles and
the court. Louis XIV, as he had guessed, was as powerless in death as his
father had been in 1643. The dynastic system and Orléans' careful preparations with his friend d'Aguesseau, Procureur Général of the Parlement,
were stronger than Louis' will and his illegitimate children. Maine would
henceforth command only those soldiers on duty guarding the King, not
the companies and regiments from which they came. In 1717 he and
Toulouse would be demoted from their rank of Princes of the Blood, back
to that of *princes légitimés*. In 1718 he was deprived of the *surintendance*
of the King's education. The elimination of Louis XIV's illegitimate son
from political life was complete.[82]

On 9 September Louis XV was taken, as Louis XIV had recommended,
to Vincennes. He travelled through Paris in a carriage with the Regent,
the Duc de Bourbon, the Maréchal de Villeroy and the Duchesse de Ventadour. He sat on her knees so that he could be seen better. In Louis XV's
first contact with Paris, Mathieu Marais saw that 'infinite' crowds cried
'Vive le roi' – so loudly that the handsome young King joined in. 'Nothing
could be added to the tenderness and acclamations of the Parisians.'[83]
Louis XV was as well received in Paris in 1715 as Louis XIV had been,
on a similar occasion and at the same age, in 1643.

*

At seven in the evening on the previous day, by the light of burning torches, a magnificent funeral procession of sixty carriages and 900 people, led by the Duc de Bourbon, princes, senior court officials and heralds in deepest mourning, had left Versailles. Eight horses pulled the funeral chariot, draped in black velvet, on which the King's embalmed body had been placed. It was escorted by Swiss and French guards beating muffled drums; Gardes du Corps; the mounted musketeers and Chevau-légers of the King's military household; Gardes de la Porte and de la Prévôté; Cent-suisses de la Garde; *aumôniers*; trumpeters; poor men – 'les pauvres' – in specially issued mourning clothes; and royal footmen carrying torches to light the way. The torches were replaced along the route so there was always enough light to guide the procession.

Watched by 'all the carriages of Paris', the funeral cortège passed over the Seine at the Pont de Sèvres, along the edge of the Bois de Boulogne to the magnificent thirteenth-century abbey of Saint-Denis, named after the first bishop of Paris who had been martyred and buried there in 250. One of the sacred sites of the French monarchy, it contained the tombs of almost all the kings since the seventh century. The procession arrived at about seven in the morning.[84]

For six weeks Louis XIV lay in state until the funeral service, in the presence of representatives of the institutions of church and state, on 23 October. 'The King is dead. Let us pray for the peace of his soul,' said the King of Arms of France, as court officials broke their wands of office and threw them on to his coffin in its vault, followed by the flags of the household troops, spurs, the sceptre, the hand of justice and the royal crown.[85] Like all Bourbons, and unlike the Valois, Louis XIV received a simple coffin in the crypt, rather than a grand royal tomb.[86] Then, as trumpets and drums sounded, the heralds proclaimed: 'Vive le Roi Louis 15e du nom, par la grâce de Dieu roi de France et de Navarre, très chrétien, très auguste, très puissant, notre très honoré seigneur et bon maître, à qui Dieu donne très longue et très heureuse vie!'[87] ('Long live King Louis, fifteenth of the name, by the grace of God king of France and Navarre, most Christian, most august, most powerful, our very honoured lord and good master, to whom may God give a very long and very fortunate life!')

At memorial services throughout France and the Spanish monarchy, from Paris to Lima, at French missions abroad from London to Aleppo, and even in the hostile capital of Vienna, preachers compared the late King to David, Solomon, Augustus and Hercules.[88] At Saint-Denis, Mgr Quiqueran de Beaujeu, Bishop of Castres, asserted, 'He almost never undertook any enterprise which did not succeed and his misfortunes themselves only served to heighten his glory,' adding, 'what was our joy and our satisfaction when we had the good fortune to see this royal table better decorated by concord than by the graces which surrounded it.' He also praised the King's 'superb palaces, prodigies of art'. His reign was superior to England's 'badly understood liberty, unending source of discord'. 'Even in dying, Louis is superior to other men.'[89]

In contrast to the funeral procession's outward dignity, however, 'on all sides' along the route from Versailles to Saint-Denis, people had been drinking, laughing, singing and playing music – as the young writer François Arouet, later known as Voltaire (who had already been imprisoned in the Bastille for a satire against Madame de Maintenon) remembered. Resentment of his wars and taxes, and oppression, was increased by the prospect of change in a new reign. Even the Master of Ceremonies Desgranges in his official register admitted, 'the people regarded it as a fête and, full of joy at having seen the living king, did not feel all the sorrow which the death of such a great King should cause.'[90] Pierre Narbonne adds: 'many people rejoiced at the death of this prince and on all sides you could hear the sound of violins.' Perhaps for fear of popular reactions, the funeral procession, unlike that of the Duc and Duchesse de Bourgogne three years earlier, did not pass through Paris.

Again poems provided a mocking counterblast to the official narrative:

> Here in the same tomb
> Lie the great Louis and the finances.
> . . . our invincible king . . . died as he lived,
> Without leaving us the
> Quarter of an écu . . .
> In Saint-Denis as at Versailles,
> He is without heart
> and without entrails.

'Our immortal king' was attacked for his taxes even more than for his wars or his absolutism. Only financiers, wrote the curé of Saint-Sulpice near Blois in his parish register, had benefited from his reign, since they acquired all the money in the kingdom.[91] Other poems called him 'the slave of an unworthy woman', the enemy of peace. 'Do not pray God for his soul. Such a monster never had one.' One called him Louis le Petit.[92]

At a solemn memorial service in the Sainte-Chapelle on the Île de la Cité in Paris, in the spiritual heart of the French monarchy, to which St Louis himself had confided what he believed to be the Crown of Thorns of Jesus Christ, one of the most respected preachers of the day, Jean-Baptiste Massillon, praised 'the father of kings, greater than all his ancestors, more magnificent than Solomon in all his glory'. However, he also mourned what he called 'an entire century of horror and carnage, the elite of the French nobility precipitated into the grave, so many ancient lines extinguished, so many inconsolable mothers who still weep for their children, our countryside deserted . . . our towns laid waste; our peoples exhausted . . . trade languishing . . . burning, bloodshed, blasphemy, abomination and all the horrors of which war is the father.' He described the glory of establishing Philip V on the throne of Spain as 'triste et amère' ('sad and bitter'); lamented that the Revocation of the Edict of Nantes had weakened the monarchy as a result of 'the escape of so many citizens' (one of the few public criticisms of their persecution); quoted the King's death-bed advice to his great-grandson to avoid wars; and deplored 'our crimes'.[93]

24

The Shadow of Versailles

After the death of Mazarin in 1661, having inherited the strongest country and army in Europe, Louis XIV had been expected to become the greatest monarch in history. By the end of his reign, however, France was no longer the supreme power in Europe. His own character was one reason. Power, leadership and hard work did not compensate for Louis XIV's love of war and lack of judgement. He overestimated French resources and underestimated European reactions.

In 1661 France had been protected by treaties with almost all the powers of Europe, except Austria – with Sweden, Denmark, Poland, Brandenburg, Bavaria, the Netherlands, England, Portugal and Spain – and by the long-standing alliance with the Ottoman Empire. As guarantor of the Treaty of Oliva in the north and the League of the Rhine in the Empire, France also had many pretexts for intervention abroad.[1] By his wars and persecutions, however, Louis XIV had helped unite Europe against France. At his death in 1715, France had no allies but Spain, Sweden, Bavaria and the Ottoman Empire.

Louis' lack of judgement led him to pick losers. His alliance with the exiled Stuarts benefited neither them nor France. Sweden lost wars against Brandenburg in 1674–8 and Russia in 1700–1721. Yet Louis remained loyal to this declining power, refusing offers of alliance from its victorious enemy Peter the Great, even asking him in 1711 (when Russia was at war with the Ottoman Empire) to return his Baltic conquests, including St Petersburg, to Sweden.[2] He continued paying subsidies to the Elector of Brandenburg when the Elector was already, in secret, allied to his enemy William III.[3]

Louis' alliance with the Elector of Bavaria, with whom he signed treaties in 1670, 1701 and 1714, also benefited neither side. Support for Bavarian ambitions led France to defeat at Blenheim, to the ravaging of the Bavarian countryside and to payment of a subsidy of 4 million livres a year to the exiled Elector, which the French treasury could ill afford.[4]

36. Louis XIV in ceremonial robes, by Hyacinthe Rigaud, 1701. In reality Louis XIV never wore these robes after his coronation in 1654 (the coronation crown can be seen on the left). The King liked this portrait so much that he hung it in Versailles, and commissioned a replica for his grandson Philip V.

37. Louise de Kéroualle, Duchess of
Portsmouth, by Pierre Mignard, 1682.
Charles II's principal mistress and
Louis XIV's agent is raising her hem to
reveal the coveted tabouret, upon
which duchesses had the privilege to
sit at ceremonies in France.

38. The Duc de Lauzun, by Alexis
Belle. After helping to organize the
flight of Mary of Modena and the
Prince of Wales to France in December
1688, Lauzun became the leading
French adviser of the exiled English
sovereigns and, as shown here, a
Knight of the Garter.

39. The family of James II, by Pierre Mignard, 1694. *Left to right*: the Prince of
Wales, later 'James III'; Mary of Modena, holding her daughter Louise Marie,
born in 1692; James II, in the robes of the Order of the Garter.

40. Leopold I, *c.* 1672. Holy Roman Emperor from 1658 to 1705, King of Hungary and Bohemia, and Louis XIV's rival as leading Catholic monarch in Europe.

41. Detail from the ceiling of the Painted Hall, Greenwich, by James Thornhill, 1707–14, showing William III and Mary II enthroned, crushing a figure of tyranny with the features of Louis XIV.

42. The apotheosis of John III Sobieski, surrounded by his family, by the workshop of Henri Gascard, *c.* 1691. Sobieski's French-born widow (*second from right*) would die forgotten in Blois in 1716; their eldest son Jakub Ludwik (*second from left*) failed to be elected king of Poland, but married his daughter Clementina to 'James III' in 1719.

43. The Marquis de Nointel (in a red robe), Louis XIV's Ambassador to the Ottoman Sultan, with his suite in Athens in 1674, part of a series attributed to Jacques Carrey, commissioned by Nointel to commemorate his embassy.

44. Reception of the Siamese ambassadors by Louis XIV, September 1686, by Charles Le Brun. The alliance with the King of Siam ended in 1689, after a failed French attempt to conquer and convert the country.

45. Président Toussaint Rose, Marquis de Coye, by François de Troy, *c.* 1684. Président Rose was Louis XIV's principal secretary, and wrote most of his official letters.

46. The Abbé Gaultier by Alexis Belle, *c.* 1712. Gaultier, a French priest living in London, was a secret intermediary during French–British negotiations in 1710–13.

47. Marie-Adélaïde de Savoie, Duchesse de Bourgogne, by Pierre Gobert, 1704. Her death in 1712 devastated the King and hastened her husband's death a week later.

48. Philip V, 1700, by Hyacinthe Rigaud. Philip V wore the traditional black dress of the Spanish court with reluctance, and, like most Spaniards, abandoned it after his victory over his Austrian rival at Almanza in 1707.

49. The taking of Mons in April 1691, print by François de Lapointe, from the *Almanach royal pour l'année 1692*. Emphasizing the military courage of the royal family, this print shows the King during the siege, surrounded by princes and, left, a soldier stunned by a cannonball.

50. *Heidelberga deleta*, medal celebrating the city's destruction, by Jérôme Roussel, 1693. Heidelberg is shown as a woman in tears, seated by a ruined wall, with the frightened River Neckar and a burning town in the distance. Other German towns were also destroyed.

51. The bombardment of the Grand-Place of Brussels, anonymous, 1695. The bombardment, lasting from 15 to 19 August 1695, destroyed most of the city centre. Vauban commented that bombardments exhausted French troops and munitions and were 'a very poor method of winning people's hearts'.

52. *La Bénédiction du ciel sur la postérité de Louis le Grand*, 25 June 1704. The Duchesse de Bourgogne can be seen in bed, after the birth of her first son the Duc de Bretagne.

53. Louis XIV with his heirs, formerly attributed to Nicolas de Largillière. *Left to right*: the Duchesse de Ventadour, the future Louis XV (in leading-strings), the Grand Dauphin, Louis XIV, his grandson the Duc de Bourgogne (father of Louis XV), whose hunchback is hidden by his wig. The Duchesse de Ventadour's family supplied five generations of Governesses of the Children of France, and she held court office for sixty years, from 1684 to 1744, longer than any other woman. Louis XV loved her and called her 'maman Ventadour'.

54. Louis XIV receives the Prince of Saxony, by Louis Silvestre, 1714. Like many foreign princes, the eldest son of Augustus II, Elector of Saxony and King of Poland, visited France during his grand tour. At Fontainebleau on 29 September 1714, he was presented by Madame (*centre*, in *grand habit*) to the King. On the right the Duchesse de Berry is wearing half-mourning, since her husband had died in May. Behind Louis is his nephew the Duc d'Orléans, later Regent. Second from right is the Cardinal de Rohan, Bishop of Strasbourg, rumoured to be a natural son of Louis XIV, to whom he would administer the last rites a year later.

55. Louis XIV in a wheelchair in the gardens of Versailles. Detail from *View of the Bassin d'Apollon and the Grand Canal of Versailles in 1713* by Pierre-Denis Martin. The King had begun to use wheelchairs in 1686 after his fistula operation.

The number and gravity of Louis' mistakes increased after Colbert's death in 1683, showing both the power of his ministers and that the famous inscription in the Galerie des Glaces 'le roi gouverne par lui-meme' was in part an illusion. The Revocation of the Edict of Nantes in 1685, the invasion of the Rhineland in 1688 (thereby helping to ensure the success of William III's invasion of England), the dispersion of French forces on different fronts in 1690–93 and the commitment to the restoration of the Stuarts were self-inflicted disasters. The bombardments of Genoa and Brussels, the persecution of the Huguenots and the devastation of the Palatinate showed the cruelty which helped turn much of Europe against France.

The year 1697, when Louis XIV ceded some of his territorial gains and failed to install his cousin the Prince de Conti as king of Poland, saw the beginning of the retreat of France. The transformations of its rivals England, Austria, Prussia and Savoy from second-rank into major powers (including England's conquest of Gibraltar and union with Scotland) were helped by Louis' wars, and in the case of England and Prussia by Huguenots fleeing his persecutions. Compared to Louis' alternations between dynasticism and nationalism, expansion and retrocession, Gallicanism and Papalism, his fellow monarchs Leopold I, William III, Victor Amadeus II and his own grandson Philip V, none of whom had Louis' initial advantages, proved more consistent and more successful.

Finance was another of Louis' weaknesses. In 1661 he had promised that 'the relief of my people is my strongest passion.' But, as he lamented on his deathbed, and as some of his subjects complained in their songs during his funeral procession, he failed in the task.[5] Both Matthew Prior and Peter the Great were shocked by the poverty and beggary they saw outside the gates of Versailles and Fontainebleau – by no means the poorest region of France – in contrast to the magnificence within.[6] Poverty weakened the quality of Louis' soldiers and his war machine. His extension of venality in the army also weakened its effectiveness – although its abolition in elite units showed his awareness of its drawbacks.[7]

Daniel Dessert has written that Louis' reign was a glorious façade, masking the continued power of financiers and beginning and ending in semi-bankruptcy.[8] Louis dismissed Fouquet in 1661, at the start of his personal reign, in order to improve French finances. For a time, with Colbert's help, he did. At the death of Colbert, France's debt had been only 240 million livres. At Louis' death, however, thirty-two years later, it was around 1.8 billion. Revenues were spent four years in advance, and the government was borrowing at 16 per cent interest or more.[9] Louis XIV's favourite courtier the Duc de Noailles, charged with reforming

French finances, wrote to Madame de Maintenon that those finances were in a far worse state than he had imagined: 'there is hardly an example of a monarchy having been in such a situation.'[10]

The King's choice and management of his servants, like his foreign and financial policies, often showed lack of judgement too. After the deaths of the able generals and ministers he had inherited from Mazarin, many of his personal appointments, such as Louvois, Chamillart and Villeroy, were unfortunate. His habit of conducting some of his wars by micro-management from Versailles, and dividing commands between rival generals, helped lead to French defeats. Louis XIV did not even choose good doctors. The attentions of his doctors led to the premature deaths of his wife, son, eldest grandson, granddaughter-in-law, two great-grandsons and, in the opinion of some courtiers, the King himself. The future Louis XV survived, as we have seen, because his Governess kept the doctors away.[11]

The King's preference for privileged families like the Noailles, Rohan and Bouillon, whom he allowed to turn court office from a favour into a birthright, began to close the court to many of the monarchy's natural supporters. In 1709 the Maréchal de Villars asked for the post of *premier gentilhomme*. The King gave it to the Duc de La Trémoille – a man whose main recommendation was his birth.[12]

Louis' reign, however, included triumphs as well as disasters. He both weakened and strengthened France. The Bourbon monarchy of Spain, which Louis established at enormous cost to France, was one of his principal legacies. After 1721 the French and Spanish Bourbons formed an effective power bloc, confirmed by treaties of alliance in 1721, 1733, 1742 and 1761. Their alliance helped a younger son of Philip V, Charles III, take Naples and Sicily from Austria in 1734, establishing, to popular applause, a third Bourbon monarchy, which would last until 1860.[13]

Three times, in 1742–8, 1761–3 and 1779–83, the French and Spanish Bourbons would fight together against Britain, as they had under Louis XIV. Their alliance helped the American colonies overthrow British rule in 1778–83; two of Louis XIV's descendants, Louis XVI and Charles III, helped found the United States. The Bourbon dynasty in Spain would outlast both its cousins in France and British control of North America; and, as Louis XIV would have been proud to observe, reigns again today.

Louis not only helped maintain Philip V on the Spanish throne, but also retained most of his conquests in the middle land between France and the Rhine: the three provinces of French Flanders, Alsace and Franche-Comté, including the cities of Dunkirk, Lille, Strasbourg and Besançon.

By respecting local traditions and authorities, ruling with a light hand, making frequent visits despite the distance from Paris and Versailles, and constructing massive fortresses (which in 1709–10 delayed Marlborough's advance long enough for a peace government to come to power in England and dismiss him), Louis proved better at incorporating French conquests, and defending France, than his republican and Bonapartist successors. He helped make Frenchmen out of Flemish, Alsatians and Burgundians and gave France its present shape.

He also provided many Frenchmen with immense emotional satisfaction, as he still does. Many were proud, like the King himself, of his wars, conquests and palaces, proud of his imposition of religious uniformity, of his hospitality to James II and of the fact that, as the lawyer M. Borelly of Nîmes wrote in his diary, 'all Europe is against our great king.'[14] In 1698 Matthew Prior noted that 'the common people of this nation have a strange veneration for their king.'[15]

In the supreme test of 1709–10, with the enemy at the gates, France, with the inglorious exception of the Cardinal de Bouillon (whom Saint-Simon called 'Cardinal Lucifer'), remained loyal.

As Louis XIV had written earlier for his son, 'reputation alone often achieves more than the most powerful armies.'[16] No one dared revolt for long. Even Saint-Simon, who hated Louis and his system, admitted that France had acquired a long habit of admiration, submission and fear of the King. Ministers felt 'la terreur du roi'. 'Never did a prince possess to such a high degree the art of reigning' – meaning his ability to win subjects' respect by his imposing manner, well-chosen words and relentless will-power.[17] Moreover some of Louis' later choices, like the Maréchal de Villars, two ministers from the Colbert clan, Torcy and Desmarets, and René d'Argenson the Lieutenant de Police de Paris, proved highly capable. If Louis ruined the monarchy's finances, he strengthened its control of its military machine. By constant attention to the prestige and effectiveness of the Maison Militaire, and to the selection and rewards of officers, he increased the loyalty of the French army to the crown.

Even more than Spain, Louis' colonies, his eastern conquests or Vauban's forts, the space by which Louis XIV is usually judged, and his most personal creation, is the enormous palace, and surrounding town, which he built at Versailles. The court's return to Versailles on 15 June 1722, after seven years in Paris, was another posthumous triumph for Louis XIV.

Versailles was believed to be healthier than Paris. The young King Louis XV loved it. Above all most people felt that, as the Paris lawyer Frédéric Barbier wrote in his diary, Versailles was 'much more superb for a king

than Paris', and a more effective symbol of the grandeur of France.[18] Thus
even the Regent Orléans, who had avoided Versailles under Louis XIV,
returned to it under Louis XV. Louis XIV had the last laugh.

From 1718 Orléans, encouraged by his former tutor the Abbé Dubois,
reasserted royal absolutism. With willpower, political intelligence and
loyal troops, Louis XIV's absolutism continued to function in France.
Like Louis XIV, Orléans used Gardes du Corps and Mousquetaires to
arrest his enemies: the Duc and Duchesse du Maine in 1718 for conspiring
with Philip V's Ambassador Prince Cellamare; and the Maréchal de Villeroy in 1722, for refusing to allow the Regent to see Louis XV alone.
Orléans was determined, he said, to return to Louis XV royal authority
in its entirety, as he had received it, and to stop the Parlements from med-
dling in affairs which were none of their business.[19]

Louis XV continued the routine of Louis XIV, as well as his absolutism: the King's *lever, coucher*, mass and councils; hunting trips to
Fontainebleau and Compiègne; balls and plays; stricter rules for presentation at court. Even more than under Louis XIV, Versailles became, with
Paris, joint capital of France. The King held *lits de justice* there, summoning members of the Parlement de Paris in 1732, 1759, 1770, 1774, 1787
and 1788, which Louis XIV had never done. Ministries of War and Foreign Affairs were built opposite the Aile des Princes in 1759–62. The
population of the town reached 70,000.

As memories of Louis XIV's wars and persecutions receded, Versailles
also inspired a growing number of foreign equivalents, often offering versions of Louis XIV's court life, with French plays, balls, ballets, music
and gardens.[20] Having failed to visit France in Louis XIV's lifetime, Peter
the Great stayed at Versailles, Trianon and Marly in May 1717 (when a
second offer of a Russian alliance was refused by the French government).
Despite his personal taste for simplicity, in 1714–23 he built a vast country
palace called Peterhof outside St Petersburg: it was partly inspired by
Versailles, with a park and fountains designed by a pupil of Le Nôtre
called J. B. le Blond, and a nearby villa named Marlia (Marly also inspired
Chatsworth in England, and Schloss Monbijou in Berlin). He also founded
on the French model an official newspaper, a tapestry factory and an
Academy of Sciences, and after 1718 introduced to his capital 'assemblies'
of men and women in the French style.[21]

Other palaces and court cities partly inspired by Versailles included
Hampton Court in England, where Charles II and his successors used a
state bedchamber, dined in public and held *levers* and council meetings;[22]
Salzdahlum and Wolfenbüttel in Brunswick; Rastatt and Karslruhe in

Baden; the enormous complex of Ludwigsburg outside Stuttgart, which after 1718 became the seat of government of the dukes of Württemberg, with an opera and a French theatre;[23] Frederick the Great's Sanssouci (1745–8, also partly inspired by Marly) and Neues Palais in Potsdam (1763–7) – he avoided Berlin almost as much as his hero Louis XIV had avoided Paris;[24] last but not least Washington DC, designed after 1791 on a similar trident plan, and incorporating a ruler's residence, government offices and a legislature, by Pierre L'Enfant, an architect from Versailles.[25]

Absolutism flourished under Cardinal Fleury. A former royal *aumônier* whom Louis XIV had chosen as his successor's tutor, Fleury was chief minister in the years 1726–43. Louis XV, however, inherited Louis XIV's problems as well as his palaces. The Comte d'Argenson, son of the Lieutenant de Police de Paris who had helped calm Paris in 1709, was a councillor of state, and later foreign minister, of Louis XV. His diary shows that Louis XV was frequently informed, often by beggars themselves, of famine and bread riots in Paris and elsewhere. Even in peacetime, in Poitou people ate grass like animals. In 1739 d'Argenson wrote: 'So people are talking of poverty at Versailles more than ever.'[26]

Louis XIV's example continued to affect French foreign policy. Fearing comparisons abroad with Louis XIV's pre-1697 acquisitions, and believing that France did not need more territory, despite his victory during the War of the Austrian Succession at Fontenoy and entry into Brussels, Louis XV refused territorial 'advantages' at the Treaty of Aix-la-Chapelle in 1748. Putting dynasty before nation like Louis XIV in 1700, he helped his son-in-law, a younger son of Philip V, establish a fourth Bourbon monarchy in Parma.[27] He wrote to his cousin the King of Spain: 'pity for my peoples and religion guided me far more than the spirit of aggrandizement.'[28]

Many Parisians, however, were dismayed by France's lack of conquests. The Maréchal de Richelieu called the peace treaty a masterpiece of stupidity. Parisians became even more hostile after Prince Charles Edward Stuart (considered a hero for his expedition to Scotland in 1745), son of 'James III', was arrested at the opera on 10 December 1748, taken with hands tied behind his back to Vincennes, then expelled from France as a condition of peace with George II.[29] D'Argenson feared that the rage of the Jacobites would cause an uprising in Paris.[30] Pamphlets attacked Louis XV as a monster and a tyrant.[31] Thus the Stuarts weakened the French monarchy internally as well as externally.

A visible symbol of the monarchy's retreat from international ambitions was the demolition of Louis XIV's Escalier des Ambassadeurs in 1752. It was replaced by the Théâtre des Petits Appartements, where Madame de Pompadour, the King's mistress, frequently performed before an admiring audience. She also assumed a major role in patronage and policymaking.[32] Madame de Pompadour became an extreme example of the female influence at Versailles which had dismayed Fénelon, and increased the court's unpopularity.[33]

In 1763, after defeats in the Seven Years War, Louis XV ceded much of the global empire of Louis XIV: India, Canada and Louisiana (although he retained the profitable Carribean colonies).[34] The peaceful acquisition of Lorraine in 1766, on the death of King Stanisław Leszczyński, and of Corsica in 1768 could not expunge the shame of defeat.

The accession of Louis XVI in 1774 temporarily restored the popularity of the monarchy. Louis XVI was the antithesis of Louis XIV. He was faithful to his wife and indifferent to his troops: he rarely reviewed them or wore uniform, ended the tradition of holding military camps at Compiègne and for reasons of economy abolished Louis XIV's beloved Mousquetaires, Chevau-légers and Gendarmes of the guard in 1775 and 1787. The bond between the crown and its troops weakened.[35]

The trigger for the revolution, however, was not famine, the unpopularity of the Austrian Queen Marie Antoinette or social tensions, but the financial system inherited from Louis XIV. Despite the prolongation of the *dixième*, the French national debt had reached 4 billion livres, and there was an annual deficit of 100 million livres. Whereas the British government could borrow at 3.5 per cent interest, the French government had to pay 6 per cent or more.[36] On 17 October 1787 the English traveller Arthur Young wrote: 'everyone agrees that bankruptcy will lead to a revolution in government.'[37]

Louis XVI had no Mazarin, no Colbert, no Villars, no Regent Orléans, to guide him through the crisis. His principal minister, who returned to power in August 1788 with the help of the Queen and the Austrian Ambassador, was Jacques Necker. This popular Anglophile banker from Geneva, whose father had served George I and whose London partner Peter Thellusson was of Huguenot descent, in practice if not intent proved to be a Protestant revenge on the Bourbons[38] (another had been the Chevalier de Jaucourt, from a Protestant family, who wrote hostile articles on Versailles, and many other subjects, for the *Encyclopédie*).[39] The great institutions which had served Louis XIV's monarchy, the nobility, the church, the army, the Parlements, began to withdraw support or demand change.

In August 1787 the Premier Président of the Parlement de Paris called for a meeting of the States General and declared forced registration of royal edicts illegal. The clergy went on a tax strike. Continuing the rivalry between their two branches of the royal family which had persisted since the reign of Louis XIV,[40] the Condé, who held the great court office of *grand maître de France*, defended the monarchy. The Duc d'Orléans (heir to the three fortunes of Monsieur, Mademoiselle and the Duc du Maine) was exiled for opposition to it. Louis XIV's gift of the Palais Royal as the Orléans' residence in Paris proved to be a time bomb. Cafés in the palace garden became meeting places for revolutionaries. In 1793 Orléans would vote for the death of Louis XVI.

The States General which finally met at Versailles in May 1789 could have regenerated the monarchy. However, instead of allying with the Third Estate, Louis XVI committed the crown to the maintenance of the noble and ecclesiastical privileges which had long weakened royal finances and which Louis XIV and Colbert had tried to limit. Attempts at conciliation between the three orders failed. Necker preferred to seek popularity rather than support the monarchy. The court's retreat to Marly from 14 to 21 June, mourning the death of Louis XVI's eldest son, encouraged a power vacuum. On 17 June, turning against the King, the radical majority of the Third Estate began to call itself the National Assembly, assumed sovereign powers and declared that it would be dispersed only by the force of bayonets.[41]

On 14 July, bread reached the highest price of the century. With weapons seized from the Invalides and the Garde Meuble (including one of the cannon sent as a present to Louis XIV by the King of Siam in 1686), mutinous Gardes Français led a Paris crowd to storm the Bastille, considered a symbol of royal tyranny. Soldiers defending it were killed. The city of Paris turned against the monarchy. The Paris National Guard, formed partly of mutinous Gardes Français, gave it an army more effective than the Paris militia during the Fronde. In the spirit of conciliation advocated by Louis XIV's enemy Fénelon, extracts from whose *Télémaque* Louis XVI had printed on his private press, the King was determined to avoid civil war. On 17 July 1789 he went to the Hôtel de Ville of Paris and accepted the Tricolour cockade from revolutionaries who had organized or applauded the murders of his soldiers and officials. The monarch helped destroy the monarchy. In the Galerie des Glaces on 17 August the National Assembly hailed Louis XVI as 'the Restorer of French Liberty'.[42]

On 5 October the Paris National Guard followed a crowd of hungry women demanding bread to Versailles: about 15,000 people in all. In its supreme crisis, Versailles proved hard to defend. Cannon, Louis XIV's 'last argument of kings', were turned on the palace by revolutionary National Guards. The royal stables' position on the Paris side of the palace, surrounded by revolutionary crowds, made the royal family's departure by carriage difficult. National Guards blocked the roads. Grooms cut the harnesses. The King ordered his troops and guards back to barracks.[43]

A crowd invaded the palace on the morning of 6 October. Hunting for the hated Austrian Queen, blamed for all the ills of France, it killed two Gardes du Corps. On Necker's advice, the King agreed to move to Paris with the National Assembly. Still trying to avoid civil war, he dismissed his Gardes du Corps and accepted in their place, as his guard, the Paris National Guards. The King said that he confided his family to the love of his good and faithful subjects. Foreign ambassadors and French officers were incredulous at his refusal to defend the monarchy.

On 6 October National Guards escorted the royal family to the Tuileries palace in Paris, with a crowd brandishing on pikes the heads of the murdered Gardes du Corps. The citizens of Versailles applauded its end as a court city. The Paris National Guard had taken control of the King, in a military coup disguised as a revolutionary *journée*.[44]

The King's escape from Paris on 20 June 1791, heading for the safety of the great Vauban fortress of Montmédy built for Louis XIV on the eastern frontier, failed, unlike Anne of Austria's escape with Louis XIV to Saint-Germain on 6 January 1649. The King was brought back to endure another year of humiliating semi-imprisonment. On 10 August 1792, badly defended by Paris National Guards, Swiss Guards and courtiers, the Tuileries palace was stormed by a revolutionary crowd. To celebrate the fall of the monarchy and the proclamation of the republic on 20 September, throughout France Louis XIV's statues were pulled off their pedestals and destroyed, while royal symbols and arms were removed from buildings, cannon and documents. On 21 January the following year, Louis XVI was guillotined.

On 14 October 1793, during the Reign of Terror, Louis XIV's corpse, with other royal corpses, was exhumed from Saint-Denis and reburied in a common grave amid 'the loud and insulting acclamations of the multitude'. The urn containing his heart, in the church of Saint-Louis in Paris, was melted down, the heart destroyed. Only his statue in Notre-Dame survived.[45]

Partly because of the legacy of Louis XIV, and the economic and social disparities he had aggravated, the French social order had been the first in Europe to be overthrown. The republic, however, proved an interlude, ended by Bonaparte's coup of 10 November 1799. In the nineteenth century both the palaces and the descendants of Louis XIV found new roles.

From 1800 to 1870, the Tuileries palace in Paris was the main winter residence of France's monarchs. Napoleon I, Louis XVIII, Charles X, Louis Philippe I and Napoleon III, their families and courts lived in rooms created in 1665–7 for Louis XIV and Marie Thérèse. Monsieur's country palace Saint-Cloud acted as the monarchs' main summer residence, the Versailles of the nineteenth century.

Napoleon I, like Louis XIV, created a centralizing monarchy (his most lasting achievement, the Code Napoléon, borrowed much from the Code Louis), made a member of his dynasty king of Spain and married a Habsburg. His use of the Grande Galerie of the Louvre, lined with pictures from the royal collection and the spoils of Europe, for his wedding procession on 4 April 1810 echoed Louis XIV's use of the Grande Galerie in Versailles. Unlike Louis XIV, however, he left France smaller than he found it.

Between 1814 and 1830, Louis XVI's brothers Louis XVIII and Charles X reigned in turn as constitutional monarchs. After Charles X's *ordonnances* trying to limit the power of the two Chambers provoked another Parisian revolution in July 1830, he was replaced by his cousin Louis Philippe, Duc d'Orléans, a descendant of Monsieur and a constitutionalist.

Versailles was too large and too charismatic to be ignored. Both Napoleon I and Louis XVIII had considered inhabiting it, and started programmes of restoration. Napoleon I occasionally stayed in Trianon. Louis Philippe also used Trianon and in June 1837 reopened Versailles as a museum of history, dedicated 'to all the glories of France': his personal project, intended as a work of national reconciliation. While the state apartments were restored, all the princes' and courtiers' apartments in the Aile des Princes and the Aile du Nord were destroyed. They were replaced by galleries of portraits and battle pictures, with particular emphasis on the Crusades, the conquest of Algeria and above all the wars of Napoleon I. The 'Citizen King' used Versailles to celebrate, not the Bourbons, but the Bonaparte dynasty which, soon after his abdication in 1848, would replace him.[46]

Some issues of Louis' reign continued to affect French politics and European diplomacy. The Franco-Prussian War in 1870–71 was partly caused by Napoleon III's refusal, like Louis XIV in 1700, to allow a king from a rival dynasty (Habsburg in 1700, Hohenzollern in 1870) to rule in Spain. It led to Napoleon III's overthrow and the establishment of a republic in September 1870. That autumn, for the first time since 1789, Versailles again became a seat of government – but for Prussia, not France. With his chancery and army headquarters, Wilhelm I of Prussia arrived there on 5 October 1870. Only Versailles could provide enough accommodation for the princes and officers accompanying the King. Moreover Versailles' strategic location, near but outside Paris, made it a suitable base from which to besiege the capital. The King stayed in the prefecture, from which flew the black and white flag of Prussia. The palace became a hospital for German soldiers. In a triumph for Protestantism which would have delighted Madame, Lutheran services were held in the chapel of Louis XIV.[47] Nightly bombardments of Paris, beginning on 27 December, lasted until 23 January. From Versailles people could see the flames of Paris.[48]

On 18 January 1871, anniversary of the self-coronation of the first King in Prussia in 1701, German princes, officers and regimental deputations crowded into the Galerie des Glaces, cleared of hospital beds, for what most of them considered the greatest event of the century. The choice of Versailles for the proclamation of the German Empire was both a tribute and a rebuke to Louis XIV, and marked the end of the French predominance in Europe for which he had worked so hard. Psalms, prayers and a Lutheran sermon denouncing the immorality of Louis XIV were followed by a Te Deum. Beneath frescoes glorifying Louis XIV, Wilhelm I accepted the crown of the German Empire. In his speech on this occasion Bismarck promised better frontiers in order to safeguard the Empire from 'new attacks by France'. Brandishing their swords, flags and helmets, the princes and the officers cheered: 'Long live His Imperial Majesty the Emperor Wilhelm!'[49]

Neither parliamentary deputies nor the King of Bavaria were present. Like Louis XIV's ally Max Emanuel, and subsequent electors of Bavaria (which, realizing a long-term ambition of Louis XIV, Napoleon I had elevated to the rank of a kingdom in 1806), Ludwig II of Bavaria had been pro-French. His armies had fought Prussia in the Austro-Prussian War of 1866. In 1870, however, he accepted a secret Prussian stipend, in return for signing a letter written for him by Bismarck, asking Wilhelm I to become German emperor.

Ludwig II spent the money he made from selling Bavarian independence on building new palaces, including Herrenchiemsee, an enlarged version of the central block of Versailles which he built beside a lake at the foot of the Alps in 1878–86. This most faithful of all imitations of Versailles has even more Ls and pictures of Louis XIV and his victories than the original, as well as a recreation of the Escalier des Ambassadeurs, and a longer version of the Galerie des Glaces. Herrenchiemsee is a tribute to Louis XIV, and Bavaria's alliance with France, from the King who ended it.[50]

Only repeated combinations of political mistakes, dynastic deaths, military defeats and eruptions of French nationalism finally created favourable conditions for a republic in France. Adolphe Thiers, leader of the new republic, signed peace preliminaries with the new German Empire at Versailles on 26 February 1871. Paris, however, was ruled by an increasingly radical and belligerent commune. On 18 March, only two weeks after the departure of Wilhelm I and Bismarck, Thiers withdrew from Paris to Versailles with the French government and army headquarters.[51] Again Versailles' strategic location made a government choose it as a temporary capital, and base from which to attack Paris, as had the Prussian government the previous year.

War with the Paris commune broke out in late March. Again Versailles watched Paris burn. Public buildings, including the Tuileries palace and the Palais Royal, were set on fire by communards, until the city was recaptured by the Versaillais during *la semaine sanglante*, 21–28 May 1871. From Versailles a French government had finally destroyed the political independence of Paris.

Under Thiers, even more than under Louis XIV or Louis XV, Versailles became the capital of France. Like Wilhelm I, Thiers lived in the prefecture. Refugees and army officers were bivouacked in houses, soldiers in the avenues.[52] Communards were imprisoned in the orangery and the stables. Ministries and the Conseil d'Etat worked in the palace. Deputies slept in the Galerie des Glaces. They met in the opera house built by Louis XV at the end of the Aile du Nord, and after 1876 in the Salle du Congrès, constructed in the Aile des Princes, where fourteen presidents of the Republic, until de Gaulle, would be elected. The Chamber of Deputies did not finally leave Versailles until 2 August 1879.[53]

The ruins of Saint-Cloud and the Tuileries, burnt in 1870 and 1871 respectively, were demolished after 1886, as a sign of the triumph of the republic over the monarchy. Sceaux, Meudon and Marly had already been demolished for building materials in 1803–11. Nothing remains of Marly except the park, stripped of its fountains and statues, and a guardhouse.[54]

Alsace and Lorraine remained contested territories, as they had been under Louis XIV. The German annexation of Alsace-Lorraine in March 1871 without a plebiscite (from fear of losing, as well as monarchical disdain), and the imposition of German as the sole official language of administration and secondary education, proved less effective in winning local loyalties than Louis XIV's respect for diversity. Over 50,000 inhabitants left for France. Having been the largest garrison town in France, Metz became the largest in Germany. Two new railway stations were built to speed the transport of German troops into France in the next war.[55]

In 1919 Versailles witnessed another nationalistic apotheosis, after a war caused in part by the previous one: by French desire to recover

Alsace-Lorraine and, as Bismarck had feared, by the hubris of the German Empire.[56] The Treaty of Versailles was prepared not by diplomats like the peace treaties of Louis XIV's reign, but by politicians. The excluded German representatives were treated with greater contempt, by the democratic French Republic and its allies, than Louis XIV's foreign enemies had been at the height of his power.

On 28 June, in another tribute to Louis XIV, the arch-republican Clemenceau arranged for the peace treaty to be signed in the Galerie des Glaces, covered for the occasion with all the King's Savonnerie carpets. Clemenceau placed himself beneath the fresco with the inscription 'le roi gouverne par lui-même'. (Germans also remembered Louis XIV; the German Foreign Minister Count Ulrich von Brockdorff-Rantzau, when asked about the friendship of his ancestor the Maréchal de Rantzau with Anne of Austria, replied, 'Oh yes, in my family the Bourbons have been considered bastard Rantzaus for three hundred years.')[57] For many Germans the word 'Versailles' became synonymous with vindictive nationalism, and a desire for revenge even fiercer than that felt by Frenchmen after 1871.

Since 1945, however, Versailles has enjoyed a gentler apotheosis. In modern Europe national divisions are less toxic, and frontiers in the middle land increasingly unimportant. Strasbourg is now a city with European as well as French, Alsatian and urban institutions. Some issues apparent in the reign of Louis XIV remain contentious: the futures of Scotland, Ireland and Catalonia (the last almost as hostile to Philip VI as it was to Philip V); the terms of global trade; the nature of relations between the states of Europe and whether they form what Louis XIV's secretary Callières called 'one same republic'.

Louis XIV, however, is now more admired than a hundred years ago. Partly in reaction to the weaknesses of the Third and Fourth Republics, since 1958 the Fifth Republic, with its powerful president elected by direct universal suffrage, is frequently described as a republican monarchy or monarchical republic. Its founder General de Gaulle came from a royalist family, with Jacobite blood, from one of Louis XIV's conquests, Lille.[58]

The General admired Louis XIV for his sense of grandeur and 'the service of the State'. His house in Colombey-les-Deux-Eglises contains two portraits of Louis XIV: one shows him in Flanders, the other in Versailles.[59] Since 1958 the President and his staff in the Elysée palace (where about 1,000 work in Crozat's hotel and nearby buildings) have had more power than the Senate and the Chamber of Deputies. Some call the Elysée the new Versailles, or 'le château', like the Tuileries before 1870. Music by Lully preceded some broadcasts of de Gaulle's press conferences in the Elysée. He sometimes stayed in the Trianon, which he returned to use as an official residence in 1966.[60] He told Alain Peyrefitte, 'Yes, we are a monarchy but it is an elective monarchy. It is of a completely different essence than the hereditary monarchy of the Ancien Régime. It has instituted a new legitimacy interrupted by the revolution, but this legitimacy depends on the people.'[61]

Under the Fifth Republic, for the first time since the Revocation of the Edict of Nantes, France has a regime accepted by all French people. It is also finally a world economic power, as Louis XIV and Colbert had hoped. Freed of the burden of international wars, its population is now as rich as England's, and its productivity greater.

With more power than in any comparable European country, the executive has won the long war with the legislature which paralysed the constitutional monarchies and the Third and Fourth Republics. France is again in some respects a court society. Despite a hundred and fifty years of republics, and the legacy of the Revolution, some structures and mentalities again owe much to the monarchy.[62] The pension systems of the republic are more extensive than those of the monarchy, and have introduced new privileges and feelings of entitlement. France has, again, more people benefiting from the system than reformers concerned to limit its abuses.

In the land of Liberty, Equality and Fraternity, under Articles 16 and 46 of the constitution the President can, in exceptional circumstances, rule by *ordonnances* bypassing the two Chambers, a power adapted from the *charte* granted by Louis XVIII in 1814.[63] Presidents occasionally use Versailles as a place for debates on constitutional change by the Senate and Chamber of Deputies, for the delivery of major speeches and for the reception of favoured foreign guests.[64]

Under the Fifth Republic, when divisions between right and left are lessening, and 'entertainment' and 'luxury', modern equivalents of Louis XIV's *divertissements*, are increasingly profitable, Versailles has global appeal. Louis XIV's role as Apollo, the dazzling patron who inspired so many musicians, dancers, writers, sculptors, painters, architects and gardeners, overshadows his crimes and failures as Mars.

Thanks to generous funding from the state and private patrons, Versailles is in better condition than at any time since the court's departure on 6 October 1789. The state apartments have been refurnished, the gardens replanted, the frescoes and the statues cleaned. As Louis XIV would have wished, his palace is visited by ever growing numbers: 7 million a year, more than any other palace except the Forbidden City in Beijing. They come from almost every country in the world, above all for the view from the terrace and the Galerie des Glaces.

The palace is not only a unique asset for French diplomacy and tourism but also a valued show room for modern French businesses, as well as the traditional luxury trades which Louis did so much to encourage.[65] Books and films and television have turned Louis XIV and Versailles into an international industry. Exhibitions have recreated most aspects of the court, from silver to science, from dining to death. The Research Centre, in the old Grand Commun, publishes new work on the court, including a database for its entire personnel from 1682 to 1789. The Académie Equestre Nationale du Domaine de Versailles has brought horses back to the Grande Ecurie. The Centre de Musique Baroque has helped rediscover the music of Louis XIV's court.

Almost every evening, more often than in other palaces, a special event – cultural, commercial or private – is held in Versailles. The violins are back. Lully Te Deums and ballets, Lalande symphonies and Campra operas are performed every weekend, round the year, in the chapel or the opera. Once a year an entire musical *Journée de Louis XIV*, including music for hunting and dining, is recreated from the *lever* to the *coucher*, in the *bosquets*, the courtyard, the chapel, the Galerie des Glaces and the King's apartments. From April to October, more often than under Louis XIV, during the *grandes eaux musicales* and *jardins musicaux*, the garden comes alive with music, fountains and fireworks. *Bals masqués* are held in the orangery, plays and serenades in the Galerie des Glaces. Three hundred years after his death, Versailles keeps Louis XIV's glory alive.

Acknowledgements

I would like to thank all those who have helped me with this book, in particular Bernard Ancer, Rosemary Baird, Andrew Barclay, Carlo Bitossi, Maxime Blin, Mark Bryant, Wolf Burchard, Andrea Canino, Georgina Capel, Juliet Carey, Matilde Cassandro-Malphettes, Edward Chaney, Frederik Dhondt, Zeki Dogan, Sven Externbrink, Laurent Ferri, Thierry Franz, Linda and Marsha Frey, Robert Frost, Antony Griffiths, Nichola Hayton, Mark Hengerer, Gordon Higgott, Leonhard Horowski, Hanns Hubach, Julian Jackson, Jérôme de La Gorce, Joy Law, Myriam Lechuiton, Henry Leremboure, Tim Llewellyn, Katharine Mac-Donogh, Giles Mandelbrote, Michael Martin, Meredith Martin, William Maufroy, Anne Mockly, Anne Motta, Claude Muller, Jonas Nordin, Alexandra Ormerod, Friedrich Polleross, Elizabeth Randall, Pierre Rhône, Eric Roussel, France de Sagazan, Diana Scarisbrick Aleksandra Skrzypietz, Jonathan Spangler, Laurent Stefanini, Corinne Thépaut, Max Tillmann, Jo Tinworth, Ferenc Toth, Floortje Tuinstra, Adriana Turpin, Bernard Vogler, Robert Wellington, Coen Wilders. Special thanks to Didier Girard for his help and kindnesses in Strasbourg and Touraine; to Charles-Eloi Vial for showing me the treasures of the Bibliothèque Nationale; and to all at the Centre de Recherche du Château de Versailles, including Mathieu da Vinha, Alexandre Maral and Béatrix Saule for their constant hospitality, encouragement and stimulation. I am deeply grateful for their help to all at Allen Lane, especially Richard Duguid, Ben Sinyor and Pen Vogler, and to all those who have read and commented on parts or all of the manuscript, including David Gelber, Candida MacDonogh, David Parrott and particularly Peter James, prince of copyeditors, and Stuart Proffitt, master of the *mot juste*. Above all I would like to express my profound gratitude to the staff at the British Library, the London Library, the Archives Nationales and the Bibliothèque Nationale, without whom this book could not have been written.

Notes

Introduction: A Thousand Years of France

1. Alexandre Gady, ed., *Jules-Hardouin Mansart*, 2010; Thierry Sarmant, *Les Demeures du soleil: Louis XIV, Louvois et la surintendance des bâtiments du Roi*, 2003   2. Mathieu da Vinha, *Les Valets de chambre de Louis XIV*, 2004; idem, *Au service du roi, dans les coulisses de Versailles*, 2015   3. Guy Rowlands, *The Financial Decline of a Great Power: War, Influence, and Money in Louis XIV's France*, 2012; cf. Daniel Dessert, *Le Royaume de Monsieur Colbert (1661–1683)*, 2007   4. Lucien Bély, *Espions et ambassadeurs au temps de Louis XIV*, 1990; idem, *L'Art de la paix en Europe: naissance de la diplomatie moderne, XVIe–XVIIIe siècles*, 2007   5. Thierry Sarmant and Mathieu Stoll, *Régner et gouverner: Louis XIV et ses ministres*, 2010   6. Guy Rowlands, *The Dynastic State and the Army under Louis XIV: Royal Service and Private Interest, 1661–1701*, 2002; cf. John A. Lynn, *The Wars of Louis XIV, 1667–1714*, 1999   7. Michèle Virol, ed., *Louis XIV et Vauban: Correspondance et agendas*, 2017   8. Charles-Edouard Levillain, *Vaincre Louis XIV: Angleterre – Hollande – France: histoire d'une relation triangulaire, 1665–1688*, 2010; Hendrik Ziegler, *Louis XIV et ses ennemis: image, propagande et contestation*, 2013   9. Alexandre Maral, *La Chapelle royale de Versailles: cérémonial, liturgie et musique*, 2010; idem, *Le Roi-Soleil et Dieu: essai sur la religion de Louis XIV*, 2012   10. Stanis Perez, *La Santé de Louis XIV: une biohistoire du Roi-Soleil*, 2010   11. Madame de Maintenon, *Lettres*, ed. Hans Bots, 7 vols., 2009–13 (henceforward ML)   12. Christophe Levantal, *Louis XIV: chronographie d'un règne*, 2 vols., 2009   13. Cf. among others, Gérard Sabatier and Béatrix Saule, eds., *Le Roi est mort: Louis XIV – 1715*, exh. cat., 2015; Alexandre Maral, *Les Derniers Jours de Louis XIV*, 2014; Joël Cornette, *La Mort de Louis XIV: apogée et crépuscule de la royauté*, 2015   14. Robert J. Knecht, *The French Renaissance Court, 1483–1589*, 2008, p. 237   15. Jean-François Solnon, *La Cour de France*, 1987, p. 22; Knecht, pp. 58–9   16. Solnon, pp. 62, 153; Knecht, p. 149, despatch by the Venetian Ambassador 1550, and pp. 161–6   17. Monique Chatenet, *La Cour de France au XVIe siècle: vie sociale et architecture*, 2002, p. 106   18. Knecht, pp. 32, 39, 42   19. Ibid., pp. xix, xx   20. Jean-Pierre Babelon, *Henri IV*, 1982, p. 708   21. Ibid., pp. 60, 247; Mathieu da Vinha, 'La Maison d'Anne d'Autriche', in Chantal Grell, ed., *Anne d'Autriche: Infante d'Espagne et reine de France*, 2009, pp. 155–85   22. William Forbes-Leith SJ, *The Scots Men-at-Arms and Life-Guards in France: From their Formation until their Final Dissolution, 1418–1830*, 2 vols., Edinburgh, 1882, I, 57   23. Père G. Daniel, *Histoire de la milice françoise*, 2 vols., Amsterdam, 1724, II, 87–8, 218   24. Philip Mansel, *Pillars of Monarchy: An Outline of the Political and Social History of Royal Guards, 1400–1984*, 1984, pp. 1, 5; cf. Chatenet, *Cour de France*, p. 141   25. Giovanni Comisso, *Les Ambassadeurs vénitiens, 1525–1792*, 1989, p. 303, relation of Sebastiano Foscarini, n.d.   26. Daniel, II, 115   27. Bibliothèque Nationale (henceforward BN) Mss. fr. 13683 f. 18, Journal de l'an 1715   28. Ivan Cloulas, *Catherine de Médicis*, 1979, p. 226   29. Knecht, p. 255   30. Pierre Chevallier, *Henri III*,

1985, p. 637   **31.** Nicolas Le Roux, *Un Régicide au nom de Dieu: l'assassinat d'Henri III*, 2006, p. 151   **32.** Nicolas Le Roux, *La Faveur du roi: mignons et courtisans au temps des derniers Valois*, 2001, p. 259   **33.** Chevallier, *Henri III*, pp. 661, 664, 666–72   **34.** Knecht, p. 333   **35.** Chevallier, *Henri III*, p. 679   **36.** Le Roux, *Régicide*, p. 231   **37.** Chevallier, *Henri III*, p. 681   **38.** Ibid., p. 701   **39.** Le Roux, *Régicide*, pp. 32, 171   **40.** Babelon, *Henri IV*, pp. 455–6, 465, 494, 503, 522, 539, 549, 552; Le Roux, *Régicide*, pp. 164–5, 184, 311   **41.** Babelon, *Henri IV*, pp. 470, 507–8, 928–9, Henri IV to Sully, 10 April 1603   **42.** Orest Ranum, *Paris in the Age of Absolutism: An Essay*, 1968, p. 44   **43.** Babelon, *Henri IV*, pp. 597, 599   **44.** Ibid., pp. 685–6   **45.** Ibid., p. 970   **46.** Jean-Christian Petitfils, *L'Assassinat d'Henri IV*, 2012, pp. 166, 171, 243   **47.** Capitaine Noël Lacolle, *Les Gardes Françaises: leur histoire, 1563–1789*, 1901, p. 80

Chapter 1: The Gift of God

1. J. H. Elliott, *Richelieu and Olivares*, 1984, p. 64   **2.** The King of Spain's full title was 'King of Castile, Leon, Aragon, of the Two Sicilies, Jerusalem, Portugal, Navarre, Granada, Toledo, Valencia, Gallicia, Mallorca, Seville, Cerdagne, Cordoba, Murcia, Iaen, of the Algarves, of Algezira, of Gibraltar, of the Canary islands, of the East and West Indies, islands and mainland of the ocean sea, Archduke of Austria, Duke of Burgundy, of Brabant and Milan, Count of Habsburg, of Flanders, of Tirol, and Barcelona, Lord of Vizcaya and of Malines etc. etc.' Later kings added 'dominator in Asia and Africa'.   **3.** Marie-Claude Canova-Green, 'Ambivalent Fictions: The Bordeaux Celebrations of the Wedding of Louis XIII and Anne d'Autriche', in Margaret McGowan, ed., *Dynastic Marriages 1612/1615*, 2013, pp. 179–200   **4.** Madame de Motteville, *Chronique de la Fronde*, 2003, pp. 41–2   **5.** Pierre de La Porte, *Mémoires de Pierre de La Porte, premier valet de chambre de Louis XIV*, 2003 edn, pp. 49, 111   **6.** Claude Dulong, *Anne d'Autriche: mère de Louis XIV*, 1980 edn, pp. 52, 87, 92   **7.** François de La Rochefoucauld, *Mémoires*, 2001 edn, p. 865; Pierre Chevallier, *Louis XIII*, 1979, pp. 389–90   **8.** Chevallier, *Louis XIII*, pp. 354, 362, 487   **9.** Ibid., pp. 472, 494   **10.** Jonathan Israel, *The Dutch Republic: Its Rise, Greatness, and Fall, 1477–1806*, 1998 edn, p. 527   **11.** Lucien Bély, 'La Diplomatie européenne et les partages de l'Empire espagnol', in Antonio Álvarez-Ossorio et al., eds., *La pérdida de Europa: la guerra de sucesión por la monarquía de España*, Madrid, 2007, pp. 631–52 at p. 632   **12.** Chevallier, *Louis XIII*, pp. 395, 466, 511, 515, despatch by Contarini, 19 August 1636, p. 537   **13.** Dulong, *Anne d'Autriche*, pp. 172, 193; Elliott, pp. 86, 97, 107, 146–7   **14.** Chevallier, *Louis XIII*, pp. 545, 579–81, 585, Angelo Correr to Venetian Senate, 5 August 1640   **15.** Martin Hume, *Queens of Old Spain*, 1906, p. 346   **16.** La Porte, pp. 47, 80; Dulong, *Anne d'Autriche*, pp. 145, 155, 159–64; Chevallier, *Louis XIII*, pp. 423, 531, 535   **17.** Chevallier, *Louis XIII*, pp. 533–7   **18.** Georges Houdard, *Les Châteaux royaux de Saint-Germain-en-Laye, 1124–1789*, 2 vols., Saint Germain-en-Laye, 1909–10, I, viii   **19.** Ruth Kleinman, *Anne of Austria, Queen of France*, Columbus, OH, 1985, p. 106   **20.** Ranum, *Paris*, p. 10   **21.** G. P. Marana, *Lettre d'un Sicilien à un de ses amis*, 1883, pp. 41, 83   **22.** Chevallier, *Louis XIII*, p. 513; René Laurentin, *Le Voeu de Louis XIII: passé ou avenir de la France*, 2004 edn, passim. On 25 March 1637 the republic of Genoa had made a similar gesture, crowning a statue of the Virgin 'Queen of Genoa' at a special ceremony, in an effort to acquire 'royal treatment', and equal status as a kingdom with its rivals Savoy and Venice.   **23.** Guillaume Kazerouni, ed., *Les Couleurs du ciel: peintures des églises de Paris au XVII siècle*, 2012, p. 43 and passim; *Louis XIV: l'homme et le roi*, exh. cat., 2009, pp. 214–15   **24.** Marina Warner, *Alone of All Her Sex: The Myth and the Cult of the Virgin Mary*, 1976, pp. 103–17; *Louis XIV à Saint-Germain, 1638–1682: de la naissance à la gloire*, Saint-Germain, 1988, pp. 21–2   **25.** Thierry Sarmant, *Louis XIV: l'homme et le roi*, 2012, p. 38   **26.** Dulong, *Anne d'Autriche*, pp. 175–6   **27.** Emmanuel Lurin, ed., *Le Château-Neuf de Saint-Germain-en-Laye*, 2010, pp. 137, 138   **28.** Chevallier, *Louis XIII*, pp. 557–8; Perez, p. 35   **29.** *Louis XIV à Saint-Germain*, p. 23   **30.** Hélène Duccini, 'Le Dauphin du miracle (5 septembre 1638)', in Bernard Barbiche et al., eds., *Pouvoirs, contestations et comportements dans l'Europe moderne*, 2005, pp. 209–25

31. Dulong, *Anne d'Autriche*, p. 185   32. Houdard, II, 165   33. Meyer, p. 138; *Louis XIV à Saint-Germain*, pp. 21, 28; Perez, pp. 38–9   34. Meyer, p. 162   35. Henri Chérot SJ, *La Première Jeunesse de Louis XIV*, Lille, 1892, p. 13, Mlle Andrieu to Mme de Sennecey, 9 April 1639   36. Dulong, *Anne d'Autriche*, pp. 217, 219   37. Comte de Beauchamp, *Louis XIII d'après sa correspondance avec le cardinal de Richelieu*, 1902, pp. 378–80, Louis XIII to Richelieu, 9, 13, 14 September 1640   38. Maximin Deloche, *La Maison du Cardinal de Richelieu: document inédit*, 1912, p. 406   39. Mansel, *Pillars of Monarchy*, pp. 8, 9; Daniel, II, 132, 153, 218; Jean Héroard, *Journal sur l'enfance et la jeunesse de Louis XIII*, 2 vols., 1868, II, 202, 212, 2 November 1616, 20 July 1617   40. Alfred Franklin, *La Cour de France et le Maréchal d'Ancre*, 1914, pp. 172, 185, 188; Rémi Masson, *Défendre le roi: la Maison Militaire au XVIIème siècle*, 2017, pp. 48, 53   41. Deloche, p. 404n   42. Ibid., pp. 381, 383, 386, 388   43. Françoise Hildesheimer, ed., *Testament politique de Richelieu*, 1995, pp. 204–6   44. Dulong, *Anne d'Autriche*, p. 188, Chavigny to Mazarin   45. Chevallier, *Louis XIII*, pp. 447, 453–4; idem, *Henri III*, p. 637   46. Chevallier, *Louis XIII*, pp. 396, 448–50, 453   47. Ibid., pp. 588–91, 594   48. Ibid., pp. 596–7; Dulong, *Anne d'Autriche*, pp. 201, 204, 221, 229   49. Chevallier, *Louis XIII*, pp. 591–2, 594, despatches by Grimaldi, 1, 8 June 1642   50. Dulong, *Anne d'Autriche*, pp. 23, 487   51. Ibid., pp. 221–2; Chevallier, *Louis XIII*, p. 597   52. Chevallier, *Louis XIII*, pp. 598–9, 613; Deloche, p. 388. After the accession of James VI to the throne of England, the Garde Ecossaise had become increasingly French: Matthew Glozier, *Scottish Soldiers in France in the Reign of the Sun King: Nursery for Men of Honour*, Leiden, 2004, pp. 33–5   53. Chevallier, *Louis XIII*, pp. 598, 610, 611, 612, Louis XIII to Séguier, 6 August 1642   54. Ibid., pp. 620–21, 625–6, despatches of the Venetian Ambassador Giustiniani, 11, 18 November 1642; Deloche, p. 409; Vicomte d'Avenel, *Lettres ... et papiers d'Etat du Cardinal de Richelieu*, 8 vols., 1853–77, VI, 7, 174; cf. Madeleine Laurain-Portemer, *Etudes Mazarines*, 2 vols., 1981–97, II, 297   55. Chevallier, *Louis XIII*, pp. 626–7, despatch of the Venetian Ambassador Giustiniani, 25 November 1642   56. Dulong, *Anne d'Autriche*, p. 227   57. Françoise Hildesheimer, *La Double Mort du Roi Louis XIII*, 2011 edn, pp. 36, 38; Chevallier, *Louis XIII*, p. 629   58. Jules Mazarin, *Carnet*, Tours, 1893, p. 13, 28 November 1649   59. Robert J. Knecht, *The French Renaissance Court, 1483–1589*, 2008, pp. 321–2   60. Madame de Motteville, *Mémoires ... sur Anne d'Autriche et sa cour*, 4 vols., 1904–11, IV, 49   61. Laurain-Portemer, II, 19, 35, 43, 49, 69, 79; Simone Bertière, *Mazarin: le maître du jeu*, 2007 edn, p. 402; Mathieu Molé, *Mémoires*, 4 vols., 1855–7, IV, 314, 12 May 1648   62. Hildesheimer, *Double Mort*, pp. 64, 69, 73   63. Ibid., pp. 107, 137, 155   64. La Rochefoucauld, *Mémoires*, p. 894   65. Solnon, p. 207. The princes' rivalry was shown throughout Louis XIV's reign in disputes over outward signs of rank, Princes of the Blood repeatedly trying to lessen differences between themselves and princes of the royal family.   66. Hildesheimer, *Double Mort*, pp. 165, 168, 171, 180, 186–7, 225   67. Levantal, *Louis XIV*, I, 44, 2 April 1643   68. Petitfils, *Assassinat d'Henri IV*, pp. 89, 98   69. *Louis XIV à Saint Germain*, p. 28.   70. Hildesheimer, *Double Mort*, pp. 188, 192   71. Ibid., pp. 103, 202   72. M. Dubois, 'Mémoire fidèle des choses qui se sont passées à la mort de Louis XIII roi de France et de Navarre', in F. Danjou, ed., *Archives curieuses de l'histoire de France*, 2nd series, vol. 5, 1838, pp. 426–7, 423   73. Laurain-Portemer, II, 149, II, 354n, Mazarin to Bartet, 27 September 1651   74. Ibid., I, 445   75. Dubois, 'Mémoire', pp. 430, 445   76. Vincent de Paul, *Lettres*, 2 vols., 1882, II, 138, Vincent de Paul to Bernard Codoing, 15 May 1643   77. Hildesheimer, *Double Mort*, p. 227   78. Suzanne d'Huart, ed., *Lettres de Turenne*, 1971, p. 382, 16 May 1643, to Mlle de Bouillon; Hildesheimer, *Double Mort*, pp. 235–6, Mazarin to Alphonse de Richelieu, 28 April 1643, p. 241   79. Hildesheimer, *Double Mort*, p. 279   80. Houdard, II, 181   81. Hildesheimer, *Double Mort*, p. 244   82. Olivier d'Ormesson, *Journal*, 2 vols., 1860–61, I, 43, 15 May 1643.

Chapter 2: Our Good City of Paris

1. Motteville, *Chronique*, p. 157; cf. Joan DeJean, *How Paris Became Paris: The Invention of the Modern City*, 2014, p. 5   2. See Jean-Pierre Babelon et al., eds., *Paris et ses rois*, 1988,

p. 42 **3.** Roland Mousnier, *La Plume, la faucille et le marteau: institutions et société en France, du Moyen Age à la Révolution*, 1970, p. 135 **4.** John Evelyn, *Diary and Correspondence*, ed. William Bray, 4 vols., 1879, I, 51, 4 January 1644; Orest Ranum, *The Fronde: A French Revolution, 1648–1652*, 1993, p. 16 **5.** A. Lloyd Moote, *The Revolt of the Judges: The Parlement of Paris and the Fronde, 1643–1652*, Princeton, 1971, pp. 8, 19, 113–14; Ormesson, *Journal*, I, 448, February 1648 **6.** Hildesheimer, *Double Mort*, pp. 40–41, 43n **7.** Beauchamp, p. 337, Louis XIII to Richelieu, 30 March 1638 **8.** Ranum, *Fronde*, pp. 100, 116, 181 **9.** Motteville, *Chronique*, p. 112 **10.** Ranum, *Paris*, p. 3 **11.** Karen Newman, *Cultural Capitals: Early Modern London and Paris*, Princeton, 2007, pp. 2, 4n **12.** Ranum, *Paris*, p. 27 **13.** Ranum, *Fronde*, pp. 55–6 **14.** Albert N. Hamscher, *The Parlement of Paris after the Fronde, 1653–1673*, 1976, pp. 9, 71, 98, 107 **15.** Evelyn, I, 47, 24 December 1643 **16.** Jean-Marie Le Gall, 'Paris à la Renaissance', in idem, ed., *Les Capitales de la Renaissance*, Rennes, 2011, pp. 59–62 **17.** Evelyn, I, 47, 24 December 1643 **18.** A. P. Faugère, ed., *Journal du voyage de deux jeunes Hollandais à Paris en 1656 et 1657*, 1899, p. 42 **19.** Mousnier, *Plume*, p. 134; Colin Jones, *Paris: Biography of a City*, 2004, p. 119; Babelon, *Paris et ses rois*, pp. 134–5 **20.** Marana, pp. 23, 43, 45 **21.** Philip Skippon, *An Account of a Journey made through Part of the Low Countries, Germany, Italy and France*, in *A Collection of Travels*, 6 vols., 1732, VI, 361–736 at 732–3 **22.** Alfred Fierro, *Histoire et dictionnaire de Paris*, 1996, pp. 358, 558; Mousnier, *Plume*, p. 127 **23.** Le Gall, 'Paris à la Renaissance', pp. 46–9 **24.** Evelyn, I, 49, 24 December 1643 **25.** Dulong, *Anne d'Autriche*, p. 193; Pierre Chevalier, *Louis XIII*, 1979, pp. 579–81 **26.** Dulong, *Anne d'Autriche*, p. 251; Sarah Hanley, *The Lit de Justice of the Kings of France: Constitutional Ideology in Legend, Ritual, and Discourse*, Princeton, 1983, pp. 308–15 **27.** Marquis de La Fare, *Mémoires et réflexions*, 1884, p. 252; Cf. Motteville, *Chronique*, 562–3, 614, 616 **28.** Motteville, *Chronique*, pp. 62, 142 **29.** Dulong, *Anne d'Autriche*, p. 263 **30.** Ormesson, *Journal*, I, 110, 119, 22 September, 4 November 1643; Dulong, *Anne d'Autriche*, p. 301; Comte de La Châtre, *Mémoires*, 1838, p. 283 **31.** Dulong, *Anne d'Autriche*, pp. 218–19 **32.** Ormesson, *Journal*, I, 216, 223, 261, September, October, November 1644; Alexandre Gady, 'Le Palais Royal sous la régence d'Anne d'Autriche', in Isabelle de Conihout and Patrick Michel, eds., *Mazarin: les lettres et les arts*, 2006, pp. 115, 119 **33.** Dulong, *Anne d'Autriche*, p. 323 **34.** Bertière, *Mazarin*, pp. 318, 324–5; Jean-Christian Petitfils, *Fouquet*, 2005, pp. 141, 151 **35.** Bertière, *Mazarin*, pp. 539–41; Dulong, *Anne d'Autriche*, pp. 393–401 **36.** Dulong, *Anne d'Autriche*, pp. 325–7; Nancy Nichols Barker, *Brother to the Sun King: Philippe, Duke of Orléans*, 1989, p. 24 **37.** Dulong, *Anne d'Autriche*, pp. 295–7; La Rochefoucauld, *Mémoires*, pp. 896, 916 **38.** Dulong, *Anne d'Autriche*, p. 273 **39.** Jules Mazarin, *Lettres du cardinal Mazarin pendant son ministère*, 9 vols., 1872–1906, II, 555, Mazarin to Marquis de Fontenay, 21 December 1647 **40.** Marie Dubois, *Moi, Marie Dubois … valet de chambre de Louis XIV*, Rennes, 1994, pp. 36–7 **41.** Dulong, *Anne d'Autriche*, p. 303 **42.** La Porte, pp. 130, 137; J. A. le Roi, ed., *Journal de la santé du roi Louis XIV de l'année 1647 a l'année 1711, écrit par Vallot, D'Aquin et Fagon*, 1862, pp. 7, 11; cf. Motteville, *Mémoires*, I, 396, 'un prince tout à fait porté à la douceur et à la bonté' **43.** La Porte, p. 142; Dubois, *Moi*, p. 38n, letter of 1 July 1647 **44.** La Porte, p. 130; Ormesson, *Journal*, I, 262, February 1645 **45.** Levantal, *Louis XIV*, I, 46, 47, 48, 2 July, 29 August 1643, 25 March 1644 **46.** Ibid., 48, 13, 23 April 1644 **47.** Claude Mignot, *Le Val-de-Grâce: l'ermitage d'une reine*, 1994, pp. 26, 34 **48.** Olivier Chaline, 'Anne of Austria, Founder of the Val-de-Grâce in Paris', in Dries Raeymaekers et al., eds., *A Constellation of Courts: The Courts and Households of Habsburg Europe, 1555–1665*, Leuven, 2014, pp. 255–66, 265 **49.** Levantal, *Louis XIV*, I, 64, 2 August 1647 **50.** Ormesson, *Journal*, I, 226, November 1644 **51.** Karen Britland, 'Exile or Homecoming? Henrietta Maria in France, 1644–1669', in Philip Mansel and Torsten Riotte, eds., *Monarchy and Exile: The Politics of Legitimacy from Marie de Médicis to Wilhelm II*, 2011, pp. 120–43 at pp. 124, 127 **52.** Jean Vallier, *Journal de Jean Vallier: maître d'hôtel du roi*, 4 vols., 1902, I, 367, July 1649 **53.** Ronald Hutton, *Charles II: King of England, Scotland and Ireland*, 1991 edn, pp. 20–21; Antonia Fraser, *King Charles II*, 2002, p. 49 **54.** Hutton, *Charles II*, pp. 30, 224 **55.** Motteville, *Chronique*, pp. 126, 135 **56.** François Bayard, 'Du rôle exact de l'argent dans le déclenchement de la Fronde', in Roger Duchêne and Pierre Ronzeaud, eds., *La Fronde en questions*, Aix-en-Provence, 1989, p. 74; Ranum, *Fronde*, p. 31 **57.** Evelyn, II, 8, 7 September 1649 **58.** Moote, pp. 78–80 **59.** Ranum, *Paris*, pp. 207–9 **60.** Ranum, *Fronde*, pp. 52, 55 **61.** Ibid., pp. 91, 92; Motteville, *Chronique*, p. 126 **62.** Ranum, *Fronde*, pp. 98, 99, 101, 109, 113; Dulong, *Anne d'Autriche*, p. 339 **63.** Dulong, *Anne d'Autriche*, p. 345; Alain Hugon, *Naples insurgée, 1647–1648: de l'événement à la mémoire*, Rennes, 2011, p. 159 **64.** Bertière, *Mazarin*, pp. 404–5 **65.** Ormesson, *Journal*, II, 2, 273, 333, 14 September 1644, March 1645, 25 November 1645; Levantal, *Louis XIV*, I, 65–6, 23 August 1647 **66.** J. Russell Major, *From Renaissance Monarchy to Absolute Monarchy: French Kings, Nobles, & Estates*, Baltimore, 1994, passim **67.** Moote, p. 136; Ranum, *Fronde*, pp. 133, 145 **68.** Ormesson, *Journal*, II, 69, 13 July 1648 **69.** Ranum, *Fronde*, p. 114 **70.** Ibid., pp. 152–5; Dubois, *Moi*, pp. 55–6 **71.** Derek A. Watts, 'La Journée des barricades racontée par les mémorialistes du temps', in Duchêne and Ronzeaud, pp. 51–62 at pp. 52, 55; Robert Descimon, 'Les Barricades frondeuses', in Duchêne and Ronzeaud, pp. 245–62 at pp. 245, 251 **72.** Ranum, *Fronde*, pp. 156, 160; Ormesson, *Journal*, I, 569, August 1648 **73.** Motteville, *Chronique*, p. 153 **74.** Derek Watts, 'Journée des barricades', p. 58 **75.** Motteville, *Chronique*, pp. 102, 218 **76.** Dubois, *Moi*, pp. 58–61 **77.** Bertière, *Mazarin*, p. 424 **78.** Christian Jouhaud, *Mazarinades: la Fronde des mots*, 1985, p. 16 **79.** Bertière, *Mazarin*, p. 538; John Lough, *France Observed in the Seventeenth Century by British Travellers*, Stocksfield, 1985, p. 140, quoting notes of Richard Symonds **80.** Molé, IV, 352–3, letters of 25, 26 July 1649 **81.** Société de l'Histoire de France, *Registres de l'Hôtel de Ville de Paris pendant la Fronde*, 3 vols., 1846–8 (henceforward *RHV*), I, 38, 26 August 1648 **82.** Dubois, *Moi*, pp. 61–3 **83.** Vallier, I, 98, 30, 31 August 1648 **84.** Dulong, *Anne d'Autriche*, pp. 350, 355–6 **85.** Motteville, *Chronique*, pp. 160–61; cf. La Rochefoucauld, *Mémoires*, p. 923 **86.** Bertière, *Mazarin*, pp. 434–5; Ranum, *Fronde*, pp. 170–71 **87.** Ranum, *Fronde*, pp. 148, 164–5, 175, 180 **88.** Hamscher, p. 17 **89.** La Grande Mademoiselle, *Mémoires*, 2005 edn, p. 71 **90.** Motteville, *Chronique*, p. 225 **91.** Grande Mademoiselle, p. 73; Motteville, *Chronique*, pp. 227–8; Claude Dulong, *Marie Mancini: la première passion de Louis XIV*, 1993, pp. 360–61 **92.** Bertière, *Mazarin*, p. 440 **93.** Ibid., p. 442; Motteville, *Chronique*, p. 232, Louis XIV to Prévôt des Marchands, 5 January 1649 **94.** Motteville, *Chronique*, pp. 243, 258 **95.** *RHV*, I, 118, 138, 252, 254, 11, 15 January, 22 February 1649; Bertière, *Mazarin*, p. 449; M. Dubuisson-Aubenay, *Journal des guerres civiles*, 2 vols., 1883–5, I, 108–14, January 1649; Ranum, *Fronde*, p. 186 **96.** Ranum, *Fronde*, pp. 183, 196 **97.** Dubois, *Moi*, p. 76; cf. Motteville, *Chronique*, p. 254 **98.** Ranum, *Fronde*, p. 184; Dulong, *Anne d'Autriche*, p. 363

Chapter 3: The Struggle for France

1. Georges Lacour-Gayet, *L'Education politique de Louis XIV*, 1898, pp. 315, 318, 324–5 **2.** Simone Bertière, *Condé: Le Héros fourvoyé*, 2014, p. 266; Major, p. 307 **3.** Major, pp. 295–6; Ranum, *Fronde*, pp. 297, 301 **4.** Philip A. Knachel, *England and the Fronde: The Impact of the English Civil War and Revolution on France*, Ithaca, NY, 1967, pp. 104n, 117 **5.** Motteville, *Chronique*, pp. 261, 277 **6.** Duchesse de Nemours, *Mémoires*, 1990, p. 86; cf. Masson, *Défendre le roi*, p. 78 **7.** Vallier, I, 75, 78, August 1648, II, 261–2, January 1651 **8.** Ibid., II, 124–5, May 1650; cf. BN Mss. fr. 4182 f.160 v, 'certification des articles accordés au nom du roy pour la satisfaction et payement des colonels et capitaines suisses', 9 May 1651 **9.** Mazarin, *Lettres*, IV, 72, Mazarin to Lionne, 14 March 1651 **10.** Bertière, *Mazarin*, p. 490 **11.** La Rochefoucauld, *Mémoires*, p. 984 **12.** Motteville, *Chronique*, pp. 626, 665 **13.** Vallier, III, 228, May 1652 **14.** Inès Murat, *Colbert*, 1980, pp. 26, 45 **15.** Nemours, p. 61 **16.** Mazarin, *Carnet*, p. 65, 18 December 1649 **17.** Bertière, *Mazarin*, p. 532, mémoire of 18 May 1651 **18.** Motteville, *Chronique*, pp. 60, 170, 205 **19.** La Rochefoucauld, *Mémoires*, pp. 985, 988, 992, 1064; Motteville, *Chronique*, p. 346 **20.** La Rochefoucauld, *Mémoires*, pp. 850, 940; Vallier, I, 127, November 1648 **21.** Archives Nationales (henceforward AN) [Cartons des Rois] K 118, 24; cf. Madame de Sévigné,

Correspondance, 3 vols., 1972–6, I, 205, to Madame de Grignan, 1 April 1671, re 'ce divin tabouret' **22.** Comte de Guilleragues, *Correspondance*, 2 vols., 1976, I, 260, Guilleragues to Louis XIV, 2 August 1680; Chevalier d'Arvieux, *Mémoires*, 6 vols., 1735, VI, 286 **23.** Guy Patin, *Lettres ... à Charles Spon*, ed. Laure Jestaz, 2 vols., 2006, II, 860n, Patin to Spon, 26 March 1652; cf. *Turenne et l'art militaire de son temps*, 1978, pp. 37, 41 **24.** Ranum, *Fronde*, p. 207; Motteville, *Chronique*, p. 233 **25.** Bertière, *Mazarin*, p. 465, Lionne to Servien, 13 March 1649 **26.** Ranum, *Fronde*, pp. 210–14; Levantal, *Louis XIV*, I, 72–4 **27.** Molé, IV, 39, Louis XIV to Molé, 28 April 1649 **28.** Motteville, *Chronique*, p. 365 **29.** Mazarin, *Lettres*, IV, 547, Mazarin to Duc de Mercoeur, 20 December 1651; Bertière, *Mazarin*, p. 478 **30.** Vallier, I, 383, 18 August 1649; cf. Chérot, pp. 39–40 **31.** Bertière, *Mazarin*, p. 467; Motteville, *Chronique*, pp. 375–7; Ormesson, *Journal*, I, 761, August 1649; *RHV*, II, 51, 18 August 1649 **32.** Ormesson, *Journal*, I, 763–4, 25 August 1649 **33.** Motteville, *Chronique*, p. 380 **34.** *RHV*, II, 62–9, 2–6 September 1649; Ormesson, *Journal*, I, 767, 5 September 1649; for the King's range of hosts, see Levantal, *Louis XIV*, I, 93, 95, 18 April, 17 May, 8 August 1651 **35.** Chérot, pp. 54, 62–5 **36.** Bertière, *Condé*, p. 229; Mademoiselle de Montpensier, *Mémoires*, 4 vols., 1891, I, 194 **37.** AN AE II 848, treaty of 2 October 1649 **38.** La Rochefoucauld, *Mémoires*, pp. 934, 939, 942; Ranum, *Fronde*, p. 241 **39.** Jérôme Fehrenbach, *La Princesse Palatine: l'égérie de la Fronde*, 2016, p. 161; Anne Blanchard, *Vauban*, 2007 edn, p. 77 **40.** Mazarin, *Carnet*, pp. 12, 28, November 1649, 94 notes **41.** Vallier, II, 29, November 1649; Bertière, *Mazarin*, p. 486 **42.** Vallier, III, 293, June 1652; Mark Bannister, *Condé in Context: Ideological Change in Seventeenth-Century France*, Oxford, 2000, pp. 41, 51, 107, 150 **43.** Bertière, *Condé*, p. 241; La Rochefoucauld, *Mémoires*, pp. 949–50 **44.** *RHV*, II, 83, 20 January 1650 **45.** Levantal, *Louis XIV*, I, 78–88; Ranum, *Fronde*, pp. 221, 243 **46.** Philippe Fortin de la Hoguette, *Lettres aux frères Dupuy et à leur entourage, 1623–1662*, 2 vols., Florence, 1997, II, 666, La Hoguette to Jacques Dupuy, 30 October 1650 **47.** Chérot, p. 72, Père Paulin to Piccolomini, 26 February 1650; cf. pp. 76, 78 for similar reactions in Burgundy **48.** Molé, IV, 393, Mazarin to Molé, 13 April 1650 **49.** Motteville, *Chronique*, p. 726 **50.** Ormesson, *Journal*, I, 768, 7 September 1649 **51.** Lacour-Gayet, pp. 160–62, quoting Venetian despatches of 24 December 1652, 21 April 1654, 259–60 **52.** Pascale Mormiche, *Devenir prince: l'école du pouvoir en France, XVIIe–XVIIIe siècles*, 2009, pp. 277, 329. In 1665 he could speak to Bernini in Italian. **53.** Hardouin de Péréfixe, *Histoire du Roi Henri le Grand*, 1816 edn, p. 4; Lacour-Gayet, pp. 146, 149–50, 205 **54.** Lacour-Gayet, pp. 96, 99n, 102, 106, 202 and passim; Mormiche, pp. 204, 423 **55.** BN Mss. fr. 3858 Carnets de Louis XIV, ff. 19, 23 and passim **56.** Lacour-Gayet, pp. 103, 114; Dubois, *Moi*, p. 30; Mormiche, pp. 203, 271, 451 **57.** Mormiche, p. 295, Comte de Chârost to Dubois, 30 June 1647 **58.** Louis-Henri de Loménie, Comte de Brienne, *Mémoires*, 3 vols., 1916–19, I, 20, 63–4; Dulong, *Anne d'Autriche*, pp. 306–7; Lacour-Gayet, p. 110n **59.** Marianne Cojannot-Le Blanc, ' "Il avoit fort dans le coeur son Alexandre ...": l'imaginaire du jeune Louis XIV d'après La Mesnardière et la peinture des Reines de Perse par Le Brun', *XVIIe Siècle*, 251, 2, 2011, pp. 371–96 **60.** Bibliothèque Interuniversitaire de la Sorbonne (henceforward BS) 1290 f. 145, Louis XIV to Maréchal de Gramont, 24 July 1667 **61.** La Rochefoucauld, *Mémoires*, p. 969; Chérot, p. 86, quoting a letter of Colbert **62.** Bertière, *Mazarin*, pp. 519–21; Vincent J. Pitts, *La Grande Mademoiselle at the Court of France*, Baltimore, 2000, p. 63; Grande Mademoiselle, p. 95 **63.** La Rochefoucauld, *Mémoires*, pp. 949, 950, 953, 976, 979, 980 **64.** Léonce Raffin, *Anne de Gonzague, Princesse Palatine, 1616–1684*, 1935, p. 145, Mazarin to Anne of Austria, 30 June 1651 **65.** La Rochefoucauld, *Mémoires*, p. 985 **66.** Motteville, *Chronique*, pp. 613, 851 **67.** Fehrenbach, pp. 167, 173, 175 **68.** Levantal, *Louis XIV*, I, 91, 5, 7 February 1651; Fehrenbach, pp. 163–7 **69.** Eveline Godley, *The Great Condé: A Life of Louis II de Bourbon, Prince of Condé*, 1915, p. 320 **70.** Maréchal du Plessis, *Mémoires*, 1676, pp. 361, 364, 365, 367; Montpensier, I, 30; Dubuisson-Aubenay, II, 16–17, 35, February, 19 March 1651 **71.** Motteville, *Chronique*, pp. 624, 627, 629; Bertière, *Mazarin*, p. 525 **72.** Montpensier, I, 301; Bertière, *Mazarin*, p. 525 and n **73.** Du Plessis, pp. 361, 364, 365, 367 **74.** Knecht, pp. 74, 265, 307 **75.** Ibid., pp. 265, 307; Margaret M. McGowan, *Dance in the Renaissance: European Fashion, French Obsession*,

2008, pp. 233–4, 237 76. Levantal, *Louis XIV*, I, 52, 27 February 1645; cf. Ormesson, *Journal*, I, 261, 26 February 1645, stating that the King dances 'avec toute l'adresse et la bonne grâce imaginables'; Mormiche, p. 317, quoting the *Gazette*, 14 April 1654, 'S.M. fit paraître de nouvelles grâces qui obligèrent les spectateurs d'avouer que ce grand monarque paraît véritablement roy en toutes ses actions'; Margaret M. McGowan, *The Court Ballet of Louis XIII: A Collection of Working Designs for Costumes, 1615–33*, 1986, passim. 77. Regine Astier, 'Louis XIV, "premier danseur"', in David Lee Rubin, ed., *Sun King: The Ascendancy of French Culture during the Reign of Louis XIV*, Washington, DC, 1992, pp. 73–102 78. Lucien Bély, ed., *Dictionnaire Louis XIV*, 2015 (henceforward *DL*), p. 588; Philippe Beaussant, *Les Plaisirs de Versailles: théâtre et musique*, 1996, p. 16; J. P. Néraudau, *L'Olympe du Roi-Soleil: mythologie et idéologie royale au Grand Siècle*, 2013, p. 122: Mormiche, p. 316 79. Levantal, *Louis XIV*, I, 91, 26 February, 2 March 1651; Sarah R. Cohen, *Art, Dance, and the Body in French Culture of the Ancien Régime*, Cambridge. 2000, pp. 15, 47–9, 80; cf. Julia Prest, *Theatre under Louis XIV: Cross-Casting and the Performance of Gender in Drama, Ballet and Opera*, 2006, pp. 89–91 80. Mazarin, *Lettres*, IV, 63, Mazarin to Servien, 9 March 1651 81. Ibid., 528, Mazarin to Senneterre, 3 December 1651 82. Adolphe Chéruel, *Histoire de France pendant la minorité de Louis XIV*, 4 vols., 1879–1880, IV, 273, 331–2 83. Levantal, *Louis XIV*, I, 94–5, June–August 1651 84. Motteville, *Chronique*, p. 777 85. Godley, p. 398 86. Ranum, *Fronde*, pp. 286, 309 87. Bertière, *Mazarin*, p. 535; Chéruel, *Minorité*, IV, pp. 369, 379 88. Bertière, *Mazarin*, p. 537; Chéruel, *Minorité*, IV, p. 402 89. Bertière, *Mazarin*, p. 543 90. Abbé Fr. Duffo, *Le Cérémonial de France à la cour de Louis XIV*, 1936, pp. 17–23, quoting Sainctot, 'Ordre de la Cérémonie touchant la Majorité du roy en 1651' 91. Evelyn, I, 26–7, 7 September 1651 92. Chérot, pp. 94–6 93. Bertière, *Mazarin*, p. 545 94. Sal Alexander Westrich, *The Ormée of Bordeaux: A Revolution during the Fronde*, Baltimore, 1972, p. 24 95. BN Mss. fr. 4182 ff. 82, 354, 364, 434, letters of 2 February, 6, 10 September 1651, 20 February 1651 96. Levantal, *Louis XIV*, I, 97 97. Du Plessis, pp. 377, 379 98. Chérot, p. 104, Mazarin to Paulin, 30 September 1651; Bertière, *Mazarin*, p. 547 99. Du Plessis, p. 379. The King had already on 9 September written to Mazarin to nullify all future declarations made against him: BN Fichier Charavay 147, Louis XIV to Mazarin, 9 September 1651 100. Ranum, *Fronde*, p. 319 101. La Porte, p. 140; James II, *Memoirs: His Campaigns as Duke of York, 1652–1660*, 1962, p. 59 102. Patin, II, 862, letter of 16 April 1652 103. Jean-Christian Petitfils, *Louis XIV*, 2008, p. 109 104. Henri d'Orléans, Duc d'Aumale, *Histoire des princes de Condé*, 8 vols., 1863–96, VI, 129–30, 132, 137, 139, 149 105. Patin, II, 820, letter of 15 January 1652; Ranum, *Fronde*, p. 299 106. Patin, II, 817n, 831, letters of 15, 30 January 1652; Bertière, *Mazarin*, p. 552n, Mazarin to Naudé, 1652 107. Eva Scott, *The King in Exile: The Wanderings of Charles II from June 1646 to July 1654*, 1905, pp. 337, 351–4, 434–5 108. Patin, II, 877, Patin to Spon, 10 May 1652; Vallier, III, 211, 26 April 1652 109. Ronald Hutton, *Charles II*, p. 83; Knachel, pp. 236–40; James II, pp. 78–80 110. Vallier, III, 280, 287, June 1652 111. Bertière, *Condé*, pp. 310, 312 112. *RHV*, II, 233, 331, Louis XIV to Ville de Paris, 6 April 1652, 12 May 1652 113. Vallier, III, 232, 294, May, June 1652 114. *RHV*, II, 322, 11 May 1652; Ranum, *Fronde*, pp. 309, 311, 313–16 115. Vallier, III, 307, July 1652; James II, p. 85 116. Ranum, *Fronde*, p. 328; James II, pp. 88, 94–100; Levantal, *Louis XIV*, I, 102, 21 August 1652 117. Vallier, III, 318, 320, 325, July 1652 118. Ibid., 341, July 1652 119. *RHV*, III, 137, letter of Ville de Paris to other cities, 29 July 1652 120. Hermann Ferrero, ed., *Lettres de Henriette Marie de France, Reine d'Angleterre à sa soeur Christine, Duchesse de Savoie*, Turin, 1881, p. 99, letter of 8 May 1652 121. Paul, II, 420, 429, 439, 449, letters of 22 May, 15 July, 16 August 1652 122. Vallier, IV, 48–9, September 1652; Nina Brière, *La Douceur du roi: le gouvernement de Louis XIV et la fin des Frondes 1648–1661*, Montreal, 2011; Ranum, *Fronde*, pp. 317, 319 123. Vallier, IV, 26, 68, September 1652 124. *RHV*, III, 285, 292, Louis XIV to Ville de Paris, 17, 28 September 1652 125. Vallier, IV, 56, September 1652; Cardinal de Retz, *Mémoires*, 2003 edn, pp. 805, 835 126. Vallier, IV, 85, October 1652; British Library (henceforward BL) Egerton mss. 1674 f. 118, 5 October 1652 127. James II, p. 112; Maréchal de Turenne, *Mémoires*, 2 vols., 1909, I, 220 128. Motteville, *Chronique*, p. 794;

Plessis, pp. 405, 422–4   **129.** Retz, p. 835; Bertière, *Mazarin*, p. 582; cf. Vallier, III, 253, 2 June 1652   **130.** Vallier, IV, 104, 21 October 1652; Jérôme Janczukiewicz, 'Gaston d'Orléans à la fin de la Fronde: la persistance dans la rébellion', in Jean-Pierre Bardet et al., eds., *Etat et société en France aux XVIIe et XVIIIe siècles*, 2000, pp. 331–45   **131.** Levantal, *Louis XIV*, I, 105; Bannister, p. 135; AN K 118, 51 'amnisties générales de tout ce qui s'est fait à l'occasion des mouvements passés, jusques à présent 22 Octobre 1652'   **132.** Vallier, IV, 106, October 1652   **133.** Levantal, *Louis XIV*, I, 107n; Bertière, *Mazarin*, pp. 587–8; see Cardinal de Retz, *Oeuvres*, 9 vols., 1870–87, VI, 456–8: Mazarin, *Lettres*, V, 497; J. H. M. Salmon, *Cardinal de Retz: The Anatomy of a Conspirator*, 1969, pp. 229, 231   **134.** Chérot, pp. 139–40, Paulin to Mazarin, 25 December 1652   **135.** Retz, pp. 857–8; Motteville, *Chronique*, p. 796   **136.** Levantal, *Louis XIV*, I, 108, 3 February 1653   **137.** Petitfils, *Louis XIV*, pp. 126–7; Lacour-Gayet, p. 161, despatch of 24 December 1652. A manuscript of the ballet is in the Rothschild collection at Waddesdon Manor, Bucks.   **138.** Isaac de Benserade, *Ballet royal de la nuit*, 1653, p. 45

Chapter 4: M. le Cardinal

1. Vallier, IV, 261–2 and n, 4 July 1653. The statue, by Gilles Guérin, is now in a courtyard of the Château de Chantilly   **2.** Motteville, *Chronique*, p. 254; cf. Vallier, III, 234n, May 1652, and Maréchal d'Estrées, *Mémoires*, 1910, p. 282, for other examples of insults to the King's livery   **3.** Vallier, IV, 292 August 1653; Mazarin, *Lettres*, IX, 546n, Mazarin to Fouquet, 12 March 1660   **4.** Montpensier, II, 335   **5.** Ranum, *Fronde*, pp. 229, 249–53, 261–2, 265, 269   **6.** Knachel, pp. 161, 193, 214, Bishop of Tulle to Mazarin, 11 August 1653; Camille Jullian, *Histoire de Bordeaux, depuis les origines jusqu'en 1895*, Bordeaux, 1895, 493–6   **7.** Vallier, IV, 279–80, July 1653   **8.** Ibid., 280–87 August 1653; Westrich, pp. 129–30; Ranum, *Fronde*, p. 346   **9.** Levantal, *Louis XIV*, I, 119, 22 February 1654; Edouard de Barthélemy, *La Princesse de Conti d'après sa correspondance inédite*, 1875, p. 8   **10.** Bertière, *Mazarin*, pp. 648–3, 659–60   **11.** Scott, *King in Exile*, p 359   **12.** Mazarin, *Lettres*, V, 626, Mazarin to Vendôme, 8 June 1653   **13.** Scott, *King in Exile*, pp. 443, 466, 490   **14.** Mazarin, *Lettres*, VI, 227, 384, Mazarin to Président de Bordeaux, 20 July, 14 November 1654, VII, 451, Mazarin to Président de Bordeaux, 14 April 1657; Fraser, *King Charles II*, p. 603   **15.** Odile Bordaz, *D'Artagnan*, 2001, p. 72, Mazarin to Bordeaux, n.d.   **16.** Mazarin, *Lettres*, IX, 64, Mazarin to Lockhart, 22 September 1658   **17.** Laurain-Portemer, I, 162, Servien to Mazarin, 22 August 1654   **18.** Richard M. Golden, *The Godly Rebellion: Parisian Curés and the Religious Fronde, 1652–1662*, Chapel Hill, NC, 1981, pp. 9, 21–4, 39, 58, 135; Bertière, *Mazarin*, p. 669   **19.** Bertière, *Mazarin*, p. 673   **20.** Dubost and Grell, pp. 87–9   **21.** See Richard A. Jackson, *Vive le Roi! A History of the French Coronation from Charles V to Charles X*, Chapel Hill, NC, 1984, p. 204 and passim   **22.** Ibid., pp. 57–8   **23.** Abbé Fr. Duffo, *Le Sacre de Louis XIV à Reims le 7 Juin 1654*, 1935, quoting the contemporary account of Nicolas Sainctot, passim   **24.** Ibid., p. 49   **25.** Ibid., p. 46; Jackson, *Vive le Roi!*, p. 97   **26.** Henri d'Avice, *La Pompeuse et magnifique cérémonie du sacre du roy Louis XIV*, 1655   **27.** Jackson, *Vive le Roi!*, p. 218   **28.** Elisabeth Oy-Marra, 'Mazarin et les fresques de Giovanni Francesco Romanelli dans l'appartement d'été d'Anne d'Autriche au Louvre', in *Mazarin: les lettres et les arts*, 2010, pp. 145–55   **29.** Christiane Aulanier, *Le Pavillon du roi: les appartements de la reine*, 1959, pp. 13, 45–7; idem, *La Petite Galerie: appartement d'Anne d'Autriche*, 1961, p. 39   **30.** Levantal, *Louis XIV*, I, 133, 16 May 1655   **31.** Dubost and Grell, p. 87; Moote, p. 359; Mazarin, *Lettres*, VI, 13 April 1655   **32.** Hamscher, p. 70, Mazarin to Fouquet, 25 May 1657, p. 89, Séguier to Mazarin, 17 August 1654   **33.** Louis Vian, 'Louis XIV au Parlement d'après les manuscrits du Parlement', in *Mémoires de la Société des sciences morales, des lettres et des arts de Seine et Oise*, Versailles, 1883, pp. 103–15   **34.** Claude Dulong, *Le Mariage du Roi-Soleil*, 1986, p. 79   **35.** F. Bouquet, ed., *Mémoires de Pierre Thomas, sieur de Fossé*, 4 vols., Rouen, 1876–9, I, 255   **36.** Dulong, *Anne d'Autriche*, p. 430; Charles de Baillon, *Henriette-Marie de France, Reine d'Angleterre*, 1877, p. 562, Henriette-Marie to

Charles II, 29 October 1655. Madame de Motteville had also called him timid: Motteville, *Mémoires*, IV, 63   37. Georgina Masson, *Queen Christina*, 1968, pp. 274–9, 281   38. Comte F. U. Wrangel, *Première Visite de Christine de Suède à la cour de France, 1656*, 1930, p. 234, Christina to Cardinal Azzolino, n.d. For further flattering opinions of Louis XIV's looks, see the Venetian Ambassadors' reports in Lacour-Gayet, pp. 243–4   39. Lacour-Gayet, p. 245   40. Chérot, pp. 117 (quoting an anonymous Mazarinade)   41. La Porte, pp. 147, 159. Cf. Bertière, *Mazarin*, p. 608n. La Porte was, however, a supporter of Condé, therefore likely to defame Mazarin: Chérot, p. 73   42. Hortense and Marie Mancini, *Mémoires*, 1987 edn, p. 39   43. Montpensier, III, 199   44. Wrangel, p. 246, Queen Christina to Cardinal Azzolino, n.d.   45. Motteville, *Mémoires*, IV, 51, 83   46. A. P. Faugère, ed., *Journal du voyage de deux jeunes hollandais à Paris en 1656–1658*, 1899, pp. 429, 432, 9 January 1658   47. Mazarin, *Lettres*, IX, 188–9, 292–3, Mazarin to Comtesse de Soissons 23 July, 8 September 1659   48. Adolphe Chéruel, *Histoire de France sous le ministère de Mazarin*, 3 vols., 1882, III, 268, anon. letters to Mazarin, October–November 1659   49. Motteville, *Mémoires*, IV, 90   50. Dulong, *Anne d'Autriche*, p. 443; Lacour-Gayet, pp. 170–71   51. Faugère, p. 416, 27 January 1658; Mazarin, *Lettres*, VIII, 359, Mazarin to Maréchal de Gramont, 18 May 1658; Primi Visconti, *Mémoires sur la cour de Louis XIV, 1673–1681*, 1988, p. 13; Comte de Bussy-Rabutin, *Mémoires*, 2010, p. 274; W. H. Lewis, *Assault on Olympus: The Rise of the House of Gramont*, 1958, pp. 89, 117, 127, 136   52. Barker, pp. 56, 6064; Montpensier, III, 213, 221, 335, 352, 354   53. Bertière, *Mazarin*, p. 703   54. Vallier, IV, 275, 277, July 1653   55. Mazarin, *Lettres*, VI, 648, Mazarin to Anne of Austria, 23 July 1653   56. M. A. Gilbert, *Le Siège de Stenay en 1654*, Bar-le-Duc, 1893, pp. 17, 59, 63, 89; Bertière, *Mazarin*, p. 610   57. Alfred Pierrot, *Histoire de Montmédy et du pays montmédien*, 2 vols., Lyon, 1910, II 73   58. Levantal, *Louis XIV*, I, 123–4, June–August 1654, 162–3, September–November 1657; MM. Vallot, d'Aquin and Fagon, *Journal de la santé du roi Louis XIV de l'année 1647 à l'année 1711*, ed. J. A. Le Roi (henceforward Vallot), 1862, p. 16, diary 1653   59. Mazarin, *Lettres*, VII, 18, 20, 22, 25, Mazarin to Anne, 24, 27, 30, 31 July 1655   60. Ibid., 264, 311, Mazarin to Turenne, 6 July, 17 August 1656; cf. ibid., VI, 211, Mazarin to Le Tellier, 8 July 1654   61. Vallot, pp. 13–15, 27–32, diary for 1653, 1655   62. Ibid., pp. 17, 19, 32, 36n, 45–6, 'digression sur l'incommodité du roi dont j'ai parlé ci-dessus', 1655   63. Ibid., p. 28n; cf. Perez, p. 55   64. Bertière, *Mazarin*, p. 745   65. Levantal, *Louis XIV*, I, 118, 8 January 1654; Faugère, pp. 54, 110, 19 January, 2 April 1657   66. Montpensier, III, 304, 313; BS 1289 f. 125, Louis XIV to Anne of Austria, 5 September 1661   67. Mazarin, *Lettres*, V, 647, Mazarin and Louis XIV to Anne, 21 July 1653   68. Ibid., VII, 107, Mazarin to Louis, 5 October 1655   69. Ibid., VIII, 575, Mazarin to Anne, 11 August 1658   70. Ibid., 553, Mazarin to Anne, 2 August 1658   71. Montpensier, III, 286; Jacques-Bénigne Bossuet, *Oraisons funèbres*, ed. Jacques Truchet, 1998, p. 114   72. Bertière, *Mazarin*, p. 711; Mazarin, *Lettres*, VIII, 484, Mazarin to Servien, 2 July 1658   73. Rev. J. S. Clarke, *The Life of James the Second . . . Collected Out of Memoirs Writ of his own Hand*, 2 vols., 1816, I, 349; James II, pp. 265–6   74. Mazarin, *Lettres*, VIII, 375, Mazarin to Anne, 27 May 1658   75. Bertière, *Mazarin*, p. 701; Mazarin, *Lettres*, VIII, 493, Mazarin to Colbert, 7 July 1658; Vallot, pp. 52–73, 'Histoire de la maladie du roi à Calais', 1658   76. Bertière, *Mazarin*, pp. 701–5   77. Mazarin, *Lettres*, VIII, 493, 499, Mazarin to Colbert 7, to Turenne 8 July 1658   78. Barker, pp. 51–3   79. Perez, p. 73   80. Bertière, *Mazarin*, pp. 631–2   81. Claude Dulong, *Mazarin et l'argent, banquiers et prête-noms*, 2002, pp. 100, 109, 229, 231, 233, 234; Vincent J. Pitts, *Embezzlement and High Treason in Louis XIV's France: The Trial of Nicolas Fouquet*, Baltimore, 2015, pp. 46, 95   82. Dulong, *Anne d'Autriche*, p. 401   83. Bertière, *Mazarin*, pp. 640–42; Dulong, *Mazarin et l'argent*, p. 229. One is now in the Rijksmuseum, the other in the Victoria and Albert Museum.   84. Montpensier, III, 234   85. F. de Fossa, *Le Château historique de Vincennes à travers les âges*, 2 vols., 1908, I, 130; Jean Chapelot, *Le Château de Vincennes*, 2003, p. 42 and passim; Daniel Séré, *La Paix des Pyrénées: vingt quatre ans de négociations entre la France et l'Espagne, 1635–1660*, 2007, p. 313   86. Montpensier, III, 309–10, 314   87. Séré, pp. 313–14, 332–5   88. Ibid., pp. 340, 376, Don Luis de Haro to Pimentel, 26 March 1659   89. Ibid., p. 424, Instructions of Condé to Jacques Caillet, 11 May 1659; Bertière,

Mazarin, p. 754   90. Séré, pp. 429, 457n, 462; E. Ducéré, *Le Mariage de Louis XIV*, Bayonne, 1903, map between pp. 56 and 57   91. Séré, pp. 395, 403–4, quoting the minutes of the Spanish Council of State, 411, 467   92. Ibid., pp. 485, 493; Hubert Delpont, *Parade pour une infante: le périple nuptial de Louis XIV à travers le Midi de la France, 1659–1660*, Bouloc, 2007 p. 74   93. Dulong, *Anne d'Autriche*, p. 436; idem, *Mariage*, p. 30   94. Motteville, *Mémoires*, IV, 83, 134   95. Mancini, p. 107   96. Pitts, *Fouquet*, p. 258   97. Montpensier, III, 328   98. Mancini, pp. 109–10   99. Séré, p. 431; Dulong, *Mariage*, pp. 41, 48   100. Dulong, *Mariage*, p. 48   101. Yves-Marie Bercé, *Le Roi absolu: idées reçues sur Louis XIV*, 2013, pp. 55–7   102. Mazarin, *Lettres*, IX, 155–6, Mazarin to Louis XIV, 28 June 1659; Jules Mazarin, *Lettres du cardinal Mazarin*, 2 vols., Amsterdam, 1745 edn, I, 2, Mazarin to Louis XIV, 29 June 1659   103. Bertière, *Mazarin*, p. 736   104. Dulong, *Mariage*, p. 57   105. Mazarin, *Lettres*, IX, 253, Mazarin to Louis XIV, 28 August 1659; Mazarin, *Lettres*, 1745 edn, I, 75, Mazarin to Louis XIV, 16 July 1659   106. Dulong, *Mariage*, pp. 62, 65–7; idem, *Marie Mancini: la première passion de Louis XIV*, 1993, pp. 66, 69   107. Mazarin, *Lettres*, 1745 edn, I, 98–103, Mazarin to Louis XIV, 29 July 1659   108. Ducéré, p. 107   109. Mazarin, *Lettres*, IX, 311, 316, to Louis XIV, 17, 20 September 1659   110. Dulong, *Marie*, pp. 60–64   111. Ducéré, p. 111   112. Delpont, pp. 26, 71, 125, 137, 215   113. Delpont, p. 64   114. *Saint-Jean de Luz: étape royale, 1660–1960*, exh. cat., Bordeaux, 1960, p. 17   115. Delpont, pp. 85, 112, 119   116. Ibid., p. 67   117. Ibid., pp. 89–93   118. Benserade, p. 95n, note from Bartet, 21 October 1659; Dulong, *Mariage*, pp. 154–5   119. Delpont, p. 154; cf. Jacques Arlet, *La Vie à Toulouse sous Louis XIV*, Portet-sur-Garonne, 2012, p. 10   120. Robert Sauzet, *Le Notaire et son roi: Etienne Borelly (1633–1718), un Nîmois sous Louis XIV*, 1998, p. 241, 9 January 1660   121. Dulong, *Mariage*, p. 163; Séré, p. 538; Bertière, *Mazarin*, pp. 766–7   122. Delpont, p. 104; Comte de Coligny, *Mémoires*, 1841, pp. 61–2   123. Delpont, pp. 106, 138   124. Ibid., pp. 105, 111; Michel Monicault, *La Basilique Sainte-Marie-Madeleine et le couvent royal dominicain*, Aix-en-Provence, 1985, p. 16   125. René Pillorget, *Les Mouvements insurrectionnels de Provence entre 1596 et 1715*, 1975, pp. 819, 821, 824   126. Adolphe Crémieux, *Marseille et la royauté pendant la minorité de Louis XIV*, 2 vols., 1917, II, 798–9, 831–2   127. Mazarin, *Lettres*, IX, 531, Mazarin to Fouquet, 6 March 1659; Delpont, p. 141   128. Crémieux, II, 835–6   129. Lough, p. 141, quoting the travels of Philip Skippon   130. Levantal, *Louis XIV*, I, 187–9, April–May 1660

Chapter 5: The Power of Queens

1. Delpont, p. 224; Ducéré, pp. 142, 148   2. Delpont, p. 246; Dulong, *Mariage*, p. 178   3. Jonathan Brown, *Velázquez: Painter and Courtier*, 1986, pp. 249, 265   4. Mazarin, *Lettres*, IX, 506, Mazarin to Colbert, 21 February 1660; Murat, p. 85   5. Montpensier, III, 457, 458, 460–61   6. Léonce Goyetche, *Saint-Jean-de-Luz historique et pittoresque*, Bayonne, 1856, pp. 109–16   7. Ducéré, pp. 188–9; Montpensier, III, 478   8. Ducéré, pp. 192–4; Motteville, *Mémoires*, IV, 202–3   9. Dulong, *Mariage*, pp. 147, 196–8; Montpensier, III, 459; Motteville, *Mémoires*, IV, 215   10. Montpensier, III, 471; Ducéré, pp. 199–204   11. Dulong, *Mariage*, p. 201   12. Ducéré, p. 208; Levantal, *Louis XIV*, I, 190; Montpensier, III, 482   13. Mazarin, *Lettres*, IX, 596, Mazarin to Marquis de Gesvres, 29 April 1660   14. Abbé Fr. Duffo, *Après le traité des Pyrénées*, 1935, pp. 18, 20, quoting M. de Brienne, 11 June 1660; Daniel de Cosnac, *Mémoires*, 2 vols., 1852, I, 284–5   15. Ducéré, pp. 212–18; Motteville, *Mémoires*, IV, 216   16. Motteville, *Mémoires*, IV, 217   17. Montpensier, III, 479   18. Motteville, *Mémoires*, IV, 218   19. Dulong, *Mariage*, pp. 171–3, 189; Montpensier, III, 455; Ducéré, p. 172   20. Montpensier, III, 469; Motteville, *Mémoires*, IV, 208   21. Jean-Baptiste Colbert, *Lettres, instructions et mémoires*, 9 vols., 1861–82, I, 422, Colbert to Mazarin, 2 March 1660   22. Mathieu Marais, *Lettre au sujet du mariage du roy*, 1660, pp. 322, 323n, 326, 329n   23. Cosnac, II, 29–30   24. François de La Rochefoucauld, *Oeuvres complètes*, 1964 edn, p. 606, to the Marquise de Sable, n.d. (1660)   25. Brown, p. 250   26. Ducéré, pp. 230–31; Levantal, *Louis XIV*, I, 191; Delplace, p. 212   27. Fossa, I,

139–44   28. Ibid., 139; René Pillorget, 'Quelques aspects de l'entrée de Louis XIV et de Marie Thérèse a Paris', in Christian Desplat and Paul Mourounneau, eds., *Les Entrées: gloire et déclin d'un cérémonial*, Biarritz, 1997, pp. 207–22; Joëlle Chevé, *Marie Thérèse d'Autriche, épouse de Louis XIV*, 2008   29. Marie-Christine Moine, *Les Fêtes à la cour du Roi-Soleil, 1653–1715*, 1984, p. 203   30. Pillorget, 'Entrée', pp. 213–17   31. Motteville, *Mémoires*, IV, 225–6   32. ML, I, 97–100, 27 August 1660   33. Pillorget, 'Entrée', pp. 208–13   34. Lawrence M. Bryant, *The King and the City in the Parisian Royal Entry Ceremony: Politics, Ritual and Art in the Renaissance*, Geneva, 1986, pp. 210–15, 276–86   35. Chevé, pp. 176–7; *L'Entrée triomphante de Leurs Majestez Louis XIV, Roy de France et de Navarre et Marie-Thérèse d'Austriche, son espouse, dans la ville de Paris . . .*, 1662, p. 31:

> Venez o reine triomphante!
> Et recevoir des voeux et nous donner des Loix,
> Venez regner sur le coeur des français;
> Et perdez sans regret le beau titre d'Infante
> Entre les bras du plus beau des roys.

36. Pillorget, 'Entrée', p. 215   37. Ibid., p. 211   38. Bertière, *Mazarin*, p. 632   39. Motteville, *Mémoires*, IV, 224   40. Bertière, *Mazarin*, pp. 794–7, 801   41. Georges Mongrédien, *Louis XIV*, 1963, pp. 260–61, report by Giovanni Battista Nani, 1660   42. Bertière, *Mazarin*, pp. 791–2, 821   43. Daniel Dessert, *Le Royaume de Monsieur Colbert (1661–1683)*, 2007, p. 43, quoting the account by Père Bissaro   44. Bertière, *Mazarin*, pp. 822, 823; Motteville, *Mémoires*, IV, 234, 240, 245–6, 248   45. BS 1289 f. 1, Louis XIV to Philip IV, 17 March 1661   46. Motteville, *Mémoires*, IV, 249   47. Séré, p. 519,   48. Ferrero, p. 121, Henrietta Maria to Duchess of Savoy, 4 June 1660   49. Mazarin, *Lettres*, IX, 625n, 630, Mazarin to Montagu, 3 July 1660   50. Forbes-Leith, II, 211–12; Glozier, *Scottish Soldiers in France*, pp. 62, 68   51. BS 1289 f. 43, Louis XIV to Charles II, 2 April 1661   52. Edouard de Barthélemy, ed., *La Galerie des portraits de Mademoiselle de Montpensier*, 1860, pp. 2–3, 'Portrait du roi par Madame la comtesse de Brégis'   53. Ibid., pp. 5–9   54. Anon., *Relation et observations du royaume de France*, Cologne, 1681, p. 520   55. Cosnac, I, 271   56. Barker, p. 69   57. Montpensier, III, 511.   58. Motteville, *Mémoires*, IV, 255–6; cf. Sir John Reresby, *Memoirs*, 1991 edn, p. 30   59. Cosnac I, 291, II, 57; cf. Montpensier, IV, 102   60. Dulong, *Marie*, pp. 115–19; Chevé, p. 183, despatch from Papal Nuncio, 25 March 1661   61. Marquis de Saint-Maurice, *Lettres sur la cour de Louis XIV*, 2 vols., 1910–12, II, 478, despatch of 31 January 1673   62. Dulong, *Marie*, pp. 203, 228–9, 336 and passim   63. Montpensier, III, 507, 513–14   64. *Être femme sous Louis XIV: du mythe à la réalité*, exh. cat., Marly, 2015, p. 10   65. Jean Le Laboureur, *Relation du voyage de la Royne de Pologne et du retour de Madame la Mareschalle de Guébriant, ambassadrice extraordinaire et surintendante de sa conduite*, 1647, passim   66. Bibliothèque Sainte-Geneviève (henceforward BSG) 2014 f. 490, Louis XIV 'à ma cousine la comtesse d'Armagnac mon ambassadrice extraordinaire en Piemont', 16 April 1663. Another female French diplomat, regularly corresponding from Brunswick or Mecklenburg with the Foreign Minister, in conscious rivalry with official male diplomats, would be Isabelle de Montmorency, Duchesse de Mecklembourg: see Nicole Reinhardt, 'Les Relations internationales à travers les femmes au temps de Louis XIV', *Revue d'Histoire Diplomatique* (henceforward RHD), 117, 3, 2003, pp. 193–230; and Paul Fromageot, *Isabelle de Montmorency, Duchesse de Chatillon et de Mecklembourg*, 1913, passim   67. Quoted in Nancy Klein Maguire, 'The Duchess of Portsmouth: English Royal Consort and French Politician, 1670–1685', in R. Malcolm Smuts, ed., *The Stuart Courts and Europe*, Cambridge, 1996, p. 259   68. Cf. Karolina Targosz, *La Cour savante de Louise-Marie de Gonzague et ses liens scientifiques avec la France, 1646–1667*, Wrocław, 1982, passim   69. Paul Sonnino, *The Search for the Man in the Iron Mask*, 2016, p. 72; Dulong, *Mazarin et l'argent*, pp. 214, 218   70. Robert I. Frost, 'The Ethiopian and the Elephant? Queen Louise Marie Gonzaga and Queenship in an Elective Monarchy, 1645–1667', *Slavonic and East European Review*, 91, 4, 2013, pp. 787–817 at pp. 790–91, 797–9, 808   71. K. Waliszewski, *Marysienka: Marie de la Grange d'Arquien,*

Reine de Pologne, 1898, p. 63, brevet of 30 November 1660 authorizing Condé's 'correspondances en Pologne'; Emile Magne, ed., *Lettres inédites du Grand Condé et du Duc d'Enghien . . . sur la cour de Louis XIV*, 1920, p. xxii   72. Fehrenbach, pp. 280–84; the treaty is in AN K 118, 119; K. Waliszewski, *Les Relations diplomatiques entre la Pologne et la France au XVII siècle, 1644–1667*, Cracow, 1889, p. 232, Lumbres to Mazarin, 28 July 1657   73. Magne, *Lettres inédites*, p. 30n, Condé to Queen of Poland, 18 April 1664   74. Louis Farges, ed., *Recueil des instructions données aux ambassadeurs et ministres de France: Pologne*, I, 1888, pp. 54, 63, 124, Instructions, 26 December 1664, 30 March 1674; Marquis de Pomponne, *Mémoires*, 2 vols., 1860–61, I, 429; Arsenal Mss. 2014, f. 473, Louis XIV to Louise Marie, April 1663   75. BS 960 f. 267, letter of 26 November 1663; cf. BS 1290 ff. 183–6, Louis XIV to Louise Marie, 6 December 1663   76. Louis André, *Louis XIV et l'Europe*, 1950, p. 51, Louis XIV to Pomponne, December 1665   77. Louis XIV, *Mémoires de Louis XIV*, ed. Jean Longnon, 2007 edn, pp. 238–9, 270   78. Anne-Marie Gasztowitt, *Une Mission diplomatique en Pologne au XVII siècle: Pierre de Bonzi à Varsovie, 1665–1668*, 1916, pp. 30, 52–3, Louis XIV to Bishop of Beziers, 24 April 1665, 8 April 1667; André, pp. 66, 77, 107   79. Bannister, pp. 165–7; Colbert, VII, 487; Enghien would also refuse an offer of the crown of Sicily in 1676: Emile Laloy, *La Révolte de Messine*, 3 vols., 1929–31, III, 19–20, 761   80. Cf. BS 961 Lettres Louis XIV ff. 405–8, Louis XIV to Grand Marshals of Poland and Lithuania, 15 December 1668   81. André, pp. 51, 107   82. BS 961 f. 375, Louis XIV to Jan Sobieski, 27 May 1668   83. Wilanów Palace Museum, *Primus Inter Pares: The First among Equals: The Story of King Jan III*, Warsaw, 2013, pp. 12, 120, 158, 171–5   84. Géraud Poumarède, ' "Fidèle sujette" ou "mauvaise française"? Marie-Casimire de la Grange d'Arquien, Reine de Pologne, sous le regard des ambassadeurs français', in Jaroslaw Dumanowski, Michel Figeac and Daniel Tollet, eds., *France–Pologne*, 2016, pp. 69–92 at p. 78   85. Waliszewski, *Marysienka*, p. 229, Louis XIV to M. de Bonzy, 17 July 1669; S. Rubinstein, *Les Relations entre la France et la Pologne de 1680 à 1683*, 1913, p. 23, Marquis de Vitry and Beauvais to Louis XIV, 8 November 1680   86. Camille Rousset, *Histoire de Louvois et de son administration politique et militaire*, 4 vols., 1863–5, III, 139, 161, 180–82, 187; Geoffrey Symcox, *Victor Amadeus II: Absolutism in the Savoyard State, 1675–1730*, 1983, pp. 81, 89   87. See the fundamental study by Robert Oresko, 'Maria Giovanna Battista of Savoy-Nemours (1644–1724): Daughter, Consort and Regent of Savoy', in Clarissa Campbell Orr, ed., *Queenship in Europe, 1660-1815: The Role of the Consort*, Cambridge, 2004, pp. 16–55   88. Harold Livermore, *A New History of Portugal*, 1976 edn, p. 194; [J. Colbatch], *An Account of the Court of Portugal during the Reign of the Present King Dom Pedro II*, 1700, pp. 45, 79, 97   89. Anon., *The history of the revolution of Portugal . . . with letters of Sir Robert Southwell during his embassy there to the duke of Ormond*, 1740, pp. 322, 327, 335, letters of 25, 28 November 1667   90. Edgar Prestage, *The Diplomatic Relations of Portugal with France, England and Holland from 1640 to 1668*, Watford, 1925, pp. 88–9, 98n; cf. Glenn J. Ames, 'A Royal Bride for Two Brothers', in *Proceedings of the Western Association for French History: Selected Papers of the 1998 Annual Meeting*, 2000, pp. 152–64 at pp. 152, 158, 164   91. See R. Francisque-Michel, *Les Portugais en France, les Français en Portugal*, 1882, pp. 220–53, including lettters of the Queen to 'Monsieur mon frère' – Louis XIV; Louis XIV, *Mémoires*, p. 238; Louis XIV, *Oeuvres*, 6 vols., 1806, V, 410, 422, Louis XIV to Queen of Portugal, 4 July 1667, 31 January 1668; VI, 399, Queen of Portugal to Princesse de Soubise, 28 September 1680   92. Anon., *Court of Portugal*, pp. 97, 106–7; cf. for more details H. de Manneville, 'Marie Françoise Elisabeth de Savoie-Nemours: une princesse française sur le trône de Portugal', *RHD*, 21, January 1931, pp. 22–46, April 1931, pp. 193–219, July 1931, pp. 294–317   93. Caroline Hibbard, 'The Role of a Queen Consort: The Household and Court of Henrietta Maria, 1625–1642', in Ronald Asch, ed., *Princes, Patronage and the Nobility: The Court and the Beginning of the Modern Age, 1450–1650*, Oxford, 1991, pp. 393–414.   94. BS 960 f. 42n, Louis XIV to Princesse de Toscane, 13 August 1664; Harold Acton, *The Last Medici*, 1980 edn, pp. 73, 82, 87, 92   95. Acton, pp. 121, 146, 214; Montpensier, IV, 527; Jean Claude Waquet, 'L'Echec d'un mariage: Marguerite-Louise d'Orléans et Côme de Médicis', in Isabelle Poutrin and Marie-Karine Schaub, eds., *Femmes et pouvoir politique:*

les princesses d'Europe, XVe–XVIIIe siècle, Rosny, 2007, pp. 120–32   **96**. Colbert, VII, 51–2n; Sévigné, I, 170, to Grignan, 27 February 1671   **97**. See Susan Shifrin, 'Subdued by a famous Roman Dame', in Julia Marciari and Catherine Macleod, eds., *Politics, Transgression, and Representation at the Court of Charles II*, New Haven and London, 2007, pp. 141–74; Cyril Hughes Hartmann, *The Vagabond Duchess*, 1926, p. 187, Courtin to Pomponne, 20 July 1676   **98**. Jean-Marie Le Gall, 'Les Pompes funèbres des souverains étrangers à Notre-Dame de Paris, XVIe–XVIIIe siècles', *Revue d'Histoire Moderne et Contemporaine*, 59-3, 3, 2012, pp. 96–123; Marquis de Dangeau, *Journal*, 35 vols., Clermont-Ferrand, 2002–14, XVIII, 236, 29 June 1705   **99**. Bercé, p. 45

Chapter 6: Fouquet's Fall

1. Jean-Marie Pérouse de Montclos, *Vaux le Vicomte*, 1997, pp. 36–41, 70–71, 135, 147 and passim; Petitfils, *Fouquet*, pp. 28, 174–88, 355–7; idem, *Louise de La Vallière*, 2011, p. 101   **2**. Daniel Dessert, *La Prise du pouvoir par Louis XIV: la construction du mythe*, 2005, pp. 227, 243–64, 245   **3**. Cornette, *Mort de Louis XIV*, pp. 72–6   **4**. Camille-Georges Picavet, *Les Dernières Années de Turenne (1660–1675)*, n.d., pp. 32–3, quoting Godefroy Hermant and Guy Patin   **5**. André, p. 31, despatch by van Beuningen, 16 March 1663; Picavet, *Turenne*, pp. 76–7, despatches of the Venetian Ambassador Giustiniani, 22 March 1666, 30 September 1664, and pp. 152–3, 156; cf. Louis XIV, *Oeuvres*, II, 447–8, for an example of Louis XIV's consultation of Turenne on foreign affairs in 1668   **6**. Colbert, II, 55, mémoire by Colbert, 1663   **7**. Sarmant and Stoll, pp. 194–9; Lucien Bély, *Les Secrets de Louis XIV: mystères d'Etat et pouvoir absolu*, 2013, pp. 225–9   **8**. Simone Bertière, *Le Procès Fouquet*, 2013, p. 141   **9**. Petitfils, *Fouquet*, pp. 139, 146–7, 151–4, 160   **10**. Ibid., pp. 225, 233–5, 293, 306, 336, 352; Murat, p. 87   **11**. Petitfils, *Fouquet*, p. 328   **12**. Sévigné, I, 48, Chapelain to Sévigné, 3 October 1661; Murat, p. 78   **13**. Motteville, *Mémoires*, IV, 282, 289, 290   **14**. Petitfils, *Fouquet*, p. 203; Bertière, *Fouquet*, p. 101   **15**. Chevé, p. 325   **16**. Bertière, *Fouquet*, p. 20; Levantal, *Louis XIV*, I, 200–204   **17**. Visconti, pp. 33, 35, 40   **18**. Ibid., p. 141   **19**. Petitfils, *La Vallière*, pp. 81–2, 89–90, 169   **20**. Motteville, *Mémoires*, IV, 281   **21**. Petitfils, *La Vallière*, pp. 94–7; idem, *Fouquet*, pp. 351–2   **22**. Louis XIV, *Mémoires*, p. 111   **23**. Petitfils, *Fouquet*, pp. 330–31   **24**. Bertière, *Fouquet*, p. 163   **25**. Petitfils, *Fouquet*, p. 337; cf. Pitts, *Fouquet*, p. 55   **26**. Dessert, *Royaume*, pp. 69, 79, 94; Colbert, I, 381, Colbert to Mazarin, 1 October 1659   **27**. Dulong, *Anne d'Autriche*, p. 463   **28**. Montclos, pp. 148, 150   **29**. Petitfils, *Fouquet*, p. 250; Colbert, I, 518–19, Fouquet to Mazarin, 6, 31 January 1660   **30**. Bertière, *Fouquet*, p. 210   **31**. Petitfils, *Fouquet*, p. 203; Bertière, *Fouquet*, pp. 183–6   **32**. Edouard de Barthélemy, *Madame d'Huxelles et ses amis*, 1881, pp. 254, 255, Madame d'Huxelles to Fouquet n.d.; Bertière, *Fouquet*, p. 101   **33**. Murat, illustrations 14–19, reproduces the relevant documents; cf. Colbert, II, clxxxix–cxcvii, notes by Colbert, 1661   **34**. Petitfils, *Fouquet*, pp. 364–71; Bertière, *Fouquet*, pp. 29–32   **35**. Louis XIV, *Oeuvres*, V, 51, Louis XIV to Anne, 5 September 1661   **36**. Bertière, *Fouquet*, p. 176   **37**. Dulong, *Anne d'Autriche*, p. 466   **38**. Petitfils, *Fouquet*, p. 390.   **39**. Pitts, *Fouquet*, pp. 75, 81, 128   **40**. Ormesson, *Journal*, II, 79, 26 January 1664   **41**. Sévigné, I, 34, Bussy-Rabutin to Sévigné, 7 October 1655   **42**. Roger Duchêne, *Madame de Sévigné*, 2002, p. 52; Petitfils, *Fouquet*, p. 434   **43**. Sévigné, I, 62, 64, 67, Sévigné to Pomponne, 26, 27 November, 2 December 1664   **44**. Ormesson, *Journal*, I, 177–9, 212, journal October–December 1664   **45**. Ibid., 231, 257, 263   **46**. Petitfils, *Fouquet*, p. 407 and n, despatch of 11 March 1664; Bertière, *Fouquet*, p. 236   **47**. Paul Sonnino, *Man in the Iron Mask*, pp. 73, 116, 119, 122, 126 and passim   **48**. Pitts, *Fouquet*, pp. 54, 70, 90, 93, 95   **49**. Colbert, VII, 399, 400, seconde note de Fouquet pour se défendre auprès du Roy; Bertière, *Fouquet*, p. 268; Pitts, *Fouquet*, p. 35   **50**. Petitfils, *Fouquet*, pp. 439, 445   **51**. Ormesson, *Journal*, II, 45, 23 August 1663   **52**. Bertière, *Fouquet*, pp. 180–82, 213; Petitfils, *Fouquet*, p. 525   **53**. Bertière, *Fouquet*, pp. 254, 285   **54**. Ormesson, *Journal*, II, 283, December 1664   **55**. Petitfils, *Fouquet*, pp. 449, 450, 478, 486, 491; Pitts, *Fouquet*, p. 161   **56**. Montclos, p. 45   **57**. Petitfils, *Fouquet*, p. 516; Pitts,

Fouquet, p. 163; Thierry Sarmant, *Louis XIV et Paris: collections du Musée Carnavalet*, 2013, p. 31; Claire Goldstein, *Vaux and Versailles: The Appropriations, Accidents, and Erasures that Made Modern France*, Philadelphia, 2008, pp. 78–80

Chapter 7: Making France Work

1. Saint-Maurice, I, 222, Saint-Maurice to Duke of Savoy, 31 August 1668, II, 403, 2 September 1672; Jeroen Duindam, *Vienna and Versailles: The Courts of Europe's Dynastic Rivals, 1550–1780*, Cambridge, 2003, pp. 154–6   2. Levantal, *Louis XIV*, I, 206, *Gazette de France*, 20 October 1661   3. Magne, *Lettres inédites*, p. 40, Enghien to Queen of Poland, 27 June 1664   4. Louis XIV's Treaty of Montmartre of 6 February 1662, adding the princes of the house of Lorraine to the French line of succession, was annulled a year later.   5. Arsenal Mss. 3568 f. 180, Louis XIV to Fabert, 30 December 1661. Later in the reign, Maréchal Catinat would refuse the honour for the same reason. Vauban, however, was happy to submit dubious 'proofs' in order to become a Chevalier du Saint-Esprit.   6. Motteville, *Mémoires*, IV, 314–18, 344, 372–4, 347–9; Sarmant, *Homme et roi*, p. 186; Ormesson, *Journal*, II, 68, December 1663; cf. Magne, *Lettres inédites*, p. 42, Enghien to Queen of Poland, 3 July 1664. The Duke was employed again in the army after 1668; the Duchess did not return to court until 1682, when Louis XIV had adopted a different moral code.   7. Ormesson, *Journal*, II, 275, December 1664   8. Colbert, II, ccxx–ccxxi, mémoire au roi, 22 July 1666   9. Ormesson, *Journal*, II, 451, 13 March 1666, 468, 23 August 1666, 328 12 March 1665   10. Saint-Maurice, II, 280, to Duke of Savoy, 27 April 1672; Hervé Drévillon, *L'Impôt du sang: le métier des armes sous Louis XIV*, 2005, pp. 41–3; AN K 119, 20/3 Caumartin to Hacqueville, 26 October 1672. Later in the reign correspondence between generals and ministers was sometimes interrupted over the question of who deserved the prefix 'Monseigneur' at the start of a letter.   11. Lough, pp. 155, 159, quoting Anthony Veryard and Joseph Shaw   12. Ibid., p. 143, quoting John Reresby   13. John Locke, *Travels in France*, ed. John Lough, 1953, pp. xliii, 31, diary, 8 February 1676   14. Saint-Maurice, I, 384, 388, to Duke of Savoy, 31 January 1670   15. John J. Hurt, *Louis XIV and the Parlements: The Assertion of Royal Authority*, Manchester, 2002 pp. 22–3, 53, 59   16. Hamscher, p. 47   17. Colbert, II, 82, Louis XIV to Colbert, 5 May 1672   18. Ibid., 264, Colbert to Chamillart, 20 January 1673   19. Anon., *Relation et observations*, pp. 509, 522   20. Colbert, VII, clxxi, despatch by Grimani, Venetian Ambassador, 1664   21. Ibid., 361, Colbert de Maulévrier to Seignelay, 5 June 1672   22. Murat, pp. 103, 109   23. Ormesson, *Journal*, II, 389, 26 August 1665   24. Dessert, *Royaume*, p. 157; Murat, pp. 63, 157   25. Francois d'Aubert, *Colbert: la vertu usurpée*, 2010, pp. 129–30   26. Murat, pp. 110, 123   27. BN Mss. fr. 6763–8 Abrégés des finances 1662–1680; cf. Jacob Soll, *The Information Master: Jean-Baptiste Colbert's Secret State Intelligence System*, Ann Arbor, 2009, pp. 60–63   28. Murat, p. 124   29. Ibid., p. 320   30. Colbert, II, 154, 164, 183, Colbert to the intendants, 28 May 1681, 7 August 1681, 8 May 1682   31. Murat, p. 158   32. Colbert, II, 204, Colbert to the intendants, 24 August 1682; II, 216, Colbert to M. Le Bret, 4 February 1683, 222, marginal note by Louis XIV, 13 June 1683   33. Ibid., IV, 153, Colbert to the Intendant of Aix, 21 January 1682   34. Ibid., 151, 152n, 158, 162, Colbert to Morant, 6 February 1682, 25 December 1681, 8 July, 17 September 1682   35. Murat, p. 151   36. Ibid., pp. 143, 378–9; Colbert, VI, 369–40, Procès verbaux des conférences tenues devant Louis XIV pour la réformation de la justice, 25 September, 11, 25 October 1665; *DL*, pp. 34–5   37. *DL*, pp. 131, 308; Levantal, *Louis XIV*, I, 260, 20 April 1667   38. Murat, p. 162; Sarmant, *Homme*, pp. 106, 127 132   39. Saint-Maurice, II, 246, Saint-Maurice to Duke of Savoy, 12 February 1672; Ormesson, *Journal*, II, 627–9, February 1672   40. Colbert, II, 427, Louis XIV to 'échevins et habitants de Marseille', 26 August 1664, 433, 16, 265   41. Centre de Recherche du Château de Versailles [henceforth CRCV], Base de données en ligne, Curia; Alfred Marie, *Naissance de Versailles: le château, les jardins*, 2 vols., 1968, I, 275   42. Magne, *Lettres inédites*, p. 85, Condé to Queen of Poland, 24 October 1664; Murat, p. 289   43. Levantal, *Louis XIV*, I, 282, 15 December 1668 and 20 March

1665; Jeremy Black, *From Louis XIV to Napoleon: The Fate of a Great Power*, 1999, p. 43 **44**. Colbert, III, part 1, 196, Colbert to d'Aguesseau, 29 November 1669 **45**. Daniel Roche, *Le Peuple de Paris au XVIIIe siècle*, 1998, pp. 279, 287 **46**. Colbert, II, cclviii, Discours sur les manufactures du royaume, 1663 **47**. Dangeau, II, 225 and n, 18 November 1687 **48**. Colbert, II, cclxxiii, Louis XIV to Colbert, 22 May 1670; I, 255, 3, 14 October 1666; V, 396, 20 November 1666 **49**. Anne Kraatz, *Lace: History and Fashion*, 1989, pp. 45, 46, 50; Louis XIV, *Mémoires*, p. 185 **50**. Colbert, II, 438, Louis XIV to Comte de La Bourlie, 6 November 1666 **51**. Kraatz, pp. 48, 50, 63-4 **52**. Sévigné, II, 154, Sévigné to Madame de Grignan, 29 July 1676 **53**. Corinne Thépaut-Cabasset, ed., *L'Esprit des modes au Grand Siècle: extraits du Mercure Galant (1672-1701)*, 2010, passim and pp. 13, 96-8, quoting *Mercure Galant*, 15 May 1678 **54**. Ibid., pp. 21, 56 **55**. Ibid., pp. 135, 150, *Mercure Galant*, October 1682, June 1687 **56**. Monique Vincent, *Le Mercure Galant: présentation de la première revue féminine d'information et de culture, 1672-1710*, 2005, pp. 45, 54 **57**. Sally-Ann Hery-Simoulin, 'Louis XIV et les mystères du justaucorps à brevet', in Pierre Arizzoli-Clémentel and Pascale Gorguet Ballesteros, eds., *Fastes de cour et cérémonies royales: le costume de cour en Europe, 1650-1800*, 2009, pp. 180-83 at p. 180; Diana de Marly, *Louis XIV and Versailles*, 1987, pp. 61-2 **58**. Philip Mansel, *Dressed to Rule: Royal and Court Costume from Louis XIV to Elizabeth II*, 2005, pp. 12-15 **59**. Béatrix Saule et al. eds., *Splendeurs de la cour de Saxe: Dresde à Versailles*, exh. cat., 2006, pp. 75, 91 **60**. Colbert, II, 610, 622, Colbert to Prévôt des Marchands et échevins de Lyon, 6 March 1671, to Madame de la Petitière, 26 June 1671 **61**. H. G. Duchesne and H. de Grandsaigne, *Histoire du Bois de Boulogne: Le Château de Madrid . . .*, 1912, pp. 83, 91 **62**. Colbert, VII, clxxiii, Extraits des relations des ambassadeurs de Venise, Giustiniani, 1668 **63**. Wolf Burchard, *The Sovereign Artist: Charles Le Brun and the Image of Louis XIV*, 2016, passim; Thomas P. Campbell, ed., *Tapestry in the Baroque: Threads of Splendour*, New York, 2007; Pascal-François Bertrand, 'Tapestry Production at the Gobelins during the Reign of Louis XIV, 1661-1715', in Campbell, *Tapestry in the Baroque*, pp. 341-55 at p. 344 **64**. *Soieries de Lyon: Commandes royales au XVIIIe siècle*, exh. cat., Lyon, 1988, p. 50; Astrid Tydén-Jordan, *Queen Christina's Coronation Coach*, Stockholm, 1988, p. 23 **65**. Corinne Thépaut-Cabasset, 'Diplomatische Agenten und der europäische Luxuswarenhandel im späten 17. Jahrhundert', in Mark Häberlein and Christof Jeggle, eds., *Materielle Grundlagen der diplomatie: Schenken, Sammeln und Verhandeln im Spätmittelalter und früher Neuzeit*, Constanz and Munich, 2013, pp. 157-75; Stéphane Castelluccio, ed., *Le Commerce du luxe à Paris aux XVIIe et XVIIIe siècles*, Bern, 2009, pp. 254-63 **66**. Colbert, VII, 250, mémoire au Roi sur les Finances, 1670 **67**. Ibid., II, 463-4, Colbert de Croissy to Pomponne, 21 March 1669 **68**. Pierre Clément, ed., *L'Italie en 1671: relation d'un voyage du marquis de Seignelay à Marseille et à Toulon*, 1867, p. 296 **69**. K. D. H. Haley, *An English Diplomat in the Low Countries: Sir William Temple and John de Witt, 1665-1672*, Oxford, 1986, pp. 148, 260, Temple to Arlington, 3 June 1666; Saint-Maurice, I, 64, Saint-Maurice to Duke of Savoy, 13 June 1667 **70**. H. H. Rowen, *John de Witt, Grand Pensionary of Holland, 1625-1672*, Princeton, 1978, p. 684; Comte d'Estrades, *Lettres, mémoires et négociations*, 6 vols., Brussels, 1709, VI, 71, Estrades to Lionne, 13 October 1667 **71**. **72**. Colbert, II, 500, 506, Colbert to Pomponne, 28 November, 27 December 1669 **73**. Jonathan Israel, *Dutch Primacy in World Trade, 1585-1740*, Oxford, 1989, pp. 223, 284, 287; René Mémain, *La Marine de guerre sous Louis XIV: le matériel: Rochefort, arsenal modèle de Colbert*, 1937, passim **74**. Paul Butel, 'France, the Antilles and Europe in the Seventeenth and Eighteenth Centuries: Renewals of Foreign Trade', in James D. Tracy, ed., *The Rise of Merchant Empires*, Cambridge, 1990, pp. 153-73 at p. 161 **75**. Jacques Savary, *Le Parfait Négociant*, ed. Edouard Richard, 2 vols., Geneva, 2011, I, 21, 22, 57 **76**. Murat, pp. 274-8 **77**. Dirk Van der Cruysse, *Le Noble Désir de courir le monde: voyager en Asie au XVIIe siècle*, 2002, p. 59 **78**. Daniel Dessert, *La Royale: vaisseaux et marins du Roi-Soleil*, 1996, pp. 201-2, 217, Louis XIV to Beaufort, 19 April 1669 **79**. Colbert, III, part 1, 104, règlement of 7 March 1669 **80**. Ibid., 230, Colbert to Matharel, April 1670; 573, Mémoire au sieur Brodat, 27 December 1675; III, part 1, 5, 244n, Colbert to Joinville, 27 March 1676, to Brodat, 21 October 1682 **81**. Ibid., III, part 1, 337, 417, Colbert to Colbert de Terron, 16 February

1671, Colbert de Croissy, 16 January 1672 **82.** Dessert, *La Royale*, p. 180 **83.** Ibid., p. 184 **84.** Colbert, III, part 1, 307, to Colbert de Terron, 6 November 1670; cf. p. 335, Louis XIV to Comte de Guiche, 27 January 1671 **85.** Levantal, *Louis XIV*, I, 219, 30 November– 6 December 1662; L. Lemaire, *Histoire de Dunkerque: des origines à 1900*, Dunkirk, 1927, p. 197 **86.** Colbert, V, 5, Colbert to M. de Chastillon, 26 November 1662; BS 1289 f. 76, Louis XIV to General de Nuquart, 26 October 1664 **87.** Laurent Dingli, *Seignelay: le fils flamboyant*, 2007, pp. 104–5 **88.** Dessert, *La Royale*, p. 19 **89.** Dessert, *La Royale*, Colbert de Maulévrier to Colbert, 27 July 1680 **90.** Bernard Cros, 'Dunkerque, port de guerre du roi soleil', *Revue Historique de Dunkerque et du Littoral*, 31, 12, 1997, pp. 49–106 **91.** Lemaire, pp. 235, 218 **92.** Ibid., pp. 209–10 **93.** Armel de Wismes, *Jean Bart et la guerre de course*, 1965, pp. 161, 180–81. Dunkirk would also be a base for French attempts to supply Prince Charles Edward in Scotland in 1745–6. Lemaire, p. 247 **94.** Colbert, III, part 1, 207, Colbert to M. Daliez de la Tour, 16 January 1670; Junko Thérèse Takeda, *Between Crown and Commerce: Marseille and the Early Modern Mediterranean*, Baltimore, 2011, pp. 31–2, 34 **95.** Takeda, pp. 98–101. After the death of Colbert, Armenians and Jews were, however, periodically expelled from Marseille. **96.** André Zysberg, *Marseille au temps du roi soleil: la ville, les galères, l'arsenal*, 2007; Regis Bertrand et al., *Marseille: histoire d'une ville*, Marseille, 2013, pp. 84, 104, 106, 108, 113, 124, 125 **97.** Zysberg, pp. 73, 76, Arnoult to Colbert, 10 March 1668 **98.** Paul W. Bamford, *Fighting Ships and Prisons: The Mediterranean Galleys of France in the Age of Louis XIV*, Minneapolis, 1973, pp. 24, 138, 142, 152–3, 156, 164, 173 **99.** Montpensier, III, 434–5 **100.** Zysberg, pp. 135–6 **101.** Ellis Veryard, *Journey through the Low Countries, France, Italy and Part of Spain*, 1701, p. 93 **102.** Zysberg, pp. 84, 115, 183 **103.** Annick Riani, 'L'Arsenal des Galériens', in *Le Siècle de Louis XIV à Marseille*, exh. cat., Marseille, 1994, pp. 30–33 **104.** Camille Gabet, *La Naissance de Rochefort sous Louis XIV, 1666–1715*, Rochefort, 1985; Konvitz, p. 87; *L'Orient arsenal XVII–XVIII siècles*, Lorient, 1983, pp. 52, 117; Yves Le Gallo, ed., *Histoire de Brest*, Toulouse, 1976, p. 70 **105.** Bernard Cros, *Toulon, l'arsenal et la ville*, 2012 **106.** Colbert, IV, 454, 498, Colbert to intendants, 28 February 1671, 9 May 1680 **107.** Chandra Mukerji, *Impossible Engineering: Technology and Territoriality on the Canal du Midi*, Princeton, 2009, pp. 61, 77, 167, 193 **108.** Colbert, IV, 148, Colbert to M. de Ris, 24 September 1681; cf. Marie-Laure Legay, *Les Etats provinciaux dans la construction de l'état moderne aux XVIIe et XVIIIe siècles*, Geneva, 2001, passim **109.** Colbert, VII, 69, Louis XIV to Colbert, 29 November 1672 **110.** Saint-Maurice, I, 158, Saint-Maurice to Duke of Savoy, 18 November 1667; Colbert, II, ccxxxi, Louis XIV to Colbert, 1 January 1673 **111.** Colbert, VI, 463–4, Louis XIV to Colbert, 19 December 1663, discusses arrangements for the birth; V, 275, Colbert to Louis XIV, 12 May 1670; Ormesson, *Journal*, II, 69–70, 19 December 1663 **112.** Sébastien Locatelli, *Voyage en France: moeurs et coutumes françaises*, 1905, p. 175, May 1665 **113.** Lough, p. 144, quoting Edward Browne **114.** Flavio Chigi, 'Relation et observation sur le royaume de France', *RHD*, 8, 2, 1894, pp. 269–79 at p. 274 **115.** Magne, *Lettres inédites*, p. 330, Enghien to Queen of Poland, 4 March 1667 **116.** Petitfils, *La Vallière*, p. 192; Montpensier, IV, 489 **117.** Louis XIV, *Mémoires*, p. 201 **118.** Colbert, VI, 466, Journal 22 April 1663 **119.** Motteville, *Mémoires*, IV, 331–4, 378 **120.** Levantal, *Louis XIV*, I, 248, 9 January 1666; Motteville, *Mémoires*, IV, 418 **121.** Motteville, *Mémoires*, IV, 394–8, 401–6, 433–9 **122.** Ibid., 447; Magne, *Lettres inédites*, pp. 245-6, Enghien to Queen of Poland, 21 January 1666; Pierre Blet, *Les Nonces du pape à la cour de Louis XIV*, 2002, p. 222, despatches of January 1666; Sarmant, *Homme et roi*, 187, 287 **123.** Louis XIV, *Oeuvres*, V, 361, Louis XIV to La Vallière, 11 February 1666; cf. Magne, *Lettres inédites*, p. 309, Enghien to Queen of Poland, 5 November 1666

Chapter 8: The Pursuit of Immortality: The Louvre and Versailles

1. Colbert, V, 537, ordonnance, 26 April 1672 **2.** DeJean, pp. 99–101, 112, 126–7, 142 and passim **3.** Francis Tallents, *Travels in France and Switzerland in the Years 1671-1673*, 2011, p. 157, 1 December 1672 **4.** Locatelli, p. 157, May 1665; Faugère, pp. 28, 110; DeJean,

p. 192   5. Anne Verdillon and Alexandre Gady, *Le Jardin des Tuileries d'André Le Notre, un chef d'oeuvre pour le Roi Soleil*, 2013, p. 78   6. Craig Koslofsky, *Evening's Empire: A History of the Night in Early Modern Europe*, Cambridge, 2011, pp. 131, 136–40. After 1697 street lighting was also introduced in French provincial cities.   7. Louis Hautecoeur, *L'Histoire des châteaux du Louvre et des Tuileries*, 1927, pp. 98–102   8. Pierre-Nicolas Sainte-Fare-Garnot, *Le Château des Tuileries*, 1988, pp. 33, 36, 47, 49   9. Geneviève Bresc-Bautier, ed., *La Galerie d'Apollon au palais du Louvre*, 2004, passim   10. Alexandre Tessier, 'Des carrosses qui en cachent d'autres: retours sur certains incidents qui marquèrent l'ambassade de Lord Denzil Holles à Paris, de 1663 à 1666', in Lucien Bély and Géraud Poumarède, eds., *L'Incident diplomatique (XVIe–XVIIe siècle)*, 2010, pp. 197–240 at pp. 228–9, 240, Holles to Arlington, 3 August 1664   11. Samuel Pepys, *Diary*, 9 vols., 1995 edn, II, p. 188, 30 September 1661; Cyril Hughes Hartmann, *The King's Friend: A Life of Charles Berkeley, Viscount Fitzhardinge, Earl of Falmouth (1630–1665)*, 1951, p. 62; Séré, p. 439n; Motteville, *Mémoires*, IV, 297–300; AN K 118 'Procès verbal contenant la Déclaration … que le marquis de la Fuente ambassadeur extraordinaire du roy catholique près du roy a faite à Sa Majesté de la part de son maître', 24 March 1662, signed Phélypeaux, Guénégaud, Le Tellier, de Loménie; cf. Louis XIV, *Mémoires*, pp. 125, 129, 131   12. Mackenzie Cooley, '"I Would Have our Courtier be a Perfect Horseman": Creating Nobility and Fashioning Horses between Mantua and Naples, 1461–1571', talk at Animals at Court conference, Munich, 9 December 2016   13. Jérôme de La Gorce, *Carlo Vigarani, intendant des plaisirs de Louis XIV*, 2005, pp. 46–8; Helen Watanabe-O'Kelly, *Triumphall Shews: Tournaments at German-Speaking Courts in their European Context, 1560–1730*, Berlin, 1992, p. 106   14. Motteville, *Mémoires*, IV, 334   15. Locatelli, pp. 124–6, 154–6, 11 November 1664, May 1665   16. Ibid., p. 179, May 1665   17. Saint-Maurice, I, 157, 11 November 1667   18. Stéphane Haffemayer, 'L'Affaire des gardes corses et l'opinion publique (20 août 1662–12 février 1664)', in Bély and Poumarède, *L'Incident diplomatique*, pp. 281–309; Maral, *Le Roi-Soleil et Dieu*, p. 122. The pyramid was demolished in 1668, after a reconciliation between the Pope and the King.   19. Maria Giulia Barberini et al., eds., *Life and the Arts in the Baroque Palaces of Rome*, New York, 1999, pp. 3, 142   20. Paul Fréart de Chantelou, *Journal de voyage du Cavalier Bernin en France*, 1981 edn, p. 51, 5 July 1665   21. Franco Mormando, *Bernini: His Life and his Rome*, 2011, p. 262   22. Chantelou, pp. 57, 160, 172, 182, 12 July, 6, 9, 13 September 1665   23. Mormando, p. 274; Chantelou, p. 199   24. Cecil Gould, *Bernini in France: An Episode in Seventeenth-Century History*, 1981, p. 39   25. Chantelou, p. 46, 27 June 1665; Gould, pp. 56, 58, 60   26. Colbert, V, xxxiv, 6 August 1665; Chantelou, pp. 59, 64, 66, 15, 22 July 1665, 122, 198, 19 August, 19 September 1665   27. Chantelou, p. 85, 30 July 1665   28. Ibid., p. 121, 19 August 1665   29. Ibid., pp. 294–5, 302, 17, 18, 19 October 1665   30. Mormando, p. 279   31. Gould, pp. 33, 34   32. Ibid., pp. 46–7, 81   33. Chantelou, pp. 113, 161, 176, 15 August, 6, 10 September 1665   34. Locatelli, pp. 126–7, 11 November 1664   35. Chantelou, pp. 223, 241, 281, 28 September, 5, 13 October 1665   36. Ibid., pp. 228, 299, 305, 306, 315, 29 September, 17, 19, 22 October 1665; Gould, p. 110   37. Chantelou, pp. 228, 299, 305, 306, 315, 29 September, 17, 19, 22 October 1665   38. Gould, p. 117   39. Mormando, pp. 286–7   40. Lough, p. 149, quoting Christopher Wren; Lisa Jardine, *On a Grander Scale: The Outstanding Career of Sir Christopher Wren*, 2003 edn, pp. 241–6   41. Sarmant, *Louis XIV et Paris*, p. 35   42. Robert W. Berger, *The Palace of the Sun: The Louvre of Louis XIV*, University Park, PA, 1993, pp. 23, 28, 75   43. Charles Perrault, *Mémoires de ma vie*, 2 vols., 1909, I, 83   44. Colbert, V, 246, observations, 1664   45. Gould, p. 121   46. Perrault, *Mémoires*, I, xxxv   47. Gould, p. 123, Colbert to Poussin, 1664   48. Guillaume Fonkenell, *Le Palais des Tuileries*, Arles, 2010, pp. 71, 102, 107, 166–7   49. Hautecoeur, pp. 98–9, 127, 137–8   50. Perrault, *Mémoires*, I, 94   51. Colbert, V, lv   52. Christiane Aulanier, *La Salle des Caryatides*, 1957, p. 41. Some academies were already meeting in the Louvre by 1665.   53. Jean-Nérée Ronfort, ed., *André-Charles Boulle, 1642–1732: un nouveau style pour l'Europe*, Frankfurt, 2009, pp. 25, 296   54. Tallents, pp. 163–5   55. Christiane Aulanier, *Le Pavillon du roi: les appartements de la reine*, 1958, pp. 64, 67, 73–4, 78; Geneviève Bresc-Bautier, *The Architecture of the Louvre*, 1995, pp. 71–3   56. Perrrault, *Mémoires*, I, 35, 37, 38, 41   57. Colbert, V,

242, Colbert to Heinsius and Vossius, 21 June 1663, 468; Henri L. Brugmans, *Le Séjour de Christian Huygens à Paris*, 1935, pp. 67, 84, 93–6. In the end however, after Colbert's death, his pension was stopped and he moved back to Holland.   **58.** Georges Dethan, *Paris au temps de Louis XIV, 1660–1715*, 1990, pp. 187–91   **59.** Sarmant, *Louis XIV et Paris*, pp. 31, 41–2   **60.** André Corvisier, *Louvois*, 1983, pp. 217–19, 208–10; Gérard Sabatier, *Le Prince et les arts*, 2010, pp. 368–9   **61.** Charles de Gaulle, *Mémoires*, 2000, p. 575   **62.** Lough, pp. 170–71   **63.** Sarmant, *Louis XIV et Paris*, pp. 43–4; Alexandre Gady, ed., *Jules Hardouin-Mansart, 1646–1708*, 2010, pp. 72–3, 85   **64.** Frédéric Tiberghien, *Versailles: le chantier de Louis XIV, 1662–1715*, 2002, pp. 76, 80, 82; Anna Keay, *The Magnificent Monarch: Charles II and the Ceremonies of Power*, 2008, pp. 101, 188   **65.** Perrault, *Mémoires*, I, 112   **66.** Ormesson, *Journal*, II, 540, 22 January 1668; cf. Jacques Saint-Germain, *Louis XIV secret*, 1970, p. 266   **67.** Jacques Levron, *Versailles, ville royale*, 1964, pp. 48–50; Burchard, passim   **68.** Jean-Pierre Samoyault, *Guide to the Museum of the Château of Fontainebleau*, 1994, pp. 20, 211 and passim   **69.** Marie-Pierre Terrien and Philippe Dien, *Le Château de Richelieu, XVIIe–XVIIIe siècles*, Rennes, 2009, pp. 42–3. **70.** Henry Kamen, *The Escorial: Art and Power in the Renaissance*, 2010, pp. 51, 57–8, 103, 143, 217, 226, 235   **71.** Jonathan Brown and J. H. Elliott, *A Palace for a King: The Buen Retiro and the Court of Philip IV*, 1980, pp. 16, 62, 142   **72.** E. Castelnuovo and W. Barberis et al., eds., *La Reggia di Venaria e i Savoia: arte, magnificenza e storia di una corte europea*, exh. cat., 2 vols., Turin, 2007, passim; Saint-Maurice, I, 377, 525, to Duke of Savoy, 27 December 1669, 19 December 1670   **73.** Colbert, V, 269–70, Colbert to Louis XIV, 28 September 1665   **74.** Ibid., 267, Palais de Versailles, raisons générales   **75.** *Musée des Archives Nationales*, 1872, p. 509   **76.** Magne, *Lettres inédites*, p. 309, Enghien to Queen of Poland, 5 November 1666   **77.** Ibid., pp. 246, 313, Enghien to Queen of Poland, 21 January, 26 November 1666   **78.** Tiberghien, pp. 133, 135, 142–3   **79.** Ormesson, *Journal*, II, 552, July 1668; Saint-Maurice, I, 211, letter of 27 July 1668; Sévigné, II, 419, Sévigné to Bussy-Rabutin, 12 October 1678; cf. Tiberghien, pp. 159, 166, for more deaths and accidents during building works in 1683 and 1684, and p. 267 for officials' criticisms of workers' low wages   **80.** Murat, p. 171, Louis XIV to Colbert, April 1672,   **81.** Colbert, V, 326n, Louis XIV to Colbert, 4 May 1672   **82.** Murat, p. 363, Colbert to d'Aguesseau, 25 May 1674; Tiberghien, pp. 198–9, 211   **83.** Pascal Julien, ed., *Marbres de Rois*, Marseille, 2013, p. 13   **84.** Mathieu da Vinha and Raphael Masson, eds., *Versailles: histoire, dictionnaire et anthologie*, 2015 (henceforward *DV*), pp. 36, 40; Burchard, p. 203; Malcolm Campbell, *Pietro da Cortona at the Pitti Palace: A Study of the Planetary Rooms and Related Projects*, Princeton, 1977, p. 177   **85.** Anthony Blunt, *Art and Architecture in France*, 1998 edn, pp. 229–30   **86.** Colbert, V, 300, Colbert to Louis XIV, 22 May 1670   **87.** Saint-Maurice, I, 507, II, 23, Saint-Maurice to Duke of Savoy, 21 November 1670, 10 February 1671; Levantal, *Louis XIV*, I, 306, 309, 29 November 1670–10 February 1671   **88.** Marquis de Sourches, *Mémoires sur le règne de Louis XIV*, 13 vols., 1882–93, I, 56n, 14 November 1681   **89.** Vallot, p. 180, d'Aquin, 'Remarques pour l'année 1687'   **90.** Levron, *Ville royale*, pp. 50–51, Louis XIV to Colbert, 22 May 1671, Declaration of 24 November 1672   **91.** Gady, *Hardouin-Mansart*, pp. 379, 381, 383; Auguste Jehan, *La Ville de Versailles: son histoire, ses monuments, ses rues*, Versailles, 1900, pp. 108–13, lists eighteen nobles' *hôtels* simply in what are now rue Colbert and rue de la Chancellerie. There were many others.   **92.** *DV*, pp. 27–8; Alfred Marie, *Mansart à Versailles*, 2 vols., 1972, I, 161   **93.** Levron, *Ville royale*, pp. 62, 66   **94.** Colbert, VI, 470, Colbert diary, 14 October 1663   **95.** Montpensier, IV, 30–32   **96.** Levantal, *Louis XIV*, I, 258; Magne, *Lettres inédites*, p. 327, Enghien to Queen of Poland, 23 February 1667; cf. ibid., pp. 196, 211, 264, Enghien to Queen of Poland, 24 July 1665, 18 September 1665, 26 March 1666   **97.** Magne, *Lettres inédites*, p. 269, Duc d'Enghien to Queen of Poland, 30 April 1666   **98.** BN Mss. fr. 7834, M. de Bizincourt, 'Les plaisirs de l'île enchantée', 6 May 1664, f. 21. A copy, given to Henrietta Maria, is at Waddesdon.   **99.** Keay, *Magnificent Monarch*, p. 91; Colbert, V, 376, Colbert to Feuquières, 15 July 1675   **100.** Koslofsky, p. 97   **101.** *Fêtes et divertissements à la cour* (henceforward *FD*), exh. cat., 2016, pp. 319–29, 348   **102.** André Félibien, *Les Fêtes de Versailles*, 2012, pp. 151, 163   **103.** Beaussant, *Plaisirs de Versailles*, p. 41; Félibien, *Fêtes de Versailles*, pp.

97, 99   104. Félibien, *Fêtes de Versailles*, pp. 35, 40, 81   105. Brugmans, pp. 78–9, account by Christian Huygens, 1668; Saint-Maurice, I, 202–9, Saint-Maurice to Duke of Savoy, 20 July 1668   106. Jean-Jacques Gautier, 'L'Imaginaire comme support du luxe: les fêtes royales de Versailles de Mai 1664', in Robert Fox and Anthony Turner, eds., *Luxury Trades and Consumerism in Ancien Régime Paris*, 2016, pp. 191–218 at pp. 212–18

Chapter 9: Conquering Flanders

1. Ormesson, *Journal*, II, 591, June 1670   2. Colbert, VI, 221, *Mémoire*, February 1663   3. Saint-Maurice, I, 122, to Duke of Savoy, 9 September 1667   4. Fernand Desmons, *La Conquête en 1667*, Tournai, 1905, p. 140   5. Picavet, *Turenne*, p. 178, Louis XIV to d'Estrades, 6 April 1663   6. Levillain, p. 96   7. Colbert, VI, 237n   8. Black, *From Louis XIV to Napoleon*, pp. 36, 41   9. Colbert, V, 627, Chapelain to Colbert, 3 December 1667   10. *Traité des droits de la reyne*, 1667, p. 1   11. Levantal, *Louis XIV*, I, 261, May 1667   12. Saint-Maurice, I, 66, to Duke of Savoy, 13 June 1667   13. Ibid., 137, to Duke of Savoy, 23 September 1667   14. Rousset, I, 249–50; Corvisier, *Louvois*, pp. 191–3, 353   15. Rousset, I, 112, Louvois to Turenne, 23 September 1667   16. Drévillon, *Impôt du sang*, p. 32   17. Picavet, *Turenne*, p. 365, Turenne to Louvois, 15 September 1673, pp. 397, 401, 429   18. La Fare, p. 172; Carl J. Ekberg, *The Failure of Louis XIV's Dutch War*, Chapel Hill, NC, 1979, pp. 70, 145–8, 150   19. Saint-Maurice, I, 89, 91, 109, to Duke of Savoy, 13 July, 18 August 1667   20. Desmons, pp. 209–15   21. Saint-Maurice, I, 105, to Duke of Savoy, 11 August 1667   22. Jean-Michel Lambin, *Quand le nord devenait français (1635–1713)*, 1980, p. 71; Levantal, *Louis XIV*, I, 267, 28 August 1667   23. Levillain, pp. 138–9, 150   24. Saint-Maurice, I, 128, 16 September 1667   25. Haley, *English Diplomat*, pp. 106, 107, 124; John Spielman, *Leopold I of Austria*, 1977, pp. 46, 54   26. Levillain, pp. 135–7; *DL*, p. 415   27. John T. O'Connor, *Negotiator out of Season: The Career of Wilhelm Egon von Fürstenberg, 1629 to 1704*, Athens, GA, 1978, p. 32   28. Haley, *English Diplomat*, pp. 150, 173, 176, 201   29. Olaf Morke, 'William III's Stadholderly Court in the Dutch Republic', in Esther Mijers and David Onnekink, eds., *Redefining William III: The Impact of the King-Stadholder in International Context*, Aldershot, 2007, pp. 227–40; for William III's French, spoken with a lisp, see Louis XIV, *Oeuvres*, VI, 520, François de Callières to the Marquise d'Huxelles, 12 November 1697   30. Haley, *English Diplomat*, p. 182; Alexander Dencher, 'The Politics of Spectacle: Imaging the Prince of Orange during the First Stadtholderless Era', *The Court Historian*, 19, 2, December 2014, pp. 163–8 at p. 166   31. Cf. Arsenal Mss. 4712 f. 134, Louis XIV to Pomponne, 3 November 1669   32. Rowen, *De Witt, Grand Pensionary*, p. 544; Estrades, I, 326–35, Estrades to Louis XIV, 8, 30 May, 5, 12 June 1664   33. Haley, *English Diplomat*, p. 176   34. Gail Bossenga, *The Politics of Privilege: Old Regime and Revolution in Lille*, Cambridge, 1991, p. 1; Lambin, pp. 49, 57   35. Alain Lottin, ed., '*Chronique immémoriale des choses mémorables par moy Pierre-Ignace Chavatte' (1657–1693): le mémorial d'un humble tisserand lillois au grand siècle*, Brussels, 2010, pp. 67, 373, August 1667, January 1685   36. Koslofsky, pp. 142–3   37. *Lille au XVIIe siècle: des Pays Bas espagnols au Roi-Soleil*, exh. cat., Lille, 2000, p. 102; Lottin, '*Chronique immémoriale*', pp. 201, May 1670, 320–22, August 1680; cf. for other conquered cities' experiences, Alain Derville, *Histoire de Saint-Omer*, Lille, 1981, p. 135; Paul Rolland, *Histoire de Tournai*, 1956, pp. 227–39; Lambin, pp. 180, 182, quoting Charles Lemaître on Valenciennes   38. Montpensier, IV, 55; Lottin, '*Chronique immémoriale*', pp. 351–2, 31 July 1683   39. Louis Trénard, ed., *Histoire de Lille, de Charles-Quint à la conquête française*, Toulouse, 1981, pp. 285–9   40. Bossenga, p. 21   41. *Lille au XVII siècle*, p. 24; Albert Croquez, *La Flandre wallonne et les pays de l'intendance de Lille sous Louis XIV*, 1912, p. 21   42. Bossenga, pp. 42–3   43. *Lille au XVIIe siècle*, p. 83; Richard Holmes, *Fatal Avenue: A Traveller's History of the Battlefields of Northern France and Flanders, 1346–1945*, 2008, p. 148   44. For example, the King's former lover the Comtesse de Soissons had tried to break up his affair with La Vallière, and had encouraged Mlle de La Mothe Houdancourt to try to seduce him in 1662; see J. Lair, *Louise de La Vallière et la jeunesse de Louis XIV*, 1881, pp. 90–91, 101–2   45. Petitfils, *La Vallière*, pp. 215–16, 220; Saint-Maurice,

I, 87, despatch of 13 July 1667   46. Jean-Christian Petitfils, *Madame de Montespan*, 1988, pp. 8, 320, 24, 63; Magne, *Lettres inédites*, p. 2, Enghien to Queen of Poland, 22 February 1664; Sourches, I, 61, 14 November 1681   47. Saint-Maurice, I, 30-31, to Duke of Savoy, 6 May 1667; Magne, *Lettres inédites*, p. 309, Enghien to Queen of Poland, 5 November 1666   48. Jean Lemoine and André Lichtenberger, *De La Vallière à Montespan*, 1903, p. 165   49. Petitfils, *Montespan*, pp. 35, 50, 52   50. Saint-Maurice, I, 112, to Duke of Savoy, 27 August 1667   51. Lemoine and Lichtenberger, *De La Vallière à Montespan*, p. 191, citing despatch of Lord St Albans to Arlington, 26 October 1667; Petitfils, *Montespan*, 59   52. Saint-Maurice, I, 133, to Duke of Savoy, 16 September 1667   53. Bussy-Rabutin, *Mémoires*, p. 293   54. Visconti, p. 40   55. Maral, *Le Roi-Soleil et Dieu*, p. 237   56. Sévigné, II, 214, to Madame de Grignan, 30 September 1676   57. Petitfils, *La Vallière*, p. 187   58. Bruno Neveu et al., *Les Demoiselles de Saint-Cyr: maison royale d'éducation, 1686-1793*, Versailles, 1999, p. 69   59. Dangeau, XXII, 30, 3 February 1709   60. Saint-Maurice, I, 370, to Duke of Savoy, 6 December 1669   61. Petitfils, *Montespan*, p. 141; Madame de Sévigné frequently refers to Montespan's alarm at the King's affair with Madame de Soubise, and to Soubise's ambition: Sévigné, II, 175, 191, 202, 574, to Grignan, 19 August, 2, 16 September 1676, 19 January 1680   62. Saint-Maurice, I, 169, to Duke of Savoy, 23 December 1667; Lewis, *Assault on Olympus*, pp. 117, 227. Madame de Maintenon made a similar remark in 1713 on the death of 'poor Madame de Soubise': ML, V, 643, Maintenon to Ursins, 10 July 1713   63. Jean-Christian Petitfils, *Lauzun ou l'insolente séduction*, 2008 edn, pp. 50, 52, 57, 59   64. Sourches, I, 49n, 12 November 1681   65. Saint-Maurice, I, 347, to Duke of Savoy, 11 October 1669   66. Magne, *Lettres inédites*, p. 200, Condé to Queen of Poland, 5 August 1665; Petitfils, *Lauzun*, pp. 77-8; Pitts, *Grande Mademoiselle*, p. 179   67. Pierre Clément, *Madame de Montespan et Louis XIV: étude historique*, 1868, p. 144n; Saint-Maurice, I, 209, to Duke of Savoy, 20 July 1668; *DV*, pp. 80-81   68. Petitfils, *La Vallière*, p. 242; Clément, *Montespan*, p. 249, Louis XIV to Colbert, 14 May 1678   69. Petitfils, *La Vallière*, p. 248; Lemoine and Lichtenberger, *De La Vallière à Montespan*, pp. 181-2   70. Saint-Maurice, II, 37, to Duke of Savoy, 20 March 1671; Petitfils, *La Vallière*, pp. 251-2   71. Barthélemy, *Huxelles*, p. 325, Madame de Louvois to Madame d'Huxelles, 29 November 1673   72. Petitfils, *Montespan*, p. 102   73. Marie-Laure de Rochebrune, ed., *La Chine à Versailles: art et diplomatie au XVIIIe siècle*, 2014, pp. 22, 30; a fan leaf with a similar decoration is in the Victoria and Albert Museum, P39-1987   74. Florian Knothe, 'Tapestry as a Medium of Propaganda at the Court of Louis XIV: Display and Audience', in Thomas P. Campbell and Elizabeth A. H. Cleland, eds., *Tapestry in the Baroque: New Aspects of Production and Patronage*, 2010, pp. 342-59   75. Sévigné, II, 246, to Madame de Grignan, 6 November 1676   76. Petitfils, *Louis XIV*, p. 255; Murat, p. 250n   77. Louis XIV, *Mémoires*, p. 271   78. Petitfils, *La Vallière*, p. 121   79. Maral, *Le Roi-Soleil et Dieu*, pp. 70-73, 77-8, 215   80. Ferdinand Belin, *La Société francaise au XVIIe siècle d'après les sermons de Bourdaloue*, Geneva, 1970, pp. 7-8, 17-18 and passim   81. Chevé, p. 409   82. Paul and Marie-Louise Biver, *Abbayes, monastères, couvents de femmes à Paris, des origines à la fin du XVIII siècle*, 1975, passim; Olwen Hufton, *The Prospect before Her: A History of Women in Western Europe*, vol. I, 1995, pp. 382-3. Other orders included Ursulines, Bénédictines Mitigées, Filles de la Conception, Filles Pénitentes du Sauveur, Filles de la Sagesse, Missionaires de la Compagnie de Marie, Soeurs Hospitalières de Saint Alexis de Limoges.   83. Jo Ann Kay McNamara, *Sisters in Arms: Catholic Nuns through Two Millennia*, 1996, p. 485   84. Petitfils, *La Vallière*, pp. 112-13, 257, 268, 271-5   85. J. B. Eriau, *Louise de La Vallière*, 1961, pp. 114, 121   86. Petitfils, *La Vallière*, pp. 294, 301, 305   87. Ibid., pp. 306, 312, 313, 319; Chevé, pp. 462-3   88. Sévigné, II, 80, Sévigné to Madame de Grignan, 29 April 1676   89. Ibid., 555-6, Sévigné to Madame de Grignan, 5 January 1680   90. Petitfils, *La Vallière*, pp. 331-5, 350

Chapter 10: Fighting the Netherlands

1. Saint-Maurice, II, 403, 472, to Duke of Savoy, 2 September 1672, 13 January 1673; Paul Sonnino, *Louis XIV and the Origins of the Dutch War*, Cambridge, 2002 edn, pp. 125-6,

172   2. Rousset, I, 22, quoting Lisola's *Bouclier d'éstat*   3. Saint-Maurice, I, 6, to Duke of Savoy, 29 April 1667   4. Sources, I, 72, 25 October 1683   5. Ibid., IV, 29n, 35, 29 April 1692, 20 May 1692; Dangeau, VI, 62, 12 May 1692; Duc de Noailles, *Histoire de Madame de Maintenon*, 4 vols., 1848–58, IV, 354–6, 391   6. Drévillon, *Impôt du sang*, pp. 15, 277, 297   7. Dina Lanfredini, *Un Antagonista di Luigi XIV: Armand de Gramont, Comte de Guiche*, Florence, 1959, p. 254, Louis XIV to Marie Thérèse, 12 June 1672   8. Rousset, I, 206–10   9. Lewis, *Assault on Olympus*, pp. 220–21   10. Sources, IV, 81n, 24 June 1692   11. Petitfils, *Louis XIV*, p. 360   12. Thierry Sarmant, *La République des médailles: numismates et collections numismatiques à Paris, du Grand Siècle au Siècle des Lumières*, 2003, pp. 97–105; Yvan Loskoutoff, ed., *Les Médailles de Louis XIV et leur livre*, Rouen, 2016, pp. 36, 159, 172 and passim   13. Sonnino, *Origins of the Dutch War*, pp. 60, 67   14. Ragnhild Hatton, ed., *Louis XIV and Europe*, 1976, p. 58; [Jean Le Clerc], *Explication historique des principales médailles frapées pour servir à l'histoire des Provinces-Unies des Pays-Bas*, Amsterdam, 1736 edn, p. 93   15. Rousset, I, 323, 379, 517, 519, 532, Louis XIV, 'Mémoire sur la campagne de 1672'   16. Colbert, VII, 89, Colbert to M. Bouchu, 22 March 1679. The fort is currently under archaeological investigation.   17. Louis XIV, *Mémoires*, pp. 178–9   18. Drévillon, *Impôt du sang*, pp. 68–9; Bertrand Fonck, *Le Maréchal de Luxembourg, et le commandement des armées sous Louis XIV*, Seyssel, 2014, p. 212   19. Jean de Plantavit de La Pause, *Mémoires*, 4 vols., Versailles, 2011–14, I, 60   20. André Corvisier, 'Les Gardes du corps de Louis XIV', in idem, *Les Hommes, la guerre et la mort*, 1985, pp. 119, 122, 127–8, 152; Drévillon, *Impôt du sang*, p. 232; Masson, *Défendre le roi*, p. 192; Louis XIV, *Mémoires*, p. 263   21. Levantal, *Louis XIV*, I, 357, 5 November 1674   22. Pieter de Groot, *Lettres ... à Abraham de Wicquefort*, ed. F. J. I. Krämer, The Hague, 1894, p. 306, March 1671   23. Dangeau, V, 153, 300, 25 January, 17 November 1691; IX, 168, 27 April 1698; Sources, IV, 16, 167, 5 March 1692, 6, 7 March 1693   24. Masson, *Défendre le roi*, pp. 191–3, 349; Dangeau, V, 297, 11 November 1691   25. John Locke, *Travels in France*, ed. John Lough, 1953, pp. 185–6, 254–5, Locke's diary, 1 February 1678, 5 January 1679   26. Saint-Maurice, I, 472, 1 August 1670   27. De Groot, pp. 65, 68, de Groot to Abraham de Wicquefort, 22 January, 5 February 1672   28. Cyril Hughes Hartmann, *The King my Brother*, 1954, pp. 32, 62, 105, 111, Charles II to Madame, 23 August, 17 October 1664   29. Ibid., pp. 243, 270, 284–5; Edward Charles Metzger, *Ralph, First Duke of Montagu, 1638–1709*, Lewiston, NY, 1987, pp. 56–9   30. Hartmann, *The King my Brother*, pp. 147, 195, 281; Haley, *English Diplomat*, pp. 104, 112   31. BS 961 f. 304, Louis XIV to Lionne, 18 April 1667   32. Metzger, pp. 55–6; Hartmann, *The King my Brother*, p. 280   33. Louis XIV, *Oeuvres*, VI, 460, Ruvigny to Louis XIV, 27 February 1676   34. Hartmann, *The King my Brother*, pp. 147, 155, 208   35. Louis XIV, *Oeuvres*, V, 35, Louis XIV to Estrades, 5 August 1661; Metzger, pp. 156, 158   36. Haley, *English Diplomat*, pp. 264–5; Hartmann, *The King my Brother*, p. 295   37. Hartmann, *The King my Brother*, pp. 304–5; Elisabetta Lurgo, *Philippe d'Orléans: frère de Louis XIV*, 2018, p. 123   38. Hartmann, *The King my Brother*, p. 311; Metzger, pp. 65–6   39. James Callow, *King in Exile: James II: Warrior, King and Saint*, 2004, p. 264   40. Haley, *English Diplomat*, pp. 228–30; Hartmann, *The King my Brother*, p. 313   41. Haley, *English Diplomat*, p. 264; cf. Ronald Hutton, 'The Religion of Charles II', in Smuts, *Stuart Court and Europe*, pp. 239, 246   42. Metzger, p. 71; Hartmann, *The King my Brother*, p. 328; Saint-Maurice, II, 451, to Duke of Savoy, 30 June 1670   43. Metzger, pp. 69–71; Bossuet, pp. 165, 168   44. Levantal, *Louis XIV*, I, 303, 23, 27 August 1670; Winifred, Lady Burghclere, *George Villiers, Second Duke of Buckingham, 1628–1687: A Study in the History of the Restoration*, 1903, pp. 221–7; de Groot, p. 49; Saint-Maurice, I, 479, to Duke of Savoy, 22 August 1670   45. Henry and George Savile, *Savile Correspondence: Letters to and from ...*, 1858, p. 34, Henry Savile to Lord Arlington, 29 October 1672   46. The following rhyme was pasted outside her chamber in Whitehall, 'Within this place a bed's appointed / For a French bitch and God's anointed': Bryan Bevan, *Charles II's French Mistress: A Biography of Louise de Kéroualle, Duchess of Portsmouth, 1649–1734*, 1972, p. 72   47. Ibid., p. 42 and passim, Colbert de Croissy to Louvois, 22 October 1671: 'we hope she will so behave that the attachment will be durable and exclude every other'; cf. Maguire, 'Duchess of Portsmouth', pp. 247–73

48. See Catherine MacLeod and Julia Marciari Alexander, eds., *Painted Ladies: Women at the Court of Charles II*, New Haven and London, 2001, pp. 44–5, 136–51; Henri Forneron, *Louise de Kéroualle, Duchesse de Portsmouth*, 1886, passim. **49.** Rosemary Baird, *Mistress of the House: Great Ladies and Grand Houses, 1670–1830*, 2003, p. 71; West Sussex Record Office, Goodwood Mss. 4, Louis XIV to Duchess of Portsmouth, 21 October 1682, 18 February 1683; Duchess of Portsmouth to Louis XIV, 18 September 1682 **50.** O'Connor, *Fürstenberg*, pp. 11, 13, 24, 47, 50, 56, 67 **51.** Saint-Maurice, II, 219, to Duke of Savoy, 6 January 1672 **52.** Louis XIV, *Oeuvres*, V, 430, to Colbert, 4 May 1672 **53.** Saint-Maurice, II, 290, to Duke of Savoy, 15 May 1672 **54.** Ibid., 294, 297, 321, 338, to Duke of Savoy, 21, 23 May, 12, 20 June 1672 **55.** See the map in Luc Panhuysen, *De Ware Vrijheid: de levens van Johan en Cornelis de Witt*, Amsterdam, 2005, p. 416 **56.** Lanfredini, p. 253, Louis XIV to Marie Thérèse, 12 June 1672; Saint-Maurice, II, 404, to Duke of Savoy, 2 September 1672 **57.** Henri and Barbara van der Zee, *William and Mary*, 1973, pp. 69, 71; M. C. Trevelyan, *William III and the Defence of Holland*, 1930, p. 169; Israel, *Dutch Republic*, pp. 796–9 **58.** Olaf van Nimwegen, *The Dutch Army and the Military Revolutions, 1588–1688*, Woodbridge, 2010, p. 441, letter of 23 June 1672 **59.** Rowen, *De Witt, Grand Pensionary*, p. 837 **60.** Trevelyan, p. 176 **61.** M. Pellisson, *Lettres historiques*, 3 vols., 1679, I, 203–10, 25 June–5 July 1672; Jean-Philippe Cénat, *Chamlay: le stratège secret de Louis XIV*, 2011, p. 17; Marquis de Ségur, *Le Maréchal de Luxembourg et le Prince d'Orange, 1668–1678*, 1902, pp. 542–3; Louis XIV, *Oeuvres*, III, 192, 203, Louis XIV to Louvois, 8 June 1672, to Maréchal de Gramont, 15 June 1672 **62.** R. P. M. Rhoen, 'Met 2,000 man informeel op bezoek: de doortocht van Lodewijk XIV door de stad Utrecht in 1671', *Oud Utrecht*, 87, 2014, pp. 24–6; S. C. J. Jessurun-ten Dam, *Utrecht in 1672 en 1673*, Utrecht, 1934, pp. 53, 73, 80–81 **63.** Corvisier, *Louvois*, pp. 258–9; Jean-Philippe Cénat, *Louvois: le double de Louis XIV*, 2015, p. 137 **64.** Trevelyan, pp. 174, 207, Godolphin to Clifford, 28 June 1672 **65.** Rowen, *De Witt, Grand Pensionary*, pp. 850–51; idem, *The Ambassador Prepares for War: The Dutch Embassy of Arnauld de Pomponne*, The Hague, 1957, p. 185, 195, 199; Lynn, *Wars*, p. 115 **66.** Nimwegen, p. 444; Rousset, I, 535 **67.** Zee, p. 72 **68.** Ibid., p. 71 **69.** Trevelyan, p. 235; M. A. M. Franken, *Coenraad van Beuningen's polieteke en diplomatieke aktiviteiten in de jaren 1667–1684*, Groeningen, 1966, p. 266 **70.** Emile Longin, *François de Lisola: sa vie, ses écrits, son testament*, Dole, 1900, p. 161; Corvisier, *Louvois*, p. 201 **71.** Wim Troost, 'To Restore and Preserve the Liberty of Europe: William III's Ideas on Foreign Policy', in David Onnekink and Gijs Rommelse, eds., *Ideology and Foreign Policy in Early Modern Europe (1650–1750)*, Farnham, 2011, pp. 283–303 at pp. 288, 295, 296, William III to Montecuccoli, November 1673, to Waldeck, 1680 **72.** Levantal, *Louis XIV*, I, 329; Louis XIV, *Oeuvres*, III, 251 **73.** Louis XIV, *Mémoires*, p. 184; BS 1290 ff. 11, 19, Louis XIV to Queen Christina, 20 August 1662, to Philip IV, 6 September 1662 **74.** Comisso, p. 272, despatch of Alvise Sagredo, 1666 **75.** Fonck, *Luxembourg*, pp. 105, 111–13, 118, 338 **76.** Corvisier, *Louvois*, p. 262, Louvois to Robert, n.d.; Rousset, II, 499, Louvois to Comte de Calvo, 14 April 1678 **77.** Rowen, *Ambassador*, p. 200 **78.** Jessurun-ten Dam, p. 114, Condé to Louis XIV, 25 April 1673 **79.** La Fare, pp. 75–7 **80.** Rousset, I, 411, Luxembourg to Condé, 7 January 1673; Ségur, *Luxembourg*, pp. 189, 209–11 **81.** Nimwegen, pp. 347, 466, Ginkel to Ginkel, 29 October 1673; Ségur, *Luxembourg*, p. 197; for the prints, see John Landwehr, *Romeyn de Hooghe as Book Illustrator*, Amsterdam, 1970, pp. 29–30 **82.** Herbert H. Rowen, *John de Witt: Statesman of the 'True Freedom'*, Cambridge, 1986, pp. 285–8; Antonin Lefèvre-Pontalis, *Jean de Witt, Grand Pensionnaire de Hollande*, 2 vols., 1884, II, 535–52; Rowen, *De Witt, Grand Pensionary*, pp. 880–82 **83.** In 1678 they left Saint-Germain on 7 February: Levantal, *Louis XIV*, I, 386 **84.** Joël Cornette, *Le Roi de guerre: essai sur la souveraineté dans la France du Grand Siècle*, 2010 edn, p. 243 **85.** Bernard Barbiche, 'La Régence de Marie Thérèse du 23 avril au 31 juillet 1672', in idem, ed., *Pouvoirs, contestations et comportements dans l'Europe moderne*, 2005, pp. 313–26 **86.** Christine Marie Peto, *When France was King of Cartography: The Patronage and Production of Maps in Early Modern France*, Plymouth, 2007, passim; Cénat, *Chamlay*, pp. 34, 37 **87.** Corvisier, *Louvois*, pp. 363–4 **88.** http://www.maastrichtvestingstad.nl/en; Carl J. Ekberg, *The Failure of Louis XIV's Dutch War*,

Chapel Hill, NC, 1979, p. 17 **89.** Louis XIV, *Oeuvres*, III, 375, Mémoires militaires, 1673 **90.** Anna Keay, *The Last Royal Rebel: The Life and Death of James, Duke of Monmouth*, 2016, p. 124 **91.** J. N. P. Watson, *Captain-General and Rebel Chief: The Life of James, Duke of Monmouth*, 1979, pp. 59–64 **92.** Keay, *Royal Rebel*, p. 117; Stephen Saunders Webb, *Lord Churchill's Coup: The Anglo-American Empire and the Glorious Revolution Reconsidered*, New York, 1995, pp. 29–31, 33, 39; Rousset, II, 5n, Lord Lockhart to Louvois, 29 March 1674 **93.** Christian Pfister, *Histoire de Nancy*, 3 vols., 1908, II, 413; III, 209, 211–12 **94.** Ekberg, pp. 95, 102 **95.** Ibid., pp. 35–6 **96.** Georges Bardot, *La Question des dix villes impériales d'Alsace depuis la paix de Westphalie jusqu'aux arrêts de réunion du conseil souverain de Brisach*, 1899, pp. 256–74 **97.** Nimwegen, pp. 458, 465; Ségur, *Luxembourg*, p. 275 **98.** Fonck, *Luxembourg*, p. 324 **99.** O'Connor, pp. 55–9; Ekberg, pp. 27, 29, 30, 34, 39–41, 69 **100.** Onno Klopp, *Der Fall des Hauses Stuart*, 14 vols., Vienna, 1875–88, I, 394, Lisola to Hocher, 3 July 1673; Maria Kroll, *Letters from Liselotte: Elisabeth-Charlotte, Princess Palatine and Duchess of Orléans, 1652–1722*, 1998, p. 211, 31 March 1718 **101.** Dangeau, I, 81, 1 December 1684 **102.** Ekberg, p. 45 **103.** See e.g. Sévigné, II, 142, to Grignan, 8 July 1676 **104.** Colbert, VII, 325, 327n, Louis XIV to Colbert, 26 September, Petit to Colbert, 6 December 1673 **105.** Petitfils, *Montespan*, p. 99; Colbert, VI, 36–7, Louis XIV to Colbert, 18, 22, 28 May, 8, 15 June 1674 **106.** Ekberg, pp. 144, 154, 163–5, Colbert de Croissy to Colbert, 30 March 1673, pp. 168–70 **107.** Rousset, II, 277, Louvois to Courtin, 23 November 1676 **108.** Charles Boutant, *L'Europe au grand tournant des années 1680: la succession palatine*, 1985, pp. 133, 138; Rousset, II, 80–81 **109.** Klaus Malettke, *Les Relations entre la France et le Saint-Empire au XVIIe siècle*, 2001, pp. 345–6; Henri Gillot, *Le Règne de Louis XIV et l'opinion publique en Allemagne*, Nancy, 1914, passim. **110.** Levantal, *Louis XIV*, I, 342, 345, 352–3; François Pernot, *La Franche-Comté espagnole à travers les archives de Simancas*, 2003, pp. 314–17 **111.** Pernot, pp. 320, 339 **112.** Maurice Gresset et al., *Histoire de l'annexion de la Franche-Comté et du Pays de Montbéliard*, Le Coteau, 1988, pp. 269–6, 272, 280–82 **113.** Darryl Dee, *Expansion and Crisis in Louis XIV's France: Franche-Comté and Absolute Monarchy, 1674–1715*, Rochester, NY, 2009, pp. 41, 44, 61 **114.** Pernot, p. 319; Gresset et al., pp. 277–9; Dee, pp. 57, 65 **115.** Dee, pp. 20, 151 **116.** Ibid., pp. 72–3, 82–4 **117.** Malettke, *Relations*, pp. 199–206; idem, 'Complots et conspirations contre Louis XIV dans la seconde moitié du XVIIe siècle', in Yves-Marie Bercé, ed., *Complots et conspirations dans l'Europe moderne*, Rome, 1996, pp. 347–71; Levillain, pp. 241, 247 **118.** Colbert, VI, 481, note of 1 November 1663 **119.** Cornette, *Mort de Louis XIV*, p. 106; Jullian, II, 506–7, 516; Rousset, II, 198–200 **120.** Laurent Coste, *Histoire des maires de Bordeaux*, 2008, pp. 202–7, 210 **121.** Petitfils, *Louis XIV*, pp. 386–7; Lynn, *Wars*, pp. 184–5 **122.** Malettke, *Relations*, p. 204 **123.** Rousset, II, 221–3; Louis XIV, *Oeuvres*, IV, 26; Corvisier, *Louvois*, pp. 198–9; Ségur, *Luxembourg*, pp. 356–7 **124.** Dangeau, XII, 63, 16 April 1699 **125.** Ségur, *Luxembourg*, pp. 439–40; Fonck, *Luxembourg*, p. 387, Louvois to Luxembourg, 13 April 1677 **126.** Visconti, p. 107 **127.** Ekberg, p. 17, Courtin to Condé, 21 May 1673 **128.** Serge Laroche, '1677: le siège victorieux de Valenciennes et la gloire de Louis XIV', in Hervé Coutau-Bégarie, ed., *Les Médias et la guerre*, 2005, pp. 184, 180–88 **129.** Levantal, *Louis XIV*, I, 378–80, 386; Louis Trénard, ed., *Histoire de Cambrai*, Lille, 1983, pp. 151, 153 **130.** Frédéric Barbier, 'L'Entrée royale de Louis XIV à Valenciennes', *Revue du Nord*, 69, 274, 1987, pp. 553–61; René Faille, 'Louis XIV devant Cambrai glorifié par les artistes de son règne', *Revue du Nord*, 58, 230, 1976, pp. 479–505 **131.** Prosper Claeys, *Pages d'histoire locale gantoise*, 3 vols., Ghent, 1885, I, 124; Joseph E. Nève et al., *Gand sous l'occupation de Louis XIV, 1678–1679, 1701–1706, 1708*, Ghent, 1929, pp. 17, 37, 60, 68; Nimwegen, pp. 506–7 **132.** Metzger, p. 154; François Mignet, *Négociations relatives à la succession d'Espagne sous Louis XIV*, 4 vols., 1835–42, IV, 318 **133.** J. A. H. Bots, ed., *The Peace of Nijmegen, 1676–1678/79*, Amsterdam, 1980, passim **134.** Nimwegen, p. 510; Fonck, *Luxembourg*, pp. 142–3, 148; Louis XIV, *Oeuvres*, IV, 171–2, Relation de la campagne de 1678; Ségur, *Luxembourg*, pp. 483, 495–8, 515 **135.** Louis XIV, *Oeuvres*, IV, 144, 146, Relation de la campagne de 1678 **136.** Ekberg, p. 21, Louis XIV to Comte d'Estrées, 30 May 1673, p. 99; Louis XIV, *Oeuvres*, IV, 144, Relation de la campagne de 1678; Rousset, I, 457   137. Faille, 'Louis XIV devant Cambrai', p. 486   138. Louis XIV, *Oeuvres*, III, 503, Colbert to Louis XIV, 26 May 1674; cf. Murat, p. 322, for similar flattery in a letter from Colbert to the King of 4 July 1673, assuring him that his wishes alone would regulate his power   139. Louis XIV, *Oeuvres*, III, 131, 136–40, 152–3 and passim   140. Picavet, *Turenne*, p. 295   141. Cénat, *Chamlay*, pp. 47–50   142. BN Mss. fr. 7891 f. 11, 12v   143. BN Mss. fr. 7892 f. 7, 10, 11v   144. BN Mss. fr. 7893 f. 16, Campagnes du roy en l'an MDCLXXVII   145. BN Mss. fr. 7894 f. 83, Campagnes du roy en l'an MDCLXXVIII   146. Isabelle Richefort, *Adam-François van der Meulen: peintre flamand au service de Louis XIV*, Rennes, 2004, p. 348

Chapter 11: To the Rhine

1. Cf. Sourches, I, 84, 18 March 1684, calling the Rhine 'la borne naturelle entre la France et l'empire'. Richelieu and Mazarin had had similar ambitions: Chevallier, *Louis XIII*, p. 481   2. Rousset, IV, 541, Vauban to Racine, 13 September 1697; Daniel Nordman, *Frontières de France: de l'espace au territoire, XVIe–XIXe siècle*, 1998, pp. 100, 148; cf. Rainer Babel, *Garde et protection. Der Königschutz in der französischen Aussenpolitick vom 15. bis zum 17. Jahrhundert*, Stuttgart, 2014, p. 189   3. Lucien Febvre, *Le Rhin: histoire, mythes et réalités*, 1997, p. 193   4. Michelle Magdelaine, *Guerre et paix en Alsace: les mémoires de voyage du sieur de l'Hermine*, Toulouse, 1981, p. 11   5. Fehrenbach, pp. 294–7, 432   6. André Lebon, ed., *Recueil des instructions données aux ambassadeurs et ministres de France depuis les traités de Westphalie jusqu'à la révolution française*, VII: *Bavière, Palatinat, Deux-Ponts*, 1889, p. 389, Louis XIV to Marquis de Béthune, 1 February 1674   7. Bertrand Jeanmougin, *Louis XIV à la conquête des Pays-Bas espagnols: la guerre oubliée, 1678–1684*, 2005, pp. 42, 47   8. Ibid., pp. 46–8   9. Christian Pfister, ed., *Sarrelouis, 1680–1930: réminiscences*, 1933, pp. 32, 34   10. Anthony F. Upton, *Charles XI and Swedish Absolutism*, 1998, pp. 95–6; Rousset, III, 30   11. Sourches, II, 52, 23 May 1687; Rousset, III, 27, 344, Louvois to Le Peletier, 18 May 1687   12. Jeanmougin, pp. 28, 29, 39, Faultrier to Louvois, 5 April 1680, p. 48, Bissy to Louvois, n.d., pp. 53–5, Abbé d'Orval to Prince de Chimay, 3 May 1681, p. 190   13. René Bour, *Histoire de Metz*, 1978, p. 151; Louis XIV, *Oeuvres*, IV, 191, Relation de la campagne de 1678   14. Magdelaine, p. 46; Georges Livet, ed., *Recueil d'instructions*, XXVIII: *L'Electorat de Trèves*, 1966; Tom Scott, *The City-State in Europe, 1000–1600*, 2012, pp. 213, 224, 228, 239 and passim; Thomas A. Brady Jr, *Turning Swiss: Cities and Empire, 1450–1550*, Cambridge, 1985, pp. 117, 135   15. Arsène Legrelle, *Louis XIV et Strasbourg*, Ghent, 1878, pp. 98, 103, 111; Bernard Vogler, 'Une Alliance manquée: Strasbourg et les XIII cantons, 1555–1789', in *Cinq siècles de relations franco-suisses*, Neuchâtel, 1984, pp. 111–21 at p. 117. The confederation was reluctant to accept Strasbourg, as another Lutheran city would upset its confessional balance.   16. Legrelle, *Louis XIV et Strasbourg*, pp. 117–18; O'Connor, p. 85   17. Sourches, I, 94n, April 1682; Legrelle, *Louis XIV et Strasbourg*, p. 221   18. Legrelle, *Louis XIV et Strasbourg*, p. 180   19. Ibid., p 232   20. Sourches, I, 23n, 1 October 1681; Legrelle, *Louis XIV et Strasbourg*, p. 175   21. Abbé Victor Guerber, *Histoire politique et religieuse de Haguenau*, 2 vols., Marseille, 1978, I, 316–18   22. Legrelle, *Louis XIV et Strasbourg*, p. 194, letter to Leopold I, 29 September 1681; Sourches, I, 23, 1 October 1681; cf. Louis Maurer, *L'Expédition de Strasbourg en septembre 1681: correspondance officielle tirée des archives de la guerre*, 1923, p. 169, magistrates of Strasbourg to Louvois, 30 September 1681   23. Legrelle, *Louis XIV et Strasbourg*, p. 194; Jean Bérenger, 'La Cour de Vienne au lendemain de la chute de Strasbourg', in Georges Livet and Bernard Vogler, eds., *Pouvoir, ville et société en Europe, 1650–1750*, p. 145   24. Legrelle, *Louis XIV et Strasbourg*, pp. 166–7   25. Maurer, p. 132, Louvois to the Marquis de La Frégeolière, 17 September 1681; Sourches, I, 22, 26 September 1681   26. Maurer, p. 164, Montclar to 'MM de Strasbourg', 28 September 1681   27. Legrelle, *Louis XIV et Strasbourg*, pp. 190–91   28. Ibid., p. 196   29. Georges Livet, ed., *Histoire de Strasbourg*, 4 vols., Strasbourg, 1980–82, III, 83–8 and n, 429; Sourches, I, 24–6, 2 October 1681; Legrelle, *Louis XIV et Strasbourg*, pp. 195–9   30. Colbert, VII,

272, Colbert to M. de la Grange, 25 July 1682 **31.** Maurer, p. 185, Louis XIV to Louvois, 2 October 1681 **32.** Sourches, I, 28–9, 8, 10 October 1681 **33.** On a visit to Dunkirk in 1671, he himself helped serve the ladies lunch, standing behind their chairs: de Groot, p. 49, to Wicquefort, February 1671 **34.** Blanchard, p. 115 **35.** Sourches, I, 33, 18 October 1681 **36.** Ibid., 35, 20 October 1681 **37.** O'Connor, pp. 92–3 **38.** Legrelle, *Louis XIV et Strasbourg*, p. 203n, letter of 21 October 1682 **39.** Ibid., pp. 203–5; Sourches, I, 37–9, 44–5, 26 October 1681 **40.** O'Connor, pp. 94–5; Bérenger, 'La Cour de Vienne', p. 145 **41.** Sourches, I, 44–5, 4 November 1681 **42.** Hanna Sonkajärvi, *Qu'est ce qu'un étranger? Frontières et identifications à Strasbourg, 1681–1789*, Strasbourg, 2008, p. 45, mémoire by the Intendant La Grange. **43.** Bernard Vogler, 'Louis XIV et les protestants alsaciens', in Louise Godard de Donville and Roger Duchêne, eds., *De la mort de Colbert à la revocation de l'édit de Nantes: un monde nouveau?*, 1984, pp. 285–91 at p. 288; Simone Herry, *Une Ville en mutation: Strasbourg au tournant du grand siècle*, Strasbourg, 1996, p. 171 **44.** Legrelle, *Louis XIV et Strasbourg*, p. 210, Louvois to Gunzer, 11 December 1681 **45.** Louis Batiffol, *Les Anciennes Républiques alsaciennes*, 1918, p. 252 **46.** Sourches, I, 76, 27 November 1683 **47.** Legrelle, *Louis XIV et Strasbourg*, pp. 211–12 and n, Chamilly to Louvois, 21 November, 23 December 1681 **48.** Maurer, p. 259, Chamilly to Louvois, 14 December 1681 **49.** Sonkajärvi, *Qu'est ce qu'un étranger?*, pp. 84–5 **50.** Legrelle, *Louis XIV et Strasbourg* (1884 edn here), p. 673; Michel Hau, *La Maison de Dietrich, de 1684 à nos jours*, Strasbourg, 1998, pp. 17, 19; Vogler, 'Louis XIV et les protestants alsaciens', p. 288 **51.** Jeanmougin, pp. 13, 58 **52.** Georges Livet, 'Strasbourg, Metz et Luxembourg: contribution à l'étude de la politique extérieure de la France sous Louis XIV', in Raymond Poidevin and Gilbert Trausch, eds., *Les Relations franco-luxembourgeoises, de Louis XIV à Robert Schuman*, Metz, 1978, pp. 1–19 at pp. 7–8, 19, Louis XIV to d'Avaux, 28 October 1683, Louvois to Maréchal d'Humières, 23 November 1683 **53.** Lottin, *'Chronique immémoriale'*, pp. 354–7, 368, Chavatte diary, 27 December 1683, 7 June 1684 **54.** Jeanmougin, pp. 81, 86, Louis XIV to Créquy, 21 March 1682 **55.** Ibid., p. 151, Louvois to Bissy, 25 January 1684; see the letters from Louvois to Vauban in Jacques Dollar, *Vauban à Luxembourg, place forte de l'Europe (1684–1697)*, Luxembourg, 1983, pp. 49–55 **56.** Dollar, pp. 53, 72, Vauban to Louvois, 4, 14 June 1684 **57.** Livet, 'Strasbourg, Metz et Luxembourg', p. 7 **58.** Dollar, pp. 91–4; Nicolas Boileau and Jean Racine, *Lettres d'une amitié: correspondence, 1687–1698*, pp. 19, 24, 91, 92, Racine to Boileau, 24 May 1687, 94 **59.** Paul Margue, 'Assujettis ou sujets? Les luxembourgeois sous Louis XIV', in Poidevin and Trausch, pp. 21–38 **60.** Cénat, *Louvois*, pp. 354–55; Blanchard, pp. 116, 131–3, 153, 189, 245–7, 433–7 **61.** Blanchard, pp. 199–201, 210, 315, 328, 332 **62.** Ibid., p. 353 **63.** Jean Glad, *Maubeuge, place de guerre, sa zone d'influence*, 2007, passim; Airey Neave, *The Flames of Calais: A Soldier's Battle*, 1940, 1972, pp. 72–3, 140, 146; cf. Bernard Crochet, *Vauban et son heritage: guide des forteresses à visiter*, Rennes, 2017, passim; and J. E. and H. W. Kaufmann, *Fortress France: The Maginot Line and French Defenses in World War II*, Westport, CT, 2006, p. 88 **64.** Dollar, p. 72 **65.** Colbert, V, 346, Louis XIV to Colbert, 8 April, 23 May 1677; Murat, p. 384, Louis XIV to Colbert, 2 August 1680 **66.** Colbert, V, xxxviii–xxxix, 382, Colbert to Louis XIV, 1 March 1678, Louis XIV to Colbert, 10 March 1678 **67.** Sarmant, *Demeures du soleil*, p. 104, Louvois to Lefèvre, 16 September 1683 **68.** *DV*, p. 135; Colbert, V, 571, mémoire of 1690, lists total expenses on Versailles in 1664–90 as 81,151,414 livres, or 87,537,989 if purchases of silver, medals and agates are included. The Machine de Marly cost 3,674,864; the works on the River Eure and Maintenon, without including related property purchases, 8,612,995. **69.** Stéphane Castelluccio, *Les Fastes de la Galerie des Glaces: recueil d'articles du Mercure Galant (1681–1773)*, 2007, pp. 100, 103, 104n **70.** Christina Strunck and Elisabeth Kieven, eds., *Europäische Galeriebauten: Galleries in a Comparative European Perspective (1400–1800)*, Munich, 2010, passim **71.** Thomas Kirchner, *Le Héros épique: peinture d'histoire et politique artistique dans la France du XVIIe siècle*, 2008, pp. 302, 452; *DV*, p. 336 **72.** Burchard, passim; Christine Albanel et al., *The Hall of Mirrors: History and Restoration*, Dijon, 2007, pp. 197–207 **73.** *DV*, p. 225 **74.** Mathieu da Vinha, *Le Versailles de Louis XIV*, 2012 edn, pp. 23–4. Saint-Simon and his wife, for example, in addition to owning an *hôtel* in the town, used the apartment of his brother-in-law the Duc de Lorges on the first floor of the Aile du Nord, until they acquired their own: Georges Poisson, *Monsieur de Saint-Simon*, 1987 edn, p. 152 **75.** Gady, *Hardouin-Mansart*, pp. 171–2, 246–56 **76.** Colbert, VII, clv, d'Ormoy to Colbert, 12 February 1682, clvii, clx–clxii, Colbert to d'Ormoy, 13, 25 March, 11 April 1682 **77.** Sourches, I, 101, 6 May 1682 **78.** Sabatier, pp. 194–9; Levantal, *Louis XIV*, II, 447–50, June–July 1683, 462, May 1684, 499–500, May 1687 **79.** Jean Chagniot, *Paris et l'armée au XVIIIe siècle*, 1985, pp. 48–9, 373; Emile Magne, *Images de Paris sous Louis XIV: d'après des document inédits*, 1939, pp. 116, 123, for the example of the Duc de Créquy, Premier Gentilhomme de la Chambre and Governor of Paris from 1676 to 1687, with houses in Paris, Versailles, Saint-Germain and Fontainebleau; Laurent Lemarchand, *Paris ou Versailles? La monarchie absolue entre deux capitales (1715–1723)*, 2014, p. 101 **80.** Perez, p. 546 **81.** Lough, pp. 322–3, quoting Martin Lister; Vincent, p. 129 **82.** Matthieu Lahaye, *Le Fils de Louis XIV: Monseigneur le Grand Dauphin (1661–1711)*, 2013, p. 365; cf. Saint-Germain, *Louis XIV secret*, pp. 264–82 **83.** Sarmant, *Louis XIV et Paris*, passim. **84.** Martin Lister, *A Journey to Paris in the Year 1698*, 1699, pp. 7, 17, 218 **85.** Sourches, I, 101, 6 May 1682; cf. Mazarin, *Lettres*, VII, 95, Mazarin to Gravel, 8 August 1657 **86.** Rodolphe Reuss, ed., *Correspondances politiques et chroniques parisiennes adressées à Christophe Güntzer, xyndic royal de la ville de Strasbourg (1681–1685)*, 1890, p. 9, 24 March 1682 **87.** Ibid., p. 19, 6 August 1682 **88.** Sourches, I, 132–3, 5, 6, August 1682; Lucy Norton, *First Lady of Versailles*, 1978, pp. 77–80; Vallot, pp. 388–94, Remarques sur l'année 1682 **89.** Jeanmougin, pp. 23–4, Mémoire by Le Peletier de Souzy, 1680; ibid., p. 95, La Vauguyon to Louis XIV, 19 August 1682 **90.** See Bernard Chevallier et al., *Saint-Cloud: le palais retrouvé*, 2013, for a full description; and Paul Micio, *Les Collections de Monsieur, frère de Louis XIV*, 2014. Monsieur also had his own Trianon at Saint-Cloud, now the International Bureau of Weights and Measures. **91.** Barker, pp. 81–3; Dangeau, IX, 29, 5 August 1695. The King used Monsieur as a source of Paris news; cf. Sévigné, I, 477, Sévigné to Grignan, 12 February 1672, for the King's remark 'Eh bien, mon frère, que dit on à Paris?' **92.** Robert Oresko, 'Homosexuality and the Court Elites of Early Modern France: Some Problems, Some Suggestions and an Example', *Journal of Homosexuality*, 16, 1988, pp. 105–28. In 1683 Monsieur's household numbered 892, compared to 620 in the Queen's: *DV*, p. 453 **93.** Maurice Lever, *Les Bûchers de Sodome*, 1985, pp. 191–2, 213–16 **94.** Jeffrey Merrick and Bryant T. Ragan Jr, *Homosexuality in Early Modern France: A Documentary Collection*, New York, 2001, pp. 43–59, reports to d'Argenson, Lieutenant Général de Police, 1702–15 **95.** Georges Minois, *Histoire de l'athéisme*, 1998, pp. 189, 333 **96.** Sourches, I, 110n, 111–12, June 1682; Jérôme de La Gorce, *Jean-Baptiste Lully*, 2002, pp. 307–9 **97.** Ezechiel Spanheim, *Relation de la cour de France en 1690*, 1882, p. 93; Sourches, I, 112, 152, June, 16 October 1682 **98.** Sourches, I, 111–12, 118n, June 1682 **99.** Saint-Simon, *Mémoires*, ed. Yves Coirault, 2 vols., 1990–94, I, 75 **100.** Cosnac, I, 359; *DL*, p. 1324 **101.** Saint-Simon, *Mémoires*, ed. Coirault, I, 72 **102.** Dirk Van der Cruysse, *Madame Palatine: Princesse européenne*, 1988, p. 176, Madame to Sophie, 7 March 1696 **103.** Louis XIV, *Oeuvres*, V, 461, Monsieur to Colbert, 2 February 1670 **104.** *DL*, pp. 1062–4; Sourches, I, 118n, June 1682 **105.** Sourches, I, 267, 12 July 1685; Sarmant, *Louis XIV: homme et roi*, pp. 410–11

Chapter 12: The King Outdoors

1. Vinha, *Valets*, p. 262 **2.** Vinha, *Versailles*, p. 28 **3.** Jane Ridley, *Fox Hunting*, 1990, pp. 101–2, 114; John Robert Christianson, 'The Hunt of Frederik II of Denmark: Structures and Rituals', *The Court Historian*, 18, 2, December 2013, pp. 165–87 **4.** Robert de Salnove, *La Vénerie royale*, 1665, Dédicace (unpaginated), and p. 1 **5.** Baron Dunoyer de Noirmont, *Histoire de la chasse en France depuis les temps les plus reculés jusqu'à la révolution*, 3 vols., 1868, II, 31–3 **6.** BSG 2015 f. 105, Louis XIV to Condé, 18 August 1668; Arsenal Mss. 3568 f. 256, Louis XIV to Duc de Tresmes, 20 October 1662 **7.** BS 960 f. 305, Louis XIV to Charles II, 27 April 1664 **8.** Ibid., 31, 57, 88 **9.** Magne, *Lettres inédites*, pp. 221,

223, Enghien to Queen of Poland, 30 October, 5 November 1665 10. William R. Newton, *Les Chevaux et les chiens du roi à Versailles au XVIIIe siècle: le grande et la petite écurie, les écuries de la reine, le grand chenil et la louveterie*, 2015, pp. 588–9; *FD*, p. 35; Dangeau, XXII, 113; XXVII, 11, 111, 11–17 January 1714 11. Newton, *Chevaux*, pp. 629, 641–7 12. Vincent Maroteaux and Jacques de Givry, *Versailles: le grand parc*, 2004, p. 54; Vincent Maroteaux, *Versailles: le roi et son domaine*, 2000, pp. 14, 17, 96 13. Faugère, p. 381, 'journal de deux jeunes hollandais', 28 December 1657 14. Duc de Saint-Simon, *Mémoires*, ed. M. Regnier and A. Chéruel, 20 vols., 1873–7, XII, 178 15. Philippe Salvadori, *La Chasse sous l'ancien régime*, 1996, pp. 202–3, 209 16. Dangeau, I, 199, 8 September 1685, III, 33, 37, 5, 19 March 1688 17. Saint-Germain, *Louis XIV secret*, p. 153. Other monarchs, such as Charles II and William III, also organized mass transport of mature trees, sometimes across the Channel: Todd Longstaffe-Gowan, *The Gardens and Parks at Hampton Court Palace*, 2005, p. 67 18. Dominique Garrigues, *Jardins et jardiniers de Versailles au Grand Siècle*, 2001, pp. 133, 135, 151–2, 284, 287; Dangeau, VIII, 190, 27 January 1695; cf. Colbert, V, 419, Colbert to Le Blanc, 6 September 1681, order for 10,000 elms from Normandy 19. Tiberghien, p. 25 20. Sourches, I, 446, 13 October 1686; Dirk Van der Cruysse, *Madame Palatine: lettres françaises*, 1989, p. 78, Madame to Duchesse de Mecklembourg, 23 January 1688 21. Reuss, p. 30, 24 October 1682 22. Dangeau, XXVI, 24, 26 January 1713, XXVII, 83, 237, 4 April, 13 September 1714; Saint-Germain, *Louis XIV secret*, p. 170 23. Hélène Delalex, *La Galerie des Carrosses: Château de Versailles*, 2016, p. 25; Dunoyer de Noirmont, I, 205; Saint-Germain, *Louis XIV secret*, p. 151 24. Dangeau, XIX, 59, 16 March 1706 25. Ibid., XVI, 73, 27 March 1703; cf. Daniel Roche et al., eds., *À Cheval! Ecuyers, amazones et cavaliers du XIVe au XXIe siècle*, 2007, pp. 126–9; Lahaye, p. 270 26. Louis XV, *Correspondance de . . . et du Maréchal de Noailles*, 2 vols., 1865, II, 204, Noailles to Louis XV, Aranjuez, 20 April 1746 27. Newton, *Chevaux*, p. 591; Dunoyer de Noirmont, I, 211–13; Ernest Jaeglé, ed., *Correspondance de Madame, Duchesse d'Orleans*, 3 vols., 1890 edn, II, 190, Madame to Electress Sophia, 16 December 1712 28. Dangeau, XII, 128, XXI, 158, 8 August 1708 29. Arsenal Mss. 3568 f. 256, Louis XIV to MM. de Bouteron, de Tillières, de la Haye, 11 August 1662 30. Jaeglé, I, 249, Madame to Raugravine Louise, 13 October 1701; Kroll, p. 73, Madame to Electress Sophia, 30 May 1694 31. *De chasse et d'épée: le décor de l'appartment du roi a Marly, 1683–1750*, exh. cat., 1999, passim 32. William R. Newton, *La Petite Cour: services et serviteurs à la cour de Versailles au XVIIIe siècle*, 2006, pp. 90–99; I am grateful to Katharine MacDonogh for additional information on royal dogs; Duindam, p. 235 33. Some of his guns and pistols are now in the Wallace Collection, London, and the Musee de l'Armée, Paris, engraved with crowns and hunting scenes. 34. Dangeau, XVII, 140, 5 June; James Christie Whyte, *History of the British Turf*, 2 vols., 1840, I, 89, 84; see e.g. Etienne Gallois, ed., *Lettres inédites des Feuquières*, 5 vols., 1845–6, II, 315, Charles XI of Sweden to Louis XIV, thanking him for a present of horses, 10 December 1673; M. de Gourville, *Mémoires*, 2 vols., 1894–5, II, 129 for Hanover; Henri Lemoine, 'Les Ecuries du roi sous l'ancien régime', *Revue de l'Histoire de Versailles*, 35, 1933, pp. 150–83 at p. 163. Most French royal horse furniture was destroyed in the revolution. 35. Daniel Roche, *Connaissances et passions: histoire de la culture équestre en France*, 2015, 258; idem, ed., *Les Ecuries royales du XVIe au XVIIIe siècle*, Versailles, 1998, pp. 49–51 36. Reuss, p. 47, 27 February 1683 37. Thomas Nugent, *The Grand Tour*, 4 vols., 1756 edn, IV, 114 38. Daniel Roche, ed., *Le Cheval et la guerre*, 2002, p. 133 39. Vicomte de Carné, *Les Pages des écuries du roi*, Nantes, 1886, p. 103 40. Chevallier, *Louis XIII*, pp. 444–5, 447 41. Patrick Daguenet, *L'Aurore du Roi-Soleil: 1661, le grand séjour de Louis XIV à Fontainebleau*, Fontainebleau, 2016, p. 148. Perhaps part of the journey was by coach. 42. Arsenal Mss. 3568 f. 92, Louis XIV to Beringhen, 19 August 1661 43. Lemoine, pp. 150, 152, 183; Newton, *Chevaux*, pp. 97, 113 44. Jonathan Spangler, *The Society of Princes: The Lorraine-Guise and the Conservation of Wealth and Power in Seventeenth-Century France*, Farnham, 2009, pp. 104, 118 45. Roche, *Ecuries*, pp. 27, 29, 30, 63–4, 66, 69, 74, 88, 90–91; Newton, *Chevaux*, pp. 147, 182 46. Louis XIV, *Mémoires*, p. 227 47. Roche, *Ecuries*, p. 84 48. Richard Creed, *Journal of the Grand Tour to Rome with the Fifth Earl of Exeter, 1699–1700*, Oundle, 2002,

p. 7, 22 October 1699 **49**. Levron, *Ville royale*, p. 123; Nugent, IV, 113 **50**. Sourches, IV, 277n, 22 October 1693; cf. Dangeau, IV, 150, 17 November 1690, V, 295, 7 November 1691, VIII, 258, 18 June 1695 **51**. Dangeau, I, 24, 29, 13, 30 June 1684, IX, 80, 4, 5 November 1695 **52**. Sévigné, I, 234, to Madame de Grignan, 24 April 1671 **53**. Dangeau, XIV, 47, 26 February 1701; cf. for similar occasions ibid., IX, 132, 8, 9 February 1696, XI, 37, 6 March 1698 **54**. Ibid., XVII, 309, 20 December 1704 **55**. Garrigues, pp. 89, 92; *Sciences et curiosités à la cour de Versailles*, exh. cat., 2010, pp. 76–86 **56**. *Sciences et curiosités*, pp. 108–19; Timothée Chevalier, *Manières de montrer Versailles: guides, promenades et relations sous le règne de Louis XIV*, 2013, p. 240, quoting *Mercure Galant*, September 1686; Tallents, p. 161, 8 December 1672 **57**. Dessert, *La Royale*, p. 81 **58**. Garrigues, pp. 202–4, 281; Chevalier, p. 239 **59**. Nicolas Jacquet, *Secrets et curiosités des jardins de Versailles: les bosquets, le domaine de Trianon, le grand parc*, 2013, p. 82; J. Fennebresque, *Versailles royal*, 1910, pp. 15, 34 **60**. Ségur, *Luxembourg*, p. 346, Luxembourg to Louvois, 1 May 1677 **61**. Garrigues, pp. 119, 223, 284, 354, 357; *Sciences et curiosités*, pp. 135–8; Jean de La Quintinie, *Instruction pour les jardins fruitiers et potagers avec un traité des orangers, suivi de quelques réflexions sur l'agriculture*, 2 vols, 1690, I, p. 3; cf. Stéphanie de Courtois, *Le Potager du Roy*, 2003, passim. John Evelyn's last publication was an English translation of La Quintinie in 1693. **62**. Martin Lister, *Travels in France*, 1809 edn, pp. 64, 67 **63**. Saint-Germain, *Louis XIV secret*, p. 97 **64**. Alexandre Maral, *Parcours mythologiques dans les jardins de Versailles*, 2012, p. 22. There are now 381 sculptures in the park and 780 'éléments sculptés' on the façade. Personal communication, Maxime Blin **65**. Jacquet, p. 53. Copies now replace the originals, which are in the Louvre. **66**. Alexandre Maral, *La Grande Commande de 1674: chefs d'oeuvre sculptés des Jardins de Versailles sous Louis XIV*, 2013, p. 9; idem, *Le Versailles de Louis XIV: un palais pour la sculpture*, Dijon, 2013, passim **67**. Alexandre Maral, *François Girardon: le sculpteur de Louis XIV*, 2015, pp. 11–12, 158, 167, 170; Castelluccio, *Fastes*, p. 103, 'parmi ces modernes nous en avons de beaucoup plus belles qu cette venus', *Mercure Galant*, August 1684 **68**. Maral, *Girardon*, pp. 114, 163–9; Jacquet, p. 60 and passim **69**. Colbert, V, 334, Colbert to Nicolas Arnoul, 16 September, 6 December 1672; Jacquet, p. 60 **70**. Jacquet, p. 29 **71**. Sourches, I, 78n, February 1682 **72**. William R. Newton, *Versailles, côté jardins: splendeurs et misères, de Louis XIV à la révolution*, 2013, pp. 53–68; Albert Mousset, *Les Francine: créateurs des eaux de Versailles, intendants des eaux et fontaines de France de 1623 à 1784*, 1930, pp. 80–88 **73**. Dangeau, I, 56, 19 October 1684; Sourches, I, 211, 24 April 1685; Sarmant, *Demeures du soleil*, pp. 141–7, 179; Chevalier, p. 311; Tiberghien, pp. 123–4 **74**. AN 261 AP 16; cf. for other criticisms from officials, Cénat, *Louvois*, pp. 336–40; Rousset, III, 414, mémoire by Chamlay **75**. The drainage and water systems are well explained in David Gaussen, *L'Île de France au temps de Louis XIV, 1661–1715*, 2005, pp. 58–65 **76**. Jacquet, p. 71 **77**. DeJean, pp. 110–11 **78**. Jérémie Benoît, *Le Grand Trianon: un palais privé à l'ombre de Versailles, de Louis XIV à Napoléon et de Louis-Philippe au général de Gaulle*, La Thuile, 2009, p. 35 **79**. Murat, p. 170, Louis XIV to Colbert, 19 May 1670 **80**. Moine, p. 200 **81**. Saint-Simon, *Mémoires*, ed. Regnier and Chéruel, VII, 287 **82**. Newton, *Versailles, côté jardins*, pp. 154–6; Benoît, *Grand Trianon*, p. 53 and passim; Philippe Beaussant, *Louis XIV artiste*, 1999, pp. 169–71; cf. Robert W. Berger, *A Royal Passion: Louis XIV as Patron of Architecture*, Cambridge, 1994 **83**. Elizabeth Hyde, *Cultivated Power: Flowers, Culture and Politics in the Reign of Louis XIV*, Philadelphia, 2005, pp. x, 137, 191, 194 **84**. See BN Mss. fr. 6995, Donnedieu de Vissé, Histoire de Louis le grand contenu dans les rapports qui se trouvent entre ses actions et les qualités et vertus des Fleurs et des Plantes **85**. Hyde, pp. 176, 180, 195 **86**. Colbert, III, part 1, 303, Colbert to Arnoul, 5 September 1670, 319; or V, 324n; Cénat, *Louvois*, pp. 336–40 **87**. Garrigues, pp. 235, 237; Benoît, *Grand Trianon*, p. 39 **88**. *Fleurs du roi: peintures, vélins et parchemins*, exh. cat., 2013, p. 72; Garrigues, p. 233; Jacquet, p. 111 **89**. Benoît, *Grand Trianon*, p. 40, quoting the Duc de Saint-Aignan in 1677 **90**. Pierre-André Lablaude, *Les Jardins de Versailles*, 1995, pp. 104, 149–54, 159; ML, I, 687, Maintenon to Comte de Jussac, 8 August 1689 **91**. J. C. Nemeitz, *Séjour de Paris*, 2 vols., Leyden, 1727, II, 507 **92**. Garrigues, pp. 290, 355 **93**. Louis XIV, *Oeuvres*, IV, 424, Louis XIV to Dauphin, 28 June 1694

94. Camille Piton, *Marly-le roi: son histoire*, 1904, p. 75n   95. Stéphane Castelluccio, *Marly: art de vivre et pouvoir, de Louis XIV à Louis XVI*, Montreuil, 2014, passim; Piton, p. 193   96. Raphaël Morera, 'Amener les eaux: entre techniques, sciences et politiques', in *Sciences et curiosités*, pp. 87–93   97. Castelluccio, *Marly*, pp. 103–5, 107, 110   98. Félibien, *Fêtes de Versailles*, pp. 76–7   99. Marquis de Torcy, *Journal inédit pendant les années 1709, 1710 et 1711*, 1884, p. x, Colbert de Croissy to Torcy, 1684   100. Leonhard Horowski, *Die Belagerung des Thrones: Machtstrukturen und Karrieremechanismen am Hof von Frankreich, 1661–1789*, Ostfildern, 2013, pp. 79 and n., 97, 134–40; Saint-Simon, *Mémoires*, ed. Regnard and Chéruel, V, 328, 334   101. Jay M. Smith, *The Culture of Merit: Nobility, Royal Service and the Making of Absolute Monarchy in France, 1600–1789*, Ann Arbor, 1996, pp. 138–9; Robert Descimon and Elie Haddad, eds., *Epreuves de noblesse: les expériences nobiliaires de la haute robe parisienne (XVIe–XVIIIe siècle)*, 2010, pp. 312–13, 331   102. Maral, *Versailles*, pp. 284–5   103. Gérard Mabille et al., *Vues des Jardins de Marly: le roi jardinier*, Montreuil, 2011, passim and plates 11, 15.   104. Ibid., plates 28, 29, 30, 31, 32   105. Dangeau, XVIII, 82, 109, 54, 105, 1703; Mabille et al., plates 7, 10, 13, 14, 15, 47, 49; Maroteaux, *Marly*, p. 166   106. Castelluccio, *Marly*, p. 79; cf. Jaeglé, I, 271, Madame to Raugravine Louise, 9 August 1702   107. N. Japikse, ed., *Correspondentie van Willem III en van Hans Willem Bentinck, eersten Graf van Portland*, 3 vols., The Hague, 1927–37, I, 240, 300, 326, Portland to William III, 1 March, 4, 28 May 1698; cf. Patricia Bouchenot-Dechin and Georges Farhat, *André Le Nôtre en perspectives*, 2013, p. 300   108. Gwenola Firmin, 'La Première Ambassade ottomane, 1721', in Daniëlle Kisluk-Grosheide and Bertrand Rondot, eds., *Visiteurs de Versailles: voyageurs, princes, ambassadeurs, 1682–1789*, 2017, pp. 174–83 at p. 182; Maroteaux, *Marly*, pp. 35–7   109. Sourches, I, 425, 14 July 1686   110. Jaeglé, II, 31, Madame to Electress Sophia, 2 August 1705; *Divertissements à Marly au temps de Louis XIV, 1686–1715*, exh. cat., Marly, 1990, passim; Saint-Simon, *Mémoires*, ed. Regnier and Chéruel, V, 327   111. Dangeau, XII, 179, 3 November 1699; cf. XI, 91, 109, 12 June, 17 July 1698   112. Torcy, *Journal*, p. 234, 30 July 1710; Spanheim, pp. 91, 96   113. Jaeglé, I, 119, Madame to Electress Sophia, 4 December 1695   114. Saint-Simon, *Mémoires*, ed. Regnier and Chéruel, III, 31; Dangeau, XIV, 124–7, 9 June 1701   115. Dangeau, XI, 200, XII, 24–6, 27 December 1698, 5 February 1699   116. Dangeau, XIII, 9, 18, 31, 7, 21, 22 January, 18 February 1700, XVI, 38, 14 February 1703, XIX, 36, 13 February 1706, XXI, 17, 19 January 1708; Castelluccio, *Marly*, p. 105   117. Dangeau, XVI, 41, 20 February 1703; Castulluccio, *Marly*, p. 122   118. Dangeau, XII, 176, 29 October 1699   119. Ibid., XV, 274, 2 November 1702   120. Ibid., XII, 182, 8 November 1699   121. Ibid., XXIII, 253, 4 December 1710   122. *DL*, p. 1146   123. Dangeau, VII, 106, 9 July 1693   124. Ibid., II, 231, 1 December 1687   125. Dangeau, XII, 114, 15 July 1699   126. Sourches, IX, 222n, 18 April 1705   127. Piton, p. 199; Dangeau, XXIV, 9, 7 January 1711   128. Nemeitz, II, 502; Masson, *Défendre le roi*, pp. 109–10   129. Dangeau, XV, 117, 2 June 1705   130. Ibid., I, 133, 13 April 1685   131. Ibid., XVII, 284, 16 November 1704; Robert W. Berger, 'Tourists during the Reign of the Sun King: Access to the Louvre and Versailles and the Anatomy of Guidebooks and Other Printed Aids', in George Mauner, ed., *Paris: Center of Artistic Enlightenment*, University Park, PA, 1988, p. 129   132. Chevalier, p. 149; Berger, 'Tourists', p. 131; Elisabeth Maisonnier, 'Les Guides de Versailles à l'usage du visiteur', in Danielle Kisluk-Grosheide and Bernard Rondot, eds., *Visiteurs de Versailles: voyageurs, princes, ambassadeurs, 1682–1789*, 2017, pp. 38–47   133. Robert W. Berger and Thomas Hedin, *Diplomatic Tours in the Gardens of Versailles under Louis XIV*, 2008, p. 17; cf. Marion E. Grew, *William Bentinck and William III*, 1924, p. 339, Portland to William III, 4 May 1698   134. Chevalier, pp. 278, 280   135. Hendrik Ziegler, '"His house at Versailles is something the foolishest in the world": la grande galerie de Versailles à travers les récits de voyageurs et d'ambassadeurs étrangers autour de 1700', in Strunck and Kieven, pp. 351–82 at pp. 353, 360, 363–4   136. Anon., *Description des châteaux et parcs de Versailles, de Trianon et de Marly*, 2 vols., Amsterdam, 1715.   137. Garrigues, p. 257; cf. Chevalier, pp. 125 (Madeleine de Scudéry, 1669), 162 (Félibien, 1674), 261 (Charles Perrault, 1687)   138. Helen Jacobsen, 'Les Ambassadeurs européens à Versailles', in Kisluk-Grosheide and Rondot, pp. 114–23 at p. 119; cf. Gordon Higgott, 'Thomas Povey's

Description of Versailles in the Spring of 1682', in *Colloque Jules Hardouin-Mansart*, forth-coming, pp. 251–61, for another admiring English account, calling Versailles and its gardens 'magnificent' and 'wonderful': 'the Grand Apartment is indeed Glorious; being burnish'd, and furnish'd to the hight of Art and Expense. The throne, Chairs, Frames, Vases, and other Vessels, are of Massy Silver' (p. 256) **139.** Lister, p. 207; Daniëlle Kisluk-Grosheide and Bertrand Rondot, 'Versailles et ses visiteurs', in Kisluk-Grosheide and Rondot, pp. 14–35 at p. 24 **140.** John Northleigh, 'Travels through France ... 1702', in John Harris, ed., *A Complete Collection of Voyages and Travels*, 2 vols., 1748 edn, p. 733 **141.** Veryard, p. 68 **142.** Nugent, IV, 113, 118, 123; cf. Duindam, p. 292. **143.** Félibien, *Fêtes de Versailles*, p. 58; Georgia J. Cowart, *The Triumph of Pleasure: Louis XIV and the Politics of Spectacle*, Chicago, 2008, p. 127 **144.** Plantavit de La Pause, III, 112–13 **145.** Mathieu Marais, *Journal de Paris*, 2 vols., Saint-Etienne, 2004, II, 320, 31 July 1722 **146.** Maral, *Versailles*, pp. 70, 228, 233, 246; cf. Alexandre Maral and Nicolas Milovanovic, eds., *Versailles et l'antique*, passim, and M. Combes, *Explication historique de ce qu'il y a de plus remarquable dans la maison royale de Versailles*, 1695 edn, 1681, p. 141, comparing it to ancient and modern Rome **147.** Jean-Luc Martinez et al., eds., *Les Antiques du Louvre*, 2004, pp. 50, 59, 61–2, 67; cf. André Félibien, *Statues et bustes antiques des maisons royales*, 1679, pas-sim **148.** Maral, *Girardon*, pp. 158, 167, 170, 175 **149.** Petitfils, *Louis XIV*, p. 426 **150.** Chevalier, p. 196 **151.** Ibid., pp. 195–6. For Guillet de Saint-Georges in 1693 Louis XIV was the greatest hero of all time, whereas Alexander was only the greatest hero of antiquity. See Kirchner, p. 298 **152.** Beaussant, *Louis XIV artiste*, p. 90; *DV*, p. 219; *DL*, p. 323; Sarmant, *Demeures du soleil*, p. 60 **153.** *DV*, p. 719, *Mercure Galant*, December 1682

Chapter 13: Inside Versailles

1. Molière, *Oeuvres complètes*, 2 vols., 2010, I, 516; Beaussant, *Louis XIV artiste*, pp. 134, 139   2. Quoted in Nicolas Le Roux, 'La Cour dans l'espace du palais: l'exemple de Henri III', in Marie-France Auzépy and Joël Cornette, eds., *Palais et pouvoir: de Constantinople à Versailles*, 2003, pp. 229–67 at p. 246   3. Dubois, *Moi*, pp. 110–11   4. Vinha, *Valets*, p. 46; Petitfils, *Lauzun*, p. 131   5. Vallot, pp. 92, 101, 1665, 1669. He also swam in rivers in hot weather.   6. Chatenet, *Cour de France*, p. 113; Saint-Simon, *Mémoires*, ed. Regnier and Chéruel, VI, 213, XII, 22; Duindam, p. 213; *DL*, pp. 764–6   7. For a recent description, see Béatrix Saule, *Versailles triomphant: une journée de Louis XIV*, 1996, pp. 32–45, 180–83; Vinha, *Valets*, p. 55; Duindam, pp. 212–13; Solnon, pp. 321–6   8. Sourches, IV, 234, 257, 1 August 1693, 10, 11, 12 September 1693   9. Locke, pp. 18, 61, 251, 254, 28 December 1678, 5 January 1679; cf. Dubois, *Moi*, p. 110, 'Nul si osé d'être debout, ni de causer ni de faire aucun bruit'   10. Dangeau, XVI, 159, 3 July 1703; Sourches, VIII, 88, 378, 18 May 1703, 30 April 1712   11. Spanheim, pp. 146–7; Vinha, *Valets*, p. 50   12. Solnon, p. 141; Chevallier, *Henri III*, p. 263; Knecht, pp. 33, 68   13. Louis XIV, *Mémoires*, p. 169   14. Visconti, pp. 50, 191; Duindam, pp. 205, 208   15. Jean Boutier, 'Les Visiteurs italiens du Roi-Soleil', in Caroline zum Kolk et al., eds., *Voyageurs étrangers à la cour de France*, Rennes, 2014, pp. 91–113 at p. 105   16. Beaussant, *Plaisirs de Versailles*, p. 120   17. Saint-Simon, *Mémoires*, ed. Regnier and Chéruel, VII, 317; cf. Saint-Maurice, I, 188, to Duke of Savoy, 25 March 1668, for Turenne battling his way through crowds for a quarter of an hour at the baptism of the Dauphin; Visconti, p. 50, for cardinals 'maintes fois heurtés dans la foule' in 1674; Sourches, I, 9, 14 February 1682, for a fight in the state apartment between a courtier and a Swiss guard; and Baron de Breteuil, *Mémoires de cour*, 2009, p. 134, for disorder in 1715   18. Spanheim, pp. 145–8, gives a full account of the *lever*; cf. Abbé de Choisy, *Mémoires pour servir à l'histoire de Louis XIV*, 1983, p. 215; Saint-Simon, *Mémoires*, ed. Regnier and Chéruel, III, 227–8   19. Visconti, p. 61; Saint-Simon, *Mémoires*, ed. Regnier and Chéruel, IX, 100–104; cf. a letter of 1658 by Président Rose describing the King's long conversations in this posture in *The Court Historian*, 7, 2, December 2002, p. 200; and Dubois, *Moi*, pp. 110, 133   20. *DL*, p. 258; *DV*, pp. 88–9; Kroll, p. 120, Madame to Sophie, 23 July 1702; cf. Perez, pp. 271–4; Lough, p. 145, John Locke on the stinking

staircase at Fontainebleau, 14 September 1677; William R. Newton, *Derrière la façade: vivre au château de Versailles au XVIIIe siècle* 2008, pp. 87, 97, estimates there were 274 *chaises percées* in Versailles in Louis XIV's reign   **21.** Corinne Thépaut-Cabasset, 'Le Service de la Garde Robe: une création de Louis XIV', in Arizzoli-Clémentel and Ballesteros, pp. 28–33   **22.** Colbert, VI, 323, Louis XIV to Colbert, 9 June 1674   **23.** Saint-Germain, *Louis XIV secret*, pp. 13, 16–17, 32   **24.** Arvieux, IV, 159   **25.** Germain Bapst, *Histoire des joyaux de la couronne de France*, 2 vols., 1889, I, 361, 402; Marc Bascou, 'Des brillants symboles de la monarchie absolue', in Arizzoli-Clémentel and Ballesteros, pp. 98–109 at p. 101   **26.** Michèle Bimbenet-Privat, 'Les Pierreries de Louis XIV: objets de collection et instruments politiques', in Bernard Barbiche and Yves-Marie Bercé, eds., *Etudes sur l'ancienne France offertes en homage à Michel Antoine*, 2003, pp. 81–96   **27.** William R. Newton, *L'Espace du roi: la cour de France au château de Versailles, 1682–1789*, 2000, pp. 140; Thépaut-Cabasset, 'Service de la garde-robe', pp. 28–33   **28.** CRCV, Base de données en ligne Curia. The figures assembled there by Caroline zum Kolk are based on different editions of *L'Estat de la France nouvellement corrigé et mis en meilleur ordre*, and include 'toutes les compagnies des gardes du roy' and 'marchands et artisans privilégiés suivans la Cour'.   **29.** *DL*, pp. 380–84   **30.** Duindam, p. 66   **31.** Knecht, pp. 299–300   **32.** Duindam, pp. 54, 74,   **33.** Vinha, *Valets*, pp. 46, 74, 124, 193   **34.** Jacques Levron, *Les Inconnus de Versailles: les coulisses de la cour*, 1968, p. 57; Vinha, *Valets*, pp. 21–3, 31–3, 39, 71, 90, 111, 117–18   **35.** Mathieu Stoll, *Servir le Roi-Soleil: Claude Le Peletier (1631-1711), ministre de Louis XIV*, Rennes, 2011, p. 232; Saint-Simon, ed. Coirault, I, 27   **36.** Comte de Forbin, *Mémoires*, 1993 edn, p. 197; Vinha, *Valets*, p. 341; cf. Maréchal de Villars, *Mémoires*, 6 vols., 1886–1904, I, 163   **37.** Vinha, *Valets*, pp. 172, 241, 265–6, 269, 326, 333; Saint-Simon, *Mémoires*, ed. Regnier and Chéruel, IV, 318–19   **38.** Spanheim, pp. 149, 151   **39.** Vinha, *Valets*, p. 225   **40.** Keay, *Magnificent Monarch*, pp. 139–43   **41.** Perez, p. 285   **42.** Roy Strong, *Feast: A History of Grand Eating*, 2002, pp. 253–5; Béatrix Saule, 'Tentative de définition du Grand Couvert', in idem, ed., *Tables royales et festins de cour en Europe, 1661–1789*, 2004, pp. 29–35; *Versailles et les tables royales en Europe: XVIIème–XIXème siècles*, exh. cat., 1993, pp. 47–52; *DL*, pp. 1144–8   **43.** Jaeglé, II, 51, Madame to Raugravine Amélie, 3 February 1707; Bernard Perrin, 'Un Professur de droit solliciteur à la cour du grand Roi, 1699–1704: Louis Monnier de Richardin', *Revue de l'Histoire de Versailles*, 55, 1964, pp. 150–206 at p. 168, 22 March 1699   **44.** Saule, 'Tentative de définition du grand couvert', p. 32   **45.** Kroll, p. 157, Madame to Sophie, 23 December 1710   **46.** Nemeitz, II, 499; Duindam, pp. 167, 175   **47.** Sourches, V, 111, 25 February 1696   **48.** Newton, *Espace*, p. 324   **49.** Lucette Fontaine-Bayer, *La Chasse-marée de Picardie sur la route du poisson*, Creil, 1993, pp. 67, 93, 117   **50.** Charles Hénin, *Fêtes et plaisirs au temps des princes de Condé*, 2015, pp. 65–6; Mathieu Deldicque, *Le Grand Condé: le rival du Roi Soleil?*, Ghent, 2016, pp. 160–61; Sévigné, I, 235–6, Sévigné to Madame de Grignan, 26 April 1671; cf. Dominique Michel, *Vatel et la naissance de la gastronomie*, 1999, p. 100   **51.** Jaeglé, II, 191, Madame to Electress Sophia, 22 January 1713   **52.** Perez, pp. 114, 226–8, 232, 239; Vallot, p. 222, remarques sur l'année 1694   **53.** Bibliothèque Municipale de Versailles, Mss. 691 ff. 128–32, 'Etat et menu général de la dépense ordinaire de la chambre aux deniers du roy, année 1691'   **54.** Strong, pp. 231, 238   **55.** Vallot, p. 218, Remarques sur l'année 1694; cf. pp. 238, 248, 267, 269, 288, 308, 325, 29 October 1698, 29 June 1701, 1703, 1704, 1706, 1708, February 1710   **56.** Perez, pp. 115–16, 238–9, 251, 255. On some days he went fifteen or sixteen times to the Garde-robe.   **57.** Vallot, p. 113, 1672   **58.** Sourches, IX, 131, 18 November 1704   **59.** Spanheim, pp. 148–9; Saint-Maurice, I, 376, to Duke of Savoy, 20 December 1669; Sharon Kettering, *Patronage in Sixteenth- and Seventeenth-Century France*, 2002, VIII, 84; Rowlands, *Dynastic State*, pp. 346–8   **60.** Forbin, pp. 257, 457; 'il faut tirer a temps' was another court proverb.   **61.** Saint-Simon, ed. Coirault, I, 308   **62.** See e.g. Dangeau, XXIII, 64, 154, 30 March 1709, 11 July 1710, for samples of such lists.   **63.** Chantelou, p. 180, 11 September 1665   **64.** Saint-Maurice, I, 197, to Duke of Savoy, 1 June 1668   **65.** Sourches, II, 321n, 29 December 1688; Dangeau, III, 39, 25 March 1688; Frédérique Leferme-Falguières, *Les Courtisans: une société de spectacle sous l'Ancien Régime*, 2007, p. 154   **66.** Saint-Maurice, I, 254, 350, to Duke of Savoy, 9 November 1668,

1 November 1669, II, 159, 18 September 1671   67. Dangeau, XVII, 261, 21 October 1704   68. Ibid., XVI, 8, 6 January 1703   69. Lanfredini, p. 84, Louis XIV to Gramont, 4 December 1673   70. Bibliothèque Municipale de Versailles, Panthéon Louis XIV, 'rôle des placets présentés au roy à Versailles le lundy 12 Juin 1702'. A typical petition was summarized thus: 'le sr Le Goux inspecteur des bâtiments du Roy, à la recommandation de Madame de Maintenon, supplie Sa Majesté de l'assister de ses bienfaits pour luy ayder à fournir la dotte [dowry] de sa fille qui désire se faire religieuse, ne pouvant y satisfaire sans secours.'   71. Jaeglé, I, 169, Madame to Electress Sophia, 18 March 1698   72. Sourches, IV, 200, 11 May 1693; Pierre Quarré, Comte d'Aligny, *Mémoires militaires*, Beaune, 1886, pp. 188, 262–4, 274   73. Perrin, 'Louis Monnier de Richardin', pp. 169, 182; cf. for a similar experience, in 1695, haunting the offices of the War Ministry, but also enjoying the music and the King's pictures in his 'cabinets', Plantavit de La Pause, III, 18–19   74. Dangeau, XII, 175, 28 October 1699   75. Petitfils, *Montespan*, pp. 81, 95, 99; idem, *Lauzun*, pp. 138–41   76. Emile Longin, *Un Franc-Comtois à Paris sous Louis XIV, 1691–92*, Vesoul, 1894, p. 37, Lallemand diary, 12 August 1691   77. Ibid., passim and pp. 46, 56, Lallemand diary, 3, 18 October 1691   78. Sourches, V, 172n, 12 August 1696; Marquis de Montglat, *Mémoires*, 1838, p. 296   79. Louis XIV, *Oeuvres*, VI, 27, Louis XIV to Maréchale de Noailles, 10 June 1694   80. BN Mss. fr. 6944, Registre des lettres, Maréchale de Noailles, passim; Marcel Langlois, *Louis XIV et la cour*, 1926, pp. 282–3   81. Newton, *Espace*, pp. 330, 382   82. Duc de Saint-Simon, *La Mort de Louis XIV*, 2007 edn, pp. 56, 326; Saint-Simon, *Mémoires*, ed. Regnier and Chéruel, XI, 280. A hundred years later Thierry de Ville d'Avray, favourite *premier valet de chambre* of Louis XVI, complained of their influence on subordinate appointments: 'MM. de Noailles ne négligent rien': Newton, *Petite Cour*, p. 233. The Noailles were also influential in Languedoc and Roussillon, where they held military commands, as was the Villeroy family in the Lyonnais: Saint-Simon, *Mémoires*, ed. Regnier and Chéruel, IV, 371   83. Savile, p. 33, letter of 27 August 1678   84. Dingli, pp. 29–33, 144; Sourches, V, 134n, 29 April 1696. His successor Pontchartrain was less ambitious, only covering the area from Bayonne to Brest.   85. Cénat, *Louvois*, pp. 176, 195, 248, 295   86. Félibien, *Fêtes de Versailles*, p. 79   87. Stéphane Pannekoucke, *Des princes en Bourgogne: les Condé gouverneurs au XVIIIe siècle*, 2010, p. 304; cf. BS 1290 f. 113, Louis XIV to Condé, 25 February 1663; BSG 2015 f. 255, Louis XIV to Duc d'Enghien [son de Condé], 24 May 1671; Mathieu Deldicque, *Le Grand Condé: le rival du Roi Soleil?*, Ghent, 2016, passim; Julian Swann, *Provincial Power and Absolute Monarchy: The Estates General of Burgundy, 1661–1790*, Cambridge, 2003, pp. 162–3.   88. See e.g. Dangeau, XVIII, 189, 1 September 1705, XXVI, 216, 9 October 1713; Sourches, X, 405, 27 September 1707; Bély, *Espions*, p. 242   89. John C. Rule and Ben S. Trotter, *A World of Paper: Louis XIV, Colbert de Torcy, and the Rise of the Information State*, Montreal, 2014, p. 214   90. BN Mss. fr. 6923 f. 9, Correspondance Amelot–Noailles 1706–9, Amelot to Duc de Noailles, 23 April 1708   91. Sévigné, II, 657, to Grignan, 19 March 1680   92. Kroll, p.256, Madame to Herr von Harling, 22 November 1721   93. *Splendeurs de la cour de Saxe: Dresde à Versailles*, exh. cat. 2006, pp. 50–51   94. *Ádám Mányoki: Actors and Venues of a Portraitist's Career*, exh. cat., Budapest, 2003, pp. 18, 23   95. Cohen, *Art, Dance, and the Body*, pp. 17–18, 35; Perez, pp. 256–7   96. Cf. Raoul Feuillet, *Chorégraphie, ou l'Art de décrire la danse par caractères, figures et signes démonstratifs avec lesquels on apprend facilement de soi-même toutes sortes de danses*, 1700   97. BN Mss. fr. 1698, André Lorin, Contre danse du roy; Wendy Hilton, *Dance of Court and Theatre: The French Noble Style, 1680–1725*, 1981, pp. 25, 29, 31, 48, 61.   98. Antoine Galland, *Journal parisien*, ed. Henri Omont, in *Mémoires de la Société de l'Histoire de Paris et de l'Île-de-France*, 46, 1919, pp. 25–156 at p. 123, 19 March 1713   99. *DL*, pp. 138–9   100. Levantal, *Louis XIV*, I, 284, 294, 13, 16 February 1669, 4 February 1670; Jean Duron, ed., *Le Prince et la musique: les passions musicales de Louis XIV*, 2009, pp. 126–9, 140; Astier, 'Louis XIV, "premier danseur" ', pp. 73–102   101. Maral, *Versailles*, p. 407; Saint-Simon, *Mémoires*, ed. Coirault, II, 302   102. ML, II, 649–50, Maintenon to M. de Noailles, 31 January 1696   103. Louis XIV, *Mémoires*, p. 170; Dangeau, XII, 38, 2, 3 March 1703   104. Moine, pp. 133, 136, 213   105. Maral, *Versailles*, p. 255   106. See e.g. Dangeau, XXIII, 245, 256, 24 November, 9 December

1710   107. Maral, *Versailles*, pp. 272-3   108. Kroll, p. 46, Madame to Wilhelmine Ernestine, 6 December 1682; *DV*, pp. 711-22, quoting *Mercure Galant*, December 1682; cf. Sévigné, II, 927, to Bussy-Rabutin, 2 February 1683   109. Kroll, p. 46, letter to Wilhelmine Ernestine, 6 December 1682; *DV*, p. 492; Catherine Arminjon, ed., *Quand Versailles était meublé d'argent*, 2007, passim. Madame de Sévigné also admired the magnificence of the furniture and courtiers' freedom to talk to the royal family: Sévigné, II, 154, 917, 29 July 1676, 12 February 1683   110. Pierre Clément, *La Police sous Louis XIV*, 1866, pp. 84-5; John Dunkley, *Gambling: A Social and Moral Problem in France, 1685-1792*, Oxford, 1985, pp. 45, 145   111. Lahaye, pp. 272, 276; Sévigné, II, 154, to Grignan, 29 July 1676; Dangeau, XII, 185, 13 November 1699; Jaeglé, I, 216, Madame to Electress Sophia, 11 February 1700   112. Sourches, V, 253, 18 March 1695; Dangeau, XII, 47, 21 March 1699, XIV, 8, 9 March 1703, XVIII, 268, 14 December 1705   113. Marcelle Benoît, *Les Evénements musicaux sous le règne de Louis XIV*, 2004, pp. 6-7; *Versailles et la musique de cour*, exh. cat., Versailles, 2007, pp. 25, 35 and passim   114. La Gorce, *Lully*, p. 741   115. Ibid., pp. 117, 204, 246, 309, 635   116. Beaussant, *Louis XIV artiste*, p. 16; *DL*, p. 961, quoting despatch of 23 March 1660. Robert de Visée dedicated his *Livre de guitare* to the King in 1682, since 'the same royal hand which gave orders for battles also touched the guitar'; cf. Comte d'Haussonville, *La Duchesse de Bourgogne et l'alliance savoyarde sous Louis XIV*, 4 vols., 1898-1908, II, 22   117. Maral, *Chapelle*, pp. 184, 188-9; Duron, p. 106   118. Duron, p. 20; Beaussant, *Plaisirs de Versailles*, p. 68; *DV*, p. 147   119. *DL*, pp. 911, 901, 997; Beaussant, *Louis XIV artiste*, p. 202   120. Dangeau, XII, 111, 122, 10, 31 July 1699   121. La Gorce, *Lully*, pp. 732-5; Maral, *Versailles*, pp. 425, 428; Maral, *Chapelle*, p. 193   122. Beaussant, *Plaisirs de Versailles*, pp. 98, 101; Duron, p. 28   123. Comte Greppi, 'Notes de voyage du Comte Giandemaria', *RHD*, 4, 3, 1890, pp. 352-67 at p. 359, 29 May 1680   124. Maral, *Chapelle*, p. 155; cf. Saint-Simon, *Mémoires*, ed. Regnier and Chéruel, XI, 187   125. Beaussant, *Plaisirs de Versailles*, p. 82   126. *FD*, pp. 89-90, 100, 104, 134   127. C. E. J. Caldicott, *La Carrière de Molière, entre protecteurs et éditeurs*, Amsterdam, 1998, pp. 81-120; Molière, *Oeuvres complètes*, II, 194   128. Charles Mazouer, 'Molière et le roi', in Denis Lopez, ed., *Le Pouvoir et ses écritures*, 2012, pp. 135-44   129. Moine, p. 123   130. Molière, *Le Bourgeois Gentilhomme*, ed. Claire Joubaire, 2016, pp. 35, 48-9; *FD*, pp. 100, 120   131. Arvieux, IV, 252-3, 281   132. Jaeglé, I, 185, Madame to Electress Sophia, 1 November 1698; Beaussant, *Plaisirs de Versailles*, p. 411   133. Néraudau, *L'Olympe du Roi-Soleil*, pp. 129-30, 195, 232   134. Raymond Picard, *La Carrière de Racine*, 1961 edn, pp. 157, 283; cf. Marie-Claude Canova-Green and Alain Viala, eds., *Racine et l'histoire*, Tübingen, 2004.   135. Picard, p. 366   136. Ibid., pp. 315, 480   137. Ibid., pp. 385-6, 393, 414, 489, 490; Beaussant, *Louis XIV artiste*, pp. 71, 78; Jean Dubu, 'Fortunes and Misfortunes of Racine the Courtier', *The Court Historian*, 7, 2, December 2002, pp. 111-33; Spanheim, pp. 402-3   138. Picard, pp. 333-5, 430-31; AN o1 34 f. 344v, brevet to 'Sr. Racine', 12 December 1690   139. Picard, pp. 413-14, 432, 443, 552; Racine, *Oeuvres complètes*, 2 vols., 1999 edn, II, 281   140. Sourches, VI, 139, 16 March 1699   141. Chantelou, p. 316, 27 October 1665   142. Alfred Baudrillart, *Philippe V et la cour de France*, 5 vols., 1890-1900, I, 234, Louis XIV to Philip V, 6 September 1705   143. Petitfils, *La Vallière*, pp. 118, 120n, 177-82; Magne, *Lettres inédites*, pp. 154, 157, 162, Condé to Queen of Poland, 19 March 1665, Enghien to Queen of Poland, 20 March 1665; cf. Anon., *Histoire galante de Madame et du comte de Guiche*, 1667, p. 325 and passim; Visconti, p. 30; Lanfredini, p. 28, Louis XIV to Maréchal de Gramont, on Guiche's death, 4 December 1673   144. Saint-Maurice, II, 381, to Duke of Savoy, 19 July 1672; cf. Dangeau, XII, 143, 6 September 1699   145. Sourches, III, 155, 13 September 1689; ML, IV, 810, Maintenon to Ursins, 11 May 1710   146. Motteville, *Mémoires*, IV, 410, 417   147. Hermann Kleber, 'Louis XIV mémorialiste: la genèse des Mémoires de Louis XIV', in Chantal Grell, Werner Paravicini and Jürgen Voss, eds., *Les Princes et l'histoire du XVIe au XVIIIe siècle*, Bonn, 1998, pp 523-33; Louis XIV, *Mémoires*, pp. 52-4, 73, 322   148. Saint-Simon, *Mémoires*, ed. Regnier and Chéruel, V, 35, 42   149. Bibliothèque Municipale de Versailles Mss. 47 (Créquy); BN Mss. fr. Papiers Noailles 6923-6   150. Sévigné, II, 170, Corbinelli to Bussy-Rabutin, 1 September 1687   151. Jaeglé, I, 173, 216, to Raugravine Louise, 17 June 1698, to Electress Sophia, 11 February 1700; Van der Cruysse, *Princesse européenne*, pp. 169, 232, 281   **152.** Van der Cruysse, *Princesse européenne*, pp. 295, 296; Jaeglé, III, 70, 80, to Raugravine Louise, 18 February 1720, 4 August 1720   **153.** Saint-Simon, *Mémoires*, ed. Regnier and Chéruel, XI, 58; Langlois, pp. 84–96; *DL*, pp. 161–2   **154.** Saint-Simon, *Mémoires*, ed. Regnier and Chéruel, V, 403–4   **155.** Petitfils, *Louis XIV*, pp. 537–8; François de Fénelon, *Lettre à Louis XIV*, 2011 edn, passim; cf. Drévillon, *Impôt du sang*, p. 99, for more criticism of the King   **156.** Fénelon, p. 82   **157.** Antony McKenna, 'Les Soupirs de la France esclave: la question de l'attribution', in Pierre Bonnet, ed., *Littérature de contestation: pamphlets et polémique du règne de Louis XIV aux lumières*, 2011, pp. 229–68   **158.** Sabine Melchior-Bonnet, *Fénelon*, 2008, pp. 171, 222–3, 248   **159.** *DL*, pp. 1122–4; Volker Kapp, *Télémaque de Fénelon: la signification d'une oeuvre littéraire à la fin du siècle classique*, Tübingen, 1982, pp. 158–9, 167–8   **160.** M. de Pontchartrain, *Correspondance de la Maison du Roi*, 2 vols., Clermont-Ferrand, 2016, I, 23, 135, 227, Pontchartrain to La Bourdonnaye, 28 January 1700, to d'Herbigny, 19 October 1701, 4 April 1703   **161.** Melchior-Bonnet, pp. 240, 322–5, 330; Saint-Simon, *Mémoires*, ed. Regnier and Chéruel, XI, 59   **162.** Abbé Oroux, *Histoire ecclésiastique de la cour de France*, 2 vols., 1727, II, 526, 528   **163.** Maral, *Versailles*, pp. 359–63   **164.** Poisson, pp. 161, 163, 214; Picard, pp. 470–71, 540   **165.** R. A. Weigert, ed., *Les Relations artistiques entre la France et la Suède, 1693–1718*, Stockholm, 1964, p. 266; cf. Alice Stroup, 'Louis XIV as Patron of the Parisian Academy of Sciences' in Rubin, pp. 221–40; Beaussant, *Louis XIV artiste*, p. 88; Maral, *Versailles*, p. 281, for the King's conversation with the painter Coypel   **166.** Bénédicte Gady and Nicolas Milanovic, eds., *Charles Le Brun (1619–1690)*, 2016, pp. 387, 394   **167.** *De Chasse et d'épée*, pp. 56, 73   **168.** Stéphane Castelluccio, *Les Collections royales d'objets d'art, de François Ier à la Révolution*, 2002, pp. 35–191. Part of Louis XIV's collection is now on display in the Galerie d'Apollon in the Louvre; the Dauphin's, inherited by Philip V, is in the basement of the Prado.   **169.** Nemeitz, II, 501; *DV*, pp. 148, 475; Thomas Hedin and Folke Sandgren, 'Deux Voyageurs suédois visitent Versailles sous le règne de roi soleil', *Versalia*, 9, 2006, pp. 86–114; cf. Creed, p. 54, describing visiting the King's 'little apartment' on 8 July 1700; Higgott, p. 257, for the Dauphin's. Helmut Lahrkamp, ed., *Lambert Friedrich Corfey: Reisetagebuch, 1698–1700*, Münster, 1977, pp. 69, 72, 77, describes this bourgeois German's visits in 1698 to Trianon, Marly (inside and out) and the King's private apartments in Versailles   **170.** *Sciences et curiosités*, pp. 165–8; Louis XIV's copy of *Traité universel des drogues simples*, 1698, by Nicolas Lémery, was on sale with the Paris dealer Camille Sourget in 2018.   **171.** AN 01 1098, Registres des ordres et lettres de mgr le duc Dantin . . . concernant les bâtiments, jardins, arts et manufactures du roy depuis 1708 jusqu'à 1732, f. 17, Antin to Poerson, 21 August 1708

Chapter 14: Inside Louis XIV

1. Perez, pp. 80, 123, 125, 128, 274, 276, quoting accounts by the royal doctors Daquin and Fagon   **2.** Ibid., pp. 336–41, quoting the *Mercure de France*   **3.** Ibid., pp. 126, 370–73, quoting Spanheim, *Relation de la cour de France*   **4.** Ibid., p. 91; Maral, *Le Roi-Soleil et Dieu*, p. 291; Colin Jones, *The Smile Revolution in Eighteenth-Century Paris*, 2014, pp. 19–21; Vallot, pp. 164, 175   **5.** Sourches, XIII, 490, April 1715   **6.** Saint-Simon, *Mémoires*, ed. Regnier and Chéruel, XII, 74–5. There were no maids at Versailles, as the work was done by men. For further confirmation of the King's politeness to women, see Comisso, p. 278, relation of Marc Antonio Giustinian, 1668: 'il se découvre toujours quand il leur adresse la parole'   **7.** Including the executions of, among many others, Monmouth, Königsmarck, the Tsarevich Alexis, Chalais and Cinq-Mars.   **8.** Lahaye, p. 148; Maral, *Le Roi-Soleil et Dieu*, p. 240   **9.** BN Mss. fr. 10261 f. 29, Louis XIV to Madame de La Mothe-Houdancourt, 19 October 1670   **10.** Levantal, *Louis XIV*, I, 278; Saint-Maurice, II, 257, to Duke of Savoy, 2 March 1672; cf. for similar grief on the death of another daughter, Comte de Lionne, *Lettres inédites*, 1877, p. 209, 18 November 1664   **11.** Van der Cruysse, *Princesse européenne*, pp. 269–70; Vincent, p. 174   **12.** Spanheim, p. xvii, Spanheim to Elector of Brandenburg,

2 August 1683   **13.** Comte de Bussy-Rabutin, *Correspondance . . . avec sa famille et ses amis*, 5 vols., 1858–9, V, 359, note by Bussy-Rabutin, 1683   **14.** *DV*, pp. 85, 210   **15.** Van der Cruysse, *Lettres françaises*, p. 56, Madame to Louis XIV, 24 May 1685   **16.** *The Collection of Autograph Letters and Historical Documents Formed by Alfred Morrison*, second series, 6 vols., 1883–92, IV, 236, Louis XIV to Madame, 11 February 1668; cf. for another loving letter to Madame, BN Fichier Charavay 382, Louis XIV to Madame, 13 September 1663   **17.** Rousset, I, 362n, Louis XIV to Condé, 31 December 1672   **18.** Louis XIV, *Oeuvres*, IV, 466, to Dauphin, 19 August 1694   **19.** Sévigné, II, 449, 452, Sévigné to Grignan, 20, 22 September 1679; Dangeau, XI, 160, 12 October 1698; Jaeglé, I, 183, Madame to Electress Sophia, 15 October 1698; Sophie de Hanovre, *Mémoires et lettres de voyage*, 1990, p. 158; Lurgo, pp. 173, 197, for his grief at the Queen of Spain's death   **20.** Dangeau, XIV, 127, 131, 9, 13 June 1701; Lurgo, pp. 297–8, 301   **21.** Lurgo, pp. 31–4, 217, 225, 297–8, 301   **22.** Dangeau, XVIII, 23, 32, 26 January, 8 February 1705; Sourches, I, 36, 2 December 1682; Saint-Simon, *Mémoires*, ed. Regnier and Chéruel, VI, 346–7   **23.** Sévigné, I, 462, to Grignan, 23 February 1672   **24.** Lurgo, p. 301   **25.** Giora Sternberg, *Status Interaction during the Reign of Louis XIV*, Oxford, 2014, pp. 18, 32, 47, 62, 84, 89, 118, 163–5   **26.** Maral, *Versailles*, pp. 249–51; Saint-Simon, *Mémoires*, ed. Regnier and Chéruel, IV, 57–8, for the King, Queen and other members of the royal family stopping visits to dukes and duchesses after 1678, and V, 323, VI, 363 for his anger over the royal status acquired by the dukes of Lorraine, Savoy and Tuscany   **27.** Jaeglé, II, 251–2, Madame to Raugravine Louise, 28 October 1717   **28.** Montpensier, IV, 92, 96; Petitfils, *Lauzun*, pp. 46, 156   **29.** Montpensier, IV, 189, 191   **30.** Ibid., 205, 209   **31.** Pitts, *Grande Mademoiselle*, pp. 198–208   **32.** Saint-Maurice, I, 517, 521, 531, to Duke of Savoy, 17, 19 December 1670   **33.** Sarmant, *Homme et roi*, p. 197; Sévigné, I, 141, to M. Coulanges, 19 December 1670   **34.** Montpensier, IV, 233–4, 236, 624–7   **35.** Paul Sonnino, *Origins of the Dutch War*, p. 137; Petitfils, *Lauzun*, pp. 137–8, 157, 165; Saint-Simon, *Mémoires*, ed. Coirault, I, 437–9; Vallot, p. 114 and n, Remarques sur l'année 1672   **36.** Matthew Gerber, *Bastards: Politics, Family, and Law in Early Modern France*, New York, 2012, pp. 13, 29, 85, 98   **37.** Alexandre Maral, *Le Roi, la cour et Versailles: le coup d'éclat permanent, 1682–1789*, 2013, pp. 276, 289, 298; Dangeau, VII, 98, 20 June 1693; cf. Sévigné, II, 597, to Grignan, 2 February 1680, for the 'tender caresses' bestowed by the King on the Princesse de Conti   **38.** Clément, *Montespan*, pp. 112–14; Petitfils, *Lauzun*, pp. 210, 213, 221, 242-3, 255.   **39.** Sourches, II, 55n, 27 May 1687   **40.** Petitfils, *Montespan*, pp. 122–5; Maral, *Le Roi-Soleil et Dieu*, pp. 242–3, 246   **41.** Sévigné, II, 265, 313, to Grignan, 11 June, 30 July 1677; Petitfils, *Montespan*, p. 134; Clément, *Montespan*, pp. 107–8   **42.** Clément, *Montespan*, pp. 90–91; Bussy-Rabutin, *Correspondance*, III, 213, note by Bussy-Rabutin, 1677, 227, Bussy-Rabutin to Jeannin de Castile, 6 March 1677, 381, Madame de Montmorency to Bussy-Rabutin, 8 October 1677   **43.** Jean Lemoine and André Lichtenberger, *Les des Oeillets: une grande comédienne, une maîtresse de Louis XIV: étude et documents*, 1938, pp. 49–51   **44.** Petitfils, *La Vallière*, pp. 183–4, 232, 235   **45.** Mark Bryant, 'The Queen of Versailles and First Lady of Louis XIV's France', typescript (kindly lent by the author), n.d., passim and p. 392, Maintenon to Noailles, 27 April 1705; Petitfils, *Montespan*, pp. 117–19, 130   **46.** Alexandre Maral, *Madame de Maintenon: à l'ombre du Roi-Soleil*, 2011, p. 15   **47.** Cf. Sévigné, I, 414, Sévigné to Grignan 13 January 1672, on the 'esprit droit' of Madame Scarron   **48.** Maral, *Maintenon*, pp. 52–6   **49.** Anne Somerset, *The Affair of the Poisons*, 2003, p. 94   **50.** Petitfils, *Montespan*, pp. 145, 147, 150; Somerset, *Poisons*, p. 105; Visconti, pp. 106–7; cf. Bussy-Rabutin, *Correspondance*, III, 205, Bussy-Rabutin to P. P. Brulart, 30 January 1677; Sévigné, II, 287, to Grignan, 7 July 1677   **51.** Bussy-Rabutin, *Correspondance*, IV, 21, Madame de Scudéry to Bussy-Rabutin, 28 January 1678   **52.** *DL*, p. 290; Saint-Simon, *Mémoires*, ed. Regnier and Chéruel, VII, 253–4   **53.** Antonia Fraser, *Love and Louis XIV: The Women in the Life of the Sun King*, 2006, p. 168; Somerset, *Poisons*, p. 106; Clément, *Montespan*, p. 95   **54.** Clément, *Montespan*, p. 251, Montespan to Duc de Noailles, April 1679   **55.** Plantavit de La Pause, I, 237n   **56.** Dangeau, XXVII, 13, 11 January 1714, note by Saint-Simon   **57.** Petitfils, *Montespan*, p. 165; Sévigné, II, 562, to Grignan, 10 January 1680   **58.** Hanovre, p. 147   **59.** Petitfils, *Montespan*, p. 218; Bussy-Rabutin, IV, 333, Bussy-Rabutin to Marquis

de Trichateau, 22 March 1679   60. Sévigné, II, 623, 649, Sévigné to Grignan, 28 February, 20 March 1680. A luxuriously decorated ebony cabinet depicting the loves of Hercules and Omphale, given to her by the King, can be seen in the Musée Jacquemart-André in Paris. 61. Ibid., 670, 681, 901, Sévigné to Grignan, 6 April, 1 May 1680, to Bussy-Rabutin, 30 June 1681   62. Petitfils, *Montespan*, p. 174   63. Ibid., p. 176   64. Cowart, p. 40   65. Somerset, *Poisons*, pp. 141, 159, 306; Cornette, *Mort de Louis XIV*, p. 262   66. Somerset, *Poisons*, pp. 203-4, 207; Sévigné, II, 582, to Grignan, 24 January 1680   67. Sévigné, II, 617, to Grignan, 23 February 1680   68. Somerset, *Poisons*, pp. 261-2, 266-7; Clément, *Montespan*, pp. 116-17   69. Somerset, *Poisons*, p. 228; Petitfils, *Montespan*, pp. 205, 212-15   70. Petitfils, *Montespan*, pp. 193, 202; Somerset, *Poisons*, pp. 181, 186; Murat, pp. 400-401, 404, 413; Cornette, *Mort de Louis XIV*, p. 264; Lemoine and Lichtenberger, *Les des Oeillets*, p. 41   71. Petitfils, *Montespan*, pp. 223-7   72. Somerset, *Poisons*, pp. 286-8; Clément, *Montespan*, pp. 120-21, mémoire of Claude Duplessis   73. Somerset, *Poisons*, pp. 216-17, 236-41; Spanheim, p. 338; Marquis de Ségur, *Le Tapissier de Notre-Dame: les dernières années du Maréchal de Luxembourg (1678-1695)*, 1903, p. 71   74. Somerset, *Poisons*, pp. 128, 221-2; Ségur, *Tapissier*, pp. 56-7; Sévigné, II, 593, to Grignan, 31 January 1680   75. Somerset, *Poisons*, pp. 269, 323-5, 331, 336, 339; cf. *DL*, pp. 1072-3; Murat, p. 400; Bussy-Rabutin, *Correspondance*, V, 49, Trichateau to Bussy-Rabutin, 1 February 1680   76. Mark Bryant, 'Romancing the Throne: Madame de Maintenon's Journey from Secret Royal Governess to Louis XIV's Clandestine Consort, 1652-1684', *The Court Historian*, 22, 2 December 2017, pp. 123-50 at p. 131; Sévigné, II, 195, to Grignan, 8 September 1676   77. Fraser, *Love and Louis XIV*, p. 194   78. Sévigné, II, 649, 717, 730, 753, 845, to Grignan, 20 March, 25 May, 5, 21 June, 11 September 1680   79. Cf. François Poullain de La Barre, *Traité de l'égalité des deux sexes* (1673)   80. Maral, *Chapelle*, pp. 114-16, 120, 277   81. Maral, *Le Roi-Soleil et Dieu*, pp. 59-68   82. Maral, *Chapelle*, p. 111; idem, *Le Roi-Soleil et Dieu*, pp. 271-2   83. Maral, *Le Roi-Soleil et Dieu*, pp. 77-80, 244-8   84. Cornette, *Mort de Louis XIV*, p. 228   85. Maral, *Le Roi-Soleil et Dieu*, pp. 66, 82, 83, 96-9   86. Louis XIV, *Oeuvres*, I, 91   87. Perez, pp. 124, 293-9; Maral, *Le Roi-Soleil et Dieu*, pp. 100-105; *DL*, p. 443. In England, Anna Keay believes that Charles II 'touched' about 3,000 people a year for the King's Evil: Keay, *Magnificent Monarch*, p. 118   88. Maral, *Le Roi-Soleil et Dieu*, p. 235   89. Ibid., pp. 252-3   90. Sévigné, II, 830, to Grignan, 28 August 1680; cf. Somerset, *Poisons*, p. 121   91. Sourches, I, 20, 25 September 1681   92. Murat, p. 414, Louis XIV to Colbert, 5 October 1681   93. Levantal, *Louis XIV*, II, 452n; Maral, *Le Roi-Soleil et Dieu*, pp. 266-9; Alexandre Maral believes that, since the location of their apartments made 'rapports intimes' difficult, it could have been a 'mariage blanc'.   94. Fraser, *Love and Louis XIV*, p. 208   95. Jaeglé, I, 205, Madame to Electress Sophia, 19 July 1699; Bryant, 'Queen', pp. 179, 316   96. ML, I, 490, Maintenon to Comte d'Aubigné, 28 September 1683   97. Bussy-Rabutin, *Correspondance*, V, 94, Bussy to Madame de Montjeu, 25 March 1680   98. Maral, *Eclat*, p. 128   99. Clément, *Montespan*, pp. 148-52, 185; Fraser, *Love and Louis XIV*, p. 83   100. Clement, *Montespan*, pp. 420-24; Petitfils, *Montespan*, p. 246; Dangeau, XX, 111, 28 May 1707; Jaeglé, I, 257, Madame to Electress Sophia, 29 December 1701   101. Bryant, 'Queen', p. 196   102. Louis XIV, *Oeuvres*, VI, 21, Louis XIV to Maintenon, April 1691   103. See e.g. ML, II, 682, to Mgr de Noailles, 18 May 1696, III, 454, to Madame de Beaulieu, 12 October 1703   104. Ibid., III, 85, 349, to Mgr de Noailles, 28 July 1698, 26 February 1702   105. Ibid., II, 611, Maintenon to Madame de Fontaines, 12 October 1695   106. Ibid., III, 608, Maintenon to Duc de Noailles, 14 May 1705, 688, to Ursins, 4 November 1709   107. Maral, *Maintenon*, pp. 64, 79, 10; Bryant, 'Queen', pp. 178-80   108. Noailles, *Maintenon*, IV, 321-3, Dauphin, Duc du Maine to Maintenon, 20, 26 March, 2, 5 April 1691   109. Bryant, 'Queen', pp. 116-20. A portrait of the King holding the plans of Saint-Cyr is at Versailles.   110. Jean-Pierre Labatut, *Les Ducs et pairs de France au XVIIe siècle*, 1972, pp. 200, 252; Sourches, VI, 18, 22, 11 March, 1 April 1698; cf. Marcel Loyau, *Madame de Maintenon et la princesse des Ursins: correspondance. 1709. Une année tragique*, 2002, p. 309, Maintenon to Ursins, 20 October 1709   111. ML, III, 352, to Comte d'Ayen, 4 March 1702   112. Norton, pp. 122, 135; Maral, *Maintenon*, p. 67; Jacques Prévot, *La Première Institutrice de France*, 1981, pp. 237, 246; cf. Louis XIV, *Mémoires*, p. 96   113.

Bryant, 'Queen', p. 144 **114.** Neveu et al., *Demoiselles de Saint-Cyr*, pp. 127, 145 **115.** Dangeau, XI, 24, 4 February 1698. Her household, however, remained modest, consisting of no more than twenty people: Bryant, 'Queen', p. 382 **116.** Bryant, 'Queen', pp. 366, 390 **117.** Olivier Chaline, *L'Année des quatre dauphins*, 2011 edn, p. 117, Madame de Maintenon to Madame de Glapion, 1705; Blet, *Nonces du pape*, pp. 155, 157–9, 186, Nuncio to Pope, 5 January 1693 **118.** Bryant, 'Queen', pp. 175–6 **119.** Georges Lizerand, *Le Duc de Beauvillier*, 1933, pp. 50, 129, 139, 151, 339 **120.** Camille-Georges Picavet, *La Diplomatie française au temps de Louis XIV*, 1933, p. 53 **121.** Newton, *Espace*, pp. 419, 426, 469 **122.** Spanheim, pp. 159, 233, 236; Dangeau, XII, 145, 10, September 1699, XVIII, 279, 1705; Levantal, *Louis XIV*, II, 675, 741, 772 **123.** AN 257 AP 2, Louis XIV to Pontchartrain, 26 October 1703 **124.** Dangeau, XI, 192, 10 December 1698, XVIII, 280, 1705 **125.** Rule and Trotter, p. 562 **126.** Sara E. Chapman, *Private Ambition and Political Alliances: The Phélypeaux de Pontchartrain Family and Government under Louis XIV*, Rochester, NY, 2004, passim; Charles Frostin, *Les Pontchartrain, ministres de Louis XIV: alliances et réseau d'influence sous l'Ancien Régime*, Rennes, 2006. *Voyage de l'Arabie heureuse*, an account of the first French expeditions to buy coffee in Moka in 1708 and 1711, was dedicated by the author Jean de La Roque in 1715 to 'Monseigneur le Comte de Pontchartrain, Ministre, et Secretaire d'Etat, Commandeur des Ordres du Roi'. Roland Mousnier, ed., *Le Conseil du roi de Louis XII à la Révolution*, 1970, pp. 134–5 **127.** Sarmant and Stoll, pp. 75, 83–4; Stoll, pp. 51, 155–7 **128.** Sourches, I, 442, 16 September 1686 **129.** Rousset, II, 565, Louvois to Louis XIV, 27 September 1679, 571, Louvois to Luxembourg, 1 October 1680; Ségur, *Tapissier*, p. 71 **130.** Duindam, pp. 100–101 **131.** Sarmant and Stoll, p. 210; Saint-Simon, *Mémoires*, ed. Regnier and Chéruel, IV, 104 **132.** Sévigné, I, 421, to Grignan, 22 January 1672 **133.** Alice Camus, 'Être reçu en audience chez le roi', *CRCV Bulletin*, 2013; Saint-Simon, *Mémoires*, ed. Regnier and Chéruel, XII, 21, 174 **134.** Sarmant, *Homme et roi*, p. 146; Picavet, *Diplomatie française*, pp. 59–67, 111, Louis XIV to French ambassadors in Sweden, Poland, 1680 **135.** Gallois, IV, 268, 292, Louis XIV to Feuquières, 23 December 1678, 27 January 1679; C. Hippeau, ed., *Correspondance inédite du Marquis d'Harcourt*, 2 vols., 1875, contains the King's frequent and lengthy letters to his Ambassador in Madrid in 1698–1700 **136.** BS 1290 f. 128–30n, 146, Louis XIV to Vivonne, 27 June, 25 July 1676; cf. Emmanuel Pénicaut, *Faveur et pouvoir au tournant du grand siècle: Michel Chamillart, ministre et secrétaire d'état de Louis XIV*, 2004, p. 172, Chamillart to Vendôme, 9 June 1702, asking for 'moindres petites nouvelles' for the King, so that he received better information from his ministers than from his courtiers **137.** Sarmant and Stoll, pp. 184, 191, 199–200, to Saint-Ruth, 23 July 1691 **138.** Colbert, III, part 2, 128, 133, 'mémoire pour mon fils', 24 August, 24 September 1673 **139.** Ibid., VI, cv; Clément, *Montespan*, p. 68n **140.** Murat, p. 368, Colbert to Louis XIV, 1680 **141.** Roland Mousnier, ed., *Un Nouveau Colbert*, 1985, p. 80, Louis XIV to Colbert, 16 March 1678; Colbert, VII, xviii–lix, Louis XIV to Colbert, 24 April 1671, xxxiii, clxxvi **142.** Colbert, VII, 43, Colbert to Duc de Chaulnes, 1 January 1667 **143.** Ibid., 141, Louis XIV to Seignelay, 2 September 1683 **144.** Colbert, VII, clxxxviiii, *Gazette de Leyde*, 14–21 September 1683, clxxxi, despatch from Foscarini, 1683; Spanheim, pp. 173, 176 **145.** Nicolas Salat and Thierry Sarmant, eds., *Lettres de Louvois à Louis XIV*, 2007, pp. 154, 171, Louis XIV to Louvois, 8, 13 November 1684 **146.** Rousset, III, 403, account by Louvois, 19 November 1686; Cénat, *Louvois*, p. 227 **147.** Perez, pp. 94–107; Vallot, p. 401, 18 November 1686 **148.** Cénat, *Louvois*, pp. 259, 260, 262 **149.** Duindam, pp. 191, 195 **150.** Sourches, II, 147, 3 March 1688 **151.** Saint-Maurice, I, 209, to Duke of Savoy, 20 July 1668 **152.** Alain Ayats, *Louis XIV et les Pyrénées catalanes de 1659 à 1681: frontière politique et frontières militaires*, Canet, 2002, p. 833; cf. Lurgo, p. 211, for Monsieur's belief in Louvois' influence on Louis XIV **153.** Rousset, II, 212, Louvois to Louis XIV, 6 April 1675 **154.** Sonnino, *Origins of the Dutch War*, p. 123 **155.** Dangeau, XXI, 173, 27 August 1708 **156.** Michèle Virol, *Louis XIV et Vauban: correspondances et agendas*, 2017, passim. **157.** See e.g. François Dumont, 'French Kingship and Absolute Monarchy in the Seventeenth Century', in Ragnhild Hatton, ed., *Louis XIV and Absolutism*, 1976, pp. 70–71 **158.** See above, p. 14, quoting Queen Christina of Sweden **159.** Spanheim, pp. 29, 255 **160.** Rousset, II, 69 **161.** Sarmant and

Stoll, p. 203   **162.** Rousset, I, 476, Courtin to Louvois, September 1673   **163.** Bussy-Rabutin, *Correspondance*, V, 189, Saint-Aignan to Bussy, 3 December 1680   **164.** Louis André, ed., *Deux Mémoires historiques de Claude Le Peletier*, 1906, 'Mémoires de mes veritables et derniers sentiments sur les affairs de l'église de l'état', pp. 145, 156, 168; Stoll, pp. 134, 135   **165.** Sarmant and Stoll, pp. 282, 561–4   **166.** AN 01 363, 2 'dépesches du secrétariat', Pontchartrain to d'Argenson, 5, 26 January, 18 February, 8 September, 18 February 1701, 1 February, 1 March 1702; AN 01 366, Pontchartrain to d'Argenson, 22 April, 3 May, 4 November, 9 December 1705   **167.** AN O1 366, Pontchartrain to Guyenet, 12 January 1705

Chapter 15: The Global King: From the Mississippi to the Mekong

1. Alfred Marie, *Naissance de Versailles: le château, les jardins*, 2 vols., 1968, II, 263–77; Burchard, pp. 197–221   **2.** Plantavit de La Pause, I, 95; Castelluccio, *Fastes*, p. 119   **3.** Meredith Martin, 'Mirror Reflections: Louis XIV, Phra Narai, and the Material Culture of Kingship', *Art History*, 38, September 2015, 652–67. Some are today in the Musée Guimet in Paris.   **4.** Sourches, I, 436–8, 446, 1 September 1686, 2 October 1686; Dirk Van der Cruysse, *Louis XIV et le Siam*, 1991, pp. 288, 399–403   **5.** Knecht, pp. 295–8   **6.** Colbert, VII, cxciii, Eloge, 19 November 1683. The Brandenburg minister Spanheim was indeed impressed by Versailles' 'ameublements superbes' and works of art: Maral, *Versailles*, p. 253   **7.** Sabatier, pp. 381, 385   **8.** Paul Roussier, *L'Etablissement d'Issiny, 1687–1702*, 1935, pp. xvii–xxx   **9.** *DL*, p. 90; Loskoutoff, p. 298   **10.** Gilles Havard and Cécile Vidal, *Histoire de l'Amérique française*, 2008 edn, p. 273   **11.** Cf. Arvieux, IV, 101 ('ils prenoient plaisir à me questioner sur les moeurs des differens Peuples que j'avais connus'), V, 40, 441, for the King's and courtiers' curiosity about the Ottoman Empire; Van der Cruysse, *Noble Désir*, pp. 61, 67, 412n. Before 1670 Louis XIV had danced as an Egyptian, an American and a Moor in court ballets: Marie-Françoise Christout, 'Louis XIV et le ballet de cour, ou le plus illustres des danseurs (1651–1670)', *Revue d'Histoire du Théâtre*, 215, 2002–3, pp. 153–78.   **12.** Van der Cruysse, *Noble Désir*, p. 281; cf. Saint-Simon, *Mémoires*, ed. Regnier and Chéruel, IV, 39, for the King's pleasure in talking during supper to a former ambassador Courtin   **13.** Van der Cruysse, *Siam*, p. 291; cf. Forbin, pp. 187, 443–5 and 453 for Louis XIV's questions at supper about naval battles   **14.** Jean-Baptiste Tavernier, *Les Six Voyages ... en Turquie, en Perse et aux Indes*, 6 vols., Rouen, 1724, II, 177, VI, ii; Anne York, 'Travels in India: Jean-Baptiste Tavernier', in Glenn J. Ames and Ronald S. Love eds., *Distant Lands and Diverse Cultures: The French Experience in Asia, 1600–1700*, Westport, CT, 2003, pp. 135–45   **15.** Guy Tachard, *Second Voyage du Père Tachard et des Jesuites envoyés par le Roy au royaume de Siam*, Amsterdam, 1689, dedication and p. 5. The King had bid farewell to these Jesuits, assuring them that their voyage was 'for the glory of God and the honour of France'.   **16.** Dangeau, XIX, 102, 12 May 1706, for Cassini at Marly   **17.** Cf. the conversations about clothes, wives and guards between African kings and French agents recorded in Tidiane Diakite, *Louis XIV et l'Afrique noire*, Arles, 2013, pp. 54–5   **18.** Arvieux, IV, 134, 159–65, 261–2; cf. Geraud Poumarède, 'Les Envoyés ottomans à la cour de France: d'une présence controversée à l'exaltation d'une alliance', in Gilles Veinstein, ed., *Turcs et Turqueries (XVIe–XVIIIe siècles)*, 2009, pp. 83–9, quoting Archives Diplomatiques (henceforward AD) CP Turquie 9 f. 226, 'l'audience donnée par Sa Majesté'   **19.** Van der Cruysse, *Siam*, p. 383   **20.** Simon de La Loubère, *Description du royaume de Siam*, 2 vols., 1692, with many illustrations and maps, dedicated to the Marquis de Torcy, Colbert's nephew and a future foreign minister, now a vital sorce for historians of Siam   **21.** Van der Cruysse, *Noble Désir*, p. 396   **22.** Tachard, *Voyage de Siam des Pères Jesuites envoyés par le Roy, aux Indes et à la Chine*, Amsterdam, 1687, pp. 166, 180, 198   **23.** La Loubère, I, 386, 408, 410; Ronald S. Love, 'Simon de La Loubère: French Views of Siam in the 1680s', in Glenn J. Ames and Ronald S. Love, eds., *Distant Lands and Diverse Cultures: The French Experience in Asia, 1600–1700*, Westport, CT, 2003, pp. 181–200 at p. 184   **24.** Jacques de Bourges, *Relation du voyage de Monseigneur l'Evêque de Beryte*, 1683, pp. 3, 108, 121; Van der Cruysse, *Siam*, p. 171. De Bourges' book was also dedicated to Louis XIV and expressed the hope that, following the examples of Charlemagne and St Louis, he would rule half the world.   **25.** Catherine Marin, ed., *La Société des missions étrangères de Paris: 350 ans à la rencontre de l'Asie, 1658–2008*, 2011, pp. 16, 20, 91   **26.** Van der Cruysse, *Siam*, p. 199   **27.** Bamford, p. 311, Louis XIV to Kings of Siam and Cochin China, 1681   **28.** BS 961 f. 125v, 1289 f. 141, Louis XIV to M. de Tracy, 18, 27 May 1665; Havard and Vidal, pp. 101, 279   **29.** Yves Cazaux, *Le Rêve Américain: de Champlain à Cavelier de La Salle*, 1988, pp. 346, 393   **30.** Pierre Margry, *Découvertes et établissemens des français dans l'ouest et dans le sud de l'Amérique Septentrionale, 1614–1754*, 4 vols., 1878, II, 354   **31.** Ibid., p. 415   **32.** W. J. Eccles, *Frontenac: The Courtier Governor*, Toronto, 1959, pp. 335–6 and n, letter from M. Tremblay, 31 May 1701; Margry, IV, 50, 294, Pontchartrain to Ducasse, 8 April 1699, pp. 308, 469, 483, mémoire sur le Mississippi, Versailles, 20 July 1701, 585, 616   **33.** Havard and Vidal, p. 219   **34.** Ibid., pp. 227, 252, 257, 366, 692   **35.** Black, *From Louis XIV to Napoleon*, pp. 200–201, 207; James Pritchard, *In Search of Empire: The French in the Americas, 1670–1730*, Cambridge, 2007 edn, pp. 16–17, 25   **36.** James Pritchard, 'Population in French America, 1670–1730', in Bradley Bond, ed., *French Colonial Louisiana and the Atlantic World*, Baton Rouge, 2005, pp. 175–203 at pp. 178, 181, 199   **37.** Guillaume Aubert, 'To Establish One Law and Definite Rules: Race, Religion and the Transatlantic Origins of the Louisiana Code Noir', in Cécile Vidal, ed., *Louisiana: Crossroads of the Atlantic World*, Philadelphia, 2014, pp. 21–43 at pp. 27–8, 33   **38.** Colbert, III, part 2, 368–9, Relation du voyage de Seignelay à Marseille et à Toulon, November 1676; Hugh Thomas, *The Slave Trade: The Story of the Atlantic Slave Trade, 1440–1870*, 1998, pp. 193–4, 228n   **39.** Joseph Roach, 'Body of Law: The Sun King and the Code Noir', in Sara E. Melzer and Kathryn Norberg, eds., *From the Royal to the Republican Body: Incorporating the Political in Seventeenth and Eighteenth-Century France*, Berkeley, 1998, pp. 113–30 at pp. 118–19; Pritchard, *In Search of Empire*, p. 90   **40.** Pritchard, *In Search of Empire*, p. 12   **41.** Sue Peabody, *'There are No Slaves in France': The Political Culture of Race and Slavery in the Ancien Régime*, Oxford, 1996, pp. 12–14   **42.** Choisy, p. 150.   **43.** Van der Cruysse, *Siam*, pp. 288, 337, 360; *Phra Narai, roi de Siam et Louis XIV*, exh. cat., 1986, p. 29, Constance Phaulkon to Chevalier de Caumont, 26 November 1685   **44.** Van der Cruysse, *Siam*, pp. 346, 349, 351, 353   **45.** Ibid., pp. 365–7, 405–7, 415, 445   **46.** Ibid., pp. 462–85   **47.** Rochebrune, pp. 18, 22, 30   **48.** Theodore N. Foss, 'The European Sojourn of Philippe Couplet and Michael Shen Fuzong, 1683–1692', in Jerome Heyndrickx, ed., *Philippe Couplet S.J. (1623–1693): The Man Who Brought China to Europe*, Nettetal, 1990, pp. 121–40 at pp. 129–30   **49.** John W. Witek Jr, 'Catholic Missions and the Expansion of Christianity', in John E. Wills, ed., *China and Maritime Europe, 1500–1800*, New York, 2011, pp. 135–82 at p. 153   **50.** Rochebrune, pp. 26, 38, 39; Liam Matthew Brockey, *Journey to the East: The Jesuit Mission to China, 1579–1724*, 2007, pp. 137, 156, 158, 182   **51.** *La Soie et le Canon: France-Chine, 1700–1860*, exh. cat., Nantes, 2010, p. 21; *DL*, p. 297; *Kangxi, Empereur de Chine, 1662–1722: la cité interdite à Versailles*, exh. cat., Versailles, 2004, passim   **52.** Brockey, p. 183   **53.** Isabelle and Jean-Louis de Vissière, eds., *Lettres édifiantes et curieuses de Chine par des missionnaires jésuites, 1702–1776*, 1979, p. 145, 20 August 1704   **54.** P. J. Bouvet, *Histoire de l'empereur de la Chine, presentée au Roy*, The Hague, 1699, pp. 6–7, 154   **55.** Witek, pp. 155–6; cf. Dangeau, XXIV, 97, XXX, 224, 242, 10 September 1707, 26 September, 23 October, 10 November 1710, for French courtiers' interest in China. Witek, pp. 158, 162–3, 166, 170   **57.** Younès Nekrouf, *Une Amitié orageuse: Moulay Ismaïl et Louis XIV*, 1987, pp. 98–101, 109, 117, 124, Moulay Ismail to Louis XIV, 14 December 1682, 145, 197   **58.** Sourches, I, 68–9, 1 January 1682   **59.** M. Pidou de Saint-Olon, *Etat présent de l'Empire de Maroc*, 1695, pp. 78–9   **60.** Eugène Plantet, *Moulay Ismaïl, Empereur du Maroc et la Princesse de Conti*, 1912, pp. 28, 49, 55, 60, 63, 76; Sourches, VI, 214, 25 December 1699; Nabil Matar, 'Abdallah ibn 'Aisha and the French Court, 1699–1701: An Ambassador without Diplomacy', *French History*, 29, 1, 2015, pp. 1–75 at pp. 62, 69   **61.** Paul Masson, *Histoire des établissements et du commerce français dans l'Afrique barbaresque (1560–1793)*, 1903, p. 217, Pontchartrain to Jourdan, 7 January 1700   **62.** Sévigné, III, 691, Madame de Sévigné to Madame de Grignan, 15

March 1690; cf. Sourches, III, 61, 237, 28 March 1689, 15 May 1690   63. Pierre Duparc, ed., *Recueil des instructions aux ambassadeurs et ministres de France*, XXIX: *Turquie*, 1969, p. 89, instruction of 10 June 1679; Colbert, III, part 2, 209, Louis XIV to Duquesne, 16 October 1681; cf. Arvieux, IV, 208, mémoire of 20 January 1670 for another reference to the alliance between France and the Ottoman Empire   64. Comte de Saint-Priest, *Mémoires sur l'ambassade de France en Turquie*, 1877, p. 238; cf. BL Mss. 2072, 'formulaire pour les lettres du roy aux princes et autres dans les pays étrangers', in which the form of address to be used for the mufti is 'très illustre et très docte seigneur'   65. Cf. Pétis de La Croix, *La Turquie Chrétienne sous la puissante protection de Louis-le-Grand, protecteur unique du christianisme en Orient*, 1695, passim   66. Henri Omont, *Missions archéologiques françaises en Orient au XVII et XVIII siècles*, 2 vols., 1902, I, 199. The view of Athens can be seen there, in the Museum of the City of Athens. The view of Jerusalem, with the Ambassador in formal French dress on horseback in front of it, was rediscovered in a Paris flat in the summer of 2018.   67. Torcy, *Journal*, p. 359, 25 January 1711   68. Bamford, pp. 145, 309; Colbert, III, part 1 (suite), p. 39, Colbert to M. Brodart, 12 November 1676; Lucette Valensi, *Ces étrangers familiers: Musulmans en Europe (XVIe–XVIIIe siècles)*, 2012, p. 115   69. Colbert, III, part 1, lii–liii and (suite), p. 154, Colbert to M. Brodart, 15 May 1679   70. John B. Wolf, *The Barbary Coast: Algiers under the Turks*, 1979, pp. 276–7   71. Jean Bérenger, 'La Politique ottomane de la France dans l'années 1680', in Rainer Babel, ed., *Frankreich im europäischen Staatensytem der Frühen Neuzeit*, Sigmaringen, 1995, pp. 87–107 at pp. 92–4; Wolf, pp. 259–66   72. Marquis de Villette, *Mémoires*, 1844, p. 65; Eugène Plantet, ed., *Correspondance des Deys d'Alger avec la cour de France, 1579–1830*, 2 vols., 1889, I, 84–5   73. Eugène Plantet, ed., *Correspondance des Beys de Tunis et des consuls de France avec la cour, 1577–1830*, 3 vols., 1893–9, III, 421, Jean-Baptiste Michel to Seignelay, June 1689; Plantet, *Deys*, I, 96n, 158   74. Wolf, pp. 267, 277   75. Filippo Casoni, *Storia del bombardamento di Genova nell'anno MDCLXXXIV*, Genoa, 1877, pp. 211–12; cf. Jacques François Blondel, *L'Art de jetter les bombes*, The Hague, 1685, dedicated to Louis XIV   76. Maximilien Misson, *A New Voyage to Italy*, 2 vols., 1699, II, 235   77. Petitfils, *Louis XIV*, p. 413; Emile Vincens, *Histoire de la république de Gênes*, 2 vols., 1842, II, 220–28   78. Chevalier de Mailly, *Histoire de la république de Gênes*, 3 vols., 1696, III, 357, 363–6, 372–82; Salvatore Rotta, 'Genova e il re sole', in Piero Boccardo and Clario di Fabbio, eds., *El siglo de los Genoveses*, Milan, 1999, pp. 286–305. I am grateful for discussion about the bombardment with Tim Llewellyn and Carlo Bitossi. Churches damaged included Madonna della Vigne, Santa Maria de Castello, San Ambrogio dei Gesuiti and four convents.   79. Plantavit de La Pause, II, 69–70, May 1685; Sourches, I, 219–22, 15 May 1685   80. Roberto Santa Maria, ed., *Palazzo Doria Spinola*, Genoa, 2011, pp. 56, 297n   81. Dangeau, I, 152–4, 156, 18, 21 May 1685; Sourches, I, 220–22, 15 May 1685   82. Eugène Sue, *Histoire de la Marine française*, 4 vols., 1845 edn, III, 460–64, M. Lenoc, 'Relation du bombardement de Gênes', 1684, 476, Mortemart to Seignelay, 15 June 1684   83. Rousset, II, 212–14n, Le Tellier to Louvois, 15 April 1676   84. Spielman, pp. 63–6, 69   85. Marie Payet and Ferenc Tóth, eds., *Mille ans de contacts: relations franco-hongroises de l'an mil à nos jours*, Szombathely, 2001, pp. 27, 30   86. Guilleragues, II, 67, 1679; Claude Michaud, 'Le Soleil, l'aigle et le croissant: l'ambassade de Guilleragues à la Porte ottomane et le siège de Vienne de 1683', in idem, *Entre croisades et révolutions: princes, noblesses et nations au centre de l'Europe (XVIe–XVIIIe siècles)*, 2010, pp. 277–92 at p. 285, Louis XIV to Guilleragues, 9 April 1682   87. André, *Louis XIV*, pp. 168, 177–8   88. Comte Renaud Przezdziecki, *Diplomatie et protocole à la cour de Pologne*, 2 vols., 1934, I, 218   89. Bérenger, 'Politique ottomane', pp. 87–107   90. Robert Paris, *Histoire du commerce de Marseille, 1660–1789: le Levant*, 1957, pp. 89–90, letter of Girardin, 23 May 1686   91. Sarmant and Stoll, p. 247, Louvois to Girardin, 12 June 1687   92. AD CP Turquie 20 f. 216, 266, Girardin to Seignelay, 20 July, 28 August 1688; *Treasure of the Holy Sepulchre*, Milan, 2013, p. 384, Mehmed IV to Louis XIV, March 1686   93. Omont, *Missions*, I, 28, instructions of 30 December 1667, 58 'Instructions pour M. Vansleben, s'en allant au Levant, le 17 mars 1671', 161, 235–6, Colbert to Nointel, 30 September 1675, 10 November 1674, 235, Arvieux to Seignelay, 10 December 1682   94. Van der Cruysse, *Noble Désir*, pp. 130,

134–5, 328   95. Claudine Cohen, *Science, libertinage et clandestinité à l'aube des Lumières*, 2011, passim   96. *DL*, p. 1083; Vicomte de Caix de Saint-Aymour, *Histoire des relations de la France avec l'Abyssinie chrétienne sous les règnes de Louis XIII et de Louis XIV*, 1886, pp. 209, 219, 248, 249, Maillet to Pontchartrain, 4 November 1707; O. G. S. Crawford, *The Fung Kingdom of Sennar*, Gloucester, 1951, pp. 229–30. Another motive for their murder may have been Italian missonaries' jealousy of French competition: Pontchartrain, II, 163, Pontchartrain to Cardinal de La Trémoille, 2 March 1707   97. Faruk Bilici, *Louis XIV et son projet de conquête d'Istanbul*, Ankara, 2004, pp. 121, 328–9, Instructions to Girardin 1685, Châteauneuf 1689, Ferriol 1692; André, *Louis XIV*, p. 200   98. René Ristelhueber, *Les Traditions françaises au Liban*, 1925 edn, pp. 130–31, Louis XIV's letters of protection, 28 April 1649   99. Albert Vandal, *Les Voyages du Marquis de Nointel*, 1900, pp. 8–9, 156, 330, Nointel to Pomponne, 17 December 1674; cf. for similar longing for 'deliverance' in Lebanon, Arvieux, II, 427–8, V, 544; in *Etat présent de la Turquie* (1675), Michel Febvre, a Capucin who had lived eighteen years in Syria, also said that local Christians regarded Louis XIV as their 'future liberator' (p. 443)   100. M. Pétis de La Croix, *Etat présent des nations et églises grecque, arménienne et maronite en Turquie*, 1715, passim; Ristelhueber, p. 212, Louis XIV to Ferriol, 20 December 1701   101. Dangeau, XIII, 143, 9 September 1700   102. Géraud Poumarède, *Pour en finir avec la croisade: mythes et réalités de la lutte contre les Turcs aux XVIe et XVIIIe siècles*, 2004, pp. 157, 196   103. Bilici, pp. 126–33; R. Clément, *Les Français d'Egypte aux XVIIe et XVIIIe siècles*, Cairo, 1960, p. 76   104. Bilici, pp. 139–46   105. Ibid., pp. 175–86, 269–76, 286, 308; cf. Henri Omont, 'Projets de prise de Constantinople et de fondation d'un empire français d'Orient sous Louis XIV', *RHD*, 7, 1893, pp. 195–246

Chapter 16: The Huguenot Cataclysm

1. André Neher, 'Principes et applications de la politique de Louis XIV à l'égard des juifs de Metz', in *Deux Siècles d'Alsace française, 1648 – 1798 – 1848*, 1948, pp. 159–73; Gilbert Roos, *Relations entre le gouvernement royal et les juifs du nord-est de la France au XVIIe siècle*, 2000, p. 149; Nathan Netter, *Vingt Siècles d'histoire d'une communauté juive: Metz et son grand passé*, Metz, 1938, pp. 52–3. His visit was followed two days later by the issue of special 'lettres patentes' of protection.   2. Patricia Behre Miskimin, *One King, One Law, Three Faiths: Religion and the Rise of Absolutism in Seventeenth-Century Metz*, Westport, CT, 2002, pp. 51, 52, 113; Pierre Birnbaum, *Un Récit de 'meurtre rituel' au grand siècle: l'affaire Raphaël Lévy, Metz, 1669*, Metz, 2008, passim; Joseph Ancillon, *Recueil journalier de ce qui s'est passé de plus mémorable dans la cité de Metz*, Metz, 2 vols., 1860, I, 69–73, January–February 1670. I am grateful for further information to M. Lang, interviewed at Metz, 2 November 2015.   3. Janine Garrisson, *L'Edit de Nantes et sa Revocation: histoire d'une intolérance*, 1985 edn, pp. 16, 102–3   4. Roger Mettam, 'Louis XIV and the Persecution of the Huguenots: The Role of the Ministers and Royal Officials', in Irene Scouloudi, ed., *The Huguenots in Britain and their French Background, 1550–1800*, Basingstoke, 1987, pp. 198–216 at p. 202; David Garrioch, *The Huguenots of Paris and the Coming of Religious Freedom, 1685–1789*, Cambridge, 2014, pp. 164–5, 264; Geoffrey Treasure, *The Huguenots*, 2014, pp. 275, 321   5. Faugère, pp. 439–40 and n, 23 February 1658, diary of MM. de Zoete van Laeke   6. Louis, XIV, *Oeuvres*, V, 46, Louis XIV to Estrades, 25 August 1661; BS 1290, Louis XIV to Duc de Saint-Aignan, 1 April 1666   7. Cénat, *Louvois*, pp. 309–10; Mettam, 'Persecution of the Huguenots', p. 206; Garrisson, p. 121; Louis XIV, *Mémoires*, p. 101   8. Matthew Glozier, *Marshal Schomberg, 1615–1690*, Brighton, 2005, pp. xviii, 3, 62, 64, 73, 87, 101   9. J. F. A. Kazner, *Leben Friederichs von Schomberg*, Mannheim, 1789, II, 102, 105   10. Trond Norén Isaksen, 'Anointing Absolutism', *The Court Historian*, 19, 1, June 2014, pp. 75–8 at p. 78   11. Charles Ancillon, *Histoire de l'établissement des François réfugiez dans les états de son altesse electorale de Brandebourg*, Berlin, 1690, dedicatory epistle   12. Garrisson, p. 128   13. Dingli, p. 84   14. Mettam, 'Persecution of the Huguenots', pp. 212–13   15. Isaac Dumont de Bostaquet, *Mémoires sur les temps qui ont précédé et suivi la Révocation de l'édit de Nantes*, 1968 edn, p. 125; cf. Cénat, *Louvois*, p. 314   16.

Savile, p. 93, Henry Savile to Lord Halifax, 5 June 1679 **17.** Sourches, I, 433, 15 August 1686 **18.** Spielman, p. 124 **19.** Rousset, III, 393n, Louvois to Condé, 27 July 1683 **20.** Sourches, V, 343n, 25 September 1697; Saint-Maurice, I, 269, 285 **21.** Salat and Sarmant, p. 46, Louvois to Louis XIV, 2 September 1679. This incident is unknown to Prince Eugène's biographers. The brothers had not been punished. **22.** Kroll, p. 142, Madame to Ameliese, 9 June 1708 **23.** Nicholas Henderson, *Prince Eugene of Savoy: A Biography*, 1964, pp. 9, 13 **24.** Duc de La Force, *Le Grand Conti*, 1948 edn, pp. 45, 55, 58, 65; Sourches, I, 283–4, 30 July 1685, IV, 325–6, 455, 23 April 1694, 15 May 1695 **25.** Bryan Cartledge, *The Will to Survive: A History of Hungary*, pp. 117–18; Spielman, p. 89 **26.** Garrisson, p. 45 **27.** Brian E. Strayer, 'The Edict of Fontainebleau and the Huguenots: Who's to Blame?', in Richard Bonney and D. J. B. Trim, eds., *Persecution and Pluralism: Calvinists and Religious Minorities in Early Modern Europe, 1550–1700*, Bern, 2006, pp. 273–94 at pp. 287–8 **28.** A. de Galtier de Laroque, *Le Marquis de Ruvigny et les Protestants à la cour de Louis XIV, 1643–85*, 1892, p. 192; Treasure, pp. 280, 324 **29.** Jean Nicolas, *La Rébellion française, 1661–1789*, 2008 edn, pp. 779, 781 **30.** Maral, *Le Roi-Soleil et Dieu*, p. 195; Garrisson, p. 149; Charles Ancillon, *L'Irrévocabilité de l'édit de Nantes*, Amsterdam, 1688, p. 274; cf. Strayer, p. 293. However, the work *Actes de l'Assemblée générale du clergé de France de MDCLXXXV concernant la religion*, by M.D.S.B., claims the clergy did not want the revocation. **31.** Edmond Esmonin, *Etudes sur la France des XVIIe et XVIIIe siècles*, 1964, p. 366, Louis XIV to Mgr d'Harcourt, 7 November 1685 **32.** Mazarin, *Lettres*, IX, 14, Mazarin to Mercoeur, 19 August 1658 **33.** Robin Briggs, *Communities of Belief: Cultural and Social Tension in Early Modern France*, Oxford, 1995 edn, p. 212; Treasure, p. 352 **34.** Esmonin, pp. 360, 361, Louis XIV to Harlay, 21 September 1685, 16 October 1685 **35.** Dingli, pp. 268–9 **36.** Garrioch, p. 50, d'Aguesseau to Pontchartrain, n.d. **37.** Strayer, pp. 277–9; Mettam, 'Persecution of the Huguenots', p. 214; Cénat, *Louvois*, p. 320; Treasure, p. 350 **38.** Maral, *Maintenon*, pp. 62–3; Strayer, pp. 280–83 **39.** Nicolas-Joseph Foucault, *Mémoires*, 2 vols., 1862, I, 115, 121, 132, 22 February 1685, 1 July 1685, Le Tellier to Foucault, 17 October 1685 **40.** Dingli, pp. 313, 316–19 **41.** Garrisson, pp. 225–7, 237 **42.** Pierre Blet, *Les Assemblées du clergé et Louis XIV, de 1670 à 1693*, Rome, 1972, pp. 468, 482 **43.** Dangeau, I, 196, 213–14, 2 September, 12, 13 October 1685; cf. Sourches, I, 318–21, 20 October 1685 **44.** Dingli, p. 271, Seignelay to La Reynie, 22 October 1685 **45.** Garrisson, pp. 11–12; Sarmant, *Homme et roi*, pp. 299–302 **46.** Treasure, p. 357 **47.** Foucault, I, 151, 161, 219, 220, 231, 288, 523, Louis XIV to Noailles, 6 November 1685, 525, Louvois to Foucault, 26 November 1685 **48.** Dingli, p. 316, Louis XIV to La Force, 30 January 1686 **49.** J. F. Thénard, *Mémoires ou livre de raison d'un bourgeois de Marseille (1674–1726)*, Montpellier, 1881, pp. 33–4, 2 November 1685 **50.** Garrisson, pp. 256, 258 **51.** Jacques Saint-Germain, *La Reynie et la police au Grand Siècle*, 1962, pp. 313–14 **52.** Sourches, I, 330, 12 November 1685 **53.** Garrioch, p. 32; Dingli, p. 327 **54.** Rousset, III, 496n, Louvois to La Trousse, 22 July 1686 **55.** Robin Gwynn, *Huguenot Heritage: The History and Contribution of the Huguenots in Britain*, Brighton, 2001 edn, p. 28 **56.** Philippe Joutard, 'The Revocation of the Edict of Nantes: End or Renewal of French Calvinism?', in Menna Prestwich, ed., *International Calvinism, 1541–1715*, Oxford, 1985, pp. 339–68 at pp. 360–61, 367–8. **57.** Garrioch, pp. 6, 10, 56; Treasure, pp. 381–3 **58.** Herbert Lüthy, *La Banque Protestante en France, de la Révocation de l'Edit de Nantes à la Révolution*, 3 vols., 1959–70, I, 77, 121–5 **59.** Jacques Saint-Germain, *Samuel Bernard, le banquier des rois*, 1960, pp. 40–41, 46 **60.** Matthew Carr, *Blood and Faith: The Purging of Muslim Spain*, 2009, pp. 1, 46, 261, 265 **61.** Rousset, III, 503, Louvois to Marquis de Lambert, 30 January 1686; Dingli, p. 336 **62.** David van der Linden, *Experiencing Exile: Huguenot Refugees in the Dutch Republic, 1680–1700*, Dorchester, 2015, pp. 11, 19, 23 **63.** Jean Migault, *Journal*, Marseille, 1978, p. 110 **64.** Dingli, pp. 108, 341–2 **65.** Information kindly communicated by Elizabeth Randall, September 2015; Pontchartrain, I, 164, Pontchartrain to Comte de La Massais, 12 April 1702; Emmanuel Jahan, *La Confiscation des biens des religionnaires fugitifs: de la Révocation de l'Edit de Nantes à la révolution*, 1959, passim **66.** Lynn, *Wars*, p. 178; Dessert, *La Royale*, p. 214 **67.** Fonck, *Luxembourg*, p. 322; Ségur, *Tapissier*, p. 350, Luxembourg to Louis XIV, 12 June 1693 **68.**

Andrew Flick, 'Jean de Robethon, a Contested Figure Behind the Throne', *Huguenot Society Journal*, xxx, April, 2016, pp. 488–502   69. Webb, pp. 57–8, 83, 97   70. Picavet, *Diplomatie française*, p. 270   71. François Charpentier, *De l'excellence de la langue française*, 1683, dedication   72. Lough, p. 309   73. Around 3,000 French Protestants settled in the English colonies in North America: Havard and Vidal, p. 27   74. Linden, pp. 55, 125; W. T. M. Frijhoff, 'Uncertain Brotherhood: The Huguenots in the Dutch Republic', in B. van Ruymbeke and R. J. Sparks, eds., *Memory and Identity: The Huguenots in France and the Atlantic Diaspora*, Columbia, SC, 2003, pp. 128–71 at p. 136   75. Hubert Bost, *Un Intellectuel avant la lettre: le journaliste Pierre Bayle (1647–1706)*, Amsterdam, 1994, passim   76. Rousset, III, 511   77. Justin Champion, *Republican Learning: John Toland and the Crisis of Christian Culture, 1696–1722*, Manchester, 2003, p. 70   78. Monique Cottret, *La Bastille à prendre: histoire et mythe de la forteresse royale*, 1986, pp. 41, 108; Constantin de Renneville, *L'Inquisition française ou l'Histoire de la Bastille*, 6 vols., Amsterdam, 1724, I, iv   79. Picavet, *Diplomatie française*, p. 194   80. Georges Pagès, *Le Grand Electeur et Louis XIV, 1660–1688*, 1905, pp. 98, 543, letter of Frederick William, 18 August 1685, 556   81. Linden, pp. 177, 202   82. MM. Erman et Reclam, *Mémoires pour servir à l'histoire des réfugiés français dans les états du roi*, 6 vols., Berlin, 1782–7, I, 104, 302, 348, 357, 360, 366–8, 371, Gaultier to William III, 3 March 1685; Derek McKay, *The Great Elector: Frederick William of Brandenburg-Prussia*, Harlow, 2001, p. 253; Ragnhild Hatton, *George I: Elector and King*, 1978, p. 73   83. Pagès, p. 541   84. Sonia P. Anderson, ed., *Report on the Manuscripts of the Late Allan George Finch, V: Secret Service Papers 1691–1693 and Naval and Military Papers to 1694*, 2004, pp. cix, 507, 612   85. Albert Waddington, *Le Grand Electeur: Frédéric Guillaume de Brandebourg*, 2 vols., 1908, II, 550–51; McKay, p. 256   86. Pagès, pp. 567, 569, letters of Frederick William, May 1686   87. Waddington, II, 564–9, letters of Rébenac, 16 August 1686, Duchess Sophie, 9 August 1686   88. Alexandre Dubois, *Journal d'un curé de campagne au XVIIe siècle*, ed. Henri Platelle, 1965, p. 70, 1685   89. Sourches, I, 359, February 1686   90. Glozier, *Schomberg*, pp. 117, 119, letter of 25 September 1687; Waddington, II, 585; AD CP Brandebourg 28, Louis XIV to Schomberg, 15 May 1687   91. Rowen, *De Witt, Grand Pensionary*, p. 746, de Groot to de Witt, 30 January 1671   92. Linda and Marsha Frey, *Frederick I: The Man and his Times*, Boulder, CO, 1984, pp. 121–6; Helmut Schnitter, 'The Refugees in the Army of Brandenburg-Prussia', in Matthew Glozier and David Onnekink, eds., *War, Religion and Service: Huguenot Soldiering, 1685–1713*, Aldershot, 2007, pp. 145–59   93. M. de la Rosière, 'Etat de la cour de Brandebourg en 1694', *RHD*, 1887, pp. 267–92, 411–24 at pp. 272, 275, 290, 411, 413   94. Eckart Birnstiel, ed., *La Diaspora des Huguenots: les réfugiés protestants de France et leur dispersion dans le monde, XVIe–XVIIIe siècles*, 2001, pp. 78, 150   95. Another Huguenot architect and pupil of Vauban, Jean de Bodt, built, in Louis XIV style, the Arsenal and part of the Schloss in Berlin, and the Japanisches Palais in Dresden, as well as forts in Brandenburg and Saxony.   96. Tim Blanning, *Frederick the Great: King of Prussia*, 2016, p. 31; Jens Häseler, 'Entre la France et le Brandebourg: la République des Lettres', in Guido Braun, ed., *Les Etats allemands et les Huguenots*, Munich, 2007, pp. 231–40 at pp. 231–9, 235. Other Huguenots at Frederick's court would include his librarian Charles Etienne Jordan and his dwarf Karl Theophilus Guichard. Other Hohenzollerns, the future Catherine II and the children of George II, also had Huguenot tutors or governesses.   97. As it had been, before 1643, for other French refugees, such as Marie de Médicis, the Duchesse de Chevreuse and the ducs de Vendôme, d'Epernon and de La Valette.   98. W. H. Manchée, *The Fouberts and their Royal Academy*, 1925, passim   99. Bernard Cottret, *Terre d'exil: l'Angleterre et ses réfugiés français et wallons, de la réforme à la révocation de l'édit de Nantes, 1550–1700*, 1985, p. 227   100. Tessa Murdoch, *The Quiet Conquest: The Huguenots, 1685–1985*, 1985, pp. 51–79   101. Laroque, p. 267; Garrisson, pp. 166–7   102. Solange Deyon, *Du loyalisme au refus: les protestants français et leur député général entre la Fronde et la Révocation*, Arras, 1976, pp. 101, 137, Ruvigny to Cardinal de Bouillon, 9 February 1686, 141–2; Randolph Vigne, '"The Good Lord Galway": The English and Irish Careers of a Huguenot Leader', in Glozier and Onnekink, pp. 59–78   103. Charles II's upholsterers and tailors had often been French. Two former ambassadors in France later became masters of the great wardrobe, responsible for the decoration of the royal palaces. Murdoch, pp. 162–3 and passim **104.** J. F. Hayward, *Huguenot Silver in England, 1688–1727*, 1959, pp. 1–7. Others were Paul Crespin and David Willaume. Silver made in London by Huguenots can be seen in the Victoria and Albert Museum and the British Museum. **105.** Murdoch, pp. ix, 12–13, 111, 183–6, 223; cf. also her talk at the Huguenot conference on 10 September 2015, 'Daniel Marot and the Louis XIV Style in England' and the Huguenot exhibition at Boughton in August 2015; Gwynn, p. 93 **106.** Alice Archer Houblon, *The Houblon Family: Its Stories and its Times*, 2 vols., 1907, I, pp. 228–41; cf. François Crouzet, 'The Huguenots and the English Financial Revolution', in idem, *Britain, France and International Commerce: From Louis XIV to Victoria*, Aldershot, 1996, I, 221–66. Other famous names included Cazalet, Bosanquet, Thellusson. Of the 542 city merchants who presented a loyal address to George II against the Pretender in 1744, 100 had French names. **107.** Murdoch, pp. 52, 280 **108.** Treasure, p. 288; Claude Badalo-Dulong, *Banquier du roi: Barthélemy Hervart, 1606–1676*, 1951, p. 153 **109.** Badalo-Dulong, pp. 198, 202, 214; Sourches, I, 330, 12 November 1685; Emma Monson, 'The Three Esthers: Noblewomen of the Huguenot Refuge', *Proceedings of the Huguenot Society of Great Britain and Ireland* XXVII, 1, 1998, pp. 1–19 **110.** E.g. *An Account of the Persecutions and Oppressions of the Protestants in France*, 1686, by Jean Claude; Pierre Jurieu, *Pastoral letters, directed to the suffering Protestants of France, groaning under the cruel persecution of the bloody tyrant Lewis XIV*, n.d., and many more **111.** Treasure, p. 365; Murdoch, pp. 40, 46; Gwynn, pp. 162–5 **112.** Hugh Trevor-Roper, 'A Huguenot Historian: Paul Rapin', in Scouloudi, pp. 3–19 **113.** Charles Littleton, 'Abel Boyer and Other Huguenot Reporters of Parliament', talk at the Huguenot conference, London, 10 September 2015 **114.** G. C. Gibbs, 'Huguenot Contributions to England's Intellectual Life and England's Intellectual Commerce with Europe, 1680–1720', in J. A. H. Bots, ed., *The Revocation of the Edict of Nantes and the Dutch Republic*, Amsterdam, 1986, pp. 181–200 **115.** Katherine Swift, 'The French Booksellers in the Strand: Huguenots in the London Book Trade, 1685–1730', *Proceedings of the Huguenot Society of Great Britain and Ireland* XXV, 2, 1990, 123–39. I am grateful for this reference to Giles Mandelbrote. **116.** Patrick Clarke de Dromantin, 'Une Noblesse atypique: les réfugiés jacobites en France au XVIIIe siècle', in J. Pontet et al., eds., *La Noblesse de la fin du XVIe au début du XXe siècle: un modèle social?*, 2 vols., Anglet, 2002, II, pp. 87–102 at pp. 89–92, 94 **117.** As recorded in an undated document by Randolph Vigne attached to the monument. **118.** Cottret, *Terre d'exil*, p. 243, Bonrepaus to Seignelay, n.d.; J. J. Jusserand, *Recueil des Instructions donnés aux ambassadeurs et ministres de France: Angleterre*, 3 vols., 1929–65, II, 327, 338, Instructions to Bonrepaus, 30 December 1685, despatch of 5 May 1686; Dingli, pp. 279, 357 **119.** *Vauban, sa famille et ses écrits, ses oisivetés et sa correspondence*, ed. Rochas d'Aiglun, 2 vols. 1910, I, 465–6, Mémoire pour le rappel des Huguenots, December 1689 **120.** Blanchard, pp. 271, 345–7 **121.** His irrational hatreds included Maine, and the Lorraine and Noailles families: Saint-Simon, *Mémoires*, ed. Regnier and Chéruel, VII, 93, 226 **122.** Ibid., 19–20, XI, 55 **123.** Alexandre Maral, *Les Derniers Jours de Louis XIV*, 2014, p. 17 **124.** Saint-Simon, *Mémoires*, ed. Regnier and Chéruel, XII, 107–8 **125.** Sauzet, pp. 212, 215–16, 228, quoting his diary for August 1681 and other years **126.** Garrioch, p. 161, quoting Bayle's *Ce que c'est que la France toute catholique*, Amsterdam, 1686 **127.** After 1715 Madame would have difficulty persuading her son the Regent to liberate Protestant galley slaves: Van der Cruysse, *Princesse européenne*, pp. 314, 550 **128.** Marianne Carbonnier-Burkard, *Comprendre la révolte des Camisards*, Rennes, 2013, pp. 29, 98–9, 30, 32, 36, 38, 40, 48, 50, 55, 61, 66, 67, 72; Jean-Christian Petitfils, *Le Régent*, 1986, p. 628 **129.** Rousset, IV, 24, Catinat to Louvois, 9 May 1686 **130.** Sévigné, III, 388, to Bussy-Rabutin, 16 March 1689 **131.** John A. Lynn, 'A Brutal Necessity? The Devastation of the Palatinate, 1688–1689', in Mark Grimsley and Clifford J. Rogers, eds., *Civilians in the Path of War*, 2002, pp. 79–100 at pp. 83–4, 100; Rousset, IV, 28, Louis XIV to Marquis d'Arcy, 8 November 1686 **132.** Rowlands, *Dynastic State*, p. 347; Dangeau, XI, 9, 8 January 1698 **133.** Isabelle Dubois et al., eds., *Place des Victoires: histoire, architecture, société*, 2003, pp. 41–7, 52, 55, 59 **134.** Sourches, I, 369–70, 25 March 1686; cf. Sabatier, p. 451 **135.** Perez, pp. 413–17; Sourches, I, 56, 14 November 1681 **136.** Dangeau, XII,

83, 18 May 1699 **137.** Michel Martin, *Les Monuments équestres de Louis XIV: une grande entreprise de propagande monarchique*, 1986, passim; Richard L. Cleary, *The Place Royale and Urban Design in the Ancien Régime*, Cambridge, 1999, pp. 1, 16–17; cf. Antoine Coutelle, *Poitiers au XVIIe siècle: les pratiques culturelles d'une élite urbaine*, Rennes, pp. 256, 263, for the erection of a statue in Poitiers **138.** Sarmant, *Louis XIV et Paris*, pp. 49–51, 54 **139.** M. Sainctot, 'Relation de ce qui s'est passé au disner du Roy dans l'Hostel de Ville le 30 janvier 1687', in Abbé Fr. Duffo, *Le Cérémonial de France à la cour de Louis XIV*, 1936, pp. 32–4; Sources, II, 14–15, 30 January 1687; Sabatier, p. 451; Perez, pp. 414–29. The visit was commemorated by a print proclaiming 'Louis le grand' 'l'amour et les délices de son peuple' and 'la terreur et l'admiration de l'univers'. **140.** Pierre Zoberman, *Les Cérémonies de la parole*, 2008, pp. 178–9 **141.** Charles Perrault, *Le Siècle de Louis le Grand*, 1687, p. 21 **142.** Spielman, p. 148 **143.** Ruth Clark, *Sir William Trumbull in Paris, 1685–1686*, Cambridge, 1938, p. 108, Trumbull to Sunderland, 3 April 1686

Chapter 17: England Changes Sides: The Flights of King James

1. Sources, III, 8, 7 January 1689; Dangeau, III, 169, 7 January 1689, XIV, 63, 76, 21 March, 4 April 1701; BN Mss. 16633 ff. 180–84, 'Cérémonies du règne de Louis XIV'; M. Sainctot, 'Arrivée de la Reyne d'Angleterre en France avec le Prince de Galles le 21 decembre 1688, et celle du Roy d'Angleterre le 2 janvier 1689', in Duffo, *Cérémonial*, pp. 37, 40 **2.** James Jones, 'French Intervention in English and Dutch Politics, 1677–88', in Jeremy Black, ed., *Knights Errant and True Englishmen: British Foreign Policy, 1660–1800*, Edinburgh, 1989, pp. 1–23 at pp. 2, 10–13; Metzger, p. 156. In the 1660s, for similar reasons, he had paid subsidies to 'certains restes de la faction de Cromwell' in order to weaken Charles II: Louis XIV, *Mémoires*, p. 261 **3.** G. C. Gibbs, 'The Reception of the Huguenots in England and the Dutch Republic, 1680–1690', in Ole Peter Grell et al., eds., *From Persecution to Toleration: The Glorious Revolution and Religion in England*, Oxford, 1991, pp. 275–306 at pp. 294–5; cf. Gwynn, pp. 181–2 **4.** Levillain, pp. 354–5; Troost, 'To Restore and Preserve', pp. 294, 296, William III to Waldeck, 18 February 1680, 23 October 1682 **5.** Nimwegen, p. 513 **6.** Louis André and Emile Bourgeois, *Recueil des Instructions données aux ambassadeurs et ministres de France*, XXI: *Hollande*, 1922, p. 394, d'Avaux to Louis XIV, 22 April 1683, 28 August 1687 **7.** Comte d'Avaux, *Négociations de Monsieur le Comte d'Avaux en Hollande, depuis 1685 jusqu'en 1688*, 6 vols., 1753, VI, 191–2, 218, 231, d'Avaux to Louis XIV, 21 August, 9, 14 September 1688; Noailles, IV, 188n, d'Avaux to Louis XIV, 29 July, 2 September 1688 **8.** Jones, 'French Intervention', pp. 3–4, 113; K. D. H. Haley, 'The Dutch, the Invasion of England and the Alliance of 1689', in Lois G. Schwoerer, ed., *The Revolution of 1688–1689: Changing Perspectives*, Cambridge, 1992, pp. 21–34 at pp. 22–4 **9.** Jones, 'French Intervention', pp. 113–17; Boutant, p. 860, Louis XIV to d'Avaux, 14 October 1688; Wout Troost, *William III: The Stadholder-King*, Aldershot, 2016, pp. 187–8 **10.** Jérôme de La Gorce, *Berain: dessinateur du Roi Soleil*, 1986, pp. 127–8 **11.** Troost, *William III*, p. 191 **12.** Jusserand, II, 409, Bonrepaus to Seignelay, 4 September 1688 **13.** Jonathan Israel, ed., *The Anglo-Dutch Moment: Essays on the Glorious Revolution and its World Impact*, Cambridge, 2003, p. 112 **14.** AD CP Prusse 32 f. 150v, Gravel to Louis XIV, 21 November 1688 **15.** Israel, *Anglo-Dutch Moment*, pp. 106–7, 109, 329; Boutant, pp. 809, 813 **16.** Peter H. Wilson, *War, State and Society in Württemberg, 1677–1793*, Cambridge, 1995, p. 113 **17.** AD CP Prusse 31 ff. 232, 242, 254, Gravel to Louis XIV, 1, 8 September 1688 **18.** AD CP Prusse 31 ff. 48v, 122, 133, 188v, Gravel to Louis XIV, 3, 28 July, 22 August 1688 **19.** AD CP Prusse 32 ff. 23, 72v, 74, Gravel to Louis XIV, 7, 16 October 1688 **20.** Sources, II, 225n, 246, 8 September, 12 October 1688 **21.** J. P. Kenyon, *Robert Spencer, Earl of Sunderland*, 1958, pp. 213–15 **22.** Noailles, IV, 203, 206, Louis XIV to Barrillon, 14, 23 September 1688, to d'Avaux, 7 October 1688; Boutant, pp. 832–3 **23.** P. Grimblot, *Letters of William III and Louis XIV, and of their Ministers*, 2 vols., 1848, II, 154, Tallard to Torcy, 9 September 1698 **24.** Avaux, VI, 175, 208, 255, d'Avaux to Louis XIV, 29 July, 2, 20 September 1688 **25.** Ibid., 257,

270, d'Avaux to Louis XIV, 23, 27 September 1688 26. Boutant, pp. 855-60 27. Van der Cruysse, *Princesse européenne*, pp. 254, 294-6; Troost, *William III*, p. 175 28. Boutant, pp. 786, 801-2 29. Avaux, VI, 268, d'Avaux, 27 September 1688 30. Ibid., 321, d'Avaux to Louis XIV, 11 November 1688 31. Ibid., 335, d'Avaux to Louis XIV, 2 December 1688 32. Ibid., 287, d'Avaux to Louis XIV, 15 October 1688 33. Troost, *William III*, pp. 194-9 34. Christoph Kampmann, 'The English Crisis, the Emperor Leopold and the Origins of the Dutch Intervention in 1688', *Historical Journal*, 55, 2, June 2012, pp. 521-32 35. André and Bourgeois, *Recueil des Instructions*, p. 395n, Louis XIV to d'Avaux, 14 October 1688 36. BN Mss. fr. 155212, 'Mémoire des raisons qui ont obligé le roy à reprendre les Armes', 24 September 1688 37. AD CP Turquie 20, Ottoman Sultan and Grand Vizier to Louis XIV, 9, 12 May 1688; Girardin to Croissy, 29 June, 28 July 1688. The letters took about seven weeks between Constantinople and Versailles. 38. AD CP Turquie 20 ff. 139, 171, 182, Girardin to Croissy, 26 May 1688 39. AD CP Turquie 20 ff. 86v, 288, 290, Girardin to Croissy, 30 September, 9 November 1688 40. AD CP Turquie 21 ff. 10-12, 86v, Girardin to Croissy, 22 October, 9 November 1688 41. AD CP Turquie 21 f. 197v, Louis XIV to Girardin, 10 September 1688 42. AD CP Turquie 21 ff. 241, 249v, Girardin to Louis XIV, 28 August 1688 43. AD CP Turquie 21 ff. 208-9, Louis XIV to Girardin, 10 September 1688. He had already made a similar promise in July 1688: Emmanuel Caron, 'Le Tournant de l'année 1683 dans la politique ottomane de Louis XIV', in Daniel Tollet, ed., *Guerres et paix: mélanges d'histoire des relations internationales offerts à Jean Bérenger*, 2003, p. 571, Louis XIV to Girardin, 31 July 1688 44. AD CP Turquie 20 ff. 269v-270, 281, Louis XIV to Girardin, 15 October, 2 December 1688 45. AD CP Turquie 20 f. 268v, Louis XIV to Girardin, 2 December 1688 46. AD CP Turquie 21 ff. 20, 41-2, Louis XIV to Girardin, 3 November 1688, 11 January 1689; cf. Caron, p. 575 47. AD CP Turquie 21 ff. 58-58v, Louis XIV to Girardin, 21 February 1689. His determination to prevent peace between Austria and the Ottoman Empire was well known. See e.g. Villars, I, pp. 361-2 48. Dangeau, III, 100, 9 October 1688; Matthew Glozier and David Onnekink 'Huguenot Soldiers in Dutch Service', in Glozier and Onnekink, pp. 111-30 at pp. 121-2 49. BN Mss. fr. 15522 ff. 10, 25, Louis XIV to Cardinal d'Estrées, 6 September 1688 50. Sévigné, II, 222, 233, Sévigné to Grignan, 22 October, 3 November 1688 51. David Davies, 'James II, William of Orange and the Admirals', in Eveline Cruickshanks, ed., *By Force or By Default? The Revolution of 1688-1689*, Edinburgh, 1989, pp. 82-108 52. Webb, pp. 117, 125, 131, 146 53. Noailles, IV, 219, Louis XIV to Barrillon, 1 November 1688 54. Clarke, II, 250; John Carswell, *The Descent on England: A Study of the English Revolution of 1688 and its European Background*, 1969, pp. 205, 209 55. Robert Beddard, *A Kingdom without a King: The Journal of the Provisional Government in the Revolution of 1688*, Oxford, pp. 37, 51; Lt Gen. Sir F. W. Hamilton, *The Origin and History of the First or Grenadier Guards*, 3 vols., 1874, I, 316; Clarke, II, 262 56. Webb, pp. 162-4 57. Beddard, p. 180; Hamilton, I, 318-19 58. Beddard, p. 60; Clarke, II, 265 59. Clarke, II, 246; Petitfils, *Lauzun*, pp. 264-81 60. Dangeau, III, 153, 23 December 1688 61. Petitfils, *Lauzun*, pp. 280-84, 329, 362; Sévigné, II, 292, 305, to Grignan, 27 December 1688, to Bussy-Rabutin, 6 January 1689. Lauzun would later advise 'James III'. 62. Callow, pp. 17, 19 63. Clarke, II, 273-7 64. Beddard, p. 44; Israel, *Anglo-Dutch Moment*, pp. 1-3 65. Ibid., pp. 134, 146, 149-50; Hamilton, I, 317-19 66. Martin Haile, *Queen Mary of Modena: Her Life and Letters*, 1905, p. 244, Abbé Melani to Grand Duke of Tuscany, February 1689, Rizzini to Duke of Modena, 2 March 1689 67. James Hogan, ed., *Négociations de M. le Comte d'Avaux en Irlande*, Dublin, 1934, p. 32, Louis XIV to d'Avaux, 12 March 1689 68. Israel, *Anglo-Dutch Moment*, p. 135; Troost, 'To Restore and Preserve', pp. 283-303, 297, 302 69. Carswell, p. 245; H. C. Foxcroft, *A Supplement to Burnet's History of my own Time*, Oxford, 1902, p. 228 70. Glozier, *Schomberg*, p. 143 71. Dubois, *Journal*, p. 76, 1690 72. Webb, p. 238; Eamonn O Ciardha, *Ireland and the Jacobite Cause: A Fatal Attachment*, Dublin, 2002, p. 83; I am grateful for this reference to Dr Andrew Barclay; Petitfils, *Lauzun*, pp. 319-20 73. Israel, *Anglo-Dutch Moment*, pp. 159, 188 74. Hogan, pp. 414, 649, Louis XIV to d'Avaux, 20 July 1689, 4 January 1690 75. Sourches, IV, 27, 20 April 1692 76. Haile, p. 288, Mary of Modena to the Superior of Chaillot, 14 June

1692   77. Edward Corp, *A Court in Exile: The Stuarts in France, 1689–1718*, 2004, p. 5   78. Ibid., pp. 105–6; *La Cour des Stuarts à Saint-Germain-en-Laye au temps de Louis XIV*, exh. cat., 1992, pp. 164, 210   79. Corp, pp. 99, 191; Callow, pp. 190, 231   80. See e.g. Madame de La Tour de Pin, *Journal d'une femme de cinquante ans*, 2 vols., 1913, I, 18, 71, 94   81. Corp, pp. 160–79   82. *Cour des Stuarts*, pp. 66–73; ML, II, 611, Maintenon to Madame de Fontaines, 12 October 1695, IV, 207, 226, Maintenon to Ursins, 1, 17 October 1707   83. ML, II, 738, Maintenon to Madame de Berval, 25 October 1696   84. Dangeau, IX, 168, 26 April 1696   85. Sourches, IV, 20, 130, 19 March, 8 October 1692   86. Ibid., III, 318, 18 October 1690   87. Sévigné, III, 310, Sévigné to Grignan, 10 January 1689   88. Jane Garrett, *The Triumphs of Providence: The Assassination Plot, 1696*, Cambridge, 1980, p. 71   89. Van der Cruysse, *Princesse européenne*, pp 325, 326; Jaeglé, I, 81, 94, Madame to Electress Sophia, 22 August 1690, 19 June 1692   90. Sévigné, III, 381, to Grignan, 12 March 1689; cf. Sourches, IV, 132, 16 October 1692   91. Sévigné, III, 337, 347, Sévigné to Grignan, 2, 10 February 1689; Aligny, p. 222; cf. Haile, p. 244, Rizzini to Duke of Modena, 2 March 1689, condemning James II for 'losing one kingdom without drawing his sword'   92. Sévigné, III, 311, 319–20, to Grignan, 10, 17 January 1689; cf. Kroll, p. 213, Madame to Luise, 29 May 1718   93. Dangeau, III, 172, 9, 10 January 1689; Sourches, III, 12, 10 January 1689   94. Dangeau, VI, 179, 11 October 1692   95. Sévigné, III, 319–20, Sévigné to Grignan, 17 January 1689   96. Haile, p. 136, Louvois to Beringhen, 1 January 1689. For example, she helped persuade Louis XIV to recognize her son in 1701 and to send an expedition to Scotland in 1708.   97. Haussonville, *Duchesse de Bourgogne*, IV, 235–8, Mary of Modena to Maintenon, 31 October, 13 February 1713   98. ML, IV, 115 to Ursins, 24 April 1707   99. Jaeglé, I, 87, 263, Madame to Electress Sophia, 10 August 1691, 6 April 1702   100. Nathalie Genet-Rouffiac, *Le Grand Exil: les Jacobites en France, 1688–1715*, 2007, p. 87; Sourches, III, 66, 3 April 1689   101. Sourches, III, 273, 27 July 1690, IV, 461, April 1695   102. Ségur, *Tapissier*, p. 214; Clément, *Police*, p. 91, Seignelay to La Reynie, 16 August 1690; Pontchartrain, I, 159, 162, Pontchartrain to d'Argenson, 22 March 1702, to Lord Middleton, 25 March 1702   103. Callow, pp. 303, 320; Clarke, II, 586   104. René Pillorget, 'Louis XIV et l'Irlande', *RHD*, 106, 1992, pp. 7–26 at p. 10; Noailles, IV, 178–9, Bonrepaus to Louis XIV, 9 October 1687, Seignelay to Bonrepaus, 29 September 1687   105. Warren C. Scoville, *The Persecution of Huguenots and French Economic Development, 1680–1720*, Berkeley, 1960, pp. 440–47   106. Corp, pp. 149–50; Callow, p. 223   107. AN oi 363 ff. 328, 337, Pontchartrain to d'Argenson, 6, 19 October 1701; oi 362, Pontchartrain to Lord Middleton, 25 March 1702   108. AN oi 366 ff. 80, 139v, d'Argenson to Caryll, 26 March, 27 May 1705   109. AN oi 363 ff. 315, 322, d'Argenson to Caryll, 25, 29 September 1705; Genet-Rouffiac, p. 325; Corp, pp. 151–7   110. Jaeglé, I, 221, Madame to Electress Sophia, 18 July 1700   111. Callow, p. 190; Paul Monod et al., eds., *Loyalty and Identity: Jacobites at Home and Abroad*, Basingstoke, 2010, pp. 211–12   112. Dangeau, XI, 27, 12 February 1698   113. Corvisier, *Louvois*, pp. 104, 186. Putting his career in the French army before his loyalty to 'James III', Berwick would refuse to follow him to Scotland in 1715: Sir Charles Petrie, *The Marshal Duke of Berwick*, 1953, p. 306, Berwick to 'James III', 3 November 1715   114. Saint-Simon, *Mémoires*, ed. Regnier and Chéruel, III, 416, V, 120   115. Ruth Clark, *Anthony Hamilton: His Life and Works and his Family*, 1921, pp. 132, 148, 217, 226; Nicholas Deakin, *Count Gramont at the Court of Charles II*, 1965, pp. 5, 10, 68, 167, 191. Madame vouched for their accuracy: Jaeglé, II, 177, 178, Madame to Electress Sophia, 1, 8 May 1712   116. Henderson, *Prince Eugene*, pp. 167–8; Gwynn, p. 116; Audrey T. Carpenter, 'J. T. Desaguliers, an 18th Century Experimental Philosopher and Freemason', *Huguenot Society Journal*, xxx, April 2016, pp. 503–18

Chapter 18: France against Europe

1. Cénat, *Louvois*, p. 73   2. Fonck, *Luxembourg*, p. 490, Luxembourg to Louvois, 4 June 1690. He was probably inspired by Turenne's remark 'Luck is always with the big battalions' ('la fortune est toujours pour les gros bataillons'): Sévigné, I, 646, Sévigné to Grignan, 22

December 1673   3. Drévillon, *Impôt du sang*, p. 277   4. André Corvisier, *Histoire militaire de la France*, 4 vols., 1997, I, 397   5. Cénat, *Louvois*, p. 59; when the 'ban' had been issued in 1674, the untrained nobles it had summoned had been dismissed as useless; Rousset, II, 98–9.   6. Rowlands, *Dynastic State*, pp. 154–5, 182; cf. Corvisier, *Louvois*, p. 325, who states that the theoretical size of the army in 1690 was 387,520   7. Rowlands, *Dynastic State*, pp. 74–7. As *surintendant* he even chose the size of nails for hanging the King's pictures: Cornette, *Mort de Louis XIV*, p. 127, Louis XIV to Louvois, 10 November 1684   8. Cénat, *Louvois*, pp. 78, 202; idem, *Chamlay*, pp. 144–9   9. Rousset, III, 299–300, 326, 331   10. Ibid., 315, 370–73   11. Langlois, p. 294, 13 July 1688; Spanheim, pp. 352–4   12. Spanheim, pp. 196–7   13. Cénat, *Chamlay*, pp. 91–3, Chamlay to Louvois, 27 October 1688   14. Emilie Dosquet, 'Le Feu et l'encre: la désolation de Palatinat: guerre et information politique dans l'Europe de Louis XIV', unpublished thesis, Sorbonne, Paris, 2 vols., 2017, I, 165, Chamlay to Louvois, 27 October 1688; Vauban had similar aims, see Blanchard, p. 365   15. Lynn, 'Brutal Necessity?', pp. 83–4, 93; Rousset, IV, 163, 164, Chamlay to Louvois, 27 October 1688, Louvois to La Grange, 17 November 1688; Michel Rousseau, *Quand Louis XIV brûlait le Palatinat: la guerre de la ligue d'Augsbourg et la presse*, 2014, pp. 39–40, 42 and passim   16. Susan Richter et al., *Heidelberg im Barock: der Wiederaufbau der Stadt nach den Zerstörungen von 1689 und 1693*, Heidelberg, 2009, passim   17. Dosquet, I, 174, 211, La Grange to Louvois, 19 April 1689, 212, 347, Louvois to La Grange, 17 November 1688; Van der Cruysse, *Princesse européenne*, p. 318   18. Bertrand Fonck, ed., *L'Âge d'or de la cavalerie*, 2015, p. 115, Mélac to Luxembourg, 17 November 1672   19. Dosquet, I, 389, Tessé to Louvois, 1 February 1689; cf. Virol, p. 363, agenda 11 March 1702; and for more praise of Mélac, Saint-Simon, *Mémoires*, ed. Regnier and Chéruel, III, 313   20. Saint-Simon, *Mémoires*, ed. Regnier and Chéruel, III, 313–14   21. Van der Cruysse, *Princesse européenne*, pp. 312, 316, 320, 322; Jaeglé, I, 67, 68, Madame to Electress Sophia, 10 November 1688, 20 March, 14 April 1689   22. Dangeau, III, 166, 5 January 1689   23. Dosquet, I, 136–9   24. Cénat, *Louvois*, p. 365, Louvois to Chamlay, 24 September 1683   25. Noailles, IV, 282n, Duras to Louvois, 21 May 1689; cf. Villars, I, 121, 161, for more denunciation by a French general of French pillaging, libertinage and marauding   26. Hélène Alexander Adda, *Liselotte von der Pfalz: Madame am Hofe des Sonnenkönigs*, 1996, pp. 31, 168; Rousset, IV, 180–83, Duras to Louvois, 21, 29 May 1689   27. Information kindly communicated by Hanns Hubach, Heidelberg, August 2016; Dangeau, XII, 38, 3 March 1699. No evidence of such a payment has been found in Speyer.   28. Boutant, pp. 141–4; Lynn, 'Brutal Necessity?', p. 79   29. Rousset, IV, 179, Chamlay to Louvois, 21 May 1689   30. Dosquet, I, 240, 315, 339, 396   31. Fonck, *Luxembourg*, p. 183   32. Sourches, III, 377, 27 March 1691; Dangeau, V, 179, 22 March 1691   33. Maurice Arnould et al., *1691: le siège de Mons par Louis XIV*, Brussels, 1991, pp. 46, 57, 83–5, 88–9, 94, 103   34. Gilles-Joseph de Boussu, *Histoire de la ville de Mons*, Mons, 1725, p. 311   35. Picavet, *Diplomatie française*, p. 45; Sarmant and Stoll, p. 98; Rowlands, *Dynastic State*, p. 59   36. Louis André, ed., *Deux Mémoires historiques de Claude Le Pelletier*, 1906, pp. 152–4   37. Rowlands, pp. 61, 62   38. Jaeglé, I, 87, Madame to Electress Sophia, 23 August 1691   39. Rowlands, pp. 65, 69; Villars, I, 145   40. Dangeau, V, 251, 255, 291, VI, 54, 15, 23 August, 28 October 1691, 28 April 1692; Fonck, *Luxembourg*, p. 435   41. Jean-Philippe Cénat, *Le Roi stratège: Louis XIV et la direction de la guerre (1661–1715)*, 2010, pp. 185, 187; Minutes of some of the King's letters to generals. Ministers and relations on military matters are in AHMG (Archives Historiques du Ministère de la Guerre) A 1 1041, 1134, 1198 and many more: Salat and Sarmant, p. xxv; cf. Virol, passim; Ségur, *Tapissier*, pp. 247–9, Maintenon to Mortemart, 24 September 1691   42. See e.g. Sourches, IV, 20, 23 March 1692 for lists of the officers he appointed in March 1692   43. ML, II, 143, Maintenon to Madame de Rochechouart, 27 September 1691   44. Masson, *Défendre le roi*, pp. 209–16, 229, 248   45. Dangeau, V, 298, 25 September 1691   46. Mss. 2320, Louis XIV to Boufflers, 31 August, 16 September, 21 October 1691   47. Ibid., Louis XIV to Boufflers, 23 October 1691; Bibliothèque Mazarine (BM) 23 July; 8 November; 12 December 1691   48. Virol, p. 138, Louis XIV to Vauban, 19 September 1693; cf. p. 250, Vauban to Le Peletier, 19 August 1695, boasting of the liberties he took with the King   49. Virol, pp. 94–5, Vauban to Maintenon, 26 April

1692   50. Cénat, *Roi stratège*, p. 12; idem, *Louvois*, p. 163   51. Ségur, *Tapissier*, pp. 247–9, Maintenon to Mortemart, 27 September 1691   52. Cénat, *Roi stratège*, p. 79   53. Ibid., pp. 105, 107, Turenne to Louis XIV, 17 May 1675   54. Ibid., pp. 27, 29   55. Fonck, *Luxembourg*, p. 467, Luxembourg to Louis XIV, 28 June 1693   56. Ibid., pp. 467–8, Louis XIV to Boufflers, 12 December 1691   57. Ibid., p. 373, Louis XIV to Luxembourg, 26 July 1692   58. Ibid., p. 568, Louis XIV to Luxembourg, 25 August 1692   59. Noailles, IV, 361, Maine to Maintenon, June 1692   60. Donneau de Visé, *Histoire du siège du château de Namur*, 1692, p. 213   61. Philippe Bragard, ed., *Vauban et Namur: le temps d'un siège, mai–juin 1692: journal de ce qui s'est passé de plus considérable à la prise de Namur, assiégée par le roi en personne, le 25 mai, et rendu à l'obéissance de sa Majesté le 29 juin 1692*, Namur, 2008, p. 181   62. André, *Le Peletier*, p. 156   63. Louis XIV, *Oeuvres*, IV, 389, Mémoires militaires année 1692   64. Petitfils, *Louis XIV*, pp. 343, 355   65. Montpensier, IV, 52   66. Louis XIV, *Oeuvres*, III, 453, Fragment sur la campagne de 1674, IV, 341, 389–90, Relation de ce qui s'est passé au siège de Namur; cf. for similar pride in French isolation, Haussonville, *Duchesse de Bourgogne*, I, 152–3, Louis XIV to Cardinal de Noailles, 10 September 1696; and BM Mss. 2326 f. 8, Instructions to Comte de Briord, 23 March 1697   67. Cénat, *Louvois*, p. 126; Sévigné, II, 655, to Grignan, 26 March 1680, 'le Roi ne peut souffrir ceux qui quittent le service'; Dangeau, XV, 104, 10 April 1702; Solnon, pp. 322, 370   68. Poisson, pp. 102, Barbezieux to Saint-Simon, 24 December 1695, 132, 156   69. Fonck, *Luxembourg*, pp. 495–7, Luxembourg to Louvois, 17 July 1691, to Louis XIV, 22 June 1693, pp. 189, 467, 526   70. Dangeau, VII, 91–2, 8, 9 June 1693; Noailles, IV, 408–10, Louis XIV to Monsieur, 8 June 1693   71. Roland Vetter, *Heidelberga Deleta*, 1989, p. 55, des Alleurs to Barbezieux, 23 May 1693; information from Nichola Hayton, 6 December 2015; Jaeglé, I, 101, Madame to Electress Sophia, 10 October 1693   72. Dangeau, IV, 47, 3 June 1689; Masson, *Défendre le roi*, p. 193   73. Noailles, IV, 292n, Maine to Maintenon, 3 July 1690; cf. Fonck, *Luxembourg*, p. 408   74. Rowlands, pp. 344–5   75. Sourches, IV, 63, 108, 13 June, 15 August 1692   76. La Force, pp. 87, 93, 96, 101; Rowlands, pp. 307–8, 340–41; Fonck, *Luxembourg*, pp. 191, 200   77. Dangeau, III, 87, 22 September 1688   78. Cénat, *Roi stratège*, pp. 33–4, Chamlay to Louvois, 16 June 1690   79. Sourches, III, 85, 2 May 1689   80. Dangeau, VIII, 223, 12, 13 April 1695   81. Sourches, IV, 238, 4 August 1693   82. Ibid., 187, 13 April 1693, 477–80, edict of April 1693; Théodore Anne, *Histoire de l'ordre royal et militaire de Saint-Louis*, 3 vols., 1860–61, I, 29–40; Drévillon, pp. 265, 295   83. Aligny, p. 224   84. Maurice Culot et al., eds., *Le Bombardement de Bruxelles par Louis XIV et la reconstruction qui s'en suivit, 1695–1700*, Brussels, 1992, pp. 42, 52, Louis XIV to Villeroy, 21 July, August 1695   85. Cénat, *Roi stratège*, p. 313; Culot et al., pp. 31, 54, 62, Villeroy to Louis XIV, 13, 14, 16, 17 August 1695   86. Culot et al., pp. 69, 71–3, Lettre de Lucifer à la France; for generals' opposition see Rousset, IV, 142   87. Swann, pp. 223, 227–9, Bourbon to Pontchartrain, 19 July 1691   88. Dubois, *Journal*, pp. 92, 93, 115   89. Sourches, IV, 333, 369, 27 May, 15 August 1694   90. *DL*, pp. 394–5   91. Corvisier, *Histoire militaire*, I, pp. 482–3, Contrôleur Général to intendants, 5 December 1686. There were also public hospitals in many towns.   92. Bryant, 'Queen', pp. 199–202   93. Dingli, p. 344; Claude Nordmann, *Grandeur et liberté de la Suède (1660–1792)*, 1971, p. 105   94. AN K 121, 21, decree of 3 August 1692   95. Levantal, *Louis XIV*, II, 596; abolished in 1697, the capitation was renewed in 1701.   96. Corp, pp. 34–6; Daniel Dessert, *Tourville*, 2002, p. 255   97. Dessert, *La Royale*, p. 143   98. Dessert, *La Royale*, pp. 195–6; Nicolas Siméon, *Louis XIV et la mer*, 2007, p. 22   99. Lynn, *Wars*, p. 88   100. Sourches, IV, 1, 2 January 1692   101. Lynn, *Wars*, pp. 84, 88   102. Dessert, *Tourville*, 256, 275   103. Wismes, pp. 106, 130   104. René Dollot, *Les Origines de la neutralité de la Belgique et le système de la Barrière, 1609–1830*, 1902, p. 287   105. M. A. Thomson, 'Louis XIV and William III, 1689–1697', in Ragnhild Hatton and J. S. Bromley, eds., *William III and Louis XIV*, Liverpool, 1968, pp. 24–48 at pp. 31–45   106. Clarke, II, 573, proclamation by James II, 8 June 1697   107. Linden, pp. 131–6, 139   108. Ibid., pp. 143, 144, 146, 150–51   109. Grew, p. 312, Portland to William III, 15 February 1698   110. John Brewer, *The Sinews of Power: War, Money and the English State, 1688–1783*, 1989, pp. 31   145. 111. Dollot, p. 325; Troost, *William III*, pp. 246–51   112. André, *Louis XIV*, p. 273; Dethan,

p. 137 113. Blanchard, pp. 354–8 114. Fonck, *Luxembourg*, p. 567, letter of 13 September 1696; Blanchard, p. 354, Vauban to Racine, 1697 115. Comte d'Haussonville, *Histoire de la réunion de la Lorraine à la France*, 4 vols., 1854–9, IV, 20, 50, instructions to Comte de La Vauguyon, 1685 116. Georges Poullet, *La Maison ducale de Lorraine: étude historique, biographique et généalogique des branches aînée, cadettes et illégitimes de cette maison*, Nancy, 1991, pp. 247–9; Anne Motta, *Echanges, passages et transferts à la cour du Duc Léopold de Lorraine*, Rennes, 2017, p. 121 117. Grimblot, I, 137, William III to Heinsius, 26 November 1697; Zee, pp. 342, 434. His entry into The Hague on 1 February 1691, as king of England and conqueror of Ireland, accompanied by princes, ambassadors and peers, had also been designed to outshine Louis XIV. Similarly the cabinet he ordered from the Antwerp furniture maker Henri van Soest to commemorate his recapture of Namur in 1695, now in the Catholic University of Leuven, is as luxurious as any of Louis XIV's. 118. Lurgo, p. 262, Marquis de La Pierre to Duke of Savoy, 14 December 1685 119. Dangeau, IX, 258, 4 November 1696; cf. Noailles, IV, 559, Louis XIV to Maintenon, 4 November 1696 120. Noailles, IV, 561–2, Louis XIV to Maintenon, 4 November 1696 121. ML, II, 745, 813, Maintenon to Duchess Dowager of Savoy, 6 November 1696, 1 July 1697 122. Nicolas Milovanovic, *Du Louvre à Versailles: lecture des grands décors monarchiques*, 2005, p. 83, note of 8 September 1699 123. Dangeau, X, 188, 190, 194, 6, 7, 11 December 1697 124. Sourches, V, 369, 11 December 1697; Castelluccio, *Fastes*, pp. 143, 148 125. Norton, pp. 141–2

Chapter 19: Spain Changes Sides: The Accession of King Philip

1. Christophe Levantal, *La Route royale: le voyage de Philippe V et de ses frères, de Sceaux à la frontière d'Espagne (décembre 1700–janvier 1701) d'après la relation du Mercure Galant*, 1996, pp. 25–6; Sourches, VI, 309, 16 November 1700, gives a different version of the King's speech 2. Catherine Désos, *Les Français de Philippe V: un modèle nouveau pour gouverner l'Espagne, 1700–1724*, Strasbourg, 2009, p. 30 3. Ibid., p. 23 4. Cénat, *Roi stratège*, p. 352 5. Ibid., pp. 342–5 6. André, *Louis XIV*, p. 287 7. Bély, *Paix*, p. 106; Grimblot, I, 271n 8. Grimblot, II, 108, Tallard to Louis XIV, 15 August 1698 9. M. A. Thomson, 'Self-Determination and Collective Security as Factors in English and French Foreign Policy, 1689–1718', in Hatton and Bromley, pp. 271–86 10. Ana Crespo Solana, 'A Change of Ideology in Imperial Spain? Spanish Commercial Policy with America and the Change of Dynasty (1648–1740)', in Onnekink and Rommelse, pp. 215–42 at pp. 226–7; John C. Rule, 'The Partition Treaties, 1698–1700: A European View', in Esther Mijers and David Onnekink, eds., *Redefining William III: The Impact of the King-Stadholder in International Context*, Aldershot, 2007, pp. 91–105 at p. 101 11. Désos, p. 46, Duc d'Escalona to Louis XIV, 29 November 1700; cf. Hippeau, *Correspondance*, II, 27–9, Harcourt to Louis XIV, 16 February 1699 12. Spielman, pp. 158, 172; Arsène Legrelle, *La Diplomatie française et la succession d'Espagne*, 6 vols., Braine-le-Comte, 1895–9 edn, IV, 131–2, Blécourt to Louis XIV, 29 October 1700; Sourches, VI, 305, 309, letters of 3, 7 November 1700 13. BL Mss. 2326 f. 120, Louis XIV to Marquis d'Harcourt, 23 December 1697 14. Grimblot, II, 49–51, Louis XIV to Tallard, 4 July 1698; Alexander Stanhope, *Spain under Charles the Second*, 1844 edn, p. 133, Stanhope to James Stanhope, 11 June 1698 15. Stanhope, p. 139, Alexander Stanhope to James Stanhope, 23 June 1698 16. Désos, p. 26 17. Carswell, pp. 146, 161n, 204 18. Grimblot, I, 216n, lists five lords, twelve pages and fifty-six footmen accompanying the Earl of Portland on his embassy to Louis XIV in 1698. After 1685 and 1688 respectively, embassy chapels were the only official places of worship for Protestants in Paris, and Catholics in London. 19. Abraham de Wicquefort, *L'Ambassadeur et ses fonctions*, Amsterdam, 1730, p. 93; Picavet, *Diplomatie française*, p. 107; Saint-Maurice, I, 204, 20 July 1668 20. Bély, *Paix*, pp. 488, 563, Louis XIV to Callières, 6 December 1696 21. Jean-Claude Waquet, *François de Callières: l'art de négocier en France sous Louis XIV*, 2005, pp. 33, 65, 67, 203, 249 and passim; Sourches, X, 40, 19 June 1706; Newton, *Petite Cour*, p. 93 22. Torcy, *Journal*, p. xv 23. Chamlay, 'Mémoire historique de ce qui s'est passé depuis 1678 jusqu'à l'an 1688', in Rousset, III, 233, 432–3

24. An extreme example would be the law of Peter the Great of Russia in 1722, which allowed the Tsar to select whom he wished as heir. He chose his second wife Catherine I, a former tavern attendant. 25. Hippeau, *Correspondance*, II, 276, Blécourt to Louis XIV, 28 September 1700 26. Marie-Françoise Maquart, *L'Espagne de Charles II et la France, 1665–1700*, 2000, pp. 119, 152 27. Marie-Françoise Maquart, 'Le Dernier Testament de Charles II', in Lucien Bély, ed., *La Présence des Bourbons en Europe, XVIe–XXIe siècle*, 2003, pp. 112–24 at pp. 120–23; Hippeau, *Correspondance*, II, 277, Blécourt to Louis XIV, 1 October 1700 28. Legrelle, *Diplomatie française*, IV, 131, Blécourt to Louis XIV, 29 October 1700 29. Désos, p. 61 30. Yves Bottineau, *L'Art de cour dans l'Espagne de Philippe V, 1700–1746*, 1993, pp. 108–10 and n; Bryant, 'Queen', pp. 222, 293 31. Dangeau, XVIII, 34, 38, 10, 16 February 1705 32. Lahaye, pp. 325, 340; Vincent, p. 157; Saint-Simon, *Mémoires*, ed. Regnier and Chéruel, VI, 422, VIII, 231, 26 33. Lahaye, p. 219 34. Ibid., pp. 242–6 35. Bottineau, p. 111, Louis XIV to Briord, 14 November 1700 36. Sourches, VI, 309, 16 November 1700 37. Grimblot, II, 477, William III to Heinsius, 16 November 1700 38. Levantal, *Route royale*, pp. 29, 37 39. Ibid., pp. 42–3 40. Sourches, VI, 326, 4 December 1700; Dangeau, XIII, 220–21, 4 December 1700; Sourches, VI, 326, 4 December 1700 41. Levantal, *Route royale*, p. 59 42. Bottineau, pp. 155–6; Levantal, *Route royale*, p. 46 43. Levantal, *Route royale*, p. 95 44. Bottineau, p. 161; Levantal, *Route royale*, p. 121 45. Désos, p. 75 and n 46. Ibid., p. 83 47. C. Hippeau, ed., *Lettres au Maréchal d'Harcourt*, Caen, 1862, p. 164 48. Bottineau, p. 162; Désos, p. 76 49. Henry Kamen, *Philip V of Spain: The King Who Reigned Twice*, 2001, pp. 5–9, 11, 22; Bottineau, p. 163 50. Baudrillart, *Philippe V*, I, 108, Philip V to Louis XIV, 18 May 1702; Kamen, *Philip V*, p. 105 51. Baudrillart, *Philippe V*, I, 87, Gramont to Maintenon, 14 June 1704; Dangeau, XVII, 417n, Vendôme to Louis XIV, 25 September 1710 52. Baudrillart, *Philippe V*, I, 112–13, Louis XIV to Philip V, 10 September 1702, Philip V to Louis XIV, 17 October 1702; Marianne Cermakian, *La Princesse des Ursins: sa vie et ses lettres*, 1969, p. 295; Saint-Simon, *Mémoires*, ed. Regnier and Chéruel, III, 469, describes d'Aubigny 53. Rule and Trotter, p. 397 54. Kroll, p. 103, Madame to Sophie, 13 November 1700 55. Kamen, *Philip V*, pp. 232–3 56. Dangeau, XIV, 155, 16 July 1701; Spielman, pp. 175–6 57. Legrelle, *Diplomatie française*, III, 389–90, Cardinal de Forbin-Janson to Louis XIV, 11 June 1697 58. Hippeau, *Lettres*, pp. 46, 48–9, Tessé to Harcourt, 15, 27 February 1701 59. Désos, p. 100 60. Hippeau, *Correspondance*, II, 424, 504, Harcourt to Louis XIV, 12 January, 23 February 1701; Désos, p. 62, Louis XIV to Blécourt, 21 November 1700, 92, 180–81 61. Dangeau, XIX, 100, 9 May 1706 62. BN NAF 12764 f. 198, Louis XIV to Philip V, 27 June 1701 (copy) 63. BN NAF 12764 f. 162, Louis XIV to Philip V, 13 July 1701; cf. for similar letters BN NAF 12764 f. 162, Louis XIV to Philip V, 6 February 1702, and Louis XIV, *Oeuvres*, VI, 107, Louis XIV to Philip V, 4 February 1703 64. Kamen, *Philip V*, pp. 21–2 65. Désos, pp. 104, 185, 194; Bottineau, p. 185; Baudrillart, *Philippe V*, I, 73–4 66. Désos, p. 139; Auguste Geffroy, ed., *Lettres inédites de la Princesse des Ursins*, 1859, p. 121, Ursins to Maréchale de Noailles, 16 December 1707 67. Levantal, *Route royale*, p. 63; Désos, p. 137 68. Désos, p. 140; Bottineau, pp. 185n, 188 69. Cf. Wilson, 1995, p. 142: the Duke of Württemberg wanted to become king of Franconia. The Duke of Lorraine claimed to be king of Jerusalem, the Duke of Savoy to be king of Cyprus, while the doges of Venice and Genoa also claimed 'royal treatment', as sovereigns of the kingdoms of Cyprus and Corsica respectively. 70. Rousset, II, 408, declaration of 15 October 1675 71. Farges, I, 222, 227, Louis XIV to Polignac, 26 July 1696, 237, Instructions to M. de Forval, 23 February 1697; Saint-Germain, *Samuel Bernard*, pp. 57–61, Polignac to Bernard, 22 April 1697 72. Dangeau, X, 62, 98, 124, 12 May, 11 July, 24 August 1697; Sourches, V, 334, 3 September 1697 73. La Force, pp. 128–9, 136; Saint-Simon, *Mémoires*, ed. Regnier and Chéruel, I, 431, 450 74. Louis XV would attempt to install as king of Poland his father-in-law Stanisław Leszczyński in 1733, even sending French troops to Danzig, as well as his favourite cousin the Prince de Conti, grandson of Louis XIV's candidate in 1697, in the 1740s. 75. Jaeglé, I, 152, Madame to Electress Sophia, 4 August 1697 76. Castelluccio, *Commerce du luxe*, pp. 274–5 77. Spielman, pp. 164–5; Tony Sharp, *Pleasure and Ambition: The Life, Loves and Wars of Augustus the Strong*,

2001, pp. 139, 141–5   **78.** La Force, pp. 138, 143; Przezdziecki, I, 233; Jerzy Lukowski, *Liberty's Folly: The Polish–Lithuanian Commonwealth in the Eighteenth Century, 1697–1795*, 1991, p. 122; Dangeau, X, 175, 194–5, 11 November, 13 December 1697. Conti remained popular in Paris and Versailles, but was never again employed by Louis XIV, until shortly before his premature death in 1709: Saint-Simon, *Mémoires*, ed. Regnier and Chéruel, VI, 272–7. I am grateful to Dr Aleksandra Skrzypietz for information about Conti's candidacy.   **79.** Dangeau, X, 117, 195, 12 August, 13 December 1697   **80.** He did, however, model some ceremonies on Versailles, and ask his resident, Spanheim, for the exact measurements of Louis XIV's wig: Frey, pp. 53, 216   **81.** Karin Friedrich and Sara H. Smart, eds., *The Cultivation of Monarchy and the Rise of Berlin*, 2010, pp. 178–9, 227, 230, 292; Waddington, II, 19, account by Regnard, 1681, 23: from 1663 the Elector was claiming through details of etiquette higher status than other electors, owing to his independent sovereignty in Prussia.   **82.** Hellmut Lorenz, 'Vienna Gloriosa', in Henry A. Millon, ed., *Circa 1700: Architecture in Europe and the Americas*, New Haven, 2005, pp. 47–64   **83.** Henderson, *Prince Eugene*, pp. 244, 257, 263–5; Marie-Louise von Plessen et al., eds., *Prince Eugene, General-Philosopher and Art Lover*, Munich, 2010, pp. 159, 172   **84.** Irmgard Harrer et al., *The Austrian National Library*, Vienna, 2015 edn, pp. 32–59   **85.** *Peter the Great, an Inspired Tsar*, exh. cat., Amsterdam, 2013, pp. 28–38, 142–54; Alexandre Orloff and Dimitri Chvidkovski, *Saint-Pétersbourg: l'architecture des tsars*, 2005 edn, pp. 22, 29, 34. Similarly Potsdam at first owed more to Dutch than to French influence: McKay, p. 235   **86.** Alfred Rambaud, ed., *Recueil des instructions données aux ambassadeurs et ministres de France: Russie*, 2 vols., 1890, I, pp. 47, 55; Sharp, pp. 245–6   **87.** Ragnhild Hatton, *Charles XII of Sweden*, 1968, p. 172; Sharp, pp. 176, 210; Jaeglé, I, 232, Madame to Electress Sophia, 2 January 1701. On his death in 1719 she called him – not Louis XIV – a hero as great as Alexander: Van der Cruysse, *Lettres françaises*, p. 603, Madame to Queen Ulrica Eleonora of Sweden, 30 April 1719   **88.** Dangeau, XVI, 125, 30 May 1702   **89.** Dr R. Doebner, ed., *Memoirs of Mary, Queen of England*, Leipzig, 1886, pp. 72, 76, William III to Electress Sophia, 28 April, 20 December 1689   **90.** Grew, pp. 400–404; Adolphus William Ward, *The Electress Sophia and the Hanoverian Succession*, 1909 edn, pp. 307, 385, 388, 395   **91.** Grimblot, II, 206, Instructions to Tallard, 17 December 1698   **92.** Ibid., 36, Bentinck to William III, 17 June 1698; cf. ibid., 161, Louis XIV to Tallard, 14 September 1698   **93.** L. G. Wickham Legg, *Matthew Prior: A Study of his Public Career and Correspondence*, Cambridge, 1921, pp. 73–4, 80, Prior to Vernon, 27 August, 1, 18 October 1698; cf. Sourches, VI, 65, 68, 10, 12 September 1698, for James II and Louis XIV reviewing troops together   **94.** Grimblot, II, 183, 186–7, Tallard to Louis XIV, 3 November 1698, Louis XIV to Tallard, 11 November 698   **95.** AN K 122, lettres patentes du roy, December 1700; Baudrillart, *Philippe V*, I, 469; Sourches, VII, 448, Déclaration du Roi en faveur du roi d'Espagne, December 1700   **96.** Philippe Hrodej, *L'Amiral du Casse: l'élévation d'un Gascon sous Louis XIV*, 2 vols., 1999, I, 293; Frostin, p. 399   **97.** Hippeau, *Correspondance*, II, 424, Harcourt to Louis XIV, 12 January 1701, 'ce commerce est très avantageux'   **98.** Frostin, p. 399, Pontchartrain to Comte de Marsin, 1 October 1701   **99.** Bottineau, p. 179; Dangeau, XV, 309, 15 December 1702; Thomas J. Schaeper, *The French Council of Commerce, 1700–1715*, Columbus, OH, 1983, pp. 88, 224, 234   **100.** Callow, p. 377   **101.** Corp, pp. 161, 164, will of James II, 5 March 1699, Louis XIV to 'James III', March 1708 (from a translated copy)   **102.** Clarke, II, 591n   **103.** Ibid., 577n; cf. Garrett, pp. 73, 143, for evidence of the continued popularity of William III, and contempt for the 'Jacks' (Jacobites), in England   **104.** Callow, p. 375; Clarke, II, 593n   **105.** Clarke, II, 598–9; Lord Perth, 'Lettres . . . au Père de La Trappe', *Revue de l'Histoire de Versailles*, October 1927, pp. 213–25 at pp. 216–17, 220, 225, Perth to Père de La Trappe, 9 October 1701; Sourches, VII, 117–18, 13–16 September 1701; Dangeau, XIV, 199, 13 September 1701   **106.** Sourches, VII, 119, 18 September 1701   **107.** Genet-Rouffiac, p. 79   **108.** Bertière, *Mazarin*, p. 655   **109.** Mazarin, *Lettres*, IX, 332, 357, 426, Mazarin to Turenne, 29 September 1659, to Le Tellier, 10 October 1659, to Turenne, 27 November 1659; cf. AD CP Angleterre 376 f. 410v, Poussin to Torcy, 24 September 1701, complaining that the recognition will 'animer la nation anglaise contre la France'   **110.** Blet, *Nonces du pape*, p. 227, despatch from

Gualtiero, 12 December 1701   111. Haile, p. 355, Manchester to Vernon, 24 September 1701; AD CP Angleterre 376 f. 210, Torcy to Poussin, 18 September 1701   112. Duke of Manchester, *Court and Society, from Elizabeth to Anne*, 2 vols., 1864, II, 196, Manchester to Blathwayt, 19 September 1701; ML, III, 316, to Philip V, 20 September 1701   113. Manchester, II, 198–200, Manchester to Blathwayt, 23, 24 September 1701; Dangeau, XIV, 214n, Manchester to Torcy, 2 October 1701   114. Corp, p. 60   115. Manchester, II, 201–3, Manchester to Blathwayt, 26, 28 September 1701   116. Charles Spencer, *Blenheim: Battle for Europe*, 2004, p. 81   117. M. A. Thomson, 'Louis XIV and the Origins of the War of the Spanish Succession', in Hatton and Bromley, pp. 140–61   118. Edward Gregg, 'Monarchs without a Crown', in Robert Oresko et al., eds., *Royal and Republican Sovereignty in Early Modern Europe*, Cambridge, 1997, pp. 382–422 at p. 401   119. Joseph Hone, 'Isaac Newton and the Medals for Queen Anne', *Huntington Library Quarterly*, 79, 1, Spring 2016, pp. 119–48

Chapter 20: The Triumph of Europe

1. Dangeau, XVII, 159–61, and 323–5, 25 June 1704. The King had also been present when his wife and daughter-in-law were in labour, staying with the Dauphine, at the birth of the Duc d'Anjou in 1683, until five in the morning: Reuss, p. 77, 22 December 1683   2. Dangeau, XVIII, 79, 16 April 1705; ML, III, 611, Maintenon to Duc de Noailles, 21 May 1705; the four generations of Bourbons are commemorated in illustration 55.   3. Dubois, *Journal*, p. 141, 25 July 1704   4. Sourches, VIII, 404, 25 June 1704; Blanchard, pp. 128, 174; Louis XIV, *Mémoires*, p. 144   5. Jérôme de La Gorce, ' "Le Triomphe de la Seine et du Tage sur les autre fleuves de l'Europe affermi par la naissance du duc de Bretagne": une fête organisée à Paris pendant la guerre de Succession d'Espagne', in Álvarez-Ossorio et al., pp. 49–63; Dangeau, XVII, 212, 28 August 1704. He also showered her with presents of gold, silver, Chinese porcelain and Persian silk, and organized a fireworks party at Marly, with a triumphal arch decorated with the words 'Pour Adélaïde': Dangeau, XVII, 195, 200, 7, 12 August 1704   6. Torcy, *Journal*, p. 144, 2 March 1710; cf. Sharp, p. 220   7. Blanning, *Frederick the Great*, pp. 13–14; Dangeau, XXI, 170, 24 August 1708   8. Richard Holmes, *Marlborough: Britain's Greatest General*, 2009 edn, pp. 216, 219, 261; Bély, *Espions*, pp. 88–91   9. Général de Vault, ed., *Mémoires militaires relatifs à la Succession d'Espagne sous Louis XIV*, 15 vols., 1835–62, X, 595, Villars to Louis XIV, 29 April 1711; Spencer, p. 264   10. Dangeau, XXII, 142–3, 1 June 1709, note by Saint-Simon   11. Spencer, p. 139   12. Ibid., pp. 197–9   13. Ibid., p. 200   14. Geoffrey Parker, *Global Crisis: War, Climate Change and Catastrophe in the Seventeenth Century*, 2013, p. 322   15. Rousset, I, 331   16. Guy Rowlands, 'Last Argument of the King, or a Step Too Far? Arms, Artillery and Absolutism under Louis XIV', talk given at the Institute of Historical Research, London, 19 May 2014; Spencer, p. 122   17. David Chandler, ed., *Military Memoirs of Marlborough's Campaigns*, 1998 edn, p. 42; Holmes, *Marlborough*, p. 387   18. Chandler, pp. 81, 89   19. Louis XIV, *Correspondance avec M. Amelot, son ambassadeur en Espagne, 1705–1709*, 2 vols., Nantes, 1864, I, 141n, Amelot to Chamillart, 22 July 1706   20. Villars, III, 290, Villars to Voysin, 29 September 1710. However, army purchase remained standard practice in the British army until 1867.   21. Dangeau, XVII, 207–8, 21, 22 August 1704; Spencer, pp. 285, 289, 291, 303–4   22. Spencer, pp. 297, 301; Holmes, *Marlborough*, p. 296   23. ML, III, 512, Maintenon to Villeroy, 23 August 1704   24. Spencer, p. 311   25. Fonck, *Luxembourg*, p. 498, Louis XIV to Luxembourg, 25 July 1691; cf. Vault, VI, 17, Louis XIV to Villeroy, 6 May 1706   26. Carbonnier-Burkard, p. 5; W. Gregory Monahan, *Let God Arise: The War and Rebellion of the Camisards*, Oxford, 2014, p. 58   27. Dangeau, XVI, 83, 96, 6, 23 April 1703. Every first Sunday in September, the Camisards are commemorated by an assembly of their descendants and admirers at the Musée du Desert, Mialet, near Nîmes.   28. Villars, III, 221, Villars to Chamillart, 9 May 1704   29. Baronne de Charnisay, *Un Gentilhomme Huguenot au temps des Camisards: le Baron d'Aigaliers*, Cahors, 1935, p. 40, Villars to Chamillart, 11 April 1704   30. Villars, II, 150   31. Sarmant, *Homme et roi*, pp. 391–3; Pénicaut, pp. 75, 79, 166;

Saint-Simon, *Mémoires*, ed. Regnier and Chéruel, VI, 217   **32.** Monahan, pp. 120, 148n, Chamillart to Julien, 3, 14 February, Chamillart note, September 1703. However, many Protestant civilians, including women, were killed on the King's orders, in order to intimidate others: Nicolas, p. 788   **33.** Sourches, IV, 167, 5 March 1693   **34.** Charnisay, pp. 158-9, 164-5, d'Aigaliers memoirs   **35.** Ibid., pp. 166, d'Aigaliers memoirs, 185, Chamillart to d'Aigaliers, 19 August 1704   **36.** Ibid., pp. 302-3, 319, 330, 332, d'Aigaliers to Chamillart, 27 November 1704   **37.** Ibid., p. 60, d'Aigaliers memoirs   **38.** Dangeau, XVII, 167, 4 July 1704   **39.** Dangeau, XVIII, 90, 28 April 1705; Sauzet, pp. 237-9; Valdo Pellegrin, *Montpellier la protestante*, Montpellier, 2012, pp. 82, 84, 87, 211   **40.** Holmes, *Marlborough*, p. 348; Masson, *Défendre le roi*, pp. 352-4   **41.** Sourches, X, 85, 26 May 1706   **42.** Dangeau, XXII, 6-7, 2, 4 January 1709. Le Quesnoy was surrendered in similar circumstances in July 1712.   **43.** ML, III, 786, Maintenon to Ursins, 4 July 1706   **44.** Saint-Simon, *Mémoires*, ed. Regnier and Chéruel, V, 9   **45.** ML, III, 798, Maintenon to Ursins, 16 July 1707   **46.** Pénicaut, p. 198, Chamillart to Vendôme, 20 August 1706   **47.** Duc de Saint-Simon, *La Mort de Louis XIV*, 2007 edn, p. 87   **48.** Louis XIV, *Oeuvres*, VI, 135, Louis XIV to Victor Amadeus II, September 1703   **49.** Vault, IV, 293, V, 129, VI, 285, Louis XIV to Orléans, 6 September 1706   **50.** Ibid., VI, 52, Louis XIV to Chamillart, 1 June 1706   **51.** Symcox, pp. 151, 227. The exterior of Blenheim is decorated with a bust of Louis XIV, military trophies and trampled fleurs-de-lys and Gallic cockerels, the interior with tapestries and frescoes of Marlborough's triumphs over Louis XIV, in a style similar to that used by Louis XIV at Versailles: James Legard, ' "Princely Glory": The 1st Duke of Marlborough, Court Culture, and the Construction of Blenheim Palace', talk to the Society for Court Studies, 18 February 2018   **52.** Holmes, *Marlborough*, p. 348   **53.** Charles W. Ingrao, *In Quest and Crisis: The Emperor Joseph I and the Habsburg Monarchy*, West Lafayette, IN, 1979, pp. 81, 98, 102, 117   **54.** Philip Attwood and Felicity Powell, *Medals of Dishonour*, 2009, pp. 18-19, 44, 51 and passim   **55.** Renger de Bruin and Maarten Brinkman, eds., *Peace was Made Here: The Treaties of Utrecht, Rastatt and Baden, 1713-1714*, Petersberg, 2013, p. 28   **56.** Holmes, *Marlborough*, pp. 277-8; Spencer, pp. 211, 216-17; Ingrao, p. 47   **57.** Dangeau, XIX, 58, 15 March 1706; cf. Didier Godard, *Le Goût de Monsieur: l'homosexualité masculine au XVIIe siècle*, 2002, p. 172, for Vendôme's relations with peasants at Anet. It was said that in 1697 he had taken Barcelona, as he caught *la vérole*, from behind.   **58.** Sourches, X, 30, 49, 13 February, 14 March 1706; Pierre Narbonne, *Journal de Police*, 2 vols., Clermont-Ferrand, 2002-3, I, 26-7, June 1712   **59.** Cénat, *Roi stratège*, p. 426   **60.** Alfred Baudrillart and Léon Lecestre, eds., *Lettres du Duc de Bourgogne au roi d'Espagne Philippe V et à la Reine*, 2 vols., 1912-16, I, pp. 198, 202, Bourgogne to Fénelon, 20 September, 3 October 1708; Norton, pp. 262-9   **61.** Norton, pp. 271, 282; Abbé Millot, *Mémoires politiques et militaires pour servir à l'histoire de Louis XIV et de Louis XV*, 1839, p. 404, Bourgogne to Maintenon, 13 July 1708   **62.** Norton, pp. 293, 297; Haussonville, *Duchesse de Bourgogne*, III, 245, 269-70   **63.** Dubois, *Journal*, p. 151, 1708   **64.** Holmes, *Fatal Avenue*, p. 393   **65.** Alain Lottin, *Les Grandes Batailles du Nord de la France*, 1984, pp. 126-30; Haussonville, *Duchesse de Bourgogne*, III, 343, quoting letters from Bourgogne to Louis XIV and Maintenon, September 1708   **66.** Vault, VIII, 399, Louis XIV to Bourgogne, 16 July 1708; cf. Norton, p. 281, Louis XIV to Bourgogne, 23 July 1708   **67.** BN Mss. fr. 6925 ff. 88, 106v, 159, Maréchal to Duc de Noailles, 26 June, 17 July, 10 September 1708   **68.** Baudrillart and Léon Lecestre, II, p. 20, Bourgogne to Philip V, 26 June 1709; Pénicaut, pp. 152, 155; Langlois, pp. 252-3; Saint-Simon, *Mémoires*, ed. Regnier and Chéruel, VI, 425-6   **69.** Maral, *Versailles*, pp. 261, 295   **70.** Sourches, XI, 26n, 21 February 1708   **71.** ML, IV, 90, 225, Maintenon to Ursins, 27 February, 17 October 1707   **72.** Norton, pp. 167, 185, 240   **73.** Haussonville, *Duchesse de Bourgogne*, II, 214   **74.** Norton, pp. 241-7; Saint-Simon, *Mémoires*, ed. Regnier and Chéruel, IV, 346, 407-8   **75.** Haussonville, *Duchesse de Bourgogne*, I, 385, II, 153, 163   **76.** Dangeau, XV, 224, 8 September 1708; Haussonville, *Duchesse de Bourgogne*, II, 188; Norton, pp. 189-92   **77.** Norton, pp. 180, 220-21   **78.** Fraser, *Love and Louis XIV*, pp. 250-51, 304; Dangeau, XII, 162, 7 October 1699   **79.** Fabrice Peyrat, ed., *Marie-Adélaïde de Savoie, Duchesse de Bourgogne, enfant terrible de Versailles*, Brussels, 2014, passim; Dangeau, XII, 168, 16 October 1699; ML, IV, 274, Maintenon to

Ursins, 22 January 1708   80. Dangeau, XI, 175, 178, 8, 13 November 1698, XII, 17, 106, 24 January, 1 July 1699, XVIII, 168, 11 August 1705   81. Fraser, *Love and Louis XIV*, p. 283; Saint-Simon, *Mémoires*, ed. Regnier and Chéruel, V, 432–3. Maintenon confirms that the King could not bear to be at Marly without the Duchesse de Bourgogne: ML, III, 867 to Ursins, 21 November 1706   82. BN Mss. fr. 6925 ff. 17–20, Maréchal to Duc de Noailles, April 1708   83. Norton, pp. 224n, 296–300; Narbonne, I, 30–31   84. Sourches, X, 136, 23 December 1710; Kroll, p. 151, to Madame, 28 September 1709; Saint-Simon, *Mémoires*, ed. Regnier and Chéruel, VI, 459–62   85. Legg, pp. 68, 73–4, 80, 103, Prior to Charles Montagu, 18 February, to James Vernon, 21 May, to Charles Montagu, 27 August, to Lord Jersey, 19 August 1699   86. Manchester, II, 145, despatch from Manchester, 22 May 1700   87. Dangeau, IX, 132, 158, 181, 18 November 1704, 8 January, 23 February 1705, V, 106–7, 12, 14 October 1690; Sourches, IX, 181, 23 February 1705   88. Dangeau, XII, 159, 1 October 1699, XVIII, 168, 11 August 1705   89. Dangeau, XVI, 8, 248, 1 March, 11 October 1703, XVIII, 257, 28 November 1705   90. However, as 'James III' would discover, these Jacobite officers often preferred serving France to serving him.   91. ML, IV, 294, 299, Maintenon to Ursins, 4, 18 March 1708   92. Rule and Trotter, p. 680; John S. Gibson, *Playing the Franco-Scottish Card: The Franco-Jacobite Invasion of 1708*, Edinburgh, 1988, pp. 38, 104–5, 119; Forbin, pp. 461, 472, 481, 489, 491; Corp, p. 64; Dangeau, XXI, 51, 54, 55, 71, 13, 16, 18 March, 10 April 1708, XXIII, 198, 15 September 1710   93. Torcy, *Journal*, pp. 63, 66–7, 11, 15 December 1709   94. Bottineau, p. 193n, Philip V to Louis XIV, 18 May 1702   95. Désos, pp. 95, 241–3; Dangeau, XVII, 46, 50, 19, 25 February 1704   96. Désos, pp. 132–3; Bottineau, pp. 195-8; Dangeau, XV, 217, 8 October 1705   97. ML, VIII, 678, Ursins to Maintenon, 3 September 1705   98. G. du Boscq de Beaumont, *La Garde Wallonne, 1702–1822: officiers français au service de l'Espagne*, 1904; Baron Guillaume, *Les Gardes wallonnes au service d'Espagne*, Brussels, 1858.   99. Geffroy, p. 76, Ursins to Maréchale de Noailles, 15 June 1700; Cermakian, pp. 204–30   100. Geffroy, p. 36n   101. Ibid., p. 86, 88, Ursins to Maréchale de Noailles, 27 December 1700   102. Saint-Simon, *Mémoires*, ed. Regnier and Chéruel, III, 79–80; Geffroy, p. 127, Ursins to Maréchale de Noailles, 14 October 1702   103. Cermakian, p. 253, Ursins to Torcy, 5 March 1702   104. Geffroy, p. 114, Ursins to Maréchale de Noailles, 12 December 1701   105. Ibid., pp. 123, 126, Ursins to Maréchale de Noailles, 7 September, 14 October 1702, p. 377, Ursins to Maintenon, 9 September 1709   106. Désos, p. 94   107. Ibid., pp. 109, 129, 131–3, 137   108. Geffroy, pp. 149, 151, Ursins to Louis XIV, 9 April 1703, Philip V to Louis XIV, 3 May 1703; Dangeau, XVI, 46, 69, 20, 2, 21 March 1703, XVII, 68, 30 March 1705   109. Cermakian, p. 309; Dangeau, XVII, 162, 217, 27 June, 1 September 1704; cf. Louis XIV, *Oeuvres*, VI, 151, Louis XIV to Abbé d'Estrées, 19 March 1704   110. Geffroy, pp. 173–4; Cermakian, pp. 323–5, quoting Torcy to Tessé, 11 January 1705; Saint-Simon, *Mémoires*, ed. Regnier and Chéruel, IV, 228–30, 242. Philip V claimed that he did not like her, but wanted to please his wife, whom he loved 'éperdument' (madly): Cermakian, p. 203, Philip V to Louis XIV, 25 December 1704   111. Cermakian, pp. 329–37; Sourches, IX, 222n, 18 April 1705   112. Geffroy, pp. 183–4   113. Cermakian, pp. 332, 335–8, 340, Ursins to Maintenon, 24 June 1707; Dangeau, XVII, 99, 20 April 1704   114. Geffroy, pp. 192–4   115. Désos, pp. 177, 182; Baudrillart, *Philippe V*, I, 230, Amelot to Louis XIV, 22 June 1705   116. Note pour M. Amelot, 1705, in Louis XIV, *Correspondance*, I, 20   117. Geffroy, pp. 296–7, 330, Ursins to Maintenon, 3 January 1707, to Torcy, 4 March 1708   118. Ibid., pp. 211, 218, 232, 252, 255, Ursins to Chamillart, 20 November, 8 December 1705, to Maintenon, February, 22 November 1706   119. János Kalmár, 'Gênes et Milan pendant la guerre de Succession d'Espagne', in Raffaele Belvederi, ed., *Rapporti Genova-Mediterraneo-Atlantica nell'eta moderna*, VIII, Genoa, 1990, pp. 443–51   120. Spielman, pp. 170, 190; William O'Reilly, 'A Life in Exile: Charles VI between Spain and Austria', in Mansel and Riotte, pp. 66–90; Sir William G. F. Jackson, *The Rock of the Gibraltarians: A History of Gibraltar*, Rutherford, NJ, 1987, pp. 113–14   121. Baudrillart, *Philippe V*, I, 264–71   122. Ibid., p. 272, Maria Luisa to Maintenon, 3 November 1706   123. Bottineau, pp. 297-8; Désos, pp. 130, 135   124. Désos, p. 161; Bottineau, p. 251   125. Baudrillart, *Philippe V*, I, 285; Dangeau, XXII, 104, Maria Luisa to Duchesse de Bourgogne, 8 April 1707; Cermakian, pp. 366, 377–9   126. Louis XIV,

Correspondance avec M. Amelot, son ambassadeur en Espagne, 1705–1709, 2 vols., Nantes, 1864, I, 163, Louis XIV to Amelot, 24 October 1706   127. Pénicaut, p. 91; Renger de Bruin and Maarten Brinkman, eds., *Peace was Made Here: The Treaties of Utrecht, Rastatt and Baden*, Petersberg, 2013, pp. 29, 30, 37   128. Sarmant and Stoll, p. 206   129. Saint-Germain, *Samuel Bernard*, p. 184, Desmarets to Bernard, 21 September 1706; Gary B. McCollim, *Louis XIV's Assault on Privilege: Nicolas Desmaretz and the Tax on Wealth*, Rochester, NY, 2012, p. 157; Stéphane Guerre, *Desmaretz: le Colbert oublié du Roi-Soleil*, 2019, p. 342   130. Rowlands, *Financial Decline*, pp. 39, 49, 229; James Macdonald, *A Free Nation Deep in Debt: The Financial Roots of Democracy*, Princeton, 2006, pp. 182–6

Chapter 21: Towards the Precipice

1. Saint-Simon, *Mémoires*, ed. Regnier and Chéruel, V, 458; Sourches, X, 216, 18 November 1706, XI, 75, 6 May 1708   2. Saint-Germain, *Samuel Bernard*, pp. 145–55, 167–9; Rowlands, *Financial Decline*, pp. 213, 234. However, after his bankruptcy in 1705, one Huguenot rival of Bernard called Huguetan led a financial war on France from England; Frostin, p. 394   3. Pierre Ménard, *Le Français qui possédait l'Amérique: la vie extraordinaire d'Antoine Crozat, milliardaire sous Louis XIV*, 2017, pp. 80, 134, 202; Fernand Braudel, *The Identity of France*, 2 vols., 1988–90, II, 572–3; cf. Pritchard, *In Search of Empire*, pp. 363, 366–7   4. Henry Kamen, *The War of the Succession in Spain, 1700–15*, 1969, pp. 183–6; Désos, p. 111   5. Ménard, p. 268   6. Haussonville, *Duchesse de Bourgogne*, IV, 19; Saint-Simon, *Mémoires*, ed. Regnier and Chéruel, VI, 310; Petitfils, *Louis XIV*, pp. 626–7   7. Dangeau, XXI, 11–12, 31, 9, 11, 12, 16, 18 January, 4 February 1709; Saint-Simon, *Mémoires*, ed. Regnier and Chéruel, VI, 253; Norton, pp. 303–4   8. Dangeau, XIX, 27, 117, 12 June 1707   9. Saint-Germain, *Samuel Bernard*, pp. 204–5, letter from Trudaine, n.d.   10. Petitfils, *Louis XIV*, pp. 626–7; Jacques Saint-Germain, *Les Financiers sous Louis XIV*, 1950, pp. 70–71, curé of Cindré to Desmarets, 1708   11. ML, IV, 464, 473, Maintenon to Ursins, 2, 23 December 1708   12. Ibid., 533, Maintenon to Ursins, 8 April 1709   13. Ibid., 542, Maintenon to Ursins, 29 April 1709   14. Ibid., 547, Maintenon to Ursins, 5 May 1709   15. Ibid., 584, 598, Maintenon to Duc de Noailles, 30 June 1709, to Ursins, 14 July 1709   16. Ibid., 610, 628, Maintenon to Duc de Noailles, 30 July 1709, to Ursins, 26 August 1709   17. Ibid., 687, Maintenon to Ursins, 4 November 1709   18. Ibid., 555, Maintenon to Ursins, 26 May 1709; the Contrôleur Général Desmarets also feared 'the most terrible revolutions': Guerre, p. 304, mémoire au roi, n.d.   19. Dangeau, XXII, 110, 115, 30 April, 2 May 1709; cf. Clément, *Police*, p. 461n, for one petition to the Dauphin   20. Dangeau, XXII, 121, 5 May 1709; Norton, p. 304   21. Nicolas, pp. 50, 226. There had been seventy-nine in 1693/4.   22. Dethan, p. 158, despatch by Mocenigo, 21 June 1709; Lemarchand, pp. 35, 41; Nicolas, pp. 360–62, 433   23. Lemarchand, pp. 30, 37, 41, 47; Rowlands, *Financial Decline*, p. 233; Sourches, XI, 313, 328, 7 April, 4 May 1709, XII, 5, 7, 5, 8 July 1709   24. ML, IV, 543   25. Nicolas, pp. 616–18, 709   26. Jane McLeod, *Licensing Loyalty: Printers, Patrons, and the State in Early Modern France*, University Park, PA, 2011, pp. 68, 103; Frédéric Barbier, ed., *Paris, capitale des livres: le monde des livres et de la presse à Paris, du Moyen Age au XXe siècle*, 2007, pp. 152, 174   27. McCollim, pp. 127, 136   28. Levron, *Ville royale*, p. 78   29. Clément, *Police*, pp. 341, 344–5, d'Argenson to Chancellor, 24 August 1702, Chancellor to d'Argenson, 31 March 1701; AN o1 notes of 26 March 1705   30. Clément, *Police*, pp. 333–4, 355, 393, d'Argenson to Desmarets, 5 April 1709   31. Dangeau, XXII, 108, 222–3, 26 April, 20–21 August 1709; Petitfils, *Louis XIV*, pp. 631, 638, 706   32. Dangeau, XXII, 108–9, 28–29 April 1709   33. Clément, *Police*, p. 461, d'Argenson to Desmarets, 4 March 1709; Jacques Saint-Germain, *La Vie quotidienne en France à la fin du grand siècle d'après les archives de Marc René d'Argenson*, 1965, pp. 194–5, d'Argenson to Desmarets, 10 September 1709   34. Clément, *Police*, p. 463, d'Argenson to Desmarets, 4 May 1709; Sourches, XI, 329, 4 May 1709   35. Clément, *Police*, pp. 464–5, d'Argenson to Pontchartrain, 4 May 1709   36. Blet, *Nonces du pape*, p. 257, despatch by the Nuncio Cusani, 29 July 1709   37. Dangeau, XXII, 116n, note of Saint-Simon, 136, 26 May

1709 38. Louis XIV, *Correspondance avec M. Amelot*, II, 143–4, Louis XIV to Amelot, 3 June 1709; McCollim, p. 124; Torcy, *Journal*, p. xxx 39. Cermakian, p. 341, Philip V to Louis XIV, 17 April 1709 40. Dangeau, XIV, 45, 24 February 1701 41. AN [Cartons des Rois], K 118, 1 Discours sur l'employ des estrangers aux charge et dignités du royaume, 1649 42. Fonck, *Luxembourg*, pp. 571–2, Louis XIV to Luxembourg, 2 August 1693. Vauban often used the word. The Colbert family motto was 'For the king often, for the fatherland always': 'Pro rege saepe, pro patria semper'. 43. Jaeglé, II, 280, Madame to Raugravine Louise, 7 August 1718 44. Petitfils, *Louis XIV*, p. 709; Torcy, *Journal*, pp. xxxi–xxxiii 45. Holmes, *Marlborough*, pp. 411, 419, letter from Cadogan, Marlborough to Heinsius, July 1709 46. Villars, III, 250, Villars to Louis XIV, 6 June 1709; Joseph Klaits, *Printed Propaganda under Louis XIV: Absolute Monarchy and Public Opinion*, Princeton, 1977, p. 219 47. Geffroy, p. 370, Ursins to Maintenon, 1 September 1709, 372n, Louis XIV to Amelot, n.d. 48. Cermakian, pp. 395, 398, 413, Ursins to Maintenon, 28 April, Maintenon to Ursins, 24 June 1709, Ursins to Maintenon, 16 December 1709; ML, IV, 711, Maintenon to Ursins, 25 November 1709 49. Cermakian, p. 390, Ursins to Noailles, 29 October 1708, to Torcy, 21 November 1708 50. Torcy, *Journal*, p. 252, 31 August 1710; cf. Saint-Simon, *Mort de Louis XIV*, p. 411, for Saint-Simon on France heading 'jusqu'au dernier bord du précipice' 51. Kroll, pp. 149–50, Madame to Sophie, 22 August 1709; Clément, *Police*, pp. 356–7, d'Argenson to Desmarets, 7 September 1709; Dangeau, XXII, 222–3, 20–21 August 1709; Sourches says three were killed: Sourches, XII, 35, 20 August 1709 52. Dethan, p. 161, Aloise Mocenigo to Senate of Venice, 23 August 1709 53. Abbé G. Esnault, *Michel Chamillart: correspondance et papiers inédits*, 2 vols., 1885, II, 137, Vendôme to Chamillart, 21 October 1706. Fénelon and Saint-Simon also favoured calling the States General: Saint-Simon, *Mémoires*, ed. Regnier and Chéruel, XI, 293 54. Loyau, pp. 261–2, 324n, 327, 342–3, Ursins to Maintenon, 30 August, 11 November 1709, Maintenon to Ursins, 25 November 1709 55. Abbé Oroux, *Histoire ecclésiastique de la cour de France*, 2 vols., 1727, II, 526, 528, 539, 543–4, Bouillon to Louis XIV, 22 May 1710; Dangeau, XXIII, 105, 25 May 1710; Torcy, *Journal*, pp. 174, 185, 3, 24 May 1710; Saint-Simon, *Mémoires*, ed. Regnier and Chéruel, XI, 96–7. He failed in his ambitions, moved to Rome and died there in 1715. 56. Dubois, *Journal*, pp. 153, 154, 168, 27 June 1709, 1711 57. Kroll, p. 151, Madame to Luise, 26 October 1709; Dethan, p. 164, Mocenigo to Senate, 30 August, 26 November 1709 58. Dubois, *Journal*, pp. 152, 158, 164, 1709, 1710; cf. Gabet, p. 192, for a similar situation on the other side of France 59. Loyau, p. 398, Princesse d'Harcourt to Maintenon, 8 September 1709 60. Raïa Zaimova, *Correspondance consulaire des ambassadeurs de France à Constantinople, 1668–1708*, 1999, pp. 100, 184, 201, Ferriol to Pontchartrain, 1 September 1701, 13 June 1704; Louis Rousseau, *Les Relations diplomatiques de la France et de la Turquie au XVIIIe siècle*, vol. I: *1700–1716*, 1908, pp. 256, 260, 261, Ferriol to Pontchartrain, 27 April 1707, to Louis XIV, 24 September 1707, to Torcy, Louis XIV, 24 September 1709 61. Marquis de Bonnac, *Mémoire historique sur l'ambassade de Constantinople*, 1894, p. 130, mémoire of Ferriol, 10 August 1711; C. Badet, 'La Crise de 1709 à Marseille: les problèmes de ravitaillement en blé (1709–1710)', in Jean-Louis Miège, ed., *Les Céréales en Méditerranée*, 1993, pp. 69–82; Dangeau, XXIII, 16, 14 January 1710 62. Vault, VI, 561, Vendôme to Louis XIV, 23 August 1706; X, 40, Louis XIV to Villars, 1 June 1710; Cénat, *Roi stratège*, p. 233 63. Vault, V, 515, Louis XIV to Villars, 1 September 1705 64. Ibid., IX, 367, Boufflers to Louis XIV, 13 September 1709; Holmes, *Marlborough*, p. 433 65. Baudrillart and Lecestre, II, 29, 32, 31 August, 16 September 1709, 39n; Dangeau, XXIII, 7, 4 January 1710; Sourches, XII, 129, 22 December 1709 66. Saint-Simon, *Mort de Louis XIV*, p. 528 67. Torcy, *Journal*, p. 69, 17 December 1709 68. McCollim, p. 158, Desmarets to Louis XIV, 26 August 1709, p. 205; Esnault, II, 215, 'Articles de demandes du Sieur Bernard', 238, Desmarets to Chamillart, 14 May 1714 69. Torcy, *Journal*, p. 86, 31 December 1709 70. Baudrillart and Lecestre, II, 35, 44, Bourgogne to Philip V, 21 October 1709, 9 February 1710 71. Torcy, *Journal*, p. 169, 30 April 1710 72. Ibid., p. 177, 9 May 1710 73. Alfred Baudrillart, 'Madame de Maintenon: son rôle politique', *Revue des Questions Historiques*, 1890, pp. 101–61 at p. 111 74. Torcy, *Journal*, pp. 122, 177, 26 January, 9 May 1710 75. Dangeau,

XIX, 253, 16 November 1706; cf. XX, 9, 8 January 1707, XXII, 160, 12 June 1709
76. AN 01 366 ff. 31, 37v, 102v, 114, 321v, Pontchartrain to d'Argenson, 28 January, 4
February, 22 April, 3 May, 9 December 1705   **77.** Dangeau, XXI, 213, 9 August 1709;
Kroll, p. 147, Madame to Electress Sophia, 9 June 1709   **78.** Dangeau, XXIII, 5, 147, 1
January, 6 June 1710; Gabriel Mareschal de Bièvre, *Georges Mareschal, seigneur de Bièvre,
chirurgien et confident de Louis XIV (1658-1736)*, 1906, pp. 239-41   **79.** McCollim, pp.
172, 176, 203, 211; Levantal, *Louis XIV*, II, 677, 12 March 1701, 805, 14 October 1710   **80.**
Villars, III, 303, Villars to Torcy, 29 July 1711   **81.** Dangeau, XXII, 179, 4 July 1709;
Saint-Simon, *Mémoires*, ed. Regnier and Chéruel, V, 374   **82.** Garrigues, pp. 226-7;
Sources, X, 398n, 12 September 1707   **83.** AN 01 1098, Registres des ordres et lettres de
Mgr. le duc d'Antin ... concernant les bâtiments, jardins, arts et manufactures du roy depuis
1708 jusqu'à 1732, f. 98, order of 3 October 1710 re marbles   **84.** *DV*, p. 205   **85.** Baudril-
lart and Lecestre, II, 56, Bourgogne to Philip V, 9 June 1710   **86.** Dangeau, XXIII, 89, 7
May 1710   **87.** Torcy, *Journal*, p. 194, 2 June 1710; Dangeau, XXIII, 109n, 29 May
1710   **88.** Breteuil, pp. 292-5; Torcy, *Journal*, p. 219, 6 July 1710; cf. for further praise of
the chapel and its music, Saint-Simon, *Mémoires*, ed. Regnier and Chéruel, XI, 187   **89.**
Dangeau, XXIII, 118n, 2 June 1710, XXV, 17; Norton, p. 328; ML, VI, 41, Maintenon
to Ursins, 1 January 1714; Saint-Simon, *Mémoires*, ed. Regnier and Chéruel, XI, 201   **90.**
Kroll, p. 172, Madame to Electress Sophia, 21 May 1712; Poisson, pp. 204, 228   **91.** Poisson, p. 277   **92.** Saint-Simon, *Mémoires*, ed. Regnier and Chéruel, X, 175   **93.** Cf. Villars'
references in 1711 and 1712 to departure from Versailles: Villars, III, 120, Villars to Maintenon, 29 July 1711, and pp. 138-9   **94.** Torcy, *Journal*, pp. 214, 222, 28 June, 16 July 1710;
Bély, *Paix*, p. 461; Villars, III, 277, Polignac to Villars, 1 June 1710, outlines allied conditions   **95.** Lahaye, p. 13   **96.** Ibid., p. 251, quoting the memoirs of Torcy   **97.** Ibid., pp. 246,
248   **98.** McCollim, p. 124; Cermakian, p. 423   **99.** Cermakian, p. 366n, Louis XIV to
Amelot, 4 November 1709; Baudrillart, *Philippe V*, I, 367, 412, 417; Torcy, *Journal*, p. 256,
3 September 1710   **100.** Torcy, *Journal*, pp. 280-81, 3 October 1710, quoting a ciphered
letter of Philip V to Louis XIV, 25 September 1710   **101.** Cermakian, pp. 341, Philip V to
Louis XIV, 17 April 1709, 355, Louis XIV to Amelot, 3 June 1709   **102.** Baudrillart and
Lecestre, II, 59, Bourgogne to Philip V, 20 September 1710; Norton, pp. 262-9   **103.** Simon
Harcourt-Smith, *Alberoni or The Spanish Conspiracy*, 1943, pp. 43, 51, 63; Cermakian, pp.
441, 501; Dangeau, XXV, 154-7n, 20 June 1712; Saint-Simon, *Mémoires*, ed. Regnier and
Chéruel, IV, 384-7   **104.** Marquis de Louville, *Mémoires secrets sur l'établissement de la
Maison de Bourbon en Espagne*, 2 vols., 1818, II, 213, 230   **105.** ML, IV, 521, Maintenon
to Ursins, 18 March 1709   **106.** Giulio Alberoni, *Lettres intimes au Comte I. Rocca*, ed.
Emile Bourgeois, 1892, p. 131, letter of 28 December 1710   **107.** Cermakian, p. 431

Chapter 22: Nemesis Averted

1. AN 257 AP 2, Louis XIV to Pontchartrain, 8 March 1708   **2.** Bruin and Brinkman, p.
30; Anne Somerset, *Queen Anne: The Politics of Passion*, 2013, p. 382; Holmes, *Fatal Avenue*,
pp. 345, 355   **3.** Edward Gregg, *Queen Anne*, 1980, pp. 336, 346   **4.** Holmes, *Marlborough*,
pp. 407-8, 436; Gregg, *Queen Anne*, pp. 275, 326-9   **5.** Holmes, *Marlborough*, pp. 414-15;
Gregg, *Queen Anne*, pp. 286-9; Ward, pp. 375, 384   **6.** Bély, *Paix*, p. 369; Gregg, *Queen
Anne*, p. 232   **7.** Dangeau, XXIII, 152, 8 July 1710, XXIV, 220, 17 October 1710   **8.**
Maréchal de Berwick, *Mémoires*, 2 vols., 1828, II, 178   **9.** Manuel Castellano Garcia, 'Fran-
çois Gaultier: un artisan de la paix d'Utrecht, (1711-1713)', 3, *RHD*, 2016, pp. 257-75   **10.**
Torcy, *Mémoires*, pp. 16-17; Bély, *Espions*, pp. 185-7   **11.** Bély, *Paix*, p. 378; Gregg, *Queen
Anne*, p. 335; Dangeau, XXV, 87, 25 March 1712   **12.** Torcy, *Journal*, pp. 347-9 and n, 21
January 1711   **13.** Gerald Cerny, *Theology, Politics and Letters at the Crossroads of Euro-
pean Civilisation: Jacques Basnage and the Baylean Huguenot Refugees in the Dutch Republic*, Dordrecht, 1987, pp. 130-40   **14.** O'Reilly, pp. 78-9   **15.** Gregg, *Queen Anne*, p.
356   **16.** Torcy, *Mémoires*, p. 121   **17.** Ibid., p. 148   **18.** Corp, p. 68.   **19.** Legg, pp. 103,
Prior to Jersey, 19 August 1699, 146-9, 156, 159 (Prior's account of his audience with Louis

XIV on 3 August 1711), 169; Charles Kenneth Eves, *Matthew Prior: Poet and Diplomatist*, New York, 1939, p. 139, Torcy to Jersey, 18 August 1699 **20.** Dangeau, XXIV, 223, 18 October 1711; Bély, *Espions*, pp. 304, 592–5 **21.** Michel Zylberberg, *Une si douce domination: les milieux d'affaires français et l'Espagne vers 1780–1808*, 1993, pp. 50–51 **22.** Rolland, pp. 227–39. The loss of Tournai was especially resented. Louis XIV had visited it in 1670, 1671, 1673, 1680, and built a citadel, a church and a Parlement building there. **23.** Ibid., pp. 341, 387; Thomas, *Slave Trade*, pp. 227–8, 231, 238; Zylberberg, p. 46 **24.** Black, *From Louis XIV to Napoleon*, pp. 90–91; Pritchard, *In Search of Empire*, pp. 148, 163, 188, 195, 402 **25.** Holmes, *Marlborough*, pp. 455–7; Fadi el Hage, *Le Maréchal de Villars: l'infatigable bonheur*, 2012, pp. 116–17 **26.** Bély, *Paix*, p. 461, 39n, Torcy to Huxelles, 29 January 1712 **27.** Ibid., p. 660; Walter Sichel, *Bolingbroke and his Times*, 1901, p. 380n; cf. the friendly letters between Villars and Ormonde in June and July 1712 in Villars, III, 311–21 **28.** Lottin, *Grandes Batailles*, pp. 141–50; Sarmant, *Homme et roi*, p. 495 **29.** El Hage, pp. 73, 135, 153 **30.** Sichel, p. 407; Dangeau, XXV, 209, 211, 21, 24 August 1712; Levantal, *Louis XIV*, II, 812; Eves, p. 244, Prior diary, August 1711, p. 266 **31.** Dangeau, XXII, 116n, note of Saint-Simon, 136, 26 May 1709 **32.** Bély, *Paix*, p. 442n **33.** Dangeau, XXVI, 117, 22 May 1713 **34.** Symcox, pp. 158, 169–71. I am grateful to John Rogister for discussion on this point. **35.** Bruin and Brinkman, p. 65 and passim; Bély, *Paix*, pp. 523, 588, 663–74 **36.** Dubois, *Journal*, p. 171, 1713 **37.** Eric Vanneufville, *Histoire de Lille: des origines au XXe siècle*, 1997, p. 144; cf. Lambin, p. 269 **38.** Troost, 'To Restore and Preserve', p. 302 **39.** Bruin and Brinkman, pp. 66, 125, 174 **40.** Bély, *Paix*, pp 724, 726; idem, *Espions*, p. 134 **41.** Waquet, *Callières*, p. 184 **42.** Grimblot, II, 267, Louis XIV to Tallard, 13 February 1699; Dollot, p. 54. Like the Duke of Lorraine when offered Milan, the Elector of Bavaria would have been happy to abandon his ancestral lands in return for richer ones. **43.** Dangeau, XXVIII, 88, 22 March 1715. His portraits of French princesses and views of Saint-Cloud still hang in Nymphenburg, his palace outside Munich. **44.** Ibid., XIX, 218, 26 September 1706 **45.** Samuel John Klingensmith, *The Utility of Splendor: Ceremony, Social Life, and Architecture at the Court of Bavaria, 1600–1800*, Chicago, 1993, pp. 61–3, 119, 121, 126, 171; Henriette Graf, 'The Apartments of Prince-Elector Charles Albert of Bavaria around 1740 and their Ceremonial Use at Court', *The Court Historian*, 22, 1, June 2017, pp. 17–37; Elmar D. Schmid et al., *Nymphenburg Palace, Park and Pavilions*, Munich, 2009, passim; Stéphane Castelluccio, ed., *Le Commerce du luxe à Paris aux XVIIe et XVIIIe siècles*, Bern, 2009, p. 249, Max Emanuel to Countess Arcos, 4 January 1705; interview with Max Tillmann, Munich, 24 September 2017. Dominique Girard, a former *fontanier* of Louis XIV, worked for the Elector in Munich from 1715 to 1738. **46.** Reginald de Schryver, *Max II Emanuel von Bayern und das spanische Erbe: die europäische Ambitionen des Hauses Wittelsbach*, Mainz, 1996, p. 210 **47.** Ingrao, pp. 124, 128, 142, 144, 149, 159; Emile Pillias, *Etudes sur François II Rákóczi, Prince de Transylvanie*, 1939, p. 14, Rákóczi to Louis XIV, 1 November 1700, Louis XIV to Villars, 9 May 1701, p. 49, Louis XIV to Bonnac, 15 November 1703 **48.** Ferenc Tóth, 'Emigré or Exile? Francis Rákóczi II and his Exile in France and Turkey', in Mansel and Riotte, pp. 91–102; Ferenc Tóth, ed., *Correspondance diplomatique relative à la guerre d'indépendance du Prince François II Rákóczi (1703–1711)*, 2012, pp. 38, 42, Bonnac to Louis XIV, 23 April 1703, 48, 60, 97, Rákóczi to Louis XIV, 6 August 1708; F. Tóth, 'Officiers français au service de l'armée du prince François II Rákóczi', in Tomasz Ciesielski, ed., *W służbie obcych monarchów i państw*, Warsaw, 2015, pp. 73–93 **49.** Saint-Simon, *Mémoires*, ed. Regnier and Chéruel, IX, 414–15; Béla Köpeczi, ed., *Correspondance diplomatique de François II Rákóczi*, Budapest, 1999, p. 153, Rákóczi to Baron de Besenval, 15 May 1713; Dangeau, XXVI, 84, 121, 146, 5 April, 29 May, 28 June 1713; Pillias, pp. 67–71 **50.** Legrelle, *Diplomatie française*, VI, 146–8. Some Catalans continue to revere 'Charles III': until 2017 his bust decorated the office of the President of Catalonia. **51.** Robert Hughes, *Barcelona*, 1992, pp. 182, 185, 189 **52.** Baudrillart, *Philippe V*, I, 652–3, Louis XIV to Philip V, 2 July, 1 August 1714. Queen Anne had also asked Louis XIV to intercede for the Catalans: Eves, p. 301, Prior to Bolingbroke, 6 December 1713 **53.** Cdt Herlaut, 'La Destruction du port de Dunkerque: la mission d'Ignace Tugghe à la cour d'Angleterre en 1713', *Revue du Nord*, 11, 41, 1925, pp. 5–35; **54.** Alberoni, I, 30–32;

Lemaire, pp. 247, 255   55. Cdt Herlaut, 'L'Intendant Le Blanc et les Anglais à Dunkerque', *Bulletin de la Société Archéologique et Historique de Dunkerque et de la Flandre Maritime*, XXII, 1925, pp. 1–187   56. Torcy, *Journal*, p. 422, 10 April 1711; Chaline, *Quatre dauphins*, pp. 60–62, 80–82; Saint-Simon, *Mémoires*, ed. Regnier and Chéruel, VIII, 244–5   57. Sourches, XIII, 87, 16 April 1711; cf. Chaline, pp. 86–9   58. And he was vexed by their daughters' grief at the death of Madame de Montespan: ML, IV, 153, Maintenon to Ursins, 26 June 1707.   59. Torcy, *Journal*, p. 424, 15 April 1711; Norton, p. 339   60. Kroll, p. 160, Madame to Sophie, 16 April 1711   61. BN Mss. fr. 6999 f. 59, Journal de la santé de Louis XIV, 14 April 1711   62. Torcy, *Journal*, p. 424, 15 April 1711; Norton, p. 339   63. Saint-Simon, *Mémoires*, ed. Regnier and Chéruel, VII, 372   64. Haussonville, *Duchesse de Bourgogne*, II, 161; Torcy, *Mémoires*, pp. 96, 100   65. Saint-Simon, *Mémoires*, ed. Regnier and Chéruel, VIII, 434–6, 446, IX, 225; Norton, p. 210   66. Chevé, p. 376; Haussonville, *Duchesse de Bourgogne*, IV, 298, 311; Dangeau, XXV, 59, 61, 18 February 1712, note of Saint-Simon; Sarmant, *Homme et roi*, p. 485   67. Norton, pp. 367–78, 386; Chaline, pp. 34, 39   68. René de Froulay de Tessé, *Lettres du maréchal de Tessé au prince Antoine Ier de Monaco*, 1917, p. 157, Tessé to Monaco, 15 February 1712; cf. Sourches, XIII, 295–8, 312, 315n, 12–16, 23 February 1712   69. ML, V, 400, 405, Maintenon to Ursins, 17, 27 March 1712; cf. Saint-Simon, *Mémoires*, ed. Regnier and Chéruel, IV, 170, for similar sentiments. Writing forty years later, he lamented 'un vide affreux qui n'a pu être diminué'.   70. Jaeglé, II, 166, 167, Madame to Electress Sophia, 14, 18 February 1712   71. Cf. Dangeau, XXV, 59, for Saint-Simon's sense of grief, and comparison of Bourgogne to Jesus Christ. He considered Bourgogne's 'pure soul' 'a reflection of the divine', and that he was 'born for the happiness of France and Europe': Saint-Simon, *Mort de Louis XIV*, p. 113   72. ML, V, 444, Maintenon to Ursins, 13 June 1712   73. Dangeau, XXV, 50, 52, 15, 18 February 1712; Saint-Simon, *Mémoires*, ed. Regnier and Chéruel, IX, 237; Sourches, XIII, 519, 520, 27 October 1712   74. Dangeau, XXV, 81, 8 March 1712   75. Ibid., XXVI, 161, 18 July 1713   76. Ibid., 223, 22 October 1713; XXVII, 24, 27, 30 January 1714   77. Ibid., XX, 10, 45, 46, 9 January, 7, 8 March 1707; Saint-Simon, *Mémoires*, ed. Regnier and Chéruel, V, 134, X, 358   78. Kroll, pp. 168, Madame to Sophie, 10 March 1712   79. Ward, pp. 410, 421–2   80. Bély, *Paix*, p. 513; Corp, pp. 71–4   81. Gregg, *Queen Anne*, pp. 375–7; Corp, p. 288   82. This view was also expressed in the treaties of 1737–8, giving Tuscany, on the death of its last Medici Grand Duke, Louis XIV's first cousin once removed Gian Gastone, to the last hereditary Duke of Lorraine, Francis Stephen, despite the superior hereditary claims of Philip V's youngest son, the future Charles III of Spain. This was a European agreement, partly devised to ensure France's ultimate acquisition of Lorraine.   83. Bély, *Paix*, p. 432   84. Baudrillart, *Philippe V*, I, 482, 527, Louis XIV to Bonnac, n.d.   85. Ibid., 517, 532; Chantal Grell, 'Philippe, prince français ou roi d'Espagne, le débat sur les renonciations', in Álvarez-Ossorio et al., eds., pp. 673–92 at pp. 675, Louis XIV to Bonnac, 24 April 1713, 677, 686   86. AN [Cartons des Rois] K 122, 21, declaration by Philip V, 7 November 1712; Dangeau, XXVI, 65, 15 March 1713, describes the ceremony   87. Bély, *Paix*, p. 553   88. S. Arthur Strong, ed., *A Catalogue of Letters ... in the Library at Welbeck*, 1903, p. 300, Prior to Oxford, 12 June 1714   89. Dangeau, XXIII, 203, 22 September 1710; Clément, *Police*, pp. 268–9; Laurence Plazenet, 'L'Anamorphose du soleil en épouvantail: Louis XIV dans l'historiographie et la littérature port-royalistes', in *Louis XIV et Port-Royal*, 2016, pp. 165–99 at p. 192   90. Cornette, *Mort de Louis XIV*, p. 244   91. Ronald Schechter, *A Genealogy of Terror in Eighteenth-Century France*, Chicago, 2018   92. Mark Bryant, ' The Catholic Church and its Dissenters, 1685–1715', in Julia Prest and Guy Rowlands, eds., *The Third Reign of Louis XIV, c. 1682–1715*, 2016, pp. 145–61   93. Maral, *Versailles*, p. 296   94. Catherine Maire, ed., *Jansénisme et révolution: actes du colloque de Versailles*, 1990, passim; Pierre Chaunu, Madeleine Foisil and Françoise de Noirfontaine, *Le Bascule-ment religieux de Paris au XVIIIe siècle: essai d'histoire politique et religieuse*, 1998, passim; Minois, pp. 222, 327   95. Marquis d'Argenson, *Journal*, 2014–, VII, 174, 301, 18 December 1751, 18 April 1752; IX, 105, 162, 200–202, 221, 21 March, 6, 19 May 1753   96. Dale Van Kley, *The Religious Origins of the French Revolution: From Calvin to the Civil Constitution, 1560–1791*, New Haven, 1996, p. 131   97. National Archives, Kew (henceforward NA) State

Papers France 78/159 f. 94v, Prior to George I, 23 August 1714, f. 97, Prior to Bolingbroke, 23 August 1714, f. 274, Prior to Townshend, 4 December 1714. The French government did, however, agree to loan James two ships to take him to England in case of a Jacobite uprising. But he also wanted troops and munitions: Daniel Szechi, *The Great Jacobite Rising*, 2006, pp. 79, 86–8 **98.** Mary, Countess Cowper, *Diary, 1714–1720*, 1864, p. 5 **99.** Torcy, *Mémoires*, p. 210 **100.** Rex A. Barrell, *Bolingbroke and France*, Lanham, MD, 1988, pp. 9–10 and passim **101.** Eveline Cruickshanks, 'The Second Duke of Ormonde and the Atterbury Plot', in Toby Barnard and Jane Fenlon, eds., *The Dukes of Ormonde, 1610–1745*, Woodbridge, 2000, pp. 243–53 at p. 245; Lord Stair, 'Extracts from Lord Stair's journal at Paris in 1715 and 1716', in Earl of Hardwicke, ed., *Miscellaneous State Papers from 1501 to 1726*, 2 vols., 1778, II, 528–54 at 538. Ormonde would plan to join Jacobite invasions of England in 1715, 1719 and 1745. **102.** Claude Nordmann, *La Crise du Nord au début du XVIIIe siècle*, 1962, pp. 40–41; Eric Schnakenbourg, 'La Politique française dans le Nord à la fin du règne de Louis XIV', *RHD*, 3, 1998, pp. 251–74; Edward Gregg, *The Protestant Succession in International Politics, 1710–1716*, 1986, pp. 161, 278–9, 286–7; Corp, p. 295. Much of the £43,500 sent by Philip V to 'James III' was lost when the ship carrying it to Scotland sank: L. B. Smith, 'Spain and the Jacobites, 1715–16', in Eveline Cruickshanks, ed., *Ideology and Jacobitism*, Edinburgh, 1982, pp. 159–78

Chapter 23: Funeral Games

1. Eves, p. 293, Prior to Bolingbroke, 7 September 1714; Legg, p. 191, Prior to Oxford, 19 January 1713, to Bolingbroke, 11 September 1714 **2.** ML, VI, 136, Maintenon to Ursins, 16 June 1714 **3.** Castelluccio, *Fastes*, p. 129; Breteuil, pp. 97–154; Dangeau, XXVIII, 57–8, 19 February 1715; Maral, *Derniers Jours*, pp. 36–40 **4.** Anne Kroell, *Louis XIV, la Perse et Mascate*, 1977, pp. 57–8; Ménard, pp. 255–6. For Louis XIV's persistent interest in Persia, see e.g. Pontchartain, II, 11, 185, Pontchartrain to Bishop of Babylon, 9 January 1704, 3 January 1710 **5.** ML, VI, 188, 242, Maintenon to Ursins, 26 August, 5 November 1714. Louis XIV had given small houses in the park of Versailles, now vanished, to the duchesses de Bourbon and d'Orléans, among others: Saint-Simon, *Mémoires*, ed. Regnier and Chéruel, III, 63. **6.** ML, VI, 215, 242, Maintenon to Ursins, 242, 30 September, 5 November 1714; Dangeau, XXVII, 199, 25 August 1714, XXVIII, 91, 28, 29 March 1715 **7.** Kroll, p. 188, Madame, 26 June 1715; Dangeau, XXV, 86, 22 March 1712: Maral, *Versailles*, p. 425 **8.** Cornette, *Mort de Louis XIV*, pp. 228–9; Dangeau, XXVII, 118, 19 May 1714, XXVIII, 143, 164, 168, 171, 8 June, 11, 16, 23 July 1715 **9.** Archives de Chantilly Série 1 11 ff. 11, 22, 26, Louis XIV to Chartres, 11 July 1693, 29 June, 10 July 1694, f. 174, Madame to Dubois, 10 August 1696 **10.** Saint-Simon, *Mémoires*, ed. Regnier and Chéruel, III, 10; Jaeglé, I, 240–41, Madame to Electress Sophia, 12 June 1701; Dangeau, XIV, 124–7 and n, 9 June 1701 **11.** ML, IV, 216, Maintenon to Ursins, 10 October 1707; Dangeau, XXIII, 9, 4 January 1710; 3, Madame to Sophie, 1 July 1711 **12.** Lurgo, pp. 281–2, 356, Madame to Dubois, 18, 21 June 1696; Dangeau, XVI, 175, 19 July 1703 **13.** ML, IV, 601, Maintenon to Ursins, 15 July 1709; Baudrillart, *Philippe V*, I, 294, 390–91, II, 57, 78–90; Claude-Frédéric Lévy, *Capitalistes et pouvoir au siècle des lumières: les fondateurs, des origines à 1715*, 1969, pp. 422–5; Petitfils, *Régent*, pp. 156–8 **14.** Geffroy, p. 384n **15.** Baudrillart, *Philippe V*, II, 96–7, Louis XIV to Philip V, 5 August 1709, Philip V to Louis XIV, 16 August 1709; Petitfils, *Régent*, pp. 156–8 **16.** Dangeau, XXII, 119n, 185, 199n, 4 May, 12, 28 July 1709 **17.** Baudrillart, *Philippe V*, I, 471; Torcy, *Journal*, p. 195, 22 June 1710. Confirmation of Orléans' dynastic ambitions would be provided in 1721 by the engagement of the eleven-year-old Louis XV to a three-year-old Spanish infanta. Thereby he hoped to delay by at least ten years Louis XV's chances of fathering a dauphin, and increased his own or his son's chances of succeeeding to the throne if the young King died. According to Villars the council feared the marriage, but dared not speak against it: the young King cried at the news. Baudrillart, *Philippe V*, II, 479; Michel Antoine, *Louis XV*, 1989, pp. 96–7 **18.** Jaeglé, II, 167, 168, 174, Madame to Electress Sophia, 20, 21 February, April 1712; Saint-Simon, *Mémoires*, ed. Regnard and Chéruel, IX,

263, 272   19. Mareschal de Bièvre, pp. 320–25   20. Dangeau, XXVIII, 138, 3 June 1715; Cornette, 1715, pp. 276–7   21. Robert Oresko, 'Bastards as Clients: The House of Savoy and its Illegitimate Children', in Charles Giry-Deloison and Roger Mettam, eds., *Patronages et clientélismes, 1550–1750 (France, Angleterre, Espagne, Italie)*, Lille, n.d., pp. 39–67   22. J. Spangler, 'A Lesson in Diplomacy for Louis XIV: The Treaty of Montmartre 1662 and the Princes of the Houses of Lorraine', *French History*, 17, 3, 2003, pp. 225–50.   23. AN AE 1/25, Testament de Louis XIV, 2 August 1714   24. BN Mss. fr. 7013 f. 414v, 416v   25. AN AE 1/25, Testament de Louis XIV, 2 August 1714   26. Baudrillart, *Philippe V*, I, 671, 679   27. Maral, *Derniers Jours*, p. 106, Philip V to Cellamare, 19 May 1715   28. Baudrillart, *Philippe V*, I, 582, del Giudice to Philip V, 4 May 1714   29. Désos, p. 330; Geffroy, p. 410n; Dangeau, XXIV, 167, 210, 29 July, 28 September 1711, XXVII, 83, 4 April 1714; Cermakian, pp. 448, 483; Baudrillart, *Philippe V*, I, 543   30. ML, VI, 70, 107, Maintenon to Ursins, 5 March, 23 April 1714   31. Cermakian, pp. 514–18   32. Ibid., pp. 521, 522–5, Ursins to Louis XIV, 10 January 1715. The Queen wrote that Ursins 'failed in all the forms of respect due to me': Duc de La Trémoille, *Madame des Ursins et la Succession d'Espagne*, 6 vols., Nantes, 1902–7, VI, 264, 'I the Queen' to Comte Pighetti, 25–30 December 1714   33. Baudrillart, *Philippe V*, I, 614, 616, Philip V to Ursins, 24, 29 December 1714, Orry to Torcy, 5 January 1715, 620, Louis XIV to Philip V, 30 April 1715; Cermakian, pp. 534, Louis XIV to Ursins, 21 January 1715, 539, 546, 582; Saint-Simon, *Mémoires*, ed. Regnier and Chéruel, XII, 62   34. Dangeau, XXVIII, 103, 12 April 1715; Stair, pp. 533–4, 24, 26 July 1715. Dubois would remain an ally of George I, twice visiting him in London in the next reign: Alexandre Dupilet, *Le Cardinal Dubois, le génie politique de la Régence*, 2015, pp. 149–55, 250   35. Stair, p. 546, 27 August 1715   36. Tessé, pp. 255–60, Tessé to Monaco, Marly, 17 June 1715   37. Dangeau, XXVIII, 117, 5 May 1715; cf., for a similar insistence in 1712, Saint-Simon, *Mémoires*, ed. Regnier and Chéruel, IX, 291   38. Levantal, *Louis XIV*, II, 850, 19 June, 6, 9, 13 July 1715; Dangeau, XXIX, 14, 7 August 1715; Narbonne, I, 41   39. Maral, *Derniers Jours*, pp. 125–6, 230; Perez, pp. 253, 377, quoting *Gazette de France*, 24 August 1715   40. Stair, pp. 539, 540, 12, 13 August 1715. 'James III' would stay in Lorraine, where he was treated as a king, until he left to invade Scotland, sailing from Dunkirk on 26 December 1715.   41. Dangeau, XXIX, 173, note of 25 August 1715   42. Jacques Anthoine, *Journal de la maladie et de la mort de Louis XIV*, 1880, pp. 11–12, 16, 13 August 1715   43. Maral, *Derniers Jours*, pp. 132, 139; Anthoine, p. 24, 17 August 1715; Saint-Simon, *Mémoires*, ed. Regnier and Chéruel, XI, 385; Perez, pp. 152–62, gives a good account of the final illness   44. Anthoine, pp. 20–21, 15 August 1715   45. Ibid., pp. 25–26, 31, 33, 16, 17, 21, 22 August 1715; Saint-Simon, *Mémoires*, ed. Regnier and Chéruel, III, 297   46. Jaeglé, II, 233, Madame to Raugravine Louise, 15 August 1715   47. Anthoine, p. 29, 20 August 1715   48. Ibid., p. 11, 12 August 1715; Perez, p. 241   49. ML, VI, 345, Maintenon to Mary of Modena, 21 August 1715   50. Anthoine, p. 36, 22 August 1715   51. Dangeau, XXIX, 150, 22 August 1715   52. Maral, *Derniers Jours*, pp. 155, 162, 166; Dangeau, XXIX, 164, 24 August 1715   53. Anthoine, p. 45, 25 August 1715   54. Cornette, *Mort de Louis XIV*, pp. 28–9; Dangeau, XXIX, 165, 175–6, 25 August 1715; Anthoine, pp. 41–2, 47, 25 August 1715   55. AN O1 (Maison du Roi) 821 f. 78, 'Pompe funèbre de Louis XIV mort à Versailles le 1er Septembre 1715'   56. AN K 136, 2ter letter by Sr Nouet, 27 August 1715   57. Dangeau, XXIX, 182, 25 August 1715; Breteuil, pp. 324–8   58. Maral, *Derniers Jours*, pp. 156–7; Dangeau, XXIX, 167, 182, 26 August 1715; Anthoine, p. 48, 25 August 1715; Saint-Simon, *Mémoires*, ed. Regnier and Chéruel, XI, 438   59. Maral, *Derniers Jours*, pp. 167–8; Dangeau, XXIX, 168, 26 August 1715   60. Maral, *Derniers Jours*, p. 181; Dangeau, XXIX, 179, 26 August 1715; Breteuil, p. 327   61. Dangeau, XXIX, 167, 176, 26 August 1715; Breteuil, p. 328   62. Maral, *Derniers Jours*, pp. 187–92; Jaeglé, II, 234, Madame to Raugravine Louise, 27 August 1715   63. Dangeau, XXIX, 169, 183–4, 187, 27, 30 August 1715   64. Ibid., 168, 184, 27 August 1715   65. Ibid., 169, 28 August 1715   66. Ibid., 185–7, 28–30 August 1715; Perez, p. 160   67. Maral, *Derniers Jours*, p. 205   68. Dangeau, XXIX, 169, 183–4, 187, 27, 30 August 1715   69. Ibid., 188, 31 August, 1 September 1715; Maral, *Derniers Jours*, pp. 209, 218   70. Jean Buvat, *Journal de la Régence*, 2 vols., 1865, I, 47, 1 September 1715; Dangeau, XXIX, 188, 1 September 1715; Mathieu Marais, *Journal de Paris*, 2 vols., Saint-Etienne, 2004, I, 45, 1 September

1715 71. AN o1 821 ff. 80–82, diary of M. Desgranges, Maître des Cérémonies 72. Ibid., ff. 83–4. In Vienna, from 1654 until 1878, Habsburgs' hearts were placed in brass or silver jars in the Augustinian church, their entrails, brains and eyes in the Cathedral of St Stephen, their bodies in the Kapuzinergruft. 73. Ibid., f. 89 74. Frédérique Leferme-Falguières, 'Les Funérailles de Louis XIV à Saint-Denis', in Sabatier and Saule, pp. 72, 273, 280 75. Stair, pp. 543–4, 23, 26 August 1715 76. Maral, *Derniers Jours*, pp. 175, 195, 206 77. Ibid., p. 149; Dangeau, XXIX, 149, 22 August 1715 78. Saint-Simon, *Mémoires*, ed. Regnier and Chéruel, XI, 333 79. Marais, *Journal*, I, 35, 2 September 1715 80. Haussonville, *Duchesse de Bourgogne*, III, 85, Duc du Maine to Chamillart, 2 August 1702 81. Marais, *Journal*, I, 62, 16 September 1715; Cornette, *Mort de Louis XIV*, pp. 285, 289, 291, 301–2 82. Cornette, *Mort de Louis XIV*, pp. 283, 285, 293–8, 306 83. Marais, *Journal*, I, 55, 9 September 1715 84. AN o1 821 ff. 95–7; Maral, *Derniers Jours*, pp. 247–9 85. AN o1 821 ff. 99–101, 23 October 1715; Levantal, *Louis XIV*, II, 854–5, 9 September, 23 October 1715 86. Jean-Marie Le Gall, 'Les Bourbons, ou le refus du tombeau', in Mark Hengerer and Gérard Sabatier, eds., *Les Funérailles princières en Europe XVIe–XVIIIe siècles*, II: *Apothéoses monumentales*, 2013, pp. 253–68 at p. 262 87. AN o1 821 ff. 114–16 88. Francis B. Assaf, *La Mort du roi: une thanatographie de Louis XIV*, Tübingen, 1999, passim; for the services in all the Catholic churches of Aleppo, with mausolea and illuminations, see Paul Lucas, *Troisième voyage . . . dans le Levant*, Saint-Etienne, 2004, p. 100 89. Abbé Migne, *Collection intégrale et universelle des orateurs sacrés*, XXXIII, 1853, pp. 1304, 1306, 1314, 1321–2; Sabatier and Saule, pp. 83–91 90. Maral, *Derniers Jours*, p. 248; AN o1 821 f. 114 91. Emile Raunié, *Chansonnier historique du XVIIIe siècle*, 10 vols., 1879–84, I, 56–7, 60–61; Cornette, *Mort de Louis XIV*, p. 62; Maral, *Louis XIV*, pp. 265–6, 270 92. Raunié, I, 61; Sabatier and Saule, p. 233 93. Jean-Baptiste Massillon, *Oraison funèbre de Louis XIV*, Grenoble, 2004, pp. 56–7, 71, 96 and passim

Chapter 24: The Shadow of Versailles

1. See e.g. Mazarin, *Lettres*, IX, 329, Mazarin to M. Silhon, 29 September 1659, for the Cardinal's sense of France's role in Europe 2. Francine-Dominique Liechtenhan, *Pierre le Grand*, 2015, pp. 255, 421 3. McKay, pp. 242–3, 253 4. McCollim, pp. 213, 215; Neil Jeffares, 'Between France and Bavaria: Louis-Joseph d'Albert de Luynes, Prince de Grimberghen', *The Court Historian*, 17, 1, June 2012, pp. 61–85 at p. 72. After 1742 the alliance with Bavaria would also help drag France, with little advantage to itself, into the War of the Austrian Succession. 5. Arsenal Mss. 13927, Louis XIV to Duc de la Meilleraye, October 1661 6. Eves, p. 111, Prior commonplace book, n.d.; Liechtenhan, p. 415 7. Leonhard Horowski, ' "Such a Great Advantage for my Son": Office-Holding and Career Mechanisms at the Court of France, 1661–1789', *The Court Historian*, 8, 2, December 2003, pp. 125–75 at pp. 138–41, 174 8. Dessert, *Royaume*, pp. 291–3 9. Rowlands, *Financial Decline*, p. 236 10. Petitfils, *Régent*, p. 357 11. Spanheim, p. xvii, 2 August 1683; Jaeglé, I, 43, II, 170, 234, Madame to Electress Sophia, 1 August 1683, to Raugravine Louise, 10 March 1712, 27 August 1715; Mareschal de Bièvre, pp. 340–43; Perez, p. 149, account by Duc d'Antin 12. Saint-Simon, *Mémoires*, ed. Regnier and Chéruel, V, 349; Villars, III, 49, cf. p. 240, Villars to Boufflers, 20 April 1708 13. Christopher Storrs, *The Spanish Resurgence, 1713–1748*, New Haven, 2016, pp. 98, 129, 188–91 14. Sauzet, pp. 246–8; cf. Sourches, I, 12, September 1681 15. Legg, p. 68, Prior to Lord Halifax, 18 February 1698 16. Louis XIV, *Oeuvres*, II, 277 17. Saint-Simon, *Mémoires*, ed. Regnier and Chéruel, III, 247, 293, XII, 49, 51 18. E. J. F. Barbier, *Journal d'un avocat de Paris*, 4 vols., Clermont-Ferrand, 2002–4, 197, 15 June 1722; Lemarchand, pp. 16, 112, 123, 255n, 259, 262, 319 19. Dupilet, p. 177; Kroll, pp. 215, 221, Madame to Luise, 14 July 1718, 5 January 1719; Petitfils, *Régent*, p. 473; Lemarchand, pp. 66, 94 20. La Gorce, *Lully*, pp. 297, 777; Braun, pp. 155, 159 21. Peter Burke, *The Fabrication of Louis XIV*, New Haven and London, 1992, p. 172; Gwenola Firmin et al., eds., *Pierre le Grand: un tsar en France 1717*, 2017, passim 22. Simon Thurley, *Hampton Court: A Social and Architectural History*, 2003, pp. 141, 153, 189, 205 23.

Wilson, pp. 126–8 **24.** Blanning, *Frederick the Great*, pp. 163, 168. In Potsdam in 1750 Frederick II recreated Louis' 1662 carousel. **25.** Cynthia Field et al., eds., *Paris on the Potomac: The French Influence on the Architecture and Art of Washington, D.C.*, Athens, OH, 2007, p. 3 **26.** Argenson, II, 63, 127, 136, 141, 151, 26 January, 3, 19, 24 May, 14 June 1739, III, 241, 243–5, 19, 23 September 1740, VII, 45, 4 October 1749, 137, 178, 200–201, 8 October 1751, 22 December 1751, 26, 27 January 1752 **27.** Black, *From Louis XIV to Napoleon*, pp. 79, 99, 108 **28.** Maral, *Versailles*, p. 179, Louis XV to Ferdinand VI **29.** Argenson, VI, 211, 233, 13, 30 December 1748, VII, 17, 81, 4 August, 14 December 1749; Laurence Bongie, *The Love of a Prince: Bonnie Prince Charlie in France*, Vancouver, 1986, pp. 248, 252, 264–6, 289–90 **30.** Argenson, VI, 211, 258, 13 December 1748, 26 January 1749, IX, 57 **31.** Ibid., VI, 149, 17 March 1750 **32.** Maral, *Versailles*, p. 203 **33.** Argenson, VII, 299, 16 April 1752 **34.** Black, *From Louis XIV to Napoleon*, pp. 14, 85, 117, 211 **35.** Guy Rowlands, 'The Maison Militaire du Roi and the Disintegration of the Old Regime', in Julian Swann and Joël Félix, eds., *The Crisis of the Absolute Monarchy: France from Old Regime to Revolution*, Oxford, 2013, pp. 245–73 **36.** Swann and Félix, p. 25 **37.** Gail Bossenga, 'Financial Origins of the French Revolution', in Thomas E. Kaiser and Dale K. Van Kley, eds., *From Deficit to Deluge: The Origins of the French Revolution*, Stanford, 2011, pp. 37–66 at pp. 37–8, 46–7, 49, 55 **38.** Cf. Nigel Aston, 'Necker and the British Connection', in Swann and Félix, pp. 127–45 **39.** Madeleine F. Morris, *Le Chevalier de Jaucourt: un ami de la terre*, Geneva, 1979, passim **40.** Argenson, I, 248, July 1738 **41.** Maral, *Derniers Jours*, pp. 448, 453–5 **42.** Maral, *Derniers Jours*, p. 385 **43.** John Hardman, *The Life of Louis XVI*, 2016, p. 346; Maral, *Derniers Jours*, pp. 486–9 **44.** Maral, *Derniers Jours*, pp. 340–422, 447, 463, 523, 565 **45.** Maral, *Derniers Jours*, pp. 279–81. The tombs of the exiled Stuarts in and outside Paris were also wrecked. **46.** *Louis-Philippe et Versailles*, exh. cat., 2018, passim **47.** Dr Moritz Busch, *Bismarck in the Franco-German War, 1870–1871*, 2 vols., 1879, I, 223, 8, October 1870; Emperor Frederick III, *War Diary, 1870–1871*, trans. and ed., A. R. Allinson, 1927, p. 151, 9 October 1870 **48.** Busch, II, 169, 27 December 1870; Michael Howard, *The Franco-Prussian War: The German Invasion of France, 1870–1871*, 1981 edn, pp. 347–9; Alistair Horne, *The Fall of Paris: The Siege and the Commune, 1870–71*, 1965, p. 217 **49.** W. H. Russell, *My Diary during the Last Great War*, 1874, p. 558, 18 January 1871; Frederick III, pp. 268–74, 18 January 1871; E. Delerot, *Versailles pendant l'occupation*, 1873, pp. 261–2 **50.** Frederick III, pp. 211–12, 2 December 1870; Jonathan Steinberg, *Bismarck: A Life*, 2011, p. 304; Gerhard Hojer, *Schloss Herrenchiemsee*, Munich, 1998, passim **51.** Pierre Guiral, *Adolphe Thiers ou De la nécessité en politique*, 1986, pp. 373–4; Robert Tombs, *The War against Paris, 1871*, Cambridge, 1981, pp. 51, 54–5 **52.** John Furley, *Struggles and Experiences of a Neutral Volunteer*, 2 vols., 1872, II, 39 **53.** Fabien Oppermann, *Le Versailles des présidents: 150 ans de vie républicaine chez le Roi-Soleil*, 2015, pp. 21, 22–31, 38; Levron, *Versailles*, p. 169; Guiral, pp. 395–6 **54.** Some statues now adorn the Cour Marly in the Louvre. **55.** Bernard Vogler, *Nouvelle Histoire de l'Alsace: une région au coeur de l'Europe*, 2003, pp. 227, 235 **56.** Prince Bismarck, *Letters to his Wife from the Seat of War, 1870–1871*, 1915, pp. 67, 83, Bismarck to Princess Bismarck, 8 October, 12 November 1870 **57.** Margaret MacMillan, *Peacemakers: The Paris Peace Conference of 1919 and its Attempt to End War*, 2001, p. 470 **58.** Julian Jackson, *A Certain Idea of France: The Life of General de Gaulle*, 2018, pp. 8, 16 **59.** Eric Roussel, *Charles de Gaulle*, 2002, p. 917 **60.** Sarmant and Stoll, pp. 565–7 **61.** Jean Lacouture, *De Gaulle: le rebelle, 1890–1944*, 1984, pp. 15–16 **62.** Jacques Revel, 'La Cour', in Pierre Nora, ed., *Les Lieux de mémoire*, 7 vols., 1984–92, III, 2, pp. 133–5, 183–6; Nicolas Charbonneau and Laurent Guimier, in *Le Roi est mort? Vive le roi! Enquête au coeur de notre monarchie présidentielle*, 2006, point out the persistence of such court traditions as rent-free 'logements de fonction', and state hunts, under the Fifth Republic. **63.** Stéphane Rials, *La Présidence de la république*, 1981, pp. 100–105 **64.** *DV*, p. 331; for example Versailles hosted a G7 summit in June 1982. President Putin came to Versailles for an exhibition on Peter the Great and France on 29 May 2017, foreign businessmen for a 'Choose France' summit on 22 January 2018. **65.** *Versailles: The Enduring Appeal of One of France's Most Iconic Monuments*, France 24, 26 July 2018

Bibliography

ARCHIVES

United Kingdom

British Library (BL)

Mss.

2072, 'formulaire pour les lettres du roy aux princes et autres dans les pays étrangers'

Egerton Mss. 1674, Lamoignon Mss. 1649–52

National Archives, Kew (NA)

State Papers France 78/159, Letters from Paris and Versailles of Matthew Prior to Bolingbroke, George I and Townshend, 1714–15

78/160, Letters from Paris and Versailles of Lord Stair to Stanhope, 1715

West Sussex Record Office

Goodwood Papers, Letters of Louis XIV to the Duchess of Portsmouth (copies)

France

Bibliothèque Nationale, Paris, Département des Manuscrits (BN)

Mss. fr.

3858, Translations from Latin 'de la main de Louis XIV'

4182, Papers of Michel le Tellier

6763–82, 'Abrégés des finances du royaume', 1661–80

6923–6, 6944, Papers of the Maréchal and Maréchale de Noailles

6995 Donnedieu de Vissé, 'Histoire de Louis le grand contenu dans les rapports qui se trouvent entres ses actions et les qualités et vertus des Fleurs et des Plantes'

6999, Journal de la santé de Louis XIV by Fagon

7013, Testament de Louis XIV

7834, 'Les plaisirs de l'île enchantée'

7891–5, Campagnes du roy, 1675–8

10261, Letters of Louis XIV to Madame de La Mothe-Houdancourt, Gouvernante des Enfants de France, 1667–93

13683, Journal de l'an 1715

155212, 'Mémoire des raisons qui ont obligé le roy à reprendre les Armes', 24 September 1688, Letter from Louis XIV to Cardinal d'Estrées, 6 September 1688

16633, M. Sainctot, 'Cérémonies du règne de Louis XIV'

15467, 15520–22, Mélanges

19188, f. 150, 'Amours du Palais Royal'

Nouvelles Acquisitions Françaises (NAF)

2038–9, Copies des lettres écrites par le roy Louis XIV, 1661–78

5132, Documents du règne de Louis XIV

12764, Letters of Louis XIV to Philip V (copies)

22818, 22896, 22936, 22938, 23006, 23093, 23179, 23180, 23864, Mélanges containing letters of Louis XIV

Fichier Charavay 147, 382, Louis XIV to Madame, 13 September 1663

Bibliothèque Interuniversitaire de la Sorbonne, Paris (BS)

960, 961, 1289, 1290, Letters of Louis XIV, 1660–76

Bibliothèque Mazarine, Paris (BM)

2320, Louis XIV to Boufflers, 1691
2326 f. 8, Instructions to Comte de Briord, 23 March 1697

Bibliothèque Sainte-Geneviève, Paris (BSG)

2014–15, 2084, Letters of Louis XIV

Bibliothèque de l'Arsenal, Paris

Mss. 2014, 2736–8, 3568, 4712, 4585, 6613, 13927, Letters of Louis XIV

Archives Nationales, Paris (AN)

[Cartons des Rois] K 118–36, Reign of Louis XIV

AE II 848, Treaty of 2 October 1649

AE 1/25, Testament de Louis XIV, 2 August 1714

O1 355–67, 'Lettres et placets, feuilles d'enregistrement du Bureau des Affaires étrangeres et des provinces', 1653-1705, with instructions and notes by Louis XIV

O1 821, 1669–1768 Registre of the maîtres des cérémonies including ff. 80–82, Diary of M. Desgranges, 'Pompe funèbre de Louis XIV mort à Versailles le 1er Septembre 1715'

O1 1098, 'Registres des ordres et lettres de mgr. le duc d'Antin . . . concernant les bâtiments, jardins, arts et manufactures du roy depuis 1708 jusqu'à 1732'

257 AP 2, Letters of Louis XIV to M. de Pontchartrain
261 AP 16, Letters of Vauban to Louvois

Musée Condé, Chantilly

I, II, Letters of Louis XIV to Turenne, 1667–73
I, vols. 2–4, Letters of Louis XIV to Chartres, Madame to Dubois, 1693–6
I, pl, plviii–plxiii, plxviii, plxi Letters of Condé and Louis XIV, 1674–86
I, II, Letters of Louis XIV and Turenne, 1667–73

Archives Diplomatiques, La Courneuve (AD)

CP Prusse 31, 32, 33 34, Despatches from the French minister in Brandenburg, 1688
CP Turquie 9, 20, 21, Correspondence between Louis XIV and Colbert de Croissy and the Ottoman Sultan and Grand Vizier, and the French ambassador in Constantinople, 1688–90
CP Angleterre 257, 262, 376, Correspondance Poussin–Torcy, 1701

Bibliothèque Municipale de Versailles

Mss. 47, Papers of the Maréchal de Créquy
Mss. 691 ff. 128–32, 'Etat et menu général de la dépense ordinaire de la chambre aux deniers du roy, année 1691'
Panthéon Louis XIV, 'rôle des placets présentés au roy à Versailles le lundy 12 Juin 1702'

BOOKS AND ARTICLES

Unless otherwise stated, all books in English are published in London, all books in French in Paris.

Acton, Harold. *The Last Medici*. 1980 edn.
Adamson, John, ed. *The Princely Courts of Europe, 1500–1750*. 2000.
Adda, Hélène Alexander and Sigrun Pass. *Liselotte von der Pfalz: Madame am Hofe des Sonnenkönigs*. Heidelberg. 1996.
Albanel, Christine et al. *The Hall of Mirrors: History and Restoration*. Dijon. 2007.
Alberoni, Giulio. *Lettres intimes au Comte I. Rocca*. Ed. Emile Bourgeois. 1892.
Aligny, Pierre Quarré, Comte d'. *Mémoires militaires*. Beaune. 1886.
Ames, Glenn J. 'A Royal Bride for Two Brothers'. In *Proceedings of the Western Association for French History: Selected Papers of the 1998 Annual Meeting*. 2000. pp. 152–64.
Ames, Glenn J. and Ronald S. Love, eds. *Distant Lands and Diverse Cultures: The French Experience in Asia, 1600–1700*. Westport, CT. 2003.
Amfreville, Marquis d'. *Histoire de la république de Gênes*. 3 vols. 1696.
Ancillon, Charles. *Histoire de l'établissement des François réfugiez dans les états de son altesse Electorale de Brandebourg*. Berlin. 1690.

Ancillon, Charles. *L'Irrévocabilité de l'édit de Nantes*. Amsterdam. 1688.

Ancillon, Joseph. *Recueil journalier de ce qui s'est passé de plus mémorable dans la cité de Metz*. 2 vols. Metz. 1860.

Anderson, Sonia P., ed. *Report on the Manuscripts of the Late Allan George Finch. V: Secret Service Papers 1691–1693 and Naval and Military Papers to 1694*. 2004.

André, Louis, ed. *Deux Mémoires historiques de Claude Le Pelletier*. 1906.

André, Louis. *Louis XIV et l'Europe*. 1950.

André, Louis and Emile Bourgeois, eds. *Recueil des instructions données aux ambassadeurs et ministres de France*. XXI: *Hollande*. 1922.

Anne, Théodore. *Histoire de l'ordre royal et militaire de Saint-Louis*. 3 vols. 1860–61.

Anon. *Description des châteaux et parcs de Versailles, de Trianon et de Marly*. 2 vols. Amsterdam. 1715.

Anon. *Histoire galante de Madame et du Comte de Guiche*. 1667.

Anon. *The history of the revolution of Portugal ... with letters of Sir Robert Southwell during his embassy there to the duke of Ormond*. 1740.

Anon. *Relation et observations du royaume de France*. Cologne. 1681.

Anthoine, Jacques. *Journal de la maladie et de la mort de Louis XIV*. 1880.

Antoine, Michel. *Louis XV*. 1989.

Ares, José Manuel de Bernardo. *Felipe V y Luis XIV a través de la correspondencia real de 1710, 1712 y 1714*. Madrid. 2017.

Ares, José Manuel de Bernardo and Elena Echeverría Pereda. *Las Cortes de Madrid y Versalles en el año 1707*. Madrid. 2011.

Ares, José Manuel de Bernardo, Elena Echeverría Peredo and Emilio Ortega Arjonilla. *De Madrid a Versalles: la correspondencia bilingüe entre el Rey Sol y Felipe V durante la Guerra de Sucesión*. Barcelona. 2011.

Argenson, Marquis d', *Journal*, 2014–.

Arlet, Jacques. *La Vie à Toulouse sous Louis XIV*. Portet-sur-Garonne. 2012.

Arminjon, Catherine. *Quand Versailles était meublé d'argent*. 2007.

Arnould, Maurice et al. *1691: le siège de Mons par Louis XIV*. Brussels. 1991.

Arvieux, Chevalier d'. *Mémoires*. 6 vols. 1735.

Assaf, Francis B. *La Mort du roi: une thanatographie de Louis XIV*. Tübingen. 1999.

Astier, Régine. 'Louis XIV, premier danseur'. In David Lee Rubin, ed. *The Sun King: The Ascendancy of French Culture during the Reign of Louis XIV*. Washington, DC. 1992.

Aston, Nigel. 'Necker and the British Connection'. In Julian Swann and Joël Félix, eds. *The Crisis of the Absolute Monarchy: France from Old Regime to Revolution*. Oxford. 2013. pp. 127–45.

Attwood, Philip and Felicity Powell. *Medals of Dishonour*. 2009.

Aubert, François d'. *Colbert: la vertu usurpée*. 2010.

Aubert, Guillaume. 'To Establish One Law and Definite Rules: Race, Religion and the Transatlantic Origins of the Louisiana Code Noir'. In Cécile Vidal, ed. *Louisiana: Crossroads of the Atlantic World*. Philadelphia. 2014. pp. 21–43.

Auger, Renée. *Louis XIV à Saint-Germain*. 1988.

Aulanier, Christiane. *Le Pavillon du roi: les appartements de la reine*. 1959.

Aulanier, Christiane. *La Petite Galerie: appartement d'Anne d'Autriche*. 1961.

Aulanier, Christiane. *La Salle des Caryatides*. 1957.

Aumale, Henri d'Orléans, Duc d'. *Histoire des princes de Condé*. 8 vols. 1863–96.

Avaux, Comte d'. *Négociations de Monsieur le Comte d'Avaux en Hollande, depuis 1685 jusqu'en 1688*. 6 vols. 1753.

Avenel, Vicomte d'. *Lettres . . . et papiers d'Etat du Cardinal de Richelieu*. 8 vols. 1853–77.

Avenel, Vicomte d'. *Richelieu et la monarchie absolue*. 4 vols. 1884–90.

Avice, Henri d'. *La Pompeuse et Magnifique cérémonie du sacre du roy Louis XIV*. 1655.

Ayats, Alain. *Louis XIV et les Pyrénées catalanes de 1659 à 1681: frontière politique et frontières militaires*. Canet. 2002.

Babel, Rainer, ed. *Frankreich im europäischen Staatensytem der Frühen Neuzeit*. Sigmaringen. 1995.

Babel, Rainer. *Garde et protection: der Königschutz in der französischen Aussenpolitik vom 15. bis zum 17. Jahrhundert*. Stuttgart. 2014.

Babelon, Jean-Pierre. *Henri IV*. 1982.

Babelon, Jean-Pierre et al., eds. *Paris et ses rois*. 1988.

Badalo-Dulong, Claude. *Le Banquier du roi: Barthélemy Hervart, 1606–1676*. 1951.

Badet, C. 'La Crise de 1709 à Marseille: les problèmes de ravitaillement en blé (1709–1710)'. In Jean-Louis Miège, ed. *Les Céréales en Méditerranée*. 1993. pp. 69–84.

Baillon, Charles de. *Henriette-Marie de France, Reine d'Angleterre*. 1877.

Baird, Rosemary. *Mistress of the House: Great Ladies and Grand Houses, 1670–1830*. 2003.

Bajou, Thierry. *Paintings at Versailles: XVIIth Century*. Paris. 1998.

Bamford, Paul W. *Fighting Ships and Prisons: The Mediterranean Galleys of France in the Age of Louis XIV*. Minneapolis. 1973.

Bannister, Mark. *Condé in Context: Ideological Change in Seventeenth-Century France*. Oxford. 2000.

Bapst, Germain. *Histoire des joyaux de la couronne de France*. 2 vols. 1889.

Barberini, Maria Giulia et al., eds. *Life and the Arts in the Baroque Palaces of Rome*. New York. 1999.

Barbiche, Bernard. 'La Régence de Marie Thérèse du 23 avril au 31 juillet 1672'. In idem, ed., *Pouvoirs, contestations et comportements dans l'Europe moderne*, 2005, pp. 313–26.

Barbier, Frédéric. 'L'Entrée royale de Louis XIV à Valenciennes'. *Revue du Nord*. 69, 274. 1987. pp. 553–61.

Barbier, Frédéric. *Paris, capitale des livres: le monde des livres et de la presse à Paris, du Moyen Age au XXe siècle*. 2007.

Bardot, Georges. *La Question des dix villes impériales d'Alsace depuis la paix de Westphalie jusqu'aux arrêts de réunion du conseil souverain de Brisach*. 1899.

Barker, Nancy Nichols. *Brother to the Sun King: Philippe, Duke of Orléans*. 1989.

Barnard, Toby and Jane Fenlon, eds. *The Dukes of Ormonde, 1610–1745*. Woodbridge. 2000.

Barrell, Rex A. *Bolingbroke and France*. Lanham, MD. 1988.

Barthélemy, Edouard de, ed. *La Galerie des portraits de Mademoiselle de Montpensier*. 1860.

Barthélemy, Edouard de. *Madame d'Huxelles et ses amis*. 1881.

Barthélemy, Edouard de. *La Princesse de Conti d'après sa correspondance inédite*. 1875.

Bascou, Marc. 'Des Brillants symboles de la monarchie absolue'. In Pierre Arizzoli-Clémentel and Pascale Gorguet Ballesteros, eds. *Fastes de cour et cérémonies royales: le costume de cour en Europe*. 2009. pp. 98–109.

Battifol, Louis. *Les Anciennes Républiques alsaciennes*. 1918.

Baudrillart, Alfred. 'Madame de Maintenon: son rôle politique'. *Revue des Questions Historiques*. 1890. pp. 101–61.

Baudrillart, Alfred. *Philippe V et la cour de France*. 5 vols. 1890–1900.

Baudrillart, Alfred and Léon Lecestre, eds. *Lettres du Duc de Bourgogne au roi d'Espagne Philippe V et à la Reine*. 2 vols. 1912–16.

Baustert, Raymond. *Un Roi à Luxembourg: édition commentée du 'Journal du voyage de Sa Majesté à Luxembourg'*. Tübingen. 2015.

Bayard, François. 'Du rôle exact de l'argent dans le déclenchement de la Fronde'. In Roger Duchêne and Pierre Ronzeaud, eds. *La Fronde en questions*. Aix-en-Provence. 1989.

Beauchamp, Comte de. *Louis XIII d'après sa correspondance avec le cardinal de Richelieu*. 1902.

Beaumont, G. du Boscq de. *La Garde wallonne, 1702–1822: officiers français au service de l'Espagne*. 1904.

Beaussant, Philippe. *Louis XIV artiste*. 1999.

Beaussant, Philippe. *Les Plaisirs de Versailles: théâtre et musique*. 1996.

Beddard, Robert. *A Kingdom without a King: The Journal of the Provisional Government in the Revolution of 1688*. Oxford. 1988.

Belin, Ferdinand. *La Société française au XVIIe siècle d'après les sermons de Bourdaloue*. Geneva. 1970.

Bély, Lucien. *L'Art de la paix en Europe: naissance de la diplomatie moderne, XVIe–XVIIIe siècles*. 2007.

Bély, Lucien, ed. *Dictionnaire Louis XIV*. 2015.

Bély, Lucien. 'La Diplomatie européenne et les partages de l'Empire espagnol'. In Antonio Álvarez-Ossorio et al., eds. *La pérdida de Europa: la guerra de sucesión por la monarquía de España*. Madrid. 2007. pp. 631–52.

Bély, Lucien. *Espions et ambassadeurs au temps de Louis XIV*. 1990.

Bély, Lucien, ed. *La Présence des Bourbons en Europe: XVIe–XXIe siècle*. 2003.

Bély, Lucien. *Les Secrets de Louis XIV: mystères d'Etat et pouvoir absolu*. 2013.

Benoît, Jérémie. *Le Grand Trianon: un palais privé à l'ombre de Versailles, de Louis XIV à Napoléon et de Louis-Philippe au général de Gaulle*. La Thuile. 2009.

Benoît, Marcelle. *Les Evénements musicaux sous le règne de Louis XIV*. 2004.

Benserade, Isaac de. *Ballet royal de la nuit*. 1653.

Bercé, Yves-Marie. *Le Roi absolu: idées reçues sur Louis XIV*. 2013.

Bérenger, Jean. 'La Cour de Vienne au lendemain de la chute de Strasbourg'. In Georges Livet and Bernard Vogler, eds. *Pouvoir, ville et société en Europe, 1650–1750*. 1985.

Bérenger, Jean. 'La Politique ottomane de la France dans les années 1680'. In Rainer Babel, ed. *Frankreich im europäischen Staatensystem der Frühen Neuzeit*. Sigmaringen. 1995.

Berger, Robert W. *The Palace of the Sun: The Louvre of Louis XIV*. University Park, PA. 1993.

Berger, Robert W. *A Royal Passion: Louis XIV as Patron of Architecture*. 1994.

Berger, Robert W. 'Tourists during the Reign of the Sun King: Access to the Louvre and Versailles and the Anatomy of Guidebooks and Other Printed Aids'. In George Mauner, ed. *Paris: Center of Artistic Enlightenment*. University Park, PA. 1988.

Berger, Robert W. and Thomas Hedin. *Diplomatic Tours in the Gardens of Versailles under Louis XIV*. 2008.

Bernier, François. *Histoire de la dernière révolution des Etats du Grand Mogul, dédiée au roi*. 1670.

Bertière, Simone. *Condé: le héros fourvoyé*. 2014.

Bertière, Simone. *Mazarin: le maître du jeu*. 2007 edn.

Bertière, Simone. *Le Procès Fouquet*. 2013.

Bertrand, Pascal-François. 'Tapestry Production at the Gobelins during the Reign of Louis XIV, 1661–1715'. In Thomas P. Campbell, ed. *Tapestry in the Baroque: Threads of Splendour*. New York. 2007. pp. 341–55.

Bertrand, Régis et al. *Marseille: histoire d'une ville*. Marseille. 2013.

Berwick, Maréchal de. *Mémoires*, 2 vols. 1828.

Bevan, Bryan. *Charles the Second's French Mistress: A Biography of Louise de Kéroualle, Duchess of Portsmouth, 1649–1734*. 1972.

Bilici, Faruk. *Louis XIV et son projet de conquête d'Istanbul*. Ankara. 2004.

Bimbenet-Privat, Michèle. 'Les Pierreries de Louis XIV: objets de collection et instruments politiques'. In Bernard Barbiche and Yves-Marie Bercé, eds. *Etudes sur l'ancienne France offertes en homage à Michel Antoine*. 2003. pp. 81–96.

Birnbaum, Pierre. *Un Récit de 'meurtre rituel' au grand siècle: l'affaire Raphaël Lévy, Metz, 1669*. Metz. 2008.

Birnstiel, Eckart, ed. *La Diaspora des Huguenots: les réfugiés protestants de France et leur dispersion dans le monde, XVIe–XVIIIe siècles*. 2001.

Bismarck, Prince. *Letters to his Wife from the Seat of War, 1870–1871*. 1915.

Biver, Paul and Marie-Louise. *Abbayes, monastères, couvents de femmes à Paris: des origines à la fin du XVIII siècle*. 1975.

Black, Jeremy. *From Louis XIV to Napoleon: The Fate of a Great Power*. 1999.

Black, Jeremy. *The Origins of War in Early Modern Europe*. Edinburgh. 1987.

Blanchard, Anne. *Vauban*. 2007 edn.

Blanning, Tim. *The Culture of Power and the Power of Culture*. Oxford. 2002.

Blanning, Tim. *Frederick the Great: King of Prussia*. 2016.

Blanning, Tim. *The Pursuit of Glory*. 2008.

Blet, Pierre. *Les Assemblées du clergé et Louis XIV, de 1670 à 1693*. Rome. 1972.

Blet, Pierre. *Le Clergé du Grand Siècle en ses assemblées, 1615–1715*. 1995.

Blet, Pierre. *Les Nonces du pape à la cour de Louis XIV.* 2002.

Blondel, Jacques François. *L'Art de jetter les bombes.* The Hague. 1685.

Blunt, Anthony. *Art and Architecture in France.* 1998 edn.

Blunt, Wilfrid. *Black Sunrise: The Life and Times of Moulay Ismaïl, Emperor of Morocco.* 1951.

Boileau, Nicolas and Jean Racine. *Lettres d'une amitié: correspondance, 1687–1698.* 2014.

Bond, Bradley, ed. *French Colony: Louisiana and the Atlantic World.* Baton Rouge. 2005.

Bongie, Laurence. *The Love of a Prince: Bonnie Prince Charlie in France.* Vancouver. 1986.

Bonnac, Marquis de. *Mémoire historique sur l'ambassade de Constantinople.* 1894.

Bonnet, Pierre. *Littérature de contestation: pamphlets et polémiques du règne de Louis XIV aux Lumières.* 2011.

Bonney, Richard and D. J. B. Trim, eds. *Persecution and Pluralism: Calvinists and Religious Minorities in Early Modern Europe, 1550–1700.* Bern. 2006.

Bordaz, Odile. *D'Artagnan.* 2001.

Bossenga, Gail. 'Financial Origins of the French Revolution'. In Thomas E. Kaiser and Dale K. Van Kley, eds. *From Deficit to Deluge: The Origins of the French Revolution.* Stanford. 2011. pp. 37–66.

Bossenga, Gail. *The Politics of Privilege: Old Regime and Revolution in Lille.* Cambridge. 1991.

Bossuet, Jacques-Bénigne. *Oraisons funèbres.* Ed. Jacques Truchet. 1998.

Bost, Hubert. *Pierre Bayle.* 1994.

Bots, J. A. H., ed. *The Peace of Nijmegen, 1676–1678/9.* Amsterdam. 1980.

Bots, J. A. H., ed. *The Revocation of the Edict of Nantes and the Dutch Republic.* Amsterdam. 1986.

Bottineau, Yves. *L'Art de cour dans l'Espagne de Philippe V, 1700–1746.* 1993.

Bouchenot-Dechin, Patricia and Georges Farhat. *André Le Nôtre en Perspectives.* 2013.

Bouquet, F., ed. *Mémoires de Pierre Thomas, sieur de Fossé.* 2 vols. Rouen. 1876.

Bour, René. *Histoire de Metz.* 1978.

Bourdieu. Pierre. *La Noblesse d'état: grandes écoles et esprit de corps.* 1989.

Bourges, Jacques de. *Relation du voyage de Monseigneur l'Evêque de Beryte.* 1683.

Boussu, Gilles-Joseph de. *Histoire de la ville de Mons.* Mons. 1725.

Boutant, Charles. *L'Europe au grand tournant des années 1680: la succession palatine.* 1985.

Boutier, Jean. 'Les Visiteurs italiens du Roi-Soleil'. In Caroline zum Kolk et al., eds. *Voyageurs étrangers à la cour de France.* Rennes. 2014. pp. 91–113.

Bouvet, P. J. *Histoire de l'empereur de la Chine, présentée au Roy.* The Hague. 1699.

Brady Jr, Thomas A. *Turning Swiss: Cities and Empire, 1450–1550.* Cambridge. 1985.

Bragard, Philippe, ed. *Vauban et Namur, le temps d'un siège (mai–juin 1692): journal de ce qui s'est passé de plus considérable à la prise de Namur, assiégée par le roi en personne, le 25 mai, et rendu à l'obéissance de sa Majesté le 29 juin 1692.* Namur. 2008.

Braudel, Fernand. *The Identity of France.* 2 vols. 1988–90.

Braun, Guido, ed. *Les Etats allemands et les Huguenots.* Munich. 2007.

Bresc-Bautier, Geneviève. *The Architecture of the Louvre.* 1995.

Bresc-Bautier, Geneviève. ed. *La Galerie d'Apollon au palais du Louvre.* 2004.

Breteuil, Baron de. *Mémoires de cour.* 2009.

Brewer, John. *The Sinews of Power: War, Money and the English State, 1688–1783.* 1989.

Brienne, Louis-Henri de Loménie, Comte de. *Mémoires.* 3 vols. 1916–19.

Brière, Nina. *La Douceur du Roi: le gouvernement de Louis XIV et la fin des Frondes 1648–1661.* Montreal. 2011.

Briggs, Robert. *Communities of Belief: Cultural and Social Tension in Early Modern France.* Oxford. 1995.

Britland, Karen. 'Exile or Homecoming? Henrietta Maria in France, 1644–1669'. In Philip Mansel and Torsten Riotte, eds. *Monarchy and Exile: The Politics of Legitimacy from Marie de Médicis to Wilhelm II.* 2011. pp. 120–43.

Brockey, Liam Matthew. *Journey to the East: The Jesuit Mission to China, 1579–1724.* 2007.

Brown, Jonathan. *Velázquez: Painter and Courtier.* 1986.

Brown, Jonathan and J. H. Elliott. *A Palace for a King: The Buen Retiro and the Court of Philip IV.* 1980.

Brugmans, Henri L. *Le Séjour de Christian Huygens à Paris.* 1935.

Bruin, Renger de and Maarten Brinkman, eds. *Peace was Made Here: The Treaties of Utrecht, Rastatt and Baden, 1713–1714.* Petersberg. 2013.

Bryant, Lawrence M. *The King and the City in the Parisian Royal Entry Ceremony: Politics, Ritual and Art in the Renaissance.* Geneva. 1986.

Bryant, Mark. 'The Catholic Church and its Dissenters, 1685–1715'. In Julia Prest and Guy Rowlands, eds. *The Third Reign of Louis XIV, c. 1682–1715.* 2016. pp. 145–61.

Bryant, Mark. 'The Queen of Versailles and First Lady of Louis XIV's France'. Typescript. N.d.

Bryant, Mark. 'Romancing the Throne: Madame de Maintenon's Journey from Secret Royal Governess to Louis XIV's Clandestine Consort, 1652–1684'. *The Court Historian.* 22, 2. December 2017. pp. 123–50.

Buckley, Veronica. *Madame de Maintenon: The Secret Wife of Louis XIV.* 2009.

Burchard, Wolf. *The Sovereign Artist: Charles Le Brun and the Image of Louis XIV.* 2016.

Burghclere, Winifred, Lady. *George Villiers, Second Duke of Buckingham, 1628–1687: A Study in the History of the Restoration.* 1903.

Burke, Peter. *The Fabrication of Louis XIV.* New Haven and London. 1992.

Busch, Dr Moritz. *Bismarck in the Franco-German War, 1870–1871.* 2 vols. 1879.

Bussy-Rabutin, Comte de, *Correspondance . . . avec sa famille et ses amis.* 5 vols. 1858–9.

Bussy-Rabutin, Comte de. *Mémoires.* 2010.

Butel, Paul. 'France, the Antilles and Europe in the Seventeenth and Eighteenth Centuries: Renewals of Foreign Trade'. In James D. Tracy, ed. *The Rise of Merchant Empires*. Cambridge. 1990. pp. 153–73.

Buvat, Jean. *Journal de la Régence*. 2 vols. 1865.

Caix de Saint-Aymour, Vicomte de. *Histoire des relations de la France avec l'Abyssinie chrétienne sous les règnes de Louis XIII et de Louis XIV*. 1886.

Caldicott, C. E. J. *La Carrière de Molière, entre protecteurs et éditeurs*. Amsterdam. 1998.

Callow, James. *King in Exile: James II: Warrior, King and Saint*. 2004.

Campbell, Malcolm. *Pietro da Cortona at the Pitti Palace: A Study of the Planetary Rooms and Related Projects*. Princeton. 1977.

Campbell, Thomas P., ed. *Tapestry in the Baroque: Threads of Splendour*, New York. 2007.

Camus, Alice. 'Être reçu en audience chez le roi'. *CRCV Bulletin*. 2013.

Canova-Green, Marie-Claude. 'Ambivalent Fictions: The Bordeaux Celebrations of the Wedding of Louis XIII and Anne d'Autriche'. In Margaret McGowan, ed. *Dynastic Marriages 1612/1615*. 2013.

Canova-Green, Marie-Claude and Alain Viala, eds. *Racine et l'histoire*. Tübingen. 2004.

Carbonnier-Burkard, Marianne. *Comprendre la révolte des camisards*. Rennes. 2013.

Carné, Vicomte de. *Les Pages des écuries du roi*. Nantes. 1886.

Caron, Emmanuel. 'Le Tournant de l'année 1683 dans la politique ottomane de Louis XIV'. In Daniel Tollet, ed. *Guerres et paix: mélanges d'histoire des relations internationales offerts à Jean Bérenger*. 2003.

Carpenter, Audrey T. 'J. T. Desaguliers, an 18th Century Experimental Philosopher and Freemason'. *Huguenot Society Journal*. xxx. April 2016. pp. 503–18.

Carr, Matthew. *Blood and Faith: The Purging of Muslim Spain*. 2009.

Carswell, John. *The Descent on England: A Study of the English Revolution of 1688 and its European Background*. 1969.

Cartledge, Bryan. *The Will to Survive: A History of Hungary*. 2011.

Casoni, Filippo. *Storia del bombardamento di Genova nell'anno MDCLXXXIV*. Genoa. 1877.

Castella, Rodolphe de. *Les Colonels généraux des Suisses et Grisons*. 1971.

Castelluccio, Stéphane. *Les Collections royales d'objets d'art, de François Ier à la Révolution*. 2002.

Castelluccio, Stéphane, ed. *Le Commerce du luxe à Paris aux XVIIe et XVIIIe siècles*. Bern. 2009.

Castelluccio, Stéphane. *Les Fastes de la Galerie des Glaces: recueil d'articles du Mercure Galant (1681–1773)*. 2007.

Castelluccio, Stéphane. *Marly: art de vivre et pouvoir, de Louis XIV à Louis XVI*. Montreuil. 2014.

Catinat, Maréchal de. *Mémoires et correspondances*. 3 vols. 1819.

Cazaux, Yves. *Le Rêve américain: de Champlain à Cavelier de La Salle*. 1988.

Cénat, Jean-Philippe. *Chamlay: le stratège secret de Louis XIV*. 2011.

Cénat, Jean-Philippe. *Louvois: le double de Louis XIV*. 2015.

Cénat, Jean-Philippe. *Le Roi stratège: Louis XIV et la direction de la guerre (1661–1715)*. 2010.

Cermakian, Marianne. *La Princesse des Ursins: sa vie et ses lettres*. 1969.

Cerny, Gerald. *Theology, Politics and Letters at the Crossroads of European Civilisation: Jacques Basnage and the Baylean Huguenot Refugees in the Dutch Republic*. Dordrecht. 1987.

Chagniot, Jean. *Paris et l'armée au XVIIIe siècle*. 1985.

Chaline, Olivier. 'Anne of Austria, Founder of the Val-de-Grâce in Paris'. In Dries Raeymakers et al., eds. *A Constellation of Courts: The Courts and Households of Habsburg Europe, 1555–1665*. Leuven. 2014.

Chaline, Olivier. *L'Année des quatre dauphins*. 2011 edn.

Chaline, Olivier. *Le Règne de Louis XIV*. 2005.

Chamillart, Michel. *Correspondance et papiers inédits*. 2 vols. 1885.

Champion, Justin. *Republican Learning: John Toland and the Crisis of Christian Culture, 1696–1722*. Manchester. 2003.

Chandler, David, ed. *Military Memoirs of Marlborough's Campaigns*. 1998 edn.

Chantelou, Paul Fréart de. *Journal de voyage du Cavalier Bernin en France*. 1981 edn.

Chapelot, Jean. *Le Château de Vincennes*. 2003.

Chapman, Sara E. *Private Ambition and Political Alliances: The Phélypeaux de Pontchartrain Family and Government under Louis XIV*. Rochester, NY. 2004.

Charbonneau, Nicolas and Laurent Guimier. *Le Roi est mort? Vive le roi! Enquête au coeur de notre monarchie présidentielle*. 2006.

Charpentier, François. *De l'excellence de la langue française*. 1683.

Charnisay, Baronne de. *Un Gentilhomme Huguenot au temps des Camisards: le Baron d'Aigaliers*. Cahors. 1935.

Chatenet, Monique. *La Cour de France au XVIe siècle: vie sociale et architecture*. 2002.

Chatenet, Monique. *Chambord*. 2013.

Chaunu, Pierre, Madeleine Foisil and Françoise de Noirfontaine. *Le Basculement religieux de Paris au XVIIIe siècle: essai d'histoire politique et religieuse*. 1998.

Chérot SJ, Henri. *La Première Jeunesse de Louis XIV*. Lille. 1892.

Chéruel, Adolphe. *Histoire de France pendant la minorité de Louis XIV*. 4 vols. 1879–80.

Chéruel, Adolphe. *Histoire de France sous le ministère de Mazarin, 1651–1661*. 3 vols. 1882.

Chevalier, Timothée. *Manières de montrer Versailles: guides, promenades et relations sous le règne de Louis XIV*. 2013.

Chevallier, Bernard et al. *Saint-Cloud: le palais retrouvé*. 2013.

Chevallier, Pierre. *Henri III*. 1985.

Chevallier, Pierre. *Louis XIII*. 1979.

Chevé, Joëlle. *Marie-Thérèse d'Autriche, épouse de Louis XIV*. 2008.

Chigi, Flavio. 'Relation et observation sur le royaume de France'. *Revue d'Histoire Diplomatique*. 8, 2. 1894. pp. 269–79.

Childs, John. *The Army of Charles II*. 1976.

Choisy, Abbé de. *Mémoires pour servir à l'histoire de Louis XIV.* 1983.

Christianson, Robert. 'The Hunt of Frederick II of Denmark: Structures and Rituals'. *The Court Historian.* 18, 2. December 2013. pp. 165–87.

Christout, Marie-Françoise. 'Louis XIV et le ballet de cour, ou le plus illustre des danseurs (1651–1670)'. *Revue d'Histoire du Théâtre.* 215. 2002–3. pp. 153–78.

Churchill, Winston S. *Marlborough: His Life and Times.* 2 vols. 1947 edn.

Ciardha, Eamonn O. *Ireland and the Jacobite Cause: A Fatal Attachment.* Dublin. 2002.

Claeys, Prosper. *Pages d'histoire locale gantoise.* 3 vols. Ghent. 1885.

Clark, Ruth S. *Anthony Hamilton: His Life and Works and his Family.* 1921.

Clark, Ruth S. *Sir William Trumbull in Paris, 1685–1686.* Cambridge. 1938.

Clarke, J. S. *The Life of James the Second King of England, etc. Collected Out of Memoirs Writ of his own Hand.* 2 vols. 1816.

Claude, Jean. *An Account of the Persecutions and Oppressions of the Protestants in France.* 1686.

Claydon, Tony and Charles-Edouard Levillain, eds. *Louis XIV Outside In.* 2016.

Cleary, Richard L. *The Place Royale and Urban Design in the Ancien Régime.* Cambridge. 1999.

Clemenceau, Georges. *Grandeurs et Misères d'une Victoire.* 1930.

Clément, Pierre, ed. *L'Italie en 1671: relation d'un voyage du Marquis de Seignelay à Marseille et à Toulon.* 1867.

Clément, Pierre. *Madame de Montespan et Louis XIV: étude historique.* 1868.

Clément, Pierre. *La Police sous Louis XIV.* 1866.

Clément, R. *Les Français d'Egypte aux XVIIe et XVIIIe siècles.* Cairo. 1960.

Cloulas, Ivan. *Catherine de Médicis.* 1979.

Cohen, Claudine. *Science, libertinage et clandestinité à l'aube des Lumières.* 2011.

Cohen, Sarah R. *Art, Dance, and the Body in French Culture of the Ancien Régime.* Cambridge. 2000.

Cojannot-Le Blanc, Marianne. ' "Il avoit fort dans le coeur son Alexandre . . .": l'imaginaire du jeune Louis XIV d'après la Mesnardière et la peinture des Reines de Perse par le Brun'. *XVIIe Siècle.* 251, 2. 2011. pp. 371–96.

[Colbatch, J.], *An Account of the Court of Portugal during the Reign of the Present King Dom Pedro II.* 1700.

Colbert, Jean-Baptiste. *Lettres, instructions et mémoires.* 9 vols. 1861–82.

Coligny, Comte de. *Mémoires.* 1841.

The Collection of Autograph Letters and Historical Documents Formed by Alfred Morrison. Second series. 6 vols. 1883–92.

Collins, James B. *The State in Early Modern France.* 2012 edn.

Combes, M. *Explication historique de ce qu'il y a de plus remarquable dans la maison royale de Versailles.* 1695 edn.

Comisso, Giovanni. *Les Ambassadeurs vénitiens, 1525–1792.* 1989.

Conihout, Isabelle de and Patrick Michel, eds. *Mazarin: les lettres et les arts.* 2006.

Cooley, Mackenzie. ' "I Would Have our Courtier be a Perfect Horseman": Creating Nobility and Fashioning Horses between Mantua and Naples, 1461–1571'. Talk given at the Animals at Court conference, Munich. 9 December 2016.

Cornette, Joël. 'Macron Ier, nouveau roi de France'. *Courrier International*. 1390. 22 June 2017.

Cornette, Joël. *La Mort de Louis XIV: apogée et crépuscule de la royauté*. 2015.

Cornette, Joël. *Le Roi de guerre: essai sur la souveraineté dans la France du Grand Siècle*. 1993.

Corp, Edward. *A Court in Exile: The Stuarts in France, 1689–1718*. 2004.

Corvisier, André. *Histoire militaire de la France*. 4 vols. 1997.

Corvisier, André. *Les Hommes, la guerre et la mort*. 1985.

Corvisier, André. *Louvois*. 1983.

Cosnac, Daniel de. *Mémoires*. 2 vols. 1852.

Coste, Laurent. *Histoire des maires de Bordeaux*. 2008.

Cottret, Bernard. *Terre d'exil: l'Angleterre et ses réfugiés français et wallons, de la réforme à la révocation de l'édit de Nantes, 1550–1700*. 1985.

Cottret, Monique. *La Bastille à prendre: histoire et mythe de la forteresse royale*. 1986.

Courtois, Stéphanie de. *Le Potager du Roy*. 2003.

Coutelle, Antoine. *Poitiers au XVIIe siècle: les pratiques culturelles d'une élite urbaine*. Rennes. 2014.

Cowart, Georgia J. *The Triumph of Pleasure: Louis XIV and the Politics of Spectacle*. Chicago. 2008.

Cowper, Mary, Countess. *Diary, 1714–1720*. 1864.

Crawford, O. G. S. *The Fung Kingdom of Sennar*. Gloucester. 1951.

Creed, Richard. *Journal of the Grand Tour to Rome with the Fifth Earl of Exeter, 1699–1700*. Oundle. 2002.

Crémieux, Adolphe. *Marseille et la royauté pendant la minorité de Louis XIV*. 2 vols. 1917.

Crochet, Bernard. *Vauban et son héritage: guide des forteresses à visiter*. Rennes. 2017.

Cros, Bernard. 'Dunkerque, port de guerre du Roi-Soleil'. *Revue Historique de Dunkerque et du Littoral*. 1997. pp. 49–106.

Cros, Bernard. *Toulon, l'arsenal et la ville*. 2012.

Croquez, Albert. *La Flandre wallonne et les pays de l'intendance de Lille sous Louis XIV*. 1912.

Crouzet, François. 'The Huguenots and the English Financial Revolution'. In idem, *Britain, France and International Commerce: From Louis XIV to Victoria*. 1996.

Cruickshanks, Eveline, ed. *By Force or by Default? The Revolution of 1688–89*. Edinburgh. 1989.

Cruickshanks, Eveline. 'The Second Duke of Ormonde and the Atterbury Plot'. In Toby Barnard and Jane Fenlon, eds. *The Dukes of Ormonde, 1610–1745*. Woodbridge. 2000. pp. 243–53.

Culot, Maurice et al., eds. *Le Bombardement de Bruxelles par Louis XIV et la reconstruction qui s'en suivit*. Brussels. 1992.

Daguenet, Patrick. *L'Aurore du Roi-Soleil: 1661, le grand séjour de Louis XIV à Fontainebleau*. 2016.

Dakhlia, Jocelyne and Bernard Vincent. *Les Musulmans dans l'histoire de l'Europe.* 2 vols. 2013.

Dangeau, Marquis de. *Journal.* 35 vols. Clermont-Ferrand. 2002–14.

Daniel, Père. *Histoire de la milice françoise.* 2 vols. Amsterdam. 1724.

Davenport-Hines, Richard. *Universal Man: The Seven Lives of John Maynard Keynes.* 2015.

Davies, David. 'James II, William of Orange and the Admirals'. In Eveline Cruickshanks, ed. *By Force or By Default? The Revolution of 1688–1689.* Edinburgh. 1989. pp. 82–108.

Deakin, Nicholas. *Count Gramont at the Court of Charles II.* 1965.

Dee, Darryl. *Expansion and Crisis in Louis XIV's France: Franche-Comté and Absolute Monarchy, 1674–1715.* Rochester, NY. 2009.

de Gaulle, Charles. *Mémoires.* 2000.

de Groot, Pieter. *Lettres . . . à Abraham de Wicquefort.* Ed. F. J. I. Krämer. The Hague. 1894.

DeJean, Joan. *How Paris Became Paris: The Invention of the Modern City.* 2014.

Delalex, Hélène. *La Galerie des Carrosses: Château de Versailles.* 2016.

Deldicque, Mathieu. *Le Grand Condé: le rival du Roi Soleil?* Ghent. 2016.

Delerot, E. *Versailles pendant l'occupation.* 1873.

Deloche, Maximin. *La Maison du Cardinal de Richelieu: document inédit.* 1912.

Delpont, Hubert. *Parade pour une infante: le périple nuptial de Louis XIV à travers le Midi de la France, 1659–1660.* 2007.

Dencher, Alexander. 'The Politics of Spectacle: Imaging the Prince of Orange during the First Stadtholderless Era'. *The Court Historian.* 19, 2. December 2014. pp. 163–8.

Derville, Alain. *Histoire de Saint-Omer.* 1981.

Descimon, Robert. 'Les Barricades frondeuses'. In Roger Duchêne and Pierre Ronzeaud, eds. *La Fronde en questions.* Aix-en-Provence. 1989. pp. 245–62.

Descimon, Robert and Elie Haddad, eds. *Epreuves de noblesse: les expériences nobiliaires de la haute robe parisienne (XVIe–XVIIIe siècle).* 2010.

Desmons, Fernand. *La Conquête en 1667.* Tournai. 1905.

Désos, Catherine. *Les Français de Philippe V: un modèle nouveau pour gouverner l'Espagne, 1700–1724.* Strasbourg. 2009.

Dessert, Daniel. *L'Argent du sel: le sel de l'argent.* 2012.

Dessert, Daniel. *La Prise du pouvoir par Louis XIV: la construction du mythe.* 2005.

Dessert, Daniel. *La Royale: vaisseaux et marins du Roi-Soleil.* 1996.

Dessert, Daniel. *Le Royaume de Monsieur Colbert (1661–1683).* 2007.

Dessert, Daniel. *Tourville.* 2002.

Dethan, Georges. *Paris au temps de Louis XIV, 1660–1715.* 1990.

Deux siècles d'Alsace française. Strasbourg. 1948.

Deyon, Solange. *Du loyalisme au refus: les protestants français et leur député général entre la Fronde et la Révocation.* Arras. 1976.

Diakite, Tidiane. *Louis XIV et l'Afrique noire.* Arles. 2013.

Diefendorf, Barbara. *From Penitence to Charity: Pious Women and the Catholic Reformation in Paris*. 2004.

Dingli, Laurent, *Seignelay: le fils flamboyant*, 2007.

Doebner, Dr R., ed. *Memoirs of Mary, Queen of England*. Leipzig. 1886.

Dollar, Jacques. *Vauban à Luxembourg, place forte de l'Europe (1684–1697)*. Luxembourg. 1983.

Dollot, René. *Les Origines de la neutralité de la Belgique et le système de la Barrière, 1609–1830*. 1902.

Dosquet, Emilie. 'Le Feu et l'encre: la désolation de Palatinat: guerre et information politique dans l'Europe de Louis XIV'. Unpublished thesis. Sorbonne. Paris. 2 vols. 2017.

Drévillon, Hervé. *L'Impôt du sang: le métier des armes sous Louis XIV*. 2005.

Drévillon, Hervé. *Le Roi absolu: Louis XIV et les Français (1661–1715)*. 2015.

Dromantin, Patrick Clarke de. 'Une Noblesse atypique: les réfugiés jacobites en France au XVIIIe siècle'. In J. Pontet et al., eds. *La Noblesse de la fin du XVIe au début du XXe siècle: un modèle social?* 2 vols. Anglet. 2002. II, pp. 87–102.

Dubois, Alexandre. *Journal d'un curé de campagne au XVIIe siècle*. Ed. Henri Platelle. 1965.

Dubois, Isabelle et al., eds. *Place des Victoires: histoire, architecture, société*. 2003.

Dubois, M. 'Mémoire fidèle des choses qui se sont passées à la mort de Louis XIII roi de France et de Navarre'. In F. Danjou, ed. *Archives curieuses de l'histoire de France*. 2nd series, vol. 5. 1838.

Dubois, Marie. *Moi, Marie Dubois . . . valet de chambre de Louis XIV*. Rennes. 1994.

Dubu, Jean. 'Fortunes and Misfortunes of Racine the Courtier'. *The Court Historian*. 7, 2. December 2002. pp. 111–33.

Dubuisson-Aubenay, M. *Journal des guerres civiles*. 2 vols. 1883–5.

Duccini, Hélène. 'Le Dauphin du miracle (5 septembre 1638)'. In Bernard Babiche et al., eds. *Pouvoirs, contestations et comportements dans l'Europe moderne*. 2005. pp. 209–25.

Ducéré, E. *Le Mariage de Louis XIV*. Bayonne. 1903.

Duchart, Heinz. *Der Friede von Rijswijk*. Mainz. 1998.

Duchêne, Roger. *Madame de Sévigné*. 2002.

Duchesne, H. G. and H. de Grandsaigne. *Histoire du Bois de Boulogne: le Château de Madrid*. 1912.

Duffo, Abbé Fr. *Après le traité des Pyrénées*. 1935.

Duffo, Abbé Fr. *Le Cérémonial de France à la cour de Louis XIV*. 1936.

Duffo, Abbé Fr. *Le Sacre de Louis XIV à Reims le 7 Juin 1654*. 1935.

Duindam, Jeroen. *Vienna and Versailles: The Courts of Europe's Dynastic Rivals, 1550–1780*. Cambridge. 2003.

Dulong, Claude. *Anne d'Autriche: mère de Louis XIV*. 1980.

Dulong, Claude. *Le Mariage du Roi-Soleil*. 1986.

Dulong, Claude. *Marie Mancini: la première passion de Louis XIV*. 1993.

Dulong, Claude. *Mazarin et l'argent, banquiers et prête-noms*. 2002.

Dumont de Bostaquet, Isaac. *Mémoires sur les temps qui ont précédé et suivi la révocation de l'édit de Nantes.* 1968 edn.

Dunkley, John. *Gambling: A Social and Moral Problem in France, 1685–1792.* Oxford. 1985.

Dunoyer de Noirmont, Baron. *Histoire de la chasse en France depuis les temps les plus reculés jusqu'à la révolution.* 3 vols. 1868.

Duparc, Pierre, ed. *Recueil des instructions aux ambassadeurs et ministres de France,* XXIX: *Turquie.* 1969.

Dupilet, Alexandre. *Le Cardinal Dubois: le génie politique de la Régence.* 2015.

Duron, Jean, ed. *Le Prince et la musique: les passions musicales de Louis XIV.* 2009.

Eccles, W. J. *Frontenac: The Courtier Governor.* Toronto. 1959.

Ekberg, Carl J. *The Failure of Louis XIV's Dutch War.* Chapel Hill, NC. 1979.

El Hage, Fadi. *Le Maréchal de Villars: l'infatigable bonheur.* 2012.

Elliott, J. H. *Richelieu and Olivares.* 1984.

L'Entrée triomphante de Leurs Majestez Louis XIV, Roy de France et de Navarre et Marie-Thérèse d'Austriche, son espouse, dans la ville de Paris . . . 1662.

Eriau, J. B. *Louise de La Vallière.* 1961.

Erman, J.-P. and P. C. F. Reclam. *Mémoires pour servir à l'histoire des réfugiés français dans les états du roi.* 6 vols. Berlin. 1782–7.

Esmonin, Edmond. *Etudes sur la France des XVIIe et XVIIIe siècles.* 1964.

Esnault, Abbé G. *Michel Chamillart: correspondance et papiers inédits.* 2 vols. 1885.

Estrades, Comte d'. *Lettres, mémoires et négociations.* 6 vols. Brussels. 1709.

Estrées, Maréchal d'. *Mémoires.* 1910.

Evelyn, John. *Diary and Correspondence.* Ed. William Bray. 4 vols. 1879.

Eves, Charles Kenneth. *Matthew Prior: Poet and Diplomatist.* New York. 1939.

Fader, Don. 'La Duchesse de Bourgogne, le mécénat des Noailles et les arts dramatiques à la cour autour de 1700'. In Fabrice Preyat, ed. *Marie-Adélaïde de Savoie (1685–1712): Duchesse de Bourgogne, enfant terrible de Versailles.* Brussels. 2014. pp. 175–90.

Faille, René. 'Louis XIV devant Cambrai glorifié par les artistes de son règne'. *Revue du Nord.* 58, 230. 1976. pp. 479–505.

Farges, Louis, ed. *Recueil des instructions données aux ambassadeurs et ministres de France: Pologne,* 2 vols. 1888.

Faugère, A. P., ed. *Journal du voyage de deux jeunes hollandais à Paris en 1656–1658.* 1899.

Febvre, Lucien. *Le Rhin: histoire, mythes et réalités.* 1997.

Febvre, Michel. *Etat présent de la Turquie.* 1675.

Fehrenbach, Jérôme. *La Princesse Palatine: l'égérie de la Fronde.* 2016.

Félibien, André, ed. *Les Fêtes de Versailles.* 2012.

Félibien, André. *Statues et bustes antiques des maisons royales.* 1679.

Fénelon, François de. *Lettre à Louis XIV.* 2011 edn.

Fennebresque, Juste. *Versailles royal.* 1910.

Ferrero, Herrmann, ed. *Lettres de Henriette-Marie de France, Reine d'Angleterre, à sa soeur Christine, Duchesse de Savoie.* Turin. 1881.

Ferriol, Comte de. *Correspondance*. Antwerp. 1870.

Feuillet, Raoul. *Chorégraphie, ou l'Art d'écrire la danse par caractères, figures et signes démonstratifs avec lesquels on apprend facilement de soi-même toutes sortes des danses*. 1700.

Field, Cynthia et al. eds. *Paris on the Potomac: The French Influence on the Architecture and Art of Washington, D.C*. Athens, OH. 2007.

Fierro, Alfred. *Histoire et dictionnaire de Paris*. 1996.

Finley-Croswhite, S. Annette. *Henry IV and the Towns*. 1999.

Firmin, Gwenola et al., eds. *Pierre le Grand: un tsar en France 1717*. 2017.

Flick, Andrew. 'Jean de Robethon, a Contested Figure behind the Throne'. *Huguenot Society Journal*. xxx, 4. 2016. pp. 488–502.

Fonck, Bertrand, ed. *L'Âge d'or de la cavalerie*. 2015.

Fonck, Bertrand. *Le Maréchal de Luxembourg et le commandement des armées sous Louis XIV*. Seyssel. 2014.

Fonkenell, Guillaume. *Le Palais des Tuileries*. Arles. 2010.

Fontaine-Beyer, Lucette. *La Chasse-marée de Picardie sur la route du poisson*. Creil. 1993.

Forbes-Leith SJ, William. *The Scots Men-at-Arms and Life-Guards in France: From their Formation until their Final Dissolution, 1418–1830*. 2 vols. Edinburgh. 1882.

Forbin, Comte de. *Mémoires*. 1993 edn.

Forneron, Henri. *Louise de Kéroualle, Duchesse de Portsmouth*. 1886.

Fortin de la Hoguette, Philippe. *Lettres aux frères Dupuy et à leur entourage, 1623–1662*. 2 vols. Florence. 1999.

Foss, Theodore N. 'The European Sojourn of Philippe Couplet and Michael Shen Fuzong, 1683–1692'. In Jerome Heyndrickx, ed. *Philippe Couplet S.J. (1623–1693): The Man Who Brought China to Europe*. Nettetal. 1990. pp. 121–40.

Fossa, F. de. *Le Château historique de Vincennes à travers les ages*. 2 vols. 1908.

Foucault, Nicolas-Joseph. *Mémoires*. 2 vols. 1862.

Foxcroft, C. *A Supplement to Burnet's History of my own Time*. 1902.

Francisque-Michel, R. *Les Portugais en France, les Français en Portugal*. 1882.

Franken, M. A. M. *Coenraad van Beuningen's politieke en diplomatieke aktiviteiten in de jaren, 1667–1684*. Groeningen. 1966.

Franklin, Alfred. *La Cour de France et le Maréchal d'Ancre*. 1914.

Fraser, Antonia. *King Charles II*. 2002.

Fraser, Antonia. *Love and Louis XIV: The Women in the Life of the Sun King*. 2006.

Frederick III, Emperor. *War Diary, 1870–1871*. Trans. and ed. A. R. Allinson. 1927.

Frey, Linda and Marsha. *Frederick I: The Man and his Times*. Boulder, CO. 1984.

Friedrich, Karin and Sara H. Smart, eds. *The Cultivation of Monarchy and the Rise of Berlin*. 2010.

Frijhoff, W. T. M. 'Uncertain Brotherhood: The Huguenots in the Dutch Republic'. In B. van Ruymbeke and R. J. Sparks, eds. *Memory and Identity: The Huguenots in France and the Atlantic Diaspora*, Columbia, SC. 2003. pp. 128–71.

Fromageot, Paul. *Isabelle de Montmorency, Duchesse de Chatillon et de Mecklembourg*. 1913.

Frost, Robert I. 'The Ethiopian and the Elephant? Queen Louise Marie Gonzaga and Queenship in an Elective Monarchy, 1645–1667'. *Slavonic and East European Review*. 91, 4. 2013. pp. 787–817.

Frostin, Charles. *Les Pontchartrain, ministres de Louis XIV: alliances et réseau d'influence sous l'Ancien Régime*. Rennes. 2014.

Furley, John. *Struggles and Experience of a Neutral Volunteer*. 2 vols. 1872.

Gabet, Camille. *La Naissance de Rochefort sous Louis XIV, 1666–1715*. Rochefort. 1985.

Gady, Alexandre, ed. *Jules Hardouin-Mansart, 1646–1708*. 2010.

Gady, Alexandre. 'Le Palais Royal sous la régence d'Anne d'Autriche'. In *Mazarin: Les Lettres et Les Arts*. 2010.

Gady, Alexandre and Anne Verdillon. *Le Jardin des Tuileries d'André Le Nôtre, un chef d'oeuvre pour le Roi Soleil*. 2013.

Gady, Bénédicte and Nicolas Milovanovic, eds. *Charles Le Brun (1619–1690)*. 2016.

Galland, Antoine. *Journal parisien*. Ed. Henri Omont. In *Mémoires de la Société de l'Histoire de Paris et de l'Île-de-France*. 46. 1919. pp. 25–156.

Gallois, Etienne, ed. *Lettres inédites des Feuquières*. 5 vols. 1845–6.

Garcia, Manuel Castellano. 'François Gaultier: un artisan de la paix d'Utrecht (1711–1713)'. *Revue d'Histoire Diplomatique*. 3. 2016. pp. 257–75.

Garrett, Jane. *The Triumphs of Providence: The Assassination Plot, 1696*. Cambridge. 1980.

Garrigues, Dominique. *Jardins et jardiniers de Versailles au Grand Siècle*. 2001.

Garrioch, David. *The Huguenots of Paris and the Coming of Religious Freedom, 1685–1789*. Cambridge. 2014.

Garrisson, Janine. *L'Edit de Nantes et sa révocation: histoire d'une intolérance*. 1985 edn.

Gasztowitt, Anne-Marie. *Une Mission diplomatique en Pologne au XVII siècle: Pierre de Bonzi à Varsovie, 1665–1668*. 1916.

Gaussen, David. *L'Île de France au temps de Louis XIV, 1661–1715*. 2005.

Gautier, Jean-Jacque. 'L'Imaginaire comme support du luxe: les fêtes royales de Versailles de Mai 1664'. In Robert Fox and Anthony Turner, eds. *Luxury Trades and Consumerism in Ancien Régime Paris*. 2016. pp. 191–218.

Geffroy, Auguste, ed. *Lettres inédites de la Princesse des Ursins*. 1859.

Genet-Rouffiac, Nathalie. *Le Grand Exil: les Jacobites en France, 1688–1715*. 2007.

Gerber, Matthew. *Bastards: Politics, Family, and Law in Early Modern France*. New York. 2012.

Gibbs, G. C. 'Huguenot Contributions to England's Intellectual Life and England's Intellectual Commerce with Europe, 1680–1720'. In J. A. H. Bots, ed. *The Revocation of the Edict of Nantes and the Dutch Republic*. Amsterdam. 1986. pp. 181–200.

Gibbs, G. C. 'The Reception of the Huguenots in England and the Dutch Republic, 1680–1690'. In Ole Peter Grell et al., eds. *From Persecution to Toleration: The Glorious Revolution and Religion in England*. Oxford. 1991. pp. 275-306.

Gibson, John S. *Playing the Franco-Scottish Card: The Franco-Jacobite Invasion of 1708*. Edinburgh. 1988.

Gilbert, M. A. *Le Siège de Stenay en 1654*. Bar-le-Duc. 1893.

Gillot, Henri. *Le Règne de Louis XIV et l'opinion publique en Allemagne*. Nancy. 1914.

Glad, Jean. *Maubeuge, place de guerre, sa zone d'influence*. 2007.

Glasgow, Vaughn, ed. *The Sun King: Louis XIV and the New World*. New Orleans. 1984.

Glozier, Matthew. *The Huguenot Soldiers of William of Orange and the Glorious Revolution of 1688*. Brighton. 2002.

Glozier, Matthew. *Marshal Schomberg, 1615–1690*. Brighton. 2005.

Glozier, Matthew. *Scottish Soldiers in France in the Reign of the Sun King: Nursery for Men of Honour*. Leiden. 2004.

Glozier, Matthew and David Onnekink. 'Huguenot Soldiers in Dutch Service'. In Matthew Glozier and David Onnekink, eds. *War, Religion and Service: Huguenot Soldiering, 1685–1713*. Aldershot. 2007. pp. 111–30.

Glozier, Matthew and David Onnekink, eds. *War, Religion and Service: Huguenot Soldiering, 1685–1713*. Aldershot. 2007.

Godard, Didier. *Le Goût de Monsieur: l'homosexualité masculine au XVIIe siècle*. 2002.

Godley, Eveline. *The Grand Condé: A Life of Louis II de Bourbon, Prince of Condé*. 1915.

Golden, Richard M. *The Godly Rebellion: Parisian Curés and the Religious Fronde, 1652–1662*. Chapel Hill, NC. 1981.

Goldstein, Claire. *Vaux and Versailles: The Appropriations, Accidents and Erasures that Made Modern France*. Philadelphia. 2008.

Gould, Cecil. *Bernini in France: An Episode in Seventeenth-Century History*. 1981.

Gourville, M. de. *Mémoires*. 2 vols. 1894–5.

Goyetche, Léonce. *Saint-Jean-de-Luz historique et pittoresque*. Bayonne. 1856.

Graf, Henriette. 'The Apartments of Prince-Elector Charles Albert of Bavaria around 1740 and their Ceremonial Use at Court'. *The Court Historian*. 22, 1. June 2017. pp. 17–37.

La Grande Mademoiselle. *Mémoires*. 2005 edn.

Gregg, Edward. 'Monarchs without a Crown'. In Robert Oresko et al., eds. *Royal and Republican Sovereignty in Early Modern Europe*. Cambridge. 1997. pp. 382–422.

Gregg, Edward. *The Protestant Succession in International Politics, 1710–1716*. 1986.

Gregg, Edward. *Queen Anne*. 1980.

Grell, Chantal, ed. *Anne d'Autriche: Infante d'Espagne et reine de France*. 2009.

Grell, Chantal. 'Philippe, prince français ou roi d'Espagne: le débat sur les renonciations'. In Antonio Álvarez-Ossorio et al., eds. *La pérdida de Europa: la guerra de sucesión por la monarquía de España*. Madrid. 2007. pp. 673–92.

Greppi, Comte. 'Notes de voyage du Comte de Giandemaria'. *Revue d'Histoire Diplomatique*. 4, 3. 1980. pp. 352–67.

Gresset, Maurice et al. *Histoire de l'annexion de la Franche-Comté et du Pays de Montbéliard*. Le Coteau. 1988.

Grew, Marion E. *William Bentinck and William III*. 1924,

Grimblot, P. *Letters of William III and Louis XIV, and of their Ministers*. 2 vols. 1848.

Guerber, Abbé Victor. *Histoire politique et religieuse de Haguenau*. 2 vols. Marseille. 1978.

Guerre, Stéphane. *Nicolas Desmaretz: le Colbert oublié du Roi-Soleil*. 2019.

Guichen, Comte de. *Crépuscule d'Ancien Régime*. 1909.

Guillaume, Baron. *Les Gardes wallonnes au service d'Espagne*. Brussels. 1858.

Guilleragues, Vicomte de. *Correspondance*. 2 vols. Geneva. 1976.

Guiral, Pierre. *Adolphe Thiers ou De la nécessité en politique*. 1986.

Gwynn, Robin. *Huguenot Heritage: The History and Contribution of the Huguenots in Britain*. Brighton. 2001 edn.

Haffemayer, Stéphane. 'L'Affaire des gardes corses et l'opinion publique (20 août 1662–12 février 1664)'. In Lucien Bély and Géraud Poumarède, eds. *L'Incident diplomatique (XVIe–XVIIe siècle)*. 2010. pp. 281–309.

Haile, Martin. *Queen Mary of Modena: Her Life and Letters*. 1905.

Haley, K. D. H. 'The Dutch, the Invasion of England and the Alliance of 1689'. In Lois G. Schwoerer, ed. *The Revolution of 1688–1689: Changing Perspectives*. Cambridge. 1992. pp. 21–34.

Haley, K. D. H. *An English Diplomat in the Low Countries: Sir William Temple and John de Witt, 1665–1672*. Oxford. 1986.

Hamilton, Lt Gen. Sir F. W. *The Origin and History of the First or Grenadier Guards*. 3 vols. 1874.

Hamscher, Albert N. *The Parlement of Paris after the Fronde, 1653–1673*. Pittsburgh. 1976.

Hanley, Sarah. *The Lit de Justice of the Kings of France: Constitutional Ideology in Legend, Ritual, and Discourse*. 1989.

Hanotin, Guillaume. *Ambassadeur de deux couronnes: Amelot et les Bourbons entre commerce et diplomatie*. Madrid. 2018.

Hanovre, Sophie de. *Mémoires et lettres de voyage*. 1990.

Harcourt-Smith, Simon. *Alberoni or The Spanish Conspiracy*. 1943.

Hardman, John. *The Life of Louis XVI*. 2016.

Hardouin de Péréfixe. *Histoire du Roi Henri le Grand*. 1816 edn.

Hardwicke, Earl of, ed. *Miscellaneous State Papers from 1501 to 1726*. 2 vols. 1778.

Harrer, Irmgard et al. *The Austrian National Library*. Vienna. 2015.

Hartmann, Cyril Hughes. *The King my Brother*. 1954.

Hartmann, Cyril Hughes. *The King's Friend: A Life of Charles Berkeley, Viscount Fitzhardinge, Earl of Falmouth (1630–1665)*. 1951.

Hartmann, Cyril Hughes. *The Vagabond Duchess*. 1926.

Häseler, Jens. 'Entre la France et le Brandebourg: la République des Lettres'. In Guido Braun, ed. *Les Etats allemands et les Huguenots*. Munich. 2007. pp. 231–40.

Hatton, Ragnhild. *Charles XII of Sweden*. 1968.

Hatton, Ragnhild. *George I: Elector and King*. 1978.

Hatton, Ragnhild, ed. *Louis XIV and Absolutism*. 1976.

Hatton, Ragnhild, ed. *Louis XIV and Europe*. 1976.

Hau, Michel. *La Maison de Dietrich, de 1684 à nos jours*. Strasbourg. 1998.

Haussonville, Comte d'. *La Duchesse de Bourgogne et l'alliance savoyarde sous Louis XIV*. 4 vols. 1898–1908.

Haussonville, Comte d'. *Histoire de la réunion de la Lorraine à la France*. 4 vols. 1854–9.

Hautecoeur, Louis. *L'Histoire des châteaux du Louvre et des Tuileries*. 1927.

Havard, Gilles and Cécile Vidal. *Histoire de l'Amérique française*. 2008 edn.

Hayward, J. F. *Huguenot Silver in England, 1688–1727*. 1959.

Hebert, François. *Memoires du curé de Versailles*. 1927.

Hedin, Thomas and Folke Sandgren. 'Deux Voyageurs suédois visitent Versailles sous le règne de Roi-Soleil'. *Versalia*. 9. 2006. pp. 86–114.

Henderson, G. D. *The Chevalier Ramsay*. 1952.

Henderson, Nicholas. *Prince Eugene of Savoy: A Biography*. 1964.

Hénin, Charles. *Fêtes et plaisirs au temps des princes de Condé*. 2015.

Herbelot, M. *Bibliothèque orientale, ou dictionnaire universel contenant généralement tout ce qui regarde la connoissance des Peuples d'orient*. 1697.

Herlaut, Cdt. 'La Destruction du port de Dunkerque: la mission d'Ignace Tugghe à la cour d'Angleterre en 1713'. *Revue du Nord*. 11, 41. 1925. pp. 5–35.

Herlaut, Cdt. 'L'Intendant Le Blanc et les Anglais à Dunkerque'. *Bulletin de la Société Archéologique et Historique de Dunkerque et de la Flandre Maritime*. XXII. 1925. pp. 1–187.

Héroard, Jean. *Journal sur l'enfance et la jeunesse de Louis XIII*. 2 vols. 1868.

Herry, Simone. *Une Ville en mutation: Strasbourg au tournant du grand siècle*. Strasbourg. 1996.

Hery-Simoulin, Sally-Ann. 'Louis XIV et les mystères du justaucorps à brevet'. In Pierre Arizzoli-Clémentel and Pascale Gorguet Ballesteros, eds. *Fastes de cour et cérémonies royales: le costume de cour en Europe*. 2009. pp. 180–83.

Hibbard, Caroline. 'The Role of a Queen Consort: The Household and Court of Henrietta Maria, 1625–1642'. In Ronald Asch, ed. *Princes, Patronage and the Nobility: The Court and the Beginning of the Modern Age, 1450–1650*. Oxford. 1991. pp. 393–414.

Higgott, Gordon. 'Thomas Povey's Description of Versailles in the Spring of 1682'. In *Colloque Jules Hardouin-Mansart*, forthcoming.

Hildesheimer, Françoise. *La Double Mort du Roi Louis XIII*. 2011 edn.

Hildesheimer, Françoise, ed. *Testament politique de Richelieu*. 1995.

Hilton, Wendy. *Dance of Court and Theatre: The French Noble Style, 1680–1725*. 1981.

Hippeau, C., ed. *Correspondance inédite du Marquis d'Harcourt*. 2 vols. 1875.

Hippeau, C., ed. *Lettres au Maréchal d'Harcourt*. Caen. 1862.

Hogan, James, ed. *Négociations de M. le Comte d'Avaux en Irlande*. Dublin. 1934.

Hojer, Gerhard. *Schloss Herrenchiemsee*. Munich. 1998.

Holmes, Richard. *Fatal Avenue: A Traveller's History of the Battlefields of Northern France and Flanders, 1346–1945*. 2008.

Holmes, Richard. *Marlborough: Britain's Greatest General*. 2009 edn.

Hone, Joseph. 'Isaac Newton and the Medals for Queen Anne'. *Huntington Library Quarterly*. 79, 1. Spring 2016. pp. 119–48.

Horne, Alistair. *The Fall of Paris: The Siege and the Commune, 1870–71*. 1965.

Horowski, Leonhard. *Die Belagerung des Thrones: Machtstrukturen und Karrieremechanismen am Hof von Frankreich, 1661–1789*. Ostfildern. 2013.

Horowski, Leonhard. ' "Such a Great Advantage for my Son": Office-Holding and Career Mechanisms at the Court of France, 1661–1789'. *The Court Historian*. 8, 2. December 2003. pp. 125–75.

Houblon, Alice Archer. *The Houblon Family: Its Stories and its Times*. 2 vols. 1907.

Houdard, Georges. *Les Châteaux royaux de Saint-Germain-en-Laye, 1124–1789*. 2 vols. Saint-Germain-en-Laye. 1909–10.

Howard, Michael. *The Franco-Prussian War: The German Invasion of France, 1870–1871*. 1981 edn.

Hrodej, Philippe. *L'Amiral du Casse: l'élévation d'un Gascon sous Louis XIV*. 2 vols. 1999.

Huart, Suzanne d', ed. *Lettres de Turenne*. 1971.

Hufton, Olwen. *The Prospect before Her: A History of Women in Western Europe*. Vol. I. 1995.

Hughes, Robert. *Barcelona*. 1992.

Hugon, Alain. *Naples insurgée, 1647–1648: de l'événement à la mémoire*. Rennes. 2011.

Hume, Martin. *Queens of Old Spain*. 1906.

Hurt, John. *Louis XIV and the Parlements: The Assertion of Royal Authority*. Manchester. 2002.

Hutton, Ronald. *Charles II: King of England, Scotland and Ireland*. 1991 edn.

Hutton, Ronald. 'The Religion of Charles II'. In R. Malcolm Smuts, ed. *The Stuart Court and Europe: Essays in Politics and Political Culture*. Cambridge. 1996. pp. 228–46.

Hyde, Elizabeth. *Cultivated Power: Flowers, Culture and Politics in the Reign of Louis XIV*. Philadelphia. 2005.

Ingrao, Charles W. *In Quest and Crisis: The Emperor Joseph I and the Habsburg Monarchy*. West Lafayette, IN. 1979.

Isaksen, Trond Norén. 'Anointing Absolutism'. *The Court Historian*. 19, 1. June 2014. pp. 75–8.

Israel, Jonathan, ed. *The Anglo-Dutch Moment: Essays on the Glorious Revolution and its World Impact*. Cambridge. 2003.

Israel, Jonathan. *Dutch Primacy in World Trade, 1585–1740*. Oxford. 1989.

Israel, Jonathan. *The Dutch Republic: Its Rise, Greatness, and Fall, 1477–1806*. 1998 edn.

Jackson, Julian. *A Certain Idea of France: The Life of General de Gaulle*. 2018.

Jackson, Richard A. *Vive le Roi! A History of the French Coronation from Charles V to Charles X*. Chapel Hill, NC. 1984.

Jackson, Sir William G. F. *The Rock of the Gibraltarians: A History of Gibraltar*. Rutherford, NJ. 1987.

Jacobsen, Helen. 'Les Ambassadeurs européens à Versailles'. In Daniëlle Kisluk-Grosheide and Bertrand Rondot, eds. *Visiteurs de Versailles: voyageurs, princes, ambassadeurs, 1682–1789*. 2017. pp. 114–23.

Jacquet, Nicolas. *Secrets et curiosités des jardins de Versailles: les bosquets, le domaine de Trianon, le grand parc*. 2013.

Jaeglé, Ernest, ed. *Correspondance de Madame, Duchesse d'Orléans*. 3 vols. 1890 edn.

Jahan, Emmanuel. *La Confiscation des biens des religionnaires fugitifs: de la Révocation de l'Edit de Nantes à la révolution*. 1959.

James II. *Memoirs: His Campaigns as Duke of York, 1652–1660*. 1962.

Janczukiewicz, Jérôme. 'Gaston d'Orléans à la fin de la Fronde: la persistance dans la rébellion'. In Jean-Pierre Bardet et al., eds. *Etat et société en France aux XVIIe et XVIIIe siècles*. 2000. pp. 331–45.

Japikse, N. ed. *Correspondentie van Willem III en van Hans Willem Bentinck, eersten Graf van Portland*. 3 vols. The Hague. 1927–37.

Jardine, Lisa. *On a Grander Scale: The Outstanding Career of Sir Christopher Wren*. 2003 edn.

Jeanmougin, Bertrand. *Louis XIV à la conquête des Pays-Bas espagnols: la guerre oubliée, 1678–1684*. 2005.

Jeffares, Neil. 'Between France and Bavaria: Louis-Joseph d'Albert de Luynes, Prince de Grimberghen'. *The Court Historian*. 17, 1. June 2012. pp. 61–85.

Jehan, Auguste. *La Ville de Versailles: son histoire, ses monuments, ses rues*. Versailles. 1900.

Jessurun-ten Dam, S. C. J. *Utrecht in 1672 en 1673*. Utrecht. 1934.

Jestaz, Bertrand. *Jules Hardouin-Mansart*. 2008.

Joly, Guy. *Traité des droits de la Reyne très chrétienne sur divers estats de la monarchie d'Espagne*. 1667.

Jones, Colin. *The Great Nation: France from Louis XIV to Napoleon*. 2003.

Jones, Colin. *Paris: Biography of a City*. 2004.

Jones, Colin. *The Smile Revolution in Eighteenth-Century Paris*. 2014.

Jones, James. 'French Intervention in English and Dutch Politics, 1677–88'. In Jeremy Black, ed. *Knights Errant and True Englishmen: British Foreign Policy, 1660–1800*. Edinburgh. 1989. pp. 1–23.

Jouhaud, Christian. *Mazarinades: la Fronde des mots*. 1985.

Joutard, Philippe. 'The Revocation of the Edict of Nantes: End or Renewal of French Calvinism?' In Menna Prestwich, ed. *International Calvinism, 1541–1715*. Oxford. 1985. pp. 339–68.

Joutard, Philippe. *La Révocation de l'édit de Nantes, ou les faiblesses d'un état*. 2018.

Julian, Pascal, ed. *Marbres de Rois*. Marseille. 2013.

Jullian, Camille. *Histoire de Bordeaux, depuis les origines jusqu'en 1895*. Bordeaux. 1895.

Jurieu, Pierre. *Pastoral letters, directed to the suffering Protestants of France, groaning under the cruel persecution of the bloody tyrant Lewis XIV*. N.d.

Jusserand, J. J. *Recueil des Instructions donnés aux ambassadeurs et ministres de France: Angleterre*. 3 vols. 1929–65.

Kaiser, Thomas E. and Dale Van Kley, eds. *From Deficit to Deluge: The Origins of the French Revolution*. Stanford. 2011.

Kalmar, Janos. 'Gênes et Milan pendant la guerre de Succession d'Espagne'. In Raffaele Belvederi, ed. *Rapporti Genova-Mediterraneo-Atlantica nell'eta moderna*. VIII. Genoa. 1990. pp. 443–51.

Kamen, Henry. *The Escorial: Art and Power in the Renaissance*. 2010.

Kamen, Henry. *Philip V of Spain: The King Who Reigned Twice*. 2001.

Kamen, Henry. *The War of the Succession in Spain, 1700–15*. 1969.

Kampmann, Christoph. 'The English Crisis, the Emperor Leopold and the Origins of the Dutch Intervention in 1688'. *Historical Journal*. 55, 2. June 2012. pp. 521–32.

Kapp, Volker. *Télémaque de Fénelon: la signification d'une oeuvre littéraire à la fin du siècle classique*. Tübingen. 1982.

Kaufmann, J. E. and H. W. *Fortress France: The Maginot Line and French Defenses in World War II*. Westport, CT. 2006.

Kazerouni, Guillaume. *Les Couleurs du ciel: peintures des églises de Paris au XVII siècle*. 2012.

Kazner, J. F. A. *Leben Friederichs von Schomberg*. Mannheim. 1789.

Keay, Anna. *The Last Royal Rebel: The Life and Death of James, Duke of Monmouth*. 2016.

Keay, Anna. *The Magnificent Monarch: Charles II and the Ceremonies of Power*. 2008.

Kenyon, J. P. *Robert Spencer, Earl of Sunderland*. 1958.

Kettering, Sharon. *Patronage in Sixteenth- and Seventeenth-Century France*. 2002.

Kirchner, Thomas. *Le Héros épique: peinture d'histoire et politique artistique dans la France du XVIIe siècle*. 2008.

Kisluk-Grosheide, Daniëlle and Bertrand Rondot. *Visiteurs de Versailles: voyageurs, princes, ambassadeurs, 1682–1789*. 2017.

Klaits, Joseph. *Printed Propaganda under Louis XIV: Absolute Monarchy and Public Opinion*. Princeton. 1977.

Kleber, Hermann. 'Louis XIV mémorialiste: la genèse des Mémoires de Louis XIV'. In Chantal Grell, Werner Paravicini and Jürgen Voss, eds. *Les Princes et l'histoire du XVIe au XVIIIe siècle*. Bonn. 1998. pp. 523–33.

Kleinman, Ruth. *Anne of Austria, Queen of France*. Columbus, OH. 1985.

Klingensmith, Samuel John. *The Utility of Splendor: Ceremony, Social Life, and Architecture at the Court of Bavaria, 1600–1800*. Chicago. 1993.

Klopp, Onno. *Der Fall des Hauses Stuart*. 14 vols. Vienna. 1875–88.

Knachel, Philip A. *England and the Fronde: The Impact of the English Civil War and Revolution on France*. Ithaca, NY. 1967.

Knecht, Robert J. *The French Renaissance Court, 1483–1589*. 2008.

Knothe, Florian. 'Tapestry as a Medium of Propaganda at the Court of Louis XIV: Display and Audience'. In Thomas P. Campbell and Elizabeth A. H. Cleland, eds. *Tapestry in the Baroque: New Aspects of Production and Patronage*. 2010. pp. 342–59.

Kolk, Caroline zum et al., eds. *Voyageurs étrangers à la cour de France*. Rennes. 2014.

Konvitz, Josef W. *Cartography in France 1660–1848: Science, Engineering and Statecraft*, Chicago. 1987.

Köpeczi, Béla, ed. *Correspondance diplomatique de François II Rákóczi*. Budapest. 1999.

Koslofsky, Craig. *Evening's Empire: A History of the Night in Early Modern Europe*. Cambridge. 2011.

Kraatz, Anne. *Lace: History and Fashion*. 1989.

Kroell, Anne. *Louis XIV, la Perse et Mascate*. 1977.

Kroll, Maria. *Letters from Liselotte: Elisabeth-Charlotte, Princess Palatine and Duchess of Orléans, 1652–1722*. 1998.

Labatut, Jean-Pierre. *Les Ducs et pairs de France au XVIIe siècle*. 1972.

Lablaude, Pierre-Andre. *Les Jardins de Versailles*. 1995.

La Châtre, Comte de. *Mémoires*. 1838.

Lacolle, Capitaine Noël. *Les Gardes Françaises: leur histoire, 1563–1789*. 1901.

Lacour-Gayet, Robert. *L'Education politique de Louis XIV*. 1898.

Lacouture, Jean. *De Gaulle: le rebelle, 1890–1944*. 1984.

La Croix, Pétis de. *Etat présent des nations et églises grecque, arménienne et maronite en Turquie*. 1715.

La Croix, Pétis de. *La Turquie chrétienne sous la puissante protection de Louis-le-Grand, protecteur unique du christianisme en Orient*. 1695.

La Fare, Marquis de. *Mémoires et réflexions*. 1884.

La Force, Duc de. *Le Grand Conti*. 1948 edn.

La Gorce, Jérôme de. *Berain: dessinateur du Roi Soleil*. 1986.

La Gorce, Jérôme de. *Carlo Vigarani, intendant des plaisirs de Louis XIV*. 2005.

La Gorce, Jérôme de. *Jean-Baptiste Lully*. 2002.

La Gorce, Jérôme de. ' "Le Triomphe de la Seine et du Tage sur les autre fleuves de l'Europe affermi par la naissance du duc de Bretagne": une fête organisée à Paris pendant la guerre de Succession d'Espagne'. In Antonio Álvarez-Ossorio et al., eds. *La pérdida de Europa: la guerra de sucesión por la monarquía de España*. Madrid. 2007. pp. 49–63.

Lahaye, Matthieu. *Le Fils de Louis XIV: Monseigneur le Grand Dauphin (1661–1711)*. 2013.

Lahrkamp, Helmut, ed. *Lambert Friedrich Corfey: Reisetagebuch, 1698–1700*. Münster. 1977.

Lair, J. *Louise de La Vallière et la jeunesse de Louis XIV*. 1881.

La Loubère, Simon de. *Description du Royaume de Siam*. 2 vols. 1692.

Laloy, Emile. *La Révolte de Messine*. 3 vols. 1929–31.

Lambin, Jean-Michel. *Quand le nord devenait français (1635–1713)*. 1980.

Landwehr, John. *Romeyn de Hooghe as Book Illustrator*. Amsterdam. 1970.

Lane, Mary Merrit and Borje Magnusson. *Nicodemus Tessin the Younger: Sources, Works, Collections, Travel Notes, 1673–1677 and 1687–88*. Stockholm. 2002.

Lanfredini, Dina. *Un antagonista di Luigi XIV, Armand de Gramont, Conte de Guiche*. Florence. 1959.

Langlois, Marcel. *Louis XIV et la cour*. 1926

La Porte, Pierre de. *Mémoires de Pierre de La Porte, Premier valet de chambre de Louis XIV*. 2003 edn.

La Quintinie, Jean de. *Instruction pour les jardins fruitiers et potagers avec un traité des orangers, suivi de quelques réflexions sur l'agriculture*. 2 vols. 1690.

Laroche, Serge. '1677: le siège victorieux de Valenciennes et la gloire de Louis XIV'. In Hervé Coutau-Bégarie, ed. *Les Médias et la guerre*. 2005. pp. 180–88.

La Rochefoucauld, François de. *Mémoires*. 2001 edn.

La Rochefoucauld, François de. *Oeuvres complètes*. 1964 edn.

Laroque, A. de Galtier de. *Le Marquis de Ruvigny et les Protestants à la cour de Louis XIV, 1643–85*. 1892.

La Rosière, M. de. 'Etat de la cour de Brandebourg en 1694'. *Revue d'Histoire Diplomatique*. 1. 1887. pp. 267–92, 411–24.

La Tour de Pin, Madame de. *Journal d'une femme de cinquante ans*. 2 vols. 1913.

La Trémoille, Duc de. *Madame des Ursins et la Succession d'Espagne*. 6 vols. Nantes. 1902–7.

Laurain-Portemer, Madeleine. *Etudes Mazarines*. 2 vols. 1981–97.

Laurentin, René. *Le Voeu de Louis XIII: passé ou avenir de la France*. 2004 edn.

[La Vallière, Louise de.] *Réflexions sur la miséricorde de Dieu, par une illustre pénitente*. 1682.

Lebon, André, ed. *Recueil des instructions données aux ambassadeurs et ministres de France*. VIII: *Bavière, Palatinat, Deux-Ponts*. 1889.

[Le Clerc, Jean.] *Explication historique des principales médailles frapées pour servir à l'histoire des Provinces-Unies des Pays-Bas*. Amsterdam. 1736 edn.

Leclercq, Henri. *Histoire de la Régence pendant la minorité de Louis XV*. 3 vols. 1922.

Leferme-Falguières, Frédérique. *Les Courtisans: une société de spectacle sous l'Ancien Régime*. 2007.

Leferme-Falguières, Frédérique. 'Les Funérailles de Louis XIV à Saint-Denis'. In *Le Roi est mort: Louis XIV – 1715*. Exh. cat. 2015.

Lefèvre-Pontalis, Antonin. *Jean de Witt, Grand Pensionnaire de Hollande*. 2 vols. 1884.

Le Gall, Jean-Marie. 'Les Bourbons, ou le refus du tombeau'. In Mark Hengerer and Gérard Sabatier, eds. *Les Funérailles princières en Europe XVIe–XVIIIe siècles*. II: *Apothéoses monumentales*. 2013. pp. 253–68.

Le Gall, Jean-Marie. *Les Capitales de la Renaissance*. 2011.

Le Gall, Jean-Marie. 'Les Pompes funèbres des souverains étrangers à Notre-Dame de Paris, XVIe–XVIIIe siècles', *Revue d'Histoire Moderne et Contemporaine*. 59-3, 3. 2012. pp. 96–123.

Le Gallo, Yves, ed. *Histoire de Brest*. Toulouse. 1976.

Legard, James. ' "Princely Glory": The 1st Duke of Marlborough, Court Culture, and the Construction of Blenheim Palace'. Talk given to the Society for Court Studies. 18 February 2018.

Legay, Marie-Laure. *Les Etats provinciaux dans la construction de l'Etat moderne aux XVIIe et XVIIIe siècles*. Geneva. 2011.

Legg, L. G. Wickham. *Matthew Prior: A Study of his Public Career and Correspondence.* Cambridge. 1921.

Legrelle, Arsène. *La Diplomatie française et la succession d'Espagne.* 6 vols. Braine-le-Comte. 1895–9 edn.

Legrelle, Arsène. *Louis XIV et Strasbourg.* Ghent. 1878.

Le Laboureur, Jean. *Relation du voyage de la Royne de Pologne et du retour de Madame la Mareschalle de Guébriant, ambassadrice extraordinaire et surintendante de sa conduite.* 1647.

Lemaire, Louis. *Histoire de Dunkerque: des origines à 1900.* Dunkirk. 1927.

Lemarchand, Laurent. *Paris ou Versailles? La monarchie absolue entre deux capitales (1715–1723).* 2014.

Lemoine, Henri. 'Les Ecuries du roi sous l'ancien régime'. *Revue de l'Histoire de Versailles.* 35. 1933. pp. 150–83.

Lemoine, Jean and André Lichtenberger. *De La Vallière à Montespan.* 1902.

Lemoine, Jean and André Lichtenberger. *Les des Oeillets: une grande comédienne, une maîtresse de Louis XIV: étude et documents.* 1938.

Le Roux, Nicolas. 'La Cour dans l'espace du palais: l'exemple de Henri III'. In Marie France-Auzépy and Joël Cornette, eds. *Palais et pouvoir: de Constantinople à Versailles.* 2003. pp. 229–67.

Le Roux, Nicolas. *La Faveur du roi: mignons et courtisans au temps des derniers Valois.* 2001.

Le Roux, Nicolas. *Un Régicide au nom de Dieu: l'assassinat d'Henri III.* 2006.

Levantal, Christophe. *Louis XIV: Chronographie d'un règne.* 2 vols. 2009.

Levantal, Christophe. *La Route royale: le voyage de Philippe V et de ses frères, de Sceaux à la frontière d'Espagne (décembre 1700–janvier 1701) d'après la relation du Mercure Galant.* 1996.

Lever, Maurice. *Les Bûchers de Sodome.* 1985.

Levillain, Charles-Edouard. *Vaincre Louis XIV. Angleterre – Hollande – France: histoire d'une relation triangulaire, 1665–1688.* 2010.

Levron, Jacques. *Les Inconnus de Versailles: les coulisses de la cour.* 1968.

Levron, Jacques. *Versailles, ville royale.* 1964.

Lévy, Claude-Frédéric. *Capitalistes et pouvoir au siècle des Lumières: les fondateurs, des origines à 1715.* 1969.

Lewis, W. H. *Assault on Olympus: The Rise of the House of Gramont.* 1958.

Lewis, W. H. *Levantine Adventurer.* 1963.

Liechtenhan, Francine-Dominique. *Pierre le Grand.* 2015.

Linden, David van der. *Experiencing Exile: Huguenot Refugees in the Dutch Republic, 1680–1700.* Dorchester. 2015.

Lionne, Comte de. *Lettres inédites.* 1877.

Lister, Martin. *A Journey to Paris in the Year 1698.* 1699.

Littleton, Charles. 'Abel Boyer and Other Huguenot Reporters of Parliament'. Talk given to the Sixth International Huguenot conference, 'Huguenot Networks in Europe', Europe House, London. 10 September 2015.

Livermore, Harold. *A New History of Portugal.* 1976 edn.

Livet, Georges, ed. *Histoire de Strasbourg.* 4 vols. Strasbourg. 1980–82.

Livet, Georges, ed. *Recueil d'instructions*, XXVIII: *L'Electorat de Trèves*. 1966.

Livet, Georges. 'Strasbourg, Metz et Luxembourg: contribution à l'étude de la politique extérieure de la France sous Louis XIV'. In Raymond Poidevin and Gilbert Trausch, eds. *Les Relations franco-luxembourgeoises, de Louis XIV à Robert Schuman*. Metz. 1978. pp. 1–19.

Lizerand, Georges. *Le Duc de Beauvillier*. 1933.

Locatelli, Sébastien. *Voyage en France: moeurs et coutumes françaises*. 1905.

Locke, John. *Travels in France*. Ed. John Lough. 1953.

Longin, Emile. *Un Franc-Comtois à Paris sous Louis XIV, 1691–92*. Vesoul. 1894.

Longin, Emile. *François de Lisola: sa vie, ses écrits, son testament*. Dole. 1900.

Longstaffe-Gowan, Todd. *The Gardens and Parks at Hampton Court Palace*. 2005.

Lorenz, Hellmut. 'Vienna Gloriosa'. In Henry A. Millon, ed. *Circa 1700: Architecture in Europe and the Americas*. New Haven. 2005. pp. 47–64.

Loskoutoff, Yvan, ed. *Les Médailles de Louis XIV et leur livre*. Rouen. 2016.

Lottin, Alain, ed. *'Chronique immémoriale des choses mémorables par moy Pierre-Ignace Chavatte' (1657–1693): le mémorial d'un humble tisserand lillois au grand siècle*. Brussels. 2010.

Lottin, Alain. *Les Grandes Batailles du Nord de la France*. 1984.

Lough, John. *France Observed in the Seventeenth Century by British Travellers*. Stocksfield. 1985.

Louis XIV. *Correspondance avec M. Amelot, son ambassadeur en Espagne, 1705–1709*. 2 vols. Nantes. 1864.

Louis XIV. *Mémoires de Louis XIV*. Ed. Jean Longnon. 2007 edn.

Louis XIV. *Oeuvres*. 6 vols. 1806.

Louis XV. *Correspondance de . . . et du Maréchal de Noailles*. 2 vols. 1865.

Louville, Marquis de. *Mémoires secrets sur l'établissement de la Maison de Bourbon en Espagne*. 2 vols. 1818.

Love, Ronald S. 'Simon de La Loubère: French Views of Siam in the 1680s'. In Glenn J. Ames and Ronald S. Love, eds. *Distant Lands and Diverse Cultures: The French Experience in Asia, 1600–1700*. Westport, CT. 2003. pp. 181–200.

Loyau, Marcel. *Madame de Maintenon et la princesse des Ursins: correspondence. 1709. Une année tragique*. 2002.

Lucas, Paul. *Troisième voyage . . . dans le Levant*. Saint-Etienne. 2004.

Lukowski, Jerzy. *Liberty's Folly: The Polish–Lithuanian Commonwealth in the Eighteenth Century, 1697–1795*. 1991.

Lurgo, Elisabetta. *Philippe d'Orléans: frère de Louis XIV*. 2018.

Lurin, Emmanuel, ed. *Le Château-Neuf de Saint-Germain-en-Laye*. 2 vols. 2010.

Lüthy, Herbert. *La Banque Protestante en France, de la Révocation de l'Edit de Nantes à la Révolution*. 3 vols. 1959–70.

Lynn, John A. 'A Brutal Necessity? The Devastation of the Palatinate, 1688–1689'. In Mark Grimsley and Clifford J. Rogers, eds. *Civilians in the Path of War*. 2002. pp. 79–100.

Lynn, John A. *The Wars of Louis XIV, 1667–1714*. 1999.

Mabille, Gérard et al. *Vues des jardins de Marly: le roi jardinier*. Montreuil. 2011.

McCollim, Gary B. *Louis XIV's Assault on Privilege: Nicolas Desmaretz and the Tax on Wealth*. Rochester, NY. 2012.

Macdonald, James. *A Free Nation Deep in Debt: The Financial Roots of Democracy*. Princeton. 2006.

McGowan, Margaret M. *The Court Ballet of Louis XIII: A Collection of Working Designs for Costumes, 1615-33*. 1986.

McGowan, Margaret M. *Dance in the Renaissance: European Fashion, French Obsession*. 2008.

McKay, Derek. *The Great Elector: Frederick William of Brandenburg-Prussia*. Harlow. 2001.

McKenna, Antony. 'Les Soupirs de la France esclave: le problème de l'attribution'. In Pierre Bonnet, ed. *Littérature de contestation: pamphlets et polémique du règne de Louis XIV aux Lumières*. 2011. pp. 229-68.

MacLeod, Catherine and Julia Marciari Alexander. *Painted Ladies: Women at the Court of Charles II*. New Haven and London. 2001.

McLeod, Jane. *Licensing Loyalty: Printers, Patrons, and the State in Early Modern France*. University Park, PA. 2011.

MacMillan, Margaret. *Peacemakers: The Paris Conference of 1919 and its Attempt to End War*. 2001.

McNamara, Jo Ann Kay. *Sisters in Arms: Catholic Nuns through Two Millennia*. 1996.

Madan, Falconer. *Stuart Papers*. 1889.

Magdelaine, Michelle. *Guerre et paix en Alsace: les mémoires de voyage du sieur de l'Hermine*. Toulouse. 1981.

Magne, Emile. *Images de Paris sous Louis XIV: d'après des document inédits*. 1939.

Magne, Emile, ed. *Lettres inédites du Grand Condé et du Duc d'Enghien . . . sur la cour de Louis XIV*. 1920.

Maguire, Nancy Klein. 'The Duchess of Portsmouth: English Royal Consort and French Politician, 1670-1685'. In R. Malcolm Smuts, ed. *The Stuart Court and Europe*. Cambridge. 1996. pp. 247-73.

Mahon, Lord, ed. *Spain under Charles II*. 1844 edn.

Mailly, Chevalier de. *Histoire de la république de Gênes*. 3 vols. 1696.

Maintenon, Madame de. *Lettres*. Ed. Hans Bots. 8 vols. 2009-16.

Maintenon, Madame de. *Proverbes dramatiques*. 2014.

Maire, Catherine, ed. *Jansénisme et révolution: actes du colloque de Versailles*. 1990.

Maisonnier, Elisabeth. 'Les Guides de Versailles à l'usage des étrangers'. In Daniëlle Kisluk-Grosheide and Bertrand Rondot, eds. *Visiteurs de Versailles: voyageurs, princes, ambassadeurs, 1682-1789*. 2017. pp. 40-44.

Major, J. Russell. *From Renaissance Monarchy to Absolute Monarchy: French Kings, Nobles, & Estates*. Baltimore. 1994.

Malettke, Klaus, 'Complots et conspirations contre Louis XIV dans la seconde moitié du XVIIe siècle'. In Yves-Marie Bercé, ed. *Complots et conspirations dans l'Europe moderne*. Rome. 1996. pp. 347-71.

Malettke, Klaus. 'L'Opposition nobiliaire sous Louis XIV, le cas du chevalier de Rohan'. In Chantal Grell and Arnaud Ramière de Fortanier, eds. *Le Second Ordre: l'idéal nobiliaire: hommage à Ellery Schalk*. 1999. pp. 217-26.

Malettke, Klaus. *Les Relations entre la France et le Saint-Empire au XVIIe siècle.* 2001.

Manchée, W. H. *The Fouberts and their Royal Academy.* 1925.

Manchester, Duke of. *Court and Society, from Elizabeth to Anne.* 2 vols. 1864.

Mancini, Hortense and Marie. *Mémoires.* 1987 edn.

Manneville, H. de. 'Une Princesse française sur le trône de Portugal: Marie Françoise Elisabeth de Savoie'. *Revue d'Histoire Diplomatique.* 21. January 1931, pp. 22–46; April 1931, pp. 193–219; July 1931, pp. 294–317.

Mansel, Philip. *The Court of France, 1789–1830.* 1989.

Mansel, Philip. *Dressed to Rule: Royal and Court Costume from Louis XIV to Elizabeth II.* 2005.

Mansel, Philip. *Pillars of Monarchy: An Outline of the Political and Social History of Royal Guards, 1400–1984.* 1984.

Maquart, Marie-Françoise. 'Le Dernier Testament de Charles II'. In Lucien Bély, ed. *La Présence des Bourbons en Europe, XVIe–XXIe siècle.* 2003. pp. 112–24.

Maquart, Marie-Françoise. *L'Espagne de Charles II et la France, 1665–1700.* 2000.

Marais, Mathieu. *Journal de Paris.* 2 vols. Saint-Etienne. 2004.

Marais, Mathieu. *Lettre au sujet du mariage du roy.* 1660.

Maral, Alexandre. *La Chapelle royale de Versailles sous Louis XIV: cérémonial, liturgie et musique.* 2010.

Maral, Alexandre. *Les Derniers Jours de Louis XIV.* 2014.

Maral, Alexandre, *Les Derniers Jours de Versailles.* 2018.

Maral, Alexandre. *François Girardon: le sculpteur de Louis XIV.* 2015.

Maral, Alexandre. *Le Grande Commande de 1674: chefs d'oeuvre sculptés des jardins de Versailles sous Louis XIV.* 2013.

Maral, Alexandre. *Madame de Maintenon: à l'ombre du Roi-Soleil.* 2011.

Maral, Alexandre. *Parcours mythologique dans les jardins de Versailles.* 2012.

Maral, Alexandre. *Le Roi, la cour et Versailles: le coup d'éclat permanent, 1682–1789.* 2013.

Maral, Alexandre. *Le Roi-Soleil et Dieu: essai sur la religion de Louis XIV.* 2012.

Maral, Alexandre. *Le Versailles de Louis XIV: un palais pour la sculpture.* Dijon. 2013.

Maral, Alexandre and Nicolas Milovanovic, eds. *Versailles et l'antique.* 2012.

Marana, Jean-Paul. *Lettre d'un sicilien à un de ses amis.* 1883.

Mareschal de Bièvre, Gabriel. *Georges Mareschal, seigneur de Bièvre, chirurgien et confident de Louis XIV (1658–1736).* 1906.

Margry, Pierre. *Découvertes et établissements des français dans l'ouest et dans le sud de l'Amérique Septentrionale, 1614–1754.* 4 vols. 1878.

Margue, Paul. 'Assujettis ou sujets? Les luxembourgeois sous Louis XIV'. In Raymond Poidevin and Gilbert Trausch, eds. *Les Relations franco-luxembourgeoises, de Louis XIV à Robert Schuman.* Metz. 1978. pp. 21–38.

Marie, Alfred. *Mansart à Versailles.* 1972.

Marie, Alfred. *Naissance de Versailles: le château, les jardins.* 2 vols. 1968.

Marin, Catherine, ed. *La Société des missions étrangères de Paris: 350 ans à la rencontre de l'Asie, 1658–2008.* 2011.

Marly, Diana de. *Louis XIV and Versailles.* 1987.

Maroteaux, Vincent. *Marly: l'autre palais du soleil.* 2002.

Maroteaux, Vincent. *Versailles: le roi et son domaine.* 2000.

Maroteaux, Vincent and Jacques de Givry. *Versailles: le grand parc.* 2004.

Martin, Meredith. 'Mirror Reflections: Louis XIV, Phra Narai, and the Material Culture of Kingship'. *Art History.* 38. September 2015. pp. 652–67.

Martin, Michel. *Les Monuments équestres de Louis XIV: une grande entreprise de propagande monarchique.* 1986.

Martinez, Jean-Luc et al., eds. *Les Antiques du Louvre.* 2004.

Massillon, Jean-Baptiste. *Oraison funèbre de Louis XIV.* Grenoble. 2004.

Masson, Georgina. *Queen Christina.* 1968.

Masson, Paul. *Histoire des établissements et du commerce français dans l'Afrique barbaresque (1560–1793).* 1903.

Masson, Rémi. *Défendre le roi: la Maison Militaire au XVIIème siècle.* 2017.

Matar, Nabil. 'Abdallah ibn 'Aisha and the French Court, 1699–1701: An Ambassador without Diplomacy'. *French History.* 29, 1. 2015. pp. 1–75.

Matar, Nabil. *Europe through Arab Eyes, 1578–1727.* New York. 2009.

Maucroix, François. *Mémoires de François Maucroix, chanoine et sénéchal de l'église de Reims.* Reims. 1842.

Maurer, Louis. *L'Expedition de Strasbourg en septembre 1681: correspondance officielle tirée des archives de la guerre.* 1923.

Mazarin, Jules. *Carnet.* Tours. 1893.

Mazarin, Jules. *Lettres du cardinal Mazarin.* 2 vols. Amsterdam. 1745 edn.

Mazarin, Jules. *Lettres du cardinal Mazarin pendant son ministère.* 9 vols. 1872–1906.

Mazouer, Charles. 'Molière et le roi'. In Denis Lopez, ed. *Le Pouvoir et ses écritures.* 2012. pp. 135–44.

Melchior-Bonnet, Sabine. *Fénelon.* 2008.

Melzer, Sara E. and Kathryn Norberg, eds. *From the Royal to the Republican Body: Incorporating the Political in Seventeenth- and Eighteenth-Century France.* Berkeley. 1998.

Mémain, René. *La Marine de guerre sous Louis XIV: le matériel: Rochefort, arsenal, modèle de Colbert.* 1937.

Ménard, Pierre. *Le Français qui possédait l'Amérique: la vie extraordinaire d'Antoine Crozat, milliardiare sous Louis XIV.* 2017.

Merrick, Jeffrey and Bryant T. Ragan Jr. *Homosexuality in Early Modern France: A Documentary Collection.* New York. 2001.

Mettam, Roger. 'Louis XIV and the Persecution of the Huguenots: The Role of the Ministers and Royal Officials'. In Irene Scouloudi, ed. The *Huguenots in Britain and their French Background, 1550–1800.* Basingstoke. 1987. pp. 198–216.

Mettam, Roger. *Power and Faction in Louis XIV's France.* Oxford. 1988.

Metzger, Edward Charles. *Ralph, First Duke of Montagu, 1638–1709*. Lewiston, NY. 1987.

Meyer, Jean. *La Naissance de Louis XIV*. 1989.

Michaud, Claude. 'Le Soleil, l'aigle et le croissant: l'ambassade de Guilleragues à la Porte ottomane et le siège de Vienne de 1683'. In idem. *Entre croisades et révolutions: princes, noblesses et nations au centre de l'Europe (XVIe–XVIIIe siècles)*. 2010. pp. 277–92.

Michel, Dominique. *Vatel et la naissance de la gastronomie*. 1999.

Micio, Paul. *Les Collections de Monsieur, frère de Louis XIV*. 2014.

Migault, Jean. *Journal*. Marseille. 1978.

Migne, Abbé. *Collection intégrale et universelle des orateurs sacrés*. XXXIII. 1853.

Mignet, François. *Négociations relatives à la succession d'Espagne sous Louis XIV*. 4 vols. 1835–42.

Mignot, Claude. *Le Val-de-Grâce: l'ermitage d'une reine*. 1994.

Mijers, Esther and David Onnekink. *Redefining William III: The Impact of the King-Stadholder in International Context*. Aldershot. 2007.

Millot, Abbé. *Mémoires politiques et militaires pour servir à l'histoire de Louis XIV et de Louis XV*. 1839.

Milovanovic, Nicolas. *Du Louvre à Versailles: lecture des grands décors monarchiques*. 2005.

Minois, Georges. *Histoire de l'athéisme*. 1998.

Miskimin, Patricia Behre. *One King, One Law, Three Faiths: Religion and the Rise of Absolutism in Seventeenth-Century Metz*. Westport, CT. 2002.

Misson, Maximilien. *A New Voyage to Italy*. 2 vols. 1699 edn.

Mitford, Nancy. *The Sun King: Louis XIV at Versailles*. 1966.

Moine, Marie-Christine. *Les Fêtes à la cour du Roi-Soleil, 1653–1715*. 1984.

Molé, Mathieu. *Mémoires*. 4 vols. 1855–7.

Molière. *Le Bourgeois Gentilhomme*. Ed. Claire Joubaire. 2016.

Molière. *Oeuvres complètes*. 2 vols. 2010.

Monahan, W. Gregory. *Let God Arise: The War and Rebellion of the Camisards*. Oxford. 2014.

Mongrédien, Georges. *La Journée des dupes*. 1961.

Mongrédien, Georges. *Louis XIV*. 1963.

Monicault, Michel. *La Basilique Sainte-Marie-Madeleine et le couvent royal dominicain*. Aix-en-Provence. 1985.

Monod, Paul et al., eds., *Loyalty and Identity: Jacobites at Home and Abroad*. Basingstoke. 2010.

Monson, Emma. 'The Three Esthers: Noblewoman of the Huguenot Refuge'. *Proceedings of the Huguenot Society of Great Britain and Ireland* XXVII. 1. 1998. pp. 1–19.

Montclos, Jean-Marie Pérouse de. *Vaux le Vicomte*. 1997.

Montglat. Marquis de. *Mémoires*. 1838.

Montpensier, Mademoiselle de. *Mémoires*. 4 vols. 1858–9.

Moote, A. Lloyd. *The Revolt of the Judges: The Parlement of Paris and the Fronde, 1643–1652*. 1971.

Morera, Raphaël. 'Amener les eaux: entre techniques, sciences et politiques'. In *Sciences et curiosités à la cour de Versailles*. 2010. pp. 87–93.

Morke, Olaf. 'William III's Stadholderly Court in the Dutch Republic'. In Esther Mijers and David Onnekink, eds. *Redefining William III: The Impact of the King-Stadholder in International Context*. Aldershot. 2007. pp. 227–40.

Mormando, Franco. *Bernini: His Life and his Rome*. 2011.

Mormiche, Pascale. *Devenir prince: l'école du pouvoir en France, XVIIe–XVIIIe siècles*. 2009.

Morris, Madeleine F. *Le Chevalier de Jaucourt: un ami de la terre*. Geneva. 1979.

Motta, Anne, *Echanges, passages et transferts à la cour du Duc Léopold de Lorraine*. Rennes. 2017.

Motteville, Madame de. *Chronique de la Fronde*. 2003.

Motteville, Madame de. *Mémoires . . . sur Anne d'Autriche et sa cour*. 4 vols. 1904–11.

Mousnier, Roland, ed. *Le Conseil du roi de Louis XII à la Révolution*. 1970.

Mousnier, Roland, ed. *Un Nouveau Colbert*. 1985.

Mousnier, Roland. *La Plume, la faucille et le marteau: institutions et société en France, du Moyen Age à la Révolution*. 1970.

Mousset, Albert. *Les Francine: créateurs des eaux de Versailles, intendants des eaux et fontaines de France de 1623 à 1784*. 1930.

Mukerji, Chandra. *Impossible Engineering: Technology and Territoriality on the Canal du Midi*. Princeton. 2009.

Murat, Inès. *Colbert*. 1980.

Murdoch, Tessa. 'Daniel Marot and the Louis XIV Style in England'. Talk given at the Sixth International Huguenot conference, 'Huguenot Networks in Europe', Europe House, London. 10 September 2015.

Murdoch, Tessa. *The Quiet Conquest: The Huguenots, 1685–1985*. 1985.

Musée des Archives Nationales. 1872.

Narbonne, Pierre. *Journal de Police*. 2 vols. Clermont-Ferrand. 2002–3.

Neave, Airey. *The Flames of Calais: A Soldier's Battle, 1940*. 1972.

Neher, André. 'Principes et applications de la politique de Louis XIV à l'égard des juifs de Metz'. In *Deux Siècles d'Alsace française, 1648 – 1798 – 1848*. 1948. pp. 159–73.

Nekrouf, Younès. *Une Amitié orageuse: Moulay Ismaïl et Louis XIV*. 1987.

Nemeitz, J. C. *Séjour de Paris*. 2 vols. Leyden. 1727.

Nemours, Duchesse de. *Mémoires*. 1990.

Néraudau, Jean-Pierre. *L'Olympe du Roi-Soleil: mythologie et idéologie royale au Grand Siècle*. 2013.

Netter, Nathan. *Vingt Siècles d'histoire d'une communauté juive: Metz et son grand passé*. Metz. 1938.

Nève, Joseph E. et al. *Gand sous l'occupation de Louis XIV, 1678–1679, 1701–1706, 1708*. Ghent. 1929.

Neveu, Bruno et al. *Les Demoiselles de Saint-Cyr, maison royale d'éducation, 1686–1793*. Versailles. 1999.

Newman, Karen. *Cultural Capitals: Early Modern London and Paris*. Princeton. 2007.

Newton, William R. *Les Chevaux et les chiens du roi à Versailles au XVIIIe siècle: le grande et la petite écurie, les écuries de la reine, le grand chenil et la louveterie*. 2015.

Newton, William R. *Derrière la façade: vivre au château de Versailles au XVIIIe siècle*. 2008.

Newton, William R. *L'Espace du roi: la cour de France au château de Versailles, 1682–1789*. 2000.

Newton, William R. *La Petite Cour: services et serviteurs à la cour de Versailles au XVIIIe siècle*. 2006.

Newton, William R. *Versailles, côté jardins: splendeurs et misères, de Louis XIV à la révolution*. 2013.

Nicolas, Jean. *La Rébellion française, 1661–1789*. 2008 edn.

Nicolson, Harold. *Peacemaking, 1919*. 1933.

Nimwegen, Olaf van. *The Dutch Army and the Military Revolutions, 1588–1688*. Woodbridge. 2010.

Noailles, Duc de. *Histoire de Madame de Maintenon*. 4 vols. 1848–58.

Nordman, Daniel. *Frontières de France: de l'espace au territoire, XVIe–XIXe siècle*. 1998.

Nordmann, Claude. *La Crise du Nord au début du XVIII siècle*. 1962.

Nordmann, Claude. *Grandeur et liberté de la Suède (1660–1792)*. 1971.

Northleigh, John. 'Travels through France . . . 1702'. In John Harris, ed. *Complete Collection of Voyages and Travels*. 2 vols. 1748 edn.

Norton, Lucy. *First Lady of Versailles*. 1978.

Nugent, Thomas. *The Grand Tour*. 4 vols. 1756 edn.

O'Connor, John T. *Negotiator out of Season: The Career of Wilhelm Egon von Fürstenberg, 1629 to 1704*. Athens, GA. 1978.

O'Reilly, William. 'A Life in Exile: Charles VI between Spain and Austria'. In Philip Mansel and Torsten Riotte, eds. *Monarchy and Exile: The Politics of Legitimacy from Marie de Médicis to Wilhelm II*. 2011. pp. 66–90.

Omont, Henri. *Missions archéologiques françaises en Orient au XVII et XVIII siècles*. 2 vols. 1902.

Omont, Henri. 'Projets de prise de Constantinople et de fondation d'un empire français d'Orient sous Louis XIV'. *Revue d'Histoire Diplomatique*. 7. 1893. pp. 195–246.

Onnekink, David and Esther Mijers, eds. *Redefining William III: The Impact of the King-Stadholder in International Context*. Aldershot. 2007.

Onnekink, David and Gijs Rommelse, eds. *Ideology and Foreign Policy in Early Modern Europe (1650–1750)*. Farnham. 2011.

Oppermann, Fabien. *Le Versailles des présidents: 150 ans de vie républicaine chez le Roi-Soleil*. 2015.

Oresko, Robert. 'Bastards as Clients: The House of Savoy and its Illegitimate Children'. In Charles Giry-Deloison and Roger Mettam, eds. *Patronages et clientélismes, 1550–1750 (France, Angleterre, Espagne, Italie)*. Lille. N.d. pp. 39–67.

Oresko, Robert. 'Homosexuality and the Court Elites of Early Modern France: Some Problems, Some Suggestions and an Example'. *Journal of Homosexuality*. 16. 1988. pp. 105–28.

Oresko, Robert. 'Maria Giovanna Battista of Savoy-Nemours (1644–1724): Daughter, Consort and Regent of Savoy'. In Clarissa Campbell Orr, ed., *Queenship in Europe, 1660–1815: The Role of the Consort*. Cambridge. 2004. pp. 16–55.

Orloff, Alexandre and Dimitri Chvidkovski. *Saint-Pétersbourg: l'architecture des tsars*. 2005 edn.

Ormesson, Olivier d'. *Journal*. 2 vols. 1860–61.

Oroux, Abbé. *Histoire ecclésiastique de la cour de France*. 2 vols. 1727.

Orr, Clarissa Campbell, ed. *Queenship in Europe, 1660–1815: The Role of the Consort*. Cambridge. 2004.

Oy-Marra, Elisabeth. 'Mazarin et les fresques de Giovanni Francesco Romanelli dans l'appartement d'été d'Anne d'Autriche au Louvre'. In Isabelle de Conihout and Patrick Michel, eds. *Mazarin: les lettres et les arts*. 2006. pp. 145–55.

Pagès, Georges. *Le Grand Electeur et Louis XIV, 1660–1688*. 1905.

Panhuysen, Luc. *De Ware Vrijheid: de Levens van Johan en Cornelis de Witt*. Amsterdam. 2005.

Pannekoucke, Stéphane. *Des princes en Bourgogne: les Condé gouverneurs au XVIIIe siècle*. 2010.

Paris, Robert. *Histoire du commerce de Marseille, 1660–1789: le Levant*. 1957.

Pariste, Ernest. *Histoire de la fabrique lyonnaise: étude sur le régime social et économique de l'industrie de la soie à Lyon, depuis le XIVe siècle*. 1901.

Parker, Geoffrey. *Global Crisis: War, Climate Change and Catastrophe in the Seventeenth Century*. 2013.

Patin, Guy. *Lettres . . . à Charles Spon*. Ed. Laure Jestaz. 2 vols. 2006.

Paul, Vincent de. *Lettres de Saint Vincent de Paul*. 2 vols. 1882.

Payet, Marie and Ferenc Tóth, eds. *Mille ans de contacts: relations franco-hongroises de l'an mil à nos jours*. Szombathely. 2001.

Peabody, Sue. *'There are No Slaves in France': The Political Culture of Race and Slavery in the Ancien Régime*. Oxford. 1996.

Pellegrin, Valdo. *Montpellier la protestante*. Montpellier. 2012.

Pellisson, M. *Lettres historiques*. 3 vols. 1679.

Pénicaut, Emmanuel. *Faveur et pouvoir au tournant du grand siècle: Michel Chamillart, ministre et secrétaire d'etat de la guerre sous Louis XIV*. 2004.

Pepys, Samuel. *Diary*. 9 vols. 1995 edn.

Perez, Stanis. *La Santé de Louis XIV: une biohistoire du Roi-Soleil*. 2010 edn.

Pernot, François. *La Franche-Comté espagnole à travers les archives de Simancas*. 2003.

Perrault, Charles. *Mémoires de ma vie*. 2 vols. 1909.

Perrault, Charles. *Le Siècle de Louis le Grand*. 1687.

Perrin, Bernard. 'Un Professeur de droit solliciteur à la cour du grand Roi, 1699–1704: Louis Monnier de Richardin'. *Revue de l'Histoire de Versailles*. 55. 1964. pp. 150–206.

Perth, Lord. 'Lettres . . . au Père de La Trappe'. *Revue de l'Histoire de Versailles.* October 1927. pp. 213–25.

Petitfils, Jean-Christian. *L'Assassinat d'Henri I V.* 2012.

Petitfils, Jean-Christian. *Fouquet.* 2005.

Petitfils, Jean-Christian. *Lauzun ou l'insolente séduction.* 2008 edn.

Petitfils, Jean-Christian. *Louis X I V.* 2008.

Petitfils, Jean-Christian. *Louise de La Vallière.* 2011.

Petitfils, Jean-Christian. *Madame de Montespan.* 1988.

Petitfils, Jean-Christian. *Le Masque de fer: entre histoire et légende.* 2003.

Petitfils, Jean-Christian. *Le Régent.* 1986.

Peto, Christine Marie. *When France was King of Cartography: The Patronage and Production of Maps in Early Modern France.* Plymouth. 2007.

Petrie, Sir Charles. *The Marshal Duke of Berwick.* 1953.

Peyrat, Fabrice, ed. *Marie-Adélaïde de Savoie, Duchesse de Bourgogne, enfant terrible de Versailles.* Brussels. 2014.

Pfister, Christian. *Histoire de Nancy.* 3 vols. 1908.

Pfister, Christian, ed. *Sarrelouis, 1680–1930: réminiscences.* 1933.

Picard, Raymond. *La Carrière de Racine.* 1961 edn.

Picavet, Camille-Georges. *Les Dernières Années de Turenne (1660–1675).* N.d.

Picavet, Camille-Georges. *La Diplomatie française au temps de Louis X I V.* 1933.

Pierrot, Alfred. *Histoire de Montmédy et du pays montmédien.* 2 vols. Lyon. 1910.

Pillias, Emile. *Etudes sur François I I Rákóczi, Prince de Transylvanie.* 1939.

Pillorget, René. 'Louis X I V et l'Irlande'. *Revue d'Histoire Diplomatique.* 106. 1992. pp. 7–26.

Pillorget, René. *Les Mouvements insurrectionnels de Provence entre 1596 et 1715.* 1975.

Pillorget, René. 'Quelques aspects de l'entrée de Louis X I V et de Marie Thérèse a Paris'. In Christian Desplat and Paul Mourounneau, eds. *Les Entrées: gloire et déclin d'un ceremonial.* Biarritz. 1997. pp. 207–22.

Piton, Camille. *Marly-le-roi: son histoire.* 1904.

Pitts, Vincent J. *Embezzlement and High Treason in Louis X I V's France: The Trial of Nicolas Fouquet.* Baltimore. 2015.

Pitts, Vincent J. *La Grande Mademoiselle at the Court of France.* 2000.

Plantavit de La Pause, Jean de. *Mémoires.* 3 vols. Versailles. 2011–13.

Plantet, Eugène, ed. *Correspondance des Beys de Tunis et des consuls de France avec la cour, 1577–1830.* 3 vols. 1893–9.

Plantet, Eugène, ed. *Correspondance des Deys d'Alger avec la cour de France, 1579–1830.* 2 vols. 1889.

Plantet, Eugène. *Moulay Ismaïl, Empereur du Maroc et la Princesse de Conti.* 1912.

Plazenet, Laurence. 'L'Anamorphose du soleil en épouvantail: Louis XIV dans l'historiographie et la littérature port-royalistes'. In *Louis X I V et Port-Royal.* 2016. pp. 165–99.

Plessen, Marie-Louise von et al., eds. *Prince Eugene, General-Philosopher and Art Lover.* Munich. 2010.

Plessis, Maréchal du. *Mémoires.* 1676.

Poisson, Georges. *Monsieur de Saint-Simon*. 1987 edn.

Pomponne, Marquis de. *Mémoires*. 2 vols. 1860–61.

Pontchartrain, M de. *Correspondance de la Maison du Roi*. 2 vols. Clermont-Ferrand. 2016.

Poullain de La Barre, François. *Traité de l'égalité des deux sexes*. 1673.

Poullet, Georges. *La Maison ducale de Lorraine: étude historique, biographique et généalogique des branches aînée, cadettes et illégitimes de cette maison*. Nancy. 1991.

Poumarède, Géraud. 'Les Envoyés ottomans à la cour de France: d'une présence controversée à l'exaltation d'une alliance'. In Gilles Veinstein, ed. *Turcs et Turqueries (XVIe–XVIIIe siècles)*. 2009. pp. 83–9.

Poumarède, Géraud. ' "Fidèle sujette" ou "mauvaise française"? Marie-Casimire de la Grange d'Arquien, Reine de Pologne, sous le regard des ambassadeurs français'. In Jaroslaw Dumanowski, Michel Figeac and Daniel Tollet, eds. *France–Pologne*. 2016. pp. 69–92.

Poumarède, Géraud. *Pour en finir avec la croisade: mythes et réalités de la lutte contre les Turcs aux XVIe et XVIIIe siècles*. 2004.

Prest, Julia. *Theatre under Louis XIV: Cross-Casting and the Performance of Gender in Drama, Ballet and Opera*. 2006.

Prestage, Edgar. *The Diplomatic Relations of Portugal with France, England and Holland from 1640 to 1668*. Watford. 1925.

Prestwich, Menna. *International Calvinism, 1541–1715*. Oxford. 1985.

Prévot, Jacques. *La Première Institutrice de France: Madame de Maintenon*. 1981.

Price, Munro. 'The Maréchal de Castries and the Pre-Revolution'. In Julian Swann and Joël Félix, eds. *The Crisis of the Absolute Monarchy: From Old Regime to Revolution*. Oxford. 2013. pp. 91–106.

Pritchard, James. *In Search of Empire: The French in the Americas, 1670–1730*. Cambridge. 2004.

Pritchard, James. 'Population in French America, 1670–1730'. In Bradley Bond, ed., *French Colonial Louisiana and the Atlantic World*. Baton Rouge. 2005. pp. 175–203.

Przezdziecki, Comte Renaud. *Diplomatie et protocole à la cour de Pologne*. 2 vols. 1934.

Racine, *Oeuvres complètes*. 2 vols. 1999.

Raeymakers, Dries et al. eds. *A Constellation of Courts: The Courts and Households of Habsburg Europe, 1555–1665*. Leuven. 2014.

Raffin, Léonce. *Anne de Gonzague, Princesse Palatine, 1616–1684*. 1935.

Rambaud, Alfred, ed. *Recueil des instructions données aux ambassadeurs et ministres de France: Russie*. 2 vols. 1890.

Ranum, Orest. *The Fronde: A French Revolution, 1648–1652*. 1993.

Ranum, Orest. *Paris in the Age of Absolutism: An Essay*. New York. 1968.

Raunié, Emile. *Chansonnier historique du XVIIIe siècle*. 10 vols. 1879–84.

Recht, Roland. *The Rhine: Culture and Landscape at the Heart of Europe*. 2001.

Reinhardt, Nicole. 'Les Relations internationales à travers les femmes au temps de Louis XIV'. *Revue d'Histoire Diplomatique*. 117, 3. 2003. pp. 193–230.

Renneville, Constantin de. *L'Inquisition française ou l'histoire de la Bastille*. 6 vols. Amsterdam. 1724.

Renneville, Constantin de. *Mémoires pour servir à l'histoires des Indes orientales*. 1688.

Reresby, Sir John. *Memoirs*. 1991 edn.

Retz, Cardinal de. *Mémoires*. 2003 edn.

Retz, Cardinal de. *Oeuvres*. 9 vols. 1870–87.

Reuss, Rodolphe, ed. *Correspondances politiques et chroniques parisiennes adressées à Christophe Güntzer, xyndic royal de la ville de Strasbourg (1681–1685)*. 1890.

Revel, Jacques. 'La Cour'. In Pierre Nora, ed. *Les Lieux de mémoire*. 7 vols. 1984–1992. III, 133–86.

Rhoen, R. P. M. 'Met 2,000 man informeel op bezoek: de doortocht van Lodewijk XIV door de stad Utrecht in 1671'. *Oud Utrecht*. 87. 2014. pp. 24–6.

Rials, Stéphane. *La Présidence de la république*. 1981.

Richefort, Isabelle. *Adam-François van der Meulen: peintre flamand au service de Louis XIV*. Rennes. 2004.

Richter, Susan et al. *Heidelberg im Barock: der Wiederaufbau der Stadt nach den Zerstörungen von 1689 und 1693*. Heidelberg. 2009.

Ridley, Jane. *Fox Hunting*. 1990.

Ristelhueber, René. *Les Traditions françaises au Liban*. 1925 edn.

Roach, Joseph. 'Body of Law: The Sun King and the Code Noir'. In Sara E. Melzer and Kathryn Norberg, eds. *From the Royal to the Republican Body: Incorporating the Political in Seventeenth and Eighteenth-Century France*. Berkeley. 1998. pp. 113–30.

Roche, Daniel et al., eds. *À Cheval! Ecuyers, amazones et cavaliers du XIVe au XXIe siècle*. 2007.

Roche, Daniel, ed. *Le Cheval et la guerre*. 2002.

Roche, Daniel. *Connaissances et passions: histoire de la culture équestre en France*. 2015.

Roche, Daniel, ed. *Les Ecuries royales, du XVIe au XVIIIe siècle*. Versailles. 1998.

Roche, Daniel. *Le Peuple de Paris au XVIIIe siècle*. 1998.

Rochebrune, Marie-Laure de, ed. *La Chine à Versailles: art et diplomatie au XVIIIe siècle*. 2014.

Rolland, Paul. *Histoire de Tournai*. 1956.

Rondot, Bertrand. 'La Première Ambassade ottomane, 1721'. In Daniëlle Kisluk-Grosheide and Bertrand Rondot, eds. *Visiteurs de Versailles: voyageurs, princes, ambassadeurs, 1682–1789*. 2017.

Ronfort, Jean-Nérée, ed. *André-Charles Boulle, 1642–1732: un nouveau style pour l'Europe*. Frankfurt. 2009.

Roos, Gilbert. *Relations entre le gouvernement royal et les juifs du nord-est de la France au XVIIe siècle*. 2000.

Rotta, Salvatore. 'Genova e il re sole'. In Piero Boccardo and Clario di Fabio, eds. *El siglo de los Genoveses*. Milan. 1999. pp. 286–305.

Rousseau, Louis. *Les Relations diplomatiques de la France et de la Turquie au XVIIIe siècle.* Vol. I: 1700–1716. 1908.

Rousseau, Michel. *Quand Louis XIV brûlait le Palatinat: la guerre de la ligue d'Augsbourg et la presse.* 2014.

Roussel, Eric. *Charles de Gaulle.* 2002.

Rousset, Camille. *Histoire de Louvois et de son administration politique et militaire.* 4 vols. 1863–5.

Roussier, Paul. *L'Etablissement d'Issiny, 1687–1702.* 1935.

Rowen, Herbert H. *The Ambassador Prepares for War: The Dutch Embassy of Arnauld de Pomponne.* The Hague. 1957.

Rowen, Herbert H. *John de Witt, Grand Pensionary of Holland, 1625–1672.* Princeton. 1978.

Rowen, Herbert H. *John de Witt: Statesman of the 'True Freedom'.* Cambridge. 1986.

Rowlands, Guy. *The Dynastic State and the Army under Louis XIV: Royal Service and Private Interest, 1661–1701.* Cambridge. 2002.

Rowlands, Guy. *The Financial Decline of a Great Power: War, Influence, and Money in Louis XIV's France.* Oxford. 2012.

Rowlands, Guy. 'Last Argument of the King, or a Step Too Far? Arms, Artillery and Absolutism under Louis XIV'. Talk given at the Institute of Historical Research, London. 19 May 2014.

Rowlands, Guy. 'The Maison Militaire du Roi and the Disintegration of the Old Regime'. In Julian Swann and Joël Félix, eds. *The Crisis of the Absolute Monarchy: France from Old Regime to Revolution.* Oxford. 2013. pp. 245–73.

Rubin, David Lee, ed. *The Sun King: The Ascendancy of French Culture during the Reign of Louis XIV.* Washington, DC. 1992.

Rubinstein, S. *Les Relations entre la France et la Pologne de 1680 à 1683.* 1913.

Rule, John C. 'The Partition Treaties, 1698–1700: A European View'. In Esther Mijers and David Onnekink, eds. *Redefining William III: The Impact of the King-Stadholder in International Context.* Aldershot. 2007. pp. 91–105.

Rule, John and Ben Trotter. *A World of Paper: Louis XIV, Colbert de Torcy, and the Rise of the Information State.* Montreal. 2014.

Russell, W. H. *My Diary during the Last Great War.* 1874.

Sabatier, Gérard. *Le Prince et les arts.* 2010.

Saint-Germain, Jacques. *Les Financiers sous Louis XIV.* 1950.

Saint-Germain, Jacques. *Louis XIV secret.* 1970.

Saint-Germain, Jacques. *La Reynie et la police au Grand Siècle.* 1962.

Saint-Germain, Jacques. *Samuel Bernard, le banquier des rois.* 1960.

Saint-Germain, Jacques. *La Vie quotidienne en France à la fin du grand siècle d'après les archives de Marc René d'Argenson.* 1965.

Saint-Maurice, Marquis de. *Lettres sur la cour de Louis XIV.* 2 vols. 1910–12.

Saint-Olon, M. Pidou de. *Etat présent de l'Empire de Maroc.* 1695.

Saint-Priest, Comte de. *Mémoires sur l'ambassade de France en Turquie.* 1877.

Saint-Simon, Duc de. *Mémoires.* Ed. Yves Coirault. 2 vols. 1990–94.

Saint-Simon, Duc de. *Mémoires.* 20 vols. 1873–7. Ed. M. Regnier and A. Chéruel.

Saint-Simon, Duc de. *La Mort de Louis XIV.* 2007 edn.

Saint-Simon, Fernand de. *La Place des Victoires.* 1984.

Sainte-Fare-Garnot, Pierre-Nicolas. *Le Château des Tuileries.* 1988.

Salat, Nicolas and Thierry Sarmant, eds. *Lettres de Louvois à Louis XIV.* 2007.

Salmon, J. H. M. *Cardinal de Retz: The Anatomy of a Conspirator.* 1969.

Salnove, Robert de. *La Vénerie royale.* 1665.

Salvadori, Philippe. *La Chasse sous l'ancien régime.* 1996.

Samoyault, Jean-Pierre. *Guide to the Museum of the Château de Fontainebleau.* 1994.

Santa Maria, Roberto, ed. *Palazzo Doria Spinola.* Genoa. 2011.

Sarmant, Thierry. *Les Demeures du soleil: Louis XIV, Louvois et la surintendance des bâtiments du Roi.* 2003.

Sarmant, Thierry. *Louis XIV et Paris: collections du Musée Carnavalet.* 2013.

Sarmant, Thierry. *Louis XIV: l'homme et le roi.* 2012.

Sarmant, Thierry. *La République des medailles: numismates et collections numismatiques à Paris, du Grand Siècle au siècle des Lumières.* 2003.

Sarmant, Thierry and Mathieu Stoll. *Régner et gouverner: Louis XIV et ses ministres.* 2010.

Satterfield, George. *Princes, Posts and Partisans: The Army of Louis XIV and Partisan Warfare in the Netherlands, 1673–1678.* Leiden. 2003.

Saule, Béatrix. 'Tentative de définition du Grand Couvert'. In idem, ed. *Tables royales et festins de cour en Europe, 1661–1789.* 2004. pp. 29–35.

Saule, Béatrix. *Versailles triomphant: une journée de Louis XIV.* 1996.

Sauzet, Robert. *Le Notaire et son roi: Etienne Borrelly (1633–1718), un Nîmois sous Louis XIV.* 1998.

Savary, Jacques. *Le Parfait Négociant.* Ed. Edouard Richard. 2 vols. Geneva. 2011.

Savile, Henry and George. *Savile Correspondence: Letters to and from . . .* 1858

Schaeper, Thomas J. *The French Council of Commerce, 1700–1715.* Columbus, OH. 1983.

Schechter, Ronald. *A Genealogy of Terror in Eighteenth-Century France.* Chicago. 2018.

Schmid, Elmar D. et al. *Nymphenburg Palace, Park and Pavilions.* Munich. 2009.

Schnakenbourg, Eric. 'La Politique française dans le Nord à la fin du règne de Louis XIV'. *Revue d'Histoire Diplomatique.* 3. 1998. pp. 251–74.

Schnitter, Helmut. 'The Refugees in the Army of Brandenburg-Prussia'. In Matthew Glozier and David Onnekink, eds. *War, Religion and Service: Huguenot Soldiering, 1685–1713.* Aldershot. 2007. pp. 145–59.

Schryver, Reginald de. *Max II Emanuel von Bayern und das spanische Erbe: die europäische Ambitionen des Hauses Wittelsbach.* Mainz. 1996.

Schwoerer, Lois G. *The Revolution of 1688–1689: Changing Perspectives.* Cambridge. 1922.

Scott, Eva. *The King in Exile: The Wanderings of Charles II from June 1646 to July 1654.* 1905.

Scott, Tom. *The City-State in Europe, 1000–1600.* 2012.

Scoville, Warren C. *The Persecution of Huguenots and French Economic Development, 1680–1720.* Berkeley. 1960.

Ségur, Marquis de. *Le Maréchal de Luxembourg et le Prince d'Orange, 1668–1678*. 1902.

Ségur, Marquis de. *Le Tapissier de Notre-Dame: les dernières années du Maréchal de Luxembourg (1678–1695)*. 1903.

Séré, Daniel. *La Paix des Pyrénées: vingt-quatre ans de négociations entre la France et l'Espagne, 1635–1660*. 2007.

Sévigné, Madame de. *Correspondance*. 3 vols. 1972–6.

Sharp, Tony. *Pleasure and Ambition: The Life, Loves and Wars of Augustus the Strong*. 2001.

Shifrin, Susan. 'Subdued by a Famous Roman Dame'. In Julia Marciari and Catherine Macleod, eds. *Politics, Transgression, and Representation at the Court of Charles II*. New Haven and London. 2007. pp. 141–74.

Sichel, Walter. *Bolingbroke and his Times*. 1901.

Siméon, Nicolas. *Louis XIV et la mer*. 2007.

Skippon, Philip. *An Account of a Journey made through Part of the Low Countries, Germany, Italy and France*. In *A Collection of Travels*. 6 vols. 1732. VI, 361–736.

Skrzypietz, Aleksandra. *Franciszek Ludwik, książę de Conti – 'obrany król Polski'. Saga rodu Kondeuszów*. Katowice. 2019.

Smith, Jay M. *The Culture of Merit: Nobility, Royal Service and the Making of Absolute Monarchy in France, 1600–1789*. Ann Arbor. 1996.

Smith, L. B. 'Spain and the Jacobites, 1715–16'. In Eveline Cruickshanks, ed. *Ideology and Jacobitism*, Edinburgh. 1982. pp. 159–78.

Smithies, Michael. *Witnesses to a Revolution: Siam, 1688*. Bangkok. 2004.

Smolar-Meynart, Arlette, ed. *Autour du bombardement de Bruxelles: désastre et relèvement*. Brussels. 1997.

Société de l'Histoire de France. *Registres de l'Hôtel de Ville de Paris pendant la Fronde*. 3 vols. 1846–8.

Solana, Ana Crespo. 'A Change of Ideology in Imperial Spain? Spanish Commercial Policy with America and the Change of Dynasty (1648–1740). In David Onnekink and Gijs Rommelse, eds. *Ideology and Foreign Policy in Early Modern Europe (1650-1750)*. Farnham. 2011. pp. 215–42.

Soll, Jacob. *Information Master: Jean-Baptiste Colbert's Secret State Intelligence System*. Ann Arbor. 2009.

Solnon, Jean-François. *La Cour de France*. 1987.

Somerset, Anne. *The Affair of the Poisons*. 2003.

Somerset, Anne. *Queen Anne: The Politics of Passion*. 2013.

Sonkajärvi, Hanna. *Qu'est ce qu'un étranger? Frontières et identifications à Strasbourg, 1681–1789*. Strasbourg. 2008.

Sonnino, Paul. *Louis XIV and the Origins of the Dutch War*. Cambridge. 2002 edn.

Sonnino, Paul. *The Search for the Man in the Iron Mask*. 2016.

Sourches, Marquis de. *Mémoires sur le règne de Louis XIV*. 13 vols. 1882–93.

Spangler, Jonathan. 'A Lesson in Diplomacy for Louis XIV: The Treaty of Montmartre 1662 and the Princes of the Houses of Lorraine'. *French History*. 17, 3. 2003. pp. 225–50.

Spangler, Jonathan. *The Society of Princes: The Lorraine-Guise and the Conservation of Wealth and Power in Seventeenth-Century France.* Farnham. 2009.

Spanheim, Ezechiel. *Relation de la cour de France en 1690.* 1882.

Spencer, Charles. *Blenheim: Battle for Europe.* 2004.

Spielman, John. *Leopold I of Austria.* 1977.

Stair, Lord. 'Extracts from Lord Stair's journal at Paris in 1715 and 1716'. In Earl of Hardwicke, ed. *Miscellaneous State Papers from 1501 to 1726.* 2 vols. 1778. Vol. II, pp. 528–54.

Stanhope, Alexander. *Spain under Charles the Second.* 1844 edn. pp. 528–54.

Steinberg, Jonathan. *Bismarck: A Life.* 2011.

Sternberg, Giora. *Status Interaction during the Reign of Louis XIV.* Oxford. 2014.

Stoll, Mathieu. *Servir le Roi-Soleil: Claude le Peletier (1631–1711), ministre de Louis XIV.* 2011.

Storrs, Christopher. *The Spanish Resurgence, 1713–1748.* New Haven. 2016.

Storrs, Christopher. *War, Diplomacy and the Rise of Savoy, 1690–1720.* 2000.

Strayer, Brian E. 'The Edict of Fontainebleau and the Huguenots: Who's to Blame?'. In Richard Bonney and D. J. B. Trim, eds. *Persecution and Pluralism: Calvinists and Religious Minorities in Early Modern Europe, 1550–1700.* Bern. 2006. pp. 273–94.

Strong, Roy. *Feast: A History of Grand Eating.* 2002.

Strong, S. Arthur, ed. *A Catalogue of Letters . . . in the Library at Welbeck.* 1903.

Stroup, Alice. *A Company of Scientists: Botany, Patronage and Community at the Seventeenth-Century Royal Parisian Academy of Sciences.* Berkeley. 1990.

Stroup, Alice. 'Louis XIV as Patron of the Parisian Academy of Sciences'. In David Lee Rubin, ed. *The Sun King: The Ascendancy of French Culture during the Reign of Louis XIV.* Washington, DC. 1992. pp. 221–40.

Strunck, Christina and Elisabeth Kieven, eds. *Europäische Galeriebauten: Galleries in a Comparative European Perspective (1400–1800).* Munich. 2010.

Sue, Eugène. *Histoire de la Marine française.* 4 vols. 1845 edn.

Swann, Julian. *Provincial Power and Absolute Monarchy: The Estates General of Burgundy, 1661–1790.* Cambridge. 2003.

Swann, Julian and Joël Félix. *The Crisis of the Absolute Monarchy: From Old Regime to Revolution.* Oxford. 2013.

Swift, Katherine. 'The French Booksellers in the Strand: Huguenots in the London Book Trade, 1685–1730'. *Proceedings of the Huguenot Society of Great Britain and Ireland* XXV. 2. 1990. pp. 123–39.

Symcox, Geoffrey. *Victor Amadeus II: Absolutism in the Savoyard State, 1675–1730.* 1983.

Szechi, Daniel. *The Great Jacobite Rising.* 2006.

Tachard, Guy. *Second Voyage du Père Tachard et des Jesuites envoyés par le Roy au royaume de Siam.* Amsterdam. 1689.

Tachard, Guy. *Voyage de Siam des Pères Jesuites, envoyés par le roy aux Indes et à la Chine.* Amsterdam. 1686.

Takeda, Junko Thérèse. *Between Crown and Commerce: Marseille and the Early Modern Mediterranean.* Baltimore. 2011.

Tallents, Francis. *Travels in France and Switzerland in the Years 1671–1673*. 2011.

Targosz, Karolina. *La Cour savante de Louise-Marie de Gonzague et ses liens scientifiques avec la France, 1646–1667*. Wrocław. 1982.

Tavernier, Jean-Baptiste. *Les Six Voyages de Jean-Baptiste Tavernier . . . en Turquie, en Perse et aux Indes*. 6 vols. 1724.

Terrien, Marie-Pierre and Philippe Dien. *Le Château de Richelieu, XVIIe–XVIIIe siècles*. Rennes. 2009.

Tessé, René de Froulay. *Lettres du maréchal de Tessé au prince Antoine Ier de Monaco*. 1917.

Tessier, Alexandre. 'Des carrosses qui en cachent d'autres: retours sur certains incidents qui marquèrent l'ambassade de Lord Denzil Holles à Paris, de 1663 à 1666'. In Lucien Bély and Géraud Poumarède, eds. *L'Incident diplomatique (XVIe–XVIIe siècle)*. 2010. pp. 197–240.

Tessier, Alexandre. *Réseaux diplomatiques et république des lettres: les correspondants de Sir Joseph Williamson, 1660–1680*. 2015.

Thénard, J. F. *Mémoires ou livre de raison d'un bourgeois de Marseille (1674–1726)*. Montpellier. 1881.

Thépaut-Cabasset, Corinne. 'Diplomatische Agenten und der europäische Luxuswarenhandle im späten 17. Jahrhundert'. In Mark Häberlein and Christof Jeggle, eds. *Materielle Grundlagen der Diplomatie: Schenken, Sammeln und Verhandeln im Spätmittelalter und früher Neuzeit*. Constanz and Munich. 2013. pp. 157–74.

Thépaut-Cabasset, Corinne. *L'Esprit des modes au Grand Siècle: extraits du Mercure Galant (1672–1701)*. 2010.

Thépaut-Cabasset, Corinne. 'Le Service de la Garde-Robe: une création de Louis XIV'. In Pierre Arizzoli-Clémentel and Pascale Gorguet Ballesteros, eds. *Fastes de cour et cérémonies royales: le costume de cour en Europe (1650–1800)*. 2009. pp. 28–33.

Thomas, Hugh. *The Slave Trade: The Story of the Atlantic Slave Trade, 1440–1870*. 1998.

Thomas, Pierre, sieur de Fossé. *Mémoires*. 4 vols. Rouen. 1876–9.

Thomson, M. A. 'Louis XIV and the Origins of the War of the Spanish Succession'. In Ragnhild Hatton and J. S. Bromley, eds. *William III and Louis XIV*. Liverpool. 1968. pp. 140–61.

Thomson, M. A. 'Louis XIV and William III, 1689–1697'. In Ragnhild Hatton and J. S. Bromley, eds. *William III and Louis XIV*. Liverpool. 1968. pp. 24–48.

Thomson, M. A. 'Self-Determination and Collective Security as Factors in English and French Foreign Policy, 1689–1718'. In Ragnhild Hatton and J. S. Bromley, eds. *William III and Louis XIV*. Liverpool. 1968. pp. 271–86.

Thuillier, Jacques. *Simon Vouet*. 1992.

Thurley, Simon. *Hampton Court: A Social and Architectural History*. 2003.

Tiberghien, Frédéric. *Versailles: le chantier de Louis XIV, 1662–1715*. 2002.

Tollet, Daniel, ed. *Guerres et paix: mélanges d'histoire des relations internationales offerts à Jean Bérenger*. 2003.

Tombs, Robert. *The War against Paris, 1871*. 1981.

Torcy, Marquis de. *Journal inédit pendant les années 1709, 1710 et 1711*. 1884.

Torcy, Marquis de. *Mémoires*. 1828.

Tóth, Ferenc, ed. *Correspondance diplomatique relative à la guerre d'indépendance du Prince François II Rákóczi (1703–1711)*. 2012.

Tóth, Ferenc. 'Emigré or Exile? Francis Rákóczi II and his Exile in France and Turkey'. In Philip Mansel and Torsten Riotte, eds., *Monarchy and Exile: The Politics of Legitimacy from Marie de Médicis to Wilhelm II*. 2011. pp. 91–102.

Tóth, Ferenc. 'Officiers français au service de l'armée du prince François II Rákóczi'. In Tomasz Ciesielski. ed. *W słuńbie obcych monarchów i państw*. Warsaw, 2015. pp. 73–93.

Treasure, Geoffrey. *The Huguenots*. 2014.

Trénard, Louis, ed. *Histoire de Cambrai*. Lille. 1983.

Trénard, Louis, ed. *Histoire de Lille, de Charles-Quint à la conquête française*. Toulouse. 1981.

Trevelyan, M. C. *William III and the Defence of Holland, 1673–1674*. 1930.

Trevor-Roper, Hugh. 'A Huguenot Historian: Paul Rapin'. In Irene Scouloudi, ed. *The Huguenots in Britain and their French Background, 1550–1800*. Basingstoke. 1987. pp. 3–19.

Troost, Wout. 'To Restore and Preserve the Liberty of Europe: William III's Ideas on Foreign Policy'. In David Onnekink and Gijs Rommelse, eds. *Ideology and Foreign Policy in Early Modern Europe (1650–1750)*. Farnham. 2011. pp. 283–303.

Troost, Wout. *William III: The Stadholder-King*. Aldershot. 2016.

Turenne, Maréchal de. *Mémoires*. 2 vols. 1909.

Turenne et l'art militaire de son temps. 1978.

Tydén-Jordan, Astrid. *Queen Christina's Coronation Coach*. Stockholm. 1988.

Ubert, Guillaume. 'To Establish One Law and Definite Rules: Race, Religion and the Transatlantic Origins of the Louisiana Code Noir'. In Cécile Vidal, ed. *Louisiana: Crossroads of the Atlantic World*. Philadelphia. 2014. pp. 21–43.

Upton, Anthony F. *Charles XI and Swedish Absolutism*. 1998.

Valensi, Lucette. *Ces Etrangers familiers: Musulmans en Europe XVIe–XVIIIe siècles*. 2012.

Vallier, Jean. *Journal de Jean Vallier: maître d'hôtel du roi*. 4 vols. 1902.

Vallot, Antoine, Antoine d'Aquin and Guy Crescent Fagon. *Journal de la santé du roi Louis XIV de l'année 1647 à l'année 1711*. Ed. J. A. Le Roi. 1862.

Vandal, Albert. *Les Voyages du Marquis de Nointel*. 1900.

Van der Cruysse, Dirk. *Louis XIV et le Siam*. 1991.

Van der Cruysse, Dirk, ed. *Madame Palatine: lettres françaises*. 1989.

Van der Cruysse, Dirk. *Madame Palatine: princesse européenne*. 1988.

Van der Cruysse, Dirk. *Le Noble Désir de courir le monde: voyager en Asie au XVI siècle*. 2002.

Van der Cruysse, Dirk. *Siam and the West, 1500–1700*. 2002.

Van Kley, Dale. *The Damiens Affair and the Unravelling of the Ancien Regime, 1750–1770*. Princeton. 1984.

Van Kley, Dale. *The Religious Origins of the French Revolution: From Calvin to the Civil Constitution, 1560–1791*. 1996.

Vanneufville, Eric. *Histoire de Lille: des origines au XXe siècle.* 1997.

Vauban, sa famille et ses écrits, ses oisivetés et sa correspondence. Ed. Rochas d'Aiglun. 2 vols. 1910.

Vault, Général de, ed. *Mémoires militaires relatifs à la Succession d'Espagne sous Louis XIV.* 15 vols. 1835–62.

Vergé-Franceschi, Michel, ed. *La Guerre de course en Mediterranée, 1515–1830.* 2000.

Vernois, Verdy du. *With the Royal Headquarters in 1870–71.* 1897.

Véry, Abbé de. *Journal.* 2 vols. Geneva. 2016.

Veryard, Ellis. *Journey through the Low Countries, France, Italy and Part of Spain.* 1701.

Vetter, Roland. *Heidelberga Deleta.* 1989.

Vian, Louis. 'Louis XIV au Parlement d'après les manuscrits du Parlement'. *Mémoires de la Société des sciences morales, des lettres et des arts de Seine et Oise.* Versailles. 1883. pp. 103–15.

Vigne, Randolph. ' "The Good Lord Galway": The English and Irish Careers of a Huguenot Leader'. In Matthew Glozier and David Onnekink, eds. *War, Religion and Service: Huguenot Soldiering, 1685–1713.* Aldershot. 2007. pp. 59–78.

Villars, Maréchal de. *Mémoires.* 6 vols. 1886–1904.

Villepin, Dominique de. *De l'esprit de cour: la malédiction française.* 2010.

Villette, Marquis de. *Mémoires.* 1844.

Vincens, Emile. *Histoire de la république de Gênes.* 2 vols. 1842.

Vincent, Monique. *Le Mercure Galant: présentation de la première revue féminine d'information et de culture, 1672–1710.* 2005.

Vinha, Mathieu da. *Au service du roi, dans les coulisses de Versailles,* 2015

Vinha, Mathieu da. 'La Maison d'Anne d'Autriche'. In Chantal Grell, ed. *Anne d'Autriche: Infante d'Espagne et reine de France.* 2009. pp. 155–85.

Vinha, Mathieu da. *Les Valets de chambre de Louis XIV.* 2004.

Vinha, Mathieu da. *Le Versailles de Louis XIV.* 2012 edn.

Vinha, Mathieu and Raphael Masson, eds. *Versailles: histoire, dictionnaire et anthologie.* 2015.

Virol, Michèle. *Louis XIV et Vauban: correspondance et agendas.* 2017.

Visconti, Primi. *Mémoires sur la cour de Louis XIV, 1673–1681.* 1988.

Visé, Donneau de. *Histoire du siège du château de Namur.* 1692.

Vissière, Isabelle and Jean-Louis, eds. *Lettres édifiantes et curieuses de Chine par des missionaires jésuites, 1702–1776.* 1979.

Vogler, Bernard. 'Une Alliance manquée: Strasbourg et les XIII cantons, 1555–1789'. In *Cinq siècles de relations franco-suisses.* Neuchâtel. 1984. pp. 111–21.

Vogler, Bernard. 'Louis XIV et les protestants alsaciens'. In Louise Godard de Donville and Roger Duchêne, eds. *De la mort de Colbert à la revocation de l'édit de Nantes: un monde nouveau?* 1985. pp. 285–91.

Vogler, Bernard. *Nouvelle Histoire de l'Alsace: une région au coeur de l'Europe.* 2003.

Waddington, Albert. *Le Grand Electeur: Frédéric Guillaume de Brandebourg.* 2 vols. 1908.

Waliszewski, K. *Marysienka: Marie de la Grange d'Arquien, Reine de Pologne.* 1898.

Waliszewski, K. *Les Relations diplomatiques entre la Pologne et la France au XVII siècle, 1644–1667.* Cracow. 1889.

Waquet, Jean-Claude. 'L'Echec d'un mariage: Marguerite-Louise d'Orléans et Côme de Médicis'. In Isabelle Poutrin and Marie-Karine Schaub, eds. *Femmes et pouvoir politique: les princesses d'Europe, XVe–XVIIIe siècle.* Rosny. 2007. pp. 120–32.

Waquet, Jean-Claude. *François de Callières: l'art de négocier en France sous Louis XIV.* 2005.

Ward, Adolphus William. *The Electress Sophia and the Hanoverian Succession.* 1909 edn.

Waresquiel, Emmanuel de. *Dans les archives secrètes du Quai d'Orsay: cinq siècles d'histoire et de diplomatie.* 2015.

Warner, Marina. *Alone of All her Sex: The Myth and the Cult of the Virgin Mary.* 1976.

Watanabe-O'Kelly, Helen. *Triumphall Shews: Tournaments at German-Speaking Courts in their European Context, 1560–1730.* Berlin. 1992.

Watson, J. N. P. *Captain-General and Rebel Chief: The Life of James, Duke of Monmouth.* 1979.

Watts, Derek A. 'La Journée des barricades racontée par les mémorialistes du temps'. In Roger Duchêne and Pierre Ronzeaud, eds. *La Fronde en questions.* Aix-en-Provence. 1989. pp. 51–62.

Webb, Stephen Saunders. *Lord Churchill's Coup: The Anglo-American Empire and the Glorious Revolution Reconsidered.* New York. 1995.

Weigert, R. A., ed. *Les Relations artistiques entre la France et la Suède, 1693–1718.* Stockholm. 1964.

Westrich, Sal Alexander. *The Ormée of Bordeaux: A Revolution during the Fronde.* Baltimore. 1972.

Whyte, James Christie. *History of the British Turf.* 2 vols. 1840.

Wicquefort, Abraham de. *L'Ambassadeur et ses fonctions.* Amsterdam. 1730.

Wiesener, Louis. *Le Régent, l'Abbé Dubois et les Anglais.* 1891.

Wills, John E., ed. *China and Maritime Europe, 1500–1800.* New York. 2011.

Wilson, Peter H. *War, State and Society in Württemberg, 1677–1793.* Cambridge. 1995.

Wismes, Armel de. *Jean Bart et la guerre de course.* 1965.

Witek Jr, John W. 'Catholic Missions and the Expansion of Christianity'. In John E. Wills, ed. *China and Maritime Europe, 1500–1800.* New York. 2011. pp. 135–82.

Wolf, John B. *The Barbary Coast: Algeria under the Turks.* 1979.

Wrangel, Comte F. U. *Première Visite de Christine de Suède à la cour de France, 1656.* 1930.

Zaimova, Raïa. *Correspondance consulaire des ambassadeurs de France à Constantinople, 1668–1708.* 1999.

Zee, Henri and Barbara van der. *William and Mary.* 1973.

Ziegler, Hendrik. ' "His house at Versailles is something the foolishest in the world": la grande galerie de Versailles à travers les récits de voyageurs et d'ambassadeurs étrangers autour de 1700'. In Christina Strunck and Elisabeth Kieven, eds. *Europäische Galeriebauten: Galleries in a Comparative European Perspective (1400–1800)*. Munich. 2010. pp. 351–82.

Ziegler, Hendrik. *Louis XIV et ses ennemis: image, propagande et contestation*. Versailles. 2013.

Zoberman, Pierre. *Les Cérémonies de la parole*. 2008.

Zoberman, Pierre. *Les Panégyriques du roi prononcés dans l'Académie française*. 1991.

Zylberberg, Michel. *Une si douce domination: les milieux d'affaires français et l'Espagne vers 1780–1808*. 1993.

Zysberg, André. *Marseille au temps du Roi Soleil: la ville, les galères, l'arsenal*. 2007.

EXHIBITION CATALOGUES

Ádám Mányoki: Actors and Venues of a Portraitist's Career. Budapest. 2003.

Castelnuovo, E. and Barberis W. et al., eds. *La Reggia di Venaria e i Savoia: arte, magnificenza e storia di una corte europea*. 2 vols. Turin. 2007.

La Cour des Stuarts à Saint-Germain-en-Laye au temps de Louis XIV. Saint-Germain. 1992.

De chasse et d'épée: le décor de l'appartment du roi à Marly, 1683–1750. 1999.

Denis, Marie-Amynthe. *Divertissements à Marly au temps de Louis XIV, 1686–1715*. Marly. 1990.

Être femme sous Louis XIV: du mythe à la realité. Marly. 2015.

Fastes de Cour et cérémonies royales: le costume de cour en Europe (1650–1800). Versailles. 2009.

Fêtes et divertissements à la cour. Versailles. 2016.

Fleurs du Roi: peintures, vélins et parchemins du Grand Trianon. Versailles. 2013.

France–Bayern: 1000 ans de relations franco-bavaroises. 2006.

Kangxi, Empereur de Chine, 1662–1722: la cité interdite à Versailles. Versailles. 2004.

Lille au XVIIe siècle: des Pays-Bas espagnols au Roi-Soleil. Lille. 2000.

Louis XIV à Saint-Germain, 1638–1682: de La naissance à la gloire. Saint-Germain. 1988.

Louis XIV: l'homme et le roi. Versailles. 2009.

Louis-Philippe et Versailles. 2018.

Maral, Alexandre and Nicolas Milovanovic. *Versailles et L'Antique*. 2012.

L'Orient arsenal XVII–XVIII siècles. Lorient. 1983.

Peter the Great, an Inspired Tsar. Amsterdam. 2013.

Phra Narai, roi de Siam et Louis XIV. 1986.

Primus Inter Pares: The First among Equals: The Story of King Jan III. Wilanów Palace Museum, Warsaw. 2013.

Riani, Annick. 'L'Arsenal des Galériens'. In *Le Siècle de Louis XIV à Marseille*. Marseille. 1994.

Sabatier, Gérard and Béatrix Saule, eds., *Le Roi est mort: Louis XIV – 1715*. Versailles. 2015.

Saint-Jean de Luz: étape royale, 1660–1960. Bordeaux. 1960.

Saule, Béatrix et al. eds. *Splendeurs de la cour de Saxe: Dresde à Versailles*. 2006.

Sciences et curiosités à la cour de Versailles. 2010.

La Soie et le canon: France-Chine, 1700–1860. Nantes. 2010.

Soieries de Lyon: commandes royales au XVIIIe siècle. Lyon. 1988.

Treasure of the Holy Sepulchre. Milan. 2013.

Versailles et la musique de cour. Versailles. 2007.

Versailles et les tables royales en Europe: XVIIème–XIXème siècles. 1993.

Vinha, Mathieu da and Alexandre Maral. *Madame de Maintenon dans les allées du pouvoir*. 2019.

Index

Moulay Ismaïl, Sultan,
291–2
Moulin, Pierre du, 311
Muiden (near Amsterdam),
171
Munich, the Residenz
at, 199
Münster, Bishop of, 149
Münster, Congress of
(1648), 183
Murat, Inès, 273*
Muscat, 429
music, 69, 216, 218, 244,
245–6, 253, 278, 458
Musketeers, 107–8

Namur, 76; siege of (1692),
351, 355
Nancy, city of, 5, 176, 359
Nangis, Marquis de, 391
Nantes, city of, 65, 107–8,
399, 415
Nantes, Edict of (1598), 11,
51, 107, 154, 302;
Revocation of (1685), 2,
304, 306–7, 308–10,
311–16, 320–23, 326,
327–8, 443, 445; clerical
opposition to, 306–7
Nantes, Mlle de
(illegitimate daughter of
King), 160, 257*, 367,
372; marries Duc de
Bourbon (1685), 218, 268
Naples, Kingdom of, 6, 38,
68, 148, 152, 363, 370,
418, 446
Napoleon I, Emperor, 169,
452, 453, 454
Napoleon III, Emperor, 453
Narbonne, Pierre, 438
Native Americans, 284, 285
Navailles, Duchesse de, 112
Navarre, Kingdom of, 8,
10, 363
navy, French: in Indian
ocean, 118; King's
attitude to, 122–3, 167;
inscription maritime,
123; shipbuilding
programme, 123;
principal naval bases,
124; galley slaves, 125–6,
291, 293–4, 357, 426;
royal galleys, 125–6, 357;
against Dutch ships, 178;
galiote à bombes, 294,
295; loss of Protestants
from, 311, 320; weakness

of, 333, 345, 357; brief
control of English
Channel (1690), 356–7;
defeat at Cap La Hogue
(1692), 357; inadequacy
of ships, 357; Tourville
sinks 'Smyrna convoy'
(1693), 357
Necker, Jacques, 450,
451, 452
Neerwinden, battle of
(1693), 352, 354, 404
Nemours, Duchesse de,
45–6
Nescambiout (American
chief), 281
Netherlands: United
Provinces in north, 15;
global empire of, 103,
289; Dutch navy, 121;
French–Dutch treaty
(1662), 121, 149, 151,
166; world trade
dominance, 121, 122,
153; collapse of Franco-
Dutch alliance, 121–2;
second Anglo-Dutch War
(1665–7), 149, 152, 166;
anti-French coalition
with England and
Sweden, 152, 166; States
General, 152–3, 172,
330, 331; 'carriage war'
(1664), 153; Louis XIV
plans war against, 162,
163, 164, 165–7; war
against France (1672–8),
169–78, 181–3, 277;
William III as
Stadholder, 172; Dutch
army atrocities (1672),
173; alliance with
Austria and Spain (1673),
176; fall of Ghent and
Ypres (1678), 182–3;
alliance with England
(1678), 183; and Chinese
blue and white porcelain,
289; Huguenot settlers
in, 312–14, 358; William
III strengthened by
Revocation, 327–8;
King's tariff war with
(1687), 328, 330; Dutch
ships/sailors in French
ports impounded (1688),
331; Louis XIV declares
war on (November 1688),
336; War of the Spanish

Succession, 380; and
Peace of Utrecht (12
April 1713), 417;
Southern Netherlands
assigned to Charles VI,
418
Neues Palais (Potsdam), 449
New York, colony of, 285
Newfoundland, 415
Newton, Isaac, 380
Nicolay, Aymard-Jean de, 38
Nijmegen, Treaty of (1678),
174, 183–4, 188, 312
Nîmes, city of, 8
Noailles family, 45, 241,
252, 272, 309, 391, 410,
436, 446; Duc de
Noailles (courtier), 145,
146, 242, 250, 309, 390,
410, 445–6; Maréchale
de Noailles (widow of
Anne-Jules), 241, 250;
Maréchal de Noailles,
242, 368, 390, 391;
Adrien Maurice de
Noailles (confidant of
King), 269, 400;
Cardinal de Noailles,
Archbishop of Paris, 381,
409, 427
nobility: Hugues Capet
elected king (987), 3; and
States General, 6, 9, 44,
451; and Queen's
household, 7; and wars
of religion, 8; legal
privileges and
exemptions, 9, 38, 81,
113, 115, 116; les
quarante-cinq, 9; and
Henri IV, 10–11; Paris as
aristocratic capital, 30;
and the Fronde, 42–3,
46, 52; powerful French
court families, 45, 241,
272, 446; princes
étrangers, 47, 112, 157,
393–4, 405–6; and revolt
in Marseille, 81–2; dress
as a political weapon,
119–20; war as
opportunity for, 162,
177; domination of
King's army, 162–3;
school at Versailles, 213;
court more exclusive
(after 1686), 220; nobles
d'épée, 220; 'Sire,
Marly?' phrase, 223;